Survival Communications
in Michigan: North and East Regions

John E. Parnell, KK4HWX

13 ISBN 978-1-62512-043-4

Cover design by:
Lynda Colón
FREELANCE GRAPHIC DESIGN &
MARKETING COMMUNICATIONS
www.hirelynda.webs.com

I do wish to acknowledge the hard work of **Angie Shirley** in putting together the database required for this book. Without her efforts, this book could not have been done.

Titles available in this series:

Survival Communications in Alabama
Survival Communications in Alaska
Survival Communications in Arizona
Survival Communications in Arkansas
Survival Communications in California
Survival Communications in Colorado
Survival Communications in Connecticut
Survival Communications in Delaware
Survival Communications in Florida
Survival Communications in Georgia
Survival Communications in Hawaii
Survival Communications in Idaho
Survival Communications in Illinois
Survival Communications in Indiana
Survival Communications in Iowa
Survival Communications in Kansas
Survival Communications in Kentucky
Survival Communications in Louisiana
Survival Communications in Maine
Survival Communications in Maryland
Survival Communications in Massachusetts
Survival Communications in Michigan
Survival Communications in Minnesota
Survival Communications in Mississippi
Survival Communications in Missouri

Survival Communications in Montana
Survival Communications in Nebraska
Survival Communications in Nevada
Survival Communications in New Hampshire
Survival Communications in New Jersey
Survival Communications in New Mexico
Survival Communications in New York
Survival Communications in North Carolina
Survival Communications in North Dakota
Survival Communications in Ohio
Survival Communications in Oklahoma
Survival Communications in Oregon
Survival Communications in Pennsylvania
Survival Communications in Rhode Island
Survival Communications in South Carolina
Survival Communications in South Dakota
Survival Communications in Tennessee
Survival Communications in Texas
Survival Communications in Utah
Survival Communications in Vermont
Survival Communications in Virginia
Survival Communications in Washington
Survival Communications in West Virginia
Survival Communications in Wisconsin
Survival Communications in Wyoming

The above titles are available from your favorite online or brick-and-mortar bookstore or directly from the publisher at Tutor Turtle Press LLC, 1027 S. Pendleton St. – Suite B-10, Easley, SC 29642.

TABLE OF CONTENTS

Survival Communications in Michigan 1
General Mobile Radio Service / Family Radio Service 1
Citizens Band Radio 1
Ham / Amateur Radio 2
Standardized Amateur Radio Prepper Communications Plan 2
Nets and Network Etiquette 3
Topics for Technician Amateur License Exam 4
Call Sign Numbers 6
Topics for General Amateur License Exam 7
Topics for Extra Amateur License Exam 9
Canadian Call Sign Prefixes 13
Common Radio Bands in the United States 14
Common Amateur Radio Bands in Canada 14
Call Sign Phonics 21
Morse Code and Ham Radio 23
International Call Sign Prefixes 24
Third Party Communications 31

Appendix A – Michigan Ham Radio Clubs

ARRL Affiliated Amateur and Ham Radio Clubs – By City

Adrian .... App A – 3
Allegan .... App A – 3
Allouez .... App A – 3
Ann Arbor .... App A – 3
Battle Creek .... App A – 3
Byron Center .... App A – 3
Cadillac .... App A – 4
Charlotte .... App A – 4
Chelsea .... App A – 4
Coldwater .... App A – 4
Comstock Park .... App A – 4
Corunna .... App A – 4
Dearborn .... App A – 4
Dollar Bay .... App A – 4
East Lansing .... App A – 4
Eben Junction .... App A – 4
Farmington Hills .... App A – 5
Flint .... App A – 5
Garden City .... App A – 5
Gaylord .... App A – 5
Gladstone .... App A – 5

Grand Haven .... App A – 5
Grand Rapids .... App A – 5
Grayling .... App A – 5
Greenville .... App A – 6
Groose Pointe Woods .... App A – 6
Hazel Park .... App A – 6
Highland .... App A – 6
Hillsdale .... App A – 6
Holland .... App A – 6
Howell .... App A – 6
Jackson .... App A – 6
Laingsuburg .... App A – 6
Lake Odessa .... App A – 7
Lake Orion .... App A – 7
Lansing .... App A – 7
Lapeer .... App A – 7
Leslie .... App A – 7
Lewiston .... App A – 7
Livonia .... App A – 7
Lowell .... App A – 7
Marquette .... App A – 8
Marysville .... App A – 8
Midland .... App A – 8
Milford .... App A – 8
Monroe .... App A – 8
Mount Clemens .... App A – 8
Muskegon .... App A – 8
Newberry .... App A – 8
Oscoda .... App A – 9
Paris .... App A – 9
Plainwell .... App A – 9
Plymouth .... App A – 9
Pontiac .... App A – 9
Port Huron .... App A – 9
Portage .... App A – 9
Prescott .... App A – 10
Ravenna .... App A – 10
Rockford .... App A – 10
Saginaw .... App A – 10
Saint Joseph .... App A – 10
Scottsville .... App A – 10
Shelby Township .... App A – 10
Sister Lakes .... App A – 10
South Lyon .... App A – 10
Southgate .... App A – 11
Spring Lake .... App A – 11

Sumner .... App A – 11
Temperance .... App A – 11
Traverse City .... App A – 11
Trenton .... App A – 11
Wetmore .... App A – 11
White Lake .... App A – 11
Ysilanti .... App A – 11

Appendix B – Michigan: North and West Regions Ham Licensees by City

Acme .... App B – 3
Ada .... App B – 3
Afton .... App B – 5
Alanson .... App B – 5
Albion .... App B – 5
Alden .... App B – 6
Allegan .... App B – 6
Allendale .... App B – 8
Allouez .... App B – 10
Alpena .... App B – 10
Alston .... App B – 12
Alto .... App B – 12
Amasa .... App B – 13
Arcadia .... App B – 13
Athens .... App B – 14
Atlanta .... App B – 14
Atlantic Mine .... App B – 15
Au Gres .... App B – 15
Au Train .... App B – 15
Augusta .... App B – 15
Baldwin .... App B – 16
Bandera .... App B – 16
Bangor .... App B – 16
Baraga .... App B – 17
Barbeau .... App B – 17
Bark River .... App B – 17
Baroda .... App B – 18
Barryton .... App B – 18
Barton City .... App B – 18
Bath .... App B – 18
Battle Creek .... App B – 19
Bay Mills .... App B – 27
Bear Lake .... App B – 28
Beaver Island .... App B – 28
Beaverton .... App B – 28

Belding .... App B – 29
Bellaire .... App B – 30
Bellevue .... App B – 31
Belmont .... App B – 31
Benton Harbor .... App B – 32
Benzonia .... App B – 34
Bergland .... App B – 34
Berrien Center .... App B – 34
Berrien Springs .... App B – 34
Bessemer .... App B – 37
Beulah .... App B – 38
Big Bay .... App B – 38
Big Rapids .... App B – 38
Bitely .... App B – 41
Black River .... App B – 41
Bloomingdale .... App B – 41
Bois Blanc Island .... App B – 41
Boon .... App B – 41
Boyne City .... App B – 41
Boyne Falls .... App B – 43
Branch .... App B – 43
Breedsville .... App B – 43
Brethren .... App B – 43
Bridgman .... App B – 43
Brimley .... App B – 44
Brohman .... App B – 44
Bronson .... App B – 44
Bruce Crossing .... App B – 44
Brutus .... App B – 45
Buchanan .... App B – 45
Buckley .... App B – 46
Burlington .... App B – 46
Burr Oak .... App B – 46
Byron Center .... App B – 46
Cadillac .... App B – 48
Caledonia .... App B – 51
Calumet .... App B – 52
Canadian Lakes .... App B – 54
Carney .... App B – 54
Carp Lake .... App B – 54
Carson City .... App B – 54
Cascade Township .... App B – 54
Casnovia .... App B – 54
Caspian .... App B – 54
Cassopolis .... App B – 54
Cedar .... App B – 55

Cedar Lake .... App B – 56
Cedar River .... App B – 56
Cedar Springs .... App B – 56
Cedarville .... App B – 58
Central Lake .... App B – 58
Centreville .... App B – 58
Ceresco .... App B – 58
Champion .... App B – 58
Channing .... App B – 59
Charlevoix .... App B – 59
Charlotte .... App B – 60
Chase .... App B – 62
Chassell .... App B – 62
Chatham .... App B – 63
Cheboygan .... App B – 63
Christmas .... App B – 65
Clare .... App B – 65
Clarksville .... App B – 65
Climax .... App B – 65
Coldwater .... App B – 66
Coloma .... App B – 68
Colon .... App B – 69
Comins .... App B – 69
Comstock .... App B – 69
Comstock Park .... App B – 69
Conklin .... App B – 70
Constantine .... App B – 71
Conway .... App B – 71
Cooks .... App B – 71
Coopersville .... App B – 71
Copemish .... App B – 72
Copper City .... App B – 72
Copper Harbor .... App B – 72
Coral .... App B – 72
Cornell .... App B – 72
Covert .... App B – 72
Covington .... App B – 72
Crystal .... App B – 72
Crystal Falls .... App B – 73
Curran .... App B – 73
Curtis .... App B – 74
Custer .... App B – 74
Cutlerville .... App B – 74
Dafter .... App B – 74
Daggett .... App B – 74
De Tour Village .... App B – 74

Decatur .... App B – 74
Deerton .... App B – 75
Delton .... App B – 75
Dewitt .... App B – 76
Dimondale .... App B – 77
Dodgeville .... App B – 78
Dollar Bay .... App B – 78
Dorr .... App B – 79
Douglas .... App B – 80
Dowagiac .... App B – 80
Dowling .... App B – 81
Drummond Island .... App B – 81
Eagle .... App B – 82
Eagle Harbor .... App B – 82
Eagle River .... App B – 82
East Grant Rapids .... App B – 82
East Jordan .... App B – 83
East Lake .... App B – 83
East Lansing .... App B – 83
East Leroy .... App B – 87
East Tawas .... App B – 87
Eastport .... App B – 88
Eaton Rapids .... App B – 88
Eau Claire .... App B – 90
Eben Junction .... App B – 90
Eckerman .... App B – 91
Edmore .... App B – 91
Edwardsburg .... App B – 91
Elberta .... App B – 92
Elk Rapids .... App B – 92
Ellsworth .... App B – 93
Elmira .... App B – 93
Elsie .... App B – 93
Empire .... App B – 93
Engadine .... App B – 94
Escanaba .... App B – 94
Evart .... App B – 96
Ewen .... App B – 96
Fairview .... App B – 96
Falmouth .... App B – 96
Farwell .... App B – 96
Felch .... App B – 97
Fennville .... App B – 97
Fenwick .... App B – 98
Ferrysburg .... App B – 98
Fife Lake .... App B – 98

Foster .... App B – 99
Fountain .... App B – 99
Fowler .... App B – 99
Frankfort .... App B – 99
Frederic .... App B – 100
Free Soil .... App B – 100
Freeport .... App B – 100
Fremont .... App B – 101
Fruitport .... App B – 102
Fulton .... App B – 102
Gaastra .... App B – 102
Galesburg .... App B – 103
Galien .... App B – 103
Garden .... App B – 103
Gaylord .... App B – 104
Germfask .... App B – 107
Gladstone .... App B – 108
Gladwin .... App B – 109
Glen Arbor .... App B – 112
Glenn .... App B – 112
Glennie .... App B – 112
Gobles .... App B – 112
Goetzville .... App B – 113
Good Hart .... App B – 113
Gould City .... App B – 113
Gowen .... App B – 113
Grand Beach .... App B – 113
Grand Haven .... App B – 114
Grand Junction .... App B – 118
Grand Ledge .... App B – 118
Grand Marais .... App B – 120
Grand Rapids .... App B – 121
Grandville .... App B – 144
Grant .... App B – 146
Grawn .... App B – 146
Grayling .... App B – 147
Greenbush .... App B – 149
·Greenville .... App B – 149
Gulliver .... App B – 151
Gwinn .... App B – 151
Hale .... App B – 152
Hamilton .... App B – 153
Hancock .... App B – 153
Harbert .... App B – 155
Harbor Springs .... App B – 155
Harrietta .... App B – 156

Harrison .... App B – 156
Harrisville .... App B – 157
Hart .... App B – 158
Hartford .... App B – 158
Hastings .... App B – 159
Hawks .... App B – 161
Hermansville .... App B – 161
Herron .... App B – 161
Hersey .... App B – 161
Hesperia .... App B – 161
Hessel .... App B – 162
Hickory Corners .... App B – 162
Higgins Lake .... App B – 162
Hillman .... App B – 163
Holland .... App B – 163
Holton .... App B – 170
Homer .... App B – 171
Honor .... App B – 171
Hopkins .... App B – 171
Houghton .... App B – 172
Houghton Lake .... App B – 174
Houghton Lake Heights .... App B – 175
Howard City .... App B – 175
Hubbard Lake .... App B – 176
Hubbardston .... App B – 176
Hubbell .... App B – 176
Hudsonville .... App B – 176
Idlewild .... App B – 179
Indian River .... App B – 179
Interlochen .... App B – 180
Ionia .... App B – 180
Iron Mountain .... App B – 181
Iron River .... App B – 183
Irons .... App B – 184
Ironwood .... App B – 185
Ishpeming .... App B – 185
Jenison .... App B – 188
Johannesburg .... App B – 190
Jones .... App B – 190
K I Sawyer AFB .... App B – 190
Kalamazoo .... App B – 190
Kaleva .... App B – 202
Kalkaska .... App B – 202
Karlin .... App B – 203
Kearsarge .... App B – 203
Kendall .... App B – 203

Kent .... App B – 203
Kent City .... App B – 203
Kenton .... App B – 204
Kentwood .... App B – 204
Kewadin .... App B – 207
Kincheloe .... App B – 207
Kingsford .... App B – 207
Kingsley .... App B – 208
Kinross .... App B – 209
Lachine .... App B – 209
Lake .... App B – 209
Lake Ann .... App B – 210
Lake City .... App B – 210
Lake George .... App B – 211
Lake Leelanau .... App B – 211
Lake Linden .... App B – 211
Lake Odessa .... App B – 212
Lakeview .... App B – 212
Lamont .... App B – 213
L'Anse .... App B – 213
Lansing .... App B – 213
Laurtum .... App B – 223
Lawrence .... App B – 224
Lawton .... App B – 224
Leland .... App B – 225
Leonidas .... App B – 225
Leroy .... App B – 225
Levering .... App B – 225
Lewiston .... App B – 226
Limestone .... App B – 227
Lincoln .... App B – 227
Little Lake .... App B – 227
Long Lake .... App B – 227
Loretto .... App B – 227
Lowell .... App B – 227
Ludington .... App B – 230
Lupton .... App B – 233
Luther .... App B – 233
Luzerne .... App B – 233
Lyons .... App B – 233
Macatawa .... App B – 233
Mackinac Island .... App B – 234
Mackinaw City .... App B – 234
Mancelona .... App B – 234
Manistee .... App B – 235
Manistique .... App B – 236

Manton .... App B – 236
Maple City .... App B – 237
Maple Rapids .... App B – 237
Marcellus .... App B – 237
Marenisco .... App B – 237
Marion .... App B – 238
Marne .... App B – 238
Marquette .... App B – 239
Marshall .... App B – 244
Martin .... App B – 245
Mattawan .... App B – 246
Mayfield .... App B – 246
McBain .... App B – 246
McBrides .... App B – 247
McFarland .... App B – 247
McMillan .... App B – 247
Mears .... App B – 247
Mecosta .... App B – 247
Mendon .... App B – 248
Menominee .... App B – 248
Merritt .... App B – 250
Merriweather .... App B – 250
Mesick .... App B – 250
Michigamme .... App B – 250
Middleville .... App B – 250
Mikado .... App B – 252
Millersburg .... App B – 252
Mio .... App B – 253
Mohawk .... App B – 254
Moline .... App B – 254
Montague .... App B – 254
Moran .... App B – 255
Morley .... App B – 255
Muir .... App B – 255
Mullett Lake .... App B – 255
Mulliken .... App B – 255
Munising .... App B – 256
Muskegon .... App B – 256
Muskegon Heights .... App B – 265
Nashville .... App B – 265
National City .... App B – 266
Naubinway .... App B – 266
Negaunee .... App B – 266
New Buffalo .... App B – 267
New Era .... App B – 267
Newaygo .... App B – 268

Newberry .... App B – 269
Niles .... App B – 270
North Muskegon .... App B – 274
Northport .... App B – 275
Norton Shores .... App B – 275
Norway .... App B – 276
Nunica .... App B – 276
Ocqueoc .... App B – 277
Oden .... App B – 277
Old Mission .... App B – 277
Olivet .... App B – 277
Omena .... App B – 277
Onaway .... App B – 277
Onekama .... App B – 277
Ontonagon .... App B – 277
Orleans .... App B – 278
Oscoda .... App B – 278
Oshtemo .... App B – 279
Ossineke .... App B – 279
Otsego .... App B – 280
Ovid .... App B – 280
Painesdale .... App B – 281
Palmer .... App B – 281
Paradise .... App B – 281
Parchment .... App B – 282
Paris .... App B – 282
Paw Paw .... App B – 282
Pelkie .... App B – 284
Pellston .... App B – 284
Pentwater .... App B – 284
Perkins .... App B – 284
Petoskey .... App B – 284
Pewamo .... App B – 287
Pickford .... App B – 287
Pierson .... App B – 287
Plainwell .... App B – 287
Pointe Aux Pins .... App B – 289
Port Sheldon .... App B – 289
Portage .... App B – 289
Portland .... App B – 293
Posen .... App B – 294
Potterville .... App B – 294
Powers .... App B – 294
Prescott .... App B – 294
Presque Isle .... App B – 295
Princeton .... App B – 295

Prudenville .... App B – 295
Pullman .... App B – 295
Quincy .... App B – 296
Quinnesec .... App B – 296
Ramsay .... App B – 296
Rapid City .... App B – 297
Rapid River .... App B – 297
Ravenna .... App B – 297
Reed City .... App B – 298
Remus .... App B – 299
Republic .... App B – 299
Rhodes .... App B – 299
Richland .... App B – 299
Riverside .... App B – 300
Rock .... App B – 300
Rockford .... App B – 300
Rodney .... App B – 303
Rogers City .... App B – 303
Roosevelt Park .... App B – 304
Roscommon .... App B – 304
Rose City .... App B – 305
Rothbury .... App B – 306
Rudyard .... App B – 306
Rumely .... App B – 306
Sagola .... App B – 306
Saint Helen .... App B – 307
Saint Ignace .... App B – 307
Saint Johns .... App B – 307
Saint Joseph .... App B – 309
Sand Lake .... App B – 312
Saranac .... App B – 312
Saugatuck .... App B – 313
Sault Sainte Marie .... App B – 313
Sawyer .... App B – 316
Schoolcraft .... App B – 316
Scotts .... App B – 316
Scottville .... App B – 317
Sears .... App B – 317
Seney .... App B – 317
Shelby .... App B – 317
Shelbyville .... App B – 318
Sheridan .... App B – 318
Sherwood .... App B – 319
Shingleton .... App B – 319
Sidnaw .... App B – 319
Sidney .... App B – 319

Six Lakes .... App B – 319
Skandia .... App B – 319
Skanee .... App B – 320
Sodus .... App B – 320
South Boardman .... App B – 320
South Branch .... App B – 320
South Haven .... App B – 320
South Range .... App B – 322
Spalding .... App B – 322
Sparta .... App B – 322
Spring Lake .... App B – 323
Springfield .... App B – 325
Spruce .... App B – 325
Stambaugh .... App B – 326
Standish .... App B – 326
Stanton .... App B – 327
Stanwood .... App B – 327
Stephenson .... App B – 328
Sterling .... App B – 328
Stevensville .... App B – 328
Sturgis .... App B – 330
Sunfield .... App B – 331
Suttons Bay .... App B – 332
Tawas City .... App B – 332
Tekonsha .... App B – 333
Thompson .... App B – 333
Thompsonville .... App B – 333
Three Oaks .... App B – 333
Three Rivers .... App B – 333
Toivola .... App B – 335
Topinabee .... App B – 335
Tower .... App B – 335
Traunik .... App B – 335
Traverse .... App B – 335
Traverse City .... App B – 335
Trenary .... App B – 345
Trout Creek .... App B – 345
Trout Lake .... App B – 345
Trufant .... App B – 345
Turner .... App B – 346
Tustin .... App B – 346
Twin Lake .... App B – 346
Twining .... App B – 347
Union .... App B – 348
Union City .... App B – 348
Union Pier .... App B – 348

Vandalia .... App B – 348
Vanderbilt .... App B – 348
Vermontville .... App B – 349
Vestaburg .... App B – 349
Vicksburg .... App B – 349
Vulcan .... App B – 350
WAFB Oscoda .... App B – 351
Wakefield .... App B – 351
Walhalla .... App B – 351
Walker .... App B – 351
Walkerville .... App B – 351
Wallace .... App B – 351
Walloon Lake .... App B – 352
Waters .... App B – 352
Watersmeet .... App B – 352
Watervliet .... App B – 354
Watton .... App B – 354
Wayland .... App B – 354
Wells .... App B – 355
Wellston .... App B – 355
West Branch .... App B – 355
West Olive .... App B – 357
Wetmore .... App B – 357
White Cloud .... App B – 358
White Pigeon .... App B – 358
White Pine .... App B – 359
Whitehall .... App B – 360
Whittemore .... App B – 361
Williamsburg .... App B – 361
Wilson .... App B – 363
Wolverine .... App B – 363
Woodland .... App B – 363
Wyoming .... App B – 363
Wyoming City .... App B – 368
Zeeland .... App B – 368

Survival Communications in Michigan

Perhaps you have prepared for WTSHTF or TEOTWAWKI with respect to food, water, self-defense and shelter. But what about communication?

Whenever there is a disaster (hurricane, earthquake, economic collapse, nuclear war, EMF, solar eruption, etc.), the normal means of communication that we're all reliant upon (cell phone, land line phone, the Internet, etc.) will probably be, at best, sporadic and at worst, non-existent.

As this author sees it, short of smoke signals and mirrors, there are three options for communication in "trying times": (1) GMRS or FRS radios; (2) CB radios; and (3) ham or amateur radio. Let's consider each of these options to come up with the most acceptable one.

GMRS (General Mobile Radio Service) / FRS (Family Radio Service)

GMRS (General Mobile Radio Service) / FRS (Family Radio Service) radios work optimally over short distances where there is minimal interference. Originally designed to be used as pagers, particularly inside a building or other such confined area, these radios are low-cost and convenient to carry. Unfortunately their small size and light weight comes with a trade-off – short range and short battery life. These radios are supposed to be able to communicate for up to 25-30 miles. Right. That's on level terrain, without buildings or trees getting in the way. While battery life technology is constantly improving, you will need spare batteries to keep communicating or someway of recharging the ones in the radio. In this author's opinion, GMRS/FRS radios are not first choice when concerned with medium or long range communication.

CB (Citizens Band)

CB (Citizens Band) radios operate in a frequency range originally reserved for ham or amateur radio operation. Because of the overwhelming number of people wishing quick, low-cost, regulation-free communication, the FCC (Federal Communication Commission) split off a portion of the frequency spectrum and allowed anyone to purchase a CB radio and start communicating. No test. No license. Just personal/business communication. Today, CB radios are readily available in such outlets as eBay and Craigslist. This author has seen them at yard/garage/tag sales and at flea markets.

CB radios come in a variety of "flavors." Fixed units, sometimes referred to as base units are intended for home use. For the most part, they derive their power from the utility company. In the event of loss of electricity, most base units can also be connected to a 12-volt battery, like that in your car/truck. If you choose to obtain a fixed unit, make sure you know how to connect the unit to the battery – ahead of time. Trying to figure this out when you're under extra stress is not a good situation.

A second type of CB radio is designed to be mobile, that is, installed in your car/truck. It gets its power from the vehicle's battery. You can either attach an antenna permanently to the vehicle or have a removable, magnetic type antenna.

The third type of CB radio is designed for handheld use. They are small and light. Most weigh less than a pound and operate on batteries. Yes, using batteries in a CB poses the same limitations as those by the GMRS/FRS radios, but have the added advantage that most handheld units come with a cigarette lighter adapter. Comes in handy when you are on the move and wish to be able to communicate both from a vehicle and also when you have to abandon it.

While they have a greater range than GMRS/FRS radios, CB radios are, legally, limited to operate on 40 channels, with a power rating of four (4) watts or less. Yes, it is possible to alter CB radios to get around these limitations, but not legally,

Ham/Amateur Radio

Ham/Amateur radio is very appealing. With a ham radio, you are not limited to less than 50 miles, but can communicate with anyone in the world (who also has access to a ham radio, of course).

Standardized Amateur Radio Prepper Communications Plan

In the event of a nationwide catastrophic disaster, the nationwide network of Amateur Radio licensed preppers will need a set of standardized meeting frequencies to share information and coordinate activities between various prepper groups. This Standardized Amateur Radio Communications Plan establishes a set of frequencies on the 80 meter, 40 meter, 20 meter, and 2 meter Amateur Radio bands for use during these types of catastrophic disasters.

Routine nets will not be held on all of these frequencies, but preppers are encouraged to use them when coordinating with other preppers on a routine basis. Routine nets may be conducted by The American Preparedness Radio Net (TAPRN) on these or other frequencies as they see fit. However, TAPRN will promote the use of these standardized frequencies by all Amateur Radio licensed preppers during times of catastrophic disaster. The promotion of this Standardized Amateur Radio Communications Plan is encouraged by all means within the prepper community, including via Amateur Radio, Twitter, Facebook, and various blogs.

Standardized Frequencies and Modes
80 Meters – 3.818 MHz LSB (TAPRN Net: Sundays at 9 PM ET)
40 Meters – 7.242 MHz LSB
40 Meters Morse Code / Digital – 7.073 MHz USB (TAPRN: Sundays at 7:30 PM ET on CONTESTIA 4/250)
20 Meters – 14.242 MHz USB
2 Meters – 146.420 MHz FM

Nets and Network Etiquette

In times of nationwide catastrophic disaster, the ability of any one prepper to initiate and sustain themselves as a net control may be limited by the availability of power and other resource shortages. However, all licensed preppers are encouraged to maintain a listening watch on these frequencies as often as possible during a catastrophic disaster. Preppers may routinely announce themselves in the following manner:

• This is [Your Callsign Phonetically] in [Your State], maintaining a listening watch on [Standard Frequency] for any preppers on frequency seeking information or looking to provide information. Please call [Your Callsign Phonetically]. Preppers exchanging information that may require follow up should agree upon a designated time to return to the frequency and provide further information. If other stations are utilizing the frequency at the designated time you return, maintain watch and proceed with your communications when those stations are finished. If your communications are urgent and the stations on frequency are not passing information of a critical nature, interrupt with the word "Break" and request use of the frequency.

For More Information

Catastrophe Network: http://www.catastrophenetwork.org or @CatastropheNet on Twitter The American Preparedness Radio Network: http://www.taprn.com or @TAPRN on Twitter

In order to use a ham radio, legally, one must be licensed to do so by the FCC (other countries have analogous governmental bodies to regulate ham radio). To obtain a license is quite easy – take a test and pay your license fee. There are currently three classes of license – Technician, General, and Amateur Extra. With each of these licenses come specific abilities.

Technician class is the beginning level. The exam consists of 35 multiple choice questions randomly drawn from a pool of 395 questions. The question pool is readily available online for free downloading (http://www.ncvec.org/downloads/Revised%20Element%202.Pdf) or in such publications at *Ham Radio License Manual Revised 2nd Edition* (ISBN 978-0-87259-097-7). The current Technician pool of questions is to be used from July 1, 2010 to June 30, 2014. Be sure the question pool you are studying from is current. You will need to score at least 26 correct to pass. (Do not worry, Morse Code is no longer on the test, although many ham operators use it anyway.) You do not need to take a formal class in order to qualify to take the exam. You can learn the material on your own. Most people spend 10-15 hours studying and then successfully take the exam. The cost of taking the exam is under $20. The exam is given in MANY locations throughout the US. Usually the exam is given by area ham clubs. You do not have to belong to the club to take the exam. Check Appendix A for a listing of clubs in Michigan.

Topics for the Technician License in Amateur Radio

The Technician license exam covers such topics as basic regulations, operating practices, and electronic theory, with a focus on VHF and UHF applications. Below is the syllabus for the Technician Class.

Subelement T1 – FCC Rules, descriptions and definitions for the amateur radio service, operator and station license responsibilities

[6 Exam Questions – 6 Groups]

T1A – Amateur Radio services; purpose of the amateur service, amateur-satellite service, operator/primary station license grant, where FCC rules are codified, basis and purpose of FCC rules, meanings of basic terms used in FCC rules

T1B – Authorized frequencies; frequency allocations, ITU regions, emission type, restricted sub-bands, spectrum sharing, transmissions near band edges

T1C – Operator classes and station call signs; operator classes, sequential, special event, and vanity call sign systems, international communications, reciprocal operation, station license licensee, places where the amateur service is regulated by the FCC, name and address on ULS, license term, renewal, grace period

T1D – Authorized and prohibited transmissions

T1E – Control operator and control types; control operator required, eligibility, designation of control operator, privileges and duties, control point, local, automatic and remote control, location of control operator

T1F – Station identification and operation standards; special operations for repeaters and auxiliary stations, third party communications, club stations, station security, FCC inspection

---

Subelement T2 – Operating Procedures

[3 Exam Questions – 3 Groups]

T2A – Station operation; choosing an operating frequency, calling another station, test transmissions, use of minimum power, frequency use, band plans

T2B – VHF/UHF operating practices; SSB phone, FM repeater, simplex, frequency offsets, splits and shifts, CTCSS, DTMF, tone squelch, carrier squelch, phonetics

T2C – Public service; emergency and non-emergency operations, message traffic handling

---

Subelement T3 – Radio wave characteristics, radio and electromagnetic properties, propagation modes

[3 Exam Questions – 3 Groups]

T3A – Radio wave characteristics; how a radio signal travels; distinctions of HF, VHF and UHF; fading, multipath; wavelength vs. penetration; antenna orientation

T3B – Radio and electromagnetic wave properties; the electromagnetic spectrum, wavelength vs. frequency, velocity of electromagnetic waves

T3C – Propagation modes; line of sight, sporadic E, meteor, aurora scatter, tropospheric ducting, F layer skip, radio horizon

Subelement T4 - Amateur radio practices and station setup

[2 Exam Questions – 2 Groups]

T4A – Station setup; microphone, speaker, headphones, filters, power source, connecting a computer, RF grounding

T4B – Operating controls; tuning, use of filters, squelch, AGC, repeater offset, memory channels

Subelement T5 – Electrical principles, math for electronics, electronic principles, Ohm's Law

[4 Exam Questions – 4 Groups]

T5A – Electrical principles; current and voltage, conductors and insulators, alternating and direct current

T5B – Math for electronics; decibels, electronic units and the metric system

T5C – Electronic principles; capacitance, inductance, current flow in circuits, alternating current, definition of RF, power calculations

T5D – Ohm's Law

Subelement T6 – Electrical components, semiconductors, circuit diagrams, component functions

[4 Exam Groups – 4 Questions]

T6A – Electrical components; fixed and variable resistors, capacitors, and inductors; fuses, switches, batteries

T6B – Semiconductors; basic principles of diodes and transistors

T6C – Circuit diagrams; schematic symbols

T6D – Component functions

Subelement T7 – Station equipment, common transmitter and receiver problems, antenna measurements and troubleshooting, basic repair and testing

[4 Exam Questions – 4 Groups]

T7A – Station radios; receivers, transmitters, transceivers

T7B – Common transmitter and receiver problems; symptoms of overload and overdrive, distortion, interference, over and under modulation, RF feedback, off frequency signals; fading and noise; problems with digital communications interfaces

T7C – Antenna measurements and troubleshooting; measuring SWR, dummy loads, feedline failure modes

T7D – Basic repair and testing; soldering, use of a voltmeter, ammeter, and ohmmeter

Subelement T8 – Modulation modes, amateur satellite operation, operating activities, non-voice communications

[4 Exam Questions – 4 Groups]

T8A – Modulation modes; bandwidth of various signals

T8B – Amateur satellite operation; Doppler shift, basic orbits, operating protocols

T8C – Operating activities; radio direction finding, radio control, contests, special event stations, basic linking over Internet

T8D – Non-voice communications; image data, digital modes, CW, packet, PSK31

Subelement T9 – Antennas, feedlines

[2 Exam Groups – 2 Questions]

T9A – Antennas; vertical and horizontal, concept of gain, common portable and mobile antennas, relationships between antenna length and frequency

T9B – Feedlines; types, losses vs. frequency, SWR concepts, matching, weather protection, connectors

Subelement T0 – AC power circuits, antenna installation, RF hazards

[3 Exam Questions – 3 Groups]

T0A – AC power circuits; hazardous voltages, fuses and circuit breakers, grounding, lightning protection, battery safety, electrical code compliance

T0B – Antenna installation; tower safety, overhead power lines

T0C – RF hazards; radiation exposure, proximity to antennas, recognized safe power levels, exposure to others

Once your name and call sign are available in the FCC database, you have the privilege of operating on all VHF (2 m) and UHF (70 cm) frequencies above 30 megahertz (MHz) and HF frequencies 80, 40, and 15 meter, and on the 10 meter band using Morse code (CW), voice, and digital mode. For a Technician license in Michigan, your call sign will consist of a two-letter prefix beginning with K or W, the number eight (8), and a three-letter suffix. The single digit number in the call sign is determined according to which area of the US you obtain your first license. Even though you may move to another state, you keep this number in your call sign. This is also true should you upgrade to a higher license and get a new call sign. The numeral portion of your call sign stays the same.

Call Sign Numbers

Below is a chart showing the various numbers and the state(s) in which you would obtain the number.

Call Sign Number	State(s)
0	CO, IA, KS, MN, MO, NE, ND, SD
1	CT, ME, MA, NH, RI, VT
2	NJ, NY
3	DE, DC, MD, PA
4	AL, FL, GA, KY, NC, SC, TN, VA
5	AR, LA, MS, NM, OK, TX
6	CA
7	AZ, ID, MT, NV, OR, WA, UT, WY
8	MI, OH, WV
9	IL, IN, WI

Residents of Alaska may have any of the following call sign prefixes assigned to them: AL0-7, KL0-7, NL0-7, or WL0-7. Likewise, residents of Hawaii may have the prefix AH6-7, KH6-7, NH6-7, or WH6-7 assigned.

Once you obtain your Technician license, do not stop there. Go and get your General license.

General is the second of three ham license classes. Like the Technician license, to get a General license, you merely have to take a 35-question multiple choice exam and pay your license fee. Passing is still at least 26 correct answers and the fee is the same (less than $20). Again the question pool is available for free online (http://www.ncvec.org/page.php?id=358). It is also available in such print publications as *The ARRL General Class License Manual 7th Edition* (ISBN 978-0-87259-811-9). The current General pool of questions is to be used from July 1, 2011 to June 30, 2015. Be sure the question pool you are using is current. Being a bit more comprehensive than the Technician license, the General license usually requires 15-20 hours of study to learn the material. Check Appendix A for a listing of clubs in Michigan where you might take your exam. Once your name and NEW call sign is listed in the FCC database, you're good to go. For a General license in Michigan, your call sign will consist of a one-letter prefix beginning with K, N or W, the number eight (8), and a three-letter suffix.

Topics for the General License in Amateur Radio

The General license exam covers regulations, operating practices and electronic theory. Below is the syllabus for the General Class.

Subelement G1 – Commission's Rules
(5 Exam Questions – 5 Groups)
G1A – General Class control operator frequency privileges; primary and secondary allocations
G1B – Antenna structure limitations; good engineering and good amateur practice, beacon operation; restricted operation; retransmitting radio signals
G1C – Transmitter power regulations; data emission standards
G1D – Volunteer Examiners and Volunteer Examiner Coordinators; temporary identification
G1E – Control categories; repeater regulations; harmful interference; third party rules; ITU regions

Subelement G2 – Operating procedures
(5 Exam Questions – 5 Groups)
G2A – Phone operating procedures; USB/LSB utilization conventions; procedural signals; breaking into a OSO in progress; VOX operation
G2B – Operating courtesy; band plans, emergencies, including drills and emergency communications
G2C – CW operating procedures and procedural signals; Q signals and common abbreviations; full break in
G2D – Amateur Auxiliary; minimizing interference; HF operations

G2E – Digital operating; procedures, procedural signals and common abbreviations

Subelement G3 – Radio wave propagation

(3 Exam Questions – 3 Groups)
G3A – Sunspots and solar radiation; ionospheric disturbances; propagation forecasting and indices
G3B – Maximum Usable Frequency; Lowest Usable Frequency; propagation
G3C – Ionospheric layers; critical angle and frequency; HF scatter; Near Vertical Incidence Sky waves

Subelement G4 – Amateur radio practices

(5 Exam Questions – 5 Groups)
G4A – Station Operation and setup
G4B – Test and monitoring equipment; two-tone test
G4C – Interference with consumer electronics; grounding; DSP
G4D – Speech processors; S meters; sideband operation near band edges
G4E – HF mobile radio installations; emergency and battery powered operation

Subelement G5 – Electrical principles

(3 Exam Questions – 3 Groups)
G5A – Reactance; inductance; capacitance; impedance; impedance matching
G5B – The Decibel; current and voltage dividers; electrical power calculations; sine wave root-mean-square (RMS) values; PEP calculations
G5C – Resistors; capacitors and inductors in series and parallel; transformers

Subelement G6 – Circuit components

(3 Exam Questions – 3 Groups)
G6A – Resistors; capacitors; inductors
G6B – Rectifiers; solid state diodes and transistors; vacuum tubes; batteries
G6C – Analog and digital integrated circuits (ICs); microprocessors; memory; I/O devices; microwave ICs (MMICs); display devices

Subelement G7 – Practical circuits

(3 Exam Questions – 3 Groups)
G7A – Power supplies; schematic symbols
G7B – Digital circuits; amplifiers and oscillators
G7C – Receivers and transmitters; filters, oscillators

Subelement G8 – Signals and emissions

(2 Exam Questions – 2 Groups)

G8A – Carriers and modulation; AM; FM; single and double sideband; modulation envelope; overmodulation
G8B – Frequency mixing; multiplication; HF data communications; bandwidths of various modes; deviation

Subelement G9 – Antennas and feed lines
(4 Exam Questions – 4 Groups)
G9A – Antenna feed lines; characteristic impedance and attenuation; SWR calculation, measurement and effects; matching networks
G9B – Basic antennas
G9C – Directional antennas
G9D – Specialized antennas

Subelement G0 – Electrical and RF safety
(2 Exam Questions – 2 Groups)
G0A – RF safety principles, rules and guidelines; routine station elevation
G0B – Safety in the ham shack; electrical shock and treatment, safety grounding, fusing, interlocks, wiring, antenna and tower safety

With a General license, you can use all VHF and UHF frequencies and most of the HF frequencies. You would have access to the 160, 30, 17, 12, and 10 meter bands and access to major parts of the 80, 40, 20, and 15 meter bands. Of course, this is in addition to all bands available to Technician license holders.

Amateur Extra is the third of three ham license classes. Like the Technician and General classes, you merely have to pass a test and pay your fee to get your Amateur Extra license. This class of license is more comprehensive than the lower license classes. The exam is longer – 50 questions – and the minimum passing score is higher – 37. However, once you get your Amateur Extra license, all ham frequencies, VHF, UHF and HF are available for your enjoyment. The Extra exam covers regulations, specialized operating practices, advanced electronics theory, and radio equipment design.

Like for the other license classes, the question pool for the Amateur Extra license is available online for downloading (http://www.ncvec.org/downloads/REVISED%202012-2016%20Extra%20Class%20Pool.doc). It is also available in print form in such publications as *The ARRL Extra Class License Manual Revised 9th Edition* (ISBN 978-0-87259-887-4).

Topics for the Extra License in Amateur Radio

Below is the syllabus for the Amateur Extra Class for July 1, 2012 to June 30, 2016.

Subelement E1 – Commission's Rules
[6 Exam Questions – 6 Groups]
E1A – Operating Standards: frequency privileges; emission standards; automatic message forwarding; frequency sharing; stations aboard ships or aircraft

E1B – Station restrictions and special operations: restrictions on station location; general operating restrictions, spurious emissions, control operator reimbursement; antenna structure restrictions; RACES operations

E1C – Station control: definitions and restrictions pertaining to local, automatic and re-mote control operation; control operator responsibilities for remote and automatically controlled stations

E1D – Amateur Satellite service: definitions and purpose; license requirements for space stations; available frequencies and bands; telecommand and telemetry operations; re-strictions, and special provisions; notification requirements

E1E – Volunteer examiner program: definitions, qualifications, preparation and admin-istration of exams; accreditation; question pools; documentation requirements

E1F – Miscellaneous rules: external RF power amplifiers; national quiet zone; business communications; compensated communications; spread spectrum; auxiliary stations; reciprocal operating privileges; IARP and CEPT licenses; third party communications with foreign countries; special temporary authority

Subelement E2 – Operating procedures

[5 Exam Questions – 5 Groups]

E2A – Amateur radio in space: amateur satellites; orbital mechanics; frequencies and modes; satellite hardware; satellite operations

E2B – Television practices: fast scan television standards and techniques; slow scan tele-vision standards and techniques

E2C – Operating methods: contest and DX operating; spread-spectrum transmissions; selecting an operating frequency

E2D – Operating methods: VHF and UHF digital modes; APRS

E2E – Operating methods: operating HF digital modes; error correction

Subelement E3 – Radio wave propagation

[3 Exam Questions – 3 Groups]

E3A – Propagation and technique, Earth-Moon-Earth communications; meteor scatter

E3B – Propagation and technique, trans-equatorial; long path; gray-line; multi-path prop-agation

E3C – Propagation and technique, Aurora propagation; selective fading; radio-path hori-zon; take-off angle over flat or sloping terrain; effects of ground on propagation; less common propagation modes

Subelement E4 – Amateur practices

[5 Exam Questions – 5 Groups]

E4A – Test equipment: analog and digital instruments; spectrum and network analyzers, antenna analyzers; oscilloscopes; testing transistors; RF measurements

E4B – Measurement technique and limitations: instrument accuracy and performance limitations; probes; techniques to minimize errors; measurement of "Q"; instrument calibration

E4C – Receiver performance characteristics, phase noise, capture effect, noise floor, image rejection, MDS, signal-to-noise-ratio; selectivity

E4D – Receiver performance characteristics, blocking dynamic range, intermodulation and cross-modulation interference; 3rd order intercept; desensitization; preselection

E4E – Noise suppression: system noise; electrical appliance noise; line noise; locating noise sources; DSP noise reduction; noise blankers

Subelement E5 – Electrical principles

[4 Exam Questions – 4 Groups]

E5A – Resonance and Q: characteristics of resonant circuits: series and parallel resonance; Q; half-power bandwidth; phase relationships in reactive circuits

E5B – Time constants and phase relationships: RLC time constants: definition; time constants in RL and RC circuits; phase angle between voltage and current; phase angles of series and parallel circuits

E5C – Impedance plots and coordinate systems: plotting impedances in polar coordinates; rectangular coordinates

E5D – AC and RF energy in real circuits: skin effect; electrostatic and electromagnetic fields; reactive power; power factor; coordinate systems

Subelement E6 – Circuit components

[6 Exam Questions – 6 Groups]

E6A – Semiconductor materials and devices: semiconductor materials germanium, silicon, P-type, N-type; transistor types: NPN, PNP, junction, field-effect transistors: enhancement mode; depletion mode; MOS; CMOS; N-channel; P-channel

E6B – Semiconductor diodes

E6C – Integrated circuits: TTL digital integrated circuits; CMOS digital integrated circuits; gates

E6D – Optical devices and toroids: cathode-ray tube devices; charge-coupled devices (CCDs); liquid crystal displays (LCDs); toroids: permeability, core material, selecting, winding

E6E – Piezoelectric crystals and MMICs: quartz crystals; crystal oscillators and filters; monolithic amplifiers

E6F – Optical components and power systems: photoconductive principles and effects, photovoltaic systems, optical couplers, optical sensors, and optoisolators

Subelement E7 – Practical circuits

[8 Exam Questions – 8 Groups]

E7A – Digital circuits: digital circuit principles and logic circuits: classes of logic elements; positive and negative logic; frequency dividers; truth tables

E7B – Amplifiers: Class of operation; vacuum tube and solid-state circuits; distortion and intermodulation; spurious and parasitic suppression; microwave amplifiers

E7C – Filters and matching networks: filters and impedance matching networks: types of networks; types of filters; filter applications; filter characteristics; impedance matching; DSP filtering

E7D – Power supplies and voltage regulators

E7E – Modulation and demodulation: reactance, phase and balanced modulators; detectors; mixer stages; DSP modulation and demodulation; software defined radio systems

E7F – Frequency markers and counters: frequency divider circuits; frequency marker generators; frequency counters

E7G – Active filters and op-amps: active audio filters; characteristics; basic circuit design; operational amplifiers

E7H – Oscillators and signal sources: types of oscillators; synthesizers and phase-locked loops; direct digital synthesizers

Subelement E8 – Signals and emissions

[4 Exam Questions – 4 Groups]

E8A – AC waveforms: sine, square, sawtooth and irregular waveforms; AC measurements; average and PEP of RF signals; pulse and digital signal waveforms

E8B – Modulation and demodulation: modulation methods; modulation index and deviation ratio; pulse modulation; frequency and time division multiplexing

E8C – Digital signals: digital communications modes; CW; information rate vs. bandwidth; spread-spectrum communications; modulation methods

E8D – Waves, measurements, and RF grounding: peak-to-peak values, polarization; RF grounding

Subelement E9 – Antennas and transmission lines

[8 Exam Questions – 8 Groups]

E9A – Isotropic and gain antennas: definition; used as a standard for comparison; radiation pattern; basic antenna parameters: radiation resistance and reactance, gain, beamwidth, efficiency

E9B – Antenna patterns: E and H plane patterns; gain as a function of pattern; antenna design; Yagi antennas

E9C – Wire and phased vertical antennas: beverage antennas; terminated and resonant rhombic antennas; elevation above real ground; ground effects as related to polarization; take-off angles

E9D – Directional antennas: gain; satellite antennas; antenna beamwidth; losses; SWR bandwidth; antenna efficiency; shortened and mobile antennas; grounding

E9E – Matching: matching antennas to feed lines; power dividers

E9F – Transmission lines: characteristics of open and shorted feed lines: 1/8 wavelength; 1/4 wavelength; 1/2 wavelength; feed lines: coax versus open-wire; velocity factor; electrical length; transformation characteristics of line terminated in impedance not equal to characteristic impedance

E9G – The Smith chart

E9H – Effective radiated power; system gains and losses; radio direction finding antennas

Subelement E0 – Safety

[1 exam question – 1 group]

E0A – Safety: amateur radio safety practices; RF radiation hazards; hazardous materials

Once your new call sign is listed in the FCC database, you are good to go. For an Amateur Extra license in Michigan, your call sign will consist of a prefix of K, N or W, the number eight (8), and a two-letter suffix, or a two-letter prefix beginning with A, N, K or W, the number eight (8), and a one-letter suffix, or a two-letter prefix beginning with A, the number eight (8), and a two-letter suffix.

Ham radio equipment can be expensive or you can do it "on the cheap." The cost will run from a couple hundred dollars to well in the thousands, depending on what you have available. eBay, and Craigslist are good places to start looking. Most ham clubs do some sort of hamfest annually wherein club members or others are willing to part with older equipment. See Appendix A for a list of clubs in Michigan.

Another excellent source of equipment, as well as advice on setting the equipment up and how to use it properly, is current ham operators. In Appendix B, the author has listed all the FCC licensed ham operators in Michigan, listed by city, and then sorted by street and house number on the street. Who knows, maybe someone who lives close to you is a ham operator. Be a good neighbor, stop by and have a chat with him/her.

Like CB radios, ham radios come in three formats – base, mobile, and handheld. They can use the electric company for power, or operate off a car battery. In the opinion of this author, in spite of the slightly higher cost of the equipment and having to take a test to legally use the equipment, ham radio is the way to go when concerned about communication during times of crisis.

Canadian Call Sign Prefixes

Because of our proximity to Canada, many times ham contact is made with our northern neighbors. Below is a chart showing the origin of Canadian call sign prefixes.

Call Sign Prefix	Provence or Territory
CY0	Sable Island
CY9	St. Paul Island
VA1, VE1	New Brunswick, Nova Scotia
VA2, VE2	Quebec
VA3, VE3	Ontario
VA4, VE4	Manitoba
VA5, VE5	Saskatchewan
VA6, VE6	Alberta
VA7, VE7	British Columbia
VE8	North West Territories
VE9	New Brunswick
VO1	Newfoundland
VO2	Labrador
VY0	Nunavut
VY1	Yukon
VY2	Prince Edward Island

Common Radio Bands in the United States

Certain radio bands are more popular with ham radio enthusiasts than others. Below is a chart showing these bands and when they are most popular.

	Band (meter)	Frequency (MHz)	Use
HF	160	1.8 – 2.0	Night
	80	3.5 – 4.0	Night and Local Day
	40	7.0 – 7.3	Night and Local Day
	30	10.1 – 10.15	CW and Digital
	20	14.0 – 14.350	World Wide Day and Night
	17	18.068 – 18.168	World Wide Day and Night
	15	21.0 – 21.450	Primarily Daytime
	12	24.890 – 24.990	Primarily Daytime
	10	28.0 – 29.70	Daytime during Sunspot highs
VHF	6	50 – 54	Local to World Wide
	2	144 – 148	Local to Medium Distance
UHF	70 cm	430 – 440	Local

Common Amateur Radio Bands in Canada

160 Meter Band - Maximum bandwidth 6 kHz

1.800 - 1.820 MHz - CW
1.820 - 1.830 MHz - Digital Modes
1 830 - 1.840 MHz - DX Window
1.840 - 2.000 MHz - SSB and other wide band modes

80 Meter Band - Maximum bandwidth 6 kHz

3.500 - 3.580 MHz - CW
3.580 - 3.620 MHz - Digital Modes
3.620 - 3.635 MHz - Packet/Digital Secondary
3.635 - 3.725 MHz - CW
3.725 - 3.790 MHz - SSB and other side band modes*
3.790 - 3.800 MHz - SSB DX Window
3.800 - 4.000 MHz - SSB and other wide band modes

40 Meter Band - Maximum bandwidth 6 kHz

7.000 - 7.035 MHz - CW
7.035 - 7.050 MHz - Digital Modes
7.040 - 7.050 MHz - International packet
7.050 - 7.100 MHz - SSB
7.100 - 7.120 MHz - Packet within Region 2
7.120 - 7.150 MHz - CW
7.150 - 7.300 MHz - SSB and other wide band modes

30 Meter Band - Maximum bandwidth 1 kHz
10.100 - 10.130 MHz - CW only
10.130 - 10.140 MHz - Digital Modes
10.140 - 10.150 MHz - Packet

20 Meter Band - Maximum bandwidth 6 kHz
14.000 - 14.070 MHz - CW only
14.070 - 14.095 MHz - Digital Mode
14.095 - 14.099 MHz - Packet
14.100 MHz - Beacons
14.101 - 14.112 MHz - CW, SSB, packet shared
14.112 - 14.350 MHz - SSB
14.225 - 14.235 MHz - SSTV

17 Meter Band - Maximum bandwidth 6 kHz
18.068 - 18.100 MHz - CW
18.100 - 18.105 MHz - Digital Modes
18.105 - 18.110 MHz - Packet
18.110 - 18.168 MHz - SSB and other wide band modes

15 Meter Band - maximum bandwidth 6 kHz
21.000 - 21.070 MHz - CW
21.070 - 21.090 MHz - Digital Modes
21.090 - 21.125 MHz - Packet
21.100 - 21.150 MHz - CW and SSB
21.150 - 21.335 MHz - SSB and other wide band modes
21.335 - 21.345 MHz - SSTV
21.345 - 21.450 MHz - SSB and other wide band modes

12 Meter Band - Maximum bandwidth 6 kHz
24.890 - 24.930 MHz - CW
24.920 - 24.925 MHz - Digital Modes
24.925 - 24.930 MHz - Packet
24.930 - 24.990 MHz - SSB and other wide band modes

10 Meter Band - Maximum band width 20 kHz
28.000 - 28.200 MHz - CW
28.070 - 28.120 MHz - Digital Modes
28.120 - 28.190 MHz - Packet
28.190 - 28.200 MHz - Beacons
28.200 - 29.300 MHz - SSB and other wide band modes
29.300 - 29.510 MHz - Satellite
29.510 - 29.700 MHz - SSB, FM and repeaters

160 Meters (1.8-2.0 MHz)

1.800 - 2.000 CW
1.800 - 1.810 Digital Modes
1.810 CW QRP
1.843-2.000 SSB, SSTV and other wideband modes
1.910 SSB QRP
1.995 - 2.000 Experimental
1.999 - 2.000 Beacons

80 Meters (3.5-4.0 MHz)

3.590 RTTY/Data DX
3.570-3.600 RTTY/Data
3.790-3.800 DX window
3.845 SSTV
3.885 AM calling frequency

40 Meters (7.0-7.3 MHz)

7.040 RTTY/Data DX
7.080-7.125 RTTY/Data
7.171 SSTV
7.290 AM calling frequency

30 Meters (10.1-10.15 MHz)

10.130-10.140 RTTY
10.140-10.150 Packet

20 Meters (14.0-14.35 MHz)

14.070-14.095 RTTY
14.095-14.0995 Packet
14.100 NCDXF Beacons
14.1005-14.112 Packet
14.230 SSTV
14.286 AM calling frequency

17 Meters (18.068-18.168 MHz)

18.100-18.105 RTTY
18.105-18.110 Packet

15 Meters (21.0-21.45 MHz)

21.070-21.110 RTTY/Data
21.340 SSTV

12 Meters (24.89-24.99 MHz)

24.920-24.925 RTTY
24.925-24.930 Packet

10 Meters (28-29.7 MHz)

28.000-28.070 CW
28.070-28.150 RTTY
28.150-28.190 CW
28.200-28.300 Beacons
28.300-29.300 Phone
28.680 SSTV
29.000-29.200 AM
29.300-29.510 Satellite Downlinks
29.520-29.590 Repeater Inputs
29.600 FM Simplex
29.610-29.700 Repeater Outputs

6 Meters (50-54 MHz)

50.0-50.1 CW, beacons
50.060-50.080 beacon subband
50.1-50.3 SSB, CW
50.10-50.125 DX window
50.125 SSB calling
50.3-50.6 All modes
50.6-50.8 Nonvoice communications
50.62 Digital (packet) calling
50.8-51.0 Radio remote control (20-kHz channels)
51.0-51.1 Pacific DX window
51.12-51.48 Repeater inputs (19 channels)
51.12-51.18 Digital repeater inputs
51.5-51.6 Simplex (six channels)
51.62-51.98 Repeater outputs (19 channels)
51.62-51.68 Digital repeater outputs
52.0-52.48 Repeater inputs (except as noted; 23 channels)
52.02, 52.04 FM simplex
52.2 TEST PAIR (input)
52.5-52.98 Repeater output (except as noted; 23 channels)
52.525 Primary FM simplex
52.54 Secondary FM simplex
52.7 TEST PAIR (output)
53.0-53.48 Repeater inputs (except as noted; 19 channels)
53.0 Remote base FM simplex
53.02 Simplex
53.1, 53.2, 53.3, 53.4 Radio remote control
53.5-53.98 Repeater outputs (except as noted; 19 channels)
53.5, 53.6, 53.7, 53.8 Radio remote control
53.52, 53.9 Simplex

2 Meters (144-148 MHz)

144.00-144.05 EME (CW)
144.05-144.10 General CW and weak signals
144.10-144.20 EME and weak-signal SSB
144.200 National calling frequency
144.200-144.275 General SSB operation
144.275-144.300 Propagation beacons
144.30-144.50 New OSCAR subband
144.50-144.60 Linear translator inputs
144.60-144.90 FM repeater inputs
144.90-145.10 Weak signal and FM simplex (145.01,03,05,07,09 are widely used for packet)
145.10-145.20 Linear translator outputs
145.20-145.50 FM repeater outputs
145.50-145.80 Miscellaneous and experimental modes
145.80-146.00 OSCAR subband
146.01-146.37 Repeater inputs
146.40-146.58 Simplex
146.52 National Simplex Calling Frequency
146.61-146.97 Repeater outputs
147.00-147.39 Repeater outputs
147.42-147.57 Simplex
147.60-147.99 Repeater inputs

1.25 Meters (222-225 MHz)

222.0-222.150 Weak-signal modes
222.0-222.025 EME
222.05-222.06 Propagation beacons
222.1 SSB & CW calling frequency
222.10-222.15 Weak-signal CW & SSB
222.15-222.25 Local coordinator's option; weak signal, ACSB, repeater inputs, control
222.25-223.38 FM repeater inputs only
223.40-223.52 FM simplex
223.52-223.64 Digital, packet
223.64-223.70 Links, control
223.71-223.85 Local coordinator's option; FM simplex, packet, repeater outputs
223.85-224.98 Repeater outputs only

70 Centimeters (420-450 MHz)

420.00-426.00 ATV repeater or simplex with 421.25 MHz video carrier control links and experimental
426.00-432.00 ATV simplex with 427.250-MHz video carrier frequency
432.00-432.07 EME (Earth-Moon-Earth)
432.07-432.10 Weak-signal CW
432.10 70-cm calling frequency

432.10-432.30 Mixed-mode and weak-signal work
432.30-432.40 Propagation beacons
432.40-433.00 Mixed-mode and weak-signal work
433.00-435.00 Auxiliary/repeater links
435.00-438.00 Satellite only (internationally)
438.00-444.00 ATV repeater input with 439.250-MHz video carrier frequency and repeater links
442.00-445.00 Repeater inputs and outputs (local option)
445.00-447.00 Shared by auxiliary and control links, repeaters and simplex (local option)
446.00 National simplex frequency
447.00-450.00 Repeater inputs and outputs (local option)

33 Centimeters (902-928 MHz)

902.0-903.0 Narrow-bandwidth, weak-signal communications
902.0-902.8 SSTV, FAX, ACSSB, experimental
902.1 Weak-signal calling frequency
902.8-903.0 Reserved for EME, CW expansion
903.1 Alternate calling frequency
903.0-906.0 Digital communications
906-909 FM repeater inputs
909-915 ATV
915-918 Digital communications
918-921 FM repeater outputs
921-927 ATV
927-928 FM simplex and links

23 Centimeters (1240-1300 MHz)

1240-1246 ATV #1
1246-1248 Narrow-bandwidth FM point-to-point links and digital, duplex with 1258-
  1260.
1248-1258 Digital Communications
1252-1258 ATV #2
1258-1260 Narrow-bandwidth FM point-to-point links digital, duplexed with 1246-1252
1260-1270 Satellite uplinks, reference WARC '79
1260-1270 Wide-bandwidth experimental, simplex ATV
1270-1276 Repeater inputs, FM and linear, paired with 1282-1288, 239 pairs every 25
  kHz, e.g. 1270.025, .050, etc.
1271-1283 Non-coordinated test pair
1276-1282 ATV #3
1282-1288 Repeater outputs, paired with 1270-1276
1288-1294 Wide-bandwidth experimental, simplex ATV
1294-1295 Narrow-bandwidth FM simplex services, 25-kHz channels
1294.5 National FM simplex calling frequency
1295-1297 Narrow bandwidth weak-signal communications (no FM)
1295.0-1295.8 SSTV, FAX, ACSSB, experimental
1295.8-1296.0 Reserved for EME, CW expansion

1296.00-1296.05 EME-exclusive
1296.07-1296.08 CW beacons
1296.1 CW, SSB calling frequency
1296.4-1296.6 Crossband linear translator input
1296.6-1296.8 Crossband linear translator output
1296.8-1297.0 Experimental beacons (exclusive)
1297-1300 Digital Communications

2300-2310 and 2390-2450 MHz

2300.0-2303.0 High-rate data
2303.0-2303.5 Packet
2303.5-2303.8 TTY packet
2303.9-2303.9 Packet, TTY, CW, EME
2303.9-2304.1 CW, EME
2304.1 Calling frequency
2304.1-2304.2 CW, EME, SSB
2304.2-2304.3 SSB, SSTV, FAX, Packet AM, Amtor
2304.30-2304.32 Propagation beacon network
2304.32-2304.40 General propagation beacons
2304.4-2304.5 SSB, SSTV, ACSSB, FAX, Packet AM, Amtor experimental
2304.5-2304.7 Crossband linear translator input
2304.7-2304.9 Crossband linear translator output
2304.9-2305.0 Experimental beacons
2305.0-2305.2 FM simplex (25 kHz spacing)
2305.20 FM simplex calling frequency
2305.2-2306.0 FM simplex (25 kHz spacing)
2306.0-2309.0 FM Repeaters (25 kHz) input
2309.0-2310.0 Control and auxiliary links
2390.0-2396.0 Fast-scan TV
2396.0-2399.0 High-rate data
2399.0-2399.5 Packet
2399.5-2400.0 Control and auxiliary links
2400.0-2403.0 Satellite
2403.0-2408.0 Satellite high-rate data
2408.0-2410.0 Satellite
2410.0-2413.0 FM repeaters (25 kHz) output
2413.0-2418.0 High-rate data
2418.0-2430.0 Fast-scan TV
2430.0-2433.0 Satellite
2433.0-2438.0 Satellite high-rate data
2438.0-2450.0 WB FM, FSTV, FMTV, SS experimental

3300-3500 MHz

3456.3-3456.4 Propagation beacons

5650-5925 MHz
5760.3-5760.4 Propagation beacons

10.00-10.50 GHz
10.368 Narrow band calling frequency 10.3683-10.3684 Propagation beacons 10.3640 Calling frequency

Now that you have your license (you do, don't you?), and your equipment, you are ready to go live. Below is a suggested start.

1) Assuming you have the HT set up to the appropriate frequency, and offset, press the mic button on the HT and say, "KK4HWX listening." Replace the KK4HWX with your own call sign, the one assigned to you by the FCC (it's the law). If no one responds to your call, you may wish to try again. Hopefully someone will respond to your call.

2) Once you get a response, it will be in the form of something like, "KK4HWX this is ??1??? in Eastport returning. My name is Florence. Back to you. ??1???" then a tone. Let us examine the response more closely. She first acknowledged your call sign (KK4HWX), then identified hers (??1???). From the 1 in her call sign, you know that she first got her license in Region 1, meaning she got it while a resident of CT, ME, MA, NH, RI, or VT. She then told you where she's transmitting from (Eastport). The term "returning" means that she is returning your call. Her name is Florence. The phrase, "Back to you" indicates that she is turning over the conversation to you. She then repeats her call sign. The tone indicates to you that it is okay to proceed with your response. BTW if she had used the term "Over" instead of "Back to you," it would mean the same thing, just fewer words.

3) At this point, press the mic button and continue with the conversation. You should restate your call sign often during the conversation (perhaps every 10 minutes or less and whenever you begin transmitting). Don't forget to say, "Over" or "Back to you" whenever you are giving Florence control of the conversation again.

4) When you are ready to stop the conversation, you should say goodbye or use the phrase "73", meaning "best wishes." Your conversation would end something like, "??1??? 73, this is KK4HWX clear and monitoring." The "clear and monitoring" indicates that you are going to continue to monitor the frequency. If you are not going to continue monitoring, you may wish to end the conversation with Florence with, "clear and QRT" instead. The QRT means that you are stopping transmissions.

Call Sign Phonics

Because of different accents of various people, sometimes it is difficult to understand call sign letters when spoken. For this reason, most ham operators verbalize their call sign using phonics. Below is a table listing the accepted phonics for letters and numbers.

A = ALFA	S = SIERRA
B = BRAVO	T = TANGO
C = CHARLIE	U = UNIFORM
D = DELTA	V = VICTOR
E = ECHO	W = WHISKEY
F = FOXTROT	X = X-RAY
G = GOLF	Y = YANKEE
H = HOTEL	Z = ZULU (ZED)
I = INDIA	1 = ONE
J = JULIETT	2 = TWO
K = KILO	3 = THREE (TREE)
L = LIMA	4 = FOUR
M = MIKE	5 = FIVE (FIFE)
N = NOVEMBER	6 = SIX
O = OSCAR	7 = SEVEN
P = PAPA (PA-PA')	8 = EIGHT
Q = QUEBEC (KAY-BEK')	9 = NINE (NINER)
R = ROMEO	0 = ZERO

The words in parentheses are the pronunciation or the alternate pronunciations for the words or numbers, but you will hear both used. With the letter Z, (ZED) is by far the most commonly used. With the number 9, NINER is the most common and easiest to understand ON THE AIR.

If you wish to use Morse code (CW) instead of voice communication, the "conversation" would follow the same steps, with a few modifications. To type out each word would require a lot of typing and translating. If you are like this author, more means more, i.e., more typing means more typos are likely. To help with this situation, CW enthusiasts have developed a language all their own – they use abbreviations for common phrases. Below is a chart showing some of these abbreviations.

Abbreviation	Use
AR	Over
de	From or "this is"
ES	And
GM	Good Morning
K	Go
KN	Go only
NM	Name
QTH	Location
RPT	Report
R	Roger
SK	Clear
tnx	Thanks
UR	Your, you are
73	Best Wishes

Morse Code and Amateur Radio

If you wish to use CW, but are concerned about accuracy, you might consider purchasing a Morse code translator. This is an electronic device that you place in front of your speakers. It takes the CW sounds and translates them into English and displays the transmission on an LCD display. For the reverse, you can pick up a CW keyboard. With the keyboard, you type in your message and it converts the text to Morse code. The translator does not need to be attached to your ham equipment, whereas the keyboard would.

For your convenience, below is a table showing the Morse code signals and their meaning.

Character	Code
A	· —
B	— · · ·
C	— · — ·
D	— · ·
E	·
F	· · — ·
G	— — ·
H	· · · ·
I	· ·
J	· — — —
K	— · —
L	· — · ·
M	— —
N	— ·
O	— — —
P	· — — ·
Q	— — · —
R	· — ·
S	· · ·
T	—
U	· · —
V	· · · —
W	· — —
X	— · · —
Y	— · — —
Z	— — · ·
0	— — — — —
1	· — — — —
2	· · — — —
3	· · · — —
4	· · · · —
5	· · · · ·

6	— · · · ·
7	— — · · ·
8	— — — · ·
9	— — — — ·
Ampersand [&], Wait	· — · · ·
Apostrophe [']	· — — — — ·
At sign [@]	· — — · — ·
Colon [:]	— — — · · ·
Comma [,]	— — · · — —
Dollar sign [$]	· · · — · · —
Double dash [=]	— · · · —
Exclamation mark [!]	— · — · — —
Hyphen, Minus [-]	— · · · · —
Parenthesis closed [)]	— · — — · —
Parenthesis open [(]	— · — — ·
Period [.]	· — · — · —
Plus [+]	· — · — ·
Question mark [?]	· · — — · ·
Quotation mark ["]	· — · · — ·
Semicolon [;]	— · — · — ·
Slash [/], Fraction bar	— · · — ·
Underscore [_]	· · — — · —

An advantage of using Morse Code is that when broadcasting CW, you are using reduced power, thereby saving your battery. Your battery is used only while actually transmitting or receiving.

International Call Sign Prefixes

As was stated earlier, all ham radio call signs begin with letters (or numbers) taken from blocks assigned to each country of the world by the *ITU - International Telecommunications Union,* a body controlled by the United Nations. The following chart indicates which call sign series are allocated to which countries.

Call Sign Series	Allocated to
AAA-ALZ	**United States of America**
AMA-AOZ	Spain
APA-ASZ	Pakistan (Islamic Republic of)
ATA-AWZ	India (Republic of)
AXA-AXZ	Australia
AYA-AZZ	Argentine Republic
A2A-A2Z	Botswana (Republic of)
A3A-A3Z	Tonga (Kingdom of)
A4A-A4Z	Oman (Sultanate of)
A5A-A5Z	Bhutan (Kingdom of)

A6A-A6Z	United Arab Emirates
A7A-A7Z	Qatar (State of)
A8A-A8Z	Liberia (Republic of)
A9A-A9Z	Bahrain (State of)
BAA-BZZ	China (People's Republic of)
CAA-CEZ	Chile
CFA-CKZ	Canada
CLA-CMZ	Cuba
CNA-CNZ	Morocco (Kingdom of)
COA-COZ	Cuba
CPA-CPZ	Bolivia (Republic of)
CQA-CUZ	Portugal
CVA-CXZ	Uruguay (Eastern Republic of)
CYA-CZZ	Canada
C2A-C2Z	Nauru (Republic of)
C3A-C3Z	Andorra (Principality of)
C4A-C4Z	Cyprus (Republic of)
C5A-C5Z	Gambia (Republic of the)
C6A-C6Z	Bahamas (Commonwealth of the)
C7A-C7Z	World Meteorological Organization
C8A-C9Z	Mozambique (Republic of)
DAA-DRZ	Germany (Federal Republic of)
DSA-DTZ	Korea (Republic of)
DUA-DZZ	Philippines (Republic of the)
D2A-D3Z	Angola (Republic of)
D4A-D4Z	Cape Verde (Republic of)
D5A-D5Z	Liberia (Republic of)
D6A-D6Z	Comoros (Islamic Federal Republic of the)
D7A-D9Z	Korea (Republic of)
EAA-EHZ	Spain
EIA-EJZ	Ireland
EKA-EKZ	Armenia (Republic of)
ELA-ELZ	Liberia (Republic of)
EMA-EOZ	Ukraine
EPA-EQZ	Iran (Islamic Republic of)
ERA-ERZ	Moldova (Republic of)
ESA-ESZ	Estonia (Republic of)
ETA-ETZ	Ethiopia (Federal Democratic Republic of)
EUA-EWZ	Belarus (Republic of)
EXA-EXZ	Kyrgyz Republic
EYA-EYZ	Tajikistan (Republic of)
EZA-EZZ	Turkmenistan
E2A-E2Z	Thailand
E3A-E3Z	Eritrea
E4A-E4Z	Palestinian Authority

E5A-E5Z	New Zealand - Cook Islands (WRC-07)
E7A-E7Z	Bosnia and Herzegovina (Republic of) (WRC-07)
FAA-FZZ	France
GAA-GZZ	United Kingdom of Great Britain and Northern Ireland
HAA-HAZ	Hungary (Republic of)
HBA-HBZ	Switzerland (Confederation of)
HCA-HDZ	Ecuador
HEA-HEZ	Switzerland (Confederation of)
HFA-HFZ	Poland (Republic of)
HGA-HGZ	Hungary (Republic of)
HHA-HHZ	Haiti (Republic of)
HIA-HIZ	Dominican Republic
HJA-HKZ	Colombia (Republic of)
HLA-HLZ	Korea (Republic of)
HMA-HMZ	Democratic People's Republic of Korea
HNA-HNZ	Iraq (Republic of)
HOA-HPZ	Panama (Republic of)
HQA-HRZ	Honduras (Republic of)
HSA-HSZ	Thailand
HTA-HTZ	Nicaragua
HUA-HUZ	El Salvador (Republic of)
HVA-HVZ	Vatican City State
HWA-HYZ	France
HZA-HZZ	Saudi Arabia (Kingdom of)
H2A-H2Z	Cyprus (Republic of)
H3A-H3Z	Panama (Republic of)
H4A-H4Z	Solomon Islands
H6A-H7Z	Nicaragua
H8A-H9Z	Panama (Republic of)
IAA-IZZ	Italy
JAA-JSZ	Japan
JTA-JVZ	Mongolia
JWA-JXZ	Norway
JYA-JYZ	Jordan (Hashemite Kingdom of)
JZA-JZZ	Indonesia (Republic of)
J2A-J2Z	Djibouti (Republic of)
J3A-J3Z	Grenada
J4A-J4Z	Greece
J5A-J5Z	Guinea-Bissau (Republic of)
J6A-J6Z	Saint Lucia
J7A-J7Z	Dominica (Commonwealth of)
J8A-J8Z	Saint Vincent and the Grenadines
KAA-KZZ	**United States of America**
LAA-LNZ	Norway
LOA-LWZ	Argentine Republic

LXA-LXZ	Luxembourg
LYA-LYZ	Lithuania (Republic of)
LZA-LZZ	Bulgaria (Republic of)
L2A-L9Z	Argentine Republic
MAA-MZZ	United Kingdom of Great Britain and Northern Ireland
NAA-NZZ	**United States of America**
OAA-OCZ	Peru
ODA-ODZ	Lebanon
OEA-OEZ	Austria
OFA-OJZ	Finland
OKA-OLZ	Czech Republic
OMA-OMZ	Slovak Republic
ONA-OTZ	Belgium
OUA-OZZ	Denmark
PAA-PIZ	Netherlands (Kingdom of the)
PJA-PJZ	Netherlands (Kingdom of the) - Netherlands Antilles
PKA-POZ	Indonesia (Republic of)
PPA-PYZ	Brazil (Federative Republic of)
PZA-PZZ	Suriname (Republic of)
P2A-P2Z	Papua New Guinea
P3A-P3Z	Cyprus (Republic of)
P4A-P4Z	Netherlands (Kingdom of the) - Aruba
P5A-P9Z	Democratic People's Republic of Korea
RAA-RZZ	Russian Federation
SAA-SMZ	Sweden
SNA-SRZ	Poland (Republic of)
SSA-SSM	Egypt (Arab Republic of)
SSN-STZ	Sudan (Republic of the)
SUA-SUZ	Egypt (Arab Republic of)
SVA-SZZ	Greece
S2A-S3Z	Bangladesh (People's Republic of)
S5A-S5Z	Slovenia (Republic of)
S6A-S6Z	Singapore (Republic of)
S7A-S7Z	Seychelles (Republic of)
S8A-S8Z	South Africa (Republic of)
S9A-S9Z	Sao Tome and Principe (Democratic Republic of)
TAA-TCZ	Turkey
TDA-TDZ	Guatemala (Republic of)
TEA-TEZ	Costa Rica
TFA-TFZ	Iceland
TGA-TGZ	Guatemala (Republic of)
THA-THZ	France
TIA-TIZ	Costa Rica
TJA-TJZ	Cameroon (Republic of)
TKA-TKZ	France

TLA-TLZ	Central African Republic
TMA-TMZ	France
TNA-TNZ	Congo (Republic of the)
TOA-TQZ	France
TRA-TRZ	Gabonese Republic
TSA-TSZ	Tunisia
TTA-TTZ	Chad (Republic of)
TUA-TUZ	Côte d'Ivoire (Republic of)
TVA-TXZ	France
TYA-TYZ	Benin (Republic of)
TZA-TZZ	Mali (Republic of)
T2A-T2Z	Tuvalu
T3A-T3Z	Kiribati (Republic of)
T4A-T4Z	Cuba
T5A-T5Z	Somali Democratic Republic
T6A-T6Z	Afghanistan (Islamic State of)
T7A-T7Z	San Marino (Republic of)
T8A-T8Z	Palau (Republic of)
UAA-UIZ	Russian Federation
UJA-UMZ	Uzbekistan (Republic of)
UNA-UQZ	Kazakhstan (Republic of)
URA-UZZ	Ukraine
VAA-VGZ	Canada
VHA-VNZ	Australia
VOA-VOZ	Canada
VPA-VQZ	United Kingdom of Great Britain and Northern Ireland
VRA-VRZ	China (People's Republic of) - Hong Kong
VSA-VSZ	United Kingdom of Great Britain and Northern Ireland
VTA-VWZ	India (Republic of)
VXA-VYZ	Canada
VZA-VZZ	Australia
V2A-V2Z	Antigua and Barbuda
V3A-V3Z	Belize
V4A-V4Z	Saint Kitts and Nevis
V5A-V5Z	Namibia (Republic of)
V6A-V6Z	Micronesia (Federated States of)
V7A-V7Z	Marshall Islands (Republic of the)
V8A-V8Z	Brunei Darussalam
WAA-WZZ	**United States of America**
XAA-XIZ	Mexico
XJA-XOZ	Canada
XPA-XPZ	Denmark
XQA-XRZ	Chile
XSA-XSZ	China (People's Republic of)
XTA-XTZ	Burkina Faso

XUA-XUZ	Cambodia (Kingdom of)
XVA-XVZ	Viet Nam (Socialist Republic of)
XWA-XWZ	Lao People's Democratic Republic
XXA-XXZ	China (People's Republic of) - Macao (WRC-07)
XYA-XZZ	Myanmar (Union of)
YAA-YAZ	Afghanistan (Islamic State of)
YBA-YHZ	Indonesia (Republic of)
YIA-YIZ	Iraq (Republic of)
YJA-YJZ	Vanuatu (Republic of)
YKA-YKZ	Syrian Arab Republic
YLA-YLZ	Latvia (Republic of)
YMA-YMZ	Turkey
YNA-YNZ	Nicaragua
YOA-YRZ	Romania
YSA-YSZ	El Salvador (Republic of)
YTA-YUZ	Serbia (Republic of) (WRC-07)
YVA-YYZ	Venezuela (Republic of)
Y2A-Y9Z	Germany (Federal Republic of)
ZAA-ZAZ	Albania (Republic of)
ZBA-ZJZ	United Kingdom of Great Britain and Northern Ireland
ZKA-ZMZ	New Zealand
ZNA-ZOZ	United Kingdom of Great Britain and Northern Ireland
ZPA-ZPZ	Paraguay (Republic of)
ZQA-ZQZ	United Kingdom of Great Britain and Northern Ireland
ZRA-ZUZ	South Africa (Republic of)
ZVA-ZZZ	Brazil (Federative Republic of)
Z2A-Z2Z	Zimbabwe (Republic of)
Z3A-Z3Z	The Former Yugoslav Republic of Macedonia
2AA-2ZZ	United Kingdom of Great Britain and Northern Ireland
3AA-3AZ	Monaco (Principality of)
3BA-3BZ	Mauritius (Republic of)
3CA-3CZ	Equatorial Guinea (Republic of)
3DA-3DM	Swaziland (Kingdom of)
3DN-3DZ	Fiji (Republic of)
3EA-3FZ	Panama (Republic of)
3GA-3GZ	Chile
3HA-3UZ	China (People's Republic of)
3VA-3VZ	Tunisia
3WA-3WZ	Viet Nam (Socialist Republic of)
3XA-3XZ	Guinea (Republic of)
3YA-3YZ	Norway
3ZA-3ZZ	Poland (Republic of)
4AA-4CZ	Mexico
4DA-4IZ	Philippines (Republic of the)
4JA-4KZ	Azerbaijani Republic

4LA-4LZ	Georgia (Republic of)
4MA-4MZ	Venezuela (Republic of)
4OA-4OZ	Montenegro (Republic of) (WRC-07)
4PA-4SZ	Sri Lanka (Democratic Socialist Republic of)
4TA-4TZ	Peru
4UA-4UZ	United Nations
4VA-4VZ	Haiti (Republic of)
4WA-4WZ	Democratic Republic of Timor-Leste (WRC-03)
4XA-4XZ	Israel (State of)
4YA-4YZ	International Civil Aviation Organization
4ZA-4ZZ	Israel (State of)
5AA-5AZ	Libya (Socialist People's Libyan Arab Jamahiriya)
5BA-5BZ	Cyprus (Republic of)
5CA-5GZ	Morocco (Kingdom of)
5HA-5IZ	Tanzania (United Republic of)
5JA-5KZ	Colombia (Republic of)
5LA-5MZ	Liberia (Republic of)
5NA-5OZ	Nigeria (Federal Republic of)
5PA-5QZ	Denmark
5RA-5SZ	Madagascar (Republic of)
5TA-5TZ	Mauritania (Islamic Republic of)
5UA-5UZ	Niger (Republic of the)
5VA-5VZ	Togolese Republic
5WA-5WZ	Samoa (Independent State of)
5XA-5XZ	Uganda (Republic of)
5YA-5ZZ	Kenya (Republic of)
6AA-6BZ	Egypt (Arab Republic of)
6CA-6CZ	Syrian Arab Republic
6DA-6JZ	Mexico
6KA-6NZ	Korea (Republic of)
6OA-6OZ	Somali Democratic Republic
6PA-6SZ	Pakistan (Islamic Republic of)
6TA-6UZ	Sudan (Republic of the)
6VA-6WZ	Senegal (Republic of)
6XA-6XZ	Madagascar (Republic of)
6YA-6YZ	Jamaica
6ZA-6ZZ	Liberia (Republic of)
7AA-7IZ	Indonesia (Republic of)
7JA-7NZ	Japan
7OA-7OZ	Yemen (Republic of)
7PA-7PZ	Lesotho (Kingdom of)
7QA-7QZ	Malawi
7RA-7RZ	Algeria (People's Democratic Republic of)
7SA-7SZ	Sweden
7TA-7YZ	Algeria (People's Democratic Republic of)

7ZA-7ZZ	Saudi Arabia (Kingdom of)
8AA-8IZ	Indonesia (Republic of)
8JA-8NZ	Japan
8OA-8OZ	Botswana (Republic of)
8PA-8PZ	Barbados
8QA-8QZ	Maldives (Republic of)
8RA-8RZ	Guyana
8SA-8SZ	Sweden
8TA-8YZ	India (Republic of)
8ZA-8ZZ	Saudi Arabia (Kingdom of)
9AA-9AZ	Croatia (Republic of)
9BA-9DZ	Iran (Islamic Republic of)
9EA-9FZ	Ethiopia (Federal Democratic Republic of)
9GA-9GZ	Ghana
9HA-9HZ	Malta
9IA-9JZ	Zambia (Republic of)
9KA-9KZ	Kuwait (State of)
9LA-9LZ	Sierra Leone
9MA-9MZ	Malaysia
9NA-9NZ	Nepal
9OA-9TZ	Democratic Republic of the Congo
9UA-9UZ	Burundi (Republic of)
9VA-9VZ	Singapore (Republic of)
9WA-9WZ	Malaysia
9XA-9XZ	Rwandese Republic
9YA-9ZZ	Trinidad and Tobago

Third-Party Communications and Amateur Radio

If all of this information about ham radios is somewhat intimidating, do not despair. "You" can still use ham radios for communications without being a licensed operator. Yes, you do have to have a ham license in order to legally transmit by ham equipment (or be under the direct supervision of someone else who is licensed), but there is an alternative – third-party communication.

Third-party communications occur when a licensed operator sends either written or verbal messages on behalf of unlicensed persons or organizations. There are two "controls" on third-party communication.

First, the communication must be noncommercial and of a personal nature. Asking a ham operator to contact another ham operator located in an area just hit by tornados and, because of being without power, phones do not work in Grandma Sally's city so you can check up on her, is okay. Asking a ham to send a message out that you have an old Chevy for sale would not be okay.

Second, the message must be going to a permitted area. Transmitting from a US location to another US location is okay, but transmitting from the US to another country may not. Because third-party communications bypass a country's normal telephone and postal systems, many foreign governments forbid such communications. In order to transmit from one country to another, the other country must have signed a third-party agreement with the US. What follows is a list of those countries that do have third-party a communications agreement with the US.

V2	Antigua / Barbuda
LU	Argentina
VK	Australia
V3	Belize
CP	Bolivia
T9	Bosnia-Herzegovina
PY	Brazil
VE	Canada
CE	Chile
HK	Colombia
D6	Comoros (Federal Islamic Republic of)
TI	Costa Rica
CO	Cuba
HI	Dominican Republic
J7	Dominica
HC	Ecuador
YS	El Salvador
C5	Gambia, The
9G	Ghana
J3	Grenada
TG	Guatemala
8R	Guyana
HH	Haiti
HR	Honduras
4X	Israel
6Y	Jamaica
JY	Jordan
EL	Liberia
V7	Marshall Islands
XE	Mexico
V6	Micronesia, Federated States of
YN	Nicaragua
HP	Panama
ZP	Paraguay
OA	Peru
DU	Philippines
VR6	Pitcairn Island

V4	St. Christopher / Nevis
J6	St. Lucia
J8	St. Vincent and the Grenadines
9L	Sierra Leone
ZS	South Africa
3DA	Swaziland
9Y	Trinidad / Tobago
TA	Turkey
GB	United Kingdom
CX	Uruguay
YV	Venezuela
4U1ITUITU	Geneva
4U1VICVIC	Vienna

Remember, before TSHTF, keep your pantry well stocked, your powder dry, and your batteries fully charged. 73

APPENDIX A

American Radio Relay League

Affiliated Amateur Radio Clubs In

Michigan

ARRL Affiliated Club	Adrian Amateur Radio Club
City	Adrian, MI
Call Sign	W8TQE
Section	MI
Links	www.W8tqe.com

ARRL Affiliated Club	Allegan County Amateur Radio Club
City	Allegan, MI
Call Sign	AC8RC
Section	MI
Links	www.Ac8rc.org

ARRL Affiliated Club	Keweenaw County Repeater Assoc. Inc.
City	Allouez, MI
Call Sign	K8MDH
Section	MI
Links	www.Kcra-Mi.Net

ARRL Affiliated Club	University Of Michigan Amateur Radio Club
City	Ann Arbor, MI
Call Sign	W8UM
Section	MI
Links	www.Umich.Edu/~Umarc

ARRL Affiliated Club	Arrow Communication Association
City	Ann Arbor, MI
Call Sign	W8PGW
Section	MI
Links	www.W8pgw.org

ARRL Special Service Club	Southern Michigan Amateur Radio Society
City	Battle Creek, MI
Call Sign	W8DF
Section	MI
Links	www.W8df.com

ARRL Affiliated Club	Battle Creek Low Banders
City	Battle Creek, MI
Call Sign	W8TOP
Section	MI

ARRL Affiliated Club	Barry Amateur Radio Assn.
City	Battle Creek, MI
Call Sign	K8BMI
Section	MI
Links	www.Qsl.Net/Kc8vto

ARRL Affiliated Club	Independent Repeater Association, Inc.
City	Byron Center, MI
Call Sign	W8IRA
Section	MI
Links	www.W8ira.org, www.W8hvg.org

ARRL Affiliated Club	Wexaukee Amateur Radio Club
City	Cadillac, MI
Call Sign	K8CAD
Section	MI
Links	www.Wexaukeearc.org

ARRL Affiliated Club	Eaton County Amateur Radio Club
City	Charlotte, MI
Call Sign	K8CHR
Section	MI
Links	www.Qsl.Net/Ecarc/

ARRL Special Service Club	Chelsea Amateur Radio Club, Inc.
City	Chelsea, MI
Call Sign	WD8IEL
Section	MI
Links	Wd8iel.Net

ARRL Affiliated Club	Branch County Amateur Radio Club
City	Coldwater, MI
Call Sign	WD8KAF
Section	MI
Links	www.Branchcountyarc.com

ARRL Affiliated Club	Michigan Amateur Radio Alliance
City	Comstock Park, MI
Call Sign	W8USA
Section	MI
Links	www.W8usa.org

ARRL Affiliated Club	Shiawassee Amateur Radio Association
City	Corunna, MI
Call Sign	W8QQQ
Section	MI
Links	www.W8qqq.org

ARRL Affiliated Club	Ford Ar League Tin Lizzy Club
City	Dearborn, MI, MI
Call Sign	K8UTT
Section	MI

ARRL Affiliated Club	Copper Country Radio Amateur Assoc. Inc.
City	Dollar Bay, MI
Call Sign	W8CDZ
Section	MI
Links	www.Ccraa.Net

ARRL Affiliated Club	Michigan State University Amateur Radio Club
City	East Lansing, MI
Call Sign	W8SH
Section	MI

ARRL Affiliated Club	Tri County Emergency Operators Association
City	Eben Junction, MI
Call Sign	K8EOC
Section	MI

ARRL Affiliated Club	Farmington Amateur Radio Club
City	Farmington Hills, MI
Section	MI

ARRL Special Service Club	Genesee County Radio Club
City	Flint, MI
Call Sign	W8ACW
Section	MI
Links	www.W8acw.org

ARRL Special Service Club	Garden City Amateur Radio Club
City	Garden City, MI
Call Sign	K8GC
Section	MI
Links	www.Gcarc.Net

ARRL Special Service Club	Top of Michigan Amateur Radio Club
City	Gaylord, MI
Call Sign	NM8RC
Section	MI
Links	www.Nm8rc.org

ARRL Affiliated Club	Delta County Amateur Radio Society
City	Gladstone, MI
Call Sign	K8PL
Section	MI
Links	www.Dcars.org

ARRL Affiliated Club	North Ottawa Amateur Radio Club
City	Grand Haven, MI
Call Sign	W8CSO
Section	MI
Links	www.Qsl.Net/Noarc/

ARRL Affiliated Club	Michigan DX Association
City	Grand Rapids, MI
Call Sign	W8DXI
Section	MI
Links	www.Mdxa1.org/

ARRL Affiliated Club	Grand Rapids Amateur Radio Association
City	Grand Rapids, MI
Call Sign	W8DC
Section	MI
Links	www.W8dc.org

ARRL Affiliated Club	Downtown Amateur Packet Radio
City	Grand Rapids, MI
Call Sign	N8DPR
Section	MI

ARRL Affiliated Club	Amateur Radio Association of Hanson Hills
City	Grayling, MI
Call Sign	N8AHZ
Section	MI
Links	www.Arahh.org

ARRL Affiliated Club	Montcalm Area Amateur Radio Club
City	Greenville, MI
Section	MI
Links	N8ma.org
ARRL Affiliated Club	South Eastern Michigan Amateur Radio Association
City	Grosse Pointe Woods, MI
Call Sign	K8BYI
Section	MI
Links	www.Semara.Us, www.Semara.Net
ARRL Affiliated Club	Hazel Park Amateur Radio Club
City	Hazel Park, MI
Call Sign	W8HP
Section	MI
ARRL Affiliated Club	Milford Amateur Radio Club
City	Highland, MI
Call Sign	W8YDK
Section	MI
Links	www.Qsl.Net/W8ydk
ARRL Affiliated Club	Hillsdale County Amateur Radio Club
City	Hillsdale, MI
Call Sign	K8HRC
Section	MI
Links	www.Hcarc.com
ARRL Affiliated Club	Holland Amateur Radio Club
City	Holland, MI
Call Sign	K8DAA
Section	MI
Links	www.Hollandarc.org
ARRL Affiliated Club	Just A Bunch of Amateurs
City	Howell, MI
Call Sign	K8JBA
Section	MI
ARRL Affiliated Club	Livingston Amateur Radio Klub
City	Howell, MI
Call Sign	W8LRK
Section	MI
Links	www.W8lrk.org
ARRL Affiliated Club	Cascades Amateur Radio Society
City	Jackson, MI
Call Sign	W8JXN
Section	MI
Links	www.W8jxn.org
ARRL Affiliated Club	Great Lakes DX/Contest Club
City	Laingsuburg, MI
Call Sign	K9PXV
Section	MI
Links	www.Qsl.Net/K9pxv

ARRL Affiliated Club	The Auto State Young Ladies
City	Lake Odessa, MI
Section	MI
Links	www.Tasyl.Net
ARRL Affiliated Club	Michigan Qrp Club
City	Lake Orion, MI
Call Sign	WQ8RP
Section	MI
Links	www.MIQRP.org
ARRL Affiliated Club	Central Michigan Amateur Radio Club
City	Lansing, MI
Call Sign	W8MAA
Section	MI
Links	www.Centralmiarc.com
ARRL Affiliated Club	Lapeer County Amateur Radio Association
City	Lapeer, MI
Call Sign	W8LAP
Section	MI
Links	www.W8lap.com
ARRL Affiliated Club	Greater Lansing DX Group
City	Leslie, MI
Call Sign	N8VYS
Section	MI
ARRL Affiliated Club	Lewiston Area Amateur Radio Club
City	Lewiston, MI
Call Sign	K8LEW
Section	MI
Links	Groups.Yahoo.com/Group/Laarc/
ARRL Affiliated Club	Livonia Amateur Radio Club
City	Livonia, MI
Call Sign	K8UNS
Section	MI
Links	www.Livoniaarc.com/
ARRL Affiliated Club	Amateur Radio Group of Youth In Lowell
City	Lowell, MI
Call Sign	K8LHS
Section	MI
Links	www.Argyl.org
ARRL Affiliated Club	Lowell Amateur Radio Club
City	Lowell, MI
Call Sign	W8LRC
Section	MI
Links	www.W8lrc.org

ARRL Affiliated Club	Hiawatha Amateur Radio Club
City	Marquette, MI
Call Sign	K8LOD
Section	MI
Links	www.Qsl.Net/K8lod

ARRL Affiliated Club	South East Michigan DX Assn.
City	Marysville, MI
Call Sign	WA8DX
Section	MI
Links	www.Semdxa.org

ARRL Special Service Club	Midland Amateur Radio Club
City	Midland, MI
Call Sign	W8KEA
Section	MI
Links	www.Qsl.Net/W8kea

ARRL Affiliated Club	Spirit Of 76 Amateur Radio Klub
City	Milford, MI
Call Sign	KC8DCS
Section	MI

ARRL Affiliated Club	Monroe County Radio Communication Assn.
City	Monroe, MI
Call Sign	W8DWL
Section	MI
Links	www.Mcrca.org

ARRL Affiliated Club	L'ANSE CREUSE Amateur Radio Club
City	Mount Clemens, MI
Call Sign	N8LC
Section	MI
Links	www.N8lc.org

ARRL Special Service Club	Utica Shelby Emergency Communication Assn.
City	Mount Clemens, MI
Call Sign	K8UO
Section	MI
Links	www.Usecaarc.com

ARRL Affiliated Club	Muskegon Area Amateur Radio Council
City	Muskegon, MI
Call Sign	W8ZHO
Section	MI
Links	www.Qsl.Net/W8zho

ARRL Affiliated Club	Luce Amateur Radio Society
City	Newberry, MI
Call Sign	W8NBY
Section	MI
Links	www.W8nby.com

ARRL Affiliated Club	Iosco City Amateur Radio Enthusiast
City	Oscoda, MI
Call Sign	W8ICC
Section	MI
Links	www.W8icc.com
ARRL Affiliated Club	Big Rapids Area Amateur Radio Club
City	Paris, MI
Call Sign	KB8QOI
Section	MI
Links	www.Bigrapidsarc.Net
ARRL Affiliated Club	MCTI Amateur Radio Club
City	Plainwell, MI
Call Sign	W8TEC
Section	MI
ARRL Affiliated Club	Plymouth Historical Museum Radio Club
City	Plymouth, MI
Call Sign	KC8SWR
Section	MI
Links	www.Qsl.Net/Kc8swr
ARRL Affiliated Club	Stu Rockafellow Amateur Radio Society
City	Plymouth, MI
Call Sign	W8NJH
Section	MI
Links	www.Qsl.Net/W8njh
ARRL Affiliated Club	Oakland County Amateur Radio Society
City	Pontiac, MI
Call Sign	W8TNO
Section	MI
Links	www.Qsl.Net/W8tno
ARRL Affiliated Club	Eastern Michigan Amateur Radio Club
City	Port Huron, MI
Call Sign	K8EPV
Section	MI
ARRL Affiliated Club	American Red Cross Amateur Radio Service
City	Port Huron, MI
Call Sign	K8ARC
Section	MI
Links	www.Qsl.Net/Arcars
ARRL Affiliated Club	Kalamazoo Amateur Radio Club
City	Portage, MI
Call Sign	W8VY
Section	MI
ARRL Affiliated Club	Southwest Michigan Amateur Radio Team
City	Portage, MI
Call Sign	K8KZO
Section	MI
Links	www.K8kzo.com

ARRL Affiliated Club	Ogemaw Arenac Amateur Radio Society
City	Prescott, MI
Call Sign	K8OAR
Section	MI
Links	www.K8oar.com
ARRL Affiliated Club	West Michigan Venturing Crew 9050 Amateur Radio Club
City	Ravenna, MI
Call Sign	KD8PGT
Section	MI
Links	www.Mcecs.Net/Venturingpg1.Htm
ARRL Affiliated Club	Midwest Traffickkers and Contesters
City	Rockford, MI
Section	MI
ARRL Affiliated Club	Saginaw Valley Amateur Radio Association
City	Saginaw, MI
Call Sign	K8DAC
Section	MI
Links	www.K8dac.com
ARRL Affiliated Club	Blossomland Amateur Radio Association
City	Saint Joseph, MI
Call Sign	W8MAI
Section	MI
Links	www.Blossomlandara.org
ARRL Affiliated Club	Mason Co. Amateur Radio Service
City	Scottville, MI
Call Sign	K8DXF
Section	MI
ARRL Special Service Club	General Motors Amateur Radio Club
City	Shelby Township, MI
Call Sign	WW8GM
Section	MI
Links	www.Gmarc.org
ARRL Affiliated Club	Michigan VHF-UHF Society
City	Shelby Township, MI
Call Sign	AD8U
Section	MI
Links	www.Ad8u.com
ARRL Affiliated Club	Catalpa Amateur Radio Society
City	Sister Lakes, MI
Call Sign	W8AG
Section	MI
ARRL Affiliated Club	South Lyon Area Amateur Radio Club
City	South Lyon, MI
Call Sign	N8SL
Section	MI
Links	www.Slaarc.com

ARRL Special Service Club	Motor City Radio Club Inc.
City	Southgate, MI
Call Sign	W8MRM
Section	MI
Links	www.W8mrm.org
ARRL Affiliated Club	West Michigan Lights Amateur Radio Club
City	Spring Lake, MI
Call Sign	KD8SET
Section	MI
ARRL Affiliated Club	Gratiot County Amateur Radio Association
City	Sumner, MI
Section	MI
ARRL Affiliated Club	River Raisin Repeater Assn.
City	Temperance, MI
Call Sign	K8RPT
Section	MI
Links	www.Mcrca.org
ARRL Affiliated Club	Cherryland Amateur Radio Club
City	Traverse City, MI
Call Sign	W8TCM
Section	MI
Links	www.Cherrylandarc.com.
ARRL Affiliated Club	Wyandotte Amateur Radio Repeater Assn.
City	Trenton, MI
Call Sign	WY8DOT
Section	MI
Links	Sites.Google.com.Site/Wy9dot/
ARRL Affiliated Club	Alger Amateur Radio Club
City	Wetmore, MI
Call Sign	KC8BAN
Section	MI
Links	www.Algerham.org
ARRL Affiliated Club	Noble Odyssey Foundation Radio Club
City	White Lake, MI
Call Sign	K8NOF
Section	MI
ARRL Affiliated Club	Mad River Radio Club
City	Ypsilanti, MI
Call Sign	K8MAD
Section	MI
Links	Madriverradioclub.org

APPENDIX B

Amateur Radio License Holders

in

Michigan: North and East Regions
(by City)

Call Sign: AA3EK
Donald T Cox
Acme MI 496100364

Call Sign: KD8JHF
Robert W Dees
Acme MI 49610

**FCC Amateur Radio
Licenses in Ada**

Call Sign: KC8DHM
Robert W Starck
8350 28th Ave
Ada MI 49301

Call Sign: KC8IZQ
Peter V Chan
6751 3 Mile Rd
Ada MI 49301

Call Sign: KC8MVN
Bryan L Clark
6246 3 Mile Rd NE
Ada MI 49301

Call Sign: KC8IYD
Daniel G Houser
7326 30th St
Ada MI 49301

Call Sign: KC8ZTW
Scott A Werkema
5695 4 Mile Rd
Ada MI 49301

Call Sign: AB8NB
Frederick A Wolfe
8385 45th St SE
Ada MI 493019227

Call Sign: KC8PZB
Dale L Wilcox
10958 5 Mile Rd
Ada MI 49301

Call Sign: AA8KE
Charles R Ritter Jr
8901 52nd St
Ada MI 49301

Call Sign: KD8RLT
Derek R Schroeder
6986 Ada Dr Dr
Ada MI 49301

Call Sign: N8IDL
Michael J Lennon
5231 Ada Dr SE
Ada MI 493017869

Call Sign: KB8VEA
Donald K Geene
507 Adapointe Dr S E
Ada MI 49301

Call Sign: KB9OSG
James W Keeth
6981 Adaside Dr SE
Ada MI 49301

Call Sign: KC8SIX
Daniel J Gillespie
6934 Adaside SE
Ada MI 49301

Call Sign: KD8IQS
Patrick R Howe
7932 Autumn Woods
Dr SE
Ada MI 49301

Call Sign: N8NEW
Roger L French
9035 Bailey Rd
Ada MI 49301

Call Sign: N8NEX
Linda J French
9035 Bailey Rd
Ada MI 49301

Call Sign: K8OQ
Thomas L Mix
9490 Bennett
Ada MI 49301

Call Sign: N8LLX
Matthew T Mix
9490 Bennett
Ada MI 49301

Call Sign: AB8ZU
Thomas L Mix
9490 Bennett

Ada MI 49301

Call Sign: W8UTE
Thomas L Mix
9490 Bennett
Ada MI 49301

Call Sign: KA5S
Cortland E Richmond
8615 Bennett St SE
Ada MI 49301

Call Sign: WM8Q
Gisele A Mix
9490 Bennett St SE
Ada MI m493019040

Call Sign: KD8IJJ
Aaron N Ebling
2887 Boynton Ave NE
Ada MI 49301

Call Sign: KB8MDW
Adam M Mix
855 Boynton Hills
Ada MI 49301

Call Sign: W8CK
Craig S Kidder
916 Bridge Crest Dr
Ada MI 49301

Call Sign: K9DH
Donald J Hruby
2111 Brookhaven Dr
SE
Ada MI 493019608

Call Sign: NB8P
Andrew M Lauppe
1596 Buttrick Ave SE
Ada MI 49301

Call Sign: KD8JTK
James W Mcfadden
3776 Buttrick Ave SE
Ada MI 49301

Call Sign: W8JWM
James W Mcfadden
Buttrick Ave SE
Ada MI 49301

Call Sign: KC8IFJ

Jonathan P Vant Hof
941 Buttrick Rd
Ada MI 49301

Call Sign: WT3U
Jonathan P Vant Hof
941 Buttrick Rd
Ada MI 49301

Call Sign: N8LUH
Timothy A Terhune
935 Buttrick SE
Ada MI 49301

Call Sign: N8FHI
Claude E McKay
6460 Channing Ct
Ada MI 49301

Call Sign: N8THA
Robert A Venlet
3014 Colchester Dr SE
Ada MI 49301

Call Sign: WB8WMX
Michael J Laemers
3054 Colchester SE
Ada MI 49301

Call Sign: N8IND
Bruce A Block
6635 Conservation NE
Ada MI 49301

Call Sign: KD8PIK
Daryn G Rollins
6667 Conservation NE
Ada MI 49301

Call Sign: KA8SLR
Daryn G Rollins
6667 Conservation NE
Ada MI 49301

Call Sign: KD8CPM
Allyson J Zuidema
9081 Conservation Rd
Ada MI 49301

Call Sign: KD8CPL
Lane T Zuidema
9081 Conservation Rd
Ada MI 49301

Call Sign: KD8CWP
Lynne A Snyder
8930 Crooked Crow
Ada MI 49301

Call Sign: N8LSK
Scott W Beardsley
11 Deer Run
Ada MI 49301

Call Sign: N9IZC
Robert W Benstein
6429 Drumlin Ct
Ada MI 49301

Call Sign: N8RWB
Robert W Benstein
6429 Drumlin Ct
Ada MI 49301

Call Sign: WI8M
Patricia M Locke
667 Duxbury Ct SE
Ada MI 493017805

Call Sign: K8SN
Samuel T Nabkey
5790 E Fulton
Ada MI 49301

Call Sign: KC8REL
Christine J Nabkey
5790 E Fulton
Ada MI 49301

Call Sign: KC8SVV
Kent County
Emergency Service
Team
5790 E Fulton
Ada MI 49301

Call Sign: KC8PCI
Christopher D Nabkey
5790 E Fulton St
Ada MI 49301

Call Sign: KB8SYQ
David B Timmick
7609 Fase St SE
Ada MI 49301

Call Sign: K8OHR
Harry J Morris

4081 Giles Ave NE
Ada MI 49301

Call Sign: KC8HLW
Travis N Sugarbaker
1920 Grand River Dr
Ada MI 49301

Call Sign: KB8UFI
Michael S Price
246 Greentree Ln NE
Ada MI 49301

Call Sign: KB8POH
Brian G Krug
5470 Hartfield Ct SE
Ada MI 49301

Call Sign: N8ZUY
Jane M Stutzman
348 Haskins Ct SE
Ada MI 49301

Call Sign: WB8NCD
Steven C Stutzman
348 Haskins Ct SE
Ada MI 49301

Call Sign: KF8PP
Steven J Boersema
1501 Hawthorne Hills
Dr SE
Ada MI 493019163

Call Sign: W8SB
Steven J Boersema
1501 Hawthorne Hills
Dr SE
Ada MI 493019163

Call Sign: WA2UBH
Mark J Shurr
5728 Highbury Dr SE
Ada MI 49301

Call Sign: KC8ZPQ
Thomas E Wodarek
2309 Honey Creek
Ada MI 49301

Call Sign: KJ8KJ
Keith B Javery
1335 Honeycreek Ave
Ada MI 49301

Call Sign: WL7GG
James W Alexander
3077 Howlett Dr SE
Ada MI 49301

Call Sign: K8JME
James W Alexander
3077 Howlett Dr SE
Ada MI 49301

Call Sign: AG8U
Phillip D Carino
2228 Knollpoint NE
Ada MI 49301

Call Sign: KC8THR
Michael W Heathfield
3400 N Applecrest Ct
SE
Ada MI 49301

Call Sign: KB8SWD
Bruce E Bjornseth
1855 Parnell Ave SE
Ada MI 493019124

Call Sign: KC8GOQ
Robert C Roberts
3350 Pettis NE
Ada MI 49301

Call Sign: KC8IFL
Robert P Roberts Jr
3350 Pettis NE
Ada MI 49301

Call Sign: W8WDF
Walter D Felver Jr
5922 Pheasant View
Dr
Ada MI 49301

Call Sign: KD8EBC
Timothy D Paver
685 Pine Meadow Ln
NE
Ada MI 49301

Call Sign: K5XF
Robert H Silkensen
6380 Redington Dr SE
Ada MI 49301

Call Sign: KD8BIF
David M Gallagher
6624 Rix SE
Ada MI 49301

Call Sign: KC8PKL
Bryan C Bestrom
252 Rollingbrook NE
Ada MI 49301

Call Sign: KC8VUF
Frederick V Gnich
45 Spring Arbor
Ada MI 49301

Call Sign: WZ8T
David M Cherba
7700 Sun Quest Ridge
Ada MI 49301

Call Sign: KC8LTO
Wendy T Cherba
7700 Sun Quest Ridge
NE
Ada MI 49301

Call Sign: N8UKE
Michael R Cherba
7700 Sun Quest Ridge
NE
Ada MI 49301

Call Sign: W8WTC
Wendy T Cherba
7700 Sun Quest Ridge
NE
Ada MI 49301

Call Sign: KC8JED
Walter D Felver Jr
4596 Sunflower Ridge
Dr
Ada MI 49301

Call Sign: KD8DKX
Robert H Berggren
4718 Sunflower Ridge
Dr
Ada MI 49301

Call Sign: K8UAJ
Kenneth R Gackler
115 Taos NE
Ada MI 49301

Call Sign: W8UGM
Louis M Goudzwaard
7938 Thornapple Club
Dr SE
Ada MI 493019413

Call Sign: KB8WGC
Anthony B Parker
7783 Timber Canyon
Ada MI 49301

Call Sign: KB8SER
Joyce M Parker
7783 Timber Canyon
SE
Ada MI 49301

Call Sign: N8BWK
G J Rottman
6321 Winter Run Ct
Ada MI 49301

Call Sign: KD8AIG
Dennis M Ford
Ada MI 49301

Call Sign: KD8RLR
Mical G Tiede
Ada MI 49301

FCC Amateur Radio
Licenses in Afton

Call Sign: KA8DOU
Burnel E Varity
7568 Montgomery Rd
Afton MI 49705

Call Sign: KN8S
John A Sullivan
297 N Silver Pl
Afton MI 49705

Call Sign: KD8HBB
Brian C Veihl
7272 Osmun
Afton MI 49705

FCC Amateur Radio
Licenses in Alanson

Call Sign: KC8TSB
Loren K Evanoff

15 1st St
Ahmeek MI 49901

Call Sign: K8YSZ
Gary L Hansen
Ahmeek MI 49901

Call Sign: KD8CGA
David S Sheffer
Ahmeek MI 49901

Call Sign: N8WLK
Catherine L Smith
9352 Banwell Rd
Alanson MI 49706

Call Sign: KC8YLJ
Herbert L Winn
6827 Cordoba 113
Alanson MI
497068220

Call Sign: KC8ZSM
Dawn M Thompson
9433 Miller Rd
Alanson MI 49706

Call Sign: KC8ZSL
Mark J Thompson
9433 Miller Rd
Alanson MI 49706

Call Sign: N8LEC
John R George
8930 Moore Rd
Alanson MI 49706

Call Sign: N8RPS
Brad D George
8950 Moore Rd
Alanson MI 49706

Call Sign: KC8HNL
Michael G Brady
2232 N Ayr Rd
Alanson MI 49706

Call Sign: KC8LJW
Catherine A Brady
2232 N Ayr Rd
Alanson MI 49706

Call Sign: WD8MJC
Martin J Beer

7963 Red Pine Trl
Alanson MI 49706

Call Sign: K8CIL
Wayne A Miller
4515 Sunny Ridge Rd
Alanson MI 49706

Call Sign: N8QVM
Geri A Szymanski
Alanson MI 49706

Call Sign: AC8AE
Geri A Szymanski
Alanson MI 49706

Call Sign: W8GER
Geri A Szymanski
Alanson MI 49706

Call Sign: N8OF
Gerald C Szymanski
Alanson MI
497060121

Call Sign: KA8HMN
Gerald C Szymanski
Alanson MI
497060121

Call Sign: N8GCS
Gerald C Szymanski
Alanson MI
497060121

FCC Amateur Radio
Licenses in Albion

Call Sign: WD8DTR
Brian D Dekoninck
17870 26 Mile Rd
Albion MI 49224

Call Sign: W8IRA
Derroll E Cortright
21931 27 1/2 Mile Rd
Albion MI 49224

Call Sign: W8IFR
Harry J Hawes Jr
14103 27 Mile Rd
Albion MI 492249459

Call Sign: WA8TIC

Gordon H Martin
15819 28 Mi Rd
Albion MI 49224

Call Sign: WD8DTH
Charles E Wixson
15980 Behling Rd
Albion MI 49224

Call Sign: N8URV
Marie O Travioli
803 Bennett St
Albion MI 49224

Call Sign: KB8USV
Charles W Center
16611 Devereaux Rd
Albion MI 49224

Call Sign: KC8OAK
David R Locke Jr
3821 Eaton Rapids Rd
Albion MI 49224

Call Sign: KC8SFO
David R Locke Sr
3821 Eaton Rapids Rd
Albion MI 49224

Call Sign: WB8BGY
George E Race
3865 Gibbs Rd
Albion MI 49224

Call Sign: WB8UWX
Barbara I Race
3865 Gibbs Rd
Albion MI 49224

Call Sign: N8LFA
Jerry A Gleason
5038 Hicks Rd
Albion MI 49224

Call Sign: N8GIV
Gregory L Gleason
5038 Hicks Rd
Albion MI 49224

Call Sign: K8TDF
Robert S Oldfield
800 Huntington Blvd
Albion MI 49224

Call Sign: KB8YQC
Leonard D Lohrke
834 Irwin Ave
Albion MI 49224

Call Sign: WA8UDN
Wilbur D Johns
27817 L Dr N
Albion MI 49224

Call Sign: W8WDX
Scott A Brown
504 Lincoln St
Albion MI 492249200

Call Sign: KC8DPX
Mark E Bollman
422 Linden
Albion MI 492242212

Call Sign: K8BJH
John F Jasienski
510 Lynn St
Albion MI 49224

Call Sign: KB8OAK
Dennis K Furrenes Sr
1025 Miller Ct
Albion MI 49224

Call Sign: WB8WXZ
Frances C Gideon
610 Orchard Dr
Albion MI 49224

Call Sign: KC8GFI
William K Engelter
1201 Pennell
Albion MI 49224

Call Sign: KC8EMH
Scott R Heath
415 Perry St
Albion MI 49224

Call Sign: WA8GEX
Fred P Scribner
14 Sunnyside Ct
Albion MI 492241956

**FCC Amateur Radio
Licenses in Alden**

Call Sign: KB8JUF

Roger L Byron
7826 Anderson Ln
Alden MI 49612

Call Sign: KA8KZW
Erik N Molby
Rfd 2 Box 49 CR 593
Alden MI 49612

Call Sign: W8COY
William D Dewey
10377 McPherson Rd
Alden MI 49612

Call Sign: KB8WOG
Donald B Ramsay Jr
474 Westwood Rd NE
Alden MI 49612

Call Sign: K8GM
Leonard R Miller
Alden MI 49612

Call Sign: W8JDR
J D Reck
Alden MI 49612

**FCC Amateur Radio
Licenses in Allegan**

Call Sign: KD8KPE
Ronald D Buzzell
2876 104th Ave
Allegan MI 49010

Call Sign: AC8RB
Ronald D Buzzell
2876 104th Ave
Allegan MI 49010

Call Sign: KC8DEG
Anna M Van Ness
3046 104th Ave
Allegan MI 49010

Call Sign: N8MOP
Robert G Rex
3162 104th Ave
Allegan MI 49010

Call Sign: N8KDC
Kenneth J Whitcomb
3072 106th Ave
Allegan MI 49010

Call Sign: KU4LJ
Kenneth S Nadell
4158 107th Ave
Allegan MI 49010

Call Sign: K8ZWR
Helen E Jones
3043 108th Ave
Allegan MI 49010

Call Sign: KB8WJU
Robert E Fisk
2886 113th Ave
Allegan MI 49010

Call Sign: WB8HNN
Joseph J Sartini
3352 116th Ave
Allegan MI 49010

Call Sign: KE5ETX
John C Keith
4347 117th Ave
Allegan MI 49010

Call Sign: KA8DYM
Mitchell J Rowe
4225 117th St
Allegan MI 49010

Call Sign: N8IGO
Donald L Miner
2411 118th Ave
Allegan MI 49010

Call Sign: WA8VGQ
Richard D St John
3834 118th Ave
Allegan MI 49010

Call Sign: KB8EQK
John M Roosenberg Jr
3472 121st Ave
Allegan MI 49010

Call Sign: KB8GKI
Solveig R Balgoyen
3615 121st Ave
Allegan MI 49010

Call Sign: KB8IWA
William G Balgoyen
3615 121st Ave

Allegan MI 49010

Call Sign: WD8AHL
Ronald R Tripp
2573 122nd Ave
Allegan MI 49010

Call Sign: KD8CJQ
Allegan County ARES
Races
3271 122nd Ave
Allegan MI 49010

Call Sign: KD8LOW
Stanley J Oetman
4464 128th Ave
Allegan MI 49010

Call Sign: KD8HEN
Joseph E Laponsie
1634 20th St
Allegan MI 49010

Call Sign: KD8NGH
Shawn M Bonnell
1753 20th St
Allegan MI 49010

Call Sign: N8MPU
John P Smith
1296 24th St Rt 7
Allegan MI 49010

Call Sign: KB8WJV
Judith A Allen
228 26th St
Allegan MI 49010

Call Sign: N8NCQ
Dennis D Survilla
228 26th St
Allegan MI 49010

Call Sign: KC8BWV
Steven J McDaniel
1299 26th St
Allegan MI 49010

Call Sign: KC8FFU
Dennis A Davidsmeyer
1138 27th St
Allegan MI 490109030

Call Sign: KC8RYB

Dorothy L Foster
1179 32nd Ave
Allegan MI 49010

Call Sign: KC8NBS
John E Foster
1179 32nd St
Allegan MI 49010

Call Sign: KC8NGE
Donald J Wallace
1203 32nd St
Allegan MI 49010

Call Sign: WB8NKB
Donald T Forster
708 32nd St Rr 6
Allegan MI 49010

Call Sign: KD8LOU
Jacob M Simsack
486 36th St
Allegan MI 49010

Call Sign: KD8EVV
Matt P Michielsen
1618 36th St
Allegan MI 49010

Call Sign: N8ACI
Richard L Bill
1738 36th St
Allegan MI 49010

Call Sign: KD8ENN
Duane J Laponsie
2044 36th St
Allegan MI 49010

Call Sign: KC8KYI
James A Ruse
2584 36th St
Allegan MI 49010

Call Sign: AB8IX
James A Ruse
2584 36th St
Allegan MI 49010

Call Sign: KC8BWR
Peter S Hetzel
630 38th St
Allegan MI 490109131

Call Sign: KC8YIC
Donna S Hetzel
630 38th St
Allegan MI 490109131

Call Sign: WB8SAF
Raymond E Lewis
320 41st
Allegan MI 49010

Call Sign: KB8VZY
James R Gillis
1917 43rd St
Allegan MI 490108942

Call Sign: AC8AG
James R Gillis
1917 43rd St
Allegan MI 490108942

Call Sign: AB8L
Bryan Lane
1815 Arrowhead Trl E
Allegan MI 490108945

Call Sign: W8CX
Richard W Boll
3347 Delano
Allegan MI 49010

Call Sign: W8CAS
Clifford A St John
3069 Dumont Rd
Allegan MI 49010

Call Sign: KB8VZE
James F Green
1203 E Village Dr
Allegan MI 49010

Call Sign: KD8FS
Allan J Chudek
314 Ely St
Allegan MI 49010

Call Sign: KD8RQJ
Michael Guttery
566 Ely St
Allegan MI 49010

Call Sign: KA0WAJ
Gina W Duckworth
743 Grand St C5
Allegan MI 49010

Call Sign: K8CJQ
William J Borgman
3066 Grand View Dr
Allegan MI 49010

Call Sign: WA4PID
Grover W Cook
200 Jackson St
Allegan MI 49010

Call Sign: KD8NGJ
Karen E Gates
243 Jackson St
Allegan MI 49010

Call Sign: KB8TDV
Helena K Yetman
4017 Lake Dr
Allegan MI 49010

Call Sign: N8ZUR
Forrest E Yetman
4017 Lake Dr
Allegan MI 49010

Call Sign: KD8ILJ
Helena K Yetman
4017 Lake Dr
Allegan MI 49010

Call Sign: KC8JBU
John A Nilles
1215 Lincoln Rd
Allegan MI 49010

Call Sign: KC8EHM
John H Schultz
1225 Lincoln Rd
Allegan MI 49010

Call Sign: N8VOS
Dean B Van Bragt
1225 Lincoln Rd
Allegan MI 49010

Call Sign: KB8OGP
Kelly A Sobanski
1830 Lincoln Rd
Allegan MI 49010

Call Sign: KD8BVX
Peter M Sobanski
1830 Lincoln Rd

Allegan MI 49010

Call Sign: N8XLX
Robert L Bailey
1260 Lincoln Rd Lot
23
Allegan MI 49010

Call Sign: N8YFK
Derek C Schroeder
234 Lowe St
Allegan MI 49010

Call Sign: WD8DRX
Jack C Schroeder
234 Lowe St
Allegan MI 49010

Call Sign: KC8CQJ
Melvin L Van Ness
1227 Martha Ct
Allegan MI 49010

Call Sign: WA8SXG
Lucille Veenkant
513 Monroe St
Allegan MI 49010

Call Sign: KB8QOK
Brenda A Morris
4338 Moore Rd
Allegan MI 49010

Call Sign: KB8QOL
Bradley C Morris
4338 Moore Rd
Allegan MI 49010

Call Sign: N8ZMD
Bradley C Morris
4338 Moore Rd
Allegan MI 49010

Call Sign: KC8FIO
Matthew A Harry
2595 N 36th St
Allegan MI 49010

Call Sign: W8FLA
Alex A Polityka
3313 Pine Tree St
Allegan MI 490108101

Call Sign: KB8YGJ

Larry J Billadeau
180 S Main St
Allegan MI 49010

Call Sign: W8LAR
Larry J Billadeau
180 S Main St
Allegan MI 49010

Call Sign: WB9LMK
Clifford E Martz
1934 Sarah St
Allegan MI 49010

Call Sign: KC8AGO
Kathleen C Sempert
551 Sherman St
Allegan MI 49010

Call Sign: K8WPQ
Martha Sempert
551 Sherman St
Allegan MI 490101452

Call Sign: K8OHC
William E Sempert
557 Sherman St
Allegan MI 49010

Call Sign: W8CJQ
Terrie L Hazekamp
107 Thompson St
Allegan MI 49010

Call Sign: KC8DXJ
Charles R Newman
3842 W 102nd Ave
Allegan MI 49010

Call Sign: KD8KYJ
Valerie G White
3470 Whispering Oaks
Allegan MI 49010

Call Sign: WB8ENA
Max R Hale
Allegan MI 49010

Call Sign: WB8SIW
James A Wades
Allegan MI 49010

Call Sign: N8UYB
Rex J Burkhead

Allegan MI 490100115

Call Sign: WA8UWJ
John L Worst
10760 52nd Ave
Allendale MI 49401

Call Sign: KD8CYF
Henry A Miller
11589 56th Ave
Allendale MI 49401

Call Sign: KD8IST
Edward Beck Jr
11440 56th Ave N
Allendale MI 49401

Call Sign: N8WUQ
Frank J Adams
10564 60th Ave
Allendale MI
494018378

Call Sign: KD8CYB
Cameron P Greinke
10166 64th Ave
Allendale MI 49401

Call Sign: WB8WIL
James P Foster
10196 64th Ave
Allendale MI 49401

Call Sign: WD8JKU
Howard E McMullin
11243 64th Ave
Allendale MI 49401

Call Sign: KC8PSZ
Seth A Thurkettle
10015 68th Ave
Allendale MI 49401

Call Sign: KC8PYN
Justin A Door
10336 68th Ave
Allendale MI 49401

Call Sign: KD8ISV
Jared Groeneveld
10577 68th Ave

Allendale MI 49401

Call Sign: W8EBQ
Arthur J Kraker
11053 68th Ave
Allendale MI 49401

Call Sign: KC8VBS
Adam M Bagley
11100 68th Ave
Allendale MI 49401

Call Sign: KA8QVR
Mary B Broeckert
11818 68th Ave
Allendale MI 49401

Call Sign: N8DCY
Hubert P Broeckert
11818 68th Ave
Allendale MI 49401

Call Sign: KC8OPU
Alfonso E Pineiro
9685 72nd Ave
Allendale MI 49401

Call Sign: KD8DBQ
Erika E Pineiro
9685 72nd Ave
Allendale MI 49401

Call Sign: KD8DBT
Rachael M Pineiro
9685 72nd Ave
Allendale MI 49401

Call Sign: KD8DBS
Sheryl A Pineiro
9685 72nd Ave
Allendale MI 49401

Call Sign: KC8QDC
Kim D Aten
9815 76th Ave
Allendale MI 49401

Call Sign: KD8CYI
Partick N Dehaan
12603 76th Ave
Allendale MI 49401

Call Sign: KD8LNQ
Jonathan B Levine

11765 78th Ave
Allendale MI 49401

Call Sign: KC8SRR
Josh L Bekkering
5897 Almari Dr
Allendale MI 49401

Call Sign: KC8SRQ
Trevor D Kuzee
6903 Aspen St
Allendale MI 49401

Call Sign: N8FYT
John M Tymensky
6930 Aspen St
Allendale MI 49401

Call Sign: KD8DAE
Cody Burger
11305 Avery St
Allendale MI 49401

Call Sign: KD8GMN
Brandon M Russell
11387 Big Bear Ct
Allendale MI 49401

Call Sign: KC8DJE
Ryan T Perna
8220 Buchanan Ave
Allendale MI 49401

Call Sign: KC8VBR
Kurtis J De Horn
6064 Crystal Dr
Allendale MI 49401

Call Sign: KE8YK
Eric L Packer
5434 Eric St
Allendale MI 49401

Call Sign: KD8LZU
Mitchell D Johnson
5780 Frostline
Allendale MI 49401

Call Sign: KC8PZF
Patrick J Glaser
5883 Frostline Dr
Allendale MI 49401

Call Sign: KD8OQH

Todd W Kirchner
5895 Frostline Dr
Allendale MI 49401

Call Sign: KC8RDG
Amanda J Fellows
11057 Gayle Ln
Allendale MI
494019388

Call Sign: KC8TKI
Connie S Zimonick
6472 Henry St
Allendale MI 49401

Call Sign: N8CON
Connie S Zimonick
6472 Henry St
Allendale MI 49401

Call Sign: N8ODP
Todd W Carter
5807 Horizon Ln
Allendale MI
494018383

Call Sign: W1TWC
Todd W Carter
5807 Horizon Ln
Allendale MI
494018383

Call Sign: KC8VBN
Aron M Dodger
11469 Hunters
Meadow Dr
Allendale MI 49401

Call Sign: N8RC
Robert C Johnston Sr
5835 Ivory Rd
Allendale MI 49401

Call Sign: W8RCJ
Robert C Johnston Jr
5835 Ivory Rd
Allendale MI 49401

Call Sign: KC8VBQ
Jennifer L Richards
6865 Joal St
Allendale MI 49401

Call Sign: KD8RVK

Ron A Wright
6943 Joal St
Allendale MI 49401

Call Sign: KB8WMO
Susan R Palma
5560 Jordan St
Allendale MI
494018305

Call Sign: N8ROJ
Carl A Palma
5560 Jordan St
Allendale MI
494018305

Call Sign: KC8ZRN
Jason M Bradley
4473 Knollwood Dr
Allendale MI 49401

Call Sign: KD8ANS
Helen M Knoper
12296 Knoper Ct
Allendale MI 49401

Call Sign: KC8VBO
Travis J Dyke
4293 Lake Michigan
Dr
Allendale MI 49401

Call Sign: KD8ISS
Jordan M Aungst
5786 Lake Michigan
Dr
Allendale MI 49401

Call Sign: KC8GDH
Robert J Tanis
7005 Lake Michigan
Dr
Allendale MI 49401

Call Sign: K8JIM
Robert J Tanis
7005 Lake Michigan
Dr
Allendale MI 49401

Call Sign: N8BIG
Scott A McConnell Sr
6692 Martinie Dr Apt
39

Allendale MI 49401

Call Sign: KD8ISU
David C Corner
10862 Melanie Dr
Allendale MI 49401

Call Sign: KC8VBT
Andrew J Cole
4435 Oakland Dr
Allendale MI 49401

Call Sign: KC8VBU
Brent K Cole
4435 Oakland Dr
Allendale MI 49401

Call Sign: KC8OMZ
Jeffrey J Dupilka
7338 Osborne Rd
Allendale MI 49401

Call Sign: WB8TGP
Clifford R Cole
7376 Osborne Rd
Allendale MI 49401

Call Sign: WD8PNG
Allendale ARC
7376 Osborne Rd
Allendale MI 49401

Call Sign: KB8BCP
Sharron K Besteman
6138 Pebble Dr
Allendale MI 49401

Call Sign: KC8SKR
Cody J Brow
6555 Peirce St
Allendale MI 49401

Call Sign: KC8NPH
Brian L Brethauer
6610 Pierce St
Allendale MI 49401

Call Sign: KD8ANU
Brian L Brethauer
6610 Pierce St
Allendale MI 49401

Call Sign: KD8ISW
Justin L Nichols

6971 Pierce St
Allendale MI 49401

Call Sign: KD8CYD
Kyle A Twiest
7794 Pierce St
Allendale MI
494019759

Call Sign: KB8GIV
David C Koch
11027 Pinecreek Ct
Allendale MI 49401

Call Sign: KD8ATR
Kent A Cogbill
11301 Prarie
Allendale MI 49401

Call Sign: KB8TDW
Robert J Beitel Jr
11394 Rosewood Ave
Allendale MI 49401

Call Sign: N8TOB
Robert J Beitel Jr
11394 Rosewood Ave
Allendale MI 49401

Call Sign: N8US
Larry R Stanton
11520 Rosewood Ave
Allendale MI
494019596

Call Sign: K8BBC
Douglas J Lemmen
11045 Stanford Ave
Allendale MI 49401

Call Sign: KD8CYE
Brett A Somero
10640 Tallpine Ln
Allendale MI 49401

Call Sign: KD8LNP
Brian M Koch
10667 Tallpine Ln
Allendale MI 49401

Call Sign: N0BMK
Brian M Koch
10667 Tallpine Ln
Allendale MI 49401

Call Sign: KA8JJN
Allan C Koch
10667 Tallpine Ln
Allendale MI 49401

Call Sign: KD8CYC
Mike J Versluis
5719 Warner St
Allendale MI 49401

Call Sign: KA8GHZ
Clifford E Vander
Hulst
6462 Warner St
Allendale MI 49401

Call Sign: N8EZS
David A Bosch
6555 Warner St
Allendale MI 49401

Call Sign: KC8WQS
David A Bosch
6555 Warner St
Allendale MI 49401

Call Sign: K8PR
David A Bosch
6555 Warner St
Allendale MI 49401

Call Sign: KB8YTQ
Wilmot J Herrick
7114 Warner St
Allendale MI 49401

Call Sign: K8MIW
Melvin E Snyder
9191 Warner St
Allendale MI 49401

Call Sign: KC8VBP
Kellen R Keck
10691 White Birch
Allendale MI 49401

Call Sign: KD8JTC
Christopher M Hollis
6565 Winans St
Allendale MI 49401

Call Sign: WA8RPB
Theodore H Slovinski

Allendale MI 49401

**FCC Amateur Radio
Licenses in Allouez**

Call Sign: K8MDH
Keweenaw County
Repeater Assn
59897 Apple St
Allouez MI 49805

Call Sign: KD8JAM
William R Labell
59897 Apple St
Allouez MI 49805

Call Sign: KB8UMZ
Yvonne Brinkman
Hc 2 Box 815
Allouez MI 498059606

**FCC Amateur Radio
Licenses in Alpena**

Call Sign: K8ZRJ
James H Sepull Sr
712 4th Ave
Alpena MI 49707

Call Sign: W8TZE
Ovide M Lee
220 Adams St
Alpena MI 49707

Call Sign: N8RIC
James J Siegel
5448 Beaver Lk Rd
Alpena MI 49707

Call Sign: KC8RIW
James M Seguin
136 Bernice Ln
Alpena MI 49707

Call Sign: KC8MVT
James E Ohlrich
3620 Bloom Rd
Alpena MI 49707

Call Sign: K8MVT
James E Ohlrich
3620 Bloom Rd
Alpena MI 49707

Call Sign: KG8JJ
Bill T Daoust
8481 Cathro Rd
Alpena MI 49707

Call Sign: K9CK
Brian R King
226 Cavanaugh St
Alpena MI 49707

Call Sign: WE8W
Kenneth M Cubilo
315 Cavanaugh St
Alpena MI 49707

Call Sign: W8OB
Kenneth M Cubilo
315 Cavanaugh St
Alpena MI 49707

Call Sign: KC8ZFO
Glenn F Campbell
10249 Chippewa Dr
Alpena MI 49707

Call Sign: KC8MMT
Gary E Seaman
450 Daisy Ln
Alpena MI 49707

Call Sign: W8KLM
Gary E Seaman
450 Daisy Ln
Alpena MI 49707

Call Sign: KC8FBQ
John D Rings
515 Dawson
Alpena MI 49707

Call Sign: KA8ZTJ
Michael S Wisenbach
533 Dawson St
Alpena MI 49707

Call Sign: KC8DOL
Vernie H Rensberry
573 Dodge Dr
Alpena MI 49707

Call Sign: KC8DOM
Pamela R Rensberry
573 Dodge Dr
Alpena MI 49707

Call Sign: KC8VHR
Bruce R Wozniak
225 E Baldwin
Alpena MI 49707

Call Sign: KD8CLG
Brady Bunch Club
225 E Baldwin St
Alpena MI 49707

Call Sign: KC8RLR
Caleb A Cross
128 E Campbell
Alpena MI 49707

Call Sign: N8TGB
Gary L Ellery
10894 E Grand Lake
Rd
Alpena MI 49707

Call Sign: KC8PWJ
Terry D Ayres
121 E Lewis St
Alpena MI 49707

Call Sign: KF8IO
Russell H Glover
203 Eagle Rd
Alpena MI 49707

Call Sign: N8RID
John F Miller
313 Elizabeth St
Alpena MI 49707

Call Sign: WB8CEC
Marc N Ouellette
2437 Emmet St
Alpena MI 497073429

Call Sign: KC8DOJ
Leonard A Johnsen
1268 Ferncliff Dr
Alpena MI 49707

Call Sign: KC8UAA
Carol F Johnsen
1268 Ferncliff Dr
Alpena MI 49707

Call Sign: AB9EV
Barbara L Terry

812 Ford Ave
Alpena MI 49707

Call Sign: KD8BJQ
Alpena ARES
3154 French Rd
Alpena MI 49707

Call Sign: N8JWH
Johnny L Thomas
3154 French Rd
Alpena MI 49707

Call Sign: KC8RCQ
David Ludlow
3326 French Rd
Alpena MI 49707

Call Sign: WA8EOE
Anthony P Fortier
5335 Irwin Rd
Alpena MI 49707

Call Sign: KB7SRB
Dale M Walenski Jr
1544 King Settlement
Alpena MI 49707

Call Sign: N8UHM
Coralee J Campbell
2990 King Settlement
Rd
Alpena MI 49707

Call Sign: W8JMP
Le Roy F Campbell
2990 King Settlement
Rd
Alpena MI 49707

Call Sign: KB8HBV
William C Blackaby
III
4181 King Settlement
Rd
Alpena MI 49707

Call Sign: WA8WPN
Wayne L Helinski
100 Klemens Dr
Alpena MI 497071119

Call Sign: KB8PDT
Raymond H Pepper

16009 Long Lake Hwy
Alpena MI 49707

Call Sign: KC8TZZ
Betty L Pepper
16009 Long Lake Hwy
Alpena MI 49707

Call Sign: KC8RCP
Jerome J Smigelski Sr
465 Long Rapids Rd
Alpena MI 497071319

Call Sign: N8JVQ
Robert L Niedzwiecki
1241 Long Rapids Rd
Alpena MI 497077918

Call Sign: KB4NTY
Gerald R Schoon
2898 Long Rapids Rd
Alpena MI 49707

Call Sign: N8XKX
Ronald K Shumaker
4710 Long Rapids Rd
Alpena MI 49707

Call Sign: KE8NJ
Richard G Tunney
4896 Long Rapids Rd
Alpena MI 49707

Call Sign: KB8HJE
Patrick C Melville
1013 Long Rapids Rd
Apt 1
Alpena MI 49707

Call Sign: N8SFV
William J Forbush
14999 Maple St
Alpena MI 49707

Call Sign: KA8EKU
Glenn K Helwig
220 McKinley Ave
Alpena MI 49707

Call Sign: KD8JFB
Jared K Helwig
220 McKinley Ave
Alpena MI 49707

Call Sign: KB8ZYZ
Hans A Stevens
316 McKinley St
Alpena MI 49707

Call Sign: KC8NHI
Barry C Buchholz
437 Minor
Alpena MI 49707

Call Sign: KA8FAA
Jerrald A Corn
1013 N 2nd Ave
Alpena MI 49707

Call Sign: N8YKG
Harold W Barnard
381 N Franklin
Alpena MI 49707

Call Sign: N8ZTM
Wendy L Barnard
381 N Franklin
Alpena MI 49707

Call Sign: KC8UWC
Dennis L Knechtel
372 N Lawn St
Alpena MI 49707

Call Sign: N8XDH
Edward W Kavanaugh
7720 N Point Shores
Dr
Alpena MI 49707

Call Sign: K8NKZ
James D Marr
270 N Ripley Blvd
Alpena MI 49707

Call Sign: KD8KUA
Robert C Morford
542 Northwood Dr
Alpena MI 49707

Call Sign: KC8WUJ
David A Rensberry
8300 Otter Tr
Alpena MI 49707

Call Sign: KB8WRN
Ellsworth R Littler

2231 Partridge Point
Rd
Alpena MI 49707

Call Sign: WB8GUL
Joseph M Mielcarek Sr
140 Patricia Ln
Alpena MI 49707

Call Sign: K8JMM
Joseph M Mielcarek Sr
140 Patricia Ln
Alpena MI 49707

Call Sign: KE8ZC
Gerald J Nowicki
3502 Piper Rd
Alpena MI 49707

Call Sign: K8GJN
Gerald J Nowicki
3502 Piper Rd
Alpena MI 49707

Call Sign: KG8N
Gerald J Nowicki
3502 Piper Rd
Alpena MI 49707

Call Sign: KC8UPZ
William J Mccrandall
Sr
1086 Pohl Rd
Alpena MI 49707

Call Sign: N8JQ
William J Mccrandall
Sr
1086 Pohl Rd
Alpena MI 49707

Call Sign: K8QBZ
Richard W Huggler
3791 Rabinette Ave
Alpena MI 49707

Call Sign: KC8CRA
David P Smith
2192 Ralph St
Alpena MI 49707

Call Sign: KB8RQQ
Kevin W Englund
2050 Riverview Dr

Alpena MI 49707

Call Sign: WB8YZD
Richard W Wiitala
1405 S 1st Ave
Alpena MI 49707

Call Sign: W1UP
Richard W Wiitala
1405 S 1st Ave
Alpena MI 49707

Call Sign: W8GRR
Daniel C Tuuri
2512 S 3rd Ave
Alpena MI 49707

Call Sign: N8UHN
Bill L Allen Jr
415 S 5th St
Alpena MI 49707

Call Sign: N8FPB
Roy M La Cross
518 S 6th Ave
Alpena MI 497072704

Call Sign: KD8RKL
Northern Michigan
ARC
441 S Brooke St Apt A
Alpena MI 49707

Call Sign: KD8KUB
Robert J Beuter
441 S Brooke St Apt A
Alpena MI 49707

Call Sign: KD8OVZ
Hugh E Jack
933 Sable St
Alpena MI 49707

Call Sign: N8YNA
Scott A Sherrill Mix
427 Saginaw St
Alpena MI 49707

Call Sign: KD8FSE
Geraldine L Dault
17707 Shubert Hwy
Alpena MI 49707

Call Sign: K1PSR

Geraldine L Dault
17707 Shubert Hwy
Alpena MI 49707

Call Sign: K9BSR
Geraldine L Dault
17707 Shubert Hwy
Alpena MI 49707

Call Sign: KB8ZZA
Robert L Fournier
209 State Ave
Alpena MI 497073835

Call Sign: KL7IYK
Douglas L Dietz
1110 Tanglewood
Alpena MI 49707

Call Sign: WD8Z
Douglas L Dietz
1110 Tanglewood
Alpena MI 49707

Call Sign: KB8UEB
Robert T Krafft
9818 US 23 N
Alpena MI 49707

Call Sign: N8ZTP
Ryan T Krafft
9818 US 23 N
Alpena MI 49707

Call Sign: KD8FSN
Michael L Tarsney
2580 US 23 S
Alpena MI 49707

Call Sign: KB8HJD
Wendy K Vander
Molen
439 Victoria Dr
Alpena MI 49707

Call Sign: KB8HMF
Tim L Vander Molen
439 Victoria Dr
Alpena MI 49707

Call Sign: KB8HJC
John J Darga
118 W Bosley St
Alpena MI 49707

Call Sign: KB8PKQ
Arden V Rensberry
7666 Wallace Rd
Alpena MI 49707

Call Sign: KC8DOK
Mary Ann Rensberry
7666 Wallace Rd
Alpena MI 49707

Call Sign: N8TQC
Gary W Chabot
2187 Werth Rd
Alpena MI 49707

Call Sign: K8NIH
Gerald S Bishop
2327 Werth Rd
Alpena MI 49707

Call Sign: W8KQ
Gerald S Bishop
2327 Werth Rd
Alpena MI 49707

Call Sign: KD8QJP
Ray L Geary
13460 White Ash St
Alpena MI 49707

Call Sign: K8PA
Thunder Bay ARC
Alpena MI 49707

Call Sign: KC8RIX
Gerard A
Tomaszewski
Alpena MI 49707

Call Sign: KC0PNG
Lorraine J Bixley
25460 Hazel Rd
Alston MI 499589217

Call Sign: N0VVR
Brian E Bixley
25460 Hazel Rd
Alston MI 499589217

Call Sign: KD8DBY
Ronald C Lindblom
8510 100th St
Alto MI 49302

Call Sign: K9KAL
Ronald C Lindblom
8510 100th St
Alto MI 49302

Call Sign: KC8WJC
Daniel C Williams
11425 60th Ave
Alto MI 49302

Call Sign: KC8PFS
Jack A Swick
11545 64th Ave
Alto MI 49302

Call Sign: KC8PFZ
Daniel L Brinks
11798 64th St
Alto MI 49302

Call Sign: KB8SOK
Marylu T Dykstra
8100 68th Ave
Alto MI 49302

Call Sign: KD8CP
Rick A Dykstra
8100 68th Ave
Alto MI 49302

Call Sign: KR8T
Rick A Dykstra
8100 68th Ave
Alto MI 49302

Call Sign: KC8VJS
Lawrence I Lanning
9075 68th St SE
Alto MI 49302

Call Sign: KC8REK
Robert S Alguire
12490 72nd St
Alto MI 49302

Call Sign: K8JJC

Paul H Geerdes
8735 76th St SE
Alto MI 49302

Call Sign: WD8IJH
Roger G Lloyd
8413 84th St
Alto MI 49302

Call Sign: KC8DHK
Clinton R Good
8798 84th St
Alto MI 49302

Call Sign: KC8OMH
Cynthia A Stout
13283 84th St
Alto MI 49302

Call Sign: WB8YEG
John W Stiegemeier
8875 84th St SE
Alto MI 49302

Call Sign: KD8LVJ
Ann M Kranenborg
7555 Alaska Ridge Pvt
Alto MI 49302

Call Sign: KD8DLN
Gerben J Kranenborg
7555 Alaska Ridge Pvt
Alto MI 49302

Call Sign: KB8OCA
Gerben J Kranenborg
7555 Alaska Ridge Pvt
Alto MI 49302

Call Sign: NF8K
Gerben J Kranenborg
7555 Alaska Ridge Pvt
Alto MI 49302

Call Sign: N2DOI
Myron Paranich
10205 Baker Ave SE
Alto MI 493029591

Call Sign: KB8YNS
Robert M McKim
6889 Braden Ct SE
Alto MI 49302

Call Sign: KD8GOX
Karl W Seper
6720 Chancery Dr SE
Alto MI 49302

Call Sign: N8OYX
Brian E Koprowski
11865 Drew Rd
Alto MI 49302

Call Sign: KT8R
Douglas W Beaudoin
11925 Drew Rd
Alto MI 49302

Call Sign: KB8TEC
Richard B Clements
8460 Dygert Dr
Alto MI 49302

Call Sign: KD8JYN
Benjamin J Pell
7441 Kettle Lake Dr
Alto MI 49302

Call Sign: KB8SUN
Patrick B Lappin
6851 McCords
Alto MI 49302

Call Sign: N8ISN
Michael L Johnson
7910 McCords SE
Alto MI 49302

Call Sign: KD8OHW
Larry R Lee
9780 Morse Lake Ave
SE
Alto MI 49302

Call Sign: WB8NDC
Roger F Greenfield
6434 Morse Lake Rd
Alto MI 49302

Call Sign: KB8PQU
Michael G Wallen
7887 Sandy Hollow SE
Alto MI 49302

Call Sign: NF8J
Paul L Van Overen
5911 Snow Ave

Alto MI 49302

Call Sign: KB8KMS
Michael H Greenfield
7225 Snow Ave
Alto MI 49302

Call Sign: KD8CPK
Caleb Z Pratt
5588 Snow Ave SE
Alto MI 49302

Call Sign: N8KGE
Christopher A
Robotham
7370 Snow Ave SE
Alto MI 49302

Call Sign: KA8TZM
Tracey L Yonker
6731 Thornapple
Alto MI 49302

Call Sign: KD8MXB
Joshua R Tozer
7974 Timpson Ave
Alto MI 49302

Call Sign: KC8OER
Nathaniel C Vos
8383 Timpson Ave
Alto MI 493029659

Call Sign: KE4ZXY
Troy C Manos
7799 Wedgemont Ct
SE
Alto MI 493029777

Call Sign: W8DA
Wolfgang Philipps
5949 Whitneyville Av
SE
Alto MI 49302

Call Sign: KB3PCF
Eberhard K Bergmann
5949 Whitneyville Av
SE
Alto MI 49302

Call Sign: AC8DK
Eberhard K Bergmann

5949 Whitneyville Av
SE
Alto MI 49302

Call Sign: K8EX
Michael J Bottema
5672 Whitneyville Ave
SE
Alto MI 49302

Call Sign: KD8RKR
Gerald B Long
9832 Windstar Dr SE
Alto MI 49302

Call Sign: KD8OPD
Paul F Jackson
7577 Wingeier Ave SE
Alto MI 49302

Call Sign: N8GHW
William R Swartz
8590 Woodland Forest
S E
Alto MI 49302

**FCC Amateur Radio
Licenses in Amasa**

Call Sign: KB8VUW
Wayne M Leppiaho
326 Hemlock Ave
Amasa MI 49903

Call Sign: KB8UKY
James E Juneau
112 Park City Cut Off
Amasa MI 49903

**FCC Amateur Radio
Licenses in Arcadia**

Call Sign: KC8MPG
Jason P Manke
17312 3rd St
Arcadia MI 49613

Call Sign: WS8Z
Gerd Hollbusch
15526 Maxey Dr
Arcadia MI 49613

Call Sign: N8KDM
Sally J Hollbusch

15526 Maxey Rd
Arcadia MI 49613

Call Sign: W8SHJ
Clarence W Lubahn
15315 St Pierre
Arcadia MI 49613

Call Sign: KB8MKB
Maxworth S Mathews
16603 Surfside Dr
Arcadia MI 49613

Call Sign: K6FC
Frederick K Crosher
1448 Watervale Rd
Arcadia MI 49613

Call Sign: N8WVD
Kent C Babcock
Arcadia MI 49613

FCC Amateur Radio Licenses in Athens

Call Sign: WA7SFE
Robert F Frederick
48 Juniper Dr
Athens MI 490119788

Call Sign: KC8LVZ
Jeffrey E Chichester
115 S Ave B
Athens MI 490110182

Call Sign: KC8LVY
Ted M Chichester
674 S Capital
Athens MI 49011

Call Sign: K8MEX
Miles D Van Orman
1196 V Dr S
Athens MI 49011

FCC Amateur Radio Licenses in Atlanta

Call Sign: KA8NAW
John S Webb
14350 Airport Rd Po 122
Atlanta MI 49709

Call Sign: KD8IHI
Christine M Moe
Herlick
9811 Big Pine St
Atlanta MI 49709

Call Sign: KD8IHM
Henry F Herlick
9811 Big Pine St
Atlanta MI 49709

Call Sign: KB8DGR
Jeffrey A Meyers
Rt 2 Box 1053
Atlanta MI 49709

Call Sign: KA8WRG
Armond H Reed
Rt 3 Box 134Ab
Atlanta MI 49709

Call Sign: N8YUM
Stanley J Streit
Rt 3 Box 300A Jewell Rd
Atlanta MI 49709

Call Sign: W8IZE
Weldon H Johnson
Rt 2 Box74A
Atlanta MI 49709

Call Sign: N8QQP
Charles E Kinzie
18335 Carter Rd
Atlanta MI 49709

Call Sign: KA8AWA
James L Krumbach
14551 Clark St
Atlanta MI 49709

Call Sign: KC8LJV
Raymond G Hinton
17800 Dobbyn Rd
Atlanta MI 497098811

Call Sign: K8CUR
Charles R Baxter
17865 Dobbyn Rd
Atlanta MI 49709

Call Sign: W1BAD
Raymond G Hinton

17800 Dobbyn Rd
Atlanta MI 49709

Call Sign: W8HRS
Irene M Steele
16985 Harwood Rd
Atlanta MI 49709

Call Sign: W8VYB
Edgar F Steele
16985 Harwood Rd
Atlanta MI 49709

Call Sign: KD8BEX
Melanie S Sides
9622 Hossler Rd
Atlanta MI 49709

Call Sign: W8LSJ
Jamie L Sides
9622 Hossler Rd
Atlanta MI 497090284

Call Sign: N8PQ
Jamie L Sides
9622 Hossler Rd
Atlanta MI 497090284

Call Sign: KD8EKI
Harry J Chapman
7265 Lutz Rd
Atlanta MI 49709

Call Sign: KC8WEJ
Charles W Isbell
8400 M 32
Atlanta MI 49709

Call Sign: KA8NVG
Robert L Robertson
10240 M 32
Atlanta MI 49709

Call Sign: KA8NCK
Eugene C Isbell
8300 M 32 Rt 2
Atlanta MI 49709

Call Sign: KC8WNT
Catherine A Isbell
8400 M 32 W
Atlanta MI 49709

Call Sign: KC8FUR

Frances M Baker
12110 M 33 N
Atlanta MI 49709

Call Sign: KE4ZRN
James L Baker
12110 M 33 N
Atlanta MI 49709

Call Sign: N8SQK
Kenneth L Dextrom
12440 Manier Rd
Atlanta MI 49709

Call Sign: N8UNA
Nancy L Dextrom
12440 Manier Rd
Atlanta MI 49709

Call Sign: WD8KPY
Harold Moore
8583 Moore Rd
Atlanta MI 49709

Call Sign: KD8LBT
Gordon R Green
11680 Pine St
Atlanta MI 49709

Call Sign: WA1KKO
Thomas E Williams
7910 Poulsen Rd
Atlanta MI 49709

Call Sign: W8TOM
Thomas E Williams
7910 Poulsen Rd
Atlanta MI 49709

Call Sign: N8YUV
Samuel M Oliver
22621 Shelton Trl
Atlanta MI 49709

Call Sign: WS8S
Richard W Stephens
17840 W Lockwood Lake Rd
Atlanta MI 48709

Call Sign: KD8GAH
Robert M Lind
Atlanta MI 49709

Call Sign: W8RML
Robert M Lind
Atlanta MI 49709

Call Sign: KC8LSJ
Jamie L Sides
Atlanta MI 497090284

Call Sign: KC8LWT
Austin D Gawne
Atlanta MI 497090284

Call Sign: KD8DUI
Austin D Gawne
Atlanta MI 497090284

FCC Amateur Radio Licenses in Atlantic Mine

Call Sign: KB8OYL
Anne E Childs
Rte 1 Box 162A
Atlantic Mine MI 49905

Call Sign: KC8LBQ
Guenther M Wilke
Rr 1 Box 191 A
Atlantic Mine MI 49905

Call Sign: WA8OAU
Joseph A Podner
13 Chippewa Dr
Atlantic Mine MI 49905

Call Sign: KC8PPI
Leanne M Hellerud
45 Coles Creek Rd
Atlantic Mine MI 49905

Call Sign: KD8DXZ
Michael J Benda
9426 Freda Rd
Atlantic Mine MI 49905

Call Sign: KB8VWZ
Jonathan E Leinonen
50520 Holman School Rd

Atlantic Mine MI 49905

Call Sign: KM4I
Martin L Young
114 B Huron St
Atlantic Mine MI 49905

Call Sign: N8CFU
Walter J Merila
10 Naumkeg
Atlantic Mine MI 49905

Call Sign: NU8V
William H White
13743 Rova Rd
Atlantic Mine MI 49905

Call Sign: K8CAS
Charles H Paavo
Box 68 Rte 1
Atlantic Mine MI 49905

FCC Amateur Radio Licenses in Au Gres

Call Sign: N8PJX
George J Caverly
700 Allen Ct
Au Gres MI 48703

Call Sign: KB8AAC
William C Beier
801 Allen Ct
Au Gres MI 48703

Call Sign: WD8CRQ
Armin C Tata
2369 Bay Ridge Dr
Au Gres MI 487039483

Call Sign: KD8CGP
Brian D Smith
784 Crescent
Au Gres MI 48703

Call Sign: KC8NFR
Robert Ameriguian
5315 E 31st St

Au Gres MI 48703

Call Sign: KA1AE
George Bullard
2862 E Booth Rd
Au Gres MI 48703

Call Sign: KD8KQS
Vernon W Looney
2673 E Gordon Rd
Au Gres MI 48703

Call Sign: W8FQT
Richard J Mondro
5145 E Michigan Ave
Au Gres MI 487039470

Call Sign: WD8JCN
Jack A Tosto
624 N Huron Rd
Au Gres MI 48703

Call Sign: K0VP
Kenneth O Schoenlein
3036 Pt Au Gres Ln
Au Gres MI 487039534

Call Sign: K8FY
Florence E Young
2634 Rumsey Rd
Au Gres MI 48703

Call Sign: W8JY
Jesse C Young
2634 Rumsey Rd
Au Gres MI 48703

Call Sign: W8OAI
Merle J Wright
1155 S Lake Ave
Au Gres MI 48703

Call Sign: N8MAI
Douglas G McDonald
3330 S Point Augres Rd
Au Gres MI 48703

Call Sign: WB8IGU
Howard G Hawkins
915 Sanford Ln
Au Gres MI 48703

Call Sign: WB8VDH
David O Swartz
5427 Whitman Rd
Au Gres MI 48703

FCC Amateur Radio Licenses in Au Train

Call Sign: K5HZ
Ronald L Rausch
East 3217 N Deer Lake Trl
Au Train MI 49806

Call Sign: KD8PYT
Sarah S Redmond
E3423 Shelter Bay Rd
Au Train MI 49806

Call Sign: KD8GJR
Duncan R Ferguson
N9260 Shore Dr
Au Train MI 49806

Call Sign: W8SAX
Gerald E Krieg
Au Train MI 49806

FCC Amateur Radio Licenses in Augusta

Call Sign: KB8NDA
Richard A Abell
15703 Ann Ln
Augusta MI 49012

Call Sign: WD8MRL
Maxwell L Schuyler
912 Augusta Dr
Augusta MI 49012

Call Sign: KB8WUC
Sharon D Weirick
15994 Augusta Dr
Augusta MI 49012

Call Sign: N8PGJ
Roger C Weirick
15994 Augusta Dr
Augusta MI 49012

Call Sign: KB8UMX
Jose A Garcia

604 E Augusta Dr
Augusta MI 49012

Call Sign: KB8QAJ
Harry W McCarty
16915 E C Ave
Augusta MI 49012

Call Sign: WA0VLU
Randall C Stout
8407 Fernwood St
Augusta MI 49012

Call Sign: KA8WQX
David B Penrod
16775 M 89
Augusta MI 49012

Call Sign: W8ISG
Bo A Thunman
4550 N 38th St
Augusta MI 49012

Call Sign: K8ICE
Albert C Schauer
6455 N 39th St
Augusta MI 49012

Call Sign: N8EVG
Phyllis J Schauer
6455 N 39th St
Augusta MI 49012

Call Sign: KD8CJA
Gary R Stratman
7880 N 40th St
Augusta MI 49012

Call Sign: KD8JGO
Kira K Hamelink
8621 N 40th St
Augusta MI 49012

Call Sign: KB8MLM
Chester C Sperry
6958 N 41st St
Augusta MI 49012

Call Sign: WA8HQD
John T Thornton
10000 N 44th St
Augusta MI 49012

Call Sign: KC8JMM

Ronda L Stace
312 N Webster St
Augusta MI 49012

Call Sign: WD8OTM
Nobile Bortolussi
705 N Webster St
Augusta MI 49012

Call Sign: KC8KZS
William O Lubitz
512 Ranson St
Augusta MI 49012

Call Sign: W8JPO
Ronald R Hutchinson
650 S Lincoln St
Augusta MI 49012

Call Sign: KB8LZY
William A Harris
308 W Jefferson Ave
Augusta MI 49012

FCC Amateur Radio Licenses in Baldwin

Call Sign: N8AGS
Leonard A Todd
555 Baldwin Ave
Baldwin MI 49304

Call Sign: KA8EBM
William Abernathy
Rt 2 Box 2178
Baldwin MI 49304

Call Sign: K8YZH
John F McGraw
R3 Box 3180B
Baldwin MI 49304

Call Sign: KB8SLL
Roy M Rockey
5018 Chief Okemos
Baldwin MI 49304

Call Sign: N8XBV
Waylon M Lambert
9105 Ironwood Dr
Baldwin MI
493048348

Call Sign: KD8EHP

David L Saunders
885 Oak St
Baldwin MI 49304

Call Sign: KD8IAD
James E Rogers Jr
5216 S Formen Rd
Baldwin MI 49304

Call Sign: KA8SKR
Daniel C Hanes
5120 S Lazy Deer Ln
Baldwin MI 49304

Call Sign: KI4ATG
Mark S Hittle
5202 S Tomahawk Trl
Baldwin MI 49304

Call Sign: N8TAB
Kenmar E Blass
692 W Blass Dr
Baldwin MI 49304

Call Sign: KD8LBI
Martin Dykstra
1689 W Centerline Rd
Baldwin MI 49304

Call Sign: KB8NUP
Karen L Kirkland
8625 W Greenbriar
Baldwin MI 49304

Call Sign: KD8EHO
Mac L Mcclellan
2535 W Hummingbird
Ln
Baldwin MI 49304

Call Sign: N8TDR
Alton D Galloup
4710 Whalen Lake
Baldwin MI 49304

Call Sign: KD8NSP
Mary A Doty
5811 Whalen Lake Dr
Baldwin MI 49304

Call Sign: KB8ZCQ
Lucinda K Dechow
4700 Whalen Lake Rd
Baldwin MI 49304

FCC Amateur Radio Licenses in Bandera

Call Sign: WA8DXM
Robert A Vidervol
1767 Bradford St N E
Bandera MI
495031323

FCC Amateur Radio Licenses in Bangor

Call Sign: KC8TZL
Elmer E Brant
65140 1st St
Bangor MI 49013

Call Sign: WD8JWY
J E Collins
55160 32nd Ave
Bangor MI 49013

Call Sign: W8AAT
Edwin G Ryba
52597 34th Ave
Bangor MI 49013

Call Sign: KC8HKD
Harold G Walworth
31230 52nd St
Bangor MI 49013

Call Sign: KC8HKH
Trena A Walworth
31230 52nd St
Bangor MI 49013

Call Sign: N8HGW
Harold G Walworth
31230 52nd St
Bangor MI 49013

Call Sign: KC8CID
Frederick R Krizan
14140 62nd St
Bangor MI 49013

Call Sign: K5PDR
Phillip H Deruiter
15725 62nd St
Bangor MI 49013

Call Sign: N8GUM

Scott A Helm
35844 62nd St
Bangor MI 49013

Call Sign: N8TFV
Peter J Stromeyer
34201 66th St
Bangor MI 49013

Call Sign: KC8EPN
Esther S Garvison
38047 66th St
Bangor MI 49013

Call Sign: WD8MWT
Paul A Reissmann
43775 66th St
Bangor MI 49013

Call Sign: KD8GLF
Alice M Reissman
43775 66th St
Bangor MI 49013

Call Sign: N8ZFT
Sherry L Ulam
104 Bangor St
Bangor MI 49013

Call Sign: N8ZFX
Charles M Schultz Sr
104 Bangor St
Bangor MI 49013

Call Sign: AJ9L
Jan M Pencik
419 Cherry Ct
Bangor MI 49013

Call Sign: NT8G
Walter L De Visser Sr
63165 CR 380
Bangor MI 49013

Call Sign: KB3QL
David W Holmes
39515 CR 673
Bangor MI 49013

Call Sign: WA8PRJ
John E Helm
32777 CR 681
Bangor MI 49013

Call Sign: WA8ZXP
Carol A Helm
32777 CR 681
Bangor MI 49013

Call Sign: WA8ZXQ
Mervin O Yeider
24722 CR 687
Bangor MI 490139450

Call Sign: WA8YYI
Wallace C Krogel
32001 CR 687
Bangor MI 49013

Call Sign: WD8MDY
Richard J Anthony Sr
310 E Cass St
Bangor MI 49013

Call Sign: NB8A
Richard J Anthony Sr
310 E Cass St
Bangor MI 49013

Call Sign: KB8DYE
William H Lindemann
29609 Eastwood Ln
Bangor MI 49013

Call Sign: AA8II
Benny F Williams
1109 Hasting St
Bangor MI 49013

Call Sign: W8RWK
Robert L Garvison
60311 M 43
Bangor MI 49013

Call Sign: N8WVF
Roy M Richmond
229 North St
Bangor MI 49013

Call Sign: N8EVA
Chelmyrle L Foltz
65574 Park Ave Drake
Sub
Bangor MI 49013

Call Sign: KE9JM
John J Toman
43400 Van Auken Dr

Bangor MI 49013

Call Sign: N9YPT
Katie Toman
43400 Van Auken Dr
Bangor MI 49013

Call Sign: AB8GL
John J Toman
43400 Van Auken Dr
Bangor MI 49013

Call Sign: KC8HBS
Michael R Todd Sr
215 W Arlington
Bangor MI 49013

Call Sign: WA8ZGR
Myrick P Wood Sr
405 W Arlington St
Bangor MI 49013

Call Sign: KB8PJU
Delores A Robinson
15 W Douglass St
Bangor MI 49013

Call Sign: N8GWT
Kim D Armstrong
832 Washington Ave
Bangor MI 49013

Call Sign: WD8RJO
Lynn L Geresy
30755 White Oak Dr
Bangor MI 49013

Call Sign: N8LLG
Lynn L Geresy
30755 White Oak Dr
Bangor MI 49013

Call Sign: K8BRC
Black River ARC
Bangor MI 49013

Call Sign: KA8JNO
Scott E Garvison
Bangor MI 49013

Call Sign: W8JUU
Black River ARC
Bangor MI 49013

FCC Amateur Radio Licenses in Baraga

Call Sign: KC8CDE
Susan B Ruddy
Rt 1 Box 202
Baraga MI 49908

Call Sign: N8XJQ
Kristine K Kuker
Rt 1 Box 202
Baraga MI 49908

Call Sign: KD8GBK
Ralph K Bemis
15404 Mission Rd
Baraga MI 49908

Call Sign: WD8ODP
Erik P Vachon
425 S US 41
Baraga MI 499089670

Call Sign: N8SRL
Brian J Ruddy
13284 US Hwy 41
Baraga MI 49908

FCC Amateur Radio Licenses in Barbeau

Call Sign: KB8YNP
Joseph P McNamara
Barbeau MI 49710

Call Sign: KB8YNR
Robert J McNamara
Barbeau MI 49710

FCC Amateur Radio Licenses in Bark River

Call Sign: KB8JCM
Joanne M Erickson
1541 13 5 Ln
Bark River MI 49807

Call Sign: N8HBK
Howard L Erickson
1541 135 Ln
Bark River MI 49807

Call Sign: N8MAK

Alan H Barra
N19297 N B1 Rd
Bark River MI 49807

Call Sign: KB8HMY
Ching Y Bezine
1226 Old Hwy 2 & 41
Bark River MI 49807

Call Sign: KB8HMW
Frank Bezine
1226 Old Hwy 2 And
41
Bark River MI 49807

Call Sign: N8AFZ
William E Baker
1000 Old US 2 41
Bark River MI 49807

Call Sign: N8XAG
Dorothy M Baker
1000 Old US 2 41
Bark River MI 49807

Call Sign: KB8VYL
Sally M Moore
1342 Old US 2 41
Bark River MI 49807

FCC Amateur Radio Licenses in Baroda

Call Sign: KD8NWV
Jerrit G Tyler
9470 Cleveland Ave
Baroda MI 49101

Call Sign: KA8IJL
Ira G Salisbury
10931 Hills Rd
Baroda MI 49101

Call Sign: WD8RQA
Wolfgang S Moneta
515 Lemon Creek Rd
Baroda MI 49101

Call Sign: KC8JUC
Luke W Galanda
1993 Lemon Creek Rd
Baroda MI 49101

Call Sign: KA8LAV

Sandra L Daignault
7232 Lincoln Ave
Baroda MI 49101

Call Sign: WA1LJY
Edward A Daignault
7232 Lincoln Ave
Baroda MI 49101

Call Sign: W8KBQ
Jack E Kessler
9141 Livengood Rd
Baroda MI 49101

Call Sign: W8GPB
Gerald E Tolsma
1580 Placid
Baroda MI 49101

Call Sign: N8BAJ
Paul F Thielen
1540 Placid Dr
Baroda MI 49101

Call Sign: KD9IU
Darryl L Council
8836 Stev Bar Rd 101
Baroda MI 49101

Call Sign: WA9WUD
Arthur A Blind
1000 W Shawnee Rd
Baroda MI 49101

FCC Amateur Radio Licenses in Barryton

Call Sign: KD8FBG
John W Carman II
5338 20 Mile Rd
Barryton MI 49305

Call Sign: KB8ZEM
Steve R Huffman
19171 30th Ave
Barryton MI 49305

Call Sign: KC8BAQ
Michael L Nicholson
19238 30th Ave
Barryton MI 49305

Call Sign: KC8DHR
Gregory R Cornell

21020 30th Ave
Barryton MI 49305

Call Sign: KC8OMJ
Lillian J Spence
21463 30th Ave
Barryton MI 49305

Call Sign: KC8LSM
Paul E Mulder
19397 35th Ave
Barryton MI 49305

Call Sign: KD5MYN
Robert D Cooley
21530 40th Ave
Barryton MI 49305

Call Sign: KB8VST
Robert W Harris
17871 55th Ave
Barryton MI 49305

Call Sign: KC8FYH
Susan R Harris
17871 55th Ave
Barryton MI 49305

Call Sign: N8VZP
Roger R Zuke
4851 Airstrip Dr
Barryton MI 49305

Call Sign: KC8WGE
Billie J Straus
3235 Hoover Rd
Barryton MI 49305

Call Sign: N8XXO
Ronald J Mackersie Jr
202 Marion Ave Box
126
Barryton MI 49305

Call Sign: KD8LAB
Lavonne M Cowan
362 Norman St
Barryton MI 49305

Call Sign: KD8DHZ
Steven L Cowan
362 Norman St
Barryton MI 49305

Call Sign: W4NKL
Patricia J Pennock
7165 Northland Blvd
Barryton MI 49305

Call Sign: W8ROD
Rodman L Bright
18336 Oxbow Dr
Barryton MI 49305

FCC Amateur Radio Licenses in Barton City

Call Sign: W8GQL
William A Bleher
2084 Trask Lake Rd
Barton City MI 48705

FCC Amateur Radio Licenses in Bath

Call Sign: KD8KYR
John A Snyder
13098 Angle Rd
Bath MI 48808

Call Sign: KA8VXA
Victor H Weipert Jr
14403 Center Rd
Bath MI 48808

Call Sign: WD8OEV
Robert L Mann
5220 Clark Rd
Bath MI 48808

Call Sign: KB8SRO
Stephen T Ward
6147 Clise Rd
Bath MI 48808

Call Sign: N8FIT
Stephanie A Ward
6147 Clise Rd
Bath MI 48808

Call Sign: KB8HTM
Scott M Rowe
7187 Drumheller Rd
Bath MI 48808

Call Sign: AB8VN
Scott M Rowe

7187 Drumheller Rd
Bath MI 48808

Call Sign: KC8CY
Donald L De Feyter
5061 E Clark Rd
Bath MI 488080073

Call Sign: W8BIT
Edward A Szuba
13981 Mead Creek Rd
Bath MI 48808

Call Sign: KB8FUF
Darrell L Ide
15605 S Chandler Rd
Bath MI 48808

Call Sign: KC5SKF
Michael S Homer
13628 Walnut St
Bath MI 48808

Call Sign: K8CWQ
Keith B Colister
14190 Webster Rd
Bath MI 48808

Call Sign: KB8IYU
Edward C Ferrigan
15449 Webster Rd
Bath MI 48808

FCC Amateur Radio Licenses in Battle Creek

Call Sign: KD8BME
Donna A Smith
16745 10 Mile Rd
Battle Creek MI 49014

Call Sign: W8USU
Gary L Kyser
20949 10 Mile Rd
Battle Creek MI 49014

Call Sign: KD8QNM
Kirk P Babcock
16800 14 Mile Rd
Battle Creek MI 49014

Call Sign: N8MVW
John P Jones

17750 14 Mile Rd
Battle Creek MI 49014

Call Sign: KB8PSG
Kenneth L Handley
116 23rd St S
Battle Creek MI 49015

Call Sign: KC8ZYM
Kenneth L Handley II
120 23rd St S
Battle Creek MI 49015

Call Sign: W8FOI
Vincent L Beck
11595 4 Mile Rd
Battle Creek MI 49015

Call Sign: N8THU
Thomas A Morris Jr
11175 8 Mile Rd
Battle Creek MI 49014

Call Sign: KF6SCE
Catherine Doubleday
13297 9 Mile Rd
Battle Creek MI 49014

Call Sign: KB8AN
Wayne F Paull
13756 9 Mile Rd
Battle Creek MI
490148286

Call Sign: K8DZN
Roland E Misner
131 Academy St
Battle Creek MI 49017

Call Sign: KA8CXS
Beverly J Williams
15202 Ackerson Dr
Battle Creek MI 49014

Call Sign: WD8LJF
Charles O Williams
15202 Ackerson Dr
Battle Creek MI 49014

Call Sign: W8NXL
Eldon L McAdams
15285 Ackerson Dr
Battle Creek MI
490178915

Call Sign: W8MGO
Daniel L Martin
126 Ansted Dr
Battle Creek MI 49015

Call Sign: WA8QBG
Hilda M Martin
126 Ansted Dr
Battle Creek MI 49015

Call Sign: KC8QNQ
Wendell K Nierman Jr
355 Ave A
Battle Creek MI 49015

Call Sign: WD8DTM
William L Collins Jr
1267 Ave A Lot 77
Battle Creek MI 49015

Call Sign: KC8UJO
Allan W Chapman
8226 B Dr N
Battle Creek MI 49014

Call Sign: KD8CPU
Stephen C Larson
7887 B Dr S
Battle Creek MI 49014

Call Sign: WB8RVT
Donald E Larkin
114 Bansill Dr
Battle Creek MI 49017

Call Sign: KD8MA
James R Keller
163 Bansill Dr
Battle Creek MI 49017

Call Sign: KD8CQN
Andrew D Rockwell
149 Barbadoes Trl
Battle Creek MI 49015

Call Sign: KA8JPR
Vernon I Tatum
95 Barney Blvd
Battle Creek MI 49017

Call Sign: KB8ZXJ
Battle Creek Academy
ARC

1265 Baseline Rd
Battle Creek MI 49017

Call Sign: KB8HRH
Alyne J Howard
5501 Bauman Rd
Battle Creek MI 49017

Call Sign: KC8WBX
James Mrozovich
225 Beachfield Dr
Battle Creek MI
490154641

Call Sign: N8UFD
Henry D Wilbur
13645 Beadle Lake Rd
Battle Creek MI 49017

Call Sign: KD8CIF
Robert A Gould
15131 Beadle Lake Rd
Battle Creek MI 49014

Call Sign: W8DOP
Richard C Hillyer
13813 Beadle Lk Rd
Battle Creek MI 49014

Call Sign: KF8U
R Craig Diederich
7071 Beaver Ridge Dr
Battle Creek MI 49014

Call Sign: K8DVG
William E Smith
304 Beckett Park
Battle Creek MI 49015

Call Sign: KC8WLD
David E Nawatny
4090 Beckley Rd
Battle Creek MI 49015

Call Sign: K8WLD
David E Nawatny
4090 Beckley Rd
Battle Creek MI 49015

Call Sign: N8SSX
Lawrence H Ruble
197 Beckwith Dr
Battle Creek MI 49015

Call Sign: N8XIP
Larry R Hatt
226 Beulah Ave
Battle Creek MI 49017

Call Sign: K8PQJ
Robert E George
35 Billy Dr
Battle Creek MI 49017

Call Sign: WD8CLF
Paul W Clark
410 Birdsall Dr S
Battle Creek MI 49017

Call Sign: KC8HSP
Daniel A Bentz
208 Bittersweet Ln
Battle Creek MI 49015

Call Sign: WB8FIZ
Henry A Gutman
214 Bittersweet Ln
Battle Creek MI 49015

Call Sign: KA8DNK
Niels M Magnusson III
200 Black Cherry Ln
Battle Creek MI
490157627

Call Sign: KC8COR
Paul J Costa
25 Bluestone Ridge
Battle Creek MI 49014

Call Sign: KB8HJ
James H Flowers
319 Bowers St
Battle Creek MI 49017

Call Sign: KA8INO
Richard J Pickard
30 Boyer Dr
Battle Creek MI
490148235

Call Sign: KD8IAO
Robert J Sharkey
258 Brentwood Dr
Battle Creek MI 49015

Call Sign: KB8MHT
David L Hlatko

153 Briars Farm Ln
Battle Creek MI 49017

Call Sign: KB8MHU
Ellen A Hlatko
153 Briars Farm Ln
Battle Creek MI 49017

Call Sign: KI4TZV
Jeff Fulcher
150 Buckley Ln
Battle Creek MI 49015

Call Sign: KC8CIF
Mark A Dill
129 Caine St
Battle Creek MI 49017

Call Sign: KC8MKB
Scott A Spaulding
1421 Capital Ave Apt
25
Battle Creek MI
490175373

Call Sign: AB8IH
Scott A Spaulding
1421 Capital Ave Apt
25
Battle Creek MI
490175373

Call Sign: KD8EPX
Dennis W Vanwinkle
600 Capital Ave NE
Battle Creek MI
490175554

Call Sign: N8UU
Russell H Beutler
1889 Capital Ave NE
Battle Creek MI 49017

Call Sign: KD8CVM
Stephanie L Halbert
20960 Capital Ave NE
Battle Creek MI 49017

Call Sign: W8AEZ
Stephanie L Halbert
20960 Capital Ave NE
Battle Creek MI 49017

Call Sign: N9KZU

Michael R Kelter
1409 Capital Ave NE 6
Battle Creek MI 49017

Call Sign: N8WDS
Larry G Allen
20699 Carpenter Dr
Battle Creek MI 49017

Call Sign: KB8VCY
Stephen R Allen
280 Carpenters Cove
Battle Creek MI
490179710

Call Sign: KC8QOR
Scott M Parker
172 Central St
Battle Creek MI 49017

Call Sign: KD8BXG
John H Phillips
262 Central St
Battle Creek MI 49017

Call Sign: KC8MUF
Howard J Westrick
22 Chambers
Battle Creek MI 49014

Call Sign: N3LRX
Randall J Berry
250 Champion St 304
Battle Creek MI
490372345

Call Sign: W8RTP
John A Heppeard
134 Chapel Hill Dr
Battle Creek MI 49015

Call Sign: KD8ILI
Timothy J Brauer
1222 Cherry Ln
Battle Creek MI 49017

Call Sign: N8AKY
Timothy J Brauer
1222 Cherry Ln
Battle Creek MI 49017

Call Sign: N8GDM
Richard V Thurtle
201 Cherry St

Battle Creek MI
490173935

Call Sign: N8SFZ
Robert C Armstrong
168 Chestnut
Battle Creek MI 49017

Call Sign: KC8SCZ
Christal G Bush
21 Clark St
Battle Creek MI 49014

Call Sign: KC8LHM
Bruce A Longanecker
382 Cliff St
Battle Creek MI 49014

Call Sign: N8AEU
Louis B Wessel
314 Clover Ln
Battle Creek MI 49015

Call Sign: WD8BVL
Gerard J Foss Sr
20756 Collier Ave
Battle Creek MI 49017

Call Sign: N8CVC
Mary E Phillips
34 Columbine Ln
Battle Creek MI 49015

Call Sign: W8JPS
John H Phillips
34 Columbine Ln
Battle Creek MI 49015

Call Sign: N8BCB
Robert W Eaton
282 Community Dr
Battle Creek MI 49014

Call Sign: KD8RCK
Thomas L Goodson
8 Cooper Ave
Battle Creek MI 49014

Call Sign: WR8G
Thomas L Goodson
8 Cooper Ave
Battle Creek MI 49014

Call Sign: KC8RHQ

Barbara L Parsons
280 Cornell Dr
Battle Creek MI 49017

Call Sign: W8RWJ
Clarence W Galen
4235 Council Crest Cir
Battle Creek MI 49017

Call Sign: WB8AAI
Clifford W Galen
396 Country Club Dr
Battle Creek MI 49015

Call Sign: KC8COT
David M Smith
35 Crosby Dr
Battle Creek MI 49014

Call Sign: W8PWE
John Dayhuff
5875B Dr S
Battle Creek MI 49017

Call Sign: WB8UUE
Mark H Lambert
222 Dream Dr
Battle Creek MI 49017

Call Sign: KD8BBG
Bush Family Radio
Club
261 E Emmett St
Battle Creek MI 49017

Call Sign: KD8DXY
Michael C Hoekstra
5240 E Halbert Rd
Battle Creek MI 49017

Call Sign: KB8CBO
Tedoric J Mohr
5270 E Halbert Rd
Battle Creek MI 49017

Call Sign: KB8YDP
Richard L Wright
4297 E Kirby Rd
Battle Creek MI 49017

Call Sign: K8IWX
Richard F Holcomb
30 E Langley Rd
Battle Creek MI 49015

Call Sign: KB8SLK
Sharon K Yeomans
1103 E Mich Ave 24
Battle Creek MI 49017

Call Sign: KC8FJG
John M Terry
368 E Michigan Ave
Battle Creek MI 49014

Call Sign: KB8UKF
Gary F Schense
1317 E Michigan Ave
Battle Creek MI 49014

Call Sign: W8IER
Gary F Schense
1317 E Michigan Ave
Battle Creek MI 49014

Call Sign: KA8IZN
Daniel J Pesch
1463 E Michigan Ave
Battle Creek MI 49017

Call Sign: KD8NOG
Daniel S Kowalewski
953 E Michigan Ave
Lot F5
Battle Creek MI 49014

Call Sign: WO8C
Robert J Bush
239 E Minges Rd
Battle Creek MI 49015

Call Sign: AB8DZ
Yoshinari Shintani
523 E Minges Rd
Battle Creek MI 49015

Call Sign: KC8MGY
Teruo Fujimoto
523 E Minges Rd
Battle Creek MI 49015

Call Sign: W8HAM
Charles E Dommer
553 E Minges Rd
Battle Creek MI 49015

Call Sign: WA8YTB
Henry R Cathcart

6258 E Morgan Rd
Battle Creek MI 49017

Call Sign: WD8OMF
Phyllis K Cathcart
6258 E Morgan Rd
Battle Creek MI 49017

Call Sign: WA8RC
Henry R Cathcart
6258 E Morgan Rd
Battle Creek MI 49017

Call Sign: KD8NJB
David M Ashbolt
7008 E Morgan Rd
Battle Creek MI
490178620

Call Sign: K8OLY
David M Ashbolt
7008 E Morgan Rd
Battle Creek MI
490178620

Call Sign: KD8BMF
Richard V Osborne
626 E Roosevelt Rd
Battle Creek MI 49017

Call Sign: N8XCN
Stephen D Cole
150 E Willard Ave
Battle Creek MI
490171826

Call Sign: WD8BZ
Jack W Cox
37 E Willard St
Battle Creek MI 49017

Call Sign: N8LS
Jack W Cox
37 E Willard St
Battle Creek MI 49017

Call Sign: W8JMZ
James M Zoss
263 Easthill Dr
Battle Creek MI 49014

Call Sign: WD8DHS
James M Zoss
263 Easthill Dr

Battle Creek MI 49017

Call Sign: KD8FJI
Bronson G Reed
277 Eaton St
Battle Creek MI 49017

Call Sign: KD8FJJ
James E Reed
277 Eaton St
Battle Creek MI 49017

Call Sign: KE4CCU
Christopher M
Cullingford
316 Eaton St
Battle Creek MI 49017

Call Sign: N8WVG
Joseph W Evankovich
Jr
12 Edgemont
Battle Creek MI 49017

Call Sign: K1RKD
Ronald F Cady
38 Elizabeth
Battle Creek MI 49017

Call Sign: KB9IAR
Donald J Prosser
155 Embury Dr
Battle Creek MI 49014

Call Sign: N8VAD
Scott L McClellan
201 Feld Ave
Battle Creek MI 49017

Call Sign: W8FOK
Jerald L Longman
123 Forest View Dr
Battle Creek MI 49015

Call Sign: KA8UVC
Theodore L Whitman
123 Foster Ave
Battle Creek MI 49015

Call Sign: KD8KZB
Ancel P Engle
55 Fountain St W
Battle Creek MI 49037

Call Sign: KC8OFU
Martin W Uitvlugt
178 Fuller Rd
Battle Creek MI 49015

Call Sign: WB8QVY
James L Keller Sr
26 Gardenia St
Battle Creek MI
490172724

Call Sign: KC8YMA
James E Hoglen
41 Garrison Ave
Battle Creek MI 49017

Call Sign: KD8PUN
Nathaniel D Klueter
92 Garrison Ave
Battle Creek MI 49017

Call Sign: N8OEC
Daniel R Klueter
92 Garrison Ave
Battle Creek MI 49017

Call Sign: KD8RCF
Chad L Hayes
5359 Glenn Valley Dr
Apt 1B
Battle Creek MI 49015

Call Sign: KC8QNY
Randy L Vallance
5084 Glenn Valley Dr
Apt 3B
Battle Creek MI 49017

Call Sign: K8LSH
Gary H Williams
40 Gordon Blvd
Battle Creek MI
490172704

Call Sign: N8QC
Gary H Williams
40 Gordon Blvd
Battle Creek MI
490172704

Call Sign: N8WVJ
Douglas W McCann
64 Gordon Blvd
Battle Creek MI 49017

Call Sign: WD8CGZ
Gerald W Coffman
609 Graham Lake Ter
Battle Creek MI 49017

Call Sign: KA8LUQ
Robert I Bursley
69 Groveland St
Battle Creek MI
490173744

Call Sign: KB8IAG
Adam B Rogers
13207 H Dr N
Battle Creek MI 49017

Call Sign: W8NZ
Duane W Kilbourn
114 Halladay Dr
Battle Creek MI 49017

Call Sign: WD8JVJ
Mike D Kilbourn
114 Halladay Dr
Battle Creek MI 49017

Call Sign: W8BWL
Mike D Kilbourn
114 Halladay Dr
Battle Creek MI 49017

Call Sign: N8BER
Gary F McKee
111 Harmony Ln
Battle Creek MI 49015

Call Sign: N8VBN
Daniel D Carlton Sr
163 Harvard Rd
Battle Creek MI 49017

Call Sign: KC8NSN
Scott A Brown
163 Harvard St
Battle Creek MI 49017

Call Sign: KB8ZGZ
James P Woodman
208 Hawthorne Ave
Battle Creek MI 49014

Call Sign: N8YJS
Jeffery L Woodman

220 Hawthorne Ave
Battle Creek MI 49017

Call Sign: KD8AJB
Douglas C Cronk
42 Hazel St
Battle Creek MI 49017

Call Sign: KC8WMN
James C Smith
112 Heather Hills Dr
Battle Creek MI 49015

Call Sign: W8SXT
James C Smith
112 Heather Hills Dr
Battle Creek MI 49015

Call Sign: AB8A
Ronald B Armour
14611 Helmer Rd S
Battle Creek MI
490158632

Call Sign: KG8BZ
Mark A Noel
10 Herman Dr
Battle Creek MI 49017

Call Sign: N8YDZ
Terralyn E Noel
10 Herman Dr
Battle Creek MI 49017

Call Sign: N8ODX
James R Doolittle
92 High St
Battle Creek MI 49017

Call Sign: KG8GZ
James R Holloway
117 Humphrey Dr
Battle Creek MI 49017

Call Sign: KC8LDQ
Rob R Brady
1255 Hunter Ridge
Battle Creek MI
490179076

Call Sign: KC8LDR
Elizabeth S Brady
1255 Hunter Ridge

Battle Creek MI
490179076

Call Sign: KB8WZ
Albert G Still
269 Hunter St
Battle Creek MI 49017

Call Sign: W8MMV
Floyd C Huggett
306 Iroquois Ave
Battle Creek MI 49015

Call Sign: KC8NZX
Kenneth J Kobes
154 Jennings Rd
Battle Creek MI 49015

Call Sign: N8AKY
Kaye J Brauer
13700 Jones Rd Mill
Lake
Battle Creek MI 49017

Call Sign: KA8LDO
Donna M Brauer
13700 Jones Rd Mill
Lake R 6
Battle Creek MI 49017

Call Sign: KC8NHM
James A Cipcic
3613 Kalamazoo Ave
Battle Creek MI
490371021

Call Sign: WA8QBH
Earl D Baxter
120 Keathley Dr
Battle Creek MI 49017

Call Sign: KD8LQM
William A Laforce IV
265 Keathley Dr
Battle Creek MI 49014

Call Sign: WX8TOR
William A Laforce IV
265 Keathley Dr
Battle Creek MI 49014

Call Sign: KB8YLH
Hayden L Roe
179 Kings Ln

Battle Creek MI 49014

Call Sign: WA8GHK
John A Stange
185 Kings Ln
Battle Creek MI 49017

Call Sign: K8YYC
Kendall L Birman
4380 Kirby Rd
Battle Creek MI 49017

Call Sign: N8BDG
William A McNally
144 Kirkpatrick
Battle Creek MI 49015

Call Sign: N8BIZ
Joan M McNally
144 Kirkpatrick Dr
Battle Creek MI 49015

Call Sign: N8XQS
Robert M Hosmer
3141 Kistler Rd
Battle Creek MI 49014

Call Sign: KW8V
Richard O Brenner
3875 Kistler Rd
Battle Creek MI 49017

Call Sign: N8EDJ
Barbara C Brenner
3875 Kistler Rd
Battle Creek MI 49017

Call Sign: WA8PVR
David T Worfel
688 Knollwood Dr
Battle Creek MI 49015

Call Sign: K8DTW
David T Worfel
688 Knollwood Dr
Battle Creek MI 49015

Call Sign: K8BWX
John J Kirkpatrick
173 Lacey Ave
Battle Creek MI 49017

Call Sign: KC8PRL
Robert G Kingsbury

324 Lakeview Ave
Battle Creek MI
490153307

Call Sign: AC8GL
Robert G Kingsbury
324 Lakeview Ave
Battle Creek MI
490153307

Call Sign: KC8NTM
Brian W Gerber
160 Leinaar Rd
Battle Creek MI 49017

Call Sign: KD8IXX
Muriel E Crow
25 Leitch Dr
Battle Creek MI 49015

Call Sign: WD8LRQ
Kenneth M Plett
215 Lois Dr
Battle Creek MI 49017

Call Sign: WB8ZLA
Donald E Tumanis
287 Lois Dr
Battle Creek MI 49017

Call Sign: KD8MNQ
James H Heckman
7 Lyda St
Battle Creek MI 49014

Call Sign: W8JTP
Edward L Haskins
155 Lynn Dr
Battle Creek MI 49017

Call Sign: W0CD
Charles E Dewey Jr
49 Lynwood Dr
Battle Creek MI
490157911

Call Sign: N8URZ
Edward H Hildebrand
20184 M 37
Battle Creek MI 49017

Call Sign: KA8ESM
Thomas E Ludwick
23738 M 78 Hwy

Battle Creek MI 49017

Call Sign: KB8GNQ
Gary D Wood
24 Magnolia St
Battle Creek MI 49017

Call Sign: N8WJQ
Anthony P Van
Ameyden
290 Marvin St
Battle Creek MI 49017

Call Sign: KD8OPA
Christopher L
Hostetler
290 Marvin St
Battle Creek MI 49017

Call Sign: KD8PKE
Christopher L
Hostetler
290 Marvin St
Battle Creek MI 49017

Call Sign: WB8KTL
Chester P Heffel
61 Massachusetts
Battle Creek MI 49017

Call Sign: KD8RMM
Larry M Tyndal
148 McCormick St
Battle Creek MI 49014

Call Sign: KD8SBJ
Mary L Tyndal
148 McCormick St
Battle Creek MI 49014

Call Sign: KC8EIC
Jesse Moreno
74 Meachem Ave
Battle Creek MI 49015

Call Sign: WA8MFL
Marion R Davidson
30 Mill Rd
Battle Creek MI 49014

Call Sign: KC8WMM
John R Davidson
30 Mill Rd
Battle Creek MI 49014

Call Sign: W8JRD
John R Davidson
30 Mill Rd
Battle Creek MI 49014

Call Sign: WA8VXE
Rosemary Davidson
30 Mill Rd
Battle Creek MI
490145718

Call Sign: WA8UYW
David H Eddy
111 Minges Cir
Battle Creek MI 49015

Call Sign: N8UFK
Dennis K Hudson
100 Minges Creek Pl
Apt C305
Battle Creek MI 49015

Call Sign: N8DWD
Eva C Plummer
151 Minges Creek Pl
K2
Battle Creek MI 49015

Call Sign: N8CP
Francis E Doyle
339 Minges Rd S
Battle Creek MI
490157918

Call Sign: N9QVK
Brian G Holmes
118 Monroe Beach Rd
Battle Creek MI 49014

Call Sign: KD8RWB
Richard C Frantz
6722 Morgan Rd
Battle Creek MI 49017

Call Sign: KD8NJA
Michael F Schmieder
7008 Morgan Rd E
Battle Creek MI 49017

Call Sign: K8JNJ
Ronald J Killian
542 Morningside Dr
Battle Creek MI 49015

Call Sign: KC8UZX
Andrea E Mills
51 Mosher Ave
Battle Creek MI 49017

Call Sign: KD8RWE
Dale W Coffman
239 N 21 St
Battle Creek MI 49015

Call Sign: N8VAE
Kenneth E Green Jr
49 N 21st St
Battle Creek MI
490151760

Call Sign: W8BAY
Elmer K Adams
146 N 21st St
Battle Creek MI
490151705

Call Sign: WD8DVQ
Gary G Criteser
174 N 21st St
Battle Creek MI 49015

Call Sign: KC8FRL
Thomas E Williams
323 N 28th St
Battle Creek MI 49015

Call Sign: KB8TNV
Daniel M Cornell
137 N 29th St
Battle Creek MI 49015

Call Sign: N8YEB
Thomas E Cornell
137 N 29th St
Battle Creek MI 49015

Call Sign: KA9ZSX
John F Wrzesinski
336 N 29th St
Battle Creek MI 49015

Call Sign: KC8IHD
Bruce J Sowles
34 N 30th
Battle Creek MI 49015

Call Sign: W8IFX

Warren E Van Zandt
37 N 31st St
Battle Creek MI 49015

Call Sign: KD8DMU
Jeremy K Yettaw
107 N 31st St
Battle Creek MI 49015

Call Sign: N8ZHR
Lyndell M Myers Jr
130 N 33rd St
Battle Creek MI 49015

Call Sign: WA8LRB
Walter J Van Nocker
410 N 34th St
Battle Creek MI 49015

Call Sign: KA5BCF
Calvin D Brooker
369 N Bedford Rd
Battle Creek MI 49016

Call Sign: KD8SBK
Scott G Riddle
450 N Bedford Rd
Battle Creek MI 49037

Call Sign: KC8QNU
Joseph A Mcjilton
22461 N Bedford Rd
Battle Creek MI 49017

Call Sign: WD8JVI
Elizabeth H Green
11893 N Dr N
Battle Creek MI 49014

Call Sign: W8RVT
Donald E Larkin
630 N Garrison Rd Apt
B
Battle Creek MI
490174545

Call Sign: KD8JJR
Zachary A Boldt
3105 N Meachem Rd
Battle Creek MI 49017

Call Sign: KA8HEA
Carol D Brenner
303 N Moorland Dr

Battle Creek MI 49015

Call Sign: WD8I
Rodger O Brenner
303 N Moorland Dr
Battle Creek MI
490153850

Call Sign: WD8CDE
Dennis B Martin
308 N Moorland Dr
Battle Creek MI
490153851

Call Sign: N8JWK
Robert J Shoens
121 N Ridgeway Dr
Battle Creek MI 49015

Call Sign: KD8CQM
Kristen L Studt
105 N Union
Battle Creek MI 49017

Call Sign: N8LLF
Daniel J Hopkins
728 North Ave
Battle Creek MI 49017

Call Sign: KB8RSU
Richard A Harris
171 Northwood Dr Rr
13
Battle Creek MI 49017

Call Sign: W8EEK
James N Palmiter
239 Oak St Oak Park
Battle Creek MI
490171299

Call Sign: KB8CEA
Elex V Baker
11749 Old Bellevue
Rd
Battle Creek MI 49014

Call Sign: KB8TIN
Idabelle J Bailey
1374 Olive St
Battle Creek MI 49014

Call Sign: WB8FBJ
Jerry L Bailey

1374 Olive St
Battle Creek MI 49014

Call Sign: KB8MYJ
Daniel W Fagan Sr
1443 Onagon Beach
Battle Creek MI 49017

Call Sign: KD8RWC
Garrett L Murray
175 Oneita St
Battle Creek MI 49037

Call Sign: KD8RVR
Angela R Makoski
447 Orchard Ln
Battle Creek MI 49015

Call Sign: KD8RVS
Paul S Makoski
447 Orchard Ln
Battle Creek MI 49015

Call Sign: WB8QIQ
Farrell V Beach
451 Orchard Ln
Battle Creek MI 49015

Call Sign: WD8NPY
Roger D Eaton
13731 P Dr N
Battle Creek MI
490148435

Call Sign: N8MVV
James L Sheldon
4869 Paradise
Battle Creek MI 49017

Call Sign: N8FBV
Ivan D Hunt
4815 Paradise Rd
Battle Creek MI 49017

Call Sign: N8TIA
Nancy G B Sheldon
4869 Paradise Rd
Battle Creek MI 49017

Call Sign: KA8PZM
Larry L Lash
5287 Paradise Rd
Battle Creek MI 49017

Call Sign: KB8BSP
Patricia A Lash
5287 Paradise Rd
Battle Creek MI 49017

Call Sign: N8QDI
Larry F Beacham
70 Parkridge Dr
Battle Creek MI 49017

Call Sign: W8RT
Residence Dx Society
271 Parkshore Dr
Battle Creek MI 49014

Call Sign: W8TOP
Battle Creek Low
Banders
271 Parkshore Dr
Battle Creek MI 49014

Call Sign: W8UVZ
George E Taft
271 Parkshore Dr
Battle Creek MI 49014

Call Sign: KC8QBY
V I Dx Club
271 Parkshore Dr
Battle Creek MI 49014

Call Sign: W8UTA
Arthur B Millar
880 Parkview Ave 45F
Battle Creek MI
490173170

Call Sign: W8VZY
Peter A Bestervelt
121 Peachtree Dr
Battle Creek MI 49017

Call Sign: KD8EYC
Robert W Secor
232 Pennbrook Tr
Battle Creek MI 49017

Call Sign: W8RZY
Larry L Payne
121 Pepperidge Ln
Battle Creek MI
490153109

Call Sign: W8LTJ

Eric R Talbot
131 Pepperidge Ln
Battle Creek MI 49015

Call Sign: KA8FLC
Robert C Hammond
507 Pettycoat Ln
Battle Creek MI 49017

Call Sign: WB8JFW
Sandra K Conant
508 Pettycoat Ln
Battle Creek MI 49017

Call Sign: KA8MZM
Jean K Kyser
20949 Pine Lake Rd
Battle Creek MI 49014

Call Sign: WD8RKW
Peter J Knight
141 Pine Ridge Rd
Battle Creek MI 49017

Call Sign: KB8YDQ
Marie Lys C
Lallemand
480 Pkwy Dr
Battle Creek MI 49017

Call Sign: KC8DBA
Shelby L Windle
119 Pleasant Ave
Battle Creek MI 49015

Call Sign: KC8CLZ
Jeff C Moran
140 Pleasantview Dr
Battle Creek MI 49017

Call Sign: N8VEI
William F Troskey
235 Post Ave
Battle Creek MI
490146351

Call Sign: KB9JSB
Rachel L West
50 Rambling Ln Apt
37B
Battle Creek MI 49015

Call Sign: WB8VCL
Thomas W Couey Jr

11203 Ridgewood Dr
Battle Creek MI 49014

Call Sign: N8EXR
Paul M Seng
281 Riverside Dr
Battle Creek MI
490152663

Call Sign: N8LOK
Kraig B Dayton
28 Riverside Pkwy
Battle Creek MI 49015

Call Sign: KD8RWF
Jamie L Findley
55 Riverview Ave
Battle Creek MI 49017

Call Sign: KA8MKG
Kent D Byrd
120 Robinwood
Battle Creek MI 49017

Call Sign: KB8VQF
Richard P Heldt
138 Roxbury Ln
Battle Creek MI 49017

Call Sign: W8EXF
Robert W Agne
208 Roxbury Ln
Battle Creek MI 49017

Call Sign: KD8DAK
Jason Johnson
168 Rustic Ln
Battle Creek MI 49017

Call Sign: KA8THR
Ancel P Engle
37 S 24th St
Battle Creek MI 49015

Call Sign: WB8WXS
Louis H Ryason
23 S 27th St
Battle Creek MI 49015

Call Sign: KC8NZY
David Kellogg
33 S 27th St
Battle Creek MI 49015

Call Sign: KC8MQU
Paul D Lopp
65 S Burdge Apt 9
Battle Creek MI 49014

Call Sign: N8RBU
Robert E Wedel
112 S Hills Dr
Battle Creek MI 49015

Call Sign: AB8JD
Brian W Gerber
13899 S M 37 Hwy
Battle Creek MI 49017

Call Sign: W8MS
Jack F Wall
279 S Minges Rd
Battle Creek MI 49015

Call Sign: KB8DLL
Pearl A Chaney
4405 S Minges Rd
Battle Creek MI
490159374

Call Sign: N8BDM
Wesley G Chaney
4405 S Minges Rd
Battle Creek MI
490159374

Call Sign: N8RRM
Elizabeth A Callan
175 S Ridgeway
Battle Creek MI 49015

Call Sign: KC8PAN
Verde L Slack
121 Sanborn
Battle Creek MI 49017

Call Sign: KC8LHL
Brenda A Hibbard
63 Saratoga Ave
Battle Creek MI 49017

Call Sign: K8AXV
Willard F Hibbard II
63 Saratoga Ave
Battle Creek MI
490172741

Call Sign: K8YZF

Roger N Warner
261 Sawyer Ave
Battle Creek MI
490148952

Call Sign: N8SW
William E Wilkey
69 Seivour
Battle Creek MI 49015

Call Sign: KA8QQF
Barbara A Wilkey
69 Seivour St
Battle Creek MI 49015

Call Sign: KD8GJP
Matthew J Davis
109 Shadowood Ln
Battle Creek MI 49014

Call Sign: WI8J
Duane J Davis
109 Shadowood Ln
Battle Creek MI 49017

Call Sign: KB8YDO
Carolyn H Bush
207 Sharon Ave
Battle Creek MI
490175435

Call Sign: N8UFB
Sammy L Wilkins
250 Sheffield Rd
Battle Creek MI 49017

Call Sign: N8TIE
Kenneth W Armstrong
492 Sheffield Rd
Battle Creek MI 49017

Call Sign: WB8ZIH
John R Loser
16 Shellenberger Ave
Battle Creek MI
490171814

Call Sign: KC8VUC
Joseph M Wohlscheid
19 Shellenberger Ave
Battle Creek MI 49037

Call Sign: KC8EUH
Kevin M Stanley

134 Sherwood Dr
Battle Creek MI 49017

Call Sign: AA8RP
Leon R Harris
283 Silver St
Battle Creek MI 49017

Call Sign: N8TSL
Alice M Harris
283 Silver St
Battle Creek MI 49017

Call Sign: N8LH
Leon R Harris
283 Silver St
Battle Creek MI
490148267

Call Sign: KB8KMM
George E Streeter Jr
175 Singletree Ln
Battle Creek MI 49017

Call Sign: KA8PFR
Louis T Marot
203 Snow Ave
Battle Creek MI 49017

Call Sign: KD8PGW
Mark J Burchard
523 Snow Ave
Battle Creek MI 49037

Call Sign: K8RKR
Mark J Burchard
523 Snow Ave
Battle Creek MI 49037

Call Sign: WD8AZR
Glenn A Birman
35 Springview Dr 201
Battle Creek MI 49017

Call Sign: N8BDL
Thomas L
Bommersbach
269 St Marys Lake Rd
Battle Creek MI 49017

Call Sign: KD8HDC
Jeffrey R Mitchell
14615 Stone Jug Rd
Battle Creek MI 49015

Call Sign: KB8WAY
Tamera S Allen
174 Strongwood
Battle Creek MI 49017

Call Sign: KB8ZCP
Joshua D Allen
174 Strongwood
Battle Creek MI 49017

Call Sign: N8ZYC
Bruce D Allen
174 Strongwood
Battle Creek MI 49017

Call Sign: KA8VNV
Raymond E Ret
120 Strongwood Ave
Battle Creek MI 49017

Call Sign: N8YFL
Jacques K Donham
Shipe
187 Summer St
Battle Creek MI
490152166

Call Sign: N8THV
Virles W White Jr
36 Summers St
Battle Creek MI 49015

Call Sign: KD8JXG
James L Orns
141 Sunnyside Dr
Battle Creek MI 49015

Call Sign: WD8PFN
William J Mrak Jr
137 Sunset Blvd E
Battle Creek MI
490175315

Call Sign: KC8HVM
Denise N Dayton
8110 Swift Rd
Battle Creek MI 49017

Call Sign: N6TLU
Terry A Dayton
8110 Swift Rd
Battle Creek MI 49017

Call Sign: K8NKP
Warren E Marsh Sr
86 Taylor Ave
Battle Creek MI 49017

Call Sign: WA8ZEE
Clark L Loyer
97 Taylor Ave
Battle Creek MI 49017

Call Sign: N8WVX
Mark P Gregory
7517 Taylor Trace
Battle Creek MI 49017

Call Sign: N8UCG
James A Edwards Jr
148 Thelma Dr
Battle Creek MI 49014

Call Sign: K8VLK
Parker H Whitney
14665 Uldricks Dr
Battle Creek MI 49017

Call Sign: KC8LWA
Barry A Gooch
22475 Uldriks
Battle Creek MI 49017

Call Sign: KD8PVK
Michael J Mckenzie
22565 Uldriks Dr
Battle Creek MI 49014

Call Sign: N8WDR
Kraig D Eaton
121 Vale St
Battle Creek MI
490146335

Call Sign: KB8YDN
Susan A McGough
62 Van Armon
Battle Creek MI 49017

Call Sign: KG8PO
John D Van De Laare
62 Van Armon
Battle Creek MI 49017

Call Sign: KC0BPH
Daniel J Poll
62 Vanarmon

Battle Creek MI 49017

Call Sign: N8WIW
Nelson R Turner
11400 Verona Rd
Battle Creek MI 49014

Call Sign: WD8JOM
Paul R Goodin
48 W Alden Ave
Battle Creek MI 49014

Call Sign: KA8YJN
Chad M Parker
4987 W Dr N
Battle Creek MI 49017

Call Sign: KB8MHV
Rebecca K Miles
8 W Grand Cir
Battle Creek MI 49015

Call Sign: KB8PWH
John H Harter
91 W Grand Cir
Battle Creek MI 49015

Call Sign: KA2HSC
William R Aikman
164 W Hamilton Ln
Battle Creek MI 49015

Call Sign: KC8PGX
Robert M Curtis
34 W Meadowlawn
Battle Creek MI 49017

Call Sign: KB8UPU
Stephen A Morgan
68 W Meadowlawn
Ave
Battle Creek MI 49017

Call Sign: WB8ILR
H Paul La Tourneau
3415 W Michigan Ave
Battle Creek MI 49017

Call Sign: KD8LPL
Kelly L Lyon
36 W Pitman
Battle Creek MI 49017

Call Sign: K8CUB

Kelly L Lyon
36 W Pitman
Battle Creek MI 49017

Call Sign: WD8CAE
Richard D Robinson Sr
1310 W River Rd
Battle Creek MI 49015

Call Sign: KC8KRL
Martin J Ftacek
1352 W River Rd
Battle Creek MI 49037

Call Sign: WD8OMJ
Gerald L Reynolds
16 W Spaulding Ave
Battle Creek MI 49017

Call Sign: K8DUE
Charles C Mead Jr
900 W Terriorlorial
108
Battle Creek MI 49015

Call Sign: N8TIG
Terry L Taplin
1738 W Territorial
Battle Creek MI 49015

Call Sign: WB8JPD
Richard L Peterson
1720 W Territorial Rd
Battle Creek MI 49015

Call Sign: KD8RVT
Matthew L Parker
105 Wabash Ave N
Battle Creek MI 49017

Call Sign: KC8LJC
Todd J Gerber
995 Wagner Dr
Battle Creek MI 49017

Call Sign: N8TJG
Todd J Gerber
995 Wagner Dr
Battle Creek MI 49017

Call Sign: W8XK
Joseph P Ohlmacher
266 Wagonwheel Ln
Battle Creek MI 49017

Call Sign: KD8RWG
Steven J Koch
548 Washington Ave
N
Battle Creek MI 49037

Call Sign: AA8KF
Bryan R Eaton
276 Wattles Rd S
Battle Creek MI 49014

Call Sign: KC8HET
Karl M Rautmann
249 Wentworth
Battle Creek MI
490153253

Call Sign: KA8FET
George H Mansfield
360 Wentworth Ave
Battle Creek MI 49015

Call Sign: KR4UT
David R Eaton
183 West St Apt 401
Battle Creek MI 49037

Call Sign: AA8KS
Douglas E Hatchett
84 Winter St
Battle Creek MI 49015

Call Sign: W8VVG
Larry R Pasman
973 Woodland Beach
Battle Creek MI 49014

Call Sign: WA8VVG
Larry R Pasman
973 Woodland Beach
Battle Creek MI 49017

Call Sign: KD8NVG
Scott W Metzgar
6282 Woodland Ct
Battle Creek MI 49014

Call Sign: N8KDK
Scott W Metzgar
6282 Woodland Ct
Battle Creek MI 49014

Call Sign: KM8U

Harlan F Jones
155 Woodridge Dr
Battle Creek MI
490179223

Call Sign: KB8QOV
Mildred B Clark
Battle Creek MI 49016

Call Sign: N8HTH
James W Yeomans
Battle Creek MI 49016

Call Sign: W8DF
Southern Michigan
ARS
Battle Creek MI 49016

Call Sign: W8INF
Alvin N Brooker
Battle Creek MI 49016

Call Sign: KB8QCB
James W Clark
Battle Creek MI 49016

Call Sign: WA8MOA
Robert P Walsh
Battle Creek MI
490160073

Call Sign: WN8P
Lawrence W Joy
Battle Creek MI
490160073

Call Sign: AD6TP
David I Sparvell
Battle Creek MI
490160073

**FCC Amateur Radio
Licenses in Bay Mills**

Call Sign: KC8QBX
James W Kinney
12607 W Wolf Ave
Bay Mills MI 49715

Call Sign: W8QBX
James W Kinney
12607 W Wolf Ave
Bay Mills MI 49715

Call Sign: N8JX
Terry J Bess
10787 Herkelrath Rd
Bear Lake MI 49614

Call Sign: KJ8W
Sandra L Ertel
13063 Hopkins Forest
Dr
Bear Lake MI 49614

Call Sign: KJ8V
David E Ertel
13063 Hopkins Forest
Dr
Bear Lake MI 49614

Call Sign: W8VVH
Edgar S O Rourke
10894 Lindeman Rd
Bear Lake MI 49614

Call Sign: KD8OGE
John M Evans
11713 Linderman Rd
Bear Lake MI 49614

Call Sign: K8GWW
Gerald E Young
7280 Potter Rd
Bear Lake MI
496140063

FCC Amateur Radio Licenses in Beaver Island

Call Sign: WB0ONE
William R Hamil Jr
26740 Barney Lake Rd
Beaver Island MI
49782

Call Sign: K8SME
Richard L Hansz
38574 Beaver Dr
Beaver Island MI
49782

Call Sign: KC8MGJ
Rick W Bucholtz

27470 Island Woods
Rd
Beaver Island MI
49782

Call Sign: N8BED
Michael G Russell
38030 Michigan Ave
Beaver Island MI
497820074

Call Sign: K8PN
Patrick J Nugent
Beaver Island MI
49782

Call Sign: WX8Z
Donovan A Langford
Jr
Beaver Island MI
497820257

FCC Amateur Radio Licenses in Beaverton

Call Sign: KB8VZS
Leah M Fitzpatrick
10505 Adams Rd
Beaverton MI
486129603

Call Sign: WA8OIK
Vernon A Fitzpatrick
10505 Adams Rd
Beaverton MI
486129603

Call Sign: KD8HIE
Kevin M Hannahs
4292 Anderson Dr
Beaverton MI 48612

Call Sign: KD8HIA
Lee W Hannahs
4292 Anderson Dr
Beaverton MI 48612

Call Sign: KD8CPG
William L Wellington
949 Badger Rd
Beaverton MI 48612

Call Sign: KD8EYD
Richard A Nephew

1250 Center Rd
Beaverton MI 48612

Call Sign: KD8LOH
Daniel F Bergman
1040 Dale Rd
Beaverton MI 48612

Call Sign: KB8HVS
Luella M Kuch
1474 Denton Cr Rd
Beaverton MI
486128747

Call Sign: KD8IWF
David A Smith
3885 Dundas Rd
Beaverton MI 48612

Call Sign: KC8VUK
Billie L Williamson
1437 Elm Blvd
Beaverton MI 48612

Call Sign: KC8YIK
Paul M Stafford
2033 Hawkins
Beaverton MI 48612

Call Sign: KC8PWK
Harold J Alburg
5691 Hunter
Beaverton MI 48612

Call Sign: WD8KUG
Gary L Stiller
2967 Jodymae St
Beaverton MI 48612

Call Sign: KB8MBB
Linda L Rybkowski
4888 Jones Rd
Beaverton MI 48612

Call Sign: KB8MBC
Norman S Rybkowski
4888 Jones Rd
Beaverton MI 48612

Call Sign: K8ZXB
Allen L McGeorge
1195 Linda Ln
Beaverton MI 48612

Call Sign: KD8PAE
Philip R Wheeler
2366 Long Rd
Beaverton MI 48612

Call Sign: KD8JSI
Terry D Whittington
4194 Oak Dr
Beaverton MI 48612

Call Sign: KB8NNP
Kenneth J Storms
4215 Oak Dr
Beaverton MI 48612

Call Sign: WD8AUM
Gerald N McLean
5323 Oakridge Dr
Beaverton MI 48612

Call Sign: W8JOH
John H Williams
5439 Oakridge Dr
Beaverton MI 48612

Call Sign: K8GEJ
Raymond O Sanford
5091 Pleasant Dr
Beaverton MI 48612

Call Sign: KB8HVR
Bernadine L Zobel
5120 Pleasant Dr
Beaverton MI
486128747

Call Sign: N8XJH
John F Pollack
837 Quillette
Beaverton MI 48612

Call Sign: KC8RRQ
Clarence R Lile
3797 Roehrs Rd
Beaverton MI 48612

Call Sign: KY8L
Clarence R Lile
3797 Roehrs Rd
Beaverton MI 48612

Call Sign: KD8KVS
Jack E Keast
1775 S River Rd

Beaverton MI 48612

Call Sign: KD8LOI
Yvette D Keast
1775 S River Rd
Beaverton MI 48612

Call Sign: KJ4PGE
Bryan P Keast
1775 S River Rd
Beaverton MI 48612

Call Sign: KA8EBR
Harry C Williams
215 Tonkin
Beaverton MI 48612

Call Sign: KC8SRV
Amanda J Donders
393 W Brown Apt 201
Beaverton MI 48612

Call Sign: KA8ZHX
Stanley Skrelunas
5968 W Dale Rd
Beaverton MI 48612

Call Sign: KB8UAJ
Margaret M Snyder
2290 W Glidden Rd
Beaverton MI 48612

Call Sign: KC8BYH
Gene Wm Gilson
4485 W Lyle Rd
Beaverton MI
486129749

Call Sign: KD8CVU
Becky S Ballard
2112 Wieman Rd
Beaverton MI 48612

Call Sign: KD8CVT
Jeffrey S Whitehead
2112 Wieman Rd
Beaverton MI 48612

**FCC Amateur Radio
Licenses in Belding**

Call Sign: N8PDO
James M Carpenter
9737 Belding Rd

Belding MI 48809

Call Sign: N8PMX
Benjamin C Carpenter
9737 Belding Rd
Belding MI 48809

Call Sign: N8UVI
Frank K Schmidt
10931 Belding Rd NE
Belding MI 488099300

Call Sign: KB8LLW
Michael P Baker
62 Belhaven
Belding MI 48809

Call Sign: KD8ECZ
Edward L Getts
8253 Bradley Rd
Belding MI 48809

Call Sign: N8HLM
Roger A Smith
404 Bricker St
Belding MI 48809

Call Sign: N8YKB
John Baker
10150 Button Rd
Belding MI 48809

Call Sign: KB8UNI
Arnold T Totch
10984 Button Rd
Belding MI 48809

Call Sign: KD8OKH
Randall A Geister
719 Charles St
Belding MI 48809

Call Sign: KD8NMJ
Stacy K Madden
7695 Dream Isle Dr
Belding MI 48809

Call Sign: KD8RLN
Shane A Madden
7695 Dream Isle Dr
NE
Belding MI 48809

Call Sign: KC8OEO

Hubert L Belding
540 E State St
Belding MI 48809

Call Sign: KB8DSM
Ray Shel R Myers
225 Elizabeth
Belding MI 48809

Call Sign: KC8KMO
Leroy E Martin
6105 Flat River Trl
Belding MI 48809

Call Sign: KC8JQN
Eugene R Getts
322 Hall St
Belding MI 48809

Call Sign: KC8SBH
Whisper S Getts
322 Hall St
Belding MI 48809

Call Sign: KC8YXF
Riverside Radio
Amateurs
313 Hanover St
Belding MI 48809

Call Sign: WA8RRA
Riverside Radio
Amateurs
313 Hanover St
Belding MI 48809

Call Sign: KD8PBZ
Angela L Sailer
313 Hanover St
Belding MI 48809

Call Sign: KB8PQZ
David R Sailer
313 Hanover St
Belding MI 488091729

Call Sign: AB8LE
David R Sailer
313 Hanover St
Belding MI 488091729

Call Sign: K8BQE
Burton A Hill
3683 Heald Rd

Belding MI 48809

Call Sign: K8DTD
Maxine F Hill
3683 Heald Rd
Belding MI 48809

Call Sign: KB8WJX
Brian J Rauch
10520 Heether Rd
Belding MI 48809

Call Sign: KB8YND
Teresa A Rauch
10520 Heether Rd
Belding MI 48809

Call Sign: KD8IQT
Travis D Rauch
10520 Heether Rd
Belding MI 48809

Call Sign: NE8K
Harley D Ridgeway
9397 Ingalls Rd
Belding MI 48809

Call Sign: KB8BK
Harley D Ridgeway
9397 Ingalls Rd
Belding MI 48809

Call Sign: N8RCZ
Bradley W McCord
501 Ionia St
Belding MI 48809

Call Sign: KB8YYW
Ronda George Gibbs
6315 Johnson Rd
Belding MI 48809

Call Sign: KB8SNC
Miles M Benedict Jr
6293 Johnson Rd
Belding MI 48809

Call Sign: W1MRZ
Marie Claire Benedict
6293 Johnson Rd
Belding MI 48809

Call Sign: KC8UZW
Lonny F Hale

6244 Kiddeville Rd
Belding MI 48809

Call Sign: N3NZC
John H Vriese
6490 Kiddville Rd
Belding MI 48809

Call Sign: KC8ZPV
Matthew S Strawser
5425 Lincoln Lake Rd
Belding MI 48809

Call Sign: KB8NMS
Rodney T Kennedy
5855 Long Lk Rd
Belding MI 48809

Call Sign: KC8ACM
Russell J Haverstick
6267 Longlake
Belding MI 48809

Call Sign: KC8SUP
Vanessa D Human
1110 Luther St
Belding MI 488091326

Call Sign: KD8PJL
Bobbie J Kelley
921 Masonic St
Belding MI 48809

Call Sign: KD8LVT
Cameron S Kelley
921 Masonic St
Belding MI 48809

Call Sign: KC8ZPI
Ryan S Kelley
921 Masonic St
Belding MI 48809

Call Sign: KC8ZPB
Andrew J Wright
913 N Marble Rd
Belding MI 48809

Call Sign: WA8ONZ
Robert H Hadden
1417 Oakwood Dr
Belding MI 48809

Call Sign: KC8MSG

Julia L Getts
5318 Ostrum Rd
Belding MI 48809

Call Sign: AB8KP
Eugene R Getts
5318 Ostrum Rd
Belding MI 48809

Call Sign: KD8EFE
Priscilla J Getts
5318 Ostrum Rd
Belding MI 48809

Call Sign: KD8KLI
Roger D Packard
6248 Palmer Rd
Belding MI 48809

Call Sign: AC8RP
Roger D Packard
6248 Palmer Rd
Belding MI 48809

Call Sign: K8BUU
Roger W Lakin
8645 Ranney Rd
Belding MI 48809

Call Sign: KC8UXN
Steven G Hyde Jr
404 S Bridge St
Belding MI 48809

Call Sign: WA8FSM
Adam Handy
817 S Broas
Belding MI 48809

Call Sign: KD8PBY
Melissa M Eerdmans
8751 Storey Rd
Belding MI 48809

Call Sign: K8MME
Melissa M Eerdmans
8751 Storey Rd
Belding MI 48809

Call Sign: KC8TOY
William D Orr
1561 W Ellis
Belding MI 48809

Call Sign: KB8FTY
Janet R Longstreet
516 W High St
Belding MI 48809

Call Sign: KB8OBO
Traci L Longstreet
516 W High St
Belding MI 48809

Call Sign: N8ILM
Matthew S Smith
321 W Isabelle St
Belding MI 48809

Call Sign: KC8ZYN
Dale M Harris
1527 W State Lot 40
Belding MI 48809

**FCC Amateur Radio
Licenses in Bellaire**

Call Sign: K8DNV
William P Edwards
116 4th St
Bellaire MI 496159419

Call Sign: K8LPP
Gary A Ciphers
8715 Alden Hwy
Bellaire MI 49615

Call Sign: KJ1B
Bruce S Marshall
8736 Bliss Rd
Bellaire MI 49615

Call Sign: KB8MCO
Alfred D Hoadley
Rt 1 Box 223
Bellaire MI 49615

Call Sign: KB8OFK
Mary A Richards
7539 Briar Ln
Bellaire MI 49615

Call Sign: W8MML
Robert G Lessard
5761 Cottage Dr
Bellaire MI 49615

Call Sign: WD8OZZ

Versile L Dawson Jr
210 Court St
Bellaire MI 496150185

Call Sign: N8OKA
Arthur W Hoadley
7538 Crystal Springs
Rd
Bellaire MI 49615

Call Sign: KC8TBU
William M Boyd
8634 Dunson Rd
Bellaire MI 49615

Call Sign: AB8HW
Thomas R Gillentine
4501 Legend Trl
Bellaire MI 49615

Call Sign: WB8YWG
Randall L Rothe
8870 Lynn Rd
Bellaire MI 49615

Call Sign: KC8TGG
Jeanine A Rothe
8870 Lynn Rd
Bellaire MI 49615

Call Sign: KC8TGH
Ian R Rothe
8870 Lynn Rd
Bellaire MI 49615

Call Sign: N8STX
William R Drollinger
603 Park St
Bellaire MI 49615

Call Sign: WD8RAR
Alphaeus R Leach
6314 River Ridge Dr
Bellaire MI 49615

Call Sign: KB8EXP
Darrell L Dewey
4889 Schuss Mt Rd
Bellaire MI 49615

Call Sign: KC8QLF
William G Bedell
2398 Vander Mark Rd
Bellaire MI 49615

Call Sign: KC8FXT
William F McIlrath Jr
108 W Hastings St
Bellaire MI 49615

Call Sign: W8LOW
Floyd M Dewey
Bellaire MI 49615

Call Sign: KD8OMG
Deanna M Shawl
Bellaire MI 49615

Call Sign: KD8GON
Steven A Shawl
Bellaire MI 49615

**FCC Amateur Radio
Licenses in Bellevue**

Call Sign: W0RUK
J Philip Holden
23900 13 Mile Rd
Bellevue MI 49021

Call Sign: KC8QNR
Randy D Sifton
14801 Bower Rd
Bellevue MI 49021

Call Sign: WB8GFN
Kent L Conant
7671 Cox Rd
Bellevue MI 49021

Call Sign: KD8BBA
Doris A Smith
7671 Cox Rd
Bellevue MI 49021

Call Sign: K8GFN
Kent L Conant
7671 Cox Rd
Bellevue MI 49021

Call Sign: KC8LDJ
Steven M Mesecar
7645 Hall Rd
Bellevue MI 49021

Call Sign: N8ZHQ
Willis E Ramer
5907 Hill Rd

Bellevue MI 49021

Call Sign: N8OCC
Keith R Haley Jr
325 Olivet Rd
Bellevue MI
490211253

Call Sign: KB8OSG
Irene E Hill
5690 S Bradley Rd
Bellevue MI 49021

Call Sign: AA8GZ
Kenneth L Hill
5690 S Bradley Rd
Bellevue MI 49021

Call Sign: KB8ZGY
Gordon W Colles
5912 S Ionia Rd
Bellevue MI 49021

Call Sign: KD8RLV
Laurie P Tucker
15254 S M 66 Hwy
Bellevue MI 49021

Call Sign: WB8VZS
Leon E Mudge
10995 Schreiner Rd
Bellevue MI 49021

Call Sign: N8HJZ
Mamie E Wilcox
12290 Schreiner Rd
Bellevue MI 49021

Call Sign: N8EHQ
Howard L Wilcox
12290 Schriener Rd
Bellevue MI 49021

Call Sign: KD8RWH
Thomas D Parsons
8480 Tasker
Bellevue MI 49021

**FCC Amateur Radio
Licenses in Belmont**

Call Sign: K8KVS
Michael T Baker
5439 5 Mile Rd NE

Belmont MI 49306

Call Sign: K8PZ
Steven J Baker
5439 5 Mile Rd NE
Belmont MI
493069010

Call Sign: KA8KFX
Douglas J Verduin
4547 7 Mile Rd
Belmont MI 49306

Call Sign: WA8ABT
Robert E Schlenker
4848 7 Mile Rd NE
Belmont MI 49306

Call Sign: KB8CDO
Patricia A Tennant
5911 7 Mile Rd NE
Belmont MI 49306

Call Sign: KD8HDL
Tamara A Habib
7619 Belmont Ave
Belmont MI 49306

Call Sign: WB8NSI
James R Foley Jr
6112 Belshire Ave NE
Belmont MI 49306

Call Sign: WD8BKA
Philip E Koelzer
6112 Belshire Ave NE
Belmont MI 49306

Call Sign: W8NSI
James R Foley Jr
6112 Belshire Ave NE
Belmont MI
493069744

Call Sign: W8DCL
Walter A Baron
6262 Belshire Ave NE
Belmont MI 49306

Call Sign: KA8WTV
Mark S Fairgrieve
6777 Blue Ridge Dr
Belmont MI
493069769

Call Sign: N8OAQ
Wayne M Knoth
6777 Blue Ridge NE
Belmont MI 49306

Call Sign: KB8RHT
Leon D Hollowell
5212 Cannonsburg Rd
Belmont MI 49306

Call Sign: KB8VUE
Sheila A Bowerman
5212 Cannonsburg Rd
Belmont MI 49306

Call Sign: W8HWN
Robert Steed
2966 Grand Island Dr
NE
Belmont MI 49306

Call Sign: KA8ART
Donald L Carlson
7220 Herrington
Belmont MI 49306

Call Sign: KD8PZI
Mark A Denslow
8004 Herrington NE
Belmont MI 49306

Call Sign: AC8JC
Mark A Denslow
8004 Herrington NE
Belmont MI 49306

Call Sign: K8GY
Mark A Denslow
8004 Herrington NE
Belmont MI 49306

Call Sign: KA8QWA
Gregory J Zimmer
2145 Hollyhock St NE
Belmont MI 49306

Call Sign: N8KUD
Daniel J Wynalda
1576 Irmamax Ct NE
Belmont MI 49306

Call Sign: KD8EHM
Patrick R Loftus

3399 Las Vegas Dr
Belmont MI 49306

Call Sign: N8LHR
Sherri L Ter Molen
3400 Las Vegas NE
Belmont MI 49306

Call Sign: KC8EGF
Mary E Nester
7312 Maize
Belmont MI 49306

Call Sign: WD8USA
Joseph G Bell
7215 Packer Dr
Belmont MI 49306

Call Sign: N8IMR
Kathleen E Bell
7215 Packer Dr
Belmont MI 49306

Call Sign: KB8EFW
Chris R Bamford
5954 Robin Hill
Belmont MI 49306

Call Sign: KD8DZR
Steven L Burns
1253 S Maize
Belmont MI 49306

Call Sign: KD8ECX
Judy K Burns
1253 S Maize Dr NE
Belmont MI 49306

Call Sign: WC8G
Paul R Zimmer Jr
6170 Viewpoint NE
Belmont MI
493069400

Call Sign: N8ALH
Laddie E Leblond
6301 Woodwater
Belmont MI 49306

**FCC Amateur Radio
Licenses in Benton
Harbor**

Call Sign: N8XSH

Steve E Lindenfeld
275 Benjamin
Benton Harbor MI
49022

Call Sign: KB8EGB
Gayle A Poe
2213 Berg St
Benton Harbor MI
49022

Call Sign: WD8IEV
William L Orvis
361 Bradford
Benton Harbor MI
49022

Call Sign: WA8EPO
Robert A Lange
1773 Broadway
Benton Harbor MI
490226519

Call Sign: KD8BUR
John E Mccoy
1865 Broadway
Benton Harbor MI
490226521

Call Sign: KD8NOH
Timothy P Richards
3218 Broderick Rd
Benton Harbor MI
49022

Call Sign: WB8RMM
Richard E Willard
233 Cherokee Trl
Benton Harbor MI
49022

Call Sign: KC8MNG
Richard J Fester
3660 Duncan Rd
Benton Harbor MI
490229703

Call Sign: N8PYV
Dale A Nafziger
5764 E Empire
Benton Harbor MI
49022

Call Sign: N8RCR

Sandra J Nafziger
5764 E Empire
Benton Harbor MI
49022

Call Sign: KB8EKW
Linda M Spencer
2088 E Empire 187
Benton Harbor MI
49022

Call Sign: N8WFT
Elizabeth D Johnson
3791 E Empire Ave
Benton Harbor MI
49022

Call Sign: W8JSJ
Jeffrey S Johnson
3791 E Empire Ave
Benton Harbor MI
49022

Call Sign: N8ZXP
Robert T Nafziger
5700 E Empire Ave
Benton Harbor MI
49022

Call Sign: KB8SWI
Scott W Bridwell
1200 E Empire Lot 24
Benton Harbor MI
49022

Call Sign: WB8UVA
Jerry M Campbell
2390 E Euclid Ave
Benton Harbor MI
49022

Call Sign: N8VHD
Mary E Shine
176 Eastern Ave
Benton Harbor MI
49022

Call Sign: KC8YSW
Daniel S Utroske
162 Elmside Rd
Benton Harbor MI
49022

Call Sign: KF8Z

Daniel S Utroske
162 Elmside Rd
Benton Harbor MI
49022

Call Sign: WB8RMR
Wilkin J Kirk
546 Eloise Dr
Benton Harbor MI
49022

Call Sign: KB8EEF
Norman L Zinn
5565 Empire St
Benton Harbor MI
49022

Call Sign: KC8CXT
Wilfred C Stapley
92049 Fairview Ave
Benton Harbor MI
49022

Call Sign: WD8KCY
Earl A Potter
421 Felton Ave
Benton Harbor MI
49022

Call Sign: KA8TMF
James F Stringer
524 Forest Pt Rd
Benton Harbor MI
49022

Call Sign: KK8G
Hobart G McLaughlin
Sr
2530 Gregory Rd
Benton Harbor MI
49022

Call Sign: N8HBH
Elizabeth R Renhack
2530 Gregory Rd
Benton Harbor MI
49022

Call Sign: KB8ZGM
Richard P Sirk
4432 Hicks Ave
Benton Harbor MI
49022

Call Sign: KC8YJV
Barbara E Sirk
4432 Hicks Ave
Benton Harbor MI
49022

Call Sign: KD8EFA
Donna M Green
4432 Hicks Ave
Benton Harbor MI
49022

Call Sign: KA8ZFE
Richard L Seymour
286 Higman Pk Rd
Benton Harbor MI
49022

Call Sign: KC8JBY
Clay R McCausland
236 Higmon Park
Benton Harbor MI
49022

Call Sign: KC8MIO
Jean W Lindenfeld
437 Hoover
Benton Harbor MI
49023

Call Sign: N8SHZ
Bela W Lindenfeld
437 Hoover Ave
Benton Harbor MI
49022

Call Sign: KD8FFV
Patrick A Fowler
2769 Kerlikowske Rd
Benton Harbor MI
49022

Call Sign: WA8ZNV
Frederick J Barnes
202 Kublick Dr
Benton Harbor MI
49022

Call Sign: KD8DMN
Michael A Momany
2372 Lora Dr
Benton Harbor MI
49022

Call Sign: KD8MAM
Michael A Momany
2372 Lora Dr
Benton Harbor MI
49022

Call Sign: WA8WNY
Milton H Zoschke
2400 Lora Dr
Benton Harbor MI
49022

Call Sign: KB8UBS
Keith A Reinbolt
68706 M 152 Hwy
Benton Harbor MI
49022

Call Sign: N8OL
Ken M Jewell
1349 Maple Ln
Benton Harbor MI
49022

Call Sign: KA8BIO
Kevin K Borgerding
3056 Maplewood St
Benton Harbor MI
49022

Call Sign: KF6PJF
Carolyn H Stockwell
276 Messner Dr
Benton Harbor MI
49022

Call Sign: KD8FFP
John E Lidstrom
1478 Miami Rd
Benton Harbor MI
49022

Call Sign: N8RYE
Richard D Boyer
3255 N Chabot Rd
Benton Harbor MI
49022

Call Sign: N8XSI
Ronald W Forrest
1565 N M 63 N Lot 88
Benton Harbor MI
49022

Call Sign: KB8EKY
Sonya M Siler
764 Nate Wells Sr Dr
Benton Harbor MI
49022

Call Sign: N8RYD
James W Maxwell
481 Nickerson
Benton Harbor MI
49022

Call Sign: W8HTH
George G Schmidt
1406 Nickerson Ave
Benton Harbor MI
49022

Call Sign: KC8HBQ
Norman L Stokes
1967 Paw Paw Ave
Benton Harbor MI
49022

Call Sign: KC8TWF
Dennis L Bakken
1452 Pipestone
Benton Harbor MI
49022

Call Sign: KD8HXE
Shirley Jetter
2464 Riverbend Dr
Benton Harbor MI
49022

Call Sign: N8MEI
Matthew L Rappette
2490 Riverbend Dr
Benton Harbor MI
49022

Call Sign: KD8GKU
Ryan J Anderson
2650 Riverside Rd
Benton Harbor MI
49022

Call Sign: KC8MNO
Ken M Jewell
2352 Roncy Rd
Benton Harbor MI
49022

Call Sign: KD8DZZ
Christopher M
Pentridge
1987 Roslin Rd
Benton Harbor MI
49022

Call Sign: WB7TGQ
Patrick H Crean
532 S Ottawa Rd
Benton Harbor MI
49022

Call Sign: KC8PK
Alton B Parrott
1227 Seneca Rd
Benton Harbor MI
49022

Call Sign: KD8LOL
Otto G Molmen Jr
1573 Shawnee Rd
Benton Harbor MI
49022

Call Sign: KB8GXG
James S Nettleton
894 Sierra Dr
Benton Harbor MI
49022

Call Sign: K8SPF
Robert H Siler Sr
1254 Summer St
Benton Harbor MI
49022

Call Sign: W8IPW
Jack F Park
2110 Sunrise Ln
Benton Harbor MI
49022

Call Sign: N8SIA
Martin A Raymond
1326 Superior
Benton Harbor MI
49022

Call Sign: WD8AAK
Ronald W Folkert
5085 Territorial Rd
Benton Harbor MI
490229409

Call Sign: N8SKH
Michael R Dryer Jr
6033 Territorial Rd
Benton Harbor MI
49022

Call Sign: WM8Z
Ronald T Oxley
7280 Territorial Rd
Benton Harbor MI
49022

Call Sign: K8BLL
Charles A Robertson
282 Villa Ln
Benton Harbor MI
49022

Call Sign: KG8NO
Shirley M Gustafson
1738 W Benson
Benton Harbor MI
49022

Call Sign: KG8YR
Donald D Gustafson
1738 W Benson
Benton Harbor MI
49022

FCC Amateur Radio Licenses in Benzonia

Call Sign: WA8FJD
Lester E Guiles
6889 Mick Rd
Benzonia MI 49616

Call Sign: KG8ZA
George E Laubach
7281 River St
Benzonia MI 49616

Call Sign: WB8GKW
Ronald L Noffsinger
7280 South St
Benzonia MI 49616

Call Sign: K8GLI
Ronald L Noffsinger
7280 South St
Benzonia MI 49616

Call Sign: KD8BXM
Terry L Crooks
Benzonia MI 49616

FCC Amateur Radio Licenses in Bergland

Call Sign: WA9KOB
Jerome A Volkmann
772 E Shore Rd
Bergland MI 49910

Call Sign: KD8MVA
Gene A Marcusen
20106 Old M 64
Bergland MI 49910

Call Sign: KD8MUZ
Kara L Marcusen
20106 Old M 64
Bergland MI 49910

Call Sign: KD8MUY
Sandra A Marcusen
20106 Old M 64
Bergland MI 49910

Call Sign: WE9C
Ronald J Warczynski
Bergland MI 49910

Call Sign: KD8GBJ
Michael L Boro
Bergland MI 49910

FCC Amateur Radio Licenses in Berrien Center

Call Sign: WB8DXM
Johanna B Simpson
7339 Dean Hill Rd
Berrien Center MI
49102

Call Sign: N8BEE
Dale H Simpson
7339 Deans Hill Rd
Berrien Center MI
49102

Call Sign: KD8GOP
John E Beal
8619 Eau Claire Rd

Berrien Center MI
49102

Call Sign: N8PYW
Clifton A Keller Jr
8701 Eau Claire Rd
Berrien Center MI
49102

Call Sign: N3MOS
Edward A Mack
9592 Fox Run
Berrien Center MI
49102

Call Sign: KU8Y
Kenneth D Simpson
10349 Jones Rd
Berrien Center MI
49102

Call Sign: N9XQG
Leroy M Rappette
6368 Oak Ct
Berrien Center MI
49102

Call Sign: N9XQH
Suz Ann M Rappette
6368 Oak Ct
Berrien Center MI
49102

Call Sign: KC7IHH
Duane E Habenicht
9368 Painter School
Rd
Berrien Center MI
49102

Call Sign: KC8PPA
Joseph E Marston
10239 Painter School
Rd
Berrien Center MI
49102

Call Sign: W8JEM
Joseph E Marston
10239 Painter School
Rd
Berrien Center MI
49102

Call Sign: N3GUN
Reginald T Swensen
9392 Park Ridge Trl
Berrien Center MI
49102

Call Sign: KD8HNR
Wanda M Swensen
9392 Park Ridge Trl
Berrien Center MI
49102

Call Sign: KB8ZGN
Joseph R Buckhanan
84 67 Pucker St
Berrien Center MI
49102

FCC Amateur Radio Licenses in Berrien Springs

Call Sign: N9DEY
Linda J Habenicht
9137 4th St
Berrien Springs MI
49103

Call Sign: N8EDH
Bethel E Habenicht
9137 4th St
Berrien Springs MI
49103

Call Sign: N8LWS
Gary L Doty
9634 Burgoyne Rd
Berrien Springs MI
49103

Call Sign: KD8GKV
Curtis L Webber
11251 Burgoyne Rd
Berrien Springs MI
49103

Call Sign: N0FIC
Jerry A Moon
10124 Castner Dr
Berrien Springs MI
49103

Call Sign: WD8OLG
James Wolfer

10173 Castner Dr
Berrien Springs MI
49103

Call Sign: KE6BOV
Lynelle M Weldon
4948 Claredon Pl
Berrien Springs MI
49103

Call Sign: N6MMC
Jerry R Weldon
4948 Claredon Pl
Berrien Springs MI
49103

Call Sign: KD8QLD
Roger K Edington
5576 Deans Hill Rd
Berrien Springs MI
49103

Call Sign: WB8QJI
Emerald L Oxley
4779 E Hillcrest Dr
Berrien Springs MI
49103

Call Sign: KC8CDM
Robert M Little III
4849 E Hillcrest Dr
Berrien Springs MI
49103

Call Sign: KB8TND
Balinda J Graham
4710-1 E Hillcrest Dr
Berrien Springs MI
49103

Call Sign: KB8MWP
Elliot C Lee
4847-2 E Hillcrest Dr
Berrien Springs MI
49103

Call Sign: KD8ALU
Donald L Bishop
2049 E Hinchman Rd
Berrien Springs MI
49103

Call Sign: W8YKS
Lowell F Dunham

215 E Lemon Creek
Rd
Berrien Springs MI
49103

Call Sign: KB6AMZ
Anita E Benson
1322 E Shawnee Rd
Berrien Springs MI
49103

Call Sign: N0CRJ
Verlyn R Benson
1322 E Shawnee Rd
Berrien Springs MI
491030251

Call Sign: KD8CZM
Jerrett C Pate
4598 E Shawnee Rd
Berrien Springs MI
49103

Call Sign: N8CPY
Gerald P Brown
1788 E Snow Rd
Berrien Springs MI
49103

Call Sign: KD8EMQ
Daniel L Hamstra
2737 E Snow Rd
Berrien Springs MI
49103

Call Sign: K8ALF
Daniel L Hamstra
2737 E Snow Rd
Berrien Springs MI
49103

Call Sign: KD8GRG
Bradley H Kerr
3604 E Snow Rd
Berrien Springs MI
49103

Call Sign: KD8GRF
Jackson H Kerr
3604 E Snow Rd
Berrien Springs MI
49203

Call Sign: KB8ZVC

Daniel P Cress
4218 E Tudor Rd
Berrien Springs MI
49103

Call Sign: KC8LHG
Lowell K George
701 Ferry St
Berrien Springs MI
49103

Call Sign: KC8SKN
Leroy D Siagian
500 Garland Ave E 26
Berrien Springs MI
49103

Call Sign: N8EXZ
Nancy J Moneta
7588 Garr Rd
Berrien Springs MI
49103

Call Sign: WA6GMH
James G Harris
10821 Garr Rd
Berrien Springs MI
49103

Call Sign: W8FEM
Richard C Sowler
8869 George Ave
Berrien Springs MI
491031407

Call Sign: N8RCO
Anna K Borchardt
8952 George Ave
Berrien Springs MI
49103

Call Sign: N8RCU
Randall N Borchardt
8952 George Ave
Berrien Springs MI
49103

Call Sign: KB8UWE
Belinda E Kent
9041 George Ave
Berrien Springs MI
49103

Call Sign: KC8SUB

Pamela J Nickel
4731 Greenfield Dr
Berrien Springs MI
49103

Call Sign: AD6BR
Ray W McAllister
8936 Grove Ave
Berrien Springs MI
49103

Call Sign: W8PQI
Ernest F Herford
8940 Grove Ave
Berrien Springs MI
49103

Call Sign: KA8MSM
Floyd A Eskridge
4862 Highland Dr
Berrien Springs MI
491031022

Call Sign: KC8NIL
Nickilos J Wolfer
4876 Highland Dr
Berrien Springs MI
49103

Call Sign: KC8LYV
Donald B Starlin
10553 Hill Point
Berrien Springs MI
49103

Call Sign: KE4CVS
Michael J Birochak
8316 Hollywood Rd
Berrien Springs MI
49103

Call Sign: KD8CZP
Ronald A Bush
2368 Honeysuckle Ln
Berrien Springs MI
49103

Call Sign: KA8MSO
Andrew C Lloyd
11432 Jones Rd
Berrien Springs MI
49103

Call Sign: W8MGW

Harry C Lloyd
11432 Jones Rd
Berrien Springs MI
49103

Call Sign: N8MYG
Celia M O Conner
4253 Lake Chapin
Bluff
Berrien Springs MI
49103

Call Sign: N8BTO
James L Ware
2738 Lakeland Dr
Berrien Springs MI
49103

Call Sign: KC8YFC
Wayne C Fuchs
6929 Long Lake Rd
Berrien Springs MI
49103

Call Sign: WA8TBL
Marvin E Budd
6953 Long Lake Rd
Berrien Springs MI
491039676

Call Sign: KR4GB
Abdias Vence
301 Madison St
Berrien Springs MI
49013

Call Sign: N8UWM
Sheri S Shimechero
550 Maplewood Ct
E71
Berrien Springs MI
49103

Call Sign: KC8SKO
Kathleen A Shoemaker
8741 Meadow Ln 2
Berrien Springs MI
49103

Call Sign: KC8LSU
Jonathan D Brauer
209B Meier Hall
Berrien Springs MI
49104

Call Sign: KH2RJ
Kevin D Bhookun
301A Meier Hall
Berrien Springs MI
49103

Call Sign: W8PYP
Mark G Evans
412 N Cass St
Berrien Springs MI
49103

Call Sign: N8WMK
Philip E Potter
316 N Harrison
Berrien Springs MI
491031005

Call Sign: KB8SVE
Marian B Potter
316 N Harrison St
Berrien Springs MI
49103

Call Sign: N9DZG
Marvin E Pelto Jr
215 N Kimmel 4
Berrien Springs MI
49103

Call Sign: KB8GNO
Homer H Halt
626 N Main St
Berrien Springs MI
49103

Call Sign: KC8MNE
Jimmy Kijai
8956 N Main St
Berrien Springs MI
49103

Call Sign: KC8YSZ
Gregg A Nicholas
524 N Mechanic St
Berrien Springs MI
49103

Call Sign: WA8TOZ
F Norman Pottle
8712 N Ridge
Berrien Springs MI
491031457

Call Sign: N8RCW
Dorothy R Hildebrand
8844 N Ridge Ave
Berrien Springs MI
49103

Call Sign: KC8WNU
Lanny G True
9659 Old US 31
Berrien Springs MI
49103

Call Sign: KB8KT
Ralph L Burlingame
10430 Old US 31s
Berrien Springs MI
49103

Call Sign: N8TYJ
Erik S La Bianca
5665 Orchard Dr
Berrien Springs MI
49103

Call Sign: W0PVA
Alexander Shepherd
4871 Pioneer Rd
Berrien Springs MI
491031454

Call Sign: KC8JGP
Marcel H Pichot
5599 Pokagon Rd
Berrien Springs MI
49103

Call Sign: KC8JIL
Kimberly S Pichiot
5599 Pokagon Rd
Berrien Springs MI
49103

Call Sign: KC9EZO
Adrian R Martin
10668 Range Line Rd
Berrien Springs MI
49103

Call Sign: KB0VJK
Tom R Shepherd
10871 Range Line Rd
Berrien Springs MI
491039620

Call Sign: AA8TT
John S Merritt
10170 Rangeline Rd
Berrien Springs MI
49103

Call Sign: KB8BTQ
Richard D Robertson
10625 Red Bud Trl
Berrien Springs MI
491039738

Call Sign: N8SAB
James A Robertson
10625 Red Bud Trl
Berrien Springs MI
491039738

Call Sign: NR8B
Elmer A Robertson Jr
10625 Red Bud Trl
Berrien Springs MI
491039738

Call Sign: KA8ZDF
John C Robertson
10625 Redbud Tr
Berrien Springs MI
49104

Call Sign: K8ROB
Robert E Moncrieff
2650 Ridgewood Trl
Berrien Springs MI
49103

Call Sign: KC8KGR
Robert E Moncrieff
2650 Ridgewood Trl
Berrien Springs MI
49103

Call Sign: N6DNN
Scott E Moncrieff
2650 Ridgewood Trl
Berrien Springs MI
49103

Call Sign: N6KPD
Lilia E Moncrieff
2650 Ridgewood Trl
Berrien Springs MI
49103

Call Sign: KB9LTO
Gerald D Alexander
2763 Ridgewood Trl
Berrien Springs MI
49103

Call Sign: N8ZXI
Benjamin R Rogers
2331 Rocky Weed Rd
Berrien Springs MI
49103

Call Sign: KB8VBX
Brian S Laird
401 Rose Hill Rd
Berrien Springs MI
49103

Call Sign: KD8NIF
Corey V Burks
7016 Rose Ln
Berrien Springs MI
49103

Call Sign: KB8SKG
Darlene V Miller
8780 S Bluffview Dr
Berrien Springs MI
49103

Call Sign: N8WOL
Gary L Miller
8780 S Bluffview Dr
Berrien Springs MI
49103

Call Sign: KC4SRD
Jon M Harris
300 S Cass St
Berrien Springs MI
49103

Call Sign: KC8AYA
Bryan T Clayton
109 S Harrison Ave
Berrien Springs MI
49103

Call Sign: N8NQZ
Bernard D Helms
417 S Main St
Berrien Springs MI
49103

Call Sign: AC8CJ
Bernard D Helms
417 S Main St
Berrien Springs MI
49103

Call Sign: N8LDA
Craig J Webster
610 S Mechanic
Berrien Springs MI
49103

Call Sign: KC8TWE
Edouard Thomas
308 S Mechanics Apt 2
Berrien Springs MI
49103

Call Sign: KB8FNB
David C Grellmann
St Clair 10179 S US 31
Berrien Springs MI
49103

Call Sign: KH2IY
Andrew D Gungadoo
9046 S US 31 Ste 1
Berrien Springs MI
49103

Call Sign: N8ZEF
Rachel A Luchak
4221 Snow Rd
Berrien Springs MI
49103

Call Sign: N8ZEG
Peter N Luchak
4221 Snow Rd
Berrien Springs MI
49103

Call Sign: AJ9I
Bradley S Bateman
6689 Snyder Rd
Berrien Springs MI
49103

Call Sign: KB8RRN
James E Tiffany
9025-2 Sunset Dr
Berrien Springs MI
49103

Call Sign: KC7GXG
Sandi R Phillips
9198 Sunset Dr
Berrien Springs MI
49103

Call Sign: KE6NUW
Gregory R Phillips
9198 Sunset Dr
Berrien Springs MI
49103

Call Sign: KC8SKM
Roman Kozlov
8785 University Blvd
Apt 7
Berrien Springs MI
49103

Call Sign: WB8RHE
Tedd Snyder
3320 US 31
Berrien Springs MI
49103

Call Sign: KD8OMF
Larry Rentfro
3320 US 31
Berrien Springs MI
49103

Call Sign: KC8YNT
Clifmond L
Shameerudeen
8715 Valley View Dr
Apt 2
Berrien Springs MI
49103

Call Sign: KB8YEH
Derek K Bradfield
405 W Union St
Berrien Springs MI
49103

Call Sign: KC8LST
C Brooks Payne
3105 Willo Dr
Berrien Springs MI
491039521

Call Sign: KD8GOJ
Roy E Puymon

3224 Willo Dr
Berrien Springs MI
49103

Call Sign: WX8Y
Donald W Sprung
5835 Windy Acres
Berrien Springs MI
49103

Call Sign: KB7NUJ
Raymond A Spoon Jr
Berrien Springs MI
49103

Call Sign: KC8PRT
Dawn M Spoon
Berrien Springs MI
49103

Call Sign: KD8QIV
Andrew Mason
Berrien Springs MI
49103

Call Sign: KF7GTT
Mari Kirk
Berrien Springs MI
49103

Call Sign: KD8QIW
Robert N Mason
Berrien Springs MI
49103

Call Sign: N6MSK
Matthew S Kirk
Berrien Springs MI
491030294

FCC Amateur Radio Licenses in Bessemer

Call Sign: KA9JTU
Monte R Hollenbeck
N11290 Black River
Rd
Bessemer MI 49911

Call Sign: KA9LAV
Winona J Hollenbeck
N11290 Black River
Rd
Bessemer MI 49911

Call Sign: KB9JNA
Scott A Spengler
508 E Iron St
Bessemer MI 49911

Call Sign: KB9MSL
Yvonne A Payne
173 Palms Location Rd
Bessemer MI 49911

Call Sign: N9OKL
Floyd M Payne
173 Palms Location Rd
Bessemer MI 49911

Call Sign: KB9RPK
Jesse F Baroka
1817 Porter St
Bessemer MI 49911

Call Sign: K8ATX
Leslie G Johnson
E 7620 Prospect Dr
Bessemer MI 49911

Call Sign: WA8DWM
Eunice L Johnson
E 7620 Prospect Dr
Bessemer MI 49911

Call Sign: KC8WNV
Blackjack ARC
E7620 Prospect Dr
Bessemer MI 49911

Call Sign: K8ATX
Blackjack ARC
E7620 Prospect Dr
Bessemer MI 49911

Call Sign: K8GXV
Ernest D Roberts
707 S Mine St
Bessemer MI
499111720

FCC Amateur Radio Licenses in Beulah

Call Sign: KE8NX
James D Mac Innes
4751 Arbutas Ln
Beulah MI 49617

Call Sign: KD8OIN
Timothy M Rockwell
11634 Brooks Trl
Beulah MI 49617

Call Sign: KB8QCF
Jeff N Wentzloff
222 Center St
Beulah MI 49617

Call Sign: N8FUN
Norman K Zink
11261 Cinder Rd
Beulah MI 496179353

Call Sign: KC8RLW
Larry F Snyder
13650 Cinder Rd
Beulah MI 49617

Call Sign: KC8RLX
Cassandra J Snyder
13650 Cinder Rd
Beulah MI 49617

Call Sign: KC8DAS
Susan M Flynn
14487 Cinder Rd
Beulah MI 49617

Call Sign: KG8CW
Michael B Flynn
14487 Cinder Rd
Beulah MI 49617

Call Sign: KC8CLL
Charles H Arington
220 Moss Rd
Beulah MI 49617

Call Sign: KC8OOC
Thomas M Davis
830 N Marshall Rd
Beulah MI 49617

Call Sign: KC8OOB
Mary K Davis
830 N Marshall Rd
Beulah MI 49617

Call Sign: K8BTE
Thomas G Schoonover
7832 Old Platte Rd

Beulah MI 49617

Call Sign: N8BKT
John M Tornow Sr
1678 Pioneer Rd
Beulah MI 496179765

Call Sign: KD8JPW
Jane A Tonn
7696 Worden Rd
Beulah MI 49617

Call Sign: KB8YPL
George D Sinclair
1427 Zimmerman
Beulah MI 49617

Call Sign: KC8AUK
Robert E Janusch
Beulah MI 49617

Call Sign: W8REJ
Robert E Janusch
Beulah MI 49617

FCC Amateur Radio Licenses in Big Bay

Call Sign: KD8DAY
Robert L Meyers
Big Bay MI 49808

Call Sign: KD8FDS
Thomas C Moran
Big Bay MI 49808

FCC Amateur Radio Licenses in Big Rapids

Call Sign: KC8GYK
Ronald A Hernden
22288 11 Mile Rd
Big Rapids MI 49307

Call Sign: KC8HVS
Matthew P Hernden
22344 11 Mile Rd
Big Rapids MI 49307

Call Sign: KB8BWW
Joel P McGorman
23763 11 Mile Rd
Big Rapids MI 49307

Call Sign: N8HZB
David R Watkins
23763 11 Mile Rd
Big Rapids MI 49307

Call Sign: KA8JGI
Jean M Engel
15511 12 Mile Rd
Big Rapids MI 49307

Call Sign: WA8AEN
Daniel D Astleford
22843 12 Mile Rd
Big Rapids MI
493079614

Call Sign: KD8SBF
Brian H Coe
19790 14 Mile Rd
Big Rapids MI 49307

Call Sign: N8CFR
Jon L Huhtala
22872 14 Mile Rd
Big Rapids MI 49307

Call Sign: KC8JQP
Rick A Dean
23717 15 Mile Rd
Big Rapids MI 49307

Call Sign: W8ZNH
William H Eckels
12322 175th Ave
Big Rapids MI
493079555

Call Sign: KC8CII
Jerrald L Buskirk
20924 175th Ave
Big Rapids MI 49307

Call Sign: KC8WFY
Christopher M Taal
12455 183rd Ave
Big Rapids MI 49307

Call Sign: KC8GDE
Edward D Augustson
22850 19 Mile Rd
Big Rapids MI 49307

Call Sign: KC8YGI

Joseph E Augustson
22850 19 Mile Rd
Big Rapids MI 49307

Call Sign: KD8ISP
Robert N Gombosh
12196 190th Ave
Big Rapids MI 49307

Call Sign: KC7GQV
William D Browers
18820 195th Ave
Big Rapids MI 49307

Call Sign: KC8BY
Lester J Richards
19060 200th Ave
Big Rapids MI 49307

Call Sign: KB8JR
Lester J Richards
19060 200th Ave
Big Rapids MI 49307

Call Sign: KB8ZSU
Gregg A McDanield
21081 205th Ave
Big Rapids MI 49307

Call Sign: N8KAY
Richard D Hunter
14845 205th St Box
214
Big Rapids MI 49307

Call Sign: KD8FBM
Michael A Lafontaine
12833 220th Ave
Big Rapids MI 49307

Call Sign: K8YHJ
Robert S Carpenter
18222 220th Ave
Big Rapids MI 49307

Call Sign: KD8EJI
Sharon K Moody
620 Birch St
Big Rapids MI 49307

Call Sign: WB8DGM
Robert W Moody Sr
620 Birch St
Big Rapids MI 49307

Call Sign: AB8NC
Robert W Moody Sr
620 Birch St
Big Rapids MI 49307

Call Sign: KC8IJV
Cynthia M Roberts
606 Bjornson D7
Big Rapids MI 49307

Call Sign: KC8JOL
Douglas J Schmidt
606 Bjornson K1
Big Rapids MI 49307

Call Sign: KC8WGA
David M Huhtala
606 Bjornson L1
Big Rapids MI 49307

Call Sign: W4OKU
Jon L Huhtala
606 Bjornson L1
Big Rapids MI 49307

Call Sign: N8ZTQ
Edward R Roberts
606 Bjornson Lod D7
Big Rapids MI 49307

Call Sign: KC8WGA
David M Huhtala
606 Bjornson Lot L1
Big Rapids MI 49307

Call Sign: K8TEE
David M Huhtala
606 Bjornson Lot L1
Big Rapids MI 49307

Call Sign: KC8MVP
Jerry L Getts
406 Bjornson St Apt 4
Big Rapids MI 49307

Call Sign: WA8TNQ
Oscar E Dennis
606 Bjornson St Lot
C11
Big Rapids MI 49307

Call Sign: KD8PUZ
Lorne H Juday

801 Campus Dr
Big Rapids MI 49307

Call Sign: KD8KQC
Calvin J Mckay
20366 Campusview Dr
Big Rapids MI 49307

Call Sign: KD8DIB
Michael J Mckay
20366 Campusview Dr
Big Rapids MI 49307

Call Sign: KD8GGD
Patricia J Mckay
20366 Campusview Dr
Big Rapids MI 49307

Call Sign: KC8OVV
John E Van Houten
14810 Chula Vista Dr
Big Rapids MI 49307

Call Sign: KD8NRO
Gregory O Woolen
14955 Chula Vista Dr
Big Rapids MI 49307

Call Sign: K4UIH
James R Woolen
14955 Chula Vista Dr
Big Rapids MI
493079055

Call Sign: KB8ZEU
John G Videtich
14891 Chulavista
Big Rapids MI 49307

Call Sign: KB8ZEN
Gregory J Videtich
14891 Chulavista Dr
Big Rapids MI 49307

Call Sign: KC8WFX
Gordon M Trute
15775 Coolidge Rd
Big Rapids MI 49307

Call Sign: W8AKJ
Gordon M Trute
15775 Coolidge Rd
Big Rapids MI 49307

Call Sign: WB8TVD
Bruce L Werner
20839 Coolidge Rd
Big Rapids MI 49307

Call Sign: KD8FBE
Peter J Kailing
9003 E 7 Mile Rd
Big Rapids MI 49307

Call Sign: WA8YWR
Dean L Luplow
21522 Forest Trl
Big Rapids MI 49307

Call Sign: KB8NBP
Lawson Kofi Adzaku
521 Fuller Ave 103A
Big Rapids MI 49307

Call Sign: KD8KPU
Tricia A Walding
Smith
521 Fuller Ave Apt
102D
Big Rapids MI 49307

Call Sign: KA8GPA
Gerald K Jordan
1135 Fuller Ave Apt 6
Big Rapids MI 49307

Call Sign: KB8ZER
Lonna J Lewis
19882 Heights Cir Dr
Big Rapids MI 49307

Call Sign: KC8KXG
Kevin J Fowler
17168 Heritage Dr
Big Rapids MI 49307

Call Sign: KC8MRS
Christopher K Fisher
420 Hutchinson
Big Rapids MI 49307

Call Sign: KI8IJ
Fred G Pins
420 Hutchinson St
Big Rapids MI 49307

Call Sign: NI8E
Fred G Pins

420 Hutchinson St
Big Rapids MI 49307

Call Sign: KB8KIR
Harry Delaney
405 Ives Ave
Big Rapids MI 49307

Call Sign: KC8ONN
Big Rapids Area ARC
21021 Madison Ave
Big Rapids MI 49307

Call Sign: KB4CCE
Peter N Chesebrough
21021 Madison Ave
Big Rapids MI
493079754

Call Sign: W8PET
Peter N Chesebrough
21021 Madison Ave
Big Rapids MI
493079754

Call Sign: KE8KL
Richard A Witzke
20879 Madison St
Big Rapids MI 49307

Call Sign: KC8ZPR
Paul A Schmidt
708 Magnolia Ct
Big Rapids MI 49307

Call Sign: KD8MMF
Jared M Paul
707 Maple St Apt
Big Rapids MI 49307

Call Sign: KD8FBO
Debra S Rolston
12966 Millpond Rd
Big Rapids MI 49307

Call Sign: N8UYE
Dwight E Rockey
14235 Millpond Rd
Big Rapids MI 49307

Call Sign: WD8MOD
Robert L Willison
7170 N Hickory Dr
Big Rapids MI 49307

Call Sign: KD8NRK
James E Bourdlais
513 N State St
Big Rapids MI 49307

Call Sign: KB8IGA
Kevin L Tucker
603 N State St
Big Rapids MI 49307

Call Sign: KD8FBI
Daniel F Farrow
929 N State St
Big Rapids MI 49307

Call Sign: KA8OLB
Jeffrey F Cross
17671 Nancy Dr
Big Rapids MI 49307

Call Sign: KI8CK
Jacob A Spence
20598 Okemos Ave
Big Rapids MI 49307

Call Sign: KB8ZYA
Western Michigan
Packet Society
20845 Okemos Dr
Big Rapids MI 49307

Call Sign: WW8Q
James O Haight
20845 Okemos Dr
Big Rapids MI 49307

Call Sign: KD8HYG
Nancy J Haight
20845 Okemos Dr
Big Rapids MI 49307

Call Sign: K8NJH
Nancy J Haight
20845 Okemos Dr
Big Rapids MI 49307

Call Sign: KD8HYA
Jessica L Schultz
237 Robin Ct
Big Rapids MI 49307

Call Sign: KB8BWX
Garnet E Zimmerman

1107 Rose Ave
Big Rapids MI 49307

Call Sign: WA4FRJ
Donald G Mac Connel
17961 Round Lake Rd
Big Rapids MI 49307

Call Sign: KD8OGC
Helen Popovich
17961 Round Lake Rd
Big Rapids MI 49307

Call Sign: KD8KPW
Megan M Bolter
203 Rust Ave
Big Rapids MI 49307

Call Sign: N8SFG
Nowell S La Rock
700 S Bronson Ave
Big Rapids MI 49307

Call Sign: KD8JRU
Neil D Beyer
414 S Steward Ave
Big Rapids MI 49307

Call Sign: KC8ZPP
Robert E Johnston
602 S Warren Ave
Big Rapids MI 49307

Call Sign: KC8OIU
Renato L Cerdena
404 Sanborn Way
Big Rapids MI 49307

Call Sign: KC8PDV
A J Clark
18025 Shamrock Blvd
Big Rapids MI 49307

Call Sign: KB8TYJ
G Thomas Behler Jr
511 Spring St
Big Rapids MI 49307

Call Sign: KC8IFP
Susan D Behler
511 Spring St
Big Rapids MI 49307

Call Sign: KC8DC

Michael T O Connor
13395 Symonds Dr
Big Rapids MI 49307

Call Sign: KC8OIV
Jens O Rick
17799 Trestle Bend Dr
Big Rapids MI
493071102

Call Sign: KL7WI
Richard A Hawley
521 W Fuller Apt 103
D
Big Rapids MI 49307

Call Sign: W8OWN
George L Rouman
300 W Pine St
Big Rapids MI 49307

Call Sign: KC8ACK
James A Beebe
715 Water Tower Rd
Apt 12
Big Rapids MI 49307

Call Sign: KD8FBF
John M Lawrence
14070 Wildwood Dr
Big Rapids MI 49307

Call Sign: KD8FBK
Dean R Krager
520 Winter Ave
Big Rapids MI 49307

Call Sign: KD8BXU
Andrew H Cline
521 Winter Ave
Big Rapids MI 49307

Call Sign: KC8MMF
Jeriel A Beard
815 Winter Ave
Big Rapids MI 49307

Call Sign: KD8IYV
Carol J Beard
815 Winter Ave
Big Rapids MI 49307

Call Sign: KD8LVC
Carol J Beard

815 Winter Ave
Big Rapids MI 49307

Call Sign: KC8CBE
Mark P Cencer
310 Woodward
Big Rapids MI 49307

Call Sign: KC8WFZ
Nathan T Miller
900 Woodward Ave
Big Rapids MI 49307

Call Sign: N8IWP
Dawn A Beamish
Big Rapids MI 49307

Call Sign: N8IWO
Rickie L Miller
Big Rapids MI 49307

Call Sign: K4APN
Alice P Nunn
Big Rapids MI 49307

FCC Amateur Radio Licenses in Bitely

Call Sign: WB9VWP
Donald L Novak
1812 Beaver Rd
Bitely MI 49309

Call Sign: WB9ZCM
Opal L Novak
1812 Beaver Rd
Bitely MI 49309

Call Sign: KD8SAY
Tim R Wagner
10973 Cedar Crest Trl
Bitely MI 49309

Call Sign: NN3U
Bruce G Rockey
8585 Lincoln St
Bitely MI 49309

Call Sign: AC8LC
Bruce G Rockey
8585 Lincoln St
Bitely MI 49309

Call Sign: KD8SAZ

Rob J Wagner
8768 N Centerline Rd
Bitely MI 49309

Call Sign: KF4JZN
Elizabeth A Barlow
11894 N Highland
Bitely MI 49309

Call Sign: W8YQJ
William B Hansen
6535 W 13 Mile Rd
Bitely MI 49309

FCC Amateur Radio Licenses in Black River

Call Sign: KD8HGV
David S Wallace
3506 E Black River
Black River MI 48721

Call Sign: KD8KUD
Jane B Wallace
3506 E Black River Rd
Black River MI 48721

Call Sign: KC8AHX
Veryl D Davis
4010 N Lake Shore Dr
Black River MI 48721

Call Sign: KC5LNV
Darryl W Bauman
4310 N US 23
Black River MI 48721

Call Sign: KC8OHJ
Bridget E Malone
4679 Sucker Creek Rd
Black River MI 48721

Call Sign: KC8TXI
Donna R Malone
4679 Sucker Creek Rd
Black River MI 48721

Call Sign: KC8UHV
Gary A Malone
4679 Sucker Creek Rd
Black River MI 48721

FCC Amateur Radio Licenses in Bloomingdale

Call Sign: KD8BRA
John P Starbuck
2298 40th St
Bloomingdale MI 49026

Call Sign: KC8NLP
Robert T Swicker
8681 46th St
Bloomingdale MI 49026

Call Sign: N8FHS
Robert Jeffries
42956 6th Ave
Bloomingdale MI 49026

Call Sign: KB8YLG
John I Taylor Jr
39787 CR 388
Bloomingdale MI 49026

Call Sign: KB8OCI
Bert G Person
3811 CR 390
Bloomingdale MI 49026

Call Sign: KD8CBY
Timothy J Essenmacher
6240 CR 665
Bloomingdale MI 49026

Call Sign: WA6KDZ
Henry J Commissaris
411 N Oak
Bloomingdale MI 49026

Call Sign: N8JH
Jerry H Hogue
605 W Kalmazoo St
Bloomingdale MI 49026

Call Sign: KC8ZRP

Alice M Noskey
Bloomingdale MI 49026

FCC Amateur Radio Licenses in Bois Blanc Island

Call Sign: WF8G
George B Whinery
Hcr 01 Box 950
Bois Blanc Island MI 497759809

FCC Amateur Radio Licenses in Boon

Call Sign: KD8OME
Jilane K Fenner
2561 S 23rd Rd
Boon MI 49618

Call Sign: KC8CZS
Floyd R Taylor
404 S 27 Rd
Boon MI 49618

Call Sign: N8ZWR
Patricia R Flynn
1730 W 26 Rd
Boon MI 49618

Call Sign: KD8FRU
Kathleen M Porter
Boon MI 49618

Call Sign: KD8APG
Robert A Porter
Boon MI 49618

FCC Amateur Radio Licenses in Boyne City

Call Sign: KD8EQV
Brady P Billings
617 Adams St
Boyne City MI 49712

Call Sign: KC8JJN
Jason R Lewis
481 Addis Rd
Boyne City MI 49712

Call Sign: KC8ZVB
Richard T May
33 Anderson Rd
Boyne City MI 49712

Call Sign: N8GXU
Dale J Heberling
175 Anderson Rd
Boyne City MI 49712

Call Sign: KC8JJO
August R Behling
3958 Behling Rd
Boyne City MI 49712

Call Sign: WB8ISG
Bryan P Shumaker
289 Blue Water Trl
Boyne City MI 49712

Call Sign: KD8KQD
Lowell D Griffin
2714 Boyne City Rd
Boyne City MI 49712

Call Sign: KA8OFC
Kenneth R Scibior
3675 Camp Sherwood
Rd
Boyne City MI 49712

Call Sign: KC8JJP
Christopher B Winkler
136 Cherry St
Boyne City MI
497121465

Call Sign: KB8RJ
John R Staats
4548 Church Rd
Boyne City MI
497129351

Call Sign: WD8KUR
Cristina N Staats
4548 Church Rd
Boyne City MI
497129351

Call Sign: KB8WFM
Barry S Maginity
610 E Court St
Boyne City MI 49712

Call Sign: KD8FBR
Tommy L Knight
465 E Crozier Rd
Boyne City MI 49712

Call Sign: KD8FJN
Debra L Bush
326 E Division 28
Boyne City MI 49712

Call Sign: W8MEH
Frank M Dolwick
409 E Lincoln
Boyne City MI 49712

Call Sign: WA9RCY
Harry A Burkart III
120 E Main St
Boyne City MI 49712

Call Sign: KA8TIL
La Verne C Rouse
220 E Morgan St
Boyne City MI
497121526

Call Sign: AB8WX
Christopher J Conroy
220 E Morgan St
Boyne City MI
497121526

Call Sign: KD8MVY
Gary B Mott
6800 Hilltop Ln
Boyne City MI 49712

Call Sign: K8ZRP
Gary B Mott
6800 Hilltop Ln
Boyne City MI 49712

Call Sign: KC8AOQ
Steven A Cavagnaro
6867 Horton Creek Rd
Boyne City MI 49712

Call Sign: N8UEC
Robert M Briede
1252 Larson Rd
Boyne City MI 49712

Call Sign: KD8CXO
Norman D Gardner

526 N Lake St Lot 74
Boyne City MI 49712

Call Sign: KD8LHJ
Nancy W Loening
3995 Pinehurst Shore
Dr
Boyne City MI 49712

Call Sign: N8CVP
John C Talboys
1128 Pleasant Ave
Boyne City MI
497129197

Call Sign: N8OR
John C Talboys
1128 Pleasant Ave
Boyne City MI
497129197

Call Sign: WB8SQT
Larry E Crain
799 Pleasant Vly Rd
Boyne City MI 49712

Call Sign: KC8NVG
Scott A Cole
514 Poplar St
Boyne City MI 49712

Call Sign: KC8POO
Lora M Cole
514 Poplar St
Boyne City MI 49712

Call Sign: KB8TVK
Archie B Cole Jr
517 Poplar St
Boyne City MI 49712

Call Sign: WB8MKH
Donald R Moore
514 S East St
Boyne City MI 49712

Call Sign: KD8ABV
Christopher J Faulknor
1905 S M 75 Hwy
Boyne City MI
497129607

Call Sign: W8EJO
Terry E O Neill

995 S Snyder Rd
Boyne City MI 49712

Call Sign: KA8SWT
Floyd W Meyers
337 Vogel
Boyne City MI 49712

Call Sign: KC8JJQ
Michael F Osment
201 W Division St
Boyne City MI
497121514

Call Sign: KC8MRF
Nancy A Holland
224 W Lincoln St
Boyne City MI 49712

Call Sign: N8QVO
William S Holland
224 W Lincoln St
Boyne City MI 49712

Call Sign: N3SNV
Susan J Stockman
6 W Main St Ste 12
Boyne City MI 49712

Call Sign: N3IWU
John R McCahan
6 W Main St Ste 12
Boyne City MI 49712

Call Sign: NZ8F
Harry D Caldecott
5481 West Rd
Boyne City MI 49712

Call Sign: KC8GHT
Danny B Monshor
2887 Wild Wood Hrd
Rd
Boyne City MI 49712

Call Sign: W9QM
Reginald R Longworth
7851 Zenith Heights
Rd
Boyne City MI 49712

Call Sign: KD8AOE
Matthew J Juszczyk
Boyne City MI 49712

Call Sign: KD8MHJ
John C Perreault
Boyne City MI 49712

Call Sign: KD8OTG
Michael J Costa
Boyne City MI 49712

Call Sign: K8MJC
Michael J Costa
Boyne City MI 49712

FCC Amateur Radio Licenses in Boyne Falls

Call Sign: KB8TKB
Ronald D Rinock
1115 Country Club Rd
Boyne Falls MI 49713

Call Sign: KC8CWI
Jeffrey S Lutz
3026 Elm St
Boyne Falls MI 49713

Call Sign: KC8MHZ
William G Holland
3415 Hill View
Boyne Falls MI 49713

Call Sign: KD8GOO
Diana R Knapp
5043 Straddling Rd
Boyne Falls MI 49713

FCC Amateur Radio Licenses in Branch

Call Sign: WA8COT
Allen J Moore
Rr 1 Box 388 S
Evergreen Rd
Branch MI 49402

Call Sign: WD8EIX
Joseph A Vaclavik
8207 E Johnson Rd
Branch MI 49402

Call Sign: KC8EGH
Douglas R Christian
6223 S Branch Rd

Branch MI 49402

Call Sign: KC8OTK
Lois M Christian
6223 S Branch Rd
Branch MI 49402

Call Sign: KC8PZG
Trevor D Peck
6407 S Branch Rd
Branch MI 49402

Call Sign: KC8PZH
Lisa M Peck
6407 S Branch Rd
Branch MI 49402

Call Sign: KC8DGY
Robert L Sullivan Sr
21 S Maple Rd
Branch MI 49402

Call Sign: K8DGY
Robert L Sullivan Sr
21 S Maple Rd
Branch MI 49402

FCC Amateur Radio Licenses in Breedsville

Call Sign: KB8ZGI
Robert K Taylor
191 E Main St
Breedsville MI
490270039

Call Sign: KB8QXI
Ronald P Taylor
Breedsville MI 49027

FCC Amateur Radio Licenses in Brethren

Call Sign: KB8FCC
David A Basil
14822 Coates Hwy
Brethren MI 49619

Call Sign: W8GJX
West Michigan
Repeater Association
10827 Johnson Rd
Brethren MI 49619

Call Sign: N8UGW
Harvey C Good Sr
10827 Johnson Rd
Brethren MI 49619

Call Sign: N8AYQ
Jim Hundley
4640 Rita Ln
Brethren MI
496199735

Call Sign: N8JIM
Marge L Hundley
4640 Rita Ln
Brethren MI
496199735

Call Sign: KB8HVD
Danielle M Baysinger
Brethren MI 49619

FCC Amateur Radio Licenses in Bridgman

Call Sign: KC8FXV
Richard W Maxam
10119 Baldwin Rd
Bridgman MI 49106

Call Sign: N8NOT
Gerald S Wight
10143 Baldwin Rd
Bridgman MI 49106

Call Sign: W8LXL
Charles Adinolfi
3397 Cedar Ln
Bridgman MI 49106

Call Sign: WB8GKL
Dieter H Kruger
9670 Circle Dr
Bridgman MI
491060232

Call Sign: KC8YTA
Charles E Davis
5122 Dogwood Ln
Bridgman MI 49106

Call Sign: N8KBG
Ronald J Ackerman
8120 Hathaway Pl

Bridgman MI 49106

Call Sign: K8PE
Harold D Gretzky
3837 Lake St
Bridgman MI 49106

Call Sign: KD8HDP
Justin D Edenfield
4139 Lake St
Bridgman MI 49106

Call Sign: K9CQX
Edmund J Blesy
3807 Michigan Ave
Bridgman MI
491069391

Call Sign: N8RMR
James P Looney
9538 Randolph St
Bridgman MI 49106

Call Sign: N8SSB
Duane K Larson
3625 Shawnee Rd
Bridgman MI 49106

Call Sign: KD8CIX
Wendy J Larson
3625 Shawnee Rd
Bridgman MI 49106

Call Sign: N9IAS
George E Shaver
4333 Snow Rd
Bridgman MI
491069363

Call Sign: KD8JJS
Michael E Skow
9798 Tower St
Bridgman MI 49106

Call Sign: W7JWE
Michael E Skow
9798 Tower St
Bridgman MI 49106

Call Sign: KB9MNW
Byron H Higgins
10096 Weko Dr
Bridgman MI 49106

Call Sign: N8JHZ
John H Braun
4222 Willard St
Bridgman MI 49106

Call Sign: WD8IES
Franklin D Lester
Bridgman MI 49106

Call Sign: KA3ZMF
Detlev D Ansinn
Bridgman MI
491060842

Call Sign: KD8NBG
Paul S Larson
Bridgman MI 49106

**FCC Amateur Radio
Licenses in Brimley**

Call Sign: KD8QDS
Eric J Sherlund
6903 S Barker St
Brimley MI 49715

Call Sign: KD8JBY
Steven W Charles
5382 S Ranger Rd
Brimley MI 49715

Call Sign: KC8WCB
Paul J Buck
8460 W 7 1/2 Mile Rd
Brimley MI 49715

Call Sign: KC8RBX
Bruce J Burdick
9658 W Rex St
Brimley MI 49715

Call Sign: KC8PAH
James W Kinney
12607 W Wolf Ave
Brimley MI 49715

**FCC Amateur Radio
Licenses in Brohman**

Call Sign: KC8UNZ
Michael B Kinney
2359 W Pierce Dr
Brohman MI 49312

**FCC Amateur Radio
Licenses in Bronson**

Call Sign: N8WGL
Joyce A Bowerman
168 Adams Rd
Bronson MI 49028

Call Sign: KE4TAN
Marlene M
Hrabowecki
579 Babcock Rd
Bronson MI 49028

Call Sign: N8JWD
Justin W Asher
579 Babcock Rd
Bronson MI 49028

Call Sign: KE4PTS
Nicholas Hrabowecki
579 Babcock Rd
Bronson MI
490289347

Call Sign: KD8JEJ
Frank E Barker
308 Buchanan St
Bronson MI 49028

Call Sign: KC8ZFT
Dennis D Brauker
1196 Burr Oak Rd
Bronson MI 49028

Call Sign: KC8ZFS
Tammy L Brauker
1196 Burr Oak Rd
Bronson MI 49028

Call Sign: KB8JAY
Aaron C Savchuk
772 Cemetary Rd
Bronson MI 49028

Call Sign: WD8JNH
Gary L Wohlers
1122 Douglas Rd
Bronson MI 49028

Call Sign: KB8EEM
Albert H Meccia
9441 Fischers
Hideaway

Bronson MI 49028

Call Sign: N8NG
James W Shaw
762 Gilead Shore Dr
Bronson MI 49028

Call Sign: KD8CYY
William A Shaw
775 Gilead Shores Dr
Bronson MI 49028

Call Sign: W8ILL
William A Shaw
775 Gilead Shores Dr
Bronson MI 49028

Call Sign: KX8R
William A Shaw
775 Gilead Shores Dr
Bronson MI 49028

Call Sign: KA8PFN
Marcia J Stewart
257 Hoopingarner Rd
Bronson MI 49036

Call Sign: KD8JEM
Kenneth E Miller
994 Hurley Rd
Bronson MI 49028

Call Sign: KD8CYT
Dustin R Brauker
124 Lyter Rd
Bronson MI 49028

Call Sign: KC8WSO
Brandon L Miller
405 N Matteson St
Bronson MI 49028

Call Sign: KG8WI
Paul J Sygnecki
100 S Matteson Lake
Rd
Bronson MI 49028

Call Sign: KB8LQO
Gene F Forsyth
334 S Walker St
Bronson MI 49028

Call Sign: KD8CMW

Brad A Mcconn
418 Shaffmaster Ave
Bronson MI 49028

Call Sign: KC8WVX
Austin D Mandoka
317 Sherman St
Bronson MI 49028

Call Sign: N8GTM
Gerald E Metzger
236 State St
Bronson MI 49028

Call Sign: N8GTO
Mary E Metzger
236 State St
Bronson MI 49028

Call Sign: W8WU
Warren I Unterkircher
971 Weaver Rd
Bronson MI 49028

Call Sign: KB8KZU
Dennis D Bakker
1006 Weaver Rd
Bronson MI 49028

**FCC Amateur Radio
Licenses in Bruce
Crossing**

Call Sign: KC8IUH
Douglas W Roberts
13565 Cemetery Rd
Bruce Crossing MI
49912

Call Sign: N8GZQ
Jeffrey K Bjurstrom
14537 N Baltimore Rd
Bruce Crossing MI
49912

Call Sign: KD8GLY
Daniel J Roberts
13616 N Paynesville
Rd
Bruce Crossing MI
49912

Call Sign: K8NYT
Stanley W Strangle

12218 Strangle Rd
Bruce Crossing MI
499120110

Call Sign: KD8GBG
William E Witt
8135 US 45
Bruce Crossing MI
49912

Call Sign: W8KP
Robert J Wittla
Bruce Crossing MI
49912

FCC Amateur Radio Licenses in Brutus

Call Sign: AB8LT
Paul T Calvelage
6600 Maple River Rd
Brutus MI 49716

Call Sign: KC8ZFN
John W Meeks
1990 Red School Rd
Brutus MI 49716

Call Sign: N8QYY
Kenneth L Sydow
1981 S Mac Hwy
Brutus MI 49716

FCC Amateur Radio Licenses in Buchanan

Call Sign: KB9AFW
Anthony L Kostreba Jr
4779 Backus Ct
Buchanan MI 49107

Call Sign: KB9AHU
Timothy D Chapman
14987 Boyle Lake Rd
Buchanan MI 49107

Call Sign: AA8IU
Bonnie L Fenn
15184 Broceus Rd
Buchanan MI 49107

Call Sign: N8NIT
Marcus A Fenn
15184 Broceus Rd

Buchanan MI 49107

Call Sign: K8ATV
Robert C Archambault
16241 Brookwood Dr
Buchanan MI 49107

Call Sign: N8MZZ
Ken W Downey
3940 Buffalo Dr
Buchanan MI 49107

Call Sign: KG8LY
Allen H Simpson
4523 Chamberlain Rd
Buchanan MI 49107

Call Sign: KB8QEC
Brian J Dickey
305 Chippewa St
Buchanan MI 49107

Call Sign: W8LHP
Robert L Mann
12597 Cleveland Ave
Buchanan MI
491079339

Call Sign: KC8MIN
Ronald S Norton
13554 Coveney Rd
Buchanan MI 49107

Call Sign: WA8ZGT
Merritt L Pinkerton
3990 Curran Rd
Buchanan MI 49107

Call Sign: N9YXV
Lisa R Buchanan
401 E Front St
Buchanan MI
491071442

Call Sign: KC8RMA
Julie A Dalson
1848 Grange Rd
Buchanan MI 49107

Call Sign: KC8ZGC
Richard A Moody
3125 Knight Dr
Buchanan MI 49107

Call Sign: K2RAM
Richard A Moody
3125 Knight Dr
Buchanan MI 49107

Call Sign: KA8BMX
Roy E Knapp Jr
508 Liberty Ave
Buchanan MI 49107

Call Sign: KD8ANE
Caleb D Schaber
3457 Little Glendora
Rd
Buchanan MI 49107

Call Sign: N8RCN
Michael R Schelkopf
14885 Mead Rd
Buchanan MI 49107

Call Sign: KD8CIV
John C Pitz
3085 Miller Rd
Buchanan MI 49107

Call Sign: KD8EAP
Julie R Pitz
3085 Miller Rd
Buchanan MI 49107

Call Sign: KC8FXO
Mary A Weldy
13888 N Red Bud Trl
Buchanan MI 49107

Call Sign: KI4HBQ
Michael Proctor
807 N Redbud Trl 14
Buchanan MI 49107

Call Sign: W8BAB
Arnold B Lemke
4882 Niles Buchanan
Rd
Buchanan MI 49107

Call Sign: WD8DAL
Patricia A Lemke
4882 Niles Buchanan
Rd
Buchanan MI 49107

Call Sign: KC8YEV

Drucilla N Wrasse
2565 Oak Forest Rd
Buchanan MI 49107

Call Sign: KC8YEW
George T Wrasse
2565 Oak Forest Rd
Buchanan MI 49107

Call Sign: KA9RDU
Chris L Smith
2645 Oak Forest Rd
Buchanan MI 49107

Call Sign: N9DYB
Glen G Ruedinger
15260 Rangeline Rd
Buchanan MI 49107

Call Sign: N8XZG
Douglas J Weldy
13888 Red Bud Trl N
Buchanan MI 49107

Call Sign: WD8DED
James J Deer
3102 Ross Dr
Buchanan MI
491079435

Call Sign: KD8MUJ
James M Mcgee
16517 Ryneanson Rd
Buchanan MI 49107

Call Sign: KA8BND
Dennis A Kettlehut
16575 Rynearson Rd
Buchanan MI 49107

Call Sign: KC8CDN
Robert G Hillebert
1965 S Bakertown Rd
Buchanan MI 49107

Call Sign: WD8NYI
R Charles Hayden
109 W Chicago St
Buchanan MI 49107

Call Sign: WA8MHU
Donald Roti Roti
309 W Front St
Buchanan MI 49107

Call Sign: KB9ZWS
Eric A Lofgren
305 W Front St
Buchanan MI 49107

Call Sign: KC8ISH
Thomas C Hoyt
609 W Front St
Buchanan MI
491071157

Call Sign: KD8CXT
Alan V White
122 W Roe St
Buchanan MI 49107

Call Sign: KD8BTP
Eugene T Wieczorek
Buchanan MI 49107

Call Sign: KA8KDR
Robert L Wades
Buchanan MI
491070192

Call Sign: KC8YGR
Curtis T Brandon
220 David
Buckley MI 49620

Call Sign: KC8OTL
Stephen P Wiltrout
8253 Fox Rd
Buckley MI 49620

Call Sign: KC8LQY
Andrew J
Langenderfer
321 Gitchegumee Dr
Buckley MI 49620

Call Sign: N8SCH
Thomas H Frohnapfel
863 Gitchegumee Dr
Buckley MI 49620

Call Sign: KB8RDB
Vernon L Duff
11391 M 37
Buckley MI 49620

Call Sign: N8XQO
David L Duff
11265 M 37 S
Buckley MI 49620

Call Sign: WB8GAF
Ronald B Elzinga
11207 N 17th Rd
Buckley MI 49620

Call Sign: K3TUC
Albin J Gietzen
Buckley MI 49620

Call Sign: KC8OLE
Peter John Junior
Sorokin
Buckley MI 49620

Call Sign: WA8NQV
Robert L Sutfin
5344 12 Mile Rd
Burlington MI 49029

Call Sign: K8OVY
Allen E Vosburg
5812 7 Mile Rd
Burlington MI 49029

Call Sign: KC8RHS
Martha K Ruggles
5997 7 Mile Rd
Burlington MI 49029

Call Sign: KB8CFT
Richard E Stormer
5997 7 Mile Rd
Burlington MI
490298701

Call Sign: KB8YNE
Kathryn D Philo
5997 7 Mile Rd
Burlington MI
490298701

Call Sign: KD8CPT
Lois J Reece
12100 M 60 E
Burlington MI 49029

Call Sign: KD8CYU
Kyle W Morris
9001 M Dr S
Burlington MI 49029

Call Sign: N8HTY
William C Brenner
8225 N Dr S
Burlington MI 49029

Call Sign: K8WCB
William C Brenner
8225 N Dr S
Burlington MI 49029

Call Sign: KB8VQG
Katherine M Hughes
233 W Main St
Burlington MI 49029

Call Sign: KD8QHL
Martin P Wendell
251 Burr Oak St
Burr Oak MI 49030

Call Sign: AC8JU
Martin P Wendell
251 Burr Oak St
Burr Oak MI 49030

Call Sign: KC8EID
Sharyl A Summey
29976 Findley Rd
Burr Oak MI 49030

Call Sign: KB7RBU
John W Pennock Sr
1038 Gunthorpe Rd
Burr Oak MI
490309504

Call Sign: KB8ESI
Sarah A Norris
31677 Kelly Rd
Burr Oak MI 49030

Call Sign: KB8AET
Lynn D Norris
31677 Kelly Rd
Burr Oak MI 49030

Call Sign: KB8AEU
Timothy S Norris
31677 Kelly Rd
Burr Oak MI 49030

Call Sign: KD8NOB
David J Markus
30781 Lafayette Rd
Burr Oak MI 49030

Call Sign: KC8IWT
Raymond A Ware
620 N 3rd St
Burr Oak MI 49030

Call Sign: N8VBM
Andrew D Phillips
1278 Round Lake Rd
Burr Oak MI 49030

Call Sign: KD8EPU
Keith I Barkman
258 Taggart Rd
Burr Oak MI 49030

Call Sign: KC0BHY
Nelson J Miller
30712 Witt Lake Rd
Burr Oak MI 49030

Call Sign: KF8IG
Richard A Miedema
945 60th St SW
Byron Center MI
49315

Call Sign: N8DCR
Cindy S Miedema
945 60th St SW
Byron Center MI
49315

Call Sign: KB8ZGK
James H Wolthuis
1440 64th St SW
Byron Center MI
49315

Call Sign: KB8ZCY
Steven J Berkenpas
3377 76th St NW
Byron Center MI
49315

Call Sign: N3CO
Russell S Tobolic
1350 76th St SE
Byron Center MI
49315

Call Sign: KD5GCR
Robert L Green
3430 84th St
Byron Center MI
49315

Call Sign: KC8JBN
Eric Venlet
2615 87th St
Byron Center MI
49315

Call Sign: KB8UMT
Gerard W Venlet II
2615 87th St
Byron Center MI
49315

Call Sign: AB8EN
Gerard W Venlet II
2615 87th St SW
Byron Center MI
49315

Call Sign: KC8GFL
James R Hook
4336 88th St SW
Byron Center MI
49315

Call Sign: WA8IGW
Ronald L Van Wieren
2092 8th Ave
Byron Center MI
493158926

Call Sign: KB8YBA
Melford C Garvin
15 92nd St SE
Byron Center MI
49315

Call Sign: KA8VBV
Phillip A Garvin
15 92nd St SE
Byron Center MI
493159316

Call Sign: KD8OFU
The Independent
Repeater Association
Inc
562 92nd St SE
Byron Center MI
49315

Call Sign: W8IRA
The Independent
Repeater Association
Inc
562 92nd St SE
Byron Center MI
49315

Call Sign: WB8ZGP
Harold A Lyday
1045 Amber Ridge Dr
Byron Center MI
49315

Call Sign: KC8ATL
Gerard W Venlet
900 Amberwood Dr W
Byron Center MI
49315

Call Sign: K8LOY
Ronald W Ricketson
Sr
1071 Amberwood Dr
WSW
Byron Center MI
49315

Call Sign: KD8ODB
Cheryl L Ricketson
1071 Amberwood Dr
WSW
Byron Center MI
49315

Call Sign: KD8DID
Milan B Greenman
10050 Burlingame
Byron Center MI
49315

Call Sign: W8MFG
James H Caris
6834 Byron Lakes Dr
Apt 1A
Byron Center MI
49315

Call Sign: KC8RTS
Morris A Braaten
6968 Byron Lakes Dr
Apt 2 B
Byron Center MI
49315

Call Sign: KC8RTT
Ann M Braaten
6968 Byron Lakes Dr
Apt 2 B
Byron Center MI
49315

Call Sign: KC8RTV
Jon E Braaten
6968 Byron Lakes Dr
Apt 2B
Byron Center MI
49315

Call Sign: KD8PGF
Luke T Sorrelle
2499 Byron Station
Byron Center MI
49315

Call Sign: KD8EOH
Nick M Kuncaitis
9656 Celery SW
Byron Center MI
49315

Call Sign: KD8QNU
Joel D Root
2674 Conifer Ct
Byron Center MI
49315

Call Sign: W8DER
Michel P Hill
2143 Creekside Dr
Byron Center MI
49315

Call Sign: WB8SCX

Dale A Bartelds
8338 E Chester Dr
Byron Center MI
49315

Call Sign: N8VWG
Victoria L Zystra
8788 Eastern Ave SE
Byron Center MI
49315

Call Sign: WB8YKH
Lloyd M Guyot II
9075 Eastern Ave SE
Byron Center MI
49315

Call Sign: WD8LWL
Jack E Goodsell
8644 Eldora Dr SW
Byron Center MI
49315

Call Sign: K8BOA
Jack R Rozema
8456 Elkwood
Byron Center MI
49315

Call Sign: WB8HDC
William Docter
698 Garden View SW
Byron Center MI
493158346

Call Sign: W8HJD
Arnold E Erickson
7018 Gardenview Ct
Byron Center MI
49315

Call Sign: W8GV
Gerard W Venlet II
1768 Hightree Dr SW
Byron Center MI
49315

Call Sign: N8EYB
Tom W Williams
10080 Ivanrest Rd SW
Byron Center MI
49315

Call Sign: N8SRU

Mark R Bogardus
1643 Lisa Dr SW
Byron Center MI
493158122

Call Sign: N8KDF
Paul A Rock
2660 Maple Creek Ln
Byron Center MI
49315

Call Sign: KD8MNX
David L Clark
6827 Marshwood Dr
SE 3 A
Byron Center MI
49315

Call Sign: KD8ECW
Mark D Lambright
8299 Merton
Byron Center MI
49315

Call Sign: KD8MDQ
Michael J Fusaro
7044 Mindew Dr SW
Byron Center MI
49315

Call Sign: KD8DDT
Raechel J Haller
9125 Monte Vista SE
Byron Center MI
49315

Call Sign: WA8UMZ
Ronald K Miedema
2281 N Whistle Vale
SW
Byron Center MI
49315

Call Sign: KD8IAQ
Ruben Allegue
546 Oldfield Dr
Byron Center MI
49315

Call Sign: KB8QAP
Jeffrey D Ver Hage
879 Perry St SW
Byron Center MI
49315

Call Sign: KC8MPI
Rebecca J Selvig
1389 Perry St SW
Byron Center MI
493159509

Call Sign: KC8EQU
Kevin J Van Singel
2110 Pleasant Pond
Byron Center MI
49315

Call Sign: KB8TEB
Owen J Smith
2276 Pleasant Pond Dr
SW
Byron Center MI
49315

Call Sign: K2WZ
John J Keeley Jr
2381 Pleasant Pond Dr
SW
Byron Center MI
49315

Call Sign: WA8IWO
John F Borgman
7587 Red Osier Dr
Byron Center MI
49315

Call Sign: KD8AFL
Robert C Grove Jr
8691 Ridgehaven SW
Byron Center MI
49315

Call Sign: KD8FF
James K Bower
1765 Spring Wind Dr
Byron Center MI
49315

Call Sign: KC8OXE
Dick Haven
7434 Whistlevale Dr
Byron Center MI
49315

Call Sign: WB8FGQ
Dick Haven
7434 Whistlevale Dr

Byron Center MI
49315

Call Sign: WB8RJU
Richard A Niles
8204 Winding Dr
Byron Center MI
49315

Call Sign: KC8ZXB
Ryan S Nabkey
8231 Woodpark SW
Byron Center MI
49315

Call Sign: W8RYN
Ryan S Nabkey
8231 Woodpark SW
Byron Center MI
49315

Call Sign: W8QAM
Rodney L Mottl
1198 Woodspointesw
Byron Center MI
49315

**FCC Amateur Radio
Licenses in Cadillac**

Call Sign: KC8WOQ
Morris H Cotton Jr
507 17th St
Cadillac MI 49601

Call Sign: AA8NL
Harry B Milton
810.5 1st Ave
Cadillac MI 49601

Call Sign: KQ8I
Harry B Milton
810.5 1st Ave
Cadillac MI 49601

Call Sign: KC5ENR
Raymond W
Scarbrough
1022 2nd Ave
Cadillac MI 49601

Call Sign: KA8LHI
Carol A Warnock
817 3rd Ave

Cadillac MI 49601

Call Sign: WB8WIV
Thomas K Warnock
817 3rd Ave
Cadillac MI 49601

Call Sign: KD8ANG
Beverly S Warnock
817 3rd Ave
Cadillac MI 49601

Call Sign: K8BEV
Beverly S Warnock
817 3rd Ave
Cadillac MI 49601

Call Sign: KD8JPU
Owen H Lloyd
821 3rd Ave
Cadillac MI 49601

Call Sign: KC8TXR
Robert E Banks
1600 40 1/2 St
Cadillac MI 49601

Call Sign: NU8L
Alton E McConnell III
4189 48 Rd W
Cadillac MI 49601

Call Sign: N8TPJ
Dale J Lyons
3736 Anna Dr
Cadillac MI 49601

Call Sign: KD8BNH
Brandon E Trowbridge
3870 Anna Dr
Cadillac MI 49601

Call Sign: KD8BNI
Greg W Trowbridge
3870 Anna St
Cadillac MI 49601

Call Sign: KC8MME
Jesse M Sisson
153 B St
Cadillac MI 49601

Call Sign: KC8HJU
Hersel W Wing

116 Blodgett St
Cadillac MI
496012002

Call Sign: KD8AZH
Shawn L Lowing
3522 Cecil Rd
Cadillac MI 49601

Call Sign: KB8WZT
Timothy J Harris
3812 Cecil Rd
Cadillac MI 49601

Call Sign: N8CFP
Beverly J Schultz
903 Chestnut St
Cadillac MI 49601

Call Sign: KA8NZD
Kenneth A Zergoski
1711 Chestnut St
Cadillac MI 49601

Call Sign: WA8EEG
Arthur T Zergoski
1711 Chestnut St
Cadillac MI 49601

Call Sign: WA8SUE
Richard J Dawson
207 Colfax
Cadillac MI 49601

Call Sign: KC8TDH
George E Shankland
101 Davidson Rd
Cadillac MI 49601

Call Sign: KD8HJT
Thomas H Grace
3665 Driftwood Dr
Cadillac MI 49605

Call Sign: KB8ZHI
William J Austin
2170 E 30 Rd
Cadillac MI
496010998

Call Sign: KD8BAI
Raymond L Hill
8360 E 30 Rd
Cadillac MI 49601

Call Sign: W8DUE
Charles R Clark
5291 E 32 Rd
Cadillac MI 49601

Call Sign: K8ATN
Warne C Stewart
6155 E 34 1/2 Rd
Cadillac MI 49601

Call Sign: WD8JYI
Joyce L Freese
2100 E 34 Rd
Cadillac MI 49601

Call Sign: WA8IPJ
Walter W Freese
2100 E 34 Rd
Cadillac MI 49601

Call Sign: KI8AU
Larry P Freese
2132 E 34 Rd
Cadillac MI 49601

Call Sign: KC8VSV
Karen J Freese
2132 E 34 Rd
Cadillac MI 49601

Call Sign: KC8SOC
Tracie M Ferguson
2211 E 34 Rd
Cadillac MI 49601

Call Sign: KC8RBQ
Jerry R Ferguson
2235 E 34 Rd
Cadillac MI 49601

Call Sign: KC4PJX
Timothy M Vaughan
10621 E 34 Rd
Cadillac MI 49601

Call Sign: KC8TDF
Donald T Mcmillan
11381 E 34 Rd
Cadillac MI 49601

Call Sign: K8AYC
Lloyd R Hewitt
7101 E 44 Rd

Cadillac MI 49601

Call Sign: KA8CBU
Dale R Fifer
5741 E 46 Mi Rd
Cadillac MI 49601

Call Sign: K8CBU
Dale R Fifer
5741 E 46 Mi Rd
Cadillac MI 49601

Call Sign: KB8RGV
Kevin M Deady
1112 E 46 Rd
Cadillac MI 49601

Call Sign: KE8VB
Patrick L Mannor
1001 E 48 Half Rd
Cadillac MI 49601

Call Sign: KD8HYE
Autumn D Hora
441 E Division St
Cadillac MI 49601

Call Sign: KC8DTW
George O Drake
802 E Division St
Cadillac MI 49601

Call Sign: KC8OTJ
William E Shier
7053 E M 115
Cadillac MI
496010669

Call Sign: KE8KU
Daniel L Schmidt
436 E Nelson St
Cadillac MI 49601

Call Sign: WA8LT
Walter K Augustat
931 Ernst St
Cadillac MI 49601

Call Sign: KC8HZR
Debbie K Erskin
404 Estate Dr
Cadillac MI 49601

Call Sign: KA8KAJ

Raymond D
Matyjaszek
9980 Freedom Rd
Cadillac MI 49601

Call Sign: KA8KAK
Elaine M Matyjaszek
9980 Freedom Rd
Cadillac MI 49601

Call Sign: W8GBV
Jonathan E
Snellenberger
115 George St
Cadillac MI 49601

Call Sign: KD8FRT
Stanley J Zaucha Jr
151 Greenridge Dr
Cadillac MI 49601

Call Sign: KC8GZE
Michael E Reilly
306 Henderson Ct
Cadillac MI 49601

Call Sign: K8MER
Michael E Reilly
306 Henderson Ct
Cadillac MI 49601

Call Sign: N8ZWU
James E Scarbrough III
414 Howard
Cadillac MI 49601

Call Sign: KD8DDP
Robert L Shankland
513 Howard St
Cadillac MI 49601

Call Sign: N8SCR
Raymond L Modders
4843 John R Rd
Cadillac MI
496019575

Call Sign: KD8LBP
Jamison R Beydoun
720 Kim Dr
Cadillac MI 49601

Call Sign: N8ACA
Jamison R Beydoun

720 Kim Dr
Cadillac MI 49601

Call Sign: KD8HXY
Matthew L Smith
8960 Lamp Lighter Ln
Cadillac MI 49601

Call Sign: KB8SYV
John A Roy
8828 Lamplighter Ln
Cadillac MI 49601

Call Sign: N8USH
Bradley J Weidemann
311 Leeson Ave
Cadillac MI 49601

Call Sign: N8PME
Kenneth V Pedersen
401 Leeson Ave
Cadillac MI
496011630

Call Sign: KC8KCW
Dallas G Horton
803 Lester St
Cadillac MI
496012352

Call Sign: AB8MD
Rick A Dean
9840 Mackinaw Trl
Cadillac MI 49601

Call Sign: KD8DRL
Julie L Bolitho
4189 Morel Dr
Cadillac MI 49601

Call Sign: K4JXN
Joseph C Munch Jr
1285 N 27 Rd
Cadillac MI 49601

Call Sign: KD8KQE
David F Maes
2192 N 27 Rd
Cadillac MI 49601

Call Sign: KC8WOO
Keith D Cox
109 Newland

Cadillac MI
496019239

Call Sign: NW8P
Dale E Soper
209 Pearl St Appt B
Cadillac MI 49601

Call Sign: KD8HXX
Nathaniel R Swiger
10534 Pine Grove Dr
Cadillac MI 49601

Call Sign: N8SWG
Nathaniel R Swiger
10534 Pine Grove Dr
Cadillac MI 49601

Call Sign: KA8FQY
James R Hanchett
2981 Pleasant Lake Sh
Dr
Cadillac MI 49601

Call Sign: KC8DTV
Michael H Kedrowski
1524 Plett Rd
Cadillac MI 49601

Call Sign: KD8FRS
George W Kumfer
138 Powers St
Cadillac MI 49601

Call Sign: KD8OMK
Greg Sabka Jr
8073 Quarter Rd
Cadillac MI 49601

Call Sign: KK5DN
Thomas P Poli
2059 S 37 Rd
Cadillac MI 49601

Call Sign: KC8FYF
Douglas R Manke
4844 S 37 Rd
Cadillac MI 49601

Call Sign: KB8PQR
Donna M Sayer
2610 S 39 Mile Rd
Cadillac MI 49601

Call Sign: N8ARJ
Roland H Sayer
2610 S 39 Mile Rd
Cadillac MI 49601

Call Sign: KG8IN
Jason A Scarbrough
3360 S 39 Mile Rd
Cadillac MI 49601

Call Sign: KG8BY
James E Scarbrough Jr
3360 S 39 Rd
Cadillac MI 49601

Call Sign: N8VLO
Jeremy L Scarbrough
3360 S 39 Rd
Cadillac MI 49601

Call Sign: KC8SIB
Tanner J Thompson
4201 S 39 Rd
Cadillac MI 49607

Call Sign: K8HFX
Jack E Brower
9101 S 47 Rd
Cadillac MI 49601

Call Sign: WD8CWL
William M Long
4660 S Birch Ln
Cadillac MI 49601

Call Sign: WB8QNG
Carlyle J Foster
10160 S Blossom Ave
Cadillac MI 49601

Call Sign: KG8VP
Michael R Sands
515 Stimson Rd
Cadillac MI 49601

Call Sign: KC8TXS
Brandy K Ruby
407 Sunnyside Dr
Cadillac MI 49601

Call Sign: KD8OLD
Tiffany M Ruby
407 Sunnyside Dr
Cadillac MI 49601

Call Sign: KD8BAA
Betty L Dumont
1113 Sunnyside Dr
Cadillac MI 49601

Call Sign: KC8VVC
Elizabeth M Dumont
1113 Sunnyside Dr
Cadillac MI
496018736

Call Sign: KB8RWI
Michael E Hammond
911 W Division St
Cadillac MI
496011733

Call Sign: KD8SBA
Ann E Solce
4720 W Lake Mitchell
Cadillac MI 49601

Call Sign: WD8RZL
Robert E Bednarick
7458 W Lake Mitchell
Dr
Cadillac MI 49601

Call Sign: N8BOB
Robert E Bednarick
7458 W Lake Mitchell
Dr
Cadillac MI 49601

Call Sign: W8PLC
Carl H Edberg
214 Wall St
Cadillac MI 49601

Call Sign: K8RWD
Robert F Hansen
9095 Windsong Ln
Cadillac MI
496019769

Call Sign: N8EYN
Robert Heinrich
Cadillac MI 49601

Call Sign: W8MIL
Stanley W Mattson
Cadillac MI
496010416

Call Sign: WB8AOV
Gerald F Van Oyen
6363 100th St
Caledonia MI 49316

Call Sign: WB8TUU
Dennis D Faist
7727 100th St SE
Caledonia MI 49316

Call Sign: K8YE
Dennis D Faist
7727 100th St SE
Caledonia MI 49316

Call Sign: KD8PDK
Micah Truax
329 144th Ave
Caledonia MI 49316

Call Sign: N8VLM
David W Dezwaan Sr
572 145th Ave
Caledonia MI 49316

Call Sign: KC8OQR
Douglas A Detmer
63 146th Ave
Caledonia MI 49316

Call Sign: KC8ZGQ
Shannon L Keizer
644 146th Ave
Caledonia MI 49316

Call Sign: N8WKK
Shannon L Keizer
644 146th Ave
Caledonia MI 49316

Call Sign: KD8ECE
Benjamin G Keizer
644 146th Ave
Caledonia MI 49316

Call Sign: N8WDY
Kevin J Keizer
644 146th Ave
Caledonia MI 49316

Call Sign: N8WKK
Kevin J Keizer
644 146th Ave
Caledonia MI 49316

Call Sign: N8WDY
Kevin J Keizer
644 146th Ave
Caledonia MI 49316

Call Sign: WA8GAE
Robert C Latta Sr
1718 68th St SE
Caledonia MI 49316

Call Sign: KD8FBS
Curtis A Trudeau
4596 6th St
Caledonia MI 49316

Call Sign: N8RRI
John H Doughty
3487 76th St
Caledonia MI 49316

Call Sign: WB8WQZ
Timothy C Reser
6536 84th SE
Caledonia MI 49316

Call Sign: N8VLL
Bradley L Waayenberg
3346 84th St
Caledonia MI 49316

Call Sign: KA8YSM
Thomas L Werkema
3547 84th St
Caledonia MI 49316

Call Sign: KB8KZH
Kathleen J Werkema
3547 84th St
Caledonia MI 49316

Call Sign: KC8IZP
Joel R Powell
3547 84th St
Caledonia MI 49316

Call Sign: KC8ZGO
Meggan M Werkema
3547 84th St
Caledonia MI 49316

Call Sign: KC8IMI
Egmont B Sturm
3547 84th St SE
Caledonia MI 49316

Call Sign: KA8GXA
Bernard L Reser
6536 84th St SE
Caledonia MI 49316

Call Sign: KD8DCK
Jeffrey M Weinstein
8953 Alanada Dr SE
Caledonia MI 49316

Call Sign: WB8HKD
Fredrick A Heileman
7975 Broadmoor
Caledonia MI 49316

Call Sign: KD8KFY
Charles A Chandler
7585 Cherry Valley
Ave
Caledonia MI 49316

Call Sign: N9UIO
Kendrick S White
9761 Cherry Valley
Ave SE
Caledonia MI 49316

Call Sign: KD8DCE
Robert S Sacha
7115 Cherry Valley SE
Caledonia MI 49316

Call Sign: KB8KBG
Christopher S
Robinson
7092 Cornerstone Dr
Caledonia MI 49316

Call Sign: N8LCV
Jay L Shook
10064 Crossroads Cir
Caledonia MI 49316

Call Sign: K8BIV
Thomas M Coleman
6026 E Fieldstone
Hills Dr SE Unit 5
Caledonia MI 49316

Call Sign: KD8DKW
Joseph P Hammer III
602 E Main St
Caledonia MI 49316

Call Sign: KA8DUY
David W Gould
4594 E Shore Dr
Caledonia MI 49316

Call Sign: KA8DUZ
Sharon E Gould
4594 E Shore Dr
Caledonia MI 49316

Call Sign: KC8MSH
Glenn D Gould
4594 E Shore Dr
Caledonia MI 49316

Call Sign: KA8DUX
Glenn D Gould
4594 E Shore Dr
Caledonia MI 49316

Call Sign: WA8UPB
Lyn D Cryderman
6527 Egan SE
Caledonia MI 49316

Call Sign: W8FLO
David C Finton
6570 Glen Hollow Dr
Caledonia MI
493168993

Call Sign: KD8RLX
Daniel J Stine
6634 Glen Hollow Dr
SE
Caledonia MI 49316

Call Sign: KF8EN
David R Church
6612 Gracepoint Dr SE
Caledonia MI 49316

Call Sign: KD8EOP
James R Johnson
8766 Grainery Ct SE
Caledonia MI 49316

Call Sign: KA2FEH

James A Brotz
8543 Grainery Rd
Caledonia MI 49316

Call Sign: AB8VI
James A Brotz
8543 Grainery Rd
Caledonia MI 49316

Call Sign: WU8P
Phillip J Mikula
6901 Hammond Ave
SE Apt B
Caledonia MI 49316

Call Sign: KF8QL
David J De Vos
8111 Hanna Lake Rd
Caledonia MI 49316

Call Sign: KB8PWJ
David A Staskiewicz
213 Johnson
Caledonia MI 49316

Call Sign: KC8RSE
Eugene L Holiday
10461 Kalamazoo Ave
Caledonia MI 49316

Call Sign: KD8PSI
Robert M Hartig
215 Maple St Apt
A301
Caledonia MI 49316

Call Sign: N8WMU
John J Coles Jr
6710 Noffke Dr
Caledonia MI 49316

Call Sign: KB8VUC
James P Kooistra
4577 Park St
Caledonia MI 49316

Call Sign: WA8NTT
Martin G Haschke
1311 Penncross Dr SE
Caledonia MI 49316

Call Sign: N8FM
Stephen M Hickel
8220 Piney Woods

Caledonia MI 49316

Call Sign: WQ8Z
Stephen M Hickel
8220 Piney Woods
Caledonia MI 49316

Call Sign: KD8NMH
Jayne E Courts
7071 Placid Pointe Ct
SE
Caledonia MI 49316

Call Sign: KD8DLR
Richard J Hodgson
7071 Placid Pt Ct SE
Caledonia MI
493169071

Call Sign: W8WO
Robert M Burton
9650 Ravine Ridge SE
Caledonia MI 49316

Call Sign: KC8EXC
Christine F Duryea
331 South St
Caledonia MI 49316

Call Sign: KD8EHH
Clarence H Kimbler
7353 Steed St
Caledonia MI 49316

Call Sign: KC8ZGR
Jeffrey D Halblaub
10580 Stirrup Dr SE
Caledonia MI 49316

Call Sign: KD5QAH
Scott D Baldwin
54 Summerwyn Dr SE
Caledonia MI 49316

Call Sign: KC8ZO
Walter A Harding
8190 Thornapple River
Caledonia MI 49316

Call Sign: N8AAZ
Walter A Harding
8190 Thornapple River
Caledonia MI 49316

Call Sign: KA8UOU
Laura R Bartleson
7520 Thornapple River
Dr
Caledonia MI 49316

Call Sign: KD8CUL
Deane A Ledsworth
2290 Vantage Ct
Caledonia MI 49316

Call Sign: KD8CUM
Nicholas D Ledsworth
2290 Vantage Ct
Caledonia MI 49316

Call Sign: KD8AZK
Chris Behm
6152 W Fieldstone
Hills Dr Apt 12
Caledonia MI 49316

Call Sign: KB8GO
William R Woolf
6511 Wood Dora Dr S
E
Caledonia MI 49316

Call Sign: KC8GKE
Jeff A Meyers
Caledonia MI 49316

Call Sign: W8DUG
Douglas A Detmer
Caledonia MI
493160425

**FCC Amateur Radio
Licenses in Calumet**

Call Sign: KC8BSR
Rodney J Mishica
334 5th St
Calumet MI 49913

Call Sign: KC8BIY
George A Kinnunen
53049 Boston Rd
Calumet MI 49913

Call Sign: WA8FZY
Rudolph C Ekdahl
R I Box 117
Calumet MI 49913

Call Sign: KC8BSQ
William S McConnell
Rr 1 Box 161 B
Calumet MI 49913

Call Sign: N8PIV
Charles W Sieders
Rt 1 Box 410
Calumet MI 49913

Call Sign: W8DQB
Leonard W Oikarinen
R 1 Box 42A
Calumet MI 49913

Call Sign: KC8BSO
Michael G Kumpula
25235 Bridge St
Calumet MI 49913

Call Sign: KD8DQO
Ralph W Wesala
25281 Bridge St
Calumet MI 49913

Call Sign: K8EK
Edwin K Kohn
57056 Calumet Ave
Calumet MI 49913

Call Sign: WD8LKD
David B Kohn
57056 Calumet Ave
Calumet MI 49913

Call Sign: KD8NSE
Michael R Sackson
57253 Calumet Ave
Calumet MI 49913

Call Sign: KC8BSK
Charles E Hein
57311 Calumet Ave
Calumet MI
499131734

Call Sign: KC8BSL
Diana M Hein
57311 Calumet Ave
Calumet MI
499131734

Call Sign: N8LAC

Daniel J Taube
892 Cambria
Calumet MI 49913

Call Sign: KB8FFT
Debra I Taube
892 Cambria St
Calumet MI 49913

Call Sign: W8ILS
Ronald M Savela
4159 Cedar Bay Rd
Calumet MI 49913

Call Sign: N8SHF
Richard D R Strieterr
Sr
54499 Cemetery Rd
Calumet MI 49913

Call Sign: KC8BST
Joanne M Polzien
55275 Cemetery Rd
Calumet MI 49913

Call Sign: N8KSO
Douglas L Polzien
55275 Cemetery Rd
Calumet MI 49913

Call Sign: KA0WII
Thomas J Helppi
56469 Cemetery St
Calumet MI 49913

Call Sign: W8WZA
Donald L Perkins Jr
25461 Center St
Calumet MI 49913

Call Sign: WA9YEF
David B Perkins
25461 Center St
Calumet MI 49913

Call Sign: KF4WDQ
Thomas M Kestie
2308 CR
Calumet MI 49913

Call Sign: KA8UZB
Kenneth V Fisher
2514 D St
Calumet MI 49913

Call Sign: KC8CDD
David J McKinstry
25570 D St
Calumet MI 49913

Call Sign: W8IDN
Gerald A Mars
59548 Dextrom Rd
Calumet MI 49913

Call Sign: WB9TNQ
Martin C
Schwamberger
52871 Dover Rd
Calumet MI 49913

Call Sign: KD8ABQ
Amber J Kemppainen
25403 E Acorn St
Calumet MI 49913

Call Sign: KC8BSN
David B Koskiniemi
25377 Elm St
Calumet MI 49913

Call Sign: WB8CBA
Edwin R Djerf
22220 Hwy M 203
Calumet MI 49913

Call Sign: KD8DKF
Philip L Baranowski
22140 Hwy M203
Calumet MI 49913

Call Sign: KD8ABP
Howard F Klann
57966 Kallio Rd
Calumet MI 49913

Call Sign: K6IPC
Richard L Bardos
25975 Lake Linden
Ave
Calumet MI 49913

Call Sign: WA8JSF
Richard T Anderson
57363 Lakeshore Dr
Calumet MI 49913

Call Sign: N8PJA

Mildred A Gasperich
58807 Lakeshore Dr
Calumet MI 49913

Call Sign: KC8FBN
Daniel N Haas
58845 Lakeshore Dr
Calumet MI 49913

Call Sign: KC8VEU
Joshua A Myles
56808 Laurium St
Calumet MI 49913

Call Sign: KB8THH
Michael W Halt
25586 Lower St
Calumet MI 49913

Call Sign: KB8THI
Gordon M Halt
25586 Lower St
Calumet MI 49913

Call Sign: KC8RFL
Steven R Foix
53096 Mulberry Ln
Calumet MI 49913

Call Sign: AA8OX
David R Murphy
2 Park Ave Apt 9
Calumet MI 49913

Call Sign: WE8D
Cecil Crider
27408 Pepin Rd
Calumet MI 49913

Call Sign: KB8QNZ
Timothy P Reilly
26298 Pine
Calumet MI 49913

Call Sign: WD8PZV
Charles D Kosovac
25210 Poplar St
Calumet MI 49913

Call Sign: KD8MFM
Ryan V Szpara
25407 Portland St
Calumet MI 49913

Call Sign: WB8ZPN
Robert L Numerick
800 Portland St
Calumet MI 49913

Call Sign: W8ZZM
Reino R Helppi
56966 Rockland St
Calumet MI 49913

Call Sign: KC8CVJ
Laura J Junkin
2009 S Calumet Ave
Calumet MI 49913

Call Sign: KB8UDD
Paul G Grabig
26105 School St
Calumet MI 49913

Call Sign: KB8ZTB
Heather L Smigowski
51760 Seebirg Dr
Calumet MI 49913

Call Sign: KC8IIH
Christina A Smigowski
51760 Seeburg Dr
Calumet MI 49913

Call Sign: N8PIZ
Judith J Smigowski
51760 Seeburg Dr
Calumet MI 49913

Call Sign: N8ILY
Paul D Smigowski
51760 Seeburg Dr
Calumet MI 49913

Call Sign: KC8ED
Donald R Gunther
30299 Sievi Rd
Calumet MI 49913

Call Sign: KB8THE
Jason E Riutta
30505 Township Park
Rd
Calumet MI 49913

Call Sign: KO8Y
Arthur A Keranen
51 US 41

Calumet MI 49913

Call Sign: KA8NLR
Matthew O Keranen
58016 US Hwy 41
Calumet MI 49913

Call Sign: KS8R
Stephen E Keranen
58016 US Hwy 41
Calumet MI 49913

Call Sign: KC8KEV
Jean C Keranen
58016 US Hwy 41
Calumet MI
499131146

Call Sign: W3GN
Lawrence T Fadner
25125 Veterans
Memorial Hwy
Calumet MI 49913

Call Sign: KC8CCW
James R Helppi
25549 Wedge St
Calumet MI 49913

Call Sign: KC8IPE
Amy J Sakkinen
25595 Wedge St
Calumet MI
499131896

Call Sign: KC8HMN
Scott P Sakkinen
25595 Wedge St
Calumet MI
499161869

Call Sign: KD8OXA
Andrew D Maine
100 Willow Ave
Calumet MI 49913

Call Sign: KD8OXB
Kevin J Nelson
100 Willow Ave
Calumet MI 49913

Call Sign: N8KME
David G Moyle
Calumet MI 49913

Call Sign: KC8OOR
Harold G Balowaara
Calumet MI 49913

Call Sign: W8UUU
Robert W Stanley Jr
9198 Elmwood Ct
Canadian Lakes MI
493469398

Call Sign: KA9LZV
Patricia A Lynch
9573 Fawn Ridge Rd
Canadian Lakes MI
49346

Call Sign: KA9LZU
Joseph N Lynch
9573 Fawn Ridge Rd
Canadian Lakes MI
493469419

Call Sign: W8RBL
Michael R Reaume
9573 Fawn Ridge Rd
Canadian Lakes MI
493469419

Call Sign: WD8LDU
Maurice D Bowman Jr
11130 Heather Ln
Canadian Lakes MI
493469768

Call Sign: N8ZH
Jon L Huhtala
6690 Sunset Ln
Canadian Lakes MI
49346

Call Sign: KB8THC
Bryan A Strahl
W3863 CR 380
Carney MI 49812

Call Sign: N8SYT
Robin L Westfall
7087 Clinton Rd
Carp Lake MI 49718

Call Sign: KD8CYS
Terry L Nielsen
3332 Elder Rd
Carp Lake MI 49718

Call Sign: KB8NNW
Melvin J Spotts
Carp Lake MI 49718

Call Sign: N8ZUN
Peter N Skeberdis
7875 S Garlock Rd 12
Carson City MI 48811

Call Sign: KD8JRT
Joshua H Peirce
3798 S Osborn Rd
Carson City MI 48811

Call Sign: WD8A
Paul L Wey
203 W Garfield St
Carson City MI 48811

Call Sign: N8NBZ
Michael D Baird
203 W Walnut St
Carson City MI 48811

Call Sign: KA8ZHN
James L Jakubiec
1981 Laraway Lake Dr
Cascade Township MI
49546

Call Sign: KB8BEU
Donald H Austin
31 East St
Casnovia MI 49318

Call Sign: N8JFX
Nina E Homrich
32 East St
Casnovia MI 49318

Call Sign: KD8FTC
Nicholas C Miller Sr
46 Grand St
Casnovia MI 49318

Call Sign: KC8OMG
Joshua C Whitehead
18330 Hall Rd
Casnovia MI 49318

Call Sign: KD8DCB
Todd A Rector Sr
Casnovia MI
493180201

Call Sign: WD8BAV
Eva M Van Poucker
104 Stanley Lk Dr
Caspian MI 499150215

Call Sign: N8AFA
Leo J Van Poucker
104 Stanley Lk Dr
Caspian MI 499150215

Call Sign: KB9TQM
Toby E Hebron
64069 Brick Church
Rd
Cassopolis MI 49031

Call Sign: N8VPZ
Daniel J Hebron
64069 Brick Church
Rd

Cassopolis MI 49031

Call Sign: KC8TSP
Ian G Sindell
21252 Bulhand Rd
Cassopolis MI 49031

Call Sign: WA9PQN
Ian G Sindell
21252 Bulhand Rd
Cassopolis MI 49031

Call Sign: N9QJD
Timothy S Osman
64183 Calvin Center
Rd
Cassopolis MI 49031

Call Sign: KA8YWK
Michael A Sumption
61250 Cass Rd
Cassopolis MI 49031

Call Sign: N8HJK
Diana L Sumption
61250 Cass Rd
Cassopolis MI 49031

Call Sign: W8MDV
Robert A Sumption
61250 Cass Rd
Cassopolis MI 49031

Call Sign: W9RAS
Robert A Sumption
61250 Cass Rd
Cassopolis MI 49031

Call Sign: KD8AXV
Diane G Leach
59941 Decatur Rd
Cassopolis MI 49031

Call Sign: WD8DJG
Grace M Carr
3279 Detroit Rd
Cassopolis MI 49031

Call Sign: N9CIC
Charles F Felton Jr
22103 Forest Hall Dr
Cassopolis MI 49031

Call Sign: W8CFF

Charles F Felton Jr
22103 Forest Hall Dr
Cassopolis MI 49031

Call Sign: WA4BYG
Wiley B Stinnett
60315 Gards Prairie
Rd
Cassopolis MI 49031

Call Sign: KD8GNR
Patrick K Cain
24756 Hospital St
Cassopolis MI 49031

Call Sign: K4FW
Albert R Kahn
21859 Howell Dr
Cassopolis MI 49031

Call Sign: N8ASE
Gerald F Arnold
17154 Lake St
Cassopolis MI 49031

Call Sign: N8YJH
Harry L McRae
61171 Lenawee Rd
Cassopolis MI 49031

Call Sign: WD8IRU
Jack R Buchalco
63200 Library Rd
Cassopolis MI 49031

Call Sign: KD8AXW
Bernadette R
Williamson
26260 M 60 W
Cassopolis MI 49031

Call Sign: KD8CJC
Connie A Swartz
23659 Monette St
Cassopolis MI 49031

Call Sign: KD8AND
James H Debruine
124 N Disbrow St
Cassopolis MI 49031

Call Sign: KD8AXU
Miriam D Bollweg
302 N Fulton St

Cassopolis MI 49031

Call Sign: K9SIG
John J Bollweg
302 N Fulton St
Cassopolis MI 49031

Call Sign: KD8BHP
Brian R Cummings
260 N Rowland
Cassopolis MI 49031

Call Sign: N8BEC
Tommy Y Leung
65491 North Dr
Shavehead Lk
Cassopolis MI 49031

Call Sign: KC8NMN
James E Luxenberger
61153 Putnam Rd
Cassopolis MI 49031

Call Sign: KD8CSV
Sandy K Swenor
104 S Broadway St
Cassopolis MI 49031

Call Sign: N3RRV
Donna N Wyland
23264 Shurte St
Cassopolis MI 49031

Call Sign: WD8PVT
Leroy Kinnison
16155 Union Rd
Cassopolis MI 49031

Call Sign: N8YUU
Kelly A Hebron
200 W State St
Cassopolis MI 49031

Call Sign: KD8GOI
Dustin L Wood
3003 White St
Cassopolis MI 49031

**FCC Amateur Radio
Licenses in Cedar**

Call Sign: K8BRX
David E Drake
1701 E Bellinger Rd

Cedar MI 49621

Call Sign: WA8OTY
George T Gauthier
1687 E CR 616
Cedar MI 49621

Call Sign: WD4FJF
Harold E Feigel
1185 E Darga Rd
Cedar MI 49621

Call Sign: KA8WTG
Stephen B Tarsa
1755 E Darga Rd
Cedar MI 49621

Call Sign: W8CHT
Albert V Travis
5988 E Hohnke Rd
Cedar MI 49621

Call Sign: WD8NRZ
Donald P Parker
4786 E Hoxie Rd
Cedar MI 49621

Call Sign: WB8VJN
Barbara J Sutton
8778 E Lincoln Rd
Cedar MI 49621

Call Sign: W8YIB
Frank N Barnes
4260 E Sugarloaf
Mountain Rd
Cedar MI 49621

Call Sign: K8AGE
Aubrey G Eggenberger
172 E Traverse Lake
Rd
Cedar MI 496219405

Call Sign: N8VZO
David A Woodcock
12859 Hwy 651
Cedar MI 49625

Call Sign: AA5WG
Charles H Pool II
7201 S Cedarview Ln
Cedar MI 49621

Call Sign: KB8GAU
Geraldine M Pool
7201 S Cedarview Ln
Cedar MI 49621

Call Sign: KC8NEJ
Lewis H Ealy
11000 S Hill Rd
Cedar MI 49621

Call Sign: KC8KXF
Jonah H Powell
2900 Schomberg
Cedar MI 49621

Call Sign: KC8GCJ
Carroll F Sattler
Cedar MI 49621

**FCC Amateur Radio
Licenses in Cedar
Lake**

Call Sign: KD8EEA
Glaa ARC
7477 Academy Rd
Cedar Lake MI 48812

Call Sign: KD8IXM
Alvin W Peterson
7640 Academy Rd
Cedar Lake MI 48812

Call Sign: KA1HDG
David L Carter
5660 Faculty Dr
Cedar Lake MI
488120142

Call Sign: KD8LOZ
Jonathan C Mcclellan
5417 Quarter Rd
Cedar Lake MI 48812

Call Sign: KC8OTU
Devon K Smith
Cedar Lake MI 48812

**FCC Amateur Radio
Licenses in Cedar
River**

Call Sign: K8ZLO
Floyd E Croy Jr

N11474 Blue Fox Ln
28 9
Cedar River MI
498139527

Call Sign: K7PAM
Pamela A Croy
N11474 Blue Fox Ln
28 9
Cedar River MI
498879527

**FCC Amateur Radio
Licenses in Cedar
Springs**

Call Sign: N8OQW
Arthur L Schultz
6220 15 Mile Rd
Cedar Springs MI
49319

Call Sign: WA8DOD
Kenneth L Zarbeck Sr
6575 15 Mile Rd
Cedar Springs MI
49319

Call Sign: KD8EVZ
Randy K Westen
7370 15 Mile Rd NE
Cedar Springs MI
49319

Call Sign: KC8LSO
Randy J Driesenga
7876 17 Mile Rd
Cedar Springs MI
49319

Call Sign: KB8ZES
Robert S Lumbert
6988 17 Mile Rd
Cedar Springs MI
49319

Call Sign: KD8LBM
Ralph S Colorado
8711 17 Mile Rd NE
Cedar Springs MI
49319

Call Sign: WD8EMC
Ralph S Colorado

8711 17 Mile Rd NE
Cedar Springs MI
49319

Call Sign: KB8KWB
Gene C Banfill
9101 18 Mile Rd
Cedar Springs MI
49319

Call Sign: KC8PKK
James E Pate
2275 18 Mile Rd NE
Cedar Springs MI
49319

Call Sign: KB8USW
Kevin E McCormick
2994 19 Mile Rd
Cedar Springs MI
49319

Call Sign: KC8TSR
Gary D Hill
6015 19 Mile Rd NE
Cedar Springs MI
49319

Call Sign: AB8AL
Terry L Hines Jr
11758 20 Mile Rd
Cedar Springs MI
49319

Call Sign: KA8SHZ
James E Norton
1850 21 Mile Rd NE
Cedar Springs MI
49319

Call Sign: N8ZFS
Jeffrey L Konkle
10987 Crawford Lake
Trl
Cedar Springs MI
49319

Call Sign: KC8UUN
Douglas E Pierce
1394 Dairy Ln NE
Cedar Springs MI
493198131

Call Sign: KD8KPR

Nathan S Stein
218 E Ash St
Cedar Springs MI
49319

Call Sign: KD8IAL
Shila J Kiander
218 E Ash St
Cedar Springs MI
49319

Call Sign: KC8ZTM
Eddie C George
12635 Edgerton
Cedar Springs MI
49319

Call Sign: KD8FTB
James M Crouch
3565 Fernfield Dr
Cedar Springs MI
49319

Call Sign: KG6R
Karl G Roersma
11699 Forestwood Dr
NE
Cedar Springs MI
493198215

Call Sign: W8KGR
Karl G Roersma
11699 Forestwood Dr
NE
Cedar Springs MI
493198215

Call Sign: KB8RHY
Jerry S Willett
12430 Heintzelman
Ave NE
Cedar Springs MI
49319

Call Sign: AC8AH
Jerry S Willett
12430 Heintzelman
Ave NE
Cedar Springs MI
49319

Call Sign: KD8FAN
Sharon G Willett

12430 Heintzelman
Ave NE
Cedar Springs MI
49319

Call Sign: AB8DT
Ronald J Karger
12727 Hoskins Ave
Cedar Springs MI
49319

Call Sign: KC8NVY
Cheryl J Karger
12727 Hoskins Ave
Cedar Springs MI
49319

Call Sign: WB8Z
Carroll J Matulis
13630 Iris Ln
Cedar Springs MI
49319

Call Sign: KC8OEU
Christopher J Dehos
4266 Ives Farm Ln
Cedar Springs MI
49319

Call Sign: KD8DCD
Shawn M Holtrop
235 Jeffrey
Cedar Springs MI
49319

Call Sign: KB8ILG
Theresa A Terpenning
433 Linda
Cedar Springs MI
49319

Call Sign: KB8KZB
Tasha J Terpenning
433 Linda
Cedar Springs MI
49319

Call Sign: KC8VDM
Jeanette Groner
3688 Mapledge Ct
Cedar Springs MI
49319

Call Sign: KC8VDN

Thomas W Groner
3688 Mapledge Ct
Cedar Springs MI
49319

Call Sign: KB8MGB
Ronald L Peterson
11781 Myers Lake
Ave
Cedar Springs MI
49319

Call Sign: KB8VOW
Timothy J Keating
14400 Myers Lake
Ave
Cedar Springs MI
49319

Call Sign: NW8J
Larry A French
12215 Myers Lake
Ave NE
Cedar Springs MI
49319

Call Sign: N8IMN
Shirley A French
12215 Myers Lake NE
Cedar Springs MI
49319

Call Sign: KC8ILN
April Guinnup
167 N Main St
Cedar Springs MI
49319

Call Sign: N8YZK
Brian D Schultz
183 Oak St
Cedar Springs MI
49319

Call Sign: KC8MVQ
Andrew M Gunneson
15250 Pine Lake Ave
NE
Cedar Springs MI
49319

Call Sign: WX8AG
Andrew M Gunneson

15250 Pine Lake Ave
NE
Cedar Springs MI
49319

Call Sign: KC8TZG
Samuel E Peterson II
12915 Podunk
Cedar Springs MI
49319

Call Sign: KC8TZF
Ricky A Byington
13586 Podunk Ave NE
Cedar Springs MI
49319

Call Sign: N8CSP
Donald E Stiles
15594 Ritchie Ave NE
Cedar Springs MI
49319

Call Sign: KD8CQC
Peter A Adamson
4100 Russell Ave
Cedar Springs MI
49319

Call Sign: KD8IFK
Miki M Cain
224 S 7th St
Cedar Springs MI
49319

Call Sign: KC8JQO
Daniel J Schilling Jr
124 S Fredrick
Cedar Springs MI
49319

Call Sign: KC8NOO
Todd H Vanderplow
12515 Shaner
Cedar Springs MI
49319

Call Sign: KC8YOE
Thomas A Parker
81 Spruce Ave
Cedar Springs MI
493198103

Call Sign: KA8KNM

Sharon A Clayton
12677 Stout Ave
Cedar Springs MI
49319

Call Sign: KB8FQE
Amanda L Clayton
12677 Stout NE
Cedar Springs MI
49319

Call Sign: N8YZL
Kathy A Scharrer
13707 Tisdel Ave
Cedar Springs MI
49319

Call Sign: N8ZEI
Allen W Scharrer
13707 Tisdel Ave
Cedar Springs MI
49319

Call Sign: KC8JEG
Sherrie E Webb
13777 Tisdel Ave
Cedar Springs MI
49319

Call Sign: N8XMX
Richard E Webb
13777 Tisdel Ave
Cedar Springs MI
49319

Call Sign: KD8QKV
Beverly A Pouget
14300 Tisdel Ave
Cedar Springs MI
49319

Call Sign: KB8OWU
Sara E Link
12445 Wabasis Ave
Cedar Springs MI
493199758

Call Sign: N8TNR
John L Link
12445 Wabasis Ave
NE
Cedar Springs MI
493199758

Call Sign: WA8SKJ
Edward O Poisson
15190 White Creek
Ave
Cedar Springs MI
49319

Call Sign: KC8IWH
Bradley A Richardson
Cedar Springs MI
49319

FCC Amateur Radio Licenses in Cedarville

Call Sign: KA8IQD
Elmer O Polzin
Rt 1 Box 55
Cedarville MI 49719

Call Sign: KG8XC
Roger W Hamel
407 E Grove St
Cedarville MI 49719

Call Sign: WD8KMN
Ralph J Duman
2245 S Crooked Tree
Cedarville MI 49719

Call Sign: KG8OK
Fredric Massena
2084 S Forest Ln
Cedarville MI 49719

Call Sign: N2CB
Harvey C Hamel
393 S Hill Island Rd
Cedarville MI 49719

Call Sign: WD8KET
Patrick C Riley
812 S Lakeside Rd
Cedarville MI 49719

Call Sign: KC8OBA
Mark S Merchberger
761 W Wilson Ave
Cedarville MI 49719

Call Sign: KC8UCA
Lance D Fisher
Cedarville MI 49719

FCC Amateur Radio Licenses in Central Lake

Call Sign: KA8TAP
Louise E Brady
Rt 1 Box 254C
Rushton Rd
Central Lake MI 49622

Call Sign: K8FX
Gary J Goetzman
10550 Highview Ln
Central Lake MI 49622

Call Sign: AG4XW
William V Perry Sr
11555 Maple Hill Rd
Central Lake MI 49622

Call Sign: AC8CN
William V Perry Sr
11555 Maple Hill Rd
Central Lake MI 49622

Call Sign: KD6IVF
James F Cook Sr
10631 Maple View Dr
Central Lake MI 49622

Call Sign: WD8DOK
Robert E Wilson
1554 N Intermediate
Lk Rd
Central Lake MI 49622

Call Sign: W8WA
Walter L Ewald
3028 NE Torch Lake
Dr
Central Lake MI 49622

Call Sign: N8EQD
Michael J Cleary
4323 Ogletree Creek
Rd
Central Lake MI 49622

Call Sign: W8VPC
Michael J Cleary
4323 Ogletree Creek
Rd
Central Lake MI 49622

Call Sign: KC8APP
Herbert R Powers
3789 Rushron Rd
Central Lake MI 49622

Call Sign: N8BEG
Robert D Younce
648 S Intermediate
Central Lake MI 49622

Call Sign: WA8OMG
John R Stein
8032 W State St
Central Lake MI 49622

Call Sign: KA8TRV
Gerald J Bronkhorst Sr
Central Lake MI 49622

Call Sign: KB8HSR
Timothy S Brockett
Central Lake MI 49622

Call Sign: W8ING
Michael E Mackiewicz
Central Lake MI 49622

FCC Amateur Radio Licenses in Centreville

Call Sign: KC8PLI
Roger A Shingledecker
309 E Ann St Apt B
Centreville MI 49032

Call Sign: WD8OIU
Gloria A Pomeroy
27519 Marvin Rd
Centreville MI 49032

Call Sign: WD8OJG
Charles C Pomeroy Jr
27519 Marvin Rd
Centreville MI 49032

Call Sign: KC8BRO
Shane Z Feek
22429 N Angling Rd
Centreville MI 49032

Call Sign: KC8VMD
Amy Lynn Feek
22429 N Angling Rd

Centreville MI 49032

FCC Amateur Radio Licenses in Ceresco

Call Sign: WB8WMW
Steven E Belson
12060 11 Mile Rd
Ceresco MI 49033

Call Sign: KG8CI
Terry J Lower
13550 A Dr N
Ceresco MI 49033

Call Sign: N8QS
Terry J Lower
13550 A Dr N
Ceresco MI 49033

Call Sign: K8GG
George A Guerin
14322 A Dr N
Ceresco MI 490338611

Call Sign: WA8HPM
Carl L Laupp
9286 B Dr S
Ceresco MI 490339762

Call Sign: N8TIL
Charles W Nachbar
9379 Division Dr
Ceresco MI 49033

FCC Amateur Radio Licenses in Champion

Call Sign: KC8EWE
Patrick A Nylander
4881 CR 478
Champion MI 49814

Call Sign: AA8QK
Jerry P Ylitalo
1039 CR C N
Champion MI 49814

Call Sign: KC8HHS
Dennis J Howe
1885 CR Ckk
Champion MI 49814

Call Sign: KC8EEA

John R Etelamaki
536 CR Fj
Champion MI 49814

Call Sign: W8ZUL
John R Etelamaki
536 CR Fj
Champion MI 49814

Call Sign: KD8RBD
John P Koski
540 CR Fnr
Champion MI 49814

Call Sign: KD8MAE
Carl J Robare
2075 CR Fx
Champion MI 49814

Call Sign: KA8VDN
Michael A La Voy
823 N Granite Lk Rd
Champion MI 49814

Call Sign: N8JSO
James D Daly
2513 US 41 W
Champion MI 49814

Call Sign: KB8CKS
Jeffrey N Kyllonen
16701 US 41 W
Champion MI 49814

Call Sign: KC8VYW
Dennis A Moro
Champion MI 49814

Call Sign: WD8OKJ
Dennis A Moro
Champion MI 49814

FCC Amateur Radio Licenses in Channing

Call Sign: KD8DJL
Rand S Hruska
N12802 E Shore Ln
Channing MI 49815

Call Sign: KE8KF
Stephen I Reese
152 Hwy M95
Channing MI 49815

Call Sign: KD8AWG
Jeff Horvat
W9130 Lake Ellen Rd
Channing MI 49815

Call Sign: N8LQ
Jeff Horvat
W9130 Lake Ellen Rd
Channing MI 49815

Call Sign: KD8DJP
David L Carey
W8560 Tosin Ln
Channing MI 49815

Call Sign: W9ALK
Arlene L Keller
Channing MI 49815

FCC Amateur Radio Licenses in Charlevoix

Call Sign: KA8ZAR
Earl L Kroll
10444 2nd St Ironton
Charlevoix MI 49720

Call Sign: KC8MWG
Richard A Knack
2015 Barnard Rd
Charlevoix MI 49720

Call Sign: KA8HLI
Brian E Brachel
6300 Bay Shore Dr W
Charlevoix MI 49720

Call Sign: K8LQ
Brian E Brachel
6300 Bay Shore Dr W
Charlevoix MI 49720

Call Sign: KK5KZ
Richard E McKee
6756 Bay Shore Dr W
Charlevoix MI 49720

Call Sign: KB8QHF
Daniel R J Hales
33 Belvedere
Charlevoix MI 49720

Call Sign: N8PVU
Kenneth V Hickman
10371 Burgess Rd
Charlevoix MI 49720

Call Sign: KB8PQQ
Gary M Ruehle Jr
10367 Burnett Rd
Charlevoix MI 49720

Call Sign: KB8YNV
Bobbie J Ruehle
10367 Burnett Rd
Charlevoix MI 49720

Call Sign: KC8CSA
David G Ruehle
10367 Burnett Rd
Charlevoix MI 49720

Call Sign: KD8RTF
Richard D Phillips
10960 Burnett Rd
Charlevoix MI 49720

Call Sign: KC8NFA
William D Huber
10970 Burnett Rd
Charlevoix MI 49720

Call Sign: KA8PYY
Donald S Couse
307 Burns Rd
Charlevoix MI 49720

Call Sign: KB8PPC
William E Burns
8264 Burns Rd
Charlevoix MI 49720

Call Sign: AA8XO
David C Burns
8661 Burns Rd
Charlevoix MI 49720

Call Sign: KC8CFP
Martin B Walker
10550 Catherine St
Charlevoix MI 49720

Call Sign: K8QPS
Hudson M Phelps
200 Cherry Ave
Charlevoix MI 49720

Call Sign: K8EET
Terry L Edger
12199 Cottage Ln
Charlevoix MI 49720

Call Sign: KB8VWV
Paul F Baron
10430 Ferry Rd
Charlevoix MI 49720

Call Sign: KD8OBL
Thomas E Schultz
13077 Golfside Dr
Charlevoix MI 49720

Call Sign: N8HXY
Robert L Omland
15976 Klooster Rd
Charlevoix MI
497209781

Call Sign: KA8NPC
Robert L Omland
15976 Klooster Rd
Charlevoix MI
497209781

Call Sign: KC8CFR
Anora M Purdy
5052 M 66 N
Charlevoix MI 49720

Call Sign: WA8ZWV
Mark C Hosler
13151 Maple St
Charlevoix MI 49720

Call Sign: W0GRS
Glenn R Snider
514 Meadow Ln
Charlevoix MI 49720

Call Sign: KC0IRS
Mary J Snider
514 Meadow Ln
Charlevoix MI 49720

Call Sign: K8OEB
J O Crawford Jr
12265 Meanderline Rd
Charlevoix MI 49720

Call Sign: WA8AMZ

Louis F Warner
211 Nettleton St
Charlevoix MI 49720

Call Sign: K8LZH
Thomas M Oleksy
516 Newman St
Charlevoix MI 49720

Call Sign: KB8KPV
Craig D Stewart
8864 Old US 31 N
Charlevoix MI 49720

Call Sign: KB8JNO
Robert E Bellairs
10431 Old US 31 N
Charlevoix MI 49720

Call Sign: KB8QAM
Lynette D Stewart
8864 Old US 31N
Charlevoix MI 49720

Call Sign: WD8ORF
Albert F Miller Jr
8730 Pincherry Rd
Charlevoix MI 49720

Call Sign: WD8O
Albert F Miller Jr
8730 Pincherry Rd
Charlevoix MI 49720

Call Sign: KC8MGH
John J Chase
12492 Pineridge
Charlevoix MI 49720

Call Sign: KF8NK
Irving L Hallett Jr
12667 Pineridge Dr
Charlevoix MI 49720

Call Sign: K8PLV
Eugene R Pittman
206 Prospect St
Charlevoix MI 49720

Call Sign: N8MPP
Dale E Buckner
8398 See Rd
Charlevoix MI 49720

Call Sign: KC5ENG
Mary Cumings
8258 Shrigley Rd
Charlevoix MI 49720

Call Sign: KC8MWE
Scott T Beatty
1003 St Johns Dr
Charlevoix MI 49720

Call Sign: N8WF
Scott T Beatty
1003 St Johns Dr
Charlevoix MI 49720

Call Sign: KD8FBJ
Ethan R Winchester
209 State St
Charlevoix MI 49720

Call Sign: KD8EQW
Lance J Daniels
8155 Susan Shores Dr
Charlevoix MI 49720

Call Sign: KD8EQY
Deborah R Peterson
8190 Susan Shores Dr
Charlevoix MI 49720

Call Sign: KD8CVQ
John A Peterson
8190 Susan Shores Dr
Charlevoix MI 49720

Call Sign: KA8DRJ
John A Peterson
8190 Susan Shores Dr
Charlevoix MI 49720

Call Sign: N8DHU
Richard C Seibert
3897 US 31 S
Charlevoix MI 49720

Call Sign: KB8WZP
William J Parton
210 W Upright St
Charlevoix MI 49720

Call Sign: N8MJE
Terrance J Roeth
504 W Upright St
Charlevoix MI 49720

Call Sign: N8MKQ
Timothy J Roeth
504 W Upright St
Charlevoix MI 49720

Call Sign: N8MKY
Martha L Roeth
504 W Upright St
Charlevoix MI 49720

Call Sign: W8COL
Chain O Lakes ARC
504 W Upright St
Charlevoix MI 49720

Call Sign: KD8CYP
Albert J Mansen
207 W Upwright
Charlevoix MI
497201348

Call Sign: K8LPR
Russell J Snyder
3611 Washington St
Charlevoix MI 49720

Call Sign: KA8PKD
C Fred Feindt
Charlevoix MI 49720

Call Sign: KC8GWA
Edward J Kaskey
680 Division St
Charlevolx MI 49720

Call Sign: KC8AUI
Beatrice K Parton
210 W Upright St
Charlevolx MI 49720

FCC Amateur Radio Licenses in Charlotte

Call Sign: KB8FSX
Michael L Vantyle
4644 Ainger Rd
Charlotte MI 48813

Call Sign: NY8Q
John A Dewey
1490 Battle Creek Rd
Charlotte MI 48813

Call Sign: KB8SGS
Douglas S Bishop
2736 Battle Creek Rd
Charlotte MI 48813

Call Sign: KB8YJR
Mark S Royston
6887 Benton Rd
Charlotte MI
488138616

Call Sign: N8JYB
William E Casey Jr
1511 Brookfield Rd
Charlotte MI 48813

Call Sign: KC8MVC
James C Burlison
8018 Brookfield Rd
Charlotte MI 48813

Call Sign: W8TGI
James R Ensign
1141 Brookfield Rd
Charlotte MI 48813

Call Sign: KD8PVW
Jacob M Longanbach
2112 Brookmead Way
Charlotte MI 48813

Call Sign: K8JML
Jacob M Longanbach
2112 Brookmead Way
Charlotte MI 48813

Call Sign: KD8PVX
William J Vallance
2112 Brookmead Way
Charlotte MI 48813

Call Sign: KC8YGO
Bryan K Woodbeck
5830 Carlisle Hwy
Charlotte MI 48813

Call Sign: KC8IQG
Brian S Kzeski
766 Casler Rd
Charlotte MI 48813

Call Sign: AB8NS
Brian S Kzeski
766 Casler Rd

Charlotte MI 48813

Call Sign: WZ8DRU
Andrew J Henderson
735 Cherry St
Charlotte MI 48813

Call Sign: KC8UOE
Elizabeth A Henderson
735 Cherry St
Charlotte MI 48813

Call Sign: W8SHY
Albert B Startup
1500 E Baseline Hwy
Charlotte MI 48813

Call Sign: WB8OUT
Keith M Sevener
1375 E Clinton Trl
Charlotte MI 48813

Call Sign: KB8NED
Brian K Roberts
2505 E Nye Hwy
Charlotte MI 48813

Call Sign: N8CPB
Thomas J McFarlane
2049 E Packard Hwy
Charlotte MI 48813

Call Sign: WD8TJM
Thomas J McFarlane
2049 E Packard Hwy
Charlotte MI 48813

Call Sign: KB8IEW
Bruce K Bailey
910 E Shaw St
Charlotte MI 48813

Call Sign: N8NZS
Kimberlee Bailey
910 E Shaw St
Charlotte MI 48813

Call Sign: WD8DJB
David G Johnson
2266 E Vermontville
Hwy
Charlotte MI 48813

Call Sign: KI8BU

Devon M Wiley
630 Emerald Dr
Charlotte MI 48813

Call Sign: KC8UAM
Jeffrey L Hall
412 Foote St
Charlotte MI 48813

Call Sign: KD8MCX
James R Dillon
1122 Gregory Ln
Charlotte MI 48813

Call Sign: WD8BKF
Robin P Reed
609 High St
Charlotte MI 48813

Call Sign: W8ATT
Scott B Tickner
2966 Island Hwy
Charlotte MI 48813

Call Sign: W8GRO
Sandy K Tickner
2966 Island Hwy
Charlotte MI 48813

Call Sign: WB8TGY
Mark D Korroch
5143 Lansing Rd
Charlotte MI 48813

Call Sign: K8PTZ
David W Huva
722 Linden St
Charlotte MI 48813

Call Sign: N8PMB
Gary W Colles
750 Linden St
Charlotte MI 48813

Call Sign: KC8IUB
Ross J Lauback
6126 Mallard Dr
Charlotte MI 48813

Call Sign: N8GBS
William D West
421 Merritt St Apt G
Charlotte MI 48813

Call Sign: KD8SU
John M Marsh
1025 Millerburg Rd
Charlotte MI 48813

Call Sign: WB8TUM
Thomas M Kremenski
6728 Mulliken Rd
Charlotte MI 48813

Call Sign: KD8FQC
Keith P Hannen
329 N Bostwick
Charlotte MI 48813

Call Sign: KC8UUG
Jon C Morrison
338 N Bostwick St Apt
3
Charlotte MI 48813

Call Sign: KC7LCT
Rebecca D Dence
6375 N Chester
Charlotte MI 48813

Call Sign: KF8HA
Steven E Bowles
454 N Clinton St
Charlotte MI 48813

Call Sign: KC8ODS
Sally M Bowles
454 N Clinton St
Charlotte MI 48813

Call Sign: KC8TJR
Matthew R Woodbeck
631 N Clinton Trl
Charlotte MI 48813

Call Sign: N8SRW
Kathleen M Bachman
5775 N Clinton Trl
Charlotte MI 48813

Call Sign: KB8TIK
Louis W Fradette III
442 N Cochran
Charlotte MI 48813

Call Sign: KD8LJE
Lon M Senko
1917 N Perkey Rd

Charlotte MI 48813

Call Sign: N8GYS
Floyd D Rush Jr
455 N Shepherd St
Charlotte MI 48813

Call Sign: KD8HTF
Dennis R Earnest
355 N Stine Rd
Charlotte MI 48813

Call Sign: AA8QC
Michael D Kehres
191 N Wheaton Rd
Charlotte MI
488138801

Call Sign: KB8SGP
Terrie J Denniston
2797 Narrow Lake Rd
Charlotte MI 48813

Call Sign: KB8WRG
Jim D Denniston
2797 Narrow Lake Rd
Charlotte MI 48813

Call Sign: K8YV
Philip J Bacon
7191 Nixon Rd
Charlotte MI 48813

Call Sign: W8HX
Philip J Bacon
7191 Nixon Rd
Charlotte MI 48813

Call Sign: KB8UYX
Scott W Jansen
2848 Old Hickory Ln
Charlotte MI 48813

Call Sign: KD8KBH
Philip N Rolfe
806 Pearl
Charlotte MI 48813

Call Sign: KD8KDZ
Rebecca M Rolfe
806 Pearl St
Charlotte MI 48813

Call Sign: KC8RWZ

Thomas L Nevai
7220 Pinch Hwy
Charlotte MI 48813

Call Sign: KD8NCO
Randy S Sherwood
1484 S Ainger Rd
Charlotte MI 48813

Call Sign: N8BVT
Bland H Reynolds
1014 S Cochran Rd
Charlotte MI 48813

Call Sign: KC8WCD
Hugh R Fuller
4160 S Cochran Rd
Charlotte MI 48813

Call Sign: K8EFS
Merlin D Anderson
4300 S Cochran Rd
Charlotte MI 48813

Call Sign: N8HEE
Jeff A Frank
330 S Sheldon
Charlotte MI 48813

Call Sign: N8MCZ
Linda D Frank
330 S Sheldon
Charlotte MI 48813

Call Sign: KC8SKF
Matthew P Frank
330 S Sheldon
Charlotte MI 48813

Call Sign: KD8KBF
Ben A Frank
330 S Sheldon
Charlotte MI 48813

Call Sign: N8KRN
William K Sherman
429 Sumpter St
Charlotte MI 48813

Call Sign: KD8RHH
Bobby D Prater
131 Thomas Dr
Charlotte MI 48813

Call Sign: AC8KK
Bobby D Prater
131 Thomas Dr
Charlotte MI 48813

Call Sign: KB8HHW
Melvin E Blair
703 Tree Top Trl
Charlotte MI 48813

Call Sign: WQ8X
Richard E Bernard
363 Vansickle Dr
Charlotte MI 48813

Call Sign: KC8SLI
Elizabeth R Bush
1944 W 5 Point Hwy
Charlotte MI 48813

Call Sign: AB8HK
David D Gerber
1944 W 5 Point Hwy
Charlotte MI 48813

Call Sign: KB8SXT
Edward F Tubbs
207 W Henry St
Charlotte MI 48813

Call Sign: KD8IFS
Eaton County ARC
250 W Kalamo
Charlotte MI 48813

Call Sign: K8ETN
Eaton County ARC
250 W Kalamo
Charlotte MI 48813

Call Sign: K8CHR
Eaton County ARC
250 W Kalamo
Charlotte MI 48813

Call Sign: N8ODR
Ladd L Riether
1057 W Kinsel
Charlotte MI 48813

Call Sign: N8PWB
Loy L Nash
1321 W Lawrence
Hwy

Charlotte MI 48813

Call Sign: KC8JGS
Richard E Garrison
1864 W Lawrence
Hwy
Charlotte MI 48813

Call Sign: KF8FD
David R Bowles Sr
423 W Lovett St
Charlotte MI 48813

Call Sign: KD8RSH
Frederick C Payne
375 W Santee
Charlotte MI 48813

Call Sign: KB8MUL
V Dale Dodds
203 W Seminary
Charlotte MI 48813

Call Sign: KC8WKA
Brian C Stults
216 W Stoddard
Charlotte MI 48813

Call Sign: N8ETC
Raymond H Black
824 Walnut St
Charlotte MI 48813

Call Sign: W8LDD
Thomas A Kelly
117 Wedgewood Dr
Charlotte MI 48813

Call Sign: KC8QYG
Ketih J Gibson
247 Wedgewood Dr
Charlotte MI 48813

Call Sign: N8QGE
Larry A Tissue
851 Wheaton Rd
Charlotte MI 48813

Call Sign: KB8TIL
David J Woodbeck
1185 Winding Way
Charlotte MI 48813

Call Sign: W6RWR

Glen H Rudesill
Charlotte MI 48813

Call Sign: K8PNT
Paul A Remer
Charlotte MI
488130438

Call Sign: WB8ZNQ
Linda M Sadler
Rt 1 Box 11 Saddler
Rd
Chase MI 49623

Call Sign: WB8ZNR
Stephen A Sadler
Rt 1 Box 11 Saddler
Rd
Chase MI 49623

Call Sign: N8MZB
William F Stankey
5221 E Marquette Trl
Chase MI 49623

Call Sign: KD8JSZ
Kymberly C Roldan
6126 Saddler Rd
Chase MI 49623

Call Sign: K9KYM
Kymberly C Roldan
6126 Saddler Rd
Chase MI 49623

Call Sign: KD8NRL
Scott M Lindsley
Chase MI 49623

Call Sign: KB8URV
Kirk N Donahue
Rt 2 Box 246
Chassell MI 49916

Call Sign: WD8ODL
Edward G Hongisto
Rt 1 Box 247 Denton
Rd

Chassell MI 49916

Call Sign: KB8FCX
Richard E Brooks Jr
21525 E Henry Rd
Chassell MI
499169139

Call Sign: KC8FUS
Jon A Brooks
21525 E Henry Rd
Chassell MI
499169139

Call Sign: KC8BSU
James P Zito
41861 Hancock St
Chassell MI
499160505

Call Sign: N8HVT
George A Uuro
39115 Hwy US 41
Chassell MI 49916

Call Sign: KC8VPF
Scott A Mcdowell
18143 Moscow Rd
Chassell MI 49916

Call Sign: W8WAY
Scott A Mcdowell
18143 Moscow Rd
Chassell MI 49916

Call Sign: KC8LBR
Kurt C Smith
42115 N Hancock St
Chassell MI 49916

Call Sign: KC7CLC
Wendy L Kohtala
39184 N Sturgeon
River Rd
Chassell MI 49916

Call Sign: KC8MMU
Kirk E Yarina
35263 Pike River Rd
Chassell MI 49916

Call Sign: KC8MVV
Tamasin R Yarina
35263 Pike River Rd

Chassell MI 49916

Call Sign: N8KLV
Stephan J Szyszkoski
25155 S Klingville Rd
Chassell MI 49916

Call Sign: WA1UJU
Glen W Rantala
37358 Tapiola Rd
Chassell MI
499169419

Call Sign: N8XJK
Daniel R Kemppainen
38770 Tapiola Rd
Chassell MI 49916

Call Sign: KB8VZU
Leigh M Kemppainen
39304 Tapiola Rd
Chassell MI 49916

Call Sign: N8BFL
John H Kemppainen
39304 Tapiola Rd
Chassell MI 49916

Call Sign: KC8PPK
Christian M Muehlfeld
20465 Upper Worham
Rd
Chassell MI 49916

Call Sign: W8NA
David C Krym
36359 US Hwy 41
Chassell MI
499169261

Call Sign: N8HVS
Betty J Uuro
39115 US Hwy 41
Chassell MI
499169278

Call Sign: KD7NPM
Jeffrey C Johnson
39927 US Hwy 41
Chassell MI 49916

Call Sign: WB8WLI
Lois A Berg
44840 US Hwy 41

Chassell MI 49916

Call Sign: KB9RQZ
Mark C Morgan
Chassell MI 49916

Call Sign: KD8CTL
Gavrielah C L
Hojnacki
Chassell MI 49916

Call Sign: WA8MAX
Maxwell P Genaw
3664 E Hallstrom St
Chatham MI 49816

Call Sign: KC8NQR
Alger Cw Marauders
3664 E Hallstrom St
Chatham MI 49816

Call Sign: NA8CW
Alger Cw Mauraders
3664 E Hallstrom St
Chatham MI 49816

Call Sign: K8PG
Paul E Genaw
3664 E Hallstrom St
Chatham MI 49816

Call Sign: KC8TOU
Bruce W Butler
N5216 Gladstone St
Chatham MI 49816

Call Sign: KC8TIL
David L Adkins
E3658 Laurich Rd
Chatham MI 49816

Call Sign: KC8VYY
Debbie K Adkins
E3658 Laurich Rd
Chatham MI 49816

Call Sign: KD8AIM
Jamie L Adkins
E3658 Laurich Rd
Chatham MI 49816

Call Sign: WA8UTB
Michael J Van Den
Branden
Chatham MI 49816

Call Sign: KD8LWB
World Flora And
Fauna Club Of
Michigan
Chatham MI 49816

Call Sign: W8WFF
World Flora And
Fauna Club Of
Michigan
Chatham MI 49816

Call Sign: KD8MAQ
U P Ufo Investigators
Club
Chatham MI 49816

Call Sign: NU8FO
U P Ufo Investigators
Club
Chatham MI 49816

Call Sign: N8NRW
Jeffery M Johnson
4016 Alpena State Rd
Cheboygan MI 49721

Call Sign: KC8UXF
Louis F Blossom
15495 Arbutus Dr
Cheboygan MI 49721

Call Sign: AB8KC
George Hugle
16 Chelsey Ln
Cheboygan MI 49721

Call Sign: KB8SVR
Edward D Truesdell III
128 Coast Guard Dr
Cheboygan MI 49721

Call Sign: N8QZD
Connie L Sexton
1214 Court St

Cheboygan MI 49721

Call Sign: KC8LSL
Gloria E Volz
4483 Dotski Rd
Cheboygan MI 49721

Call Sign: KB8VNW
Henry W Rose
400 Duncan Apt 417
Cheboygan MI
497212160

Call Sign: W8LKE
Thomas C Romanauski
328 Duncan Ave Apt 5
Cheboygan MI 49721

Call Sign: W8IPQ
Cheboygan County
Amateur Repeater
Assoc
4225 E Burt Lake Rd
Cheboygan MI 49721

Call Sign: WB8DEL
Del M Reynolds
4225 E Burt Lake Rd
Cheboygan MI 49721

Call Sign: N8QZB
George W Grawey
1119 Fremont St
Cheboygan MI 49721

Call Sign: WB8AWY
Frank J Sines
485 Garfield Ave
Cheboygan MI 49721

Call Sign: KB8SDN
Gerald L Gross
14561 Goebel Rd
Cheboygan MI 49721

Call Sign: KC8ZSP
John W Hutchinson
955 Hancock St
Cheboygan MI 49721

Call Sign: KD8OHR
Robin S Moran
536 James St
Cheboygan MI 49721

Call Sign: KC8DTX
Bernard E Beethem
6020 Levering Rd
Cheboygan MI 49721

Call Sign: KC8EJG
Timothy L Beethem
6020 Levering Rd
Cheboygan MI 49721

Call Sign: K8ZI
Bernard E Beethem
6020 Levering Rd
Cheboygan MI 49721

Call Sign: N0CJA
Douglas L Schrag
1006 Loomis St
Cheboygan MI 49721

Call Sign: KA8TUA
Allen R Moberly
7271 McDonald Rd
Cheboygan MI 49721

Call Sign: N4YVE
Dennis J Dombroski
4990 Mullett Burt Rd
Cheboygan MI 49721

Call Sign: KC8MBI
Raymond Michalik
1372 N Black River Rd
Cheboygan MI 49721

Call Sign: KC8SSM
David B Crist
1477 N Black River Rd
Cheboygan MI 49721

Call Sign: N8YCT
Denise K Bohn
11432 N Black River
Rd
Cheboygan MI 49721

Call Sign: KC8QIH
Greg R Spencley
8901 N M 33 Hwy
Cheboygan MI 49721

Call Sign: W8GAG
Greg R Spencley

8901 N M 33 Hwy
Cheboygan MI 49721

Call Sign: KB8RVM
Steven L Schalow
1273 Nicolet Dr
Cheboygan MI 49721

Call Sign: KC8RKJ
Dawn J Shepherd
1909 Nicolet Dr
Cheboygan MI 49721

Call Sign: KB8NNN
Janice R Girard
897 Old Mackinaw Rd
Cheboygan MI 49721

Call Sign: N8QZC
Richard D Phillips
704 Palmyra St
Cheboygan MI 49721

Call Sign: KF8WW
Thomas A Palmer
3651 Polish Line Rd
Cheboygan MI 49721

Call Sign: KI4IKP
Michael T Rooksberry
112 S Ball
Cheboygan MI 49721

Call Sign: K8GUG
William E De May
3337 S Extension Rd
Cheboygan MI 49721

Call Sign: WB8AQY
Patrick J Sullivan
604 S Huron St
Cheboygan MI 49721

Call Sign: KC8CLQ
James R Prodan
4158 S River Rd
Cheboygan MI 49721

Call Sign: N8VOT
Kip A Thibeault
8084 S River Rd
Cheboygan MI 49721

Call Sign: KC8RRF

James A Norcross
14360 Scenic Ct
Cheboygan MI 49721

Call Sign: KD8BST
James F Davis
14407 Scenic Ct
Cheboygan MI 49721

Call Sign: KE6JEH
Dennis H Garside
1176 Shore Dr
Cheboygan MI 49721

Call Sign: N8SYR
Chuck R Burgtorf
5350 Stempky Rd
Cheboygan MI 49721

Call Sign: KD8GGX
Dale C Noble
313 Todd St
Cheboygan MI 49721

Call Sign: W8MI
Dennis P Havlena
3305 Tryban Rd
Cheboygan MI 49721

Call Sign: KC8QIJ
Del M Reynolds
4460 US 23
Cheboygan MI 49721

Call Sign: WB8MWR
Gary Lee Williams
13957 US 23 E
Cheboygan MI 49721

Call Sign: N8RVC
Kathy I Stoker
2653 Vanyea Rd Lot
75
Cheboygan MI 49721

Call Sign: KD8KTA
Ned O Workman
665 W Lincoln Ave
Cheboygan MI 49721

Call Sign: KD7GGH
Cheryl L Jankoviak
1315 W State St
Cheboygan MI 49721

Call Sign: WA8WTE
George M Ewing
3477 Wartella Rd
Cheboygan MI 49721

Call Sign: KB8TNX
Thomas S Shepherd
199 Western Ave
Cheboygan MI 49721

Call Sign: WD8KQC
Silas W Wallace
2161 Westwood Dr
Cheboygan MI 49721

Call Sign: WA8QOJ
Fred M Daeschler
Cheboygan MI 49721

FCC Amateur Radio Licenses in Christmas

Call Sign: K8PMD
Robert L Nelson
E 8010 Northpole
Christmas MI 49862

Call Sign: K8QHB
Jesse E Wilder Jr
136 Santa Ln
Christmas MI 49862

FCC Amateur Radio Licenses in Clare

Call Sign: KD8KQG
Elizabeth J Ringelberg
5986 E Dover Rd
Clare MI 48617

Call Sign: KC8FEX
Charles D Fachting
2612 E Herrick Rd
Clare MI 48617

Call Sign: KA8DIZ
J George Teeter
2137 E Ludington Dr
Clare MI 48617

Call Sign: KB8HJK
Lesa K Witbeck
1674 E N Co Line Rd

Clare MI 48617

Call Sign: KC8RSC
Virgil E Graham
312 Forest Ave
Clare MI 48617

Call Sign: WD8DVB
Donald R Peterson
704 Forest St
Clare MI 48617

Call Sign: K8NGA
Bryan T McKinney
10093 Grant Rd
Clare MI 48617

Call Sign: KC8ZKW
David T Prawdzik
411 John R
Clare MI 48617

Call Sign: KD8CVV
Dwight D Mcclain
2020 S Clare Ave
Clare MI 48617

Call Sign: KC8DIH
Kurt H Snider
3210 S Clare Ave
Clare MI 48617

Call Sign: KA8ZHO
Robert L Pryor
10365 S Grant Ave
Clare MI 48617

Call Sign: W8CCX
Robert L Pryor
10365 S Grant Ave
Clare MI 48617

Call Sign: WD8LGL
James A Seiter
10918 S Grant Ave
Clare MI 48617

Call Sign: KD8RMI
Lori S Lickly
9901 Tobacco Dr
Clare MI 48617

Call Sign: KC8MUC
Andrew J Weiss

211 W 1st St Apt 2E
Clare MI 48617

Call Sign: KW8A
Jon A Paetschow
521 Wilcox Pkwy
Clare MI 48617

FCC Amateur Radio Licenses in Clarksville

Call Sign: KD8EOJ
William M Oakley III
9932 Bell Rd
Clarksville MI 48815

Call Sign: KJ4QNL
Kyle L Eveleth
10502 Bell Rd
Clarksville MI 48815

Call Sign: WD8AFI
Leo L Pepper Jr
264 Broad St Box 55
Clarksville MI 48815

Call Sign: W8QOY
Donna J Burch
179 E Ferney St Apt 107
Clarksville MI 48815

Call Sign: KD8GBY
Benjamin J Veltman
10363 Hastings Rd
Clarksville MI 48815

Call Sign: KC8KTO
Bradley D Nicholas
6455 W Clinton Trl
Clarksville MI 48815

FCC Amateur Radio Licenses in Climax

Call Sign: K8TOU
Frank Cooley Jr
355 E Maple St
Climax MI 49034

Call Sign: K8UYN
Ala F Cooley
355 E Maple St

Climax MI 49034

Call Sign: WA8FYZ
Glenn S Seybert
12976 E P Ave
Climax MI 49034

Call Sign: KC8IRR
Scott A Torrance
120 Maple Cir
Climax MI 49034

Call Sign: K8YTZ
Charles A Fleming
16451 Mercury Dr
Climax MI 49034

Call Sign: K8DVF
Edwin W Smith
129 N Main St
Climax MI 49034

Call Sign: KD8OXR
Jay Jarrett
5103 S 36th St
Climax MI 49034

Call Sign: KD8AUU
Daryl L Meloche
5545 S 36th St
Climax MI 49034

Call Sign: WD8DLG
Michelle V Strauss
7561 S 45th St
Climax MI 49034

Call Sign: KC8UMQ
Richard C Clark
1600 S 46th St
Climax MI 49034

Call Sign: K8WUF
Henry F Sowles
5245 Sandstone
Climax MI 49034

Call Sign: K8WUI
Brenda K Sowles
5245 Sandstone
Climax MI 49034

Call Sign: K8OXD
Donald G Sowles

5227 Sandstone Dr
Climax MI 490349742

Call Sign: KZ8RSQ
Richard C Clark
220 Sunflower Dr
Climax MI 49034

Call Sign: KB0TQH
Darby L Felton
Climax MI 49034

FCC Amateur Radio Licenses in Coldwater

Call Sign: KD8JEG
Mayann R Worley
310 Airport Dr
Coldwater MI 49036

Call Sign: KC8ZFQ
Alvin R Worley
310 Airport Rd
Coldwater MI 49036

Call Sign: KO8R
Alvin R Worley
310 Airport Rd
Coldwater MI 49036

Call Sign: KB8GRN
Joe E Millard Jr
64 Bater Rd
Coldwater MI 49036

Call Sign: KB8EXK
Brent A Fazekas
645 Block Rd
Coldwater MI 49036

Call Sign: N8KBS
Norman P Marks
831 Buccaneer Ln
Coldwater MI 49036

Call Sign: KB8EXJ
James A Winebrenner
Jr
100 Burch Rd Lot 84
Coldwater MI 49036

Call Sign: KD8JEL
Justin A Lopshire
97 Coombs Ave

Coldwater MI 49036

Call Sign: N8CTI
Steven C Williams
228 Cutter Ave
Coldwater MI 49036

Call Sign: KW8YZ
Richard C Rowe
94 Cynthia Dr
Coldwater MI 49036

Call Sign: KD8CYV
Mark A Rogers
286 Cynthia Dr
Coldwater MI 49036

Call Sign: KD8ATL
Patrick A Beeman
62 Daugherty St
Coldwater MI 49036

Call Sign: N8VM
Patrick A Beeman
62 Daugherty St
Coldwater MI 49036

Call Sign: KD8JEI
Albert M Miller
338 Dylan Dr
Coldwater MI 49036

Call Sign: KD8EPY
Robert R Neer
299 E Chicago St
Coldwater MI 49036

Call Sign: KD8LEK
Aaron M King
550-31 E Chicago St
Coldwater MI 49036

Call Sign: KC8UGV
James A King
550 E Chicago St 31
Coldwater MI 49036

Call Sign: KC8GRM
Gary L Forgette
32 E Pointe Dr
Coldwater MI 49036

Call Sign: KD8PQI

Super Cub Contest
Club
284 E Rose Rd
Coldwater MI 49036

Call Sign: W8CUB
Super Cub Contest
Club
284 E Rose Rd
Coldwater MI 49036

Call Sign: KC8TEX
James R Cunningham
387 E Southern Rd
Coldwater MI 49036

Call Sign: WA8S
Richard C Wilcox
22 Edison Ct
Coldwater MI 49036

Call Sign: N8FUP
Gary L Stechschulte
37 Gruner Dr
Coldwater MI 49036

Call Sign: KD8BUG
Duane M Robbins
6 Hooker St
Coldwater MI 40936

Call Sign: KI8BM
Randy L Kruger
22 Hull St
Coldwater MI 49036

Call Sign: KC8WWB
Randy T Kruger
22 Hull St
Coldwater MI 49036

Call Sign: KC8OFV
Theresa V Peterson
67 Hull St
Coldwater MI 49036

Call Sign: W0SPB
Theresa V Peterson
67 Hull St
Coldwater MI
490361635

Call Sign: KC8ZFP

William Richard
Acock III
156 Jackson St
Coldwater MI 49036

Call Sign: K8AXN
Paul B Herman
262 Lake Dr
Coldwater MI 49036

Call Sign: KC8VFI
Michael J Jepson
791 Lake Dr
Coldwater MI 49036

Call Sign: K8TIY
Walter W Wright
703 Lott Rd
Coldwater MI 49036

Call Sign: KC8ZLB
Michael J Spencer
765 Marias Dr
Coldwater MI 49036

Call Sign: N8MRK
Richard R Guisinger
151 Marshall St
Coldwater MI 49036

Call Sign: KD8JGF
Branch County ARES
Races Club
242 Marshall St
Coldwater MI 49036

Call Sign: KI8BN
Arnold W Hayward
242 Marshall St
Coldwater MI 49036

Call Sign: NS8T
Arnold W Hayward
242 Marshall St
Coldwater MI 49036

Call Sign: WD8RKM
William J Miller
205 N Batavia Rd
Coldwater MI 49036

Call Sign: W8RCR
Richard C Rowe
265 N Fiske Rd

Coldwater MI 49036

Call Sign: N9XZC
Dennis R O Keefe
183 N Fremont St
Coldwater MI 49036

Call Sign: KB8ZGX
Lawrence L Hughes
204 N Hudson St
Coldwater MI 49036

Call Sign: KA1YIP
Jose Rodriguez
364 N Hudson St
Coldwater MI 49036

Call Sign: N0CHE
Jose Rodriguez
364 N Hudson St
Coldwater MI 49036

Call Sign: KA8QDQ
Deborah J Sterling
219 N Marshall Rd
Coldwater MI 49036

Call Sign: KB8PTI
Donald J Sullivan
99 N Michigan Ave
Coldwater MI 49036

Call Sign: KA8JDO
Dallas Rockwell
543 N Union City Rd
Coldwater MI 49036

Call Sign: K8ROK
Dallas Rockwell
543 N Union City Rd
Coldwater MI 49036

Call Sign: KC8SOW
Jonathan D Voss
603 N Union City Rd
Coldwater MI 49036

Call Sign: WV0SS
William J Voss
603 N Union City Rd
Coldwater MI 49036

Call Sign: N8GTH
Peggy J Voss

603 N Union City Rd
Coldwater MI 49036

Call Sign: K8SST
Jonathan D Voss
603 N Union City Rd
Coldwater MI 49036

Call Sign: KD8NAL
Darrell D Carr
767 N Union City Rd
Coldwater MI 49036

Call Sign: WB8R
Larry E Camp
71 Oakdale Ln
Coldwater MI 49036

Call Sign: WD8KAF
Branch County ARC
Inc
71 Oakdale Ln
Coldwater MI 49036

Call Sign: N8UDJ
Dianne L Pavka
57 Patricia Dr
Coldwater MI 49036

Call Sign: N8JHE
Christopher Pavka
530 Patricia Dr
Coldwater MI 49036

Call Sign: WB8RYR
Max W Benjamin
21631 Pearl Beach
Coldwater MI 49036

Call Sign: KD8MTO
James T Hadfield
15 Peckham St
Coldwater MI 49036

Call Sign: K7CHL
James T Hadfield
15 Peckham St
Coldwater MI 49036

Call Sign: K8CHS
Thomas D Twite
321 Penn Dr
Coldwater MI 49036

Call Sign: WA8DGG
David R Angle
496 Pinecrest Dr
Coldwater MI 49036

Call Sign: KA8MMW
Patrick C Angle
496 Pinecrest Dr
Coldwater MI 49036

Call Sign: WD8ICC
Donald G Behnke
446 Pleasant View Dr
Coldwater MI
490369768

Call Sign: W8CWX
Gary L Stechschulte
371 Rohloff Dr
Coldwater MI 49036

Call Sign: KD8EPW
Robert W Morford
66 Rose St
Coldwater MI 49036

Call Sign: N8YUT
Tamara L Davis
597 S Angola Rd
Coldwater MI 49036

Call Sign: KC8WWC
Christopher R Peters
844 S Angola Rd
Coldwater MI 49036

Call Sign: KD8RQE
Michael Delong
130 S Centennial Rd
Coldwater MI 49036

Call Sign: KE9RL
Stephen L Runyon
519 S Fremont Rd
Coldwater MI 49036

Call Sign: KE8LV
John J Sistanich
265 S Hawley Dr
Coldwater MI 49036

Call Sign: KC8PWB
Eugene R Miller
282 S Jefferson St

Coldwater MI 49036

Call Sign: WA8GJR
Bernard D Coy
889 Seminole Dr
Coldwater MI 49036

Call Sign: K8TZI
Harold L Sissem
31 Sherman St
Coldwater MI
490362134

Call Sign: N8KNM
James M Blackman
64 Sherman St
Coldwater MI
490362138

Call Sign: KD8CYX
Nancy L Slade
762 Tomahawk Tr
Coldwater MI 49036

Call Sign: WD8MGF
William A Slade
762 Tomahawk Trl
Coldwater MI 49036

Call Sign: KC8QT
John R L Boyer
16251 Treasure Cove
Coldwater MI 49036

Call Sign: KS8D
William J Voss
1008 Union City Rd
Coldwater MI 49036

Call Sign: W8SST
William J Voss
1008 Union City Rd
Coldwater MI 49036

Call Sign: KB8IYQ
David A Sharpley
96 Vans Ave
Coldwater MI 49036

Call Sign: WD8OUO
Dennis E Jaques
3B Victoria Dr
Coldwater MI
490361068

Call Sign: WA8LGO
Amos Fleming
353 W Colon Rd
Coldwater MI 49036

Call Sign: KG8TX
Steven T Unroe
298 W Lockwood Rd
Coldwater MI 49036

Call Sign: KD8HLP
Robert E Murray
318 W Pearl St
Coldwater MI 49036

Call Sign: KC8NDK
Stephen D Andrews
28 W State St Apt19
Coldwater MI 49036

Call Sign: KD8NSN
Laura E Bowers
86 Waterman Ave
Coldwater MI 49036

Call Sign: N8JWC
Matthew D Godell
95 Waterman Ave
Coldwater MI
490361353

Call Sign: KC8TOO
Godells H F Packet
Club
95 Waterman Ave
Coldwater MI
490361353

Call Sign: KC8GTD
David L Strang
571 White Dr
Coldwater MI 49036

Call Sign: WV8Q
Jack L Asher
266 Woods Ln
Coldwater MI 49036

Call Sign: KD8NSO
Timothy B Dempsey
Coldwater MI 49036

Call Sign: KO3P

Timothy B Dempsey
Coldwater MI 49036

FCC Amateur Radio
Licenses in Coloma

Call Sign: N8WMI
Daniel J Sadler
82060 45th Ave
Coloma MI 49038

Call Sign: KD8DZY
Patricia N Crenshaw
5075 Anderson Dr
Coloma MI 49038

Call Sign: KD8MBL
Christopher J Immoos
278 Apple St
Coloma MI 49038

Call Sign: KB8WZN
Susan M Ridge
2450 Bainbridge Ctr
Rd
Coloma MI 49038

Call Sign: K8BLU
Susan M Ridge
2450 Bainbridge Ctr
Rd
Coloma MI 49038

Call Sign: WB8JJM
Fred W Munchow
5142 Becht Rd
Coloma MI 49038

Call Sign: N8XLY
Laurence G Eyerly
5258 Becht Rd E
Coloma MI 490389551

Call Sign: WB8MFI
Robert C Knapp
5749 Beechwood
Coloma MI 49038

Call Sign: N8LVM
Florence A Wolff
6846 Blue Star Hwy
Coloma MI 49038

Call Sign: N8KYK

James R Collis Sr
6555 Brunden Pl
Coloma MI 49038

Call Sign: N8RYH
Joseph F Littleton
6726 Buena Vista Dr
Coloma MI 49038

Call Sign: N8UD
Walter J Williams
5430 Carmody Rd
Coloma MI 490389742

Call Sign: KB8ZVF
Robert L Rogers
45083 CR 703
Coloma MI 49038

Call Sign: WW9E
Patrick E McPherson
6860 Hagar Shore Rd
Coloma MI 49038

Call Sign: KB9YSQ
Carmella D Mcpherson
6860 Hagar Shore Rd
Coloma MI 49038

Call Sign: KC8MNH
Lynda H Nybro
5410 Interlochen Rd
Coloma MI 49038

Call Sign: KC8MNJ
Rosetta F T Nybro
5410 Interlochen Rd
Coloma MI 49038

Call Sign: N8PYT
Dennis L Nybro
5410 Interlochen Rd
Coloma MI 49038

Call Sign: KD8FFU
Corey M Mccarty
5782 Johnson Rd
Coloma MI 49038

Call Sign: KD8FFT
Nathan R Conrad
3072 Kerlikowske Rd
Coloma MI 49038

Call Sign: K8EGR
Charles R Shine
5264 M 63 N
Coloma MI 49038

Call Sign: WB9JGU
William J Zeilenga Sr
5019 Maple Ct
Coloma MI 49038

Call Sign: KE6GPE
Robert L Doornbos
5449 Marquette Dr
Coloma MI 49038

Call Sign: N4HTT
Daniel E King
5691 Meadow Ln
Coloma MI 49038

Call Sign: AC8CK
Daniel E King
5691 Meadow Ln
Coloma MI 49038

Call Sign: KD8DZW
Monica R Dolby
5314 Morning Aire Ln
Coloma MI 49038

Call Sign: KD8FFS
Caryn J Dolby
5314 Morning Aire Ln
Coloma MI 49038

Call Sign: KD8FFR
David E Dolby
5314 Morning Aire Ln
Coloma MI 49038

Call Sign: N8ZXQ
David A Vance
5768 Mountain Rd
Coloma MI 49038

Call Sign: WA8NUE
Warren W Haynes
4672 Paw Paw Lake
Rd
Coloma MI 490389666

Call Sign: KC8LOA
Martin P Immoos
7470 Paw Paw Lk Rd

Coloma MI 49038

Call Sign: N8PPG
Charles D Kibler IV
7110 Ryno Rd
Coloma MI 49038

Call Sign: KC8SWY
Kenneth L Schneider
6400 Sycamore Bluff
Coloma MI 49038

Call Sign: KD8DZX
Casey M Timm
5169 Taube Rd
Coloma MI 49038

Call Sign: KC8MIQ
Kathy S White
5941 Taylor St
Coloma MI 49038

Call Sign: KC8MIP
Richard K White
5941 Taylor St
Coloma MI 49038

Call Sign: KC8IXA
Harry L Johnson
377 Timber Dr
Coloma MI 49038

Call Sign: WW4BPH
Blossomland Youth
ARC
302 W St Joseph
Coloma MI 49038

Call Sign: N8MEK
Kenneth C Warner
5642 Wendzel Dr
Coloma MI 49038

Call Sign: KG8SV
Milton T Shaw
4701 Wil O Paw
Coloma MI 49038

Call Sign: KB8YOX
Fern C Shaw
4701 Wil O Paw Dr
Coloma MI 490389534

Call Sign: N8YO

Michael W Knapp
4749 Wil O Paw Dr
Coloma MI 49038

Call Sign: KB8COA
Jeff L Vanderboegh
221 Wilson St
Coloma MI 49038

Call Sign: KD8FFM
Amy D Warczynski
Coloma MI 49038

Call Sign: KD8ALT
Bertha L Nicholas
Coloma MI 49038

Call Sign: KD8FFL
Ronald G Warczynski
Coloma MI 49038

Call Sign: K9RON
Ronald G Warczynski
Coloma MI 49038

Call Sign: KC8QNS
Gerald L Barnes
427 E State St
Colon MI 49040

Call Sign: WB8TYH
James V Martin
219 Frank
Colon MI 49040

Call Sign: KC8WKB
Clayton A Walters
59332 Lakeshore Dr
Colon MI 49040

Call Sign: KB8AEV
Jo A Mitchell
59359 Lakeshore Dr
Colon MI 49040

Call Sign: KG8WL
Ralph A Mitchell
59359 Lakeshore Dr
Colon MI 49040

Call Sign: W8JWC

David J Volosky
60392 S Burr Oak Rd
Colon MI 49040

Call Sign: W8BFD
William G Ernst
16300 Campbell Rd
Comins MI 48619

Call Sign: KD8PFP
Starlynn A Maple
Comins MI 48619

Call Sign: K9JNY
Starlynn A Maple
Comins MI 48619

Call Sign: KB8SUV
Milford D Waddle
5708 E Ml Ave
Comstock MI 49041

Call Sign: KB8PSQ
Russell H Wright II
Comstock MI 49041

Call Sign: WY8X
Lloyd J Gosa
Comstock MI 49041

Call Sign: K8LAB
Marty A Johnson
Comstock MI 49041

Call Sign: KD8OBQ
Jacob A Johnson
Comstock MI 49041

Call Sign: KD8LSN
Joshua E Johnson
Comstock MI 49041

Call Sign: KD8FQO
Thomas V Oram
Proudfoot
Comstock MI 49041

Call Sign: WA8HC
Harry N Coates
1471 10 Mile Rd NE
Comstock Park MI
49321

Call Sign: KD8SK
Robert J Koss
579 4 Mile Rd NW
Comstock Park MI
49321

Call Sign: N8KVX
Steven L Burns
4256-6 Alpenhorn Dr
Comstock Park MI
49321

Call Sign: KA6RAM
Sandy A Wyche
4263 12 Alpenhorn Dr
Comstock Park MI
49321

Call Sign: N6MVH
Linda L Cope
4263 12 Alpenhorn Dr
Comstock Park MI
493218745

Call Sign: WD8BET
Edward G Bowe
5820 Baumhoff NW
Comstock Park MI
49321

Call Sign: KB8AKV
Gary A Springfield
435 Biddeford Ct
Comstock Park MI
49321

Call Sign: N8NIJ
Daniel L Markowski
343 Brandywyne NW
Comstock Park MI
49321

Call Sign: K8GAP
Mark A Nieman

1240 Buth Dr NE
Comstock Park MI
493219501

Call Sign: N8FBI
Edward D Birdsley II
431 Chasseral Dr NW
Apt 1A
Comstock Park MI
493219153

Call Sign: KD8BTV
Matthew M Satonin
5057 Division Ave N
Comstock Park MI
493218225

Call Sign: NF8P
John C Visser
4897 Gretchen Ave
NW
Comstock Park MI
49321

Call Sign: W8KBI
Keith O Connor
7109 Hass Dr
Comstock Park MI
49321

Call Sign: N8IDX
John R Gardner Jr
4783 Kittery Dr NW
Comstock Park MI
49321

Call Sign: KB8NUA
Sharon L Berry
50 Lana Ln Ct NE
Comstock Park MI
49321

Call Sign: KC8HZO
John H Velting
4064 Luxford Ave
Comstock Park MI
49321

Call Sign: KC8IJS
Marie L Velting
4064 Luxford NW
Comstock Park MI
49321

Call Sign: KG8OI
Michael J Adkins
651 Marway NW
Comstock Park MI
49321

Call Sign: AB8HD
Michael J Adkins
651 Marway NW
Comstock Park MI
49321

Call Sign: KD8KEY
Neal A Rusche
135 Meadowfield Ln
Comstock Park MI
49321

Call Sign: KD8PSJ
Jeffrey L Thompson
3630 Megan Ct NW
Comstock Park MI
49321

Call Sign: N8NIB
Dennis A Dixon
8990 Nestor
Comstock Park MI
49321

Call Sign: KC8FUW
Brian R Pawloski
606 Netherfield
Comstock Park MI
49321

Call Sign: WD8MSC
Lloyd J De Young Jr
432 Netherfield NW
Comstock Park MI
49321

Call Sign: KC8THQ
William O Baron II
5357 Pendleton Ct
Comstock Park MI
49321

Call Sign: N8YEM
Frederick T Bliss
5412 Pine Island Dr
NE
Comstock Park MI
49321

Call Sign: WD9JIV
Mickey L McLaren
6881 Pine Island Dr
NE
Comstock Park MI
493219538

Call Sign: N8KBU
Irwin V Tiejema
4158 Robert St
Comstock Park MI
49321

Call Sign: WD8RER
Thomas M Updike
5834 Rollaway Dr
Comstock Park MI
49321

Call Sign: KC8YOA
Comstock Park Ham
Radio Club
1250 Skyhills NE
Comstock Park MI
49321

Call Sign: KA8OND
Elizabeth A Wonders
1250 Skyhills NE
Comstock Park MI
49321

Call Sign: KD8QQ
Stephen L Wonders Sr
1250 Skyhills NE
Comstock Park MI
49321

Call Sign: WD8LBR
James C Schaefer
4705 Stony Creek
Comstock Park MI
49321

Call Sign: KC8EIL
Nathan L Bultman
5175 Wallingford
Comstock Park MI
49321

Call Sign: KC8TTF
Donald L Schuitman
Sr

4546 Westshire Dr
NW
Comstock Park MI
49321

Call Sign: KD8OPW
James H Neider III
4678 Westshire Dr
NW
Comstock Park MI
49321

Call Sign: KC8BLS
Chad D Sikora
3714 Wilmington Dr
Comstock Park MI
49321

Call Sign: KC8DRD
Kenneth A Howe
3881 Yorkland Dr Apt
12
Comstock Park MI
49321

Call Sign: KD8LBK
Adam M Howe
3917 Yorkland Dr Apt
7
Comstock Park MI
49321

Call Sign: WI8W
Thomas E Durfee Jr
3877-08 Yorkland Dr
NW
Comstock Park MI
49321

Call Sign: N8LCD
Robert J Moy
Comstock Park MI
49321

**FCC Amateur Radio
Licenses in Conklin**

Call Sign: WD8EMI
Barry T Heintz
18224 Elder Dr
Conklin MI 49403

Call Sign: W8EMI
Barry T Heintz

18224 Elder Dr
Conklin MI 49403

Call Sign: KD8IXW
Richard L Griggs Sr
16436 Juniper Dr
Conklin MI 49403

Call Sign: KC8VBV
Cory K Thompson
17550 Juniper Dr
Conklin MI 49403

Call Sign: KC8HLP
Benjamin H Hogston
19702 Maple Ave
Conklin MI 49403

Call Sign: KC8OVT
Amanda K Garvey
19702 Maple Ave
Conklin MI 49403

Call Sign: KB8TEF
Donald A McCallum
3439 Truman St
Conklin MI 49403

FCC Amateur Radio Licenses in Constantine

Call Sign: K8TCK
Albert J Smith
64264 Constantne Rd
Constantine MI 49042

Call Sign: N8JTE
Delbert J Cole
17130 Featherstone Rd
Constantine MI
490429738

Call Sign: KA8JET
Dennis W Rumsey
14177 Garber Rd
Constantine MI 49042

Call Sign: KB8VKJ
Fred E Miller
17560 Mintdale Rd
Constantine MI 49042

Call Sign: KB8VKK

Sandra L Miller
17560 Mintdale Rd
Constantine MI 49042

Call Sign: KB8GLR
Ryan D Schnepp
1518 River Heights Rd
Constantine MI 49042

Call Sign: WD8AAR
Mikeal D Skelton
720 Riverside Dr
Constantine MI 49042

Call Sign: KD8BHQ
Charles F Fisher
13076 Riverside Dr
Constantine MI 49042

Call Sign: W8AMR
Charles F Fisher
13076 Riverside Dr
Constantine MI 49042

Call Sign: K8IQC
Walter M Johansen
13506 Riverside Dr
Constantine MI 49042

Call Sign: W8MAW
Frederick N Carlisle
13789 Timm Rd
Constantine MI 49042

Call Sign: N8SM
Olley R Wise III
15710 Withers Rd
Constantine MI 49042

Call Sign: KA8QIH
Sandra K Smith
Constantine MI 49042

Call Sign: N8SGL
David H Erickson
Constantine MI 49042

FCC Amateur Radio Licenses in Conway

Call Sign: KB8KNM
Matthew J Merchant
Conway MI 49722

Call Sign: WD8MJB
Joseph F Werden
Conway MI 49722

FCC Amateur Radio Licenses in Cooks

Call Sign: KB8OFB
Brad M Jones
10475 W Peterson
Cooks MI 498179700

Call Sign: KD8PRP
Robert J Kok
11138 W Tanquay Rd
Cooks MI 49817

FCC Amateur Radio Licenses in Coopersville

Call Sign: W8ZV
Kim M Herron
16141 24th Ave
Coopersville MI 49404

Call Sign: KA8ZHR
Gary D Rollenhagen
16931 56th Ave
Coopersville MI 49404

Call Sign: KA8CLD
Calvin J Posthuma
13430 60th Ave
Coopersville MI 49404

Call Sign: KC8NF
John D Sedine
17429 64th Ave
Coopersville MI 49404

Call Sign: KA8RKU
Pamela A Bennink
14410 68th Ave
Coopersville MI 49404

Call Sign: KD8LXS
Jason D Vonroy
14564 84th Ave
Coopersville MI 49404

Call Sign: KD8HRC
Ruth E Wyant
222 Ann St

Coopersville MI 49404

Call Sign: KC8OJY
Thomas I Wyant Sr
222 Ann St
Coopersville MI 49404

Call Sign: WF8A
David L Roersma
241 Ann St
Coopersville MI 49404

Call Sign: KC8AMZ
Dewey E Mourer
129 Burr Oak Dr
Coopersville MI 49404

Call Sign: NE8KE
Boyd D Mason
8297 Cleveland W
Coopersville MI 49404

Call Sign: N8YQC
Jacqueline J Jara
57 Eastmanville
Coopersville MI 49404

Call Sign: KC8VBY
Robert E Smith
179 Eastmanville St
Coopersville MI 49404

Call Sign: WB8AIN
Barry R Kantz
17525 Egan St
Coopersville MI 49404

Call Sign: N8UMO
Paul S Malarik
493 Harrison St
Coopersville MI 49404

Call Sign: KD8LSZ
William E Eureka IV
8265 Hayes St
Coopersville MI 49404

Call Sign: WB8USV
Richard C Weise
9846 Leonard Rd
Coopersville MI 49404

Call Sign: KC8SRP
Jason M Kisner

4559 Leverette St
Coopersville MI 49404

Call Sign: N4MQQ
David W Bowden
221 Main St Apt B
Coopersville MI 49404

Call Sign: K8IFU
Lawrence R De Kiep
5327 Mill Rd
Coopersville MI 49404

Call Sign: KD8NMI
Frits Hartgers
9339 Oriole Dr
Coopersville MI 49404

Call Sign: WD8KPQ
Bruce D Reffeor
718 Ridgefield Dr
Coopersville MI
494049665

Call Sign: WD8LGN
Charlotte H Reffeor
718 Ridgefield Dr
Coopersville MI
494049665

Call Sign: KA8UQR
Howard W Slaughter
280 River St
Coopersville MI 49404

Call Sign: KF8TP
Roberto Jara Jr
423 W Randall St
Coopersville MI 49404

Call Sign: KC8MGL
Larry E Hard
11806 Wilson S8
Coopersville MI 49404

Call Sign: W8JJD
George E Martin
10550 Wilson St
Coopersville MI 49404

FCC Amateur Radio Licenses in Copemish

Call Sign: WA8BYA

William E Boyd Sr
18551 Bigge Rd
Copemish MI 49625

Call Sign: KB8ELN
Shawn L Gaylord
22266 Faylor Rd
Copemish MI 49625

Call Sign: KB8EOA
Shannon D White
17630 Litzen Rd
Copemish MI 49625

Call Sign: KX8LL
John C Doneth
15853 Marilla Rd
Copemish MI 49625

Call Sign: KX8CW
John C Doneth
15853 Marilla Rd
Copemish MI 49625

FCC Amateur Radio Licenses in Copper City

Call Sign: KB8VZV
Lawrence H Blahnik
Copper City MI 49917

FCC Amateur Radio Licenses in Copper Harbor

Call Sign: N8CSF
Thomas A Boost
11 Gratiot St US 41
Copper Harbor MI
49918

Call Sign: KA8L
Richard M Powers
15834 US 41
Copper Harbor MI
49918

Call Sign: K9SJ
Michael J Musiel
15504 US Hwy 41
Copper Harbor MI
49918

Call Sign: NN9NN
Paul J La Vanway Sr
Copper Harbor MI
499180059

FCC Amateur Radio Licenses in Coral

Call Sign: N8FOH
Victoria L Matulis
4288 Fogison
Coral MI 49322

Call Sign: KD8FSY
Barbara K Heath
4741 Gravel Ridge Rd
Coral MI 49322

Call Sign: KB8ZEO
Teresa C Howe
13152 Lake Montcalm
Coral MI 49322

Call Sign: KB8YPY
Ken G Howe
13152 Lake Montcalm
Coral MI 49322

Call Sign: N8HDJ
Michael A Towns Sr
4655 Oak St
Coral MI 49322

Call Sign: N8OHI
Brian A Miller
13595 W McBride
Coral MI 49322

FCC Amateur Radio Licenses in Cornell

Call Sign: KB8RJX
James E Owens
435 Cedardale 28Rd
Rd
Cornell MI 49818

FCC Amateur Radio Licenses in Covert

Call Sign: WD8CSW
Fred L Davis Jr
75859 40th Ave
Covert MI 49043

Call Sign: KD8FFW
Sarah B Mort
44759 76th St
Covert MI 49043

FCC Amateur Radio Licenses in Covington

Call Sign: KC8RMP
Bruce H Hackett
Covington MI 49919

FCC Amateur Radio Licenses in Crystal

Call Sign: N8UVJ
Richard L Thomas
1524 Beach Dr
Crystal MI 48818

Call Sign: KD8EOM
Jennifer L Depue
3653 Miner Rd
Crystal MI 48818

Call Sign: K9JAK
Jennifer L Depue
3653 Miner Rd
Crystal MI 48818

Call Sign: KD8CEO
Andrew E Kasdorf
979 Mt Hope Rd
Crystal MI 48818

Call Sign: KC8SID
Steven R Meinhardt
1801 N Shore Dr
Crystal MI 488189723

Call Sign: KB8TYG
Phillip J McCracken
717 Parker St
Crystal MI 48818

Call Sign: KD8PPD
Jonathan P Nyenhuis
554 Richard Dr
Crystal MI 48818

Call Sign: KC8YDZ
Loyal E Beard
215 S Main St

Crystal MI 48818

Call Sign: K8WKR
A La Vern Frost
520 S Main St
Crystal MI 48818

Call Sign: W8BK
Lester D Stowell
1208 S Main St
Crystal MI 48818

Call Sign: KD8HYD
Amanda J Kasdorf
979 S Mount Hope Rd
Crystal MI 48818

Call Sign: WA8ABM
Dean M Horak
2411 S Shore Dr
Crystal MI 48818

Call Sign: KA8SNL
Larry R Miller
1113 Senator
Crystal MI 48818

Call Sign: WD8KEZ
John A Eggleston
2198 Straittow
Crystal MI 48818

Call Sign: W8LXK
Oliver C Benham Sr
1911 Waterview Way
Crystal MI 48818

FCC Amateur Radio Licenses in Crystal Falls

Call Sign: KA8QGQ
Allan P Stacy
122 Alto Rd
Crystal Falls MI 49920

Call Sign: KC7TXB
John E Larsen
117 Briar Hill
Crystal Falls MI 49920

Call Sign: KC8JLZ
Robert H Erickson
124 Bristol St

Crystal Falls MI
499201001

Call Sign: AB8KO
John L Ponchaud Jr
Phd
325 Carpenter Rd
Crystal Falls MI 49920

Call Sign: KD8PPC
Tammy L Marks
325 Carpenter Rd
Crystal Falls MI 49920

Call Sign: KC8UYT
Lone Wolf Hf ARS
333 Carpenter Rd
Crystal Falls MI 49920

Call Sign: N8OWM
John L Ponchaud Jr
333 Carpenter Rd
Crystal Falls MI 49920

Call Sign: K8VC
Lone Wolfe Pack High
Frequency ARS
333 Carpenter Rd
Crystal Falls MI 49920

Call Sign: KB8KLD
Nathan W Clark
720 Crystal Ave
Crystal Falls MI 49920

Call Sign: KB8TOR
William R Winton
131 E Stager Lk Dr
Crystal Falls MI 49920

Call Sign: W8UL
Eugene C Sedberry
120 Good Fortune Ln
Crystal Falls MI 49920

Call Sign: KA9GRC
Roger E Gussy
526 Idlewild Rd
Crystal Falls MI
499209147

Call Sign: N8WQG
Le Roy E Anderson
126 Indian Lake Dr

Crystal Falls MI 49920

Call Sign: WD9DZU
Peter D Oss
124 Kaski Rd
Crystal Falls MI 49920

Call Sign: KA9BLA
Gerald P Jensen
121 Kohon Rd
Crystal Falls MI 49920

Call Sign: K9PWD
Gerald P Jensen
121 Kohon Rd
Crystal Falls MI 49920

Call Sign: N8OYO
Ronnie R Curnow
225 Lincoln
Crystal Falls MI 49920

Call Sign: KC8ZOO
John L Faccin
431 Lind Rd
Crystal Falls MI 49920

Call Sign: KD8BPN
Elizabeth A Bradish
203 N 6th St
Crystal Falls MI 49920

Call Sign: KC8MXP
Douglass B Showers
415 Oswald St
Crystal Falls MI 49920

Call Sign: WB8CHJ
John W Riverside
147 Pentoga Trl
Crystal Falls MI 49920

Call Sign: KB8TOW
Daniel J Benishek
802 Pentoga Trl
Crystal Falls MI 49920

Call Sign: W9GZZ
John L Glaze
189 Phelan Rd
Crystal Falls MI 49920

Call Sign: W8ZNK
Arnold W Kaarlela

170 Ravnio Rd
Crystal Falls MI 49920

Call Sign: KB8HFH
Curtis M Bacon
835 Runkle Lk Rd
Crystal Falls MI 49920

Call Sign: W8YNY
Wilbur J Kuure
440 Sheltrow Rd
Crystal Falls MI 49920

Call Sign: W8IFI
James O Rye
129 Sheridan Dr
Crystal Falls MI 49920

Call Sign: KA8RVU
William R McCarthy
795 Urban Ave
Crystal Falls MI 49920

Call Sign: KB9DLV
Richard R Glasson
1743 US 2 W
Crystal Falls MI 49920

Call Sign: KC8KLM
Bruce J Holm
107 W Townline Rd
Crystal Falls MI 49920

Call Sign: KB9HAH
Ralph W Haugen
181 W Townline Rd
Crystal Falls MI
499209211

FCC Amateur Radio Licenses in Curran

Call Sign: KC8CFA
Ben F Phetteplace
2306 M 65
Curran MI 48728

Call Sign: WD8JRT
Warren D Cross
2880 N Lake Rd
Curran MI 487289708

Call Sign: KC8HXK
Denise F Botkin

2188 Reeves Rd
Curran MI 48728

Call Sign: KC8HXL
Paul E Botkin Jr
2188 Reeves Rd
Curran MI 48728

Call Sign: N8JR
Paul E Botkin Jr
2188 Reeves Rd
Curran MI 48728

Call Sign: KC8BKG
Timothy J London
8506 W Deer Rd
Curran MI 48728

FCC Amateur Radio
Licenses in Curtis

Call Sign: KC8SZE
Alfred V Gage
W 16332 Sandtown Rd
Curtis MI 49820

Call Sign: KD8QJE
Betty J Gage
W16332 Sandtown Rd
Curtis MI 49820

Call Sign: N8SUI
Michael J Griffin
W16311 Sandtown Rd
Curtis MI 49820

Call Sign: KC8CWT
Joseph J Ruelle
Curtis MI 498200081

Call Sign: K8CWT
Joseph J Ruelle
Curtis MI 498200081

FCC Amateur Radio
Licenses in Custer

Call Sign: KB8HG
John F Nelson
1268 E Lone Pine Rd
Custer MI 49405

Call Sign: KB8AEM
Leon C Kenfield

3138 E US 10
Custer MI 49405

Call Sign: WA8YEW
Leonard P Smedberg
390 Monroe St
Custer MI 49405

Call Sign: KC8HMD
George F Ohse
218 N Schoenherr Rd
Custer MI 49405

Call Sign: N8KRD
George A Allison
1955 S Custer Rd
Custer MI 49405

Call Sign: WA8YLZ
Harold R Smedberg
Custer MI 49405

FCC Amateur Radio
Licenses in
Cutlerville

Call Sign: N8NCM
Tim E Lomas
7485 Sunview SE
Cutlerville MI 49548

FCC Amateur Radio
Licenses in Dafter

Call Sign: KC8KSZ
Richard B Walker
10625 S Mackinaw Trl
Dafter MI 49724

Call Sign: KD8QYR
Matt C Giordano
8916 W 10 1/2 Mile
Rd
Dafter MI 49724

Call Sign: W8SIG
Matt C Giordano
8916 W 10 1/2 Mile
Rd
Dafter MI 49724

Call Sign: KC8BZE
Timothy R Kymes
Dafter MI 497240025

FCC Amateur Radio
Licenses in Daggett

Call Sign: KD8BEM
Nita K Gomske
N9802 0 3 Ln
Daggett MI 49821

Call Sign: KD8BMH
Ronnie S Te Beest
W6386 CR 358
Daggett MI 49821

Call Sign: N9QPJ
Andreas Michels Jr
N11824 Dellfosse Ln
Daggett MI 49821

Call Sign: KC8ZRS
Gabriel A Savage
N 11107 Effa Ln
Daggett MI 49821

Call Sign: K8MML
Gabriel A Savage
N 11107 Effa Ln
Daggett MI 49821

Call Sign: KC8HOR
Lisa R Christophersen
N 12006 Hwy 41
Daggett MI 49821

Call Sign: N8OSR
Gregory A
Christophersen
N 12006 Hwy US 41
Daggett MI 49821

Call Sign: KA9ZRR
David C Christenson
W4317 Oakwood Rd
Daggett MI 49821

Call Sign: W9SGD
David C Christenson
W4317 Oakwood Rd
Daggett MI 49821

FCC Amateur Radio
Licenses in De Tour
Village

Call Sign: K8NFR
Michael C
Buschbacher
Hc54 Box 101
De Tour Village MI
49725

Call Sign: AD8Z
Robert H Bryan
Hc54 Box 39
De Tour Village MI
49725

Call Sign: KL7RG
Charles R Mayward
15203 E M 134 63E
De Tour Village MI
49725

Call Sign: WB8GUD
Craig R Luplow
486 N Division
De Tour Village MI
49725

Call Sign: KB8TS
Kenneth W Gates
603 N Division
De Tour Village MI
497250326

Call Sign: KC8JLH
Dale R Johnson
37099 S Hazelwood
Ln
De Tour Village MI
49725

Call Sign: WD8EKK
Charles A Lanning
37109 S Lakewood Ln
De Tour Village MI
49725

Call Sign: N3NLS
Walter V Smith Jr
37 Woodsman Trl
De Tour Village MI
49725

FCC Amateur Radio
Licenses in Decatur

Call Sign: N8TPA

Eric O Richardson
75780 46th St
Decatur MI 490458120

Call Sign: WB9RIC
Herbert R Mead
90820 Celery Center
Rd
Decatur MI 49045

Call Sign: N8RCT
Allen D Dill
85920 Cherry Ln
Decatur MI 49045

Call Sign: N8RYF
Patricia A Dill
85920 Cherry Ln
Decatur MI 49045

Call Sign: KC8TWW
Robert A Smith
38391 CR 669
Decatur MI 49045

Call Sign: KC8TWX
Bonnie L Stearns
38391 CR 669
Decatur MI 49045

Call Sign: KD8NPX
Tony A Hemenway
39197 CR 669
Decatur MI 49045

Call Sign: WB8UJO
Richard F Gordenier
46971 Delta Dr Shady
Shores Sub
Decatur MI 49045

Call Sign: N8LRK
Ronald C Chapman
311 E Delaware
Decatur MI 49045

Call Sign: KC8UQE
John E Johnson
42615 Evergreen Dr
Decatur MI 49045

Call Sign: KB8OSC
George R Wilder
46611 Lakeview Dr

Decatur MI 49045

Call Sign: KF8ZF
Stephen F Rajzer
82382 M 51 N
Decatur MI 49045

Call Sign: KD8DMB
Thomas J Haselberger
77841 N M 51 Hwy
Decatur MI 49045

Call Sign: KD8KXZ
Jillana M Ross
510 Rosewood Ave
Decatur MI 49045

Call Sign: KB6WJ
Albert M Walkling
Decatur MI 490450038

FCC Amateur Radio Licenses in Deerton

Call Sign: KC8CVU
Bettie Jo Deyoung
Patrie
Deerton MI 49822

FCC Amateur Radio Licenses in Delton

Call Sign: K8GEA
Harry M Phelps
5035 1st St
Delton MI 490469515

Call Sign: WA8ZKR
John E Arnold
5043 4th St
Delton MI 49046

Call Sign: W8III
David L Burk
8394 Corey Dr
Delton MI 490469714

Call Sign: K9AAA
David L Burk
8394 Corey Dr
Delton MI 490469714

Call Sign: N8GIN
Otis L Roberts

6635 Delton Rd
Delton MI 49046

Call Sign: KD8CBZ
Brent R Sovjak
6677 Delton Rd
Delton MI 49046

Call Sign: KC8RSU
Brent A Cravens
314 E Orchard St
Delton MI 49046

Call Sign: N8NXC
Joseph S Kiraly
7844 Enzian Rd
Delton MI 49046

Call Sign: N8KJD
George L Tyler Jr
11745 Fair Lake Dr
Delton MI 49046

Call Sign: KC8NTX
Ruth A Tyler
11745 Fair Lake Dr
Delton MI 490469539

Call Sign: KD8HXB
Robert J Trader
9781 Ford Rd
Delton MI 49046

Call Sign: KG8US
Donald E Hardy
112 Guernsey Lake
Delton MI 49046

Call Sign: KC8OXW
Ronald L Wilson
597 Harrington Rd
Delton MI 49046

Call Sign: KC8MCE
Kevin R Downs
6682 Lammers Rd
Delton MI 49046

Call Sign: WA8QWI
Paul A Voegtler
7761 Leeward Shores
Dr
Delton MI 49046

Call Sign: N8JJD
Norman C Risk
7904 Leeward Shores
Dr
Delton MI 490467773

Call Sign: KA8HBI
Cheryl A Shea
4998 Lindsey Rd
Delton MI 49046

Call Sign: W8YMG
Clifford R L Esperance
6720 Lindsey Rd
Delton MI 49046

Call Sign: W8QOQ
Emma V L Esperance
6720 Lindsy Rd
Delton MI 49046

Call Sign: KC8UJA
Arveda J Yeo
11690 Manning Lake
Rd
Delton MI 49046

Call Sign: W8LEQ
William E Collick
8320 Milo Rd
Delton MI 49046

Call Sign: KB8LKY
Rick J Baker
10751 N Shore Dr
Delton MI 49046

Call Sign: KA8VVM
Robert G Mousseau
9400 Norris Rd
Delton MI 49046

Call Sign: KC8DPL
Michael J Flesee Jr
10209 Norris Rd
Delton MI 49046

Call Sign: K8UJF
Michael J Fleser
10209 Norris Rd
Delton MI 49046

Call Sign: N8TKO
Karl M Smith

3189 Osborne Rd
Delton MI 49046

Call Sign: KD8GDM
Arend B Ackles
5110 Osborne Rd
Delton MI 49046

Call Sign: KD8FLP
William Anderson
2484 Pifer Rd
Delton MI 49046

Call Sign: K8CFO
Raymond A Trumm
8998 S Enzian Rd
Delton MI 49046

Call Sign: WA8HZB
Marguerite Trumm
8998 S Enzian Rd Rte
1
Delton MI 49046

Call Sign: AC8I
Steven A Wickham
9910 S Kingsbury Rd
Delton MI 490469528

Call Sign: KD8KYM
Christopher M Haas
8484 S M 43 Hwy
Delton MI 49046

Call Sign: KD8CDV
Robert F Hills
8620 S M 43 Hwy
Delton MI 49046

Call Sign: K8RFH
Robert F Hills
8620 S M 43 Hwy
Delton MI 49046

Call Sign: W8AW
Maurice J Garrett Jr
11717 S M 43 Hwy
Delton MI 49046

Call Sign: W8JOK
Helen M Garrett
11717 S M 43 Hwy
Delton MI 490469415

Call Sign: KD8KYL
Robert G Mousseau
9400 S Norris Rd
Delton MI 49046

Call Sign: KA8WBN
Jon S Duflo
3873 S Shore Dr
Delton MI 49046

Call Sign: WB8SAN
Myron L Edgerton
7133 S Shore Dr
Delton MI 49046

Call Sign: KA8EOS
Frances K Edgerton
7133 S Shore Dr
Delton MI 49046

Call Sign: KA8VES
June E Vander Wall
11301 Shultz Dr
Delton MI 49046

Call Sign: N8DLR
William G Vander
Wall Jr
11301 Shultz Dr Fair
Lk
Delton MI 49046

Call Sign: KB8RFP
Leigh M Tsuji
11334 Sprague Rd
Delton MI 49046

Call Sign: W8JGK
George R Leonard
9220 State Hwy M43
Delton MI 49046

Call Sign: KB8UMU
William F Nordmark
12995 Stuck Rd
Delton MI 49046

Call Sign: KB8WLA
Geoff G Hook
14220 Stuck Rd
Delton MI 49046

Call Sign: KC4ILG
Charles R Elden
4309 Ballentine Rd
Dewitt MI 48820

Call Sign: WB8PPB
Donald E Hunsaker
13595 Blackwood Dr
DeWitt MI 488209324

Call Sign: AE8E
Donald T Dew
614 Cedarwood Dr
Dewitt MI 48820

Call Sign: KC8ZHC
Douglas W Farrell
4233 Driftwood Dr
Dewitt MI 48820

Call Sign: N8JW
John M White
4234 Driftwood Dr
DeWitt MI 48820

Call Sign: N8OQD
Scott E Rokely
1800 E Alward
DeWitt MI 48820

Call Sign: KC8WHC
Nick B Katxman
31316 E Round Lake
Rd
Dewitt MI 48820

Call Sign: N8WKZ
Lois M Davis
14108 Everett St
Dewitt MI 488209645

Call Sign: NA8D
Jerry L Davis
14108 Everett St
Dewitt MI 488209645

Call Sign: KE8IP
Richard H Monroe
9840 Faust
Dewitt MI 48820

Call Sign: KD8GLK
Carl F Hunt

9701 Forest Hill Rd
Dewitt MI 48820

Call Sign: N8QPS
Richard R McKinley
13150 Hitching Post
Rd 77
DeWitt MI 48820

Call Sign: WD8RMS
David A Hunsaker
713 Larchmont
DeWitt MI 48820

Call Sign: K8ILF
David A Hunsaker
713 Larchmont
DeWitt MI 48820

Call Sign: KC8TIY
Jeffrey L Baumann
1351 Linden Cove
Dewitt MI 48820

Call Sign: KC8FDP
Lisa A Kelly
10670 Lowell Rd
Dewitt MI 48820

Call Sign: KC8CPF
Kristen M Kelly
10670 Lowell Rd
Dewitt MI 488208018

Call Sign: KD8IUJ
Bobby H Adam
3265 Luroma
Dewitt MI 48820

Call Sign: KC8VJR
Matthew K Trombley
1094 Oakwood Dr
Dewitt MI 48820

Call Sign: KB8PQP
William R Wing
13096 Old Hickory Trl
DeWitt MI 48820

Call Sign: W2PMH
William R Wing
13096 Old Hickory Trl
DeWitt MI 488209633

Call Sign: KC8LWG
Tyler G Head
105 Rivergate Ln
Dewitt MI 48820

Call Sign: KC8WHD
James G Sanderson
1237 S Geneva Dr
Dewitt MI 488209531

Call Sign: AA8LF
John W Kelly
10670 S Lowell Rd
DeWitt MI 48820

Call Sign: AA8NC
Nancy D Kelly
10670 S Lowell Rd
DeWitt MI 48820

Call Sign: KC8SXP
Abraham D Kimball
9855 S Wacousta Rd
Dewitt MI 48820

Call Sign: W8ABE
Abraham D Kimball
9855 S Wacousta Rd
Dewitt MI 48820

Call Sign: KA8ODQ
James O Macklin
13220 Shadybrook Ln
Dewitt MI 48820

Call Sign: KD8DJH
Donald J Hinkle
13155 Starwood Ln
Dewitt MI 48820

Call Sign: KD8IKO
Jean A Serviss
13121 Tucker Dr
Dewitt MI 48820

Call Sign: KD8HHN
William J Serviss
13121 Tucker Dr
Dewitt MI 488209351

Call Sign: KD8GLJ
Robert L Rose
1130 Turner Rd
Dewitt MI 48820

Call Sign: N8MAZ
Robert L Rose
1130 Turner Rd
Dewitt MI 48820

Call Sign: KE8CK
Dale A Wey
1204 Turner Rd
Dewitt MI 488208117

Call Sign: WA8GMD
Robert J Olance
14229 Turner St
DeWitt MI 48820

Call Sign: KB8QPA
James G Miller
11340 US 27 N
Dewitt MI 48820

Call Sign: KC8QWL
David E Zischke
4468 W Chadwick Rd
Dewitt MI 48820

Call Sign: N5ODZ
David E Zischke
4468 W Chadwick Rd
Dewitt MI 48820

Call Sign: WB8MWG
David C Ouellette
6148 W Cutler Rd
DeWitt MI 48820

Call Sign: KD8HFR
Clinton County A R P
S C
6148 W Cutler Rd
Dewitt MI 48820

Call Sign: W8CLI
Clinton County A R P
S C
6148 W Cutler Rd
Dewitt MI 48820

Call Sign: KD8DHO
Zachary O Dvorak
8450 W Cutler Rd
Dewitt MI 48820

Call Sign: KC8TIZ

Tim B Sullivan
900 W Geneva Dr
Dewitt MI 48820

Call Sign: KC8WHB
Jeff L Lawton
615 W Main St
Dewitt MI 48820

Call Sign: WA8ZJP
John M Hanley
1654 W Pratt Rd
Dewitt MI 48820

Call Sign: K8HJ
John M Hanley
1654 W Pratt Rd
Dewitt MI 48820

Call Sign: N8ERH
Bobbie S Dougherty
1451 W Webb Rd
Dewitt MI 48820

Call Sign: WB8PPG
Robert A Reynolds
4100 Westwind Ln
Dewitt MI 48820

Call Sign: WB8GXN
Lloyd R Mox
10804 Williams Rd
DeWitt MI 48820

Call Sign: KC8YKG
David D Barnett
402 Wilson St
Dewitt MI 48820

**FCC Amateur Radio
Licenses in
Dimondale**

Call Sign: WD8MJH
David M Steinman
6741 Aberdeen Dr
Dimondale MI 48821

Call Sign: AC8M
David M Steinman
6741 Aberdeen Dr
Dimondale MI
488219401

Call Sign: N8LWX
Stephen L Whiting
231 Bridge St
Dimondale MI 48821

Call Sign: N8CFK
Michael L Morey
444 Burr Oak Dr
Dimondale MI
488219553

Call Sign: KD8QZX
James L Miller Jr
10175 Carol Ln
Dimondale MI 48821

Call Sign: N8LNU
Reza J Beha
6390 Cheshire
Dimondale MI 48821

Call Sign: N8BPI
Matthew W Beha
6390 Cheshire Dr
Dimondale MI 48821

Call Sign: KD8HPX
Kenneth E Jones
6550 Cheshire Dr
Dimondale MI 48821

Call Sign: K8YRD
Dale L Moore
571 Creyts Rd
Dimondale MI 48821

Call Sign: WB8ZVK
Sharon R Moore
571 Creyts Rd
Dimondale MI 48821

Call Sign: KC8NFT
Amanda N Lamp
7405 Creyts Rd
Dimondale MI 48821

Call Sign: K1CJN
Keegan W Lamp
7405 Creyts Rd
Dimondale MI 48821

Call Sign: N8LRB
Candis R Cummings
7442 Creyts Rd

Dimondale MI 48821

Call Sign: AC8EX
Candis R Cummings
7442 Creyts Rd
Dimondale MI 48821

Call Sign: N9CVU
Roger W Cummings
7442 Creyts Rd
Dimondale MI 48821

Call Sign: KC8SXQ
Chelsea J Cummings
7442 Creyts Rd
Dimondale MI 48821

Call Sign: N9UV
Roger W Cummings
7442 Creyts Rd
Dimondale MI 48821

Call Sign: KD8OT
David W Karn
7276 E Vermontville
Hwy
Dimondale MI 48821

Call Sign: WD8BDL
James R Hein Jr
10036 Hart Hwy
Dimondale MI 48821

Call Sign: K8DZG
Silo F Rodriguez
11942 Holt Rd
Dimondale MI
488219619

Call Sign: WD8OOB
Paul L Bailor
5536 Jimson Dr
Dimondale MI 48821

Call Sign: N8SVK
Steven C Dexter
5579 Jimson Dr
Dimondale MI 48821

Call Sign: N8SVL
Bonnie L Dexter
5579 Jimson Dr
Dimondale MI 48821

Call Sign: WD8AZF
Raymond L Ettinger Jr
5579 Jimson Dr
Dimondale MI 48821

Call Sign: WD8MFY
Lynn A Ettinger
5579 Jimson Dr
Dimondale MI 48821

Call Sign: KC8WZF
David G Courey
4920 Knapp
Dimondale MI 48821

Call Sign: K8MX
Jeffery Cripps
4035 M 99
Dimondale MI 48821

Call Sign: KB8DSV
Daniel L Morey
333 Maple St
Dimondale MI 48821

Call Sign: KB8EFU
Betty J Morey
524 N Kensington Dr
Dimondale MI 48821

Call Sign: N8BOE
Robert A Van Antwerp
11842 Ransom Hwy
Dimondale MI 48821

Call Sign: KC8SET
Albert A Etheridge
8020 Rossman Hwy
Dimondale MI 48821

Call Sign: WB8LZG
Gregg C Mulder
7251 Saratoga Way
Dimondale MI 48821

Call Sign: KC8QYU
Jordon J Mulder
7251 Saratoga Way
Dimondale MI 48821

Call Sign: KC8QZE
Kevin C Mulder
7251 Saratoga Way
Dimondale MI 48821

Call Sign: N8EOP
Stanley W Smith
503 Sheffield Rd
Dimondale MI 48821

Call Sign: N8OSW
Patricia J Smith
503 Sheffield Rd
Dimondale MI 48821

Call Sign: KB8DQQ
Robert W Strobel
10901 Skinner Hwy
Dimondale MI 48821

Call Sign: KC8DYW
Matthew T Kelly
798 Tanbark
Dimondale MI 48821

Call Sign: N8JFY
Chad C Lycos
376 Tanbark Dr
Dimondale MI
488219789

Call Sign: WD8SBF
Tracy A Sisco
784 Tanbark Dr
Dimondale MI 48821

Call Sign: KC8BNC
Eric E Lantzer
209 W Jefferson
Dimondale MI 48821

Call Sign: K8UHF
James R Hein Jr
530 W Jefferson St
Dimondale MI 48821

Call Sign: KC8AGA
Joseph D Hinojosa
331 Walnut St
Dimondale MI 48842

Call Sign: KA8CPA
Gary L Titus
9210 Windsor Hwy
Dimondale MI 48821

Call Sign: N8TSI
David F Leeak

Dimondale MI 48821

Call Sign: N8VID
Cindy R Basto
651A Hildebrant St
Dodgeville MI 49921

Call Sign: N8HZH
Jon A Herlevich Sr
46629 Main St
Dodgeville MI
499219745

Call Sign: KB8VZR
Patricia M Halkola
102 Ave E Box 376
Dollar Bay MI 49922

Call Sign: N8XJV
Paul P Halkola
102 Ave E Box 376
Dollar Bay MI 49922

Call Sign: N8BYR
Risto S Vuorinen
111 Ave F Box 196
Dollar Bay MI 49922

Call Sign: N8SHD
Dale A Odgers
407 Ave G
Dollar Bay MI 49922

Call Sign: KC8EKW
Francis R Gariepy
26477 E Grosse Pt Box
585
Dollar Bay MI 49922

Call Sign: W8DAO
Dale A Odgers
23270 Granite Ave
Dollar Bay MI 49922

Call Sign: N8XJS
Dale A Junkin

49990 Hwy M26
Mason
Dollar Bay MI 49922

Call Sign: W8RAP
Roy A Peltoniemi
49079 M 26
Dollar Bay MI
499220317

Call Sign: N8XJP
Judy K Odgers
Dollar Bay MI 49922

Call Sign: KA8WLG
Alan L Olson
Dollar Bay MI 49922

Call Sign: KB8TOT
Scott G Hiltunen
Dollar Bay MI 49922

Call Sign: KC8QEB
Joel D Boutin
Dollar Bay MI 49922

Call Sign: KC8IAY
Ronald E Lamanen
Dollar Bay MI 49922

Call Sign: N8XLF
Brian D Engman
Dollar Bay MI 49922

Call Sign: W8CDZ
Copper Country Radio
Amat Assn
Dollar Bay MI
499220217

Call Sign: WB8ZYL
Roy A Peltoniemi
Dollar Bay MI
499220317

**FCC Amateur Radio
Licenses in Dorr**

Call Sign: KD8AFK
Thomas E Zomberg
1822 138th Ave
Dorr MI 49323

Call Sign: W8TEZ

Thomas E Zomberg
1822 138th Ave
Dorr MI 49323

Call Sign: W8EMD
Maurice E Hope
2023 138th Ave
Dorr MI 49323

Call Sign: KB8YTT
Denise M Miklusicak
2523 138th Ave
Dorr MI 49323

Call Sign: W8AJU
Wayne R Dial
2228 141st Ave
Dorr MI 49323

Call Sign: WB8SQJ
Jay P Hoppe
2380 142nd Ave
Dorr MI 49323

Call Sign: KD8LLI
Andrew D Egeler
1742 143rd Ave
Dorr MI 49323

Call Sign: N8XKK
Brian L Kleeves
1557 144th Ave
Dorr MI 49323

Call Sign: W8JAS
Jeffrey A Swainston
2589 144th Ave
Dorr MI 49323

Call Sign: KD8KBA
Jeffrey A Swainston
2589 144th Ave
Dorr MI 49323

Call Sign: KD8FCA
Mark E Buskirk
2719 144th Ave
Dorr MI 49323

Call Sign: KC8CKY
Daniel J Beute
4680 19th St
Dorr MI 493239763

Call Sign: W8WXD
Daniel J Beute
4680 19th St
Dorr MI 493239763

Call Sign: KC8FQL
Timothy J Beute
4705 19th St
Dorr MI 49323

Call Sign: KB8KZM
David L Hoppe
4430 27th St
Dorr MI 49323

Call Sign: W8ATS
Paul M Loew
4488 32nd Ave
Dorr MI 49323

Call Sign: KD8LOV
Marty C Loew
4488 32nd St
Dorr MI 49323

Call Sign: KD8KLS
Douglas C Pastoor
1711 Agnes Ave
Dorr MI 49323

Call Sign: N8JXM
Ronald M Russell
4347 Alpine Dr
Dorr MI 49323

Call Sign: WD8CKM
Dale C McClellan
2960 Braden Blvd
Dorr MI 49323

Call Sign: KD8KLU
Donald W Myrick Jr
4279 Bramblewood Ct
Dorr MI 49323

Call Sign: KB8GPN
Joseph J Palmer
1762 Deerfield Ct
Dorr MI 49323

Call Sign: KD8MCG
Steve S Garrett
1763 Deerfield Ct
Dorr MI 49323

Call Sign: KC8PCN
Dale J Pausinga II
2802 Fairway Dr
Dorr MI 49323

Call Sign: KC8PCO
Dale J Pausinga
2802 Fairway Dr
Dorr MI 49323

Call Sign: KC8SLH
Paula R Pausinga
2802 Fairway Dr
Dorr MI 49323

Call Sign: W8VBV
Dale J Pausinga
2802 Fairway Dr
Dorr MI 49323

Call Sign: KD8CYA
John J Pausinga III
2802 Fairway Dr
Dorr MI 49323

Call Sign: KC8UPB
Tamara J Pausinga
2802 Fairway Dr
Dorr MI 49323

Call Sign: N8JMU
Brian K Peters
1696 Heather Ct
Dorr MI 49323

Call Sign: KD8SBO
Kenneth W Kensington
1691 Heather Hills Ct
Dorr MI 49323

Call Sign: N8JWZ
Christopher J Hoppe
3822 Hidden Forest Dr
Dorr MI 49323

Call Sign: KD8JTD
Paul M Vandentoorn
4055 Kay Dr
Dorr MI 49323

Call Sign: KD8IAA
David A Everts
4166 Litchfield

Dorr MI 49323

Call Sign: W8CRT
David A Everts
4166 Litchfield
Dorr MI 49323

Call Sign: N8ODO
David J Van Oeveren
1721 Margaret Dr
Dorr MI 49323

Call Sign: WB8GIC
William N Kirby
4295 Medie Lot 9
Dorr MI 493239734

Call Sign: KD8CHT
Ronald L Miller
4174 Radgtock
Dorr MI 49323

Call Sign: KD8DBR
Randy L Wilson
4165 Radstock Dr
Dorr MI 49323

Call Sign: KD8RQB
Allegan County Search
And Rescue
4174 Radstock Dr
Dorr MI 49323

Call Sign: AC8SR
Allegan County Search
And Rescue
4174 Radstock Dr
Dorr MI 49323

Call Sign: KD8PUQ
Timothy J Oudbier
4136 Ranchero Dr
Dorr MI 49323

Call Sign: KD8DLP
Paul A Bodnar
1981 Red Pine Dr
Dorr MI 49323

Call Sign: N8VFI
Darla J Lane
2973 Secluded Acres
Dr
Dorr MI 49323

Call Sign: K8YNO
Jeffrey A Lane
2973 Secluded Acres
Dr
Dorr MI 49323

Call Sign: KD8PVS
John A Kotecki
1679 Slater Ave
Dorr MI 49323

Call Sign: KG8YO
James J Phillips Jr
1910 Sycamore Dr
Dorr MI 49323

Call Sign: N8RRJ
Hosea J Haralson
1778 Tumbleweed
Dorr MI 49323

Call Sign: N8ROC
Janice K Haralson
1778 Tumbleweed Dr
Dorr MI 49323

Call Sign: WB8ZFJ
Hosea J Haralson
1778 Tumbleweed Dr
Dorr MI 493239561

Call Sign: KB8OIB
Brian L Van Wyhe
1807 Walnut
Dorr MI 49323

Call Sign: N8YJU
Robert D Calhoun
4120 White Pine Dr
Dorr MI 49323

**FCC Amateur Radio
Licenses in Douglas**

Call Sign: N8ZXH
Luther E Lee
170 Mixer St
Douglas MI 49406

**FCC Amateur Radio
Licenses in Dowagiac**

Call Sign: WA8PST

Kenneth J Barker
503 3rd Ave
Dowagiac MI 49047

Call Sign: KD8PVN
Bonnie M Swan
56100 92nd Ave
Dowagiac MI 49047

Call Sign: KB8PFT
Brian G Darlas
718 Alma St
Dowagiac MI 49047

Call Sign: KC8GGS
Richard T Ashley
27806 Burmax Park
Dowagiac MI 49047

Call Sign: KD8CSU
Thomas D Ashley
27806 Burmax Park
Dowagiac MI 49047

Call Sign: KD8HON
Bryan M Lewandowski
50020 Circle Dr
Dowagiac MI 49047

Call Sign: KD8JAV
Frank Kuiken
4270 Clawson Rd
Dowagiac MI 49047

Call Sign: KC8MNK
Derek B Sheppler
9256 Columbia Rd
Dowagiac MI 49047

Call Sign: KC8MNL
Vince L Sheppler
9256 Columbia Rd
Dowagiac MI 49047

Call Sign: KD6RXT
Gary V Smith
107 Courtland St
Dowagiac MI 49047

Call Sign: KC8UEU
Margaret P Smith
107 Courtland St
Dowagiac MI 49047

Call Sign: W6GVS
Gary V Smith
107 Courtland St
Dowagiac MI 49047

Call Sign: KC8PQW
George A Losey
410 Courtland St
Dowagiac MI 49047

Call Sign: KD8FJQ
Corey M Maxedon
33419 Crystal Springs
Dowagiac MI 49047

Call Sign: KD8CSR
Shawn D Sirk Sr
58030 Dailey Rd
Dowagiac MI 49047

Call Sign: KB8PVA
William F Brock
52845 Decatur Rd
Dowagiac MI 49047

Call Sign: KD8CSW
Walter G Yaw
438 E Division St
Dowagiac MI 49047

Call Sign: KA8PHY
Roe A Woodruff
407 E Prairie Ronde St
Dowagiac MI 49047

Call Sign: KD8CZL
Guy H Evans
204 E Wayne St
Dowagiac MI 49047

Call Sign: KA8LGP
Robert W Haas
22790 Fosdick St
Dowagiac MI 49047

Call Sign: KA8LUU
Larry Conrad
23973 Gage St
Dowagiac MI 49047

Call Sign: KC8POX
Ranjit S Diol
608 Green St
Dowagiac MI 49047

Call Sign: W8JBM
Michael Bobik
207 Hamilton Ave
Dowagiac MI 49047

Call Sign: KD8PHP
George D Markham
52834 Indian Lake Rd
Dowagiac MI 49047

Call Sign: N8JRF
John O Arnold Sr
205 Indiana Ave
Dowagiac MI 49047

Call Sign: N8JRG
Robyn J Arnold
205 Indiana Ave
Dowagiac MI 49047

Call Sign: KD8IGF
Lawrence D
Mcdonnell
31949 Jones Dr
Dowagiac MI 49047

Call Sign: KC8JLW
Jerry L Yaw
52813 Lake View Dr
Dowagiac MI 49047

Call Sign: KD8IXN
Dawn R Tyrakowski
52525 Lakeshore Dr
Dowagiac MI 49047

Call Sign: WB8MFN
Bernard A Herold Jr
33203 Lakeview Ave
Dowagiac MI
490479378

Call Sign: KC8SOV
Mimi S Yaw
52813 Lakeview Dr
Dowagiac MI 49047

Call Sign: WB8MNZ
Ruth D Laszynski
211 Lester Ave
Dowagiac MI 49047

Call Sign: KC8POZ

Duane M Wright
29650 M 152
Dowagiac MI 49047

Call Sign: K8ADS
Darwin E Evans
66427 M 152 Hwy W
Dowagiac MI 49047

Call Sign: KD8BHM
Troy M Foreman
29530 M 152 Lot 18
Dowagiac MI 49047

Call Sign: KD8FWT
James L Jerue
28895 Middle Crossing
Dowagiac MI 49047

Call Sign: KC8HHV
Brian L Howard
25388 Morton St
Dowagiac MI 49047

Call Sign: K8STS
Vern L Murphy
610 Orchard Dr
Dowagiac MI 49047

Call Sign: KD8AYA
Michael C Schrader
32857 Peavine St
Dowagiac MI 49047

Call Sign: KD8AXZ
James E Scholz
50525 Pleasant St
Dowagiac MI 49047

Call Sign: N8HID
James E Wilson
30720 Pokagon Hwy
Dowagiac MI 49047

Call Sign: KA8TBW
David A Davidson
128 S Front St Apt 1
Dowagiac MI 49047

Call Sign: KD8KXY
Edward D Goodman
55718 Sink Rd
Dowagiac MI 49047

Call Sign: KA9VHZ
George S Haley
50109 Sister Lakes Rd
Dowagiac MI 49047

Call Sign: KD8JAO
Becky J Kelly
31761 Sunrise Ave
Dowagiac MI 49047

Call Sign: KD8JAR
Patrick S Kelly
31761 Sunrise Ave
Dowagiac MI 49047

Call Sign: KD8BHL
Richard A Tyrakowski
52525 Twin Lake
Shore Dr
Dowagiac MI 49047

Call Sign: WU6B
Allison M Farkas
Dowagiac MI 49047

Call Sign: KD8ANC
Leon D Comstock III
Dowagiac MI 49047

**FCC Amateur Radio
Licenses in Dowling**

Call Sign: AF4IK
Steven G Ehrhardt
11900 Bird Rd
Dowling MI 49050

Call Sign: WA8CZD
Frederic L Halbert
2721 Bristol Lake Rd
Dowling MI 49050

Call Sign: KA8JZL
James M Hilton
10265 Case Rd
Dowling MI 49050

Call Sign: KC8GXP
William J Gray
11877 Cisco Bay Dr
Dowling MI 49050

Call Sign: K8GTK
Vern S Weage

521 Clear Lake
Dowling MI 49050

Call Sign: KB8PAV
Jeremy T Strait
1700 Clearlake
Dowling MI 49050

Call Sign: KC8LLT
David D Gerber
8021 North Ave
Dowling MI 49050

Call Sign: KA7UIU
Albert E Hashley
8811 S Gurd Rd
Dowling MI
490509717

Call Sign: KB8FYI
Donna M Hashley
8811 S Gurd Rd
Dowling MI
490509717

Call Sign: KD8RWJ
Donald D Eddy
8915 S M 37 Hwy
Dowling MI 49050

Call Sign: KD8BFQ
Jacob P Bower
1210 W Dowling Rd
Dowling MI 49050

**FCC Amateur Radio
Licenses in
Drummond Island**

Call Sign: KA9TBP
William A Faville
Hc 53 Box 540
Drummond Island MI
49726

Call Sign: WA8HQW
Richard L Benson
25864 E Channel Rd
Drummond Island MI
497269439

Call Sign: W8QYT
Thomas W Brum
27017 E Channel Rd

Drummond Island MI
49726

Call Sign: WB8CZB
Michael L Helfand
30420 E Johnswood
Rd
Drummond Island MI
49726

Call Sign: KC8ZQK
Richard H Borth
34972 Fairbank Point
Rd
Drummond Island MI
49726

Call Sign: KC8JLC
Arthur V Kelsey
34616 S Fairbank Pt
Rd
Drummond Island MI
49726

Call Sign: KD8MC
Frank J Arnold Jr
31196 S Maxton Rd
Drummond Island MI
49726

Call Sign: N8IDV
Phillip R Stites
32884 S Maxton Rd
Drummond Island MI
49726

Call Sign: KA8IKM
Ruth A Powell
38878 S McKenzie Pt
Rd
Drummond Island MI
49726

Call Sign: KA8IQJ
Edsel R Powell
38878 S McKenzie Pt
Rd
Drummond Island MI
49726

FCC Amateur Radio
Licenses in Eagle

Call Sign: KA8OEY

Thompson H Haigh
11497 Bauer Rd
Eagle MI 48822

Call Sign: KD8RVV
Bruce E Erlandson
11200 Eden Trl
Eagle MI 48822

Call Sign: KB8RTO
Reynolds C Brokob
13525 Hawaii Ave
Eagle MI 48822

Call Sign: W8BRV
Reynolds C Brokob
13525 Hawaii Ave
Eagle MI 48822

Call Sign: KC8SAS
Robert L Winstanley
9660 Herbison Rd
Eagle MI 48822

Call Sign: KC8NJI
Susan M Motz
13110 Hinman
Eagle MI 48822

Call Sign: KC8WGF
Diana S Cooper
9150 Howe Rd
Eagle MI 48822

Call Sign: KI8JW
Charles K Cullimore
15571 S Tallman Rd
Eagle MI 48822

Call Sign: KA8FHU
Robert C Johnston Jr
11055 S Wright Rd
Eagle MI 48822

Call Sign: K8AJC
Lester K Hosford
9893 Tallman Rd
Eagle MI 488229752

Call Sign: KC8MAE
Charles K Cullimore
15571 Tallman Rd
Eagle MI 48822

Call Sign: N8RBR
Robert L Braley
14900 W Grand River
Eagle MI 48822

Call Sign: KA4ZSM
James L Retzlaff Sr
14900 W Grand River
Hwy
Eagle MI 488229612

Call Sign: KC8TIS
Timothy W Barney
10670 W Herbison Rd
Eagle MI 488229503

Call Sign: KA8PME
Michael L Mather
10914 W Herbison Rd
Eagle MI 48822

Call Sign: KC8POB
David O Work
Eagle MI 48822

Call Sign: KB8SXK
Jeffery S Oberg
Eagle MI 488220062

FCC Amateur Radio
Licenses in Eagle
Harbor

Call Sign: N8DBJ
Terry J Cauvin
8146 Eliza Creek Ln N
Eagle Harbor MI
49950

FCC Amateur Radio
Licenses in Eagle
River

Call Sign: KD8DYP
Jonathan R Hopper
Hc1 Box 680
Eagle River MI 49950

Call Sign: AB8WU
Jonathan R Hopper
Hc1 Box 680
Eagle River MI 49950

Call Sign: KD8DYN

Katrina Hopper
Hc1 Box 680
Eagle River MI 49950

Call Sign: KB8QOA
Charles R Hopper
25 W Main St
Eagle River MI 49924

Call Sign: KD8JAJ
Charles R Hopper
4957 W Main St
Eagle River MI 49950

FCC Amateur Radio
Licenses in East
Grand Rapids

Call Sign: W8IKO
John F Dunn
2217 Audobon Dr SE
East Grand Rapids MI
49506

Call Sign: KB8VEB
Joshua A Meekhof
2426 Gilmour St SE
East Grand Rapids MI
49506

Call Sign: N8QOG
Kent A Williamson
525 Gladstone
East Grand Rapids MI
49506

Call Sign: WA9REY
Evan L Morris
1660 Pontiac Rd SE
East Grand Rapids MI
49506

Call Sign: W8EW
Edward D Wells
741 San Jose Dr SE
East Grand Rapids MI
49506

Call Sign: K8AQZ
Donald F Firlik
1609 Seminole Rd Se
East Grand Rapids MI
49506

Call Sign: KF8RN
Rockwell F Slaski
1725 Warwick Rd SE
East Grand Rapids MI
49506

FCC Amateur Radio Licenses in East Jordan

Call Sign: KD8ESG
Eugene T Plite
621 6th St
East Jordan MI 49727

Call Sign: KE8HN
Donald E Brownell
2474 Adams Rd
East Jordan MI 49727

Call Sign: KC8GTZ
Joseph E Ignatowski
4775 Boyne City E
Jordan Rd
East Jordan MI 49727

Call Sign: KD8IFR
Matthew D Uler
3285 Bridge Dr
East Jordan MI 49727

Call Sign: W8ABB
Matthew D Uler
3285 Bridge Dr
East Jordan MI 49727

Call Sign: KC0NYT
Matthew D Uler
3285 Bridge Dr
East Jordan MI 49727

Call Sign: K8LIT
Robert A Hawkins
3320 Chula Vista Dr
East Jordan MI 49727

Call Sign: K8QER
Larry G Trumble
8710 Dutchman Bay
Rd
East Jordan MI 49727

Call Sign: KE8TB
James D Beswetherick

9339 Graham Rd
East Jordan MI 49727

Call Sign: WA8JTM
Arthur E Weinschenk
II
5925 Hosler Leisure
Ln
East Jordan MI 49727

Call Sign: KC8QNZ
Chain O Lakes ARC
2131 M 66 S
East Jordan MI 49727

Call Sign: KD8OHP
Herbert A Mcguire IV
506 Main St
East Jordan MI 49727

Call Sign: WB8TPM
Edward E Clark
604 Maple St
East Jordan MI
497279779

Call Sign: N8UN
Edward E Clark
604 Maple St
East Jordan MI
497279779

Call Sign: KA8RUI
George D Nelson
4041 Miles Rd
East Jordan MI
497278904

Call Sign: WD8JFP
Herschel C Young
5055 Miles Rd
East Jordan MI 49727

Call Sign: KA8ARY
William G McArthur
Jr
5742 Miles Rd
East Jordan MI 49727

Call Sign: KD8FQY
Kay E Harper
311 N Lake St
East Jordan MI 49727

Call Sign: N8PV
Scott M Harper
311 N Lake St
East Jordan MI 49727

Call Sign: KA8DCQ
Donald L Metcalf
3612 Nelson Rd
East Jordan MI 49727

Call Sign: WB8CTU
George Buxmann
8264 Nelson Rd
East Jordan MI 49727

Call Sign: K8MKJ
Joseph E Ponchart
3820 Nelson Rd N
East Jordan MI 49727

Call Sign: KC8IIJ
Michael R Sladewski
8465 Rogers Rd
East Jordan MI 49727

Call Sign: K8IUV
Jack P Moran
2131 S M 66
East Jordan MI 49727

Call Sign: N8CVB
Robert H Draves Jr
459 S Peninsula Rd
East Jordan MI 49727

Call Sign: KC8TS
William C Vaughan
198 S Peninsula Rd
East Jordan MI 49727

Call Sign: N9RZN
Daniel A Buchanan
4322 Sloop Rd
East Jordan MI 49727

Call Sign: KB8KVE
Scott M Harper
East Jordan MI 49727

Call Sign: KD8EVB
Nelson W Ogden
East Jordan MI 49727

Call Sign: W8NWO

Nelson W Ogden
East Jordan MI 49727

Call Sign: AB8VR
Scott M Harper
East Jordan MI 49727

Call Sign: KC8TX
James H Clark
East Jordan MI
497270481

FCC Amateur Radio Licenses in East Lake

Call Sign: N8UVE
Todd S Hundley
373 3rd St
East Lake MI 49626

Call Sign: WD8MDX
Richard J Siemion Sr
East Lake MI
496260067

FCC Amateur Radio Licenses in East Lansing

Call Sign: KB8RTM
Alfred J Fortino
1145 Abbott Rd
East Lansing MI 48823

Call Sign: KC8WGW
James W Seelhoff
736 Alton
East Lansing MI 48823

Call Sign: KC8WHA
Don D Batch
1717 Ann St
East Lansing MI 48823

Call Sign: KD8BDK
Douglas P Hines
417 Bailey St
East Lansing MI 48823

Call Sign: W8WZH
Thomas N Tabler
5310 Bear Lake Dr
East Lansing MI 48823

Call Sign: K8YI
Thomas N Tabler
5310 Bear Lake Dr
East Lansing MI 48823

Call Sign: KC8IOD
James R Nuttall
941 Bedford Rd
East Lansing MI 48823

Call Sign: KB8IBX
Matthew D Cohen
101 Bessemaur Dr
East Lansing MI 48823

Call Sign: KA8MZE
John F Fox
1259 Blanchette Dr
East Lansing MI 48823

Call Sign: W8EGI
Donald L Devendorf
5380 Blue Haven Dr
East Lansing MI 48823

Call Sign: AA8YS
Alan E Grunewald
304 Brookfield Cir
East Lansing MI 48823

Call Sign: KC8MCZ
John D Overhouse
1841 Burrwood Cir
East Lansing MI 48823

Call Sign: KU6I
Pit Schmidt
1857 Burrwood Cir
East Lansing MI 48823

Call Sign: KD8GTD
John M Glandon
B 322 Butterfield Hall
East Lansing MI
488251021

Call Sign: KD8DAR
Michael O King Jr
1551 Cambria Dr
East Lansing MI 48823

Call Sign: KA8YXS
Ronald J Trosty
6218 Captains Way

East Lansing MI 48823

Call Sign: KC8YJG
Richard P Estill
3834 Caracara Ln
East Lansing MI 48823

Call Sign: KC8PAZ
Ruth E Schaar
6206 Carino Ct
East Lansing MI 48823

Call Sign: KC8OTY
Lucas J Schaar
6206 Carino Ct
East Lansing MI 48823

Call Sign: KD8HPZ
Ryan M Blair
6060 Carriage Hill Dr
23
East Lansing MI 48823

Call Sign: KB0HAF
Susan M Prepejchal
6060 Carriage Hill Dr
Apt 26
East Lansing MI 48823

Call Sign: K8LZF
Tom D Russell
1320 Cedarhill Dr
East Lansing MI 48823

Call Sign: WA8ZWR
Robert E Lindberg
16240 Center Rd
East Lansing MI 48823

Call Sign: KB8LAC
Celina G Wille
915 C Cherry Ln
East Lansing MI 48823

Call Sign: KC8IQJ
Youngsun Chun
921K Cherry Ln
East Lansing MI 48823

Call Sign: KC8ZHA
Ahmet Turkmen
810 Cherry Ln Apt C
East Lansing MI 48823

Call Sign: N8WJO
Yonas Fisseha
809 F Cherry Ln Apts
East Lansing MI 48823

Call Sign: KC8TIP
Jereme D Warner
350 Chesterfield Pkwy
East Lansing MI
488234113

Call Sign: KC8TIQ
Douglas W Warner
350 Chesterfield Pkwy
East Lansing MI
488234113

Call Sign: N8VZS
Peter L Ford
241 Clarendon
East Lansing MI 48823

Call Sign: KB8VCD
Timothy A Akin
9490 Clark Rd
East Lansing MI 48823

Call Sign: KB0BBE
Carl D Nelson
6150 Cobblers Dr 104
East Lansing MI 48823

Call Sign: WB8ZIG
Earl R Goodrich II
7465 Coleman Rd
East Lansing MI 48823

Call Sign: K8KSX
Hazel I Rickerd
7480 Coleman Rd
East Lansing MI 48823

Call Sign: N8VKV
Daniel A Carleton
6241 Coleman Rd R 7
East Lansing MI 48823

Call Sign: K8HD
H David Wenger
718 Collingwood Dr
East Lansing MI 48823

Call Sign: WA8UWG
Donald O Foster

551 Cornell Ave
East Lansing MI 48823

Call Sign: KD8DAQ
Celina G Wille
1811 Cricket Ln
East Lansing MI 48823

Call Sign: W8WCP
Carl W Preston
524 Curtis Rd
East Lansing MI
488232006

Call Sign: N8UTA
Anna E Peter
1200 E Grand River 18
East Lansing MI 48823

Call Sign: KD8KOC
Dawn M Bezanson
1404 E Grand River
Ave 38
East Lansing MI 48823

Call Sign: KC8ICR
Bruce J Serven
2843 E Grand River
Ave Ste 250
East Lansing MI 48165

Call Sign: KD8MMN
Richard A Siersma
460 E McDonel
East Lansing MI 48825

Call Sign: N8WTD
James N Kallis
568 E McDonel
East Lansing MI 48825

Call Sign: WB9TOW
Steven A Marquie
1155 E Saginaw
East Lansing MI 48823

Call Sign: N8LJO
Wendy S Zauderer
211 E Shaw Hall MSU
East Lansing MI 48825

Call Sign: W8MSU
Msu Vhf Association
2121 Engineering Bldg

East Lansing MI 48824

Call Sign: W8SH
Michigan State
University Ama Rad
Club
2121 Engineering Bldg
East Lansing MI 48824

Call Sign: W8TJQ
William W Chapman
614 Forest Ave
East Lansing MI 48823

Call Sign: KE6VIS
Lynn A Baril
1757 Fox Croft Rd
East Lansing MI 48823

Call Sign: KA8OIM
Juan C Posada
1760 Foxcroft
East Lansing MI 48823

Call Sign: K8KU
Costas Kouklis
6031 Gibson
East Lansing MI 48823

Call Sign: N8SR
Steven R Rentschler
5248 Golden Cir
East Lansing MI 48823

Call Sign: N8NOO
Robert F Golaszewski
6165 Gossard
East Lansing MI 48823

Call Sign: W8VJC
Richard M Thomas
2360 Haslett Rd
East Lansing MI
488232915

Call Sign: KD8HNS
Jennifer L Wolfe
2651 Heather Dr
East Lansing MI 48823

Call Sign: KD8EHI
Daniel R Young
227 Highland Ave
East Lansing MI 48823

Call Sign: KC8SDB
William A Zlotek
6024 Horizon Dr
East Lansing MI 48823

Call Sign: KC8ODK
Emily L Shanblatt
1018 Huntington
East Lansing MI 48823

Call Sign: W8ELS
Emily L Shanblatt
1018 Huntington Rd
East Lansing MI 48823

Call Sign: K8MAS
Michael A Shanblatt
1018 Huntington Rd
East Lansing MI
488234126

Call Sign: KB8SSM
Frank E McBath
621 Kedzie
East Lansing MI 48823

Call Sign: KC8BFM
Robert J Peck
326 Kedzie St
East Lansing MI 48823

Call Sign: WA9GPH
Douglas A Limbaugh
2351 Kings Cross
East Lansing MI
488237735

Call Sign: KA1LUV
Scott H Harrison
1078 Lilac Ave
East Lansing MI 48823

Call Sign: KC8SOU
Clifton W Brown
1841 Linden St
East Lansing MI 48823

Call Sign: W8QS
Gerald L Park
2530 Maiffett Rd Apt
240
East Lansing MI 48823

Call Sign: N8DWI
Charles J Stahl
2663 Mansfield Dr
East Lansing MI 48823

Call Sign: N8YQJ
Ralph C Riggs Jr
6083 Maple Ln
East Lansing MI 48823

Call Sign: KC8EDD
Carolyn M Au
253 Maplewood
East Lansing MI 48823

Call Sign: N8QGV
Terry J Swick
2700 Marfitt Apt 320
East Lansing MI
488236338

Call Sign: KB8FPE
Stephen M Wagner
1530 Meadowbrook
East Lansing MI 48823

Call Sign: KA4TBG
Silas B Yates Jr
1560 Mt Vernon
East Lansing MI 48823

Call Sign: WB8IOV
Walter M Williams
1260 Mulberry Ln
East Lansing MI 48823

Call Sign: KC8QZA
Mengmeng Yu
371 N Case Hall
East Lansing MI 48825

Call Sign: KF8HZ
Jeffrey M Wille
1617 N Hagadorn
East Lansing MI 48823

Call Sign: K8NNZ
Robert O Marklewitz
5125 N Okemos Rd
East Lansing MI 48823

Call Sign: KC8ORS
Kimberly R Carpenter
6148 N Raindrop

East Lansing MI 48823

Call Sign: KC8IRN
Ahmad Nazir Atassi
2761 Northwind Dr 18
East Lansing MI 48823

Call Sign: N8YCN
Thomas H Weiss
1275 Oak Ridge 14
East Lansing MI
488233979

Call Sign: KC8ZAT
Renee M Mcconahy
239 Oakhill Ave
East Lansing MI 48823

Call Sign: KC8TLE
Hal W Hepler
5331 Panda Bear Cir
East Lansing MI 48823

Call Sign: K8EXH
Hal W Hepler
5331 Panda Bear Cir
East Lansing MI 48823

Call Sign: WA8IAL
Jack E Wiswasser
15625 Park Lake Rd
East Lansing MI 48823

Call Sign: WD8OVL
Bernhart B Barker
15721 Park Lake Rd
East Lansing MI
488239434

Call Sign: WB8BWT
Jack E Balzer
16117 Park Lake Rd
East Lansing MI 48823

Call Sign: WA8TIA
William M McAuliffe
16430 Park Lake Rd
Lot 214
East Lansing MI 48823

Call Sign: W8LBQ
Kenneth Corey
5968 Parklake Rd Apt
315

East Lansing MI 48823

Call Sign: N8ZSX
Dylan A Constan Wahl
1538 Parkvale Ave
East Lansing MI 48823

Call Sign: WA8ZTQ
John B Kreer
1834 Pinecrest Dr
East Lansing MI 48823

Call Sign: KC8RWW
Paul J Donahue
6063 Porter Ave
East Lansing MI 48823

Call Sign: KD8IEG
Ingham County D Star
Group
6187 Porter Ave
East Lansing MI 48823

Call Sign: KD8INM
Scientific Electronic &
Technical Exploration
Club
6187 Porter Ave
East Lansing MI 48823

Call Sign: W1RLS
Scientific Electronic &
Technical Exploration
Club
6187 Porter Ave
East Lansing MI 48823

Call Sign: KB8ZQZ
Dennis R Boone
6187 Porter Ave
East Lansing MI 48823

Call Sign: WB8CQM
Lansing Civil Defense
Repeater Association
6187 Porter Ave
East Lansing MI 48823

Call Sign: KD8RQW
Daniel P Smith
6309 Porter Ave
East Lansing MI 48823

Call Sign: W9WSW

Walter S Westerman
III
1085 Prescott Dr
East Lansing MI 48823

Call Sign: WB8YOX
Alan J Shaw
637 Puffin Pl
East Lansing MI 48823

Call Sign: KD8GIV
Jeanne M Pellegrino
409 Rosewood Ave
East Lansing MI 48823

Call Sign: WA8VBY
Richard H Mason
2506 Royce Ct
East Lansing MI 48823

Call Sign: KC8PUM
Robert H Smith
4908 S Hagadorn 24
East Lansing MI 48823

Call Sign: KD8NKH
Gordon S Mayes
16540 Sanctuary Cir
East Lansing MI 48823

Call Sign: N8PWC
Ethel S Goodman
Anthony
2343 Sapphire Ln
East Lansing MI 48823

Call Sign: KD8MMO
Courtney N Macdonald
1265 Scott Dr
East Lansing MI 48823

Call Sign: KA8YIW
Donald H Ebert
6030 Skyline Dr
East Lansing MI 48823

Call Sign: KD8DAS
Rudolph N Band
5854 Smithfield Ave
East Lansing MI 48823

Call Sign: W8LUX
Daniel T Davis
1672 Snyder Rd

East Lansing MI 48823

Call Sign: N9IWN
Craig W Tucker
1420 Somerset Close
St
East Lansing MI
488232436

Call Sign: N8WVC
Paul D Schneider
2819 Southwood Ave
East Lansing MI 48823

Call Sign: KB8UZA
Scott R Johnston
1542B Spartan Village
East Lansing MI 48823

Call Sign: KC8RHL
Clay B Reimann
821 Sunset Dr
East Lansing MI 48823

Call Sign: KB8YHO
Richard A Corner
835 Sunset Ln
East Lansing MI 48823

Call Sign: W8GQ
Kevin R Peterson
6404 Timber View Dr
East Lansing MI 48823

Call Sign: KC8YBW
James G Hilty
6309 Towar Ave
East Lansing MI 48823

Call Sign: N8WQP
Hiroshi Ochi
1108J University
Village
East Lansing MI 48823

Call Sign: KC8UDK
Gabrial S Gersten
1307 University
Village Apt G
East Lansing MI 48823

Call Sign: AC6MC
Minoru Tanigaki

1303 University
Village Apt I
East Lansing MI 48823

Call Sign: N9XAM
Laurence G Battin
1107 University
Village K
East Lansing MI 48823

Call Sign: KD8EZL
Chun -I Wu
258 W Owen Hall Msu
East Lansing MI 48825

Call Sign: KD8MMR
Shangyan Shi
142 W Shaw Hall
East Lansing MI 48825

Call Sign: KD8EHQ
Christopher L Hagist
1875 W Shore Dr C 2
East Lansing MI 48823

Call Sign: N8CEM
Sky R Weatherly
1522 Walnut Hts
East Lansing MI 48823

Call Sign: N8ZND
James A Miller
420 Wayland Ave
East Lansing MI 48823

Call Sign: KD8MVZ
Mark A Mckeel
464 Wayland Ave
East Lansing MI 48823

Call Sign: AA0JV
Charles L Roche
5763 Westminster Way
East Lansing MI 48823

Call Sign: N8JAK
Barbara R Hollstein
345 Whitehills Dr
East Lansing MI 48823

Call Sign: N8JWM
Werner Hollstein
345 Whitehills Dr
East Lansing MI 48823

Call Sign: W8IWA
David R Rovner
633 Whitehills Dr
East Lansing MI 48823

Call Sign: KC8GXM
Nathan J C Russell
637 Whitehills Dr
East Lansing MI 48823

Call Sign: KC8GXN
Marc A Russell
637 Whitehills Dr
East Lansing MI 48823

Call Sign: KC8HGG
Samuel M J Russell
637 Whitehills Dr
East Lansing MI 48823

Call Sign: KC8KBJ
Brenda S Russell
637 Whitehills Dr
East Lansing MI 48823

Call Sign: N5NBT
Jeffrey I Richards
938 Wildwood Dr
East Lansing MI 48823

Call Sign: W8EO
Edward A Oxer
1968 Winchester Dr
East Lansing MI 48823

Call Sign: KD8HQA
Antoni D Williams
1408 Wolf Ct
East Lansing MI 48823

Call Sign: N8PWA
Edward W Thomas
1707 Woodside Dr
East Lansing MI 48823

Call Sign: KC8NEZ
Joseph C Leshock
5903 York Way
East Lansing MI 48823

Call Sign: KA8OGK
Ruth E Hess
East Lansing MI 48826

Call Sign: N8WJN
Eric S Bak
East Lansing MI 48826

Call Sign: WB8YDZ
Alex Azima
East Lansing MI 48826

Call Sign: KC8QWK
Imad H Elhajj
East Lansing MI 48826

Call Sign: K8ZKC
Ted G Daniel
East Lansing MI 48826

Call Sign: W8KAR
Michael A Volz
East Lansing MI
488261371

Call Sign: KC8OXS
Kirt D Livernois
East Lansing MI
488266340

FCC Amateur Radio Licenses in East Leroy

Call Sign: N8MOR
Paul D Farmer
9085 1 1/2 Mile Rd
East Leroy MI 49051

Call Sign: KB8UPD
James K Camp
6263 2 Mile Rd
East Leroy MI 49051

Call Sign: W8DQK
Paul L Frederick
6336 4 Mile Rd
East Leroy MI 49051

Call Sign: KC8AXD
Charles G Green
10678 4 Mile Rd
East Leroy MI 49051

Call Sign: N8YEA
Ervin G Green
10687 4 Mile Rd
East Leroy MI 49051

Call Sign: KD8RVP
Julie M Seifke
8934 5 Mile Rd
East Leroy MI 49051

Call Sign: WD8OIG
Gloria L Mowry
6705 6 1/2 Mile Rd
East Leroy MI 49051

Call Sign: KD8CDT
David T Sootsman
2241 H Dr S
East Leroy MI 49051

Call Sign: W8MYU
Robert A Hibbard
3541 H Dr S
East Leroy MI 49051

Call Sign: W8IPZ
Laurence D Chapman
3548 H Dr S
East Leroy MI 49051

Call Sign: WA8A
Ronald K Gore
5045 N Dr S
East Leroy MI 49051

FCC Amateur Radio Licenses in East Tawas

Call Sign: KD8BDZ
Tyler D Rood
200 Adams St
East Tawas MI 48730

Call Sign: N8CJK
Gregory J Dahlstrom
72 Baldwin Resort Rd
East Tawas MI 48730

Call Sign: KD8PVC
Robert C Otwell III
2664 Brooks Rd
East Tawas MI 48730

Call Sign: KC8FDO
Richard W Kalinowski
109 Church St Apt 401

East Tawas MI
487301165

Call Sign: KD8KVT
Henry F Bacon
544 Cornett
East Tawas MI
487309727

Call Sign: WD8JSC
James A Carl
3645 Crescent Dr
East Tawas MI 48730

Call Sign: KC8ZOH
Gerald C Atkin
620 Curtis Rd
East Tawas MI 48730

Call Sign: WB8TQL
Arnold O Heier
901 E Franklin
East Tawas MI 48730

Call Sign: K8TXA
Frederick W Besancon
910 E Galion Rd
East Tawas MI 48730

Call Sign: KC2GFV
Phillip R Michaelis
2475 E Huron Rd
East Tawas MI 48730

Call Sign: KG8IR
Ronald J Epacs
2769 E Huron Rd
East Tawas MI 48730

Call Sign: KC8WHF
Todd Essary
2298 E US 23
East Tawas MI 48730

Call Sign: K8TOD
Todd Essary
2298 E US 23
East Tawas MI 48730

Call Sign: W8GZF
John A Alexander
327 E Washington St
East Tawas MI
487301418

Call Sign: KB8VII
Sharon A Musolf
808 Kunze Rd
East Tawas MI 48730

Call Sign: N8NJY
Thomas C Musolf
808 Kunze Rd
East Tawas MI 48730

Call Sign: K8PPO
Emil E Sass
513 Main St
East Tawas MI 48730

Call Sign: KC3HC
Van D Olmstead
1026 N Ottawas Ln
East Tawas MI 48730

Call Sign: W8VJ
Robert N Hogaboam
1010 N Tawas Lake
Rd
East Tawas MI 48730

Call Sign: KB8RB
Julia C Brainard
855 N US 23
East Tawas MI 48730

Call Sign: N8EYU
Aaron D Brainard
855 N US 23
East Tawas MI 48730

Call Sign: KD8PVD
Lauren K Reynolds
1185 N US 23
East Tawas MI 48730

Call Sign: KC8EHU
Alan K Kontak
606 Newman St
East Tawas MI
487301250

Call Sign: KC8EYK
Kenneth D Murphy
475 Old State Rd
East Tawas MI 48730

Call Sign: KB8VGI

David L Papas
524 Rainbow Dr
East Tawas MI 48730

Call Sign: W8KZK
David L Papas
524 Rainbow Dr
East Tawas MI 48730

Call Sign: KC8IPJ
Thomas E Hurd
2667 Tac Trl
East Tawas MI 48730

Call Sign: KC8ZOJ
Chad M Meyer
72 W Anderson Rd
East Tawas MI
487309740

Call Sign: KC8EYN
Bruce T Meyer
226 W Anderson Rd
East Tawas MI 48730

Call Sign: N8VSJ
Terry L Hartley
729 Wadsworth
East Tawas MI 48730

Call Sign: K8ACQ
Robert J Knop
2922 Wolverine St
East Tawas MI
487309533

Call Sign: KB0ONB
John J Daly
158 Wood Ave
East Tawas MI 48730

Call Sign: KA8UQV
Edwin J Rivers
3405 Zudell Ct
East Tawas MI
487309559

Call Sign: KA8HPQ
William T Roy
5988 N M 88 Hwy
Eastport MI 49627

Call Sign: KB8RRV
Otto H Bretz
Eastport MI 49627

Call Sign: KD8KFE
Clyde A Atkinson
Eastport MI 49627

Call Sign: W8PDL
Clyde A Atkinson
Eastport MI 49627

Call Sign: W8IEA
Walter J Sattler
Eastport MI
496270237

Call Sign: N8NTV
Terry L Becker
7413 5 Point Hwy
Eaton Rapids MI
48827

Call Sign: WA8AFV
Dennis E Csondor
2775 Ackley Rd
Eaton Rapids MI
488279020

Call Sign: KE8SZ
Steven J Kratzer
1181 Arch Rd
Eaton Rapids MI
488279216

Call Sign: KC8DZL
Joseph R Wessling
1552 Arch Rd
Eaton Rapids MI
48823

Call Sign: KA8HOM
Terence E Conklin
9905 Barnes Hwy
Eaton Rapids MI
48827

Call Sign: KC8PKA
Terence E Conklin

9905 Barnes Rd
Eaton Rapids MI
48827

Call Sign: WA8CFV
Ottmar L Holley
312 Blake St
Eaton Rapids MI
48827

Call Sign: KC8JAF
Darren H Fether
211 Broad St
Eaton Rapids MI
48827

Call Sign: KC8JAG
Michelle M Fether
211 Broad St
Eaton Rapids MI
48827

Call Sign: N8UCI
Robert N Carpenter
228 Brook St
Eaton Rapids MI
48827

Call Sign: N8YVY
Roy B Detwiler
10609 Bunker Hwy
Eaton Rapids MI
48827

Call Sign: KB8SHK
Stephen C Klink
11682 Bunker Hwy
Eaton Rapids MI
48827

Call Sign: W8OCK
Gordon D Main
6111 Bunker Rd
Eaton Rapids MI
48827

Call Sign: WA8CXR
Clayton J Mahan
527 Canal St
Eaton Rapids MI
48827

Call Sign: N8YAH
Ida M Dennis

5656 Clinton Tr
Eaton Rapids MI
48827

Call Sign: K8ATS
David M Dennis
5600 Clinton Trl
Eaton Rapids MI
48827

Call Sign: N9ASG
James L Nestell
9279 Columbia Hwy
Eaton Rapids MI
48827

Call Sign: KD8JJQ
James A Deagan
11825 Columbia Hwy
Eaton Rapids MI
48827

Call Sign: KC8HLV
Richard E Bernard
5802 Durfee Rd
Eaton Rapids MI
48827

Call Sign: KB8WEG
Bill M Kelly
4390 E Clinton Trl
Eaton Rapids MI
48827

Call Sign: K8ESA
Nancy E Dennis
5600 E Clinton Trl
Eaton Rapids MI
48827

Call Sign: KF8VH
David A Dennis
5608 E Clinton Trl
Eaton Rapids MI
48827

Call Sign: KC8POA
Mike D Baker
601 E Knight
Eaton Rapids MI
48827

Call Sign: N8XME
Donald A Clark

130 Frost
Eaton Rapids MI
48827

Call Sign: KC8TCS
Peter D Strank
2145 Gale Rd
Eaton Rapids MI
488279604

Call Sign: N8UCH
Steve E Mahan
320 Grand St
Eaton Rapids MI
48827

Call Sign: N8HQ
Steve E Mahan
320 Grand St
Eaton Rapids MI
48827

Call Sign: WJ8A
Steve E Mahan
320 Grand St
Eaton Rapids MI
48827

Call Sign: N8CDP
Alden J Smith
420 Haven St 12
Eaton Rapids MI
48827

Call Sign: NI8A
Robert M De Meester
8836 Houston Rd
Eaton Rapids MI
48827

Call Sign: KD8JGK
Todd A Gardner
8255 Island Hwy
Eaton Rapids MI
48827

Call Sign: KB8ZXP
Kim E Morgan
124 Lansing St
Eaton Rapids MI
48827

Call Sign: KA8NRI
Hugh M Betz

4628 Mahan Hwy
Eaton Rapids MI
48827

Call Sign: WD8BDT
Ronald L Beckwith
403 McArthur Riv Dr
Eaton Rapids MI
48827

Call Sign: WD8BDU
Joan S Beckwith
403 McArthur River
Dr
Eaton Rapids MI
48827

Call Sign: KC8ODO
John R Schultz
1303 Montgomery Dr
Eaton Rapids MI
48827

Call Sign: W8VRV
William Winters
1314 Montgomery Dr
Eaton Rapids MI
48827

Call Sign: KC8VXG
Donald E West
2236 N Canal Rd
Eaton Rapids MI
48827

Call Sign: KD8NOD
James L Hamilton
7331 Peck Rd
Eaton Rapids MI
48827

Call Sign: KF8WD
Dean E Dennis
10262 Plains Hwy
Eaton Rapids MI
48827

Call Sign: KC8TJB
Thomas R Rostorfer
11182 Plains Hwy
Eaton Rapids MI
48827

Call Sign: KD8JGN

Adam C Collard
11553 Plains Rd
Eaton Rapids MI
48827

Call Sign: KC8AFJ
Ottmar L Holley II
7706 Royston Rd
Eaton Rapids MI
48827

Call Sign: KC8PGW
Mary E Holley
7706 Royston Rd
Eaton Rapids MI
48827

Call Sign: N8XHN
William T Sands
240 S Canal Rd
Eaton Rapids MI
48827

Call Sign: WD8LCV
Steven D Gramling
105 S Donegal St B
Eaton Rapids MI
48827

Call Sign: KB8VLV
James E Masters
569 S Gallery Dr
Eaton Rapids MI
48827

Call Sign: N8JFB
John F Imeson
1420 S Onondaga Rd
Eaton Rapids MI
48827

Call Sign: N8JI
John F Imeson
1420 S Onondaga Rd
Eaton Rapids MI
48827

Call Sign: KC8VNZ
Cassandra A Imeson
1420 S Onondaga Rd
Eaton Rapids MI
48827

Call Sign: KD8GAB

Joseph L Ellsworth
1811 S Royston Rd
Eaton Rapids MI
488279094

Call Sign: KA8GWU
Susan M Lampman
6888 S Royston Rd
Eaton Rapids MI
48827

Call Sign: N8OBZ
Douglas M Morgan
5276 Spicerville Hwy
Eaton Rapids MI
488279035

Call Sign: N8NSS
Gary A Williams
7351 Spicerville Hwy
Eaton Rapids MI
48827

Call Sign: N8OCB
Luann Williams
7351 Spicerville Hwy
Eaton Rapids MI
48827

Call Sign: KC8ULD
Randy R Kissee
8708 Spicerville Hwy
Eaton Rapids MI
48827

Call Sign: KD8QNT
Christine M Bean
5225 Stimson Rd
Eaton Rapids MI
48827

Call Sign: KC8EHR
Clint Kelly Hannahs
5700 Stimson Rd
Eaton Rapids MI
48827

Call Sign: WC8LAN
Lansing Michigan
Arpsc
5700 Stimson Rd
Eaton Rapids MI
48827

Call Sign: KC8ODU
David R Kenyon
8289 Stub Hwy
Eaton Rapids MI
48827

Call Sign: KC8DJH
Jaymes S Kenyon
8289 Stub Hwy
Eaton Rapids MI
488279319

Call Sign: KD8RQU
Mark L Anderson
11930 Vfw Rd
Eaton Rapids MI
48827

Call Sign: KD8KUN
Matthew J Mcmillan
6463 W Columbia
Hwy
Eaton Rapids MI
48827

Call Sign: WB8KWQ
Matthew J Mcmillan
6463 W Columbia
Hwy
Eaton Rapids MI
48827

Call Sign: KC8KUF
Noah A Crites
3631 Whittum Rd
Eaton Rapids MI
48827

Call Sign: W8NAC
Noah A Crites
3631 Whittum Rd
Eaton Rapids MI
48827

Call Sign: WA8CSU
Horace K Whittum
4708 Whittum Rd
Eaton Rapids MI
48827

Call Sign: KD8RXN
Thomas M Stumpfig
261 Winding Acres Ln

Eaton Rapids MI
48827

Call Sign: KN8W
Roger A McNutt
540 Wood Ave
Eaton Rapids MI
48827

FCC Amateur Radio Licenses in Eau Claire

Call Sign: KD8JAQ
Rick F Pletz
6645 Black Lake Rd
Eau Claire MI 49111

Call Sign: W8BYC
Blossomland Youth
ARC
7555 E Main St
Eau Claire MI 49111

Call Sign: N8MS
Matthew T Severin
7555 E Main St
Eau Claire MI 49111

Call Sign: KD8JAU
Bryan L Huggins
54632 Estates Ln
Eau Claire MI 49111

Call Sign: K8RQG
John J O Toole
33666 Indian Trl
Eau Claire MI 49111

Call Sign: N8KTJ
Margaret A O Toole
33666 Indian Trl
Eau Claire MI 49111

Call Sign: WA8MIW
Vincent M Lyons
3301 Michael Rd
Eau Claire MI 49111

Call Sign: KB3AID
John P Kent
6514 Naomi Rd
Eau Claire MI 49111

Call Sign: KH6TS
C Murray Robinson
5840 Shanghai Rd
Eau Claire MI 49111

Call Sign: N8RCV
Hilary J Robinson
5840 Shanghai Rd
Eau Claire MI 49111

Call Sign: N8KVT
David W J Robinson
5840 Shanghi Rd
Eau Claire MI 49111

Call Sign: KA8AIW
Rita M Young
6369 W Berrien
Eau Claire MI
491110116

Call Sign: K8HYG
Charles E Young
6369 W Berrien St
Eau Claire MI
491119473

Call Sign: KD8QLU
Matthew J Harrison
Eau Claire MI 49111

FCC Amateur Radio Licenses in Eben Junction

Call Sign: KD8JYJ
Kena M Mceachern
E 3281 Haapala Rd
Eben Junction MI
49825

Call Sign: KD8PHM
Tri County Emergency
Operators Association
E3281 Haapala Rd
Eben Junction MI
49825

Call Sign: K8EOC
Tri County Emergency
Operators Association
E3281 Haapala Rd
Eben Junction MI
49825

Call Sign: KD8KFM
Joshua M Johnson
E3281 Haapala Rd
Eben Junction MI
49825

Call Sign: N8TLD
Brian K McEachern
E3281 Haapala Rd
Eben Junction MI
49825

Call Sign: KD8NPH
Jessica L Johnson
Eben Junction MI
49825

FCC Amateur Radio Licenses in Eckerman

Call Sign: KA8KGR
Daniel D Reattoir
Star Rt 81 Box 20
Eckerman MI 49728

Call Sign: KD8DD
David B Hopper
Star Rt 81 Box 32
Eckerman MI 49728

Call Sign: WD8DKE
Norman J Burlison
5292 N M 123
Eckerman MI 49728

Call Sign: KC8PDT
Manistique Amateur
Radio Association
27872 W M 28
Eckerman MI 49728

Call Sign: KB8MBA
Martha J Baker
32650 W North Shore
Dr
Eckerman MI 49728

FCC Amateur Radio Licenses in Edmore

Call Sign: KC8LIL
Lanny G Graham
8426 Cedar Lake Rd N

Edmore MI 48829

Call Sign: KD8OMH
Jessica M Peterson
949 Cutler NW
Edmore MI 48829

Call Sign: KC8LEQ
Michael A Peterson
949 Cutler NW
Edmore MI 488299750

Call Sign: WB8VWK
Raymond R Peterson
949 Cutler Rd NW
Edmore MI 488299750

Call Sign: WD8NQB
Linda J Peterson
949 Cutler Rd NW
Edmore MI 488299750

Call Sign: N6URK
Thomas M Brun
4603 E Deaner Rd
Edmore MI 48829

Call Sign: N8DE
Donald J Havlicek
1897 E Edgar Rd
Edmore MI 48829

Call Sign: KC8OLQ
Johnmichael B Ayers
1897 E Edgar Rd
Edmore MI 48829

Call Sign: KC8ZMO
Paul R Odem
412 E Forrest St
Edmore MI 48829

Call Sign: KB8DSR
Susan D Hansen
504 E Gilson
Edmore MI 48829

Call Sign: KD8IXL
Alex B Hansen
504 E Gilson
Edmore MI 48829

Call Sign: KD8EMP
Ryan E Williams

6039 E Lake
Montcalm Rd
Edmore MI 48829

Call Sign: KC8KRF
Shawn M Walker
222 N 3rd St
Edmore MI 48829

Call Sign: KC8LIM
Daniel W Graham
7077 N Deja Rd
Edmore MI 48829

Call Sign: KD8LCG
Paul D Wanty Jr
4043 N Waldron Rd
Edmore MI 48829

Call Sign: K8SLG
John L Willard
505 S 2nd St
Edmore MI 48829

Call Sign: W8VIP
Ricky A Byington
1900 Water Wheel
Edmore MI 48829

Call Sign: W6UF
Residence Contesting
Association
Edmore MI 48829

Call Sign: W8OZ
Washtenaw Amateur
Radio Transmitting
Society
Edmore MI 48829

Call Sign: KF4BKC
Brenton C Rogers
Edmore MI 488290521

FCC Amateur Radio Licenses in Edwardsburg

Call Sign: KD8AYD
Douglas L Stickney
68825 8th St
Edwardsburg MI
49112

Call Sign: WD8PRD
Edward E Switalski
70423 Adamsville Rd
Edwardsburg MI
49112

Call Sign: KC7QYL
Jeremy J Fiedler
71090 Brande Creek
Dr
Edwardsburg MI
49112

Call Sign: W8EGK
Robert A Long
68668 Cass St
Edwardsburg MI
491120272

Call Sign: KD8KOR
David J Kiefer Jr
21504 Channel Pkwy
Edwardsburg MI
49112

Call Sign: WA8AZX
Edward B Dowiat
68319 Channel Pkwy
Edwardsburg MI
49112

Call Sign: KA8SMG
Walter R Stitt Sr
69400 Christiana Lake
Rd
Edwardsburg MI
49112

Call Sign: N8FGO
James E Slager
68880 Circle Dr
Edwardsburg MI
49112

Call Sign: WD8IZF
Dawn L Schlamersdorf
66788 Conrad Rd
Edwardsburg MI
49112

Call Sign: WD8IZG
John M Schlamersdorf
66788 Conrad Rd

Edwardsburg MI
49112

Call Sign: WA9YXI
George L Krauser
68396 Dailey Rd
Edwardsburg MI
49112

Call Sign: K9TW
Terry L Wagoner
70341 Elkhart Rd
Edwardsburg MI
49112

Call Sign: KB8YAC
Robert W Newton
69205 Garver Lake Rd
Lot 3
Edwardsburg MI
49112

Call Sign: N9TOT
James W Taylor
69205 Garver Lake Rd
Lot 72
Edwardsburg MI
491129483

Call Sign: KC8PVZ
Richard J Tripp Jr
26843 Hamilton St
Edwardsburg MI
49112

Call Sign: WD8IZH
William A Griffin
67445 Hess Rd
Edwardsburg MI
49112

Call Sign: WA9GZL
Douglas C Fetters
27201 Indigan Ln
Edwardsburg MI
49112

Call Sign: N9MVV
Terry L Gaskill
70034 Kenmore Dr
Edwardsburg MI
491146544

Call Sign: WB8LJD

Douglas R
Stringfellow
67256 M 62
Edwardsburg MI
49112

Call Sign: N8UCQ
Sue Ann Stringfellow
67256 M 62
Edwardsburg MI
49112

Call Sign: WB8ZSW
Jess G Whiting
69425 M 62 E77
Edwardsburg MI
49112

Call Sign: N8URS
Lyle L Pontius
23491 May St
Edwardsburg MI
49112

Call Sign: KC8OMN
Craig Kirkwood
67583 N Shore Dr
Edwardsburg MI
49112

Call Sign: KC8VLW
Dennis A Kroeg
68549 Oak Springs
Edwardsburg MI
49112

Call Sign: KC8VLX
Margie Mark
68549 Oak Springs
Edwardsburg MI
49112

Call Sign: N8UCR
Carolyn L Knoll
70930 Ridgewood Dr
Edwardsburg MI
49112

Call Sign: N8UCS
Sally M Cornwall
70930 Ridgewood Dr
Edwardsburg MI
49112

Call Sign: N8URT
Norma M Wesoloski
70930 Ridgewood Dr
Edwardsburg MI
49112

Call Sign: N0CWY
Gordon K Prieb
21865 Rodway Rd
Edwardsburg MI
49112

Call Sign: W9NCH
Alton D Floyd
23126 S Shore Dr
Edwardsburg MI
49112

Call Sign: KA8GAT
Russel R Eslinger
19992 State Line Rd
Edwardsburg MI
49112

Call Sign: WA8YYH
Charles R Pitts
17301 US 12
Edwardsburg MI
49112

Call Sign: NM9C
Barry L Oberling
25772 US 12
Edwardsburg MI
49112

Call Sign: WB8OMM
Raymond S Homo
22322 US 12 E
Edwardsburg MI
49112

Call Sign: KB8NYT
Jay R Penny
24144 US 12 E
Edwardsburg MI
49112

Call Sign: KD8NIG
James A Houshoulder
19311 US Hwy 12 Lot
26
Edwardsburg MI
49112

Call Sign: KC8KRK
Scott T Doane
25850 Yankee St
Edwardsburg MI
49112

Call Sign: N8UCP
Kevin M English
25850 Yankee St
Edwardsburg MI
49112

Call Sign: N8VZI
Robin K English
25850 Yankee St
Edwardsburg MI
49112

Call Sign: N8XHI
Sabrina H English
25850 Yankee St
Edwardsburg MI
49112

Call Sign: KD8PUK
Charles V Hart
Edwardsburg MI
49112

Call Sign: KD8MYW
John R Beckwith
Edwardsburg MI
49112

FCC Amateur Radio Licenses in Elberta

Call Sign: N8NCW
Paul C Schram
744 Lincoln Ave
Elberta MI 49628

Call Sign: N8YZN
Theodore A McClellan
Sr
705 Washington Ave
Elberta MI 49628

FCC Amateur Radio Licenses in Elk Rapids

Call Sign: W8TEE

Clayton J Heller
613 Maplewood
Elk Rapids MI 49629

Call Sign: N8YAY
Walter W Hensler
822 Miller Park Rd
Elk Rapids MI 49629

Call Sign: K8UEU
Roland P Jones
7958 N Bayshore Dr
Elk Rapids MI 49629

Call Sign: K8WQK
Peter D Van Den
Berge
405 Pine St
Elk Rapids MI 49629

Call Sign: KD8OAK
Phillip P Vandenberge
405 Pine St
Elk Rapids MI 49629

Call Sign: KB8PZV
Richard D Gotts
716 Pine St
Elk Rapids MI 49629

Call Sign: KC8PHL
Brandon C Soule
909 S Bayshore Dr
Elk Rapids MI 49629

Call Sign: KB8WZQ
Kevin B Nelson
6683 Timberlake Dr
Elk Rapids MI 49629

Call Sign: K8OTA
Jeffrey L Miller
Elk Rapids MI 49629

FCC Amateur Radio Licenses in Ellsworth

Call Sign: KJ4OAH
John R Winfield
7026 Best Rd
Ellsworth MI 49729

Call Sign: N8LUL
Kenneth A Semproch

10484 Church Rd
Ellsworth MI 49729

Call Sign: KA8ARL
Alan C Vanniman
Box 29 Essex Rd
Ellsworth MI 49729

Call Sign: N8MJC
Leon J Clancy
9332 N Main St
Ellsworth MI 49729

Call Sign: W8CYO
Elvis E Allen
7247 Rushton Rd
Ellsworth MI 49729

Call Sign: WD8EOU
Ronald R Drenth
88 Sunrise Dr
Ellsworth MI 49729

Call Sign: WD8OHU
Marcia F Drenth
88 Sunrise Dr
Ellsworth MI 49729

Call Sign: WD8MGD
Calvin P Kern
7405 White Pine Dr
Ellsworth MI 49729

FCC Amateur Radio Licenses in Elmira

Call Sign: KA8ZXL
Rosabelle R Hand
3873 Patterson Rd
Elmira MI 49730

Call Sign: KB8PHP
Thomas E McClusky
9618 Valleyway Dr
Elmira MI 49730

Call Sign: KC8TGC
Christopher M Davis
8378 Van Tyle Rd
Elmira MI 49730

Call Sign: KD8CHH
Jeanne M Davis
8378 Van Tyle Rd

Elmira MI 49730

Call Sign: KD8FQP
Northern Michigan
ARES
8378 Van Tyle Rd
Elmira MI 497309717

Call Sign: NM8ES
Northern Michigan
ARES
8378 Van Tyle Rd
Elmira MI 497309717

Call Sign: KC8NTE
James E Davis
8378 Van Tyle Rd
Elmira MI 497309717

Call Sign: KD8CHF
Melissa M Meadows
8607 Van Tyle Rd
Elmira MI 49730

Call Sign: KD8CCS
Donald E Meadows
8607 Van Tyle Rd
Elmira MI 49730

Call Sign: KD8IHJ
Daniel A Morris
3829 Webster Rd
Elmira MI 49730

Call Sign: N8YDA
Charles A Ulmer
10763 Woodward Rd
Elmira MI 49730

Call Sign: KB8PHQ
Andrew J Le Pain
Elmira MI 49730

FCC Amateur Radio Licenses in Elsie

Call Sign: WB8JLR
Lowell V Lockwood
126 E Pine
Elsie MI 48831

Call Sign: KA8OOH
Blair V Daley
421 S Ovid St

Elsie MI 48831

Call Sign: KB8MAE
Evelyn N Kern
8145 S Shepardsville
Rd
Elsie MI 48831

Call Sign: N8GPZ
Gary M Burton
8030 W Henderson Rd
Elsie MI 48831

Call Sign: KD8EYP
Timothy G Dunsmore
20185 W Peet
Elsie MI 48831

Call Sign: KD8EYM
Melissa M Ferrante
20185 W Peet Rd
Elsie MI 48831

FCC Amateur Radio Licenses in Empire

Call Sign: KD8GOM
David W Brockette Sr
16759 Pettengill
Empire MI 49630

Call Sign: KC8WRV
Ian J Wagner
12855 S Coleman Rd
Empire MI 49630

Call Sign: W8HPJ
David W Jeris
11391 S Hermies Pass
Empire MI 49630

Call Sign: N8KKA
Carolyn J Ballmer
11042 S Lacore
Empire MI 49630

Call Sign: K8NTK
Robert B Ballmer
11042 S Lacore
Empire MI 49630

Call Sign: N2LAH
George W McCue Jr
11886 S Lake St

Empire MI 49630

Call Sign: KF8KK
John S Martin
5375 W Beeman Rd
Empire MI 49630

Call Sign: N8NCO
Edward J Martin
5375 W Beeman Rd
Empire MI 49630

Call Sign: KD8PUT
Cynthia S Pomerleau
Empire MI 49630

Call Sign: W2AXO
Cynthia S Pomerleau
Empire MI 49630

Call Sign: K8EV
Ovide F Pomerleau
Empire MI 49630

Call Sign: K8SRO
Jane L Hastings
Lot 33 Block C
Engadine MI 49827

Call Sign: KC8ZHF
Peter J Poole
N 7531 Pleasant Ave
Engadine MI 49827

Call Sign: KC8ZYL
Sallee A Poole
N 7531 Pleasant Ave
Engadine MI 49827

Call Sign: W8PVU
Frank F Hastings
Engadine MI 49827

Call Sign: K8RRD
Allan C Erno
Engadine MI 49827

Call Sign: WA8LKW
Audrey J Erno
Engadine MI 49827

Call Sign: KD8IGY
Dennis E Menard
4542 12th Rd
Escanaba MI 49829

Call Sign: N8GWM
Bruce G Taylor
5027 12th Rd
Escanaba MI 49829

Call Sign: KA8WOF
Denise A Sayklly
2911 14th Ave S
Escanaba MI 49829

Call Sign: KA8WOH
Edward J Sayklly
3117 14th Ave S
Escanaba MI 49829

Call Sign: K8GMW
Donald R Brackenbury
1636 16th Ave S
Escanaba MI 49829

Call Sign: KD8DKA
Michael J Brackenbury
1636 16th Ave S
Escanaba MI 49829

Call Sign: KD8NPG
Matthew G Spreitzer
1619 17th Ave S
Escanaba MI 49829

Call Sign: KB8BTI
Bonnie A Hakkola
1707 17th Ave S
Escanaba MI 49829

Call Sign: KB8BWV
Jack L Hakkola
1707 17th Ave S
Escanaba MI 49829

Call Sign: KA8IHT
Leonard A Gerou Sr
2323 18th Ave S
Escanaba MI 49829

Call Sign: WD8IXZ

Sandra L Chapman
4739 18th Rd
Escanaba MI 49829

Call Sign: WD8IYA
Eric W Chapman
4739 18th Rd
Escanaba MI 49829

Call Sign: N8YFY
Scott A Williams
4788 18th Rd
Escanaba MI 49829

Call Sign: KD8BDL
Jesse L Pepin
4860 18th Rd
Escanaba MI 49829

Call Sign: W8KBH
Orville M Jensen
2701 1st Ave S Apt
321
Escanaba MI 49829

Call Sign: N8HUX
John V La Porte
2127 21st Ave S
Escanaba MI 49829

Call Sign: WA8KEF
Edward H Gadnis
421 2nd Ave S
Escanaba MI
498293935

Call Sign: KD8NDP
Cory J Kennedy
2004 5th Ave S
Escanaba MI 49829

Call Sign: KB8FCV
Terry A Anderson
1722 8th Ave S
Escanaba MI 49829

Call Sign: KC8OJQ
John S Merki
5050 Alyssa 17 04 St
Escanaba MI 49829

Call Sign: KD8NSS
Stephen W Merki
5050 Alyssa 17 04 St

Escanaba MI 49829

Call Sign: KD8KKO
John S Merki
5050 Alyssa St
Escanaba MI 49829

Call Sign: WD8RCN
John A Sviland
310 And Ave S
Escanaba MI 49829

Call Sign: KD8PRR
William J Gartner
4673 Bayberry 16 65
Dr
Escanaba MI 49829

Call Sign: KG8SQ
Lysle L Elder
6985 G 75 Ln
Escanaba MI 49829

Call Sign: WA8LE
Lysle L Elder
6985 G 75 Ln
Escanaba MI 49829

Call Sign: N8XAI
Thomas A McGugan
4087 Hwy US 2 And
41
Escanaba MI 49829

Call Sign: N8JOP
Robert M Taylor
5566 J 5 Rd
Escanaba MI 49829

Call Sign: WB8ZLP
Raymond L Erickson
5619 J Rd
Escanaba MI 49829

Call Sign: KC8SFL
Richard C Deno
5386 K Ln
Escanaba MI 49829

Call Sign: KC8HGC
Patrick R Ness
3723 L 15 Ln
Escanaba MI 49829

Call Sign: N8PN
Patrick R Ness
3723 L 15 Ln
Escanaba MI 49829

Call Sign: KD8KKT
Roy P Chenier
6954 L 5 Ln
Escanaba MI 49829

Call Sign: WA9KEU
James M Meinken
404 Lake Shore Dr
Escanaba MI 49829

Call Sign: W8KEU
James M Meinken
404 Lake Shore Dr
Escanaba MI 49829

Call Sign: KD8KKP
Richard L Hendrickson
516 Lake Shore Dr
Escanaba MI 49829

Call Sign: KD8KKU
Marilyn H Kinsey
630 Lake Shore Dr
Escanaba MI 49829

Call Sign: KD8MK
Marilyn H Kinsey
630 Lake Shore Dr
Escanaba MI 49829

Call Sign: N8ZBI
William A Harris
1005 Lake Shore Dr
Escanaba MI 49829

Call Sign: N8MCO
Terry L Allis
2515 Lake Shore Dr
Escanaba MI 49829

Call Sign: N8MCP
Rosalind E Allis
2515 Lake Shore Dr
Escanaba MI 49829

Call Sign: W8CQG
Sergio F Dreon
5044 Ln 17 7 Dr
Escanaba MI 49829

Call Sign: N8XAH
Mark D Seymour
2425 Ludington St 251
Escanaba MI
498291328

Call Sign: KB8QYH
Scott A Coppock
4387 M Rd
Escanaba MI 49829

Call Sign: W8LSZ
Rene A Marcoe
5227 N 1785 Kurth Dr
Escanaba MI 49829

Call Sign: KA8JLS
Robert E Farrell
1221 N 18th St
Escanaba MI 49829

Call Sign: KA8EBY
Sherrie A Johnson
500 N 19th St
Escanaba MI 49829

Call Sign: N8MCS
David W Johnson
500 N 19th St
Escanaba MI 49829

Call Sign: N8YP
Jeremy R Reese
1401 N 23rd St 153
Escanaba MI 49829

Call Sign: KA8PCE
Edward T Reynolds
215 Ogden Ave
Escanaba MI 49829

Call Sign: WU8S
Dean L Nelson
517 Ogden Ave
Escanaba MI 49829

Call Sign: KD8DKC
Ken D Leduc
6376 Poplar St
Escanaba MI 49829

Call Sign: KD8DKB
Michael S Leduc

6376 Poplar St
Escanaba MI 49829

Call Sign: W8ZMQ
Jack W Foster
1004 S 10th St
Escanaba MI 49829

Call Sign: N8NFO
Wyatt E Dean
800 S 11th St Apt C4
Escanaba MI 49829

Call Sign: KD8IGU
Grant W Heslip
808 S 13th St
Escanaba MI 49829

Call Sign: K8MJK
Thomas F Elegeert
1403 S 13th St
Escanaba MI 49829

Call Sign: N8XAJ
James C Bauer
806 S 14th St
Escanaba MI 49829

Call Sign: N8KFR
Mike R Duchaine
1600 S 14th St
Escanaba MI 49829

Call Sign: KC8ZDY
Steve A Fritz
510 S 15th St
Escanaba MI 49829

Call Sign: KA8ECK
Mark L Carter
1607 S 15th St
Escanaba MI 49829

Call Sign: KA9EVK
Roy D Hebert
916 S 16th St
Escanaba MI 49829

Call Sign: KD8KKQ
Jason R Germain
212 S 17th St
Escanaba MI 49829

Call Sign: W8ZMN

Henry C Olsen
818 S 19 St
Escanaba MI 49829

Call Sign: W8HTK
James F Sarasin
604 S 20th St
Escanaba MI 49829

Call Sign: KC8MSW
John A Martin Jr
1600 S 30th Lot 152
Escanaba MI 49829

Call Sign: KA8IHU
Rex V Coulter
1600 S 30th Lot 21
Escanaba MI 49829

Call Sign: K8QHA
James R Emerson
1600 S 30th St 49
Escanaba MI 49829

Call Sign: KD8PRQ
John M Izzi
314 S 8th St
Escanaba MI 49829

Call Sign: NK8N
Gerald D Shapy
520 S 8th St
Escanaba MI 49829

Call Sign: KB8URY
Justin L Olsen
509 S 9th St
Escanaba MI 49829

Call Sign: N8VBA
Marshall C Seawright
5256 S Kurth Dr
Escanaba MI 49829

Call Sign: K8IKC
Ronald D Mantel
500 Stephenson
Escanaba MI 49829

Call Sign: N8JCC
Edward F Christensen
5077 View Dr 17 5
Escanaba MI 49829

Call Sign: KB8TOS
David E Linnee
4935 Whisper 18 8 Ln
Escanaba MI 49829

Call Sign: KB8FCU
Warren L Isaacson
1110 Willow Creek Rd
Escanaba MI 49829

Call Sign: KD8KKS
Norbert B Berg
1620 Willow Creek Rd
Lot E127
Escanaba MI 49829

Call Sign: AA8DE
Leon E Kinasiewicz
Escanaba MI 49829

Call Sign: KB9BQX
Robert J Derbisz
Escanaba MI 49829

Call Sign: KD8LWU
Jennifer M Derbisz
Escanaba MI 49829

Call Sign: KD8FIX
Ronald A Derbisz Sr
Escanaba MI 49829

FCC Amateur Radio Licenses in Evart

Call Sign: KC0WJO
Mark J Carey
12550 110th Ave
Evart MI 49631

Call Sign: KC8VSA
G Lenore Snyder
3858 125th Ave
Evart MI 49631

Call Sign: KB8FJB
Albert J Snyder
3858 125th Ave
Evart MI 496311003

Call Sign: AA8WD
Leo J Rosneck
6444 70th Ave
Evart MI 49631

Call Sign: N8HVR
James L Jennings
20670 70th Ave
Evart MI 49631

Call Sign: KA8EFG
Richard J Mann
9781 Cheynne Trl
Evart MI 49631

Call Sign: K8IXP
Dale V Dennis
12273 N 30th
Evart MI 49631

Call Sign: KD8EHK
Samantha J Cass
236 N Pine
Evart MI 49631

Call Sign: W8NPC
Neal E Beach
11177 S River Rd
Evart MI 49631

Call Sign: KD8KPY
Wayne W Stevens
308 W 6th St
Evart MI 49631

FCC Amateur Radio Licenses in Ewen

Call Sign: AA8YF
Ted A Trudgeon
Rt 1 Box 7
Ewen MI 49925

Call Sign: KC8SZV
Heather R Trudgeon
Rte 1 Box 7
Ewen MI 49925

Call Sign: KC8NUH
Sean P Trudgeon
20126 Trudgeon
Ewen MI 49925

Call Sign: KC8PRP
Scott P Trudgeon
20126 Trudgeon Rd
Ewen MI 49925

FCC Amateur Radio Licenses in Fairview

Call Sign: W8HML
Russell C Watrous
2150 E Helmer Lake
Rd
Fairview MI 48621

Call Sign: KD8EHF
Allen G Mitchell
1888 Esch Dr
Fairview MI 48621

Call Sign: N8ISV
Linda M Volz
1323 N Abbe Rd
Fairview MI 48621

Call Sign: WT8G
Gerald R Volz
1323 N Abbe Rd
Fairview MI
486219730

Call Sign: WB8UDI
James A Lupo
819 N Perry Creek Rd
Fairview MI 48621

Call Sign: KD8KNN
Thomas H Jenkins
2219 Pearsall Rd
Fairview MI 48621

Call Sign: KB8KLX
David L Diener
Fairview MI 48621

Call Sign: KB8TMP
Jon W Longacre
Fairview MI 48621

Call Sign: KD8BTN
Ruth A Miller
Fairview MI 48621

FCC Amateur Radio Licenses in Falmouth

Call Sign: KC8OHC
Robert J Ray
2649 9 Mile Rd
Falmouth MI 49632

Call Sign: KC8WON
Terry E Laughlin
4100 S 9 Mile
Falmouth MI 49632

FCC Amateur Radio Licenses in Farwell

Call Sign: N8POY
William R Clark
3183 Apple Tree Ln
Farwell MI 48622

Call Sign: N8TFA
Darryl W Johns
1899 Autumn Dr
Farwell MI 48622

Call Sign: KA8UCK
Carleton A German
2954 Birch Isle
Farwell MI 48622

Call Sign: W8YNV
Edmund T Hines
8608 Coolidge
Farwell MI 48622

Call Sign: KG8XS
Donald R Shepard
2124 E Surrey Dr
Farwell MI 486220262

Call Sign: KE8WI
Russell E Kuespert
300 E Surrey Rd
Farwell MI 48622

Call Sign: KA8AUQ
George P Zemke
3250 Juniper Dr
Farwell MI 48622

Call Sign: KC8ZWO
Dennis J Rhoads
393 Mill St Apt H
Farwell MI 48622

Call Sign: N8ARI
Harold D Lockwood
3060 N Co Line Rd
Farwell MI 48622

Call Sign: N8GDJ
Richard C Glass
5421 Oak Run
Farwell MI 48622

Call Sign: W8ALO
James D Hart
2257 Oakridge Dr
Farwell MI 48622

Call Sign: KB8NPE
Marcella J Lewis
2155 Pine St
Farwell MI 48622

Call Sign: WD8MQR
Lawrence C Witbeck
9990 S Harrison Ave
Farwell MI 48622

Call Sign: KC8PPP
Keith C Campbell
10113 S Harrison Ave
Farwell MI 48622

Call Sign: KC8AZE
David G Fullerton
4363 W Battle
Farwell MI 48622

Call Sign: KD8AXH
David K Fullarton
3958 W Beck Rd
Farwell MI 48622

Call Sign: K8DKF
David K Fullarton
3958 W Beck Rd
Farwell MI 48622

Call Sign: KB8PBQ
Sharon A Glass
3501 W Coleman Rd
Farwell MI 48622

Call Sign: K8GUS
Gustave H Glass
3501 W Coleman Rd
Farwell MI 48622

Call Sign: N8VYQ
Gustave H Glass
3501 W Coleman Rd
Farwell MI 486229508

Call Sign: AA8RO
Frank G Kuhles Jr
1809 W Grass Lake Rd
Farwell MI 486229530

Call Sign: W8PZQ
Howard J Klinger
3131 W Huckleberry R
1
Farwell MI 48622

Call Sign: N8YBF
Barry C Babcock
1979 W Maple Grove
Rd
Farwell MI 48622

Call Sign: KA8ROS
Patricia L Francis
2610 W Washington
Farwell MI 48622

Call Sign: WB8ZNO
Terrell L Francis
2610 W Washington
Farwell MI 48622

Call Sign: N8FHK
Kenneth L Hardin
441 Washington Rd
Farwell MI 486229402

Call Sign: N8XJG
John M Wegner
7501 White Birch Dr
Farwell MI 48622

Call Sign: N5MUS
Robert J Mannion
7711 White Birch Dr
Farwell MI 48622

Call Sign: N8YVX
James R Kennedy
1050 Ziggy Rd
Farwell MI 48622

Call Sign: KC8YZP
Areca
Farwell MI 48622

Call Sign: KA8TGC
Phyllis L Palmer

Farwell MI 48622

Call Sign: NE8I
Lloyd J Ellsworth
Farwell MI 486220202

Call Sign: KB8VEN
Linda Y Le Quia
N7531 Lucas Rd
Felch MI 498318834

Call Sign: WD9HDP
F D Le Quia
N7531 Lucas Rd
Felch MI 498318834

Call Sign: KB8FFY
Philip E Logsdon
6550 113th Ave
Fennville MI 49408

Call Sign: NN8C
Dennis M Dodge
6981 116th Ave
Fennville MI 49408

Call Sign: KD8BBM
Debbie C Dodge
6981 116th Ave
Fennville MI 49408

Call Sign: WB8FAL
Debbie C Dodge
6981 116th Ave
Fennville MI 49408

Call Sign: N8UYD
John M Byrne
5601 120th Ave
Fennville MI 49408

Call Sign: KC8OOV
William B Brownlee
6339 122nd Ave
Fennville MI 49408

Call Sign: KB8VZB
Billy P Baty

6645 122nd Ave
Fennville MI 49408

Call Sign: N8GJA
Cletus W Jones
6661 122nd Ave
Fennville MI 49408

Call Sign: KC8EGK
Dick H Miles
5328 123rd Ave
Fennville MI 49408

Call Sign: KD8ATT
David M Baarman
6414 127th Ave
Fennville MI 49408

Call Sign: KE8JA
Douglas J Patosky
6676 129th Ave
Fennville MI 49408

Call Sign: WB3AXR
James M Lytle
2746 54th St
Fennville MI 49408

Call Sign: KA8JXY
William D Childs
1311 56th St
Fennville MI 49408

Call Sign: KC8HBR
Leslie G Morehead Jr
2923 56th St
Fennville MI 49408

Call Sign: WD9DPP
James P Mastalerz
2960 57th St
Fennville MI 49408

Call Sign: KD8PJP
Scott C Batey
2331 58th St
Fennville MI 49408

Call Sign: KB8ZCX
Daniel L Westveld
2714 58th St
Fennville MI 49408

Call Sign: WB8ASK

Richard A Guilfoil
2908 62nd St Rte 2
Box 14
Fennville MI 49408

Call Sign: KB8SOH
Paul Sisson
2483 63rd St
Fennville MI 49408

Call Sign: KC8UUO
Norman H Slimmer Jr
2895 63rd St
Fennville MI
494089606

Call Sign: W2DKX
Norman H Slimmer Jr
2895 63rd St
Fennville MI
494089606

Call Sign: N8FWG
James R Marshall
1326 66th St
Fennville MI 49408

Call Sign: AK8A
Steven Batema
1567 66th St
Fennville MI 49408

Call Sign: N8EMV
Paula L Batema
1567 66th St
Fennville MI 49408

Call Sign: WA8DEX
Alfred J Van Til
1857 70th St
Fennville MI 49408

Call Sign: WA8OCD
Marion A Van Til
1857 70th St
Fennville MI 49408

Call Sign: W8PQO
Charles E Spencer
705 E Main St
Fennville MI
494080173

Call Sign: KI8JH

Daniel G Keuhs
463 Hickory Dr
Fennville MI 49408

Call Sign: AB8VK
Daniel G Keuhs
463 Hickory Dr
Fennville MI 49408

Call Sign: WB3BRA
Thomas L Konvolinka
6530 Leos Ln
Fennville MI 49408

Call Sign: N8ZFZ
Vaughn M Faust
2562 N 58th St
Fennville MI 49408

Call Sign: KD8HEM
Kyle A Nelson
2680 Old Allegan Rd
Fennville MI 49408

Call Sign: N8SKA
James H Bailey
2722 Old Allegan Rd
Fennville MI 49408

Call Sign: N8YFJ
Kathy Bailey
2722 Old Allegan Rd
Fennville MI 49408

Call Sign: KC8FWL
Richard P Betz
65-1 Wiley Ct
Fennville MI 49408

Call Sign: W8QBY
Theodore Chinalski
Fennville MI 49408

Call Sign: KB8YTR
James R Johnson
Fennville MI 49408

**FCC Amateur Radio
Licenses in Fenwick**

Call Sign: WD8CXE
Daniel L Pettengill
9300 Amsden Rd
Fenwick MI 48834

Call Sign: KB8NLT
Robert A Parks I
10670 S Brown Rd
Fenwick MI 48834

Call Sign: KC8CUQ
George M Deible
11202 S Vickeryville
Rd
Fenwick MI 48834

Call Sign: KC8FAT
Gaynell Deible
11202 S Vickeryville
Rd
Fenwick MI 48834

**FCC Amateur Radio
Licenses in
Ferrysburg**

Call Sign: KB8ODB
Donald A Meyer
Ferrysburg MI 49409

**FCC Amateur Radio
Licenses in Fife Lake**

Call Sign: KC8ELH
Warren J Brown
12281 13 Mile Rd
Fife Lake MI 49633

Call Sign: KD8BOC
Rodney A Schema
662 Birgy Rd
Fife Lake MI 49633

Call Sign: K8VAJ
William E Harvey Jr
1011A Creighton Rd
Fife Lake MI 49633

Call Sign: N8FD
Russ M Rinckey
8611 E Sparling Rd
Fife Lake MI 49633

Call Sign: N8STU
Suzanne M Rinckey
8611 E Sparling Rd
Fife Lake MI 49633

Call Sign: KC8NXI
Jason E Rinckey
8611 E Sparling Rd
Fife Lake MI 49633

Call Sign: KB8RIW
Jeanine R Ritter
5200 Gallatin Rd SW
Fife Lake MI 49633

Call Sign: KE5HF
David L Ritter
5200 Gallatin Rd SW
Fife Lake MI 49633

Call Sign: KD8FRV
Chad R Lytle
13716 Grand Kal
Fife Lake MI 49633

Call Sign: N8STV
David W Gill
12359 Grecian Rd SW
Fife Lake MI 49633

Call Sign: WD8ELC
Leonard E
Nowakowski
1266 Hatley Rd SE
Fife Lake MI 49633

Call Sign: KC8LFN
Elmer L Minthorn
7352 Ingersoll Rd
Fife Lake MI 49633

Call Sign: KC8NOZ
Matthew L Flaska
3776 Ingersoll Rd SW
Fife Lake MI 49633

Call Sign: WD8MPQ
Allan D Scott
7126 Ingersoll Rd SW
Fife Lake MI 49633

Call Sign: KC8HEC
Michael W Keeley
3081 Lund Rd SW
Fife Lake MI 49633

Call Sign: KD8BGZ
Michael W Keeley
3081 Lund Rd SW

Fife Lake MI 49633

Call Sign: KD8CVO
Donald M Blake
9775 M 66 SE
Fife Lake MI 49633

Call Sign: KD8BNM
Kurt T Mcginess
10672 M 66 SW
Fife Lake MI 49633

Call Sign: K8TTE
North Country
Amateur Radio
Association
9396 Raspberry Rdg
SW
Fife Lake MI 49633

Call Sign: KT8L
David M Gillahan
9396 Raspberry Ridge
SW
Fife Lake MI 49633

Call Sign: KD8KQA
John W Hulbert
3366 Seneca Ln SE
Fife Lake MI 49633

Call Sign: KC8AUE
David O Calkins
2627 Sharon Rd SE
Fife Lake MI 49633

Call Sign: N8ZRZ
Alfred A Rugenstein
11184 Shippy Rd SW
Fife Lake MI 49633

Call Sign: WA8WFA
Pamela L McNamara
13663 Spring Creek
Rd
Fife Lake MI 49633

Call Sign: N8ISQ
Mervin D Twigg
8678 Twiff Cir
Fife Lake MI 49633

Call Sign: KC8ZAU
Richard J Matley

8738 Vallad Rd
Fife Lake MI 49633

Call Sign: KG8CU
Johnny R North
10680 Vans Ln
Fife Lake MI 49633

Call Sign: W8KAL
Johnny R North
10680 Vans Ln
Fife Lake MI 49633

Call Sign: KC8QAO
Daniel T Hough
1473 W Sharon Rd SE
Fife Lake MI 49633

Call Sign: KC8SZX
Matt D Hough
1473 W Sharon Rd SE
Fife Lake MI 49633

Call Sign: KC8UPV
David J Briggs
11485 Waterhole Crk
Fife Lake MI 49633

Call Sign: KC8LFQ
Patrick J Stuck
4410 Willow Creek Ln
Fife Lake MI 49633

Call Sign: W0RJW
Edward E Hungness
Fife Lake MI 49633

FCC Amateur Radio Licenses in Foster City

Call Sign: KC8CKX
James L Faulkner
W2692 Finntown Rd
Foster City MI 49834

FCC Amateur Radio Licenses in Fountain

Call Sign: WB8ZFE
Robert S Buckley
7154 E Hansen Rd
Fountain MI 49410

Call Sign: KD8IIJ
Amel Posner IV
6463 E Stolberg Rd
Fountain MI 49410

Call Sign: WS9H
Michael W Schaefer
6145 Griffin Rd
Fountain MI 49410

Call Sign: KA8ATV
Norman L Hankins
2007 N Benson Rd
Fountain MI 49410

Call Sign: KC8OTI
Allen D Alter
1940 N Campbell
Fountain MI 49410

Call Sign: AA8PT
Otto W Wendt
6717 N Claeys Dr
Fountain MI 49410

Call Sign: AA8WC
Rogene A Wendt
6717 N Claeys Dr
Fountain MI
494109775

Call Sign: KD8LVO
Bruce A Tamulis
5180 N Ford Lake Rd
Fountain MI 49410

Call Sign: KC8CDW
Daniel L Miller
4827 N Larson Rd
Fountain MI 49410

Call Sign: K8HU
Daniel L Miller
4827 N Larson Rd
Fountain MI 49410

Call Sign: N8WEU
Jenice E Heckman
3945 N Morse Rd
Fountain MI 49410

Call Sign: WG0W
Joseph A Jurkowski
3945 N Morse Rd

Fountain MI 49410

Call Sign: N8FXT
Robert Rickert
6725 Sugar Grove Rd
Fountain MI 49410

FCC Amateur Radio Licenses in Fowler

Call Sign: WD8ONK
Francis J Martin
5729 S Jones Rd
Fowler MI 48835

FCC Amateur Radio Licenses in Frankfort

Call Sign: KC8LBP
Benjamin R Mac Rae
2977 Forrester Rd
Frankfort MI 49635

Call Sign: N8ACX
Benjamin R Mac Rae
2977 Forrester Rd
Frankfort MI 49635

Call Sign: KD8CJV
Jeanne L Amond
1960 Frankfort Hwy
Frankfort MI 49635

Call Sign: KC8ONA
Kerry D Swisher
4882 Joyfield Rd
Frankfort MI 49635

Call Sign: KD8BXK
Dorothy J Meier
5570 Lake Ridge Tr
Frankfort MI 49635

Call Sign: KD8BXJ
Theodore J Meier
5570 Lake Ridge Tr
Frankfort MI 49635

Call Sign: N8CG
Gene E Hutson
641 Michigan Ave 206
Frankfort MI 49635

Call Sign: N8KMH

Shannon W Fisk
2292 Pilgrim Hwy
Frankfort MI
496359502

Call Sign: AA4R
William C Parris
1409 S Shore E
Frankfort MI 49635

Call Sign: N4NPT
Joetta R Parris
1409 S Shore E
Frankfort MI 49635

Call Sign: KJ4RZH
John L O'Neal
261 Standish Rd
Frankfort MI 49635

Call Sign: N8XSK
Thomas C Warren
Frankfort MI 49635

Call Sign: KC8YVX
Benzie Amateur Radio
Friends
Frankfort MI 49635

Call Sign: W8NBZ
Benzie Amateur Radio
Friends
Frankfort MI 49635

Call Sign: W8BNZ
Benzie Amateur Radio
Friends
Frankfort MI 49635

Call Sign: KB8MAW
John W Seymour
Frankfort MI 49635

Call Sign: KH2KD
Birchard H Ohlinger
Frankfort MI 49635

Call Sign: WB8PDV
Lucius E Smith
Frankfort MI 49635

Call Sign: KC8SZA
John W Seymour
Frankfort MI 49635

Call Sign: KC8SZM
Luann E Sheridan
Seymour
Frankfort MI 49635

Call Sign: AB8MM
John W Seymour
Frankfort MI 49635

Call Sign: KD8QYE
Richard C Bayer
Frankfort MI 49635

Call Sign: W8VWY
Marion J Stoner
Frankfort MI
496352220

FCC Amateur Radio Licenses in Frederic

Call Sign: KB8LDN
Bryan D Scott
Rt 1 Box 108 Old 27
Frederic MI 49733

Call Sign: KD8ORS
Donna J Pratt
7448 Evans St
Frederic MI 49733

Call Sign: KD8ORT
David J Pratt
6512 Hazelwood Ln
Frederic MI 49733

Call Sign: KB8YBR
Carl G Dallmann
6769 Hiawatha
Frederic MI 49733

Call Sign: WB8CEU
Donald G Hewson
6885 N Hiawatha Dr
Frederic MI 49733

Call Sign: N8ECF
Katherine E Cauvin
6461 N Uppnorthe Dr
Frederic MI 49733

Call Sign: N8ORZ
James R Stevens

7449 W Batterson Rd
Frederic MI 49733

Call Sign: KB8TNZ
Jordan A Hall
Frederic MI 49733

Call Sign: KC8ELI
James R Owens
Frederic MI 49733

Call Sign: KC8GCG
Ivan Kirko
Frederic MI 49733

Call Sign: KD8OWC
Bennie J Pratt
Frederic MI 49733

Call Sign: KD8OTJ
Judy K Hammond
Frederic MI 49733

FCC Amateur Radio Licenses in Free Soil

Call Sign: KD8LBO
John Thomas
1894 E Gajeski Rd
Free Soil MI 49411

Call Sign: KD8LBN
Kim M Thomas
1894 E Gajeski Rd
Free Soil MI 49411

Call Sign: N8HVG
Richard L Persinger
304 E Hoague Rd
Free Soil MI 49411

Call Sign: KA9RLF
Michael A Beres
6939 N Poplar Rd
Free Soil MI 49411

Call Sign: K9SDL
Michael A Beres
6939 N Poplar Rd
Free Soil MI 49411

Call Sign: N9DNE
Richard D Blanchong
Sr

6922 N US 31
Free Soil MI 49411

Call Sign: WA8AZB
George E Ward
10553 N US 31
Free Soil MI 49411

Call Sign: KC8TSD
Deborah A Reed
5040 S County Line
Rd
Free Soil MI 49411

Call Sign: WD8DID
Chris D Williams
5040 S County Line
Rd
Free Soil MI 49411

Call Sign: WB8CPW
Kenneth G Rosenow Jr
725 W Freesoil Rd
Free Soil MI 49411

Call Sign: WB8FFB
Elizabeth M Rosenow
725 W Freesoil Rd
Free Soil MI 49411

FCC Amateur Radio Licenses in Freeport

Call Sign: KA8SVV
Orelo C Kohl
Rr 1 Box 287A Eckert
Rd
Freeport MI
493259801

Call Sign: N8RGL
Linda K Robinson
377 Cherry St
Freeport MI 49325

Call Sign: KC8RO
Fred E Korevec
220 Cressey St
Freeport MI 49325

Call Sign: N8DOI
Vivian M Korevec
220 Cressey St
Freeport MI 49325

Call Sign: N8LCU
Ivan F Bourn
7301 Solomon Rd
Freeport MI 49325

Call Sign: KD8AYB
James R Yarger
1451 W Sisson Rd
Freeport MI
493259710

Call Sign: K8JRY
James R Yarger
1451 W Sisson Rd
Freeport MI
493259710

FCC Amateur Radio Licenses in Fremont

Call Sign: KA8EYP
Robert J Pinder
3315 Baldwin Ave
Fremont MI 49412

Call Sign: WB9AFJ
Carol A Frodey
4345 Chippewa Trl
Fremont MI 49412

Call Sign: WB8MCR
Ray C Frodey
4345 Chippewa Trl
Fremont MI 49412

Call Sign: KC8HSW
Victoria S Wilkinson
206 Connie Ave
Fremont MI 49412

Call Sign: WB8VSP
Harry H Schultz
6406 Croswell
Fremont MI 49412

Call Sign: N8KYI
John L Webster
621 E Oak St
Fremont MI
494121766

Call Sign: KC8NCA
Philip R Wilcox

6060 Fitzgerald Ave
Fremont MI 49412

Call Sign: KB8BCU
John C Evanick
5653 Green Ave
Fremont MI 49412

Call Sign: KB8TWT
David M Brake
1801 Kparson
Fremont MI 49412

Call Sign: W8VN
Clarence O Henderson Jr
7254 Lake Dr
Fremont MI 49412

Call Sign: WA8NNL
Leslie M Lee II
459 Mary Ln
Fremont MI 49412

Call Sign: N8EJH
Douglas A Woodring
20 Meadow Hills Ln
Fremont MI 49412

Call Sign: WD8DCA
Leo J Woodard
304 N Stone Rd
Fremont MI 49412

Call Sign: KB8PHR
Thomas D Oliver
7538 Orchard Cir
Fremont MI 49412

Call Sign: KB8KGK
Ronald L Mercer
2960 Parson Ave
Fremont MI 49412

Call Sign: KD8EBB
Philip D Deur
6150 Pat St
Fremont MI 49412

Call Sign: N8KCH
Melvin E Wilcox
9311 S Brucker
Fremont MI
494129137

Call Sign: KC8NFP
Deborah Wilcox
9311 S Bruckner
Fremont MI 49412

Call Sign: KB8VCB
Leanne M Black
3538 S Croswell
Fremont MI 49412

Call Sign: KG8XW
Andrew R Black
3538 S Croswell
Fremont MI 49412

Call Sign: KC8HSZ
Floyd J Franklin
3551 S Gordon Ave
Fremont MI 49412

Call Sign: KC8RZR
Kenneth J Stroven
1284 S Green Ave
Fremont MI 49412

Call Sign: KC8JNJ
Bruce J Soloway
4124 S Green Ave
Fremont MI 49412

Call Sign: KB8PHU
Richard E Schondelmayer
4453 S Green Ave
Fremont MI 49412

Call Sign: KA8CMO
Neal A Tedford
6211 S Green Ave
Fremont MI 49412

Call Sign: K8SHP
Neal A Tedford
6211 S Green Ave
Fremont MI 49412

Call Sign: KC8JNG
Scott Woodring
3515 S Osborn
Fremont MI 49412

Call Sign: KC8RQQ
Darlene R Woodring

3515 S Osborn
Fremont MI 49412

Call Sign: KA8KAW
Bruce R Barton
4365 S Parsons Ave
Fremont MI 49412

Call Sign: AB8QH
Linda L Rosenthal
1490 S Stone Rd
Fremont MI 49412

Call Sign: WA8M
Linda L Rosenthal
1490 S Stone Rd
Fremont MI 49412

Call Sign: AB8SC
William Fries Jr
1490 S Stone Rd
Fremont MI 49412

Call Sign: NA8M
William Fries Jr
1490 S Stone Rd
Fremont MI 49412

Call Sign: KC8HTA
Angela B Morton
8510 S Warner Ave
Fremont MI 49412

Call Sign: KA8CUT
Nancy K Wilkinson
8510 S Warner Ave
Fremont MI
494120281

Call Sign: N8ACL
James O Wilkinson
8510 S Warner Ave
Fremont MI
494120281

Call Sign: W8MHM
Robert L Zeller Sr
3947 Shorewood Dr
Fremont MI 49412

Call Sign: KD8AR
Gerald L Woodring
604 State St 1
Fremont MI 49412

Call Sign: KD8JZL
Kevin E Johnson
845 Valley Ave
Fremont MI 49412

Call Sign: KB8BCS
Curt A Crandell
428 Vista Ln
Fremont MI 49412

Call Sign: KB6VHJ
Glenn H Hymer
8885 W 32nd St
Fremont MI
494129549

Call Sign: WD8AQS
Lewis J Bishop Jr
7649 W 48th
Fremont MI 49412

Call Sign: KC8TBX
William Fries Jr
6910 W 48th St
Fremont MI 49412

Call Sign: N8PXH
Ron Maike
40 W Elm
Fremont MI 49412

Call Sign: N8IGN
Charles A Kempf
36 W Main St
Fremont MI 49412

Call Sign: WB8PKU
Charles M Erickson
16 W Sheridan
Fremont MI 49412

Call Sign: KD8ABM
Garrett R Blanchard
28 Wood Row
Fremont MI 49412

Call Sign: KC8NCZ
Zoua L Lee
Fremont MI 49412

Call Sign: KC8RQZ
Corrie J Richard
Fremont MI 49412

**FCC Amateur Radio
Licenses in Fruitport**

Call Sign: W8FDX
Louis O Myrmel
19 Circle Dr
Fruitport MI 49415

Call Sign: KC8UEX
Bonnie C Cooper
4200 E Pontaluna Rd
Fruitport MI 49415

Call Sign: KC8JHZ
Cecil J Stone Jr
5997 E Sternberg Rd
Fruitport MI 49415

Call Sign: KA8FOP
Daniel J Vryhof
6125 E Summit Rd
Fruitport MI 49415

Call Sign: KB8AHX
David A Burel
5610 Fairview Ct
Fruitport MI 49415

Call Sign: K8DAB
David A Burel
5610 Fairview Ct
Fruitport MI 49415

Call Sign: KD8MJW
Brian M Retzlaff
2956 Fruitport Rd
Fruitport MI 49415

Call Sign: WA8NCC
Benjamin H Gustafson
Sr
5900 Heights Ravenna
Rd
Fruitport MI 49415

Call Sign: KA8PJN
Clarence H Smith Jr
13732 Hickory Rd
Fruitport MI 49415

Call Sign: KB8YNA
William G Schmidt
13855 Hickory St

Fruitport MI 49415

Call Sign: KB8BLX
Frederick M Schmidt
Sr
13855 Hickory St
Fruitport MI 49415

Call Sign: KB8WXK
Fred M Schmidt Jr
13855 Hickory St
Fruitport MI 49415

Call Sign: KB8WXO
Adam J Schmidt
13855 Hickory St
Fruitport MI 49415

Call Sign: KB8YNL
Carol M Schmidt
13855 Hickory St
Fruitport MI 49415

Call Sign: K8UDY
Alan C Fletcher
374 N 6th Ave
Fruitport MI 49415

Call Sign: N8OCT
John N Van Epps
370 Pine St
Fruitport MI 49415

Call Sign: KC8NPG
Stirling N Cousins
3058 Pleasantwood Dr
Fruitport MI 49415

Call Sign: KC8DOH
Nikole A Leenhouts
6425 Red Pine Ct
Fruitport MI 49415

Call Sign: KD8QVV
Jacob W Frame
48 S 2nd Ave
Fruitport MI 49415

Call Sign: KD8EOO
George P Brewster
271 S 3rd Ave
Fruitport MI 49415

Call Sign: KC8HLN

Joseph C Irwin
6288 Walker Rd
Fruitport MI 49415

Call Sign: KD8KLG
Spencer D Weiland
6422 Windwood Dr
Fruitport MI 49415

Call Sign: KC8OJZ
Timothy G Smith
Fruitport MI 49415

**FCC Amateur Radio
Licenses in Fulton**

Call Sign: KA8CSJ
William Van
Middlesworth
12087 44th St
Fulton MI 49052

Call Sign: KJ8T
James N Standley
16005 E Tu Ave
Fulton MI 49052

Call Sign: KC8QNT
Wyatt R Thompson
13381 E Yz Ave
Fulton MI 49052

Call Sign: KC8TFS
Douglas G Kent
13896 Whitelawn
Fulton MI 49052

**FCC Amateur Radio
Licenses in Gaastra**

Call Sign: N8OXW
Martin J Penkivech
27 2nd St
Gaastra MI 49927

Call Sign: KC8MFQ
Josh L Penkivech
46 Maple Wood Ave
Gaastra MI 49927

Call Sign: N8IEQ
Paul R Penkivech
46 Maplewood Ave
Gaastra MI 49927

Call Sign: N8OXV
Michaeline Penkivech
46 Maplewood Ave
Gaastra MI 49927

Call Sign: NW8K
John W Sullivan Jr
154 Scott Lake Rd
Gaastra MI 49927

Call Sign: KC8OOS
Dale P Hookenson
Gaastra MI 49927

FCC Amateur Radio Licenses in Galesburg

Call Sign: W8LFW
Alan F Gooch
9932 Beth Anne
Galesburg MI 49053

Call Sign: KC8VFJ
John Gajor
3837 Briarpatch Cir
Galesburg MI 49053

Call Sign: W7REX
Derek J Sheehan
4049 Broken Ridge Cir
Galesburg MI 49053

Call Sign: KB0JNE
Brian D Marsh
9559 Candytuft Ln
Galesburg MI 49053

Call Sign: WB8MKR
James R Mcintosh
4818 Cascade Ct
Galesburg MI 49053

Call Sign: W8MKR
James R Mcintosh
4818 Cascade Ct
Galesburg MI 49053

Call Sign: KC8AAE
Robert A Turner Sr
4929 Catskill
Galesburg MI 49053

Call Sign: KB8SFR

Charles W Chapman
80 Division St
Galesburg MI 49053

Call Sign: KC8MUW
Line Of Sight Team
80 Division St
Galesburg MI 49053

Call Sign: KB8UWA
John H Chapman
135 E Beckwith
Galesburg MI 49053

Call Sign: K8BMP
James D Lynn
10075 E H J
Galesburg MI 49053

Call Sign: KC8ATG
Darnetta A Cotyk
10520 E Mn Ave
Galesburg MI 49053

Call Sign: WB8THH
Andrew L Cotyk
10520 E Mn Ave
Galesburg MI 49053

Call Sign: KC9AXJ
Shashi C Shah
8421 Fawn Meadow
Trl
Galesburg MI 49053

Call Sign: KB8WRO
Dale C Winling
9635 Firefly
Galesburg MI 49053

Call Sign: KB8MCE
Cecil A Curtiss
12156 Ft Custer Dr
Galesburg MI 49053

Call Sign: N8WOU
Andrew J Wayne
35 Grove Ave
Galesburg MI 49053

Call Sign: KC8SSK
James Drenthe
102 N 30th St Lot 19

Galesburg MI
490534897

Call Sign: KG8BE
Douglas C Waggoner
102 N 30th St Lot 56
Galesburg MI 49053

Call Sign: KC5ZPV
Matthew J Burton
2831 N 33rd St
Galesburg MI 49053

Call Sign: KC8QNX
David K Glenn
1981 N 36th St
Galesburg MI 49053

Call Sign: KA8GKA
Albert G Ahlrich
2644 N 37th St
Galesburg MI 49053

Call Sign: WA8ZXO
John R Garrod
2555 S 35th St
Galesburg MI 49053

Call Sign: KC8RHR
Christopher J Garrod
2555 S 35th St
Galesburg MI 49053

Call Sign: K8WJY
Lawrence L Jenkins
1767 S 44th St
Galesburg MI 49053

Call Sign: KD8SAW
James R Hill
9176 Shade Tree Cir
Galesburg MI 49053

Call Sign: KD8DTV
Ruth M Bates Hill
9176 Shade Tree Cir
Galesburg MI 49053

Call Sign: WB8VEV
Ruth M Bates Hill
9176 Shade Tree Cir
Galesburg MI 49053

Call Sign: WY8Z

Garth H Stoltz Jr
10228 Shadowlane
Ave
Galesburg MI 49053

Call Sign: KC8TLD
Arend B Ackles
540 Streemside Dr
Galesburg MI 49053

Call Sign: KC8MVM
Christina M Payne
161 W Michigan Ave
Galesburg MI 49053

FCC Amateur Radio Licenses in Galien

Call Sign: KB8QPV
Orson J Chapel
17570 Batten Rd
Galien MI 49113

Call Sign: WB8ZBJ
Ronald R Groshans
17422 Gardner Rd
Galien MI 49113

Call Sign: WD8JIB
Russell K Logston
201 N Cleveland Ave
Galien MI 49113

Call Sign: KD8ANI
Gregory A Briney
16746 N Cleveland
Ave
Galien MI 49113

Call Sign: KC8UXR
Roy G Smith
18880 Rickerman
Galien MI 49113

FCC Amateur Radio Licenses in Garden

Call Sign: KA8PCD
Nancy L Lang
12912 9 5 Rd
Garden MI 49835

Call Sign: KD8KW
Gary M Lang

12912 9 5 Rd
Garden MI 49835

Call Sign: N9NPD
Kathleen Bates
6157 Garden Bay Nn
15 Ln
Garden MI 49835

Call Sign: N8ULA
Douglas G Smith Jr
5471 Nn Rd
Garden MI 49835

Call Sign: KA8OCU
Alfred W Swanson
Garden MI 49835

Call Sign: KD8FWL
Alfred W Swanson
Garden MI 49835

Call Sign: KD8FWM
Zandra M Swanson
Garden MI 49835

FCC Amateur Radio Licenses in Gaylord

Call Sign: N8YVW
William R Brown
397 Al Do Ro Va Dr
Gaylord MI 49735

Call Sign: N8RDV
Billie S Zinke
1640 Altorf Strasse
Gaylord MI
497358303

Call Sign: KC8WIG
Zach T Stevens
1900 Altorf Strasse
Gaylord MI 49735

Call Sign: KD8CHK
Austin W Loper
1494 Arow Head Tr
Gaylord MI 49735

Call Sign: W1BIC
Harrison S Bicknell
5624 Arrowroot
Gaylord MI 49735

Call Sign: N8SBC
Gregory N Evans
7423 Arrowroot Tr
Gaylord MI 49735

Call Sign: W9KBI
Keith B Smith
1336 Beacon Sq Ln
Gaylord MI 49735

Call Sign: KB8VYH
Brian M Lawnichak
1060 Benson Dr
Gaylord MI 49735

Call Sign: KB8VYD
Hal G Lawnichak
1060 Benson Rd
Gaylord MI 49735

Call Sign: KC8TXV
Renee M Snyder
109 Brandywine Ln
Gaylord MI 49735

Call Sign: AA8PQ
William N Hughes
153 Brandywine Ln
Gaylord MI 49735

Call Sign: KB8RIU
William N Hughes
153 Brandywine Ln
Gaylord MI 49735

Call Sign: KB8VRC
Cathy M Hughes
153 Brandywine Ln
Gaylord MI 49735

Call Sign: KD8MTM
Todd B Hopp
870 Briar Ln
Gaylord MI 49735

Call Sign: N8VKS
Renee S Matlock
862 Butcher Dr
Gaylord MI 49735

Call Sign: KC8BJX
Howard A Grosser
1639 Calcite

Gaylord MI 49735

Call Sign: N8XKW
Thomas W Bates
1615 Chippewa Trl
Gaylord MI 49735

Call Sign: KB7SZW
Donald R Johnson
7267 Compton Dr
Gaylord MI 49735

Call Sign: W8YBK
Neil A Baer
398 Crestwood Dr
Gaylord MI 49735

Call Sign: K8PDN
Eric J Rusak
454 Crestwood Dr
Gaylord MI 49735

Call Sign: KD8KCV
David E Peck
3513 Deer Trl
Gaylord MI 49735

Call Sign: KE8GX
Joseph T Sarzynski
6848 Dogwood Ct
Gaylord MI
497359072

Call Sign: KC8AIR
Dale F Lesatz
2689 Dorothy Dr
Gaylord MI 49735

Call Sign: KB8NNU
Richard D Eagle
321 E 3rd St
Gaylord MI 49735

Call Sign: N8JIL
Mary A McClure
501 E 3rd St
Gaylord MI 49735

Call Sign: WA7OEH
Walter C Feole Jr
510 E Delweiss Trl
Gaylord MI 49735

Call Sign: W8MAT

Glenn W Steiner
345 E Felshaw
Gaylord MI 49735

Call Sign: WB8LUH
James F Volant
1604 E Heart Lake
Gaylord MI 49735

Call Sign: AB8VU
James F Volant
1604 E Heart Lake
Gaylord MI 49735

Call Sign: KB8BRA
Daniel F Walsh
500 E Huron Rd
Gaylord MI 49735

Call Sign: KD8CRQ
Tina J Sly
315 E Main St
Gaylord MI 49735

Call Sign: N8VCQ
Richard V Rider
220 E Mitchell
Gaylord MI 49735

Call Sign: KC8FWM
Christina J Nelson
551 E Petoskey St
Gaylord MI 49735

Call Sign: KC8UKI
David L Tober
4233 E Vail Ln
Gaylord MI 49735

Call Sign: KC8QWB
Nicholas R Reichert
1157 Estelle Rd
Gaylord MI 49735

Call Sign: KC8QWC
Larry J Reichert
1157 Estelle Rd
Gaylord MI 49735

Call Sign: N8GWN
James E Robb
2225 Evergreen
Gaylord MI 49735

Call Sign: KD8RTA
Raymond F Neubecker
121 Felshaw St
Gaylord MI 49735

Call Sign: KD8IET
William R Lavalle III
4309 Fowler Lake Rd
Gaylord MI 49735

Call Sign: KD8EUX
David C Goosen II
7786 Frist Ct Ave
Gaylord MI 49735

Call Sign: KC8KEL
William L Pearson
1713 Geres N St
Gaylord MI 49735

Call Sign: WD4FDL
James L Potter
864 Goslow Rd
Gaylord MI 49735

Call Sign: W8JLP
James L Potter
864 Goslow Rd
Gaylord MI 49735

Call Sign: KJ8P
James L Potter
864 Goslow Rd
Gaylord MI 49735

Call Sign: KB8KLU
Brandon E Krol
780 Grove St
Gaylord MI 49735

Call Sign: KE8BY
Glen E Boger
1634 Groveland Ave
Gaylord MI 49735

Call Sign: KD8LHM
Thomas M Shaltry
3890 Hallenius Rd
Gaylord MI 49735

Call Sign: KD8RTZ
Eugene M Branigan II
2300 Hallock Rd
Gaylord MI 49735

Call Sign: N8JVF
Richard R Blackmore
1767 Hayes Tower Rd
Gaylord MI 49735

Call Sign: KD8AOY
Robert A Rau
4301 Hayes Tower Rd
Gaylord MI 49735

Call Sign: K8MTN
William A Ackerman
4931 Hayes Tower Rd
Gaylord MI 49735

Call Sign: KC8AAB
Patricia A Ackerman
4931 Hayes Tower Rd
Gaylord MI 49735

Call Sign: WN8V
Richard B Ross
6724 Hayes Tower Rd
Gaylord MI 49735

Call Sign: KC8HUD
Brian M Ackerman
4931 Hayes Tower Rd
Gaylord MI 49735

Call Sign: KC8TBV
George A Lake Jr
2266 Hickorywood Dr
Gaylord MI 49735

Call Sign: N8QVN
Paula L Birdsall
1868 John St
Gaylord MI 49735

Call Sign: KD8FHA
Harold D Crow
212 Karlee Ave
Gaylord MI 49735

Call Sign: KD8IHN
Rodger D Munson
6213 Karslake Rd
Gaylord MI 49735

Call Sign: W8RRM
Rodger D Munson
6213 Karslake Rd

Gaylord MI 49735

Call Sign: KC8MHY
Michael G Eme
9833 Keewanee Trl
Gaylord MI 49735

Call Sign: KC8YGM
Michael J Kasprzak
771 Krystal Meadows
Ln
Gaylord MI 49735

Call Sign: WB8UYO
Carol S Kasper
1089 Kubacki Rd
Gaylord MI 49735

Call Sign: WB8UYP
Bryan J Kasper
1089 Kubacki Rd
Gaylord MI 49735

Call Sign: KC8OLD
Charles E Weinheimer
1398 Kubacki Rd
Gaylord MI 49735

Call Sign: KD8HLG
Robert T Stimble
4002 Lake Manuka Rd
Gaylord MI 49735

Call Sign: W8NTD
Robert T Stimble
4002 Lake Manuka Rd
Gaylord MI 49735

Call Sign: KC8SUS
Shawn N Addis
2101 Lonepine St
Gaylord MI 49735

Call Sign: KA8ZUO
Trevor J Bast
9955 Lower Chub Lk
Rd
Gaylord MI 49735

Call Sign: W8OBX
Trevor J Bast
9955 Lower Chub Lk
Rd
Gaylord MI 49735

Call Sign: KC8TGF
Bernard A Bast
9955 Lower Club Lake
Rd
Gaylord MI 49735

Call Sign: KD8PTW
Larry A Stuck
5964 M 32 E
Gaylord MI 49735

Call Sign: W8LAS
Larry A Stuck
5964 M 32 E
Gaylord MI 49735

Call Sign: KC8FFR
John C Kirby
2645 Maggie Ln
Gaylord MI 49735

Call Sign: AB8VT
John C Kirby
2645 Maggie Ln
Gaylord MI 49735

Call Sign: KD8FYF
Terry G Repp
4474 Manuka Lake Rd
Gaylord MI 49735

Call Sign: KD8RTX
William J Blanzy
3089 Marquardt Rd
Gaylord MI 49735

Call Sign: AB8MT
Michael F Currie
780 Michaywe Dr
Gaylord MI 49734

Call Sign: WB8AKH
Richard J Nelson
1283 Michaywe Dr
Gaylord MI 49735

Call Sign: N8VAI
Stephen L Sederquist
1831 Michaywe Dr
Gaylord MI 49735

Call Sign: N8IVW
George G Woloskie

694 Michaywe Dr
Gaylord MI 49735

Call Sign: KD8JPL
Austin D Gawne
4191 Mulberry Ln
Gaylord MI
497358965

Call Sign: N8JTQ
Joseph M Hickerson
1593 Murner Rd
Gaylord MI 49735

Call Sign: N8VPS
Michele E Hickerson
1593 Murner Rd
Gaylord MI 49735

Call Sign: N8YKD
Roger D Mench
72 N Alpine Ct
Gaylord MI 49735

Call Sign: KB8TOA
David F Mihalyfy
1431 N Heart Lake Dr
Gaylord MI 49735

Call Sign: KC8NFU
Michael L Mihalyfy
1431 N Heart Lake Dr
Gaylord MI 49735

Call Sign: WB8NIG
Richard W Heater
813 N Ohio Ave
Gaylord MI 49735

Call Sign: KC8KLH
James M Harrington
403 N Otsego
Gaylord MI 49735

Call Sign: KD8FQZ
Jean L Brown
2702 N Townline Rd
Gaylord MI 49735

Call Sign: N8QAJ
Robert A Brown Jr
2702 N Townline Rd
Gaylord MI
497359270

Call Sign: KC8FNS
Debra L Johnston
650 Nancy Ln
Gaylord MI 49735

Call Sign: KI8CU
Chad W Johnston
650 Nancy Ln
Gaylord MI 49735

Call Sign: KB8LYJ
Oliver E Greggs Jr
6677 Nightingale
Gaylord MI 49735

Call Sign: KB8SFQ
Doris L Greggs
6677 Nightingale
Gaylord MI 49735

Call Sign: KD8FRB
David E Peck Jr
3314 Nina Rd
Gaylord MI 49735

Call Sign: AC8AY
David E Peck Jr
3314 Nina Rd
Gaylord MI 49735

Call Sign: N8MVB
Robert A Nowak
4480 Nowak Rd
Gaylord MI 49735

Call Sign: N8VPU
Sandy L Nowak
4480 Nowak Rd
Gaylord MI 49735

Call Sign: N8PZW
Lawrence P O Dell
1928 Old 27 S
Gaylord MI 49735

Call Sign: KC8DMB
Timothy Raybould
3036 Otsego Land Dr 6
Gaylord MI 49735

Call Sign: KC8UMC
John F TRUE
1343 Park Meadow Dr

Gaylord MI 49735

Call Sign: KC8TGE
Tabitha E Walther
2635 Parmater Rd
Gaylord MI 49735

Call Sign: KD8JMA
John D Thompson
5175 Parmater Rd
Gaylord MI 49735

Call Sign: WX8APX
National Weather
Service Forecast Office
8800 Passenheim Rd
Gaylord MI 49735

Call Sign: KC8NVN
National Weather
Service Forecast Office
Gaylord Mi
8800 Passenheim Rd
Gaylord MI 49735

Call Sign: KC8OBB
Eric W Kennedy
670 Pearl Ln
Gaylord MI 49735

Call Sign: KD8GOV
John D Leckner
971 Pine Briar Ln
Gaylord MI 49735

Call Sign: KB8SJQ
Sandra R Davis
4186 Pine Hollow Ct
Gaylord MI 49735

Call Sign: N8MJM
Michael J Morse
5562 Pueblo Trl M 7
Gaylord MI 49735

Call Sign: KC8APQ
Steven A Heintz Jr
462 Ramblewood Dr
Gaylord MI 49735

Call Sign: KD8EUY
Brett J Hopp
2288 Ramona Trl
Gaylord MI 49735

Call Sign: W8IAR
Floyd N Churchill
384 Roberts Ave Apt 2
Gaylord MI 49735

Call Sign: KB8VYI
Jan D Martin
410 S Center St Apt 10
Gaylord MI 49735

Call Sign: KI8EA
Joseph T McCormick
Sr
524 S Court Ave
Gaylord MI 49735

Call Sign: KC8QPQ
George Hugle
118A S Elm St
Gaylord MI 49735

Call Sign: KC8QPS
Loretta M Hugle
118-A S Elm St
Gaylord MI 49735

Call Sign: KF8QH
Paul E Modrzynski
1636 S Geres St
Gaylord MI 49735

Call Sign: N8PTX
Harold J Luebs Jr
115 S Maple Rd
Gaylord MI 49735

Call Sign: KD8INP
Barbara J Fuzi
421 S Oak Ave
Gaylord MI 49735

Call Sign: KD8JYG
Darcie A Fuzi
421 S Oak Ave
Gaylord MI 49735

Call Sign: KD8INQ
Mark J Fuzi
421 S Oak Ave
Gaylord MI 49735

Call Sign: KC8QWA
Lance M Holmes

286 S Pinecrest Dr
Gaylord MI 49735

Call Sign: KC8QWE
Joe M Holmes
286 S Pinecrest Dr
Gaylord MI 49735

Call Sign: WD8RDZ
Phillip Slotwinski
974 S Summitview Dr
Gaylord MI 49735

Call Sign: KB8TAS
Jerald A Cokewell
3336 Sawyer Rd
Gaylord MI 49735

Call Sign: KB8YYB
Deborah A Cokewell
3336 Sawyer Rd
Gaylord MI 49735

Call Sign: AB8VV
Jerald A Cokewell
3336 Sawyer Rd
Gaylord MI 49735

Call Sign: KA8JWQ
Everett L Brown
5062 Seneca Tr Rt 7
Gaylord MI 49735

Call Sign: N8OIX
Rudi D Edel
5234 Seymore Rd
Gaylord MI 49735

Call Sign: KA8ADB
Richard R Boik
1219 Shady Brook Ln
Gaylord MI 49735

Call Sign: KC8QVY
Elaine A Harre
831 Ski View Trl
Gaylord MI 49735

Call Sign: KC8QVZ
William C Harre
831 Ski View Trl
Gaylord MI 49735

Call Sign: KC8TLL

Gerald F Januzzi
7271 Snow Goose Cir
Gaylord MI 49735

Call Sign: KD8HOI
Michael J Harbin
4874 Starlight Trl
Gaylord MI 49735

Call Sign: WB8REH
James T Theisen
4692 Theisen Rd
Gaylord MI 49735

Call Sign: KA8UEY
Susan E Theisen
4692 Theisen Rd
Gaylord MI 49735

Call Sign: KC8BQM
Laurence F Monshor Jr
1541 Thumm
Gaylord MI 49735

Call Sign: KF8SF
John L Libertine
1019 Timberline Trl
Gaylord MI 49734

Call Sign: KD8EUZ
Gregory V Smith
5678 Turkyfoot Tr
Gaylord MI 49735

Call Sign: KD8PVA
Nila I Kietzman
1665 Twin Pine Ave
Gaylord MI 49735

Call Sign: KD8CHG
Donald N Storing
1746 Valais Strasse
Gaylord MI 49735

Call Sign: KC9ON
John W Clements
2240 Van Tyle Rd
Gaylord MI 49735

Call Sign: KG1CW
James P Toler
3070 Van Tyle Rd
Gaylord MI 49735

Call Sign: KD4RMQ
Joel G Petz
320 W Congdon Rd
Gaylord MI 49735

Call Sign: N8JCR
Thomas A Dickinson
2216 W Dixon Lake
Dr
Gaylord MI 49735

Call Sign: N8JCN
Vincent J La Rosa II
2272 W Dixon Lk Dr
Gaylord MI 49735

Call Sign: KB8EYS
Michael W Green
110 W Sheldon
Gaylord MI 49735

Call Sign: KC8MTX
Joseph C Walker
3771 Wequas Rd
Gaylord MI 49735

Call Sign: W8JCW
Joseph C Walker
3771 Wequas Rd
Gaylord MI 49735

Call Sign: W8JCW
Joseph C Walker
3771 Wequas Rd
Gaylord MI 49735

Call Sign: WW8R
Russell D Bresser
513 West St
Gaylord MI
497358305

Call Sign: KB8DUK
Scott W Ruebel
7682 White Cloud Trl
Gaylord MI 49735

Call Sign: KC8WEK
Jack L Bigelow
7970 White St
Gaylord MI 49735

Call Sign: KC8WEL
Kody C Bigelow

7970 White St
Gaylord MI 49735

Call Sign: WA8VQL
Ralph N Nutter III
2789 Wilkinson Rd
Gaylord MI 49735

Call Sign: KB8EYO
Christopher O
Guggisberg
Gaylord MI 49734

Call Sign: KE8DP
Gary J Merritt
Gaylord MI 49734

Call Sign: KD8DHY
Clifford C Loughrige
Gaylord MI 49734

Call Sign: KD8FYG
Eremal L Repp
Gaylord MI 49734

Call Sign: KD8AFE
Top Of Michigan ARC
Gaylord MI 49735

Call Sign: NM8RC
Top Of Michigan ARC
Gaylord MI 49735

Call Sign: KB8TOB
Sarah E Early
Gaylord MI 49735

Call Sign: N8PZX
Dennis J Early
Gaylord MI 49735

**FCC Amateur Radio
Licenses in Germfask**

Call Sign: KC8GKJ
Charles G Davis II
Rt 1 Box 31
Germfask MI 49836

Call Sign: KC8KMB
Charles H Helzer Sr
Germfask MI
498360153

Call Sign: K8IJQ
Bernard R Maynard
5159 19 85 Ln
Gladstone MI 49837

Call Sign: KA8IHS
Lynn F Maynard
5159 19 85 Ln
Gladstone MI 49837

Call Sign: KA8SBH
Dwaine J Taylor
3782 Co 416 20th Rd
Gladstone MI 49837

Call Sign: KA8EBZ
Gloria J Kanerva
5622 25th Rd
Gladstone MI 49837

Call Sign: W8WK
Walter O Kanerva
5622 25th Rd
Gladstone MI 49837

Call Sign: N8ZGA
John P D Broeders
5698 25th Rd
Gladstone MI 49837

Call Sign: WA8DHB
Aileen J Gagnon
9159 Bay Shore Dr
Gladstone MI
498372762

Call Sign: KD8DVL
Kenneth M Pillera Jr
9103 Bayshore Dr
Gladstone MI 49837

Call Sign: KB8PTF
Scott B Thompson
9560 Chaison N 5 Rd
Gladstone MI 49837

Call Sign: N8OYR
Richard I Thompson
9560 Chaison N 5 Rd
Gladstone MI 49837

Call Sign: KA8RPB
Lowell D Seeley
235 Chaison Rd
Gladstone MI 49837

Call Sign: W8DJT
Dwaine J Taylor
3782 Co 416 20th Rd
Gladstone MI 49837

Call Sign: W8JNL
James N Love
6029 Country Club 19
25 Ln
Gladstone MI 49837

Call Sign: KD8IGX
James N Love
6029 Country Club
1925 Ln
Gladstone MI 49837

Call Sign: WD8ARJ
Betty M Palmgren
6132 CR 420 21st Rd
Gladstone MI 49837

Call Sign: WB8OIY
David C Palmgren
6132 CR 420 21st Rd
Gladstone MI 49837

Call Sign: N8DP
David C Palmgren
6132 CR 420 21st Rd
Gladstone MI 49837

Call Sign: K8PL
Delta County ARS
6132 CR 420 21st Rd
Gladstone MI
498378815

Call Sign: K8ZAS
Delta County ARS
6132 CR 420 21st Rd
Gladstone MI
498378815

Call Sign: KD8DVN
Mark E Hallfrisch
5026 CR 426 21st Rd
Gladstone MI 49837

Call Sign: KD8KKR
Joshua D Hallfrisch
5026 CR 426 21st Rd
Gladstone MI 49837

Call Sign: KB8QFI
Paul R Sanford
1116 Dakota Ave
Gladstone MI 49837

Call Sign: KA8PCA
Bernard J Coleman
217 Dakota Ave Apt
317
Gladstone MI
498371943

Call Sign: KD8BJD
Steven D Soderman
6207 Days River 245
Rd
Gladstone MI 49837

Call Sign: WA8ASJ
Robert W Salmi
515 Delta Ave
Gladstone MI 49837

Call Sign: N8MDM
Terry G La Count
6398 E Side 23 2 Dr
Gladstone MI 49837

Call Sign: N8MEH
Cory J La Count
6398 E Side 23 2 Dr
Gladstone MI 49837

Call Sign: N8GOH
Walter G Hantsch
6466 E Side Dr
Gladstone MI 49837

Call Sign: WB8FUW
Lee G Anderson
5993 Horseshoe 223
Dr
Gladstone MI 49837

Call Sign: KB8FFG
Sean H Cote
7270 Lake Bluff 19 4
Rd
Gladstone MI 49837

Call Sign: K8OVG
Thomas L Wilson
7292 Lake Bluff 194
Rd
Gladstone MI 49837

Call Sign: KD8PK
Arthur T Pope
1204 Lakeshore Dr
Gladstone MI 49837

Call Sign: N8HUW
Michael K Delke
6185 M 35
Gladstone MI 49837

Call Sign: K8EMS
Michael K Delke
6185 M 35
Gladstone MI 49837

Call Sign: WD8DXN
Michael C La Fleur
7633 M 5 Co 426 Rd
Gladstone MI 49837

Call Sign: KD8IRE
Jason P Erickson
8399 M 5 Rd
Gladstone MI 49837

Call Sign: WD8IXY
Margaret L Hagman
8422 M 5 Rd
Gladstone MI 49837

Call Sign: KE8GG
Duane A Puro
8672 M 5 Rd
Gladstone MI 49837

Call Sign: K8AO
Duane A Puro
8672 M 5 Rd
Gladstone MI 49837

Call Sign: KA8IQQ
Albert J Johnson Sr
417 Mich Ave
Gladstone MI 49837

Call Sign: WD8IXW
Tom J Elegeert

1228 Michigan Ave
Gladstone MI 49837

Call Sign: KC8UCZ
Joseph R Thompson
602 Montana Ave
Gladstone MI 49837

Call Sign: KC8ZYI
Joseph R Thompson
602 Montana Ave
Gladstone MI 49837

Call Sign: W8JRT
Joseph R Thompson
602 Montana Ave
Gladstone MI 49837

Call Sign: KD8FWN
Natalie K Thompson
602 Montana Ave
Gladstone MI 49837

Call Sign: K8NKT
Natalie K Thompson
602 Montana Ave
Gladstone MI 49837

Call Sign: WB8AKY
Walter C Johnson
801 Montana Ave
Gladstone MI 49837

Call Sign: KC8OVL
Joseph R Thompson
602 Montana Ave
Gladstone MI 49837

Call Sign: KA8WOG
Floyd L Swift
728 N 16th St
Gladstone MI 49837

Call Sign: KA8EBW
Joan O Hereau
1228 N Bluff Dr
Gladstone MI 49837

Call Sign: KA8ECL
Victor Hereau Sr
1228 N Bluff Dr
Gladstone MI 49837

Call Sign: KD8NST

Mitchel R West
7697 N Lake 0 5 Bluff
Dr
Gladstone MI 49837

Call Sign: KD8NQI
Richard K West
7697 N Lake Bluff O 5
Dr
Gladstone MI 49837

Call Sign: N0ATB
Erik M Rubright
6772 Oak Bluff 237 Dr
Gladstone MI 49837

Call Sign: KD8KKN
Patrick G Pierron
636 Railway Ave
Gladstone MI 49837

Call Sign: N1PWW
Philip M Howard
5983 Rivers 22nd Rd
Gladstone MI 49837

Call Sign: N8MDX
Gary E Stiles
21 S 3rd St
Gladstone MI 49837

Call Sign: WB8VKR
Howard E St John
22 S 3rd St
Gladstone MI 49837

Call Sign: W8HSJ
Howard E St John
22 S 3rd St
Gladstone MI 49837

Call Sign: KA0AID
Lois J McIntosh
408 S 7th St
Gladstone MI 49837

Call Sign: KB8JET
John Erdody IV
7440 S Lake Bluff 0 5
Dr
Gladstone MI 49837

Call Sign: WD8PEK
John P Erdody III

7440 S Lake Bluff 0 5
Dr
Gladstone MI 49837

Call Sign: KD8KKV
Caleb M Cox
9156 Stagecoach Q 5
Ave
Gladstone MI 49837

Call Sign: N8MCN
Randal L Rice
7746 Summit 19 55 Dr
Gladstone MI 49837

Call Sign: KD8DKE
James T Moore
1002 Superior Ave
Gladstone MI 49837

Call Sign: KA9YEB
Jody D Purvis
7622 Tipperary Rd
Gladstone MI 49837

Call Sign: KD8IGW
John S Trotter
8343 Venture P2 Ln
Gladstone MI 49837

Call Sign: KD8HDG
Rick G Williams
5140 William 19 7 Dr
Gladstone MI 49837

Call Sign: KB8QYI
Steven C Heitman
1006 Wisconsin Ave
Gladstone MI
498371524

Call Sign: KD8DKD
Walter P Aho
1206 Wisconsin Ave
Gladstone MI 49837

Call Sign: K8WLT
Walter P Aho
1206 Wisconsin Ave
Gladstone MI 49837

Call Sign: N8ZHC
Allan C Pierron
1417 Wisconsin Ave

Gladstone MI 49837

Call Sign: KC8RCJ
Ronald T Maxam
5882 Alice Dr
Gladwin MI 48624

Call Sign: WB8RM
Ronald T Maxam
5882 Alice Dr
Gladwin MI 48624

Call Sign: WA8FRE
Andrew J Wlotkowski
1190 Birch Ridge Rd
Gladwin MI 48624

Call Sign: KB8SQZ
Lawrence G Belloli
480 Black Creek Rd
Gladwin MI 48624

Call Sign: KB8NVZ
Jason L Kidd
5221 Butman Rd
Gladwin MI 48624

Call Sign: KB8OWA
Nick E Le Vasseur
5868 Butman Rd
Gladwin MI 48624

Call Sign: WB8BYS
Ronald R Rees
4777 Buxton Ct
Gladwin MI 48624

Call Sign: KB8RPD
Matthew R Lauer
1230 Chatterton
Gladwin MI 48624

Call Sign: KC8QAQ
Randall Peck
1171 Chatterton St
Gladwin MI 48624

Call Sign: KB8BIN
John E Buswell
1400 Clarwin
Gladwin MI 48624

Call Sign: KC8QAL
Patrick C Barz
157 Clendening
Gladwin MI 48624

Call Sign: KD8EJF
Leo J Gary
5437 Darby Way
Gladwin MI 48624

Call Sign: KB8TLS
Robert J Clarke
1753 Dutcher Rd
Gladwin MI
486248632

Call Sign: KC8QAS
David P Springborn
435 E Maple St
Gladwin MI 48624

Call Sign: KB8NVY
Rayme R La Bean
912 E Ridge Rd
Gladwin MI 48624

Call Sign: KB8NVS
Brian E Taylor
3823 Eagleson Rd
Gladwin MI 48624

Call Sign: KB8OVZ
Dan J Stepaniak Jr
3873 Eagleson Rd
Gladwin MI 48624

Call Sign: K8WXJ
Stanley E Smith
4900 Eagleson Rd
Gladwin MI 48624

Call Sign: W8SES
Stanley E Smith
4900 Eagleson Rd
Gladwin MI 48624

Call Sign: KC8NPC
Daniel F Spencer
6267 Elk Lk Rd
Gladwin MI 48624

Call Sign: KB8QOS
Joseph E Anthony

9235 Evergreen
Gladwin MI 48624

Call Sign: KB8NVT
Floyd L Starr
5615 Fitzwater Rd
Gladwin MI 48624

Call Sign: KD8RS
Grant Stevens
1580 Hi Acre
Gladwin MI 48624

Call Sign: KB8NWE
Tanya L Garrison
4365 Howard Rd
Gladwin MI 48624

Call Sign: K8AYZ
Lanse Creuse ARC
5280 Huntington Way
Gladwin MI 48624

Call Sign: K8EO
Ted M Bak
5280 Huntington Way
Gladwin MI 48624

Call Sign: N8YKF
Judy A Cywinski
5339 Jerry Rd Rt 5
Gladwin MI 48624

Call Sign: N1CLJ
Cathy L Johnson
4667 Keswick Ct
Gladwin MI 48624

Call Sign: N1SJ
Steven W Johnson
4667 Keswick Ct
Gladwin MI 48624

Call Sign: KA8RTT
Lawrence K Raby Sr
2616 Lakeshore Dr
Gladwin MI 48624

Call Sign: W8AQD
Ralph C Turner
4746 Lancelot Ct
Gladwin MI 48624

Call Sign: KB8NWC

Erik W Huber
284 Lockwood Dr
Gladwin MI 48624

Call Sign: N4GTW
David W Miller
1572 Manchester Way
Gladwin MI
486248522

Call Sign: N8ZWY
David W Miller
1572 Manchester Way
Gladwin MI
486248522

Call Sign: KB8OWB
Todd M McKenna
820 Martin Rd
Gladwin MI 48624

Call Sign: KA9PSR
Paul D Walters
7322 Muma Rd
Gladwin MI 48624

Call Sign: KB8OLM
Adam R Ball
401 N Antler
Gladwin MI 48624

Call Sign: KB8NVV
Collin M Riffert
1309 N Antler
Gladwin MI 48624

Call Sign: KB8RPE
Christian V Riffert
1309 N Antler
Gladwin MI 48624

Call Sign: KB8UAK
John A Stansfield
324 N Antler St
Gladwin MI 48624

Call Sign: KB8RPC
Derek J Brown
3280 N Bard
Gladwin MI 48624

Call Sign: WT8J
Harvey E Wice
3015 N Bard Rd

Gladwin MI 48624

Call Sign: KD8EJH
Mickie L Duby
3535 N Clarwin Ave
Gladwin MI 48624

Call Sign: KD8EJG
Robert J Duby II
3535 N Clarwin Ave
Gladwin MI 48624

Call Sign: KB8OLN
Ryan W Ritchie
551 N Clarwin Rd
Gladwin MI 48624

Call Sign: KB8NWG
Mike J Cook
509 N Hockaday
Gladwin MI 48624

Call Sign: KB8RPG
Joseph E Dinkel
1986 N Hockaday
Gladwin MI 48624

Call Sign: KC8QNG
Richard L Dorn
2504 N M 18
Gladwin MI 48624

Call Sign: KB8NVM
Scott T Zietz
2769 N Nickless Rd
Gladwin MI 48624

Call Sign: KC8HXP
Matthew D Pahl
5419 N Oberlin Rd
Gladwin MI 48624

Call Sign: KC8QAP
Nicholas J Pahl
5419 N Oberlin Rd
Gladwin MI 48624

Call Sign: KB8NWB
Chris D James
1093 N Shaw Rd
Gladwin MI 48624

Call Sign: KB8ZSC
Morgan K Lee

1305 N Spring St Lot 14
Gladwin MI 48624

Call Sign: KB8ZSB
Andrew R Keen
1200 Nickless Rd
Gladwin MI 48624

Call Sign: KC8QAR
Rick A Snider
2981 Nickless Rd
Gladwin MI 48624

Call Sign: KA8HHJ
Emerson L Guilliat
1573 Oakwood Dr
Gladwin MI 48624

Call Sign: KC8QAN
Matt D Good
821 Oberlin Rd
Gladwin MI 48624

Call Sign: KB8NWF
Brad E De Vries
1300 Oberlin Rd
Gladwin MI 48624

Call Sign: KB8NWH
Jason J Cassiday
4368 Pratt Lake Rd
Gladwin MI 48624

Call Sign: KC8YXQ
Todd J Bonham
4485 Pratt Lake Rd
Gladwin MI 48624

Call Sign: W8SYU
Harold B Marble
4996 Prince Ct
Gladwin MI
486248220

Call Sign: KB8NVN
Mark D Wilson
1064 Ranger Dr
Gladwin MI 48624

Call Sign: KB8NVQ
Frederick W Weiss III
1286 Recreation Dr
Gladwin MI 48624

Call Sign: KB8NVR
Steven M Walters
1109 Ritchie Rd
Gladwin MI 48624

Call Sign: KB8OLP
Kenett C Kelly
230 S Antler
Gladwin MI 48624

Call Sign: N8ZIE
Keith W Sleeper
701 S Arcade
Gladwin MI 48624

Call Sign: KA8KIY
David C Sleeper
701 S Arcade
Gladwin MI
486242111

Call Sign: N8ES
James F Volant
220 S Bailey Lake Ave
Gladwin MI 48624

Call Sign: WD8PKR
Jack D Kehoe
150 S Bowery Ave
Gladwin MI 48624

Call Sign: K8BZ
Steven C Wuelfing
240 S Hockaday Rd
Gladwin MI 48624

Call Sign: KB8NVX
Jon R Lyons
879 S M 18
Gladwin MI 48624

Call Sign: KD8BUL
Judith M Ford
150 Saint Andrews Dr
Gladwin MI
486247627

Call Sign: K8KIU
Judith M Ford
150 Saint Andrews Dr
Gladwin MI
486247627

Call Sign: W8KIU
Earl E Ford
1505 Saint Andrews Dr
Gladwin MI
486247627

Call Sign: KD8JSW
James C Wright Sr
562 Sergent Rd
Gladwin MI 48624

Call Sign: KB8NWA
Brian W Johnson
1060 Shaw Rd
Gladwin MI 48624

Call Sign: KB8NVO
Jason M Wilhelm
1053 Siesta Dr
Gladwin MI 48624

Call Sign: KB8NVW
Shayn D McFarland
617 Stacey Ct
Gladwin MI 48624

Call Sign: KA8PJA
Wilbert C Hammond
6434 Sylvan Dr
Gladwin MI 48624

Call Sign: KB8NWI
David A Beam
3987 W Branch Dr
Gladwin MI 48624

Call Sign: KB8UAL
Edward L Cline
1201 W Cedar Av Apt B9
Gladwin MI 48624

Call Sign: KD8EJJ
Larry L Eagleson
4373 W M 61
Gladwin MI 48624

Call Sign: KA8URU
Lloyd R Bowen
4846 W M 61
Gladwin MI 48624

Call Sign: N8GAN

Kenneth L Koch
5740 W M 61
Gladwin MI 48624

Call Sign: KB8NWD
Raymond P Hoermann
1444 W Ridge Rd
Gladwin MI 48624

Call Sign: KB8NVP
Chad A White
3588 W Wagarville Rd
Gladwin MI 48624

Call Sign: KC8LNA
Thomas F Kareus
2936 W Wirtz Rd
Gladwin MI 48624

Call Sign: KB8NVU
Chris M Robinson
5052 W Ziemer Rd
Gladwin MI 48624

Call Sign: N8UEA
John L Welt Sr
2535 Wagarville Rd
Gladwin MI 48624

Call Sign: AA8HY
Eugene S Fritcher
5009 Wagarville Rd
Gladwin MI 48624

Call Sign: KC8QAM
Howard P Bigham
1494 Weber Rd
Gladwin MI 48624

Call Sign: KL0DN
Sharron R Walcutt
4890 Wild Wood Dr
Gladwin MI 48624

Call Sign: N8LYL
Bruce D Wagner
Gladwin MI 48624

Call Sign: KC8NPX
Nancy R Wagner
Gladwin MI 48624

Call Sign: KD8HIG
David R Sicard

Gladwin MI 48624

Call Sign: W8MPB
Harvey N Heinz
Gladwin MI 48624

Call Sign: W8GDW
Gladwin Area ARC
Gladwin MI
486249998

Call Sign: KB8ZML
Gladwin Area ARC
Gladwin MI
486249998

FCC Amateur Radio Licenses in Glen Arbor

Call Sign: N8EJI
Daniel J Semple
4615 Northwood
Glen Arbor MI 49636

Call Sign: K8LSK
David M Baldwin
5600 W MacFarlane
Rd
Glen Arbor MI 49636

Call Sign: KC8FEV
Frank G Siepker Jr
6896 W MacFarlane
Rd
Glen Arbor MI 49636

Call Sign: K2YAZ
Robert G Senk
Glen Arbor MI 49636

Call Sign: KD8AWF
David M Watt
Glen Arbor MI
496360111

Call Sign: N8BTD
David M Watt
Glen Arbor MI
496360111

FCC Amateur Radio Licenses in Glenn

Call Sign: KC8DE
Robert E Decker Sr
1438 West Ln
Glenn MI 49416

FCC Amateur Radio Licenses in Glennie

Call Sign: KD8PTD
David R Dee
3523 Bissonette Rd
Glennie MI 48737

Call Sign: K9DRD
David R Dee
3523 Bissonette Rd
Glennie MI 48737

Call Sign: KC8JPA
Barry D Wilson
4870 Cody Rd
Glennie MI 48737

Call Sign: KA8CKL
Melvin L Armstrong
4897 Cody Rd
Glennie MI 487379757

Call Sign: N8HA
Clifford R Dolliver
3636 F 30
Glennie MI 48737

Call Sign: KA8QBB
Edward D Williams
4612 Ford Rd
Glennie MI 48737

Call Sign: N8GVH
Darrell G Busch
4842 Fraser Rd
Glennie MI 48737

Call Sign: KC8ELP
Clifford R Dolliver
3636 Glennie Rd
Glennie MI 48737

Call Sign: W8ICC
Iosco County Amateur
Radio Enthusiasts
3636 Glennie Rd
Glennie MI 48737

Call Sign: KB8RWG
Kelly F Karpp
4321 W F30
Glennie MI 48737

Call Sign: WD8PIK
George R Porter
3560 W Glennie Rd
Glennie MI 48737

FCC Amateur Radio Licenses in Gobles

Call Sign: N8TPE
Jim Amos
27177 27 1/2 St
Gobles MI 49055

Call Sign: KB8NCL
Fred A Stap
19470 27th St
Gobles MI 49013

Call Sign: N8OKU
Allen J Stap Sr
19470 27th St
Gobles MI 49055

Call Sign: N8RPF
Lovedia J Stap
19470 27th St
Gobles MI 49055

Call Sign: KC8TZK
Allen J Stap Jr
19470 27th St
Gobles MI 49055

Call Sign: AC8DX
Allen J Stap Sr
19470 27th St
Gobles MI 49055

Call Sign: N8PYS
Ray L Hoogenboom Jr
15710 29th St
Gobles MI 49055

Call Sign: KD8JBI
Lawrence J Kancauski
15201 31st St
Gobles MI 49055

Call Sign: KD8CIM

Daniel J Ellis
6163 35th St
Gobles MI 49055

Call Sign: KD8ERM
Michael P Markus
25804 Chaty Ln
Gobles MI 49055

Call Sign: N8UFG
Allen J Cassada
28220 CR 388
Gobles MI 49055

Call Sign: N8YFM
Brian S Pritchard
1450 CR 653
Gobles MI 49055

Call Sign: KA8AOI
David W Hurley
28252 E 20th Ave
Gobles MI 49055

Call Sign: WA8QAA
Roger W Norman
409 E Exchange St
Gobles MI 49055

Call Sign: KC8VUD
Donald J Emmons
605 E Vanburen St
Gobles MI 49055

Call Sign: KG4NGL
Norbert Mcguire
7784 M 40
Gobles MI 49055

Call Sign: WB8YXA
Bernard L Clark Jr
119 Merson Rd Lot 22
Gobles MI 49055

Call Sign: KA8AOH
Elton E Ransler
304 Orchard Cir
Gobles MI 49055

Call Sign: KA8SLC
Alice K Ransler
304 Orchard Cir
Gobles MI 49055

Call Sign: N8UFJ
Janet M McColl
3722 S Dock Lake Dr
Gobles MI 49055

Call Sign: N8TFZ
Laurence A Snyder
3722 S Duck Lake Dr
Gobles MI 49055

Call Sign: KB8DGS
John C Ross
28098 S Shore Dr
Gobles MI 49055

Call Sign: N8PCC
Richard E Cook
116 S State St
Gobles MI 49055

Call Sign: KD8PJQ
Michael Fenton
13881 W Brookwood
Gobles MI 49055

Call Sign: K8TTO
Michael Fenton
13881 W Brookwood
Gobles MI 49055

Call Sign: W8AGW
Myrtle M Goff
201 W Exchange St
Gobles MI 49055

Call Sign: W8CJP
Richard L Goff
Gobles MI 49055

Call Sign: W8SCS
Robert W High
Gobles MI 49055

FCC Amateur Radio Licenses in Goetzville

Call Sign: KC8TMO
Robert J Tunney Jr
13387 E Nicole Ln
Goetzville MI 49736

Call Sign: KC8RBW
Floyd J Wilson
13405 Nicole Ln

Goetzville MI 49736

Call Sign: WD8OST
Michael S Yonan
13405 Nicole Ln
Goetzville MI 49736

FCC Amateur Radio Licenses in Good Hart

Call Sign: KB8UOF
Walter M Methven
999 Lake Shore Dr
Good Hart MI 49737

FCC Amateur Radio Licenses in Gould City

Call Sign: N8WI
Daniel R Perry
N5201 Fisher Ln
Gould City MI 49838

FCC Amateur Radio Licenses in Gowen

Call Sign: KC8AGS
Debbie L Rauch
12787 16 Mile Rd
Gowen MI 49326

Call Sign: KB8VOU
Taylor A Lance
14383 17 Mile Rd
Gowen MI 49326

Call Sign: KC8PQI
Michelle L Taylor
14383 17 Mile Rd
Gowen MI 49326

Call Sign: KD8DQD
Jeff A Macdonald
14010 18 Mile Rd
Gowen MI 49326

Call Sign: KB8IKI
Gloria A Beach
13033 19 Mile Rd Lot 84
Gowen MI 49326

Call Sign: KD8KTP
James F Knapp
15110 Carsen Ave
Gowen MI 49326

Call Sign: N8WUN
Rex K Baird
13033 E 19 Mi M99
Gowen MI 49326

Call Sign: KB8UPS
Carlton H Rauch
12787 E16 Mile Rd R 1
Gowen MI 49326

Call Sign: KC8FQE
Andrew C Cody
12779 Elton St
Gowen MI 49326

Call Sign: N8ZMZ
David C Scears
13701 Jewett
Gowen MI 49326

Call Sign: KB8PBD
Ryan A Sauber
12551 Lincoln Lake Ave
Gowen MI 493269720

Call Sign: KE8FJ
Gary A Wood
13255 Lincoln Lake Rd
Gowen MI 49326

Call Sign: N8HRS
Pamela J Wood
13255 Lincoln Lk Ave
Gowen MI 49326

Call Sign: N8HOL
Neil H Schmachtenberger
4128 Montcalm NE
Gowen MI 49326

Call Sign: KB8JZL
Jack A Hicks
12900 Morgan Mills Ave
Gowen MI 49326

Call Sign: KD8RTY
Joyce A Stevens
2316 S Satterlee Rd
Gowen MI 49326

Call Sign: W8TWA
Peter E Hansen
13680 Sprague St
Gowen MI 49326

Call Sign: N8HFV
Jerry W McCoy
10435 W Colby Rd
Gowen MI 49326

Call Sign: N8HDH
Anne H McCoy
10435 W Colby Rd
Gowen MI 49326

Call Sign: KB8PIQ
Mary E Palmer
11109 W Colby Rd
Gowen MI 49326

Call Sign: N8BSF
Alec W Palmer
11109 W Colby Rd
Gowen MI 49326

Call Sign: N8UWH
Judith J Asiala
11624 W Pakes Rd
Gowen MI 49326

Call Sign: K8GOU
Donald R Van Sickle
Gowen MI 49326

Call Sign: KB8PJT
Robert J Horak
Gowen MI 49326

FCC Amateur Radio Licenses in Grand Beach

Call Sign: N8EAT
James D Conerty
49208 Perkins Blvd
Grand Beach MI 49117

Call Sign: KC8YOB
Thomas A Johnson
13504 120th Ave
Grand Haven MI
49417

Call Sign: KC8PMM
Andrew R Young
14484 124th Ave
Grand Haven MI
49417

Call Sign: W8GP
Gregory S Poel
12410 128th Ave
Grand Haven MI
49417

Call Sign: WA8BJP
Barbara J Poel
12410 128th Ave
Grand Haven MI
49417

Call Sign: KD8ATU
Joseph J Veldhuis
12403 136th Ave
Grand Haven MI
494179608

Call Sign: KB8YTU
Paul A Vander Ploeg
13930 136th Ave
Grand Haven MI
49417

Call Sign: KB8TOG
Faith A Kettler
13124 144th Ave
Grand Haven MI
49417

Call Sign: KB8ODC
Eugene A Camfield
14579 154th Ave
Grand Haven MI
49417

Call Sign: KB8GNM
Donald D Thompson

14590 154th Ave
Grand Haven MI
49417

Call Sign: KB8HEY
Bryan P Thompson
14590 154th Ave
Grand Haven MI
49417

Call Sign: KI8DZ
James M Green
14142 155th Ave
Grand Haven MI
49417

Call Sign: KA8FXG
Robert P Brunais
15105 160th Ave
Grand Haven MI
49417

Call Sign: WB8ZNP
Richard L Borgman
15108 160th Ave
Grand Haven MI
49417

Call Sign: KC8OPL
Randy D Goldberg
15588 164th Ave
Grand Haven MI
49417

Call Sign: WB9ZPL
Larry H McLauchlin
12341 168th Ave
Grand Haven MI
49417

Call Sign: KD8FCW
Denver J Todd Jr
1501 Barbara Ct
Grand Haven MI
49417

Call Sign: WD8PDT
Daniel O Fett
1715 Barbara Ct
Grand Haven MI
49417

Call Sign: KB8VXV
Ronald J Pataky

1616 Beacon Blvd
Grand Haven MI
49417

Call Sign: AB2AO
Walter L Brink
17591 Beech Hill Dr
Grand Haven MI
49417

Call Sign: K8RNW
Walter L Brink
17591 Beech Hill Dr
Grand Haven MI
49417

Call Sign: N8WUZ
Pamela S De Witt
13641 Bittersweet Dr
Grand Haven MI
49417

Call Sign: KC8ZCN
Robert B Ennenga
14315 Briarfield Ln
Grand Haven MI
49417

Call Sign: N8IKI
Robert B Ennenga
14315 Briarfield Ln
Grand Haven MI
49417

Call Sign: KC8QCP
Gregory L Gleason
11497 Buchanan St
Grand Haven MI
494179730

Call Sign: N8KYG
Carl W Treutler
17287 Burkshire Dr
Grand Haven MI
49417

Call Sign: KE8FO
Mark J Brooky
14905 Canary Dr
Grand Haven MI
49417

Call Sign: KC8TOD
Gregory T Villerot

15900 Cedar Ave
Grand Haven MI
49417

Call Sign: KA8ZLG
Daniel M Tlachac
15333 Cherry St
Grand Haven MI
49417

Call Sign: KD8GEM
Steven J Czadzeck
400 Clinton St
Grand Haven MI
49417

Call Sign: KD8OHX
Janice M Forrest
15032 Coleman Ave
Grand Haven MI
49417

Call Sign: W8QOR
Stanley E Kuczmera
15168 Coleman Ave
Grand Haven MI
49417

Call Sign: WD8BWF
J Warren Billett
1424 Colfax Ave
Grand Haven MI
49417

Call Sign: WB8GCQ
James S Ceton
1350 Columbus
Grand Haven MI
49417

Call Sign: KC8WFV
David J Ceton
1350 Columbus St
Grand Haven MI
49417

Call Sign: KC8WYV
David J Ceton
1350 Columbus St
Grand Haven MI
49417

Call Sign: N8PGM
Donnie F Ennenga

16110 Comstock
Grand Haven MI
49417

Call Sign: N8YQD
John F Sundstrom
17933 Comstock St
Grand Haven MI
49417

Call Sign: NQ8M
William E Franks
166 Crescent Dr
Grand Haven MI
49417

Call Sign: K8BIL
William E Franks
166 Crescent Dr
Grand Haven MI
49417

Call Sign: N8KKF
Kenneth E Sanders
15280 David Ave
Grand Haven MI
494172910

Call Sign: N8HDB
Raymond R Miller Jr
520 Elliott Ave
Grand Haven MI
49417

Call Sign: KC8WCP
Penni A Dewitt
15338 Ferris St
Grand Haven MI
49417

Call Sign: KD8NWZ
Michael A Sabatino
17317 Ferris St
Grand Haven MI
49417

Call Sign: K8SAB
Michael A Sabatino
17317 Ferris St
Grand Haven MI
49417

Call Sign: KB8ZBR
Melissa W Jaeger

625 Franklin Ave
Grand Haven MI
49417

Call Sign: KB8ZBS
George F Jaeger
625 Franklin Ave
Grand Haven MI
49417

Call Sign: KC8MVR
Jane M McGregor
1644 Franklin Ave
Grand Haven MI
49417

Call Sign: WA8QIE
Robert A Ogle
1425 Franklin St
Grand Haven MI
49417

Call Sign: W8RAO
Robert A Ogle
1425 Franklin St
Grand Haven MI
49417

Call Sign: KC8DOI
Michael B Smith
1528 Franklin St
Grand Haven MI
49417

Call Sign: KC8GDF
Brad D Smith
1528 Franklin St
Grand Haven MI
49417

Call Sign: N8HCS
Donald E Smith Jr
1528 Franklin St
Grand Haven MI
49417

Call Sign: W8ESZ
Joseph L Kolenic
218 Friant St
Grand Haven MI
49417

Call Sign: KD8FCV
James R Miller

700 Fulton St 2
Grand Haven MI
49417

Call Sign: KD8KYI
Kyle G Doyon
551 Gidley Dr Apt G
Grand Haven MI
49417

Call Sign: KC6PHX
Douglas D Beecham
551 Gidley Dr Unit H
Grand Haven MI
49417

Call Sign: N8PHA
Harold F Jones
555 Gidley Dr Unit I
Grand Haven MI
49417

Call Sign: KD8JMD
Douglas G Furton
1722 Gladys Ave
Grand Haven MI
49417

Call Sign: K8EXB
Douglas G Furton
1722 Gladys Ave
Grand Haven MI
49417

Call Sign: K8CRC
Craig R Christilaw
1800 Gladys Ave
Grand Haven MI
49417

Call Sign: KD8KAP
Antonia R Clive
1805 Gladys Ave
Grand Haven MI
49417

Call Sign: KD8KAQ
Robert N Clive
1805 Gladys Ave
Grand Haven MI
49417

Call Sign: NF8L
Richard J Tanis

1811 Gladys Ave
Grand Haven MI
494172565

Call Sign: KC8YMJ
George F Verduin
1706 Gladys St
Grand Haven MI
49417

Call Sign: K8RRA
George F Verduin
1706 Gladys St
Grand Haven MI
49417

Call Sign: KD8FCT
Bradley J Fisher
525 Grand Ave
Grand Haven MI
49417

Call Sign: WB8ZFS
Donald J Theleen
1139 Grand Ave
Grand Haven MI
49417

Call Sign: N8MNS
Kenneth G Allen
15718 Grand Point Dr
Grand Haven MI
49417

Call Sign: W8NRY
Archie L Edwards
209 Grandview
Grand Haven MI
49417

Call Sign: N8JTM
Charles E Sessoms Sr
1038 Grant
Grand Haven MI
49417

Call Sign: KD8JCQ
Norman Williams
414 Grant Ave
Grand Haven MI
49417

Call Sign: KC8TOE
Andrew K Macleod

802 Grant Ave
Grand Haven MI
49417

Call Sign: KC8TOF
Rory D Macleod
802 Grant Ave
Grand Haven MI
49417

Call Sign: KC8TSW
Evan P Macleod
802 Grant Ave
Grand Haven MI
49417

Call Sign: N3WJF
David B Cross
1117 Grant Ave
Grand Haven MI
49417

Call Sign: WA8DLW
John E Sloan
1213 Grant St
Grand Haven MI
49417

Call Sign: KB8DWR
Todd J Green
14894 Groesbeck
Grand Haven MI
49417

Call Sign: KC8UBR
Mike H Meyer
120 Henley Dr
Grand Haven MI
49417

Call Sign: KF8JG
David A De Witt
13502 Hidden Creek
Ct
Grand Haven MI
49417

Call Sign: KD8EVW
Frederick J Kellaway
13583 Hidden Creek
Ct
Grand Haven MI
49417

Call Sign: WA8PYL
Kennith C Retzlaff
1306 Hillcrest Ave
Grand Haven MI
49417

Call Sign: W8CCC
Clifford T Bee
1605 Hillcrest Ave
Grand Haven MI
49417

Call Sign: KE8DL
George H Vander
Weide
1815 Hillcrest Ave
Grand Haven MI
49417

Call Sign: KF8IL
Devere R Van Oordt
616 Hillock Ct
Grand Haven MI
49417

Call Sign: KA8LEP
Seth H Holt
15404 Hofma Dr
Grand Haven MI
49417

Call Sign: W8CSO
North Ottawa ARC
14703 Indian Trl
Grand Haven MI
49417

Call Sign: N8GNA
Thomas R Nuyens
14703 Indian Trls
Grand Haven MI
49417

Call Sign: W8VH
John S Vander Heide
Jr
12491 Jansma Dr
Grand Haven MI
49417

Call Sign: KB8KGS
Edward L Cech
11621 Johnson St

Grand Haven MI
49417

Call Sign: KB8TXC
Julie C Cech
11689 Johnson St
Grand Haven MI
49417

Call Sign: N8PMD
Dan R Cech
11689 Johnson St
Grand Haven MI
49417

Call Sign: KB8WMA
Coreen A Walling
13549 Killdeer
Grand Haven MI
49417

Call Sign: KC5LNG
David J De Young
400 Lafayette Ave
Grand Haven MI
49417

Call Sign: W8GVK
Henry E Riekels Jr
619 Lake Ave
Grand Haven MI
49417

Call Sign: KC9DZG
Eric J Repaal
13672 Lake Shore Dr
Grand Haven MI
49417

Call Sign: KC8DEI
Mark A Moss
13615 Lakeshore Dr
Grand Haven MI
49417

Call Sign: N8VWH
Dennis J Berens
12239 Limberlost Ln
Grand Haven MI
49417

Call Sign: KC8PNV
Matthew D Urick
13843 Lincoln St

Grand Haven MI
49417

Call Sign: KB8LOG
Scott M Heinen
15075 Lukas Ct Apt
134
Grand Haven MI
49417

Call Sign: KF8NS
Dean F Whitney
1242 Marion Ave
Grand Haven MI
49417

Call Sign: N8KCW
Daniel L Whisman
15355 Meadowwood
Dr
Grand Haven MI
49417

Call Sign: KB8TOE
Joan L Blasky
15934 Mercury Dr
Grand Haven MI
49417

Call Sign: N8QEC
Renee K Blasky
15934 Mercury Dr
Grand Haven MI
49417

Call Sign: N8QED
Mark E Blasky
15934 Mercury Dr
Grand Haven MI
494179127

Call Sign: W8DEJ
Raymond F Brooks
15142 Mitchell
Grand Haven MI
49417

Call Sign: WB8SOE
Jack V Den Braber
13575 Pebblebrook Ct
Grand Haven MI
494179565

Call Sign: WB8FYT

Theodore H
McConnell Sr
744 Pennoyer Ave
Grand Haven MI
49417

Call Sign: N8ARY
Andrew R Young
1023 Pennoyer Ave
Grand Haven MI
49417

Call Sign: KD8HRF
Lynnette C Maddox
1023 Pennoyer Ave
Grand Haven MI
49417

Call Sign: KC8OKA
Linda M Smith
1520 Pennoyer Ave
Grand Haven MI
49417

Call Sign: KC8THP
Richard L Macdonald
15326 Pine St
Grand Haven MI
49417

Call Sign: KB8TOH
Tim P Kettler
13259 Pinewood Dr
Grand Haven MI
49417

Call Sign: KC8HXO
Gregory M Schippers
13171 Rich St
Grand Haven MI
49417

Call Sign: KC8NCG
Bonnie K Schippers
13171 Rich St
Grand Haven MI
49417

Call Sign: KC8TOI
James H Schippers
13171 Rich St
Grand Haven MI
49417

Call Sign: KC8WCO
Jeffrey T Markovicz
18000 Robbins Rd
Grand Haven MI
49417

Call Sign: WA8HLX
Dewayne G Juhnke
16600 Robbins Rd 139
Grand Haven MI
49417

Call Sign: KD8HRI
Robert L Sinke
1700 Robbins Rd 408
Grand Haven MI
49417

Call Sign: W9LNU
Wilburn S Rudd Sr
1700 Robbins Rd Lot
432
Grand Haven MI
49417

Call Sign: KB8CPZ
James J Haan Jr
1700 Robbins Rd Lot
451
Grand Haven MI
49417

Call Sign: KC8HLU
Casey J Haan
1700 Robbins Rd Lot
451
Grand Haven MI
49417

Call Sign: K8RFT
Douglas J Vander Laan
16092 Robrick St
Grand Haven MI
49417

Call Sign: KD8IAF
Daniel C Hendrick
15650 Ronny Rd
Grand Haven MI
48417

Call Sign: KC8UNY
John T Fischer
309 S 3rd St

Grand Haven MI
49417

Call Sign: KC8DHQ
Mark T Smith
205 S 5th
Grand Haven MI
49417

Call Sign: KB8WYC
Lawrence J McFadden
1500 S Ferry Apt 416
Grand Haven MI
49417

Call Sign: KA8UQT
Gordon W Stockhill
914 S Ferry St
Grand Haven MI
49417

Call Sign: WB8BSZ
Jack E Olger
1500 S Ferry St 520
Grand Haven MI
49417

Call Sign: K8BOL
William T Mackay Sr
1500 S Ferry St
Pinewood Pl Apt 402
Grand Haven MI
49417

Call Sign: W8LHM
Larry H McLauchlin
16863 Shady Dunes
Pvt
Grand Haven MI
49417

Call Sign: KB8UYO
Elizabeth M Westra
1734 Sheldon Dr
Grand Haven MI
49417

Call Sign: N8RCX
Luke A Westra
1234 Sheldon Rd
Grand Haven MI
49417

Call Sign: N8ONK

Michael A Westra
1234 Sheldon St
Grand Haven MI
49417

Call Sign: KD8INY
Joel P Nic
13098 Sikkema Dr
Grand Haven MI
49417

Call Sign: W8JPN
Joel P Nic
13098 Sikkema Dr
Grand Haven MI
49417

Call Sign: W8DUT
Joel P Nic
13098 Sikkema Dr
Grand Haven MI
49417

Call Sign: KC8VEW
Marc R Spetoskey
13186 Sikkema Dr
Grand Haven MI
49417

Call Sign: WA8ITM
Lawrence Y Park
414 Slayton Ave
Grand Haven MI
49417

Call Sign: WA8QIS
Roy E Close Jr
1435 Slayton Ave
Grand Haven MI
49417

Call Sign: W8REC
Roy E Close Jr
1435 Slayton Ave
Grand Haven MI
494172036

Call Sign: KD8NMM
Craig M Mason
12255 Sleeper St
Grand Haven MI
49417

Call Sign: W8BVA

Robert G Japenga
1350 Taylor St
Grand Haven MI
49417

Call Sign: N8PMA
Dan P Westra
1407 Taylor St
Grand Haven MI
49417

Call Sign: KB3HGR
Bart A Brummans
13896 Twin Oaks Dr
Grand Haven MI
49417

Call Sign: KC8JWE
Richard J Zintek
1954 US 31
Grand Haven MI
49417

Call Sign: KC8OQF
Richard J Zintek
11954 US 31
Grand Haven MI
49417

Call Sign: KC8KAW
Leroy Ramos Jr
520 Washington Apt
1W
Grand Haven MI
49417

Call Sign: N8LAV
Allan C TRUE
1150 Washington Ave
Grand Haven MI
49417

Call Sign: N8CUE
Robert V Plants
101 Washington Ave
193
Grand Haven MI
49417

Call Sign: KC8OVS
Jason J Mackay
14793 Williams Way
Grand Haven MI
49417

Call Sign: K8LLG
Gary L Tripp
15497 Winchester Cir
Grand Haven MI
49417

Call Sign: KD8KZE
Craig S Otto
13415 Winding Creek
Dr
Grand Haven MI
49417

Call Sign: KD8CI
William Masselink
1425 Woodlawn Cmns
Grand Haven MI
49417

Call Sign: AB8CN
David I Bodey
12974 Woodrush Ct
Grand Haven MI
49417

Call Sign: WB9OMG
Mark R Yoder
12987 Woodrush Ct
Grand Haven MI
49417

Call Sign: W8IYK
William M Booth
Grand Haven MI
49417

Call Sign: WB8SAL
Steven P Polasky
Grand Haven MI
494170714

FCC Amateur Radio
Licenses in Grand
Junction

Call Sign: KA8DVL
Richard E Neumann
4743 102nd Ave
Grand Junction MI
49056

Call Sign: KD8OPK
Robert L Suhr

6096 104th Ave
Grand Junction MI
49056

Call Sign: N9HXQ
Colin Duncan
47054 16th Ave
Grand Junction MI
490569413

Call Sign: N8RKH
Robert L Shearer
49822 2nd Ave
Grand Junction MI
49056

Call Sign: KD8QDR
Richard James Jura
13980 47th St
Grand Junction MI
49056

Call Sign: KB8NXP
John R Austin
720 49th St
Grand Junction MI
49056

Call Sign: N8WNM
Norma E Kasinger
738 49th St
Grand Junction MI
49056

Call Sign: KD8EMO
Joshua M Szynkowski
13121 52nd St
Grand Junction MI
49056

Call Sign: N8RDY
Elkin T Daniels
6268 59th St
Grand Junction MI
49056

Call Sign: N8NNV
Beder Rayborn Jr
46853 CR 384
Grand Junction MI
49056

Call Sign: KB9BMC
James P Davis

50216 CR 384 Saddle
Lake
Grand Junction MI
49056

Call Sign: KC8QPR
Jonathan L Van Ness
48042 CR 388
Grand Junction MI
49056

Call Sign: KD8KRX
David A Yohnka
2530 CR 681
Grand Junction MI
49056

Call Sign: KC8EYI
Belva Lou Krizan
13118 CR 681
Grand Junction MI
49056

Call Sign: KC8PV
Albert H Baerren
8786 W Shore Dr
Grand Junction MI
49056

Call Sign: WA8QGS
John R Williams
Grand Junction MI
49056

Call Sign: KC8CQI
Richard D Kasinger
Grand Junction MI
49056

FCC Amateur Radio
Licenses in Grand
Ledge

Call Sign: KC8UXY
Charles W Johnson Jr
10 Ballans Dr Apt 4
Grand Ledge MI
48837

Call Sign: WA8TAU
William C Myers Jr
13624 Benton Rd
Grand Ledge MI
48837

Call Sign: KF4ALD
Jeremy K Handley
435 Burch St
Grand Ledge MI
48837

Call Sign: KB8SHJ
Erik G Frimodig
12953 Chippewa Dr
Grand Ledge MI
48837

Call Sign: KC8KBI
Robert S Shaefer Jr
8940 Clark Rd
Grand Ledge MI
48837

Call Sign: W8KCJ
Theodore R Watson
6247 E Mt Hope Hwy
Grand Ledge MI
48837

Call Sign: KC8MA
James M Slater
2037 E St Joe Hwy
Grand Ledge MI
48837

Call Sign: WD8JAN
Mark A Schaefer
4646 E St Joseph Hwy
Grand Ledge MI
48837

Call Sign: N8CE
Geoffrey E Richardson
13313 Forest Hill Rd
Grand Ledge MI
48837

Call Sign: WD8PEN
Leslie E Tompkins
12945 Georgia Ave
Grand Ledge MI
48837

Call Sign: W8QQC
Le Roy J Morgan
1155 Grand Ledge
Hwy

Grand Ledge MI
48837

Call Sign: KB8RXQ
Ronald E Berghorst II
164 Grand Manor Dr
Grand Ledge MI
48837

Call Sign: KC8ODP
Bazella G Rainey III
6055 Grand River Dr
Grand Ledge MI
488378916

Call Sign: KA8VMO
Sean D Royston
620 Green
Grand Ledge MI
48837

Call Sign: KC8OXT
Clifford L Jones
119 High St
Grand Ledge MI
48837

Call Sign: N8DEF
Mark R Humphreys
7790 Jon Scott Dr
Grand Ledge MI
48837

Call Sign: N8DEH
Marilyn M Humphreys
7790 Jon Scott Dr
Grand Ledge MI
48837

Call Sign: N8WTH
David S Humphreys
7790 Jon Scott Dr
Grand Ledge MI
488379279

Call Sign: KD8GLI
John C Elder Jr
316 Lamson
Grand Ledge MI
48837

Call Sign: W8CRH
Stephen C Dible
12936 Legend Dr

Grand Ledge MI
488379451

Call Sign: K8YQQ
Richard L Hadfield
9899 Looking Glassbrk
Rd 3
Grand Ledge MI
48837

Call Sign: KC8SDU
Thomas E Hynes
217 Maple St
Grand Ledge MI
48837

Call Sign: N8MYD
Julianna J Routhier
515 Maple St Apt 6
Grand Ledge MI
488371440

Call Sign: WD8ISH
Ned A Kilmer III
916 McDiarmid Ln
Grand Ledge MI
48837

Call Sign: N8MZX
Jeffrey S Sweet
147 McMillan St
Grand Ledge MI
48837

Call Sign: KS8B
Jerome Maslowski
6875 Mt Hope R 2
Grand Ledge MI
48837

Call Sign: KC8QWJ
Brian D Monaghan
402 N Clinton St
Grand Ledge MI
48837

Call Sign: KB8YRB
Joseph S Lentz
7212 N River Hwy
Grand Ledge MI
48837

Call Sign: KC8CBN
Alicia M Houseman

6991 N River Rd
Grand Ledge MI
48837

Call Sign: KC8CBO
Brooke N Pierce
7080 N River Rd
Grand Ledge MI
48837

Call Sign: KB8IEX
Terry L Chamberlin
9681 N Royston Rd
Grand Ledge MI
48837

Call Sign: KC8YPO
Margaret J Johnson
10649 Nixon Rd
Grand Ledge MI
48837

Call Sign: W8FEV
Leighton A Tiedeman
11840 Nixon Rd
Grand Ledge MI
48837

Call Sign: N8RBX
Carl L Lance
113 Old Mill Pond 18
Grand Ledge MI
48837

Call Sign: WA8UGA
Gary R Cook
101 Old Mill Pond Rd
Apt 7
Grand Ledge MI
488375801

Call Sign: N8BIC
Michael J Fernholz
12954 Oneida Rd
Grand Ledge MI
488379495

Call Sign: KC8HOF
Timothy V Shunsky
803 Oneida Woods Tr
Grand Ledge MI
48837

Call Sign: W8KWD

Karl W Dickert Jr
7401 Pine Manor Dr
Grand Ledge MI
48837

Call Sign: KG8EN
David J Vanderwall
9214 Riverside Dr
Grand Ledge MI
48837

Call Sign: N8HFJ
Dan L Fuller
9075 Royston Rd
Grand Ledge MI
488379414

Call Sign: W8VVR
Dan L Fuller
9075 Royston Rd
Grand Ledge MI
488379414

Call Sign: N8LLP
Jerome T Ballard Sr
11095 Stoney Brook
Dr
Grand Ledge MI
48837

Call Sign: N8NRO
Teresa S Ballard
11095 Stoney Brook
Dr
Grand Ledge MI
48837

Call Sign: K8VXS
Douglas A Barnes
1116 Timber Creek Dr
Unit 30
Grand Ledge MI
48837

Call Sign: KE4BIO
Kenneth J Hooper
12948 Townsend Dr
312
Grand Ledge MI
488378712

Call Sign: KC8FXS
Phillip A Dowker
15543 W Eaton Hwy

Grand Ledge MI
48837

Call Sign: KC8WGZ
Nicholas M Dowker
15543 W Eaton Hwy
Grand Ledge MI
48837

Call Sign: KD8GLM
John C Elder Sr
855 W Jefferson 176
Grand Ledge MI
48837

Call Sign: KB8WVI
Peter D Manley
516 W Main St
Grand Ledge MI
48837

Call Sign: KD8KEA
Ronald M Pioch
1060 W Main St
Grand Ledge MI
48837

Call Sign: KB8TIM
Theodore J Nixon
12842 W Melody Ln
Grand Ledge MI
48837

Call Sign: WD8RQH
Richard H McCubbin
20 W Mt Hope
Grand Ledge MI
48837

Call Sign: KC8UUK
Matthew T McCubbin
20 W Mt Hope
Grand Ledge MI
48837

Call Sign: K8MTM
Matthew T McCubbin
20 W Mt Hope
Grand Ledge MI
48837

Call Sign: KC8UUL
Peter L McCubbin
20 W Mt Hope

Grand Ledge MI
48837

Call Sign: KB8FQH
Jeremy P McCubbin
20 W Mt Hope
Grand Ledge MI
48837

Call Sign: N8YAF
Kurt R Stauffer
212 W Scott St
Grand Ledge MI
48837

Call Sign: KA8KUF
Thomas G Davage
13701 W State Rd
Grand Ledge MI
48837

Call Sign: KD8QFE
Cheryl C Davage
13701 W State Rd
Grand Ledge MI
48837

Call Sign: KD8DAP
Jason D Bingham
15273 Wacousta Rd
Grand Ledge MI
48837

Call Sign: KD8DAU
Lawrence E Bingham
15273 Wacousta Rd
Grand Ledge MI
48837

Call Sign: KB8LBT
John E McEnhill
6271 Willow Hwy
Grand Ledge MI
48837

Call Sign: KC8SDA
William M Carney
6346 Willow Hwy
Grand Ledge MI
48837

Call Sign: WC8GOP
William M Carney
6346 Willow Hwy

Grand Ledge MI
48837

Call Sign: KC8EUE
Amanda L Burnett
1139 Willow St
Grand Ledge MI
488372132

Call Sign: KB8HWT
Maxwell L Stauffer
Grand Ledge MI
48837

Call Sign: KC8GBI
Michael A Smallwood
Grand Ledge MI
48837

Call Sign: KD8CFJ
Cheryl C Smallwood
Grand Ledge MI
48837

Call Sign: W8RQ
Michael A Smallwood
Grand Ledge MI
48837

**FCC Amateur Radio
Licenses in Grand
Marais**

Call Sign: KD8DBF
Howard A Baker
N-14268 McMillan St
Grand Marais MI
49839

Call Sign: KA5NHU
Lee G Durrwachter
E21743 Randolph St
Grand Marais MI
498390117

Call Sign: W8ENX
Harold R Meldrum
Box 307 Wilson St
Grand Marais MI
49839

Call Sign: K5UNZ
Park G Ogden Jr

Grand Marais MI
49839

Call Sign: W8HFA
Hugh C Mehlenbacher
Grand Marais MI
49839

Call Sign: KD8FPJ
Charles C Cardinal
Grand Marais MI
49839

Call Sign: K8CCC
Charles C Cardinal
Grand Marais MI
49839

Call Sign: KD8FPL
Edward E Marx
Grand Marais MI
49839

Call Sign: KD8BMR
Joseph B Mcdonald
Grand Marais MI
49839

Call Sign: KD8FDJ
Richard N Janney
Grand Marais MI
49839

**FCC Amateur Radio
Licenses in Grand
Rapids**

Call Sign: KC8NEQ
Kim D Karr
O-10883 12th Ave
Grand Rapids MI
49544

Call Sign: KC8CUT
James E Dohm
726 144th Ave
Grand Rapids MI
49316

Call Sign: KC8WBQ
Cathy M Nowell
812 1st NW Apt 2
Grand Rapids MI
49504

Call Sign: N8QOK
Robert S Lynton
3645 28th St SE 190
Grand Rapids MI
49512

Call Sign: KA8CHD
Edward G Szymanski
Jr
O 10823 2nd Ave NW
Grand Rapids MI
49544

Call Sign: KD8DBU
Eric Kiander
1541 3 Mile NE
Grand Rapids MI
49505

Call Sign: W8WMR
Frank Myers
641 3 Mile Rd
Grand Rapids MI
49505

Call Sign: K8BCZ
Robert E Quick
644 3 Mile Rd NE
Grand Rapids MI
49505

Call Sign: N8FKO
Raymond J Westra Jr
653 3 Mile Rd NE
Grand Rapids MI
49505

Call Sign: W8PDL
Donald O Parker
987 3 Mile Rd NE
Grand Rapids MI
49505

Call Sign: K9BOJ
Paul C Hummel
1017 3 Mile Rd NE
Grand Rapids MI
49505

Call Sign: N4KJH
Jerry R Strunk
1452 3 Mile Rd NE

Grand Rapids MI
49505

Call Sign: KC8RWL
Jeffrey A Norder
2582 3 Mile Rd NE
Grand Rapids MI
49525

Call Sign: N0EET
Charles N Keller
1462 32nd St SE
Grand Rapids MI
49508

Call Sign: KB8THF
Ronald S Mills
1067 4 Mile Rd NE
Grand Rapids MI
49525

Call Sign: KD8JJE
Robert A Osborn
1950 4 Mile Rd NE
Grand Rapids MI
49525

Call Sign: KB8DEY
Eileen S Royer
984-2C 4 Mile Rd NW
Grand Rapids MI
49504

Call Sign: KD8JTF
Daniel S Teelander
1008 4 Mile Rd NW
Apt 2B
Grand Rapids MI
49544

Call Sign: KD8NSY
Peter J Vawter
317 43rd St SE
Grand Rapids MI
49548

Call Sign: KD7PDA
Rebecca L Slater
2169 43rd St SE Apt
C10
Grand Rapids MI
49508

Call Sign: KC6CJY

Jeff L Burghgraef
2115 43rd St SE Apt I6
Grand Rapids MI
49508

Call Sign: KC8FAV
Donald P Lomonaco
2017 43rd U 3
Grand Rapids MI
49508

Call Sign: KD8PWA
Alfred I Lazo
1088 44th St SE
Grand Rapids MI
49508

Call Sign: W8AXA
Donald R Turney
0-10231 4th Ave
Grand Rapids MI
49544

Call Sign: KC8SIY
Jason M Guminski
1856 4th NW
Grand Rapids MI
495044816

Call Sign: KC8PCM
William P Jones
634 4th St Apt 2
Grand Rapids MI
49504

Call Sign: N8WUI
Kenneth J Novakowski
826 4th St NW
Grand Rapids MI
49504

Call Sign: N8WVM
Fredrick E Castro
1529 4th St NW
Grand Rapids MI
49504

Call Sign: K8TSU
Gordon W Oster
1052 51st St SE
Grand Rapids MI
49508

Call Sign: KD8LZO

Lee A Jones Sr
410 5th NW
Grand Rapids MI
49504

Call Sign: KD8LZP
Katherine M Frary
410 5th St NW
Grand Rapids MI
49504

Call Sign: W8AKI
Edward Wisniewski
5795 60th St SE
Grand Rapids MI
49512

Call Sign: N8AOP
James R Vinkemulder
6700 60th St SE
Grand Rapids MI
49512

Call Sign: KG8GH
Ken Nanzer
7035 60th St SE
Grand Rapids MI
49512

Call Sign: N8GND
Ken Nanzer
7035 60th St SE
Grand Rapids MI
49512

Call Sign: KB8VHA
Arthur D Visser Jr
883 61 St SE
Grand Rapids MI
49508

Call Sign: KA8GVC
Mike E Wittmer
28 68th St SW
Grand Rapids MI
49548

Call Sign: N8EBO
Gerald R Orange
564 76th St SE
Grand Rapids MI
49508

Call Sign: KD8FSR

Vicki L Huffman
1841 7th NW
Grand Rapids MI
49504

Call Sign: KD8RVL
Troy B Bergsma
13051 8th Ave
Grand Rapids MI
49534

Call Sign: KC8TSU
Carl D Bolthouse
0-12615 8th Ave NW
Grand Rapids MI
49504

Call Sign: KB8ILI
Evelyn J Thompson
0-12657 8th Ave NW
Grand Rapids MI
49504

Call Sign: WA8AAT
Carl A Thompson
0-12657 8th Ave NW
Grand Rapids MI
49504

Call Sign: N8IWQ
Martin F Sabraw
5785 Ada Dr SE
Grand Rapids MI
49506

Call Sign: KC8HBU
Jason T Zawodny
6391 Ada Dr SE
Grand Rapids MI
49546

Call Sign: KD8PVZ
Dustin G Olsen
500 Adams SE
Grand Rapids MI
49507

Call Sign: KB8TDY
Brad K Sleighter
1183 Alger SE
Grand Rapids MI
49507

Call Sign: N8QOI

Mark E Veenstra
2460 Almont SE
Grand Rapids MI
49507

Call Sign: KC8UUJ
James M Tumbling Sr
1717 Alpine Ave NW
Grand Rapids MI
49504

Call Sign: KB8INS
Jack Heeringa
630 Alta Dale SE
Grand Rapids MI
49546

Call Sign: KC8CBW
Ronald W Ricketson
Sr
1071 Amberwood Dr
WSW
Grand Rapids MI
49509

Call Sign: KD8HHL
John M Winstanley
245 Ann St NE
Grand Rapids MI
49505

Call Sign: KC8VJQ
Steffen Froehlich
7165 Aqua Fria Ct
Grand Rapids MI
49546

Call Sign: AA8TN
Leena Mammen
1819 Argentina Dr SE
Grand Rapids MI
49506

Call Sign: KD8RVH
Kenneth M Hoffman
2320 Argentina Dr SE
Grand Rapids MI
49506

Call Sign: N8TFX
Daryl S Boersema
857 Argo Ave SE
Grand Rapids MI
49546

Call Sign: KB8WXQ
Todd B Korn
836 Arianna NW
Grand Rapids MI
49504

Call Sign: KB8YNJ
Bonnie R Korn
836 Arianna NW
Grand Rapids MI
49504

Call Sign: N8IJN
David S Hoffer
477 Arrowhead Ave
SE
Grand Rapids MI
49546

Call Sign: K8ECB
Mark V Wittkoski
2217 Ashcreek Ct NW
Grand Rapids MI
49534

Call Sign: N8SRQ
Laurence M
Halberstadt
2232 Audobon Dr SE
Grand Rapids MI
49506

Call Sign: KC8WBO
Daniel C Tuuri
1833 Avondale Dr SE
Grand Rapids MI
49506

Call Sign: WS8K
Timothy E Steenwyk
3178 Baldwin St
Grand Rapids MI
49426

Call Sign: KC8SWV
Timothy Scott Sanford
1131 Baldwin St SE
Grand Rapids MI
49506

Call Sign: KC8BZI
Anthony P Naujalis
1935 Ball Ave

Grand Rapids MI
49505

Call Sign: KC8OVY
Paula L Naujalis
1935 Ball Ave
Grand Rapids MI
49505

Call Sign: KD8HLF
Kent County ARES
Races
701 Ball Ave NE
Grand Rapids MI
49509

Call Sign: WB8WMP
Roy E Vrba
1525 Ball NE
Grand Rapids MI
49505

Call Sign: KC8LGF
Michael T Schulte
354 Ball Park Blvd
Grand Rapids MI
49504

Call Sign: KD8PVV
William E Bailey
1339 Banbury Ave NE
Grand Rapids MI
49505

Call Sign: KB8ZSW
Stephen N Marouchoc
1442 Barke NE A
Grand Rapids MI
49506

Call Sign: WW8K
Ted A Nowak
555 Bayberry Pt Dr
NW Apt B
Grand Rapids MI
49534

Call Sign: KD8GJU
Michael G Miller
226 Baynton NE
Grand Rapids MI
49503

Call Sign: KB8WZI

Adam G Twork
1913 Bayou Ct NE
Grand Rapids MI
49505

Call Sign: KC8CKZ
Viktors A Miske Jr
4016 Baywood Dr SE
Grand Rapids MI
495462212

Call Sign: N8ACO
James G Sproul
4385 Baywood SE
Grand Rapids MI
49546

Call Sign: K8ACE
Harold W Reick
1653 Beard Dr SE
Grand Rapids MI
49546

Call Sign: WA8WLK
Sara Jean Feistamel
O 106 Begole SW
Grand Rapids MI
49534

Call Sign: WA8VNI
John S Feistamel
O 106 Begole SW
Grand Rapids MI
49544

Call Sign: KD8GSZ
Robert D Woodhill
3249 Behler Dr SE
Grand Rapids MI
49546

Call Sign: W4FMS
Frank M Scutch III
3271 Behler Dr SE
Grand Rapids MI
49546

Call Sign: KC8FGV
Trannie P Carter II
1252 Bemis SE
Grand Rapids MI
49506

Call Sign: KC8GYN

Kenneth W Van
Prooyen II
930 Benjamin Ave SE
Grand Rapids MI
49506

Call Sign: KD8PVP
David L Homant
1964 Benjamin NE
Grand Rapids MI
49505

Call Sign: KD8PVM
Heidi J Vereecken
2745 Birchcrest Dr SE
Apt 501
Grand Rapids MI
49506

Call Sign: N8WKN
Robert J Gage
2910 Bird Ave
Grand Rapids MI
49525

Call Sign: KC8PKP
Kyle A Curtis
3131 Bird NE
Grand Rapids MI
49525

Call Sign: KD8NRB
David W Jolly
1770 Bloomfield Dr
SE
Grand Rapids MI
49508

Call Sign: K8DWJ
David W Jolly
1770 Bloomfield Dr
SE
Grand Rapids MI
49508

Call Sign: KB8TWW
Alphonse P Sekeet
1320 Blossom SE Apt
I
Grand Rapids MI
49508

Call Sign: KD8OSB
Charles S Cairns

177 Bona Vista Dr NW
Grand Rapids MI
49504

Call Sign: K8BJP
Robert H Barnhart
1845 Boston St SE Ste
201
Grand Rapids MI
49506

Call Sign: W8PFL
Alfred N Gwinn
115 Bowne St NE
Grand Rapids MI
49505

Call Sign: KD8DEE
Michael J Steele
4830 Boyd Ln NE
Grand Rapids MI
49525

Call Sign: KC8UX
Ronald D Houtman
2219 Bradford Ct NE
Grand Rapids MI
495056406

Call Sign: KC8HZP
Christopher M Grow
4285 Bradford NE
Grand Rapids MI
49525

Call Sign: K8WU
Richard G Kirkpatrick
2500 Breton Woods Dr
Apt 3041
Grand Rapids MI
49512

Call Sign: K8ALJ
William I Jones Jr
2500 Breton Woods Dr
S E Apt 3065
Grand Rapids MI
495129132

Call Sign: W8POK
Dale S Vennen
416 Briar Ln NE
Grand Rapids MI
49503

Call Sign: N8KFO
Phillip C Medawar
317 Briar Wood SE
Grand Rapids MI
49506

Call Sign: N8HNI
Robert T Flannery
1458 Bridge NW
Grand Rapids MI
49504

Call Sign: N8YEO
Lloyd B Little
1925 Bridge NW Apt
602
Grand Rapids MI
49504

Call Sign: KB8ECB
Mark V Wittkoski
1719 Bridge St NW
Grand Rapids MI
495044918

Call Sign: KB8NFU
Blake Braesicke
1006 Bridge St NW
Grand Rapids MI
49504

Call Sign: KC8WIK
Blake Braesicke
1006 Bridge St NW
Grand Rapids MI
49504

Call Sign: KC8VMU
Briana M Asmus
2025 Bridgeport Rd
100
Grand Rapids MI
49505

Call Sign: KC8UUI
Michael W York
2025 Bridgeport Rd
NE Apt 100
Grand Rapids MI
49505

Call Sign: KC8RJE
Brian J Veen

7450 Bridle Path
Grand Rapids MI
49546

Call Sign: KG8PI
William C Dells
3531 Briggs Blvd NE
Grand Rapids MI
49505

Call Sign: KB8WJW
Helen S Dells
3531 Briggs Blvd NE
Grand Rapids MI
49525

Call Sign: KD8DEC
Stephen D Cornelius
2305 Brighton Dr SE
Grand Rapids MI
49506

Call Sign: KC8EGM
Douglas E Phillips
2761 Brisam
Grand Rapids MI
49505

Call Sign: N8JGV
Kenneth W
Montgomery
O - 11770 Brisben NW
Grand Rapids MI
49544

Call Sign: N8KGM
Jerry L Yntema II
2522 Bristol Ave NW
Grand Rapids MI
495441412

Call Sign: KC8PKN
Jack H Kunnen
312 Bristol NW
Grand Rapids MI
495044928

Call Sign: KC8QKC
Jack H Kunnen
312 Bristol NW
Grand Rapids MI
495044928

Call Sign: KC8PKN

Jack H Kunnen
312 Bristol NW
Grand Rapids MI
495044928

Call Sign: AB8ND
Jack H Kunnen
312 Bristol NW
Grand Rapids MI
495044928

Call Sign: KB8SEU
David L Nylen
1700 Bristol NW
Grand Rapids MI
49504

Call Sign: WB8AEO
Norman A Weber
630 Broadview SE
Grand Rapids MI
49507

Call Sign: KC8WBP
Paul E Longoria
419 Broadway
Grand Rapids MI
49504

Call Sign: KC8IFO
Jeff A Steinport
600 Broadway Ave
NW Ste 406
Grand Rapids MI
49504

Call Sign: N8VDJ
Donald L Davis Jr
1063 Broadway NW
Apt 2
Grand Rapids MI
49504

Call Sign: KB8TLZ
Stephen R Falk
3370 Brook Trls SE
Grand Rapids MI
49508

Call Sign: N8EQ
Stephen R Falk
3370 Brook Trls SE
Grand Rapids MI
49508

Call Sign: KD8LVP
Gregory J Folkert
4948 Buchanan Ave
SW
Grand Rapids MI
49548

Call Sign: KC8HGD
Rohn P Kunnen
933 Burke Ave NE
Grand Rapids MI
49503

Call Sign: KC8KVQ
Richard L Riessen
106 Burr Oak NE
Grand Rapids MI
49505

Call Sign: KD7PAF
Phillip E Hall
3190 Burton SE
Grand Rapids MI
49546

Call Sign: WJ8F
Ted A Dekker
1738 Burton St SE
Grand Rapids MI
49506

Call Sign: KB8MGG
Daniel W Foster
3811 Butterworth St
Grand Rapids MI
495446655

Call Sign: KC8WBN
Donald F Barsema
1458 Byron St SE
Grand Rapids MI
49506

Call Sign: N8NIK
Robert G Bulten
2226 Cambridge SE
Grand Rapids MI
49506

Call Sign: WB8SKJ
Anton F Buczek Jr
29 Canyon Dr NW

Grand Rapids MI
49504

Call Sign: WB2ZQR
Thomas F Schwanda
6125 Capitan SE
Grand Rapids MI
49546

Call Sign: KB8MGE
Stacy M Hazeltine
1431 Carlton Ave NE
Grand Rapids MI
49505

Call Sign: KC8VTZ
Amy J Westhouse
1214 Carlton NE
Grand Rapids MI
49505

Call Sign: KC8JYG
Stephen M Conrad
1431 Carlton NE
Grand Rapids MI
49505

Call Sign: WB9VJW
Vicki L Conrad
1431 Carlton NE
Grand Rapids MI
49505

Call Sign: WN8S
Thomas D Conrad
1431 Carlton NE
Grand Rapids MI
49505

Call Sign: K8VOJ
Sandra L Biziorek
940 Carpenter NW
Grand Rapids MI
49504

Call Sign: K8VOL
Steven J Biziorek
940 Carpenter NW
Grand Rapids MI
49504

Call Sign: KD8CKR
Thomas J Gerger Jr
1332 Cedar NE

Grand Rapids MI
49503

Call Sign: KC8FGO
Michael E Price
2851 Central Pkwy
102
Grand Rapids MI
49505

Call Sign: N8QBK
Christiane E Warsinski
2839 Central Pkwy NE
Apt 202
Grand Rapids MI
49505

Call Sign: WB8VON
Howard J Broekema
3435 Chamberlain SE
Grand Rapids MI
49508

Call Sign: KA8TWP
Gordon J Buys
3628 Chamberlain SE
Grand Rapids MI
49508

Call Sign: KD8JTE
Falon E Gray
688 Charlotte Ave NW
Grand Rapids MI
49504

Call Sign: KD8MSN
Falon E Gray
688 Charlotte Ave NW
Grand Rapids MI
49504

Call Sign: KD8OVF
Donald M Jansen
831 Charlotte NW
Grand Rapids MI
49504

Call Sign: WB8MRC
Robert J Koetsier
959 Charlotte NW
Grand Rapids MI
49504

Call Sign: KC8KMN

Thomas H Stocks
1035 Cheerywood NE
Grand Rapids MI
49506

Call Sign: KF6HSP
Wolfgang Philipps
5862 Christie Ave SE
Grand Rapids MI
49508

Call Sign: KF8DBT
Wolfgang Philipps
5862 Christie Ave SE
Grand Rapids MI
49508

Call Sign: KD8JSY
Robin L Blanton
6979 Christmas Ln
Grand Rapids MI
49548

Call Sign: KC8KGS
Charles P Allen III
7776 Cidermill Dr SE
Grand Rapids MI
495087606

Call Sign: W9TA
Richard F Roll
6878 Cimarron Dr SE
Grand Rapids MI
495467220

Call Sign: N8HNQ
Thomas D Mettler
536 Clinton NW
Grand Rapids MI
49544

Call Sign: KC8BWU
Scott M Poggi
2251 Clover Dr
Grand Rapids MI
49504

Call Sign: KC8EST
Kent County
Emergency Service
Team
2851 Clyde Park
Grand Rapids MI
49501

Call Sign: KA8DDZ
Timothy A Hynde
1388 Cobb Dr SE 2A
Grand Rapids MI
49508

Call Sign: N8VWI
William J Zaidel
1036 Cogswell St NW
Grand Rapids MI
495442819

Call Sign: N8WKQ
Connie S Zaidel
1036 Cogswell St NW
Grand Rapids MI
495442819

Call Sign: KC8EWV
Andrew M Kasul
766 Coif NE
Grand Rapids MI
49503

Call Sign: W8COF
Alfred K Howes
1524 Coit Ave NE
Grand Rapids MI
49505

Call Sign: KC8AYD
Russell J Anthony
2912 Coit Ave NE
Grand Rapids MI
49505

Call Sign: KC8BAY
Melissa T Anthony
2912 Coit Ave NE
Grand Rapids MI
49505

Call Sign: KB8PQY
Vicki L Sorensen
2317 Coit N E
Grand Rapids MI
49505

Call Sign: KB8NFJ
Thomas B McDonniel
5575 Coit NE
Grand Rapids MI
49505

Call Sign: KC8PPL
Jason R Rudd
1106 Coldbrook St NE
Grand Rapids MI
49503

Call Sign: KC8LGG
Daniel A De Ruiter
6708 College Ave
Grand Rapids MI
49548

Call Sign: KC8UAT
Andrew J Felde
459 Collindale NW
Grand Rapids MI
49504

Call Sign: AF8U
Andrew J Felde
459 Collindale NW
Grand Rapids MI
49504

Call Sign: KD8QXB
Timothy C Van
Reenen
115 Colrain St SW
Grand Rapids MI
49548

Call Sign: N8OCR
Douglas A Post
2901 Colt NE
Grand Rapids MI
49505

Call Sign: W8FSW
David C Boyce
3623 Cook Valley
Blvd SE
Grand Rapids MI
49546

Call Sign: KC8HVT
David J Buffington
2875 Coppergrove Ct
Grand Rapids MI
49525

Call Sign: KB8VEJ
Sheryl R Van Den
Akker

1635 Country Club
Grand Rapids MI
49505

Call Sign: KC8FMT
Richard D Brown
6660 Creekstone Ln
Apt 304
Grand Rapids MI
495487851

Call Sign: KC8LXN
Lori Beck
6660 Creekstone Ln
Apt 304
Grand Rapids MI
495487851

Call Sign: KD8LVS
Timothy R Jones
6640 Creekstone Ln
SW Apt 302
Grand Rapids MI
49548

Call Sign: KC8WBR
Robert E Cardwell
235 Crescent NE 1
Grand Rapids MI
49503

Call Sign: WA8YYY
Albert R Lane
726 Crescent St NE
Grand Rapids MI
49503

Call Sign: N8EJJ
Thomas J Mogilnicki
1139 Crescent St NE
Grand Rapids MI
495033621

Call Sign: KC8LLV
Alvin E Tillman
5560 Crippen SW
Grand Rapids MI
49548

Call Sign: KG8QH
Kenneth W Van
Weerdhuizen
990 Culpepper SE

Grand Rapids MI
49508

Call Sign: W8SIN
Walter R Peterson
4605 Curwood SE
Grand Rapids MI
49508

Call Sign: KA8SAG
Julio H Noriega
2111 Darwin Ave SW
Grand Rapids MI
495072319

Call Sign: W8AXD
Wilbur J Adams Jr
924 Dayton SW
Grand Rapids MI
49504

Call Sign: N8INE
Jeremy P Nachbar
1100 Dayton SW
Grand Rapids MI
495046113

Call Sign: WB9NIR
Robert B Arbetman
6064 Del Cano Dr SE
Grand Rapids MI
49546

Call Sign: KC8LTV
Clifford W Walker
131 Delaware St SE
Grand Rapids MI
49507

Call Sign: KC8MZW
Roger A Hill
1455 Derby Dr NW
Grand Rapids MI
495042622

Call Sign: KD8DKY
Adam B Gillette
1486 Dewberry Pl NE
Apt 6
Grand Rapids MI
495055891

Call Sign: KC8WCQ
Mitchell R Payne

1444 Dewberry Pl NE
Apt 7
Grand Rapids MI
49505

Call Sign: KC8NJV
Michael J Howard
1255 Diamond NE
Grand Rapids MI
49505

Call Sign: N8ARG
Gregory J Jaglowski
1909 Diamond NE
Grand Rapids MI
49505

Call Sign: KC8CBZ
Patrick W Laundra
44 5 Division S Apt 73
Grand Rapids MI
49503

Call Sign: N8DDE
Erik K Taube
1742 Dorais Ct NE
Grand Rapids MI
49505

Call Sign: N8HAQ
Eric Taube
1742 Dorais Ct NE
Grand Rapids MI
49505

Call Sign: KB8AXZ
Biruta Taube
1742 Dorais Ct NE
Grand Rapids MI
495252801

Call Sign: KD8PIZ
Ronald E Easley
3115 Dorais Dr NE
Grand Rapids MI
495252802

Call Sign: KA8BCI
Donald E Hazelswart
833 Dorroll
Grand Rapids MI
49505

Call Sign: KD8AUO

Andrew J Pariwozik
721 Dorroll NE
Grand Rapids MI
49505

Call Sign: KA8ZCO
Randall S Barrett
759 Douglas
Grand Rapids MI
49504

Call Sign: KA8OVT
Maryjo K Barrett
759 Douglas NW
Grand Rapids MI
49504

Call Sign: KA8RIV
Gwen K Barrett
759 Douglas NW
Grand Rapids MI
49504

Call Sign: NE8E
Franklin D Barrett
759 Douglas NW
Grand Rapids MI
49504

Call Sign: KB8AOJ
William D Johns
1015 Douglas NW
Grand Rapids MI
49504

Call Sign: KF4GJK
Christopher M Bolek
2673 Dunnigan Ave
NE
Grand Rapids MI
49525

Call Sign: N8SAN
R Henckel
2301 E Beltline NE
Grand Rapids MI
495259779

Call Sign: KC8LZL
Benjamin W Johnson
985 E Beltline NE
Campus
Grand Rapids MI
49525

Call Sign: KF8IT
Christopher G Goron
1019 E Fulton
Grand Rapids MI
49503

Call Sign: KC8WRW
Louis R Craig
500 E Fulton 383
Grand Rapids MI
49503

Call Sign: KC8JEE
Kevin W Greene
1849 E Fulton St
Grand Rapids MI
495033804

Call Sign: KC8UHQ
Bob Jones
313 E Fulton St 1
Grand Rapids MI
49503

Call Sign: W8ALA
Merlin J Applegate
3604 E Fulton St Apt
336
Grand Rapids MI
495461428

Call Sign: K8DKD
Dwight K Dodge
535 E Fulton St Ste Ii
Grand Rapids MI
49503

Call Sign: KC8DYU
Justin T W Gustafson
4682 E Meadows Dr
Grand Rapids MI
49546

Call Sign: WA3LKN
David R Pennes M D
2059 E Wyndham Hill
Dr NE Apt 303
Grand Rapids MI
495056358

Call Sign: KF8VY
Robert A Bonner

2072 Eastcastle SE Apt
Dd7
Grand Rapids MI
495048764

Call Sign: KC8PZC
Dustin L Amerson
7068 Eastern Ave
Grand Rapids MI
495087434

Call Sign: KC8PZI
Christian Dahlke
7068 Eastern Ave
Grand Rapids MI
495087434

Call Sign: KD8NSW
Howard A Weatherly
3347 Eastern Ave NE
Grand Rapids MI
49525

Call Sign: KD8QFC
John M Smith
1346 Eastern Ave SE
Grand Rapids MI
49507

Call Sign: KG8ZO
Mark S Robart
2533 Eastern Ave SE
Grand Rapids MI
49507

Call Sign: KD8GSX
Robert B Simonson Jr
6648 Eastern Ave SE
Grand Rapids MI
49508

Call Sign: KC8SWL
John R Stinson Jr
516 Eastern NE
Grand Rapids MI
49503

Call Sign: K8TWN
Ralph Ter Beek
6981 Edgeview
Grand Rapids MI
49509

Call Sign: N8MXJ

Daniel P Vanderhorst
2009 Edgewood NE
Grand Rapids MI
49505

Call Sign: N8ZTS
Donald J Schmuker
205 Edison Park NW
Grand Rapids MI
49504

Call Sign: W8JLJ
Raymond L Ritchey
913 Edna SE
Grand Rapids MI
49507

Call Sign: N8PQK
James H Van Prooyen
943 Edna SE
Grand Rapids MI
495073703

Call Sign: N8UXS
Jeffrey G Boris
320 Eleanor NE
Grand Rapids MI
49505

Call Sign: KB8NFF
William S Thomas
520 Eleanor NE
Grand Rapids MI
49505

Call Sign: KD8LZT
Robert G Hardin
945 Eleanor St NE
Grand Rapids MI
49505

Call Sign: N8VLJ
John S Kay
1000 Elliot SE
Grand Rapids MI
49505

Call Sign: N8QOL
Bob E Deboer
1000 Elliot SE
Grand Rapids MI
49507

Call Sign: KB8RHW

Robert E Guth
1361 Elmdale NE Apt
103
Grand Rapids MI
49505

Call Sign: N8PGW
Edward J Kindl
2275 Elmridge NW
Grand Rapids MI
49504

Call Sign: N8FCE
Richard L Sutherland
12 Elmwood NE
Grand Rapids MI
49505

Call Sign: N8LVH
Scott A Haga
2845 Englewood
Grand Rapids MI
495081557

Call Sign: KD8KLJ
Eric H Smith
1410 Escott Ave NW
Grand Rapids MI
49504

Call Sign: N8DJE
Eric H Smith
1410 Escott Ave NW
Grand Rapids MI
49504

Call Sign: KD8PJJ
Christopher J Kragt
415 Ethel Ave NE Apt
2
Grand Rapids MI
49506

Call Sign: KD8EFC
Suzanne A Bratt
2321 Everest SE
Grand Rapids MI
49507

Call Sign: WA8DFP
Charles R Edmunds
1028 Evergreen St SE
Grand Rapids MI
49507

Call Sign: KD8LQJ
Matthew J Slachter
580 Fairfield NW
Grand Rapids MI
49504

Call Sign: N8DGD
Thomas M Hansen
632 Fairview Ave
Grand Rapids MI
49503

Call Sign: KB8UYQ
Thomas E Borgir
526 Fairway NW
Grand Rapids MI
49504

Call Sign: WA8SQX
Donald J Faber
2616 Falcon Pointe Dr
NW
Grand Rapids MI
49544

Call Sign: WB5VHB
Clayton E Wittman
3659 Falling Leaf Dr
Grand Rapids MI
49512

Call Sign: KD8JDA
Donald D Giese
483 Faraday Dr SE
Grand Rapids MI
49548

Call Sign: N8WKI
Kevin J Knibbe
4540 Fennessy
Grand Rapids MI
49504

Call Sign: WA8YUH
Donald R Turney Jr
0-561 Fennessy SW
Grand Rapids MI
49534

Call Sign: AC8IM
Philip M Haines
1556 Fern Pl NE

Grand Rapids MI
49505

Call Sign: N8STG
David H Zemmer
421 Ferndale NW
Grand Rapids MI
49504

Call Sign: KB8UKB
Randy L Weener
1522 Ferndale SW
Grand Rapids MI
49504

Call Sign: KD8DEA
Tyler A Maleport
6988 Festival Dr
Grand Rapids MI
49548

Call Sign: W8CCE
Harold R Millgard Sr
2115 Finsbury Ln NW
Grand Rapids MI
49504

Call Sign: KD8RLQ
Anne M Thompson
4789 Firefly Dr
Grand Rapids MI
49525

Call Sign: KD8RLU
Leo P Thompson
4789 Firefly Dr NE
Grand Rapids MI
49525

Call Sign: W8IQD
Leon E Fosner
3738 Fitzhugh Ave NE
Grand Rapids MI
49505

Call Sign: KC8FGP
Dan M Fowler
2462 Fletcher Dr NE
Grand Rapids MI
49506

Call Sign: KV8V
Melbourne Frontjes
2420 Fletcher NE

Grand Rapids MI
49506

Call Sign: KA8AXK
Max Bailey
1055 Forest Hill Ave
SE Apt 145
Grand Rapids MI
49546

Call Sign: WA8VYL
Bernard P Kool
1910 Forest Shore SE
Grand Rapids MI
49506

Call Sign: KC8BAS
Richard G Laninga
2115 Fox Ridge NE
Grand Rapids MI
49505

Call Sign: W8TZC
William P Boss
1551 Franklin St SE
Apt 2098
Grand Rapids MI
495063356

Call Sign: KC8PFR
Todd E Walton
960 Fremont Ave NW
Grand Rapids MI
495044368

Call Sign: N8QPY
Daniel P Mish
1707 Fremont Ave
NW
Grand Rapids MI
495042838

Call Sign: N8QZR
Kelaine L Mish
1707 Fremont NW
Grand Rapids MI
495042838

Call Sign: KC8OZD
Kenneth P Bosma
3270 Fuller Ave S E
Grand Rapids MI
49508

Call Sign: KD8DDY
Deborah L Trowbridge
843 Fuller Ave SE
Grand Rapids MI
49506

Call Sign: KD8DDV
Rachael A Scholten
843 Fuller Ave SE
Grand Rapids MI
49506

Call Sign: N8LEZ
Peter D Patsakos
831 Fuller NE
Grand Rapids MI
49503

Call Sign: KD8LYN
Satern
1215 Fulton St SE
Grand Rapids MI
49503

Call Sign: W8SAT
Wmni Satern
1215 Fulton St SE
Grand Rapids MI
49503

Call Sign: KA8DCS
Silvia G Rittenhouse
1835 Fulton W
Grand Rapids MI
49504

Call Sign: WB8VOJ
John R Rittenhouse
1835 Fulton W
Grand Rapids MI
49504

Call Sign: KD8DCH
Benjamin D Palmerlee
1258 Garfield Ave NE
Apt 2
Grand Rapids MI
49504

Call Sign: KD8FSS
Gillian L Jacques
1430 Garfield Ave NW
Grand Rapids MI
49504

Call Sign: KD8LXT
Robert G Bunker Jr
1038 Garfield NW
Grand Rapids MI
49504

Call Sign: KB8YNC
David E Rittenhouse
1120 Garfield NW
Grand Rapids MI
49504

Call Sign: NZ8V
Douglas R Smith
2554 Garfield NW
Grand Rapids MI
495441822

Call Sign: KA8RTS
Anthony R Krzykwa
1275 Gentian Dr SE
Grand Rapids MI
49508

Call Sign: KD8MDJ
Ronald L Decker
1252 Gentian SE
Grand Rapids MI
495086266

Call Sign: KC8EKJ
John H Pinkerton
1027 Gibson
Grand Rapids MI
49507

Call Sign: W8JHP
John H Pinkerton
1027 Gibson
Grand Rapids MI
49507

Call Sign: KD8RLG
Tella Minkkinen
745 Gladstone
Grand Rapids MI
49506

Call Sign: WA8DWX
William J Hakeem
7135 Gladys Dr SE
Grand Rapids MI
49546

Call Sign: AC8EZ
Mary K Hakeem
7135 Gladys Dr SE
Grand Rapids MI
49546

Call Sign: WB8COB
Hervey E Sherd
5630 Glen Cove SE
Grand Rapids MI
49506

Call Sign: KD3Y
G Edward Lambert
1282 Glen Ellyn Dr SE
Grand Rapids MI
49546

Call Sign: KD8PNL
Emily M Potter
4849 Glen Meadow Ct
SE
Grand Rapids MI
49546

Call Sign: K1GRS
Gregory R Snow
2219 Godwin Ave SE
Grand Rapids MI
49507

Call Sign: KA9JKA
Michael G Winnowski
8 Gold Ave SW
Grand Rapids MI
49504

Call Sign: K8QS
Quentin J Schultze
2607 Golfridge Dr SE
Grand Rapids MI
49546

Call Sign: W8USA
Michigan Amateur
Radio Alliance
812 Grace Land NE
Grand Rapids MI
495054363

Call Sign: K8JX
Richard M Ranta
812 Graceland NE

Grand Rapids MI
49505

Call Sign: WB8HJX
Richard M Ranta
812 Graceland NE
Grand Rapids MI
49505

Call Sign: K8JX
Richard M Ranta
812 Graceland NE
Grand Rapids MI
49505

Call Sign: KC8YXG
Michigan Amateur
Radio Telegraphers
Society
812 Graceland NE
Grand Rapids MI
495054363

Call Sign: KC8DWE
James J Lepech
1656 Graham Ct NW
Grand Rapids MI
49504

Call Sign: KC8UXO
Timothy J Ham
3423 Grand River Dr
NE
Grand Rapids MI
49525

Call Sign: KC8BMD
Michael C Poplawski
2456 Greenings NE
Grand Rapids MI
49505

Call Sign: N8SRN
Paul A Daverman
1555 Gridley Ave NW
Grand Rapids MI
495342482

Call Sign: N8ZUU
Douglas G Luurs
1030 Griswold St SE
Grand Rapids MI
49507

Call Sign: KD8EAU
Thomas J Gottschalk
35 Guild NE
Grand Rapids MI
49505

Call Sign: W8QBA
Roland R Beineman
136 Guild St
Grand Rapids MI
49505

Call Sign: KD8KTQ
Caleb A Hoover
4474 Hackley Dr NE
Grand Rapids MI
49525

Call Sign: KD8GUX
Don P Hoover
4474 Hackley Dr NE
Grand Rapids MI
49525

Call Sign: AC8EG
Don P Hoover
4474 Hackley Dr NE
Grand Rapids MI
49525

Call Sign: KD8DBZ
Terrence L Groesser
5408 Hall SE
Grand Rapids MI
49546

Call Sign: W8TLG
Terrence L Groesser
5408 Hall SE
Grand Rapids MI
49546

Call Sign: KD8DLM
Jan T Fair Jr
5822 Hall St SE
Grand Rapids MI
49546

Call Sign: K8EGU
Philip L Burton
3939 Hall St SW
Grand Rapids MI
49544

Call Sign: KC8LJT
Richard P Strayer
5025 Hendershot Ave
NW
Grand Rapids MI
49544

Call Sign: N8OAR
William J Wisneski
1845 Herrick Ave NE
Grand Rapids MI
495054866

Call Sign: KD8EFF
Don J Fehsenfeld
1318 Herrick NE
Grand Rapids MI
49505

Call Sign: W9BOO
William Parzyszek III
4760 Hickory Way SE
Grand Rapids MI
495466321

Call Sign: K8RAF
Robert A Frans
3332 Hidden Hills Ct
Grand Rapids MI
49546

Call Sign: KC8BAP
Robert A Frans
3332 Hidden Hills Ct
SE
Grand Rapids MI
49546

Call Sign: KC8EFK
Arie C Nobel
619 High St SW
Grand Rapids MI
49509

Call Sign: N8BBW
James G Paulsen
2131 Highbluff Dr NE
Grand Rapids MI
49505

Call Sign: KD8PVT
Carla L Heavilon
2306 Highland View
Cir S

Grand Rapids MI
49506

Call Sign: KD8LZQ
Ronald J Reitsma
2528 Highridge Hills
Ln
Grand Rapids MI
49546

Call Sign: KD8IYK
Joel C Schmitz
2538 Highridge Ln SE
Grand Rapids MI
49546

Call Sign: N8QNY
Donald L Goris
760 Hill St NW
Grand Rapids MI
49504

Call Sign: KB8YXE
Donald H Glaum
1310 Hillburn Ave
NW
Grand Rapids MI
49504

Call Sign: K8HYB
James V Jeltema
1359 Hillcrest NW
Grand Rapids MI
49504

Call Sign: KC8JQL
Daniel B Diephouse
1961 Hillsboro
Grand Rapids MI
495469791

Call Sign: KE4YAO
Janice A Javery
1648 Hillsboro Ave
Grand Rapids MI
49546

Call Sign: KC8PFV
Charles B Brown
1430 Holborn Dr NW
Grand Rapids MI
49504

Call Sign: KC8RMK

Robert L Franzen
1033 Hollywood NE
Grand Rapids MI
49505

Call Sign: W8AFQ
Henry J Elgersma Sr
100 Holmdene Blvd
NE
Grand Rapids MI
49503

Call Sign: KD8GWE
Ann E Ed
2383 Holtman Ave
Grand Rapids MI
49525

Call Sign: KD8GWF
David W Ed
2383 Holtman Ave Dr
NE
Grand Rapids MI
49525

Call Sign: AC8AB
David W Ed
2383 Holtman Ave Dr
NE
Grand Rapids MI
49525

Call Sign: WB9YKB
Paul J Fricke
4146 Holyoke Dr SE
Grand Rapids MI
49508

Call Sign: KA4NYN
James L McKinley
1256 Hope SE
Grand Rapids MI
49506

Call Sign: KC8EKG
Lori D Rowe
2206 Horton SE
Grand Rapids MI
49507

Call Sign: WD8JMF
Scott M Rowe
2206 Horton SE

Grand Rapids MI
49507

Call Sign: N8YZM
Douglas L Applegate
4792 Hunsberger NE
Grand Rapids MI
49505

Call Sign: N8SAM
Jason C Blodgett
4452 Hyde Park Ave
SW
Grand Rapids MI
495484140

Call Sign: N8UMN
Michael L Burgess
46 Indiana SW
Grand Rapids MI
49504

Call Sign: W8MLB
Milton L Burgess
46 Indiana SW
Grand Rapids MI
49504

Call Sign: W8ZP
Milton L Burgess
46 Indiana SW
Grand Rapids MI
49504

Call Sign: KB8QAW
Laurie A Berens
341 Indiana SW
Grand Rapids MI
49504

Call Sign: KC8EIJ
Richard M Rempalski
Jr
716 Innes NE
Grand Rapids MI
49503

Call Sign: KG8BU
Jonathan Swets
63 Iris Pl
Grand Rapids MI
49503

Call Sign: KB8VUA

Michael J Thompson
347 James Sc
Grand Rapids MI
49503

Call Sign: KC8VUA
Candace A Benson
2059 Jefferson
Grand Rapids MI
49507

Call Sign: KF8IJ
George Groenleer
1521 Jennette Ave NW
Grand Rapids MI
49504

Call Sign: KC8EXB
Russell J Johnson
1907 Jerome SW
Grand Rapids MI
49507

Call Sign: KA8DNQ
Michael R Krenz
2132 Kalamazoo SE
Grand Rapids MI
49507

Call Sign: K8MRK
Michael R Krenz
2132 Kalamazoo SE
Grand Rapids MI
49507

Call Sign: K8IUE
Ernest D Yeager
3785 Keeweenaw Dr
NE
Grand Rapids MI
49505

Call Sign: KD8EOK
Patricia J Malski
631 Kellogg St SE
Grand Rapids MI
49503

Call Sign: KB8WXD
Mike P Palma
943 Kelsey NE
Grand Rapids MI
49505

Call Sign: KC8YIQ
Paul S Wittkoski
1025 Kendalwood NE
Grand Rapids MI
49505

Call Sign: W8MSK
Jerome V Wittkoski
1025 Kendalwood NE
Grand Rapids MI
495053231

Call Sign: N8AYP
James D Fugitt
1041 Keneberry Way
SE
Grand Rapids MI
49506

Call Sign: KC8TBY
Thomas K Lane
2014 Kenning NW
Grand Rapids MI
495044744

Call Sign: K8DJA
David J Abraczinskas
4295 Kentridge Dr SE
Grand Rapids MI
49508

Call Sign: W8HVG
Raymond J
Abraczinskas
4295 Kentridge SE
Grand Rapids MI
49508

Call Sign: KC8IFH
Scott R Docter
1034 Kentwood Dr NE
Grand Rapids MI
49505

Call Sign: W8KQM
Anthony G Gibbons
1035 Kentwood Dr NE
Grand Rapids MI
49505

Call Sign: WD8ONJ
Robert D Meyer
1018 Kentwood NE

Grand Rapids MI
49505

Call Sign: WB7EXA
Conrad C Rustenburg
1816 Keyhill Ave SE
Grand Rapids MI
49546

Call Sign: KC8YWM
Ryan J Meissner
4164 Kings Row Dr
Grand Rapids MI
49544

Call Sign: KC8ASZ
Frederick B Malefyt
1978 Kingston Dr SE
Grand Rapids MI
49508

Call Sign: WD8MWR
Harry E McClurken
681 Kinney Ave
Grand Rapids MI
49544

Call Sign: WA8ZXZ
Harry E McClurken
681 Kinney Ave NW
Grand Rapids MI
49534

Call Sign: N8DXC
Vernon E Bergman
532 Kinney NW
Grand Rapids MI
49504

Call Sign: KB8AAI
Nathan F Leichty
946 Knapp NE
Grand Rapids MI
49505

Call Sign: AA8MW
Ronald J Harkai
2557 Knapp NE
Grand Rapids MI
49505

Call Sign: N8HAH
Cora L Miller
841 Knapp St NE

Grand Rapids MI
49505

Call Sign: KC8ANC
Rachel A Harkai
2557 Knapp St NE
Grand Rapids MI
49505

Call Sign: N8WUJ
Barbara A Harkai
2557 Knapp St NE
Grand Rapids MI
49505

Call Sign: KD8IFL
James M Pouillon
350 Lafayette Ave SE
4th Fl
Grand Rapids MI
49503

Call Sign: KC8ORU
Robert J Long IV
211 Lafayette NE
Grand Rapids MI
495033306

Call Sign: WB9PCO
Leo E Patin
1260 Lafayette NE
Grand Rapids MI
49505

Call Sign: W8VOM
Charles A Lemarbre
O-947 Lake Michigan
Dr
Grand Rapids MI
49534

Call Sign: W8SPX
Leonard M Schaafsma
2243 Lake Michigan
Dr NW
Grand Rapids MI
49504

Call Sign: K8ILR
Charles P Ausberger
2421 Lake Michigan
Dr NW
Grand Rapids MI
49504

Call Sign: KB8KGD
Jeremy N Grey
3683 Lake Michigan
Dr NW
Grand Rapids MI
49534

Call Sign: KD8RQL
Ralph Tanner
2510 Lake Michigan
Dr NW Apt F208
Grand Rapids MI
49504

Call Sign: KD8NME
Senez O Rodriguez
1515 Lancashire Dr SE
Grand Rapids MI
49508

Call Sign: W8PEM
Walter J Wnuk
126 Langdon NE
Grand Rapids MI
49503

Call Sign: W8HRT
Richard G Waldner
1225 Langley SE
Grand Rapids MI
49508

Call Sign: NP2HA
Brenda C Russell
559 Laurel Ave SE
Grand Rapids MI
49506

Call Sign: W8BB
James C Corbett
2502 Lawncrest Dr NE
Grand Rapids MI
49505

Call Sign: WA8IGY
Ransom B Perkins
251 Lawndale NE
Grand Rapids MI
49503

Call Sign: KC8PNP
James W Karczewski

1768 Leffingwell Ave
NE
Grand Rapids MI
49525

Call Sign: KC8POQ
James W Karczewski
1768 Leffingwell Ave
NE
Grand Rapids MI
49525

Call Sign: N8JSL
Brian J Van Order
2650 Leffingwell Ave
NE
Grand Rapids MI
49525

Call Sign: N8HNK
Thomas D Fitzgerald
1701 Leffingwell NE
Grand Rapids MI
49525

Call Sign: W8NZW
Edmund J
Lomasiewicz
271 Lenora NW
Grand Rapids MI
49504

Call Sign: KD8NSX
Michael N King
301 Lenora NW
Grand Rapids MI
49504

Call Sign: KC8JIN
Donna B Wild
1008 Leonard NE
Grand Rapids MI
49503

Call Sign: W8DMW
Donna B Wild
1008 Leonard NE
Grand Rapids MI
49503

Call Sign: WA8HZN
Philip D Latta Sr
2110 Leonard NE Apt
314

Grand Rapids MI
49505

Call Sign: KB8PHV
James N Veneklasen
Sr
1911 Leonard NW
Grand Rapids MI
49504

Call Sign: N8IPL
George E Hamilton
0-1016 Leonard NW
Grand Rapids MI
49544

Call Sign: N8JXB
Robert D Wild
1008 Leonard St NE
Grand Rapids MI
495031232

Call Sign: WC8O
Robert D Wild
1008 Leonard St NE
Grand Rapids MI
495031232

Call Sign: KD8QHA
The Geek Group
902 Leonard St NW
Grand Rapids MI
49504

Call Sign: KD8OHU
Teresa R Farah
4061 Leonard St NW
Grand Rapids MI
495342117

Call Sign: N8WDV
Edgar P Brotherton
4091 Leonard St NW
Grand Rapids MI
49544

Call Sign: W8MRD
Michael R Dryer Sr
0-1418 Leonard St
NW
Grand Rapids MI
495349540

Call Sign: WB8CWE

Michael R Dryer Sr
O-1418 Leonard St
NW
Grand Rapids MI
495449540

Call Sign: KB8MGF
Donna J Janke
1436 Lewison NE
Grand Rapids MI
49505

Call Sign: KT8G
Jeffrey R Janke
1436 Lewison NE
Grand Rapids MI
49505

Call Sign: K8ADA
Floyd E Wooden
1533 Lewison NE
Grand Rapids MI
49505

Call Sign: KB8UYT
Kevin S Jung
1554 Lewison NE
Grand Rapids MI
495055420

Call Sign: N9GWZ
Robert P Draperi
164 Lichfield Lot 69
Grand Rapids MI
49548

Call Sign: KD8GJL
Deborah G Hill
1044 Lincoln NW Apt
2
Grand Rapids MI
49504

Call Sign: WA8SUW
William R Schall
2438 Linden Ave SE
Grand Rapids MI
49507

Call Sign: KD8NMK
Douglas S Dekam
7051 Linden Ave SE
Grand Rapids MI
49548

Call Sign: K8DDK
Douglas S Dekam
7051 Linden Ave SE
Grand Rapids MI
49548

Call Sign: KG8NT
Jeffrey A Kludy
1634 Lockhart NW
Grand Rapids MI
49504

Call Sign: KD8MDI
Harold O Varnedoe
7196 Lodge Pole Dr
SE
Grand Rapids MI
49548

Call Sign: N8LRF
Raymond E Larabee
612 London SW
Grand Rapids MI
49503

Call Sign: KD8LZN
Manuel Duran
751 London SW
Grand Rapids MI
49503

Call Sign: K8EMO
Mark E Van Halsema
1920 Lotus Ave SE
Grand Rapids MI
49506

Call Sign: KC8PSX
Mark E Van Halsema
1920 Lotus Ave SE
Grand Rapids MI
49506

Call Sign: KD8BIH
Robert D Johnson Sr
46 Lowell
Grand Rapids MI
49503

Call Sign: KB8PHT
Raymond F Gallagher
Jr
106 Lowell NE

Grand Rapids MI
49503

Call Sign: WA8PAU
Wayne W Wyman
2172 Luce SW
Grand Rapids MI
49534

Call Sign: WA8EBM
Michael J Penkas
259 Luray NW
Grand Rapids MI
49504

Call Sign: NZ8I
Charles F Schuler
5060 Luxemburg St SE
Grand Rapids MI
49546

Call Sign: W8FCP
John E Warner
1603 Lyon NE
Grand Rapids MI
49503

Call Sign: N8YEF
David J Van Houten
1709 Lyon St NE
Grand Rapids MI
49503

Call Sign: KC8EQW
Jacob Clouse
546 Lyon St NE Apt 2
Grand Rapids MI
49503

Call Sign: KD8FHM
Tommy R Ray
1588 Mac Nider SE
Grand Rapids MI
49546

Call Sign: WD8AHB
Michael L
Maciejewski
2765 Maguire Ave NE
Grand Rapids MI
49525

Call Sign: KD8DDW
Nathan C Smith

4171 Maguire Ct NE
Grand Rapids MI
49525

Call Sign: KD8NCS
Nathan C Smith Ncs
4171 Maguire Ct NE
Grand Rapids MI
49525

Call Sign: KD8MD
Michael D Castleman
2626 Maguire NE
Grand Rapids MI
495259605

Call Sign: WB8VVE
Gerrit W Sheeres
2023 Mallard Dr SE
Grand Rapids MI
495465797

Call Sign: WD8PBV
Thomas R Vander
Molen
1021 Malta St NE
Grand Rapids MI
49503

Call Sign: KC8PCK
Edward L Buck
308 Manhattan Rd SE
Grand Rapids MI
49506

Call Sign: KD8MEY
Steven B Haueisen
73 Manzana Ct Apt 3D
Grand Rapids MI
49534

Call Sign: KD8EQJ
Christopher P Furner
5166 Maple Creek Ave
SE
Grand Rapids MI
49508

Call Sign: KD8DCI
Dirk E Holmberg
1102 Maple Ln NW
Grand Rapids MI
49534

Call Sign: KC8GDG
Donald M Endres II
1053 Maplegrove Dr
NW
Grand Rapids MI
49504

Call Sign: KG8LM
Andrew G Longfellow
1310 Maplerow
Grand Rapids MI
49504

Call Sign: KG8NS
Charles A Longfellow
1310 Maplerow NW
Grand Rapids MI
49534

Call Sign: N8ILU
Michael P Bowen
552 Marcia St SW
Grand Rapids MI
49509

Call Sign: KD8HRG
Kenn Andrus
1444 Mark NE
Grand Rapids MI
49525

Call Sign: KC8OZX
Richard J Thomas
74 Market SW
Grand Rapids MI
49503

Call Sign: KC8OPO
Michael E Geukes
450 Marsh Ridge Dr
Apt 105
Grand Rapids MI
49504

Call Sign: KC8CUO
Steven D Nichols
6954 Marshall Ave SE
Grand Rapids MI
495087439

Call Sign: KB8MKD
Patrick G Hall
2868 Marshall Rd Apt
C 11

Grand Rapids MI
49508

Call Sign: KA8YTC
Jason T Vander Kodde
2315 Marshall SE
Grand Rapids MI
49507

Call Sign: KB8UWJ
Kevin M Crouse
2125 Martindale
Grand Rapids MI
49509

Call Sign: KC8DRH
David H Hoffmann
3455 Mason Ridge Dr
Grand Rapids MI
495259499

Call Sign: KC8DWG
Adam G Collier
1619 Matilda
Grand Rapids MI
49503

Call Sign: KC8HVN
Kendall G Hewitt
1324 Maude NE
Grand Rapids MI
49505

Call Sign: KC8TCC
Robert W Smith
1850 Mayberry St SE
Grand Rapids MI
49508

Call Sign: K8QC
Robert W Smith
1850 Mayberry St SE
Grand Rapids MI
49508

Call Sign: KC8IFM
Christine M Cooper
3870 Mayfield 2B
Grand Rapids MI
49525

Call Sign: KD8NMR
Andrew G Johnson
2721 Mayfield Ave

Grand Rapids MI
49505

Call Sign: WB8MIW
Patrick I Gillespie
105 Mayfield NE
Grand Rapids MI
49503

Call Sign: W8WZN
John M Hauser
1341 Mayfield NE
Grand Rapids MI
49505

Call Sign: N8MUY
Timothy J Elzinga
195 Maynard Ave SW
Grand Rapids MI
49504

Call Sign: KD8BSY
Kathy J Smith
1560 McDonald NW
Grand Rapids MI
49504

Call Sign: KC8WJA
Michael W Smith
1560 McDonald NW
Grand Rapids MI
49504

Call Sign: KB8SEV
Richard H Dean
2343 McKee Ave SW
Grand Rapids MI
49509

Call Sign: KC8EWT
Richard E James Sr
2350 McKee Ave SW
Grand Rapids MI
495091580

Call Sign: KC8PFU
Rofugio Ortiz
1115 McReynolds NW
Apt 1
Grand Rapids MI
49504

Call Sign: KA8EIT
Robert J Doornbos

2237 Meadowglen Dr
NE
Grand Rapids MI
49505

Call Sign: N8INC
Ronald E Linkfield
2346 Meadowglen NE
Grand Rapids MI
49505

Call Sign: N8NJF
Gerald D McNamara
2016 Melita NE
Grand Rapids MI
49505

Call Sign: N8LCW
Daniel D Vander Haar
1918 Menominee St
Grand Rapids MI
49506

Call Sign: WA8HZL
David W Johnson
2108 Merlin NE
Grand Rapids MI
495052866

Call Sign: KC8DJ
David W Johnson
2108 Merlin NE
Grand Rapids MI
495252866

Call Sign: K8PUJ
Lawrence J Kozal Jr
2500 Michigan St NE
Grand Rapids MI
495061237

Call Sign: W8UJ
Lawrence J Kozal Jr
2500 Michigan St NE
Grand Rapids MI
495061237

Call Sign: NE8Q
Leonard A O'Kelly
2536 Michigan St NE
Grand Rapids MI
49506

Call Sign: W8CFZ

Carl E Hainer
3940 Michigan St NE
Grand Rapids MI
495253400

Call Sign: KD8DUS
Rick W Pocklington
4209 Michigan St NE
Grand Rapids MI
49525

Call Sign: KC8THU
Norwin B Peirce
1704 Millbank St SE
Grand Rapids MI
495082668

Call Sign: KB8OGQ
Henry R Smitter
1836 Millbrook St SE
Grand Rapids MI
49508

Call Sign: WA8NHL
Joseph J Rinkevich
2432 Miller Ave NW
Grand Rapids MI
49544

Call Sign: KB8WMJ
Phil K Ratzsch
1325 Milton Ave
Grand Rapids MI
49506

Call Sign: KC8AMU
Timothy M Schliewtz
2650 Moerland Dr
Grand Rapids MI
49504

Call Sign: N8INF
Gordon C Piatt
2613 Moerland Dr NW
Grand Rapids MI
49504

Call Sign: KD8RLO
Amy C Colby
4148 Mohler St NW
Grand Rapids MI
49534

Call Sign: W8IAE

Stanley A Jensen
1953 Monroe Ave NE
Grand Rapids MI
49503

Call Sign: KD8AAG
Zachary M Steindler
60 Monroe Center NW
Ste 11C
Grand Rapids MI
49503

Call Sign: KD8KPD
Grand Rapids Eco
Radio Club
1 Monroe Cn NW
Grand Rapids MI
49503

Call Sign: K8GRP
Grand Rapids Eco
Radio Club
1 Monroe Cn NW
Grand Rapids MI
49503

Call Sign: KC8FGQ
James M Cordes
1235 Morgan NW
Grand Rapids MI
49504

Call Sign: KC8MHX
Michigan Dx
Association
1235 Morgan NW
Grand Rapids MI
49504

Call Sign: KI8JD
James M Cordes
1235 Morgan NW
Grand Rapids MI
49504

Call Sign: KC8OTW
Cynthia L Cordes
1235 Morgan NW
Grand Rapids MI
49504

Call Sign: W8DXI
Michigan Dx
Association

1235 Morgan NW
Grand Rapids MI
49504

Call Sign: N8WEE
Joel D Swets
1243 Morgan NW
Grand Rapids MI
49504

Call Sign: W8ONC
Charles L Sheffield
1916 Morningside Dr
Grand Rapids MI
49506

Call Sign: W8MFB
Robert L McKay
205 Morris Ave SE
Grand Rapids MI
49503

Call Sign: KB8WMI
Jeremiah D Ellis
238 Morris SE
Grand Rapids MI
495034604

Call Sign: KC8SIW
Garrett J Albert
10921 Mtn Ash Ave
NW
Grand Rapids MI
49544

Call Sign: N8VYX
Edward J Kerschen II
6801 Muirfield Ct SE
Grand Rapids MI
49546

Call Sign: WD8LWK
Theodore L Nikodem
415 Mulford Dr SE
Grand Rapids MI
495073568

Call Sign: KB8WXJ
William N Sneller
450 N Center 2B
Grand Rapids MI
49544

Call Sign: KB8TWY

Stephen J Smitter
915 N Park Ct
Grand Rapids MI
49505

Call Sign: KB8TWX
Pamela J Smitter
915 N Park Ct NE
Grand Rapids MI
49505

Call Sign: KD8IQU
Robert C Baker
2110 N Quail Crest Ct
SE
Grand Rapids MI
49546

Call Sign: KC8PQJ
Garry L Hall
4849 N Quail Crest Dr
SE
Grand Rapids MI
49546

Call Sign: N8ZCW
Daniel B Schultz
1306 N White
Grand Rapids MI
49504

Call Sign: KB8ILK
Joseph G French
848 Nagold NW
Grand Rapids MI
49504

Call Sign: WW8L
Charles J Jonkman
1827 Nelson SE
Grand Rapids MI
49507

Call Sign: KD8HHI
Ken L Hurt
910 Nevada SE
Grand Rapids MI
49507

Call Sign: AB8IW
Columbus Stewart
2516 Nomandy Dr S E
Apt 301C

Grand Rapids MI
49506

Call Sign: KC8IRL
Steven R Dennis
3869 Nordic Ave
Grand Rapids MI
49544

Call Sign: KC8IRJ
Robert A Dennis
3869 Nordic Ave
Grand Rapids MI
49544

Call Sign: KC8IRK
Kathryn M Dennis
3869 Nordic Ave
Grand Rapids MI
49544

Call Sign: WX8BOB
Robert A Dennis
3869 Nordic Ave
Grand Rapids MI
49544

Call Sign: KD8KLK
Hollie L Dennis
3869 Nordic Ave NW
Grand Rapids MI
49544

Call Sign: KC8TFO
Phillip E Hall
2538 Norfolk Rd
Grand Rapids MI
49506

Call Sign: WD8ELY
Mark A Crane
2504 Normandy Dr SE
113B
Grand Rapids MI
495067902

Call Sign: KB8TEH
Ovidiu Daniel
Amarandei
2516 Normandy SE
102 C
Grand Rapids MI
49506

Call Sign: N8ETM
Kenneth S Rosloniec
4351 Northgate NE
Grand Rapids MI
49525

Call Sign: WA8VST
David W Elbrecht
918 Northlawn St NE
Grand Rapids MI
495053720

Call Sign: N8LPU
Katherine A Truax
2718 Northvale Dr Apt
101
Grand Rapids MI
49505

Call Sign: N8LSO
Jonathan C Truax
2718 Northvale Dr NE
Grand Rapids MI
49505

Call Sign: KB8IIQ
Michael J Hendricks
4815 Northview NE
Grand Rapids MI
49505

Call Sign: W8IDP
Jerome S Miller
4842 Northview NE
Grand Rapids MI
49505

Call Sign: KC8TKH
Richard W Lunger
2669 Northville Dr NE
Grand Rapids MI
495251760

Call Sign: KD8XI
William J Moran
2751 Northville Dr NE
Grand Rapids MI
49505

Call Sign: K8WM
William J Wisneski
2863 Northville Dr NE
Grand Rapids MI
495251791

Call Sign: KB8RWT
David J De Graw
1110 Northwood NE
Grand Rapids MI
49505

Call Sign: N8ODV
Bruce F Sommer
7115 Nottingham SW
Grand Rapids MI
495487191

Call Sign: KA8ASZ
Donald W Pulte
2581 O Brien Rd SW
Grand Rapids MI
49534

Call Sign: K8YKI
Randall J Hekman
1932 Oak Hollow Rd
NW
Grand Rapids MI
49504

Call Sign: KB8TWS
Melanie A Vanderhorn
1241 Oaklawn NE
Grand Rapids MI
49505

Call Sign: W8QMF
Roland R Petersen
1124 Oaklawn St
Grand Rapids MI
49505

Call Sign: KB8QAX
Justin G De Fouw
1257 Oakleigh NE
Grand Rapids MI
49504

Call Sign: K8CGD
Paul Boris
1939 Observatory SE
Grand Rapids MI
49506

Call Sign: KC8CUZ
Chris S Brower
2326 Okemos

Grand Rapids MI
49506

Call Sign: K9ZUT
John R Brocker
3876 Old Elm Dr SE
Grand Rapids MI
49512

Call Sign: KD8OXL
Chris E Kolenda
2736 Olderidge Ct NE
Grand Rapids MI
49525

Call Sign: KB8QXH
Roe W Van Fossen
3484 Olderidge Dr NE
Grand Rapids MI
49505

Call Sign: K8SSA
H William Bouwkamp
2216 Ontonagon SE
Grand Rapids MI
49506

Call Sign: KD8NRN
David J O'Brien
7103 Oran Dr
Grand Rapids MI
49546

Call Sign: KC8UPA
Brian J Van Order
1334 Orville SE
Grand Rapids MI
49507

Call Sign: N8OGD
Kragh J Hertel
62 Oswego Dr NW
Grand Rapids MI
49504

Call Sign: N8SVV
John E Huizinga
631 Ottillia SE
Grand Rapids MI
49507

Call Sign: KD8MMS
Josiah R Clemence
1114 Ottillia St SE

Grand Rapids MI
49507

Call Sign: KD8NRP
Gregory J Stoike
28 Page St NE Apt 2
Grand Rapids MI
49505

Call Sign: KB8OUW
Jack E Williams
2231 Palace SW
Grand Rapids MI
49507

Call Sign: KC8AMX
Arthur Steenwyk
850 Paradise Lk Dr SE
Grand Rapids MI
49546

Call Sign: KC8AMY
Judy A Steenwyk
850 Paradise Lk Dr SE
Grand Rapids MI
49546

Call Sign: KC8RTX
Rohn P Kunnen
4645 Paramount Dr
NE
Grand Rapids MI
49525

Call Sign: WD8IMJ
Candice S Knepper
4848 Paramount Dr
NE
Grand Rapids MI
49525

Call Sign: N8XPM
David H Burgess
1144 Paris Ave NE
Grand Rapids MI
495031141

Call Sign: W8SHT
John J Kalishevich
1265 Paris NE
Grand Rapids MI
49505

Call Sign: K8JJK

John Joseph
Kalishevich
1265 Paris NE
Grand Rapids MI
49505

Call Sign: N8JJK
John J Kalishevich
1265 Paris NE
Grand Rapids MI
49505

Call Sign: N8BBB
John J Kalishevich
1265 Paris NE
Grand Rapids MI
49505

Call Sign: K8FCC
John J Kalishevich
1265 Paris NE
Grand Rapids MI
49505

Call Sign: N8JJK
John J Kalishevich
1265 Paris NE
Grand Rapids MI
49505

Call Sign: K8FCC
John J Kalishevich
1265 Paris NE
Grand Rapids MI
49505

Call Sign: N8JJK
John J Kalishevich
1265 Paris NE
Grand Rapids MI
49505

Call Sign: K8FCC
John J Kalishevich
1265 Paris NE
Grand Rapids MI
49505

Call Sign: W8HJK
John Kalishevich
1265 Paris NE
Grand Rapids MI
495055182

Call Sign: KC8GOK
James R Talen
323 Paris SE
Grand Rapids MI
495034716

Call Sign: N8HNV
Raymond G Lantinga
416 Paris SE
Grand Rapids MI
49503

Call Sign: N8NKC
Martin J Schreur
2204 Paris SE
Grand Rapids MI
49507

Call Sign: N8PQL
James P Miller
1148 Patterson SE
Grand Rapids MI
49546

Call Sign: KD8DEF
Timothy R Alkema
1050 Patton Way
Grand Rapids MI
49504

Call Sign: WB8QNX
David J Van Holstyn
3442 Peach Ridge NW
Grand Rapids MI
49544

Call Sign: KC8CUS
Gordon L Wyant
1325 Penn Ave NE
Grand Rapids MI
49505

Call Sign: WD8EMD
Harold J Wisneski
159 Pershing Dr NE
Grand Rapids MI
49505

Call Sign: KE8QH
Richard L Voit
2360 Pheasant Ct SE
Grand Rapids MI
49506

Call Sign: KC8SBI
Christopher A Driskell
1658 Philadelphia SE
Grand Rapids MI
49507

Call Sign: N8JUT
Joseph R O Brien
1828 Philadelphia SE
Grand Rapids MI
495072839

Call Sign: KD8EON
Marie Claire O Camp
943 Pine Ave NW
Grand Rapids MI
49504

Call Sign: N8JPR
John P Ruiz
962 Pine Ave NW
Grand Rapids MI
49504

Call Sign: KB8WMD
Kenneth P Fuss
5649 Pinebrook Ave
SE
Grand Rapids MI
495485952

Call Sign: KC8NWC
Brentford J
Rittenhouse
2909 Pioneer Rd
Grand Rapids MI
49506

Call Sign: AB8HC
Brentford J
Rittenhouse
2909 Pioneer Rd
Grand Rapids MI
49506

Call Sign: K8SO
Brentford J
Rittenhouse
2909 Pioneer Rd SE
Grand Rapids MI
49506

Call Sign: K8UYA

Benjamin F
Vanderhorst
4605 Poinsettia SE
Grand Rapids MI
49508

Call Sign: K8PRH
Patrick R Howe
3029 Poplar Creek Dr
SE Unit 103
Grand Rapids MI
49512

Call Sign: KC8OMK
Jason C Sperry
1340 Portland
Grand Rapids MI
49505

Call Sign: KD8KLQ
Judy L Hebert
753 Powers Ave NW
Grand Rapids MI
49504

Call Sign: WB8DQO
Jerry L Daverman
1050 Powers Ct
Grand Rapids MI
49544

Call Sign: N8IMS
Charles L Jones
2405 Powers NW
Grand Rapids MI
49504

Call Sign: KD8JOM
James D Warfield
1425 Preston Ridge
Apt C11
Grand Rapids MI
49504

Call Sign: KD8IYA
Rebecca A Rubante
313 Prospect Ave NE
Grand Rapids MI
49503

Call Sign: KB8TWU
Sean D Crombez
508 Prospect NE

Grand Rapids MI
49503

Call Sign: KD8DMF
Paul L Meyer
1914 Prospect SE
Grand Rapids MI
49507

Call Sign: NX8D
Raymond J Dondzila
7806 Quail Run W SE
Grand Rapids MI
49508

Call Sign: N8UXN
Edward J Novakowski
Jr
1547 Quarry NW
Grand Rapids MI
49504

Call Sign: KC8TSV
Daniel J Novakowski
1547 Quarry NW
Grand Rapids MI
49504

Call Sign: KA9PFV
Timothy S Ashbaugh
338 Quimby NE
Grand Rapids MI
49505

Call Sign: KC8RQU
Michael A Johnson
531 Quimby St NE
Grand Rapids MI
49505

Call Sign: KB8VEF
Thomas W Purcell
6868 Quincy SW
Grand Rapids MI
49548

Call Sign: N7RXW
William D Zeilstra
2269 Radcliff Cir SE
Grand Rapids MI
49546

Call Sign: WJ8LC
Daniel D Vander Haar

2334 Radcliffe Village
Dr
Grand Rapids MI
49546

Call Sign: W7PG
Andrew A Gusack
1852 Ranch Dr NW
Grand Rapids MI
49504

Call Sign: N8PWR
Ralph W Ortwig
5407 Ranger Hills Dr
SE
Grand Rapids MI
49546

Call Sign: W8KYN
Clifford J Hayes
50 Ransom Ave NE
Grand Rapids MI
45403

Call Sign: KB4OKK
Martin C Kooistra Sr
2105 Ray Brook Ave
SE Apt 4026
Grand Rapids MI
49546

Call Sign: WD8AVW
Evan W Runner
2111 Raybrook SE
1017
Grand Rapids MI
495467719

Call Sign: K8RDO
Elmer J Roossien
2111 Raybrook SE
2013
Grand Rapids MI
49506

Call Sign: N8CZF
Martha H Felton
2105 Raybrook St
2032
Grand Rapids MI
495467737

Call Sign: W8YCI
Wilbur A Carrington

2121 Raybrook St SE
340
Grand Rapids MI
49546

Call Sign: KB8ILH
Glen G Holt Jr
2504 Red Maple Dr SE
Grand Rapids MI
495129101

Call Sign: N8XHP
Eric M Hutchinson
O-104 Redolent Run
NW
Grand Rapids MI
49534

Call Sign: KD8DMH
Sharyl L Hutchinson
O-104 Redolent Run
NW
Grand Rapids MI
49534

Call Sign: N8PUQ
Duane N Denhof Sr
1226 Regina St NE
Grand Rapids MI
49505

Call Sign: WA4QBJ
Eino Karppinen
668 Rehoboth Dr NE
Grand Rapids MI
49505

Call Sign: KC8WJD
Randal K Roberts
4350 Remembrance Rd
NW 122
Grand Rapids MI
49544

Call Sign: AC8DT
Andrew J Witte
315 Richard Ter SE
Grand Rapids MI
49506

Call Sign: N8NEK
Leonard Gongalski
214 Richards NW

Grand Rapids MI
49504

Call Sign: KD8GBX
Ronald H Weinrick
2326 Richmond NW
Grand Rapids MI
495042529

Call Sign: KD8QXQ
Ronald J Vigh
2777 Richmond NW
Grand Rapids MI
49504

Call Sign: KC8LZK
Dennis H Tanner
3080 Richmond St NW
Grand Rapids MI
49534

Call Sign: KD8IAE
Joseph E Morris
2167 Ridgecrest Dr SE
Apt 7
Grand Rapids MI
49546

Call Sign: N8NIG
Brian A Snider
2505 Rimrock Ct NE
Grand Rapids MI
49525

Call Sign: AA8EP
Joel D Hainer
2721 Roanoke Dr NE
Grand Rapids MI
49525

Call Sign: K8CUP
William J Connelly III
2752 Robinson Rd SE
Grand Rapids MI
49506

Call Sign: WA8QJM
Eleanor M Connelly
2752 Robinson Rd SE
Grand Rapids MI
49506

Call Sign: KC8YWN
Roland L Forward

2787 Rock Valley Ct
NE
Grand Rapids MI
49525

Call Sign: KD8PZH
Chris A Boden
612 Rosewood SE
Grand Rapids MI
49506

Call Sign: KC8PCL
David M Smith
1652 Rossman SE
Grand Rapids MI
49507

Call Sign: N8ROK
John P Bazen Jr
1430 Rothbury NE
Grand Rapids MI
49505

Call Sign: KC8GYO
Christopher J Sillers
2060 Rowland 303
Grand Rapids MI
49546

Call Sign: N8JUW
Bert Block Jr
1906 Rowland Ave
Grand Rapids MI
49546

Call Sign: N8HNT
Michael E Hack
1926 Rowland SE
Grand Rapids MI
49506

Call Sign: KB8HHH
Bernard D Clemens Jr
11388 Rugby Dr NW
Grand Rapids MI
49504

Call Sign: N8HNR
Russell L Shearer
0-11335 Rugby Dr
NW
Grand Rapids MI
49504

Call Sign: KD8EBE
John A Gracki
220 Russwood NE
Grand Rapids MI
49505

Call Sign: N8DCQ
Glen W Sironen Sr
3139 Rypens Dr NW
Grand Rapids MI
49504

Call Sign: W8BRI
Brian R Pawloski
476 S Amber
Grand Rapids MI
495486844

Call Sign: WX8GRR
West Michigan
Skywarn Team
4899 S Complex Dr
Grand Rapids MI
49512

Call Sign: KC8JEF
Mark A Tew
4899 S Complex Dr SE
Grand Rapids MI
49512

Call Sign: KB8CJ
Thomas L Haynes
3325 S Creek Dr SE
Apt 302
Grand Rapids MI
49512

Call Sign: KC8WWW
Phillip E Hall
60 S Division 439
Grand Rapids MI
49503

Call Sign: KB8OPD
Nancy F Morrison
2048 S Eventide Dr
NE
Grand Rapids MI
49505

Call Sign: WD8OTL
David H Morrison

2048 S Eventide Dr
NE
Grand Rapids MI
49505

Call Sign: W8AGT
Russell H Van Vlack
1757 S Greenfield Cir
NE Apt 302
Grand Rapids MI
49505

Call Sign: KD8AFI
Curt D Baragar
4157 S Norway SE
Grand Rapids MI
49546

Call Sign: KC8PQG
Franklin H Alexander
1338 Saffron Ln SE
Apt 2B
Grand Rapids MI
495087345

Call Sign: WW8GR
Albert J Flowers
4171 Sand Creek Dr
Grand Rapids MI
495449714

Call Sign: WA8IKP
David A Linderman
2700 Sandalwood Ct N
E
Grand Rapids MI
495251358

Call Sign: W8HM
Herbert G Eastwood
1772 Sandra St NW
Grand Rapids MI
49504

Call Sign: KD8EOU
Joshua D Smith
4162 Sawkaw Dr Apt
203
Grand Rapids MI
49525

Call Sign: WH6LY
John J Vander Stel Jr
4171 Sawkaw Dr NE

Grand Rapids MI
49525

Call Sign: KD8EOT
Christian R Komor
1665 Seminde Rd SE
Grand Rapids MI
49506

Call Sign: N8IML
Floyd H Miltz
4921 Sequoia SE
Grand Rapids MI
49512

Call Sign: W8CGR
Floyd H Miltz
4921 Sequoia SE
Grand Rapids MI
49512

Call Sign: KB8OHV
Ted J Ooyevaar
3443 Shady Pl NE
Grand Rapids MI
49525

Call Sign: N8OQV
Edward V Connors
1702 Shangraila Dr SE
Grand Rapids MI
49508

Call Sign: N4SC
Roman J Downer
2110 Shawnee Dr SE
Grand Rapids MI
49506

Call Sign: KC8YYI
Jonathan T Peters
861 Sheffield St SW
Grand Rapids MI
49503

Call Sign: KC8AKH
Clark Radio Club Of
The Clark Retirement
Comm
1516 Sherman SE
Grand Rapids MI
49506

Call Sign: AA8PW

Lloyd R Hansen
1516 Sherman SE
Grand Rapids MI
495062715

Call Sign: W8CRC
Clark Radio Club
1516 Sherman SE
Grand Rapids MI
495062715

Call Sign: KC8GOO
Terry R Risch
1517 Sherwood Dr
Grand Rapids MI
49506

Call Sign: KD8KLH
Martin L Whittemore
2118 Shetland Dr NE
Grand Rapids MI
49505

Call Sign: W8MLW
Martin L Whittemore
2118 Shetland Dr NE
Grand Rapids MI
49505

Call Sign: KE8GQ
Harold W Morrison
2207 Shetland Dr NE
Grand Rapids MI
495056390

Call Sign: KD8NMQ
Kyle J Young
553 Shirley NE
Grand Rapids MI
49503

Call Sign: KD8IFJ
Curt L Novitsky
1711 Sibley NW
Grand Rapids MI
49504

Call Sign: KC8FGR
Joseph J Swierbut
1719 Sibley NW
Grand Rapids MI
49504

Call Sign: W8WOP

Ronald J Wilson
2640 Sidney St SW
Grand Rapids MI
49509

Call Sign: KD8QXC
Frank D Thompson
2040 Sinclair Ave NE
Grand Rapids MI
49505

Call Sign: K8UGM
Alan L Bishop
744 Sligh Blvd NE
Grand Rapids MI
49505

Call Sign: K8ITT
I T T Grand Rapids
ARC
4020 Sparks Dr St
Grand Rapids MI
49546

Call Sign: KC8QYK
I T T Grand Rapids
ARC
4020 Sparks Dr St
Grand Rapids MI
49546

Call Sign: KA6JSD
Richard I Sharp
545 Spencer NE
Grand Rapids MI
49505

Call Sign: NA8RS
Richard I Sharp
545 Spencer NE
Grand Rapids MI
49505

Call Sign: N8SOT
Brian S Flynn
427 Spencer St NE Apt
2
Grand Rapids MI
49505

Call Sign: KC8UEV
Bruce A Rittenhouse
3132 Spring Brook
NW

Grand Rapids MI
49544

Call Sign: N8IRW
Bruce A Rittenhouse
3132 Spring Brook
NW
Grand Rapids MI
49544

Call Sign: KD8CWM
Edward C Czyzyk Jr
876 Spring St
Grand Rapids MI
49503

Call Sign: KD8LVI
Kevin J Van Horn
1170 Springwood Dr
SE
Grand Rapids MI
49508

Call Sign: KB8WJZ
Elizabeth A Ronda
Deboer
4162 Spruce Hollow
Dr NE
Grand Rapids MI
49525

Call Sign: K8GWJ
Gary W James
591 St Andrews Ct S E
Grand Rapids MI
49546

Call Sign: KA9HJR
Laraine G Anderson
1476 Stark Ave NW
Grand Rapids MI
49534

Call Sign: WB9SFK
Barry R Anderson
1476 Stark Ave NW
Grand Rapids MI
49534

Call Sign: N8PUD
David A Steigenga
225 Stewart SW
Grand Rapids MI
49507

Call Sign: K8DOG
Robert P McClymont
3661 Stilesgate Ct
Grand Rapids MI
49508

Call Sign: K5MRO
Bert B Bouma
1610 Stilesgate SE
Grand Rapids MI
49508

Call Sign: KC8JEH
Thomas R Hultquist
1104 Stonebrook Ct
NE
Grand Rapids MI
49505

Call Sign: N8DQW
Judith A Gardner
3788 Stowe NW
Grand Rapids MI
49504

Call Sign: N8DLN
John R Gardner Sr
3788 Stowe NW
Grand Rapids MI
49544

Call Sign: N8MQS
Daniel J Vickers
43 Straight Ave SW
Grand Rapids MI
495046334

Call Sign: KC8EQV
John Spielmaker
828 Summer Creek Ct
SE
Grand Rapids MI
49508

Call Sign: NR8E
Lois M Mateer
4552 Summer Creek
Ln SE
Grand Rapids MI
49508

Call Sign: K8OOK
Michael J Eilers

3648 Sundance Ln NE
Grand Rapids MI
49525

Call Sign: N8IPG
Nancy L Eilers
3648 Sundance Ln NE
Grand Rapids MI
49525

Call Sign: N8XHQ
William R Annable III
1365 Sunnyside NE
Grand Rapids MI
49525

Call Sign: KD8QMW
Brian M Howell
978 Sunrise Ln NW
Grand Rapids MI
49534

Call Sign: KC8JMZ
Kenneth L Boyd
1217 Sylvan Ave SE
Grand Rapids MI
49506

Call Sign: KD8DLC
Michelle K Palma
3912 Tallman Creek
Dr NW
Grand Rapids MI
49534

Call Sign: KB8UMY
Michael W Seekman
1119 Tamarack Ave
NW
Grand Rapids MI
49504

Call Sign: AB8TB
Michael W Seekman
1119 Tamarack Ave
NW
Grand Rapids MI
49504

Call Sign: KD8KLY
Joshua C Kovach
513 Tamarack Trl Apt
3A

Grand Rapids MI
49544

Call Sign: N8HKM
Kenneth J Baas
2130 Tecumseh Dr SE
Grand Rapids MI
49506

Call Sign: W8GWQ
Peter Vander Meer
1467 Tenby Ct NE
Grand Rapids MI
49505

Call Sign: KD8RPV
Brian J Ebbers
1473 Tenby Ct NE
Grand Rapids MI
49505

Call Sign: WD8CMR
Corinne J Strauss
7734 Thornapple
Bayou
Grand Rapids MI
49508

Call Sign: KD8KUQ
Jacob R Stoutjesdyk
5545 Thornapple River
Dr
Grand Rapids MI
49512

Call Sign: N3YNG
Raymond L Belknap
3081 Thorncrest Dr SE
Grand Rapids MI
495467346

Call Sign: KC8TCB
Lynn C Van Note
3315 Thorncrest Dr SE
Grand Rapids MI
49546

Call Sign: KA8URQ
Cornelius R
Vanderweele
2900 Thornhills Ave
SE Apt 210
Grand Rapids MI
49546

Call Sign: KD8RPX
David I Stycos
1610 Timberlane Ln
NE
Grand Rapids MI
49505

Call Sign: WD8REQ
Donald E Holm Sr
151 Tottenham SW
Grand Rapids MI
49548

Call Sign: KC8OXE
Dick Haven
4557 Trail View
Grand Rapids MI
49525

Call Sign: NN8D
Roger L
Grossenbacher
3475 Trail West Dr NE
Grand Rapids MI
49525

Call Sign: N8TKL
Charlie D Whitley
2142 Trailridge
Grand Rapids MI
49508

Call Sign: N8UML
Sherry J Whitley
2142 Trailridge Ct SE
Grand Rapids MI
49507

Call Sign: KC8CUY
Katherine A Piirala
128 Travis Rd
Grand Rapids MI
49505

Call Sign: KC8CUX
Jerald D Piirala
128 Travis St NE
Grand Rapids MI
49505

Call Sign: KC8BWT
Paul Garvin

7774 Tree Swallow Dr
SE
Grand Rapids MI
49508

Call Sign: KC8NCW
April A Anderson
7501 Treeline Dr
Grand Rapids MI
49546

Call Sign: KC8ZOD
Union High School
Radio Club
1800 Tremont Blvd
NW Rm 150
Grand Rapids MI
49504

Call Sign: KB8BIV
Jennifer A Gray
1260 Troon Ct SE
Grand Rapids MI
49506

Call Sign: K8SG
Speed Gray
1260 Troon Ct SE
Grand Rapids MI
49546

Call Sign: KB8BDI
Ellen B Gray
1260 Troon Ct SE
Grand Rapids MI
49546

Call Sign: WA8DGN
Thomas C Newton
319 Trowbridge NE
Grand Rapids MI
495031620

Call Sign: K8PEP
Paul E Phelps
2649 Union Ave SE
Grand Rapids MI
49507

Call Sign: K8PLP
Penny L Phelps
2649 Union Ave SE
Grand Rapids MI
49507

Call Sign: N8DKB
Roger D Russ
1921 Union SE
Grand Rapids MI
49507

Call Sign: N8HNP
Mary E Austin
2021 Valentine Blvd
NE
Grand Rapids MI
495252922

Call Sign: WD8OZS
Robert D Moe
2235 Valentine Blvd
NE
Grand Rapids MI
49525

Call Sign: AC8ZX
Robert D Moe
2235 Valentine Blvd
NE
Grand Rapids MI
49525

Call Sign: KA8PWB
Lawrence M Austin
2021 Valentine NE
Grand Rapids MI
49505

Call Sign: KJ5AI
Michael A Zeeff
2821 Valley Ave NW
Grand Rapids MI
49544

Call Sign: KC8BMI
Matthew A Overholt
900 Van Ess
Grand Rapids MI
49504

Call Sign: KB8MXV
William K Roberts
745 Veto NW
Grand Rapids MI
49504

Call Sign: KG8LN
Eric A Bartlett

863 Veto NW
Grand Rapids MI
49504

Call Sign: W8UBF
Mitchell A Paniwozik
1053 Veto St NW
Grand Rapids MI
49504

Call Sign: K8IWI
Louis Van Duyn
6071 W Amber SE
Grand Rapids MI
49548

Call Sign: K8WMD
Wayne M Dowling
2442 W Collier Ave
SE
Grand Rapids MI
49546

Call Sign: W8GVU
Grand Valley State
Univ Amat Rad
Council
301 W Fulton St
Grand Rapids MI
49504

Call Sign: K8QFH
Robert E Inman
1617 W Kentview Dr
Grand Rapids MI
495054834

Call Sign: KC8YXS
David J Yarington
0-1710 W Leonard Rd
NW
Grand Rapids MI
49544

Call Sign: K4DJY
David J Yarington
0-1710 W Leonard Rd
NW
Grand Rapids MI
49544

Call Sign: KB8UKD
Chester R Kondracki
3321 W River Dr

Grand Rapids MI
49504

Call Sign: N8RYB
Carl M Egner
1524 Wakeley
Grand Rapids MI
49505

Call Sign: KB8NFK
Randy S Greenland
1131 Walker St
Grand Rapids MI
49504

Call Sign: KB8KZD
Debra L Nabkey
57 Wallasey SW
Grand Rapids MI
49548

Call Sign: N8NET
Timothy F Mullen
37 Wallinwood Ave
NE
Grand Rapids MI
49503

Call Sign: N8LUF
Perry L Zimonick
37 Wallinwood N E
Grand Rapids MI
49503

Call Sign: N8KAQ
Shirley A Cochran
48 Wallinwood NE
Grand Rapids MI
49503

Call Sign: KD8KOU
Miguel A Acuna
1434 Walnut St NE
Grand Rapids MI
49503

Call Sign: KC8AMV
Gary W James
1070 Waltham Sr
Grand Rapids MI
49546

Call Sign: KC8QAV
Patrick D Mcbride

1673 Watermark Dr
SE
Grand Rapids MI
49546

Call Sign: KB8NAK
Daniel J Barr
1645 Webster St NW
Grand Rapids MI
49504

Call Sign: KB8MCW
Eric P La Pointe
7187 Wellingborough
SW
Grand Rapids MI
49548

Call Sign: KD8DCC
Matt J Groesser
6509 Wendell St SE
Grand Rapids MI
49546

Call Sign: KB8UFG
Michael P Zaharakos
2520 Westboro Dr NE
Grand Rapids MI
49506

Call Sign: WB8NWY
Edward A McCready
Jr
2447 Westboro NE
Grand Rapids MI
49506

Call Sign: WA8MDC
James D Vander Werp
2551 Westbrook
Grand Rapids MI
49504

Call Sign: KD8FBU
Jeff D Greenop
2521 Westbrook Dr
NW
Grand Rapids MI
49504

Call Sign: KD8DCG
Patrick P Clarin
4350 Westchester Dr
SE

Grand Rapids MI
49546

Call Sign: WA8ZXY
Thomas S Shutich
1209 Westend Dr NW
Grand Rapids MI
49504

Call Sign: KD8MCW
James A Berger
9 Westmont Dr NW
Grand Rapids MI
49504

Call Sign: KC8HAW
Kevin J Snoap
541 Westway Dr
Grand Rapids MI
49544

Call Sign: W8YPK
Richard L Moored
1830 Weymouth SE
Grand Rapids MI
49508

Call Sign: W8UFS
Nelson K Hurst
3974 Whispering Way
SE
Grand Rapids MI
49546

Call Sign: KC8EDC
Joseph P Ripley
2171 Wildfield Dr N E
Grand Rapids MI
49505

Call Sign: WA8IIK
Marc H Boogaard
3234 Wildridge Dr NE
Grand Rapids MI
49505

Call Sign: KC8KVR
Larry L Dells
4317 Willow Dr NE
Grand Rapids MI
49525

Call Sign: KD8OKG
Walter L Colley

575 Wilson Ave SW
Grand Rapids MI
49534

Call Sign: N8LSI
Charles R Davis
3422 Winterberry SE
Grand Rapids MI
49546

Call Sign: KB8WME
Tex V Woods
53 Withey SW
Grand Rapids MI
49507

Call Sign: KC8YNH
Judyth A Hakala
3024 Woodbridge SE
Apt 304
Grand Rapids MI
49512

Call Sign: KC8AVW
Grand Rapids
Community College
Amat Rad Club
6405 Woodbrook SE
Grand Rapids MI
49546

Call Sign: KD8KMB
Patric R Spence
2125 Woodburn SE 12
Grand Rapids MI
49546

Call Sign: W8VV
Calvin J Miller Sr
2080 Woodcliff Ave
SE
Grand Rapids MI
49506

Call Sign: N8IMF
Jeri S Dondzila
1826 Woodcliff SE
Grand Rapids MI
49506

Call Sign: WB8QZS
Timothy H Friske
4575 Woodcreek Dr
SE

Grand Rapids MI
495467903

Call Sign: KF4EJA
Zeus P Duites
6157 Woodfield Pl SE
1
Grand Rapids MI
49548

Call Sign: WB8CCV
Robert L Sheneman
0 11616 Woodgate Dr
NW
Grand Rapids MI
495343321

Call Sign: KC8GEC
Gerrit A Peddemors
1813 Woodlawn Ave
SE
Grand Rapids MI
49506

Call Sign: KC8TST
Harold D Morgan
0-13391 Woodrow
NW
Grand Rapids MI
49544

Call Sign: KD8ODA
Michael J Brockette
7482 Woodvale
Grand Rapids MI
49546

Call Sign: KA8ZAZ
Peter L Van
Duivendyk
1501 Woodworth NE
Apt 201
Grand Rapids MI
495252305

Call Sign: WA8DJN
Kenneth C Achard
1333 Worcester Dr NE
Grand Rapids MI
49505

Call Sign: N8ALV
Lawrence A Patin
1253 Worcester NE

Grand Rapids MI
49505

Call Sign: N8MYY
Sharon L Harrington
Grand Rapids MI
49510

Call Sign: K8FM
Fulton Amateur Radio
Transmitting Soc
Grand Rapids MI
49501

Call Sign: AB9DY
Walter E Postava II
Grand Rapids MI
49501

Call Sign: KD8CDG
Donn K Mendricks
Grand Rapids MI
49501

Call Sign: KD8QHQ
Max L Buhler
Grand Rapids MI
49501

Call Sign: WB8NWY
Raymond F Gallagher
Jr
Grand Rapids MI
49501

Call Sign: KD8IWR
Paula Triplett
Grand Rapids MI
49505

Call Sign: KB8OE
Paul G Muller
Grand Rapids MI
49509

Call Sign: N8LOP
Ned A Greenop
Grand Rapids MI
49514

Call Sign: KC8MZX
Mark A Ranney
Grand Rapids MI
49514

Call Sign: N7MUT
Steven F Kaney
Grand Rapids MI
49515

Call Sign: KB8QAU
Bradley W Kallio
Grand Rapids MI
49516

Call Sign: KC8WIU
Downtown Amateur
Packet Radio Grand
Rapids Mi
Grand Rapids MI
495012428

Call Sign: N8DPR
Downtown Amateur
Packet Radio Grand
Rapids Mi
Grand Rapids MI
495012428

Call Sign: W1LMN
Linda M Nordstrand
Grand Rapids MI
495012428

Call Sign: W8IPN
Ivan P Nordstrand Jr
Grand Rapids MI
495012428

Call Sign: W8DC
Grand Rapids Amateur
Radio Assn
Grand Rapids MI
495013282

Call Sign: W9CFL
Leonard A O'Kelly
Grand Rapids MI
495168165

Call Sign: AA8QL
Michael D Zandee
Grand Rapids MI
495230611

Call Sign: WI8P
Michael D Zandee

Grand Rapids MI
495230611

Call Sign: NG8W
Michael D Zandee
Grand Rapids MI
495230611

Call Sign: KC7NJC
David R Crepin
Grand Rapids MI
495888811

FCC Amateur Radio Licenses in Grandville

Call Sign: KB0RNT
Jason A Werick
3057 27th St
Grandville MI 49418

Call Sign: K8KDK
Kim D Karr
3754 30th St
Grandville MI 49418

Call Sign: W8IP
Jeffrey W Emery
3388 34th St SW
Grandville MI 49418

Call Sign: KE8EN
Sally A Emery
3388 34th St SW
Grandville MI 49418

Call Sign: W8GEH
Dale Wolters
4594 36th St SW
Grandville MI
494182254

Call Sign: KB8VG
Kenneth A McClurken
4088 42nd St
Grandville MI
494182359

Call Sign: K8ZKU
Robert W Stratford
3849 44th St SW
Grandville MI 49418

Call Sign: KC8YMF
Ken D De Jonge
2911 52nd SW
Grandville MI 49418

Call Sign: K8NTE
Robert H Pinder
3511 56th Ave
Grandville MI 49418

Call Sign: KD8FBV
Aaron D Mitchell
5138 Alexandria
Grandville MI 49418

Call Sign: KD8FBQ
Andrew J Mitchell
5138 Alexandria
Grandville MI 49418

Call Sign: KD8JZK
Kyle T Poeller
5788 Barcroft Dr
Grandville MI 49418

Call Sign: N8GTT
J Richard Wolf Jr
3727 Basswood
Grandville MI 49418

Call Sign: KC8PWD
Dina M Bailey
5898 Bayberry Farms
Dr Apt 1
Grandville MI 49418

Call Sign: KD8NMP
Kara L Sturgis
5856 Bayberry Farms
SW Apt 6
Grandville MI 49418

Call Sign: K8ILS
Kara L Sturgis
5856 Bayberry Farms
SW Apt 6
Grandville MI 49418

Call Sign: N8IMA
Beverly R Kloostra
4573 Blackfoot SW
Grandville MI 49418

Call Sign: N8IMB

Jack A Kloostra
4573 Blackfoot SW
Grandville MI 49418

Call Sign: WA8JOB
David J Van Randwyk
7047 Bliss Ct
Grandville MI 49418

Call Sign: K8OK
Robert J Becker
4560 Bremer St SW
Grandville MI 49418

Call Sign: KC8JEC
Rod A Cox
4290 Brookcrest Dr
SW
Grandville MI 49418

Call Sign: N8ISD
Richard W Oren
4337 Brookcrest Dr
SW
Grandville MI 49418

Call Sign: N8ISE
Carol J Oren
4337 Brookcrest Dr
SW
Grandville MI 49418

Call Sign: K9CJO
Carol J Oren
4337 Brookcrest Dr
SW
Grandville MI
494189745

Call Sign: KD8KLW
Michael S Mol
22 Brookmeadow N
Ln Apt 2
Grandville MI 49418

Call Sign: KB8WY
Frank L Packard
6680 Brookwood Dr
Grandville MI 49418

Call Sign: WD8OKT
Peter Bida
3825 Bruce Dr
Grandville MI 49418

Call Sign: N8ITD
Gregory S Deacon
2954 Chicago Dr
Grandville MI 49418

Call Sign: KC8EQY
Theodore H Buesching
2974 Chicago Dr SW
Apt 3
Grandville MI 49418

Call Sign: W8MRX
Carl E Lynema
4350 Crest Creek Ct
Grandville MI 49418

Call Sign: KE7NXY
Katie M Glennemeier
5341 Crooked Pine Dr
Grandville MI 49418

Call Sign: N8XPO
Scott L St Pierre
5286 Debbie Ct SW
Grandville MI 49418

Call Sign: KD8JZM
Brent W Willyard
4358 Del Mar Dr SW
Grandville MI 49418

Call Sign: KC8JUB
Charles A Cobb
3487 Fairwood Ct SW
Grandville MI
494181542

Call Sign: KD8KLP
Daniel S Wierenga
2930 Gable St
Grandville MI 49418

Call Sign: KA8VHQ
James D McIntyre Jr
4030 Grandview Ter
Grandville MI 49418

Call Sign: KC8IFN
Ryan D Schnepp
4477 Happy Hollow
Dr
Grandville MI 49418

Call Sign: N8IJE
Ronald D Schnepp
4477 Happy Hollow
Dr
Grandville MI 49418

Call Sign: N8VFN
Rose M Schnepp
4477 Happy Hollow
Dr
Grandville MI 49418

Call Sign: KI8BW
Jeffrey W Emery
3949 Honeybrook
Grandville MI 49418

Call Sign: KD8IFE
Brian L Fredrick
3840 Ivanrest Ave SW
Grandville MI 49418

Call Sign: N8YBJ
Leonard J Buursma
4354 Jack Alan
Grandville MI 49418

Call Sign: K8BJG
Elliott M Myers
4575 Jacob St
Grandville MI 49418

Call Sign: KD8NMB
Bobby J Ramsey
6731 Kenowa SW
Grandville MI 49418

Call Sign: KB8UYP
William C Adams
4084 Lila St SW
Grandville MI 49418

Call Sign: KC8FJX
Roger W Hartsig
3157 Locke
Grandville MI 49418

Call Sign: KD8EFB
D J Parkin
2888 Locke SW 3
Grandville MI 49418

Call Sign: KD8DLA
Erin N Wiseman

2888 Locke SW 3
Grandville MI 49418

Call Sign: KD8RPP
Ralph E Gady
5576 Marian Ct
Grandville MI 49418

Call Sign: KC8FHI
Gregg A Rozeboom
1185 McClelland St
Grandville MI 49418

Call Sign: KC8SHC
Daniel Rozeboom
1185 McClelland St
Grandville MI 49418

Call Sign: KC8JHP
Eric J Rozeboom
1185 McClelland St
Grandville MI 49418

Call Sign: KD8CKM
Paul S Foguth
4342 Mill St
Grandville MI 49418

Call Sign: NY8X
Leon E St Pierre
4358 Mill St
Grandville MI 49418

Call Sign: K8UXK
Marvin E Ditmar
4232 Mohawk Ave
SW
Grandville MI 49418

Call Sign: W8LEI
Raymond M Hamacher
3903 Navaho SW
Grandville MI 49418

Call Sign: KC8NGF
Lawrence S Brumwell
3824 Oakes
Grandville MI 49418

Call Sign: WA8LZD
John H Briel Jr
5388 Palmair
Grandville MI 49418

Call Sign: W8WOH
Eugene J Kowalski
6453 Par 5 Dr SW
Grandville MI 49418

Call Sign: KA8KBK
Robert D Bagby
3118 Pine Meadow
Grandville MI 49418

Call Sign: K8AAI
Robert D Bagby
3118 Pine Meadow
Grandville MI 49418

Call Sign: WB8DKA
James C Leese Sr
4025 Pineview W
Grandville MI 49418

Call Sign: N8XHA
Robert L Hammond
0-461 Port Sheldon Rd
Grandville MI 49418

Call Sign: WD8ELT
Malcolm K Palmer
2920 Porter Ct
Grandville MI 49418

Call Sign: N8WDZ
Jerry D Lester
461 Pt Sheldon Rd
Grandville MI 49418

Call Sign: N8ZSV
John Molegraaf
4386 Red Bush
Grandville MI 49418

Call Sign: KC8ZPY
Gerard A Rudy
4245 Red Bush Dr SW
Grandville MI 49418

Call Sign: KJ4QIS
Roger W Dickey Jr
2885 Sanford Ave SW
12784
Grandville MI 49418

Call Sign: KC0SYZ
Theodore B Byrd

2885 Sanford Ave SW
16567
Grandville MI 49418

Call Sign: N8AV
Robert E Robart
3977 Sante Fe Ct
Grandville MI 49418

Call Sign: KB8YEG
Scott P Muller
2831 Shady Oaks Ct
Grandville MI 49418

Call Sign: KB8YXA
Deanna B Mitchell
3741 Shoshone
Grandville MI 49418

Call Sign: WB8YQK
Dwain M Mitchell
3741 Shoshone Dr
Grandville MI
494181849

Call Sign: KD8NMF
James J Kastelz
3675 Shoshone Dr SW
Grandville MI 49418

Call Sign: WB8NWC
Edwin J Vander Ploeg
Jr
109 Stonehenge Dr
SW
Grandville MI 49418

Call Sign: KS8P
C B Moberly
178 Sunnyview SW
Grandville MI 49418

Call Sign: N8EZD
Steven R Vredevoogd
2840 Timberlane Dr
Grandville MI 49418

Call Sign: KB8EHM
Lyle F Griffin
3224 Town Crossing
Dr
Grandville MI 49418

Call Sign: KB8TEE

William M Crowner
3159 Vermont
Grandville MI 49418

Call Sign: KC8GDD
Geoffrey D Kooistra
3155 Wallace
Grandville MI 49418

Call Sign: N8HNW
Janet M Schuiling
4200 White Dr
Grandville MI 49418

Call Sign: N8YZH
Harold J Schuiling
4200 White St
Grandville MI 49418

Call Sign: N8ZTR
Ronald G Schuiling
4200 White St
Grandville MI 49418

Call Sign: KB8FVW
Thelma I McClurken
3471 Wilson Ave SW
Grandville MI 49418

Call Sign: WA8ZXZ
Archie McClurken
3471 Wilson Ave SW
Grandville MI
494181878

Call Sign: N8GHJ
Frances M Klein
4279 Windcrest Dr
Grandville MI 49418

Call Sign: W8ALV
Norman E Klein
4279 Windcrest Dr
Grandville MI
494189700

Call Sign: W8VTG
Arthur J Freyling
3670 Yellowstone Dr
Grandville MI 49418

Call Sign: KC8KRO
Stanley C Osmolinski
Jr

Grandville MI 49468

Call Sign: KC8QKA
Rolland F Mullin
4415 E 104 St
Grant MI 49327

Call Sign: WD8PLM
Ronald M Hilden
4285 E 106
Grant MI 49327

Call Sign: KJ8C
Robert W Boyink
1751 Hess Lake Dr
Grant MI 49327

Call Sign: WA8EOW
Doran A Ditlow
12635 Luce Ave
Grant MI 493279635

Call Sign: W8KGV
Ralph H Gould
12396 McClelland Ave
Grant MI 49327

Call Sign: WB8NNC
Leland C Godfrey
7495 W 108th St
Grant MI 49327

Call Sign: KC8ANE
James R Renney
2380 W 120th St
Grant MI 49327

Call Sign: N8IMV
Jack L Southland
5960 W 124th St
Grant MI 49327

Call Sign: W2UHI
Frank B Lumney
6275 W 124th St
Grant MI 49327

Call Sign: KB8RDT

Thomas A McMillan
2414 Birch Rd
Grawn MI 49637

Call Sign: KC8CBG
Shannon M McMillan
2414 Birch Rd
Grawn MI 49637

Call Sign: KB8ZPF
Kennith A Schug
7511 Birch St
Grawn MI 49637

Call Sign: N8QVQ
Justin J Cascagnett
5893 Blair Town Hall
Grawn MI 49637

Call Sign: KC8DYZ
Scott A Sanderson
1811 Compton Ct
Grawn MI 496379637

Call Sign: KB8IIC
Brian F Steinebach
3816 E Shore Dr
Grawn MI 49637

Call Sign: KA8QVH
Edward L Irwin
4625 Fouch Rd
Grawn MI 49637

Call Sign: KB8RRW
Victor L Bartlette
4710 Fouch Rd
Grawn MI 49637

Call Sign: W8EYC
Michael M Glasser
4102 Peninsular Shores
Dr
Grawn MI 49637

Call Sign: KC8TDL
Andrew K Barth
5088 S M 37
Grawn MI 49637

Call Sign: KL2WF
Robert P Gunnerfeldt
6266 US Hwy 31 S
Grawn MI 49637

Call Sign: KB8WZW
Bernard R Bossert Jr
5170 Vance Rd
Grawn MI 49637

Call Sign: KC8LTR
Richard J Cieslik
5698 Vance Rd
Grawn MI 49637

Call Sign: KB8IJP
Tanya Pickard
5772 Vance Rd
Grawn MI 49637

Call Sign: N8KAT
Teresa J Pickard
5772 Vance Rd
Grawn MI 49637

Call Sign: KC8UPX
Michael J Mckenna
1699 Walter Dr
Grawn MI 49637

Call Sign: KB8ZPC
Kip G Burns
Grawn MI 49637

**FCC Amateur Radio
Licenses in Grayling**

Call Sign: KC8WBZ
Faye Tackett
214 Alexia Ln
Grayling MI 49738

Call Sign: N8RYU
Michelle M Adamski
115 Barbara St
Grayling MI
497388655

Call Sign: N8TPN
Thomas S Adamski
115 Barbara St
Grayling MI
497388655

Call Sign: KC8JRZ
Harvey J Smale
7031 Beasley Ave
Grayling MI 49738

Call Sign: W8PCY
Rex E Shattuck Jr
15745 Beaver Bank Trl
Grayling MI 49738

Call Sign: WD8AHF
Vernon R Cecil
6663 Beaver Rd
Grayling MI 49738

Call Sign: WD8POU
Tom C Loomis Jr
10201 Beech Ter
Grayling MI 49738

Call Sign: KD8OWD
Pamela S Rohr
1844 Black Antler Ct
Grayling MI 49738

Call Sign: AK8M
Ronald L Joyce
1540 Bow Bend Trl
Grayling MI
497389049

Call Sign: KB8MNY
Richard W Febey
Rt 1 Box 2340
Grayling MI 49738

Call Sign: W8JKM
Michael R Cerven
Rr 2 Box 2505 Wakely
Bridge Rd
Grayling MI 49738

Call Sign: N8XDI
Kevin T McMurphy
Rt 3 Box 3695
Grayling MI 49738

Call Sign: KB8ZHQ
Fred B Hinkle
Rt 5 Box 5389
Grayling MI 49738

Call Sign: N8SUB
Timothy W Febey
Rr 1 Box Kw2340
Grayling MI 49738

Call Sign: WB8YOY

William R Summitt
8535 Clough Dr
Grayling MI 49738

Call Sign: KD8LHK
Joan L Eddy
277 Dale St
Grayling MI 49738

Call Sign: KD8LZG
Steve L Eddy
277 Dale St
Grayling MI 49738

Call Sign: WD8ORV
Ronald R Yon
6177 Deerfield Dr
Grayling MI 49738

Call Sign: WD8OTR
Robert A Yon
6177 Deerfield Dr
Grayling MI 49738

Call Sign: KD8BNO
William E Hartig
4234 E Beaver Island
Rd
Grayling MI 49738

Call Sign: KD8HTI
Will T Schultz
3729 E Branch Rd
Grayling MI 49738

Call Sign: W8YSS
Will T Schultz
3729 E Branch Rd
Grayling MI 49738

Call Sign: N8AHZ
Amateur Radio Assn
Of Hanson Hills
3729 E Branch Rd
Grayling MI 49738

Call Sign: KC8DME
Chad J Schultz
3729 E Branch Rd
Grayling MI 49738

Call Sign: N8YSS
Jon F Schultz
3729 E Branch Rd

Grayling MI 49738

Call Sign: N8ZKG
Ben E Schultz
3729 E Branch Rd
Grayling MI 49738

Call Sign: KD8HXZ
Katie L Schultz
3729 E Branch Rd
Grayling MI 49738

Call Sign: K8YSS
Katie L Schultz
3729 E Branch Rd
Grayling MI 49738

Call Sign: KC8TOA
Ronald R Lukas
3997 E Railroad Tr
Grayling MI 49738

Call Sign: KC8BJY
Timothy R Butzin
305 Elm St
Grayling MI 49738

Call Sign: KB8GT
Laurence D Smith
1982 Evelyn Ave
Grayling MI 49738

Call Sign: K1HBM
Harmon E Brammer
1365 Falcon Ave
Grayling MI 49738

Call Sign: K8BOR
David H Borkowski
332 Goline Rd
Grayling MI 49738

Call Sign: N8ZMJ
Thomas W Hammond
2713 Hammond Trl
Grayling MI 49738

Call Sign: N8YBQ
Albert R Ingalls Sr
1049 Heather Ln
Grayling MI 49738

Call Sign: N8YBR
Joyce E Ingalls

1049 Heather Ln
Grayling MI 49738

Call Sign: KC8FCJ
Robert F Bovee
505 Ingham
Grayling MI
497380151

Call Sign: WA8IWV
Roger P Wisniewski
125 Jeannette St
Grayling MI 49738

Call Sign: K8CWC
Lyle K Keipinger
5782 Keipinger Trl
Grayling MI 49738

Call Sign: KC8PIQ
Robert E Orr
5844 Keipinger Trl
Grayling MI 49738

Call Sign: KC8PWT
Sherie L Orr
5844 Keipinger Trl
Grayling MI 49738

Call Sign: WA8QMC
Lawrence J Lipinski
2482 Kirkland Dr
Grayling MI 49738

Call Sign: K8MV
Marty A Van De Ven
810 Little John Ave
Grayling MI 49738

Call Sign: KD8FZJ
Vincent E Robertson
5734 Loeffler Dr
Grayling MI 49738

Call Sign: KC8ELJ
Shirley M Galleck
15688 M 72
Grayling MI 49738

Call Sign: KC8DMF
Teresa D Raybould
229 M 72 E
Grayling MI 49738

Call Sign: KB8VFQ
Frederick W Raybould
229 M 72 E
Grayling MI 49738

Call Sign: N8ZKE
Clara M Gibbs
306 Madsen St
Grayling MI 49738

Call Sign: N7AJZ
Carolyn R Wilske
7436 Merrio Rd
Grayling MI 49738

Call Sign: WB8GOY
David A McCarthy
6334 Old Lake Rd
Grayling MI
497386428

Call Sign: NM8L
Melvin R Moore
4522 Orbit Dr
Grayling MI 49738

Call Sign: KB8TDN
Leon F D Amour
605 Ottaws
Grayling MI 49738

Call Sign: KA8BFA
Leslie R Hunter
505 Park Ave
Grayling MI 49738

Call Sign: KD8GJE
James W Baker
406 Park St
Grayling MI 49738

Call Sign: KD8CXI
Robert H Marcereau
11540 Red Pine Dr
Grayling MI 49738

Call Sign: N8YH
Robert H Marcereau
11540 Red Pine Dr
Grayling MI 49738

Call Sign: N8YSR
Jack C Mahank
9270 Romany Ave

Grayling MI 49738

Call Sign: KD8OTH
Gary T Rapelje
2168 Rosalind Ave
Grayling MI 49738

Call Sign: KC8KHB
Ronald E Wood
6662 S Military Rd
Grayling MI
497389782

Call Sign: W8IOK
Robert C Schmidt Sr
1779 Schmidt Trl
Grayling MI
497380664

Call Sign: N8ZKD
Jack M Campbell
302 Scott St
Grayling MI 49738

Call Sign: W8CA
Kenneth D Wright
3568 Serenity Trl
Grayling MI 49738

Call Sign: WA8SCO
George E Brand III
10223 Shupac Lake Rd
Grayling MI 49738

Call Sign: KC8NXH
Hunter C Brand
10223 Shupac Lake Rd
Grayling MI 49738

Call Sign: KC8HCM
Jack H Woodward
1387 Stephan Bridge
Rd
Grayling MI 49738

Call Sign: WB8JRQ
Edwin M Underwood
1472 Stephen Bridge
Rd
Grayling MI 49738

Call Sign: KC8CEZ
Stephen J Doyle
1549 Sunfish Ave

Grayling MI 49738

Call Sign: KD8IHL
George C Wilson
1550 Swamp Rd
Grayling MI 49738

Call Sign: KB8QWK
Peter A Funck
110 Vilas St
Grayling MI 49738

Call Sign: KB8VYE
John L Welt Jr
4632 W 5 Mile Rd
Grayling MI 49738

Call Sign: N8HEM
Richard O Lee
2716 W Jones Lake Rd
Grayling MI 49738

Call Sign: N8YSQ
Dave B Niederer
1103 W M 72 Hwy E
Of Grayling
Grayling MI 49738

Call Sign: N8OCW
Steven R Jackson
Grayling MI 49738

Call Sign: KA8AAW
Robert F Woodland
Grayling MI 49738

Call Sign: WD8LUM
Marshall D Damoth
Grayling MI 49738

Call Sign: KD8PTC
Jack H Woodward
Grayling MI 49738

Call Sign: KD8RTW
John L Chad
Grayling MI 49738

Call Sign: KB8VYF
Louis J Baker II
Grayling MI
497381039

Call Sign: WD8ELH
Jared M Freeman
3625 Cedar St
Greenbush MI 48738

Call Sign: KD8FQN
Charles W Kitchen
2413 Running Brook
Greenbush MI 48738

Call Sign: WA0SXX
Robert G Saner
3576 S US 23
Greenbush MI 48738

Call Sign: KC8FBS
Charles L Major Jr
4457 W Cedar Lake
Rd
Greenbush MI 48738

Call Sign: KC8HNN
James E Gruba
1550 Wade Trl
Greenbush MI 48738

Call Sign: KC8ZAN
John C O Donald
12790 14 Mile Rd
Greenville MI 48838

Call Sign: N8HOE
Lawrence P Vos
14380 14 Mile Rd
Greenville MI 48838

Call Sign: K8OFL
Ronald J High
990 Arloa Dr
Greenville MI 48838

Call Sign: KA8ZKD
Jay A Wood
819 Baldwin St
Greenville MI 48838

Call Sign: KA8VTK

Bruce W Beauvais
12974 Beardslee
Greenville MI 48838

Call Sign: KA8YQY
Susan K Beauvais
12974 Beardslee
Greenville MI 48838

Call Sign: N8WLF
Bruce W Beauvais
12974 Beardslee
Greenville MI 48838

Call Sign: K8SKB
Susan K Beauvais
12974 Beardslee
Greenville MI 48838

Call Sign: KB8SWA
Scott E Masengale
7125 Briker Rd
Greenville MI 48838

Call Sign: N8FUA
W Donovan Shroll
10766 Carson City Rd
SW
Greenville MI 48838

Call Sign: N8JIQ
Robert E Harp Jr
13595 Claude Ave
Greenville MI 48838

Call Sign: KD8DLO
Gary V Norris
10185 Connelley Ave
NE
Greenville MI 48838

Call Sign: K8USB
Gary V Norris
10185 Connelley Ave
NE
Greenville MI 48838

Call Sign: KB8VED
Scott E Dakin
218.5 E Benton
Greenville MI 48838

Call Sign: KD8CDI
Dennis R Vander Zand

313 E Cass St SE
Greenville MI 48838

Call Sign: W8JYG
Harry O Caulk
320 E Oak St
Greenville MI 48835

Call Sign: WD8RZZ
Joseph H Greenwood
919 E Oak St
Greenville MI
488382025

Call Sign: KD8LNR
Thomas M Rydahl
911 E Pearl St
Greenville MI 48838

Call Sign: KC8HDH
Eugene G Holsted
210 E Summit Apt 2
Greenville MI 48838

Call Sign: KB8JMV
Carmen D Baker
205 E Summit St
Greenville MI 48838

Call Sign: WD8KFA
James D Irish
920 E Van Deinse St
Greenville MI 48838

Call Sign: N8WKO
Steven L Burgtorf
609 E Washington St
Greenville MI 48838

Call Sign: K8HE
Harry W Eldridge
745 Eureka St
Greenville MI 48838

Call Sign: KC8NUS
Century Club Truckers
Club
745 Eureka St
Greenville MI 48838

Call Sign: KB8EII
Leslie G Rice
11622 Harlow Rd
Greenville MI 48838

Call Sign: N8ILV
Jack N Rice
11622 Harlow Rd
Greenville MI 48838

Call Sign: KD8IQW
Cheryl A Jean
1005 Hawthorne Ct
Greenville MI 48838

Call Sign: KB8VEI
Michael D Winegard
8815 Hebert Dr
Greenville MI 48838

Call Sign: N8KKO
Ricky D Beach
5595 Johnson Rd
Greenville MI 48838

Call Sign: KB8RWV
Daniel C Ferguson
13801 Keiber
Greenville MI 48838

Call Sign: KB8VEG
Jeramie J Ferguson
13826 Keiber NE
Greenville MI 48838

Call Sign: N8HNU
Sally J Stephens
13925 Keiber Rd
Greenville MI 48838

Call Sign: WD8MPN
Charles M Stephens
13925 Keiber Rd
Greenville MI 48838

Call Sign: KB8SVX
Deborah D Ferguson
13801 Keiber St
Greenville MI 48838

Call Sign: K8AYL
Francis S Wirtz
10745 Kickland Rd
Greenville MI 48838

Call Sign: N8HOK
Darlene I Wirtz
10745 Kickland Rd

Greenville MI 48838

Call Sign: KB8QZU
Phillip G Symonds
10353 Leland Dr
Greenville MI 48838

Call Sign: KD8PKS
Greenville ARC
13425 Lynn Dr
Greenville MI 48838

Call Sign: WX8GRN
Greenville ARC
13425 Lynn Dr
Greenville MI 48838

Call Sign: KD8RXD
Greenville ARC
13425 Lynn Dr
Greenville MI 48838

Call Sign: KB8ZGL
Mike J Wolthuis
13425 Lynn Dr
Greenville MI 48838

Call Sign: K8CRI
Walter L Peacock
3642 Morgan Dr
Greenville MI 48838

Call Sign: KB8VQH
Michael C Malone
13660 Moss Ave
Greenville MI 48838

Call Sign: WD8ALP
George C Lewis
205 N Bower
Greenville MI 48838

Call Sign: K8WJQ
Jeanette R Christensen
1022 N Edgewood St
Greenville MI 48838

Call Sign: N8WC
Wilbur W Christensen
1022 N Edgewood St
Greenville MI 48838

Call Sign: N8OKY
Deborah A Rich

201 N Luray St
Greenville MI 48838

Call Sign: KC8ZPG
Edward V Minion
803 N Osmun St
Greenville MI 48838

Call Sign: W8OTM
Edward V Minion
803 N Osmun St
Greenville MI 48838

Call Sign: KC8ZPD
Jeff R Keene
621 N Walnut St 34
Greenville MI 48838

Call Sign: K8BOG
Jack E Casterline
13230 Old 14 Mile Rd
Greenville MI 48838

Call Sign: KB8KIX
Donald C Grunow
600 Pearl St
Greenville MI 48838

Call Sign: N8LWK
Dayle F Grunow
600 Pearl St
Greenville MI 48838

Call Sign: N8WVL
Robert J Adams
10604 Roy Dr
Greenville MI 48838

Call Sign: N8YEE
Daniel S Poeder
11123 S Bailey Valley
Dr
Greenville MI 48838

Call Sign: KC8OLP
Chris M Myers
10226 S Greenville Rd
Greenville MI 48838

Call Sign: KC8OET
Joseph A Collins
4757 S Greenville Rd
Apt A
Greenville MI 48838

Call Sign: K8RTM
Robert L Heintzelman
1120 S Lafayette St
Greenville MI 48838

Call Sign: KB8DSN
Rolfe E Kogelschatz
5840 Shearer Rd
Greenville MI 48838

Call Sign: N8KKU
Cynthia J Harp
10972 Simpson W Pvt
Greenville MI 48838

Call Sign: KB8FUA
Jammie L Watson
10972 Simpson W Pvt
Greenville MI 48838

Call Sign: KD8FAL
Kevin M Mccarthy
1206 Tamarack Ct
Greenville MI 48838

Call Sign: WD8KXA
Juergen E Dellenbusch
10210 Van Hoose Rd
Greenville MI
488389375

Call Sign: N8YJP
Lindsey D Shelden
1125 Vining Rd
Greenville MI 48838

Call Sign: KB8FUB
Roy S Jibson
14211 W 14 Mile Rd
Greenville MI 48838

Call Sign: KC8UUM
Wendi L Sellers
310 W Congress St
Greenville MI 48838

Call Sign: N8VYU
Rodney A Sellers
310 W Congress St
Greenville MI 48838

Call Sign: KC8OUD
Alicia F Ranney

513 W Grove St
Greenville MI 48838

Call Sign: WD8KEY
Paul B Irish
308 W Judd
Greenville MI 48838

Call Sign: N8MA
Montcalm Area ARC
200 W Montcalm St
Greenville MI
488380312

Call Sign: WA8LKL
Camp Tuhsmeheta
ARC
200 W Montcalm St
Greenville MI 48838

Call Sign: WA8QCW
Roberta L Alman
200 W Montcalm St
Greenville MI 48838

Call Sign: KC8PSY
Dennis P Partridge
109 W Oak
Greenville MI 48838

Call Sign: KC8EGJ
Roger B Gough
214 W Orange St
Greenville MI 48838

Call Sign: W8RBG
Roger B Gough
214 W Orange St
Greenville MI 48838

Call Sign: KC8SZD
Westley C Ely
521 W Orange St
Greenville MI 48838

Call Sign: KD8RLK
Charles M Hill
521 W Ornage St
Greenville MI 48838

Call Sign: N8IBM
Mark W Watson
8985 Wabasis Ave NE
Greenville MI 48838

Call Sign: N8JIR
Gilbert L Jewell Sr
1120 Wellington Ct
Apt 201
Greenville MI 48838

Call Sign: KA8CAU
Roberta L Alman
Greenville MI 48838

Call Sign: KB8QZT
Bettye J Link
Greenville MI 48838

Call Sign: N8RO
John A Link Jr
Greenville MI 48838

Call Sign: WA8QCW
Larry L Alman
Greenville MI 48838

Call Sign: KC8NOM
Bonnie L Symonds
Greenville MI 48838

Call Sign: WB8ABC
Harry W Eldridge
Greenville MI 48838

Call Sign: NX8O
Century Club Truckers
Club
Greenville MI 48838

Call Sign: W8WR
Larry L Alman
Greenville MI
488381744

Call Sign: KD8FWJ
Robert H Johnson
828N E Gulliver Lake
Rd
Gulliver MI 49840

Call Sign: KB8MJO

Thomas E Robinson
483 Adams St S
Gwinn MI 49841

Call Sign: KC8FGM
Jeff S Wiersma
109 Banshee
Gwinn MI 49841

Call Sign: AB8KI
Jeff S Wiersma
109 Banshee
Gwinn MI 49841

Call Sign: KC8UGZ
Jeff J Chappa
100 Crusader
Gwinn MI 49841

Call Sign: WB8KYC
Harvey S Miser
805 E Airfield Rd
Gwinn MI 49841

Call Sign: WB8ODO
Bonnie L Miser
805 E Airfield Rd
Gwinn MI 49841

Call Sign: KD8IZL
Richard D Papkey
661 E M 35 Apt 19
Gwinn MI 49841

Call Sign: KC8CVQ
James A Jackson
Rr 70 E Sands St
Gwinn MI 49841

Call Sign: AB8NF
James A Jackson
Rr 70 E Sands St
Gwinn MI 49841

Call Sign: AA8FZ
Donald A Siebert
520 E Slough Lake Rd
Gwinn MI 498410583

Call Sign: KC5BNT
Beverley I Harwood
747 E State Hwy M35
Gwinn MI 498419012

Call Sign: W5WTX
Ted G Harwood
747 E State Hwy M35
Gwinn MI 498419012

Call Sign: KB8SNN
Kory S Dykstra
152 Elm
Gwinn MI 49841

Call Sign: KD8PTG
Joseph E Haapapuro
247 Explorer St
Gwinn MI 49841

Call Sign: N9PAR
Nick J Mills
210 Fortress
Gwinn MI 49841

Call Sign: KD8NJO
Matthew D Hodgins
507 Jupiter St
Gwinn MI 49841

Call Sign: WD8CLA
Edward A Gosselin
1365 Knudsen Rd
Gwinn MI 49841

Call Sign: WD8ALT
Gareth B Todd
520 Laramie Rd
Gwinn MI 498418752

Call Sign: K7LTU
Matthew D Hodgins
411 Liberator
Gwinn MI 49841

Call Sign: KC8CVV
Gary F Filizetti
217 N Ash St
Gwinn MI 498419617

Call Sign: KC8STM
Dale A Akerley
359 N Bertrand Lake
Rd
Gwinn MI 49841

Call Sign: ND8A
Dale A Akerley

359 N Bertrand Lake
Rd
Gwinn MI 49841

Call Sign: N8HCA
Ronald K Timock
280 N Boulder St
Gwinn MI 49841

Call Sign: KD8BJC
Leona D Rowe
128 N Crestview Dr
Gwinn MI 49841

Call Sign: WD8CYB
Duane K Ross
216 N Elm St
Gwinn MI 49841

Call Sign: WD8RCD
Patsy A Ross
216 N Elm St
Gwinn MI 49841

Call Sign: KC8OXH
Gwendolyn Akom
28 N Mitchell St
Gwinn MI 49841

Call Sign: KC8OXJ
Terance A Dejuliannie
259 N Pine
Gwinn MI 49841

Call Sign: KC8DIG
Joseph S Shafer
497 N River Dr
Gwinn MI 49841

Call Sign: KB8YJU
Joseph L Duckworth Jr
497 N River Dr
Gwinn MI 49841

Call Sign: W8AXI
Robert G Weingartner
30 N Seass Dr
Gwinn MI 49841

Call Sign: KC8EED
Arlene A Johnson
131 N Serenity Dr
Gwinn MI 49841

Call Sign: W8YV
Richard L Johnson
131 N Serenity Dr
Gwinn MI 49841

Call Sign: KB5VDM
Carolyn J Lowe
530 Old CR 553
Gwinn MI 49841

Call Sign: AB9BA
David J Hodgins
133 Provider St
Gwinn MI 49841

Call Sign: N8SGZ
David P York
112 Provider Str
Gwinn MI 498412726

Call Sign: N8WBI
Claire J Easley
9 S Blue Lake Dr
Gwinn MI 49841

Call Sign: K8BHZ
Brian W Mattson
1800 S CR 557
Gwinn MI 498419256

Call Sign: KD8NPF
Mary K Morris
520 S Mackinac Ln
Gwinn MI 49841

Call Sign: WA8DOF
David R Van Denburg
140 Station Rd
Gwinn MI 49841

Call Sign: N9XTY
Joy M Ward
251 Thunderchief
Gwinn MI 49841

Call Sign: W8ABX
Alton D Sunday
629 Valkyrie
Gwinn MI 49841

Call Sign: KA8DNA
Eric A Anderson
460 W Adams St S
Gwinn MI 49841

Call Sign: N8XBI
Holland L Werner
3119 W Albert Ln
Gwinn MI 49841

Call Sign: KD8SCB
Ronald S Hewson
228 W Flint
Gwinn MI 49841

Call Sign: KD8JIQ
Michelle R Grund
2110 W Horsehoe
Lake Dr
Gwinn MI 49841

Call Sign: NV8N
Upper Peninsula Dx
And Contest Club
1139 W Little Shag
Lake Rd
Gwinn MI 49841

Call Sign: N8RY
Ryan W Fountain
1139 W Little Shag
Lake Rd
Gwinn MI 49841

Call Sign: KC8CVW
Judith M Parlato
456 W M 35
Gwinn MI 49841

Call Sign: N8TES
Terry P Parlato
456 W M 35
Gwinn MI 49841

Call Sign: KD8SCD
Russell W Ransom
2133 W M 35
Gwinn MI 49841

Call Sign: KG8JW
John W Wright
190 Youngs Rd
Gwinn MI 49841

Call Sign: KG8JX
Linda L Wright
190 Youngs Rd
Gwinn MI 49841

Call Sign: N8PCK
Joel B Blixt
Gwinn MI 49841

Call Sign: KD8ASQ
Upper Peninsula Dx
And Contest Club
Gwinn MI 49841

Call Sign: KB8PEM
Rita E Savola
Gwinn MI 49841

Call Sign: N8XAE
Robert A Savola
Gwinn MI 49841

Call Sign: KC8UGY
Julie L Akerley
Gwinn MI 49841

Call Sign: KD8FPO
Delan S Dravland
Gwinn MI 49841

Call Sign: KC8VYX
William L Olson
Gwinn MI 49841

Call Sign: W8SQ
William L Olson
Gwinn MI 49841

**FCC Amateur Radio
Licenses in Hale**

Call Sign: W8HHD
Herbert H Watts
4137 Chippewa Dr
Hale MI 48739

Call Sign: KC8HXM
Clarence E Bosley
800 Crammond Rd
Hale MI 48739

Call Sign: WT8X
Daniel J Leonard
6875 Curtis Rd
Hale MI 48739

Call Sign: WD8OWN
Robert D Leonard

6838 E Curtis Rd
Hale MI 48739

Call Sign: K8SPE
Robert J Shuman
5779 Frolic Trl
Hale MI 48739

Call Sign: KC8JQJ
John M Miller
6381 Grace Dr
Hale MI 48739

Call Sign: KD8HNM
Dion T Jordan
4939 Iroquois St
Hale MI 48739

Call Sign: N8IGM
Joe C Glover
4690 Lakeside Blvd
Hale MI 48739

Call Sign: N8GPW
George W Beckley Jr
3613 Mill Station Rd
Hale MI 48739

Call Sign: K8HRL
Raymond H Bialk
204 N Lake St
Hale MI 48739

Call Sign: KB8HOK
Harry E Head Jr
5820 Orchard St
Hale MI 48739

Call Sign: KW8L
Jack L Mccurdy
8795 Riley Rd
Hale MI 48739

Call Sign: N8SXT
David A Zsidi
1344 S Sage Lake Rd
Hale MI 48739

Call Sign: KC8GXS
Daniel A Mitchell
6245 Slosser Rd
Hale MI 48739

Call Sign: KD8JSL

Dale L Wheeler
4831 Stahlbush Rd
Hale MI 48739

Call Sign: KB8KTV
Charles E Brodie
6612 Terry Ln
Hale MI 487399098

Call Sign: KC8MXD
George W Schrage
304 Victoria Ave
Hale MI 48739

Call Sign: KA8ZNM
Dale F Bissonnette
7901 W Esmond Rd
Hale MI 48739

Call Sign: KD8PSZ
Tim J Larabell
6559 Wickert Rd
Hale MI 48739

FCC Amateur Radio Licenses in Hamilton

Call Sign: KD8OYD
Benjamin A Roels
4147 132nd Ave
Hamilton MI 49419

Call Sign: KD8OYC
Ross E Harris
5030 136th Ave
Hamilton MI 49419

Call Sign: KA4CFQ
Henry Bierling
3866 136th Ave Rt 3
Hamilton MI 49419

Call Sign: KC8QDE
John H Hanse
4680 137th Ave
Hamilton MI 49419

Call Sign: AC8HZ
John H Hanse
4680 137th Ave
Hamilton MI 49419

Call Sign: K6JAA
Jeffrey A Amundsen

4682 137th Ave
Hamilton MI 49419

Call Sign: WD9GGG
Anthony S Phillips
3529 38th St
Hamilton MI 49419

Call Sign: N8QEO
Donald R Dekker
4119 38th St
Hamilton MI 49419

Call Sign: KC8KKG
Kirk A Oswald
3624 47th St
Hamilton MI
494199723

Call Sign: KB8GFP
David L Timmer
3871 47th St
Hamilton MI 49419

Call Sign: KC8JQQ
Brenda M Williams
3174 60th St
Hamilton MI 49419

Call Sign: N8NXB
Steven L Williams
3174 60th St
Hamilton MI 49419

Call Sign: N8UMS
Orval J Essink
3677 E Volkers
Hamilton MI 49419

Call Sign: KD8OHV
Eric E Burmeister
4138 Meyer Dr
Hamilton MI 49419

Call Sign: KD8OHZ
Adam R Pickworth
4177 Meyer Dr
Hamilton MI 49419

Call Sign: WB8EEI
Clifford L Sale
3408 Spruce Dr
Hamilton MI 49419

Call Sign: N8UXP
Donald D Robinson
3569 Walnut Park Dr
Hamilton MI 49419

FCC Amateur Radio Licenses in Hancock

Call Sign: KD8IJV
Denise M Talcott
50617 4th St
Hancock MI 49930

Call Sign: KD8IJW
Jeffrey T Talcott
50617 4th St
Hancock MI 49930

Call Sign: N8ITG
Paul R Taddeucci
1215 Anthony St
Hancock MI 49930

Call Sign: KC8CCT
Ruth L Angove
49048 Arcadian St
Hancock MI 49930

Call Sign: AA8YL
Gary J Angove
49048 Arcadian St
Hancock MI 49930

Call Sign: KC8IIG
Dale K Dewald
49595 Blessent Rd
Hancock MI 49930

Call Sign: K8VXB
Paul P Ekdahl
Rt 1 Box 297 Paavola
Loc
Hancock MI 49930

Call Sign: KB8URX
Anders E Maki
Rte 1 Box 337A
Hancock MI 49930

Call Sign: KB8URW
Aaron S Janke
Rt 1 Box 338E
Hancock MI 49930

Call Sign: KD8CGB
Jacob M Hults
49034 Burt St
Hancock MI 49930

Call Sign: N8UKL
Erik N Janners
1300 Cedar St
Hancock MI 49930

Call Sign: N8GWO
William A Schoos
21771 Coal Dock Rd
Hancock MI 49930

Call Sign: N8PBK
Laurie A Curran
22446 Coal Dock Rd
Hancock MI 49930

Call Sign: KC8CDC
James A La Haie
1033 Crestwood Glade
Hancock MI 49930

Call Sign: KC8CDB
Anne Marie L La Haie
1033 Crestwood Glade
Hancock MI
499301154

Call Sign: KC8AIA
Ronald Gnadinger
23820 E Lakeview Tr
Hancock MI 49930

Call Sign: WA8NUP
Kenneth E Manninen
903 Elm St
Hancock MI 49930

Call Sign: W8LTL
James R Carstens
918 Elm St
Hancock MI 49930

Call Sign: KC8KC
Peter G Kilpela
920 Elm St
Hancock MI 49930

Call Sign: WD8AFX
Phillip J Verville II
1213 Emery St

Hancock MI 49930

Call Sign: KD8DYM
Javier Fernandez
615 Finn St
Hancock MI 49930

Call Sign: KB8FCW
Edward W Maki
23745 Forsman Rd
Hancock MI 49930

Call Sign: KC8TSA
Scott L Mcneil
513 Hancock St
Hancock MI 49930

Call Sign: KC8ZNF
Kenneth D Cygan
317 Harris Ave
Hancock MI 49930

Call Sign: KC8JXU
Paul D Peterson
1203 Hecla St
Hancock MI
499301036

Call Sign: WA8MAM
Robert E Zulinski
1221 Hecla St
Hancock MI
499301036

Call Sign: KC8NPI
John E Dueweke Jr
21522 Hwy M 26
Hancock MI 49930

Call Sign: KB8ZCD
Paul M Christensen
49938 Hwy M 26
Hancock MI
499309730

Call Sign: W9VLM
Paul M Christensen
49938 Hwy M 26
Hancock MI
499309730

Call Sign: KC8SFM
Gerald N Huffman
1112 Ingot St

Hancock MI 49930

Call Sign: KB8XI
Roland B Burgan
2161 Jasberg St
Hancock MI 49930

Call Sign: KC8EKZ
William L Yarroch
621 Lake Ave
Hancock MI 49930

Call Sign: KC8MVX
Scott A Linna
19785 Lakeview Dr 8
Hancock MI
499302145

Call Sign: KD8MFO
Jason E Socha
309 Montezuma St
Hancock MI 49930

Call Sign: KD8FPM
Joshua P Olson
934 N Elevation St
Hancock MI 49930

Call Sign: WQ8G
Donald R Van Uum
49336 N Grosse Point
Shores Rd
Hancock MI 49930

Call Sign: KD8ELN
Michael K Blaser
730 N Lincoln Dr
Hancock MI 49931

Call Sign: KC8YDU
Mark S Konczel
804 N Lincoln Dr
Hancock MI 49930

Call Sign: KD8BJA
Vickie M Fortier
804 N Lincoln Dr
Hancock MI 49930

Call Sign: N8FHF
Howard D Junkin
22074 New St
Hancock MI 49930

Call Sign: N8PBD
Jean E Junkin
22074 New St
Hancock MI 49930

Call Sign: KC8RGL
Aric J Asti
1004 Prospect St
Hancock MI 49930

Call Sign: KB8VZP
John F Kroll
1607 Quincy
Hancock MI 49930

Call Sign: KC8NFW
Steven P Hemp
1301 Quincy St Apt 3
Hancock MI 49930

Call Sign: W8SDT
Paul R Hinzmann
1150 Roberts St
Hancock MI 49930

Call Sign: KD8OWX
Jordan R Schulze
20566 Royce Rd
Hancock MI 49930

Call Sign: KD8HZB
Justin C Izzard
915 S Lincoln Dr
Hancock MI 49930

Call Sign: W8IZZ
Justin C Izzard
915 S Lincoln Dr
Hancock MI 49930

Call Sign: KD8AWC
Mark R Lamotte
1035 S Lincoln Dr
Hancock MI 49930

Call Sign: KC8FLK
Paul A Kemppainen
55345 Salo Rd
Hancock MI 49930

Call Sign: KG4GGJ
Gustavo F Bourdieu
25 Shafter St
Hancock MI 49930

Call Sign: K8OOI
Gustavo F Bourdieu
25 Shafter St
Hancock MI 49930

Call Sign: W8MHJ
Edward C Hoyer
1107 Summit St
Hancock MI 49930

Call Sign: KC8PPJ
Shawn M Len
1215 Summit St
Hancock MI 49930

Call Sign: N8SHB
David J Doyle
817 Up Hancock St
Hancock MI 49930

Call Sign: N8ZBJ
Andrew C Kangas
21240 Waasa Rd
Hancock MI 49930

Call Sign: KD8GBH
David O Torrey Jr
23490 Woodside Ln
Hancock MI 49930

Call Sign: WA8QNF
Glenn P Ekdahl
Hancock MI
499300465

FCC Amateur Radio Licenses in Harbert

Call Sign: KB6SIJ
Lynne C Haman
7250 Knaute Rd
Harbert MI 491150154

FCC Amateur Radio Licenses in Harbor Springs

Call Sign: KB8RE
Bernie B Slotnick
630 Ann St
Harbor Springs MI
49740

Call Sign: N8KHQ
Gerald A Haan Jr
564 Arbor St
Harbor Springs MI
49740

Call Sign: N9FEI
Richard A Lent
22 L Arbre Croche
Harbor Springs MI
49740

Call Sign: N8IT
David G Wright
2193 Catob Rd
Harbor Springs MI
49740

Call Sign: N8QVY
Desiree L Wright
2193 Catob Rd
Harbor Springs MI
49740

Call Sign: N8TIW
James R Wright III
2193 Catob Rd
Harbor Springs MI
49740

Call Sign: KC8SDX
Emmett ARC
2193 Catob Rd
Harbor Springs MI
49740

Call Sign: W8IN
Desiree L Wright
2193 Catob Rd
Harbor Springs MI
49740

Call Sign: W8ON
Emmet ARS
2193 Catob Rd
Harbor Springs MI
49740

Call Sign: KD8HOF
Thomas W Andrews II
171 Church Rd
Harbor Springs MI
49740

Call Sign: N8LGH
Kenneth W Oliver
2850 E Lake Rd
Harbor Springs MI
49740

Call Sign: KC8GHR
Maria L Dentel
296 E Lk
Harbor Springs MI
49740

Call Sign: K8ZQB
Edwin J Strojny
4695 Gully Rd
Harbor Springs MI
49740

Call Sign: KC8NVI
Clifford S Rosebohm
7574 Hedrick Rd
Harbor Springs MI
49740

Call Sign: KC8QII
Arlene A Rosebohm
7574 Hedrick Rd
Harbor Springs MI
49740

Call Sign: N8AY
Mort A Neff
535 Hoyt
Harbor Springs MI
49740

Call Sign: KB8PQW
Bradley S Swiss
7671 Hoyt Rd
Harbor Springs MI
49740

Call Sign: N8ZPD
Jack L Burley
6918 M 119 Hwy
Harbor Springs MI
49740

Call Sign: N8MJH
Glenn J Chilson
860 Meadow Ln
Harbor Springs MI
49740

Call Sign: N8SXE
George L Tippett
4321 Middle Rd
Harbor Springs MI
49740

Call Sign: WB8RUV
Mario N Kaminski
8969 Mink Rd
Harbor Springs MI
49740

Call Sign: KC8DVN
Little Traverse Bay
ARC
1986 N Lakeshore Dr
Harbor Springs MI
49740

Call Sign: KG8CS
Floyd A Davis
1986 N Lakeshore Dr
Harbor Springs MI
49740

Call Sign: WA6OKT
Lloyd D Pedersen
3165 Petes Run
Harbor Springs MI
49740

Call Sign: KC8LJX
De Wayne E Holmes
4047 Quarter Mile Rd
Harbor Springs MI
49740

Call Sign: KC8WXN
Maxine A Holmes
4047 Quarter Mile Rd
Harbor Springs MI
49740

Call Sign: KC8FFQ
Henry B Joy IV
7156 Rolling Meadow
Trl
Harbor Springs MI
497400278

Call Sign: N8XYR
Kenneth R Barkley
7361 S State Rd

Harbor Springs MI
49740

Call Sign: KC8NVH
Charice R Baughman
152 Snyder St
Harbor Springs MI
49740

Call Sign: KC8VXJ
Samuel R Baughman
152 Snyder St
Harbor Springs MI
49740

Call Sign: WB8TCR
Kenneth A Parada
7645 Tamarac Trl
Harbor Springs MI
49740

Call Sign: KD8CLI
David J Beattie
6008 Teillium Trl
Harbor Springs MI
49740

Call Sign: K8OWM
David J Beattie
6008 Trillium Trl
Harbor Springs MI
49740

Call Sign: W9IEH
Glenn L Kendrick
150 W Main St
Harbor Springs MI
49740

Call Sign: KC8IPO
James C Neff
7943 W Robinson Rd
Harbor Springs MI
49740

Call Sign: W8CSL
Edmund A Unger
137 Zoll St
Harbor Springs MI
49740

**FCC Amateur Radio
Licenses in Harrietta**

Call Sign: KA1ZLQ
Warren D Gionet
1074 S 7 1/2 Rd
Harrietta MI
496389417

Call Sign: WG1WG
Warren D Gionet
1074 S 7 1/2 Rd
Harrietta MI
496389417

**FCC Amateur Radio
Licenses in Harrison**

Call Sign: KD8KQF
William E Felix
2291 Beatrice Rd
Harrison MI 48625

Call Sign: KD8CYK
Gerald E Galloway
2930 Cedar Rd
Harrison MI 48625

Call Sign: KD8QAO
Jack K Hutchinson
1601 Center St
Harrison MI 48625

Call Sign: KA8PPG
Miles H House
4510 Clarence Rd
Harrison MI 48625

Call Sign: KD8QVY
Casarah A Nance
4266 Dan Dr
Harrison MI 48625

Call Sign: KD8QVX
Thomas J Nance
4266 Dan Dr
Harrison MI 48625

Call Sign: WD8CEY
Robert Wagner
2545 Deer Lake Rd
Harrison MI 48625

Call Sign: N8YYW
Johnnie J Keel
778 Dodge Lake Ave
Harrison MI 48625

Call Sign: N8YW
Johnnie J Keel
778 Dodge Lake Ave
Harrison MI 48625

Call Sign: W8VVR
Kenneth A Fuller
2779 E Lake George
Dr
Harrison MI 48625

Call Sign: KB8EAD
Ava J Lyvere
3025 E Lansing St
Harrison MI 48625

Call Sign: KB8GCU
John F Horvat Sr
4560 E Mostetler
Harrison MI 48625

Call Sign: KB8GEW
John F Horvat Jr
4560 E Mostetler
Harrison MI 48625

Call Sign: N8KQT
Charles L Johnson
600 E Temple Dr
Harrison MI 48625

Call Sign: KA8DCJ
Richard J Johnson
1924 Edwin Rd
Harrison MI 48625

Call Sign: KC8ZWN
Nancy J Johnson
1924 Edwin Rd
Harrison MI 48625

Call Sign: KB8UON
Spencer H Watterson
4600 Finley Lk Ave
Harrison MI 48625

Call Sign: KD8OYP
Al O Loucks
2916 Hamilton Dr
Harrison MI 48625

Call Sign: WA8UWW
Al O Loucks

2916 Hamilton Dr
Harrison MI 48625

Call Sign: KD8DOF
Allen J Tessman
3560 Hamilton Dr
Harrison MI 48625

Call Sign: NE8F
John C Iadipaolo
8599 Jackson
Harrison MI 48625

Call Sign: N8KJC
Joseph R Davidowicz
4255 Jeffery Rd
Harrison MI 48625

Call Sign: WD8BHD
Norman J Burlew
4935 Lakepoint Dr
Harrison MI 48625

Call Sign: KD8ALL
Richard D Tackett
4779 Lakewood Dr
Harrison MI 48625

Call Sign: KB8VOD
Les E Smith
5742 Lily Lk Rd
Harrison MI 48625

Call Sign: NY8Y
Robert A Klimkiewicz
2600 Mostetler Rd Lot
19
Harrison MI 48625

Call Sign: N8NUD
Robin R Hamilton
2600 Mostetler Rd Lot
43
Harrison MI 48625

Call Sign: KB8VPV
Robert W Bess
4503 N Athey Ave
Harrison MI 48625

Call Sign: KB8VPW
Careene E Craft
4503 N Athey Ave
Harrison MI 48625

Call Sign: KD8HLN
Jeffery D Schefke
5825 N Ball Ave
Harrison MI 48625

Call Sign: KD8HLO
Jerome L Schefke Jr
5825 N Ball Ave
Harrison MI 48625

Call Sign: KF8EQ
Samuel S Sellers
225 N Clare Ave
Harrison MI
486259587

Call Sign: KD8QLE
Dale R Roth
5954 N Eberhart Ave
Harrison MI 48625

Call Sign: N8AZT
George F Mough
3031 N Harrison Ave
Harrison MI
486259101

Call Sign: KB8MMA
Glee Y Gorka
3720 Norway Ln
Harrison MI 48625

Call Sign: N8HG
Henry J Gorka
3720 Norway Ln
Harrison MI 48625

Call Sign: N8XTR
William H Common
4121 Oak Flats Rd
Harrison MI
486259603

Call Sign: N8XOD
William J Larson
299 Parklane Dr
Harrison MI
486259115

Call Sign: WA8IZM
Ronald F Bertrand
6415 Redman Rd
Harrison MI 48625

Call Sign: KC8DQY
Dennis L Fairbanks
652 Rodgers Rd
Harrison MI 48625

Call Sign: WA8DJI
Marvin C Copenhaver
Sr
1540 S Coolidge
Harrison MI 48625

Call Sign: W8JXB
Oliver F Nash
2875 S Harrison Ave
Harrison MI 48625

Call Sign: KC8UTH
John L Tobey III
398 S Lake St
Harrison MI 48625

Call Sign: W8JLT
John L Tobey III
398 S Lake St
Harrison MI 48625

Call Sign: KB8GCV
Evelyn M Harris
6979 S Ruby
Harrison MI 48625

Call Sign: N8GCD
Kenneth J Wolfe
5450 Shawnee Dr
Harrison MI 48625

Call Sign: NJ8S
Billy R Pennington
1160 W Clarence
Harrison MI 48625

Call Sign: KB8NIK
Ellen Wagner
Harrison MI 48625

Call Sign: KI8GJ
Paul W Cronstrom
Harrison MI 48625

**FCC Amateur Radio
Licenses in
Harrisville**

Call Sign: KC8OLL
Brandon W Smith
209 1st St
Harrisville MI 48740

Call Sign: KC8EYL
Mark R Sullivan
5050 Clark Rd
Harrisville MI 48740

Call Sign: KC8NGT
Arthur K Laatz
5151 Clark Rd
Harrisville MI
487409797

Call Sign: K8AKL
Arthur K Laatz
5151 Clark Rd
Harrisville MI
487409797

Call Sign: KD8BRJ
Kevin R Newland
4105 Clemens Rd
Harrisville MI 48740

Call Sign: KC8RJA
Robert C Flood
4764 Dean Rd
Harrisville MI 48740

Call Sign: KC8NGU
John R Jones
4765 Dean Rd
Harrisville MI 48740

Call Sign: KD8IMJ
Cori R Upper
3273 E Clark Rd
Harrisville MI 48740

Call Sign: KD8GFH
Allan M Neumann Jr
4615 E Clark Rd
Harrisville MI 48740

Call Sign: KD8JUB
Dean L Morris
2715 E Dewar Rd
Harrisville MI 48740

Call Sign: W8DLM
Dean L Morris

2715 E Dewar Rd
Harrisville MI 48740

Call Sign: KC8ZWL
Alex F Brown
3650 E Quick Rd
Harrisville MI 48742

Call Sign: KC8NYM
Harold R Truman
2137 Fowler Rd
Harrisville MI 48740

Call Sign: K8PGJ
David O Thomas
112 Huron Ave
Harrisville MI 48740

Call Sign: N8AVX
James H Smith II
4722 M 72
Harrisville MI 48740

Call Sign: W8JIU
Russell M Pickelmann
2140 McKechnie Rd
Harrisville MI
487409775

Call Sign: KC8RIY
John J Parsons
1628 Mill Rd
Harrisville MI 48740

Call Sign: KC8OLK
Nathan R Prince
3131 N Huron Rd
Harrisville MI 48740

Call Sign: WD8OWM
Stanley L Darmofal
888 N Lake Huron
Shore Dr
Harrisville MI
487400015

Call Sign: W8SZ
Stanley L Darmofal
888 N Lake Huron
Shore Dr
Harrisville MI
487400015

Call Sign: KC8ZOI

Terrence C Boucher
4262 Rolling Hills
Harrisville MI 48740

Call Sign: WD8APL
Charles J Spitznagel
1225 S Campbell Rd
Harrisville MI 48740

Call Sign: WB2NSE
David N Huff
106 S F 41
Harrisville MI 48740

Call Sign: KC8NGR
Christopher C Susan
435 S US 23
Harrisville MI 48740

Call Sign: WD8PXP
Terry L Young
1530 S US 23
Harrisville MI 48740

Call Sign: KC8OHG
Tiffany R Wilson
214 Swamp Rd
Harrisville MI 48740

Call Sign: WA8PRK
John L Wittenberg
Harrisville MI 48740

Call Sign: KD8BRH
Elizabeth M Smith
Harrisville MI 48740

Call Sign: KC8NGV
Sandra A Darmofal
Harrisville MI
487400015

FCC Amateur Radio Licenses in Hart

Call Sign: WZ8S
Thomas A Fitzpatrick
2919 56th Ave
Hart MI 49420

Call Sign: N8DB
Douglas J Barker
123 Apple St
Hart MI 49420

Call Sign: W0MVR
Virgil K Linke Jr
514 Church St
Hart MI 494201378

Call Sign: KD8BGO
Marsha A Hildreth
505 E Main St
Hart MI 49420

Call Sign: N8SRV
Morris A Norton
4900 Fox Rd R 3
Hart MI 49420

Call Sign: KB8RXG
Lewis E Stone
510 Hart St
Hart MI 49420

Call Sign: KC8DGX
Ruth F Stone
510 Hart St
Hart MI 49420

Call Sign: KB8CAM
Marilyn A Schumaker
134 Lake St
Hart MI 49420

Call Sign: N8NCS
Herbert T Buckley
2100 N 112th Ave
Hart MI 49420

Call Sign: KD8HBJ
Titus J Vandezande
2073 N 122nd Ave
Hart MI 49420

Call Sign: KD8IGT
Timothy R
Vandezande
4401 N 144th Ave
Hart MI 49420

Call Sign: W8VTM
Fred L Richter
2646 N 72nd Ave
Hart MI 49420

Call Sign: KD8BGN
Margaret M Richter

2646 N 72nd Ave
Hart MI 49420

Call Sign: KC8FCU
Merle S Lindsay
3858 N 72nd Ave
Hart MI 494208543

Call Sign: AB8NT
Merle S Lindsay
3858 N 72nd Ave
Hart MI 494208543

Call Sign: KC8SHZ
Don L Brown
6044 N 72nd Ave
Hart MI 49420

Call Sign: KC8RZS
Ann R Herrygers
2315 N 84th
Hart MI 49420

Call Sign: KC8NEX
Betty L Root
42 Orchard Ave
Hart MI 494201038

Call Sign: KC8HSY
Robert L Tozer
3654 W Southern2
Hart MI 49420

Call Sign: KF4YUH
Don L Brown
341 Westwood Dr Box
24
Hart MI 49420

Call Sign: N8PFC
Bradley R King
Hart MI 49420

FCC Amateur Radio Licenses in Hartford

Call Sign: W8MBW
Robert G Sisson
84575 2nd St
Hartford MI 49057

Call Sign: N8LEB
Allen H Prouty
61925 52nd Ave

Hartford MI 49057

Call Sign: KB8PUY
Frederick C Simpson
44321 CR 687
Hartford MI 49057

Call Sign: N8XIM
Roger D Gordon
49938 CR 687
Hartford MI 49057

Call Sign: N8HFA
Frank S Colman Jr
126 Michigan Ave
Hartford MI 49057

Call Sign: W8AMB
Clifford G Swift
322 N Center St
Hartford MI 49057

Call Sign: KC8RVU
Paul J Smith
310 Olds Ave
Hartford MI 49057

Call Sign: KD8NPB
Richard A Meister Jr
110 Paras Hill Dr
Hartford MI 49057

Call Sign: N8TFY
Bill J Nimmo
59127 Red Arrow Hwy
Hartford MI 49057

Call Sign: N8TYK
Donna J Justice
59127 Red Arrow Hwy
Hartford MI 49057

Call Sign: KB9FVL
Scott E Rumley
68158 Red Arrow Hwy
Hartford MI 49057

Call Sign: KA8GJF
Maureen C Nichols
102 Wendell Ave
Hartford MI 49057

Call Sign: KD8JAS
Leroy F Whelan Jr

Hartford MI 49047

Call Sign: KD8JAT
Nancy J Whelan
Hartford MI 49057

**FCC Amateur Radio
Licenses in Hastings**

Call Sign: KB8VLX
Frank W Wilkey
1813 Biddle Rd
Hastings MI 49058

Call Sign: N8TYZ
Robert V Former
1932 Buehler Rd
Hastings MI 49058

Call Sign: KC8LCC
Daniel E Ringleka
4745 Buehler Rd
Hastings MI 49058

Call Sign: N8VWW
Russell T Craven
1658 Center Rd
Hastings MI 49058

Call Sign: N8VXH
Ralph J Payne
3825 Center Rd
Hastings MI 49058

Call Sign: KB8UJF
Floyd E Gates
931 Cloverdale Rd
Hastings MI 49058

Call Sign: WB8HAO
Carl Grashuis
4396 Coats Grove Rd
Hastings MI 49058

Call Sign: KA8IBD
James J Barnum Jr
3083 Culbert Dr
Hastings MI 49058

Call Sign: KA8IBE
Loraine M Barnum
3083 Culbert Dr
Hastings MI 49058

Call Sign: WD8DJH
Raymond J Volosky
1324 David Dr
Hastings MI 49004

Call Sign: KC8ORR
Chad M Cusack
1111 E Center Rd
Hastings MI 49058

Call Sign: N8FIO
Nancy L Dingledine
5597 E Center Rd
Hastings MI 49058

Call Sign: KB8HZV
Donald H Scott
317 E Lincoln St
Hastings MI
490581334

Call Sign: KC8TJS
Kenneth A Wood
2370 E M 43 Hwy
Hastings MI 49058

Call Sign: KC8QKE
Chad M Cusack
526 E Madison St
Hastings MI 49058

Call Sign: KC8DHS
Andrew D Lewis
628 E Mill St
Hastings MI 49058

Call Sign: KB8YGO
Matthew S Miles
644 E Mill St
Hastings MI 49058

Call Sign: WA8JGV
Lindsay E Hutt
1591 E Quimby Rd
Hastings MI 49058

Call Sign: KC8PKB
Edward R White
529 E State Rd
Hastings MI 49058

Call Sign: KB8YGQ
Adam L Miles
621 E Thorn St

Hastings MI 49058

Call Sign: WD8NZQ
Martin C Allerding
602 Gaskill Rd
Hastings MI 49058

Call Sign: KC8HJV
Clarence H Coy
4507 Goodwill Rd
Hastings MI 49058

Call Sign: W8FZL
Clarence H Coy
4507 Goodwill Rd
Hastings MI 49058

Call Sign: WD8KWX
Bud Z Knuppenburg
4725 Headlake Rd
Hastings MI 49058

Call Sign: KC8YCF
Michael D Sams
2836 Heath Rd
Hastings MI 49058

Call Sign: WB8IBB
Kenneth L Tinker
2964 Heath Rd
Hastings MI 49058

Call Sign: KD8YX
James M Boyer
4580 Heath Rd
Hastings MI
490588277

Call Sign: K8SWR
Brian W Gerber
5582 Henry Rd
Hastings MI 49058

Call Sign: WB8BTC
James G Densberger
1892 Iroquois Trl
Hastings MI 49058

Call Sign: KC8EGO
Thad E Burger
6475 Irving Rd
Hastings MI 49058

Call Sign: KB8QFJ

Jack D Fox
2977 Loehrs Landing
Dr
Hastings MI 49058

Call Sign: KD8LNM
Todd D Fox
2977 Loehrs Landing
Dr
Hastings MI 49058

Call Sign: W8RVO
Vernon V Alger
931 Maple Cir
Hastings MI
490581669

Call Sign: KB8UMM
Robert D Ward
330 Meadow Ln
Hastings MI 49058

Call Sign: KB8UMV
Kal B Ward
330 Meadow Ln
Hastings MI 49058

Call Sign: KD8UMM
Robert D Ward
330 Meadow Ln
Hastings MI 49058

Call Sign: KD8EAS
Craig A Veldheer
4021 Mindi Lynne Dr
Hastings MI 49058

Call Sign: KD8EAZ
Kimberly L Veldheer
4021 Mindi Lynne Dr
Hastings MI 49058

Call Sign: N0SIK
Marilyn J Ridenour
505 Molly Dr
Hastings MI 49058

Call Sign: KB8ETY
Raymond L Ridenour
505 Molly Dr
Hastings MI
490588323

Call Sign: KB8UGE

Ronald W Hinkle
3380 N Broadway
Hastings MI 49058

Call Sign: K8OLD
Ronald W Hinkle
3380 N Broadway
Hastings MI 49058

Call Sign: KB8VZD
Barbara S Edmonds
828 N East St
Hastings MI 49058

Call Sign: WA8HYX
Hugh C Edmonds
920 N Ferris
Hastings MI 49058

Call Sign: KA9FON
Milton Poulos
920 N Ferris St
Hastings MI 49058

Call Sign: KB8UIM
Thomas M Edmonds
627 N Hanover
Hastings MI 49058

Call Sign: KB8YGN
Stephen L Miller
1225 N Mich Ave
Hastings MI 49058

Call Sign: KB8SES
Larry E Wallace
623 N Wilson
Hastings MI 49058

Call Sign: W7DTT
James R Rutledge
1905 Nashville Rd
Hastings MI
490589163

Call Sign: KB8TAQ
Gary L Hill
4229 S Bedford Rd
Hastings MI 49058

Call Sign: KB8VLW
Dawn I Hill
4229 S Bedford Rd
Hastings MI 49058

Call Sign: N5MXT
Glen A Brasseur
1722 S Broadway
Hastings MI 49058

Call Sign: KD8AXX
Stephen J Johncock
221 S Broadway St
Apt 3
Hastings MI 49058

Call Sign: N8XJX
Phyllis J Brumm
1750 S Charlton Park
Rd
Hastings MI 49058

Call Sign: K8LHM
Douglas B Brumm
1750 S Charlton Park
Rd
Hastings MI
490589123

Call Sign: KC8NZZ
James H Pyle
2715 S M 37 Hwy
Hastings MI 49058

Call Sign: KA8ZPN
Brenda K Sidney
6035 S M 43 Hwy
Hastings MI 49058

Call Sign: WB8JZN
Wilbert W Sidney
6035 S M 43 Hwy
Hastings MI 49058

Call Sign: KD8EBR
Emily A Hart
923 S Michigan Ave
Hastings MI 49058

Call Sign: KD8EEB
Eric R Hart
923 S Michigan Ave
Hastings MI 49058

Call Sign: N8IZB
John E Mullenix
1212 S Michigan Ave
Hastings MI 49058

Call Sign: KD8GJM
James R Ewer
1340 S Montgomery St
Hastings MI 49058

Call Sign: AC8AZ
James R Ewer
1340 S Montgomery St
Hastings MI 49058

Call Sign: N4HBJ
Donald R Turner Jr
1980 Starr School Rd
Hastings MI 49058

Call Sign: KC8WIY
Shawna M Allerding
51 Sundago Park
Hastings MI 49058

Call Sign: KD8PGG
Daniel C Trigg
2442 Thunder Valley
Dr
Hastings MI 49058

Call Sign: KC8LLS
Michael R Turnes
4950 Upton Rd
Hastings MI 49058

Call Sign: KD8DED
Robert P Kelley
4950 Upton Rd
Hastings MI 49058

Call Sign: W8MBM
Frank C Weyerman
317 W Green St
Hastings MI 49058

Call Sign: KC8OXX
Justin H Brehm
625 W Green St
Hastings MI 49058

Call Sign: WD8PUQ
Gerald L
Knickerbocker
3002 W M 179 Hwy
Hastings MI 49058

Call Sign: KD8AUP

Kevin C Hirons
3159 W M 179 Hwy
Hastings MI 49058

Call Sign: KB8YGP
Jonathan C Miles
2819 W Quimby Rd
Hastings MI 49058

Call Sign: AB8HN
Jonathan C Miles
2819 W Quimby Rd
Hastings MI 49058

Call Sign: KB8YLD
Christopher J
Hammond
110 W Sager Rd
Hastings MI 49058

Call Sign: KD8CDU
Robert W Bishop
314 W State Rd
Hastings MI 49058

Call Sign: KC8LCB
James D Archambeau
2110 W State Rd
Hastings MI 49058

Call Sign: KC8VBZ
James D Archambeau
2110 W State Rd
Hastings MI 49058

Call Sign: N8JFX
James D Archambeau
2110 W State Rd
Hastings MI 49058

Call Sign: KD8AXY
Terry J Swisher
1576 Whiskey Run Dr
Hastings MI 49058

Call Sign: WB8UNB
Vernon L Macy
490 Willitts Rd
Hastings MI 49058

Call Sign: KB8SEM
Jerry M Edmonds Sr
4493 Wood School Rd
Hastings MI 49058

Call Sign: K8YPW
Jack Hill
Hastings MI 49058

Call Sign: KC8UQN
Susan L Hill
Hastings MI 49059

Call Sign: N8DXR
Daniel T Smith
Hastings MI
490580369

FCC Amateur Radio Licenses in Hawks

Call Sign: KB8FKQ
Mary Alice Y Lefebvre
6982 CR 441
Hawks MI 49743

Call Sign: KB8FKR
Robert J Lefebvre
7010 CR 441
Hawks MI 49743

Call Sign: N8RIB
Glen A Paull
9537 F 21
Hawks MI 49743

Call Sign: KB8LWN
Kenneth C McNealy Sr
8170 Rasche Rd
Hawks MI 49743

FCC Amateur Radio Licenses in Hermansville

Call Sign: KA8ZSU
Harley J Baribeau
N16052 CR 388
Hermansville MI
49847

Call Sign: W8IJB
John C Lungerhausen
N 16628 N 4 Rd
Hermansville MI
49847

FCC Amateur Radio Licenses in Herron

Call Sign: KE4NEP
John R Walters
1131 Emerson Rd
Herron MI 49744

Call Sign: AB8TE
John R Walters
1131 Emerson Rd
Herron MI 49744

Call Sign: W8CX
John R Walters
1131 Emerson Rd
Herron MI 49744

Call Sign: KC8FBT
Joshua D Cohoon
10178 Harrison Rd
Herron MI 49744

FCC Amateur Radio Licenses in Hersey

Call Sign: K8JTS
Donald R Gillett
2884 170th Ave
Hersey MI 49639

Call Sign: KC8IFI
Edward R Stuart Jr
13495 23 Mile Rd
Hersey MI 49639

Call Sign: KD8HXW
Michelle E Wayne
103 4th St
Hersey MI 49639

Call Sign: KC8JOM
Robert J Tyson
23191 Holiday Dr
Hersey MI 496399619

Call Sign: KC5YAA
Willow S Robinson
23277 Holiday Dr
Hersey MI 49639

Call Sign: KC5YAB
Larry M Robinson
23277 Holiday Dr

Hersey MI 49639

Call Sign: KD8HYC
Abigail B Marek
214 Mill Site Rd
Hersey MI 49639

Call Sign: KD8IAM
Valarie J Antor
17849 Old Logging Rd
Hersey MI 49639

Call Sign: KC8UB
Richard A Osborne
17317 Rapids Dr
Hersey MI 49639

Call Sign: KB8ESO
Barbara A Simons
17653 Rapids Dr
Hersey MI 49639

Call Sign: N8IJH
James D Simons
17653 Rapids Dr
Hersey MI 49639

Call Sign: KC8VUE
Clyde J Yencer
1672 Riverview Dr
Hersey MI 49639

Call Sign: N8LPR
William E Jeffrey
16365 Roaring Brook
Dr
Hersey MI 496398403

Call Sign: WB8WIA
Gary N Atteberry
115 S Main St
Hersey MI 49639

Call Sign: KC8IJU
Susan M Roberts
16326 Schofield Rd
Hersey MI 49639

Call Sign: N8YZF
Thomas E Roberts
16326 Schofield Rd
Hersey MI 49639

Call Sign: KD8HYJ

Jack L Boden
16376 Schofield Rd
Hersey MI 49639

Call Sign: WD8PFC
Beverly J Callewaert
18197 Stonehouse Rd
Hersey MI 49639

Call Sign: KD8FBD
Virginia L Watkins
210 W 1st St
Hersey MI 49639

FCC Amateur Radio Licenses in Hesperia

Call Sign: N8GVS
Madeline A Bowers
8165 1 Mile Rd
Hesperia MI 49421

Call Sign: WA8UAN
Eugene N Bowers
8165 1 Mile Rd
Hesperia MI 49421

Call Sign: KB8BCT
James M Kelley
8665 1 Mile Rd
Hesperia MI 49421

Call Sign: N8HUB
Andrew Suszka
1772 176th
Hesperia MI 49421

Call Sign: W8JEG
Ronald E Boughton
1385 186th Ave
Hesperia MI 49421

Call Sign: KB5CCR
Barbara E Aber
1391 186th Ave
Hesperia MI 49421

Call Sign: KB8FGT
Kevin Eldred
7655 8 Mile Rd
Hesperia MI 49421

Call Sign: KB8FGV
Nancy Eldred

7655 8 Mile Rd
Hesperia MI 49421

Call Sign: N8WUL
Patricia D Phelps
316 Adams St
Hesperia MI 49421

Call Sign: W8DGD
James F Campbell Sr
R 2 Box 111
Hesperia MI 49421

Call Sign: KA6OXA
Richard V Huston Sr
53 Cook St
Hesperia MI 49421

Call Sign: KC8HTD
Kenneth E Scissons
921 Daniel St
Hesperia MI 49421

Call Sign: KE8VY
Valentine S Kish
3798 E Baker Rd
Hesperia MI
494219392

Call Sign: KD8NBL
Frank B Florka
8830 E Buchanan Rd
Hesperia MI 49421

Call Sign: N8UKH
David V Robertson
6355 E Gale Rd
Hesperia MI 49421

Call Sign: KC8MSE
Tim A Deater
6344 E Garfield Rd
Hesperia MI 49421

Call Sign: AB8UO
Mike A Banfill
8866 E Loop Rd
Hesperia MI 49421

Call Sign: KD8NOL
Carol L Neal
3147 E M 20
Hesperia MI 49421

Call Sign: WB8CCS
Gary R Dawkins
8366 E M 20
Hesperia MI 49421

Call Sign: KD8ANT
Samuel E Routley
1420 Garfield Rd
Hesperia MI 49421

Call Sign: KC8HVV
Heidi M Davis
471 Grosbeck
Hesperia MI 49421

Call Sign: KC8PWR
Franklin A Tinkham
657 Grosdeck Ave
Hesperia MI 49421

Call Sign: KD7TOO
John B Wolford
397 Michigan Ave
Hesperia MI
494218562

Call Sign: KC8YME
Mike A Banfill
54 N Elm St
Hesperia MI 49421

Call Sign: KD8MFN
Zachary J Sponhauer
1536 S 148th Ave
Hesperia MI 49421

Call Sign: KD8NBM
Mary J Debrot
2200 S 172nd Ave
Hesperia MI 49421

FCC Amateur Radio
Licenses in Hessel

Call Sign: KC8OBC
Frank E Arnold
330 N 3 Mile
Hessel MI 49745

Call Sign: KC8HES
Ethan S Lamoreaux
6015 N Simmons Rd
Hessel MI 49745

Call Sign: KE8KY
Gerald T Stein
4071 N St Martins Pt
Hessel MI 49745

Call Sign: K8SFF
Jerome E Knight
N 3874 St Martins Pt
Hessel MI 49745

Call Sign: KB8SVQ
Karen R Dutcher
Hessel MI 49745

Call Sign: KB8SVS
Wilma J Schalow
Hessel MI 49745

FCC Amateur Radio
Licenses in Hickory
Corners

Call Sign: KC8NBA
Wayne P Baroch
14410 Brooklodge Rd
Hickory Corners MI
49060

Call Sign: N8JG
James H Gorka
1282 Burlington Dr
Hickory Corners MI
49060

Call Sign: KG8CG
Gary L Gesmundo
3840 E Gull Lake Dr
Hickory Corners MI
49060

Call Sign: N8TIF
Larry D Burdick
3170 Hickory Rd
Hickory Corners MI
49060

Call Sign: KB8ZVG
Scott E Howes
4121 Hickory Rd
Hickory Corners MI
49060

Call Sign: KB8YPZ
Reed M Tittle

15075 Marshfield
Hickory Corners MI
49060

Call Sign: K8YPZ
Reed M Tittle
15075 Marshfield
Hickory Corners MI
49060

Call Sign: WA8OFW
Karen A Longman
15928 Noodlawn
Beach Dr
Hickory Corners MI
490609737

Call Sign: KD8PUL
Lori A Philips
4647 W Hickory Rd
Hickory Corners MI
49060

Call Sign: K8IZN
Marion H Longman
15928 Woodlawn
Beach Dr
Hickory Corners MI
49060

Call Sign: W8DA
Ernest R Longman
15928 Woodlawn
Beach Dr
Hickory Corners MI
49060

FCC Amateur Radio
Licenses in Higgins
Lake

Call Sign: N8KIL
Ronald G Kiersey
5720 E Shady Grove
Ln
Higgins Lake MI
48627

Call Sign: KC8QBB
John E Szewc
426 Pine Acres Dr
Higgins Lake MI
48627

Call Sign: KA8OFU
Shirley A Hacker
427 Sam O Set
Higgins Lake MI
48627

Call Sign: WA8CTY
Robert L Hacker
427 Sam O Set
Higgins Lake MI
48627

Call Sign: KD8JIJ
Jason E Trautz
Higgins Lake MI
48627

Call Sign: KD8HDM
Karen L Trautz
Higgins Lake MI
486270030

FCC Amateur Radio Licenses in Hillman

Call Sign: KC8TC
Earl W Elowsky
17574 Avalon Dr
Hillman MI
497468243

Call Sign: N8UPT
Robert L Mann
22811 Cohoon Rd
Hillman MI 49746

Call Sign: N8UPU
Mary L Mann
22811 Cohoon Rd
Hillman MI 49746

Call Sign: KD8JWJ
Everett R Swift
17535 CR 451
Hillman MI 49746

Call Sign: K8IUN
Paul A Neiderer
Grosinsky Rd
Hillman MI 49746

Call Sign: N8SYB
Stacey M Oesch
8384 Klein Rd

Hillman MI 49746

Call Sign: KB8CZL
Karen R Heft
22410 Lake Avalon Rd
Hillman MI 49746

Call Sign: K8CIT
Arthur W Heft
22410 Lake Avalon Rd
Hillman MI 49746

Call Sign: N8SCY
Thomas H Oesch
23900 M 32 S
Hillman MI 49746

Call Sign: N8BLT
Don M Hamilton
18651 Pleasant Valley
Rd
Hillman MI
497469061

Call Sign: KX8D
Duane L Durflinger
14946 Royston Rd
Hillman MI 49746

Call Sign: N8JML
Barbara J Durflinger
14946 Royston Rd
Hillman MI 49746

Call Sign: KB8RWH
Fred C Webber
Hillman MI 49746

FCC Amateur Radio Licenses in Holland

Call Sign: KC8YPX
Chad A Vander Kooi
5025 108th Ave
Holland MI 49424

Call Sign: KC8YOD
Jeremy J Werner
3392 112th Ave
Holland MI 49424

Call Sign: KC8ZCM
Keith A Bonnes
7397 120th Ave

Holland MI 49424

Call Sign: KB9OBV
Gregory W Heinen
2651 132nd Ave
Holland MI 49424

Call Sign: N8UJE
Kenneth J Cooper
3876 140th Ave
Holland MI 494249454

Call Sign: KC8DWI
Mark A Benson
3979 142nd Ave
Holland MI 49424

Call Sign: KC8HVP
Lori B Benson
3979 142nd Ave
Holland MI 49424

Call Sign: KD8NPC
Nathan A Silva
4788 142nd Ave
Holland MI 49423

Call Sign: WO8C
Nathan A Silva
4788 142nd Ave
Holland MI 49423

Call Sign: K8NMV
Elmer J Rowder
A6375 143rd Ave
Holland MI 49423

Call Sign: KB8AZI
James M Knoll
A6209 144th Ave
Holland MI 49423

Call Sign: N8JFR
Rochelle D Knoll
A6524 144th Ave
Holland MI 49423

Call Sign: K8TVZ
Laryn D Lohman
5918 146th Ave
Holland MI 49423

Call Sign: W8BBJ
Gordon O Cogswell

174 159th Ave
Holland MI 49424

Call Sign: KB8TWE
Paul C Duckworth
224 159th Ave
Holland MI 49424

Call Sign: KC8WBS
Mary P Byrne
128 170th Ave
Holland MI 49424

Call Sign: N8UYC
Robert G Byrne
128 170th Ave
Holland MI 49424

Call Sign: KC8CWF
Ralph E Corning
139 170th Ave
Holland MI 49424

Call Sign: WD5GET
James H Moore
A4224 47th St
Holland MI 49423

Call Sign: WA8EIM
Robert J Van Vuren
A4584 47th St
Holland MI 49423

Call Sign: N8JDO
Ronald J Wegrzyn
4351 60th St
Holland MI 49423

Call Sign: KD8IFB
Laura J Mokma
4623 60th St
Holland MI 49423

Call Sign: KD8IFD
Wayne A Mokma
4623 60th St
Holland MI 49423

Call Sign: N8KSH
Webb Van
Dokkumburg
A4061 62nd St
Holland MI 49423

Call Sign: N8DWT
Vern Tinholt
A4703 64th Ave
Holland MI 49423

Call Sign: N8EOO
Steven R Lemson
A4351 64th St
Holland MI 49423

Call Sign: KD8HSD
Rich J Munson
4135 65th St
Holland MI 49423

Call Sign: AC8GV
Rich J Munson
4135 65th St
Holland MI 49423

Call Sign: K8TUC
Jarvin H Kleiman
A4115 65th St
Holland MI 49423

Call Sign: K9DV
David M McCormick
14662 Anchor Ct
Holland MI 49424

Call Sign: WD8BXQ
James J Nash
192 Aniline Ave
Holland MI 49424

Call Sign: N8UJD
Steven J Vander Hill
2003 Basin Ct
Holland MI 49424

Call Sign: K8HKQ
James E Coulter
1760 Bay Ct
Holland MI 49424

Call Sign: KB8IRF
Stephen F Zachev
334 Beeline Apt 4
Holland MI 49424

Call Sign: KB8OKS
John S Mattias
2581 Beeline Rd
Holland MI 49424

Call Sign: KC8NWD
Michael U Avery
A3954 Beeline Rd
Holland MI 49423

Call Sign: AC8GN
Michael U Avery
A3954 Beeline Rd
Holland MI 49423

Call Sign: K8EMU
Ivan J De Witt
160 Beth St
Holland MI 494242175

Call Sign: KD3WC
Daniel Szalay
186 Beth St
Holland MI 49424

Call Sign: KD8FVC
Alan S Hughes
1210 Birdie Ln
Holland MI 49423

Call Sign: KC8KKF
Patrick L Battaglia
194 Blaine St
Holland MI 494242515

Call Sign: N8IGJ
Armando Mercado
13078 Blair St
Holland MI 49424

Call Sign: K8RXB
David R Chase
11339 Blue Heron
Pkwy
Holland MI 49424

Call Sign: KD8NWY
William W Smith
6392 Blue Jay Ln
Holland MI 49423

Call Sign: KD8QVA
Paul A Den Uyl
2268 Brighton
Holland MI 49424

Call Sign: W1PDU
Paul A Den Uyl

2268 Brighton
Holland MI 49424

Call Sign: N8XIN
Carolyn E Geoffroy
3611 Butternut Dr 197
Holland MI 49424

Call Sign: N8RPG
Robert F Geoffroy
3611 Butternut Dr Lot
197
Holland MI 49424

Call Sign: N8DGU
Kenneth J Van Holstyn
3611 Butternut Dr Lot
3
Holland MI 49424

Call Sign: W8EEB
James Jimae
4705 Cardinal Dr
Holland MI 49423

Call Sign: KC8OPB
Carl L Selover
644 Central Ave
Holland MI 49423

Call Sign: N8HET
Michael Matuz
284 Chatham Ave
Holland MI 49423

Call Sign: KD8MGJ
Glenn D Pomp
4736 Chautauqua
Ridge
Holland MI 49423

Call Sign: K8GDP
Glenn D Pomp
4736 Chautauqua
Ridge
Holland MI 49423

Call Sign: K8YBZ
Burton J Borr
896 Clarewood Ct
Holland MI 49423

Call Sign: WD8PUO
Dave A Posthuma

3293 Clearview Dr
Holland MI 49424

Call Sign: N8HNJ
Albertus Derks
145 Columbia Ave Apt
531
Holland MI 49423

Call Sign: W8REN
John D Benedict
145 Columbia Ave Apt
672
Holland MI 494232987

Call Sign: N8ACK
Douglas W Beverly
145 Columbia Ave Apt
718
Holland MI 494232987

Call Sign: W8EL
Ernest H Lloyd
145 Columbia Ave Apt
766
Holland MI 49423

Call Sign: W8LUH
Charles W Denk
145 Columbia Ave Apt
766
Holland MI 49423

Call Sign: N8CME
Norman R Heinrich
1681 Columbus St
Holland MI 49423

Call Sign: WB8BNX
Gerard R Szymczak
775 Concord Dr
Holland MI 49423

Call Sign: KC8GOV
Brent M Barkel
229 Country Club Rd
Holland MI 49423

Call Sign: WB8GON
Simon Sybesma
884 Creekridge Dr
Holland MI 49423

Call Sign: KD8CUK

Randall J Schregardus
714 Crestview St
Holland MI 49423

Call Sign: KD6QMS
Gary R Phillips
743 Crestview St
Holland MI 494237317

Call Sign: KD8IFC
Gayle Wilson
761 Crestview St
Holland MI 49632

Call Sign: KD8NWX
Richard L Stowe
169 Dartmouth Ave
Holland MI 49423

Call Sign: N8CMR
David G Hekman
14059 Deer Cove Dr
Holland MI 49423

Call Sign: KA8MAA
Dan A Kolean
4230 Defeyter Ave
Holland MI 49424

Call Sign: KD8OYB
Mike D Tuka
420 Donann Dr
Holland MI 49424

Call Sign: KD8PUR
Mike D Tuka
420 Donann Dr
Holland MI 49424

Call Sign: K8MDT
Mike D Tuka
420 Donann Dr
Holland MI 49424

Call Sign: KD8NXA
Alfredo Gonzalez Jr
298 E 14th St
Holland MI 49423

Call Sign: KD8IFF
Philip D Chapman
137 E 17th St
Holland MI 49423

Call Sign: KC8KML
Howard H Fitzgerald
III
111 E 18th St
Holland MI 49423

Call Sign: KD8MDL
Jessica A Fitzgerald
111.5 E 18th St
Holland MI 49423

Call Sign: KD8PHR
West Michigan ARC
246 E 18th St
Holland MI 49423

Call Sign: KD8LLJ
Jack R Smits
246 E 18th St
Holland MI 49423

Call Sign: W8KJS
Jack R Smits
246 E 18th St
Holland MI 49423

Call Sign: N8HYU
Bruce W Deacon Jr
242 E 1912 St
Holland MI 49423

Call Sign: KC8TBZ
Linda L Rosenthal
94-1/2 E 23rd St
Holland MI 49423

Call Sign: N8KID
Marvin R Laeger
111 E 24th
Holland MI 49423

Call Sign: N8ZJX
Garold J Van Beek
77 E 25th St
Holland MI 49423

Call Sign: KD8MDG
Michael E Byrne
194 E 27th St
Holland MI 49423

Call Sign: WB8BZF
Edwin A Comstock
68 E 29th St

Holland MI 49423

Call Sign: N8UJG
Andrew Van Slot
68 E 29th St
Holland MI 494235126

Call Sign: KC8TKE
Nancy O Chamness
122 E 30th St
Holland MI 49423

Call Sign: KC8ZCL
James W Geuder
83 E 31st St
Holland MI 49423

Call Sign: N8KUC
Gregory T Caskey
114 E 31st St
Holland MI 49423

Call Sign: KB8PQS
Robin D Williams
186 E 32nd
Holland MI 49423

Call Sign: WB8WQR
Elden J Sumerix
14 E 32nd St
Holland MI 49423

Call Sign: KC8TSZ
Christopher J
Samuelson
160 E 38th St
Holland MI 494237065

Call Sign: KF8UJ
Daniel W Coltrane
204 E 38th St
Holland MI 49423

Call Sign: N8CTL
James L Tibbitts
155 E 48th St Lot 71
Holland MI 49423

Call Sign: KB8EPI
Delwyn J Langejans
23 E 8th Ave
Holland MI 49423

Call Sign: KB8WCH

Ignacio E Perez
3169 E Crystal Waters
Dr Unit 5
Holland MI 49424

Call Sign: KC8OPC
Kirstie K Perez
3169 E Crystal Waters
Dr Unit 5
Holland MI 49424

Call Sign: N8AGF
Philip D Sherman
333 E Lakewood Blvd
Lot 278
Holland MI 494242054

Call Sign: N8XHE
Mark A Nickel
333 E Lakewood Lot
424
Holland MI 49424

Call Sign: W5UCS
Ronald J Weerstra
16985 Eagle Lake Dr
Holland MI 49424

Call Sign: KC8QPW
Eric L Krontz
289 Eastmont Ave
Holland MI 49424

Call Sign: N9NYS
Steven H Miller
14416 Edmeer Dr
Holland MI 49424

Call Sign: KC8CVH
Richard A Campbell
14518 Edmeer Dr
Holland MI 49424

Call Sign: KD8JOB
Sarah J Dinkelmann
3261 Elderswood Ave
Holland MI 49424

Call Sign: KA8COB
Henry L Dinkelmann
3261 Elderwood
Holland MI 49424

Call Sign: K8HLD

Henry L Dinkelmann
3261 Elderwood
Holland MI 49424

Call Sign: KA8EFO
Leo J Scannell
3346 Elderwood Dr
Holland MI 49423

Call Sign: KC8ACN
James C Hotchkiss
14293 Essenburg Dr
Holland MI 49424

Call Sign: KA8RSN
Mary K Rich
373 Fairhill Ct
Holland MI 49423

Call Sign: W8HJB
Charles L Rich
373 Fairhill Ct
Holland MI 49423

Call Sign: KD8JHE
Philip E Bohlander
4625 Forest Ln
Holland MI 49423

Call Sign: NZ4M
John R Parker
1103 1 Fountainview
Cir
Holland MI 49423

Call Sign: NW8G
John R Parker
1103 1 Fountainview
Cir
Holland MI 49423

Call Sign: KC5EDM
Richard A Slotman
13970 Fox Trl Dr
Holland MI 49424

Call Sign: N8ZJV
Daniel S Brasier
206 Glendale Ave
Holland MI 49423

Call Sign: KD8FVB
Nadine Braiser
206 Glendale Ave

Holland MI 49423

Call Sign: KC8GAO
Alex K Burrell
719 Goldenrod Ave
Holland MI 49423

Call Sign: KC8BSE
James C Hook III
364 Hamilton Ave
Holland MI 49424

Call Sign: K8HJI
Robert A Durdle
3352 Harbor Ct
Holland MI 49424

Call Sign: W8DLE
Robert A Durdle
3352 Harbor Ct
Holland MI 49424

Call Sign: KC8JBW
Michael D Olson
727 Harrington Ave
Holland MI 49423

Call Sign: KB8WJR
Donald B Hillebrands
724 Harrison Ave
Holland MI 49423

Call Sign: N8KFB
Dean A Parrott
683 Hayes St
Holland MI 49424

Call Sign: N2OWU
James R Pavlinik
1268 Heather Ct
Holland MI 49423

Call Sign: WB8UYU
David J Knoll
1194 Heather Dr
Holland MI 49423

Call Sign: KD8NWW
David S Sheldon
11843 Hidden Harbor
Holland MI 49424

Call Sign: KD8KAN
Shaun M Bell

11843 Hidden Harbor
Holland MI 49424

Call Sign: N9SSA
Peter R Hoffswell
395 Highbanks Ct
Holland MI 49424

Call Sign: KC8VUG
William H Nelson
1604 Highland Ave
Holland MI 494236713

Call Sign: KB8LU
Ronald W Flynn
796 Holly Creek Dr
Holland MI 494237807

Call Sign: N8ILK
Randall D Bierema
17133 Inavale St
Holland MI 49424

Call Sign: KC8YYX
Mi American Red
Cross Ottawa County
270 James St
Holland MI 49424

Call Sign: N8LCT
Mark E Logsdon
16528 James St
Holland MI 49424

Call Sign: KD8CUJ
Steven J Vander
Zwaag
16762 James St
Holland MI 49424

Call Sign: WA8NIW
Nelson L Molenaar
11907 James St
Holland MI 49424

Call Sign: KC8SWX
Kendra J Snyder
580 Jasmine Dr
Holland MI 49423

Call Sign: K8KJS
Kendra J Snyder
580 Jasmine Dr
Holland MI 49423

Call Sign: KD8HDS
William J Topp
1511 Jerome St
Holland MI 49423

Call Sign: W8EGR
James E Coulter
2835 Jewel Ct
Holland MI 49424

Call Sign: WA8YGP
Wilson G Meredith
481 Julius St
Holland MI 494241629

Call Sign: N8ZJW
Brian J Borr
815 Knollcrest Ave
Holland MI 49423

Call Sign: W8QT
James D Van Putten Jr
4031 Lakeridge Dr
Holland MI 49424

Call Sign: KC8LLU
David Q Boone
4267 Lakeshore Dr
Holland MI 49424

Call Sign: WB8WHN
Charles L Hozer
5750 Lakeshore Dr
Holland MI 49423

Call Sign: ND8Q
Allen D Walters
600 Lawn Ave
Holland MI 49424

Call Sign: N8GWA
Ronald Mokma
882 Lincoln Ave
Holland MI 49423

Call Sign: KC8YZY
William L King Jr
1358 Linwood Dr
Holland MI 49424

Call Sign: K8WLK
William L King Jr
1358 Linwood Dr

Holland MI 49424

Call Sign: KC8OVR
Ronald D Post
199 Lizbeth Dr
Holland MI 49423

Call Sign: N8UJF
Kurt W Pott
251 Lizbeth Dr
Holland MI 49423

Call Sign: KC8OPH
James A Dewaard
639 Lugers
Holland MI 49423

Call Sign: KC8OPJ
Jason E Dewaard
639 Lugers Rd
Holland MI 49423

Call Sign: KB8DVM
Pamela S Van Dyke
202 Maple Ave
Holland MI 49423

Call Sign: N8MHJ
Charles W Saylor
637 Maple Creek Dr
Holland MI 49423

Call Sign: WA8NHM
Cornelius J Steketee
288 Marquette Ave
Holland MI 494242620

Call Sign: N8KER
Robert E Eller
780 Mary Ave
Holland MI 49424

Call Sign: WD8LTC
Charles M Vanden
Berg
751 Marylane Dr
Holland MI 49423

Call Sign: KC8ZCJ
Lisa D Zwagerman
336 Mayfair St
Holland MI 494241735

Call Sign: KD8AZJ

Tim J Zwagelman
336 Mayfair St
Holland MI 49424

Call Sign: KC8KE
Jim A Lamberts
2442 Meadow Creek
Ln
Holland MI 49424

Call Sign: KC7LIM
Michael B Rose
775 Meadowbrook
Holland MI 494237327

Call Sign: KC8HZL
Donald A Afton
614 Michigan Ave
Holland MI 49423

Call Sign: WB8NBV
Ned Joldersma
833 Millbridge Ave
Holland MI 49423

Call Sign: KD8JNY
Cody A Brewer
493 Myra Ln
Holland MI 49424

Call Sign: N8KDV
Steven R Lare
733 Myrtle Ave
Holland MI 49423

Call Sign: W6SWL
Steven R Lare
733 Myrtle Ave
Holland MI 49423

Call Sign: W8LAI
Elmer S Barkel
394 N 120 Ave
Holland MI 49423

Call Sign: KB8IDQ
James A Hays
3909 N 168 Ave
Holland MI 494241146

Call Sign: KB8TWF
Rudolph J Vedovell
6697 N Cherry
Holland MI 49423

Call Sign: KD8MGM
Ross J Flamboe
100 N Division
Holland MI 49424

Call Sign: N8ZMD
Lindell F Morris
311 N Division
Holland MI 49424

Call Sign: KB8HLW
Keith D Parrott
447 N Division
Holland MI 49424

Call Sign: N8TGX
Joseph C Campbell
10413 Northfield Dr
Holland MI 49424

Call Sign: KD8CAL
David J Slater
479 Northridge Dr
Holland MI 49423

Call Sign: K9EMT
Allan G Brattset
1921 Ottawa Beach Rd
Holland MI 49424

Call Sign: KD8OHY
Trevor J Lee
12136 Parkview Ln
Unit 2 B
Holland MI 49423

Call Sign: N8CCS
Bill R Bush
2200 Perry
Holland MI 49424

Call Sign: KE8TR
Steven L Geerlings
1561 Perry St
Holland MI 49424

Call Sign: KC8FAW
Donald L Bareman
631 Pine Ave
Holland MI 49423

Call Sign: K3FD
Murray K Leshner

725 Pine Bay Ave
Holland MI 49424

Call Sign: KC8NGD
Benjamin H Yanis
14323 Pine Creek Ct
Holland MI 49424

Call Sign: N8YME
Eric R Yagerlener
14397 Pine Creek Ct
Holland MI 49424

Call Sign: KC8UOY
Angela E Olsen
4684 Pine Dr
Holland MI 49423

Call Sign: KC8SUO
Loren H Howard
4764 Pine Hollow
Holland MI 49423

Call Sign: K8LHH
Loren H Howard
4764 Pine Hollow
Holland MI 49423

Call Sign: AB8ZZ
Loren H Howard
4764 Pine Hollow
Holland MI 49423

Call Sign: KC8SWZ
Micah A Howard
4764 Pine Hollow Rd
Holland MI 49423

Call Sign: K8MAH
Micah A Howard
4764 Pine Hollow Rd
Holland MI 49423

Call Sign: KC8WBT
Karen E Howard
4764 Pine Hollow Rd
Holland MI 49423

Call Sign: K8KEH
Karen E Howard
4764 Pine Hollow Rd
Holland MI 49423

Call Sign: WD8JMD

Sandra L Koedoot
334 Pine View Ln
Holland MI 49424

Call Sign: KC8JHV
Scott A Hansen
447 Pinewood Ct
Holland MI 49424

Call Sign: AB8JS
Scott A Hansen
447 Pinewood Ct
Holland MI 49424

Call Sign: KC8TKF
Alex S Hansen
447 Pinewood Ct
Holland MI 49424

Call Sign: N8FZE
Raymond H Crockford
Jr
1468 Post Ave
Holland MI 494242505

Call Sign: KB8YTS
Wayne L Postma
14849 Quincy St
Holland MI 49424

Call Sign: N8NZK
Bruce R De Wit
16780 Ransom St
Holland MI 49424

Call Sign: KD4ZLO
David L Eaton
13308 Riley St
Holland MI 49424

Call Sign: N8UXB
William R Rininger
14250 Rose Park Dr
Holland MI 49424

Call Sign: WA8HNM
Leon Beyer
711 Ruth Ave
Holland MI 49423

Call Sign: KC8OOY
Stephen M Shoup
616 S 160th Ave
Holland MI 49423

Call Sign: WB8SHM
Harry G Derks
600 S 96th Ave
Holland MI 49424

Call Sign: KD8HDR
Michael T Mcmahon
12233 S Crystal
Waters Dr Unit 8
Holland MI 49424

Call Sign: K8YLB
Rae E Du Mez
925 S Shore Dr
Holland MI 49423

Call Sign: WB8VVH
Bill R Du Mez
925 S Shore Dr
Holland MI 49423

Call Sign: WB8NGF
Ronald D Looman
1179 S Shore Dr
Holland MI 49423

Call Sign: KB8EKR
Gerry C Eggebrecht
1987 S Shore Dr
Holland MI 49923

Call Sign: N8HYW
Thomas E Buis
1125 S Store Dr
Holland MI 494234463

Call Sign: KC8MVA
Ronald J Martin
121 S Waverly Rd F 5
Holland MI 494233085

Call Sign: KD8JTJ
Michael W Dekam
611 Sand Hollow Dr
Holland MI 49423

Call Sign: KD8MDT
Matthew W Dekam
611 Sand Hollow Dr
Holland MI 494239169

Call Sign: W8MDK
Matthew W Dekam

611 Sand Hollow Dr
Holland MI 494239169

Call Sign: KD8MDK
Michael W Dekam
611 Sand Hollow Dr
Holland MI 494239169

Call Sign: K8MDK
Michael W Dekam
611 Sand Hollow Dr
Holland MI 494239169

Call Sign: KD8KMA
John D Kuiphof
258 Sea Esta Ave
Holland MI 49424

Call Sign: KD8JOA
Megan L Heyl
1380 Seminole Dr
Holland MI 49424

Call Sign: WO0MEG
Megan L Heyl
1380 Seminole Dr
Holland MI 49424

Call Sign: KD8MGL
Derrick D Noland
1380 Seminole Dr
Holland MI 49424

Call Sign: W8DDN
Derrick D Noland
1380 Seminole Dr
Holland MI 49424

Call Sign: N8QMD
James R Heyl
1380 Seminole Dr
Holland MI 49424

Call Sign: KB8VXT
Edith M Spencer
815 Shadybrook
Holland MI 49424

Call Sign: N8ROL
Louis M Spencer
815 Shadybrook
Holland MI 49424

Call Sign: KD8FVD

Todd W Mathews
1314 Shoshone Walk
Holland MI 49423

Call Sign: N8FNE
Edward L Speyers
664 Sleepy Hollow Ln
Holland MI 49423

Call Sign: WB8RCE
James W Higgins
618 Spring Ln
Holland MI 494234627

Call Sign: KC8ZPC
Michael T Veldheer
11267 Starflower Dr
Holland MI 49424

Call Sign: KD4ALC
Ricky W Willbanks
11274 Starflower Dr
Holland MI 49424

Call Sign: AD4H
Jonathan L Compton
1355 Sundance Ct
Holland MI 49424

Call Sign: K8NFT
William F Rocker Sr
127 Sunrise Dr
Holland MI 49423

Call Sign: W8IQF
John R Du Mez
2349 Sunset Bluff Dr
Holland MI 49424

Call Sign: KC8CWD
Joseph M Filcik
14259 Sunview Dr
Holland MI 49424

Call Sign: KD8GMQ
David J Van Doorne
662 Tennis Ct
Holland MI 49424

Call Sign: WD8BXP
Thomas L Caldwell
3341 Terrace Ct
Holland MI 494249819

Call Sign: KD8JBG
Nicholas J Roush
13338 Terri Lyn Ln
Apt 4
Holland MI 49424

Call Sign: KD8JSO
Marian Boyer
2920 Thistle Ct
Holland MI 49424

Call Sign: N9GXR
Ed Link
115 Tiffany Ridge Dr
Holland MI 49424

Call Sign: WB8ZAU
Robert C Philipps
495 Timberlake Dr W
Holland MI 49424

Call Sign: KC8ZCK
Paul H Dalman
480 Timberlake E
Holland MI 494245340

Call Sign: K8CKK
Roger Dale Van Den
Berg
375 Tr Trl
Holland MI 49424

Call Sign: KB8UFO
Thomas G Ryl
2285 Tunnel Breeze Ct
Holland MI 49424

Call Sign: N8STM
Gene Geib
3561 Twin Oaks Ln
Holland MI 49424

Call Sign: KC8DIE
Chris J Nienmuis
11349 Tyler Dr
Holland MI 49924

Call Sign: K8GMO
Lawrence C England
17062 Ventura Dr
Holland MI 49424

Call Sign: N8ZMH
Paul L Bradford

17157 Ventura Dr
Holland MI 49424

Call Sign: NJ8U
Le Roy Mohn
17158 Ventura Dr
Holland MI 49423

Call Sign: KF8GR
William H Leonard Jr
273 W 12th St
Holland MI 49423

Call Sign: KC8ZCG
Cheryl L Leonard
273 W 12th St
Holland MI 49423

Call Sign: KC8ZCI
James D Leonard
273 W 12th St
Holland MI 49423

Call Sign: KC8ZCH
Scott W Leonard
273 W 12th St
Holland MI 49423

Call Sign: KC5PND
James L Boyd
296 W 15th St
Holland MI 49423

Call Sign: KC8UER
Thomas W Harris Jr
295 W 19th
Holland MI 49423

Call Sign: WB8WQL
John F Dinkel
458 W 20th St
Holland MI 49423

Call Sign: WD8BWK
John S Seidelman
46 W 21st St
Holland MI 49423

Call Sign: KC8RQS
Susan M Seidelman
46 W 21st St
Holland MI 49423

Call Sign: KC8PHF

David W Prins
192 W 21st St
Holland MI 49423

Call Sign: N8UJH
David W Prins
192 W 21st St
Holland MI 49423

Call Sign: N8EOH
Donald E Hovenga
241 W 21st St
Holland MI 49423

Call Sign: N5EDG
Kenneth C Perry
651 W 21st St
Holland MI 49423

Call Sign: N8AAE
Kenneth C Perry
651 W 21st St
Holland MI 49423

Call Sign: KD8DAD
Gordon W Kossen
134 W 23rd St
Holland MI 49423

Call Sign: KB8TWG
William J Eyre
80 W 24th
Holland MI 49423

Call Sign: KB8YC
James H Huisman
653 W 27th St
Holland MI 49423

Call Sign: WA8VLU
Ronald F Breuker
19 W 28th St
Holland MI 49423

Call Sign: KC8OOZ
Philip A Foreman
84 W 29th St
Holland MI 49423

Call Sign: KC8OPE
Daniel D Foreman
84 W 29th St
Holland MI 49423

Call Sign: KC8OPI
Gwen L Foreman
84 W 29th St
Holland MI 49423

Call Sign: KC8OPA
Josiah E Foreman
84 W 29th St
Holland MI 49423

Call Sign: WB8WTZ
Charles E O Connor Sr
234 W 29th St
Holland MI 494236905

Call Sign: KC4RDW
Juan E Lira
449 W 31st St
Holland MI 494237227

Call Sign: KD4DFF
Raquel E Lira
449 W 31st St
Holland MI 494237227

Call Sign: N8AU
Kaye D Hoogerhyde
363 W 32nd St
Holland MI 49423

Call Sign: W8MRR
James H Jipping
559 W 32nd St
Holland MI 49423

Call Sign: KC8QXY
Philip J Van Huis
707 W 32nd St
Holland MI 49423

Call Sign: K8PVH
Philip J Van Huis
707 W 32nd St
Holland MI 49423

Call Sign: N8UJH
David W Prins
811 W 32nd St
Holland MI 49423

Call Sign: KC8YIR
Mitchel D Bortner
309 W 33rd St
Holland MI 49423

Call Sign: N8AFW
Lance C Reidsma
46 W 39th
Holland MI 49423

Call Sign: WA8TVZ
Laryn D Lohman
466 W 48th St
Holland MI 49423

Call Sign: KC8QPV
Earl E Krontz
130 W 9th St
Holland MI 49423

Call Sign: KC8MNU
John M Eldred
643 W Lakewood Blvd
Holland MI 49424

Call Sign: KD8JXF
Joseph S Eldred
643 W Lakewood Blvd
Holland MI 49424

Call Sign: KD8DAF
Michael J Eldred
643 W Lakewood Blvd
Holland MI 49424

Call Sign: N8IBL
Carl V Seif
953 W Lakewood Blvd
Holland MI 49424

Call Sign: WB8VVF
Jan F A Veen
1055 W Lakewood
Blvd
Holland MI 49424

Call Sign: KA8TEY
Larry R Saylor
1257 W Lakewood
Blvd
Holland MI 49424

Call Sign: KD8PWZ
Jennifer L Johnson
3030 W Meadow
Springs Dr 3
Holland MI 49424

Call Sign: AB9Z
Bradley S Smith
3035 W Springview Dr
Apt 2
Holland MI 49424

Call Sign: KC8LBA
Mark A Rokus
1136 Warwick Ct
Holland MI 49424

Call Sign: KA8DSS
Craig W Brumels
1481 Waukazoo Dr
Holland MI 49424

Call Sign: KD8OPZ
Reid F Pinkham
1571 Waukazoo Dr
Holland MI 49424

Call Sign: WA8IWL
Robert L Reed
1722 Waukazoo Dr
Holland MI 49424

Call Sign: KD8MGK
Paul K Pearl
3334 Waverly Park
Holland MI 49424

Call Sign: KD8IFG
Brian Artwick
11739 Waverly Shores
Holland MI 49424

Call Sign: KC8USP
Robert A Holton
1220 Wellington Rd
Holland MI 49423

Call Sign: KC8GOT
Jay M McDowell
13073 Westland Ct
Holland MI 494249100

Call Sign: KC5IIN
Betty J Gorton
332 Westmont
Holland MI 49424

Call Sign: KC8CQH
Greg S Meadowcroft
678 Whitman Ave

Holland MI 49423

Call Sign: KC8HVX
Marlene M
Meadowcroft
678 Whitman Ave
Holland MI 49423

Call Sign: W8GCW
Charles E Rich
300 Wildwood Dr
Holland MI 49423

Call Sign: KD8HDQ
Mark W Hyde
4762 Wildwood Rd
Holland MI 49423

Call Sign: KB8TWH
Edward P Walters
6494 Wildwood Rd
Holland MI 49423

Call Sign: WB8IXM
Lawrence E Pierce
2650 William Ave
Holland MI 49423

Call Sign: AI8G
R Dean Rosendahl
345 Winterpine Way
Holland MI 49424

Call Sign: KC8JBV
Thomas R Olson
1605 Woodlawn Ave
Holland MI 49423

Call Sign: KC8OPK
Pamela K Olson
1605 Woodlawn Ave
Holland MI 49423

Call Sign: KC8OPM
Michael D Olson
1605 Woodlawn Ave
Holland MI 49423

Call Sign: KC8ORC
Andrew B Olson
1605 Woodlawn Ave
Holland MI 49423

Call Sign: KC8AGP

Marc H Van Dis
Holland MI 49422

Call Sign: K9SKP
Michael P Mitchell
Holland MI 49422

FCC Amateur Radio Licenses in Holton

Call Sign: KC8OTV
Matthew L David Sr
2772 Brunswick
Holton MI 49425

Call Sign: KC8ZTR
Clarissa M Hicks
2772 Brunswick
Holton MI 49425

Call Sign: K8MLD
Matthew L David Sr
2772 Brunswick
Holton MI 49425

Call Sign: WC8OTV
Dawn M Leon
2772 Brunswick Rd
Holton MI 49425

Call Sign: K8DMD
Dawn M Leon
2772 Brunswick Rd
Holton MI 49425

Call Sign: N8DWY
Wendy S Hubbard
5295 E Crystal Lake
Rd
Holton MI 494250283

Call Sign: N8FYV
David A Hubbard
5295 E Crystal Lk Rd
Holton MI 49425

Call Sign: WD8MKG
William D Hubbard
5295 E Crystal Lk Rd
Holton MI 49425

Call Sign: N8DWZ
Linda L Hubbard
5295 E Crystal Rd

Holton MI 494250283

Call Sign: WA8NDV
Robert Hanke
8050 Holton Duck
Lake Rd
Holton MI 49425

Call Sign: N8WRW
Joseph J Johnson
7798 Holton Rd
Holton MI 49425

Call Sign: N8WRX
Homer L Johnson
7798 Holton Rd
Holton MI 49425

Call Sign: W0WCH
Theodore M Gergen Jr
2307 Meinert Rd
Holton MI 49425

Call Sign: KD8FBY
Barbara L Grob
2508 Meinert Rd
Holton MI 49425

Call Sign: K9BLG
Barbara L Grob
2508 Meinert Rd
Holton MI 49425

Call Sign: KD8FXE
Gary S Evans
8323 S 200th Ave
Holton MI 49425

Call Sign: N8GMZ
John A Swierczewski
Sr
6765 Schow Rd
Holton MI 49425

Call Sign: KD8CBJ
Paul S Seyferth
6610 Skeels Rd
Holton MI 49425

Call Sign: KC8RDF
Edward Hanke
8655 W 112
Holton MI 49425

Call Sign: N8XNP
George B Davis
Holton MI 49425

Call Sign: N8XSC
Esther M Davis
Holton MI 49425

Call Sign: KC8WCS
Dawn M Hicks
Holton MI 49425

**FCC Amateur Radio
Licenses in Homer**

Call Sign: NJ8D
Thomas L Stewart
8225 20 Mile Rd
Homer MI 49245

Call Sign: KB8IGH
Charles D Martin
8229 25 1/2 Mi Rd
Homer MI 49245

Call Sign: KA8JMD
Bernard L Gorsline
5546 25 1/2 Mile Rd
Homer MI 49245

Call Sign: KD8NSL
Julie A Biggs
24345 County Line Rd
Homer MI 49245

Call Sign: KA8JTV
Carolyn M Gorsline
23971 F Dr S
Homer MI 49245

Call Sign: N8BGB
Gerald L Gorsline
23971 F Dr S
Homer MI 49245

Call Sign: KB8RTF
Robert E Towery
26325 J Dr S
Homer MI 49245

Call Sign: N4CIX
Thomas G O Connor Jr
21100 T Dr S
Homer MI 492458610

Call Sign: KC8DZV
Russell L Wilson
24036 T Dr S
Homer MI 49245

Call Sign: W8KI
Russell L Wilson
24036 T Dr S
Homer MI 49245

Call Sign: KC8QGI
Joe H Johnson
27035 V Dr S
Homer MI 49245

Call Sign: W8JNT
Joe H Johnson
27035 V Dr S
Homer MI 49245

Call Sign: KC8HEF
Gary A Newsome
215.5 W Main St
Homer MI 49245

**FCC Amateur Radio
Licenses in Honor**

Call Sign: KD8HRK
Phillip A Jeannot
7107 Dead Stream Rd
Honor MI 49640

Call Sign: W8JXE
Verrol R Conklin
10858 Main St Box
205
Honor MI 49640

Call Sign: WA8IIN
Thomas E Nejelske Sr
10655 Riverside Dr
Honor MI 496400164

Call Sign: KC8BBI
William M Saddington
2272 Scenic Spur
Honor MI 496409438

Call Sign: KD8NXJ
Terry K Smith
3400 Valley Rd
Honor MI 49640

Call Sign: KC8LPK
Jeffrey M Lepke
7931 Woodland Dr
Honor MI 496400012

Call Sign: KB8VZF
Martha D Garber
Honor MI 49640

Call Sign: KM4PK
Anthony M Elliott
Honor MI 496400266

**FCC Amateur Radio
Licenses in Hopkins**

Call Sign: KB8WGE
Willard T Steffens
1736 126th Ave
Hopkins MI 49328

Call Sign: N8WKM
Daniel G Thompson
1844 126th Ave
Hopkins MI 49328

Call Sign: N8JMY
David E Kaylor
1380 130th Ave
Hopkins MI 49328

Call Sign: N8YJO
Kimberly S Kaylor
1380 130th Ave
Hopkins MI 49328

Call Sign: WB8FGR
Robert G Veenstra
1387 130th Ave
Hopkins MI 49328

Call Sign: WB8FGS
Ethel M Veenstra
1387 130th Ave
Hopkins MI 49328

Call Sign: KD8QNX
Jason L Veenstra
2187 132nd Ave
Hopkins MI 49328

Call Sign: N8PDN
Jeffrey A Lane

2705 134th Ave
Hopkins MI 49328

Call Sign: N8ZUX
Mark A Holman
1853 135th Ave
Hopkins MI
493289715

Call Sign: AB8RU
Mark A Holman
1853 135th Ave
Hopkins MI
493289715

Call Sign: N8FHL
Kenneth L Josey
3271 13th St
Hopkins MI 49328

Call Sign: WB8YNU
Benjamin G Laseur
2751 16th St
Hopkins MI 49328

Call Sign: KB8YNB
Roger L Havens
2920 21st St
Hopkins MI 49328

Call Sign: KD8FLS
Robert T Zapolnik
2944 22nd St
Hopkins MI 49328

Call Sign: KD8FNN
Robert T Zapolnik
2944 22nd St
Hopkins MI 49328

**FCC Amateur Radio
Licenses in Houghton**

Call Sign: KC8VEQ
David R Tripp
200 2nd St
Houghton MI 49931

Call Sign: KC8YXN
Nathan G Whiting
200 2nd St Front
Houghton MI 49931

Call Sign: KC8TRV

Todd O Arney
1005 6th Ave
Houghton MI
499311433

Call Sign: KJ4M
William M Strome
602 7th Ave
Houghton MI
499311721

Call Sign: KB8IXA
William S Shapton
1200 8th Ave
Houghton MI 49931

Call Sign: KC8LSH
Jacob T Eastman
212 Blanche St
Houghton MI 49931

Call Sign: KC8YXM
Jason P J Shim
220 Blanche St
Houghton MI 49931

Call Sign: KC8YXL
Jayavanan R Vijayen
220 Blanche St
Houghton MI 49931

Call Sign: KB8ZTC
C David Pulse
Rt 1 Box 31
Houghton MI
499319703

Call Sign: KB8THB
Michael J Stone
Rt 1 Box 395
Houghton MI 49931

Call Sign: KB8QMY
Brett A Crawford
Rt 1 Box 88
Houghton MI 49931

Call Sign: KA3KSO
Joan Z Suits
1502 Brookside Dr
Houghton MI 49931

Call Sign: WB8WKN
Bryan H Suits

1502 Brookside Dr
Houghton MI 49931

Call Sign: N8SWY
Sherman R Foster III
302 Calverley Ave
Houghton MI 49931

Call Sign: AA8D
David C Krym
49186 Canal Rd
Houghton MI
499319252

Call Sign: N8WGS
Scott D Carlborn
53394 Canal Rd
Houghton MI 49931

Call Sign: KC8ARL
Douglas J Coffman
701 Cedar Bluff Dr
Apt 6
Houghton MI
499311932

Call Sign: W9VKG
Warren O Weingarten
216 Clark St
Houghton MI 49931

Call Sign: KD8RBB
Clayton C Doyle
1109 College Ave
Houghton MI 49931

Call Sign: KD8CFV
Alexander W Kennedy
1206 College Ave
Houghton MI 49931

Call Sign: KD8CFW
John A Horgos
1206 College Ave
Houghton MI 49931

Call Sign: KC8CVN
Jonathan M Tallon
153 Dhh 1700
Townsend Dr
Houghton MI
499311194

Call Sign: KD8RBE

John J Pastore Jr
407 Dodge St
Houghton MI 49931

Call Sign: KD8RBC
Matthew J Gardeski
407 Dodge St
Houghton MI 49931

Call Sign: W8ZIV
Robert E Kurtti
920 Dodge St Apt 414
Houghton MI 49931

Call Sign: KB8DWA
Timothy D Gard
213 Douglass
Houghton Hall
Houghton MI 49931

Call Sign: N8WAV
John C Swift
105 E Douglass Ave
Houghton MI
499312005

Call Sign: KB8BCB
Jess H Pike
103 E Houghton Ave
Houghton MI 49931

Call Sign: KD8ALF
Chris H Hock
809 E Houghton Ave
Houghton MI 49931

Call Sign: KD8CFZ
Mark A Szaroletta
809 E Houghton Ave
Houghton MI 49931

Call Sign: KD8JAK
Henry Lovett Doust
1013 E Houghton Ave
Houghton MI 49931

Call Sign: KD8LWV
Henry Lovett Doust
1013 E Houghton Ave
Houghton MI 49931

Call Sign: KC8RFN
Nicholas J Mehl
1016 E Houghton Ave

Houghton MI 49931

Call Sign: N8HXP
Jon M Davis
210 E Jacker Ave
Houghton MI 49931

Call Sign: N3WGA
Allen J Kempke
403 E Jacker Ave
Houghton MI 49931

Call Sign: KD8NSD
Daniel M Hamilton
1011 E Lakeshore Dr
Houghton MI 49931

Call Sign: KC8VEP
Joshua P Wrucke
900 E Lakeshore Dr
Apt 9
Houghton MI 49931

Call Sign: KD8HRM
Brock D Nummerdor
705 E Montezuma
Houghton MI 49931

Call Sign: KD8RAW
Andrew J Hoekstra
111 E Montezuma Ave
Houghton MI 49931

Call Sign: KC8ULB
Nicholas A Manor
810 E South Ave
Houghton MI 49931

Call Sign: KD8QCK
Aaron J Wendzel
210 E St Apt 2
Houghton MI 49931

Call Sign: N8SRR
Rajendra K Damle
247 E Wadsworth Hall
Houghton MI 49931

Call Sign: KC8YMS
Andrew J Hildebrand
203 Emerald St
Houghton MI 49931

Call Sign: KB8PPB

Jeremy M Parkinson
201 Ermeald St
Houghton MI 49931

Call Sign: KB8QMZ
Gunawan Witjaksono
204 Franklin St
Houghton MI 49931

Call Sign: KD8DYO
Adam J Herman
405 Garnet
Houghton MI 49931

Call Sign: KC8RGN
Sean I Ford
600 Garnet Apt D
Houghton MI 49931

Call Sign: KD8CFY
John T Mancini
600 Garnet St Apt W
Houghton MI 49931

Call Sign: KC8WOG
Jerry J Gedvillas
49645 Gedvillas Rd
Houghton MI 49931

Call Sign: KC8DIF
Dorothy B Pollack
1273 Hickory Ln
Houghton MI 49931

Call Sign: KB8THD
Denis W Skoglund
1274 Hickory Ln
Houghton MI 49931

Call Sign: KB8ZCC
Charles G Nottoli
Houghton Canal Rd
Houghton MI 49931

Call Sign: KA0IMU
David A Olson
211 Hubbell
Houghton MI 49931

Call Sign: N8NNG
Neil R Peplinski
225 Hubbell St Apt 3
Houghton MI 49931

Call Sign: KB8QMX
Peter A Larsen
2106 Hunters Ln
Houghton MI 49931

Call Sign: KC8NFX
Thomas J Guzek
711 Jacker Ave
Houghton MI 49931

Call Sign: W8NAV
Thomas J Guzek
711 Jacker Ave
Houghton MI 49931

Call Sign: KB9YNR
David J Gunderson Jr
20092 James St
Houghton MI 49931

Call Sign: KC8VPD
Chad A Arney
48355 Jefferson St
Houghton MI 49931

Call Sign: KA8UEL
James W Clingersmith
900 Lake St Apt 4
Houghton MI 49931

Call Sign: KC8FLO
Paul T Sulisz
47300 Main St
Houghton MI 49931

Call Sign: KC8QWQ
Ginger W Sulisz
47300 Main St
Houghton MI 49931

Call Sign: KC8JRN
Steven M Mainville
32 Mill Rd Apt 2
Houghton MI 49931

Call Sign: KC8RFK
Jeffrey C Cunningham
32 Mill Rd Apt H
Houghton MI 49931

Call Sign: KC8RGO
Vance B Nelson
17419 Osma Plat Rd
Houghton MI 49931

Call Sign: KC8VET
Donald N Bowlby
202 Prospect St
Houghton MI 49931

Call Sign: KF8TI
Charles T Young
208 Prospect St
Houghton MI 49931

Call Sign: KC8VER
Dean W Seefeldt
404 Quincy St
Houghton MI 49931

Call Sign: KD8RAU
Eddy H Trinklein
506 Quincy St Apt 2
Houghton MI 49931

Call Sign: W8ZKV
Jack W Keck
22182 Ridge Rd
Houghton MI 49931

Call Sign: KB8HFT
Mike Mabington
1207 Ruby
Houghton MI 49931

Call Sign: KB8ZCF
Elizabeth A Strachan
1002 S Franklin Apt A
Houghton MI 49931

Call Sign: KC8BSP
Joseph W Lett
18956 Sermon Rd
Houghton MI 49931

Call Sign: KB8URU
Dallas K Bates
1270 Sharon Ave
Houghton MI 49931

Call Sign: KD8OWY
Andrew P Mauragis
500 Sharon Ave Apt
32
Houghton MI 49931

Call Sign: KC8RGP
Pey Hann Ooi

407 Shelder Ave Apt 8
Houghton MI 49931

Call Sign: KD8HZA
Mariusz P Nowak
2107 Sherwood Dr
Houghton MI 49931

Call Sign: W8TJH
Thomas J Heltunen
2106 Spruce Ln
Houghton MI 49931

Call Sign: N8GPM
Thomas J Heltunen
2106 Spruce Ln
Houghton MI 49931

Call Sign: W8GQM
Michael R Neuman
42579 Superior Rd
Houghton MI 49931

Call Sign: W8YY
Husky ARC
Ee Dept Mtu 1400
Townsend
Houghton MI 49931

Call Sign: KC8RFO
Sean A Tabacsko
1701 Townsend Dr
308E Wadsworth Hall
Houghton MI 49931

Call Sign: KD8JPR
David M Brown
1701 Townsend Dr
312E
Houghton MI 49931

Call Sign: KD8ELK
Weston H Thomas
1703 Townsend Dr
Wht Rm 419 W
Wadsworth Hall
Houghton MI 49931

Call Sign: KD8FPN
Nancy L Banfield
512 W Edwards Ave
Houghton MI 49931

Call Sign: KC8JGD

Alan D Karna
711 W Edwards Ave
Houghton MI
499312420

Call Sign: KD8MFL
Jason P Mack
805 W Edwards Ave
Houghton MI 49931

Call Sign: KC8TRX
Kevin D Michaelson
210C W Sharon Ave
Houghton MI 49931

Call Sign: KD8GKD
Luke L Sanner
405 W South Ave
Houghton MI 49931

Call Sign: KD8QGO
William C Bettendorf
IV
1801 Woodland Dr
Apt 205C
Houghton MI 49931

Call Sign: ND8V
William C Bettendorf
IV
1801 Woodland Dr
Apt 205C
Houghton MI 49931

Call Sign: KB8FFS
Lloyd A Heldt
8 Woodland Rd
Houghton MI 49931

Call Sign: W8ERB
Walter T Anderson
21927 Woodland Rd
Houghton MI
499319710

Call Sign: KD9CW
Howard H Bixby
21955 Woodland Rd
Houghton MI 49931

Call Sign: KB8HFV
Max K Kicherer
8A Woodland Rd
Houghton MI 49931

Call Sign: KD8CFX
Peter W Corbett
1812D Woodmar Dr
Houghton MI 49931

Call Sign: N8XBG
Jeffrey P Winkler
1903D Woodmar Dr
Houghton MI 49931

Call Sign: KB8WOZ
Jae H Hotaling
1907 D Woodmar Dr
Houghton MI 49931

Call Sign: N8SRP
Alwood P Williams Jr
2002B Woodmar Dr
Houghton MI 49931

Call Sign: KC8TRW
Sheri L Ripke
2002-B Woodmar Dr
Houghton MI 49931

Call Sign: KC8NFY
William Frey
2104B Woodmar Dr
Houghton MI
499311029

Call Sign: N8IWT
William H Hillard Jr
2104H Woodmar Dr
Houghton MI 49931

Call Sign: N7XFZ
Jacob P Fugal
2010 B Woodmar Dr
Houghton MI
499311009

Call Sign: KC8YMT
Orrin S Davis
442 Wwh 1703
Townsend Dr
Houghton MI 49931

Call Sign: KA0PIC
Mark W Kwilinski
Houghton MI 49931

Call Sign: KB8JIH

Douglas E Wilken
Houghton MI 49931

Call Sign: KC8VES
Nathaniel P Rutterbush
Houghton MI 49931

Call Sign: KD8QAA
Tim D Nelson
Houghton MI 49931

FCC Amateur Radio Licenses in Houghton Lake

Call Sign: NA2G
Larry L Moeggenberg
105 Bryan J
Houghton Lake MI
48629

Call Sign: N8CGY
Kenneth A Miller Jr
136 Cadillac Ave
Houghton Lake MI
48629

Call Sign: N8ZZF
Patrick A Talbert
126 Dodge Dr
Houghton Lake MI
486298997

Call Sign: W8ELK
Donald W Miller
4413 E Houghton Lake
Dr
Houghton Lake MI
48629

Call Sign: WA8LNL
Laurence L Tallman
7049 E Houghton Lake
Dr
Houghton Lake MI
48629

Call Sign: WB9OFE
Eric T Woodings
7683 E Houghton Lake
Dr
Houghton Lake MI
48629

Call Sign: WB8VLF
Ralph B Hall
8404 E Houghton Lake
Dr
Houghton Lake MI
48629

Call Sign: KA8CPV
Carmon W Wheeler
9385 Elizabeth Rd
Houghton Lake MI
48629

Call Sign: KB8RNP
Daniel F Davis
406 Erie Ave
Houghton Lake MI
48629

Call Sign: KC8KQD
James W Thomas
205 Fairbanks Dr
Houghton Lake MI
48629

Call Sign: WB8IZM
Gregory K Bodker
138 Frisco
Houghton Lake MI
486290969

Call Sign: WD8DWH
Dennis S Barke
311 Houghton Heights
Manor
Houghton Lake MI
48629

Call Sign: W8DSD
David F Lemma
312 Huntington
Houghton Lake MI
48629

Call Sign: N8RSI
Guy W Williams
1481 Loxley
Houghton Lake MI
48629

Call Sign: KB8PRU
Charles T Flynn
224 Mallard Ave

Houghton Lake MI
482699553

Call Sign: W8GQZ
Leo W Brandt
131 Michelson Rd
Houghton Lake MI
48629

Call Sign: WA8TUO
Robert C Harris Sr
142 Oak Marr Dr
Houghton Lake MI
48629

Call Sign: K8AEV
James R Clewley
505 Old Trail Dr
Houghton Lake MI
486299381

Call Sign: WD8QDR
Thomas B King Jr
2757 Owens Rd
Houghton Lake MI
486299026

Call Sign: KA8TCU
Robert F Armstrong
139 Pinecrest Dr
Houghton Lake MI
48629

Call Sign: KC8BVZ
Eli S Cogar
206 Redwine Dr
Houghton Lake MI
48629

Call Sign: W8NRU
Neil F Johnson
6376B Rhodes Rd
Houghton Lake MI
48629

Call Sign: WD8RPV
James E Holmes
117 Russell Ave
Houghton Lake MI
48629

Call Sign: KD8MJM
Deborah I Gouin
1525 S Harrison Ave

Houghton Lake MI
48629

Call Sign: K8DML
Roy E Peters
340 Sandhill Manor
Apt 2
Houghton Lake MI
48629

Call Sign: N2XBQ
Richard A Olivar
200-7 Sandhill Manor
Dr
Houghton Lake MI
48629

Call Sign: N8YKE
Theodore D Farquhar
108 Sunset Dr
Houghton Lake MI
48629

Call Sign: KD8GSH
Daniel K Laginess Jr
6222 W Emery Rd
Houghton Lake MI
48629

Call Sign: KD8SAD
Daniel K Laginess Jr
6222 W Emery Rd
Houghton Lake MI
48629

Call Sign: N8WDI
John E Pawlik
2989 W Houghton
Lake Dr 1
Houghton Lake MI
48629

Call Sign: W8EYK
James R Deamud
4419 W Nestel Rd
Houghton Lake MI
48629

Call Sign: KC8GMO
Clare A Gee
113 Washington Ave
Houghton Lake MI
48629

Call Sign: KD4ZAR
Clarence M Adams
108 Whitebirch
Houghton Lake MI
486290845

Call Sign: KD8LVY
Michael G Allumi
231 Whitebirch Dr
Houghton Lake MI
48629

Call Sign: N8NCD
Robert A Farr Jr
147 Wooden Key Dr
Houghton Lake MI
48629

Call Sign: KB8YLA
Darcee M Miller
Houghton Lake MI
48629

Call Sign: KC8QBD
Kurt D Kareus
Houghton Lake MI
48629

FCC Amateur Radio Licenses in Houghton Lake Height

Call Sign: KU8H
William R Cromwell
105 Ferris Ave
Houghton Lake Height
MI 48630

Call Sign: WB8QXH
Ricky L Ratza
301 Sanford Ave
Houghton Lake Height
MI 48630

FCC Amateur Radio Licenses in Howard City

Call Sign: KD8GTC
Andrew C Harwood
7901 104th St
Howard City MI 49329

Call Sign: KD8HYF

Kyle O Harwood
7901 104th St
Howard City MI 49329

Call Sign: KC8LLW
John D Branton
8745 112th St
Howard City MI 49329

Call Sign: WV8K
Joseph B Hondalus
22718 Almy Rd
Howard City MI 49329

Call Sign: KA8GFQ
Lola J Burley
7803 Amy School Rd
Howard City MI 49329

Call Sign: KA8GFP
Thomas E Burley
7803 Amy School Rd
Howard City MI 49329

Call Sign: KD8RQD
Chad M Davis
9991 Beech Ave
Howard City MI 49329

Call Sign: KD8FAK
Allen S Brooks
8130 Cherokee
Howard City MI 49329

Call Sign: KD8RQC
Shaughna H Langerak
17715 Chippewa Trl
Howard City MI 49329

Call Sign: KD8FPD
Leanne M Crites
8491 Cochise Dr
Howard City MI 49329

Call Sign: N5MDM
David L Crites
8491 Cochise Dr
Howard City MI 49329

Call Sign: KD8EAW
Shane A Willholt
21897 Cutler Rd
Howard City MI 49329

Call Sign: KD8FBN
Chuck Delaney
790 Cypress
Howard City MI 49329

Call Sign: KD8NMC
Brian D Milligan
7776 Green Rd
Howard City MI 49329

Call Sign: KB8VXX
Tom L Olsen
15902 M 46
Howard City MI 49329

Call Sign: NB9N
Joel W Cooper
9921 Reed Rd
Howard City MI 49329

Call Sign: KG8IS
Fred I Fisher Sr
17175 Seneca Dr
Howard City MI 49329

Call Sign: N8AFC
Lawrence A Wahoski
6855 Suzanne Ct
Howard City MI 49329

Call Sign: AA8R
Randy L Hatt
7878 W County Line
Rd
Howard City MI 49329

Call Sign: KD8IXJ
Patricia L Hatt
7878 W County Line
Rd
Howard City MI 49329

Call Sign: W8TAX
Patricia L Hatt
7878 W County Line
Rd
Howard City MI 49329

Call Sign: KC8WQP
Jeffrey M Humphreys
510 Walnut
Howard City MI 49329

Call Sign: KD8DTP
Evonne M Cooke
116 1st St
Hubbard Lake MI
49747

Call Sign: N8UHL
Norman W Ghiata
6230 Cedar Dr
Hubbard Lake MI
49747

Call Sign: KC8UHW
Paul J Coleman
11768 Hubbard Lake
Rd
Hubbard Lake MI
49747

Call Sign: W8NWX
Richard J Heiss
12140 Indian Res Rd
Hubbard Lake MI
49747

Call Sign: KC8ZOK
Ryan R Mathewson
2151 Mathewson Rd
Hubbard Lake MI
49747

Call Sign: KC8OHK
Eric R Nelson
5845 Mt Maria Rd
Hubbard Lake MI
49747

Call Sign: KD8KUC
Donald G Bone
6228 Mt Maria Rd
Hubbard Lake MI
49747

Call Sign: KC8WUI
William F Rensberry
9605 Wolf Creek Rd
Hubbard Lake MI
49747

Call Sign: KC0LWK
Cynthia R Carollo
15250 Maple Rapids
Hubbardston MI 48845

Call Sign: WD8ANB
Harland L Heimke
609 Spruce St
Hubbell MI 499340297

Call Sign: KA8SFF
Russell C Clouthier
26958 W 22nd St
Hubbell MI 49934

Call Sign: KA8ZEY
James D Matson
Hubbell MI 49934

Call Sign: N8PIW
Mary K Herlevich
Hubbell MI 49934

Call Sign: KC8YDV
Raymond E Dube
Hubbell MI 49934

Call Sign: KB8ERI
Paul S Roth
6223 14th Ave
Hudsonville MI 49426

Call Sign: N8ALI
John G Van Baren
2731 16th Ave
Hudsonville MI 49426

Call Sign: KC8QCX
Michael J Peuler
6748 28th Ave
Hudsonville MI 49426

Call Sign: KD8PVU

Oren J Londo
6757 28th Ave
Hudsonville MI 49426

Call Sign: KC8UEP
David M Tencate
7115 28th Ave
Hudsonville MI 49426

Call Sign: WA8SRY
Laurence R Gibson
5527 32nd Ave
Hudsonville MI 49426

Call Sign: KB8UMW
James A Mudget
6391 36th Ave
Hudsonville MI 49426

Call Sign: KD8OIA
Joshua W Hinken
6890 36th Ave
Hudsonville MI 49426

Call Sign: WD8JMI
Leonard Schut
7331 48th Ave
Hudsonville MI 49426

Call Sign: KD8PVQ
Ryan J Dornbos
6717 56th Ave
Hudsonville MI 49426

Call Sign: KD8GRT
Brett D Barton
7350 56th Ave
Hudsonville MI 49426

Call Sign: KD8DDU
Matthew A Blythe
9014 56th Ave
Hudsonville MI 49426

Call Sign: KC8CWH
Paula J Olsen
5373 72nd Ave
Hudsonville MI 49426

Call Sign: KB8WXM
Karl R Stephens
8825 72nd Ave
Hudsonville MI 49426

Call Sign: KB8AXX
Brenda L Larzabal
3320 Allen St
Hudsonville MI 49426

Call Sign: KB8UKX
Fernando E Larzabal
3320 Allen St
Hudsonville MI 49426

Call Sign: KB8RHR
Michael S
Bartosiewicz
4827 Baldwin Ave
Hudsonville MI 49426

Call Sign: KC8QPU
Christopher S Holiday
3466 Baldwin St
Hudsonville MI 49426

Call Sign: WB8ZSI
Douglas C Dykstra
4885 Barnsley Dr
Hudsonville MI
494269286

Call Sign: KD8ENO
David A Lynema
2358 Barry St
Hudsonville MI 49426

Call Sign: N8JGM
David A Lynema
2358 Barry St
Hudsonville MI 49426

Call Sign: KC8OPG
Joe E Hop
6923 Barry St
Hudsonville MI 49426

Call Sign: WD8KFF
Terrence E Vos
5811 Bauer Rd
Hudsonville MI 49426

Call Sign: N8FOX
William T Mac Kay
1368 Bent Tree Ct
Hudsonville MI 49426

Call Sign: KB8BOW
Wilbert C Dick

4033 Blair St
Hudsonville MI 49426

Call Sign: K8IHY
John E Meyer
1840 Byron Rd
Hudsonville MI 49426

Call Sign: KA8ONM
Lois B Meyer
1840 Byron Rd R 2
Hudsonville MI 49426

Call Sign: KC8LJA
Andrew T Roon
4076 Cambridge Dr
Hudsonville MI 49426

Call Sign: N8ATR
Andrew T Roon
4076 Cambridge Dr
Hudsonville MI 49426

Call Sign: KC8RLB
Hudsonville
Emergency Services
3275 Central Blvd
Hudsonville MI
494261450

Call Sign: KB8VZG
Steven L Schellenberg
2558 Cleveland Ct
Hudsonville MI 49426

Call Sign: KB8TWV
Steve L Morren
4258 Creekview Dr
Hudsonville MI 49426

Call Sign: N8BCC
Jack R Folkema
4273 Crestlane Dr
Hudsonville MI 49426

Call Sign: AB8HB
Jack R Folkema
4273 Crestlane Dr
Hudsonville MI 49426

Call Sign: KD8OGF
Debra L Secor
3637 Curtis
Hudsonville MI 49426

Call Sign: KD8FBX
Jeffrey B Secor
3637 Curtis St
Hudsonville MI
494261225

Call Sign: WB8MUV
Martin L Koppenol
6625 Dale Ave SW
Hudsonville MI 49426

Call Sign: N8QOJ
Patrick S Wilde
4148 Dale Ct
Hudsonville MI 49426

Call Sign: KA8DPR
David M Driggs
7112 Deep Rose Ct
Hudsonville MI
494268847

Call Sign: K8RW
Robert C Wallison
4920 Faringdom Grove
Dr
Hudsonville MI
494269189

Call Sign: KD8QHE
Rudolph A Schulte II
6933 Gettsburg Dr
Hudsonville MI 49426

Call Sign: KA9NAM
Debby A Lenz
917 Greenly St
Hudsonville MI 49426

Call Sign: KB9NK
Kenneth C Lenz Jr
917 Greenly St
Hudsonville MI 49426

Call Sign: KD8IYO
Ronald L Terpstra Jr
3732 Greenly St
Hudsonville MI 49426

Call Sign: KC8FGN
Lloyd E Dipple
4244 Heritage Dr
Hudsonville MI 49431

Call Sign: KC8WQQ
Sheri A Detrick
2965 Highbrook Cir
Hudsonville MI 49426

Call Sign: KC8VDO
William M Detrick
2965 Highbrook Cr
Hudsonville MI 49426

Call Sign: KD8EGT
Timothy B Zimmer
3563 Kiel St
Hudsonville MI 49426

Call Sign: W8TBZ
Timothy B Zimmer
3563 Kiel St
Hudsonville MI 49426

Call Sign: N8JMJ
Evelyn J Kooistra
166 Laramy Ln
Hudsonville MI 49426

Call Sign: N8IMK
Martin C Kooistra Jr
1626 Laramy Ln
Hudsonville MI 49426

Call Sign: KD8AZL
David A Dahl Jr
4985 Laurelwood Dr
Hudsonville MI 49426

Call Sign: W8ALF
Raymond D Hamstra
5801 Lincoln Ct
Hudsonville MI 49426

Call Sign: K8ZU
Romulo P Campos
3142 Maplepond Dr
Hudsonville MI 49426

Call Sign: AB8YH
Richard C Harder
2848 Mason Rd
Hudsonville MI 49426

Call Sign: KC8UEQ
John A Klaassen
3148 Mason Rd

Hudsonville MI 49426

Call Sign: KC8KN
Daniel S Ruiter
7106 Michael Dr
Hudsonville MI 49426

Call Sign: N8SBD
James E Meekhof Sr
6766 N Wentward Ct
Hudsonville MI 49426

Call Sign: K8EFK
Arlen J Dykema
6160 Nellie Ave
Hudsonville MI 49426

Call Sign: W8VMB
Roger D Conley
2974 Perry St
Hudsonville MI 49426

Call Sign: KC8TFM
Valerie R Conley
2974 Perry St
Hudsonville MI 49426

Call Sign: KA8SSN
John Van Abbema
3015 Perry St
Hudsonville MI 49426

Call Sign: N8ZMC
Chris H Vuyst
5375 Port Sheldon
Hudsonville MI 49426

Call Sign: KD8EBA
Julie A Vruggink
4644 Port Sheldon St
Hudsonville MI 49426

Call Sign: N8IRP
Carl L Shearer
3160 Quincy St
Hudsonville MI 49426

Call Sign: WA8MTJ
Glenn Hinkle
3140 Raintree Ct
Hudsonville MI 49426

Call Sign: KC8GOR
Edward Mosley Jr

4455 B Ridgeville Ct
Hudsonville MI
494269161

Call Sign: KA8TLN
Jeffry R Stam
7053 Rolling Hills Dr
Hudsonville MI 49426

Call Sign: KC8IJP
Michael J Hefferan
3060 Rosewood Ave
Hudsonville MI 49426

Call Sign: KI8JF
Michael J Hefferan
3060 Rosewood Ave
Hudsonville MI 49426

Call Sign: KC8M
Michael J Hefferan
3060 Rosewood Ave
Hudsonville MI 49426

Call Sign: WA8URE
Thomas L Bosscher
3148 Rosewood Ave
Hudsonville MI 49426

Call Sign: K8IIE
Thomas L Bosscher
3148 Rosewood Ave
Hudsonville MI 49426

Call Sign: K8TB
Thomas L Bosscher
3148 Rosewood Ave
Hudsonville MI 49426

Call Sign: KC8UEO
Sheila K Bosscher
3148 Rosewood Ln
Hudsonville MI 49426

Call Sign: WD8URE
Sheila K Bosscher
3148 Rosewood Ln
Hudsonville MI 49426

Call Sign: W8IIE
Sheila K Bosscher
3148 Rosewood Ln
Hudsonville MI 49426

Call Sign: K8AJ
Sheila K Bosscher
3148 Rosewood Ln
Hudsonville MI 49426

Call Sign: K8TRD
Larry D Ver Hage
5222 Rosewood Ln
Hudsonville MI
494269740

Call Sign: KB8ZDC
Christopher T Postmus
7194 Royal Oak Dr
Hudsonville MI 49426

Call Sign: KD8QHB
Tim Hower
6367 Rush Creek Ct
Hudsonville MI 49426

Call Sign: KC8CUB
Duane T Becksvoort
7483 Russell Dr
Hudsonville MI 49426

Call Sign: WD8BVM
Melvin F Clouse
7271 Ryan Ct
Hudsonville MI 49426

Call Sign: WD8NTH
Gayle E Clouse
7271 Ryan Ct
Hudsonville MI 49426

Call Sign: W8MEL
Melvin F Clouse
7271 Ryan Ct
Hudsonville MI 49426

Call Sign: KC8UEN
Douglas J Lemmen
5526 School Ave
Hudsonville MI
494261122

Call Sign: KD8HZZ
John J Lawrence Jr
7789 Schoolside Dr
Hudsonville MI 49426

Call Sign: N7DOC
Robert A Swayze

6166 Sheldon Dr
Hudsonville MI 49426

Call Sign: KD8RQM
William G Miller
6210 Sheldon Dr
Hudsonville MI 49426

Call Sign: K9HXO
William G Miller
6210 Sheldon Dr
Hudsonville MI 49426

Call Sign: KC8TTA
August L Lukow Jr
6213 Sheldon Oak Dr
Hudsonville MI 49426

Call Sign: WA8RFK
Myron R Wernette
7489 Sleepy Hollow
Dr
Hudsonville MI 49426

Call Sign: W8RFK
Myron Wernette
7489 Sleepy Hollow
Dr
Hudsonville MI 49426

Call Sign: KD8FXD
Richard J Brand
5290 Southbrook Ct 48
Hudsonville MI 49426

Call Sign: KR8B
Richard J Brand
5290 Southbrook Ct 48
Hudsonville MI 49426

Call Sign: KB8QAS
James A Soles
1445 Spencer
Hudsonville MI 49426

Call Sign: W8QOL
Horace G Timmer
6314 Springmont Dr
Hudsonville MI 49426

Call Sign: KB8KZE
Kevin L Guyot
5511 Stevendale Dr
Hudsonville MI 49428

Call Sign: N8FQL
Jack A De Graaf
3474 Stonyridge Dr
Hudsonville MI 49426

Call Sign: KD8RGB
Ian R Miller
7196 Tory Dr
Hudsonville MI 49426

Call Sign: W8AOP
Robert F Gornick
1925 Van Buren St
Hudsonville MI 49426

Call Sign: WA8UJA
Joan P Gornick
1925 Van Buren St
Hudsonville MI 49426

Call Sign: KD8DQC
Joshua D Vollink
1904 Vanburen St
Hudsonville MI 49426

Call Sign: N8JRA
D Scott Guthrey
6872 Vintage Dr
Hudsonville MI 49426

Call Sign: KD8DDX
Patrick S Coombs
4142 Wood Duck Ln
Hudsonville MI 49426

Call Sign: N8GDR
David A Thompson
7548 Woodside Dr
Hudsonville MI 49426

Call Sign: KB8SUW
Debra E Martin
4243 Yorkshire Dr
Hudsonville MI 49426

Call Sign: KA8LOV
James F Zeman
7302 Yorkshire Dr
Hudsonville MI 49426

Call Sign: N8YTV
Harry R Gerow III
Hulbert MI 49748

**FCC Amateur Radio
Licenses in Idlewild**

Call Sign: KD8HYH
Jeffrey L Davenport
5325 E 68th St
Idlewild MI 49642

Call Sign: KB8AJW
Dale N Bowen
42 St
Idlewild MI 49642

Call Sign: KD8PWU
Michael Applewhite
Idlewild MI 49642

**FCC Amateur Radio
Licenses in Indian
River**

Call Sign: WB8IFW
Zeal McGrew
6870 Barbara Ave
Indian River MI 49749

Call Sign: KC8OTN
David G Hare
1889 Bowersock Rd
Indian River MI
497499508

Call Sign: KC8OIB
William L Howe
6443 Burchfield
Indian River MI
497490130

Call Sign: K8INI
George J Waldvogel
5837 Diane Dr
Indian River MI 49749

Call Sign: KB8FPN
Marianne L Solomon
6045 Goose Lake Rd
Indian River MI 49749

Call Sign: KC8AFO
Birgitta Brown
6045 Goose Lake Rd
Indian River MI 49749

Call Sign: WG8W
Rodney R Brown
6045 Goose Lake Rd
Indian River MI 49749

Call Sign: KE8OS
John E Gibson
25 Grandview Beach
Rd
Indian River MI 49749

Call Sign: N8NXO
John L Coon
37 S Straits Hwy
Indian River MI 49749

Call Sign: KD8CHJ
Dianne L Myers
2274 W Hackleburg
Rd
Indian River MI 49749

Call Sign: KA2UDA
Jon E Lembke
Indian River MI 49749

Call Sign: N8PZZ
Thomas D Clementson
Indian River MI 49749

Call Sign: N8UCD
Susan M Coon
Indian River MI 49749

Call Sign: W8IAC
Edward Prested
Indian River MI 49749

Call Sign: W8LSH
Ross B Pobanz
Indian River MI 49749

Call Sign: KD8CHI
Patricia L Wilcox
Indian River MI 49749

Call Sign: W6KIS
James W Dryden
Indian River MI
497490926

Call Sign: KD8GDE
Charlevoix Cheboygan
Emmet Counties

Public Service
Communication
Organization
Indian River MI
497493026

Call Sign: W8CCE
Charlevoix Cheboygan
Emmet Counties
Public Service
Communication
Organization
Indian River MI
497493026

Call Sign: KD8GQL
Charlevoix Cheboygan
Emmet Counties
Public Service
Communication
Organization
Indian River MI
497493026

Call Sign: W8AGB
Charlevoix Cheboygan
Emmet Counties
Public Service
Communication
Organization
Indian River MI
497493026

Call Sign: KC8OAZ
John R Wilcox
Indian River MI
497493041

**FCC Amateur Radio
Licenses in
Interlochen**

Call Sign: KC8QEE
Donald C Inman
4689 Betsie River Rd
Interlochen MI 49643

Call Sign: W8DCI
Donald C Inman
4689 Betsie River Rd
Interlochen MI 49643

Call Sign: KD8BXI
Mary E Miller

19466 Bronson Lake
Rd
Interlochen MI 49643

Call Sign: KA8WUF
Patty Heinz
19973 Bronson Lk Rd
Interlochen MI 49643

Call Sign: KB8QCH
James S Jorgenson
10825 Cedar Hedge
Trl
Interlochen MI 49643

Call Sign: N8STO
Eric L Send
843 Cedar Trl
Interlochen MI 49643

Call Sign: N8TC
Brian J Cox
11542 Diamond Park
Rd
Interlochen MI 49643

Call Sign: W8NMC
Northwestern
Michigan Amateur
Radio Asso
11542 Diamond Park
Rd
Interlochen MI 49643

Call Sign: KD8OTX
Eugene T Tanke II
6344 Eagle Valley Dr
Interlochen MI 48768

Call Sign: KD8RTC
Joseph G Clark
2368 Fashion Ave
Interlochen MI 49643

Call Sign: KB8PGD
Patrick A Mahar
2566 Gonder Rd
Interlochen MI 49643

Call Sign: KD8NEJ
Shane R Brosier
2270 Griner Pkwy
Interlochen MI 49643

Call Sign: KC8PHK
Terry M Stevens
9558 Innwood W
Interlochen MI 49643

Call Sign: KC8NJS
David A Gary
9743 Innwood W
Interlochen MI 49643

Call Sign: K7XK
Richard W Yager
4081 Jeri Rd
Interlochen MI 49643

Call Sign: AA8AA
Richard W Yager
4081 Jeri Rd
Interlochen MI 49643

Call Sign: K7XK
Richard W Yager
4081 Jeri Rd
Interlochen MI 49643

Call Sign: K8UK
Richard W Yager
4081 Jeri Rd
Interlochen MI 49643

Call Sign: N8UUJ
Marilyn H Shenk
5604 Lakeview Dr
Interlochen MI 49643

Call Sign: W8PIT
William G Shenk
5604 Lakeview Dr
Interlochen MI 49643

Call Sign: KC8JEX
James S Andersen
912 Lodge Trl
Interlochen MI 49643

Call Sign: KC8UPW
Francis J Long
10037 Mud Lake Rd
Interlochen MI 49643

Call Sign: KC8YYG
Jacqueline A Long
10037 Mud Lake Rd
Interlochen MI 49643

Call Sign: W8VPW
Thomas A Borsos
10210 Mud Lake Rd
Interlochen MI 49643

Call Sign: KB8QOU
Marvin E Knecht
1537 N Lamb Rd
Interlochen MI 49643

Call Sign: K8YCU
Robert D Randall
2871 N Lamb Rd
Interlochen MI 49643

Call Sign: KD8MKX
Christopher D Parrish
2511 Reynolds Rd
Interlochen MI 49643

Call Sign: KD8MTT
Christopher D Parrish
2511 Reynolds Rd
Interlochen MI 49643

Call Sign: KD8OXX
Katrina M Parrish
2511 Reynolds Rd
Interlochen MI 49643

Call Sign: KD8FUS
Kyle P Monteith
1126 S Long Lake Rd
Interlochen MI 49643

Call Sign: KD8UX
Phillip M Cuchetti
9580 Toni Tr
Interlochen MI 49643

Call Sign: KB8CIG
Gary G Lucchetti
19251 US 31
Interlochen MI 49643

**FCC Amateur Radio
Licenses in Ionia**

Call Sign: K8ILN
Myriam R Gregg
129 Arnold
Ionia MI 488462009

Call Sign: KD8OHT
Christopher M Sallek
403 Baldie St
Ionia MI 488461505

Call Sign:
WW4WWW
Christopher M Sallek
403 Baldie St
Ionia MI 488461505

Call Sign: WA8ZXI
James E Huntley
515 Beresford St
Ionia MI 488461477

Call Sign: WA8JKP
Lewis A Guernsey
555 Beresford St
Ionia MI 48846

Call Sign: KD8ODR
Issac J Beeman
319 Colby St
Ionia MI 48846

Call Sign: KD8KLL
Penny A Beeman
319 Colby St
Ionia MI 48846

Call Sign: N8PNY
Penny A Beeman
319 Colby St
Ionia MI 48846

Call Sign: KD8KLV
Scott A Beeman
319 Colby St
Ionia MI 48846

Call Sign: AC8EU
Scott A Beeman
319 Colby St
Ionia MI 48846

Call Sign: NE8E
Scott A Beeman
319 Colby St
Ionia MI 48846

Call Sign: KD8OND
William M Sandborn
641 Cyrus St

Ionia MI 48846

Call Sign: KC8ILK
Adel C Wentworth
517 E Main St
Ionia MI 48846

Call Sign: WD8ROK
William L Kime
3640 E Stage Rd
Ionia MI 48846

Call Sign: KC8ZHD
Janette L Crandell
360 E Tuttle Rd 333
Ionia MI 48846

Call Sign: KB8SEQ
Donald W Ishman
360 E Tuttle Rd 97
Ionia MI 499468622

Call Sign: N8RRK
David W Oliver
931 E Washington
Ionia MI 48846

Call Sign: K8KCF
Ralph C Furman
270 E Washington 1
Ionia MI 48846

Call Sign: KD8QNQ
George F Fox
915 Hackett St
Ionia MI 48846

Call Sign: KD8PJK
James C Angus
1150 Haynor Rd
Ionia MI 48846

Call Sign: K1ION
James C Angus
1150 Haynor Rd
Ionia MI 48846

Call Sign: N8FAU
Robert C Rogers
747 Johnson Rd
Ionia MI 488469540

Call Sign: KC8ZPE
Daniel D Lutz

1919 Kelsey
Ionia MI 48846

Call Sign: N8EOJ
Charles A Peterson
6664 Kelsey Hwy
Ionia MI 48846

Call Sign: KB8IUN
Douglas G Bormann
522 Lafayette St
Ionia MI 48846

Call Sign: K8CJR
Richard L Letts
695 Lawton St
Ionia MI 48846

Call Sign: KC8ZTX
Jason L Miller
129 Mill St
Ionia MI 48846

Call Sign: KD8PJM
Andrea C Lask
526 N Jackson St
Ionia MI 48846

Call Sign: K8MKH
William H Burras
412 Nicholson
Ionia MI 48846

Call Sign: KD8IYG
Louis E Wolthuis
4264 Nickleplate Rd
Ionia MI 48846

Call Sign: KD8IYI
William E Wolthuis Sr
4264 Nickleplate Rd
Ionia MI 48846

Call Sign: KC8DWK
Kelly J Jean
324 Pearl
Ionia MI 48846

Call Sign: KC8DYV
Matthew B Hallead
137 Reimer Dr
Ionia MI 48846

Call Sign: N8VWD

Matt S Kidder
407 Rice
Ionia MI 48846

Call Sign: KC5JRF
Thomas P Rossbottom
640 S Bellamy Rd
Ionia MI 48846

Call Sign: KB2MVF
David P Felzke
751 Valley View Dr
Apt 205
Ionia MI 48846

Call Sign: N8PNR
Kim R Sherrick
819 W Lincoln Ave
Ionia MI 48846

Call Sign: KE4ZIW
Ruth A Ring
236 Yeomans St
Ionia MI 48846

Call Sign: KD8JTH
Gary L Betz
1133 Yeomans St Lot
159
Ionia MI 48846

Call Sign: WD8OAO
Larry E Kline
Ionia MI 48846

FCC Amateur Radio Licenses in Iron Mountain

Call Sign: KB8ETJ
Yvonne M Bafile
401 3rd St
Iron Mountain MI
49801

Call Sign: KD8KUG
Corissa L Stachowicz
521 7th St Apt B
Iron Mountain MI
49801

Call Sign: KC8JRI
Gordon J Reed Jr
N3775 Bass Lake Rd

Iron Mountain MI
49801

Call Sign: W8HFS
Jay C Jennings
W 9260 Beverly St
Iron Mountain MI
49801

Call Sign: KB8ETK
Joseph A Komblevicz
W8568 Collins Rd
Iron Mountain MI
49801

Call Sign: N8ZAL
Judith I Komblevicz
W8568 Collins Rd
Iron Mountain MI
49801

Call Sign: KD8DJJ
Sheila M Caswell
N5832 CR 607
Iron Mountain MI
49801

Call Sign: KE9L
Arthur A Caswell
N5832 CR 607
Iron Mountain MI
49801

Call Sign: KA8TFF
Scott R Jarmusch
705 E A St
Iron Mountain MI
49801

Call Sign: WA8AYG
Donald P Schettler
901 E Blaine St
Iron Mountain MI
49801

Call Sign: KD8KUI
Dennis V Adam
723 E C Ave
Iron Mountain MI
49801

Call Sign: KD8KWP
Joe L Gerwig
605 E E St

Iron Mountain MI
49801

Call Sign: N8MNZ
Ken Runsat
910 E E St
Iron Mountain MI
49801

Call Sign: KC8CDA
Michael J Kusz
921 E E St
Iron Mountain MI
49801

Call Sign: KB8TOV
Mark L Capra
1131 E E St
Iron Mountain MI
49801

Call Sign: WB8UUB
Douglas L Villa
909 E G St
Iron Mountain MI
49801

Call Sign: K8CIV
Dudley E Brown
1315 E Grant
Iron Mountain MI
49801

Call Sign: KE7PNM
Travis J Quick
419 E Grant St
Iron Mountain MI
49801

Call Sign: KD8DJN
Robert M Olson
630 E H St Apt 3
Iron Mountain MI
49801

Call Sign: KD8GXN
Andrew S Van Sickle
600 E Main St Apt 3
Iron Mountain MI
49801

Call Sign: KD8KUH
Mark D Schultz
1023 E Margaret St

Iron Mountain MI
49801

Call Sign: N8ZHB
Nathan A Raiche
N3026 Fumee Lake Dr
Iron Mountain MI
49801

Call Sign: KB8IMA
John A De Amicis
W 9460 H Lucas Dr
Iron Mountain MI
49801

Call Sign: N8OYN
Brenda W De Amicis
W 9460 H Lucas Dr
Iron Mountain MI
49801

Call Sign: KB8XK
Lloyd K Sundberg
W8869 Lakeview Dr
Iron Mountain MI
49801

Call Sign: N5QPC
Michael D Havens
1300 Michigan Ave
Trlr 60
Iron Mountain MI
49801

Call Sign: KB8PHX
William D Wicklund
429 Millie St Apt A
Iron Mountain MI
49801

Call Sign: N9VWK
Bruce V Gray
N3672 Moonlake Dr
Iron Mountain MI
49801

Call Sign: KC8RYY
Steve R Johnson
728 N Kimberly
Iron Mountain MI
49801

Call Sign: KC8SZP
Debra A Johnson

728 N Kimberly
Iron Mountain MI
49801

Call Sign: N9TNH
Theresa A Johnson
106 N Kimberly St
Iron Mountain MI
49801

Call Sign: WA9QIM
Gordon W Munsche
300 N Lake St
Iron Mountain MI
49801

Call Sign: KB8ETO
Beverly J Munsche
300 N Lake St
Iron Mountain MI
498016834

Call Sign: K8ABS
James M Riverside
W9390 Nocerini Rd
Iron Mountain MI
49801

Call Sign: WD8LVN
Betty M Beaudoin
1530 Oslo Ave
Iron Mountain MI
49801

Call Sign: WB9TNG
Frank J Tehako
N3941 Pine Mountain
Rd
Iron Mountain MI
49801

Call Sign: KB8PTH
James G Wilcheck
1200 S Hemlock St
Iron Mountain MI
49801

Call Sign: KA8VDY
James M Young
705 S Kimberly Ave
Iron Mountain MI
49801

Call Sign: KB8JNH

Karen E Whitenack
1256 S Kimberly Ave
Iron Mountain MI
49801

Call Sign: W8DXS
Charles G Steinke
1628 S Park Ave
Iron Mountain MI
49801

Call Sign: N8LT
Lee T Michaud
W7921 S US 2
Iron Mountain MI
49801

Call Sign: KC8LVD
Rudolph M Pratl Jr
W8079 S US 2 Lot 97
Iron Mountain MI
49801

Call Sign: W5CQY
John G Clark
N 7040 Smith Ln
Iron Mountain MI
49801

Call Sign: K8TKH
Boris S Tchokreff
W6884 Sportsman
Iron Mountain MI
498019519

Call Sign: KL2MK
Robert C Filipczak
1113 Vulcan St Apt 13
Iron Mountain MI
49801

Call Sign: WA8HBP
Douglas G Villa
1509 W A St
Iron Mountain MI
498012523

Call Sign: W8JWN
Thomas R Martin Sr
812 W B St
Iron Mountain MI
49801

Call Sign: KD8DJO

Edwin R Armbrust
918 W B St
Iron Mountain MI
49801

Call Sign: W8XBO
Edwin R Armbrust
918 W B St
Iron Mountain MI
49801

Call Sign: KB8EYF
Norman B Cornelia
507 W C St
Iron Mountain MI
49801

Call Sign: KD8DJQ
Rebecca L Rowell
413 W D St
Iron Mountain MI
49801

Call Sign: KB8UWF
Mickey J Grunlund
217 W E St
Iron Mountain MI
49801

Call Sign: W9UOI
Charles F Dickinson
900 Wells St
Iron Mountain MI
49801

Call Sign: KC8JRJ
Karen R Hoffman
N3369 Woodland Dr
Iron Mountain MI
49801

Call Sign: WA9TDI
Duane E Hoffman
N3369 Woodland Dr
Iron Mountain MI
49801

Call Sign: AA8DJ
Anthony C Hoynacke
512 Woodward Ave
Iron Mountain MI
49801

Call Sign: WB8UFL

James R Bertoldi
Iron Mountain MI
49801

Call Sign: KC8TH
Thomas W Heyboer
Iron Mountain MI
49801

Call Sign: KC8LKO
Thomas W Heyboer
Iron Mountain MI
49801

FCC Amateur Radio Licenses in Iron River

Call Sign: KC8YAX
David R Hill
201 2nd St
Iron River MI 49935

Call Sign: KD8GJW
David R Hill
201 2nd St
Iron River MI 49935

Call Sign: KB8UCO
Jerry G Hooper
718 4th Ave
Iron River MI 49935

Call Sign: W7HZO
Wilhart N Altonen
105 9th Ave
Iron River MI 49935

Call Sign: N8XSZ
William E Walsh
Bates Gaastra Rd
Iron River MI 49935

Call Sign: KC8VOE
John M Mastie
762 Baumgartner Rd
Iron River MI 49935

Call Sign: AB8ST
John M Mastie
762 Baumgartner Rd
Iron River MI 49935

Call Sign: N8OK

John M Mastie
762 Baumgartner Rd
Iron River MI 49935

Call Sign: KA9RAB
Michael P Nies
109 Campbell Rd
Iron River MI 49935

Call Sign: N8SLI
Beth A Nies
109 Campbell Rd
Iron River MI 49935

Call Sign: KD8FIT
Charles D Sledge
163 Caspian Cutoff Rd
Iron River MI 49935

Call Sign: KB9IVE
Daryl R Waters
417 Cherry St
Iron River MI 49935

Call Sign: KC8LNI
Kelly M Waters
417 Cherry St
Iron River MI 49935

Call Sign: KC8AXJ
Steve J Holm
1606 Davidson St
Iron River MI 49935

Call Sign: KA8FFM
Vincent N Tarnowski
218 E Hill Rd
Iron River MI 49935

Call Sign: KC8MFP
John D Stachowicz
605 E Hunter Rd
Iron River MI 49935

Call Sign: N9NLN
Robert W Heinritz Jr
437 E Siding Rd
Iron River MI
499359775

Call Sign: AA9JG
Dan R Waters
3338 E US Hwy 2
Iron River MI 49935

Call Sign: N9XTX
Mary R Waters
3338 E US Hwy 2
Iron River MI 49935

Call Sign: N8LVQ
Iron Range ARC
3338 E US Hwy 2
Iron River MI 49935

Call Sign: N8OYP
Peggy A Cronkright
208 Gibbs City Rd
Iron River MI 49935

Call Sign: N8OYQ
Duane A Cronkright
208 Gibbs City Rd
Iron River MI 49935

Call Sign: N8FZU
George W Peterson
277 Gibbs City Rd
Iron River MI 49935

Call Sign: N8LIQ
Edward C Jones
144 Lakso Rd
Iron River MI 49935

Call Sign: K8VXC
Sylvester A Nocerini
907 Lalley Rd
Iron River MI 49935

Call Sign: WD9FIH
Margaret M Dahn
141 Larson Rd
Iron River MI 49935

Call Sign: WD9FIG
Charles C Dahn
141 Larson Rd
Iron River MI 49935

Call Sign: WD8KQF
Donald R Smith
213 M 73
Iron River MI 49935

Call Sign: KC8LNG
Nathan J Drier
196 Meadow View Dr

Iron River MI 49935

Call Sign: KC8LNH
Linda A Drier
196 Meadow View Dr
Iron River MI 49935

Call Sign: KC8LNF
Roger E Drier
196 Meadowview Dr
Iron River MI 49935

Call Sign: KA8PNL
Earl H Luck
1428 N 2nd Ave
Iron River MI 49935

Call Sign: KC8UHX
Kenneth M Uznanski
133 N 8th Ave
Iron River MI
499351609

Call Sign: WD9JHW
Robert A Charter
1828 N Verona Ave
Iron River MI 49935

Call Sign: KA8RKZ
Waino T Lahti
108 Noren Rd
Iron River MI 49935

Call Sign: N8DMD
Mark C Smitham
2347 Ottawa Lake Rd
Iron River MI 49935

Call Sign: KC8IZT
Kevin D Drier
2319 Ottawa Lk Rd
Iron River MI 49935

Call Sign: KB8HCB
Joseph D Flood III
511 Roosevelt Ave
Iron River MI 49935

Call Sign: KC8YIO
Daniel L Baumgartner
II
409 Spruce St
Iron River MI 49935

Call Sign: KC8ZIM
Alma L Baumgartner
409 Spruce St
Iron River MI 49964

Call Sign: KB0JPW
Joel M Serbinski
302 Stambaugh Ave
Iron River MI 49935

Call Sign: KG0BH
Michael D Serbinski
302 Stambaugh Ave
Iron River MI 49935

Call Sign: KC8UWE
Joel M Serbinski
302 Stambaugh Ave
Iron River MI 49935

Call Sign: KM8S
Michael D Serbinski
302 Stambaugh Ave
Iron River MI 49935

Call Sign: KF6JVI
Bruce H Hackett
516 Stambaugh Ave
Iron River MI 49935

Call Sign: KA8FEF
Garold R Ward Jr
1005 Stambaugh Ave
Iron River MI 49935

Call Sign: KC8ZIL
Dorothy J Hookenson
Apartment 106
Stambaugh Ave
Iron River MI 49935

Call Sign: KD8KFL
Allan Wickstrom
333 State Hwy M73
Iron River MI 49935

Call Sign: N8KXR
Lydia A Haack
196 Tamarack Lake Rd
Iron River MI 49935

Call Sign: KC8MEC
Iron Range ARC
339 W Division St

Iron River MI 49935

Call Sign: N8OWL
Thomas W Stephenson
339 W Division St
Iron River MI
499351635

Call Sign: KB9MLN
James E Meier
404 W Hagerman Lake
Rd
Iron River MI 49935

Call Sign: N8WIS
Ronald J Simmons
133 W Silver Lake Dr
Iron River MI 49935

Call Sign: KB8ORI
Roger W Bofinger
Iron River MI 49935

Call Sign: KB8ORJ
Jonathan W Bofinger
Iron River MI 49935

Call Sign: N9ZVJ
Dale A Noth
Iron River MI 49935

Call Sign: KB8ZIN
Frank S Stanich
Iron River MI
499350348

FCC Amateur Radio
Licenses in Irons

Call Sign: KD8CKQ
Phil R Waybrant Jr
11088 N Merrillville
Rd
Irons MI 49644

Call Sign: AA8WS
Sue Witkowski
11545 N Midget Lake
Dr
Irons MI 49644

Call Sign: N8SJD
Chester J Witkowski

11545 N Midget Lake
Dr
Irons MI 49644

Call Sign: N8GTP
Annette King
7370 W 6 Mile Rd
Irons MI 496448962

Call Sign: KD8GRE
Keith A Cantrell
6970 W 8 Mile Rd
Irons MI 49644

Call Sign: KC8UXX
Frederick B Wayward
6634 W Wayward Ct
Irons MI 49644

Call Sign: KC8DGW
Ronald A Hartzell
Irons MI 496440270

FCC Amateur Radio Licenses in Ironwood

Call Sign: KC8BKE
Lawrence R Maki
249 E Ash St
Ironwood MI 49938

Call Sign: KD8EBO
Andrew J Tait
407 E Bonnie St
Ironwood MI 49938

Call Sign: AB8ZJ
Andrew J Tait
407 E Bonnie St
Ironwood MI 49938

Call Sign: W8ZJA
George F Oberlander
217 E Ridge Rd
Ironwood MI 49938

Call Sign: KD8FKP
Doug L Mead
1135 Florence St
Ironwood MI 49938

Call Sign: K8DLM
Doug L Mead
1135 Florence St

Ironwood MI 49938

Call Sign: WD8JKN
Russell W Maki
E4561 Lake Rd
Ironwood MI 49938

Call Sign: KD8PFU
Jeremy J Balduc
101 N Lowell St
Ironwood MI
499382066

Call Sign: KD8PGY
Jeremy J Balduc
101 N Lowell St Apt L
Ironwood MI
499382066

Call Sign: WD8BOA
Dean A Olson
N10753 Olson Rd
Ironwood MI 49938

Call Sign: WD8QJC
Betty A Olson
E 4511 Orchard Rd
Ironwood MI 49938

Call Sign: K8UTI
Jack R Olson
E4511 Orchard Rd
Ironwood MI 49938

Call Sign: KD8NSF
Derek A Etheridge
106 S Curry St
Ironwood MI 49938

Call Sign: KC8SKJ
Gerald N Huffman
130 W Aurora St Apt 1
Ironwood MI 49938

Call Sign: N8PBH
Alan N Harrison
210 W Ayer
Ironwood MI 49938

Call Sign: KB9IV
William J Marvin
302 W Birch St
Ironwood MI 49938

Call Sign: K9MLD
Joel E Eschmann
116 W Coolidge Ave
Ironwood MI 49938

Call Sign: N9KDO
Linda A Eschmann
116 W Coolidge Ave
Ironwood MI 49938

Call Sign: W0EZI
Michael T Weigel
141 W Coolidge Ave
Ironwood MI 49938

Call Sign: W8EZI
Michael T Weigel
141 W Coolidge Ave
Ironwood MI 49938

Call Sign: KB8TNF
William G Cloon Jr
125 W Francis St
Ironwood MI 49938

Call Sign: KA0BUM
George W Mead
351 W Midland Ave
Ironwood MI
499381030

Call Sign: KA8CNA
Robert L Koski
104 W Pewabic
Ironwood MI 49938

FCC Amateur Radio Licenses in Ishpeming

Call Sign: KC8BLB
Elizabeth A Nevala
S327 1st Ave
Ishpeming MI 49849

Call Sign: KD8IZM
Ryan C Foster
563 3 Mile Rd
Ishpeming MI 49849

Call Sign: KD8KDH
Robert P Sihtala
230 Aspen Dr
Ishpeming MI 49849

Call Sign: N8XLG
Brian D Nap
1545 Aspen Dr
Ishpeming MI 49849

Call Sign: KC8MGT
Laurie A Wirtanen
118 Bessemer St
Ishpeming MI 49849

Call Sign: W8DOG
Michael P Wirtanen
118 Bessemer St
Ishpeming MI 49849

Call Sign: KB0P
Paul W Racine
19 Birch Ln
Ishpeming MI 49849

Call Sign: KD8LAG
Chad A Racine
19 Birch Ln
Ishpeming MI 49849

Call Sign: N8RFB
Dean E Rushford
Rr 1 Box 1958
Ishpeming MI 49849

Call Sign: KC8QWN
Louis J Bertucci
Rt 1 Box 2
Ishpeming MI 49849

Call Sign: KC8WAD
Timothy R Swanson
151 Cooper Lake Rd
Ishpeming MI 49849

Call Sign: N8QKH
Julie A Szenina
1135 Cooper Lake Rd
Ishpeming MI 49849

Call Sign: KC8OND
Thomas G Rogers
1216 Cooper Lake Rd
Ishpeming MI 49849

Call Sign: N8HDT
Donald J Szenina
1135 Cooper Lake Rd
Ishpeming MI 49849

Call Sign: KC8EEF
David S Emanuelson
250 Cord Pbp
Ishpeming MI 49849

Call Sign: N8DJU
Gary W Robinson
1000 Country Ln Ste
300
Ishpeming MI 49849

Call Sign: KG8LA
Timothy T Teall
13151 CR Cf
Ishpeming MI 49849

Call Sign: K8ET
Arthur R Troumbly
601 CR Crf
Ishpeming MI 49849

Call Sign: W8ART
Judith M Troumbly
601 CR Crf
Ishpeming MI 49849

Call Sign: WB8NNG
Daniel L Cloninger
320 CR Pae
Ishpeming MI 49849

Call Sign: KD8LMU
Bert D Hill
5115 CR Pb
Ishpeming MI 49849

Call Sign: KC8MPC
Michael J Cox
7100 CR Pg
Ishpeming MI 49849

Call Sign: N8ZIG
Roger A Pietro
880 CR Prg
Ishpeming MI 49849

Call Sign: KC8VQV
Carol A Bertucci
17 Deer Lake Rd
Ishpeming MI 49849

Call Sign: K8UPA
Louis J Bertucci

17 Deer Lake Rd
Ishpeming MI 49849

Call Sign: W8BZM
Peter J Lammi
4034 Deer Lake Rd
Ishpeming MI 49849

Call Sign: KC8EWD
William F Dowe
154 Douglas
Ishpeming MI 49849

Call Sign: KE9LL
Joseph G Rayome
241 Douglas St
Ishpeming MI 49849

Call Sign: WB8HKX
Gary L Sundblad
821 E Empire St
Ishpeming MI 49849

Call Sign: KA8SBN
David G Lehtinen
831 E Empire St
Ishpeming MI 49849

Call Sign: WB8IEH
James J Delongchamp
834 E Maurice
Ishpeming MI 49849

Call Sign: W8HV
Theodore Kangas
648 Elliott St
Ishpeming MI 49849

Call Sign: N8ZWB
Michael M Bjorne
1785 Ellsworth St
Ishpeming MI 49849

Call Sign: KB8PLQ
Kevin J De Loughary
409 Excelsior
Ishpeming MI 49849

Call Sign: W8CBZ
Leonard N Olgren
285 Gold St
Ishpeming MI
498492612

Call Sign: KD8FDU
Betsie L Bush
102 Graham St
Ishpeming MI 49849

Call Sign: KD8FDT
Raymond K Bush
102 Graham St
Ishpeming MI 49849

Call Sign: K8UXB
David S Kakkuri
125 Helen St
Ishpeming MI 49849

Call Sign: KD8HOS
Justin A Carlson
1156 Highland Dr
Ishpeming MI 49884

Call Sign: WB8BIL
Gregg C Anderson
247 Hill St
Ishpeming MI 49849

Call Sign: WA8MZY
Joseph G Mahoski
2009 Jackson Ave
Ishpeming MI 49849

Call Sign: KD8OIR
Aaren A Joki
12 Lawer Dr
Ishpeming MI 49849

Call Sign: KG8ZL
Randy R Teall
641 Little Perch Lake
Ishpeming MI 49849

Call Sign: KD8NDA
Jon L Compton
1312 N 2nd Ave
Ishpeming MI 49849

Call Sign: KD8OAH
Michael D Byers
912 N 3rd St
Ishpeming MI
498491102

Call Sign: KC8BAK
Fred W Saari
604 N 4th Ave

Ishpeming MI 49849

Call Sign: KC8BAM
Judith S Saari
604 N 4th St
Ishpeming MI 49849

Call Sign: KD8BPC
Norman W Duman
404 N Main Apt 4
Ishpeming MI 49849

Call Sign: W8NWD
Norman W Duman
404 N Main Apt 4
Ishpeming MI 49849

Call Sign: KB8VMB
Joseph G Youren
908 N Main St
Ishpeming MI 49849

Call Sign: N8RSC
Michael A Ollila
215 N Maple St
Ishpeming MI 49849

Call Sign: N8HPF
Gary J Paveglio
1465 N Westwood Cir
Ishpeming MI 49849

Call Sign: N8NBJ
Kristina L Paveglio
1465 N Westwood Cir
Ishpeming MI 49849

Call Sign: KC8CCX
Michael R Helppi
1105 N Westwood Dr
Ishpeming MI 49849

Call Sign: KD8DRD
Stuart A Skauge
458 Oak St
Ishpeming MI 49849

Call Sign: N8TER
Keith M Whittington
619 Park St
Ishpeming MI 49849

Call Sign: N1HJK
David J Williams

723 Park St
Ishpeming MI 49849

Call Sign: W8HSE
David J Williams
723 Park St
Ishpeming MI 49849

Call Sign: WB8NJP
Bruce G Bureau
742 Poplar St
Ishpeming MI 49849

Call Sign: KO8U
Ronald S Sihtala
1836 Prairie Ave
Ishpeming MI 49849

Call Sign: N8NBO
Susan C Sihtala
1836 Prairie Ave
Ishpeming MI 49849

Call Sign: N8QBL
Laura S Sihtala
1836 Prairie Ave
Ishpeming MI 49849

Call Sign: WA8GJD
Gregory E Mahoski
1909 Prairie Ave
Ishpeming MI 49849

Call Sign: KB8DNS
Rodney T Wallberg
1740 Rosewood Ln
Ishpeming MI 49849

Call Sign: KI8DJ
Gary A Nevala
327 S 1st
Ishpeming MI 49849

Call Sign: KC8VJZ
James E Nevala
327 S 1st St
Ishpeming MI 49849

Call Sign: KD8CCP
Stephen J Skauge
213 S Angeline
Ishpeming MI 49849

Call Sign: KC8BAL

Don E Loven
241 S Angeline St
Ishpeming MI 49849

Call Sign: KC8RJI
Timothy J Saxwold
275 S Camp Rd
Ishpeming MI 49849

Call Sign: KG8NK
Louis A Gembolis
130 S Daisy St
Ishpeming MI 49849

Call Sign: AB8GM
Louis A Gembolis
130 S Daisy St
Ishpeming MI 49849

Call Sign: KG8NK
Louis A Gembolis
130 S Daisy St
Ishpeming MI 49849

Call Sign: KD8EDS
Sheree A Gembolis
130 S Daisy St
Ishpeming MI 49849

Call Sign: N8HXG
Ralph C Watters
165 S Pansy St
Ishpeming MI 49849

Call Sign: KC8PKF
John R Peterson
400 S Rose St
Ishpeming MI 49849

Call Sign: KD8OXE
Gregg C Anderson
1555 S Westwood Cir
Ishpeming MI 49849

Call Sign: WB8BIL
Gregg C Anderson
1555 S Westwood Cir
Ishpeming MI 49849

Call Sign: N8NHJ
Angela L Mason Epper
1665 S Westwood Cir
Ishpeming MI 49849

Call Sign: W8JXJ
Viola M Lehtinen
200 Saginaw Dr
Ishpeming MI
498493003

Call Sign: KA8AFW
Tommy J Harvala
1710 Southwood Dr
Ishpeming MI 49849

Call Sign: KD8EM
Richard S Harvala
1710 Southwood Dr
Ishpeming MI 49849

Call Sign: N8PUM
Brandon T Anderson
1935 Southwood Dr
Ishpeming MI 49849

Call Sign: W8AFD
John A Williams
250 Steel St
Ishpeming MI 49849

Call Sign: KB8VYN
Chad D Vuorinen
315 Stoneville Rd
Ishpeming MI 49849

Call Sign: WD8PAJ
Laurence B Dube
380 Stoneville Rd
Ishpeming MI 49849

Call Sign: KC8ABS
Scott W Patrick
575 Stoneville Rd
Ishpeming MI 49849

Call Sign: KD0LJE
Stephen J Hansen
1080 Suncliff Dr
Ishpeming MI 49849

Call Sign: KC8HXZ
Daniel J Filbrandt
60 Sunny Side Est
Ishpeming MI 49849

Call Sign: KC8NIC
Robert A Uren
62 Sunnyside Estates

Ishpeming MI
498493029

Call Sign: N8YCB
Gregory S Self
122 W Barnum St
Ishpeming MI 49849

Call Sign: N8QHI
Stuart A Skauge Jr
416 W Empire St
Ishpeming MI 49849

Call Sign: N8SLH
Charles W Waters
426 W Empire St
Ishpeming MI
498491404

Call Sign: KB8VEQ
Wendy L Rautio
814 Wabash St
Ishpeming MI 49849

Call Sign: KD8BPB
Michael R Rautio
814 Wabash St
Ishpeming MI 49849

Call Sign: KD8OIQ
Todd S Noordyk
109 Zorza Dr
Ishpeming MI 49849

Call Sign: KA8WHO
Alger L Blau
Ishpeming MI 49849

Call Sign: KB8EZS
Bruce A Collick
Ishpeming MI 49849

Call Sign: KB8EZT
Michele J Collick
Ishpeming MI 49849

Call Sign: KC8ONC
Robert J Saxwold
Ishpeming MI 49849

Call Sign: KC8TIM
Joseph R Rose
Ishpeming MI 49849

Call Sign: KD8IYJ
Thaddeus C Ward
7522 21st Ave
Jenison MI 49428

Call Sign: KC8WTI
Carri L Dykstra
7407 22nd Ave
Jenison MI 49428

Call Sign: N8LRA
Robert K Schober
7502 22nd Ave
Jenison MI 49428

Call Sign: KB8SEW
Graham C Merrill
7407 22nd Ave
Jenison MI 49428

Call Sign: WB8GQG
Harvey J Huberts
7166 23rd Ave
Jenison MI 49428

Call Sign: KC8ZXC
Timothy T Vander
Meer
8168 Amelia Dr
Jenison MI 49428

Call Sign: WO8F
Alan L Bierema
6471 Arthur Ave
Jenison MI 49428

Call Sign: N8RAW
Michael J Kasper
8684 Astro Dr
Jenison MI 49428

Call Sign: KD8LU
Craig S Rockwell
1628 Baldwin St
Jenison MI 49428

Call Sign: KD8EQI
William R Shea
2557 Baldwin St
Jenison MI 49428

Call Sign: W1HBZ
Gale R Ecenbarger
725 Baldwin St Apt
3030
Jenison MI 49428

Call Sign: KH6IKH
Anthony L Lillo
725 Baldwin St Apt
D23
Jenison MI 494287945

Call Sign: WD8IZS
Daniel E Betz
6909 Belhurst
Jenison MI 49428

Call Sign: N8UMM
Kyle J Maxim
7421 Belvue Ln
Jenison MI 49428

Call Sign: KA8FCH
John G Smeda
7523 Belvue Ln
Jenison MI 49428

Call Sign: KC8KRM
Michael S Hansen
7991 Birchwood
Jenison MI 49428

Call Sign: N8LKZ
Kenneth F Linscott
8355 Birchwood
Jenison MI 49428

Call Sign: KC4VEF
Timothy A Losch
1587 Broadview
Jenison MI 494288507

Call Sign: WD8SEZ
John C Bry III
1734 Broadview
Jenison MI 49428

Call Sign: W8QAX
Lester J Wallinga
2741 Cedar Grove N
Jenison MI 49428

Call Sign: KC8PIM
Roger D Conley

8833 Cedar Lake Dr
Jenison MI 49428

Call Sign: KC8KQ
Bruce A Withrow
9066 Cedarview Ave
Jenison MI 49428

Call Sign: W2SDL
Richard A Cade
7570 Cherry Ave
Jenison MI 49428

Call Sign: KB8UYM
Paul K Smith
6635 Cherrywood St
SW
Jenison MI 494289223

Call Sign: KB8VEH
Nancy J Smith
6635 Cherrywood St
SW
Jenison MI 494289223

Call Sign: KG8BK
Lionel M Owen
7685 Chickadee SW
Jenison MI 49428

Call Sign: KB8EIZ
Kathy G Burmeister
1066 Coral
Jenison MI 49428

Call Sign: KC8DNP
Loc V Nguyen
1618 Cotton Dr
Jenison MI 49428

Call Sign: AH2AV
Roger C Van Haitsma
7471 Eastlane Ave
Jenison MI 49428

Call Sign: N9ZSW
Ronald D James
7023 Eastwood Ave
Jenison MI 49428

Call Sign: KD8BGK
Tami M James
7023 Eastwood Ave
Jenison MI 49428

Call Sign: N8SAJ
Philip J Van Zalen
7304 Edgewood Ave
Jenison MI 49428

Call Sign: N8SAL
Brenda J Van Zalen
7304 Edgewood Ave
Jenison MI 49428

Call Sign: KC8QDD
Kim A Lobert
2649 Fairbrook Dr
Jenison MI 494288718

Call Sign: N8KAL
Kim A Lobert
2649 Fairbrook Dr
Jenison MI 494288718

Call Sign: KI8HR
Alan R Van Oort
7749 Fairlawn Ave
Jenison MI 49428

Call Sign: WD8JTO
Spencer A Angers
3000 Fillmore St
Jenison MI 49428

Call Sign: WD8BZN
Martin Buikema Jr
7366 Glendora
Jenison MI 49428

Call Sign: KG8WO
Frederick S Otto
7502 Glendora Ave
Jenison MI 49428

Call Sign: KD8LPA
Andrew Leffler
6841 Glenview Ave
Jenison MI 49428

Call Sign: KD8OMJ
Richard G Leffler
6841 Glenview Ave
Jenison MI 49428

Call Sign: WD8PUP
Marvin G Kloostra
871 Glenwood

Jenison MI 49428

Call Sign: KB8UFK
Mark J Nickerson
7408 Green Tree Dr
Jenison MI 49428

Call Sign: KC8UUQ
Matthew T Young
8038 Grove Dr
Jenison MI 49428

Call Sign: KC8PQH
Brent N South
2815 Hagerview Ct
Jenison MI 49428

Call Sign: K8BNS
Brent N South
2815 Hagerview Ct
Jenison MI 49428

Call Sign: KD8BCU
Joseph A Jones
7323 Harmon Ln
Jenison MI 494288716

Call Sign: N8DMO
Richard Carter
8259 Hearthway
Jenison MI 49428

Call Sign: N8EZG
Shirley V Carter
8259 Hearthway
Jenison MI 49428

Call Sign: N8COS
Christian J Hagen
7734 Hickory
Jenison MI 49428

Call Sign: KI8GT
Paul J Longoria I
1789 Jason Ct
Jenison MI 49428

Call Sign: KD8NFB
Terence R Mahone
7767 Lamplight Dr
Jenison MI 49428

Call Sign: W8IMA
Richard J Corey

7652 Lilac Dr
Jenison MI 49428

Call Sign: N8WKP
Mark A Dannenberg
1940 Mulberry Ln
Jenison MI 49428

Call Sign: KD8LLK
Steven J Meines
1664 Oakbrook
Jenison MI 49428

Call Sign: KD8QHR
Kenneth J Meines
1664 Oakbrook Dr
Jenison MI 49428

Call Sign: KB8MZR
Lawrence V Ambruz
2288 Olde Farm Dr
Jenison MI 49428

Call Sign: KA8PNA
Leonard D Roe
6539 Orchid Dr
Jenison MI 49428

Call Sign: N8ROM
Jacob C Mol Jr
7638 Park Ridge Dr
Jenison MI 49428

Call Sign: KC8DHO
Matthew J Mol
7638 Parkridge Dr
Jenison MI 49428

Call Sign: KC8TZJ
Samuel J Mol
7638 Parkridge Dr
Jenison MI 49428

Call Sign: N8CPU
Brian T Deuby
2665 Parkside Dr
Jenison MI 49428

Call Sign: W8UND
Brian T Deuby
2665 Parkside Dr
Jenison MI 49428

Call Sign: KD8OQE

Chris A Beauchene
1903 Parkwood
Jenison MI 49429

Call Sign: KC8CEK
Jacob C Mol III
7394 Pinegrove Dr
Jenison MI 49428

Call Sign: KB8MBD
David J McKenzie Sr
2467 Pinewood
Jenison MI 49428

Call Sign: WD8PAP
Larry A De Blaay
7796 Ridgewood Dr
Jenison MI 49428

Call Sign: KD8PZJ
Brian S Deblaay
7796 Ridgewood Dr
Jenison MI 49428

Call Sign: N8NIF
Richard K Seeley
1549 Rosewood Ave
Jenison MI 49428

Call Sign: N8NKE
Michael D Mazure
2339 Rosewood Ave
Jenison MI 49428

Call Sign: KB8PDD
Philip C McMillen
2694 Rosewood Ave
Jenison MI 49428

Call Sign: KE6ZVL
Gary L Goudzwaard
1656 Rosewood St
Jenison MI 49428

Call Sign: WD8JMA
John Huizinga
7050 S Wood
Jenison MI 49428

Call Sign: N8RMJ
John L Haralson
7665 Sally Dr
Jenison MI 49428

Call Sign: WB8STQ
Donald L Upp
7335 Shadbleau Dr
Jenison MI 49428

Call Sign: K8DMR
Ronald J Fredricks
8900 Stonepoint Ct
Jenison MI 49428

Call Sign: N8EHN
Roger G See
615 Summerset Dr
Jenison MI 494287938

Call Sign: N8LVG
Ronald L Bell
7053 Sunset Dr
Jenison MI 49428

Call Sign: KB8ILC
Craig W Christian
7423 Terrace Ln
Jenison MI 49428

Call Sign: N8CUF
Dennis C Christian
7423 Terrace Ln
Jenison MI 49428

Call Sign: N8EZL
Mary L Christian
7423 Terrace Ln
Jenison MI 49428

Call Sign: K8CXI
Ronald E Holkeboer
8575 Thornbrook Dr
Jenison MI 49428

Call Sign: N8HNN
Ronald F Yaw
2213 Timberlane
Jenison MI 49428

Call Sign: WB2JRY
Evan A Iacoboni
1912 Tulip Ln
Jenison MI 494287739

Call Sign: KC8BMF
Michael A Huene
1927 Tulip Ln
Jenison MI 49428

Call Sign: KD8LDV
Brian J Brunsting
9132 Victor Ave
Jenison MI 49428

Call Sign: KD8JOU
Rolland C Trowbridge
9132 Victor Ave
Jenison MI 49428

Call Sign: K8PUG
David E Gale
2537 Wagonwheel Dr
Jenison MI 49428

Call Sign: WA8CRV
James M Wieland
7520 Westlane Ave
Jenison MI 49428

Call Sign: N8ARK
Richard R Roberds
7287 Westwood Dr
Jenison MI 49428

Call Sign: W8DAQ
Burton E Jones Jr
7257 Windgate
Jenison MI 49428

Call Sign: KG8BL
Nelson M
Haydamacker
7506 Windgate Dr
Jenison MI 49428

Call Sign: KB0BIJ
Paul E Gansberger
6521 Wrenwood
Jenison MI 49428

Call Sign: KB8TYH
Ross H Pike
Jenison MI 49429

Call Sign: WA8MQM
John T Myers
Jenison MI 494290485

Call Sign: W8KJU
John T Myers
Jenison MI 494290485

Call Sign: KC8VIT
Douglas M Stewart
6975 Bear Lake Dr
Johannesburg MI
49751

Call Sign: K8VIT
Douglas M Stewart
6975 Bear Lake Dr
Johannesburg MI
49751

Call Sign: KD8POF
Philip R Smith
6606 Crystal Rd
Johannesburg MI
49751

Call Sign: KC8EOW
Debbie L Janisch
7392 Finnegan Rd
Johannesburg MI
49751

Call Sign: KC8WPA
Michael R Burley
1357 Gingell Rd
Johannesburg MI
49751

Call Sign: K8NT
Edward C Talik
1764 M 32
Johannesburg MI
49751

Call Sign: N8QFW
Jeffrey Briley
13938 M 32
Johannesburg MI
497519561

Call Sign: N8PTZ
William Latuszek
10951 M 32 E
Johannesburg MI
49751

Call Sign: KB8GBO
Dawn M Aisthorpe

13722 Sparr Rd
Johannesburg MI
49751

Call Sign: K8DMC
Joseph R Anderson
11047 Sparr Rd
Johannesburg MI
49751

Call Sign: W8LDS
Samuel E Smith
Johannesburg MI
49751

Call Sign: KD8BHN
John J Mclain II
61933 M 40
Jones MI 49061

Call Sign: KD8BHO
Arthur E Forrester
62021 M 40
Jones MI 49061

Call Sign: WB8RLD
Jeanne Guy D Perreau
Jones MI 49061

Call Sign: WD8MGC
Ryan W Cermak
Psc 1 Box 1156
K I Sawyer AFB MI
49843

Call Sign: N8UAK
Steven W McNitt
329 Dart
K I Sawyer AFB MI
49843

Call Sign: KB4BTN
Frank W Stepongzi
507 Invader
K I Sawyer AFB MI
49843

Call Sign: KD8SBZ
Kyle W Lipscomb
39886 22nd St
Kalamazoo MI 49009

Call Sign: WB8RCU
Warren L Haan
1114 4th St
Kalamazoo MI 49001

Call Sign: KB8SOF
Mildred S Jennings
3611 Adams St
Kalamazoo MI 49008

Call Sign: KB8UOJ
Jessica J Velasquez
3611 Adams St
Kalamazoo MI 49008

Call Sign: N8MOU
John P De Winter
2110 Alamo Ave
Kalamazoo MI
490061605

Call Sign: KD8BSB
Michael J Hillard
2421 Applelane Ave
Kalamazoo MI 49008

Call Sign: KD9BG
Dennis J Berkebile
5167 Atwater Ct
Kalamazoo MI 49009

Call Sign: K8VIF
Stanton C Smart
1904 Autumn Crest Ln
Kalamazoo MI 49008

Call Sign: KC8HEV
Ralph F Shibler
525 Axtell Apt 3
Kalamazoo MI 49008

Call Sign: N8JOX
Robert A Woodford II
2907 Bard Ave
Kalamazoo MI 49004

Call Sign: WW8BOB
Robert A Woodford II
2907 Bard Ave
Kalamazoo MI 49004

Call Sign: KD8FZZ
Robert J Norwood
Charlier
3001 Bard Ave
Kalamazoo MI 49008

Call Sign: KC8QFF
Thomas M Oliver
2631 Barkwood Ln
Kalamazoo MI 49004

Call Sign: KD8QNL
Christoph Hartel
7141 Baton Rouge
Kalamazoo MI 49009

Call Sign: N8HQI
John P Phillips II
2951 Belle Chase Blvd
Kalamazoo MI 49009

Call Sign: K9IRO
Paul A Jursinic
5643 Blue Jay Dr
Kalamazoo MI 49009

Call Sign: N8NSW
John A Walker
2658 Bluestone Cir
Kalamazoo MI
490096762

Call Sign: KC8DQ
John W Winkler
3620 Borgess Dr
Kalamazoo MI 49048

Call Sign: KD8EFD
David P Seaman
6025 Briarcliff Path C
Kalamazoo MI 49009

Call Sign: KA8IOK
Harold G Cronk
2837 Briarwood Dr
Kalamazoo MI 49004

Call Sign: N8QWF

Cathy A Krieg
2815 Bronson Blvd
Kalamazoo MI 49008

Call Sign: N8UAC
Lowell B Mason Jr
3621 Bronson Blvd
Kalamazoo MI 49008

Call Sign: N8UXW
Joan A Mason
3621 Bronson Blvd
Kalamazoo MI 49008

Call Sign: W8KMR
Richard A Hunt
1700 Bronson Way
Kalamazoo MI 49009

Call Sign: WA8OWB
Charles N Tanton
1700 Bronson Way
Kalamazoo MI
490091072

Call Sign: W8FGK
Max A Van Den Berg
1700 Bronson Way
266
Kalamazoo MI 49009

Call Sign: KC8FQF
Edward R Sova Jr
2902 Brook Dr
Kalamazoo MI 49004

Call Sign: KK8Q
David H Bradshaw
328 Buchanan Ave
Kalamazoo MI 49001

Call Sign: KC8JGQ
Harold M Boyer
721 Buchanan Ave 1
Kalamazoo MI 49008

Call Sign: KB2UI
La Verne L Hoag
6374 Buckham Wood
Dr
Kalamazoo MI 49009

Call Sign: KB8LH
La Verne L Hoag

6374 Buckham Wood
Dr
Kalamazoo MI 49009

Call Sign: K8TXC
Roy W Chenery Jr
1702 Buena Vista
Kalamazoo MI 49001

Call Sign: AA8DF
Carroll R Seats
1264 Bunker Hill
Kalamazoo MI 49009

Call Sign: KC8MKC
Shawn J Rodrigues
1218 California Ave C
104
Kalamazoo MI 49006

Call Sign: N8IQD
Ted J Brooks Sr
1127 California Rd
Kalamazoo MI 49007

Call Sign: KD8RXO
Kim F Ross
1309 Cambridge Dr
Kalamazoo MI 49001

Call Sign: WA8HBL
Paul J Bede
2815 Cameron St
Kalamazoo MI 49001

Call Sign: N8SHX
Jordon E Laird
436 Campbell Apt 4
Kalamazoo MI 49006

Call Sign: W8VMI
Walter L Fuller
1002 Campbell Ave
Kalamazoo MI
490063082

Call Sign: N8KCR
George Bennett
3324 Canterbury
Kalamazoo MI 49007

Call Sign: WD8MLR
Stanley M Petkus
4710 Canterbury Ave

Kalamazoo MI 49007

Call Sign: KA8BLO
Charles F Burgstahler
6658 Carlisle
Kalamazoo MI 49001

Call Sign: KA8AOB
Jack R Price Jr
1511 Center St
Kalamazoo MI 49001

Call Sign: N8ODT
James L Stewart
814 Central Pl
Kalamazoo MI 49002

Call Sign: KD8IRW
Andrew L Gahan
5076 Century Ave
Kalamazoo MI 49006

Call Sign: KC8MGO
Peter J Van Bruggen
5895 Chandra Dr
Kalamazoo MI
490049100

Call Sign: KD8CIZ
Richard N Boehme
2225 Chevy Chase
Kalamazoo MI 49008

Call Sign: KC8ZYD
Simon J Boehme
2225 Chevy Chase
Kalamazoo MI 49008

Call Sign: KD8FVG
Brian J Stannard
2310 Chevy Chase
Kalamazoo MI 49008

Call Sign: W8TZJ
Carl E Lee
1902 Chevy Chase
Blvd
Kalamazoo MI 49008

Call Sign: KB8RFS
Jonathan L Ryskamp
2231 Chevy Chase
Blvd
Kalamazoo MI 49008

Call Sign: N8VFH
Brett W Robbins
5339 Chickadee
Kalamazoo MI 49002

Call Sign: AI4SJ
Frank A Wood
2611 Cimarron
Kalamazoo MI 49004

Call Sign: KC8OUZ
Lois E Wood
2611 Cimarron Dr
Kalamazoo MI 49004

Call Sign: N8FAW
Frank A Wood
2611 Cimarron Dr
Kalamazoo MI 49004

Call Sign: N8LEW
Lois E Wood
2611 Cimarron Dr
Kalamazoo MI 49004

Call Sign: WB8YZH
Raymond M Clark
3914 Clarnin St
Kalamazoo MI 49004

Call Sign: KD8PCI
Charles S Crane
3914 Clarnin St
Kalamazoo MI 49004

Call Sign: AC8IG
Charles S Crane
3914 Clarnin St
Kalamazoo MI 49004

Call Sign: KC8DEJ
John M Clark
3914 Clarnin St
Kalamazoo MI
490041723

Call Sign: KB8CHG
Brian P Bell
3321 Claxton St
Kalamazoo MI 49001

Call Sign: KC8OFR
Zachary M Lassiter

4707 Claybourne Dr
Kalamazoo MI 49009

Call Sign: AA8WN
Richard A Weirick Jr
1022 Claymoor Dr Apt
1D
Kalamazoo MI 49009

Call Sign: KC8FWX
Kathryn L Weirick
1022 Claymoor Dr Apt
1D
Kalamazoo MI 49009

Call Sign: KB8VKQ
Eva M Raifsnider
516 Clinton Ave
Kalamazoo MI 49001

Call Sign: KC8GQH
Eric R Raifsnider
516 Clinton Ave
Kalamazoo MI 49001

Call Sign: KC8GQI
Erron W Raifsnider
516 Clinton Ave
Kalamazoo MI 49001

Call Sign: KD8PCJ
Michael C Mendez
910 Clinton Ave
Kalamazoo MI 49001

Call Sign: KD8GYG
Gundars Elksnis
404 Clubview Dr
Kalamazoo MI 49009

Call Sign: WX8ZAC
Zachary M Lassiter
1912 Colgrove Ave
Apt 212
Kalamazoo MI 49048

Call Sign: KA8VAF
Janice F Blackmun
601 Collette St
Kalamazoo MI 49001

Call Sign: KC8TZI
Scott D Perin
5403 Collingwood Ave

Kalamazoo MI 49004

Call Sign: KD8BYG
Chris J Hansen
1308 Concord Pl 2C
Kalamazoo MI 49009

Call Sign: KD8EQH
Jeremy N Hall
1510 Concord Pl Dr
Apt 2C
Kalamazoo MI 49009

Call Sign: KB8OBF
Matt E Schley
428 Coolidge
Kalamazoo MI 49006

Call Sign: N8UEZ
William R Schley Jr
428 Coolidge
Kalamazoo MI 49006

Call Sign: KC8NTN
Leeann A Heinert
1495 Coolidge Ave
Kalamazoo MI 49006

Call Sign: KC8NTO
William L Heinert
1495 Coolidge Ave
Kalamazoo MI 49006

Call Sign: KI8HF
James R Gardner
620 Coolidge Ave
Kalamazoo MI 49006

Call Sign: KD8KUO
Gregory L Farrer Jr
2348 Crane Ave
Kalamazoo MI 49001

Call Sign: KC8PNB
Allan L Lapekas
6411 Crestwood
Kalamazoo MI 49004

Call Sign: KG8V
Earl L Clason
1112 Crown St
Kalamazoo MI 49006

Call Sign: KD8LLG

Joshua D Homet
5200 Croyden Ave
9202
Kalamazoo MI 49009

Call Sign: WA8SWV
Sylvester D Randall
2232 Cumberland
Kalamazoo MI
490061375

Call Sign: KD4ZLT
Kathleen A Anlage
6789 Cypress Bay Dr
Kalamazoo MI 49009

Call Sign: KB8JBI
Thomas F Smith
729 Darby Ln
Kalamazoo MI 49007

Call Sign: N8EEB
Herman C Brown
5725 De Ave E
Kalamazoo MI 49004

Call Sign: WD8AIB
David W Elliott
5148 Deep Point Dr
Kalamazoo MI 49002

Call Sign: KC8VHS
Alice L Bodnar
1107 Denway Dr
Kalamazoo MI 49008

Call Sign: KC8VHT
Paul Bodnar
1107 Denway Dr
Kalamazoo MI 49008

Call Sign: AB8QK
Paul Bodnar
1107 Denway Dr
Kalamazoo MI 49008

Call Sign: K8BLO
Charles F Burgstahler
1103 Denway Dr
Kalamazoo MI 49008

Call Sign: KA8OSV
Michael B Atkins
3311 Donnegal Ave

Kalamazoo MI 49007

Call Sign: KC8VPG
Blake W Naftel
1229 Douglas Apt B
Kalamazoo MI 49007

Call Sign: WB8CFV
Douglas G Burke
8550 Douglas Ave
Kalamazoo MI 49007

Call Sign: N8URO
Monica M Marlett
227 Douglas Ave 2
Kalamazoo MI 49007

Call Sign: N8QEP
Joseph S West
227 Douglas Ave Apt
2
Kalamazoo MI 49007

Call Sign: N8KVK
James H Egerton
1004 Douglas Ave Apt
610
Kalamazoo MI 49007

Call Sign: KD8LVM
Thomas C Sivak
4620 Dover Hills Dr
303
Kalamazoo MI 49009

Call Sign: WD8NSJ
Hazel J Tiefenthal
3020 Duke St
Kalamazoo MI 49008

Call Sign: WA8GTG
Lew L Graham
1821 E Cork
Kalamazoo MI 49001

Call Sign: KB8RFQ
Tony B Johnson
1710 E Cork St Apt 3C
Kalamazoo MI 49001

Call Sign: KC8BUB
Chris C Ronfeldt
4422 E D Ave

Kalamazoo MI
490049612

Call Sign: KC8HHU
Bruce P Ives
254 E D Ave 33
Kalamazoo MI 49004

Call Sign: N8XCP
Frank N Guarisco
5043 E De Ave
Kalamazoo MI 49004

Call Sign: N8SRS
Carl G Bryant
6080 E F Ave
Kalamazoo MI 49004

Call Sign: N8WDW
Wade A Bryant
6080 E F Ave
Kalamazoo MI 49004

Call Sign: KD8RSJ
Todd A Braysher
3416 E G Ave
Kalamazoo MI 49004

Call Sign: N8KYU
Daniel D Stersic
5670 E H Ave
Kalamazoo MI 49001

Call Sign: KB8QJH
Garry R Blaskie
6500 E H Ave
Kalamazoo MI 49036

Call Sign: N8VDK
Glenn A Wegner
6569 E H Ave
Kalamazoo MI 49048

Call Sign: N8QQG
Joseph M Lalleman
5285 E H Ave Apt 214
Kalamazoo MI
490011191

Call Sign: KC8RGC
Jerry K Turben
5740 E L Ave
Kalamazoo MI 49048

Call Sign: WD8KWK
Larry M Meyer
3308 E Main Ave
Kalamazoo MI
490012287

Call Sign: K8DLJ
Frank G Rector
7204 E Michigan Ave
Kalamazoo MI 49001

Call Sign: N8SHW
Scott A Baldwin
1072 E Mosel
Kalamazoo MI 49004

Call Sign: K8OAD
Richard E Smith Sr
5259 E P Ave
Kalamazoo MI 49001

Call Sign: N8ZSJ
William D Van Lester
210 E Prouty St
Kalamazoo MI 49007

Call Sign: KC8RCK
Rick J Baker
471 E Stockbridge
Kalamazoo MI 49001

Call Sign: N8DWE
Marion J Sheen
813 E Walnut
Kalamazoo MI 49001

Call Sign: KC8KRQ
John K Bolt
105 E Walnut St Apt
3211
Kalamazoo MI
490075255

Call Sign: KC8KRN
Shelley M Seifer
105 E Walnut St Apt
3406
Kalamazoo MI
490076105

Call Sign: KD8RCE
Carl L Scamp
3394 E Wembley Ln
Kalamazoo MI 49009

Call Sign: W8OXQ
H Douglas Lewis
3624 E Wembley Ln
Kalamazoo MI 49009

Call Sign: KG8UI
Thomas R Gillentine
6190 Eagle Ridge Dr
Kalamazoo MI 49004

Call Sign: AA8PI
Donald F Mac Phee
8251 Earl Ct
Kalamazoo MI 49009

Call Sign: N8ISX
Ronald P Austin Sr
2105 Eckner Dr
Kalamazoo MI 49002

Call Sign: K0NS
Romolo H Russo
1230 Edgemoor
Kalamazoo MI 49008

Call Sign: KD8ODQ
Robert H Emerson
222 Edgemoor Ave
Kalamazoo MI 49001

Call Sign: KD8DFZ
Michael J Newberger
741 Edison St
Kalamazoo MI 49004

Call Sign: KC8DXH
Richard A Nivala
9391 El Dorado Ave
Kalamazoo MI
490096720

Call Sign: K8BKB
Gary F Franklin
1010 Eldridge Dr
Kalamazoo MI 49006

Call Sign: KC8BKN
WMU ARC
Electrical & Computer
Eng Wmu
Kalamazoo MI 49008

Call Sign: WA8YOX

William Meyer
1438 Elkerton Ave
Kalamazoo MI 49001

Call Sign: KD8RMU
Thomas E Foor
2902 Emerald Dr
Kalamazoo MI 49001

Call Sign: W8HJL
James A Milvert
1517 Fairbanks Ct
Kalamazoo MI 49001

Call Sign: N8RKG
Schuyler T Barnum
2246 Fairfield Ave
Kalamazoo MI 49004

Call Sign: W8JCY
Allen R Lewis
6070 Far Hills Way
Kalamazoo MI 49009

Call Sign: W8TXY
Howard K McCoy
3804 Ferndale Ave
Kalamazoo MI 49001

Call Sign: K8JCS
John C Schneider
32184 Fish Hatchery
Rd
Kalamazoo MI 49009

Call Sign: KD8LZ
James M Hastings
4641 Fountain Sq Dr
Kalamazoo MI
490099542

Call Sign: KB8LVC
Robert K Krieg
4931 Fountain Sq Dr
Kalamazoo MI 49009

Call Sign: KD8AFD
Daniel J Swodzinski
2420 Frederick Ave
Kalamazoo MI 49008

Call Sign: N5TRF
Martin B Draznin
5476 Gatwick Ct

Kalamazoo MI 49009

Call Sign: WA8LSY
Ronald A Kent
708 Gayle Ave
Kalamazoo MI 49048

Call Sign: WD8BWB
Randall W Stewart
1907 Glendale Blvd
Kalamazoo MI 49004

Call Sign: N8VLS
Stanley C Macey
2217 Glendale Blvd
Kalamazoo MI 49004

Call Sign: KC8OQO
Jerald P Conroy
2415 Glendale Blvd
Kalamazoo MI 49004

Call Sign: KD8RMD
Gary K Thompson
1713 Golfview Ave
Kalamazoo MI 49001

Call Sign: KD8NPV
Jeffrey R Romence
1226 Grand Pre Ave
Kalamazoo MI 49006

Call Sign: WB8ZZV
James L Pyle
4216 Gray St
Kalamazoo MI 49002

Call Sign: KB8CSH
William E Robinson
5100 Green Meadow
Kalamazoo MI 49001

Call Sign: N8ITS
Steven R Heystek
5134 Green Meadow
Kalamazoo MI 49009

Call Sign: W8DM
Edward Van Peenen
5210 Green Meadow
Dr
Kalamazoo MI 49009

Call Sign: W8HMK

James T Welch
5270 Green Meadow
Dr
Kalamazoo MI 49009

Call Sign: W8YIA
John W Nelson
1921 Greenlawn Ave
Kalamazoo MI
490064324

Call Sign: KD8BYJ
Brian C Ferrell
3721 Greenleaf Cir
Apt 107
Kalamazoo MI 49008

Call Sign: WD8AWQ
Dennis R Fleck
1804 Greenview
Kalamazoo MI 49002

Call Sign: KD8LHC
Matthew W Mason
1400 Greenwood Ave
7
Kalamazoo MI 49006

Call Sign: KD8ONH
Katie E French
5548 Gull Prairie Way
Kalamazoo MI 49048

Call Sign: KD8AMH
Axel J Anderson
740 Hawley St
Kalamazoo MI 49007

Call Sign: KD8PXR
Eric W Wolfe
130 Haymac Dr
Kalamazoo MI 49004

Call Sign: WA8ZEW
Kent A Spencer
911 Hays Pk
Kalamazoo MI 49001

Call Sign: KC8GPM
Amir R Khillah
3025 Heatherdowns Ln
Kalamazoo MI 49001

Call Sign: KC8WMO

Kenneth J Hawley
1429 Henderson Dr
Kalamazoo MI 49006

Call Sign: WA8HDR
David C Doubleday
1709 Henley Ave
Kalamazoo MI 49002

Call Sign: KD8KRV
Noah Klugman
661 Hicks Center
Kalamazoo MI 49006

Call Sign: KB8UPT
Daniel R Wilson
1498 Highland Hills
Dr
Kalamazoo MI 49007

Call Sign: KC8IUP
Glenn E Noonan
1722 Hillshire Dr
Kalamazoo MI 49008

Call Sign: N8XLZ
Curtis T Simmons
1216 Homecrest Ave
Kalamazoo MI 49001

Call Sign: N8YNX
Patricia A Simmons
1216 Homecrest Ave
Kalamazoo MI 49001

Call Sign: WA8WXZ
Robert A Hoffman
1818 Homecrest Ave
Kalamazoo MI 49001

Call Sign: KB8OGK
Brian G Phipps
1940 Howard 422
Kalamazoo MI 49008

Call Sign: KC8JEJ
Mark J Holloway
161 Hughes St
Kalamazoo MI 49001

Call Sign: WB8EKU
Robert F Struble
2915 Hunters Pl
Kalamazoo MI 49048

Call Sign: KC8KTP
Christopher S Collins
168 Imperial St
Kalamazoo MI 49001

Call Sign: KB8JDQ
Todd E Martin
810 Ira Ave
Kalamazoo MI 49048

Call Sign: WA8REM
Carl L Motter
831 Ira St
Kalamazoo MI 49001

Call Sign: K8RQU
Judy J Deroo
3311 Iroquois Trl
Kalamazoo MI
490062030

Call Sign: W8KZO
Michael J Campbell
1602 Jefferson Ave
Kalamazoo MI
490063136

Call Sign: N8UFA
Marion D Webster
715 Jenks Blvd
Kalamazoo MI 49006

Call Sign: KB8KBV
Harris D Webster
715 Jenks Blvd
Kalamazoo MI 49007

Call Sign: KC8AAF
John R Felcyn
4302 Jody Ln
Kalamazoo MI 49007

Call Sign: KD8QHM
Samantha L Turner
3541 Kenbrooke Ct
Kalamazoo MI 49006

Call Sign: N8YRV
Richard C Wenban
5178 Kitz Way
Kalamazoo MI 49009

Call Sign: WD8BWP

Bruce V Colson
530 La Salle
Kalamazoo MI 49002

Call Sign: KD8HQZ
Pramod Mallipaddi
4024 Lake Crest Cir
1B
Kalamazoo MI 49048

Call Sign: KB0OM
David S Roe
4020 Lake Crest Cir
Apt 3B
Kalamazoo MI 49048

Call Sign: KD8BYF
Eric D Jennings
430 Lake Forest Blvd
Kalamazoo MI 49006

Call Sign: KD8PXU
Patrick D Hug
438 Lake Forest Blvd
Kalamazoo MI 49006

Call Sign: KB8TVI
Shigeru Toda
4307 Lake Forest Dr
Kalamazoo MI 49008

Call Sign: KD8ODV
Greg Kolich
1218 Lake St
Kalamazoo MI 49001

Call Sign: KA8RUA
Kenneth G Losey
2825 Lake St
Kalamazoo MI 49048

Call Sign: KB8SVJ
Robert J Barrons
3324 Lake St
Kalamazoo MI 49001

Call Sign: WC8AAJ
Kalamazoo County
Races
4414 Lakeforest
Kalamazoo MI 49008

Call Sign: W8JAA
Robert W Rogers

1921 Lakeway
Kalamazoo MI 49001

Call Sign: KG8KX
Steven F Jennings
4853 Landing Way Dr
Kalamazoo MI 49048

Call Sign: KC8FZY
Brian S Perkins
5166 Lands End Dr
Kalamazoo MI 49009

Call Sign: KC8DWR
Anna C Kamphaus
5849 Larkwood Ct Apt
1B
Kalamazoo MI 49048

Call Sign: WB8IRU
Robert J Laylon
1317 Lay Blvd
Kalamazoo MI 49001

Call Sign: W8NWW
Elmer C Sanborn
7031 Leawood St
Kalamazoo MI 49002

Call Sign: WA8JQV
Rick L Hayner
4410A Lilac Ln Apt
144
Kalamazoo MI 49006

Call Sign: KC8WLE
John E Corey
3412 Lincolnshire
Blvd
Kalamazoo MI 49001

Call Sign: N8IYF
Alan A Halpern
1400 Low Rd
Kalamazoo MI 49008

Call Sign: KC8RGB
Cynthia A Verhage
3518 Madison
Kalamazoo MI
490082619

Call Sign: N4NQH
Theodore J Haveman

3612 Madison
Kalamazoo MI 49008

Call Sign: KD8AGQ
Ronald D Kaul
3412 Madison St
Kalamazoo MI 49008

Call Sign: KC8OQM
Donald L Verhage
3518 Madison St
Kalamazoo MI
490082619

Call Sign: KB8UBA
Roy V Zimmer
1343 Manor Dr
Kalamazoo MI 49006

Call Sign: WB8DSR
Norman C Miller
1326 Manor St
Kalamazoo MI 49006

Call Sign: N8RZY
Lisa C Wilder
2730 McKinley Ave
Kalamazoo MI 49004

Call Sign: KC8DEF
Robert E Tindle
3046 McKinley Ave
Kalamazoo MI 49004

Call Sign: KA8AOC
Edwin M Curry
4114 Mead St
Kalamazoo MI 49004

Call Sign: N3TFM
Todd A Putman
3150 Meadowcroft Ln
Kalamazoo MI 49004

Call Sign: WD8OAR
James R Smith
6326 Medford Way
Kalamazoo MI 49009

Call Sign: KB8QGF
Andrew C Robins
1529 Miles Ave
Kalamazoo MI 49001

Call Sign: KC8RYA
Dorothy M Robins
1529 Miles Ave
Kalamazoo MI 49001

Call Sign: KC8MMS
Fred De Vries
816 Miller Rd
Kalamazoo MI
490014312

Call Sign: AC8ED
Fred De Vries
816 Miller Rd
Kalamazoo MI
490014312

Call Sign: KB8JQK
Kerry S Kupka
1210 Miller Rd
Kalamazoo MI 49001

Call Sign: KD8RCJ
George Davidson III
156 Monroe St
Kalamazoo MI 49006

Call Sign: K6WRD
George W Davidson
III
156 Monroe St
Kalamazoo MI 49006

Call Sign: KD8RLI
Daniel L Selvidge
608 Montrose Ave
Kalamazoo MI 49008

Call Sign: KB8UPW
Joseph F Hurlbert
2913 Morgan
Kalamazoo MI 49001

Call Sign: KA8TGN
William D Moerdyk
3018 Morgan St
Kalamazoo MI 49001

Call Sign: KE8AK
Terril E Jarvis
6634 Morningstar
Kalamazoo MI 49009

Call Sign: WB8WGG

Richard M Bergells
5571 Mt Olivet
Kalamazoo MI 49004

Call Sign: KC8PQX
Clifford E Bodine Jr
2934 Mt Olivet Rd
Kalamazoo MI 49004

Call Sign: KC8ZNG
Jeremy S Sanderson
411 Myrtle St
Kalamazoo MI 49007

Call Sign: WA9ZMO
Robert E A Adams
6354 N 12th St
Kalamazoo MI 49009

Call Sign: W8DAB
Dennis A Boersema
7820 N 14th St
Kalamazoo MI 49009

Call Sign: K8WPI
James R Buchanan
9549 N 17th St
Kalamazoo MI 49004

Call Sign: KB8GUW
Ronnie D Bickings
5867 N 20th
Kalamazoo MI 49004

Call Sign: N3YPA
Charles M Long
6117 N 24th St
Kalamazoo MI 49004

Call Sign: KC8ZAM
Ben C Pinkowski
8721 N 24th St
Kalamazoo MI 49004

Call Sign: KB8GUV
Doris L Bell
156 N 28th Apt 3
Kalamazoo MI 49001

Call Sign: K8DNP
David N Pomeroy
921 N 2nd St
Kalamazoo MI 49009

Call Sign: KB8ZDA
Cayce L Wilcox York
5115 N 2nd St
Kalamazoo MI 49009

Call Sign: WB8YOF
Gregory W York
5115 N 2nd St
Kalamazoo MI 49009

Call Sign: KF8DX
Thomas N Weller
6293 N 2nd St
Kalamazoo MI 49009

Call Sign: KC8WOE
Debora J Weller
6293 N 2nd St
Kalamazoo MI 49009

Call Sign: N9ULD
Donald R Johnson
1767 N 3rd St
Kalamazoo MI
490098591

Call Sign: KC8CIC
Edwin L Allen
2690 N 3rd St
Kalamazoo MI 49009

Call Sign: KN8N
Larry A Boekeloo
2985 N 3rd St
Kalamazoo MI 49009

Call Sign: WB8VWW
James L Butcher
3146 N 5th St
Kalamazoo MI 49009

Call Sign: N8IYQ
Dennis E King
2422 N 5th St
Kalamazoo MI
490098510

Call Sign: W8BGZ
Merrill T See
5651 N 8th St
Kalamazoo MI 49009

Call Sign: KC8SDS
Harry W Hahn III

2069 N 9th St
Kalamazoo MI 49009

Call Sign: KC8PLJ
Wayne K Wood
1623 N Burdick St
Kalamazoo MI 49007

Call Sign: N8SHO
James H Teeters
448 N Burdick St 43
Kalamazoo MI 49007

Call Sign: KE8N
Joe A Jackson
132 N Clarendon St
Kalamazoo MI 49007

Call Sign: W8DO
David M Clark
167 N Crooked Lake
Dr
Kalamazoo MI 49009

Call Sign: N8EYD
Leighton C Brown
610 N Dartmouth St
Kalamazoo MI 49007

Call Sign: KC8LF
Paul W Bartholomew
1400 N Drake 314
Kalamazoo MI
490061970

Call Sign: WD9AHV
Kathryn G Mohney
3520C N Drake Apt
117
Kalamazoo MI 49007

Call Sign: W8DUA
James A Mac Gregor
710 N Fletcher Ave
Kalamazoo MI
490063303

Call Sign: WB8BMM
Warren H Fritz
2516 N Hills Ct W
Kalamazoo MI 49007

Call Sign: AB8DQ
William B Franklin

9222 N Riverview Dr
Kalamazoo MI 49004

Call Sign: KC8ECZ
Shirley M Tinney
1525 Nassau
Kalamazoo MI 49001

Call Sign: KD8LR
Robert H Tinney
1525 Nassau
Kalamazoo MI 49001

Call Sign: K8LR
Robert H Tinney
1525 Nassau St
Kalamazoo MI
490481487

Call Sign: N8URK
Charles D Wegner
1319 Nazareth Rd
Kalamazoo MI 49001

Call Sign: K8JON
Jon G Blackburn
1320 Nazareth Rd
Kalamazoo MI 49001

Call Sign: K8MPH
James T Oliver
2038 Nazareth Rd
Kalamazoo MI 49001

Call Sign: WB8ZXL
Kirk G Hart
3722 New Farm St
Kalamazoo MI 49048

Call Sign: WA8CDU
William C Robbins
6960 Northstar Dr
Kalamazoo MI 49009

Call Sign: KD8RCI
Scott J Lemmer
713 Norton Dr
Kalamazoo MI 49001

Call Sign: N9DSW
David S Weir
2622 Oakland Dr
Kalamazoo MI 49008

Call Sign: K8DSW
David S Weir
2622 Oakland Dr
Kalamazoo MI 49008

Call Sign: WD8CCX
Arlene J Colson
7331 Oakland Dr
Kalamazoo MI 49002

Call Sign: KD8IJK
Timothy R Tindall
6205 Oatman Dr
Kalamazoo MI 49004

Call Sign: KC8SZL
Alex E Turton
5331 Old Douglas
Kalamazoo MI
490095423

Call Sign: KI6NE
Loren D Carlson
3812 Old Field Pl
Kalamazoo MI 49008

Call Sign: W8QPB
Thomas L Baden
6151 Old Post Rd
Kalamazoo MI 49009

Call Sign: WA8YLI
Robert F Struble
6480 Ormada
Kalamazoo MI 49004

Call Sign: KC8WLC
James D Mitchell
2513 Outlook St
Kalamazoo MI
490016150

Call Sign: KB8KCO
Robert W Frick
6580 Owen Dr
Kalamazoo MI 49009

Call Sign: KE8LW
Michael R Bell
6936 Owen Dr
Kalamazoo MI 49009

Call Sign: KA8SAX
Robert J Gasperini

1915 Paddington
Kalamazoo MI 49001

Call Sign: K8GAS
Robert J Gasperini
1915 Paddington
Kalamazoo MI 49001

Call Sign: KC8ECY
Kenneth C Thies
2031 Paddington
Kalamazoo MI 49001

Call Sign: KD8BU
John J Rice
2225 Paddington Rd
Kalamazoo MI 49001

Call Sign: KA8RWL
Richard Bass
1524 Palmer Ave
Kalamazoo MI 49001

Call Sign: N8HOP
L Michael Ruzicka
1106 Par 4 Cir
Kalamazoo MI 49008

Call Sign: KA8QML
John E Allgaier Jr
1740 Park Ave
Kalamazoo MI
490041650

Call Sign: W8OAY
Hubert T Schnotala
404 Parker Ave
Kalamazoo MI 49001

Call Sign: KX8J
Martin J Bedecs Jr
614 Parker Ave
Kalamazoo MI 49008

Call Sign: KC8WVY
Megan P Davis
2513 Parkwyn Dr
Kalamazoo MI 49008

Call Sign: N8XWD
Edward J Doris
7648 Paso Fino Ct
Kalamazoo MI 49009

Call Sign: KC8HEI
Bruce E Hutt
6164 Pheasant Ln
Kalamazoo MI
490091886

Call Sign: KC8ZVU
Brian J Craig
2728 Pine Ridge Rd
Kalamazoo MI 49008

Call Sign: N8UXU
Martha Beverly
529 Pinehurst Blvd
Kalamazoo MI 49006

Call Sign: WG8J
Bill Beverly
529 Pinehurst Dr
Kalamazoo MI
490063095

Call Sign: KD8KLT
Benjamin Jackson
610 Pleasent Ave
Kalamazoo MI 49006

Call Sign: KC8BGQ
Timothy C James
3902 Pontiac Ave
Kalamazoo MI
490061928

Call Sign: W8GFK
Joel W Perry
10934 Portage Rd
Kalamazoo MI 49002

Call Sign: WB8BOB
Harry W Spencer
11247 Portage Rd
Kalamazoo MI 49002

Call Sign: W8ZZA
Francis L Morse
2300 Portage St Apt
322
Kalamazoo MI
490016505

Call Sign: KD8PGX
Martin J Spaulding
119 Prairie Ave
Kalamazoo MI 49006

Call Sign: KZ8KZO
Martin J Spaulding
119 Prairie Ave
Kalamazoo MI 49006

Call Sign: N8KBK
Lois Kirks
6393 Queens Way
Kalamazoo MI 49009

Call Sign: N8URM
Carl R Olson
6415 Queens Way
Kalamazoo MI 49009

Call Sign: WA8F
Ivan D Smith
2624 Rambling Rd
Kalamazoo MI 49008

Call Sign: K8IDS
Ivan D Smith
2624 Rambling Rd
Kalamazoo MI 49008

Call Sign: KD8JBH
Justin J Vanorder
4600 Ravine Rd
Kalamazoo MI 49006

Call Sign: KC8AIS
Ronald L Holmes
6319 Ravine Rd
Kalamazoo MI 49009

Call Sign: KC8LHN
Michael J Campbell
1411 Red Maple Ln
Kalamazoo MI
490043315

Call Sign: KB8UBD
Una M Campbell
1616 Reed
Kalamazoo MI
490032883

Call Sign: KD8KBP
Lukasz G Krawczyk
703 Regency Sq Apt
301
Kalamazoo MI 49008

Call Sign: KB8UMS
Julius D Payne
179 Rex
Kalamazoo MI 49001

Call Sign: N8URN
Robert L Mitchell
3813 Rockwood
Kalamazoo MI 49004

Call Sign: NP4C
Luis G Ortiz
4019 Rockwood
Kalamazoo MI 49004

Call Sign: AA8KB
Michael A La Bond
5352 Rocky Mountain
Kalamazoo MI 49009

Call Sign: KY8D
Gan U Starling
224 Rose Pl
Kalamazoo MI
490012617

Call Sign: KB8VGF
Robert R Besser
228 Rose Pl
Kalamazoo MI 49001

Call Sign: KB8YVR
Cheryl A Besser
228 Rose Pl
Kalamazoo MI 49001

Call Sign: N8TPD
Clayton W Robbins
906 Royce Ave
Kalamazoo MI 49001

Call Sign: N8ZSF
William J Vande
Werken
1234 Royce Ave
Kalamazoo MI 49001

Call Sign: KC8EDB
Joel E Triemstra
1607 Royce Ave
Kalamazoo MI 49001

Call Sign: KD8PXW
David W Mcmorrow

2431 Russet Dr
Kalamazoo MI 49008

Call Sign: K8TMD
David W Mcmorrow
2431 Russet Dr
Kalamazoo MI 49008

Call Sign: KC8IDX
Theresa M Gooch
31 S 1st St
Kalamazoo MI 49009

Call Sign: AA8YE
John L Gooch
31 S 1st St
Kalamazoo MI 49009

Call Sign: KC8JSM
David G De Waters
5974 S 1st St
Kalamazoo MI 49009

Call Sign: KC8YJO
Eric V Blough
36295 S 23rd St
Kalamazoo MI 49009

Call Sign: WB8LGO
Cornelius Van De
Biezen Jr
6622 S 25th St
Kalamazoo MI 49001

Call Sign: W8JVP
Kenneth M Irish Jr
2651 S 4th St
Kalamazoo MI 49009

Call Sign: N8TGA
Thomas J Allen
4301 S 5th St
Kalamazoo MI 49001

Call Sign: K8KMI
Casper Hegedus
2583 S 6th St
Kalamazoo MI 49009

Call Sign: N8WVH
Scott J Davis
3001 S 6th St
Kalamazoo MI 49009

Call Sign: KB8QXJ
Wallace C De Forest
7475 S 6th St
Kalamazoo MI 49009

Call Sign: KK9Q
Michael J Wendland
1903 S 8th St
Kalamazoo MI 49009

Call Sign: W8RTY
George N Harvey
2997 S 8th St
Kalamazoo MI 49009

Call Sign: KA8SSZ
Alfred J Hettinga
8962 S 8th St
Kalamazoo MI 49009

Call Sign: KB8DHJ
Robert C McKnight
2253 S 9th St
Kalamazoo MI 49009

Call Sign: KC8PLK
Craig L Rosenbloom
145 S Berkley
Kalamazoo MI
490064312

Call Sign: KB8UIN
John R Howard
712 S Burdick Apt 1
Kalamazoo MI 49007

Call Sign: KC8ANH
Richard W Darling
1539 S Crooked Lake
Dr
Kalamazoo MI
490099798

Call Sign: KC8EFT
Wendy L Holforty
4090 S Deadwood Dr
Kalamazoo MI 49002

Call Sign: WJ8L
Philip J Schmitt
800 S Kendall Ave
Kalamazoo MI 49007

Call Sign: W8WMU

Philip J Schmitt
800 S Kendall Ave
Kalamazoo MI 49007

Call Sign: WJ8L
Philip J Schmitt
800 S Kendall Ave
Kalamazoo MI 49007

Call Sign: KD8CJB
James L Stewart
922 S Park Apt 1 S
Kalamazoo MI 49001

Call Sign: KB8BXY
Curtis J Harding
1143 S Park Ave
Kalamazoo MI 49001

Call Sign: N8DRA
Chauncey H Scarlett
4033 S Rose St Apt
202
Kalamazoo MI 49001

Call Sign: N8ZFW
Michael V Baber
820 S Westnedge Ave
Kalamazoo MI 49008

Call Sign: KB8JZJ
Joshua A Locke
2207 S Westnedge Ave
Kalamazoo MI 49008

Call Sign: KD8FWD
Allen L Dell
7084 Saginaw Dr
Kalamazoo MI 49048

Call Sign: KM8L
Joseph W Kremer
1983 Sandy Cove Dr
Kalamazoo MI 49048

Call Sign: KC8IPV
Ryan A Breisach
6327 Saybrook Dr
Kalamazoo MI 49009

Call Sign: N8YUI
Randall J Tarantino
5814 Scenic Way Dr
Kalamazoo MI 49009

Call Sign: KC8IPW
David S Roe
2507 Schippers Ln
Kalamazoo MI 49048

Call Sign: WB0JNV
Martin S Roe
2507 Schippers Ln
Kalamazoo MI 49048

Call Sign: K8AVD
Robert H Cutler
2623 Schippers Ln
Kalamazoo MI 49001

Call Sign: N8EID
Nellie J Walters
1328 Seminole Dr
Kalamazoo MI 49007

Call Sign: KT8T
Thomas R Hodapp
1415 Seminole Dr
Kalamazoo MI 49006

Call Sign: K8CFP
Ronald E Walters
1328 Seminole St
Kalamazoo MI 49007

Call Sign: WM8H
Raymond D Mitscher
3470 Senne
Kalamazoo MI 49001

Call Sign: WB8CXS
Dale H Beebe
3496 Senne
Kalamazoo MI 49001

Call Sign: KC8AAG
David M Moss
4118 Sequoia
Kalamazoo MI
490061323

Call Sign: KB8WUE
Steve G Schauer
5104 Shepherds Glen
Kalamazoo MI 49009

Call Sign: N8LLI
David M Johnson

1103 Southern Ave
Kalamazoo MI 49001

Call Sign: KD8AAE
Kimberly C Kerekes
745 Springwood Dr
Kalamazoo MI 49009

Call Sign: KB8MOB
Allen V Buskirk
3324 St Antoine Ave
Kalamazoo MI 49007

Call Sign: WA8QCT
Herman N Harms Jr
8401 Stadium Dr
Kalamazoo MI 49009

Call Sign: KD8CIW
Michel A Mussche
3757 Starchief St
Kalamazoo MI 49048

Call Sign: KC9LVT
Garrett J Kaltenbach
7666 Stermer Dr
Kalamazoo MI 49048

Call Sign: N8UFH
Charlie Krenek
2003 Stevens Ave
Kalamazoo MI 49008

Call Sign: N8FYM
William A Hamlin
2321 Stevens Ave
Kalamazoo MI 49008

Call Sign: KC8UAU
Jeremy T Franklin
923 Stockbridge Apt 2
Kalamazoo MI 49001

Call Sign: AB8HU
Piran Mohazzabi
4529 Stonebrook Ave
Kalamazoo MI
490091121

Call Sign: KD8BS
Piran Mohazzabi
4529 Stonebrooke Ave
Kalamazoo MI
490091121

Call Sign: KD8DFX
Paul R Baker
4160 Stoney Hill Dr
Kalamazoo MI 49009

Call Sign: KZ8OEM
Paul R Baker
4160 Stoney Hill Dr
Kalamazoo MI 49009

Call Sign: KB8FDZ
Jill George
2490 Strathmore
Kalamazoo MI 49009

Call Sign: N8IYR
Tim R Dunham
6424 Sturbridge Dr
Kalamazoo MI 49004

Call Sign: KD8MBF
Shawn M Avery
5527 Summer Ridge
Ln Apt H
Kalamazoo MI 49009

Call Sign: WA8PGR
Andrew Lapekas
2386 Summerdale Dr
Kalamazoo MI 49004

Call Sign: N8WUH
Nathan M Vandenbos
802 Sunnock
Kalamazoo MI 49001

Call Sign: WA8YPD
Frederic H McAlister
902 Sunnock
Kalamazoo MI 49001

Call Sign: KC8KZD
John A Kapenga
4260 Sunnybrook Dr
Kalamazoo MI 49008

Call Sign: KD8EIB
Michael E Boersma
9803 Sunnywood Dr
Kalamazoo MI 49009

Call Sign: W9ATU
Donald G Klein

5655 Swallow Ave
Kalamazoo MI 49009

Call Sign: N8CML
Ronald A Schubot
2632 Taliesin Dr
Kalamazoo MI 49008

Call Sign: N8LQR
Janis Maldups
2661 Taliesin Dr
Kalamazoo MI 49008

Call Sign: WD8KSD
Hugh Street
2128 Tamrack
Kalamazoo MI 49006

Call Sign: KD8PXQ
Wilfred B Staufer
5620 Texas Dr
Kalamazoo MI 49009

Call Sign: K9AMY
Amy L Widenhofer
6133 Thunderbluff
Kalamazoo MI 49009

Call Sign: KB8CRS
Robert J Krum
279 Timber Ridge Dr
Kalamazoo MI 49007

Call Sign: KA8URC
Richard J Ross
6262 Torrington Rd
Kalamazoo MI 49009

Call Sign: N8YNY
Susan K Wilson
1416 Trimble Ave
Kalamazoo MI 49048

Call Sign: WB8LOE
George F Farmer
1417 Trimble Ave
Kalamazoo MI
490011619

Call Sign: N9FKB
Kyle A Furge
7124 Turkey Glen Trl
Kalamazoo MI 49009

Call Sign: KD8RCH
Theodore E Davis
6113 Twilight Ave
Kalamazoo MI 49048

Call Sign: N8GHR
Richard L
Genschoreck
6279 Twilight Ave
Kalamazoo MI 49048

Call Sign: KD8PXS
Harold I Minor
6411 Twilight Ave
Kalamazoo MI 49048

Call Sign: KD8PXT
Karena A Minor
6411 Twilight Ave
Kalamazoo MI 49048

Call Sign: N0OKA
Robert H Emerson
2421 University Ave
Kalamazoo MI 49008

Call Sign: WA8CZE
Walker H Sisson
2507 University Ave
Kalamazoo MI 49008

Call Sign: W8UUS
Walker H Sisson
2507 University Ave
Kalamazoo MI 49008

Call Sign: KC8EDE
Joseph R Eby
115 Upjohn
Kalamazoo MI 49001

Call Sign: KD8IHB
Michael S Richey
4016 Valley Ridge Apt
4
Kalamazoo MI 49006

Call Sign: AB8SO
David A Murphy
4131 Valley Ridge Dr
Apt 2
Kalamazoo MI 49006

Call Sign: K8GAR

George A Robinson
1122 Vassar Dr
Kalamazoo MI 49001

Call Sign: KA8ITP
Forrest R Frederick Jr
1328 Vassar Dr
Kalamazoo MI 49001

Call Sign: KB8IGS
Dennis A Boersema
127 Velvet
Kalamazoo MI 49002

Call Sign: W8VY
Kalamazoo ARC
5640 Venture Ct
Kalamazoo MI 49009

Call Sign: KC8HPS
Bryan P Burrma
2838 Virginia Ave
Kalamazoo MI 49004

Call Sign: W8NXV
Wendell C Zeluff
4049 W B Ave
Kalamazoo MI 49009

Call Sign: WA8PKH
Stephen G Zeluff
4515 W B Ave
Kalamazoo MI
490099021

Call Sign: N8ZSK
Eric R Raifsnider
8368 W C Ave
Kalamazoo MI 49009

Call Sign: WD8CLM
Dorsey C Van Horne
1720 W D Ave
Kalamazoo MI 49007

Call Sign: KC8TIN
Brian S Kloack
2694 W D Ave
Kalamazoo MI 49009

Call Sign: K8CDK
Nathaniel L Chapman
2820 W D Ave
Kalamazoo MI 49007

Call Sign: K8CJV
Nathaniel E Chapman
2870 W D Ave
Kalamazoo MI 49007

Call Sign: N8AXF
Adrian C Van Kesteren
9085 W D Ave
Kalamazoo MI 49009

Call Sign: N8NXI
Paul D Rahn
1031 W E Ave
Kalamazoo MI 49009

Call Sign: WF8Q
Joan M Rahn
1031 W E Ave
Kalamazoo MI
490049310

Call Sign: WA8PRY
William P Young
1810 W E Ave
Kalamazoo MI 49004

Call Sign: KD8GJQ
Katelynd R Dreger
1047 W F Ave
Kalamazoo MI 49009

Call Sign: KC8YYJ
Brenda K Macomber
7591 W F Ave
Kalamazoo MI 49009

Call Sign: KB8JCD
Scott D Schneider
6981 W G Ave
Kalamazoo MI 49009

Call Sign: KA8YHN
Patrick L Van Zile
8292 W G Ave
Kalamazoo MI 49009

Call Sign: KC8KAP
Lois A Ketchum
9282 W G Ave
Kalamazoo MI 49009

Call Sign: KC8HKF
James A Ketchum

9282 W G Ave
Kalamazoo MI 49009

Call Sign: N8PHC
Thomas L Fletcher
8775 W H Ave
Kalamazoo MI 49009

Call Sign: KC8JBJ
Louis C Dooley
9303 W H Ave
Kalamazoo MI 49009

Call Sign: WA8PLM
David W Gordon
742 W Kilgore Apt
305
Kalamazoo MI 49008

Call Sign: KD8BXB
Micah A Lillrose
7820 W Kl Ave
Kalamazoo MI 49009

Call Sign: KB8WAP
Michael D Parker
8315 W Long Lake Dr
Kalamazoo MI 49048

Call Sign: N9MUU
Matthew W Mason
724 W Lovell 1
Kalamazoo MI 49007

Call Sign: KC8TGD
William J Cherup
2421 W Main St
Kalamazoo MI 49006

Call Sign: KB8JPA
David I Stycos
3430 W Main St Apt 5
Kalamazoo MI 49007

Call Sign: N8IQH
Theodore J Brooks II
1401 W Maple St
Kalamazoo MI 49008

Call Sign: N8LFL
Leslie J Mills Brooks
1401 W Maple St
Kalamazoo MI
490081849

Call Sign: KD8RHG
Terry D Palmatier
7268 W Ml Ave
Kalamazoo MI 49009

Call Sign: WA8ORW
Robert P Mulder
7774 W N Ave
Kalamazoo MI
490098122

Call Sign: N8ZRK
Thomas A Wesseling
7933 W N Ave
Kalamazoo MI 49009

Call Sign: KC8IIX
Harold E Nutter Jr
7944 W Q Ave
Kalamazoo MI 49009

Call Sign: KB8VOC
Terry W Eisenhauer
7960 W Q Ave
Kalamazoo MI
490098927

Call Sign: WA8CQU
James R Forden
7830 W R Ave
Kalamazoo MI 49009

Call Sign: KB5BGC
Gary F Runcie
915 W Vine St
Kalamazoo MI 49008

Call Sign: KD8GTH
Barbara L Runcie
915 W Vine St
Kalamazoo MI 49008

Call Sign: KC8JOF
Thomas F Ahlrich
314 W Vine St Apt 4
Kalamazoo MI 49001

Call Sign: KB8PAX
Michael A Osborne
229 W Walnut Apt 1
Kalamazoo MI 49007

Call Sign: N8OXE

Marty P Franz
525 W Walnut St
Kalamazoo MI 49007

Call Sign: N8UFI
Amy Proni
530 W Walnut St
Kalamazoo MI 49007

Call Sign: KE8TJ
Jack L Koole
3780 W Wembley
Kalamazoo MI 49009

Call Sign: N8RKI
Leslie E Dodson
1836 Waite Ave
Kalamazoo MI 49008

Call Sign: N8KDB
Mark A Russell
8349 Warbler Dr
Kalamazoo MI 49002

Call Sign: KC8HSN
Ronald W Ryan
534 Wealthy Ave
Kalamazoo MI 49006

Call Sign: KC8UHS
Ronald W Ryan
534 Wealthy Ave
Kalamazoo MI 49006

Call Sign: KC8NBU
John L Hazel
1009 Westmoreland Dr
Kalamazoo MI
490065567

Call Sign: WD8QXP
Helmut Schinkel
4707 Weston Ave
Kalamazoo MI 49006

Call Sign: KB8HBU
Eric M Summerer
5072 Whippoorwill
Kalamazoo MI 49002

Call Sign: KA8RST
Frank W Sanders
312 Whitcomb St
Kalamazoo MI 49001

Call Sign: WA8OEP
Philip W Holm
3121 Windhell
Kalamazoo MI 49008

Call Sign: K8BKE
De Forrest C Franklin
3310 Windmill Ln
Kalamazoo MI 49004

Call Sign: KG8IP
William C Toepper
3125 Winter Wheat Rd
Kalamazoo MI
490043364

Call Sign: K8AHX
Kenneth C Sowles
3310 Winter Wheat Rd
Kalamazoo MI 49004

Call Sign: K8HQY
Mary J Sowles
3310 Winter Wheat Rd
Kalamazoo MI 49004

Call Sign: KC8GQG
William L Godfrey
1414 Winters Dr
Kalamazoo MI 49002

Call Sign: N8WVK
Cornelius Baden
3711 Wolf Dr
Kalamazoo MI 49009

Call Sign: W8FDB
Howard M Gage
3506 Woodhams Dr
Kalamazoo MI 49002

Call Sign: W8EPN
Robert F Farmer
5229 Woodmont Dr
Kalamazoo MI 49001

Call Sign: KD8PXV
Richard J Milliman
5663 Woodsage St
Kalamazoo MI 49009

Call Sign: KA8IOF
David A Weese

6426 Wright St
Kalamazoo MI 49001

Call Sign: K8TDJ
James E Walker
Kalamazoo MI 49003

Call Sign: KR8W
Donald M Pyne
Kalamazoo MI 49005

Call Sign: N8JKP
Anthony Bolden
Kalamazoo MI 49005

Call Sign: N8YNW
Dorman E Wilson II
Kalamazoo MI 49004

Call Sign: KS8F
Eleanor C Pyne
Kalamazoo MI 49005

Call Sign: K8EME
Luis G Ortiz
Kalamazoo MI
490191495

FCC Amateur Radio Licenses in Kaleva

Call Sign: KD8FHC
James G Gauthier
7616 Adamson Lake
Rd
Kaleva MI 49645

Call Sign: KD8NXM
Tyler J Gauthier
7616 Adamson Lake
Rd
Kaleva MI 49645

Call Sign: KD8RAZ
Matthew D Berryhill
8653 Adamson Lake
Rd
Kaleva MI 49645

Call Sign: KA8RWM
Jim S Desy
9620 Jouppi Rd
Kaleva MI 49645

Call Sign: N8RDE
Gaylord A Knapp
9900 Jouppi Rd
Kaleva MI 49645

Call Sign: W8ZN
William L Little
16777 Lindroos Rd
Kaleva MI 49645

Call Sign: WD8NZU
Anice M Little
16777 Lindroos Rd
Kaleva MI 49645

Call Sign: N8ZWW
Charles R Stryker
16325 Sedlar Rd
Kaleva MI 49645

Call Sign: KC8SXS
William S Wittig
7721 Wilson Rd
Kaleva MI 49645

Call Sign: K8SKY
William S Wittig
7721 Wilson Rd
Kaleva MI 49645

FCC Amateur Radio Licenses in Kalkaska

Call Sign: AA8ZV
Everett L Homan Jr
173 Aller Rd
Kalkaska MI 49646

Call Sign: KC8KEM
Monica J Homan
173 Aller Rd'
Kalkaska MI 49646

Call Sign: KC8CLR
Michael N Ruppert
3421 Bear Ln NE
Kalkaska MI 49684

Call Sign: N8MKC
Earl A Lopinski
R 1 Box 309 E Bear
Lake Rd
Kalkaska MI 49646

Call Sign: KD8EL
Douglas J Peterson
Rt 3 Box 455C Rogers
Rd
Kalkaska MI 49646

Call Sign: N8KMY
Craig C Duprey
8398 Centrall Ave NE
Kalkaska MI 49646

Call Sign: KC8UPU
Duncan K Paschall
309 Chestnut St
Kalkaska MI 49646

Call Sign: KD8CCW
Necole A Flanigan
3909 Cool Rd
Kalkaska MI 49646

Call Sign: KD8FHB
William A Ingels
3419 CR 571 NE
Kalkaska MI 49646

Call Sign: N8SCK
Tod E Dehmel
7356 CR 612
Kalkaska MI 49646

Call Sign: N8EHV
Emberly N Johnson
11715 CR 612 NE
Kalkaska MI
496469034

Call Sign: N8BAR
Edward N Johnson
11715 CR 612 NE
Kalkaska MI
496469034

Call Sign: WT8WW
Duane Delorey
1851 Darke Rd NE
Kalkaska MI 49646

Call Sign: KD8BYQ
Dennis J Choike
1274 Flashaar Ln NE
Kalkaska MI 49646

Call Sign: KB8AF

Robert L Ricketts
1576 Island Lake Rd
NW
Kalkaska MI 49646

Call Sign: KB8RCZ
Robert R Bowersox
4601 Kniss Rd
Kalkaska MI 49646

Call Sign: K8RCZ
Robert R Bowersox
4601 Kniss Rd
Kalkaska MI 49646

Call Sign: AA8UE
Jack E Thomas
959 Lake Dr
Kalkaska MI 49646

Call Sign: KC8LSP
James A Shaner
3915 Lincoln Dr NE
Kalkaska MI 49646

Call Sign: N8HBU
William W Kitti
2860 Log Lake Rd NE
Kalkaska MI 49646

Call Sign: N8HGP
Lawrence E Barnard
95 Mitchell Rd SE
Kalkaska MI 49646

Call Sign: K8AMB
Anna M Bell
508 N Coral
Kalkaska MI 49646

Call Sign: W8KAL
Dave J Bell
508 N Coral
Kalkaska MI 49646

Call Sign: K8DJB
Dave J Bell
508 N Coral
Kalkaska MI 49646

Call Sign: NN8J
Dave J Bell
508 N Coral
Kalkaska MI 49646

Call Sign: KD8JWH
David Bell
2710 N Sharon Rd
Kalkaska MI 49646

Call Sign: KC8DIX
David R Headapohl
106 N Walnut St
Kalkaska MI 49646

Call Sign: N8YBO
Robert L Larsen
509 N Walnut St
Kalkaska MI 49646

Call Sign: W8SKS
Stanley K Summers
933 Old M 72
Kalkaska MI 49646

Call Sign: W8HIW
Donald J Chase
308 S Cedar St
Kalkaska MI 49646

Call Sign: KD8JKQ
Michigan 45Th
Parallel Radio Club
407 S Cherry St
Kalkaska MI 49646

Call Sign: WB8HSL
Michigan 45Th
Parallel Radio Club
407 S Cherry St
Kalkaska MI 49646

Call Sign: N8HGM
Virginia H Yost
407 S Cherry St
Kalkaska MI 49646

Call Sign: NM8R
Scott M Yost
407 S Cherry St
Kalkaska MI 49646

Call Sign: KC8EVJ
Raymond L Thorne
503 S Coral St
Kalkaska MI
496460503

Call Sign: KC8YLK
Sue A Mccauley
108 S Walnut St
Kalkaska MI 49646

Call Sign: WA8VGW
Charles G Clark
215 S Walnut St
Kalkaska MI 49646

Call Sign: KF8EA
Terry L Anderson
4099 Saunders Rd SE
Kalkaska MI 49646

Call Sign: WB8EYM
Donald A Holloway
7667 Shore Dr NE
Kalkaska MI 49646

Call Sign: WA8QGU
Harold D Sheffer
1277 Spencer Rd SE
Kalkaska MI 49646

Call Sign: N8CVX
Timothy C Liljestrand
3967 Tyler Rd SE
Kalkaska MI 49646

Call Sign: WB6LFG
Timothy C Liljestrand
3967 Tyler Rd SE
Kalkaska MI 49646

Call Sign: N8VZA
Elizabeth A Edwards
2054 Valley Rd
Kalkaska MI 49646

Call Sign: KC8KPO
Tom S Blanshan
Kalkaska MI 49646

Call Sign: KC8KPP
Brenda L Blanshan
Kalkaska MI 49646

Call Sign: N8JCO
Elizabeth A Turanski
Kalkaska MI 49646

Call Sign: KC8NOP
Mary J Shaner

Kalkaska MI 49646

Call Sign: KC8QLB
Graham S Yost
Kalkaska MI 49646

Call Sign: KC8QLC
Jesse S Yost
Kalkaska MI 49646

Call Sign: KC8YLL
Michael Mccauley
Kalkaska MI 49646

FCC Amateur Radio Licenses in Karlin

Call Sign: KA8WKJ
Judith M Schmansky
7614 Wilson St
Karlin MI 49643

Call Sign: KB8PY
Norman E Schmansky
7614 Wilson St
Karlin MI 496439415

FCC Amateur Radio Licenses in Kearsarge

Call Sign: WA8ZYB
Earl R Lark Sr
68 2nd Ave
Kearsarge MI 49942

Call Sign: NV8P
Charles D Peterson
36 Smith Ave
Kearsarge MI 49942

Call Sign: N8XJJ
Helen I Peterson
27510 Smith Ave
Kearsarge MI 49913

FCC Amateur Radio Licenses in Kendall

Call Sign: KD8TK
Guy A Leversee
27062 Lake St Box 6
Kendall MI 49062

FCC Amateur Radio Licenses in Kent

Call Sign: KC8CEQ
Edward D Birdsley II
2920 Newton Ave SE
Kent MI 495081537

FCC Amateur Radio Licenses in Kent City

Call Sign: N8PMH
Dale E Stream
3530 19 Mile Rd
Kent City MI 49330

Call Sign: KB8QFK
Norman E Hall II
3353 22 Mile Rd
Kent City MI 49330

Call Sign: KA8ZXJ
James N Stellema
13595 Big John Ct
Kent City MI
493309146

Call Sign: W8ONJ
Melvin A H Saur
87 College St
Kent City MI 49330

Call Sign: WB8RXS
Gerald G Lerch
13232 Kenowa Ave
Kent City MI 49330

Call Sign: K8GGL
Gerald G Lerch
13232 Kenowa Ave
Kent City MI 49330

Call Sign: N8EUX
David M Goodson
12823 N Sparta Ave
Kent City MI 49330

Call Sign: K8VQJ
Alfred P Earley
11 North St
Kent City MI 49330

Call Sign: N8ELT
Raymond D Hockstra

13535 Paine Ave
Kent City MI 49330

Call Sign: KC8EFJ
John W Price
15812 Peach Ridge
Ave
Kent City MI 49330

Call Sign: KC8GOM
Dennis D Cooper
16320 Red Pine Dr
Kent City MI 49330

Call Sign: KC8REG
Harold Loveland
14122 Sparta Ave
Kent City MI 49330

Call Sign: KC8RWO
Rita J Loveland
14122 Sparta Ave
Kent City MI 49330

Call Sign: KD8RFQ
Christopher L
Hathaway
665 Truman Rd
Kent City MI 49330

Call Sign: KD8DBV
Brian W Klawiter
4660 Wild Locust St
Kent City MI 49330

**FCC Amateur Radio
Licenses in Kenton**

Call Sign: KA8UEC
R Kenton Leksell
Kenton MI 49943

**FCC Amateur Radio
Licenses in Kentwood**

Call Sign: KC8HZS
Susan E Cody
692 44th St 4
Kentwood MI 49548

Call Sign: KB8UNE
Tony Phan
1441 48th SE
Kentwood MI 49508

Call Sign: KB8UYU
Nguyet M Phan
1441 48th St SE
Kentwood MI 49508

Call Sign: KB8UYV
Hanna Phan
1441 48th St SE
Kentwood MI 49508

Call Sign: KF8AN
Columbus Stewart
1997 52nd SE
Kentwood MI 49518

Call Sign: N8COV
Dennis A Schmidt
1105 59th St SE
Kentwood MI 49508

Call Sign: KD8EHL
Ava J Grover
1041 60th SE
Kentwood MI 49508

Call Sign: N8DAL
Phillip J Doezema
1325 60th St S E
Kentwood MI 49508

Call Sign: N7BQH
Theo G Morrison
705 60th St SE
Kentwood MI 49548

Call Sign: K8CCT
Charles T Snyder
697 Andover SE
Kentwood MI
495487608

Call Sign: KD8DAI
Jack A Deyoung
5677 Bellewood Ct
Kentwood MI 49548

Call Sign: KF8CN
Rodney P Brown
5608 Bentbrook Dr SE
Kentwood MI 49508

Call Sign: N8FZB
Michael J Ward

4630 Bonnie SE
Kentwood MI 49508

Call Sign: KA8TPX
Steven P Harrod
1350 Bowdoin
Kentwood MI 49508

Call Sign: N8JTV
Darrell A Mortensen
1954 Bridle Creek SE
Kentwood MI 49508

Call Sign: KD8BCS
Cheryl L Mortensen
1954 Bridle Creek SE
Kentwood MI 49508

Call Sign: N8LUD
Joseph D Sarber Jr
1342 Brookmark
Kentwood MI 49508

Call Sign: KC8ZFI
Thomas M Driesenga
4518 Brookmeadow Ct
SE
Kentwood MI 49512

Call Sign: KC8CDG
Todd M Vanderwoude
5414 Bunker Hill Ct
Kentwood MI 49508

Call Sign: KD8DLH
Andrew D Schultz
5337 Christie Ave
Kentwood MI 49508

Call Sign: W8ADS
Andrew D Schultz
5337 Christie Ave
Kentwood MI 49508

Call Sign: KD8ECV
Katherine M Schultz
5337 Christie Ave SE
Kentwood MI 49508

Call Sign: KD8DLE
Bradford E Schultz
5337 Christie Ave SE
Kentwood MI 49508

Call Sign: KA0SQN
Jacob E Dockter
5932 Christie Ave SE
Kentwood MI 49508

Call Sign: N8WKS
Paul D Kennedy
5547 Claudia SE
Kentwood MI 49548

Call Sign: KB8TAO
Robert R Thomas
1240 Cobb SE Apt 2B
Kentwood MI 49508

Call Sign: KC8EXE
Todd C Rogers
2137 Countrywood SE
Kentwood MI 49508

Call Sign: KB8TDZ
Jacquelyn L Sato
4449 Curwood Ave SE
Kentwood MI
495084669

Call Sign: KD8AZM
Gary R Lauff
4721 Curwood Ave SE
Kentwood MI 49508

Call Sign: KG8L
Gary R Lauff
4721 Curwood Ave SE
Kentwood MI 49508

Call Sign: W8GL
Gary R Lauff
4721 Curwood Ave SE
Kentwood MI 49508

Call Sign: KD8IAJ
Krystal D Grau
4701 Drummond Blvd
Apt 104
Kentwood MI 49508

Call Sign: KD8MCZ
Brian C Toronyi
5384 E Heathwood
Kentwood MI 49512

Call Sign: KA8IDJ
David N Kutter

1206 Edsel St SE
Kentwood MI 49508

Call Sign: KC8WBV
Donald L Eakins
2013 Fawnwood Dr SE
Kentwood MI 49508

Call Sign: N8PNV
Richard J Chadbourne
6180 Fordwick SE
Kentwood MI
495486818

Call Sign: N8YEN
Charles F Sears
4069-1C Forest Creek
Kentwood MI 49512

Call Sign: KD8DLI
John R Baylo
4361 Forest Way Ave
SE 32
Kentwood MI 49512

Call Sign: KD8ABL
Ilie Vidican
4363 Forest Way Dr 32
Kentwood MI 49512

Call Sign: N8YZJ
David M Gould
4309 Forestway Dr 21
Kentwood MI 49512

Call Sign: KC8KK
John D Knoper
4832 Fuller
Kentwood MI 49508

Call Sign: KA8ZBR
Debra L Knoper
4832 Fuller Ave SE
Kentwood MI 49508

Call Sign: KC8UES
Travis C Knoper
4832 Fuller SE
Kentwood MI 49508

Call Sign: W8TLD
Terry L Decker Jr
1250 Gentian Dr SE
Kentwood MI 49508

Call Sign: KC8WQN
Audra J Decker
1250 Gentian Dr SE
Kentwood MI 49508

Call Sign: KB8SVV
Mark C Phleeger
1404 Gentian Dr SE
Kentwood MI 49508

Call Sign: KC8YOC
Barry A Graham
1801 Gentian SE
Kentwood MI 49508

Call Sign: N8DGK
Daniel G Keuhs
1844 Gerda SE
Kentwood MI 49508

Call Sign: KC8NON
Richard Dryer
4662 Grantwood
Kentwood MI 49508

Call Sign: N8KQX
Randy L Chelette
5517 Greenboro Dr
Kentwood MI 49508

Call Sign: WB8WNR
John J Troost Sr
5473 Greenboro SE
Kentwood MI 49508

Call Sign: KC8BIH
Cris M Plyer
2740 Harbor Dr SE
103
Kentwood MI 49512

Call Sign: W8AFL
Terry L Harvey
424 Harp St SE
Kentwood MI 49548

Call Sign: K8KWT
Robert A Daniels
1033 Harvester Dr SE
Kentwood MI 49508

Call Sign: KC8THO
Ernest J Ostuno

5768 Hickory Hill
Kentwood MI 49512

Call Sign: KN8JDN
Hiram A Le Pard
4740 Hickory Way SE
Apt 1
Kentwood MI 49546

Call Sign: N8JLN
Margaret A Le Pard
4740 Hickory Way SE
Apt 1
Kentwood MI 49546

Call Sign: N9WAI
Ryan R Hullah
4340 Hidden Lakes Dr
SE 103
Kentwood MI 49512

Call Sign: KB8YNN
Warren Jackson
2091 Highlander Dr
SE
Kentwood MI 49508

Call Sign: W8AYC
Warren Jackson
2091 Highlander Dr
SE
Kentwood MI 49508

Call Sign: AB8WT
John C Bradley
2311 Jamestown Dr SE
Kentwood MI
495086581

Call Sign: N8NLJ
Gene Brott
4447 Jefferson SE
Kentwood MI 49548

Call Sign: KC0VQA
David J Meyer
5685 Juanita Dr SE
Kentwood MI 49508

Call Sign: AC8CV
David J Meyer
5685 Juanita Dr SE
Kentwood MI 49508

Call Sign: KB8ZSV
Kevin D Porter
142 Kellogg Woods Pk
Dr 102
Kentwood MI 49548

Call Sign: KC8UBT
Jonathan T Buist
4843 Kimball St
Kentwood MI 49508

Call Sign: KC8VMX
Dorothy K Gergen
4677 Lantana Dr SE
Kentwood MI 49512

Call Sign: K8BZL
Harold G Timmer
4730 Larkwood Dr
Kentwood MI 49508

Call Sign: KB8OPC
Maurice J Buskers
5953 Leisure S Dr SE
Kentwood MI 49548

Call Sign: KC8PWS
Thomas M Hammen
1802 Lockmere SE
Kentwood MI 49508

Call Sign: KD8CAN
James R Leys
4480 Madison
Kentwood MI 49548

Call Sign: KB8UNG
Douglas A Slopsema
1509 Maple Hollow
SE
Kentwood MI 49508

Call Sign: WD8REV
Susan Woolf
4728 Meadow Lake Dr
SE
Kentwood MI 49512

Call Sign: KD8RPS
Eric M Nugent
3639 Merrimont Ct SE
Kentwood MI 49512

Call Sign: N8COX

Edward R Boorsma
45 Montebello SE
Kentwood MI 49548

Call Sign: N8NBU
David R De Winter
128 Montebello SE
Kentwood MI 49548

Call Sign: KD8LL
Melvin R Holloway
5226 Newcastle Dr SE
Kentwood MI 49508

Call Sign: N8HOD
Kimberly S Holloway
5226 Newcastle Dr SE
Kentwood MI 49508

Call Sign: KB8DT
James B Harrison
5249 Newcastle SE
Kentwood MI 49508

Call Sign: KC8YKD
Chris M Gage
2312 Old Dominion Ct
Kentwood MI 49508

Call Sign: KB7DAJ
John F Keller
3861 Old Elm
Kentwood MI 49512

Call Sign: WA8UDE
Steven D Price
3896 Old Elm Dr SE
Kentwood MI 49512

Call Sign: KA9YGJ
Ronnie J Hessman
3108 Old Kent Rd SE
Kentwood MI
495122777

Call Sign: KD8NEX
David E Brace
4394 Overlook Ter SE
Kentwood MI 49512

Call Sign: W8RUZ
David E Brace
4394 Overlook Ter SE
Kentwood MI 49512

Call Sign: KB8MFH
Dalbert G Schuelke
4875 Pamela SE
Kentwood MI 49548

Call Sign: KC8SUN
Greg S Webb
128 Parkbrook
Kentwood MI 49508

Call Sign: N8HMD
Charles A Whitfield
887 Pembroke SE
Kentwood MI 49508

Call Sign: KC8UPY
Patricia A Whitfield
887 Pembroke SE
Kentwood MI 49508

Call Sign: WB8ICX
Paul W Bennink
1418 Pickett St SE
Kentwood MI 49508

Call Sign: N8YEJ
Kenneth J Hoort
380 Pine NEedles Ct
Kentwood MI 49548

Call Sign: N8VDI
Doug W Zandstra
5358 Pinebrook
Kentwood MI 49548

Call Sign: N8EOM
Erik J Nelson
4757 Poinsettia
Kentwood MI 49508

Call Sign: KD8DLG
Michael S Ayers
4646 Poinsettia SE
Kentwood MI 49508

Call Sign: KB8UNH
Douglas M Bigelow
460 Prince Albert
Kentwood MI 49548

Call Sign: WA8IKO
Byron A Scully
339 Ridgewood St SE

Kentwood MI
495484357

Call Sign: KD8IAI
Jennifer E Bechtel
2654 Rum Creek Dr
SE
Kentwood MI 49508

Call Sign: KC8YPW
Eric A Hultman
2721 Rum Creek Dr
SE
Kentwood MI 49508

Call Sign: KD8DLL
Nathan E Deppe
2754 Rum Creek Dr
SE
Kentwood MI 49508

Call Sign: KC8VMY
Randy J Caris
3308 S Creek Dr Apt
104
Kentwood MI 49512

Call Sign: N8XHB
Kendall S Jung
3301 S Creek Dr SE
Apt 102
Kentwood MI 49512

Call Sign: AB8WN
Peter M Sobanski
3325 S Creek Dr SE
Apt 301
Kentwood MI 49512

Call Sign: WB8YEH
Paul M Vant Hof
5082 Southglow Ct SE
Kentwood MI 49508

Call Sign: WB8YEI
Jeanette F Vant Hof
5082 Southglow Ct SE
Kentwood MI 49508

Call Sign: KA8YXJ
Eric J Sturgis
24A Spear
Kentwood MI 49548

Call Sign: N8UMK
Elizabeth K Bonner
734 Springwood Dr SE
Kentwood MI 49548

Call Sign: WB8WZU
James R Leland
2057 Stanford SE
Kentwood MI 49508

Call Sign: KC8BKR
Robert T Harvey
5494 Stowehill Dr SE
Kentwood MI 49508

Call Sign: WS8W
Dawn M Moreno
4552 Summer Creek
Ln SE
Kentwood MI 49508

Call Sign: N8LOB
Louis J Janicki
819 Summertime Ave
SE
Kentwood MI 49508

Call Sign: KC8PJE
Nicholas A Foster
2569 Sunnycreek
Kentwood MI 49508

Call Sign: WA8RUV
Jason B Herron
4513 Terry Dr SE
Kentwood MI 49512

Call Sign: KC8ULY
David C Putney
4527 Terry Dr SE
Kentwood MI 49512

Call Sign: K0TEA
Matthew S Hodges
4589 Torrington Ave
SE
Kentwood MI 49512

Call Sign: AF6VN
Dennis L Bieber
2621 Trails End SE
Kentwood MI 49546

Call Sign: KD8HHJ

Michael H Farr
3895 Villa Montee Dr
SE
Kentwood MI 49512

Call Sign: KB8VOZ
Wayne M Dowling
2442 W Collier Ave
SE
Kentwood MI 49546

Call Sign: N7OUF
Steven L Becker
5429 W Rosebud Ct
SE
Kentwood MI 49512

Call Sign: KD8ATP
Kurt A Hulst
4711 Walma Ave Apt
201
Kentwood MI 49512

Call Sign: K8YAM
Lyman P Wenger
2305 Whisper Cove Dr
S E
Kentwood MI 49508

Call Sign: KD8FHN
Joseph L Mattson
6160 Woodfield Dr
Apt 12 SE
Kentwood MI 49548

**FCC Amateur Radio
Licenses in Kewadin**

Call Sign: N8UGU
Karol M Vanderhoff
13344 Chippewa Trl
Kewadin MI 49648

Call Sign: KE8QZ
Robert G Swanson
634 Golden Beach Dr
Kewadin MI
496489223

Call Sign: AG8E
Richard D Russell
12020 Hjelte Rd
Kewadin MI 49648

Call Sign: WA8OWN
Charles S McDowell
3358 Joe Marks Trl
Kewadin MI 49648

Call Sign: WA8UNK
Raymond W Stiles
4868 Juniper Dr
Kewadin MI 49648

Call Sign: W8UAN
Timothy S Brockett
3009 N 31
Kewadin MI 49648

Call Sign: K8BVC
Edward P Juras
3970 NW Torch Lake
Dr
Kewadin MI 49648

Call Sign: KC8OIA
Dennis Mcquillan
3865 Sutter Ln
Kewadin MI 49648

Call Sign: KC8QXJ
Randy D Harlan
Kewadin MI 49648

**FCC Amateur Radio
Licenses in Kincheloe**

Call Sign: KD8NHS
Fred W Mcclendon
3 Birch Pl
Kincheloe MI 49788

Call Sign: KJ4JBI
Pat R McMahon
6 Countrywood Dr
Kincheloe MI 49788

Call Sign: KC8HEP
Dale J Petkus
34 Hope Ln
Kincheloe MI 49788

Call Sign: KD8EOW
Tim I Mckee
71 Kincheloe Dr
Kincheloe MI 49788

Call Sign: KC8HEQ

Timothy R Carnahan
91 Parkside Dr
Kincheloe MI 49788

Call Sign: KD8KYA
Richard L Maki Jr
93 Partridge Dr
Kincheloe MI 49788

Call Sign: KC8QIA
Roger A Merchberger
9 Tamara Lynn Cir
Kincheloe MI 49788

Call Sign: AB8KK
Roger A Merchberger
9 Tamara Lynn Cir
Kincheloe MI 49788

Call Sign: KC8ZGB
Ronald L Munro
25 Tamara Lynn Cir
Kincheloe MI 49788

Call Sign: W8ARS
Eastern Upper
Peninsula Amateur
Radio Service
4657 W Industrial Park
Dr
Kincheloe MI 49788

**FCC Amateur Radio
Licenses in Kingsford**

Call Sign: KD8AIT
Dennis J Beurjey
612 Balsam St
Kingsford MI 49802

Call Sign: K8SWX
Dennis J Beurjey
612 Balsam St
Kingsford MI 49802

Call Sign: KB8JSY
Susan K Knutson
417 Beech St
Kingsford MI 49801

Call Sign: KB9CQY
Debbie K Costa
501 Birch St
Kingsford MI 49802

Call Sign: KD8GLO
Arthur W Costa
501 Birch St
Kingsford MI
498026105

Call Sign: KB8UGK
Dennis D Ryan
301 Cleveland Ave
Kingsford MI
498024329

Call Sign: KD8POR
Dana L Bey
608 Crest St
Kingsford MI 49802

Call Sign: KB8ETP
James C Ries
400 E Sagola Ave
Kingsford MI 49801

Call Sign: N8ZAN
Jason P Sawall
628 E Sagola Ave
Kingsford MI 49801

Call Sign: KC8MYF
Floyd C Kucharski
554 Everton
Kingsford MI 49802

Call Sign: N8UKD
Mark J Lewis
412 Fairmount St
Kingsford MI 49802

Call Sign: KB8HHQ
Dennis J Nelson
316 Fox Dr
Kingsford MI 49802

Call Sign: KB8SBP
William A Bertoldi Jr
Jr
709 Hamilton Ave
Kingsford MI 49801

Call Sign: KB8VUV
Charles J Harris
712 Hazel Pl
Kingsford MI 49801

Call Sign: KC8QYP
Jon D Mott
217 Hooper St
Kingsford MI 49802

Call Sign: KC8QYS
Donna L Mott
217 Hooper St
Kingsford MI 49802

Call Sign: W9HNJ
William D Wicklund
704 John St
Kingsford MI 49802

Call Sign: K8IFC
Genevieve C Olson
405 Maple St
Kingsford MI 49801

Call Sign: K8IFD
Russell N Olson
405 Maple St
Kingsford MI 49801

Call Sign: KA8KTU
Carl R E Olson
405 Maple St
Kingsford MI 49801

Call Sign: KB8KY
Kelvin A Olson
405 Maple St
Kingsford MI 49801

Call Sign: N8ZAM
Kristine H Olson
405 Maple St
Kingsford MI 49801

Call Sign: KB8PEJ
Robert G Koski
824 Maplewood Ct
Kingsford MI 49801

Call Sign: KD8KUF
Paul A Schultz
325 Osage St
Kingsford MI 49802

Call Sign: KD8PWE
Stephanie M Mieras
200 Ripley St
Kingsford MI 49802

Call Sign: KD8GLP
Nathan G Mieras
200 Ripley St
Kingsford MI 49802

Call Sign: N8MJR
Walter F Tomasoski Jr
616 Roycroft
Kingsford MI 49801

Call Sign: KA8FMG
Robert E Wells
572 S Hemlock St
Kingsford MI 49801

Call Sign: KB8HNE
David J Knutson
929 Superior Ave
Kingsford MI 49802

Call Sign: KC8QHM
Anthony G Paquette II
1037 Superior St
Kingsford MI 49802

Call Sign: KD8DJM
Stephen E Coughlin
925 Turner Rd
Kingsford MI 49802

Call Sign: KB9PLR
Sally A Steidl
416 Waverly St
Kingsford MI 49802

Call Sign: KB8ODP
Earl R Poisson
617 Wilson Ave
Kingsford MI 49801

Call Sign: N8XSY
Dennis W Ziemba
1713 Woodward Ave
Kingsford MI 49802

Call Sign: K4WUN
Edward S Marshall Jr
Kingsford MI 49801

Call Sign: KE8PD

Frederick P Hastings
1101 Clous Rd
Kingsley MI 49649

Call Sign: KB8RDI
Steven C Weaver
3303 County Line Rd
Kingsley MI 49649

Call Sign: KC8EXD
Lisa G Weaver
3303 County Line Rd
Kingsley MI 49649

Call Sign: KB8LIX
Donald R Flegel
8765 Dell Rd
Kingsley MI 49649

Call Sign: KA8ZXN
Victor R Rioux
2582 E M 113
Kingsley MI 49649

Call Sign: KC8GZK
Michael T Huskins
852 Eden St
Kingsley MI 49649

Call Sign: KB8TBZ
Lyle D Lehn
5387 Garfield Rd
Kingsley MI 49649

Call Sign: KD8OLA
Keith A Tampa
2295 Gregory Ln
Kingsley MI 49649

Call Sign: KD8OLB
Kimberly S Reynolds
2295 Gregory Ln
Kingsley MI 49649

Call Sign: KC8JOH
Christopher S Brow
3375 Harrand Estates
Pvt
Kingsley MI 49649

Call Sign: KC8ZAP
Mark J Kristof
3768 Harrand Rd
Kingsley MI 49649

Call Sign: KD6LOB
Catherine M Jedlicka
5782 Johnson Rd
Kingsley MI 49649

Call Sign: KD6NIB
Jason M Pinion
5782 Johnson Rd
Kingsley MI 49649

Call Sign: KD6LOC
Robert C Jedlicka
5782 Johnson Rd
Kingsley MI
496499252

Call Sign: KC8OLF
Kevin K Knight Sr
7347 M 113 E
Kingsley MI 49649

Call Sign: KA8CVF
Fred A Leishman
5808 Margaret Dr
Kingsley MI 49649

Call Sign: N8STY
Brian L Fouch
4266 Marsh Rd
Kingsley MI 49649

Call Sign: KD8NEI
Joel M Shivey
7200 Marshalltown Trl
Kingsley MI 49649

Call Sign: KC8UPT
Michael C Schoech
5247 Old CR 611
Kingsley MI 49649

Call Sign: KD8HTH
David H Edgecombe
3780 Red School Rd
Kingsley MI 49649

Call Sign: KD8EPQ
Thomas B Bennett
1475 S Winds Ct
Kingsley MI 49649

Call Sign: WB8ILB
Richard K Stiner

2785 Sparling Dr
Kingsley MI 49649

Call Sign: WA8PXD
Anthony A Raschi
2785 Sparling Rd
Kingsley MI 49649

Call Sign: W8KHZ
Brian F Steinebach
2829 W M 113
Kingsley MI 49649

**FCC Amateur Radio
Licenses in Kinross**

Call Sign: N8WLJ
Michael P Neal
Rt 1 Fair St Box 65
Kinross MI 49752

Call Sign: KC8WYQ
Robert D Baker
6518 W Feole
Kinross MI 49752

**FCC Amateur Radio
Licenses in Lachine**

Call Sign: KC8LZF
Charles A Oncina
1768 Bean Creek Rd
Lachine MI 49753

Call Sign: W8KEF
Kendall E Fader
16845 Jakes Rd
Lachine MI 49753

Call Sign: KD8QZA
Charles M Bigelow
11200 Jakob Ln
Lachine MI 49753

Call Sign: WB8ZIQ
Kenneth L Bigelow Sr
11200 Jakob Ln
Lachine MI 497539379

Call Sign: KD8JKD
Gary D Mcintire
16301 Long Rapids Rd
Lachine MI 49753

Call Sign: KB8PGC
James M Metivier
15121 McEwan Rd
Lachine MI 49753

Call Sign: KC8FDC
Rebecca K Metivier
15121 McEwan Rd
Lachine MI 49753

Call Sign: KD8LPR
Krista M Creekmore
16690 Moores Landing
Rd
Lachine MI 49753

Call Sign: K8WLZ
Krista M Creekmore
16690 Moores Landing
Rd
Lachine MI 49753

Call Sign: KC0RQL
Willie Creekmore
16690 Moores Landing
Rd
Lachine MI 49753

Call Sign: W0KLZ
Willie Creekmore
16690 Moores Landing
Rd
Lachine MI 49753

Call Sign: KD8OWA
Jerrald A Corn
11545 Standen Rd
Lachine MI 497539791

Call Sign: KA8FAA
Jerrald A Corn
11545 Standen Rd
Lachine MI 497539791

Call Sign: WD8RDL
Graydon K Choate Jr
Lachine MI 49753

**FCC Amateur Radio
Licenses in Lake**

Call Sign: N8WTA
Gary E Goudie
6603 Bear Lake Dr

Lake MI 48632

Call Sign: KC8ZYY
Donald J Alter
160 Big Stone Lake Rd
Lake MI 48632

Call Sign: AB8AU
Jerome E Burger
748 Connie Dr
Lake MI 48632

Call Sign: N8WUR
Joseph L Stragea
571 Hillcrest Ave
Lake MI 48632

Call Sign: KA8WJJ
Alton W Rapin
10922 Lake Station
Lake MI 48632

Call Sign: KF3CT
Homer L Weaver
6584 Ludington Dr
Lake MI 48632

Call Sign: KC8NGM
Dale W Haskell
8245 Maple Grove Rd
Lake MI 48632

Call Sign: KC8TDJ
Cora L Jones
11801 N Rolland Rd
Lake MI 48632

Call Sign: AA8TM
Joseph H Jones
11801 N Rolland Rd
Lake MI 486329407

Call Sign: N8ZEL
Edward F Raths Sr
11103 N Sherman Rd
Lake MI 48632

Call Sign: K8MW
Richard S Larsen
10777 N Shore Dr
Lake MI 486329037

Call Sign: WB8NEW
Grant K Allen

4689 Rustic Hills Rd
Lake MI 48632

Call Sign: KA8YWT
Douglas E Meeboer Jr
11295 S Alpine Dr
Lake MI 48632

Call Sign: KB8AUB
Nellieann A Hebert
11295 S Alpine Dr
Lake MI 48632

Call Sign: N8TWZ
Rebecca J Hebert
11295 S Alpine Dr
Lake MI 48632

Call Sign: WA8SDM
Russell F Hebert
11295 S Alpine Dr
Lake MI 48632

Call Sign: K8VSO
Walter M Wall
11942 S Lake Sta Ave
Lake MI 48632

Call Sign: KB3CCO
Ryan D Jarmon
8856 Smith St
Lake MI 48632

Call Sign: WD8MNQ
George D Kline
8421 W Beck Rd
Lake MI 48632

Call Sign: KB8VJG
Richard M Johnson
4509 W Coleman Rd
Lake MI 48632

Call Sign: KA8GUN
Annabel M Schrock
8628 W Colemand Rd
Lake MI 486329670

Call Sign: KA8QKW
Steven M Howe
8145 W Maple Grove
Rd
Lake MI 48632

Call Sign: N8HGU
Leo M Guzowski
Lake MI 48632

Call Sign: N8DMV
Dennis A Taetsch
8345 Bent Pine Dr
Lake Ann MI 49650

Call Sign: KB8UFS
Michael A Jean
8380 Easy St
Lake Ann MI 49650

Call Sign: KD8RTD
Gerald G Mckay
6291 Hardwood Dr
Lake Ann MI 49650

Call Sign: KC8CLM
Norman J Brown
5442 Maple Grove Rd
Lake Ann MI 49650

Call Sign: K8CLM
Norman J Brown
5442 Maple Grove Rd
Lake Ann MI 49650

Call Sign: KC8GGR
Richard J Marth
20359 Maple St
Lake Ann MI 49650

Call Sign: N8EMS
Richard J Marth
20359 Maple St
Lake Ann MI 49650

Call Sign: KC8LTQ
Jarrel L Dell
11826 N Long Lake
Rd
Lake Ann MI 49650

Call Sign: KC8ABY
Frederick H Feiger
4690 Oakwood Dr
Lake Ann MI 49650

Call Sign: KD8APF

Glenn M Onken
4710 Oakwood Dr
Lake Ann MI 49650

Call Sign: N8EV
Edward W Vick
19640 Pleasant View
Rd
Lake Ann MI 49650

Call Sign: KC8CLT
Richard G Wheaton
20153 Richardson Rd
Lake Ann MI 49650

Call Sign: KB8SGJ
Patricia L Jean
19239 Ridge View Ln
Lake Ann MI 49650

Call Sign: NK8R
Richard G Jean
19239 Ridge View Ln
Lake Ann MI 49650

Call Sign: KD8NXK
Richard N Weishaar
Lake Ann MI 49650

Call Sign: K8TAO
Richard N Weishaar
Lake Ann MI 49650

Call Sign: W8HAW
Allen H Krafve
145 Duck Point Dr
Lake City MI 49651

Call Sign: KA8ABM
Dennis W Aldrich
855 E Walker Rd
Lake City MI 49651

Call Sign: KC8GZH
Robert B Peckham II
116 Huron St
Lake City MI
496510720

Call Sign: KC8CZR
David L Ostrander Sr

212 Kalkaska St
Lake City MI 49651

Call Sign: KC8FYG
Michelle R Ostrander
212 Kalkaska St
Lake City MI 49651

Call Sign: KB8WPX
William J Richards
9461 Kelly Rd
Lake City MI 49651

Call Sign: KD8POI
Christopher G Raden
3394 Lachance Rd
Lake City MI 49651

Call Sign: K8MML
Melvin M La Grone
437 Lakeshore Dr
Lake City MI 49651

Call Sign: KC8MMG
David B Schweikhart
10006 Lindsy Dr
Lake City MI 49651

Call Sign: KA8YPP
Marvin C Bolles
385 Meadowlark
Lake City MI 49651

Call Sign: N8GFL
Gordon L Baldwin
121 N Al Moses Rd
Lake City MI 49651

Call Sign: W8GLB
Gordon L Baldwin
121 N Al Moses Rd
Lake City MI 49651

Call Sign: W8CT
Gordon L Baldwin
121 N Al Moses Rd
Lake City MI 49651

Call Sign: W8AMA
Cheryl K Baldwin
121 N Al Moses Rd
Lake City MI
496510116

Call Sign: KC4ETH
Richard J Bombard
129 N Canal St
Lake City MI 49651

Call Sign: KC4HZV
Frances A Bombard
129 N Canal St
Lake City MI 49651

Call Sign: KC8CZV
Charles A Goodman
122 N Huron Rd
Lake City MI 49651

Call Sign: KC8HJO
William J Beaudette III
85 N Park St A
Lake City MI 49651

Call Sign: N8KWR
Raymond A Pastula
7070 N Pioneer Rd
Lake City MI 49651

Call Sign: KD8BNG
David E Kutzbach
330 N Vander Meulen
Rd
Lake City MI 49651

Call Sign: NS8Q
George J Wade
8841 N Vandermuelen
Rd
Lake City MI 49651

Call Sign: WA8EEF
Maurice J Patterson
102 Prospect
Lake City MI 49651

Call Sign: NX8S
Ted N Turanski
4940 River Woods Rd
Lake City MI 49651

Call Sign: KD8AZI
Anthony E Harris
186 S Carolyn Dr
Lake City MI 49651

Call Sign: N8ML
Melvin M La Grone

437 S Lakeshore Dr
Lake City MI 49651

Call Sign: KC8JQS
Curt A Helmer
605 S Lakeshore Dr
Lake City MI 49651

Call Sign: N8BCA
Lonnie D Cowley
1246 S Vandermeulen
Rd
Lake City MI 49651

Call Sign: N8PMF
Joseph J Erickson
8880 Turnerville Rd
Lake City MI 49651

Call Sign: KC8KQK
Jerry P Jessel
7590 Vandermeulen
Rd
Lake City MI 49651

Call Sign: WB8AFU
William D Wade
6766 W Broadway St
Lake City MI 49651

Call Sign: W5VWR
John W Forsythe
6431 W Circle Dr
Lake City MI 49651

Call Sign: N8OVB
Liguori M Shortsle
1150 W Houghton Lk
Rd
Lake City MI 49651

Call Sign: KC8QEC
Richard L Grant
2188 W Jennings Rd
Lake City MI 49651

Call Sign: KC8QLH
Richard L Grant
2188 W Jennings Rd
Lake City MI 49651

Call Sign: W8YTV
Richard L Grant
2188 W Jennings Rd

Lake City MI 49651

Call Sign: KG8QY
Larry D Johnson
7250 W Jennings Rd
Lake City MI 49651

Call Sign: KB8WZO
John Richards Jr
8951 W Jennings Rd
Lake City MI 49651

Call Sign: KB8WZL
Ollie L Sayers
9363 W Kelly Rd
Lake City MI 49651

Call Sign: KB8ZDZ
Nancy J Richards
9461 W Kelly Rd
Lake City MI 49651

Call Sign: KA8PRV
Raymond T Rising
444 W Lane Dr
Lake City MI 49651

Call Sign: WA9QFS
Kirkland W Merley
9537 W Oak Dr
Lake City MI 49651

Call Sign: KC8NK
Reuben R Johnson
9010 W Oak Ln
Lake City MI 49651

Call Sign: KC8CBF
Raymond L Hatt Sr
6200 W Randall Rd
Lake City MI 49651

Call Sign: WD8CYP
Robert A Bolda
6670 W Redman Dr
Lake City MI 49651

Call Sign: K8PUU
Paul R Nelson
Lake City MI 49651

Call Sign: N8FVJ
James W Benedict
Lake City MI 49651

Call Sign: N8JCM
Cheryl K Baldwin
Lake City MI
496510116

FCC Amateur Radio
Licenses in Lake
George

Call Sign: KB8GCW
Chadrick D Mahaffey
6673 Mannsiding
Lake George MI 48633

Call Sign: KC8ZYJ
George J Bowles Jr
Lake George MI 48633

Call Sign: KC8ZYK
Marcia L Bowles
Lake George MI 48633

Call Sign: KC8ZYJ
Marcia L Bowles
Lake George MI 48633

FCC Amateur Radio
Licenses in Lake
Leelanau

Call Sign: N8JKV
Evan D Birch
1201 CR 643 Box 608
Lake Leelanau MI
49653

Call Sign: KC8OZL
Michael J Steffens
7717 E Alpers Rd
Lake Leelanau MI
49653

Call Sign: KF6YIO
Adam R Emerick
3091 E Gousty Knowe
Ln
Lake Leelanau MI
49653

Call Sign: K8DT
Joseph L Panyard
111 Meinard St

Lake Leelanau MI
49653

Call Sign: KC8KCV
Joseph L Panyard Jr
111 Meinrad St
Lake Leelanau MI
49653

Call Sign: N8RRQ
Le Roy E Martin
94 N Eagle Hwy
Lake Leelanau MI
49653

Call Sign: KA3PIO
Robert Turner
2639 N Lake Leelanau
Dr
Lake Leelanau MI
49653

Call Sign: N8VVG
John F Rutherford
2462 S French Rd
Lake Leelanau MI
49653

Call Sign: KD8QAP
Timothy C Mcneil
2796 S Popp Rd
Lake Leelanau MI
49653

Call Sign: KD8RSY
John S Shanklin III
1720 S Schomberg Rd
Lake Leelanau MI
49653

Call Sign: KB8RDC
Mark A Galla
411 St Joseph St
Lake Leelanau MI
49653

FCC Amateur Radio
Licenses in Lake
Linden

Call Sign: W8KUU
Juliette M High
Rr 1 Box 2 Post Rd
Lake Linden MI 49945

Call Sign: N8PIX
Vicki A Englund
503 Calumet St
Lake Linden MI 49945

Call Sign: KD8RBA
Alex J Smith
120 Calumet St Apt 5
Lake Linden MI 49945

Call Sign: KC8FSN
John J Krause
343 Front St Apt 214
Lake Linden MI 49945

Call Sign: N8NNT
Rebecca J Koski
43 Gregory
Lake Linden MI 49945

Call Sign: KA0WIL
Arthur A Koski
43 Gregory St
Lake Linden MI 49945

Call Sign: KC8EKX
Aleda M Savolainen
26660 Kuusisto Rd
Lake Linden MI 49945

Call Sign: KC8EKY
Dawn M Savolainen
26660 Kuusisto Rd
Lake Linden MI 49945

Call Sign: WB8FCY
Charles F Savolainen
26660 Kuusisto Rd
Lake Linden MI 49945

Call Sign: KE5PX
Samuel W Coates
51683 Paradise Ln
Lake Linden MI
499459605

Call Sign: W8KUV
Robert D High
Rr 1 Post Rd
Lake Linden MI
499459802

Call Sign: WB8QJZ

Stanley F La Muth
30284 Rice Lake Rd
Lake Linden MI 49945

Call Sign: KB8THG
Donald M Koskiniemi
30821 Ricelake Rd
Lake Linden MI 49945

Call Sign: KC8CCY
Brent A Henney
159 School Craft St
Lake Linden MI 49945

Call Sign: N4LAN
Eldon W Jones
27570 W 34th St
Lake Linden MI 49945

Call Sign: KB8SGG
John A McPherson
Lake Linden MI 49945

**FCC Amateur Radio
Licenses in Lake
Odessa**

Call Sign: KD8KLZ
Brent D Schipper
650 1st St
Lake Odessa MI 48849

Call Sign: KC8BXY
Sally J Pepper
742 5th Ave
Lake Odessa MI 48849

Call Sign: KC8BXZ
Larry J Pepper
742 5th Ave
Lake Odessa MI 48849

Call Sign: N8BXK
William J Renkema
846 Beech St
Lake Odessa MI 48849

Call Sign: KC8QKB
Sylvia K Hutchinson
9145 Bliss Rd
Lake Odessa MI 48849

Call Sign: K8SYL
Sylvia K Hutchinson

9145 Bliss Rd
Lake Odessa MI 48849

Call Sign: K8CH
Charles L Hutchinson
9145 Bliss Rd
Lake Odessa MI
488499732

Call Sign: KB0POV
James L Peabody
2961 E Tupper Lake
Lake Odessa MI 48849

Call Sign: WD8AIM
Katherine L Baine
1008 Lake View Dr
Lake Odessa MI 48849

Call Sign: KC8YHT
Jim Brandt
1016 Lakeview Dr
Lake Odessa MI 48849

Call Sign: KD4VGA
Darrin L Johnson
1318 Pearl St
Lake Odessa MI 48849

Call Sign: KI8DO
Mark L Lepard
1317 Pleasant St
Lake Odessa MI 48849

Call Sign: KD8COM
Peter T French
14805 Willowbrook Dr
Lake Odessa MI 48849

**FCC Amateur Radio
Licenses in Lakeview**

Call Sign: W8SNB
Mary Ellen Lewis
210 105th Ave
Lakeview MI 48850

Call Sign: N8PUG
James E Orlowski
10386 5 Mile Rd
Lakeview MI 48850

Call Sign: WA8QAB
Cesar H Colon Bonet

6457 Cutler Rd
Lakeview MI
488509156

Call Sign: KB8PHS
Rebecca S Wilson
667 Fern Dr
Lakeview MI 48850

Call Sign: KD8LMN
Julia D Carter
4648 Hillman Rd
Lakeview MI 48850

Call Sign: KC8LIK
Jamy M Johnston
6063 Honeymoon Dr
Lakeview MI 48850

Call Sign: KC8DTU
Chris L Maxfield
8875 Jefferson Rd
Lakeview MI 48850

Call Sign: KC0LNK
Michael W Matthews
10731 Jefferson Rd
Lakeview MI 48850

Call Sign: KB8TEA
Michael J Maxfield Jr
7725 Johnson Rd
Lakeview MI 48850

Call Sign: KC8OML
Carrie L Maxfield
7725 Johnson Rd
Lakeview MI 48850

Call Sign: WA8KOF
Elwood C Carpenter
400 Lake Dr
Lakeview MI 48850

Call Sign: N8JIP
Robert B Bates
205 Mill St
Lakeview MI 48850

Call Sign: KB8DSP
Joyce L Bates
205 Mill St
Lakeview MI 48850

Call Sign: KA8EZF
Warren D Ostrander
4303 N Backus Rd
Lakeview MI 48850

Call Sign: KB8TXB
Juanita J Stokely
6023 Tamarack Rd
Lakeview MI 48850

Call Sign: KB8WMC
Michael J Maxfield
6023 Tamarack Rd
Lakeview MI 48850

Call Sign: N8XHG
Jeffery E Wilson
7508 Townline Rd
Lakeview MI 48850

Call Sign: KB8PZZ
Roy F Burmeister
5380 Vining Rd
Lakeview MI 48850

Call Sign: KC8FNR
Gail P Bly
5380 Vining Rd
Lakeview MI 48850

Call Sign: KB8SBV
Kenneth S Brodie
8565 W Cannonsvillle
Rd
Lakeview MI 48850

Call Sign: N8OCS
Mark J Stevens
810 Washington Ave
Lakeview MI 48850

Call Sign: KB8ZTD
Lowell Amateur Radio
Youth Club
9918 Wilcox
Lakeview MI
488509467

Call Sign: KB8RHZ
William F Wales Jr
Lakeview MI 48850

Call Sign: KD8GZG
Matthew S Rynd
13216 44th Ave
Lamont MI 49430

Call Sign: KC8EKL
Gregory A Nickel
4601 Leonard
Lamont MI 49430

Call Sign: W8GAN
Gregory A Nickel
4601 Leonard
Lamont MI 49430

Call Sign: KC8AMW
John A Brooke
O 4654 Leonard St
Lamont MI 49430

Call Sign: KB8VEP
Paul E Moore
Hcr 2 Box 660 B
L'Anse MI 49946

Call Sign: KB8TLX
Melvin J Taisto
Rt 2 Box 769
L'Anse MI 49946

Call Sign: WD8ODO
Stuart L Lahti Sr
Rt 2 Box 807
L'Anse MI 49946

Call Sign: KC8DIA
Dave A Heltunen
Rt 1 Box 83
L'Anse MI 49946

Call Sign: KB8QYE
Larry E Cowling
Hc 03 Box 914
L'Anse MI 49946

Call Sign: N8JSJ
Jennifer A Peters
Rte 2 Box 930
L'Anse MI 49946

Call Sign: N8TET
William S Morrow
233 Center St
L'Anse MI 49946

Call Sign: N8VIC
James A Penokie
701 E Broad St
L'Anse MI 49946

Call Sign: AC8LE
Mark E Skidmore
20384 Keranen Rd
L'Anse MI 49946

Call Sign: N8QBJ
Jeffrey W Summers
17137 Lystila Rd
L'Anse MI 49946

Call Sign: KC8QEA
James H Bertagnoli
110 Spruce St
L'Anse MI 49946

Call Sign: N8BNC
Robert J Oakes
16117 Tailor Rd
L'Anse MI 49946

Call Sign: N8JSI
Cynthia L Parker
16111 Tailor Rd
L'Anse MI 49946

Call Sign: KD8HRO
Randall F Bell
13080 Townline Rd
L'Anse MI 49946

Call Sign: K8HRO
Randall F Bell
13080 Townline Rd
L'Anse MI 49946

Call Sign: N8RSH
Michael D Hokenson
L'Anse MI 49946

Call Sign: KD8DKG
John P Tembreull
L'Anse MI 49946

Call Sign: N8PWK
Roger L Smith
15479 Airport Rd
Lansing MI 48906

Call Sign: KB8LCY
Michael G Bond
2815 Alfred Ave
Lansing MI 48906

Call Sign: WD8NYW
William E Cote
1633 Alpha St
Lansing MI 48910

Call Sign: KD8OQY
Robert W Leder
1308 Alsdorf St
Lansing MI 48910

Call Sign: WA8VFV
Robert W Leder
1308 Alsdorf St
Lansing MI 48910

Call Sign: N8ECL
Douglas D Goodrich
5121 Applewood Dr
Lansing MI 48917

Call Sign: KD8DSX
James S Richardson
836 Armstrong Rd
Lansing MI 48911

Call Sign: KC8TIR
Richard L Shirely
2830 Aurelius Rd
Lansing MI 489103704

Call Sign: W8JOO
Claude M Watson
1922 Autumn Ln
Lansing MI 48912

Call Sign: N8QIC
David F Kroft
3024 Avalon
Lansing MI 48911

Call Sign: K8UJC

Wardell Flourry Sr
4510 Ballard Rd
Lansing MI 48911

Call Sign: KB8QZW
Lester C Conarton
328 Banberry S
Lansing MI 48906

Call Sign: N8OBV
Monty L Decess
916 Banghart St
Lansing MI 48906

Call Sign: N8RZK
David L Ford
2202 Barstow
Lansing MI 48906

Call Sign: N8WGX
Steven W Wood
2913 Bascom Cir
Lansing MI 48912

Call Sign: KD8HPW
Joshua T Ackley
5714 Bearcreek
Lansing MI 48917

Call Sign: KD8LJG
James E Byers
6240 Beechfield Dr
Lansing MI 48911

Call Sign: N8GNN
James E Byers
6240 Beechfield Dr
Lansing MI 48911

Call Sign: WA8FAK
Gerald L Hosford
1520 Bennett Rd
Lansing MI 489061878

Call Sign: K8ARM
Floyd J May Jr
1245 Bensch St
Lansing MI 48912

Call Sign: KC8WGY
William S Whiddon
1525 Berkeley Dr
Lansing MI 48910

Call Sign: KB8LVG
Marilyn R Wulfekuhler
11070 Bishop Hwy
Lansing MI 489116201

Call Sign: W8LEW
Louis E Wulfekuhler
11070 Bishop Hwy
Lansing MI 489116201

Call Sign: KB8LEN
Louis E Wulfekuhler
11070 Bishop Hwy
Lansing MI 489116201

Call Sign: KT8Q
Gregory H Hussey
14263 Boichot Rd
Lansing MI 48906

Call Sign: N8RPT
Donald G Wright
1515 Born Trl
Lansing MI 48911

Call Sign: K8EGT
Shirley K Frantz
2424 Boston Blvd
Lansing MI 48910

Call Sign: KC8IIM
Richard K Bruce Jr
2614 Boston Blvd
Lansing MI 48910

Call Sign: W8AB
Michael T Cooper
1925 Bowker Dr
Lansing MI 48911

Call Sign: KD8ID
Ronald B Alexander
2204 Boxwood Ln
Lansing MI 48917

Call Sign: KC5VMF
Duane L Howard Sr
310 Brandywine Pl
Lansing MI 48906

Call Sign: K8SSX
Sam J Belsito
800 Bretton Woods Rd
Lansing MI 48917

Call Sign: W8QG
Harold J Mahlke
1341 Briarfield Dr
Lansing MI 489106106

Call Sign: N8UVC
Marian D Stoddard
1502 Briarwood Rd
Lansing MI 48917

Call Sign: W8KLN
Ashman C Stoddard
1502 Briarwood Rd
Lansing MI 48917

Call Sign: W8BRV
Forrest O Robinson
11558 Broadbent Rd
Lansing MI 48917

Call Sign: KC8VEI
Robert J Harshey
12449 Broadbent Rd
Lansing MI 48917

Call Sign: N8QOM
Stephen T Kochin
801 Brookside Dr 113
Lansing MI 48917

Call Sign: KA8PKZ
Donald F Miller
6727 Bunker Hill
Lansing MI 48906

Call Sign: K8DYH
Lyle F Wight
4723 Burchfield Ave
Lansing MI 489105266

Call Sign: KB8VRQ
William E Wood
4814 Burchfild Ave
Lansing MI 48910

Call Sign: KD8GLN
Gerald L Waite
2816 Cabot Dr
Lansing MI 48911

Call Sign: KD8HHK
Sharon M Waite
2816 Cabot Dr

Lansing MI 489112303

Call Sign: W8FSZ
Currin L Skutt
101 Cadgewith E
Lansing MI 48906

Call Sign: WA8FHI
Boyd A Shumaker
2924 Canarsie Dr
Lansing MI 48910

Call Sign: KB8EJA
Danny L Griffin
5511 Central Cir
Lansing MI 48911

Call Sign: N8OQT
Gail L Griffin
5511 Central Cir
Lansing MI 48911

Call Sign: W8HNI
Kenneth L Faiver
509 Chanticleer Trl
Lansing MI 48917

Call Sign: WB8ZTA
William D Wallace
7446 Chellmar Dr
Lansing MI 489179103

Call Sign: KC8YQH
Deborah A Frank
612 Cherry St
Lansing MI 48933

Call Sign: N8NSR
John A Brodberg
4007 Chickory Ln
Lansing MI 48910

Call Sign: N8OUL
Laurie E Lane
4007 Chickory Ln
Lansing MI 48910

Call Sign: KC8BFL
Matthew J McNenly
3306 Christine
Lansing MI 48911

Call Sign: KB8FHU
Danny L Jorgensen

1410 Christopher Dr
Lansing MI 48906

Call Sign: KB8LFU
Wendell W Parsons
2125 Clearview Ave
Lansing MI 48917

Call Sign: WD8RIS
Christopher T Jenkins
1137 Cleo St
Lansing MI 48915

Call Sign: N4PFO
Lewey Kennedy
1512 Clifton Ave
Lansing MI 48910

Call Sign: W8SZW
J Raymond Wilson
2024 Clifton Ave
Lansing MI 48910

Call Sign: W8GOU
Harland R Mingus
2932 Clinton Rd
Lansing MI 48906

Call Sign: N8JVT
Gary W Rue
3809 Coachlight
Common
Lansing MI 48911

Call Sign: KC8RME
Mary S Rue
3809 Coachlight
Common
Lansing MI 489114411

Call Sign: KC8RMF
John E Shaner
3809 Coachlight
Common
Lansing MI 489114411

Call Sign: WD8PVS
Charles J Culton
734 Community St
Lansing MI 48906

Call Sign: W8TCY
Elbert C Monkman
2207 Coolidge St

Lansing MI 48906

Call Sign: KD8MOH
Shannon M Ranes
1728 Cooper Ave
Lansing MI 48910

Call Sign: WA2NVK
Shannon M Ranes
1728 Cooper Ave
Lansing MI 48910

Call Sign: KC8CAJ
Christopher E Ranes
1728 Cooper Ave
Lansing MI 48910

Call Sign: KD8GKG
Ernest W Lamp
6425 Cooper Rd
Lansing MI 48911

Call Sign: K8OGR
Ernest W Lamp
6425 Cooper Rd
Lansing MI 48911

Call Sign: KB1OLI
Keegan W Lamp
6425 Cooper Rd
Lansing MI 48911

Call Sign: N8FTK
Raymond E Platt
6736 Cooper Rd
Lansing MI 48911

Call Sign: KB8MUN
Ron E Meddaugh
333 Corral Path
Lansing MI 48917

Call Sign: KB8LKC
Mark Q Lynch
6236 Coulson
Lansing MI 48911

Call Sign: N8QLL
Faye L Blink
5930 Coulson Ct
Lansing MI 48911

Call Sign: N8WKY
Steve C Montague

6324 Coulson Ct
Lansing MI 48911

Call Sign: KC8LBN
Jason R Bates
810 Crown Pt Dr
Lansing MI 489174312

Call Sign: KB8PRM
Christopher P
Wilkinson
6415 Culver Dr Rt 7
Lansing MI 48823

Call Sign: AA8DQ
Douglas L Nelson
6021 Daft St
Lansing MI 48911

Call Sign: KB8TTU
Russell L Nelson
6021 Daft St
Lansing MI 48911

Call Sign: N8YAG
Allison A Dennis
6039 Daft St
Lansing MI 48911

Call Sign: KA8OBO
Milton S Connor
15161 Daggott Rd
Lansing MI 48906

Call Sign: KA8UAI
George L Stark
15201 Daggott Rd
Lansing MI 48906

Call Sign: K8DHN
John E Hewitt
4310 Darron Dr
Lansing MI 489173503

Call Sign: N8PGB
George A Albrecht
1607 David St
Lansing MI 48912

Call Sign: K8ZRX
Duard L Jones
4815 Delbrook Ave
Lansing MI 48910

Call Sign: K8ZRY
Leonteen Jones
4815 Delbrook Ave
Lansing MI 48910

Call Sign: KD8IAP
Jamie R Kahler
1843 Delevan Ave
Lansing MI 48910

Call Sign: KC8OYS
Jennifer S Lacluyze
4356 Dell Rd Apt F
Lansing MI 48911

Call Sign: KC8OYR
Aaron P Lacluyze
4356 Dell Rd Apt F
Lansing MI 48911

Call Sign: N8FPR
Edward K Fitzgerald
2211 Delta River Dr
Lansing MI 48906

Call Sign: KD8ICK
Gregory A Sprout
3324 Delta River Dr
Lansing MI 48906

Call Sign: W8RXY
Alan L Conn
6502 Delta River Dr
Lansing MI 48906

Call Sign: N8LLC
John W Crawford
2523 Dier St
Lansing MI 489105819

Call Sign: KI0RZ
Richard D Pestrue
160 Donald Ave
Lansing MI 48906

Call Sign: KB8QZY
Lance L Rodberg
1141 Dorchester Cir 17
Lansing MI 48910

Call Sign: KC8IWA
Terry A Grost
2524 E Cavanaugh Rd
Lansing MI 48910

Call Sign: N8SHR
David S Gardner
1584 E Clark Rd
Lansing MI 48906

Call Sign: KD8GIF
Lyle Laylin
204 E Grand River
Ave
Lansing MI 48906

Call Sign: KD6KCX
John T Tyree
517.5 E Grand River
Ave 1
Lansing MI 48606

Call Sign: K8USY
Charles J Shawnee
12223 E Greenfield
Lansing MI 48917

Call Sign: N8CYY
Charles J Shawnee Jr
12223 E Greenfield Rd
Lansing MI 489179710

Call Sign: KC8NTS
Jeffrey L Cressman
308 E Greenlawn Ave
Lansing MI 48910

Call Sign: N8JHO
Alice M Counterman
515 E Howe Ave
Lansing MI 48906

Call Sign: KB8SKV
Charles L Keep Jr
1816 E Irvington
Lansing MI 48910

Call Sign: KF8HD
Evelyn C Wright
235 E Jackson St
Lansing MI 48906

Call Sign: W8QN
Robert E Wright Jr
235 E Jackson St
Lansing MI 48906

Call Sign: KB8TTW

Philip L Larson
2315 E Jolly Rd Apt
11
Lansing MI 48910

Call Sign: K8NOP
Fred W Butler
3020 E Lafayette Cir
Lansing MI 48906

Call Sign: KB8MOW
Mary Ann Wesley
807 E Miller Rd
Lansing MI 48911

Call Sign: KA8FKT
R G Curtiss Jr
2500 E Mt Hope
Lansing MI 48910

Call Sign: WD8PJX
Stonewall J Cross
530 E Paulson
Lansing MI 48906

Call Sign: KC8IHV
Randall L Stortz
220 E Syringa Dr
Lansing MI 48910

Call Sign: K8VY
Randall L Stortz
220 E Syringa Dr
Lansing MI 489107444

Call Sign: KD8JHZ
Mark E Brink
1100 E Thomas L
Pkwy
Lansing MI 48917

Call Sign: KC8MEB
Mark E Brink
1100 E Thomas L
Pkwy
Lansing MI 48917

Call Sign: WR8S
Kenneth W Hull
545 E Willard
Lansing MI 48910

Call Sign: N8OHJ
Dale A Burgess

2700 Eaton Rapids Rd
113
Lansing MI 48911

Call Sign: KB8LTR
Shirley G Pittenger
730 Edgemont Blvd 1
Lansing MI 489172219

Call Sign: KD8QFF
Nathan R Cunningham
1308 Edmond St
Lansing MI 48910

Call Sign: KD8RQS
William T Bradley
1203 Edwards St
Lansing MI 48910

Call Sign: WD8BDR
Max A Grove
542 Elmshaven
Lansing MI 48917

Call Sign: KD8QZW
Richard K Gargett
507 Elmshaven Dr
Lansing MI 48917

Call Sign: AE8AE
Richard K Gargett
507 Elmshaven Dr
Lansing MI 48917

Call Sign: KD8AKW
Timothy W Marshall
8513 Ember Glen Pass
Lansing MI 48917

Call Sign: N8MTE
William P Williams
2215 Fairfax Rd
Lansing MI 489102417

Call Sign: KB8ZRF
Peter E Schneider
813 Fayette St
Lansing MI 48910

Call Sign: AC8FK
Victor Iacobescu
3114 Felt St
Lansing MI 48906

Call Sign: N8KAD
Steven C Texley
3303 Felt St
Lansing MI 48906

Call Sign: KD8MMP
Edwin L Poling Jr
2508 Fielding Dr
Lansing MI 48910

Call Sign: KC8CGH
Roger Young
2631 Forest Rd
Lansing MI 489103764

Call Sign: KD8NZM
Brian Baldus
3105 Forest Rd 201
Lansing MI 48910

Call Sign: KC8MHN
Brian M Fish
519 Galahad
Lansing MI 48906

Call Sign: KD8QBF
Daniel H Cameron
1024 Garfield Ave
Lansing MI 48917

Call Sign: WA8VPG
Michael E Ellis
5035 Geraldine Dr
Lansing MI 48917

Call Sign: KD8EKY
Wayne A Conklin
7329 Golf Gate
Lansing MI 48917

Call Sign: W8CPN
Craig P Naranjo
1033 Gordon Ave
Lansing MI 48910

Call Sign: K8TKV
Thomas A Kelley
2929 Grandell Ave
Lansing MI 48906

Call Sign: KD8NUX
Kevin M Vanderhoof
419 Green Meadows
Dr

Lansing MI 48917

Call Sign: NG8L
John A Ingraham
2807 Greenbriar Ave
Lansing MI 48912

Call Sign: KA8DGR
Preston D Snow
4707 Gull Rd 48
Lansing MI 48917

Call Sign: KA8DGS
Marjane Snow
4707 Gull Rd 48
Lansing MI 48917

Call Sign: KC8MVD
Charles C Hoffmeyer
517 Hamilton Ave
Lansing MI 48910

Call Sign: KD8QLO
Harold D Gary Jr
4036 Hartford Rd 12
Lansing MI 48911

Call Sign: WC8ING
Ingham County
Michigan Arpsc
314 Hathaway
Lansing MI 48910

Call Sign: N8JEB
John E Barber Jr
314 Hathaway St
Lansing MI 48917

Call Sign: KB8QJC
John E Barber Jr
314 Hathaway St
Lansing MI 48917

Call Sign: NO8T
John E Barber Jr
314 Hathaway St
Lansing MI 48917

Call Sign: KC8DQD
Donald L Ward
4009 Heathgate Dr
Lansing MI 489112515

Call Sign: N8PWE

Ronald D Merchant
1023 Hickory St
Lansing MI 489121710

Call Sign: W8WDA
Allan E Budden
1105 Hillgate Way
Lansing MI 48912

Call Sign: KC8NSB
Tyler D Whitney
1142 Hillgate Way
Lansing MI 48912

Call Sign: KD8HLM
David D Smith
5825 Hilliard
Lansing MI 48911

Call Sign: KC8DPY
Glenn A Knapp
6216 Hilliard
Lansing MI 48911

Call Sign: KD8HBA
Jason D Southwell
6229 Hilliard Rd
Lansing MI 48911

Call Sign: KD8FPF
Jason D Watson
2101 Holly Way
Lansing MI 48910

Call Sign: KD8IUL
Brian C Adams
2635 Hopkins Ave
Lansing MI 48912

Call Sign: KB8IS
Lowel L Nash
5861 Horstmeyer Rd
Lansing MI 48911

Call Sign: KD8HLS
Lowel L Nash
5861 Horstmeyer Rd
Lansing MI 48911

Call Sign: K8LPD
Lowel L Nash
5861 Horstmeyer Rd
Lansing MI 48911

Call Sign: KB8GOY
James R Kuerbitz
4804 Hughes Rd
Lansing MI 48910

Call Sign: KC8ZYE
Tyler D Bergstrom
4804 Hughes Rd
Lansing MI 48910

Call Sign: N8JM
Joseph M Marrah
642 Hunter Blvd
Lansing MI 48910

Call Sign: N8ERM
Terry A Morgan
722 Hunter Blvd
Lansing MI 48910

Call Sign: N8KPL
Glenda F Andre
118 Huron St
Lansing MI 489151748

Call Sign: KG8LE
Glenn W Sommerfeldt
2324 Hyman Dr
Lansing MI 489123418

Call Sign: KA8LEQ
Thomas M Jacobs
14834 Idylcrest Dr
Lansing MI 48906

Call Sign: KC8ARI
Ronald J McCormick
3809 Ingham St
Lansing MI 48911

Call Sign: N9BRB
Brian R Bowman
5303 Ivan Dr Apt 215
Lansing MI 48917

Call Sign: N8LWZ
Wayne G Wood
1521 Jerome St
Lansing MI 48912

Call Sign: KC8VEH
Jason W Hoyland
600 Jesop Ave
Lansing MI 48910

Call Sign: KD8GJF
Tammy L Hoyland
600 Jessop Ave
Lansing MI 48910

Call Sign: N8NMT
Martin W Davis
209 Julie Dr
Lansing MI 48906

Call Sign: K5TTS
William J Mathews
5505 Kaynorth 8
Lansing MI 48911

Call Sign: N8PVZ
Bernard F Gaffney Jr
1020 Kendon Dr
Lansing MI 489105638

Call Sign: W8BFG
Bernard F Gaffney Jr
1020 Kendon Dr
Lansing MI 489105638

Call Sign: KD8EOR
Nathan A Simon
2345 Kensington Rd
Lansing MI 48910

Call Sign: KC8GAK
Roxanna L Hannahs
5010 Kessler Dr
Lansing MI 48910

Call Sign: KC8QEU
Lansing Michigan
Arpsc
5010 Kessler Dr
Lansing MI 48910

Call Sign: KC8RLD
Ingham County
Michigan Arpsc
5010 Kessler Dr
Lansing MI 48910

Call Sign: KC8FSK
Jane L Hosford
7057 Kieppes Ct
Lansing MI 48911

Call Sign: KC8QZB

John C Hosford
7057 Kieppes Ct
Lansing MI 48911

Call Sign: N8FLK
Kerby H Rials
3308 Kilberry Rd
Lansing MI 48911

Call Sign: K4FPH
Larry G Sullivan
416 La Salle Blvd
Lansing MI 489124129

Call Sign: KA8OBS
Rowena M Elrod
111 Lancelot Pl
Lansing MI 48906

Call Sign: KB9GIY
Philip G Willis
1416 Lansing Ave
Lansing MI 48915

Call Sign: WA8MFQ
Theodore D Sadilek
2718 Lasalle Gardens
Lansing MI 489124133

Call Sign: KC8HVU
Marcus C Anderson
3227 Lawdor
Lansing MI 48911

Call Sign: K8RDN
Robert L Berger
6130 Lerner Way
Lansing MI 489116001

Call Sign: KD8QMY
Nicholas C Blackledge
559 Lincoln Ave
Lansing MI 48910

Call Sign: KD8QVR
Todd E Bertolozzi
812 Loa St
Lansing MI 48910

Call Sign: KC8YMM
Robert M Britton
1511 Lockbridge Dr
Lansing MI 48911

Call Sign: W8PSD
Robert L Reid
900 Long Blvd 463
Lansing MI 48911

Call Sign: N8BII
Walter G Heinritzi
1520 Lotipac Pl
Lansing MI 48917

Call Sign: KD8DAT
Michael D Keeney
1910 Lourder Ct
Lansing MI 48910

Call Sign: KB8NPH
Donald E Peavey
15344 Lowell Rd
Lansing MI 48917

Call Sign: KC8YKF
Brian Taylor
1813 Lyons Ave
Lansing MI 48910

Call Sign: KB8AKZ
Craig A Goble
12056 Madonna Dr
Lansing MI 48917

Call Sign: KB8ZRG
Tillie J Turner
2214 Maple Wood Ave
Lansing MI 48910

Call Sign: KA8TPQ
William O Anderson Jr
1427 Mark Twain
Lansing MI 48911

Call Sign: KC8WJY
Joseph D Caswell
1216 McCullough St
Lansing MI 48912

Call Sign: N8DHR
Debra A Hethorn
6818 Meese Dr
Lansing MI 48910

Call Sign: KM8X
Chris G Hethorn
6818 Meese Dr
Lansing MI 48911

Call Sign: WB8NUS
Donald L Tillitson
2910 Meister Ln
Lansing MI 489069010

Call Sign: N8GAQ
Roy E Uchigashima
2854 Memory Ln
Lansing MI 48910

Call Sign: W8LPK
Devern A Chubb
2801 Mersey Ln Apt C
Lansing MI 489111475

Call Sign: N8TSP
Anthony K Jones
6760 Mill Stream Ln
Lansing MI 48911

Call Sign: KD4NDK
Roger A Barnhill
6840 Mill Wheel Dr
Lansing MI 48911

Call Sign: KD8BDI
Deanna M Barnhill
6840 Mill Wheel Dr
Lansing MI 48911

Call Sign: W8MAA
Central Michigan ARC
Inc
6840 Mill Wheel Dr
Lansing MI 489117066

Call Sign: KD8BZL
James R Lakin
528 Monroe St
Lansing MI 48906

Call Sign: WD8BYC
Howard D Brown
Unit D Montevideo Dr
Lansing MI 48917

Call Sign: KB8DQP
Jennifer M Quinn
1015 Moores River Dr
Lansing MI 48910

Call Sign: KB8UKR
L Susan Carter

1710 Moores River Dr
Lansing MI 48910

Call Sign: N8GSK
Robert P Dale
328 N Canal Rd
Lansing MI 48917

Call Sign: N8DEF
Delta Township
811 N Canal Rd
Lansing MI 48917

Call Sign: K8IFI
Helen E Burl
215 N Canal Rd L 22
Lansing MI 48917

Call Sign: KA8YNB
Charles E Kissee
215 N Canal Rd Lot 87
Lansing MI 48917

Call Sign: KB8IBF
Ruth A Tepin
236 N Catherine
Lansing MI 489174902

Call Sign: K8JNZ
Richard C Stortz
1112 N Creyts Rd
Lansing MI 48917

Call Sign: KC8BFK
Jan L Bradfield
621 N Deerfield Ave
Lansing MI 48917

Call Sign: KA4MCK
Laura D Black
604 N Dexter Dr
Lansing MI 48910

Call Sign: W8DSH
Kenneth G Noyce
726 N Fairview
Lansing MI 48912

Call Sign: KC8SOT
Richard F Mccreight
801 N Foster
Lansing MI 48912

Call Sign: WD8DGV

Cathy J Siebert
811 N Foster
Lansing MI 48912

Call Sign: KC8WVZ
John L Gibson
601 N Foster Ave
Lansing MI 48912

Call Sign: KY8V
Inez W Pearson
1926 N Genessee
Lansing MI 48915

Call Sign: KC8WW
James W Brooks
5026 N Grand River
Lansing MI 48906

Call Sign: W8NRE
Edward C Liebler
2611 N Grand River
Ave
Lansing MI 48906

Call Sign: KD8BWL
Louis B Larche
1425 N Hayford
Lansing MI 48912

Call Sign: KD8ICJ
Keith S Watson
224 N Jenison
Lansing MI 48915

Call Sign: KB8LJC
Bryan J Tetreau
1107 N Magnolia
Lansing MI 48912

Call Sign: N8XMF
Donald H Ashland
1417 N Magnolia
Lansing MI 48912

Call Sign: KD8BDJ
Kay V Clark
4084 N Pine Dell
Lansing MI 489116126

Call Sign: N8PWD
Forrest B Clark Jr
4084 N Pine Dell Dr
Lansing MI 489116126

Call Sign: KC8NBT
Kevin M Ellis
325 N Sycamore
Lansing MI 48933

Call Sign: KB8YQZ
Paul F Keefer
6059 Nancy St
Lansing MI 489116458

Call Sign: KC8SVM
Thomas G Stenske
2201 Northampton
Way
Lansing MI 48912

Call Sign: KC8QYT
James M Kutz
4921 Northlane Dr
Lansing MI 489174423

Call Sign: N8NKZ
Janice K Harper
3000 Norwich Rd
Lansing MI 48911

Call Sign: W8JWW
Willis L Nielsen Sr
3024 Norwich Rd
Lansing MI 48911

Call Sign: W8AAX
Kenneth A Kruger
1539 Ohio Ave
Lansing MI 48906

Call Sign: KC8RQV
John H Hayes II
4311 Old Castle Cir
Lansing MI 48911

Call Sign: AK8G
John H Hayes II
4311 Old Castle Cir
Lansing MI 48911

Call Sign: KC8TMP
Robin L Hayes
4311 Old Castle Cir
Lansing MI 48911

Call Sign: KD8CLU
John Hayes III
4311 Old Castle Cir
Lansing MI 48911

Call Sign: AB8ZL
Christopher R Reusch
5256 Old Lansing Rd 1
Lansing MI 48917

Call Sign: KD8CC
Fred Demske Jr
4900 Ora St
Lansing MI 489105383

Call Sign: KB8ZRB
John C Hernly
3425 Palmer Sr
Lansing MI 48910

Call Sign: KD8LVH
Brook D Babcock
1803 Pattengill
Lansing MI 48910

Call Sign: N8XHO
Artis L White
1806 Pepper Tree Ln
Lansing MI 48912

Call Sign: K8SP
Steve A Pollo
3404 Pickwick Pl
Lansing MI 48917

Call Sign: N7JBY
Shannon R Pollo
3404 Pickwick Pl
Lansing MI 48917

Call Sign: KC8KED
James L Greiner
3603 Pkwy Dr
Lansing MI 489100706

Call Sign: KB8WNG
Ronald R Blonshine
4110 Pleasant Grove
Rd
Lansing MI 48910

Call Sign: KC8PEJ
Lansing Community
College ARC
7240 Police And
Public Safety
Lansing MI 48901

Call Sign: W8LCC
Lansing Community
College ARC
7240 Police And
Public Safety
Lansing MI 48901

Call Sign: WB8QWS
William E Bauer
2951 Quincy Ln
Lansing MI 48910

Call Sign: KD8OQT
Samuel Fitzgerald
3506 Ramsgate Dr
Lansing MI 48906

Call Sign: N8FPR
Samuel E Fitzgerald
3506 Ramsgate Dr
Lansing MI 48906

Call Sign: N8FZ
Russell E Fitzgerald
3506 Ramsgate Dr
Lansing MI 48906

Call Sign: KC8ALL
William S Torrence Jr
208 Redner
Lansing MI 489113742

Call Sign: N8RBP
Burton G Pickens
240 Renker
Lansing MI 48917

Call Sign: KC8VEJ
Douglas J Aves
1734 Reo Rd
Lansing MI 48910

Call Sign: KC8VEK
Tamara L Aves
1734 Reo Rd
Lansing MI 48910

Call Sign: WH6CKJ
Robert M Smith
118 Richard Ave
Lansing MI 48917

Call Sign: KB8SI
Peter J Cremeans
554 Riley St
Lansing MI 48910

Call Sign: KC8NMS
Holly C Gaffney
5312 River Ridge Dr
Lansing MI 48917

Call Sign: N8BET
Billie R Richmond
719 Robert St
Lansing MI 48910

Call Sign: N8ECU
Robert C Higdon
900 Robins Rd
Lansing MI 48917

Call Sign: N8KRF
David H Petrilli
2014 Rock Way
Lansing MI 48910

Call Sign: N8QZF
Deborah L Petrilli
2014 Rockway
Lansing MI 48910

Call Sign: KC8UUF
Douglas E Sitterson Sr
6329 Rosedale Rd
Lansing MI 48911

Call Sign: KC8YMN
Evelyn J Sitterson
6329 Rosedale Rd
Lansing MI 48911

Call Sign: WA8LAY
Harold J Bell
1430 Roseneath
Lansing MI 48915

Call Sign: KD8MOK
Randolph A Williams
Sr
2421 Rossiter Pl
Lansing MI 48911

Call Sign: N8NJX
Donald W Page
423 Roundtop Rd

Lansing MI 48917

Call Sign: KE5GBR
Darrell J Demartino
1153 Runaway Bay Dr
Apt 3D
Lansing MI 48917

Call Sign: KC8OTX
Alexander S Roig
505 Ryder Rd Apt 706
Lansing MI 48917

Call Sign: KC8NJL
Alice W Mailhot
601 S Butler 4
Lansing MI 48915

Call Sign: KE8YI
Kris J Krycinski
407 S Clemens
Lansing MI 48912

Call Sign: N8WTG
Robert H Storey
507 S Detroit St
Lansing MI 48912

Call Sign: AE8A
Gene A Garrage
14560 S Dewitt Rd
Lansing MI 48906

Call Sign: W8SFA
Richard B Pennington
728 S Dexter Dr
Lansing MI 489104642

Call Sign: KC8QYV
Kurt R Niemeyer
129 S Foster Ave
Lansing MI 48912

Call Sign: N0JOR
Katrina D Ramsell
566 S Park Blvd
Lansing MI 48910

Call Sign: N8YQR
Juan R Pizano Sr
4810 S Pennsylvania
Ave
Lansing MI 489105612

Call Sign: KC8VKB
Derek M Halliwill
4823 S Pennsylvania
Ave Apt 7
Lansing MI 48910

Call Sign: KD8PSG
Arnaldo Vaca
500 S Pine St Apt 417
Lansing MI 48933

Call Sign: KB8TIJ
Brian S Moles
6813 S Washington
Lansing MI 48911

Call Sign: N9VQB
Kevin L Kenyon
6762 S Washington
Ave Lot 15
Lansing MI 48911

Call Sign: KC8GXO
Marlene M Harger
6433 S Washington Rd
Lansing MI 48911

Call Sign: W8BCI
Daniel G Harger
6433 S Washington Rd
Lansing MI 48911

Call Sign: KD8HHM
Robert C Kerr
714 Sawyer Rd
Lansing MI 48911

Call Sign: KC8IKO
Michael F Kovalchick
3011 Scarborough
Lansing MI 48910

Call Sign: KC8DQC
Edward A Schweifler
3017 Scarborough Rd
Lansing MI 48910

Call Sign: KB8KYR
Raymond S Rokita Jr
3816 Schlee St
Lansing MI 489104435

Call Sign: KB8NBM
Brian K Stipanuk

933 Seymour Ave
Lansing MI 48906

Call Sign: KD8EZM
Daniel J Martin
1423 Shannon Ln
Lansing MI 48917

Call Sign: KB8FIX
Clifford C Dible
3423 Snowglen Ln
Lansing MI 48917

Call Sign: W8PRL
Theodore A Chartrand
3504 Snowglen Ln
Lansing MI 48917

Call Sign: K8WEX
Louis H Smith
5008 Southgate Ave
Lansing MI 48910

Call Sign: WB3BSJ
Arthur Bell III
3430 Springbrook Ln
Lansing MI 48917

Call Sign: KC8ARG
Lowell T Hoyland
533 Sprucewood
Lansing MI 48910

Call Sign: KC8FFW
Theodore G Blanchard
533 Sprucewood
Lansing MI 48910

Call Sign: KC8SEQ
Jim E Crites
3227 Stabler St
Lansing MI 48910

Call Sign: KC8VKC
Steven T Brooks
4010 Stabler St
Lansing MI 48910

Call Sign: KC8SEP
Amy K Crites
3227 Stadler St
Lansing MI 48910

Call Sign: KC8FFX

John R Marty
3035 Staten Ave Apt 9
Lansing MI 489103796

Call Sign: KB8SFI
Lawrence A Scott
4912 Stillwell
Lansing MI 48911

Call Sign: W8UDA
Dorothy A Scott
4912 Stillwell
Lansing MI 48911

Call Sign: KD8EBS
Kevin M Johnson
1826 Stirling Ave
Lansing MI 48910

Call Sign: KD8LDN
John C Fisher
1812 Stoney Point Dr
Lansing MI 48917

Call Sign: KD8LDM
Sean C Fisher
1812 Stoney Point Dr
Lansing MI 48917

Call Sign: KA8JDJ
Renee M Patterson
1918 Stoney Point Dr
Lansing MI 48917

Call Sign: KC8MMD
Timothy W Rowan
2324 Strathmore
Lansing MI 48910

Call Sign: KB8YQW
Paul E Carpenter III
168 Susan Dr
Lansing MI 48906

Call Sign: KB8IBP
Ronald J Hicks
5633 Taffey Park Way
Lansing MI 48911

Call Sign: KB8FHS
Nicholas A Nelson
3424 Tecumseh River
Rd
Lansing MI 48906

Call Sign: KD8MGX
Gregory J Martin
2107 Teel Ave
Lansing MI 48910

Call Sign: K8FSQ
Gregory J Martin
2107 Teel Ave
Lansing MI 48910

Call Sign: KC8BFJ
Emile Alhaddad
2407 Teel Ave
Lansing MI 489103122

Call Sign: KD8MB
Alton G Stoddard
5001 Tenny St
Lansing MI 48910

Call Sign: KA8DDQ
James L Harvey
3919 Tennyson Ln
Lansing MI 489112167

Call Sign: KB8QEZ
Herbert A Terbrack
4132 Thackin Dr
Lansing MI 48911

Call Sign: KF7DYU
Adrian J Flynn
634 Tilsdale Rd
Lansing MI 489103312

Call Sign: KC8AYF
Christopher N Larock
3019 Timber Dr
Lansing MI 48917

Call Sign: KC8FCX
Mary J Larock
3019 Timber Dr
Lansing MI 48917

Call Sign: KB8FTR
Mark A Martin
218 Tinley Dr
Lansing MI 48911

Call Sign: KM8K
Peter W Lycos
601 Tisdale Ave

Lansing MI 48910

Call Sign: KB8LFT
Joanie R Birdsall
608 Tisdale Ave
Lansing MI 48910

Call Sign: KC8YWO
Chris J Borchard
7619 Trestlewood Dr
Apt 3A
Lansing MI 48917

Call Sign: KD8FLL
Chris J Borchard
7619 Trestlewood Dr
Apt 3A
Lansing MI 48917

Call Sign: KA8BCL
Raymond G Gustafson
14165 Trumpeter Ln
Lansing MI 489069224

Call Sign: K1GTO
James B Hein
3919 Truxton Ln
Lansing MI 48911

Call Sign: N8TSM
John W Hallett
3301 Turner Rd
Lansing MI 48906

Call Sign: KC8ULF
Richard J Wahl
3463 Twilight Ave
Lansing MI 48906

Call Sign: N8WTI
Richard W Keck
415 Valley Rd
Lansing MI 48906

Call Sign: KC8CEM
Raymond C Wilkinson
2012 Vermont Ave
Lansing MI 48906

Call Sign: WB8YYG
Jeffrey A Hall
2921 Vermont St
Lansing MI 48906

Call Sign: N8LMU
Michael J Dokter
728 Vernon Ave
Lansing MI 48910

Call Sign: KD8MOI
Jennifer C Frank
834 Vernon Ave
Lansing MI 48910

Call Sign: N8VWA
Paul J Waters
1307 Victor Ave
Lansing MI 48910

Call Sign: K8GHX
George J Wood
2237 Victor Ave
Lansing MI 48910

Call Sign: K8HLX
Gary D Wood
2237 Victor Ave
Lansing MI 489111731

Call Sign: KD8HCO
Matthew D Warncke
333 Village Dr
Lansing MI 48911

Call Sign: KB8QOY
Gayle M Vallad
901 Vincent Ct
Lansing MI 48910

Call Sign: WD8NOY
Betty J Hack
625 W Barnes Ave
Lansing MI 48910

Call Sign: N8ELF
Phillip D Morris
238 W Fairfield
Lansing MI 48906

Call Sign: KC8HJQ
Jane M Newton
220 W Gier St
Lansing MI 48906

Call Sign: N8LNA
Victor Iacobescu
318 W Grand River 9
Lansing MI 48906

Call Sign: W8AIH
William A Mueller
12478 W Greenfield
Lansing MI 48917

Call Sign: WD8NZC
Gerald F Nestell
215 W Hodge
Lansing MI 48910

Call Sign: KB8PKY
Robert C Sasser
2908 W Holmes Rd
Lansing MI 48911

Call Sign: KB8YYN
Ted M McDaniel
200 W Jackson St
Lansing MI 48906

Call Sign: KC8NOI
Marie M Watson
2031 W Jolly Rd
Lansing MI 48910

Call Sign: KC8MAD
Garry L Watson
2031 W Jolly Rd
Lansing MI 489105153

Call Sign: KA8RYE
Stephany A Wills
Boyd
1132 W Lenawee St
Lansing MI 48915

Call Sign: WB8OIP
Marvin W Sommer
2706 W Libbie Dr
Lansing MI 48917

Call Sign: KD8LCE
David J Cohoon
5414 W Michigan Apt
203
Lansing MI 48917

Call Sign: KD8OIC
Michael T Corbin
1318 W Michigan Ave
Lansing MI 48915

Call Sign: KA8GKW

Raymond N Langley
3309 W Michigan Ave
Lansing MI 48917

Call Sign: KC8ZLQ
Michael N Bofysil
1008 W Miller Rd
Lansing MI 48911

Call Sign: KC8ZSR
Stacey L Armstrong
1008 W Miller Rd
Lansing MI 48911

Call Sign: KC8AYE
Gregory L Hartman
3121 W Mt Hope
Lansing MI 48911

Call Sign: K8DRB
Dennis R Beckner
3407 W Mt Hope Ave
A25
Lansing MI 48911

Call Sign: KD8HLR
Richard L Greeson
508 W Northrup St
Lansing MI 48911

Call Sign: KD8PA
Gregory L Wesley
933 W Northrup St
Lansing MI 48911

Call Sign: KC8TOZ
John P O Donnell
424 W Paulson St
Lansing MI 489063049

Call Sign: KD8WP
Henry J Lewandoski
1318 W Rundle Ave
Lansing MI 489102526

Call Sign: KC8QOU
Delta Township
7614 W Saginaw Hwy
Lansing MI 48917

Call Sign: KD8EPZ
Linda C Conklin
5859 W Saginaw Hwy
303

Lansing MI 48917

Call Sign: K8JBJ
Robert Handy
4416 W St Joe
Lansing MI 48917

Call Sign: KD8PI
Irving W Graham
4646 W St Joe
Lansing MI 48917

Call Sign: N8VGM
Donald D Dixon
5889 W State Rd
Lansing MI 48906

Call Sign: WA8NHD
Ralph R Chapman
5359 W Stoll Rd
Lansing MI 48906

Call Sign: KC8UBM
Angela N Zischke
5621 W Stoll Rd
Lansing MI 48906

Call Sign: KD8BD
Donald M Cote
100 W Syringa Dr
Lansing MI 489105378

Call Sign: N8SGV
Philip C Sims
424 W Willard
Lansing MI 48910

Call Sign: N8YCE
Bruce J Squires
2715 W Willow Apt 4
Lansing MI 48917

Call Sign: AA8DU
Charles H Witt
5002 W Willow Hwy
Lansing MI 48917

Call Sign: KC8ERD
Charles R Sipes
5405 W Willow Hwy
Lansing MI 48917

Call Sign: KA8EDW
James P Charles

5520 W Willow Hwy
Lansing MI 48917

Call Sign: W8WHU
Robert Stahl
305.5 W Willow St
Lansing MI 48906

Call Sign: KB8ZQY
Jeffrey B Baker
2430 Wabash Rd
Lansing MI 48910

Call Sign: KC8DPW
Julia K Baker
2430 Wabash Rd
Lansing MI 48910

Call Sign: KD8OIB
Daniel V Ruger
1212 Walsh
Lansing MI 48912

Call Sign: KB8QEY
Ellis W Whitehead
3343 Wardell Rd
Lansing MI 48917

Call Sign: N8AVE
Dennis D Defore
2352 Washington Rd
Lansing MI 48911

Call Sign: KC8ICT
David J Timmer
3434 Wayside Ter
Lansing MI 48917

Call Sign: KB8UKC
Steven L Hunt
2838 Webster Rd
Lansing MI 489069005

Call Sign: KC8UAK
Robert F Stahl
327 West St
Lansing MI 48915

Call Sign: KC8UAL
Nicholas D Clark
327 West St
Lansing MI 48915

Call Sign: KD8ONE

Dennis R Van Wormer
4910 Westhill Dr
Lansing MI 48917

Call Sign: WA8WFB
Thomas J McNamara
4930 Westhill Dr
Lansing MI 48917

Call Sign: KC8PIK
Pamela L Mcnamara
4930 Westhill Dr
Lansing MI 48917

Call Sign: KD8ONF
Andrew L Grabenstein
318 Westmoreland Dr
Lansing MI 48915

Call Sign: K8ZLP
Bert L Carter
3122 Westwood Ave
Lansing MI 489062867

Call Sign: KD8DMC
Joseph B Wachter
5330 Wexford Rd
Lansing MI 489113312

Call Sign: W8KQQ
James L Frazer
3010 White Oaks Dr
Lansing MI 48906

Call Sign: WB8QKR
Daniel W Poorman
3730 Wilson Ave
Lansing MI 48906

Call Sign: W8TCC
Troy C Creed
1715 Windsor St
Lansing MI 489062878

Call Sign: KB8NPO
Paul D Parkanzky
825 Wisconsin Ave
Lansing MI 48915

Call Sign: N8OBP
Frank C McLaughlin
900 Wisconson Ave
Lansing MI 489152115

Call Sign: KB8WXG
Scott A Van Walsum
1314 Wolf Run Dr
Lansing MI 48917

Call Sign: WA8YQB
Martin H Onstad
6053 Woodgate Dr
Lansing MI 48910

Call Sign: KC8TIO
Donald J Quillan
2614 Woodview Dr
Lansing MI 48911

Call Sign: KB8OVM
Paul R Binkowski
6321 Worhtmore Rd
Lansing MI 48917

Call Sign: KD8KJU
Ericka A Kahler
Lansing MI 48901

Call Sign: KC8YYO
Jonathan L Mire
Lansing MI 48901

Call Sign: KD8MVX
Joseph Burke
Lansing MI 48901

Call Sign: W4USD
Joseph Burke
Lansing MI 48901

Call Sign: N8CLS
Luke A Sandel
Lansing MI 48901

Call Sign: KC8YPN
Travis M Mccolgan
Lansing MI 48901

Call Sign: KC8NQM
Edward F Hartwick
Lansing MI 48901

Call Sign: K8CIA
Paul C Harmer
Lansing MI 48908

Call Sign: WA8BEN
Benjamin M Holcomb

Lansing MI 48908

Call Sign: KF5DGW
Gordon T Satoh
Lansing MI 48909

FCC Amateur Radio Licenses in Laurium

Call Sign: W8CSI
John P Sincock
95 2nd St
Laurium MI 49913

Call Sign: WA8ICV
Henry M Somero
723 7th St
Laurium MI 49913

Call Sign: WD8QEK
Frank H Underdown Jr
747 7th St
Laurium MI 49913

Call Sign: KC8FLJ
Daniel S Hein
207 Amygdaloid St
Laurium MI 49913

Call Sign: N8XJU
Steven C Hein
207 Amygdaloid St
Laurium MI 49913

Call Sign: KC8CCV
Allison M Hein
207 Amyodaloid St
Laurium MI 49913

Call Sign: WD8SCR
John Meyers
151 Calumet St
Laurium MI 49913

Call Sign: N8IMU
Harold R Bekkala
137 Florida St
Laurium MI 49913

Call Sign: N8QBH
Michael E Bekkala
137 Florida St
Laurium MI 49913

Call Sign: KB8W
Danny L Miller
300 Florida St
Laurium MI 49913

Call Sign: N8FOP
John J Lanyon
309 Florida St
Laurium MI 49913

Call Sign: KC8BSM
Charyl A Johnson
606 Florida St
Laurium MI 49913

Call Sign: KC8CCZ
Terry L Johnson
606 Florida St
Laurium MI 49913

Call Sign: W8QLT
Charyl A Johnson
606 Florida St
Laurium MI 49913

Call Sign: W8FMR
Terry L Johnson
606 Florida St
Laurium MI 49913

Call Sign: N8XJT
James M Johnson
200 Iroquois St
Laurium MI 49913

Call Sign: N8SRK
Joseph P Maurer
317 Iroquois St
Laurium MI 49913

Call Sign: W8FWG
George R Thurner
225 Kearsarge St
Laurium MI
499132109

Call Sign: KA8UZI
Steven J Clark
149 N Florida St
Laurium MI 49913

Call Sign: N8XLH
Joanne L Hannula
323 N Florida St

Laurium MI 49913

Call Sign: N8XLI
Clifford A Hannula
323 N Florida St
Laurium MI 49913

Call Sign: KD8ELM
Erik J Johnson
117 N Pewabic St
Laurium MI 49913

Call Sign: N8OOM
Alfred J Brewer
417 Osceola St
Laurium MI 49913

Call Sign: N8OPO
Judy A Brewer
417 Osceola St
Laurium MI 49913

Call Sign: KC8YMR
Andrew J Diepen
347 Pewabic St
Laurium MI 49913

Call Sign: N8XJY
Brian O Berghefer
26487 Quincy St
Laurium MI 49913

Call Sign: N8PIU
Kurt E Erkkila
138 S Pewabic St
Laurium MI 49913

Call Sign: KD8QCI
Branden R Ghena
100 Willow Ave
Laurium MI 49913

**FCC Amateur Radio
Licenses in Lawrence**

Call Sign: N8IZW
Robert C Kurzrock
41738 46th St
Lawrence MI 49064

Call Sign: WB8BNU
Clark W Tyler
47463 48th Ave
Lawrence MI 49064

Call Sign: KI8Z
Edward E Alderman
56500 48th Ave
Lawrence MI 49064

Call Sign: N8GPG
Cynthia E Alderman
56500 48th Ave
Lawrence MI 49064

Call Sign: KD8GLE
Ryan E Alderman
56500 48th Ave
Lawrence MI 49064

Call Sign: KC8FFT
Judith M Vanderboegh
57747 48th Ave
Lawrence MI 49064

Call Sign: KA9BUW
William D Hollenbeck
38973 48th St
Lawrence MI 49064

Call Sign: KA9JTT
Edna L Hollenbeck
38973 48th St
Lawrence MI 49064

Call Sign: KC8FJC
Glen E Cowles
40040 48th St
Lawrence MI 49064

Call Sign: KC8IIY
Ruth E Cowles
40040 48th St
Lawrence MI 49064

Call Sign: K8ZXT
William J Heldt
43796 48th St
Lawrence MI 49064

Call Sign: KC8OFT
John R Utter
58370 50th St
Lawrence MI 49064

Call Sign: KC8TZM
David J Garvison
44988 52nd St

Lawrence MI 49064

Call Sign: KA8GNW
Lester F Lennemann
64185 52nd St
Lawrence MI 49064

Call Sign: WD8KGR
Sewell J Mason
46914 64th Ave
Lawrence MI 49064

Call Sign: KC8BPC
Ronald G Anderson
50121 Cir 673
Lawrence MI 49064

Call Sign: KB9IGJ
William A Brown
51884 CR 215
Lawrence MI 49064

Call Sign: N8FAH
Robert R Small Sr
47880 CR 374
Lawrence MI 49064

Call Sign: N8ZGC
Colin G Lindel
48516 Red Arrow Hwy
Lawrence MI 49064

**FCC Amateur Radio
Licenses in Lawton**

Call Sign: N8UFM
Ann Wuis
66122 32nd St
Lawton MI 49065

Call Sign: KB8UPG
Irene A Golike
29032 60th Ave
Lawton MI 49065

Call Sign: KC8OAA
Billy T Kidd
30673 64th Ave
Lawton MI 49065

Call Sign: K8SWD
Rudolph M Marcelletti
30764 64th Ave
Lawton MI 49065

Call Sign: KC8MOM
Dale W Sherburn
32660 64th Ave
Lawton MI 49065

Call Sign: KD8FLR
Gary A Losey
35763 92nd Ave
Lawton MI 490659444

Call Sign: K8CRH
Allen A McNeil
32323 CR 352
Lawton MI 49065

Call Sign: KA8SHU
Robert J Boyd Sr
79028 CR 652
Lawton MI 49065

Call Sign: W8TE
Richard B Ackerman
31981 CR 669
Lawton MI 490659344

Call Sign: AB8DS
David L Schneider
27125 Drape Rd
Lawton MI 49065

Call Sign: N8YJR
Adam C Hess
27125 Drape Rd
Lawton MI 49065

Call Sign: KB8QGJ
William K Hilmert
123 Durkee St
Lawton MI 49065

Call Sign: W8MUD
William K Hilmert
123 Durkee St
Lawton MI 49065

Call Sign: KC8ZGS
Melvin A Clark Jr
217 E Bitely St
Lawton MI 49065

Call Sign: N8LTN
Sherrill S Coady
27118 Lake Dr

Lawton MI 49065

Call Sign: N8BFI
Marilyn J Hazelton
75075 M 40
Lawton MI 49065

Call Sign: N8GH
Gary L Hazelton
75075 M 40
Lawton MI 49065

Call Sign: N9HKR
Richard M Kohn
62595 Oak Shadows
Rd
Lawton MI 490659602

Call Sign: KB8CRR
William B Hughey
855 S Main St
Lawton MI 49065

Call Sign: N8WME
Forrest B Duddles
851 S Nursery St
Lawton MI 49065

Call Sign: KL0TE
David N Pomeroy
29371 Shaw Rd
Lawton MI 49065

Call Sign: KC8AIQ
Larry L Homan
28373 Spring Brook
Dr
Lawton MI 49065

Call Sign: KC8TWY
Jody L Briggs
9954 W Tu Ave
Lawton MI 49065

Call Sign: KC8CK
Donald G Cochran
Lawton MI 49065

Call Sign: KC8QED
Andrew L Hollibaugh
18351 130th Ave

Le Roy MI 49655

Call Sign: KD8PUX
Jacob A Gregory
16657 140th Ave
Le Roy MI 49655

Call Sign: KD8PUY
Mark A Gregory
16657 140th Ave
Le Roy MI 49655

Call Sign: KC5FUP
Ronald D Hanes
18573 140th Ave
Le Roy MI 49655

Call Sign: KD8CVK
Ronald D Hanes
18573 140th Ave
Le Roy MI 49655

Call Sign: KB8ZSR
Mary J Deady
20745 16 Mile Rd
Le Roy MI 49655

Call Sign: KC8DTY
James F Deady
20745 16 Mile Rd
Le Roy MI 49655

Call Sign: WB8UGU
Richard D Mol Jr
23525 17 Mile Rd
Le Roy MI 49655

Call Sign: KD8NRJ
Ronald J Brissette
13913 170th Ave
Le Roy MI 49655

Call Sign: WR8J
Carlin J Belville
15345 220th Ave
Le Roy MI 49655

Call Sign: KD8LBJ
Barbara R Booth
122 Beach Cir Dr
Le Roy MI 49655

Call Sign: KD8IWE
Paul A Booth

122 Beach Cir Dr
Le Roy MI 49655

Call Sign: WY8H
Paul A Booth
122 Beach Cir Dr
Le Roy MI 49655

Call Sign: WD8KOX
Louis Fekete
R 1 Box 80 Lakola
Le Roy MI 49655

Call Sign: KD8FRW
Zachary R Neely
119 Osceola Ledge
Le Roy MI 49655

Call Sign: W8NEV
Kenneth L Baker
12019 Pearl St
Le Roy MI 49655

Call Sign: KD8PUW
Jerry W Cornell
143 Plateau Cir
Le Roy MI 49655

Call Sign: KC8KF
Jerry L Terpstra
13867 Robinhood Ln
Le Roy MI 49655

Call Sign: KC8SBP
Gary M Townsend III
Le Roy MI 49655

Call Sign: KA8UDX
Edward J Collins Jr
512 Mill St
Leland MI 496540593

Call Sign: KC8BQN
Lowell V Jacobsen
521 Mill St
Leland MI 496540837

Call Sign: W9AL
Thurber G Bombaugh
4157 Oxford Dr
Leland MI 49654

Call Sign: K9TNT
James L Duff
302 S Main St
Leland MI 49654

Call Sign: KA8FSP
Anton De Kok
Leland MI 49654

Call Sign: N8PGE
Theda A Morris
30614 E Michigan Ave
Leonidas MI 49066

Call Sign: KC8COS
John C Feek
53730 Olney Rd
Leonidas MI 49066

Call Sign: KC8NFO
Melissa L Feek
53730 Olney Rd
Leonidas MI 49066

Call Sign: N8VEJ
Scott M Niswander
6600 Canby Rd
Levering MI 49755

Call Sign: KC8CGD
Melony G O Neal
293 E Lakeview Rd
Levering MI 49755

Call Sign: N8PVV
Charles L Jett
6597 E Levering
Levering MI
497559744

Call Sign: KI8BG
Walter J Sowles
2443 Levering Rd
Levering MI 49755

Call Sign: N8VEL
David L Bohn

9103 Munro Lake
Access Rd
Levering MI 49755

Call Sign: N8QYZ
Glen F Lewis
2250 Schmalzried Rd
Levering MI 49755

Call Sign: N8IUF
Carl L Hoyt
7533 Sommers Rd
Levering MI 49755

Call Sign: KC8ZSO
Mike R Reed II
7525 Valley Rd
Levering MI 49755

Call Sign: WB8UCE
Peter A Wenk
21 W Levering Rd
Levering MI
497559320

Call Sign: KB8PNK
Robert Barley
10961 Weadock Rd
Levering MI 49755

FCC Amateur Radio Licenses in Lewiston

Call Sign: KD8EKE
Eugene E Agren
5355 Agren Rd
Lewiston MI 49756

Call Sign: KD8EKD
Thomas H Agren
5355 Agren Rd
Lewiston MI 49756

Call Sign: KC8WII
Daniel B Hughes
4875 Andergood Rd
Lewiston MI 49756

Call Sign: KC8TXK
Richard E Deska
2885 Birch St
Lewiston MI 49756

Call Sign: WB8POL

William F Rudorf
Rt 1 Box 4G
Lewiston MI 49756

Call Sign: W8GPP
John T Streeter Sr
3111 Cobb Rd
Lewiston MI 49756

Call Sign: N8MHT
Kirk D Revitzer
4950 Comstock Trl
Lewiston MI 49756

Call Sign: WB8DIV
Kirk D Revitzer
4950 Comstock Trl
Lewiston MI 49756

Call Sign: AB8UP
Kirk D Revitzer
4950 Comstock Trl
Lewiston MI 49756

Call Sign: KD8EKC
John R Vancoillie
3125 CR 489
Lewiston MI 49756

Call Sign: KC8WCA
Mike D Coy
7775 CR 491
Lewiston MI 49756

Call Sign: KC8OEK
Douglas E Agren
2986 CR 612
Lewiston MI 49756

Call Sign: KC8CEY
John P Lamoria Sr
5080 CR 612
Lewiston MI 49756

Call Sign: KC8SWB
Kent A Balogh
10911 CR 612
Lewiston MI 49756

Call Sign: KD8GAC
Wendall J Alexander
3662 Dorothy St
Lewiston MI 49756

Call Sign: KC8VQF
Doug Cady
6735 Goldenrod Rd
Lewiston MI 49756

Call Sign: KD8EKJ
Jennifer E Cady
6735 Goldenrod Rd
Lewiston MI 49756

Call Sign: KC8OEJ
Paul R Cole
1800 Halberg Rd
Lewiston MI 49756

Call Sign: KA8VGG
Ronald J Parker
2600 Mary Ann
Lewiston MI 49756

Call Sign: N8KOB
Mark A Lesar
5610 Mellbery Ln
Lewiston MI 49756

Call Sign: KD8KMC
Michael L Hegwood
5850 Mellbery Ln
Lewiston MI 49756

Call Sign: KD8EUR
Earl J Osburn
3570 N Marion
Lewiston MI 49756

Call Sign: KD4SUW
Carol M Ryckman
5210 N Townline Rd
Lewiston MI 49756

Call Sign: KD4VJD
Randy C Ryckman
5210 N Townline Rd
Lewiston MI 49756

Call Sign: KC8CMQ
John H Shearer Sr
5213 N Townline Rd
Lewiston MI 49756

Call Sign: KC8CUC
Shari L Shearer
5213 N Townline Rd
Lewiston MI 49756

Call Sign: KC8OEZ
Roger J Haworth Sr
5190 Pinecrest Dr
Lewiston MI 49756

Call Sign: KC8OFD
Diane M Haworth
5190 Pinecrest Dr
Lewiston MI 49756

Call Sign: KD8EKH
Robert J Haworth
5190 Pinecrest Dr
Lewiston MI 49756

Call Sign: W8WOW
Dennis R Martin
5315 Pinecrest Dr
Lewiston MI 49756

Call Sign: KC8YOX
David L Fogle
3375 Thornapple Trl
Lewiston MI 49756

Call Sign: KD8KNQ
David C Mcintire
4042 W Kneeland Rd
Lewiston MI 49756

Call Sign: N8IFV
Paul J Stone
4140 W Kneeland Rd
Lewiston MI 49756

Call Sign: KC8WIH
Brian D Agren
6331 Winkelman Dr
Lewiston MI 49756

Call Sign: N8QAA
Robert J Setchell
Lewiston MI 49756

Call Sign: KD8AEM
Montmorency
Emergency Radio
Services
Lewiston MI 49756

Call Sign: KD8NAR
Lewiston Area ARC
Lewiston MI 49756

Call Sign: K8LEW
Lewiston Area ARC
Lewiston MI 49756

Call Sign: KD8EKG
Gregory M Arbogast
Lewiston MI 49756

Call Sign: KD8EKF
Linda R Arbogast
Lewiston MI 49756

Call Sign: KC8WIJ
Robby A Koons
Lewiston MI 49756

FCC Amateur Radio Licenses in Limestone

Call Sign: WD8RJQ
Stephen H Wolfe
Hcr 1 Box 178
Limestone MI 49816

Call Sign: KC8DQG
Frank A Pernak Jr
E 3440 Brisson Rd
Limestone MI 49816

FCC Amateur Radio Licenses in Lincoln

Call Sign: W8HUF
David N Huff
210 Alger St
Lincoln MI 487420075

Call Sign: KA8ESE
Herbert R Sinclair
4250 Elder Rd
Lincoln MI 48742

Call Sign: KC8NSP
Joshua J Desmet
208 Hawley St
Lincoln MI 48742

Call Sign: K8NCP
Nicolas C Palazzolo
3010 N Barlow Rd F41
Lincoln MI 48742

Call Sign: KC8OHI

Patricia J Idema
2280 Quick Rd
Lincoln MI 48742

Call Sign: N8ZTN
Karen A Sharboneau
1709 Ritchie Rd
Lincoln MI 48742

Call Sign: N8ZTO
Dale J Sharboneau
1709 Ritchie Rd
Lincoln MI 48742

Call Sign: KC8TXL
Larry G Duby
781 Somers Rd
Lincoln MI 48742

Call Sign: KD8BRK
Joshua N Geiersbach
2061 Trask Lake Rd
Lincoln MI 48742

FCC Amateur Radio Licenses in Little Lake

Call Sign: KB8NDH
Leonard A Bodenus Jr
253 N Bodenus Dr
Little Lake MI 49833

Call Sign: KB8PEO
Robert A Wadhams
613 Prince St Apt 1
Little Lake MI 49866

FCC Amateur Radio Licenses in Long Lake

Call Sign: K8TJB
Bruce W Bonnell
8511 Kokosing Rd
Long Lake MI 48743

FCC Amateur Radio Licenses in Loretto

Call Sign: KC8IME
Ernest M Johnson
223 Dean Ave
Loretto MI 49852

Call Sign: KC8ISP
D Joann Johnson
W3880 Dean St
Loretto MI 49852

Call Sign: N8YFZ
Christine L Peterson
N1771 River Ave
Loretto MI 49852

Call Sign: N8ZAO
Christine L Peterson
N1771 River Ave
Loretto MI 49852

FCC Amateur Radio Licenses in Lowell

Call Sign: WD8ONL
Dean A Alger
13401 3 Mile Rd
Lowell MI 49331

Call Sign: KC8MNI
Ryan M Hoffman
12631 36th St
Lowell MI 49331

Call Sign: N8ED
Edward I Brubaker
12888 36th St
Lowell MI 49331

Call Sign: W8HXZ
Walter G Nickless
13597 36th St
Lowell MI 49331

Call Sign: KB8KKY
Danne L Gordon
12350 36th St SE
Lowell MI 49331

Call Sign: N8OHG
Esther M Gordon
12350 36th St SE
Lowell MI 49331

Call Sign: KC8WJB
Michael W Pretzel
11859 4 Mile Rd
Lowell MI 49331

Call Sign: KD8KUP
Christopher E Mokma
10798 52nd St
Lowell MI 49331

Call Sign: KA8DMP
Merritt Wissman Jr
12955 52nd St
Lowell MI 49331

Call Sign: AA8JR
James E Jaworowicz
1365 Alden Nash
Lowell MI 49331

Call Sign: KD8ABN
Linzy A Zylstra
3043 Alden Nash
Lowell MI 49331

Call Sign: WA4SXT
Jeffery J Morgenthaler
1366 Alden Nash NE
Lowell MI 49331

Call Sign: N8PFK
Richard G Jean Jr
12665 Alder Meadows
Lowell MI 49331

Call Sign: KC8MGK
Timothy V Dimmick
160 Bahala
Lowell MI 49331

Call Sign: KD8GJK
Dylan J Dues
11569 Bailey Dr
Lowell MI 49331

Call Sign: KF8LX
Thomas R Andrews
11598 Barnsley Rd
Lowell MI 49331

Call Sign: KD8JCH
Brenden J Kettner
11100 Bennett SE
Lowell MI 49331

Call Sign: KD8NLF
Harold G Kettner
11100 Bennett SE
Lowell MI 49331

Call Sign: KD8NYR
Patrick G Kettner
11100 Bennett SE
Lowell MI 49331

Call Sign: KD8EGU
Andrew J Bewell
2650 Bewell Ave
Lowell MI 49331

Call Sign: KD8RLM
Steven J Mcbride
3330 Bewell Ave
Lowell MI 49331

Call Sign: KC8AGC
Virginia Tyler
13980 Bieri Dr
Lowell MI 49331

Call Sign: W8GIH
Marvin C Tyler
13980 Bieri Dr
Lowell MI 49331

Call Sign: KC8WYU
Bobby A Onan
11600 Blue Water
Hwy
Lowell MI 49331

Call Sign: KD8NSV
Daniel J Onan
11600 Blue Water
Hwy
Lowell MI 49331

Call Sign: KD8KUR
Jeffrey D Onan
11600 Bluewater Hwy
Lowell MI 49331

Call Sign: KC8ZTL
Aric D Newsted
11521 Boulder Dr Apt
177
Lowell MI 49331

Call Sign: WW8WW
Allan L Eckman
725 Bowes Rd Apt K6
Lowell MI 49331

Call Sign: KC8EWU
Tony W Tymes
13325 Burroughs
Lowell MI 49331

Call Sign: KC8UET
William B Moore
1545 Carol Lynne Dr
Lowell MI 49331

Call Sign: KD8BPH
Zachary D Steckler
2045 Conservation Tr
Lowell MI 49331

Call Sign: KC8ZOX
Derek J Chopp
82 Countryview
Lowell MI 49331

Call Sign: KC8ZOZ
Devon A Chopp
82 Countryview
Lowell MI 49331

Call Sign: KC8ZOY
Theresa A Chopp
82 Countryview
Lowell MI 493319877

Call Sign: N8SRO
Travis H Briggs
2990 Court Dr
Lowell MI 49331

Call Sign: KD8CYG
Anthony J Freeburg
13838 Covered Bridge
Rd
Lowell MI 49331

Call Sign: KD8BCT
Nicholas R Freeburg
13838 Covered Bridge
Rd
Lowell MI 49331

Call Sign: AB8VO
Nicholas R Freeburg
13838 Covered Bridge
Rd
Lowell MI 49331

Call Sign: NI0CK

Nicholas R Freeburg
13838 Covered Bridge
Rd
Lowell MI 49331

Call Sign: KC8ZPA
Parker G Liu
13520 Crestwood Dr
Lowell MI 49331

Call Sign: KB8TXA
Phillip K Smith
927 Cumberland
Lowell MI 493319641

Call Sign: N8WVO
Louis G Smith
927 Cumberland SE
Lowell MI 49331

Call Sign: N8YZG
Terry K Smith
927 Cumberland SE
Lowell MI 49331

Call Sign: KC8PGA
Meghan A Carigon
1501 Deborah Dr Apt
113
Lowell MI 49331

Call Sign: KC8EGP
Michael R Carigon
1501 Deborah Dr Apt
113
Lowell MI 493311266

Call Sign: KD8DZS
Timothy D Hollister
10890 Deerwood Ct
Lowell MI 49331

Call Sign: N9TJJ
Robert M Gruendel
11005 Deerwood Dr
Lowell MI 49331

Call Sign: KB8YGK
Susan K McGlamery
321 Donna
Lowell MI 49331

Call Sign: N8ZUS
Michael S McGlamery

321 Donna
Lowell MI 49331

Call Sign: KC8ZTN
Alisha S Mcglamery
321 Donna
Lowell MI 49331

Call Sign: KC8ZPU
Cody A Kastanek
333 Donna Dr
Lowell MI 493311217

Call Sign: KA8ONK
Darlene C Wessling
11761 Downes NE
Lowell MI 49331

Call Sign: N8WUO
Barbara A Anderson
12360 Downes NE
Lowell MI 49331

Call Sign: WB8VFR
Brian G Anderson
12360 Downes NE
Lowell MI 49331

Call Sign: W8LRC
Lowell ARC
11535 E Fulton Ste
101
Lowell MI 493319609

Call Sign: KD8NRM
Paul R Parnofiello
218 E Main St
Lowell MI 49331

Call Sign: KD8NLE
Jesse A Schmidt
826 E Main St
Lowell MI 49331

Call Sign: WA8ZJT
Thomas H Adams Jr
1111 Fero Ave
Lowell MI 49331

Call Sign: KD8IJI
Bob A Schreur
538 Flat River Dr
Lowell MI 49331

Call Sign: KC8REJ
Jared J Huffman
995 Flat River Dr
Lowell MI 49331

Call Sign: KC8RMN
David M Huffman
995 Flat River Dr
Lowell MI 49331

Call Sign: KD8CSK
Derek A Mixon Jr
516 Forstrom Dr
Lowell MI 49331

Call Sign: KD8NEZ
Austin H Gittins
732 Godfrey St
Lowell MI 49331

Call Sign: KC8RML
Matt J Amidon
10876 Grand River
Ave
Lowell MI 49331

Call Sign: KC8RMM
Bradley D Amidon
10876 Grand River
Ave
Lowell MI 49331

Call Sign: KC8ZTS
Nathaniel D Clements
12654 Grand River Dr
Lowell MI 49331

Call Sign: N8YJY
Timothy S McCaul
13515 Grand River Dr
Lowell MI 49331

Call Sign: KC8REE
Joshua L Morrison
220 Grant St
Lowell MI 49331

Call Sign: KC8PGC
Brian A Mccaul
819 Grindle Dr
Lowell MI 49331

Call Sign: N8FIK

Anna E Greidanus
Probes
2960 Gulliford Dr
Lowell MI 493318955

Call Sign: ND8S
Lawrence M Probes
2960 Gulliford Dr
Lowell MI 493318955

Call Sign: KC8REI
Drew J Morrison
3328 Gulliford Dr
Lowell MI 49331

Call Sign: KC8RSF
Drew J Morrison
3328 Gulliford Dr
Lowell MI 49331

Call Sign: WE2RD
Drew J Morrison
3328 Gulliford Dr
Lowell MI 49331

Call Sign: KC8SIV
Tim C Jurmo
3700 Heron Hollow
Lowell MI 49331

Call Sign: N8YEH
Ronnie A Sheldon
12934 Hillcrest Dr
Lowell MI 49331

Call Sign: KD8DZU
William C Thompson
720 Hillside Ct
Lowell MI 49331

Call Sign: KD8CQB
Sierra A Moore
4191 Hilton Ave SE
Lowell MI 49331

Call Sign: KC8DWH
Mark R Fritsma
5671 Hotchkiss Rd
Lowell MI 493319210

Call Sign: KC8UHR
Tyler A Barkacs
229 Jefferson
Lowell MI 49331

Call Sign: KC8ZPL
Shaun R Hale
709 Lafayette
Lowell MI 493311128

Call Sign: KD8RVJ
James B Jorgensen
865 Lincoln Lake Ave
NE
Lowell MI 49331

Call Sign: KB8ZSX
Ann M Ingersoll
1554 Lincoln Lake
Ave NE
Lowell MI 493319711

Call Sign: KD8NQY
John L Giberson
484 Lincoln Lake Ave
SE
Lowell MI 49331

Call Sign: K8AI
Curtis Benjamin
47 Lincoln Lake NE
Lowell MI 49331

Call Sign: KC8LZH
Cornelius J Kerner
730 Lincoln Lake Rd
Lowell MI 49331

Call Sign: KA8SBU
Robert E Reyburn
2502 Lowellview
Lowell MI 49331

Call Sign: K0ZRD
Jean M Carlson
11345 Mary Jane St
Lowell MI 493319662

Call Sign: KC9QO
Stephen L Platt
11171 McPherson NE
Lowell MI 493319766

Call Sign: KC8RJF
Andrew D Platt
11171 McPherson Rd
Lowell MI 49331

Call Sign: KD8AJD
Nicholas A Comdure
11641 McPherson Rd
Lowell MI 49331

Call Sign: KC8ZOU
Gus J Geldersma
12465 McPherson Rd
Lowell MI 49331

Call Sign: KC8ZOV
Benjamin K Geldersma
12545 McPherson Rd
Lowell MI 49331

Call Sign: KD8POK
Michael K Smith
605 Montcalm Ave NE
Lowell MI 49331

Call Sign: KD8AII
Ian A Blodger
151 Montcalm Ave SE
Lowell MI 49331

Call Sign: K8CBW
Charles T Csolkovits
275 Montcalm Ave SE
Lowell MI 49331

Call Sign: KC8ZPH
Britta B Cieslak
3935 Murray View Dr
Lowell MI 49331

Call Sign: KC8IXY
Gail P Lowe
3935 Murray View Dr
Lowell MI 49331

Call Sign: KC7ZXY
Donald P Watkins Jr
3853 Murray View Dr
NE
Lowell MI 49331

Call Sign: KD8HNF
Robert L Robinson
130 N Center St
Lowell MI 49331

Call Sign: KC8RWM
Rob Cilley
960 N Washington

Lowell MI 49331

Call Sign: KD8AIH
Maxwell E Stormzand
1020 N Washington
Lowell MI 49331

Call Sign: KC8ZTV
Nick J Myaard
413 N Washington St
Lowell MI 49331

Call Sign: KD8OHS
Franklin C Mcclelland
306 N West St
Lowell MI 49331

Call Sign: KD8QNS
Bonnie E Van
Spronsen
790 Parnell Ave NE
Lowell MI 49331

Call Sign: KC8FGL
Christopher W Borton
10027 Peck Lake Rd
Lowell MI 49331

Call Sign: KC8TCA
Melissa M Borton
10027 Peck Lake Rd
Lowell MI 49331

Call Sign: KC8GDJ
Wayne H Borton
10111 Peck Lake SW
Lowell MI 49331

Call Sign: N8CMQ
Jeffrey L Young
11840 Potters Rd
Lowell MI 49331

Call Sign: KC8SWW
James J Mclarty
5533 Pratt Lake SE
Lowell MI 49331

Call Sign: KA8WGF
Rudolph S Sauber
1726 Rhoda
Lowell MI 493319669

Call Sign: N8USY

Stefano A M Lassini
13011 Ryan Ridge Dr
Lowell MI 493319494

Call Sign: KB8EJY
Robert J Davis
119 S Grove
Lowell MI 49331

Call Sign: KC8REH
Charles T Putney
11350 Shiela Lot 178
Lowell MI 49331

Call Sign: KD8RLL
Eric J Johnson
11372 Shiela St
Lowell MI 49331

Call Sign: KD8MMU
Charles L Hayden
1304 Sibley St
Lowell MI 49331

Call Sign: KD8OXK
Charlotte R Haden
1304 Sibley St
Lowell MI 49331

Call Sign: KB8ZCZ
Scott A Treglia
1672 Stonewood Dr
Lowell MI 49331

Call Sign: KD8BLO
Kelsey M Stickney
9609 Tanglewood Ct
Lowell MI 49331

Call Sign: KD8AKM
Derek A Fountaine
9716 Tanglewood Ct
Lowell MI 49331

Call Sign: KK9T
Timothy L Rife
2673 Tyler Trl
Lowell MI 49331

Call Sign: KD8KNZ
Austin M Rife
2673 Tyler Trl
Lowell MI 49331

Call Sign: K8KXN
Austin M Rife
2673 Tyler Trl
Lowell MI 49331

Call Sign: K8LHS
Lowell Amateur Radio
Youth Club
11700 Vergennes Rd
Lowell MI 49331

Call Sign: KB8HWN
David A Tanner
12932 Vergennes Rd
Lowell MI 49331

Call Sign: N8WDG
Germaine R Thompson
Jr
13208 Vergennes Rd
Lowell MI 49331

Call Sign: KC8ZOW
Joshua S Gerard
13254 Vergennes Rd
Lowell MI 49331

Call Sign: KD8KLM
Eric P Nelson
12920 Vergennes St
Lowell MI 49331

Call Sign: KD8AIJ
Jacob A Mcvey
13306 Vergennes St
Lowell MI 49331

Call Sign: KD8AIK
Nicholas S Mcvey
13306 Vergennes St
Lowell MI 49331

Call Sign: NY8D
Jack C Amelar
13110 Victory Woods
Dr NE
Lowell MI 493318857

Call Sign: KC8CUP
Stacy R Mourer
1800 W Main 97
Lowell MI 49331

Call Sign: KC8VMR

Robin A Putney
1800 W Main Lot 31
Lowell MI 49331

Call Sign: KD8KLO
Gregory A Nelson
11057 Wildlife Dr
Lowell MI 49331

Call Sign: KC8FAU
Elizabeth A Geene
11102 Woodbushe Dr
Lowell MI 49331

Call Sign: WA8YUA
John T Walker
1760 Woodrun Ct SE
Lowell MI 49331

Call Sign: N1TNU
Casey K Brown
Lowell MI 49331

FCC Amateur Radio
Licenses in Ludington

Call Sign: WD8CNB
John L Sonefeld
4390 1st St
Ludington MI 49431

Call Sign: KB8CJR
Diane L Sonefeld
4390 1st St
Ludington MI 49431

Call Sign: WA8ORC
Amy L Dewey
702 3rd St
Ludington MI 49431

Call Sign: N8QOZ
Frank C Tomasik
703 6th St
Ludington MI 49431

Call Sign: N8TFO
Mila C Tomasik
703 6th St
Ludington MI 49431

Call Sign: KA8FAO
Alice L Swan
4839 Beaune Rd

Ludington MI 49431

Call Sign: WB8ERN
Nicholas D Swan
4839 Beaune Rd
Ludington MI 49431

Call Sign: K7LEE
Lincoln E Engwall
1027 Daisy Ln 1
Ludington MI
494311256

Call Sign: WE8SIX
Lincoln E Engwall
1027 Daisy Ln 1
Ludington MI
494311256

Call Sign: KA8WOM
John C Quillan
606 E Court St
Ludington MI 49431

Call Sign: NN8L
Harold E Genter
401 E Danaher St
Ludington MI 49431

Call Sign: K8VXO
Albert J Meny
707 E Foster St
Ludington MI 49431

Call Sign: N8OPW
John H Yax
811 E Foster St
Ludington MI 49431

Call Sign: KC8POR
Otis H Jarvie
723 E Loomis
Ludington MI 49431

Call Sign: KC8MWF
Gary C Berk
909 E Ludington Ave
Ludington MI 49431

Call Sign: KC8BHZ
Steven M Rakczynski
930 E Maple St
Ludington MI 49431

Call Sign: KD8BWT
Steven M Rakczynski
930 E Maple St
Ludington MI 49431

Call Sign: W8BHK
Harcourt E Quick Jr
808 E Melendy St
Ludington MI 49431

Call Sign: KC8TSG
Jane Krolczyk
5563 Hazelwood Dr
Ludington MI 49431

Call Sign: WB8CRA
John C Covert
6916 Illinois Rd
Ludington MI
494319503

Call Sign: WB8BJP
Phyllis J Covert
6916 Illinois St
Ludington MI 49431

Call Sign: KB8CRX
Robert V Nash Sr
6580 Jagger Rd
Ludington MI 49431

Call Sign: KB8RRX
Charles R Pollard
1111 Kenowa
Ludington MI 49431

Call Sign: WB8PSF
Lavern E Hanson
7260 Kildeer Ln
Ludington MI
494319764

Call Sign: KA8DID
Bonnie J Gorzynski
323 Lewis St
Ludington MI 49431

Call Sign: KG8PW
Gary W Nelson
2843 N Canal Rd
Ludington MI 49431

Call Sign: N8CHI
August P Engblade II

317 N Delia
Ludington MI 49431

Call Sign: KD8YJ
Howard D Olson Sr
816 N Emily
Ludington MI 49431

Call Sign: WB8OZX
Maurice J McCormick
719 N Emily St
Ludington MI 49431

Call Sign: KA8WON
William S Olson
816 N Emily St
Ludington MI 49431

Call Sign: N8KCG
Ned R Hutchinson
1036 N Ferry St
Ludington MI
494311322

Call Sign: KC8HJN
William R Merkey
704 N Gaylord Ave
Ludington MI
494311324

Call Sign: KG8HQ
Robert C Bachman
714 N Gaylord Ave
Ludington MI 48813

Call Sign: KB8RRY
Greg A Dykestra
510 N Harrison
Ludington MI 49431

Call Sign: WN8HFN
L Gardiner Miller
313 N Harrison St
Ludington MI 49431

Call Sign: WA8CID
Louis W Carlson
1303 N Ivanhoe Rd
Ludington MI 49431

Call Sign: KC8REP
Michael J Koudelka
210.5 N James St
Ludington MI 49431

Call Sign: W8BUS
Michael J Koudelka
210.5 N James St
Ludington MI 49431

Call Sign: W0UV
Larry E McKiernan
2410 N Lakeshore Dr
Ludington MI 49431

Call Sign: KC8JWB
Michael P Collins
2828 N Lena Sr Lot
542
Ludington MI 49431

Call Sign: K8DID
Ronald L Gorzynski
323 N Lewis
Ludington MI 49431

Call Sign: KC8OD
Norman J
Schoenmaker
1933 N Lincoln Rd
Ludington MI 49431

Call Sign: WB8WIU
Leo H Schumaker
413 N Rath Ave
Ludington MI
494311666

Call Sign: N8HBC
James W McMaster
812 N Rath Ave
Ludington MI 49431

Call Sign: W8TJW
Theodore C Schultz
820 N Rath Ave
Ludington MI 49431

Call Sign: WB8FIW
Philip F Eckley
910 N Rath Ave
Ludington MI 49431

Call Sign: N8FNG
Gregory L Andersen
404 N Robert St
Ludington MI 49431

Call Sign: K8RE
Robert E Engblade
1034 N Robert St
Ludington MI 49431

Call Sign: W8QPR
H David Flickinger
1042 N Robert St
Ludington MI 49431

Call Sign: WD0FGF
Frank P Longmore
305 N Robert St
Ludington MI 49431

Call Sign: N8KBZ
Wayne D Melin
303 N Rowe St
Ludington MI 49431

Call Sign: KB8FP
Harold E Knight
2041 N Sherman Rd
Ludington MI
494319597

Call Sign: KC8SKL
Thomas L Nash
501 N Washington
Ave Apt 3
Ludington MI 49431

Call Sign: K8TLN
Thomas L Nash
501 N Washington
Ave Apt 3
Ludington MI 49431

Call Sign: WD8KAU
Virgil J Horner Sr
1144 Pine Way
Ludington MI 49431

Call Sign: KC8TSH
David W Rafter
1065 Pineway St
Ludington MI 49431

Call Sign: WD8KQT
Thomas W Mitchell
5505 Raccoon Trl
Ludington MI 49431

Call Sign: KG8I

Robert J Matthews
4784 S Brye Rd
Ludington MI 49431

Call Sign: WD8MZM
David J Bortell
5528 S Lake Shore
Ludington MI 49431

Call Sign: K5ESK
Esther S Karp
4745 S Lakeshore Dr
Ludington MI 49431

Call Sign: KD5AAY
Patrick W Karp
4745 S Lakeshore Dr
Ludington MI 49431

Call Sign: KD5HHX
Matthew P Karp
4745 S Lakeshore Dr
Ludington MI 49431

Call Sign: KD8CUN
Patrick W Karp
4745 S Lakeshore Dr
Ludington MI 49431

Call Sign: KD8CUO
Esther S Karp
4745 S Lakeshore Dr
Ludington MI
494319755

Call Sign: K8PVC
Peter A Mars
2716 S Tamarac Dr
Ludington MI 49431

Call Sign: KC8JJM
Harland L Babcock
702 Saint Catherine
Ludington MI 49431

Call Sign: W8ZKZ
Harland L Babcock
702 Saint Catherine
Ludington MI 49431

Call Sign: N8ASN
Christine D Blalock
6533 Sassafras St

Ludington MI
494319430

Call Sign: WB8PSE
Robert E Overholt
903 Seminole Dr Box
555
Ludington MI 49431

Call Sign: KB9ZJD
Hale F Lemmer Jr
1833 Tall Oaks Dr E
Ludington MI 49431

Call Sign: KD8QFD
Jennifer A Fritton
5839 W Decker Rd
Ludington MI 49431

Call Sign: N8BMH
Theodore J Le Sarge
6027 W Decker Rd
Ludington MI
494319453

Call Sign: KE8YM
Walter D Johnson
6266 W Decker Rd
Ludington MI 49431

Call Sign: KB8VCW
Dale B White
4935 W Deren Rd
Ludington MI
494319748

Call Sign: K8VHF
Sharon M Spencer
6144 W Dewey Rd
Ludington MI 49431

Call Sign: W8VHF
Elmer C Spencer
6144 W Dewey Rd
Ludington MI 49431

Call Sign: KB4ENN
Charles J Derler
204 W Fitch St
Ludington MI 49431

Call Sign: K8EBE
Wilfred J Fortier
3749 W Forest Hill Cir

Ludington MI 49431

Call Sign: KB8PTE
Sarah L Kanitz
3108 W Fountain Rd
Ludington MI 49431

Call Sign: AC8FO
George J Kelen
3750 W Hansen Rd
Ludington MI 49431

Call Sign: KC8UBX
W William Westphal
III
5353 W Hesslund Rd
Ludington MI
494319326

Call Sign: KB8RRZ
Jeff C Schindler
3275 W Johnson Rd
Ludington MI 49431

Call Sign: WB8UFM
Ronald W Van Dyke
2785 W Kinney Rd
Ludington MI 49431

Call Sign: WB8MYX
Thomas J Kibildis Jr
6660 W Lane Ave
Ludington MI 49431

Call Sign: K8SOM
Harvey B Washer Jr
406 W Lowell St
Ludington MI 49431

Call Sign: N0PJF
Paul J Yost
706 W Ludington Ave
Ludington MI 49431

Call Sign: N8MNK
David D Van Arsdale
6785 W Timberlane
Ludington MI 49431

Call Sign: KA9ZAK
James G Jones
Ludington MI 49431

Call Sign: KC8JQK
Laura A Snyder
3286 Ash St
Lupton MI 48635

Call Sign: KB8UGW
Neil Hulsether
2835 Chippewa Trl
Lupton MI 48635

Call Sign: KB8DDI
Phillip G Boussie
4121 Deckerville Rd
Lupton MI 48635

Call Sign: KC8HTG
Robert A McElroy
2359 E Rose City Rd
Lupton MI 48635

Call Sign: AB8IY
Thomas M Wilcox
143 Eastside Dr
Lupton MI 48635

Call Sign: KC8GMN
Thomas M Wilcox
2980 Heath Rd
Lupton MI 48635

Call Sign: W8DMI
Daniel C Karbginsky
3257 Rose City Rd
Lupton MI 48635

Call Sign: N8TQB
Sally J Horton
882 Sages Dr
Lupton MI 48635

Call Sign: WM5AA
Steven J Gillis
1249 Sensabaugh Rd
Lupton MI 48635

Call Sign: KC8RGH
Chris M Hartwell
758 Sunset Dr
Lupton MI 48635

Call Sign: KD8EUD

Terry L Hassell
827 Sunset Dr
Lupton MI 48635

Call Sign: W1CKK
Lila J De Maw
4061 N Douglas Rd
Luther MI 49656

Call Sign: W1FB
Milton F De Maw
4061 N Douglas Rd
Luther MI 49656

Call Sign: N8GCJ
Reita L Craddock
Luther MI 49656

Call Sign: N8ISB
Linda D Wesolowski
3543 Chevy Dr
Luzerne MI 48636

Call Sign: KC8IGK
Marlynne L Crawford
1356 Cripps Rd
Luzerne MI
486360308

Call Sign: K8GER
Gerald A Crawford
1356 Cripps Rd
Luzerne MI
486360308

Call Sign: KD8EHD
Craig A Mitchell
2043 E Dumont Dr
Luzerne MI 48636

Call Sign: KD8EHA
Nikole A Mitchell
Fisher
2372 Royce Haven Dr
Luzerne MI 48636

Call Sign: KD8EGX
Bruce J Fisher

2372 Roycehaven Dr
Luzerne MI 48640

Call Sign: KD8EGW
Bruce E Dorsett Jr
1290 Schmall Rd
Luzerne MI 48636

Call Sign: N8PWU
Donald F Fox
1938 W Oak
Luzerne MI 48636

Call Sign: KD8EHE
Joe D Mitchell
Luzerne MI 48636

Call Sign: KD8EHG
Kathleen T Mitchell
Luzerne MI 48636

Call Sign: KD8EHC
Klint K Mitchell
Luzerne MI 48636

Call Sign: KF4GEE
Teresa J Craft
300 Baldwin St
Lyons MI 48851

Call Sign: WB8VAV
Gary A Grabenstein
3926 Divine Hwy
Lyons MI 48851

Call Sign: KC8RQW
Kathryn M
Grabenstein
3926 Divine Hwy
Lyons MI 48851

Call Sign: K8CKW
Gary A Grabenstein
3926 Divine Hwy
Lyons MI 488519809

Call Sign: KD8IAS
Roy E Conrad
4308 E Riverside Dr
Lyons MI 48851

Call Sign: N8FUF
Daniel M Holcomb
4406 E Riverside Dr
Lyons MI 48851

Call Sign: KC8BMG
David W Coon
4855 E Riverside Dr
Lyons MI 48851

Call Sign: WA8JLW
Lucille E Meyers
4937 E Riverside Dr
Lyons MI 48851

Call Sign: KD8NQX
Devon Dewey
8340 E Sunset Dr
Lyons MI 48851

Call Sign: KD8QNR
David J Holcomb
7395 Kimball
Lyons MI 48851

Call Sign: WB8TUD
Joan H Boog
8807 Murphy Rd
Lyons MI 48851

Call Sign: WB8TUE
Michael J Boog
8807 Murphy Rd
Lyons MI 48851

Call Sign: KA8CUY
Roger K Thomas
1451 Somers Rd
Lyons MI 48851

Call Sign: KD8IWQ
Jimmy W Dunahoo
8340 Sunset Dr
Lyons MI 48851

Call Sign: KD8KXI
Daniel L Taylor Jr
Macatawa MI 49434

Call Sign: KD8MDO
Phillip B Hill

Macatawa MI 49434

Call Sign: KB8VQE
Kenneth A Salmon
Market St Box 263
Mackinac Island MI
49757

Call Sign: KB8VNV
William B Bernard
Mackinac Island MI
49757

Call Sign: KD8KHS
Stephen H Humphrey
Mackinac Island MI
49757

Call Sign: N8NYR
Stephen T Metz
301 Ethrington
Mackinaw City MI
49701

Call Sign: KB8TVM
Charles K Heilman
211 Henry St Box 8
Mackinaw City MI
49701

Call Sign: KA8IOW
William J Morrison
812 Lakeside Dr
Mackinaw City MI
497010042

Call Sign: K8NUN
Laurence W Davis
814 Lakeside Dr
Mackinaw City MI
497010182

Call Sign: KC8JXG
Albert R Cowell
1060 Lakeside Dr

Mackinaw City MI
497010091

Call Sign: N8IX
Eric J Campbell
306 N Huron Ave
Mackinaw City MI
497010893

Call Sign: KB8VNZ
Edward M Wilk
827 Pond
Mackinaw City MI
49701

Call Sign: N8VWT
Joseph F Havlena
408 W Etherington
Mackinaw City MI
49701

Call Sign: N8NXP
Charles J Brew
Mackinaw City MI
49701

Call Sign: N8OIW
Robert F Desy
Mackinaw City MI
49701

Call Sign: KB8FWN
Terrance L Bamford
Mackinaw City MI
49701

Call Sign: N8HGZ
Kathleen A Morse
Arnold
9162 Blue Lake Rd NE
Mancelona MI 49659

Call Sign: N8HBQ
Frederick J Morse
9164 Blue Lake Rd NE
Mancelona MI 49659

Call Sign: KB8UAD
Timothy L Finch
5781 Cedar River

Mancelona MI 49659

Call Sign: WD8LFH
Melvin A Meadows Sr
126 Downey St
Mancelona MI 49659

Call Sign: KC8NIS
Gregory M Parsons
409 E Division St
Mancelona MI 49659

Call Sign: KB8VNY
Richard E Callesen
1188 Elder Rd
Mancelona MI 49659

Call Sign: KD8QJD
Matthew R Milnickel
9550 Lake Of The
Woods Rd
Mancelona MI 49659

Call Sign: N8XCO
Brian A Lewis
2101 Lee Derrer Rd
Mancelona MI 49659

Call Sign: KC8FWN
Ward J Rathbun
10393 Montrose Ave
Mancelona MI 49659

Call Sign: KD8GKE
Sean A Homan
1345 N Limits
Mancelona MI 49659

Call Sign: N8YDB
Randy K Homan
113 N Maple
Mancelona MI 49659

Call Sign: KC8TDK
Keith L Deyoung
4610 Oslund Rd
Mancelona MI 49659

Call Sign: N8HBZ
James L Mott Sr
9782 Park St
Mancelona MI 49659

Call Sign: KD8LHL

Wilhelm F Von
Preussen II
6671 Pineview Dr
Mancelona MI 49659

Call Sign: KF8SM
Richard S Kler Jr
11626 Priest Rd
Mancelona MI 49659

Call Sign: KB8YNQ
Kim R Thorman
3850 S M 66
Mancelona MI 49659

Call Sign: KB8UAE
William J Callesen
6805 Satterly Lk Rd
Mancelona MI 49659

Call Sign: KD8FQX
Kevin L Julian
9610 Starvation Lake
Rd
Mancelona MI 49659

Call Sign: N8GYV
Larry P Medley
2236 Twin Lake Rd
Mancelona MI 49659

Call Sign: W8EGB
Clyde S Niles
10259 Twin Lk Rd NE
Mancelona MI
496599211

Call Sign: KD8LVW
Caleb T Marquard
6626 Wilderness Dr
Mancelona MI 49659

Call Sign: KB8SWJ
Eugene R Miles
7918 Willowbrook Cir
Mancelona MI 49659

Call Sign: KD8HFG
David A Montgomery
10337 Wyndwood
Mancelona MI 49659

Call Sign: N8SXD
Everett L Homan

Mancelona MI 49659

Call Sign: KC8ZOQ
Lester B Hasse III
Mancelona MI
496590220

**FCC Amateur Radio
Licenses in Manistee**

Call Sign: WB8DRM
William O Hund
391 11th St
Manistee MI
496602123

Call Sign: AA8AE
Margaret V Cloutier
232 1st Ave
Manistee MI 49660

Call Sign: NY8R
Le Roy F Gramza
1113 25th St
Manistee MI 49660

Call Sign: KC8SBR
Paul F Burns
343 2nd St
Manistee MI 49660

Call Sign: KC8QLG
Lemuel O Granada Jr
351 2nd St
Manistee MI
496601747

Call Sign: N8YKH
Ross T Duprey
429 2nd St
Manistee MI 49660

Call Sign: WB8BGQ
Stephen P Cole
488 4th St
Manistee MI 49660

Call Sign: WD8RYS
Jane P Cole
488 4th St
Manistee MI
496601629

Call Sign: W8GJX

Helen H Schmock
273 6th Ave 502
Manistee MI 49660

Call Sign: KD8MCJ
West Michigan
Repeater Association
273 6th Ave Apt 407
Manistee MI 49660

Call Sign: NL7VA
Michael R Pratt
363 6th St
Manistee MI 49660

Call Sign: KC8WWX
Michael R Pratt
363 6th St
Manistee MI 49660

Call Sign: WD8DEW
Keith R Brown
334 7th St
Manistee MI
496601944

Call Sign: KC8EUI
Zachary M
Tomaszewski
463 8th St
Manistee MI 49660

Call Sign: KA9JLE
Andrew J Richards
1865 Blossom Trl
Manistee MI 49660

Call Sign: KB8YED
Helmut Henn
606 Broad Ave
Manistee MI 49660

Call Sign: AA8PC
Donald D Grant
1412 Brown Rd
Manistee MI 49660

Call Sign: KC8YEB
Kenneth L Schulz
597 Browning Ave
Manistee MI 49660

Call Sign: KS8B
Kenneth L Schulz

597 Browning Ave
Manistee MI 49660

Call Sign: KB8DSL
Barry R Heinzel
100 Charter Ct
Manistee MI 49660

Call Sign: N8OVA
Thomas R Johnson
306 Condon Rd
Manistee MI 49660

Call Sign: KD8HRH
Elizabeth I Johnson
306 Condon Rd
Manistee MI 49660

Call Sign: WB8TAM
Richard C Uible
2046 Crescent Beach
Rd
Manistee MI 49660

Call Sign: KA8PXD
Elmer E Stamp
2710 Filer City Rd
Manistee MI 49660

Call Sign: K8YRJ
Henry P Rozmarek
1669 Fruit Ridge
Manistee MI 49660

Call Sign: KD8HRJ
Shane M Gillespie
6303 Kerry Rd
Manistee MI 49660

Call Sign: W8IAZ
Donald R Harter
3084 Lake Shore Rd
Manistee MI 49660

Call Sign: KC8UBL
Jonathan D Behring
3695 Lakeshore Dr
Manistee MI 49660

Call Sign: N8CFJ
Roger G Vogelsang
2303 Marzinski Rd
Manistee MI 49660

Call Sign: KD8RLZ
Zachary R Chisholm
4475 Milarch Rd
Manistee MI 49660

Call Sign: WD8NGU
Jean R Wheeler
651 Piney Rd
Manistee MI 49660

Call Sign: KB8BIT
Michael C La Prise Sr
2721 Red Apple Rd
Manistee MI
496609673

Call Sign: KC8ZIT
Edward M Thomas
1605 Snow Trls Dr
Manistee MI 49660

Call Sign: N8PVT
Walter A Smart
2141 Suida Rd
Manistee MI 49660

Call Sign: KC8ALA
Stephanie A Smart
2141 Suida Rd
Manistee MI 49660

Call Sign: AB0NQ
William A Schnurr
3142 W Fox Farm Rd
Manistee MI 49660

Call Sign: WZ8N
Richard H Mark
1659 W Merkey Rd
Manistee MI 49660

Call Sign: N8DJO
Madelyn J Klusowski
3522 Wildwood Dr
Manistee MI 49660

Call Sign: WA8V
Edward M Klusowski
3522 Wildwood Rd
Manistee MI 49660

Call Sign: KD8FJG
David N Geerlings
3720 Wildwood Rd

Manistee MI 49660

Call Sign: W8END
David N Geerlings
3720 Wildwood Rd
Manistee MI 49660

Call Sign: N8LEN
James W Plummer
Manistee MI 49660

Call Sign: KD8QJJ
Christian J Bennett
Manistee MI 49660

Call Sign: WA4HEI
Peter C Markham
416 Alger Ave
Manistique MI 49854

Call Sign: WA8KHA
George C Phillipp
R 1 Box 1554P
Manistique MI 49854

Call Sign: WG8E
Robert G Keefer Sr
Hc 01 Box 3035E
Manistique MI
498549508

Call Sign: WD8IBT
Debra K Barton
Hcr 01 Box 3065
Manistique MI 49854

Call Sign: WA8OTH
Harold A Neumann Sr
704 Cattaragus
Manistique MI 49854

Call Sign: N8OXX
Aretta T Neumann
704 Cattaragus
Manistique MI 49854

Call Sign: KC8ABU
Kimberly A Kronos
623 Deer St
Manistique MI 49854

Call Sign: KB8YJT
Eric E Sherbinow
207 Deer St 2
Manistique MI 49854

Call Sign: KA8WDQ
Gary F Koschmider
807 Garden Ave
Manistique MI 49854

Call Sign: KC8UMB
Jeffrey S Osterhout
844 Garden Ave
Manistique MI 49854

Call Sign: KD8QCU
Gail I Sulander
30735 Little Harbor Rd
Manistique MI 49854

Call Sign: KD8QCT
Kate A Steider
30735 Little Harbor Rd
Manistique MI 49854

Call Sign: N8RSB
Mark B McCune
110 N CR 455
Manistique MI 49854

Call Sign: KB8YUS
Manistique Amateur
Radio Assn
200 N Houghton Ave
Manistique MI 49854

Call Sign: W8NI
Henry F Brolin
200 N Houghton Ave
Manistique MI 49854

Call Sign: K0JRC
James R Cunningham
1183 N Oak St
Manistique MI 49854

Call Sign: N8WAY
Richard D Beckman
126 New Delta
Manistique MI 49854

Call Sign: WA8JNZ
Frederick A Cota

523 Oak St
Manistique MI 49854

Call Sign: W8ORR
Lyle M Kotchon
526 Oak St
Manistique MI 49854

Call Sign: KI8CL
Roger U Beauchamp
2023 S Little Harbor
Manistique MI 49854

Call Sign: KC8NNZ
Karen E Beauchamp
2023 S Little Harbor
Manistique MI 49854

Call Sign: W8NI
Manistique Amateur
Radio Association
2023 S Little Harbor
Rd
Manistique MI 49854

Call Sign: KA8JST
Pamela Toncray
7855 W Evergreen Rd
Manistique MI 49854

Call Sign: KC8ARK
Mark A Latva
7621 W Hiawatha St
Rd
Manistique MI 49854

Call Sign: KB8QGI
Charles N Hilmert
8009 W Quarter Mile
Rd
Manistique MI 49854

Call Sign: N8QXZ
Rudolph F Evonich Jr
7557 W Riverview Dr
Manistique MI 49854

Call Sign: W8LS
Larry J Snyder
6774 W Smith Lake Dr
Manistique MI 49854

Call Sign: WD8MIB
Linda J Ritchie

Manistique MI 49854

Call Sign: K8MRC
Marcus R Cheuvront
Manistique MI 49854

Call Sign: N8SVO
Joshua P Farrell
5913 E 12 1/2 Rd
Manton MI 49663

Call Sign: KD8GGC
Kelly J Whitehead
11151 E 12 Rd
Manton MI 49663

Call Sign: KB8YLC
Dennis P Downey
5052 E 14 Rd
Manton MI 49663

Call Sign: KC8PVQ
Jill L Raymer
8360 E 20 Rd
Manton MI 49663

Call Sign: KC8TZO
Jeffrey D Sutton
10860 E 22 Rd
Manton MI 49663

Call Sign: KD8FSL
Brandon R Musselman
9368 E M 42
Manton MI 49663

Call Sign: KD8GGF
Kelly D Whitehead
10485 E M 42
Manton MI 49663

Call Sign: K8WZS
Richard G Hockridge
10585 E M 42
Manton MI 49663

Call Sign: N8ZWT
Michael R Lovelace Jr
7015 Elm Dr
Manton MI 49663

Call Sign: N8IYH
Jarvis T Wood
2828 N 41 1/2 Rd
Manton MI 49663

Call Sign: KD8AGH
Carla M Sparks
7225 N 45 1/2 Rd
Manton MI 49663

Call Sign: K8NML
Helen L Sherman
3151 N Hilbrand Rd
Manton MI 49663

Call Sign: KD8BRL
Robert E Blackford Jr
11045 Packingham Rd
Manton MI 49663

Call Sign: KA8GIG
Eugene H St Onge
223 Pine St
Manton MI 496639128

Call Sign: KA8HSU
Richard H Morris
206 Randolph
Manton MI 49663

Call Sign: KD8BNK
Dale L Perry
505 Roberts St
Manton MI 49663

Call Sign: KB0CWW
James W Davlantes
401 W Main St
Manton MI 49663

Call Sign: N8PML
John J Bivens
7897 W Moorestown
Rd
Manton MI 49663

Call Sign: KD8AZG
Edward J Aten
7640 W Walker Rd
Manton MI 49663

Call Sign: KD8BNL
Clayton P Helsel
8744 W Walker Rd

Manton MI 49663

Call Sign: W8UJH
George A Reynolds
407 Wenonah Trl
Manton MI 49663

Call Sign: W8BSC
Camp Greilick Boy
Scout Camp
Manton MI 49663

Call Sign: KC8RUR
Camp Greilick Boy
Scout Camp
Manton MI 49663

Call Sign: KC8TDI
Jay A Raymer
Manton MI 49663

Call Sign: KB8EZR
Nathan A Tarsa
Rt 1 Box 110
Maple City MI 49664

Call Sign: KB8PZU
William A Phillips
8338 S Coleman Rd
Maple City MI 49664

Call Sign: K8DVM
John E Binsfeld
8944 S Dunns Farm Rd
Maple City MI 49664

Call Sign: KB8VCQ
Marc D Alderman
10697 S Newman Rd
Maple City MI 49664

Call Sign: KD8PCG
Charles L Schaeffer Jr
1776 W Burnley Ln
Maple City MI 49664

Call Sign: W8WFN
Gerald A Gorrell
3596 W Trumbull Rd

Maple City MI
496649756

Call Sign: KC8ADO
Jodi R Schmidt
250 W Union St
Maple Rapids MI
488530081

Call Sign: KB8ZRE
William H Schmidt
250 W Union St
Maple Rapids MI
488530081

Call Sign: WA8KDP
James C Hamilton
Maple Rapids MI
48853

Call Sign: W9EFL
Noel O Kindt
90888 Bluff Dr
Marcellus MI 49067

Call Sign: KD8KOQ
Kenneth R Hutchins
50775 Burlington Rd
Marcellus MI 49067

Call Sign: N8MUT
Guy D Pound III
10466 Cranberry Lake
Rd
Marcellus MI 49067

Call Sign: N8BFA
Jeanne A Kaylor
54003 Day Rd
Marcellus MI 49067

Call Sign: N8ABY
Jack V Huss
451 Elm St
Marcellus MI 49067

Call Sign: N8GEJ

Richard B Martin
50199 M 40
Marcellus MI 49067

Call Sign: KC8DEH
Rebecca S Cowham
13836 Marcellus Hwy
Marcellus MI 49067

Call Sign: KC8NZO
Patrick B Baker
14490 Marcellus Hwy
Marcellus MI 49067

Call Sign: K8NZO
Patrick B Baker
14490 Marcellus Hwy
Marcellus MI 49067

Call Sign: K8LCF
Jarett F Alwine
16415 Marcellus Hwy
Marcellus MI 49067

Call Sign: KD8EKX
Rand J Eddy
12595 N Ct
Marcellus MI 49067

Call Sign: KD8CST
Michael J Dwyer
450 S Maple Rd
Marcellus MI 49067

Call Sign: KD8CIY
David G Graham
13460 Shannon St
Marcellus MI 49067

Call Sign: WD8JUP
Kenneth C Kaylor
400 South St Lot 41
Marcellus MI 49067

Call Sign: KB8GXU
Lee Forzer
Marcellus MI 49067

Call Sign: KB8FII
Jeremy W Gerrits
Hc 1 Box 211

Marenisco MI 49947

Call Sign: N8JUP
Arthur Pardi Jr
N10986 St Hwy M 64
Marenisco MI 49947

Call Sign: KC9AMX
John L Armata Sr
E-13543 Stateline Lake
Rd
Marenisco MI
499479767

Call Sign: KC9DNE
Kenneth T Tworek
E13565 Stateline Lake
Rd
Marenisco MI 49947

Call Sign: KD8DDL
Edward W Dracht
23350 100th Ave
Marion MI 49665

Call Sign: WA8ONH
Oral J Christie
2751 19 Mile Rd
Marion MI 49665

Call Sign: KC8OHD
Michael L Hoadley
4847 19 Mile Rd
Marion MI 49665

Call Sign: KF8KP
Lester L Alberts
7371 19 Mile Rd
Marion MI 49665

Call Sign: KD8DDO
Darren L Kamphouse
8460 22 Mile Rd
Marion MI 49665

Call Sign: KD8DUR
Richard L Christie
19689 40th Ave
Marion MI 49665

Call Sign: KC8DGQ

Jeffrey C Merrifield
17828 50th Ave
Marion MI 49665

Call Sign: KC8WZR
Jeffrey D Bressler
13045 5th Ave
Marion MI 49665

Call Sign: KC8WZQ
Sabrina K Bressler
13045 5th Ave
Marion MI 49665

Call Sign: K8CAD
Wexaukee ARC
133 6th St
Marion MI 49665

Call Sign: N8NJA
William R Kelso
133 6th St
Marion MI 49665

Call Sign: N8EIX
Gary A Hultgren
305 6th St
Marion MI 49665

Call Sign: KB8IUT
Terry R Chesney
19396 70th Ave
Marion MI 49665

Call Sign: KD8DDK
Jerry D Kamphouse
23726 95th Ave
Marion MI 49665

Call Sign: KD8BNJ
Kenneth Kamphouse
23726 95th Ave
Marion MI 49665

Call Sign: KD8DOJ
Jack D Kamphouse
23880 95th Ave
Marion MI 49665

Call Sign: WD8LVZ
David A McAlpine
11227 Clam River Rd
Marion MI 49665

Call Sign: KC8CZT
Aaron J Michell
2767 E 14 Mile Rd
Marion MI 49665

Call Sign: KD8FRY
Adam M Southwick
8715 E 22 Mi Rd
Marion MI 49665

Call Sign: KC8FYE
Sarah A Fox
9870 Forest Rd
Marion MI 49665

Call Sign: WD8MXH
Elwin A Pritchard
309 Morton Dr
Marion MI 49665

Call Sign: KD8DDH
Jason L Huttenga
23953 N 5th Ave
Marion MI 49665

Call Sign: N8ETS
Homer R Montgomery
106 N Case St
Marion MI 49665

Call Sign: KC8WOM
Todd A Hamilton
9420 Pine Rd
Marion MI 49665

Call Sign: KC4SZD
Neal E Beach
11340 S 8 Mile
Marion MI 49665

Call Sign: KC8ZRU
Brian K Bouma
107195 S Turnerville
Rd
Marion MI 49665

Call Sign: KC8TXT
Brian L Polk
13826 Serenity Dr
Marion MI 49665

Call Sign: KD8NXN
Claude F Dean
411 West Ln

Marion MI 49665

Call Sign: WB8NDB
Stanley K Williams
14204 12th Ave
Marne MI 494359704

Call Sign: K8RB
Roger A Bergman
12544 24th Ave
Marne MI 49435

Call Sign: KD8RVM
Joshua M Westgate
14593 32nd Ave
Marne MI 49435

Call Sign: W8KIZ
Alan W Scott
13799 8th Ave
Marne MI 49435

Call Sign: K8EB
Erwin V Beemer
953 Garfield St
Marne MI 49435

Call Sign: WB8YKJ
Godwin Heights
Amateur Radio Assn
0-2204 Hayes NW
Marne MI 49435

Call Sign: K8XL
Robert S Czachorski Jr
0-2204 Hayes St NW
Marne MI 49435

Call Sign: WA8WEE
Dale R Scholten
3324 Johnson Rd
Marne MI 49435

Call Sign: WB8QLB
George T Frazee
0-15623 Kenowa Ave
Marne MI 49435

Call Sign: KB8ILP
Patricia E Mallory
4333 Leonard Rd

Marne MI 49435

Call Sign: WA8CAS
William S Mallory
4333 Leonard Rd
Marne MI 49435

Call Sign: KE4CQQ
Roger K Tomkins
Marne MI 494350067

FCC Amateur Radio Licenses in Marquette

Call Sign: N8UAI
Gordon D Gill
1320 2nd St
Marquette MI 49855

Call Sign: WX8MQT
National Weather
Service Marquette Mi
Skywarn Association
112 Airpark Dr S
Marquette MI 49866

Call Sign: KD8CGJ
William H Dupras
2246 Allen Rd
Marquette MI 49855

Call Sign: N8RRZ
Eric L Smith
1024 Allouez Rd
Marquette MI 49855

Call Sign: KC8RSW
Jordan R Smith
1024 Allouez Rd
Marquette MI 49855

Call Sign: KD8IAX
Adam R Smith
1024 Allouez Rd
Marquette MI 49855

Call Sign: KB8THA
Susan S Syria
1024 Allouez Rd
Marquette MI
498555206

Call Sign: KC8HYB

Jackson L Pellett
1042 Allouez Rd
Marquette MI 49855

Call Sign: W8JMN
Harry D Pedakis
1047 Allouez Rd
Marquette MI 49855

Call Sign: N8RSE
John S Veiht
1609 Altamont
Marquette MI 49855

Call Sign: K8VLD
Paul O Donovan
127 Aspen Dr
Marquette MI 49855

Call Sign: KD8DQY
Jonathan M Rose
524 Baraga Apt 1
Marquette MI 49855

Call Sign: KD8DQZ
Mindy C Gaetz
524 Baraga Ave Apt 1
Marquette MI 49855

Call Sign: N8PKN
Robert H Serfas
1600 Bayview Dr
Marquette MI 49855

Call Sign: KC8ULA
Debra L Smith
1600 Bayview Dr
Marquette MI 49855

Call Sign: KC8IIF
Jeanne M Friesen
780 Bishop Woods Rd
Marquette MI
498558623

Call Sign: KI8DK
Gary M Friesen
780 Bishop Woods Rd
Marquette MI
498558623

Call Sign: KC8AUM
Douglas G Cook
Hc01 Box 280

Marquette MI 49855

Call Sign: KB8YJS
Wilbert C Wagner
412 Cherry Creek Rd
Marquette MI 49855

Call Sign: KC8ABZ
Carl R Wagner
412 Cherry Creek Rd
Marquette MI 49855

Call Sign: WD8PAI
James A Petrella
449 Cherry Creek Rd
Marquette MI 49855

Call Sign: W3KGW
Donald J Anlauf
2492 Cherry St
Marquette MI 49855

Call Sign: KC8CVS
Arthur J Brabbs
100 Cheryl Ct
Marquette MI 49855

Call Sign: KD8OAG
Robert T Doonan
120 Chocolay River
Trl
Marquette MI 49855

Call Sign: KB8QFG
Louis O Carr
1100 Cleveland Ave
Marquette MI 49855

Call Sign: KD8NDD
Wilfred L Barber
1246 Cleveland Ave
Marquette MI 49855

Call Sign: KD8NPJ
Scott J Machalk
1040 CR 480
Marquette MI 49855

Call Sign: N8QBI
Rudy F Evonich
1470 CR 492
Marquette MI 49855

Call Sign: KD8DRC

Stanley E Wittler
124 CR 545
Marquette MI 49855

Call Sign: KB9WCL
Teresa M Smith
5089 CR 550
Marquette MI 49855

Call Sign: KB9QKW
James W Smith
195B CR 550
Marquette MI 49855

Call Sign: W8AAC
Douglas G Cook
448 CR Kch
Marquette MI 49855

Call Sign: KC8NN
Allan J Meeves
604 Craig St
Marquette MI 49855

Call Sign: NH6CN
James E Belles
136 Dandelion Ln
Marquette MI 49855

Call Sign: N8NAV
James E Belles
136 Dandelion Ln
Marquette MI 49855

Call Sign: KD8MER
Andrea L Clark
1120 Divdision
Marquette MI 49855

Call Sign: KC8NCJ
Dexter D Clark
1120 Division St
Marquette MI 49855

Call Sign: KD8LRQ
Alisha A Wells
103 Dobson Pl
Marquette MI 49855

Call Sign: WA8GDW
Jon E Wennerberg
509 Dukes Rd
Marquette MI
498551054

Call Sign: KC8ZYH
Terrance M Laforge
203 E Anda St
Marquette MI 49855

Call Sign: W8GGO
Theodore G Graphos
309 E Arch St
Marquette MI 49855

Call Sign: KB8CKV
Karen A La More
329 E Arch St
Marquette MI 49855

Call Sign: KC8UXJ
Karen A Lamore
329 E Arch St
Marquette MI 49855

Call Sign: KC8EWF
Robert H Botsford
116 E College Ave
Marquette MI 49855

Call Sign: KD8SCC
Andrew R Norris
400 E College Ave
Marquette MI 49855

Call Sign: N8UZQ
Robert D Hogg
329 E Crescent St
Marquette MI 49855

Call Sign: KC8YIV
Jeffrey A Hoffman
336 E Crescent St
Marquette MI 49855

Call Sign: KC8LKY
Bruce W Kobie
440.5 E Crescent St
Marquette MI 49855

Call Sign: KC8RSX
Penny K Pederson
525 E Hewitt Ave
Marquette MI 49855

Call Sign: KL1TU
Keith H Norton
318 E Kaye Ave

Marquette MI 49855

Call Sign: KB8VEL
Trevor O Dupras
177 E Main St
Marquette MI 49855

Call Sign: N4SP
Stephen Paull
451 E Michigan St
Marquette MI 49855

Call Sign: N8MOT
Randy O Ryan
2 E Nicolet Blvd
Marquette MI 49855

Call Sign: KC8FEW
Timothy P Shandonay
311 E Park St
Marquette MI 49855

Call Sign: N8WAU
Sam J Dyer
37 Elder Dr
Marquette MI 49855

Call Sign: KC8LVV
Over The Air Rad Clb
Upr Peninsula Chldrn
Mus
47 Elder Dr
Marquette MI 49855

Call Sign: N8MOS
Howard B Schweppe
47 Elder Dr
Marquette MI 49855

Call Sign: N8WBJ
Julie K Schweppe
47 Elder Dr
Marquette MI 49855

Call Sign: K8OV
Howard B Schweppe
47 Elder Dr
Marquette MI 49855

Call Sign: KC8EEE
Jon R Pederson
1802 Erie Ave
Marquette MI 49855

Call Sign: WL7OS
Harold B Hildebrand
135 Fassbender Rd
Marquette MI 49855

Call Sign: KT5L
Samuel K Culp II
148 Fassbender Rd
Marquette MI 49855

Call Sign: KB8PFB
David G Aldrich
37 Feather Ridge Rd
Marquette MI 49855

Call Sign: KD8COR
Adam R Reichel
146 Fisher St
Marquette MI 49855

Call Sign: KC8CVY
Daniel S Sackett
1733 Fitch Ave
Marquette MI 49855

Call Sign: W8YRT
Daniel S Sackett
1733 Fitch Ave
Marquette MI 49855

Call Sign: KC8IQD
Stuart P Sarasin
225 Forest Hills Dr
Marquette MI 49855

Call Sign: AJ8MH
Joseph M Hutchens
633 Forest Park Dr
Marquette MI 49855

Call Sign: KD8KMN
Pamela A Hutchens
633 Forest Park Dr
Marquette MI 49855

Call Sign: KC8TIK
Eric A Lautanen
900 Garfield Ave 16
Marquette MI 49855

Call Sign: KA8ZGW
Michael P Bennett
350 Genesee Rd
Marquette MI 49855

Call Sign: KD0FBI
Justin I Titus
1021 Hancock St Apt 7
Marquette MI 49855

Call Sign: KB8UCM
David S Stobbelaar
530 Harrison Ave
Marquette MI 49855

Call Sign: KD8SCA
Joel E Tapio
9 Heather Ln
Marquette MI 49855

Call Sign: KD8BJX
Kari C Fleegel
20 Heather Ln
Marquette MI 49855

Call Sign: KD8LMS
Carol S Steinhaus
708 Hennepin Rd
Marquette MI 49855

Call Sign: N8KCF
David O Peterson
4 Hidden Creek Tr
Marquette MI 49855

Call Sign: WK8D
Yvonne S Peterson
4 Hidden Creek Trl
Marquette MI 49855

Call Sign: KD8LMW
Jean E Schultz
325 High St
Marquette MI 49855

Call Sign: KD8LMT
William W Thum
508 Hillside Dr
Marquette MI 49855

Call Sign: K8NMU
Joseph L Duckworth Jr
2012 Huron St
Marquette MI 49841

Call Sign: KD8RXT
John T Mahan
2202 Huron St

Marquette MI 49855

Call Sign: N8JRN
John R Nelson
2 Jack St
Marquette MI 49855

Call Sign: KD8DBE
Robert L Taylor
204 Jean St
Marquette MI 49855

Call Sign: K8ACT
Robert L Taylor
204 Jean St
Marquette MI 49855

Call Sign: KD8RXR
Patrick J Gimse
205 Jean St
Marquette MI 49855

Call Sign: N8GGN
Michael A Neiger
313 Jonathan Carver
Rd
Marquette MI 49855

Call Sign: K8CEE
Arthur B Neiger
319 Jonathan Carver
Rd
Marquette MI 49855

Call Sign: KF8UC
James P Collins
201 Judy St
Marquette MI 49855

Call Sign: KE8IL
Michael E Hoffman
132 Juliet St
Marquette MI 49855

Call Sign: N8ITK
Judy J Hoffman
132 Juliet St
Marquette MI 49855

Call Sign: KC8RSV
Philip M Hoffman
132 Juliet St
Marquette MI 49855

Call Sign: K8SAX
Gary T Krieg
3050 Lakeshore Blvd
Marquette MI 49855

Call Sign: N8JIK
Robert C Stow Sr
29 Lakeview Dr
Marquette MI 49855

Call Sign: W8ILW
Charles H Marvin
243 Lakewood Ln
Marquette MI 49855

Call Sign: KB8VER
Christopher K White
370 Lakewood Ln
Marquette MI 49855

Call Sign: N8FQF
John D Wojcik
381 Lakewood Ln
Marquette MI 49855

Call Sign: WA2HEQ
John D Wojcik
381 Lakewood Ln
Marquette MI 49855

Call Sign: KC8VCD
Edward C Fenelon
385 Lakewood Ln
Marquette MI 49855

Call Sign: KD8NCZ
Ryan V Salo
271 Little Lake Rd
Marquette MI 49855

Call Sign: KD8NDB
Sam A Salo
271 Little Lake Rd
Marquette MI 49855

Call Sign: KD8PTE
Lucille T Scotti
500 Little Lake Rd
Marquette MI 49855

Call Sign: KB8PEL
Donald A Salo Jr
271 Little Lake Rd
Marquette MI 49855

Call Sign: KB8VEK
Karla M Salo
271 Little Lake Rd
Marquette MI 49855

Call Sign: KD8RXS
Brian C Thill
360 Little Lake Rd
Marquette MI 49855

Call Sign: W8BP
John C Wasmuth
505 Lost Creek Dr
Marquette MI 49855

Call Sign: WJ5MH
Joseph M Hutchens
1514 Lynn Ave
Marquette MI 49855

Call Sign: K8CED
Jeffrey M Glass
2048 M 28
Marquette MI 49855

Call Sign: KB8GHT
Donald J Oakes Jr
1523 M 28 E
Marquette MI 49855

Call Sign: N8IYB
Donald J Oakes
1523 M 28 E
Marquette MI 49855

Call Sign: KD8NDC
George F Hough
418 M 553 W
Marquette MI 49855

Call Sign: KC8UUC
David G Petrovich
101 Meadow Ln
Marquette MI 49855

Call Sign: KD8OXD
Gary L Lambert
214 Mesnard St
Marquette MI 49855

Call Sign: KD8IVK
Kurt J Bell
2433 Montgomery St

Marquette MI 49855

Call Sign: KC8HYD
Daniel P Carilli
8 Morgan Meadows
Marquette MI 49855

Call Sign: KC8PYD
Donald K Ohman
420 N 3rd St
Marquette MI 49855

Call Sign: KC7YGQ
John B Carroll
420 N 3rd St
Marquette MI 49855

Call Sign: KD8JXZ
Kevin D Czupinski
623 Northland Dr
Marquette MI
498554427

Call Sign: KF8RV
Mark A Robertson
1803 Norwood St
Marquette MI 49855

Call Sign: WD8SBW
Lynn E Miller
34 Oak Hill Dr
Marquette MI 49855

Call Sign: KB8YJO
Chris R Cappuccio
55 Oak Hill Dr
Marquette MI 49855

Call Sign: KB8HLZ
Ted A Balzarini
3 Oakridge Dr
Marquette MI 49855

Call Sign: KB8HOJ
Kristina A Balzarini
3 Oakridge Dr
Marquette MI 49855

Call Sign: KD8DBB
Jean V Adams
1009 Old Little Lake
Rd
Marquette MI 49855

Call Sign: KD8DBC
John W Heinrich
1009 Old Little Lake
Rd
Marquette MI 49855

Call Sign: KB8SBR
David R Northey
860 Orianna Dr
Marquette MI 49855

Call Sign: KB8SNO
Carolyn C Northey
860 Orianna Dr
Marquette MI 49855

Call Sign: KB8HQH
William J Sawaski
32 Pine Acres
Marquette MI 49855

Call Sign: KD8SCE
Peter A Klanderud
316 Pine Apt 215
Marquette MI 49855

Call Sign: W8NEY
Dale D Massoglia
777 Pioneer Rd Lot 73
Marquette MI 49855

Call Sign: KC8OXI
John L Rice
110 Poplar Trl
Marquette MI 49855

Call Sign: KC8FPV
Samuel L Peano
2133 Presque Isle
Marquette MI 49855

Call Sign: WD8DJA
James F Jacobson
105 Raymbault Dr
Marquette MI 49855

Call Sign: W8QQE
James F Jacobson
105 Raymbault Dr
Marquette MI 49855

Call Sign: KC8GKH
Lyn L Nelson
1 Ridge Rd

Marquette MI 49855

Call Sign: KD8PTF
Paul E Motter
108 Ridgewood Dr
Marquette MI 49855

Call Sign: KD8IAT
Donna L Campbell
104 Riverdale Rd
Marquette MI 49855

Call Sign: KD8FPK
Mark M Campbell
104 Riverdale Rd
Marquette MI 49855

Call Sign: KC8WZS
Steve D Macdonald
203 A Rt 550
Marquette MI 49855

Call Sign: KB8VGL
Jordan M Povich
1066 S Lake St
Marquette MI 49855

Call Sign: KD8BPA
Delbert E Storms
1084 S Lake St
Marquette MI 49855

Call Sign: KC8TII
Robin J Turner
49 S Tracie Ln
Marquette MI 49855

Call Sign: KC8QWO
Michael J Cauley
945 S Willow Rd
Marquette MI 49855

Call Sign: N8KEX
William A Sweeney
104 Sandy Ln
Marquette MI 49855

Call Sign: N8WAX
Todd A Miilu
Box 200B Saux Head
Lk Rd
Marquette MI 49855

Call Sign: KC8PYC

Carol E Hicks
360 Shot Point Dr
Marquette MI 49855

Call Sign: KD8DVM
Cathy A Sleeter
302 Silver Creek Rd
Marquette MI 49855

Call Sign: KD8DRE
Terry W Sleeter
302 Silver Creek Rd
Marquette MI 49855

Call Sign: KC8DTD
Sarah J Schwenke
21 Smith Ln
Marquette MI 49855

Call Sign: K8LOD
Hiawatha Amateur
Radio Assn Inc
46 Smith Ln
Marquette MI 49855

Call Sign: N8GBA
Richard E B Schwenke
46 Smith Ln
Marquette MI 49855

Call Sign: KD8DZV
John David A Forslin
8 Southfork St
Marquette MI 49855

Call Sign: KD8DKU
Lake Effect ARC
36 Southfork St
Marquette MI 49855

Call Sign: KC8ULE
John J Forslin
36 Southfork St
Marquette MI 49855

Call Sign: KD8AIL
Marjorie A Forslin
36 Southfork St
Marquette MI 49855

Call Sign: WB8EOH
Gary T Bourgois
429 Spring St
Marquette MI 49855

Call Sign: KB8JUZ
Peter H Goodrich
517 Spruce St
Marquette MI 49855

Call Sign: KB8JVA
Andrew S Goodrich
517 Spruce St
Marquette MI 49855

Call Sign: KC8TIJ
Patricia L Anderson
599 State Hwy 553
Marquette MI 49855

Call Sign: AB8RE
Patricia L Anderson
599 State Hwy 553
Marquette MI 49855

Call Sign: KG8YT
Bruce M Anderson
599 State Hwy M 553
Marquette MI 49855

Call Sign: KB8PWP
Kendall M Cox
1910 Sugarloaf 40
Marquette MI 49855

Call Sign: KD8DAZ
John R Nelson
124 Surrey Ln
Marquette MI 49855

Call Sign: KD8JIP
Fred E Mouser
190 Timber Ln
Marquette MI 49855

Call Sign: NJ8H
Gary D French
6220 US 41 S
Marquette MI 49855

Call Sign: KD8DRA
Jon M Carlson
6417 US 41 S 1
Marquette MI 49855

Call Sign: KJ4GIH
Paul E Millen

3224 US Hwy 41 W
Pmb 135
Marquette MI 49855

Call Sign: KD8HOQ
Ronald A Raisanen
109 Veda St
Marquette MI 49855

Call Sign: KC8QWR
Carl A Wozniak
1055 Vistanna Dr
Marquette MI 49855

Call Sign: KD8DVO
Matthew J Gagnon
524 W Baraga Apt 3
Marquette MI 49855

Call Sign: KC8ABV
Lisa A La Course
818 W College Ave
Marquette MI 49855

Call Sign: N8XBH
Chris A Danek
34 W Elder Dr
Marquette MI 49855

Call Sign: N8YGA
Andrea L Danek
34 W Elder Dr
Marquette MI 49855

Call Sign: N8UZP
Steven W Lindberg
1911 W Fair Ave
Marquette MI 49855

Call Sign: KD8HLZ
Christopher M Nelson
2273 W Fair Ave
Marquette MI 49855

Call Sign: KI8AF
Gregory L Hanson
624 W Hampton St
Marquette MI 49855

Call Sign: KU2D
Yi-Min Huang
624 W Hampton St
Marquette MI 49855

Call Sign: KD8MBB
Arun-Prakash
Periasamy
624 W Hampton St
Marquette MI 49855

Call Sign: KD8OVL
Binesh Unnikrishnan
624 W Hampton St
Marquette MI 49855

Call Sign: KD8MAZ
Ching-Lin Liou
624 W Hampton St
Marquette MI 49855

Call Sign: AC8HO
David J Lo
624 W Hampton St
Marquette MI 49855

Call Sign: KK6K
David J Lo
624 W Hampton St
Marquette MI 49855

Call Sign: KD8MBC
Eric P Chen
624 W Hampton St
Marquette MI 49855

Call Sign: KC2TRF
Jen-Chieh Hsing
624 W Hampton St
Marquette MI 49855

Call Sign: KD8MBA
Jeng-Shiou Wu
624 W Hampton St
Marquette MI 49855

Call Sign: KI6RYJ
Long-Rong Yang
624 W Hampton St
Marquette MI 49855

Call Sign: KC2TRB
Pao-Yun Chang
624 W Hampton St
Marquette MI 49855

Call Sign: KD8MBE
Randson Huang
624 W Hampton St

Marquette MI 49855

Call Sign: WJ2I
Randson Huang
624 W Hampton St
Marquette MI 49855

Call Sign: KD8OVK
Thiagarajan
Soundappan
624 W Hampton St
Marquette MI 49855

Call Sign: KC2TQZ
Yao-Pin Tsai
624 W Hampton St
Marquette MI 49855

Call Sign: KI6RYP
Yi-Min Huang
624 W Hampton St
Marquette MI 49855

Call Sign: KD8MBD
Yogeswaran
Umasankar
624 W Hampton St
Marquette MI 49855

Call Sign: NY3W
Yogeswaran
Umasankar
624 W Hampton St
Marquette MI 49855

Call Sign: KC2TRD
Chien-Chung Wu
624 W Hampton St
Marquette MI
498555037

Call Sign: KC2TRC
Chung-Hung Chang
624 W Hampton St
Marquette MI
498555037

Call Sign: KI6RYO
Jini Lin
624 W Hampton St
Marquette MI
498555037

Call Sign: KC2TRA

Li-Cheng Liu
624 W Hampton St
Marquette MI
498555037

Call Sign: KC2TRE
Ming-Hsien Wang
624 W Hampton St
Marquette MI
498555037

Call Sign: KI6RYM
Ping-Tsun Hsu
624 W Hampton St
Marquette MI
498555037

Call Sign: W8WNT
Roy S Anderson
700 W Kaye Ave
Marquette MI 49855

Call Sign: KB8CKR
Mary E Anderson
700 W Kaye Ave
Marquette MI
498550759

Call Sign: K8CZO
Mary Jane Akkala
810 W Kaye Ave
Marquette MI 49855

Call Sign: W8AT
John M Akkala
810 W Kaye Ave
Marquette MI 49855

Call Sign: KB8PEI
Mary A Treml
725 W Magnetic
Marquette MI 49855

Call Sign: KB8PGM
Jacqueline N Treml
725 W Magnetic
Marquette MI 49855

Call Sign: KC8HYC
William C Chesney
810 W Magnetic
Marquette MI 49855

Call Sign: KB8CKU

Heidi L Treml
725 W Magnetic St
Marquette MI 49855

Call Sign: K8PT
B Peter Treml
725 W Magnetic St
Marquette MI
498552730

Call Sign: KD8DRF
David L Thomas
311 W Main St
Marquette MI 49855

Call Sign: KD8NCY
Brandon M Rasmussen
312 W Ohio Rd
Marquette MI 49855

Call Sign: KD8JXE
John W Robertson
323 W Park St
Marquette MI 49855

Call Sign: W8BJP
Donald J Vajda
1532 W Ridge 50
Marquette MI 49855

Call Sign: WD8RWV
Joseph H Meyskens
415 W Ridge St
Marquette MI 49855

Call Sign: WD8MDD
Emil H Vajda
1540 W Ridge St Apt
18
Marquette MI 49855

Call Sign: KC8UGX
Steven M Rehn
1534 W Ridge St Apt
40
Marquette MI 49855

Call Sign: KA8CDT
Jeffrey A Selesky
517 W Spring St
Marquette MI 49855

Call Sign: W8HAV
Zelma V Neault

854 W Washington
Marquette MI 49855

Call Sign: N8CDZ
Walter J McClintock
1801 Waldo St
Marquette MI 49855

Call Sign: W8VJD
Eugene A Cole
203 Westkaye Ave
Marquette MI 49855

Call Sign: KB8CNK
Bruno J Bicigo
1616 Woodland Ave
Marquette MI 49855

Call Sign: WD8BYU
Marvin C Oysti
1708 Woodland Ave
Marquette MI 49855

Call Sign: N8HLH
Julius C De Falico Jr
1350 Woodridge
Marquette MI 49855

Call Sign: KC8KJG
Karl J Harmon
1802 Wright St
Marquette MI
498551530

Call Sign: KB8PEN
Patricia An Kohl
Marquette MI 49855

Call Sign: KC8CZX
Arnold J Rohen
Marquette MI 49855

Call Sign: N8BTS
Frederick R Anderson
Marquette MI 49855

Call Sign: N8NRG
William J Beitel III
Marquette MI 49855

Call Sign: KC8EEB
Todd Pasanen
Marquette MI 49855

**FCC Amateur Radio
Licenses in Marshall**

Call Sign: KA8HQN
Beverly J Russell
7700 15 1/2 Mile Rd
Marshall MI
490689243

Call Sign: W8MGR
Michael G Russell
7700 15 1/2 Mile Rd
Marshall MI
490689243

Call Sign: KC8COQ
Mary L Findley
15784 15 Mile Rd
Marshall MI 49068

Call Sign: KD8RWI
Sarah G Findley
15784 15 Mile Rd
Marshall MI 49068

Call Sign: KG8HD
Oscar G Findley
15784 15 Mile Rd
Marshall MI 49068

Call Sign: WA8VRA
Arnold E Tew
17703 15 Mile Rd
Marshall MI 49068

Call Sign: KD8RWD
Bryan S Miller
14999 15 Mile Rd Apt
6
Marshall MI 49068

Call Sign: KC8OZW
Karen L Loyer
18500 17 1/2 Mile Rd
Marshall MI 49068

Call Sign: KC8OVK
Barton O Loyer
18500 17 1/2 Mile Rd
Marshall MI 49068

Call Sign: N8OBW
Enos E Christie
10801 17 Mile Rd

Marshall MI 49068

Call Sign: KG4SBB
Daniel J Jezowski
6631 18 1/2 Mile Rd
Marshall MI 49068

Call Sign: AB8PZ
Daniel J Jezowski
6631 18 1/2 Mile Rd
Marshall MI
490689231

Call Sign: N0MRX
Richmond A Offerson
16009 18 Mile Rd
Marshall MI
490689463

Call Sign: KD8NKJ
Harry C Hedges
14878 A Dr N
Marshall MI 49068

Call Sign: KD8NAJ
Harry C Hedges
14878 A Dr N
Marshall MI 49068

Call Sign: KC8HEU
David A Goedde
15525 A Dr N
Marshall MI 49068

Call Sign: WA8GVM
Lucile E Moore
22821 B Dr N
Marshall MI 49068

Call Sign: W8AQU
Louellis D Cain
321 Boyer Ct
Marshall MI 49068

Call Sign: W8ZEJ
Albert B Cain
321 Boyer Ct
Marshall MI 49068

Call Sign: KB9WHD
Beatrice A Deppe
121 Chauncey Ct
Marshall MI 49068

Call Sign: KA8LXI
Jacqueline R
Malinowski
20577 Division Dr
Marshall MI 49068

Call Sign: N8BGM
John R Malinowski
20577 Division Dr
Marshall MI 49068

Call Sign: KB9AAZ
Hope A Rodenbarger
223.5 E Michigan Ave
Marshall MI 49068

Call Sign: K8AEM
Walter J Wilson
14249 Eden St
Marshall MI 49068

Call Sign: KB8END
Forest E Hills
16515 F Dr N
Marshall MI 49068

Call Sign: AA8PO
Vernon J Hills
16625 F Dr N
Marshall MI 49068

Call Sign: KF8AB
John F Hanfland
20580 F Dr N
Marshall MI 49068

Call Sign: WS8F
John F Hanfland
20580 F Dr N
Marshall MI 49068

Call Sign: N8BIA
James C Tompkins
17895 F Dr S
Marshall MI 49068

Call Sign: KA9LUJ
Peter F Weston
742 Forest St
Marshall MI 49068

Call Sign: KI8KP
Peter F Weston
742 Forest St

Marshall MI 49068

Call Sign: WA8GGF
Larry Eccleston
18565 G Dr N
Marshall MI 49068

Call Sign: WA8HVS
John D Horsman Jr
22111 H Dr N
Marshall MI 49068

Call Sign: AB8I
Scott A Spaulding
18575 Homer Rd
Marshall MI 49068

Call Sign: KC8ZNJ
Timothy E Cathcart
14635 L Dr N
Marshall MI 49068

Call Sign: K8UCQ
Earl R Goodrich
110 Lyon Lake Rd
Marshall MI 49068

Call Sign: K8UCY
Donna L Goodrich
110 Lyon Lake Rd
Marshall MI 49068

Call Sign: WA8PNX
Alan Vandenburg
739 Lyon Lake Rd
Marshall MI 49068

Call Sign: KD8JBV
Douglas J Mathewson
21496 M Dr N
Marshall MI 49068

Call Sign: KD8JBU
Sharon M Mathewson
21496 M Dr N
Marshall MI 49068

Call Sign: KB7YQY
Anthony G Newton
16868 N Dr N
Marshall MI 49068

Call Sign: KF6ARI
Karen R Newton

16868 N Dr N
Marshall MI 49068

Call Sign: KA7FAN
David E Harris
219 N Eagle
Marshall MI 49068

Call Sign: W8OCC
Maurice H Henker
623 N Gordon St
Marshall MI 49068

Call Sign: WA8UHJ
Dennis R Mattis
525 N Kalamazoo Ave
Marshall MI 49068

Call Sign: WD8KBI
Richard K Day
548 N Madison
Marshall MI 49068

Call Sign: KB8TON
Stephen M Ward
346 N Marshall Ave
Marshall MI 49068

Call Sign: W8IWJ
Hubert D Butcher
514 North Dr E
Marshall MI 49068

Call Sign: KC8DBB
Blane E Quilhot
16600 Old 27 N
Marshall MI 49068

Call Sign: KD8BYD
Craig M Kimerer
15087 S Dr N
Marshall MI 49068

Call Sign: WB8UEJ
James H Kelly
223 S Liberty St
Marshall MI 49068

Call Sign: KA8MDA
Luther K McPherson
15488 Tau Rd
Marshall MI 49068

Call Sign: KD8QLT

Andrew D Smith
16147 US Hwy 27 N
Marshall MI 49068

Call Sign: N8MVH
Ginger E Williams
606 Ventura Way
Marshall MI 49068

Call Sign: WB8TRL
Brent A Williams
606 Ventura Way
Marshall MI 49068

Call Sign: W8NXY
Charles W Lutz
820 Verona Rd
Marshall MI
490681040

Call Sign: KB8QAI
Kenneth D Eagle
207 W Prospect St
Marshall MI 49068

Call Sign: WB8BPO
Paul A Rauth
372 Westbrook Ct
Marshall MI 49068

**FCC Amateur Radio
Licenses in Martin**

Call Sign: N8JBN
Sandra L Davidson
1394 10th St
Martin MI 49070

Call Sign: N8EQR
Wallace P Davidson Sr
1394 10th St
Martin MI 490709725

Call Sign: KD8GTF
Steven D Herlein
1972 10th St
Martin MI 49070

Call Sign: KC2BNC
Nathaniel L Edison
526 116th Ave
Martin MI 49070

Call Sign: N2AYW

Lawrence W Edison
526 116th Ave
Martin MI 49070

Call Sign: AJ8N
Joseph B Maley
1939 8th St
Martin MI 49070

Call Sign: N8AWN
Gail B Maley
1939 8th St
Martin MI 49070

Call Sign: N8BEQ
Paul R McFarland
906 E Allegan St
Martin MI 49070

Call Sign: K8DFI
Ward E Dean
922 E Allegan St
Martin MI 49070

FCC Amateur Radio Licenses in Mattawan

Call Sign: KB8WQB
Christy E Kubin
24468 2nd St
Mattawan MI 49071

Call Sign: KC8KEH
Chad W Robertson
24414 3rd Ave
Mattawan MI 49071

Call Sign: KB8EUL
Croffort E Lumpkin Jr
23220 44th Ave
Mattawan MI 49071

Call Sign: K8CQP
William R Hamilton
45745 CR 652
Mattawan MI 49071

Call Sign: KC8PGQ
John L Van Wagner
55687 Giddings Ct
Mattawan MI 49071

Call Sign: K8EMT
James D Kirklin

57737 Hamilton Ave
Mattawan MI
490719502

Call Sign: KB8SUO
Arthur R Townsley
48327 Hickory Ln
Mattawan MI 49071

Call Sign: KB8ZVL
Wade B Lawrence
48915 Hickory Ln
Mattawan MI 49071

Call Sign: KD8GTX
Michael F Greis
49960 Kiawah Trl
Mattawan MI 49071

Call Sign: KC8FZX
Catherine S Oliver
25316 Mac Arthur
Mattawan MI 49071

Call Sign: W8LAO
Karel R Slatmyer Jr
25374 Mac Arthur Dr
Mattawan MI 49071

Call Sign: KD8LZR
Russell J Johnson
58120 Main St Apt 1
Mattawan MI 49071

Call Sign: N8DFW
Carl S Diehl
49300 Meadow Oak
Trl
Mattawan MI 49071

Call Sign: KC8OYT
Richard G Anderson
10688 Pennycress
Mattawan MI 49071

Call Sign: KG8QD
Robert E Lawson
25472 Pershing Dr
Mattawan MI
490719308

Call Sign: KC8OFS
Carolyn A Perreau
8403 S 2nd

Mattawan MI 49071

Call Sign: K8RLD
Jeanne Guy D Perreau
8403 S 2nd St
Mattawan MI 49071

Call Sign: KB8ZVK
Dina M Wells
9673 S 2nd St
Mattawan MI 49071

Call Sign: KC8ZKM
Ira Bilancio
7416 S 4th St
Mattawan MI 49071

Call Sign: N8DXB
James M Hoffman
39862 Sparrow St
Mattawan MI 49071

Call Sign: N8IFG
Dorotha E Hoffman
39862 Sparrow St
Mattawan MI 49071

Call Sign: KA8FVE
Wayne A Copenhaver
10705 W P Ave
Mattawan MI 49071

Call Sign: KC8CIH
Russell L Shafer
10307 W Rs Ave
Mattawan MI 49071

Call Sign: KC8ORE
Rushford W Hotchkiss
10437 W S Ave
Mattawan MI 49071

Call Sign: N8ZFU
Gaylen D Stecker
57777 Western Ave
Apt R2A
Mattawan MI 49071

Call Sign: W8GDS
Gaylen D Stecker
57777 Western Ave
Apt R2A
Mattawan MI 49071

Call Sign: KC8OQQ
Alain E Svilpe
59210 Whitewood Dr
Mattawan MI 49071

Call Sign: KC8JVH
Steve D Hyde
59213 Whitewood Dr
Mattawan MI 49071

Call Sign: WB8YXI
Frederick P Skalski
59224 Whitewood Dr
Mattawan MI 49071

Call Sign: KD8PVO
Tamiko L Buckles
46795 Woodfield Dr
Mattawan MI 49071

Call Sign: KD8NOA
Richard T Jackson
Mattawan MI 49071

Call Sign: N8TPB
Norman H Orr
Mattawan MI
490710063

FCC Amateur Radio Licenses in Mayfield

Call Sign: KD8POC
Eugene R Bland
4210 Main St
Mayfield MI 49666

FCC Amateur Radio Licenses in McBain

Call Sign: KD8GZP
Adam D Gilde
7194 Jamie Dr
McBain MI 49657

Call Sign: KD8DDI
Keith J Rozeveld
11023 S Laces Rd
McBain MI 49657

Call Sign: KD8DDN
James D Kamphouse
10079 S Lucas Rd
McBain MI 49657

Call Sign: KD8DDM
William H Rozeveld
11023 S Lucas Rd
McBain MI 49657

Call Sign: KD8DDJ
Kevin G Pluger
11608 S Lucas Rd
McBain MI 49657

Call Sign: N8TAA
Daniel J Winkel
8119 S Morey
McBain MI 49657

Call Sign: KD8FRX
Gary J Yonkman
353 W Finkle
McBain MI 49657

Call Sign: KD8DOI
Jeff G Quist
810 W Geers Rd
McBain MI 49657

Call Sign: KD8GAQ
James H Yonkman
960 W Geers Rd
McBain MI 49657

Call Sign: KD8AGI
Randall W Kroes
9458 W McIntyre Ave
McBain MI 49657

Call Sign: KD8POH
Benjamin A Dekraker
McBain MI 49657

Call Sign: KD8POE
Phillip J Dekraker
McBain MI 49657

FCC Amateur Radio Licenses in McBride

Call Sign: KC8GYM
Louis K Borton
4163 Division Box 43
McBride MI 48852

Call Sign: KC8KAT
Nathan S Inbody

4141 Division St
McBride MI
488520125

FCC Amateur Radio Licenses in McFarland

Call Sign: KC8CVR
William J Schram
2898 R F Rd
McFarland MI 49880

FCC Amateur Radio Licenses in McMillan

Call Sign: WD8EIB
Della L Carver
Rt 3 Box 2266 Cr 438
McMillan MI 49853

Call Sign: N8GAU
Norman Carver
Rr 3 Box 2266 Rd 438
Luce Co
McMillan MI 49853

Call Sign: KA8SCG
James P Parker
County Rd 459 Box
2465B
McMillan MI 49853

Call Sign: KC8QZL
Jeremy A Bragiel
Rr 3 Box 2493 C
McMillan MI 49853

Call Sign: WD8QGX
Peter D Rahilly Jr
21365 CR 135
McMillan MI 49853

Call Sign: KD8OXC
Peter D Costa
1675 CR 370
McMillan MI 49853

Call Sign: K8PDC
Peter D Costa
1675 CR 370
McMillan MI 49853

Call Sign: WA8ALR

Jimmie L Marquardt
2758 CR 413
McMillan MI 49853

Call Sign: KD8BMO
Margaret A Mattingly
24352 CR 438
McMillan MI 49853

Call Sign: KD8BMN
Gerald R Fighter
5044 CR 461
McMillan MI 49853

Call Sign: KD8BMM
Lois J Fighter
5044 CR 461
McMillan MI 49853

Call Sign: KD8MAD
Zachary J Hilliard
6308 Florence Dr
McMillan MI 49853

Call Sign: KC8QZH
Richard T Majinska
7073 Hwy 415
McMillan MI 49853

Call Sign: KA8K
David B Hopper
22926 Maple Dr
McMillan MI 49853

FCC Amateur Radio Licenses in Mears

Call Sign: WD8MQQ
Sydney J Stooke Sr
5933 4th Box 78
Mears MI 49436

Call Sign: KC8ZM
Robert L De Haan
1756 Morrison Ave
Mears MI 49436

Call Sign: KG8WS
Blain D Highland
2165 N 56th Ave
Mears MI 49436

Call Sign: KD8EVC
Richard A Hale

697 N Golden Sands
Dr
Mears MI 49436

Call Sign: KC8TZH
Carl W Thoreson
4700 N Lakeshore Dr
Mears MI 49436

Call Sign: K8CWT
Carl W Thoreson
4700 N Lakeshore Dr
Mears MI 49436

Call Sign: KE4ABS
John M Carpenter
1530 N Shore Dr
Mears MI 49436

Call Sign: KC8FQJ
Lynette A Nicholson
5832 W 5th St
Mears MI 49436

Call Sign: KC8TRZ
Jordan T Vanliere
8250 W Duck Rd
Mears MI 49436

Call Sign: W8BXS
Howard R Reece
8227 W Taylor
Mears MI 49436

Call Sign: KA8ZWL
Robert S Simonson
5786 W Taylor Rd
Mears MI 49436

Call Sign: N8KAS
Charles F Gresens
Mears MI 49436

FCC Amateur Radio Licenses in Mecosta

Call Sign: KC8KRY
Cris L Dewolf
8145 13 Mile Rd
Mecosta MI
493320357

Call Sign: WB8G
Robert D Macauley

9656 90th Ave
Mecosta MI 49332

Call Sign: KC8WGH
Justin C Macauley
9656 90th Ave
Mecosta MI 49332

Call Sign: N8KDR
Terry W Moore
11450 90th Ave
Mecosta MI 49332

Call Sign: KD8PVB
Terry W Moore Jr
11450 90th Ave
Mecosta MI 49332

Call Sign: KC8ZKV
Anthony W Colton
11780 90th Ave
Mecosta MI 49332

Call Sign: W8LFO
Anthony W Colton
11780 90th Ave
Mecosta MI 49332

Call Sign: N8YJX
Russell E Clinton
5356 Birch Haven Dr
Mecosta MI 49332

Call Sign: W8ZNG
Carl R Brockdorf
9100 Buchanan Rd Apt
207
Mecosta MI 49332

Call Sign: N8TWJ
Jeremy J McNamara
10580 E Blue Lake Dr
Mecosta MI 49332

Call Sign: K8HHL
Dominic W Theodore
14550 E Horsehead
Lake Dr
Mecosta MI 49332

Call Sign: N8PUA
Robert A Rawlinson
16785 Myrtle Dr
Mecosta MI 49332

Call Sign: W8SUE
Shirley L Metcalf
10690 Round Lake Dr
Mecosta MI 49332

Call Sign: KC8NYQ
Sandra L Lane
9345 W School
Section Lake Rd
Mecosta MI 49332

Call Sign: KC8LVM
Larry L Olsson
298 Webber St
Mecosta MI 49332

Call Sign: W8SO
Deborah K Macauley
Mecosta MI
493320104

Call Sign: W8KMS
Kathleen M Setina
363 E State St
Mendon MI 49072

Call Sign: KC8MCC
Edward A Klein
27401 Smith Rd
Mendon MI 49072

Call Sign: KD8JEH
Amanda M Klein
27401 Smith Rd
Mendon MI 49072

Call Sign: KD8GEN
Olley R Wise III
208 W Jackson St
Mendon MI 49072

Call Sign: KB8OYB
Richard R Chaltry
N 2357 0 1 Dr
Menominee MI 49858

Call Sign: KC8RGD
Ronald J Skufca
1016 10th Ave
Menominee MI 49858

Call Sign: KD8OVR
Douglas W Dooley
2316 13th Ave
Menominee MI 49858

Call Sign: KB8YQG
Charles W Johnson
5000 13th St 209
Menominee MI 49858

Call Sign: N8OQU
William D Meyst
2010 14th St
Menominee MI 49858

Call Sign: AC8IO
William D Meyst
2010 14th St
Menominee MI 49858

Call Sign: KD8CHL
Tearlach F Sinclair
1500 15th Ave
Menominee MI 49858

Call Sign: W8SCO
Tearlach F Sinclair
1500 15th Ave
Menominee MI 49858

Call Sign: KD8BYT
Tri Cities Contest Club
1821 15th Ave
Menominee MI 49858

Call Sign: NG9T
Tri Cities Contest Club
1821 15th Ave
Menominee MI 49858

Call Sign: K8IR
James R Callow
1821 15th Ave
Menominee MI 49858

Call Sign: KB8YQF
Richard J Edquist
1101 16th Ave
Menominee MI 49858

Call Sign: W8NZV
John H Edquist
1101 16th Ave
Menominee MI 49858

Call Sign: W8NZV
Richard J Edquist
1101 16th Ave
Menominee MI 49858

Call Sign: KC8KXE
Adam M Blair
2000 16th Ave
Menominee MI 49858

Call Sign: KD8EYA
Menominee Dar Radio
Club
2100 16th Ave
Menominee MI 49858

Call Sign: K8DAR
Menominee Dar Radio
Club
2100 16th Ave
Menominee MI 49858

Call Sign: KG8CX
Edward L Engleman
2100 16th Ave
Menominee MI 49858

Call Sign: KB8AGV
Robert C Anderson
3012 16th St
Menominee MI 49858

Call Sign: N8JHF
William P Kakuk
1712 17th Ave
Menominee MI 49858

Call Sign: AA8UT
Robert E Johnson
1901 17th Ave
Menominee MI 49858

Call Sign: KB8PCQ
James J Armstrong
1106 18th Ave
Menominee MI 49858

Call Sign: KD8ESH

Mark S Erickson
1705- 18th Ave
Menominee MI 49858

Call Sign: KB8HQV
Nancy C Callow
1900 18th St
Menominee MI 49858

Call Sign: KC9PBI
Dustin R Kurath
1201 1st St
Menominee MI 49858

Call Sign: W8NCC
Dustin R Kurath
1201 1st St
Menominee MI 49858

Call Sign: W8ZPU
Howard W Sorensen
1710 1st St
Menominee MI 49858

Call Sign: K8ICO
Thomas E Zeratsky
W6619 2 5 Ln
Menominee MI 49858

Call Sign: KC8DOA
James E Swanson
1108 20th St
Menominee MI 49858

Call Sign: KD8FUE
Michael A Lemke
3204 22nd St
Menominee MI 49858

Call Sign: KC8ZVC
Jason M Lauzer
1609 25th Rd
Menominee MI 49858

Call Sign: KD8ESI
Dallas S Blair
1509 27th Ave
Menominee MI 49858

Call Sign: K8BKA
Kurt Berge
1700 28th Ave
Menominee MI 49858

Call Sign: KF9XV
Robert A Arends
1501 30th Ave
Menominee MI 49858

Call Sign: AB8MC
Robert A Arends
1501 30th Ave
Menominee MI 49858

Call Sign: KC9III
Diann E Hallam
2100 30th Ave
Menominee MI 49858

Call Sign: KD8IGH
Thomas C Barrington
2100 30th Ave
Menominee MI 49858

Call Sign: W8DXX
David J Arnold
1801 32nd Ave
Menominee MI 49858

Call Sign: KD8ECU
Brendan J Jenquin
1600 36th Ave
Menominee MI 49858

Call Sign: KB8HCN
Jodi R Beacom
806 46th Ave
Menominee MI 49858

Call Sign: KD8ELF
Erin M Eichhorn
822 46th Ave
Menominee MI 49858

Call Sign: KC8UHU
Frederick W Sorensen
W5774 5Pt25 Ln
Menominee MI 49858

Call Sign: N8YWB
John A Mans
804 6th Ave
Menominee MI 49858

Call Sign: KD8IJQ
Hunter L Mans
804 6th Ave
Menominee MI 49858

Call Sign: K8MBI
Hunter L Mans
804 6th Ave
Menominee MI 49858

Call Sign: N8RFF
Donald F Balthazore
4300 6th St
Menominee MI 49858

Call Sign: KD8FUF
Joshua M Marcin
N 34 99 M 35
Menominee MI 49858

Call Sign: WB8SNQ
Harold C Plong
1220 9th Ave Apt 210
Menominee MI 49858

Call Sign: KD8DQR
Ashley A Linsmeier
W6061 Evergreen Ln
Menominee MI 49858

Call Sign: WA8LRU
Larry C Campbell
W7719 Fernwood Dr
Menominee MI 49858

Call Sign: N9JFC
Terrance A Dobrzenski
N 2450 Hwy 577
Menominee MI 49858

Call Sign: WA8FVD
Ronald S Zurawski
N2240 Hwy 577
Menominee MI
498589770

Call Sign: KC8YZB
Paul H Sorensen
N1149 Hwy M 35
Menominee MI 49858

Call Sign: NS8V
Paul H Sorensen
N1149 Hwy M 35
Menominee MI 49858

Call Sign: N8LHB
Thomas B Rynish

N 2158 Hwy M35
Menominee MI 49858

Call Sign: N8OSK
Lynne F Rynish
N 2158 Hwy M35
Menominee MI 49858

Call Sign: KB8DAG
Steven K Hohl
N 1529 M 35
Menominee MI 49858

Call Sign: N8YVZ
William C Durow Sr
N 3633 M 35
Menominee MI 49858

Call Sign: KD8BEN
Joyce A Dehne
W4977 Million Dollar
Rd
Menominee MI 49858

Call Sign: KD8DQQ
Nicholas M Smith
W6333 N 2 Rd
Menominee MI 49858

Call Sign: KD8IXS
Jake T Ziemba
W6896 N 2 Rd
Menominee MI 49858

Call Sign: KD8IXR
Zack J Ziemba
W6896 N 2 Rd
Menominee MI 49858

Call Sign: WW9Q
Robert A Arends
4017 N Shore Dr
Menominee MI
498580353

Call Sign: KD8FUG
Bradley D Sellers
N1410 Oak Park Dr
Menominee MI 49858

Call Sign: KC8WJN
Earl E Bramschreiber
N1234 R 3 Dr
Menominee MI 49858

Call Sign: KC8DOB
Jim A Morrison
N 143 River Dr
Menominee MI 49858

Call Sign: N8YWA
James A Morrison
N 143 River Dr
Menominee MI 49858

Call Sign: KB8VQR
Constance I Fletcher
N 256 River Dr
Menominee MI 49858

Call Sign: WB8PFB
Ronald G Sobay
N1453 State Hwy M35
Menominee MI 49858

Call Sign: N8YWC
Lester J Poquette
W5350 Twin Creek Rd
Menominee MI 49858

Call Sign: KB8MBS
Robert C Niemann
W 5429 Willow Rd
Menominee MI 49858

Call Sign: W8JKZ
Roy C Ihde
W 5664 Willow Rd
Menominee MI 49858

Call Sign: KD8ODP
Blake V Borski
W5566 Willow Rd
Menominee MI 49858

Call Sign: KD8NAZ
Brett E Borski
W5566 Willow Rd
Menominee MI 49858

Call Sign: KE4JBO
Raymond A Molkentin
Menominee MI 49858

Call Sign: N9WOC
Mari M Arends
Menominee MI 49858

Call Sign: KC8WAI
Valerie D Hallam
Menominee MI 49858

FCC Amateur Radio Licenses in Merritt

Call Sign: WA8QHI
Walter W Akerly Jr
11653 Burns Rd
Merritt MI 49667

Call Sign: N8NBW
Victor P Vercruysse
8385 Davis Rd
Merritt MI 49667

FCC Amateur Radio Licenses in Merriweather

Call Sign: K9RON
Ronald J Warczynski
122 Superior Ave
Merriweather MI
499479625

Call Sign: KC8ZJK
Judith A Boze
122 Superior Ave
Merriweather MI
49947

FCC Amateur Radio Licenses in Mesick

Call Sign: KC8LTK
Marty L Roberson
12828 Litzen Rd
Mesick MI 49668

Call Sign: KD8QEC
Joseph S Essex
5425 N 15th Rd
Mesick MI 49668

Call Sign: KC8LTM
John J Hakes
5815 N 19 Rd
Mesick MI 49668

Call Sign: KC8OIC
Edith M Hakes
5815 N 19 Rd

Mesick MI 49668

Call Sign: W8LWH
Scott M Hawkins
6737 W 18 Rd
Mesick MI 49668

Call Sign: KB8TEG
Mark L Maxfield
1325 W 20 Rd
Mesick MI 49668

Call Sign: KD8DOH
Anthony J Liuzzo
1435 W 20 Rd
Mesick MI 49668

Call Sign: W8LOS
George M Tice
6201 W 20 Rd
Mesick MI 49668

Call Sign: KB8FXY
Danny G Spicer
9400 W M 115
Mesick MI 49668

Call Sign: KB8FYS
Matthew H Spicer
9400 W M 115
Mesick MI 49668

Call Sign: KC8WZK
Douglas G Boonstra
915 W M 42
Mesick MI 49668

Call Sign: KC8WZJ
Robin A Boonstra
915 W M 42
Mesick MI 49668

Call Sign: KD8BXH
Frank Zinger
3921 Wm42
Mesick MI 49668

Call Sign: KC8CZU
Craig A Smith
Mesick MI 496680433

FCC Amateur Radio Licenses in Michigamme

Call Sign: KB8STY
Alan R Larsen
Hcr 1 Box 350
Michigamme MI
49861

Call Sign: KB8HMC
Jean L Guster
Michigamme MI
49861

Call Sign: KC8YTW
James O Phillips
Michigamme MI
49861

FCC Amateur Radio Licenses in Middleville

Call Sign: KD8LNO
Floyd A Hopewell Jr
7658 108th Ave
Middleville MI 49333

Call Sign: KC8MGX
Paul E Geddes
8863 108th St
Middleville MI 49333

Call Sign: KB8OYH
Tony Sclafani
618 Bernard St
Middleville MI 49333

Call Sign: KD8WD
Donald R Smith
7255 Bouman Dr
Middleville MI 49333

Call Sign: KB8OYK
Jeffrey H Hernandez
315 Charles St
Middleville MI 49333

Call Sign: KA8DTH
Edward K Cisler Sr
428 Cider Mill Dr
Middleville MI 49333

Call Sign: KC8NGG
Mike Wolowicz
11555 Cobb Lk Rd

Middleville MI 49333

Call Sign: KH2VB
Holly A Beech
5716 Duncan Lake Rd
Middleville MI 49333

Call Sign: KD8RPQ
Janet L Moody
6222 Duncan Lake Rd
Middleville MI 49333

Call Sign: AB8WF
Lucinda K Moody
6222 Duncan Lake Rd
Middleville MI 49333

Call Sign: N8XOF
David A Moody
6222 Duncan Lake Rd
Middleville MI
493339732

Call Sign: KD8CDW
Wayne L Bishop
505 Edward St
Middleville MI 49333

Call Sign: KQ8Z
Lyle E Gillespie
3624 Elmwood Beach
Middleville MI 49333

Call Sign: KD8GTA
Frances A Jones
516 Grand Rapids St
Middleville MI 49333

Call Sign: KD8DLD
Michael A Jones
516 Grand Rapids St
Middleville MI 49333

Call Sign: KB0EWU
Adam E Canfield
1020 Greenwood
Middleville MI 49333

Call Sign: WB0RKQ
Jim S Canfield
1020 Greenwood
Middleville MI 49333

Call Sign: KD8IYS

Philip L Clinton
824 Greenwood St
Middleville MI 49333

Call Sign: W8HSQ
Donald H Shipman
10838 Hermitage Point
Rd
Middleville MI 49333

Call Sign: KB8OYI
Anthony L Hernandez
119 High St
Middleville MI 49333

Call Sign: KB8RFX
Peter P Hernandez Jr
119 High St
Middleville MI 49333

Call Sign: KB8QF
David W Goron
7225 Irving Rd
Middleville MI 49333

Call Sign: KF8MP
Kenneth W Schad
6460 Ivan Trl
Middleville MI 49333

Call Sign: KD8RZO
Anne K O'Riley
312 Lloyd Ct
Middleville MI 49333

Call Sign: KD8GGG
Michael J O' Riley
312 Lloyd Ct
Middleville MI 49333

Call Sign: WY8F
Michael J O' Riley
312 Lloyd Ct
Middleville MI 49333

Call Sign: KB8QHI
Gale F Wilcox
7121 Loop Rd
Middleville MI 49333

Call Sign: KB8QOM
Roberta J Wilcox
7121 Loop Rd
Middleville MI 49333

Call Sign: WB8WWP
Donald C Coffman
1188 Lynn Dr
Middleville MI 49333

Call Sign: WD8MOF
Larry R Stolsonburg
1242 Lynn Dr
Middleville MI 49333

Call Sign: WD8MOE
Kay L Stolsonburg
1242 Lynn Dr
Middleville MI 49333

Call Sign: KA8WRM
Carlyle Borck
130 Manor Dr
Middleville MI 49333

Call Sign: KD8CIU
Jake T Brower
2525 McCann Rd
Middleville MI 49333

Call Sign: KD8CDX
Thomas G Brower
2525 McCann Rd
Middleville MI 49333

Call Sign: KC8ANB
James E Thompson
209 Meadowlark
Middleville MI 49333

Call Sign: KB8SLO
John D Fredenburg Jr
7363 Middleville Rd
Middleville MI 49333

Call Sign: KA8NWD
Bruce W Johnson
3311 N Johnson Rd
Middleville MI 49333

Call Sign: WD8KWM
Milton R Lawrence
2644 N Loop Rd
Middleville MI 49333

Call Sign: WB8ZEY
Lee A Shumway
2900 N M 37 Hwy

Middleville MI 49333

Call Sign: KD8OXO
Scott A Shumway
2900 N M 37 Hwy
Middleville MI 49333

Call Sign: N8RGM
William T Roszell
7623 N Moe Rd
Middleville MI 49333

Call Sign: K8BMI
Barry Amateur Radio
Association
3232 N Nagle
Middleville MI 49333

Call Sign: KC8VTO
Barry Amateur Radio
Association
3233 Nagle
Middleville MI 49333

Call Sign: KC8THT
Pamela A Davis
3232 Nagle Rd
Middleville MI 49333

Call Sign: WB8T
Pamela A Davis
3232 Nagle Rd
Middleville MI 49333

Call Sign: KC8BZG
James R Duryea
5338 Parmalee Rd
Middleville MI 49333

Call Sign: KD8MTV
Paul G Herreran
6325 Parmalee Rd
Middleville MI 49333

Call Sign: N8VWC
Chris K Otto
7156 Parmalee Rd
Middleville MI 49333

Call Sign: KC8FIU
Christopher J Veenstra
9358 Parmalee Rd
Middleville MI 49333

Call Sign: KD8QLF
Michael S Bekius
3160 Patterson Rd
Middleville MI 49333

Call Sign: KD8IYL
Anna M Ward
4602 Patterson Rd
Middleville MI 49333

Call Sign: W8FMX
Mike Wolowicz
524 Payne Ridge Dr
Middleville MI 49333

Call Sign: KC8KZE
Leonard R Daniels
894 Pepperwood Pl
Middleville MI 49333

Call Sign: KD8AVZ
Kenneth L Bohn
1059 Quail Run Dr
Middleville MI 49333

Call Sign: K8OIE
Kenneth L Bohn
1059 Quail Run Dr
Middleville MI 49333

Call Sign: KA8BHK
Walter E Rott
4072 Robertson Rd
Middleville MI 49333

Call Sign: WD8NSK
Emily A Rott
4072 Robertson Rd
Middleville MI 49333

Call Sign: W8NSH
David R Parker
10946 Shady Ln
Middleville MI 49333

Call Sign: N8YZI
Astrid J M Strait
9445 Spring Creek Ct
Middleville MI 49333

Call Sign: WM8C
Todd A Strait
9445 Spring Creek Ct
Middleville MI 49333

Call Sign: KB8PAU
Joshua T Strait
228 Stadium Dr
Middleville MI 49333

Call Sign: KC8NCX
James A Clark
5095 Staurolite Ln
Middleville MI 49333

Call Sign: KC8NDB
Lisa M Clark
5095 Staurolite Ln
Middleville MI 49333

Call Sign: KC8MSD
Christel N Clark
5095 Staurolite Ln
Middleville MI 49333

Call Sign: KF4VZK
Patrick Walsh Jr
5095 Staurolite Ln
Middleville MI 49333

Call Sign: KC8NDU
Susan J Clark
5095 Staurolite Ln
Middleville MI 49333

Call Sign: N9YDP
Michael D Gerke
4125 Thornapple Hills
Dr
Middleville MI 49333

Call Sign: W8JRH
James R Hamlin
4611 Thornbird
Middleville MI 49333

Call Sign: KB8OYJ
Timothy J Wilkins
406 Thornton St
Middleville MI 49333

Call Sign: N8LDR
Timothy J Wilkins
406 Thornton St
Middleville MI 49333

Call Sign: KD8PZN
Andrew J Kursch

5875 W Crane Rd
Middleville MI 49333

Call Sign: KC8OMI
Andrew C Ordway
1025 W Main St
Middleville MI 49333

Call Sign: N8SRT
Grant E Rath
6905 Whitneyville Rd
Middleville MI 49333

Call Sign: N8UCK
Kendrick Barker
225 Yankee Springs
Rd
Middleville MI 49333

Call Sign: KC8OPS
Nick P Barker
225 Yankee Springs
Rd
Middleville MI 49333

Call Sign: WB8VOL
Douglas K Shumway
2820 Yankee Springs
Rd
Middleville MI 49333

Call Sign: KC8OPF
Michael J Souter
Middleville MI 49333

FCC Amateur Radio
Licenses in Mikado

Call Sign: KC8TXM
David Holthaus
2935 Coville Rd
Mikado MI 48745

Call Sign: KC8TXN
Adam Holthaus
2935 Coville Rd
Mikado MI 48745

Call Sign: KG8QI
Robert M Henwood
185 E F 30
Mikado MI 48745

Call Sign: KD8DTQ

Jacob A Wade
804 E F 30
Mikado MI 48742

Call Sign: KC8FBR
Burt A Ostby
2424 F 30
Mikado MI 48745

Call Sign: KD8BRG
Casey T Travis
1378 Goddard Rd
Mikado MI 48745

Call Sign: KC8OHH
Leonard P Mcneill
2094 Poor Farm Rd
Mikado MI 48745

Call Sign: KC8JEP
Robert B Cain
1835 S London Rd
Mikado MI 48745

FCC Amateur Radio
Licenses in
Millersburg

Call Sign: N8HBA
Donald E Pomeroy
16128 Beach Hwy
Millersburg MI 49759

Call Sign: KD8DPN
Kenneth R Goetz
14532 Beach Ln
Millersburg MI 49759

Call Sign: KB8CRH
Carol J Kelly
10439 Golden Trl
Millersburg MI
497599621

Call Sign: KC8GWC
Robert T Brown
13905 N Shore Dr
Millersburg MI 49759

Call Sign: W8CAG
Robert T Brown
13905 N Shore Dr
Millersburg MI 49759

Call Sign: WB8AIC
Harry K Scott
18464 Osage Ln
Millersburg MI 49759

Call Sign: W8HIB
Jerome Heron
4577 S Ocqueoc Rd
Millersburg MI 49759

Call Sign: KB8FNV
Greg A Robbins
Millersburg MI 49759

**FCC Amateur Radio
Licenses in Mio**

Call Sign: KC8LLO
James L Sherwood
308 9th St Box 101
Mio MI 48647

Call Sign: K8OMH
Marcella H Lewis
1596 Camp 10
Mio MI 48647

Call Sign: KB8TGM
William G Phetteplace
2670 East Dr
Mio MI 48647

Call Sign: KA8YWV
Tim F Morgan
1120 Gerber Rd
Mio MI 48647

Call Sign: KB8WJF
Robert M Dobski Sr
774 Green Dr
Mio MI 48647

Call Sign: KA8BDJ
Donald E Robinson Sr
1408 Helmer Lake Rd
Mio MI 48647

Call Sign: WA8AAG
Bennie G Blanchard
831 Hillcrest Ct
Mio MI 48647

Call Sign: KD8BTM
Peggy A Nietiedt

34 James Dr
Mio MI 48647

Call Sign: W8KIM
Kim B Babcock
894 Joeli Dr
Mio MI 48647

Call Sign: N8MBV
Diane V Gates
884 Lahman Trl
Mio MI 48647

Call Sign: KA8YWH
Steven K Gates
884 Lahman Trl
Mio MI 48647

Call Sign: W8MIO
Robert C Miller
164 Larry Joe Dr
Mio MI 48647

Call Sign: KA8VQR
Daniel M Belanger
318 M 33
Mio MI 48647

Call Sign: KB8AXB
James Peters
122 Maple St Apt 19
Mio MI 486479447

Call Sign: KD8BRM
Susan L Avery
1288 Marsh Rd
Mio MI 48647

Call Sign: N8JVU
Robert D McGregor
975 McKinley Rd
Mio MI 48647

Call Sign: KD8CLM
Allan D Bickford
2675 Mishler Rd
Mio MI 48647

Call Sign: KD8EUF
Diane G Bickford
2675 Mishler Rd
Mio MI 48647

Call Sign: WB6FUZ

Diane G Bickford
2675 Mishler Rd
Mio MI 48647

Call Sign: W8QJL
George B Risler
1237 N Mt Tom Rd
Mio MI 48647

Call Sign: KC8VOW
Jan S Rauhauser
868 N Perry Creek Rd
Mio MI 486479714

Call Sign: WI8L
John F Miller
134 Oak Lake Rd
Mio MI 48647

Call Sign: N8IHK
George C Zimowske
2860 Pierce Rd
Mio MI 48647

Call Sign: KB8YMU
Walter Dreffs
49 Popps Rd
Mio MI 48647

Call Sign: KB8YMV
Judy A Dreffs
49 Popps Rd
Mio MI 48647

Call Sign: KE7ARV
T Stone
206 Randall
Mio MI 48647

Call Sign: KD8ELJ
Jonathon A Welters
29 S Mount Tom
Mio MI 48647

Call Sign: N8DTZ
Michael P Gates
107 S Mt Tom
Mio MI 48647

Call Sign: KD8FSA
Elizabeth K Galer
2051 Stitt Rd
Mio MI 48647

Call Sign: K9FSR
Elizabeth K Galer
2051 Stitt Rd
Mio MI 48647

Call Sign: KD8EHB
Carol A Mitchell
912 W 11th St
Mio MI 48647

Call Sign: KD8EGZ
Terry A Mitchell
912 W 11th St
Mio MI 48647

Call Sign: KC8GPL
Cassie L Booth
1101 W 14th St
Mio MI 48647

Call Sign: N8QVW
John J Felts
271 W 15th St
Mio MI 486479183

Call Sign: WA8JAY
John J Felts
271 W 15th St
Mio MI 486479183

Call Sign: KD8JST
Alesia J Willobee
2239 W Kittle Rd
Mio MI 48647

Call Sign: AA7KR
Christopher Gennick
222 W Miller Rd
Mio MI 48647

Call Sign: KB8PLL
Sharon L Antepara
Mio MI 48647

Call Sign: WD8PMV
Randy C Underhill
Mio MI 48647

Call Sign: KD8CLH
David A Schleicher
Mio MI 48647

Call Sign: KB8MCR
James F Colson Sr

Mio MI 486470598

Call Sign: K9GIR
Dennis H Royce
Hc 1 Box 281
Mohawk MI 49950

Call Sign: N8PIY
Shannie J Tuoriniemi
304 Fulton
Mohawk MI 49950

Call Sign: KC8FLL
Carol I Schneiderhan
5770 Gay Lac La Belle
Rd
Mohawk MI 49950

Call Sign: KC8FLM
Edward J Schneiderhan
5770 Gay Lac Labelle
Rd
Mohawk MI 49950

Call Sign: K9JCO
Carroll K Crist
13290 M 26
Mohawk MI 49950

Call Sign: N8JAB
Brian R Isaacson
429 Manhattan
Mohawk MI 49950

Call Sign: N8OTA
Mark R Isaacson
431 Manhattan
Mohawk MI 49950

Call Sign: W9AGX
Camillus F Hogan
128 Stanton Ave
Mohawk MI
499500386

Call Sign: KD8PKW
Alan J Church
7164 State Hwy M26
Mohawk MI 49950

Call Sign: KC8DYG

Lee J Royce
Mohawk MI 49950

Call Sign: KC8BMH
Scott A Bredeweg
4415 12th Ave
Moline MI 49335

Call Sign: KC8BZH
Brent A Winger
1279 144th Ave
Moline MI 49335

Call Sign: AA8AG
Don L Moore
4377 Linda St
Moline MI 49335

Call Sign: K8QCY
Linda L Moore
4377 Linda St
Moline MI 49335

Call Sign: KC8IAU
Nelson C Thumser
8763 Blaine St
Montague MI 49437

Call Sign: N8IU
Nelson C Thumser
8763 Blaine St
Montague MI 49437

Call Sign: KC8LPS
Richard W La Pree
8050 Cook St Apt A1
Montague MI 49437

Call Sign: KC8FJB
James E Hain Jr
8344 Flower Creek Rd
Montague MI 49437

Call Sign: KC8MDA
Raymond L Hall Jr
5893 Hancock Rd
Montague MI
494379332

Call Sign: KC8MUE
Robert W Bush II
6025 Hancock Rd
Montague MI 49437

Call Sign: KB8WMM
Brian W Giddis
7942 Hill St
Montague MI 49437

Call Sign: K8YJK
David J Bedau Jr
6540 Indian Point
Montague MI 49437

Call Sign: KA8DLV
Walter J Andersen
10870 Kubon Rd
Montague MI 49437

Call Sign: WB8FIV
Frank R Andersen
10870 Kubon Rd
Montague MI 49437

Call Sign: WB8RNJ
Frank R Andersen
10870 Kubon Rd
Montague MI 49437

Call Sign: N8XML
Roy D Struven
5915 Lake Shore Dr
Montague MI 49437

Call Sign: KD8JJG
Dion A Stumpo
5123 Lakeview St
Montague MI
494371464

Call Sign: K8KPU
David A Brow
6667 Lau Rd
Montague MI 49437

Call Sign: KC8JNM
Jane A Pallay
7761 N Old Channel
Trl
Montague MI 49437

Call Sign: KC8JHX

Daniel W Walsh
8690 Oceana Dr
Montague MI 49437

Call Sign: N8HX
Daniel W Walsh
8690 Oceana Dr
Montague MI 49437

Call Sign: KC8MDD
James B Cole
7704 Old Channel Trl
Montague MI 49437

Call Sign: NS8S
David W Fleming
8104 Old Channel Trl
Montague MI 49437

Call Sign: KC8FJA
Joshua D Craymer
8652 Old Channel Trl
Montague MI 49437

Call Sign: KC8FLX
David D Craymer
8652 Old Channel Trl
Montague MI 49437

Call Sign: KD8FXF
Raymond S Berry
5914 Post Rd
Montague MI 49437

Call Sign: KB8WXE
Phillip L Hall
6572 Post Rd
Montague MI 49437

Call Sign: KB8YNH
Margaret A Hall
6572 Post Rd
Montague MI 49437

Call Sign: KA8WMH
Jeffrey A Hanson
8734 Sheridan St
Montague MI 49437

Call Sign: KC8UBY
Dale Kroll
8843 Staple St
Montague MI 49437

Call Sign: KC8MSI
David P Caughey
2711 W Webster Rd
Montague MI 49437

Call Sign: N8YQB
Everett F Lehman
9954 Walsh Rd
Montague MI 49437

Call Sign: KC8UEW
John E Bowden
8930 Water St Apt 3
Montague MI
494372210

Call Sign: KD8AKD
Sharon A Mclouth
9121 Whitbeck Rd
Montague MI 49437

Call Sign: KC8YTG
Merle D Mclouth
9121 Whitbeck Rd
Montague MI 49437

Call Sign: W8OOD
Merle D Mclouth
9121 Whitbeck Rd
Montague MI 49437

**FCC Amateur Radio
Licenses in Moran**

Call Sign: N8DDX
Billie N Townsend
440 Church St
Moran MI 49760

Call Sign: KB9VYT
Henry J Michaels
W1882 Dukes Rd
Moran MI 49760

Call Sign: KD8NNJ
Mackinac Area Digital
ARC
W2015 Dukes Rd
Moran MI 49760

Call Sign: K8EUP
Mackinac Area Digital
ARC
W2015 Dukes Rd

Moran MI 49760

Call Sign: WA8OOH
Ronald J Peterka
2015 W Dukes Rd
Moran MI 49760

Call Sign: W8DR
Ronald J Peterka
2015 W Dukes Rd
Moran MI 49760

**FCC Amateur Radio
Licenses in Morley**

Call Sign: N8ETN
Daniel L McLaughlin
20148 1 Mile Rd
Morley MI 49336

Call Sign: KD8QVB
Darryll E Hall
4557 155th Ave
Morley MI 49336

Call Sign: N8PUB
Jeffery A Smith
3942 180th Ave
Morley MI 49307

Call Sign: KD8KPV
Susan M Bachinski
2198 215th Ave Apt 1
Morley MI 49336

Call Sign: KI8DP
Kenneth D Paulson
19316 3 Mile Rd
Morley MI 49336

Call Sign: KC8HJT
Jeff A Hernden
21602 3 Mile Rd
Morley MI 49336

Call Sign: KC8HVR
Delcy A Hernden
21602 3 Mile Rd
Morley MI 49336

Call Sign: KD8GGA
Jonathan A Hernden
21602 3 Mile Rd
Morley MI 49336

Call Sign: KD8GGB
Monica R Hernden
21602 3 Mile Rd
Morley MI 49336

Call Sign: KC8RBR
Nathan M Moore
11974 Federal Rd
Morley MI 49336

Call Sign: KA8MVR
Delbert A Wilcox
19747 Jefferson Rd
Morley MI 49336

Call Sign: W8LEU
Virgil L Groff
17580 Kent Ave
Morley MI 493369436

Call Sign: N8FR
Fred C Radford
16491 Monroe Rd
Morley MI 49336

Call Sign: K8SHX
Vincent T Panicci
2557 Northland Dr
Morley MI 49336

Call Sign: KC8SGB
Douglas T Chicora
11300 Paris Rd
Morley MI 49336

Call Sign: N8LSJ
William A Gillis
18434 W Cotler Rd
Morley MI 49336

Call Sign: KD8KPS
Joseph L Aldrich
17544 W River Dr
Morley MI 49336

Call Sign: KB8WMH
Lawayne M Hill
Morley MI 49336

Call Sign: KB8WMK
Terry D Plank
Morley MI 49336

**FCC Amateur Radio
Licenses in Muir**

Call Sign: KC8EXA
Michael L Brooks
315 Blanchard St
Muir MI 48860

Call Sign: W8MLB
Michael L Brooks
315 Blanchard St
Muir MI 48860

Call Sign: KD8QQZ
Randy C Hoppes
6376 E Blue Water
Hwy
Muir MI 48860

Call Sign: KC8ZTT
Michael K Van Houten
5919 Olmstead Rd
Muir MI 48860

Call Sign: WD8LCW
Richard J Hanchett
1978 Struble
Muir MI 48860

**FCC Amateur Radio
Licenses in Mullett
Lake**

Call Sign: W8IPQ
James A Sweetland
871 Patricia Ave
Mullett Lake MI 49761

Call Sign: WA8LNE
Robert T Johnson
Mullett Lake MI 49761

**FCC Amateur Radio
Licenses in Mulliken**

Call Sign: KC8KCT
Paula M Meaton
7689 Dow Rd
Mulliken MI 48861

Call Sign: KI8FF
Jeffrey C Meaton
7689 Dow Rd
Mulliken MI 48861

Call Sign: WB8GTT
Raymond N Ingersoll
9141 Eaton Hwy
Mulliken MI 48861

Call Sign: KC8SKE
John P Vassel
357 French St
Mulliken MI 48861

Call Sign: K8RFD
John P Vassel
357 French St
Mulliken MI 48861

Call Sign: KA8KRQ
Johnnie F Cathcart
2351 Grandledge Hwy
Mulliken MI 48861

Call Sign: KD8DJA
Alfred F Newell Jr
209 Ionia St
Mulliken MI 48861

Call Sign: WD8OHD
Helen L Cathcart
2351 M 43 Hwy
Mulliken MI 48861

Call Sign: KD8GAA
Steve Kamm
382 Potter St
Mulliken MI 48861

Call Sign: KD8EQK
Randolph C Sauber
4942 Saginaw Hwy
Mulliken MI 48861

Call Sign: WB8CKA
John H Marsh
4040 W Mt Hope Hwy
Mulliken MI
488619724

Call Sign: KE4NJR
Michael T Dence
5055 W Strange Hwy
Mulliken MI 48861

Call Sign: K3SRK
Steve R Kamm

Mulliken MI 48861

| FCC Amateur Radio Licenses in Munising |

Call Sign: KI8CF
Harold C Cook
N7651 Carmody Rd
Munising MI
498629126

Call Sign: W8SUZ
Susan M Cook
N7651 Carmody Rd
Munising MI
498629126

Call Sign: WA8QXW
Gerald F Beacham
1442 Center St
Munising MI 49862

Call Sign: N8TNM
Kenneth A Rieli
E 10074 CR H58
Munising MI 49862

Call Sign: N8TNN
Pamela A Rieli
E 10074 CR H58
Munising MI 49862

Call Sign: KA8URA
Carlene C Harwick
E9526 E Munising
Ave
Munising MI 49862

Call Sign: KA8URB
George D Harwick
E9526 E Munising
Ave
Munising MI 49862

Call Sign: N8WRM
Miracle R Lester
E10074 H58
Munising MI 49862

Call Sign: N8WRP
Michael T Lester
E10074 H58
Munising MI 49862

Call Sign: WD8IOQ
Phillip C Ford
N7930 Koski Rd
Munising MI 49862

Call Sign: KD8NPK
Theodore J Woodaz
E9501 Lehnen Rd
Munising MI 49862

Call Sign: KC8LKZ
John R Cromell
E8402 M 94
Munising MI 49862

Call Sign: K8KIR
Lester M Flake
E 9725 Old Indiantown
Rd
Munising MI
498629237

Call Sign: W9UJC
William Gibson
1616 Sand Pt Rd
Munising MI 49862

Call Sign: KC8BAN
Gregory J Revord
308 W Chocolay
Munising MI 49862

Call Sign: KD8QCS
Jim D Eklund
1430 Washington St
Munising MI 49862

Call Sign: KD8NLN
Robert H Beauprey Jr
Munising MI 49862

| FCC Amateur Radio Licenses in Muskegon |

Call Sign: N8MMH
Susan L Mills
1173 4th St
Muskegon MI 49441

Call Sign: KC8UWK
Heath A Scarbrough
1174 4th St
Muskegon MI 49441

Call Sign: KB9PPF
Jason A Stephenitch
1191 7th St
Muskegon MI
494401020

Call Sign: KB8TOD
Scott A McConnell
1665 Ada Ave
Muskegon MI 49442

Call Sign: KC8MDE
Richard D Grimard
1671 Ada Ave
Muskegon MI 49442

Call Sign: W8WAK
Robert C Thompson
4133 Airline Rd
Muskegon MI 49444

Call Sign: KC8AGR
Howard R Strait
619 Allen Rd
Muskegon MI 49442

Call Sign: WB8DBP
Frank H Walsworth
920 Andree Rd
Muskegon MI 49445

Call Sign: KC8VTW
Michael P Kelly
1615 Ann St
Muskegon MI 49445

Call Sign: KG8KU
John D Benson
1821 Antisdale
Muskegon MI 49441

Call Sign: KG8CF
Owen Bickford
588 Apple Ave
Muskegon MI 49442

Call Sign: KC8YID
Muskegon Technical
Academy Radio Club
2900 Apple Ave
Muskegon MI 49442

Call Sign: W8MTA

Muskegon Technical
Academy Radio Club
2900 Apple Ave
Muskegon MI 49442

Call Sign: N8JTL
Margaret F Worra
2233 Arbor Ave
Muskegon MI 49441

Call Sign: KD8OIO
Clay A Creswell
4382 Armstrong
Muskegon MI 49441

Call Sign: KD8IX
Charles P Carroll
730 August Rd
Muskegon MI 49441

Call Sign: KC8ZSU
Robert S Hildreth
2849 Bailey St
Muskegon MI 49444

Call Sign: KB8XG
David H Deitrick
1548 Bayview
Muskegon MI 49441

Call Sign: WD8ACL
Lynette L Lawrence
1542 Beardsley
Muskegon MI 49441

Call Sign: KC8MDC
Justin P Calkins
1690 Becker Rd
Muskegon MI 49445

Call Sign: KD8HBI
Daniel J Browe
1724 Beidler St 1
Muskegon MI 49441

Call Sign: KD8BPJ
Ryan D Lubbers
1645 Benjamin
Muskegon MI 49445

Call Sign: KD8MMT
Melanie J Wisneski
4087 Bexley Dr
Muskegon MI 49444

Call Sign: N8NFY
Darrell C Zang
4161 Bexley Dr
Muskegon MI 49444

Call Sign: KC8UWL
Ronald L Minzey
3271 Birchwood
Muskegon MI 49442

Call Sign: KC8ECU
Kristoffer M Hain
5329 Bittersweet Dr
Muskegon MI 49445

Call Sign: KD8PWO
Stanley A Rop
2328 Bloomfield Ct
Muskegon MI 49441

Call Sign: N8AGW
Leroy T Olson
3936 Bobby Ln
Muskegon MI
494426576

Call Sign: N8CUV
Jeffrey L Hagenbuch
1686 Bonneville Dr
Muskegon MI 49441

Call Sign: W9IS
Leroy M Stevenson
1804 Bonneville Dr
Muskegon MI 49441

Call Sign: WB9SYW
Elinore P Stevenson
1804 Bonneville Dr
Muskegon MI 49441

Call Sign: KB8ZCU
David D Mckee
4888 Brookdale Blvd
Muskegon MI 49441

Call Sign: KB8ZCR
Randy W Feister
3157 Brooks
Muskegon MI 49444

Call Sign: KC8TEJ
Amos L Daniels

3411 Butler Dr
Muskegon MI 49441

Call Sign: N8PFJ
Harry E Huston Jr
3209 Butternut
Muskegon MI 49444

Call Sign: WA8URR
Thomas V Reed
1185 Calgary Dr
Muskegon MI 49444

Call Sign: W8URR
Thomas V Reed
1185 Calgary Dr
Muskegon MI 49444

Call Sign: KD8NBK
James R Duplissis
2456 California Ave
Muskegon MI 49445

Call Sign: W8TQZ
William H Belden
1925 Calvin Ave
Muskegon MI 49442

Call Sign: KB8GIL
Arnold W Tammen
535 Cambridge Dr
Muskegon MI 49441

Call Sign: WA8YCN
Harold Cavanaugh
960 Carlton St
Muskegon MI 49442

Call Sign: KD8BWO
Dustin J Chilson
1900 Catalina Dr 422
Muskegon MI
494447777

Call Sign: KD8FXC
Lester L Price
4431 Cedar Ln
Muskegon MI 49441

Call Sign: KI8EP
Patrick D Herman
759 Center St
Muskegon MI 49442

Call Sign: K8CMA
Patrick D Herman
759 Center St
Muskegon MI 49442

Call Sign: W8DNM
Frank M Meyers
2665 Chateau Dr
Muskegon MI 49441

Call Sign: KC8ZXI
Tyler Wellman
1015 Cheboygan
Muskegon MI 49445

Call Sign: N8NNB
Edwin E Needham
3410 Chippewa Dr
Muskegon MI 49441

Call Sign: KD8BIG
Mark D Strait
966 Clark St
Muskegon MI 49442

Call Sign: KB8TLY
Alan C Anderson
1293 Clayton Ave
Muskegon MI 49441

Call Sign: WB8QCY
Robert A Voyt
4915 Clearwater Ct
Muskegon MI 49441

Call Sign: KC0CXC
Christopher J Schulte
1611 Columbus Ave
Muskegon MI 49441

Call Sign: KC8ZSJ
Christopher J Schulte
1611 Columbus Ave
Muskegon MI 49441

Call Sign: AB8WO
Christopher J Schulte
1611 Columbus Ave
Muskegon MI 49441

Call Sign: KD8IGR
Thomas M Labelle
2145 Columbus Ave
Muskegon MI 49441

Call Sign: KB8VEE
Thomas J Vander Mel
1651 Columbus Ave
Muskegon MI
494413733

Call Sign: K8BDL
Charles H Heskett
1894 Commerce St
Muskegon MI 49441

Call Sign: WB8VEY
De Wayne P Carlson
1378 Cornell Rd
Muskegon MI 49441

Call Sign: KG9GI
Ralph D May
2951 Country Club Dr
Muskegon MI 49441

Call Sign: KC8ZMH
Harland W Hansen
3121 Country Club Dr
Muskegon MI 49441

Call Sign: KD8DAH
Frank E Thomas
581 Courtland
Muskegon MI 49442

Call Sign: KD8OQS
Norman S Hakes
1181 Creekview Dr
Muskegon MI 49441

Call Sign: WD8LUD
George W Siler
565 Creston St
Muskegon MI 49442

Call Sign: KA7UGH
David M Compton
1874 Crestwood Ln
Muskegon MI 49441

Call Sign: K8CJC
Gerrit W Van
Donkelaar
2048 Dangl Rd
Muskegon MI 49442

Call Sign: KB8DVR

Constance M
Goodnough
5404 Davis Rd
Muskegon MI 49441

Call Sign: KB8DVS
Sean P Mullally
5404 Davis Rd
Muskegon MI 49441

Call Sign: KA8WNN
Michael D Kamerad
2830 Dawes
Muskegon MI 49441

Call Sign: WB8HUM
Ronald P Eckert
2902 De Vowe
Muskegon MI 49444

Call Sign: K8UA
Norman K Medendorp
2269 Deanna Dr
Muskegon MI 49444

Call Sign: AB8QL
Darrell M Fuglseth Jr
3152 Donald
Muskegon MI 49442

Call Sign: KC8LSQ
Norman A Bayle Sr
4219 Doral Dr
Muskegon MI 49442

Call Sign: KB8GEL
Gabe W Skofic
1080 Drent Rd
Muskegon MI 49442

Call Sign: KD8NJM
Way Point Academy
ARC
2900 E Apple Ave
Muskegon MI 49442

Call Sign: KC8ZAS
Sherwood T Nickisch
3329 E Apple Ave
Muskegon MI 49442

Call Sign: W8AMZ
Sherwood T Nickisch
3329 E Apple Ave

Muskegon MI 49442

Call Sign: KC9GNV
James D Main
2280 E Apple Ave Apt
A
Muskegon MI 49442

Call Sign: KC8MDK
Richard R Ronning
1039 E Byron Rd
Muskegon MI 49441

Call Sign: KC8WSG
Deborah J Ronning
1039 E Byron Rd
Muskegon MI 49441

Call Sign: W8LGP
Richard R Ronning
1039 E Byron Rd
Muskegon MI 49441

Call Sign: KA8PZG
Sharon L Godfrey
1254 E Catherine Ave
Muskegon MI 49442

Call Sign: KD8CJX
Keith A Johnson
2400 E Columbia Ave
Muskegon MI 49444

Call Sign: KB8BCN
Kevin J Palsrok
1117 E Dale Ave
Muskegon MI 49442

Call Sign: N8JOO
Janice A Palsrok
1117 E Dale Ave
Muskegon MI 49442

Call Sign: KA4VRP
Rosemary C
Hockenberry
1093 E Giles Rd
Muskegon MI
494452615

Call Sign: K3SWB
Richard G
Hockenberry
1093 E Giles Rd

Muskegon MI
494452625

Call Sign: KD8KGV
Kelly K Cooper
71 E Isabella Ave
Muskegon MI 49442

Call Sign: KB8BET
John Contrady
5720 E Jefferson
Muskegon MI 49442

Call Sign: K8BHY
William W Sutton
2755 E Mararebecah
Ln
Muskegon MI 49442

Call Sign: KD8IQV
Timothy J Dunn
2765 E Riley
Thompson Rd
Muskegon MI 49445

Call Sign: K8EEZ
Timothy J Dunn
2765 E Riley
Thompson Rd
Muskegon MI 49445

Call Sign: KB8WKC
Martin C Shalifoe
1367 E Summit
Muskegon MI 49444

Call Sign: KB8ZCW
Randy L Wood
4315 E Summit
Muskegon MI 49444

Call Sign: KD8QKU
Lyndel Berry
4431 E Summit Ave
Muskegon MI 49444

Call Sign: K8CYV
Jack L Maciejewski
2113 E Virginia Dr
Muskegon MI 49444

Call Sign: KD8EH
Willie H Simmons
175 E Walton Ave

Muskegon MI 49443

Call Sign: N8RWT
Keith R De Young
1381 Eastwood Dr
Muskegon MI 49442

Call Sign: KB8UFF
Mark A Derby
5081 Edenbrook Ct
Muskegon MI 49441

Call Sign: K8MHZ
Mark A Derby
5081 Edenbrook Ct
Muskegon MI 49441

Call Sign: KD8BGM
Nicole M Austin
5081 Edenbrook Ct
Muskegon MI 49441

Call Sign: K0LEY
Nicole M Austin
5081 Edenbrook Ct
Muskegon MI 49441

Call Sign: N8ZST
Steven J Drewes
383 Ellen St
Muskegon MI 49444

Call Sign: KC8JWC
Richard A Marsh
1095 Elliot St
Muskegon MI 49442

Call Sign: KD8DLQ
James R Wolffis
166 Elm Ct
Muskegon MI 49445

Call Sign: KD8NBJ
Guy T Hinton
422 Elsa
Muskegon MI 49445

Call Sign: KZ1GUY
Guy T Hinton
422 Elsa
Muskegon MI 49445

Call Sign: KD8NQZ
Marc T Medendorp

3767 Evaline Dr
Muskegon MI 49444

Call Sign: KC8VMS
Pat J Murphy
1252 Evanston Ave
Muskegon MI 49442

Call Sign: KC8FLZ
Scott A Zawlocki
2127 Evanston Ave
Muskegon MI 49442

Call Sign: KC8NND
Kerry A Wood
2625 Evanston Ave
Muskegon MI 49442

Call Sign: K8KAW
Kerry A Wood
2625 Evanston Ave
Muskegon MI 49442

Call Sign: K8BGS
H Keith Crankshaw
3414 Evanston Ave
Muskegon MI 49442

Call Sign: KD8KGT
Barbara A Zulauf
4010 Fenner Rd
Muskegon MI 49445

Call Sign: KD8AKB
Nathan A Hyrns
4288 Ford Rd
Muskegon MI 49440

Call Sign: N8HRN
Nathan A Hyrns
4288 Ford Rd
Muskegon MI 49445

Call Sign: KB8GYC
Lee M Marsh
1070 Fordham Ct
Muskegon MI 49441

Call Sign: KC8CLU
Bernard C Wildgen
1427 Forest Park Rd
Muskegon MI 49441

Call Sign: KC8VDP

Matthew J Hassen
1712 Forest Park Rd
Muskegon MI 49441

Call Sign: KB2SWK
George P Maniates
2124 Forest Park Rd
Muskegon MI 49441

Call Sign: KA8BXL
Amy K Hodson
1666 Francis Ave
Muskegon MI 49442

Call Sign: KD4CKM
Roni L Bowers
3408 Fulton Ave
Muskegon MI 49441

Call Sign: KD4CKN
James A Bowers
3408 Fulton Ave
Muskegon MI 49441

Call Sign: WA8FLL
Charles M George
3418 Fulton Ave
Muskegon MI 49441

Call Sign: K8YNO
Vernon A Lane
1855 Furhman
Muskegon MI 49441

Call Sign: N8VMM
Francine E Harmsen
1855 Furhman
Muskegon MI
494413715

Call Sign: KA8YHI
Robert A Holcomb
2089 Garland Dr
Muskegon MI 49441

Call Sign: KC8IQU
David G Bonfoey
2463 Geenwood St
Muskegon MI
494471214

Call Sign: W8FDE
Cornelius G Smith
1395 Glen

Muskegon MI 49441

Call Sign: KC8TEI
Tyrone Hill
500-3A Glen Oak Dr
Muskegon MI 49442

Call Sign: KC8DTK
Michael L Lamb
3317 Glendale St
Muskegon MI
494442918

Call Sign: K8PIX
Lloyd E Pixley
1214 Gordon St
Muskegon MI
494425468

Call Sign: KC8OVQ
Susan L Ronning
1144 Green St
Muskegon MI 49442

Call Sign: KD8PWS
Kris L Cyr
3091 Griesbach St
Muskegon MI 49441

Call Sign: W8GXD
Edwin J Homa
2515 Grove St
Muskegon MI
494411239

Call Sign: WB8RCV
Franklin D Clark
2301 Hadden St
Muskegon MI 49441

Call Sign: WB8TKA
Orchard View Middle
School Rad Clb
2301 Hadden St
Muskegon MI 49441

Call Sign: KC8ETN
Marvin F Frein III
3760 Hall Rd
Muskegon MI 49442

Call Sign: WD8AGX
James V Grimard Sr
4115 Hall Rd

Muskegon MI 49442

Call Sign: WB8FEM
Gayle A Vanderwier
926 Hampden Rd
Muskegon MI 49441

Call Sign: KA8VID
William T Mann
1034 Hampton Blvd
Muskegon MI 49441

Call Sign: N8JLY
Eric A Anderson
1213 Harbor Point Dr
Muskegon MI 49441

Call Sign: N8LMP
Carl D Eigenauer
3940 Harbor Point Dr
Muskegon MI 49441

Call Sign: WA8QVP
Glen R Cryderman
2230 Harding Ave
Muskegon MI 49441

Call Sign: K8TYO
James A Reed
4528 Harding Ct
Muskegon MI 49441

Call Sign: WA8HMV
William P Myers Jr
1523 Haverhill Dr
Muskegon MI
494413812

Call Sign: KC8DOD
James W Surge
1629 Helen Dr
Muskegon MI
494415733

Call Sign: KB8AZD
Kenneth R Kadrovich
1345 Hendrick Rd
Muskegon MI 49441

Call Sign: K8BGQ
Gerald L Broge
1459 Hendrick Rd
Muskegon MI 49441

Call Sign: KD8RQK
Andrew Patten
1556 Hendrick Rd
Muskegon MI 49441

Call Sign: KD8MGI
Jonathan C Truax
4716 Henry
Muskegon MI 49441

Call Sign: W8MU
Joseph E Pascavis
1593 Henry St
Muskegon MI 49441

Call Sign: KD8BFP
Michael D Breeding
4330 Henry St
Muskegon MI 49441

Call Sign: WB9FLC
Robert R Tejchma
5649 Henry St
Muskegon MI 49441

Call Sign: W8NWV
Robert R Tejchma
5649 Henry St
Muskegon MI 49441

Call Sign: KB8OCA
Russell P La Belle
3424 Hiawatha Dr
Muskegon MI 49441

Call Sign: KA8SMH
Henry J Palsrok
4420 Hickory Ln
Muskegon MI 49441

Call Sign: KB8OPJ
Frank O Sundquist Jr
1017 Hidden Creek Dr
Muskegon MI 49441

Call Sign: KD8PWP
Steven W Rop
3722 Highgate Rd
Muskegon MI 49441

Call Sign: KB8VXU
Lyle L Norton
1321 Hillcrest Ave
Muskegon MI 49442

Call Sign: K8CBT
Maurice W Carlson
2189 Horton Rd
Muskegon MI 49445

Call Sign: KB8AMQ
August W Panici
2137 Hudson St
Muskegon MI 49441

Call Sign: NS8Z
Wilmer R Osborne
3235 Hulka St
Muskegon MI 49444

Call Sign: KC8FLY
Daniel J Zawlocki
1928 Interwood St
Muskegon MI 49442

Call Sign: KD8LMR
William G Slocum
1077 Jefferson St Apt
610
Muskegon MI 49440

Call Sign: WA8SCS
William H Sprecken
1355 Kitchener Dr
Muskegon MI 49444

Call Sign: WM8F
Douglas E Hawkins
248 Lake Dr
Muskegon MI 49441

Call Sign: W8HRZ
Paul C Van Wyck
605 Lake Forest Ln
Apt G7
Muskegon MI 49441

Call Sign: KB8IXY
Walter P Edmondson
3875 Lake Harbor Rd
Muskegon MI 49441

Call Sign: K8WP
Wayne E Pickler
5167 Lake Harbor Rd
Muskegon MI 49441

Call Sign: AA8CE

Keith H Rumley
6532 Lake Harbor Rd
Muskegon MI
494416130

Call Sign: KD8HCY
Francis M Booth
1760 Lee Ave
Muskegon MI 49444

Call Sign: KC8OEP
Allen L Degroot
1674 Leif Ave
Muskegon MI 49442

Call Sign: KC8MDH
Jared D Juntunen
1461 Leonard Ave
Muskegon MI 49442

Call Sign: WB8IXV
Robert L Pulsifer
3884 Linda St
Muskegon MI 49444

Call Sign: KD8KGO
Terry L Zahniser
1385 Linden St
Muskegon MI 49442

Call Sign: KC8GKC
Ronald Lee Barrett
872 Linter
Muskegon MI 49442

Call Sign: W8LOJ
Alan K Gittins
69 Locust Ct
Muskegon MI 49445

Call Sign: WB8UQY
Scott A Mund
2351 Mac Arthur Rd
Muskegon MI 49442

Call Sign: KD8HSC
Paul Phillips
2690 Macarther Rd
Muskegon MI 49442

Call Sign: W8EHO
Gerald E Heykoop
1335 Madison St
Muskegon MI 49442

Call Sign: N8NSE
Janice S La Brenz
2172 Mann St
Muskegon MI 48441

Call Sign: WB8I
Donald L La Brenz II
2172 Mann St
Muskegon MI 49441

Call Sign: KA8WDI
Jennifer E La Brenz
2172 Mann St
Muskegon MI 49441

Call Sign: KD8RFO
Gerald T Place
2276 Marlette Lot 134
Muskegon MI 49442

Call Sign: KD8PWQ
Kevin H Dean
2306 Marquard Ave
Muskegon MI 49445

Call Sign: KC8NCE
Jonathan M Bunda
1138 Marquette Dr
Muskegon MI 49442

Call Sign: W8MRW
Dayton R Maggert
1233 Marquette Dr
Muskegon MI 49442

Call Sign: WB8OQT
Robert G Carter
4431 Marshall Rd
Muskegon MI 49441

Call Sign: KD8MRD
Thomas R Reed
2016 Marvin Ave
Muskegon MI 49442

Call Sign: W8WXM
Thomas R Reed
2016 Marvin Ave
Muskegon MI 49442

Call Sign: KD8OTT
Bryon L Thornton
5183 McDowell Rd

Muskegon MI 49441

Call Sign: K8JEO
Roger J Filius Sr
5155 McDowell St
Muskegon MI 49441

Call Sign: WB6WDO
Robert C Phelps
1722 McLaughlin Ave
Muskegon MI
494424228

Call Sign: W8CJ
Frederick E Castenholz
1530 McLaughlin Ave
Apt 333
Muskegon MI 49442

Call Sign: WB8MYZ
Gary A Fletcher
3276 Medema St
Muskegon MI
494444301

Call Sign: KD8GCX
Randal P Hughey
2899 Memorial Dr
Muskegon MI 49445

Call Sign: K8RPH
Randal P Hughey
2899 Memorial Dr
Muskegon MI 49445

Call Sign: KD8LMQ
Michael A Sanford
3797 Michael St
Muskegon MI 49444

Call Sign: KD8KMU
Gregory M Holman
1449 Michillinda Rd
Muskegon MI 49445

Call Sign: NU8E
John W Barkel
3224 Millard
Muskegon MI 49441

Call Sign: KB8IRL
Stephen E Rumley
2360 Milton Ave
Muskegon MI 49442

Call Sign: KB8IQG
Laura D Rumley
2360 Milton Ave
Muskegon MI 49442

Call Sign: KF8GW
Peter A Rumley
2360 Milton Ave
Muskegon MI 49442

Call Sign: N8PFL
Michael J Reynolds
1944 Miner
Muskegon MI 49441

Call Sign: KC8JNI
Karen M Reynolds
1944 Miner Ave
Muskegon MI 49441

Call Sign: KD8RFP
Walter S Johnston
2309 Monica Ln
Muskegon MI 49442

Call Sign: WD8COG
David H Jirikovic
126 Moss Breeze Rd
Muskegon MI 49444

Call Sign: KC8TOG
Bradly D Fett
1887 Muirfield Way
Muskegon MI 49442

Call Sign: KB8LQH
Bart A Nielsen
1653 Mulder Dr
Muskegon MI 49445

Call Sign: KD8QPD
Daniel P Van Beek
61 N Kenwood St
Muskegon MI 49442

Call Sign: KC8VVK
James L Cloutier
2154 N Manitou Cir
Muskegon MI 49441

Call Sign: KC8BZK
Robert D Pickard
1711 N Roberts Rd

Muskegon MI
494451802

Call Sign: KD8MUE
Jordan T Sabo
968 N Sandalwood Cir
Muskegon MI 49441

Call Sign: KF8VU
James R Collins
1829 N Weber Rd
Muskegon MI 49445

Call Sign: N8WRV
Malcolm B McKee
1360 Nelson St
Muskegon MI 49441

Call Sign: WB8IUI
Robert J Yost Jr
1917 Nevada
Muskegon MI 49441

Call Sign: K8IUI
Robert J Yost Jr
1917 Nevada
Muskegon MI 49441

Call Sign: KB8IXX
Edward E Maycroft
2240 New Moon
Muskegon MI 49442

Call Sign: K8CCG
Robert A Swett
1935 Nielwood Dr
Muskegon MI 49445

Call Sign: KB8WAA
Marcy J Grayson
4088 Nobhill Dr
Muskegon MI 49441

Call Sign: KB8VZZ
Douglas A Grayson
4088 Nobhill Dr
Muskegon MI
494414546

Call Sign: W8CPD
Max E Aley
1415 Nolan Ave
Muskegon MI 49441

Call Sign: K8WNJ
Muskegon County
Emergency Services
1611 Oak Ave
Muskegon MI 49442

Call Sign: KB8RID
Harold E Miller
2368 Oak Ave
Muskegon MI 49442

Call Sign: KF8YP
Darrell M Fuglseth Jr
1424 Oaklea
Muskegon MI 49442

Call Sign: W8NXD
Ronald A Mann Sr
3937 Palm Harbor Ln
Muskegon MI 49442

Call Sign: KC8GKD
Paul T Bourne
2020 Park St
Muskegon MI 49444

Call Sign: KA8KRV
Timothy L Kies
2475 Patriot Ln
Muskegon MI 49442

Call Sign: KC8MDF
Ronald D Groteler
1539 Peterson Rd
Muskegon MI 49445

Call Sign: KC8MEX
Sharon M Groteler
1539 Peterson Rd
Muskegon MI 49445

Call Sign: ND8O
Clifton W Martin
570 Porter Rd
Muskegon MI 49441

Call Sign: N8RCY
David M Barrick
586 Porter Rd
Muskegon MI 49441

Call Sign: KB8GP
Melvin L Dykstra
1747 Princess Ln

Muskegon MI
494451739

Call Sign: KD8DHK
Wilbur L Greene
2817 Quarterline Rd
Muskegon MI 49444

Call Sign: KC8WBL
Craig Vanvolkinburg
1931 Queens Ct
Muskegon MI 49445

Call Sign: KC8WBM
Kristine A
Vanvolkinburg
1931 Queens Ct
Muskegon MI 49445

Call Sign: KC8BAT
Christopher S Lamrock
2044 Rambling Oak Dr
Muskegon MI 49445

Call Sign: WD8AGV
Marjory J Horness
643 Ranch Rd
Muskegon MI 49441

Call Sign: KA8SDF
Thomas A Shreve Sr
3548 Reginald Dr
Muskegon MI 49444

Call Sign: KB8GAZ
Robert S Waite
2097 Reneer Ave
Muskegon MI 49441

Call Sign: N8RXD
Eldon B Taylor
5713 Richmond Ave
Muskegon MI 49442

Call Sign: KC8MJT
Heidi D Hagen
1990 Riegler Rd
Muskegon MI 49445

Call Sign: KC8LLY
Michael D Hagen
1990 Riegler Rd
Muskegon MI 49445

Call Sign: KB8ZCO
Diane K Vanderstelt
1850 Ritter Hills Dr
Muskegon MI 49441

Call Sign: NV8B
Jeffrey D Vanderstelt
1850 Ritter Hills Dr
Muskegon MI 49441

Call Sign: NR9B
William K Schneider
1928 Ritter Hills Dr
Muskegon MI
494414552

Call Sign: K8WSN
William K Schneider
1928 Ritter Hills Dr
Muskegon MI
494414552

Call Sign: WO8D
Herman A Hudson
1255 Roberts
Muskegon MI 49442

Call Sign: N8YQA
Casey Kay
3280 Rockland Rd
Muskegon MI 49441

Call Sign: KC8HUC
Bruce A Schouten
5370 Rood Rd
Muskegon MI 49441

Call Sign: KB8PMA
Robert L Friel
2897 Roosevelt Rd
Muskegon MI 49441

Call Sign: KD8PWX
Christopher J Dean
3246 Roosevelt Rd Apt
Y11
Muskegon MI 49441

Call Sign: KB8VXZ
Pamela D Asplund
81 S Broton Rd
Muskegon MI 49442

Call Sign: WD8MKY

James E Bovenkerk
81 S Broton Rd
Muskegon MI 49442

Call Sign: K8SQP
Raymond J Jasicki
1415 S Carr Rd
Muskegon MI 49442

Call Sign: KB8EKL
Jody L Schultz
1416 S Dangl
Muskegon MI 49442

Call Sign: WB8NHX
Lee R Klemetti
3269 S Dangl
Muskegon MI 49444

Call Sign: N8FV
James D Main
4427 S Dangl Rd
Muskegon MI 49444

Call Sign: KC8JQM
Alan E Gascho
149 S Hilton Park Rd
Muskegon MI 49442

Call Sign: KB8RIC
Jonathan R Plyler
339 S Mill Iron Rd
Muskegon MI 49442

Call Sign: AB8RD
Jonathan R Plyler
339 S Mill Iron Rd
Muskegon MI 49442

Call Sign: KC8WSF
Matthew D Plyler
339 S Mill Iron Rd
Muskegon MI
494422730

Call Sign: KD8AXG
Samuel J Plyler
339 S Milliron Rd
Muskegon MI 49442

Call Sign: KD8KTO
Mcc Criminal Justice
221 S Quarterline Rd
Muskegon MI 49442

Call Sign: K8RKO
Robert K Outwin
2621 S Sheridan Dr
Muskegon MI 49444

Call Sign: N8HTU
Edward L Norris
2680 S Sheridan Dr
Muskegon MI 49444

Call Sign: WA8CTK
Michael N Martens
4372 S Sheridan Dr
Muskegon MI 49444

Call Sign: KC8EGG
Jill R Lamrock
4674 S Sheridan Rd
Muskegon MI 49444

Call Sign: N8IDP
Deborah J Deuster
3210 S Walker Rd
Muskegon MI 49444

Call Sign: N8MRI
Chris L Carter
3249 S Walker Rd
Muskegon MI 49444

Call Sign: W8RVE
Theodore W Bensinger
3432 Sand Dock Ct
Muskegon MI
494416405

Call Sign: N8WFS
Paula M Andersen
1485 Sarnia
Muskegon MI 49441

Call Sign: WB8ZOS
Donald J Wilson
1448 Saskatoon Ave
Muskegon MI 49444

Call Sign: KD8KGS
Robert B Skeels
1390 Sauter St
Muskegon MI 49442

Call Sign: W8TBP
Robert B Skeels

1390 Sauter St
Muskegon MI 49442

Call Sign: KD8LMP
Robert M Wygant Sr
1287 Scenic Dr
Muskegon MI 49445

Call Sign: KB8DPS
Duane S Davis
2733 Scenic Dr
Muskegon MI 49445

Call Sign: KD8DUT
Charles B Morton
1527 Scranton Dr
Muskegon MI 41449

Call Sign: N8KQQ
Charles B Morton
1527 Scranton Dr
Muskegon MI 49441

Call Sign: N8LWO
Laurel S Morton
1527 Scranton Dr
Muskegon MI 49441

Call Sign: KC4RF
Jerry L Bigsby
1947 Seminole Rd
Muskegon MI 49441

Call Sign: KD8FBW
Gail A Merrill
2080 Seminole Rd
Muskegon MI 49441

Call Sign: WA0YFX
Dennis J Stroh
3582 Sheringer Rd
Muskegon MI 49444

Call Sign: W8KNV
Henry C Tomasiewicz
3036 Sherwood Ct
Muskegon MI 49441

Call Sign: N8UKF
Michael L Cameron
1222 Shettler Rd
Muskegon MI 49444

Call Sign: KB8ZCS

Ronald C Feister
1825 Shettler Rd
Muskegon MI 44944

Call Sign: KC8KFN
Brad L Feister
1825 Shettler Rd
Muskegon MI 49444

Call Sign: N8FGZ
Michael K Harrison
2500 Shettler Rd
Muskegon MI 49444

Call Sign: N8WTK
Arthur Syperda
1653 Shorewood Dr
Muskegon MI 49441

Call Sign: W8VN
Dennis W Dufford
1896 Shorewood Dr
Muskegon MI 49441

Call Sign: W8HJE
Joseph P Roth
1735 Southland Dr
Muskegon MI 49442

Call Sign: KC8PFA
Edward L George
2147 Southwood Ave
Muskegon MI 49441

Call Sign: KD8KGQ
Selene A Mack
864 Spring St Apt 707
Muskegon MI 49442

Call Sign: KA8KAP
Ronald E Jacobs
3294 Springhill Dr
Muskegon MI 49444

Call Sign: N5HIT
Roger W Hulett
4268 Sqaw Creek Trl
Muskegon MI 49442

Call Sign: KB8ZCN
Bertha L Bacheller
860 Sternberg
Muskegon MI
494416054

Call Sign: WB8HAM
Leo Bacheller
860 Sternberg Rd
Muskegon MI
494416054

Call Sign: KB8HAM
Bertha L Bacheller
860 Sternberg Rd
Muskegon MI
494416054

Call Sign: N8BVU
William N Finlay
107 Stewart
Muskegon MI 49442

Call Sign: KD8QYZ
Matthew M
Milkowsky
4188 Tean Mar Ave
Muskegon MI 49444

Call Sign: KD8CJW
Walter F Love
4056 Teanmar Ave
Muskegon MI
494443638

Call Sign: KD8HBH
John J Stauffer
4363 Teanmar Ave
Muskegon MI 49444

Call Sign: KC8HPE
Michael J Strait
1671 Terrace St
Muskegon MI 49442

Call Sign: KC8IJT
Wayne P Firestone
2343 Timber Ln
Muskegon MI 49445

Call Sign: WB8ZXZ
David L Swanson
2240 Torrent St
Muskegon MI 49441

Call Sign: N8FPO
Robert J Jackson
2334 Tryon Ave
Muskegon MI 49444

Call Sign: KC8KLI
Nicholas F Deville
3693 Tuck A Way Ter
Muskegon MI 49444

Call Sign: W8QAY
Lester L Price
1041 Vick Rd
Muskegon MI 49441

Call Sign: KA8KGL
Scott W Mann
740 W Bard Rd
Muskegon MI 49445

Call Sign: WB8ASB
Michael H Hansen
757 W Dale
Muskegon MI 49441

Call Sign: KC8AZR
John M Field
1191 W Dale
Muskegon MI 49441

Call Sign: KD8PWM
Fred R Silvis
988 W Dale Ave
Muskegon MI 49441

Call Sign: N8CWO
Leon C Conklin Jr
1212 W Dale Ave
Muskegon MI 49441

Call Sign: KA8ATC
James A Churchill
935 W Fenwood Cir
Muskegon MI 49445

Call Sign: KC8YTE
Frank R Towsley
1070 W Forest
Muskegon MI 49441

Call Sign: WA7VLH
Frank R Towsley
1070 W Forest Ave
Muskegon MI 49441

Call Sign: KD8AKC
Susan A Towsley
1070 W Forest Ave

Muskegon MI 49441

Call Sign: KC8JNH
David L Barnhart
1208 W Giles Rd
Muskegon MI 49445

Call Sign: KC8YJP
Ronald A Mann Jr
287 W Hile Rd
Muskegon MI 49441

Call Sign: KA9UMB
Bob Lenz
1385 W Hill Rd
Muskegon MI 49441

Call Sign: KC8JHY
Thomas A Tretheway
981 W Larch Ave
Muskegon MI 49441

Call Sign: KD8YL
John W Hulka
1028 W Larch Ave
Muskegon MI 49441

Call Sign: KC8VTY
Susan M Hewitt
1103 W Mt Garfield
Rd
Muskegon MI 49441

Call Sign: K8CCJ
Jerome J Novotny
120 W Pontaluna Rd
Muskegon MI 49444

Call Sign: KC8NBY
Thomas J Ericksen
544 W River Rd
Muskegon MI 49445

Call Sign: KC8NBZ
Douglas V Ericksen
544 W River Rd
Muskegon MI 49445

Call Sign: KC8NCB
Kenneth M Juntunen
701 W River Rd
Muskegon MI 49445

Call Sign: KC8NCF

Colleen M Juntunen
701 W River Rd
Muskegon MI 49445

Call Sign: KC8KAU
Vicky L Skofic
933 W River Rd
Muskegon MI 49445

Call Sign: KD8KZD
Dona J David
1346 W River Rd
Muskegon MI 49445

Call Sign: KD8CMK
Scott R Pawlowski
1200 W Sternberg Rd
Muskegon MI 49441

Call Sign: W8NVY
Muskegon Co Red
Cross Ar Comm Gp
313 W Webster Ave
Muskegon MI 49440

Call Sign: WB8QIR
James C Fletcher
3731 Waalkes St
Muskegon MI 49444

Call Sign: KB8QCM
David J Ladd
1415 Wagner Ave
Muskegon MI 49445

Call Sign: KB8APS
Robert B Wright
3160 Walker Rd
Muskegon MI 49444

Call Sign: WB8QGZ
Theodore P Sebranek
1043 Washington Ave
Apt 2
Muskegon MI 49441

Call Sign: NT8Q
Howard E Camp
930 Washington Ave
Unit 2F
Muskegon MI 49441

Call Sign: W8HEC
Howard E Camp

930 Washington Ave
Unit 2F
Muskegon MI 49441

Call Sign: KB8ZGO
Chris A Robbins
2345 Weber Rd
Muskegon MI 49445

Call Sign: W8LZ
Laurence E Zawlocki
2035 Wesley Ave
Muskegon MI 49442

Call Sign: N8GEQ
Kenneth W Arnold
2479 Wesley St
Muskegon MI 49442

Call Sign: KC8NY
Charles S Russell
2444 Westwood Dr
Muskegon MI 49441

Call Sign: KD8PWL
Andrew D Busard
2361 Westwood Rd
Muskegon MI 49441

Call Sign: WD8ICY
Edna H Krause
3672 Whispering
Woods Dr
Muskegon MI 49444

Call Sign: KD8OQR
John R Armstrong
1831 Whisperwood
Way E
Muskegon MI 49442

Call Sign: W8EVV
John R Armstrong
1831 Whisperwood
Way E
Muskegon MI 49442

Call Sign: W8CJS
Christopher J Schulte
4096 Whisperwood
Way S
Muskegon MI 49442

Call Sign: K8CBL

Thomas J Montambo
1554 Wildwood Dr
Muskegon MI 49445

Call Sign: KC8WQM
Michael J Capman
4929 Wilfred St
Muskegon MI 49444

Call Sign: K8MIC
Michael J Capman
4929 Wilfred St
Muskegon MI 49444

Call Sign: W8DMZ
Michael J Capman
4929 Wilfred St
Muskegon MI 49444

Call Sign: KC8LLN
Bernard P Shreve
854 Wilson Ave
Muskegon MI
494413073

Call Sign: KC8SRO
Henry O Braspenning
924 Wilson Ave
Muskegon MI 49441

Call Sign: N8YPQ
Timothy A Govan
959 Wilson Ave
Muskegon MI 49441

Call Sign: K8UDM
Frank S Koteles
1357 Winchester Dr
Muskegon MI 49441

Call Sign: WB8TNE
Peter P Moyer
1381 Winchester Dr
Muskegon MI
494413251

Call Sign: N8KQP
Timothy D Gray
1391 Winchester Dr
Muskegon MI 49441

Call Sign: N8YKC
Jason E Jespersen
1195 Witham Dr

Muskegon MI 49445

Call Sign: KC8NCC
Susan M Jespersen
1195 Witham Rd
Muskegon MI 49445

Call Sign: KD8OCZ
David D Thill
521 Wood St
Muskegon MI 49442

Call Sign: N8GMY
Ross B Gates
169 Woodslee Ct
Muskegon MI 49444

Call Sign: KC8AKM
Albert J Teunis
1169 Yorkshire St
Muskegon MI 49441

Call Sign: N8JLX
Mark A Anderson
4758 Zuder St
Muskegon MI 49441

Call Sign: KD8KKW
Zho Sub Club Uss
Silversides
Muskegon MI 49441

Call Sign: N8SUB
Zho Sub Club Uss
Silversides
Muskegon MI 49441

Call Sign: KD8LGU
Lst393 Radio
Operators Club
Muskegon MI 49441

Call Sign: N8LST
Lst393 Radio
Operators Club
Muskegon MI 49441

Call Sign: KC5DBY
T Joseph Fitzgerald
Muskegon MI 49441

Call Sign: KC8GKF
Jeffrey L Ross
Muskegon MI 49443

Call Sign: W8ZHO
Muskegon Area
Amateur Radio
Council
Muskegon MI 49443

Call Sign: KD8CBH
Joshua M Charney
Muskegon MI 49443

Call Sign: N1ASS
Joshua M Charney
Muskegon MI 49443

Call Sign: N1JMC
Joshua M Charney
Muskegon MI 49443

FCC Amateur Radio Licenses in Muskegon Heights

Call Sign: W8NWY
Guadalupe Alviar
55 E Delano Ave
Muskegon Heights MI
49444

Call Sign: KA8ZEV
Robert F Hughes Jr
2628 Riordan St
Muskegon Heights MI
49444

FCC Amateur Radio Licenses in Nashville

Call Sign: KB8ZL
Thomas R Cain
324 Center Ct
Nashville MI 49073

Call Sign: WB8YAC
Sharon L Cain
324 Center Ct
Nashville MI 49073

Call Sign: N8GWD
Carolyn J Cooper
7385 Curtis
Nashville MI 49073

Call Sign: KA8UDT

Jeffrey C Cooper
7385 Curtis Rd
Nashville MI 49073

Call Sign: WB8VPM
William L Eastman
201 Kellogg St
Nashville MI 49073

Call Sign: N8CC
Jeffrey P Benson
9325 M 66
Nashville MI 49073

Call Sign: KC8WZG
Judy K Bidinger
9939 Maple Grove Rd
Nashville MI 49071

Call Sign: AA8GR
Daniel M Smith
9939 Maple Grove Rd
Nashville MI 49073

Call Sign: W8BMZ
Daniel M Smith
9939 Maple Grove Rd
Nashville MI 49073

Call Sign: N8KRG
David A Reese
9939 Maple Grove Rd
Nashville MI 49073

Call Sign: N8LLH
Carolyn S Smith
9939 Maple Grove Rd
Nashville MI 49073

Call Sign: K8OFE
Robert A Wood
330 Philadelphia St
Nashville MI 49073

Call Sign: K8ZRL
Clovis D Cathcart
8197 S Clark Rd
Nashville MI 49073

Call Sign: KB8GWH
Diana M Hammond
3811 S Curtis Rd
Nashville MI 49073

Call Sign: KB8GWI
Dwaine L Hammond
3811 S Curtis Rd
Nashville MI 49073

Call Sign: KD8FUV
Nathan A Glass
6336 S M 66
Nashville MI 49073

Call Sign: KB8IBB
Robbin L Glass
6336 S M 66 Hwy
Nashville MI 49073

Call Sign: KD8IZP
Aaron O Shaver
268 W Casgrove Rd
Nashville MI 49073

Call Sign: N0FKX
Jon E Miller
Nashville MI 49073

Call Sign: KA8ZAG
Mark J Fawley
Nashville MI 49073

FCC Amateur Radio Licenses in National City

Call Sign: WA8EMK
Robert J Stock
1770 Cowan Dr
National City MI
48748

Call Sign: N0RJS
Robert J Stock
1770 Cowan Dr
National City MI
48748

Call Sign: W8ILN
Ronald E Korthals
2164 Essex Rd
National City MI
48748

Call Sign: KD8LXQ
David W Finley
3372 Genesee St

National City MI
48748

Call Sign: KD8PIY
Michael B Granger
3755 Jay St
National City MI
48748

Call Sign: WB8GNH
Carroll B Range
2106 Latham
National City MI
48748

Call Sign: KB8IKC
John A Thompson
1378 N National City
Rd
National City MI
48748

Call Sign: N8GXI
Robin L Castonguay
1205 N Sand Lake Rd
National City MI
48748

Call Sign: K8RNT
James O Trinkle
3758 Saginaw Dr
National City MI
48748

FCC Amateur Radio Licenses in Naubinway

Call Sign: N8MMJ
John C Browning Sr
St Rt Box 160
Naubinway MI 49762

Call Sign: KA8CVE
Donald R Frazier
Naubinway MI 49762

FCC Amateur Radio Licenses in Negaunee

Call Sign: KC8RJG
National Weather
Service Marquette Mi
Skywarn

112 Airpark Dr S
Negaunee MI 49866

Call Sign: KB8QNY
Jonathan R Hopper
927 Baldwin Ave
Negaunee MI 49866

Call Sign: K8EU
Glenn S Bath
945 Baldwin Ave
Negaunee MI 49866

Call Sign: KB8UCR
Kurt M Jandron
812 Burt St
Negaunee MI 49866

Call Sign: KC8ABR
Dan K Rose
633 Carr
Negaunee MI 49866

Call Sign: N9MDE
Bruce A Carlson
94 Cedar Ln
Negaunee MI 49866

Call Sign: KD8FPH
Jeremy C Carlson
94 Cedar Ln
Negaunee MI 49866

Call Sign: KB8DFO
Jason R Stott
213 Cliff St
Negaunee MI 49866

Call Sign: KD8IAV
Lindsay A Demers
7889 CR 510
Negaunee MI 49866

Call Sign: KD8HOP
Nathan S Demers
7889 CR 510
Negaunee MI 49866

Call Sign: N8NJW
Mike A Larson
49 CR Mu
Negaunee MI 49866

Call Sign: KA8RAS

John G Meier
166 E Buffalo Rd
Negaunee MI 49866

Call Sign: N8RRY
Elmer O Rinehart
133 E Lincoln St
Negaunee MI 49866

Call Sign: KA8PVM
Janice C Anderson
1309 E Maas St
Negaunee MI 49866

Call Sign: WD8NLM
Rolf H Anderson
1309 E Maas St
Negaunee MI 49866

Call Sign: KD8QIS
John T Richardson
716 Everett St
Negaunee MI 49866

Call Sign: WB8CTX
Darrel L Fezatt
49 Forest Dr
Negaunee MI 49866

Call Sign: KD8FPG
Herbert G Helsel III
136 Maple Ridge Dr
Negaunee MI 49866

Call Sign: KD8FPI
Mathias M Munger
100 McClure Dam Rd
Negaunee MI
498669699

Call Sign: K8PEK
Mathias M Munger
100 McClure Dam Rd
Negaunee MI
498669699

Call Sign: WB8SML
James P Anthony
173 Midway Dr
Negaunee MI 49866

Call Sign: W8JOM
Graham A Hopper
655 Mitchell Ave

Negaunee MI
498661319

Call Sign: KD8QIR
Gary J Kivela
197 N Basin Dr
Negaunee MI 49866

Call Sign: KC8IZS
Andrew K Kotila
185 Neejee Rd
Negaunee MI 49866

Call Sign: KC8YTX
Peter M Kotila
185 Neejer Rd
Negaunee MI 49866

Call Sign: W9VKI
Wayne E Weingarten
1105 Owaissa St
Negaunee MI 49866

Call Sign: N8MLI
Steven S Etelamaki
14 Perala Ct
Negaunee MI 49866

Call Sign: KD8LMV
Nicholas D Francisco
Sr
709 Prince St
Negaunee MI 49866

Call Sign: KD8PTH
Robert J Coolidge
204 Rail St Apt 3
Negaunee MI 49866

Call Sign: KC8PKH
Lowell A Larson Jr
14 River Run Rd
Negaunee MI 49866

Call Sign: KC8GKG
Robert D Kangas
Box 392 Rte 1
Negaunee MI 49866

Call Sign: WD8LHT
Richard W Kauppila
158 S Basin Dr
Negaunee MI 49866

Call Sign: W8LHT
Richard W Kauppila
158 S Basin Dr
Negaunee MI 49866

Call Sign: KA8YEF
Pamela S Kauppila
158 S Basin Dr
Negaunee MI 49866

Call Sign: KD8EFY
Matthew K Zika
105 Takken Dr
Negaunee MI 49866

Call Sign: KB8RJV
Bruce J Lawry
416 12 Teal Lake Ave
Negaunee MI 49866

Call Sign: KC8HHR
Timothy J Akom
107 Valley Rd
Negaunee MI 49866

Call Sign: N8YGB
Michael J Bath
321 Victoria Ave
Negaunee MI 49866

Call Sign: N8TEV
Eric J Pellinen
113 W Clark St
Negaunee MI 49866

Call Sign: W8GEV
Charles E Swanson
312 W Peck St
Negaunee MI 49866

Call Sign: KC8HYA
Martin Terzaghi
318 W Pek St
Negaunee MI 49866

Call Sign: KC8CLI
Wayne H Weidlich
142 White Bear Dr
Negaunee MI 49866

Call Sign: KO4FB
Mimmie Weidlich
142 White Bear Dr
Negaunee MI 49866

Call Sign: KB8EYE
James A Nagy
4112 Choctaw Box 11
New Buffalo MI 49117

Call Sign: KA8UGB
Anthony M Fields
13226 Country Ln
New Buffalo MI
491178860

Call Sign: N8KCZ
Debra A Fields
13226 Country Ln
New Buffalo MI
491178860

Call Sign: AA8AX
David A Kurz
401 E Jefferson St
New Buffalo MI
491171730

Call Sign: KD8RCM
Andrew J Cherrone
19270 Laporte Rd Apt
1
New Buffalo MI 49117

Call Sign: KD8BGA
Kenneth R Maynard Jr
11354 Marquette Dr
New Buffalo MI 49117

Call Sign: W8KRM
Kenneth R Maynard Jr
11354 Marquette Dr
New Buffalo MI 49117

Call Sign: WD8QHG
Simon J Phillips
11125 Marquette Rd
New Buffalo MI 49117

Call Sign: K9WMM
Rudolph A Monkewich
126 N Barton St
New Buffalo MI 49117

Call Sign: W9FZA
Gerald M Pals
410 Oselka Dr Unit
121
New Buffalo MI 49117

Call Sign: KC9UPP
Daniel J Kolavo
10 Pokagon Trl
New Buffalo MI 49117

Call Sign: KA8BMW
Frank Vorel
121 S Barker St
New Buffalo MI 49117

Call Sign: W8BPG
William White
19400 S Lakeside Rd
New Buffalo MI 49117

Call Sign: KD8KDN
Frank S Wetterow
11850 Wilson Rd
New Buffalo MI 49117

Call Sign: N8JXE
Anthony J Felan
351 Aa1 Cleveland Rd
New Era MI 49446

Call Sign: KA8WJR
Dorothy M Kamrowski
2111 W Fish Rd
New Era MI 49446

Call Sign: KC8MDB
Lori A Hogston
2650 W M 20
New Era MI 49446

Call Sign: AB8AZ
Darrell A Hogston
2650 W M 20
New Era MI 49446

Call Sign: KA8OHV
David D Hegarty
8425 W Stony Lake Rd
New Era MI 49446

Call Sign: KC8LCD
Nathanael P Thomas
2268 68th St
Newaygo MI 49337

Call Sign: N8FWC
Judith L Hoolihan
395 Allen St
Newaygo MI 49337

Call Sign: KB8ZSP
Michael J Hikade
160 Barton Dr
Newaygo MI 49337

Call Sign: KG8TE
Stanley R Brookman
5560 Butternut
Newaygo MI 49337

Call Sign: W8AJX
Caryl A Schaefer
5447 Centerline Rd
Newaygo MI 49337

Call Sign: KC8PFT
David O Campbell
5267 Chestnut
Newaygo MI 49337

Call Sign: N8TKM
David L Mortensen
8474 Cypress Ave
Newaygo MI 49337

Call Sign: KC8RQY
Amy L Deater
5997 E 48th St
Newaygo MI 49337

Call Sign: KB8IGY
Terrence R Thomas
449 E 56th St
Newaygo MI 49337

Call Sign: KB8IGZ
Clifanne J Thomas
449 E 56th St
Newaygo MI 49337

Call Sign: KB8IHA

Tracy L Thomas
449 E 56th St
Newaygo MI 49337

Call Sign: AL7JB
Donald J Werkema
3735 E 72nd St
Newaygo MI 49337

Call Sign: N8UMR
Arthur W Westgate
5661 E 76th St
Newaygo MI 49337

Call Sign: N8UMQ
Katherine A Westgate
5773 E 76th St
Newaygo MI 49337

Call Sign: N8WMH
Allen K Westgate
5917 E 76th St
Newaygo MI 49337

Call Sign: KB8ZDD
Ronald F Cook
3791 E 82nd St
Newaygo MI 49337

Call Sign: WB8EET
Nick J Filonow
4567 E 82nd St
Newaygo MI 49337

Call Sign: KB8OQV
Lucille L Hole
2559 E 88th
Newaygo MI 49337

Call Sign: N8ALF
Richard L Hole
2559 E 88th St
Newaygo MI 49337

Call Sign: N8RL
Richard L Hole
2559 E 88th St
Newaygo MI 49337

Call Sign: KC8MVS
Thomas K Porter
5090 E 92 St
Newaygo MI 49337

Call Sign: N8GTQ
Diane L Betts
5785 E 92nd
Newaygo MI 49337

Call Sign: KD8QKT
Wilford John Presler
IV
5015 E 96th St
Newaygo MI 49337

Call Sign: KC8ENP
Gregory L Gerard
6822 E Carrigan
Newaygo MI 49337

Call Sign: KC8AKX
Lee J Grandon
870 E Hummingbird
Ln
Newaygo MI 49337

Call Sign: KC8AKY
Chris M Grandon
870 E Hummingbird
Ln
Newaygo MI 49337

Call Sign: N8IMM
Dawn R Korytkowski
6784 Evergreen
Newaygo MI 49337

Call Sign: KC8KRP
Kathleen E Osmolinski
308 Ewing St
Newaygo MI 49337

Call Sign: N9WKR
Ted E Sulikowski
5414 Front St
Newaygo MI 46552

Call Sign: KB8BCR
Kathleen J Van
Popering
5170 Gordon
Newaygo MI 49337

Call Sign: WA8UAS
Richard J Van
Popering
5170 Gordon Ave
Newaygo MI 49337

Call Sign: WA8ZMS
Henry C Rowe
6264 Gordon Ave
Newaygo MI 49337

Call Sign: KB8FHG
Delbert B Cook
3456 Johnson Rd
Newaygo MI 49337

Call Sign: KC8AGD
Ronald F Cook II
3456 Johnson Rd
Newaygo MI 49337

Call Sign: N8UAJ
Lorraine K Harju
5568 King St
Newaygo MI 49337

Call Sign: WD8JME
Ronald L Rowe
2497 Main St
Newaygo MI 49337

Call Sign: KD8RWY
Francis Dall'Acqua
5846 Oak Ave
Newaygo MI 49337

Call Sign: KD8SBG
Matthew G Carpenter
9818 Oak Ave
Newaygo MI 49337

Call Sign: KA8PGB
Thomas A Burgess
5740 Pear Ave
Newaygo MI 49337

Call Sign: KE6LLW
Betty S Tremblay
5450 Pear Ave
Newaygo MI 49337

Call Sign: KK7YO
W Joseph Schlientz
381 Quarterline St
Newaygo MI 49337

Call Sign: KI8KQ
W Joseph Schlientz
381 Quarterline St

Newaygo MI 49337

Call Sign: W8QM
W Joseph Schlientz
381 Quarterline St
Newaygo MI 49337

Call Sign: N8PDM
James W Pendergast
9177 Redwood Dr
Newaygo MI 49337

Call Sign: KD8MMV
Michael J Gregory
3990 S Beech Ave
Newaygo MI 49337

Call Sign: KC8OPW
Thomas A Burgess
5901 S Carrigan
Newaygo MI 49337

Call Sign: N8AJE
Carl D Clayton
5779 S Croton Hardy
Dr
Newaygo MI 49337

Call Sign: KC8UBV
Carol A Posler
4275 S Pine Ave
Newaygo MI 49337

Call Sign: KC8UBW
Michael Posler
4275 S Pine Ave
Newaygo MI 49337

Call Sign: KC8DHW
Fletcher P Newfer
6390 S Pine Ave
Newaygo MI 49337

Call Sign: N8DRN
Lester W Van Essen
5467 Shady Dr
Newaygo MI 49337

Call Sign: N8EOL
Larry J Berwald
9575 Spruce St
Newaygo MI 49337

Call Sign: KD8KFC

Douglas G Cobb
6981 Stephen Miller
Dr
Newaygo MI 49337

Call Sign: WA8LKG
Alice B Aldrich
5275 Stray Dr
Newaygo MI 49337

Call Sign: N8OKR
Terry E Krontz
9516 Timberline Ct
Newaygo MI 49337

Call Sign: KC8LGD
Shawn R Gibson
3377 W 80th St
Newaygo MI 49337

Call Sign: KC8JYF
Jeanette J Newfer
157 W Barton St Apt 4
Newaygo MI
493378516

Call Sign: KC8CUW
Paul R Newfer
782 W Brooks St Apt
225
Newaygo MI
493378853

Call Sign: W8SRN
Scott R Newfer
141 W Pine Lake Dr
Apt G
Newaygo MI 49337

Call Sign: KB8OVN
Harold G Mercer
42 Washington St
Newaygo MI 49337

Call Sign: N8TGY
Cheryl L Corey
11600 Whitefish Rd
Newaygo MI 49337

Call Sign: N8TGZ
Mark L Corey
11600 Whitefish Rd
Newaygo MI 49337

Call Sign: KB8JYD
Edith C Toy
Newaygo MI 49337

Call Sign: ND8M
Barbara E Counterman
Newaygo MI 49337

Call Sign: NG8J
Richard M
Counterman
Newaygo MI 49337

Call Sign: KC8EGI
Terry L Jackson
Newaygo MI 49337

Call Sign: KE6LLV
Philip D Tremblay Jr
Newaygo MI 49337

Call Sign: KC8ULZ
Jonathon M Hikade
Newaygo MI 49337

Call Sign: WA8NXX
Donald L Betts
Newaygo MI 49337

FCC Amateur Radio Licenses in Newberry

Call Sign: W8GTP
Ralph E Vitale
R1 Box 502 Charles
Rd
Newberry MI 49868

Call Sign: KC8DYT
Ryan C Fahler
Rr 4 Box 742
Newberry MI 49868

Call Sign: KD8EVA
Tim R Maskus
13894 Cherry Hill Dr
Newberry MI 49868

Call Sign: W8TRM
Tim R Maskus
13894 Cherry Hill Dr
Newberry MI 49868

Call Sign: KB8RIT

James R Reynolds
15449 CR 402
Newberry MI
498687991

Call Sign: KC8ZHG
Linda K Walker
12479 CR 408
Newberry MI 49868

Call Sign: KD8LMB
Luce ARS
6401 CR 441
Newberry MI 49868

Call Sign: W8NBY
Luce ARS
6401 CR 441
Newberry MI 49868

Call Sign: KC8QZG
David D Dake
6401 CR 441
Newberry MI 49868

Call Sign: KC8HER
Linda R Grant
6017 CR 457
Newberry MI 49868

Call Sign: KD8QJG
Kimball J Eddy
6017 CR 457
Newberry MI 49868

Call Sign: KC8QZJ
Scott M Mctiver
18519 CR 458
Newberry MI 49868

Call Sign: K8VOB
Robert E Miller
18776 CR 458
Newberry MI 49868

Call Sign: KD8BMP
Gregory J Padgham
408 E John St
Newberry MI 49868

Call Sign: N8FDM
Elva E McCutcheon
903 E Limits St

Newberry MI
498680328

Call Sign: KB8FHH
Robert W Farr
410 E McMillan
Newberry MI 49868

Call Sign: KC8MJV
Jack A Olson
407 E Truman St
Newberry MI
498681034

Call Sign: N8ATS
Samuel E Holmes
401 E Victory Way
Newberry MI 49868

Call Sign: N8WKK
Evelyn R Keizer
Hamilton Lk Rd
Newberry MI 49868

Call Sign: K8ZNU
George A Moulder
Maple Hill Rd
Newberry MI 49868

Call Sign: KA8KQR
Peter D Rahilly
219 W Ave A
Newberry MI 49868

Call Sign: KC8OKR
Jean M Rahilly
403 W Ave C
Newberry MI 49868

Call Sign: N8FJK
Robert E McCutcheon
506 W Ave C
Newberry MI
498681709

Call Sign: KC8QHZ
Ted E Hendricks
516 W Ave C
Newberry MI 49868

Call Sign: KC8CVP
Samuel E Holmes
106 W Ave D
Newberry MI 49868

Call Sign: KA8CEP
Michael V Kalnbach
302 W Harrie St
Newberry MI 49868

Call Sign: WD8JGL
Carl L Bergman
204 W Helen St
Newberry MI 49868

Call Sign: KD8QJF
Nathan C Neeb
13937 Woodland Dr
Newberry MI 49868

Call Sign: KA8CEO
Michael B Ennis
Newberry MI 49868

Call Sign: N8DVT
Edward L McCutcheon
Newberry MI 49868

Call Sign: KC8QZK
Paul F List
Newberry MI 49868

Call Sign: AB8LX
Paul F List
Newberry MI 49868

Call Sign: KD8DBA
Eric S Laroue
Newberry MI 49868

Call Sign: KD8BMQ
John P Ross
Newberry MI 49868

Call Sign: KD8QJI
Joseph D Bennett
Newberry MI 49868

Call Sign: KD8QJH
Sheila M Laroue
Newberry MI 49868

**FCC Amateur Radio
Licenses in Niles**

Call Sign: KB8LUT
David P Kloko
1950 13th St 34

Niles MI 49120

Call Sign: K8KED
Hector C Brown
1251 Airport Rd
Niles MI 49120

Call Sign: N8MJL
Gregory J Miars
2707 Alane St
Niles MI 49120

Call Sign: KB8UXD
Judith K Johnson
1068 Bame Ave
Niles MI 49120

Call Sign: WB9WYR
Kenneth A Kuespert
185 Bell Rd
Niles MI 49120

Call Sign: KD8NID
Richard L Critchlow Jr
2303 Bicknell
Niles MI 49120

Call Sign: N8VNP
Gordon J Young
2207 Bicknell Ave
Niles MI 491204436

Call Sign: KC8KTN
Charles T Rodgers
2211 Bicknell St
Niles MI 49120

Call Sign: WB8ZCS
Robert E Thompson
2527 Bond St
Niles MI 49120

Call Sign: KA8LDQ
James W Schroeder Sr
2716 Bond St
Niles MI 49120

Call Sign: WD8PFE
Robert E Clark
1775 Burton Rd
Niles MI 49120

Call Sign: KD8PPK
Eleanor S Hein

943 Carberry Rd
Niles MI 49120

Call Sign: KD8PPL
Ronald D Hein
943 Carberry Rd
Niles MI 49120

Call Sign: N8ZEH
Lisa D Tittle
1097.5 Carberry Rd
Niles MI 49120

Call Sign: WB8OWQ
Mark D Thompson
214 Carter Ave
Niles MI 49120

Call Sign: W8LIA
Robert W Bell
70764 Carter Ave
Niles MI 49120

Call Sign: KD8EIG
William K McCraner
251 Cass St Apt 101
Niles MI 49120

Call Sign: KD8FFY
Windell L Phillips
1807 Cedar St
Niles MI 49120

Call Sign: WA8DAL
William L Kromer
2649 Center Ave
Niles MI 49120

Call Sign: WB8BVP
Camden M Miars
305 Christiana Dr
Niles MI 49120

Call Sign: N9SBV
Robert E Stephenson
1435 Clarendon Ave
Niles MI 49120

Call Sign: KA9JVV
Michael A Malisa
725 Colonyct Apt 2
Niles MI 49120

Call Sign: KD8ZX

Jaime A Aravena
1411 Country Club Dr
Niles MI 491204229

Call Sign: KB8ONQ
Bonnie J Beaird
1401 Dewberry
Niles MI 49120

Call Sign: N8GED
Donald L Beaird
1401 Dewberry
Niles MI 49120

Call Sign: KC8DUF
Brian K Turrell
1514 E Bertrand
Niles MI 49120

Call Sign: N8XBB
Douglas A Domokos
2330 E Main Lot 13
Niles MI 49120

Call Sign: K8STR
Roy G Peters
1521 E Main St
Niles MI 49120

Call Sign: W8LSP
Raymond Canfield
1823 E Main St
Niles MI 49120

Call Sign: W8UCB
Robert D Ashcraft
1922 E Winn Rd
Niles MI 49120

Call Sign: WK8K
Garrott W Elghammer
1602 Echo Valley Dr
Niles MI 49120

Call Sign: KF4KKQ
Jerry G Beaird
1547 Ferndale Blvd
Niles MI 49120

Call Sign: KC8UBK
Jerry G Beaird
1547 Ferndale Blvd
Niles MI 49120

Call Sign: N5GBM
Michael D Martin Sr
185 Fir Rd
Niles MI 49120

Call Sign: N8NUQ
Paul A Boggs Jr
71195 Fir Rd
Niles MI 491205960

Call Sign: KD8PPM
Troy M Thompson
1419 Florence Ave
Niles MI 49120

Call Sign: K8VO
Brian J Mcintosh
118 Forest Ave
Niles MI 49120

Call Sign: KC5AJU
David W Ward
3825 Gateway Ln
Niles MI 49120

Call Sign: KC5AXR
Carrie D Ward
3825 Gateway Ln
Niles MI 49120

Call Sign: N8MGD
Sharon L Urquhart
121 Green Gable
Niles MI 49120

Call Sign: KD8LOX
Esther J Lucas
107 Hatfield Rd
Niles MI 49120

Call Sign: K8GNA
Douglas R Wise
175 Hatfield Rd
Niles MI 49120

Call Sign: WA8EFN
Karen T Wise
175 Hatfield Rd
Niles MI 49120

Call Sign: WA8EPL
Harold R Hosler
1427 Howard
Niles MI 49120

Call Sign: WA8EFQ
Lucille E Robinson
1709 Howard St
Niles MI 49120

Call Sign: KW8E
Louis G Konopinski
1124 Hyrne
Niles MI 491209534

Call Sign: AA8FG
Brian K McGrath
1970 Jay St
Niles MI 49120

Call Sign: N8UIA
Carl V Lowell Jr
826 Kensington Dr
Niles MI 49120

Call Sign: KD8NIE
William R Coleman
2532 Lakeshore Dr
Niles MI 49120

Call Sign: KC8OVZ
William A Casper
2571 Lakeshore Dr
Niles MI 49120

Call Sign: KB8WKS
Gregory M D Haeze
1868 Lewis Dr
Niles MI 49120

Call Sign: KC8BRS
Four Flags ARC
1883 Lewis Dr
Niles MI 49120

Call Sign: WA8ZPD
Michael K Stueber
1883 Lewis Dr
Niles MI 49120

Call Sign: WB8SXN
Donald A Garling
1893 Lewis Dr
Niles MI 49120

Call Sign: KB8OGB
Rebekah S Finn
2012 Lewis Dr

Niles MI 49120

Call Sign: KC8NAP
Gary R Crouch
2139 Lewis Dr
Niles MI 49120

Call Sign: KB8OEG
Freddie P Bailey Sr
2466 Lone Elm St
Niles MI 49120

Call Sign: K6KZ
Harvey J Lawrence
1984 M 51 N
Niles MI 491209103

Call Sign: WA6AQA
Ruth S Lawrence
1984 M 51 N
Niles MI 491209103

Call Sign: KD8KTC
Jack E Henry
2729 Madison St
Niles MI 49120

Call Sign: KD8KTB
Kathleen S Henry
2729 Madison St
Niles MI 49120

Call Sign: KC8TLO
Charles O Ziegler
2236 Maple Ln
Niles MI 49120

Call Sign: KA8OXZ
Mary A Poplewski
119 Matthew Rd
Niles MI 49120

Call Sign: KC8IV
David V Poplewski
119 Matthew Rd
Niles MI 49120

Call Sign: N8FPD
Charles F Felty
2450 Mayflower Rd
Niles MI 49120

Call Sign: KB8UPP
Daniel C Snow

1124 Miami Rd
Niles MI 49120

Call Sign: N8YMI
Daniel C Finch
1414 Michigan St
Niles MI 49120

Call Sign: K8UZC
Robert W Rose
1644 Michigan St
Niles MI 49120

Call Sign: WD8BQH
William A Best
1815 Miller Dr
Niles MI 49120

Call Sign: WD9GOL
Robert J Hagenberg
1294 Missions E Dr
Niles MI 49120

Call Sign: N8BXY
Virgil C Warner
401 Monroe St
Niles MI 49120

Call Sign: KG8YP
Robert D Vernon
1715 N 11th St
Niles MI 49120

Call Sign: KC8LVC
Leonard V Lawver
1502 N 12th
Niles MI 49120

Call Sign: KA8OCL
Robert B Loughin
221 N 15th St
Niles MI 49120

Call Sign: KA8MJD
Dorothy L Bolinger
515 N 17th St Apt 6
Niles MI 491202061

Call Sign: N8HOI
Edgar E Haase
2720 N 5th St
Niles MI 49120

Call Sign: KD8BTQ

Ralph E Arnold
2945 N 5th St
Niles MI 49120

Call Sign: KC8DUE
Kenneth F Seifert
3119 N 5th St
Niles MI 49120

Call Sign: KB0YLA
Traci D Lewis
135 N Fairview
Niles MI 49120

Call Sign: KB9JBA
William S Rahiser
110 N Philip Rd
Niles MI 491201496

Call Sign: KD8GOH
Adrian C Sarli
1906 Niles Buchanan
Rd
Niles MI 49120

Call Sign: AC8CA
Adrian C Sarli
1906 Niles Buchanan
Rd
Niles MI 49120

Call Sign: KD8HOX
Nathan M Sarli
1906 Niles Buchanan
Rd
Niles MI 49120

Call Sign: KD8IYC
Nathan M Sarli
1906 Nilcs Buchanan
Rd
Niles MI 49120

Call Sign: KD8HOW
Rocco V Sarli
1906 Niles Buchanan
Rd
Niles MI 49120

Call Sign: KD8HMB
Walter Hess
1310 Oak St
Niles MI 49120

Call Sign: KD8ANF
Douglas W Michels
236 Ontario Rd
Niles MI 49120

Call Sign: N8XOB
George A Wolf
2006 Ontario Rd Box
53
Niles MI 49120

Call Sign: N8XOA
Patricia H Wolf
2006 Ontario Rd Lot
53
Niles MI 49120

Call Sign: N8MAU
Pennie A Messner
1012 Pine St
Niles MI 49120

Call Sign: KD8BTR
Leonard E Whittaker
501 Platt St
Niles MI 49120

Call Sign: KB9IYC
Jennifer L Boyer
3120 Portage Rd
Niles MI 49120

Call Sign: K8STT
Edward L Schadler
2554 Prospect Pt
Niles MI 49120

Call Sign: N5SDZ
Steven R Sowder
10953 Pucker St
Niles MI 49120

Call Sign: KB8LGV
Howard P Lenhardt
2441 Rebecca Ln
Niles MI 49120

Call Sign: KC8BBM
Joyce E Laskus
3010 Red Field Rd
Niles MI 49120

Call Sign: KD8CGQ
John J Dykema

2895 Redbud Trl
Niles MI 49120

Call Sign: KA8WWV
Helen M Brooks
2223 Redfield Rd
Niles MI 49120

Call Sign: N8CNM
Joseph E Ingle
2289 Redfield Rd
Niles MI 49120

Call Sign: KD8FWV
Eric R Renken
31301 Redfield Rd
Niles MI 49120

Call Sign: W8KSX
Richard T Simons
923 Regent
Niles MI 49120

Call Sign: W8ZXC
Marion N Skinner
1515 Regent
Niles MI 49120

Call Sign: KC8BH
David W Rice
1625 Regent St
Niles MI 49120

Call Sign: KC8QMD
Christopher T Phillips
1817 Regent St
Niles MI 49120

Call Sign: KA8HCA
James O Bell
1716 River Bluff Rd
Niles MI 49120

Call Sign: KC8MB
Lavall Lane
275 Roosevelt Rd
Niles MI 49120

Call Sign: KC8MY
Ethan J Mittan
1001 Ruth Layne
Niles MI 49120

Call Sign: KD8IAY

Justin S Pontius
2315 S 13th St
Niles MI 49120

Call Sign: W8JCU
Dwayne H Cusick
2608 S 13th St
Niles MI 49120

Call Sign: WB8UHO
Leonard E Booth
3123 S 13th St
Niles MI 49120

Call Sign: KC8LKI
Anthony S Lake
1240 S 14th St
Niles MI 49120

Call Sign: KB8HMS
James J Granning
831 S 15th St
Niles MI 49120

Call Sign: KB8IQF
William A Hayes
2232 S 21st
Niles MI 49120

Call Sign: KD8ANH
Larry L Griffith
509 S 5th St
Niles MI 49120

Call Sign: W8UES
Donald C Camp
308 S Barrett St
Niles MI 491203115

Call Sign: KE4PM
Larry M Prelog
10 S Fairview Ave
Niles MI 49120

Call Sign: WA8LKI
Andrews University
ARC
10 S Fairview Ave
Niles MI 49120

Call Sign: KC9TT
Michael E Ruedinger
327 S Philip Rd
Niles MI 49120

Call Sign: WA8LKC
Richard D Wilcox
2415 S Redbud Trl
Niles MI 491208601

Call Sign: WA8LHM
Frederick H Lindenfeld
443 S St Joseph Ave
Niles MI 49120

Call Sign: KC8NIK
Eric D Neff
436 S State St
Niles MI 49120

Call Sign: KA0SLK
Mark W Ludwig
1165 Sassafras Ln
Niles MI 49120

Call Sign: KD8GQI
Duane L Rule
1141 Sassafrass Ln
Niles MI 49120

Call Sign: KA8SKW
Winafred M Smith
1114 Scott St
Niles MI 49120

Call Sign: KC8LM
Roger Smith
1114 Scott St
Niles MI 49120

Call Sign: W4INS
Brian J Mcintosh
1615 Sheridan Ave
Niles MI 49120

Call Sign: KD8GZN
Steven J Mann
149 Silverbrook
Niles MI 49120

Call Sign: KC8KXZ
David B Witham
803 Skyline Dr
Niles MI 49120

Call Sign: KC8PUL
Rhonda S Witham
803 Skyline Dr

Niles MI 49120

Call Sign: K8RPF
Roger D Mais
205 Sorin St
Niles MI 42910

Call Sign: KC8ICH
Seth A Weldy
1305 South St
Niles MI 49120

Call Sign: K8UYH
Richard L Born
520 Springfield Cr
Niles MI 49120

Call Sign: KD8RHJ
James L Todd
71467 Stags Leap Ct
Niles MI 49120

Call Sign: N8JDV
Albert W Simons
1611 Stateline Rd
Niles MI 49120

Call Sign: KD8CSQ
David H Reits
2659 Terminal
Niles MI 49120

Call Sign: KE8BO
Walter L Biggs Jr
1229 Thomson Rd
Niles MI 49120

Call Sign: WA8TTX
Robert W Jorgensen
1353 Thomson Rd
Niles MI 49120

Call Sign: WA8EGS
Keith B Fisher
2267 Thunderbird Ln
Niles MI 49120

Call Sign: AA8FP
John C Huffman
925 Tomahawk Ln
Niles MI 49120

Call Sign: WB8HWH
Scott H Kasler

615 Topinabee Rd
Niles MI 49120

Call Sign: KA8DQP
Jack B Thatcher
621 Topinabee Rd
Niles MI 49120

Call Sign: KB8ZVE
Ronald L Johnson
7126 True Rd
Niles MI 49120

Call Sign: W8AIJ
Kenneth L Geideman
2276 US 12 E
Niles MI 49120

Call Sign: KD8AYG
Janice E Irwin
2915 US 31 N
Niles MI 49120

Call Sign: WB4PBM
John R Christie
91 W Bayberry
Niles MI 49120

Call Sign: W8NLO
Harold L Treesh
526 W Main St
Niles MI 49120

Call Sign: KD8NIC
Rodney C Woods
2717 West St
Niles MI 49120

Call Sign: WA8ZCY
Robert L Ashcraft
2274 White St
Niles MI 49120

Call Sign: WD8OHT
Charles G Bower
2509 White St
Niles MI 49120

Call Sign: W8WQS
Robert F Hand
2678 White St
Niles MI 49120

Call Sign: K8THZ

John F Schadler
7959 Wright Rd
Niles MI 491209035

Call Sign: WD8QZZ
Dorothy F Ferguson
8724 Wright Rd
Niles MI 49120

Call Sign: WD8RAA
Forrest W Ferguson
8724 Wright Rd
Niles MI 49120

Call Sign: WB8WGX
Thomas N Pinard
2316 Yankee
Niles MI 49120

Call Sign: WB8WGW
Ronald E Bell
2563 Yankee St
Niles MI 49120

Call Sign: KI8FO
Dale R Vernon
3058 Yankee St
Niles MI 49120

Call Sign: KD8LPO
Jonathan B Estabrook
2394 Yankee St Apt 2
Niles MI 49120

Call Sign: KD8RGE
Wayne G Shearier
Niles MI 49120

Call Sign: WA8YNE
Wayne G Shearier
Niles MI 49120

Call Sign: KD8CSS
John J Light
Niles MI 491200113

Call Sign: KD8BNW
The Salvation Army
Niles Eds Satern
Niles MI 491201150

**FCC Amateur Radio
Licenses in North
Muskegon**

Call Sign: WD8OHB
Carolyn L Botbyl
182 Apple Ct
North Muskegon MI
49445

Call Sign: AC8U
M Ronald Miccoli
569 Bear Lake Rd
North Muskegon MI
49445

Call Sign: KC8JNN
Noah H Hogston
2827 Clelery Ln
North Muskegon MI
49445

Call Sign: N8UAL
Richard E Strach
800 Franklin St
North Muskegon MI
49445

Call Sign: KC8NOQ
Charles A Hermanson
1725 Manistee Rd
North Muskegon MI
49445

Call Sign: KC8VTX
Robert E Duplissis
233 McConnell Ave
North Muskegon MI
49445

Call Sign: N9AUY
Robert E Duplissis
233 McConncll Ave
North Muskegon MI
49445

Call Sign: KA8NJG
William R Damm
2577 Memorial Dr
North Muskegon MI
49445

Call Sign: W8UD
David E Nygren
3395 Memorial Dr
North Muskegon MI
49445

Call Sign: N8XPP
Donald S Munski
810 Miller Dr
North Muskegon MI
49445

Call Sign: N8PPQ
Daniel B Mills
1817 Mills Ave
North Muskegon MI
49445

Call Sign: NA8B
Paul T Cummings
2205 Mills Ave
North Muskegon MI
49445

Call Sign: KA8NTX
Richard D Hallberg Sr
2222 Mills Ave
North Muskegon MI
49445

Call Sign: KI8EP
Patrick D Herman
2314 Mills Ave
North Muskegon MI
49445

Call Sign: KI8UM
Patrick D Herman
2314 Mills Ave
North Muskegon MI
49445

Call Sign: N8KSW
Daniel W Lenz
1321 Moulton Ave
North Muskegon MI
49445

Call Sign: WA8ULC
Michael Simerick Jr
177 N Green Creek
North Muskegon MI
49445

Call Sign: KC8PLM
Michael Simerick Jr
177 N Green Creek Rd
North Muskegon MI
49445

Call Sign: KA8OXG
Stanley J Hale
1523 N Green Creek
Rd
North Muskegon MI
49445

Call Sign: KV8X
Allen J Pepping
2283 N Hyde Park Rd
North Muskegon MI
494459302

Call Sign: N8PPM
Jerry A Fore
1693 N Roberts Rd
North Muskegon MI
49445

Call Sign: WD8AHA
Virginia H Carr
651 Penn Ln
North Muskegon MI
49445

Call Sign: KC8YTF
Jon Dean
555 Plymouth Dr
North Muskegon MI
49445

Call Sign: N8YJT
Tom Porritt
1321 Ruddiman
North Muskegon MI
49445

Call Sign: K8EOD
Tom Porritt
1321 Ruddiman
North Muskegon MI
49445

Call Sign: KC7NEC
Damon S Talbot
1642 Ruddiman
North Muskegon MI
49445

Call Sign: N8RXB
Gregory J Hoffman
435 Ruddiman Dr

North Muskegon MI
49445

Call Sign: WD8QWU
David K Wilson
1471 Scenic Dr
North Muskegon MI
49445

Call Sign: KC8MDL
Charles C Stark
668 Straley St
North Muskegon MI
49445

Call Sign: W8CCS
Charles C Stark
668 Straley St
North Muskegon MI
49445

Call Sign: KD8CBG
Charles A Stark
668 Straley St
North Muskegon MI
49445

Call Sign: KA8NQV
Ellen R Bisson
1475 Sunview St
North Muskegon MI
49445

Call Sign: KF8QT
William R Bowman
1784 W Bard Rd
North Muskegon MI
49445

Call Sign: KD8DKV
Jayne L Pyle
3350 W Bard Rd
North Muskegon MI
49445

Call Sign: KD8DKZ
Roger H Pyle
3350 W Bard Rd
North Muskegon MI
49445

Call Sign: N8WQK
James T Litton
543 W Chadwick Dr

North Muskegon MI
49445

Call Sign: WA8RTL
Joseph F Firlit
335 W Circle Dr
North Muskegon MI
49445

Call Sign: K8FLY
William J Skofic
933 W River Rd
North Muskegon MI
49445

Call Sign: KC8KAV
Sandra L Dail
4776 W River Rd
North Muskegon MI
494450906

Call Sign: AA8JZ
Richard L Dial
4776 W River Rd
North Muskegon MI
49445

FCC Amateur Radio
Licenses in Northport

Call Sign: N8RTE
Bill F Cain
9081 E Onomonee Rd
Northport MI 49670

Call Sign: K8SZN
Edward A Ketterer III
15155 N Cathead Bay
Dr
Northport MI 49670

Call Sign: N8JIB
Linda E Ketterer
15155 N Cathead Bay
Dr
Northport MI 49670

Call Sign: KB8IWO
Vernon F Lawson
13651 N Forest Beach
Shores Rd
Northport MI 49670

Call Sign: W8BZA

Philip E Johnson
11920 N Foxview Dr
Northport MI
496709510

Call Sign: KD8HHW
James L Duff
6971 N Manitou Trl
Northport MI 49670

Call Sign: AC8DG
James L Duff
6971 N Manitou Trl
Northport MI 49670

Call Sign: N8KV
Roger J Cameron
8571 N Manitou Trl
Northport MI 49670

Call Sign: KC8LRB
Nathaniel G Cheatham
8571 N Manitou Trl
Northport MI
496709403

Call Sign: WB8HBJ
Roger J Cameron
8571 N Manitou Trl
Northport MI
496709403

Call Sign: W8RXL
Charles F Plachetzki
10733 N Shore Box 72
Northport MI 49670

Call Sign: W8GVS
Isaac N Hagen
609 Ransom
Northport MI
496709392

Call Sign: N8ROV
Philip N Loud
Northport MI 49670

Call Sign: W8IOY
Richard H Hanson
Northport MI 49670

Call Sign: KD8NXI
Laura L Cameron
Northport MI 49670

Call Sign: KD8OGD
Paul S Cameron
Northport MI 49670

FCC Amateur Radio
Licenses in Norton
Shores

Call Sign: KD8HSE
Kirk D Nygren
1705 Bonneville Dr
Norton Shores MI
49441

Call Sign: W8GXT
Kirk D Nygren
1705 Bonneville Dr
Norton Shores MI
49441

Call Sign: KO8Z
Kirk D Nygren
1705 Bonneville Dr
Norton Shores MI
49441

Call Sign: KD8GUY
David J Purchase
1035 Brookway Ct
Norton Shores MI
49444

Call Sign: KD8KLR
Cheryl A Brandt
3653 Courtland Dr
Norton Shores MI
49441

Call Sign: KC8PCJ
James P Meyers
1283 Crestbrook Ave
Norton Shores MI
494444220

Call Sign: WA9TGD
Karel A Snoble
1016 Edinborough Dr
Norton Shores MI
49441

Call Sign: KB8TMA
Robert J Smeed
1788 Forest Park Rd

Norton Shores MI
49441

Call Sign: KC8ZMF
Richard E Johnson
1529 Getz
Norton Shores MI
49441

Call Sign: KB8DPR
Katherine L Gietzen
1709 Lawnel Ave
Norton Shores MI
494413740

Call Sign: WA8HDG
William D Gietzen
1709 Lawnel Ave
Norton Shores MI
494413740

Call Sign: KC8WSD
Randy L Miller
1848 Lawnel Ave
Norton Shores MI
494413743

Call Sign: KC8MDM
Donald L Vanderkooi
4484 Marshall Rd
Norton Shores MI
494415125

Call Sign: N8RYP
Denise L Meyer
5450 Martin Rd S
Norton Shores MI
49441

Call Sign: KC8AOR
Scott A King
3427 McCracken
Norton Shores MI
49441

Call Sign: W8SWX
Jeffrey D Stapel
4504 McKinley Ct
Norton Shores MI
49441

Call Sign: KD8FXA
Jeffrey D Stapel
4504 McKinney Ct

Norton Shores MI
49441

Call Sign: KD8FBT
Zachary L Sparks
5133 Melmax St
Norton Shores MI
49441

Call Sign: KB8RHQ
Karl J Spielberger
4651 Rood Rd
Norton Shores MI
49441

Call Sign: KD8BHV
Linda L Fisher
529 Tournament Cir
Norton Shores MI
49444

Call Sign: KC8DYA
Muskegon County
Amateur Radio
Emergency Service
530 W Hile Rd
Norton Shores MI
49441

Call Sign: KC8MDJ
Joseph J Kinnucan
530 W Hile Rd
Norton Shores MI
49441

Call Sign: KC8LBZ
Edward C Summers
1534 Westwood Dr
Norton Shores MI
49441

Call Sign: W0MZA
John J Hoekstra
6841 Windwater Ct
Norton Shores MI
494447736

Call Sign: WB8SZI
Paul A Hintz
407 2nd Ave
Norway MI 49870

Call Sign: KB8HJL
John M Nelson Jr
1707 7th Ave
Norway MI 49870

Call Sign: KB8YET
Gerald D Girard
120 Beckstrom
Norway MI 49870

Call Sign: KE8MX
Philip H Bekkala
208 Forest Dr
Norway MI 49870

Call Sign: KC8NQI
Michelle A Bekkala
208 Forest Dr
Norway MI 49870

Call Sign: WB8SYA
Walter F Peters
128 Iron St
Norway MI 49870

Call Sign: KB8YEU
Jack D O Brion
108 Mine St
Norway MI 49870

Call Sign: KB8YEV
Robert G Norton
317 Norway St
Norway MI 49870

Call Sign: KC8EMF
Patrick M Servia
2226 Pearny Ln
Norway MI 49870

Call Sign: KC8JRH
Peter C Schlitt
W5786 Piers Gorge Rd
Norway MI 49870

Call Sign: KC8QYQ
David A Tinti
N2625 Valley View
Rd
Norway MI 49870

Call Sign: N8III
John H Fuller
15868 132nd Ave
Nunica MI 494489729

Call Sign: N8JKS
Judith K Fuller
15868 132nd Ave
Nunica MI 494489729

Call Sign: KD8KAM
Anthony L Gould
17781 136th Ave
Nunica MI 49448

Call Sign: W8TKW
Lester D Timmerman
9958 Cleveland Rd
Rfd 2
Nunica MI 49448

Call Sign: KC8ACS
George A Homoly
12013 State Rd
Nunica MI 49448

Call Sign: KC8JWD
Kimberly D Reminder
13294 State Rd
Nunica MI 49448

Call Sign: KC8JWA
Beverly J Traxler
13625 State Rd
Nunica MI 49448

Call Sign: KC8MZE
Robert W Traxler
13625 State Rd
Nunica MI 49448

Call Sign: KC8ZMG
Dennis R David
6500 Sullivan Rd
Nunica MI 49448

Call Sign: KB6RLA
Douglas C Dixon
6575 Sullivan Rd
Nunica MI 49448

Call Sign: N8RXE
Donald E McGregor

Nunica MI 49448

Call Sign: KC8LYT
James T Gillen
16243 Beach Hwy
Ocqueoc MI 49759

Call Sign: KB8MDP
Kathryn I Damon
18348 Cherokee Ln
Ocqueoc MI 49759

Call Sign: KC8EJF
Duane P Freel
4644 N Ocqueoc Rd
Ocqueoc MI 49759

Call Sign: AB8EM
Duane P Freel
4644 N Ocqueoc Rd
Ocqueoc MI 49759

Call Sign: W8PIC
H Robert George
Oden MI 49764

Call Sign: KC8OFA
Lyndon D Scott
Old Mission MI 49673

Call Sign: KC8SBT
Lyndon D Scott
Old Mission MI 49673

Call Sign: AB8LS
Lyndon D Scott
Old Mission MI 49673

Call Sign: WD8CUO
Davis W Allen

23240 26 Mile Rd
Olivet MI 49076

Call Sign: KD8CSB
Peter K Brown
2758 Butterfield
Olivet MI 49076

Call Sign: KD8RSI
Lewis A Ellwanger
115 Court St
Olivet MI 49076

Call Sign: KB8VIC
Gerald Rydzewski
231 E Green St
Olivet MI 49076

Call Sign: KA8CLR
Richard E Toncray
6471 Morse Dr
Olivet MI 49076

Call Sign: KD8CSC
Michael J Barnes
7936 S Ainger
Olivet MI 49076

Call Sign: KC8DHV
Daniel M Forrester
5344 S Ainger Rd
Olivet MI 49076

Call Sign: KC8DQB
Jamie L Scheib
139 Washington St
Olivet MI 49076

Call Sign: KD8ONG
Randall R Smith
112 Westridge St
Olivet MI 49076

Call Sign: N8STQ
Kathleen A Shelton
Omena MI 49674

Call Sign: KE8SB
John H Mulligan
Omena MI 49674

Call Sign: N8NLQ
Timothy A White
19378 Hackett Lake
Hwy
Onaway MI 49765

Call Sign: KC8UKG
Kimberlee A White
19378 Hackett Lake
Hwy
Onaway MI 49765

Call Sign: KD8KNP
Jeanne D Mcdowell
10046 M 33
Onaway MI 49765

Call Sign: KD8KNO
Rick H Mcdowell
10046 M 33
Onaway MI 49765

Call Sign: KB8YNT
Ross K Brooke
10743 Mason Rd
Onaway MI 49765

Call Sign: WA8IUT
Roy T Money
Box 157A Rt 2
Onaway MI 49765

Call Sign: KB8WPR
Adam M Donaldson
4504 Prospect St
Onekema MI 49675

Call Sign: W8UXG
Robert M Reid
101 3rd St
Ontonagon MI 49953

Call Sign: KB8FBC
Donald G Danks

105 3rd St
Ontonagon MI 49953

Call Sign: WA8AHX
Ernest R Baullinger
702 Cane Ct
Ontonagon MI 49953

Call Sign: WB8RVK
John K Parker
33523 Halfway River
Rd
Ontonagon MI 49953

Call Sign: WB8QKF
Stanley V Lanker Jr
125 Hibbeln Rd
Ontonagon MI 49953

Call Sign: AB8GN
Stanley V Lanker Jr
125 Hibbeln Rd
Ontonagon MI 49953

Call Sign: KC8RPP
Ontonagon County
Amateur Radio
Association
145 Hokkanen Rd
Ontonagon MI 49953

Call Sign: KC8OCK
Alfred R Trainer III
26715 Hokkanen Rd
Ontonagon MI 49953

Call Sign: K8ONT
Ontonagon County
Amateur Radio
Associati
26715 Hokkanen Rd
Ontonagon MI 49953

Call Sign: KC8ZNI
Threman E Julian
312 Hubbell St
Ontonagon MI 49953

Call Sign: KC8DCF
Thomas J Worgull
36675 Kujala Rd
Ontonagon MI 49953

Call Sign: KB8OBH

Carol L Fetsch
1025 Lakeshore Dr
Ontonagon MI 49953

Call Sign: KA8ZPM
Bernard E Spotton
1276 M 38
Ontonagon MI 49953

Call Sign: KB8HMB
Richard A Tandlund
738 Michigan Ave Apt
2
Ontonagon MI 49953

Call Sign: N8AQ
William R Meador
19253 Mtn View Rd
Ontonagon MI 49953

Call Sign: KC8RFJ
Michael R Badgero
512 Mulock St
Ontonagon MI 49953

Call Sign: W6LOO
David N Danks
115 Pennsylvania Ave
Ontonagon MI 49953

Call Sign: WD6CLY
Marie J Danks
115 Pennsylvania Ave
Ontonagon MI 49953

Call Sign: KC8DCE
James H Norris
284 Quarterline Rd
Ontonagon MI 49953

Call Sign: KC8WJ
Wesley E Hoover
341 Seward Ave
Ontonagon MI
499539643

Call Sign: N8KGB
Robert L Fitze
515 Spar St
Ontonagon MI 49953

Call Sign: KD8LAH
John B Groop
38529 Strang Rd

Ontonagon MI 49953

Call Sign: KC8ABQ
James L Waters
35781 US Hwy 45
Ontonagon MI 49953

Call Sign: KC8CDF
Charles W Silver
24677 W State Hwy M
64
Ontonagon MI 49953

Call Sign: W8HYQ
Jack D Watt
112 Watt Rd
Ontonagon MI 49953

FCC Amateur Radio Licenses in Orleans

Call Sign: KD8NFA
Susan J Halliwill
8272 3rd Ave
Orleans MI 48865

Call Sign: K8DCF
Walter E Reeves
915 Belding Rd
Orleans MI 48865

Call Sign: WA8KCP
Lucy M Reeves
915 Belding Rd
Orleans MI 488659603

Call Sign: KC8YDR
William D Doty
5072 Orleans Rd
Orleans MI 48865

Call Sign: W8WDD
William D Doty
5072 Orleans Rd
Orleans MI 48865

Call Sign: K8BZD
Maurice A Clements
5663 Orleans Rd
Orleans MI 48865

Call Sign: N8SFE
Jerry W Brown
7081 Orleans Rd

Orleans MI 48865

Call Sign: KB8ZKS
Nicholas B Smith
2835 W Long Lake Rd
Orleans MI 48865

Call Sign: KC8ACR
Russell A Smith
2835 W Long Lake Rd
Orleans MI 48865

Call Sign: KC8KNL
Gordon D Lanting
3490 W Long Lake Rd
Orleans MI 49565

Call Sign: KB8KHT
Jim D McRoberts
1169 Youngs Rd
Orleans MI 48865

FCC Amateur Radio Licenses in Oscoda

Call Sign: KC8GXV
Richard S Raesly Jr
6580 Ahrens St
Oscoda MI 48750

Call Sign: N8TVK
Homer H Rudolph
5512 Alvin Rd
Oscoda MI 48750

Call Sign: KC8ZOF
Linda J Gillam
Ostrander
2152 Bisssomotte Rd
Oscoda MI 48750

Call Sign: KC8TXO
Anton J Orso
6391 Cedar Lake Rd
Oscoda MI 48750

Call Sign: KC8THB
Thomas E Rudolph
6890 Cedar Lake Rd
Oscoda MI 48750

Call Sign: KC8TGY
Christine J Rudolph
6890 Cedar Lake Rd

Oscoda MI 487509438

Call Sign: KD8AOF
Joseph W Knuth
5035 Cedar Lake Rd
Apt 23
Oscoda MI 48750

Call Sign: N8DQU
Allan J Duncan
5035 Cedar Lake Rd
Apt 5
Oscoda MI 48750

Call Sign: N8ZLN
Doug O Barnowski
417 Chester Rd
Oscoda MI 48750

Call Sign: N8ENU
Gregory M Praiss
7042 Colbath Rd
Oscoda MI 48750

Call Sign: KB8BEA
William T Schultz
1201 Cooke Dam Rd
Oscoda MI 48750

Call Sign: KD8GVL
Daniel D Kimerer
4612 Del Rosa
Oscoda MI 48750

Call Sign: KC8ZWM
Jeffrey A Shue
805 E Bissonette Rd
Oscoda MI 48750

Call Sign: KF8BM
Donald J Stech
6164 F 41 Box 278
Oscoda MI 48750

Call Sign: K8ILJ
Ralph H Ferber
4176 Forest Rd
Oscoda MI 48750

Call Sign: WD6EMR
Robert G Kowalak
4518 Hillcrest Ave
Oscoda MI 48750

Call Sign: WB8WPN
Frank A Schaller
7610 Hillcrest Dr
Oscoda MI 48750

Call Sign: KC8PRQ
Dale E Smith
4775 Kingswood Ln
Oscoda MI 48750

Call Sign: WD8KQD
Donald P Turner
7558 Lakewood Dr
Oscoda MI 48750

Call Sign: K8LJU
Frederick A Van Cleve
6399 Loud Dr
Oscoda MI 487509680

Call Sign: KB8PAL
Marilyn E Van Cleve
6399 Loud Dr
Oscoda MI 487509680

Call Sign: KB8UEA
Donald R Cobley
6793 Loud Dr
Oscoda MI 48750

Call Sign: N0RBN
Danny C Althouse
6938 Loud Dr
Oscoda MI 48750

Call Sign: KA8MZT
Bjorg Garn
7525 Loud Dr
Oscoda MI 48750

Call Sign: KA8VPF
Charles D Stone
4655 Mackenzie
Oscoda MI 48750

Call Sign: KB8ZYY
Raymond H Knuth
4143 Maple Rd
Oscoda MI 487500271

Call Sign: KB8BAM
John Barta
9741-B Massachusetts
St

Oscoda MI 48750

Call Sign: KF8XM
Milton E Abell
5559 Melanie Ln
Oscoda MI 48750

Call Sign: WA8JOI
Raymond J Gasiewicz
3777 N US 23
Oscoda MI 48750

Call Sign: KC8YMX
Iosco County ARES
Races Group
2874 N US Hwy 23
Oscoda MI 48750

Call Sign: KC8QNE
James C Kuerbitz
2874 N US Hwy 23
Oscoda MI 48750

Call Sign: KD8PTB
James S Mcintyre
6176 Norway Rd
Oscoda MI 48750

Call Sign: KC8TXJ
Bruce D Bailey
4531 Oakridge Dr
Oscoda MI 48750

Call Sign: KD8AFY
Joseph A Langan
113 Pack 209
Oscoda MI 48750

Call Sign: KA8ZIN
Thomas A Stalker Jr
4643 River St
Oscoda MI 48750

Call Sign: W8AGK
Frederick F Stewart
6758 Roanoak Rd
Oscoda MI 487508713

Call Sign: KC8YVM
Frederick L Rogel
6815 Roanoak Rd
Oscoda MI 48750

Call Sign: KA9TVP

Marjorie E Mork
5641 Schaeffer St
Oscoda MI 48750

Call Sign: KA9TVO
Forrest J Mork
5641 Schaeffer St
Oscoda MI 48750

Call Sign: KD8PTA
Harvey R Larabell
4589 Shady Ln
Oscoda MI 48750

Call Sign: W8LML
Robert W Sanderson
10201 Tennessee St
Oscoda MI 48750

Call Sign: K8LIN
Richard M Lanz
216 W Michigan Ave
Oscoda MI 48750

Call Sign: N9GBL
James L Cadieux
7050 Wentworth Rd
Oscoda MI 48750

Call Sign: KF6WDA
Robert D Roughley
6010 Westshore Rd
Oscoda MI 48750

Call Sign: KC8CLB
Robert B Zimmerman
4702 Wildflower Ct
Oscoda MI 48750

Call Sign: K8IBE
William B Summers
6613 Woodlea
Oscoda MI 48750

Call Sign: KC8EYM
Nancy E Summers
6613 Woodlea
Oscoda MI 48750

Call Sign: KD8FSD
Clarence David Wright
III
7535 Woodlea Rd W
Oscoda MI 48750

Call Sign: K9GSR
Clarence David Wright
III
7535 Woodlea Rd W
Oscoda MI 48750

Call Sign: KD8HBK
Iosco ARES
Oscoda MI 48750

Call Sign: KC8SUE
Iosco County Amateur
Radio Enthusiast
Oscoda MI 48750

Call Sign: KD8NWG
Gerrilinn F Tepfer
Oscoda MI 48750

FCC Amateur Radio Licenses in Oshtemo

Call Sign: KE8QB
Dennis J Raher
Oshtemo MI 49077

Call Sign: WD8AWV
Robert A Hull
Oshtemo MI 49077

FCC Amateur Radio Licenses in Ossineke

Call Sign: N8RDO
Robert A Crandall
9548 Piper Rd
Ossineke MI 49766

Call Sign: K8BZH
Jay G Baker
6505 US 23 S
Ossineke MI 49766

Call Sign: WA8ENP
Adeline M Baker
6505 US 23 S
Ossineke MI 49766

Call Sign: WB8ZIR
Robert J Colarusso
1001 W Nicholson Hill
Rd

Ossineke MI
497669735

Call Sign: N4AHK
Mack A Proszek
Ossineke MI 49766

Call Sign: KD8PWD
John P Bolen
1998 101st Ave
Otsego MI 49078

Call Sign: KD8SBN
Julie A Buck
2165 101st Ave
Otsego MI 49078

Call Sign: N8DAG
James R McEwen
2007 102nd Ave
Otsego MI 49078

Call Sign: WB8BQX
Harry J Brainard
2377 103rd Ave
Otsego MI 49078

Call Sign: KC8FSS
Gene C Hollon
1852 104th Ave
Otsego MI 49078

Call Sign: KD8MNY
Brandon P Weber
1727 106th Ave
Otsego MI 49078

Call Sign: KD8MNP
Lee A Lancaster
2050 108th Ave
Otsego MI 49078

Call Sign: KB8FMX
Floyd H McEwen
1425 112th St
Otsego MI 49078

Call Sign: KD8PUO
Keith D Cunningham
956 19th St
Otsego MI 49078

Call Sign: WB8HGJ
Melvyn H Hyman
1878 Ames
Otsego MI 49078

Call Sign: KA8BCP
Kenneth R Brown
1362 E 723 Lot 168
Otsego MI 49078

Call Sign: KE4PYP
Larry I Charson
123 E Franklin St
Otsego MI 49078

Call Sign: WB8IHN
Arlene P Magierka
543 E Hammond St
Otsego MI 49078

Call Sign: WB8IHO
Thomas E Magierka
543 E Hammond St
Otsego MI 49078

Call Sign: KA8BRV
Cletus H Ewing
317 Garfield Ave
Otsego MI 49078

Call Sign: N8NGY
Robert A Paradine Sr
216 Helen Ave
Otsego MI 49078

Call Sign: KC8CBV
Keith D Cunningham
1833 Jefferson Rd
Otsego MI 49078

Call Sign: WD8NZD
Christopher L Maley
856 N 16th St
Otsego MI 49078

Call Sign: W8RFQ
Matthew Ogrin
1030 N 16th St
Otsego MI 490789733

Call Sign: KD8OGB
Jacob Belknap
392 Rolling View Dr

Otsego MI 49078

Call Sign: KD8NNP
Jeremy L Belknap
392 Rolling View Dr
Otsego MI 49078

Call Sign: N8RWS
Jeffrey L Belknap
392 Rollingview
Otsego MI 49078

Call Sign: KC8WYJ
Christopher M Harris
Sr
810 S Farmer St Apt 7
Otsego MI 49078

Call Sign: KB8WKB
Donald R Warden
10523 W Ab Ave
Otsego MI 49078

Call Sign: KD8KHT
Dwayne J Bills
239 W Franklin St
Otsego MI 49078

Call Sign: KC8VUY
Elaine K Sheehan
439 W Franklin St
Otsego MI 49078

Call Sign: KC8OZG
William S Simpson
439 W Franklin St
Otsego MI 49078

Call Sign: WD8MBT
Steven R Motter
708 W Franklin St
Otsego MI 49078

Call Sign: AC8RC
Allegan County ARC
708 W Franklin St
Otsego MI 49078

Call Sign: KB8PFJ
Nancy E Motter
708 W Franklin St
Otsego MI 49078

Call Sign: KC8ITU

Allegan County ARC
708 W Franklin St
Otsego MI 49078

Call Sign: KD8FVF
Peter J Blowers
209 W Orleans St
Otsego MI 49078

Call Sign: W8BUX
Peter J Blowers
209 W Orleans St
Otsego MI 49078

Call Sign: AA8L
Peter J Blowers
209 W Orleans St
Otsego MI 49078

Call Sign: WD8RAW
Wayne L Moorlag
530 W Orleans St
Otsego MI 49078

Call Sign: W8DZQ
William F Bibbings
260 Water St
Otsego MI 49078

Call Sign: WB8YJX
Roy H Steunenberg
1573 Wood Lea Dr
Otsego MI 49078

Call Sign: WD8KNW
William N Cool
Otsego MI 49078

Call Sign: KD8BPI
Jack O Buck Jr
Otsego MI 49078

Call Sign: W8PPM
Jack O Buck Jr
Otsego MI 49078

Call Sign: KD8KRU
Richard D Lyon II
Otsego MI 49078

Call Sign: WC8CLI

Clinton County
Amateur Association
2990 Birmingham Rd
Ovid MI 48866

Call Sign: KD8AGP
Cindy L Cosgrove
2990 Birmingham Rd
Ovid MI 48866

Call Sign: KB8QZX
Richard L Cosgrove
2990 Birmingham Rd
Ovid MI 488669664

Call Sign: N8TSK
Mark F Cosgrove
2990 Brimingham Rd
Ovid MI 488669664

Call Sign: KC8ESN
Robert M Dobski Jr
202 E Clinton St
Ovid MI 48866

Call Sign: K8EAG
Gilbert J Cross
7660 Krouse Rd
Ovid MI 48866

Call Sign: KA8YGF
Roy L Elwood Sr
405 McBride Rd
Ovid MI 48866

Call Sign: KB8NOW
Troy D Zell
5221 Meridian Rd
Ovid MI 48866

Call Sign: KA8DEH
Ann M Ferden
1638 N Shepardsville
Rd
Ovid MI 48866

Call Sign: KF8IV
Francis C Ferden
1638 N Shepardsville
Rd
Ovid MI 48866

Call Sign: W8RRW
Francis C Ferden

1638 N Shepardsville
Rd
Ovid MI 48866

Call Sign: KD8DRN
Loren D Hunt
1987 N Warren Rd
Ovid MI 48866

Call Sign: KC5NDA
Jeffery A Swan
212 N West Ct St
Ovid MI 48866

Call Sign: N8ZNG
Patsy A Sheldon
8701 Pond View Dr
Ovid MI 48866

Call Sign: NU8J
Richard P Johnson
3250 S Balcom Rd
Ovid MI 48866

Call Sign: KC8WGX
Dennis G Gunning
1849 S Hollister Rd
Ovid MI 48866

Call Sign: N8EUH
David H Bough
333 W High
Ovid MI 48866

Call Sign: WD8QLG
William J Brooks
6225 W Krouse Rd
Ovid MI 48866

Call Sign: K8QY
Neil D Schultz
9868 W M 21
Ovid MI 48866

Call Sign: ND8S
Neil D Schultz
9868 W M 21
Ovid MI 48866

Call Sign: N8MID
Robby L Elwood
203 W Pearl St
Ovid MI 48866

Call Sign: KD8FUZ
Robert Heinrich
304 W Williams St
Ovid MI 48866

Call Sign: KA8LGW
Howard E Bryant
305 West St
Ovid MI 48866

Call Sign: KI8FR
Paul A Shaw
9200 Wilkinson
Ovid MI 48866

Call Sign: KD8GLL
Marie S Richmond
Ovid MI 488660356

FCC Amateur Radio Licenses in Painesdale

Call Sign: WD8ODQ
Raymond A Bosley Sr
29 Goodell Ave
Painesdale MI 49955

Call Sign: N8PIT
Carl B Olson
15308 Highland St
Painesdale MI 49955

Call Sign: KB8FDA
Donald J Heikkila Sr
42607 Hubbard Ave
Painesdale MI 49955

Call Sign: W8ZDO
Werner R Hartel
Painesdale MI 49955

Call Sign: N8QYB
Richard C Schulze
Painesdale MI 49955

FCC Amateur Radio Licenses in Palmer

Call Sign: WD8CYA
Edwin A Holappa
410 Isabella
Palmer MI 49871

Call Sign: W8EOI
Wilhart R Etelamaki
Isabella Ave
Palmer MI 49871

Call Sign: W8KT
August Erickson Sr
408 Kirkpatrick
Palmer MI 49871

Call Sign: W8HK
John E Lammi
411 Kirkpatrick
Palmer MI 49871

Call Sign: KB8THJ
Michelle M Kemp
203 Kirkpatrick Ave
Palmer MI 498710191

Call Sign: N8FDI
Kenneth E Kemp
203 Kirkpatrick St
Palmer MI 498710191

FCC Amateur Radio Licenses in Paradise

Call Sign: KA8GZD
Gaile F Simpson
Star Rte 48 Box 71A
Paradise MI 49768

Call Sign: KC8RPG
Richard J Erickson
Maple Block Rd
Paradise MI 49768

Call Sign: KA8NLQ
Carl C Clark
8236 N M 123
Paradise MI
497680200

Call Sign: KD8BMV
Gary D Huttenstine
Paradise MI
497680024

Call Sign: KC8RPH
Chris R Lavoy
Paradise MI 49768

Call Sign: KC8AIP
William A Arnold
808 Amsterdam
Parchment MI 49004

Call Sign: KB8RRM
Michael A Guernsey
5217 N 20th
Parchment MI 49004

Call Sign: KD8AJC
James B Newton
4249 Pine Knoll
Parchment MI 49004

Call Sign: WB8MTF
Margaret A Lovins
2480 Summerdale Dr
Parchment MI 49004

Call Sign: ND8V
Michael E Guernsey Sr
2026 Travis Rd
Parchment MI 49004

Call Sign: KZ8O
Michael E Guernsey Sr
2026 Travis Rd
Parchment MI 49004

Call Sign: KC8BUA
Ronald D Larson
1953 W C Ave
Parchment MI
490049342

Call Sign: KC8AND
Diane M Marshall
22480 220th Ave
Paris MI 49338

Call Sign: KC8BZF
Linda L Marshall
22480 220th Ave
Paris MI 49338

Call Sign: KD8FBP

Irene J Kasbohm
23885 23 Mile Rd
Paris MI 49338

Call Sign: WD8NIO
George V Esterle
23870 230th Ave
Paris MI 49338

Call Sign: KC8SIA
Edward T Neubeck
17642 Indian Village
Rd
Paris MI 49338

Call Sign: WA8EZR
Victor N Kidder
401 Lincoln St
Paris MI 49338

Call Sign: KC8BHY
Joni K Blanchard
14167 N Newcosta
Paris MI 49338

Call Sign: KB8ZEQ
Danny D Gramer
14167 N Newcosta
Paris MI 493380046

Call Sign: N8PXP
Richard A Rasmussen
Sr
11375 N Pine Ave
Paris MI 49338

Call Sign: KD8HBF
Big Rapids Area ARC
Paris MI 49338

Call Sign: KD8HBG
Big Rapids Area ARC
Paris MI 49338

Call Sign: KD8ILD
Big Rapids Area ARC
Paris MI 49338

Call Sign: K8FSU
Big Rapids Area ARC
Paris MI 49338

Call Sign: K8MEC
Big Rapids Area ARC

Paris MI 49338

Call Sign: K8OSE
Big Rapids Area ARC
Paris MI 49338

Call Sign: KB8QOI
Big Rapids Area ARC
Paris MI 49338

Call Sign: N8OE
Big Rapids Area ARC
Paris MI 49338

Call Sign: KY8W
William G Camburn
46217 30th St
Paw Paw MI 49079

Call Sign: KC8LLR
Billy G Elmore
46171 34 1/2 St
Paw Paw MI 49079

Call Sign: N8BPH
Clarence B Allgor Jr
39898 35 1/2 St
Paw Paw MI 49079

Call Sign: N8JUQ
Robert K Tompsett
50984 3550 St
Paw Paw MI
490798653

Call Sign: N8DAN
Randall J Hofmeyer
30639 38 Ave
Paw Paw MI 49079

Call Sign: KC8MON
Lois E Richardson
27803 38th Ave
Paw Paw MI 49079

Call Sign: NC8J
John D Richardson
27803 38th Ave
Paw Paw MI 49079

Call Sign: K8DUU

John D Richardson
27803 38th Ave
Paw Paw MI 49079

Call Sign: KC8ALK
Kathy J Hofmeyer
30639 38th Ave
Paw Paw MI 49079

Call Sign: K9PZL
Charles L Uridil
63171 40th St
Paw Paw MI 49079

Call Sign: N8KDO
James J Bos
62252 41st
Paw Paw MI 49079

Call Sign: WD8AWS
Robert L Gaudio
31439 42nd Ave
Paw Paw MI 49079

Call Sign: N8KKL
Stephen D Krefman
70060 42nd St
Paw Paw MI 49079

Call Sign: KE8VJ
Edmond G Jaco Sr
31277 45th Ave
Paw Paw MI 49079

Call Sign: KB8GBC
Carl W Weis
35284 51st Ave
Paw Paw MI 49079

Call Sign: KG8QE
Letitia A Bates
29155 58th Ave
Paw Paw MI 49079

Call Sign: KB8VHO
Neal A Elgersma Sr
52700 Ackley Ter
Paw Paw MI 49079

Call Sign: WE8U
Ronald C Holter
35538 Bellware Blvd
Paw Paw MI 49079

Call Sign: KB8QGH
Gregory J Yost
35678 Bellware Blvd
Paw Paw MI 49079

Call Sign: KD8RMO
Christopher D Yost
35678 Bellware Blvd
Paw Paw MI 49079

Call Sign: KD8HEU
Michael B Wierenga
35760 Bellware Blvd
Paw Paw MI 49079

Call Sign: N7DPM
David P Miller
34259 Bond Dr
Paw Paw MI 49079

Call Sign: KD8QKD
David P Miller
34259 Bond Dr
Paw Paw MI 49079

Call Sign: WB8BGW
Jerome W Miller
55843 Cedar Ln
Paw Paw MI 49079

Call Sign: KB8HMG
Joseph M Soule
40975 CR 358
Paw Paw MI 49079

Call Sign: N8XIQ
John P Szewczyk
50780 CR 653
Paw Paw MI 49079

Call Sign: KD8BLP
Jeff S Whitfield
52555 CR 657
Paw Paw MI 49079

Call Sign: KC8CIE
Timothy B Smith
32210 CR 665
Paw Paw MI 49079

Call Sign: KC8VDK
Nicole L Smith
32210 CR 665
Paw Paw MI 49079

Call Sign: KB8KBU
Gary N Osbon
104 E St Joseph
Paw Paw MI 49079

Call Sign: KD8HYL
Jason T Atteberry
625 Elm St
Paw Paw MI 49079

Call Sign: KD8DRQ
Toshia E Williams
114 Elm St Apt 3
Paw Paw MI 49079

Call Sign: KA8RCQ
Albert M Anthony
56585 Fairway Dr
Paw Paw MI 49079

Call Sign: KC8DPP
Donna A Stahlbaum
39475 Fisk Lake Rd
Paw Paw MI 49079

Call Sign: KC8HVQ
Donald A Stahlbaum
39475 Fisk Lake Rd
Paw Paw MI 49079

Call Sign: K8WMF
William R Russ
725 Hazen St
Paw Paw MI 49079

Call Sign: KD8MZW
Mary E Walters
30245 Hidden Pines
Paw Paw MI 49079

Call Sign: N8FYZ
Jeffrey M Kowalczyk
30245 Hidden Pines
Paw Paw MI
490798557

Call Sign: KC8FBL
Gregory A Smith
43124 M 43 Lot 108
Paw Paw MI 49079

Call Sign: KC8VGB
Jenettia Smith

43124 M 43 Lot 108
Paw Paw MI 49079

Call Sign: KF7BRC
Steven J Cherrone
43124 M 43 Lot 328
Paw Paw MI 49079

Call Sign: KD8RCG
Suzan M Cherrone
43124 M 43 Lot 328
Paw Paw MI 49079

Call Sign: KA8VXQ
Tamara L Kowalczyk
600 N Gremps
Paw Paw MI 49079

Call Sign: N8BSE
Charles E Fross Jr
31592 N M 40
Paw Paw MI
490798519

Call Sign: N8NPH
Carol J Jager
34425 North St
Paw Paw MI 49079

Call Sign: KD8AJF
Robert R Fuentes
69940 Palmer Dr
Paw Paw MI 49079

Call Sign: KB9NUR
James P Nearn
36771 Paw Paw Rd
Paw Paw MI 49079

Call Sign: N8OKS
Michael A Wood
38798 Paw Paw Rd
Paw Paw MI 49079

Call Sign: KC8HHX
Kenneth J Madison
41118 Paw Paw Rd
Paw Paw MI 49079

Call Sign: K8FDX
Kenneth J Madison
41118 Paw Paw Rd
Paw Paw MI 49079

Call Sign: N8OXN
Christina A Krizan
32586 Red Arrow Hwy
Paw Paw MI 49079

Call Sign: N8OXO
Richard W Krizan
32586 Red Arrow Hwy
Paw Paw MI 49079

Call Sign: KB8SOJ
Dennis W Fitzpatrick
610 Ridge Rd
Paw Paw MI
490791707

Call Sign: KR8U
Dennis W Fitzpatrick
610 Ridge Rd
Paw Paw MI
490791707

Call Sign: N8ZFV
Michael A Kolosar
527 River Rd
Paw Paw MI 49079

Call Sign: KC8PCG
Carolyn Ball
58975 S Lagrave Lot 8
Paw Paw MI 49079

Call Sign: KO8J
Donald L Klein
33164 Thelma Ave
Paw Paw MI 49079

Call Sign: N8ZGD
John R Greene
48522 Valley Ct
Paw Paw MI 49079

Call Sign: N8ECS
Judith L Klein
211 Woodman St
Paw Paw MI 49079

Call Sign: KB8YLI
Mary L Lee
Paw Paw MI 49079

Call Sign: KG8QM
James M Lee
Paw Paw MI 49079

Call Sign: W6POK
Hugh R Paul
Paw Paw MI 49079

Call Sign: KC8QFG
Roark Consolatti
Paw Paw MI 49079

Call Sign: N8XJR
Thomas R Koponen
R 1 Box 20
Pelkie MI 49958

Call Sign: KB8VZT
Mari L Koponen
Rte 1 Box 20
Pelkie MI 49958

Call Sign: WA8CZT
Melvin L Velmer
Rte 1 Box 29 Eilola Rd
Pelkie MI 49958

Call Sign: KC8ZNK
Tom J Babbitt
16453 Horoscope Rd
Pelkie MI 49958

Call Sign: W8KQB
Tom J Babbitt
16453 Horoscope Rd
Pelkie MI 49958

Call Sign: KB8VZQ
Timothy J Jurmu
10856 Larson Rd
Pelkie MI 49958

Call Sign: WA8PLA
Ronald W Mantila
501 Mantila Rd
Pelkie MI 49958

Call Sign: KB8YNF
James P Bialas
32461 Naasko Rd
Pelkie MI 49958

Call Sign: KC8SAI
Matt Mikus
11321 Douglas Lake
Rd
Pellston MI 497699137

Call Sign: W8IZS
Thomas M Sorrick
6446 E Main Box 416
Pellston MI 497690416

Call Sign: KC8VIU
Bruce E Emaus
6038 E Robinson Rd
Pellston MI 49769

Call Sign: WA8EFE
Leonard J Miller
371 N Ayr Rd
Pellston MI 497699210

Call Sign: KB8PNX
Andrew V Wasaquam
6118 Pell St
Pellston MI 49769

Call Sign: KC8UKH
Gregory L Specht
39 S Park St
Pellston MI 49769

Call Sign: KF8US
William H Thatcher
375 Townline Rd
Pellston MI 49769

Call Sign: KA8SAT
Frank P Zulski
2625 Zulski Rd
Pellston MI 49769

Call Sign: WB8YDO
Alvin E Grover
6761 Lake St
Pentwater MI
494499662

Call Sign: KA8HZO
Vaughn E Somerville
9557 N Montgomery

Pentwater MI 49449

Call Sign: KA8ZZM
Jane E Somerville
9557 N Montgomery
Pentwater MI 49449

Call Sign: KA9ZDO
Raymond S Hasil
541 N Morris St
Pentwater MI 49449

Call Sign: AA8DT
Marc H Wiener
299 N Wythe
Pentwater MI 49449

Call Sign: N8OCU
Thomas F Sturr
319 Old St Rd
Pentwater MI 49449

Call Sign: WC8A
Leo C Middendorf
1155 Park St
Pentwater MI 49449

Call Sign: KD8NBI
John R Collins
6599 S Lakeshore Dr
Pentwater MI 49449

Call Sign: WD9AKB
Mark E Erenburg
6821 S Mack Rd
Pentwater MI 49449

Call Sign: WI9SAM
Samuel W Morrison
101 S Wythe
Pentwater MI
494490603

Call Sign: KB8WWG
Brock S Deanda
4906 W Birch Ln
Pentwater MI 49449

Call Sign: KB8XA
Jerry C Moser
5008 W Birch Ln
Pentwater MI 49449

Call Sign: N8XQJ

Richard K Schober
1746 W Marrison Rd
Pentwater MI 49449

Call Sign: N8DLU
Eugene S Killian
5285 W Monroe Rd
Pentwater MI 49449

Call Sign: N9AWY
James M Harlan
Pentwater MI 49449

Call Sign: KC8NUR
Antony R Marietta
12388 N 0 1 La
Perkins MI 49872

Call Sign: KC8NEV
Jack M Vantreese
1516 Atkins Rd
Petoskey MI 49770

Call Sign: KD8CNS
William R Dunstan
1018 Atkins St
Petoskey MI 49770

Call Sign: WA8DVD
Dennis A McClure
1120 Autumn Ln
Petoskey MI 49770

Call Sign: N8FPZ
Herman J Stein
149 Balsam
Petoskey MI 49770

Call Sign: N8HBT
Irene Stein
149 Balsam Apt 10
Petoskey MI 49770

Call Sign: KD8CKS
Walker C Van
Wagoner
201 Bayview Ave
Petoskey MI 49770

Call Sign: KA8HGS
Dennis F Hoshield
424 Beech St
Petoskey MI 49770

Call Sign: KC8TU
Richard L Jersey
2768 Berger Rd
Petoskey MI 49770

Call Sign: W8HCS
Russell F Pichlik
904 Blackbird Rd
Petoskey MI 49770

Call Sign: WA8ZQM
Louis Price
11 Bridge St
Petoskey MI 49770

Call Sign: KC8LCI
James F Kargol Jr
4141 Brubaker Rd
Petoskey MI 49770

Call Sign: KO8P
James F Kargol
4141 Brubaker Rd
Petoskey MI 49770

Call Sign: KA8QJJ
Borge R Reimer
4049 Cedar Bluff Dr
Petoskey MI 49770

Call Sign: KB8PNW
Tarreg A Mawari
1316 Cedar Valley Rd
Petoskey MI 49770

Call Sign: KC8LSI
Scott P Burrows
3191 Cedar Valley Rd
Petoskey MI 49770

Call Sign: KC8ZSK
Harley I Vaughan
2274 Cemetery Rd
Petoskey MI 49770

Call Sign: K8AJK
Gerald A Gadowski
7301 Channel Dr

Petoskey MI
497709624

Call Sign: KI8IU
John G Kafer
421 Charlevoix Ave
Petoskey MI 49770

Call Sign: KC8VOD
John W Hall
1142 Charlevoix Ave
Petoskey MI 49770

Call Sign: KC8IFQ
Carol Lynn Dwan
2504 Charlevoix Ave
Petoskey MI 49770

Call Sign: KC8VOC
Margaret A Hall
1142 Charlevoix Ave 6
Petoskey MI 49770

Call Sign: K8GGC
Oliver E Todd Jr
3444 Cliffs Dr
Petoskey MI 49770

Call Sign: N8XUH
Justin R Drenth
3737 Country Club Rd
Petoskey MI 49770

Call Sign: K8HHM
Thomas R Kirk
Curtis Ln Rt 1
Petoskey MI 49770

Call Sign: K8KJP
Arthur V Francis
1755 E Gruler Rd
Petoskey MI 49770

Call Sign: KD8QCC
Charlevoix Cheboygan
Emmet Counties
Public Service
Communication
120 E Lake St
Petoskey MI 49770

Call Sign: KD8QCD
Charlevoix Cheboygan
Emmet Counties

Public Service
Communication
120 E Lake St
Petoskey MI 49770

Call Sign: KB8UII
Sakthi P Vadivel
120 E Lake St
Petoskey MI
497702440

Call Sign: W8BTX
Carlin L Peck
809 E Lake St
Petoskey MI 49770

Call Sign: KG4DXC
Andrew H Teklinski
706 E Mitchell
Petoskey MI 49770

Call Sign: N8ZKF
David B Scott
2068 E Mitchell Apt
C4
Petoskey MI 49770

Call Sign: KA8FAW
Ronald E Beer
2196 E Mitchell Rd
Petoskey MI 49770

Call Sign: KB8ZPG
Richard R Ruffe
1023 Emmet St
Petoskey MI 49770

Call Sign: KD8LVX
Chester M Mitchell
1211 Emmet St
Petoskey MI 49770

Call Sign: KC8WXM
Steven A Sutton
1231 Emmet St
Petoskey MI 49770

Call Sign: KD8BBR
Dawn M Gilmore
1044 Eppler Rd
Petoskey MI 49770

Call Sign: N5GKZ
Michael D Gilmore

1044 Eppler Rd
Petoskey MI 49770

Call Sign: K8RVR
Michael D Gilmore
1044 Eppler Rd
Petoskey MI 49770

Call Sign: N8IZF
Robert P Cook
107 Fulton St
Petoskey MI 49770

Call Sign: KG8JK
Dirk J Esterline
3106 Greenfield Dr
Petoskey MI 49770

Call Sign: W8GQN
Straits Area ARC
3106 Greenfield Dr
Petoskey MI 49770

Call Sign: WD8KBD
Thomas D Swiger
4228 Greenwood
Petoskey MI 49770

Call Sign: WA8AA
Thomas D Swiger
4228 Greenwood
Petoskey MI 49770

Call Sign: W8UMK
Arnold Windmueller
2086 Greenwood Ch
Rd
Petoskey MI 49770

Call Sign: KB8TKC
John K Tillotson
4640 Greenwood
Church Rd
Petoskey MI 49770

Call Sign: KC8AUJ
Stephen W Tillotson
4640 Greenwood
Church Rd
Petoskey MI 49770

Call Sign: KD8ABU
Craig A Schoenith
4596 Greenwood Rd

Petoskey MI 49770

Call Sign: KC8ZSN
James E Schoenith
4596 Greenwood Rd
Petoskey MI 49770

Call Sign: KC8ZLN
Keith J Schoenith
4596 Greenwood Rd
Petoskey MI 49770

Call Sign: KC8ZLO
Luke A Tillotson
4640 Greenwood Rd
Petoskey MI 49770

Call Sign: KD8BSS
Tempest M Tillotson
4640 Greenwood Rd
Petoskey MI 49770

Call Sign: KE8DI
William A Moss
715 Harvey
Petoskey MI 49770

Call Sign: N8LQY
Edward McCune
510 Harvey St
Petoskey MI 49770

Call Sign: N8MWF
Mark S Wieland
6154 Hastings Ave
Petoskey MI 49770

Call Sign: WD8JVQ
Richard E Buckstiegel
1237 Hazelton St
Petoskey MI
497703210

Call Sign: N8FHO
Kent J Cartwright
2415 Hemlock Ln
Petoskey MI 49770

Call Sign: KX8M
Kent J Cartwright
2415 Hemlock Ln
Petoskey MI 49770

Call Sign: WA8HNW

Homer J Moore
575 Hillcrest Ave
Petoskey MI 49770

Call Sign: KC8QMX
Robert E Hoover
4095 Howard Rd
Petoskey MI 49770

Call Sign: KC8TFV
Barbara H Hoover
4095 Howard Rd
Petoskey MI 49770

Call Sign: W8MUB
Raymond W
Kalbfleisch
4832 Howard Rd
Petoskey MI 49770

Call Sign: KC8VXI
John W Felton
107 Howard St 1
Petoskey MI 49770

Call Sign: KD7MZX
Colby M Mckethen
1515 Howard St 313
Petoskey MI 49770

Call Sign: KD8EQX
Dorothy L Felton
107 Howard St Apt 1
Petoskey MI 49770

Call Sign: KD8CYR
Robert L Mclellan
934 Intertown Rd
Petoskey MI 49770

Call Sign: KD8HLH
Jody A Van
Slembrouck
1682 Kemp Rd
Petoskey MI 49770

Call Sign: KC8GWB
Thomas E Hansen
907 Kolinski
Petoskey MI 49770

Call Sign: WB8DYG
James D Glynn

301 Lafayette Ave Apt
F302
Petoskey MI 49770

Call Sign: KD8NVU
Neal R Touran
5136 Lake Grove
Petoskey MI 49770

Call Sign: KC8NTF
Ismael Huerta
1121 Lears Rd Lot 32
Petoskey MI
497709253

Call Sign: KB5DPX
David W Rodgers
1003 Lockwood Ave
Petoskey MI
497703155

Call Sign: KD8HRN
Brent L Woodard
711 Michigan St
Petoskey MI 49770

Call Sign: KA2ZXA
Ronald T Griffin
7450 Mitchel Rd
Petoskey MI 49770

Call Sign: KC8QIG
James J Godzik
309 Monroe St Apt 2
Petoskey MI 49770

Call Sign: W8FF
Maurice C Karriger
3010 Oden Isl Dr
Petoskey MI 49770

Call Sign: W8JMQ
Nancy A Karriger
3010 Oden Isl Dr
Petoskey MI 49770

Call Sign: N8VEK
Linda L Coon
7463 Old US 31 Lot 37
Petoskey MI 49770

Call Sign: WD8ASH
Ricky J Pagel

7463 Old US 31 Lot 42
Bay Shore Est
Petoskey MI 49770

Call Sign: KD8MXI
Bravo 6Bn
372 Orchard Ridge Dr
Petoskey MI 49770

Call Sign: K2CGA
Bravo 6Bn
372 Orchard Ridge Dr
Petoskey MI 49770

Call Sign: KD8MNW
James H Buller
372 Orchard Ridge Dr
Petoskey MI
497708414

Call Sign: K9JHB
James H Buller
372 Orchard Ridge Dr
Petoskey MI
497708414

Call Sign: KD8RHZ
Michael A Sears
1053 Owen Dr
Petoskey MI 49770

Call Sign: KB8TVL
Dennis M Rinock
4608 Pickerel Lake Rd
Petoskey MI 49770

Call Sign: N8OIV
Harry E Leiber Jr
5300 Pickerel Lake Rd
Petoskey MI 49770

Call Sign: KB8QWE
Carol J Leiber
5300 Pickerel Lake Rd
Petoskey MI 49770

Call Sign: N8JXC
Christopher J Conroy
7968 Pickerel Lake Rd
Petoskey MI 49770

Call Sign: KC8FAR
Jerry J Hollopeter

11091 Pickerel Lake
Rd
Petoskey MI 49770

Call Sign: KC8LJU
Patrick E Wilson
10400 Pickrell Lake
Rd
Petoskey MI 49770

Call Sign: KB8ZPD
Dale W Rhea
4104 River Rd
Petoskey MI 49770

Call Sign: KB8YNU
Zachery J Bruin Slot
1916 Roy Rd
Petoskey MI 49770

Call Sign: KD8CYQ
Robert J Still
5990 Rustic
Petoskey MI 49770

Call Sign: K8RJS
Robert J Still
5990 Rustic
Petoskey MI 49770

Call Sign: AL7RV
James E Cook III
3020 School Rd
Petoskey MI 49770

Call Sign: W8RHD
John E Gibes
602 State St
Petoskey MI 49770

Call Sign: KC8KLG
Kurt W Olsen
620 Still Rd
Petoskey MI 49770

Call Sign: KC8PSH
Michael J Sypniewski
7040 Stolt Rd
Petoskey MI 49770

Call Sign: KC8PBL
Joseph P Sypniewski
7040 Stolt Rd
Petoskey MI 49770

Call Sign: KC8PBM
Adam J Sypniewski
7040 Stolt Rd
Petoskey MI 49770

Call Sign: WA8KHB
Kenneth W Dorrien
790 Surrey Ln
Petoskey MI 49770

Call Sign: N8DNX
Charles P Scott
1105 Tall Pines Ct
Petoskey MI 49770

Call Sign: KC8NEW
Janice M Schwinke
1105 Tall Pines Ct
Petoskey MI 49770

Call Sign: KB8QHA
Ricky L Trudell Sr
801 W Sheridan
Petoskey MI 49770

Call Sign: KC8LFC
Thomas R Kullik
143 W Sheridan St
Petoskey MI
497702813

Call Sign: KC8NEY
Robert R Rasmussen
6591 White Tail Ln
Petoskey MI
497708887

Call Sign: N8VKT
Charles A Cigrand
Petoskey MI 49770

Call Sign: KC8GEA
Charles L Cook
Petoskey MI 49770

FCC Amateur Radio
Licenses in Pewamo

Call Sign: KC8FYW
Denise M Schafer
240 N State St
Pewamo MI 48873

Call Sign: N8ZMT
John A Schafer
240 N State St
Pewamo MI 48873

FCC Amateur Radio
Licenses in Pickford

Call Sign: KC8GCI
Vern H Roe
Hc 46 Box 529 A
Pickford MI 49774

Call Sign: KD8IHO
Gordon R Earl
15523 S Riverside Dr
Pickford MI 49774

Call Sign: KC8JLF
Gary B Switzer Sr
19947 S Riverside Dr
Pickford MI 49774

Call Sign: W8KPC
George L Kehoe
20338 S Riverside Dr
Pickford MI 49774

Call Sign: K8YHR
Clyde R Ernst
23190 S Rocky Pt Rd
Pickford MI 49774

Call Sign: N7ZUW
Kimberly D Cummins
23673 SE Bay Rd
Pickford MI 49774

Call Sign: AL7GJ
Virgil L Ball
4974 W Nettleton Ln
Pickford MI
497749171

Call Sign: KC8PSC
Robert L Clawson
Pickford MI 49774

Call Sign: K8OZZ
Robert L Clawson
Pickford MI 49774

Call Sign: KC8PWF
Micheline L Clawson

Pickford MI 49774

FCC Amateur Radio
Licenses in Pierson

Call Sign: KC8IDY
Beverly C Honeysette
21030 McBride Rd
Pierson MI 49339

Call Sign: KE8TS
Robert M Hamlin
3890 Newcosta Rd
Pierson MI 49339

Call Sign: WB8VOQ
John G McNay
21805 Oak Dr
Pierson MI 49339

Call Sign: W8DBE
Robert M Hamlin
3890 W County Line
Rd
Pierson MI 493399501

FCC Amateur Radio
Licenses in Plainwell

Call Sign: KB8FWS
Jeremy I Stoepker
320 106th Ave
Plainwell MI 49080

Call Sign: KB8MZE
Barbara K Cripe
320 106th Ave
Plainwell MI 49080

Call Sign: WB8THO
Mervin R Cripe
320 106th Ave
Plainwell MI 49080

Call Sign: KD8HXC
Walter A Wolf
907 11th St
Plainwell MI 49080

Call Sign: KB8FQJ
Carl T Flickinger
343 12th St Apt 3
Plainwell MI 49080

Call Sign: KD8NPU
Andrew J Flickinger
343 12th St Apt 3
Plainwell MI 49080

Call Sign: KD8LVR
Bruce J Lenardson
445 6th St
Plainwell MI 49080

Call Sign: KD8IYF
Cynthia J Sweeter
590 8th St
Plainwell MI 49080

Call Sign: KB8JZK
Olga L Hulsebus
573 9th St
Plainwell MI 49080

Call Sign: KB8DRB
Georgia L Edgerton
33 Alber Dr
Plainwell MI 49080

Call Sign: KB8SOG
Nicholas R Balcerak
Alber Dr
Plainwell MI 49080

Call Sign: KD8AYF
Scott Corbin
313 Anns Ct
Plainwell MI 49080

Call Sign: K8KUB
Stephen M Kantz
334 Bayview Ln
Plainwell MI 49080

Call Sign: KC8AAD
Timothy L Marsh
226 Colfax St
Plainwell MI 49080

Call Sign: K8JRS
James R Smith
11851 Doster Rd
Plainwell MI 49080

Call Sign: N8OYB
John G Erickson
14300 Doster Rd
Plainwell MI 49080

Call Sign: KA8BVN
Douglas C Sorenson
3342 E B Ave
Plainwell MI
490808904

Call Sign: K1AZL
Paul A Wolfson
323 E Bridge St
Plainwell MI
490801721

Call Sign: KC8BWS
Benjamin J Cance
215 E Plainwell St
Plainwell MI 49080

Call Sign: KC8ORF
Andy J Cance
215 E Plainwell St
Plainwell MI 49080

Call Sign: KC8JSY
Karen P Cance
215 E Plainwell St
Plainwell MI 49080

Call Sign: KG8UO
James E Cance
215 E Plainwell St
Plainwell MI 49080

Call Sign: AB8SF
James E Cance
215 E Plainwell St
Plainwell MI 49080

Call Sign: AB8SD
Karen P Cance
215 E Plainwell St
Plainwell MI 49080

Call Sign: NJ8O
William B Thommes
38 Eagle Greens Ct
Plainwell MI 49080

Call Sign: N8WVI
David B Stein
142 Flora Glynn Dr
Plainwell MI 49080

Call Sign: KD8GTG

Diane L Stein
142 Flora Glynn Dr
Plainwell MI 49080

Call Sign: K8DLS
Diane L Stein
142 Flora Glynn Dr
Plainwell MI 49080

Call Sign: WB8DWO
Carl H Brainard
954 Gainder Rd
Plainwell MI 49080

Call Sign: KF8A
Sven U Bohm
9855 Graham Rd
Plainwell MI 49080

Call Sign: KC8UOZ
James K Berg Jr
602 Hicks St
Plainwell MI 49080

Call Sign: KA8AOE
Eugene S Murphy
329 Highland Ct
Plainwell MI 49080

Call Sign: KD8MCF
Jacob M Steele
360 Horseshoe Ct
Plainwell MI 49080

Call Sign: KC8LPP
Randall S Mac Neil
1214 Keith
Plainwell MI 49080

Call Sign: WA6OUX
Charles A Slocum
367 Kenneth Dr
Plainwell MI 49080

Call Sign: KD8FWE
Terry T Steele
282 Lesa
Plainwell MI 49080

Call Sign: KC8DJG
Brett C Mort
7841 Lindsey
Plainwell MI 49004

Call Sign: KC8DJF
Scott R Corstange
7869 Lindsey
Plainwell MI 49080

Call Sign: KB8SY
Clinton G Williams
8246 Lindsey Rd
Plainwell MI 49080

Call Sign: KC8TSQ
Jennings G Heilig
11250 Longpoint Rd
Plainwell MI 49080

Call Sign: N8UFL
Thomas R Bolf
634 Marsh Rd
Plainwell MI 49080

Call Sign: W8JFU
George R Riley
333 Midlakes Blvd
Plainwell MI 49080

Call Sign: KD8NGI
Gary D Blanchard
10402 N 8th St
Plainwell MI 49080

Call Sign: KB8WJY
Diane L Stein
1188 N Peach Ct
Plainwell MI 49080

Call Sign: KD8JXT
Mcti ARC &
Rehabilitation Services
11611 Pine Lake Rd
Plainwell MI 49080

Call Sign: W8TEC
Mcti ARC &
Rehabilitation Services
11611 Pine Lake Rd
Plainwell MI 49080

Call Sign: KA8CTF
Gregory A McNeil
329 Prince
Plainwell MI 49080

Call Sign: N8XIO
Matthew D Davies

10226 Riverview Dr
Plainwell MI 49080

Call Sign: KD8FLQ
Linda S Burd
224 Russet Dr
Plainwell MI 49080

Call Sign: WB3LHU
Dennis R Burd
224 Russett Dr
Plainwell MI 49080

Call Sign: N8ZUZ
Jeffrey D Waltermire
1022 Taylor Dr
Plainwell MI 49080

Call Sign: KC8QLZ
Sheila A Waltermire
1022 Taylor Dr
Plainwell MI 49080

Call Sign: WD8ENA
Donald L Sutton
10755 W 4 Mile Rd
Plainwell MI 49080

Call Sign: KD5JNX
Marcus L Martin
12215 W 9 Mile Rd
Plainwell MI 49080

Call Sign: KD8CKT
Leon J Caleo Jr
11611 W Pine Lake Rd
664
Plainwell MI 49080

Call Sign: KC8WYT
Nancy N Clark
11611 W Pinelake Rd
Plainwell MI 49080

Call Sign: KD8MCH
Jill E Rantz
418 Walnut Ct
Plainwell MI 49080

FCC Amateur Radio
Licenses in Pointe
Aux Pins

Call Sign: N8NFZ

Serge R Lisk
406 Huron
Pointe Aux Pins MI
49775

Call Sign: WA8WLE
Michael E Radala
Pointe Aux Pins MI
49775

FCC Amateur Radio
Licenses in Port
Sheldon

Call Sign: WB9JSR
John P Wehmer
17277 Rolling Dunes
Dr
Port Sheldon MI 49460

FCC Amateur Radio
Licenses in Portage

Call Sign: WB9JLN
Charles O Jensen
2130 Albatross Ct 1B
Portage MI 49024

Call Sign: N8QOH
James C Cotton
4664 Andover Woods
Ct
Portage MI 49024

Call Sign: KA8LEV
George E Myers
7645 Andrea
Portage MI 49002

Call Sign: KC8FZW
Richard V Medonis
7801 Andrea
Portage MI 49024

Call Sign: KC8FWY
Stephanie M Carlin
10883 Andrews
Portage MI 49002

Call Sign: KA8VKM
Jeff L L Esperance
7406 Angling Rd
Portage MI 49024

Call Sign: KC8YZZ
Shaun M Stecker
1729 Apple St
Portage MI 49002

Call Sign: KD8DLF
Joshua M Trumpie
6077 Applegrove Ln
Portage MI 49024

Call Sign: KA8UQL
Joyce W Johnson
7545 Arborcrest
Portage MI 49002

Call Sign: KB8YVP
Christopher J Bradford
3900 Arbutus Tr
Portage MI 49002

Call Sign: KD8RHC
Albert A Ramudo
7807 Ashton Woods
Dr
Portage MI 49024

Call Sign: KB8PZK
Vernon N Schurter
3545 Austrian Pine
Way 10C
Portage MI 49024

Call Sign: KC8OIM
Sandra J Bender
7125 Austrian Pine
Way 9C
Portage MI 49024

Call Sign: KA8RUO
Richard D Simmer II
718 Bacon Ave
Portage MI 49002

Call Sign: N8DEO
Michael P O Bryan
1525 Bacon Rd Apt 9
Portage MI 49081

Call Sign: KC8JVI
William C Dawson
5249 Bala Cynwyd
Portage MI 49024

Call Sign: KB8SVG

Michael D Burdick
231 Barberry Ave
Portage MI 49002

Call Sign: KD8NAK
Scott A Herron
5280 Barrymore St
Portage MI 49024

Call Sign: KB8JYB
Hollis B Locke III
3834 Biscayne Ave
Portage MI 49002

Call Sign: KB8EQI
Charles E Klinkner
415 Boston
Portage MI 49081

Call Sign: W8KSZ
Norman C Peterson
6738 Bratcher
Portage MI 49024

Call Sign: N8TPG
Donald G Paulsen
5166 Burning Tree
Portage MI 49002

Call Sign: KC8RQP
Stephen M Welsh
4209 Cabot St
Portage MI 49002

Call Sign: KD8DKR
Brian J Kincaid
1231 Carriage Pl
Portage MI 490245730

Call Sign: KD8FFX
Harold A Thomas
7755 Chippewa St
Portage MI 49024

Call Sign: N8HAL
Harold A Thomas
7755 Chippewa St
Portage MI 49024

Call Sign: KD8IHA
Melissa M French
7755 Chippewa St
Portage MI 49024

Call Sign: KD8IGZ
Sheryl L Thomas
7755 Chippewa St
Portage MI 49024

Call Sign: KB8MVG
Alan F Freed
1711 Colchester
Portage MI 49002

Call Sign: N8LPL
Kenneth F Way
311 Colonial
Portage MI 49002

Call Sign: KC8RZ
Walter R Skeels
6600 Constitution Blvd
Apt 414
Portage MI 490248902

Call Sign: KB8RHA
Keri L Schmitt
6833 Cornell
Portage MI 49002

Call Sign: KD8EAO
Thomas R Singer
7367 Cottage Oak Dr
Portage MI 49024

Call Sign: W8TRS
Thomas R Singer
7367 Cottage Oak Dr
Portage MI 49024

Call Sign: KB8HMQ
Robert C Moore
5743 Cranston St
Portage MI 49002

Call Sign: KC8AAH
Amanda M Sielatycki
6803 Cromwell
Portage MI 49002

Call Sign: KC8SSJ
William G Nikitas
6835 Cromwell St
Portage MI 49024

Call Sign: KC8PCH
Mike Ball
4055 Crumps Rd

Portage MI 49002

Call Sign: KC8RJM
Kimberly A Ball
4055 Crumps Rd
Portage MI 49002

Call Sign: KC8WVP
Nathaniel A Enyedi
6390 Cullys Trl
Portage MI 490241775

Call Sign: KD8EMD
Nathaniel A Enyedi
6390 Cullys Trl
Portage MI 490241775

Call Sign: WA8EOV
Peter Bax
7855 Currier Dr
Portage MI 49001

Call Sign: WD8AIA
Hal R Millgard Jr
6719 Cypress St
Portage MI 49024

Call Sign: KB8AOT
John K Adams
8912 Dolphin
Portage MI 49024

Call Sign: KD8DFW
Robert M Hudson
10177 Doves Hollow
Ct
Portage MI 49002

Call Sign: KD8BPW
Michael F Brye
5728 Downing St
Portage MI 49024

Call Sign: WA8EIP
Michael F Brye
5728 Downing St
Portage MI 49024

Call Sign: N8FTZ
Edward L Schumann
809 Dukeshire St
Portage MI 49008

Call Sign: AA8SS

James J Pike Jr
7300 Dunross
Portage MI 49024

Call Sign: WB8RXT
La Monte W Norton
4747 E Milham Apt P
Portage MI 49001

Call Sign: WB8CDT
Robert M Shane
728 E Osterhout Ave
Portage MI 49002

Call Sign: WA8TSN
John D Crago
9728 E Shore Dr
Portage MI 490027482

Call Sign: KC8AAC
Vilnis Sulcs
3109 E T Ave
Portage MI 49002

Call Sign: W9MTX
Stafford H Thomas
7815 Elk St
Portage MI 49002

Call Sign: KD8RHF
Antony A Low
4613 Fox Valley Dr
Apt 1A
Portage MI 49024

Call Sign: K8AAL
Antony A Low
4613 Fox Valley Dr
Apt 1A
Portage MI 49024

Call Sign: KC8LZN
Phillip E Sanders
4807 Foxfire Trl
Portage MI 49024

Call Sign: KG8HN
John J O Keefe
5010 Garden Rd
Portage MI 49002

Call Sign: KD8BYI
Joe A Wall
711 Gladys St Apt 1A

Portage MI 49002

Call Sign: WD8IDJ
Donald R Eikhoff
5826 Grand Traverse
Ln
Portage MI 49002

Call Sign: KA8POB
Kathryn M Eikhoff
5826 Grand Traverse
Ln
Portage MI 49024

Call Sign: KC8TQM
Phillip T Eikhoff
5826 Grand Traverse
Ln
Portage MI 49024

Call Sign: KB8NMZ
Paul J Bruneau
1918 Greenbriar Dr
Portage MI 49024

Call Sign: NP2F
Blair S Balden
1734 Greenbriar Dr
Portage MI 49024

Call Sign: KC8EPO
Leroy Klose III
7706 Hampton Oaks
Dr
Portage MI 49024

Call Sign: AB8YQ
Leroy Klose III
7706 Hampton Oaks
Dr
Portage MI 49024

Call Sign: NX9D
Helmut S Bader
2205 Hemlock Ave
Portage MI 490241105

Call Sign: KC8JSL
Laura L Gifford
2223 Hemlock Ave
Portage MI 49024

Call Sign: N8EG
Eric M Gifford

2223 Hemlock Ave
Portage MI 490241105

Call Sign: KB8SJS
Abner D Doubleday
1709 Henley Ave
Portage MI 490242537

Call Sign: K8DCD
David C Doubleday
1709 Henley Ave
Portage MI 490242537

Call Sign: WB8TNN
James D Steffey
6825 Hickory Point Dr
W
Portage MI 49002

Call Sign: N8GOK
William E Hamlin
2601 Hillanbrook Dr
Portage MI 49008

Call Sign: N8UXY
Ronald W Kelley
2916 Hillanbrook Dr
Portage MI 49024

Call Sign: N8OKP
Robert W Richards
5914 Iowa Ave
Portage MI 49002

Call Sign: KB8YVQ
Brian K Perry
6727 Isabelle
Portage MI 49002

Call Sign: KG8PQ
Geoffrey M Miller
1397 Jennifer St
Portage MI 49024

Call Sign: KB8OAY
Kimberly J Larson
1435 Jennifer St
Portage MI 49024

Call Sign: KC8YKE
Richard J Hewitt
2732 Kalarama Ave
Portage MI 49024

Call Sign: K8DHN
Richard J Hewitt
2732 Kalarama Ave
Portage MI 49024

Call Sign: KX8L
Ernest P Mullinax
7996 Kenmure Dr
Portage MI 49024

Call Sign: N8EIC
Betty L Mullinax
7996 Kenmure Dr
Portage MI 49024

Call Sign: KC8AAJ
Levi D Boldt
6755 Keystone
Portage MI 49002

Call Sign: WB8MPA
Raymond A Liby
809 Lakeview Dr
Portage MI 49002

Call Sign: WD8NTW
Donald W Garthe
1123 Lakeview Dr
Portage MI 49081

Call Sign: KC0UZC
Aaron G Gruber
1408 Lakeview Dr
Portage MI 49002

Call Sign: WG8V
Patrick T Kulikowski
7830 Lakewood Dr
Portage MI 49002

Call Sign: KB8WAO
Jack W Cotton
428 Landsdowne
Portage MI 490015533

Call Sign: KC8ZTJ
John M Mathieson
1926 Lauralwood
Portage MI 49002

Call Sign: AC8JW
John M Mathieson
1926 Lauralwood
Portage MI 49002

Call Sign: KB8OAX
Janet A Tucker
2024 Lauralwood
Portage MI 49002

Call Sign: WB8ZVV
John D Tucker
2024 Lauralwood Ave
Portage MI 49002

Call Sign: KC8NDL
Daniel A Tucker
2024 Laurel Wood
Portage MI 49002

Call Sign: KB8TDU
Michael G Blodgett
361 Lawton Ct
Portage MI 49024

Call Sign: KB4UAZ
Molly A Carrico
7296 Leawood St
Portage MI 49024

Call Sign: KB8UAZ
Molly A Carrico
7296 Leawood St
Portage MI 49024

Call Sign: KD8NNZ
Jonathan E Orweller
4607 Lexington Ave
Portage MI 49002

Call Sign: N8MOM
Lawrence A Thomas
10233 Lloy St
Portage MI 49002

Call Sign: KC8EDG
Emily A Tower
7535 Mac Arthur Ln
Portage MI 49002

Call Sign: NC8O
Sam Kurlandsky
5124 Maple Ridge Dr
Portage MI 49024

Call Sign: N8CCE
Melvin G Marsley
415 Marigold

Portage MI 49002

Call Sign: KC8NLO
Gerald D Carpenter II
4205 Monroe Ave
Portage MI 49002

Call Sign: KD8EKW
Gary L Kamrowski
5717 Mt Vernon
Portage MI 49024

Call Sign: WA8WJO
Gary L Kamrowski
5717 Mt Vernon
Portage MI 49024

Call Sign: KD8RKP
Robert W Forgey
3109 Muirfield Dr
Portage MI 49024

Call Sign: KD8RHE
Robert D Van Hover
5606 Oakland Dr
Portage MI 49024

Call Sign: KC0DWU
Samuel D Borrello
7296 Oakland Dr
Portage MI 490244100

Call Sign: W8UH
Joseph A Borrello
7296 Oakland Dr
Portage MI 490244100

Call Sign: W8SEY
Wayne C Roe
7330 Oakland Dr
Portage MI 49024

Call Sign: KB8VGE
Cindy S Givens
10632 Oakland Dr
Portage MI 49002

Call Sign: KB8VGZ
Leon L Givens
10632 Oakland Dr
Portage MI 49002

Call Sign: WA8WZN
Dick A Lovins

8790 Oakland Hills Cir
Portage MI 49024

Call Sign: N8NOR
Kenneth D Mac Leod
1529 Orchard Dr
Portage MI 490025637

Call Sign: KC8OGP
Jimmie D Ball
10357 Periwinkle
Portage MI 49024

Call Sign: KD8SAX
Jim J West
1910 Pleasant Dr
Portage MI 49002

Call Sign: KB8RFT
Joseph S Whisman
723 Rainbow Ave
Portage MI 49002

Call Sign: KC8JSJ
Ronald H Franklin
2110 Ramona Ave
Portage MI 49002

Call Sign: KC8DEK
Lei Ditch
7545 Ravenswood Dr
Portage MI 49002

Call Sign: KD8JSG
Edward J Knauss
2816 Rolling Hill Ave
Portage MI 49024

Call Sign: KC8SPU
Richard O Purk
1504 Romence
Portage MI 49024

Call Sign: KB8CRT
Mindy M Tai
1620 Romence Rd
Portage MI 49024

Call Sign: WD8AXA
Charles D Agosti
1723 Romence Rd
Portage MI 49024

Call Sign: N8QHZ

Vicki J Locke
2627 Romence Rd
Portage MI 490244009

Call Sign: WB8ALW
Hollis B Locke II
2627 Romence Rd
Portage MI 490244009

Call Sign: NK8X
Arthur G Snapper
5326 S 12th St
Portage MI 49024

Call Sign: KC8QXZ
James W Johnston
6178 S 12th St
Portage MI 49024

Call Sign: KC8QYA
Jerilyn F Johnston
6178 S 12th St
Portage MI 49024

Call Sign: K8JWJ
James W Johnston
6178 S 12th St
Portage MI 49024

Call Sign: K8JFJ
Jerilyn F Johnston
6178 S 12th St
Portage MI 49024

Call Sign: W8XQ
J D Wilder
7589 S 12th St
Portage MI 49024

Call Sign: WA2CWU
Thomas V Oram
Proudfoot
7731 S 12th St
Portage MI 49024

Call Sign: KB8WAQ
Mary K Derr
643 S Evergreen St
Portage MI 49002

Call Sign: AC6QX
Matthew D Jensen
9844 S Sprinkle Rd
Portage MI 49002

Call Sign: WA8WVV
Everett L Floyd
10546 S Westnedge
Portage MI 49002

Call Sign: W8RUS
James O Stewart
10075 S Westnedge
Ave
Portage MI 49002

Call Sign: K8WGN
Scott A Herron
6749 S Westnedge Ave
Ste K 101
Portage MI 49002

Call Sign: KC8KVP
Ron E Marzett
6749 S Westwedge
Apt K 277
Portage MI 49002

Call Sign: KC8FMS
Anthony M Gettig
10721 Schuur St
Portage MI 49024

Call Sign: N6JHN
Larry H Hulsebos
1402 Sherry Dr
Portage MI 49002

Call Sign: AA8BF
Wray I Marshall
6745 Shoreham Ave
Portage MI 49002

Call Sign: KD8HPF
Amy S Houghtaling
6343 Silver Fir St
Portage MI 49024

Call Sign: NU8N
Bryan E Garfoot
3255 Stonebridge Ct 8
Portage MI 49931

Call Sign: KC8KEG
Richard A Van Trease
4278 Suffield Woods
Ave
Portage MI 490025888

Call Sign: KD8AHA
Kathryn L Ankenbauer
6574 Sunburst Dr
Portage MI 49024

Call Sign: KB1IMF
Thomas G Ankenbauer
6574 Sunburst Dr
Portage MI 49024

Call Sign: KD8EBU
Melvin D Freeland
2621 Tall Trees Dr
Portage MI 49024

Call Sign: N8ZUV
Michael R Miller
2825 Tall Trees Dr
Portage MI 490246686

Call Sign: K8AZO
Michael R Miller
2825 Tall Trees Dr
Portage MI 490246686

Call Sign: K8KCX
Dan A Van Loo
1720 Tamfield
Portage MI 49002

Call Sign: KC8VGC
Thomas M Bennett
1201 Tanglewood Dr
Portage MI 49024

Call Sign: KB8YRZ
Richard C Fenner
1927 Thrushwood Ave
Portage MI 49002

Call Sign: KA8RWK
John C Ongley
8620 Tozer Ln
Portage MI 49081

Call Sign: N8UGD
Matthew P Robbins
6511 Trotwood
Portage MI 49024

Call Sign: KC8CYM
Gerald F Kimble Sr
4128 Twin Ter

Portage MI 49002

Call Sign: KC8ATF
Em Ward
1715 Valleywood Ct 3
Portage MI 490025248

Call Sign: KA8TGK
Marinus P Van Brugge
3130 Vanderbilt Rd
Portage MI 490246062

Call Sign: W8OPA
Marinus P Van Brugge
3130 Vanderbilt Rd
Portage MI 490246062

Call Sign: KD8PUP
Bruce L Billedeaux
7697 Vernard Cir
Portage MI 49024

Call Sign: KC8OQN
Ryan L Cousins
525 Victoria Ct 6
Portage MI 49024

Call Sign: KB8RXS
John A Spaeth
8329 W Long Lake Dr
Portage MI 49002

Call Sign: KC9IUD
Rachel L Johnston
235 W Melody Ave
Portage MI 49024

Call Sign: N8URJ
Sandra Wood
108 W Osterhout
Portage MI 49024

Call Sign: N8GYN
Theresa J Wegner
108 W Osterhout Rd
Portage MI 490247381

Call Sign: N8GYO
David C Wegner
108 W Osterhout Rd
Portage MI 490247381

Call Sign: N8URL
Janet M Vantilburg

5198 W Valley Cir
Portage MI 49002

Call Sign: KC8HKG
Ronald G Harrington
505 W Van Hoesen
Blvd
Portage MI 49024

Call Sign: N4INU
Albert P D Errico
715 W Vanhoesen
Portage MI 49024

Call Sign: W2INU
Marilyn F D Errico
715 W Vanhoesen
Portage MI 49024

Call Sign: KC8FGU
Dave E Seitz
3816 Wedgwood
Portage MI 49024

Call Sign: KC8FHD
Jeannette C Seitz
3816 Wedgwood
Portage MI 49024

Call Sign: AD4UR
Benjamin P Vlug
10312 Westminster St
Portage MI 49002

Call Sign: N8IIO
Preston M Givens Jr
6417 Westshire St
Portage MI 49024

Call Sign: KD8AJE
Barry H Vanderweele
6538 Westshire St
Portage MI 49024

Call Sign: KD8TH
Michael Eady
7635 Whispering
Brook Apt B16
Portage MI 49002

Call Sign: KD8IFH
Michael Eady
7635 Whispering
Brook Apt B16

Portage MI 49024

Call Sign: KD8KRW
Raymond A Gabriel
Ojo
7590 Whispering
Brook Dr Apt A3
Portage MI 49024

Call Sign: WD8NRG
James R Miyagawa
1529 Woodland Dr
Portage MI 490244133

Call Sign: KA8ZUK
Romeo E Phillips
5132 Woodmont Dr
Portage MI 49002

Call Sign: KB8CUK
Arthur J H Phillips
5132 Woodmont Dr
Portage MI 49002

Call Sign: K8KZO
Southwestern
Michigan Ama Rad
Team
Portage MI 49081

Call Sign: KE4MET
Andrew D Galo III
Portage MI 49081

Call Sign: WB8IKJ
Kenneth R Appleman
Portage MI 49081

Call Sign: WB8RWV
Lynn D Clark
Portage MI 49081

Call Sign: KD8HDB
Sharon L Dekorte
White
Portage MI 49081

Call Sign: WB8NNI
Archie W Keyes
Portage MI 490241287

FCC Amateur Radio
Licenses in Portland

Call Sign: KD8DVV
H Michael Pierce
535 Church St
Portland MI
488751009

Call Sign: K8VEB
William R Sherman
13701 Clintonia Rd
Portland MI 48875

Call Sign: KC8FJW
John W Leyrer
6330 Divine Hwy
Portland MI 48875

Call Sign: W8VJW
John W Leyrer
6330 Divine Hwy
Portland MI 48875

Call Sign: KD8IZR
Charles J Shawnee Jr
7954 E Grand River
Ave
Portland MI 48875

Call Sign: KB8GVE
Thomas E Simmons
103 East St
Portland MI 48875

Call Sign: KC8JRM
Bryan N Gehrcke
7136 Friend Rd
Portland MI 48875

Call Sign: WD8BOX
Steven D Kelley
11815 Grand River
Ave
Portland MI 48875

Call Sign: WB8VKL
Raymond H Wardwell
8233 Grand River Trl
Portland MI
488759402

Call Sign: K9IUF
William D Brossmann
10854 Grand River Trl
Portland MI 48875

Call Sign: KD8LPG
Keith A Thibeault
238 Hill St
Portland MI 48875

Call Sign: KA5GST
Wayne N Hyland
815 Kent St
Portland MI 48875

Call Sign: KA5HBL
Dolores M Hyland
815 Kent St
Portland MI 48875

Call Sign: W8JIK
Richard S De Mello
536 Lyons Rd
Portland MI 48875

Call Sign: WA8RD
Ward J McGinnis
937 Lyons Rd
Portland MI 48875

Call Sign: N8EUQ
Michael F Manning
311 N West St
Portland MI
488751159

Call Sign: K8TLC
Ronald J Blakeman
9117 Peake Rd
Portland MI
488759428

Call Sign: KA8VMM
Mark D Haworth
9194 Peake Rd
Portland MI 48875

Call Sign: K8TES
Thomas E Simmons
103 S East St
Portland MI 48875

Call Sign: AB8RX
Roger A Barnhill
12641 Turner Rd
Portland MI 48875

Call Sign: W8UN
Daryl H Kiebler

Portland MI 48875

Call Sign: WB8YIG
Edward E Teckman
14965 Bolton Rd
Posen MI 497769724

Call Sign: KD8OIM
Kenneth J Ciarkowski
9543 Polaski Rd
Posen MI 49776

Call Sign: KA8TLC
James F Stoddard
4499 E Gresham Hwy
Potterville MI 48876

Call Sign: N8MVJ
Rodney D Parks
117 Elizabeth Way
Potterville MI 48876

Call Sign: W8SWR
Rodney D Parks
117 Elizabeth Way
Potterville MI 48876

Call Sign: N8EUZ
Harold A Degner
4723 Hartel Rd Lot 34
Potterville MI 48876

Call Sign: KD8OOS
Matthew T Miller
4613 Llama Ln
Potterville MI 48876

Call Sign: WD8RCF
Dennis G Little
121 N Church St
Potterville MI 48876

Call Sign: KD8EXU
Michael E Bockrath
3802 Nixon Rd
Potterville MI 48876

Call Sign: KC8FQD

Aaron D Parks
4784 Pine Hill Dr
Potterville MI 48876

Call Sign: WB8GEG
Allen J West
242 S Church St
Potterville MI 48876

Call Sign: KD8CCY
Michael J Larson
225 W Vermontville
Hwy
Potterville MI 48876

Call Sign: KC8QWG
Scott B Tickner
5765 Windsor Hwy
Potterville MI 48876

Call Sign: K8SBT
Scott B Tickner
5765 Windsor Hwy
Potterville MI 48876

Call Sign: KC8TFQ
Sandy K Tickner
5765 Windsor Hwy
Potterville MI 48876

Call Sign: WD8AFM
Aaron J St John
W 4024 Quarry Rd
Powers MI 49874

Call Sign: N8HMM
James E Christie
3977 Barbra Dr
Prescott MI 48756

Call Sign: WD8BIO
Ford F La Pointe
5525 Cranberry
Prescott MI 48756

Call Sign: KD8FQE
Kathryn L David

1935 Henderson Lake
Rd
Prescott MI 48756

Call Sign: KB8HIO
Valerie A Ernest
2172 Lake View Ave
Prescott MI 48756

Call Sign: KB8VOT
Dan P Ernest
2172 Lakeview Ave
Prescott MI 48756

Call Sign: KC8JIJ
William G Hroba
2321 Peterson Rd
Prescott MI 48756

Call Sign: AB8BU
Dale E Mondeau
5049 Turner Pine Dr
Prescott MI 48756

Call Sign: WB8YXX
Kay A Mitchell
510 W Harrison
Prescott MI 48756

Call Sign: WB8UJB
Robert W Mitchell
510 W Harrison
Prescott MI 487569123

Call Sign: KC8QND
Richard D Beattie
4076 William S Dr
Prescott MI 48756

Call Sign: AB8YG
Richard D Beattie
4076 William S Dr
Prescott MI 48756

Call Sign: KC8VUZ
Ogemaw Arenac ARS
Prescott MI 48756

Call Sign: K8OAR
Ogemaw Arenac ARS
Prescott MI 48756

Call Sign: KD8AXA
Alexander H Smith

Prescott MI 48756

Call Sign: AC8BG
Alexander H Smith
Prescott MI 48756

FCC Amateur Radio Licenses in Prescott Isle

Call Sign: KD8FQM
Robert A Carr
16531 Bay Height Dr
Presque Isle MI 49777

Call Sign: KG8WD
John L Douglas
7120 Belfair Dr
Presque Isle MI 49777

Call Sign: KC8WUK
John L Campbell
10213 Maple St
Presque Isle MI 49777

Call Sign: N8YDY
Thomas R Le Monds
17761 Pineview Dr
Presque Isle MI 49777

Call Sign: WA8EUD
John M Porter
16216 Renwick Cir W
Presque Isle MI 49777

Call Sign: KB7IPT
Kathleen P Vidoni
15876 Spruce Dr
Presque Isle MI
497778707

Call Sign: KB4L
Daniel E Fitch
6128 Timberway Ct
Presque Isle MI
497770003

Call Sign: KD8OOO
James A Mendham Sr
24055 US 23 Hwy S
Presque Isle MI 49777

Call Sign: WB8THB
James M Mendham

24055 US 23 S
Presque Isle MI 49777

Call Sign: N8YNB
Greg F Mulka Jr
6620 Whitesand Dr
Presque Isle MI 49777

Call Sign: KB8RQP
Gregory A Mulka Sr
6620 Whttesand Dr
Presque Isle MI 49777

FCC Amateur Radio Licenses in Princeton

Call Sign: W8CYA
Ryan C Foster
2110 W Horseshoe
Lake Dr
Princeton MI 49841

FCC Amateur Radio Licenses in Prudenville

Call Sign: KB8L
Philip D Freebold
345 Bright Angel Dr
Prudenville MI 48651

Call Sign: N8BNS
Barbara J Freebold
345 Bright Angel Dr
Prudenville MI 48651

Call Sign: KF8UR
Cynthia J Brown
105 Deer Run Blvd
Prudenville MI 48651

Call Sign: WF8R
Mark L Marsh
105 Deer Run Blvd
Prudenville MI 48651

Call Sign: KD8LBQ
Sharon R Marsh
105 Deer Run Blvd
Prudenville MI 48651

Call Sign: KC8NNW
Royal N Waltz
505 Deer Run Blvd

Prudenville MI 48651

Call Sign: ND8D
Michael E Kenley Sr
857 Deer Run Blvd
Prudenville MI 48651

Call Sign: N8AWH
Vahan Kapagian
325 Hawthorne Ranch
Rd
Prudenville MI 48651

Call Sign: N8POR
Diana L Kapagian
325 Hawthorne Ranch
Rd
Prudenville MI 48651

Call Sign: KB5HVO
Donna M Detmer
607 Houghton View
Dr
Prudenville MI 48651

Call Sign: N8LCO
Gary J Bosnak
133 Indian Oaks Trl
Prudenville MI 48651

Call Sign: AB8NM
Gary J Bosnak
133 Indian Oaks Trl
Prudenville MI 48651

Call Sign: KB8DPT
Dorman J Holder
507 Iroquois Ave
Prudenville MI 48651

Call Sign: KG8MZ
Shawn J Sellen
581 Lake James Dr
Prudenville MI 48651

Call Sign: KC8INU
Richard S Dupon
102 Northland Dr
Prudenville MI 48651

Call Sign: K8QFS
Robert S Hicks
115 Tuscaroras Trl
Prudenville MI 48651

Call Sign: KC8PKJ
Michael F Currie
131 Valley Ave
Prudenville MI 48651

Call Sign: KC8PRR
Ellen L Currie
131 Valley Ave
Prudenville MI 48651

Call Sign: W8HFZ
Ronald M Baker
115 Valley Dr
Prudenville MI 48651

Call Sign: W8MCE
Walter W Konrad
102 Vegas Ct
Prudenville MI 48651

Call Sign: KA8DKS
Edwin A Lumley
207 Widdis Dr
Prudenville MI
486519569

Call Sign: N8IIR
Agnes S Sear
Prudenville MI 48651

Call Sign: N8OLA
Leonard Sear
Prudenville MI 48651

Call Sign: KC8PWL
Barry J Fisher
Prudenville MI
486510921

Call Sign: K8TKF
Barry J Fisher
Prudenville MI
486510921

Call Sign: N8DAD
Barry J Fisher
Prudenville MI
486510921

FCC Amateur Radio Licenses in Pullman

Call Sign: KC8DSE

Terry R Davis
5778 108th Ave
Pullman MI 49450

Call Sign: K8AJD
Kenneth L Mills
4708 112th Ave
Pullman MI 49450

Call Sign: K8PMN
Patrick M Nolan
952 4th St
Pullman MI 49450

Call Sign: KG8K
John S Braunz
1218 60th St
Pullman MI
494509777

Call Sign: KM8E
June A Braunz
1218 60th St Rt 1
Pullman MI 49450

Call Sign: KB8RRL
Gregory P Sisson
921 64th St
Pullman MI 49450

Call Sign: N8ZXF
Stephen P Leach
Oak Haven 52 St
Pullman MI 49450

Call Sign: KC8ZEM
Dustin L Kellogg
Pullman MI 49450

Call Sign: KC8ZTO
Sasha M Kellogg
Pullman MI 49450

Call Sign: KC8TRN
Benjamin M Miller
180 Brocklebank Rd
Quincy MI 49082

Call Sign: N8TID
Gerald B Whitney Sr
1092 Burbank Rd

Quincy MI 49082

Call Sign: N8WOF
Dianne E Schlueter
182 Castlepine
Quincy MI 490829592

Call Sign: KA8OLT
Richard L Schlueter
182 Castlepine Dr
Quincy MI 49082

Call Sign: W8ARM
Philip W Sattler
690 Clarendon
Quincy MI 490829477

Call Sign: KD8CYW
Jan E Hayden
979 Clarendon Rd
Quincy MI 490829467

Call Sign: N8QCT
Gordon J Phair Jr
882 Craft Rd
Quincy MI 49082

Call Sign: KC8EIB
Daniel L Dickerson
103 Crockett Dr
Quincy MI 49082

Call Sign: KC8PRM
Donald G Cook
442 Doris St
Quincy MI 49082

Call Sign: KB8JAZ
Donald A Michael
61 E Chicago St
Quincy MI 49082

Call Sign: KD8HLQ
Larry D Ware
1225 E Chicago St
Quincy MI 49082

Call Sign: AC8GD
Larry D Ware
1225 E Chicago St
Quincy MI 49082

Call Sign: KA8MQK
Clarence E Lenon

206 Lakeside Dr
Quincy MI 49082

Call Sign: KC8ZFR
David L Smith
277 Lakeside Dr
Quincy MI 49082

Call Sign: KC8ATC
Janice E Kubiac
129 Lukesport Dr
Quincy MI 49082

Call Sign: KB8VWI
William H Kubiac
129 Lukesport Dr
Quincy MI 49082

Call Sign: KC8IWW
Mark A Eifrid
48 Miller Dr
Quincy MI 490829743

Call Sign: KB8IYO
Jeanne A Asher
465 N Ridge Rd
Quincy MI 49082

Call Sign: KB8IYP
Jo Ellen A Asher
465 N Ridge Rd
Quincy MI 49082

Call Sign: WD8ARD
Ronald D Smith
416 Potter Rd
Quincy MI 490829700

Call Sign: N7VEY
Eugene G Hesse
1065 Quincy Grange
Rd
Quincy MI 49082

Call Sign: KD8NVC
Brenton Allen
7 W Jefferson St
Quincy MI 49082

Call Sign: KA8MMY
Norrita L Geiman
49 W Jefferson St
Quincy MI 49082

Call Sign: WA8HMG
Edgar D Geiman
49 W Jefferson St
Quincy MI 49082

Call Sign: W8URR
F Gordon Adams
1025 Wildwood Rd
Quincy MI 49082

Call Sign: KD8GHG
Roger A Aho
855 Christine Ct
Quinnesec MI 49876

Call Sign: WB8EBS
Burton W Armbrust Sr
693 Cliff St
Quinnesec MI 49876

Call Sign: KC8TWG
Robert J Uren
849 Colleen Cir Dr
Quinnesec MI 49876

Call Sign: KB8FJI
William L Recla
1030 Division St Box
856
Quinnesec MI 49876

Call Sign: KB0OSW
Scott R Blackberg
1214 Lake Ave
Quinnesec MI 49876

Call Sign: KC8VC
Meyer M Wolfe
4775 Lincoln
Quinnesec MI 49876

Call Sign: N8RSD
Kathleen D Wolfe
4775 Lincoln St
Quinnesec MI 49876

Call Sign: KC8TG
David X Zazeski

141 Main St
Ramsay MI 49959

Call Sign: N9EZ
John A Forslund
N10275 Spring St
Ramsay MI 49959

FCC Amateur Radio Licenses in Rapid City

Call Sign: KG6HBV
Vern E White
7195 Aarwood Trl NW
Rapid City MI 49676

Call Sign: KD8KCO
Mark W Width
8067 Aarwood Trl NW
Rapid City MI 49676

Call Sign: KC8VSU
Toby S Way
12839 Bussa Rd
Rapid City MI 49676

Call Sign: K2MHE
Lawrence E Mitchell
6524 Crystal Beach Rd
Rapid City MI 49676

Call Sign: W1TYQ
Victor L Crawford
9566 Fowler Ln
Rapid City MI 49676

Call Sign: KB8PWU
Edward D Jenney
3721 Morrison Rd NW
Rapid City MI 49676

Call Sign: W8THH
Harold R Dewey
9830 Rapid City Rd
NW
Rapid City MI 49676

Call Sign: W8DDN
Harold E Wilke
10495 W Torch Lake
Dr
Rapid City MI 49676

Call Sign: KD8BZQ
Douglas P Strong
6964 Walker Rd
Rapid City MI 49676

FCC Amateur Radio Licenses in Rapid River

Call Sign: WA8JWP
Lawrence H Blahnik
7960 30th Rd
Rapid River MI 49878

Call Sign: KA5JEM
Carl E Person
8099 30th Rd
Rapid River MI 49878

Call Sign: WB5WRD
Penelope L Person
8099 30th Rd
Rapid River MI 49878

Call Sign: WA8MDI
Robert J Utterback
9919 Bay Shore Dr
Rapid River MI 49878

Call Sign: KD8FWI
Michael C Racine
8547 CR 509 Y Rd
Rapid River MI 49878

Call Sign: KD8MCR
Michael C Racine
8547 CR 509 Y Rd
Rapid River MI 49878

Call Sign: KA8JZX
Phyllis A Belongie
6292 Mirons 16 8 Ln
Rapid River MI 49878

Call Sign: KD6ASN
Daniel J Beggs
8808 N Lakeside T 5
Dr
Rapid River MI 49878

Call Sign: N8ITH
Timothy B Smigowski
10717 Q 5 Ln
Rapid River MI 49878

Call Sign: K8TNZ
Allen F Salmi
10637 Q5 Ln
Rapid River MI 49878

Call Sign: KB8HMX
Brad A Salmi
10637 Q5 Ln
Rapid River MI 49878

Call Sign: WD8BVO
Robert R Simonson
10727 S 75 Rd
Rapid River MI 49878

Call Sign: WB8IGP
Edward N Belland
8605 S Lakeside T 5
Dr
Rapid River MI 49878

Call Sign: K8GWY
William J Arnold
7399 Sunset Ln
Rapid River MI 49878

Call Sign: KB8FCT
George J Holzworth
7249 Twin Springs Pk
20 5 Ln
Rapid River MI 49878

Call Sign: KA8PCF
Lisa M Blau
7417 Twin Springs Rd
20 5 Ln
Rapid River MI 49878

Call Sign: ND8X
Mark E Blau
7417 Twin Springs Rd
20 S Ln
Rapid River MI 49878

Call Sign: WB2MFO
Lorne J Davey Sr
10526 U 25 Rd
Rapid River MI 49878

Call Sign: WB8WAJ
Dwight A Cochran
9151 U 5 Ln
Rapid River MI 49878

Call Sign: N8JWT
Todd B Berg
10244 US 2
Rapid River MI 49878

Call Sign: KA8IHR
Dwight H Seger
11297 US 41 Sunny
Brook Ln
Rapid River MI 49878

Call Sign: N8IPU
Christopher C Parrett
House 7876
Washington St
Rapid River MI 49878

Call Sign: W8WRL
Christopher C Parrett
House 7876
Washington St
Rapid River MI 49878

Call Sign: KC8AS
Paul N Roberts
Rapid River MI 49878

Call Sign: KA8ECC
Scott A Roberts
Rapid River MI 49878

FCC Amateur Radio Licenses in Ravenna

Call Sign: KC8IWE
Benjamin J Trute
11609 Cline Rd
Ravenna MI 49451

Call Sign: KC8IWF
Heather Trute
11609 Cline Rd
Ravenna MI 49451

Call Sign: KB8ZCV
Robert D Hurtubise
3643 Conklin St
Ravenna MI 49451

Call Sign: KD8RVU
William L Smith
11780 Haymeadow Ct
Ravenna MI 49451

Call Sign: KD8FWY
Daniel R Mosack
8303 Laketon
Ravenna MI 49451

Call Sign: WD8MXL
Robert J Coon
3474 Main St
Ravenna MI 49451

Call Sign: K8KWF
John Leatherman
436 N Trent Rd
Ravenna MI 49451

Call Sign: KB8MGC
Roland E Metcalf
6376 Rollenhagen Rd
Ravenna MI
494519103

Call Sign: KA8ANS
Wendy S Reffeor
6135 S Ravenna Rd
Ravenna MI 49451

Call Sign: KA8BXE
Randy W Woirol
1384 Squires Rd
Ravenna MI 49451

Call Sign: KD8DHJ
Karen M Strait
1479 Sullivan Rd
Ravenna MI 49451

Call Sign: KD8IVJ
Kayla M Strait
1479 Sullivan Rd
Ravenna MI 49451

Call Sign: KD8PWT
Luke A Strait
1479 Sullivan Rd
Ravenna MI 49451

Call Sign: KD8BGQ
Richard E Strait
1479 Sullivan Rd
Ravenna MI 49451

Call Sign: AC8AL
Richard E Strait

1479 Sullivan Rd
Ravenna MI 49451

Call Sign: KD8AKL
Betty S Lebeck
4215 Truman Rd
Ravenna MI 49451

Call Sign: KC8ZGP
Douglas F Lebeck
4215 Truman Rd
Ravenna MI 49451

Call Sign: KD8PGT
West Michigan
Venturing Crew 9050
ARC
Ravenna MI 49451

Call Sign: KC8IWG
Christopher D
Bombardier
Ravenna MI 49451

**FCC Amateur Radio
Licenses in Reed City**

Call Sign: KC8OIF
Thomas G Kiser III
22762 11 Mile Rd
Reed City MI 49677

Call Sign: KC8PQK
John R Kiser
22762 11 Mile Rd
Reed City MI 49677

Call Sign: KC8RBN
Mary L Clark
7516 170th Ave
Reed City MI 49677

Call Sign: KD8INC
Norman W Wolffis
6880 200th Ave
Reed City MI 49677

Call Sign: KC8EGL
Lynda A Remus
4263 220th Ave
Reed City MI 49677

Call Sign: WA8BGN
Nelson R Bregg

Rt 3 Box 259B
Reed City MI 49677

Call Sign: WA8YTY
Lawrence C Conrad
8790 Crestview
Reed City MI 49677

Call Sign: K8MXC
Robert L Sikkila
20416 Crestview Dr
Reed City MI 49677

Call Sign: KC8RKI
James S Deady
11215 E 72nd
Reed City MI 49677

Call Sign: N8YIQ
Gary A Patteen
29 Greensboro Ct
Reed City MI 49677

Call Sign: N8ZPL
Julie A Patteen
29 Greensboro Ct
Reed City MI 49677

Call Sign: N0IKB
David E Williams
319 N Higbee
Reed City MI 49677

Call Sign: KD8SBE
Annamaria J Herrera
319 N Higbee St
Reed City MI 49677

Call Sign: N8JCP
William L Brown
4666 Park Ave
Reed City MI 49677

Call Sign: WB8GAO
Walter A Nalezyty Jr
10401 Schwys Cir
Reed City MI 49677

Call Sign: KD8LBH
Dennis W Nalezyty
10401 Schwyz Cir
Reed City MI 49677

Call Sign: WB8YPG

Robert L Croaker
10411 Schwyz Cir
Reed City MI 49677

Call Sign: N8PQZ
William P Steelman
10114 W 2 Mile Rd
Reed City MI 49677

Call Sign: KD8FBH
Kathaleen R Yost
613 W Church Ave
Reed City MI 49677

Call Sign: KD8SBH
James C Anderlohr
628 W Lipton Ave
Reed City MI 49677

Call Sign: KD8HYI
Diane M Bush
Vandergiff Good
246 W Slosson A
Reed City MI 49677

Call Sign: KC8BAR
John W Mcdowell
138 W Slosson Ave
Reed City MI 49677

Call Sign: KD8PHK
David A Belden
222 W Slosson Ave
Reed City MI 49677

Call Sign: N8CYA
David A Belden
222 W Slosson Ave
Reed City MI 49677

Call Sign: KC8CBX
Mark A Watkins
561 W Slosson Ave
Reed City MI 49677

Call Sign: KB8VUB
James D Hulliberger
623 W Slosson Ave
Reed City MI 49677

Call Sign: KD8DIE
Larry G Bell
435 W Upton
Reed City MI 49677

Call Sign: N8QQH
John R Neahr II
711 Werth Dr
Reed City MI 49677

Call Sign: KB8SKB
Edward M Galloup
Rt 4 Wild Turkey Tr
Reed City MI 49677

FCC Amateur Radio Licenses in Remus

Call Sign: KD8RBW
Donald R Blough Jr
4881 11 Mile Rd
Remus MI 49340

Call Sign: N8IHY
Leon L Mac Donald Jr
10504 30th Ave
Remus MI 49340

Call Sign: WD8LUW
Robert B Ruetz
2155 9 Mile Rd
Remus MI 49340

Call Sign: KC8ZKU
Carol E Hegyi
232 N Sheridan Ave
Remus MI 49340

Call Sign: KB8ZSS
Elvin D Eagleson
3540 Quarterline Rd
Remus MI 49340

Call Sign: KB8OSY
William E Russell
5917 S Lake Shore Dr
Remus MI 49340

Call Sign: N8YOQ
Robert S Sherwood
8281 W Pickard
Remus MI 49340

Call Sign: WA8UVQ
Ward F Diehl
7520 W Remus Rd
Remus MI 49340

FCC Amateur Radio Licenses in Republic

Call Sign: KB8PTG
Robert Larson
Rr 1 Box 95
Republic MI 49879

Call Sign: KH6JSD
Frederick H Nannestad
Republic MI
498790447

FCC Amateur Radio Licenses in Rhodes

Call Sign: KD8ILS
William J Leonard Jr
2688 Cody Estey Rd
Rhodes MI 48652

Call Sign: KC8HBF
Neil R Libbrecht
3640 Katzer Rd
Rhodes MI 48652

Call Sign: WD8PUG
Jay R Horton Sr
3488 School Rd
Rhodes MI 48652

FCC Amateur Radio Licenses in Richland

Call Sign: KD8CTY
Paul R Edwards
7855 Broadhill
Richland MI 49083

Call Sign: KC8MFX
Peter K Jacobson
9324 Bunker Hill
Richland MI 49083

Call Sign: KC8MSF
John E Dillworth Jr
9170 Cotters Ridge Rd
Richland MI
490839583

Call Sign: KC8ETW
Dennis E Phillips
10453 Country Club
Dr

Richland MI 49083

Call Sign: KD8OSO
Ronald T Baden
6096 E B Ave
Richland MI 49083

Call Sign: W8RTB
Ronald T Baden
6096 E B Ave
Richland MI 49083

Call Sign: KF8PB
Jeffrey D Webster
8475 E D Ave
Richland MI 49083

Call Sign: N8FTI
Robert G Wagner
12318 E D Ave
Richland MI 49083

Call Sign: K8ZQV
Harold M Seelye
8905 E D Ave Box 126
Richland MI 49083

Call Sign: WB8PGK
James P McCann
10168 E De Ave
Richland MI 49083

Call Sign: WD8JAR
Edward J Green
6291 E E Ave
Richland MI 49083

Call Sign: KD8DFY
John C Greenfield
6695 E E Ave
Richland MI 49083

Call Sign: KD8RZN
Timothy J Walker
9584 E Gullway
Richland MI 49083

Call Sign: N8TPF
Sandra M Gorka
7914 Foxwood
Richland MI 49083

Call Sign: WA8YWL
Jay J De Nooyer

7820 Foxwood St
Richland MI 49083

Call Sign: KA8ZHT
Richard C Brookins
333 Gull Lake Dr S
Richland MI 49083

Call Sign: K8CIS
John B Hogan
371 Gull Lake Dr So
Richland MI
490839383

Call Sign: W8IPB
Fredrick A Kendall
345 Gull Lk Dr S
Richland MI 49083

Call Sign: N8ASA
Donald K McNee
8361 Harvest
Richland MI 49083

Call Sign: KB8KBT
Leopold T Zawol
2201 Idlewild
Richland MI 49083

Call Sign: WA8DNZ
John W Budnick
1977 Idlewild Dr
Richland MI 49083

Call Sign: W8UNF
Murray M Cooper
9800 N 24th St
Richland MI
490839515

Call Sign: WA8VFO
Stanley B Luykx
8528 N 27th St
Richland MI 49083

Call Sign: KB8WUD
Douglas M Densmore
6141 N 28th St
Richland MI 49083

Call Sign: N8SJV
Dacon M Pilbeam
5258 N 32nd
Richland MI 49083

Call Sign: KD8JBT
Gary W Bleyer
6553 N 37th St
Richland MI 49083

Call Sign: KB8MDS
James D Warren
1411 Shoal Dr
Richland MI 49083

Call Sign: KB8WHS
Timothy E Riley
10396 W Gull Lake Dr
Richland MI 49083

Call Sign: K8DVR
Donald J Van Tilburg
11938 Yorkshire Dr
Richland MI 49083

Call Sign: N8UFF
Tracy McNeil
Richland MI 49083

FCC Amateur Radio Licenses in Riverside

Call Sign: WB8VKA
Craig M Christian
3148 Coloma Rd
Riverside MI
490840081

FCC Amateur Radio Licenses in Rock

Call Sign: WD8RLG
Edward A Bruhnke
3314 Finn Hall 38th
Rd
Rock MI 49880

Call Sign: N8CKT
Randall P Parr
2592 Maple Ridge Dr
Rock MI 498809541

Call Sign: KC8PDU
Jeremy R Reese
12645 Old M 35
Rock MI 49880

Call Sign: KC8SFK

Lawrence R Pierce
3877 Saint Nicholas
31st Rd
Rock MI 49880

Call Sign: WA8LRI
Daniel Z Lupinski
4473 Trombly 35th Rd
Rock MI 49880

FCC Amateur Radio Licenses in Rockford

Call Sign: KA8ARU
Wilfred B Paull
5501 10 Mile Rd
Rockford MI 49341

Call Sign: W8CBH
William A Gerber
3210 10 Mile Rd NE
Rockford MI 49341

Call Sign: KD8RLP
Allan D Rau
7195 10 Mile Rd NE
Rockford MI 49341

Call Sign: KD8JTG
Jerry L Wineland
8847 11 Mile Rd
Rockford MI 49341

Call Sign: KD8KLX
James P Kovach
2286 11 Mile Rd NE
Rockford MI 49341

Call Sign: N8XX
Henry R Greeb
5727 11 Mile Rd NE
Rockford MI
493419502

Call Sign: KB8GOW
Kenneth C Gager
10975 12 Mile Rd
Rockford MI 49341

Call Sign: N8IMJ
John M O Rourke
2640 13 Mile Rd
Rockford MI 49341

Call Sign: KC8NJW
Howard J Bosscher
3333 13 Mile Rd NE
Rockford MI
493419140

Call Sign: KC8KKE
Lynne A Marihugh
11050 14 Mile Rd
Rockford MI 49341

Call Sign: N8LLR
Michael A Le Baron
10984 14 Mile Rd NE
Rockford MI
493418664

Call Sign: N8LLS
Darla Jo Le Baron
10984 14 Mile Rd NE
Rockford MI
493418664

Call Sign: N8FMV
Lucas J Tonneberger
10905 Algoma Ave
Rockford MI 49341

Call Sign: KA8UNK
Roger M Hockstra
9039 Algoma Ave NE
Rockford MI 49341

Call Sign: KC8ZAO
Wayne R West
9047 Algoma Ave NE
Rockford MI 49341

Call Sign: AB8UG
Wayne R West
9047 Algoma Ave NE
Rockford MI 49341

Call Sign: KD8JME
Chris A Orent
9051 Algoma Ave NE
Rockford MI 49341

Call Sign: N8ZUW
David A Grant
3545 Ancliff St NE
Rockford MI 49341

Call Sign: KC8NVX

Marion K Mikula
10648 Aquarius Dr NE
Rockford MI 49341

Call Sign: N8ITY
Phillip J Mikula
10648 Aquarius Dr NE
Rockford MI
493418421

Call Sign: N8IFL
Lorie J Roersma
10406 Aquila St NE
Rockford MI
493417885

Call Sign: N8OQE
Michael S Mieras
6090 Arroyo Vista
Rockford MI 49341

Call Sign: WB8QCD
Rick A Norman
6210 Arroyo Vista
Rockford MI 49341

Call Sign: KD8DVX
James A Allore
6179 Arroyo Vista NE
Rockford MI 49341

Call Sign: N7LLL
Ronald D Grew Sr
6635 Bella Vista Dr
NE
Rockford MI 49341

Call Sign: W8MAN
Ronald D Grew Sr
6635 Bella Vista Dr
NE
Rockford MI 49341

Call Sign: W8RDG
Ronald D Grew Sr
6635 Bella Vista Dr
NE
Rockford MI 49341

Call Sign: WD8BFI
Gerald S Hockstra
7501 Blakely Dr
Rockford MI 49341

Call Sign: N8BKS
David J Bergren
6257 Blanca
Rockford MI 49341

Call Sign: KD8AAH
David H Fast
6243 Blanca Dr NE
Rockford MI 49341

Call Sign: KD8EBF
Ryan D Fast
6243 Blanca Dr NE
Rockford MI 49341

Call Sign: N8WEI
Todd W Powers
172 Cahill Dr
Rockford MI
493411105

Call Sign: K8YAL
Ronald E Howard
7155 Camino Del Rey
Rockford MI 49341

Call Sign: KB8ERV
Bruce J Fawley
4951 Castle Hill Ct NE
Rockford MI 49341

Call Sign: KC6HOK
Kipp C Bronk
6764 Childsdale
Rockford MI 49341

Call Sign: N8GNL
John J Jailor
6901 Childsdale
Rockford MI 49341

Call Sign: KC8DRF
Jesse R Steed
6907 Childsdale
Rockford MI 49341

Call Sign: KC8HLT
Remington J Steed
6907 Childsdale
Rockford MI
493419232

Call Sign: KC8KMP
Alexandra M Steed

6907 Childsdale Ave
Rockford MI
493419232

Call Sign: KB4BWI
Nicholas H
Wetherington
6933 Childsdale Ave
NE
Rockford MI
493418397

Call Sign: KC8YIS
Patricia J Heldt
186 Childsdale NE
Rockford MI 49341

Call Sign: KC8YPV
Klay D Watson
188 Childsdale NE
Rockford MI 49341

Call Sign: N8AJJ
John R Steed
6907 Childsdale NE
Rockford MI 49341

Call Sign: WD8RJN
James R Babcock
6915 Childsdale NE
Rockford MI 49341

Call Sign: KD8EFH
Lois-Kaye Dusendang
6933 Childsdale NE
Rockford MI 49431

Call Sign: W8KVH
John H Schams
6537 Courtland Dr
Rockford MI 49341

Call Sign: KC8LTU
Tomas A Sturr
160 Courtland St
Rockford MI 49341

Call Sign: KD8DLK
Tim Crothers
7153 Cuesta Way Dr
Rockford MI 49341

Call Sign: WD8DXG
John T Moran

7441 Davies Dr
Rockford MI 49341

Call Sign: KC8IFK
Glen P Van Orman
7649 Deer Grove Ct
Rockford MI 49341

Call Sign: WD8OBB
Constantine Scooros
190 E Main St
Rockford MI 49341

Call Sign: KD8GKI
Steve J Rousos
190 E Main St
Rockford MI 49341

Call Sign: KD8PIU
Jilian S Rakow
10525 Edgerton Ave
NE
Rockford MI 49341

Call Sign: K9LGO
Jilian S Rakow
10525 Edgerton Ave
NE
Rockford MI 49341

Call Sign: WA8QFB
Donald R Stuart
6158 Egypt Valley
Rockford MI 49341

Call Sign: KB8TWZ
Vicki S Smitter
6773 Elmview NE
Rockford MI 49341

Call Sign: KD8GBW
Randall C Kriscunas
7110 Fox Meadow Dr
NE
Rockford MI 49341

Call Sign: W8RCK
Randall C Kriscunas
7110 Fox Meadow Dr
NE
Rockford MI 49341

Call Sign: WA8NGJ
Douglas H Williamson

5120 Gahan NE
Rockford MI 49341

Call Sign: NN8Y
Louis F Heline
10303 Garden Ln NE
Rockford MI 49341

Call Sign: KD8HGA
Colin T Cady
3306 Gateshead St NE
Rockford MI 49341

Call Sign: N8VS
Anthony M Elliott
20 Gibraltar Dr NE
Rockford MI 49341

Call Sign: KD8OQQ
Kevin L Vermerris
7 Gibralter Dr NE
Rockford MI 49341

Call Sign: KC8NWG
Karen S Cloherty
5079 Giles Ave NE
Rockford MI 49341

Call Sign: KD8RPT
Kanda S Carey
186 Glen Eagle Dr
Rockford MI 49341

Call Sign: KC8UBU
Jason R Bradley
379 Glen Wood Ct
Rockford MI 49341

Call Sign: KD8DCF
Andrew M Vandusen
141 Hawthorne Ct
Rockford MI 49341

Call Sign: K8AMV
Andrew M Vandusen
141 Hawthorne Ct
Rockford MI 49341

Call Sign: N8OSS
Jeffrey S Vander Klipp
4446 Hillrise Ct
Rockford MI 49341

Call Sign: N8CMX

Darryn B Hansen
1383 Hollow Ridge Rd
Rockford MI 49341

Call Sign: KB8KB
Michael A Stark
58 James Dr
Rockford MI 49341

Call Sign: KD8EBG
Thomas D Smith
88 James St
Rockford MI 49341

Call Sign: WB8SYX
Howard R Babcock
7700 Jericho Rd NE
Rockford MI 49341

Call Sign: KD8NDQ
Evan J Smith
3345 Knollwood
Rockford MI 49341

Call Sign: KB8BLZ
William A Zahradnik
Jr
8321 Kreuter
Rockford MI 49341

Call Sign: KB8BMA
William Zahradnik
8321 Kreuter Rd
Rockford MI 49341

Call Sign: KD8AIF
Kelly M Vandenberg
4656 Kroes St NE
Rockford MI 49341

Call Sign: KC8WQL
Stephen T Provost
6845 Kuttshills Dr NE
Rockford MI 49341

Call Sign: WA8NEZ
Donald J Burtnick
12017 Lappley Ave
NE
Rockford MI
493419526

Call Sign: K8AHM
Andrew J Laing

577 Legacy Ct
Rockford MI 49341

Call Sign: KE9WX
William B Hansen
336 Lewis St
Rockford MI 49341

Call Sign: KD8MCY
Elizabeth F Berryhill
9060 Loveless Dr
Rockford MI 49341

Call Sign: N8LWV
John E Chickering
6605 Majestic Way Dr
Rockford MI 49341

Call Sign: W0OBP
Monty A Williams
4868 Maple Shade Ct
NE
Rockford MI 49341

Call Sign: KD8DCJ
Tim Kraai
8964 Marabella Ct NE
Rockford MI 49341

Call Sign: N8SGT
Timothy E Kraai
8964 Marabella Ct NE
Rockford MI 49341

Call Sign: KC8UXP
James E Gibson
4503 Mercury
Rockford MI 49341

Call Sign: N8QT
Royce E Tuck
4411 Moonlite Ln NE
Rockford MI
493418170

Call Sign: KC8FQK
Keith L Eadie Jr
10506 Morning Star
Way
Rockford MI 49341

Call Sign: KC8ZYW
Gerald R Dominowski

8150 Muscatay Grove
NE
Rockford MI 49341

Call Sign: N2JPZ
Gerald R Dominowski
8150 Muscatay Grove
NE
Rockford MI 49341

Call Sign: KC8FAX
Robert M Wolford
7852 Myers Lake
Rockford MI 49341

Call Sign: N8NHK
Genevieve I Van
Prooyen
8330 Myers Lake
Rockford MI 49341

Call Sign: K8OO
Wendell M Broome
9350 Myers Lake Ave
Rockford MI 49341

Call Sign: KB8UFD
Michael A Gunneson
11390 Myers Lake
Ave
Rockford MI 49341

Call Sign: K8TXH
William A Annable
10585 Myers Lake Rd
Rockford MI 49341

Call Sign: K8KWD
Leonard H Van
Prooyen
8330 Myers Lake Rd
NE
Rockford MI 49341

Call Sign: KB8KQB
Mandy E Mikita
161 N Monroe St
Rockford MI 49341

Call Sign: N8XMD
Brooks A Filonow
161 N Monroe St
Rockford MI 49341

Call Sign: KB8AFS
Timothy M Courtier
10431 Neptune St
Rockford MI 49341

Call Sign: WA8IIG
Robert E Swider
210 Northland Dr
Rockford MI 49341

Call Sign: KC8DHL
Steven P Nastaj
8960 Old Belding Rd
Rockford MI 49341

Call Sign: KD8JTI
Baron A Baldwin
9580 Parmeter Ave
Rockford MI 49341

Call Sign: N8UXO
Emily J Densberger
8314 Peach Tree
Rockford MI 49341

Call Sign: KD8MDB
William M Pribble
148 Pearl St
Rockford MI 49341

Call Sign: KD8LX
David Y Yoshida
8573 Pebble Dr NE
Rockford MI 49341

Call Sign: N8OSP
Eugene W Debevic
6889 Peninsula Dr
Rockford MI 49341

Call Sign: W8GGN
Ralph J Bennett
7061 Peninsula Dr
Rockford MI 49341

Call Sign: WY8P
Alan D Wever
6823 Petersen Valley
NE
Rockford MI 49341

Call Sign: KD8NMO
Mark A Garnsey
4333 Porter Hollow Dr

Rockford MI 49341

Call Sign: K8ZAJ
William B Glaske Jr
4420 Porter Hollow Rd
Rockford MI 49341

Call Sign: W8TLW
Terry L Winright
6590 Ramsdell
Rockford MI 49341

Call Sign: KD8CGR
Douglas J McCarty
7370 Ramsdell Dr
Rockford MI 49341

Call Sign: KC8PKO
Terry L Winright
6590 Ramsdell Dr NE
Rockford MI 49341

Call Sign: KC6TRK
Donald H Byers
12749 Ramsdell Dr NE
Rockford MI 49341

Call Sign: KC8EKI
Douglas J Wolford
7233 Russet Trl
Rockford MI 49341

Call Sign: KD6RGX
David R Snow Sr
159 S Lincoln St
Rockford MI 49341

Call Sign: KD6UMX
Theresa A Snow
159 S Lincoln St
Rockford MI 49341

Call Sign: WD8LDC
Richard A Sivins Jr
3726 Senna Dr NE
Rockford MI
493419282

Call Sign: KC8NWE
Scott A Hansen
10737 Shaner Ave NE
Rockford MI 49341

Call Sign: AA8VU

Richard C Bronk
7006 Silver Lake Dr
Rockford MI
493419409

Call Sign: W8OET
Richard C Bronk
7006 Silver Lake Dr
Rockford MI
493419409

Call Sign: KM0W
Stuart A Malafa
8261 Squires St NE
Rockford MI
493419326

Call Sign: N8SRF
Richard J Guzorek
11301 Summit St
Rockford MI 49341

Call Sign: K8CHA
Louis G Anderson
9977 Swem
Rockford MI 49341

Call Sign: NS8X
Boyce D Evans
10538 Swem Ave NE
Rockford MI 49341

Call Sign: KB8SET
Mary J De Boe
10590 Swem Rd NE
Rockford MI 49341

Call Sign: N8YKA
David L Herrema
10588 Swem St NE
Rockford MI 49341

Call Sign: KC8DHX
Thomas E Warren
7476 Tillicum Tr
Rockford MI 49341

Call Sign: N8ZWI
Greg A Kolander
6914 Verde Vista
Rockford MI 49341

Call Sign: WD5GXO
Steven P Engel

8131 Vista Royale Ln
NE
Rockford MI
493418823

Call Sign: KD8QNP
Arthur A Ward Sr
8585 Wabasis Ave
Rockford MI 49341

Call Sign: KD8QNO
Anna K Ward
8585 Wabasis Ave NE
Rockford MI 49341

Call Sign: WB8MFG
Philip J Hamlin
9174 Walnut Grove Dr
NE
Rockford MI 49341

Call Sign: KC8KHH
Carl J Hessler
8418 Whittall
Rockford MI
493419323

Call Sign: N8KCQ
Wilma J Droge
7138 Wilkinson NE
Rockford MI 49341

Call Sign: N8JSP
David A Malin
4297 Wintercress Dr
NE
Rockford MI 49341

Call Sign: N7DAM
David A Malin
4297 Wintercress Dr
NE
Rockford MI 49341

Call Sign: KB8FDH
David A Malin Jr
4297 Wintercress Dr
NE
Rockford MI
493418914

Call Sign: KD8PWC
Scott D Spencer
9045 Young Ave NE

Rockford MI 49341

Call Sign: K8SDS
Scott D Spencer
9045 Young Ave NE
Rockford MI 49341

Call Sign: W8BCL
Norman Karlberg
8580 Young NE
Rockford MI 49341

FCC Amateur Radio Licenses in Rodney

Call Sign: KC8MGN
Bryan E Nevins
15460 16 Mile Rd
Rodney MI 493429625

Call Sign: KD8KPZ
Christopher L Wall
15750 16 Mile Rd
Rodney MI 49342

Call Sign: KA8MOM
Lavail E Hull
9053 19 Mile Rd
Rodney MI 49342

Call Sign: KA8OUY
Jeanne M Barstow
12630 Wilson Rd
Rodney MI 49342

Call Sign: WD8DLK
Jefferson W Barstow
12630 Wilson Rd
Rodney MI 49342

FCC Amateur Radio Licenses in Rogers City

Call Sign: KC8WEM
Robert M Taylor Jr
6867 40 Mile Pt Rd
Rogers City MI 49779

Call Sign: KD8BY
Paul D Rase
1165 Birch St
Rogers City MI 49779

Call Sign: AB8LO
Randall D Martens
6134 Cheyenne Ct
Rogers City MI 49779

Call Sign: AA8PQ
Neal R Hughes
3682 CR 451
Rogers City MI 49779

Call Sign: WB8TQZ
Michael J Horn
6988 CR 646
Rogers City MI 49779

Call Sign: N8JIH
John A Nordin
1299 Dettloff
Rogers City MI 49779

Call Sign: KC8CFQ
John R Leszinske
239 E Orchard St
Rogers City MI 49779

Call Sign: W8PCE
Leonard R Stone
6037 Huron Shore Rd
Rogers City MI 49779

Call Sign: KD8LBU
David L Miller
6381 Huron Shore Rd
Rogers City MI 49779

Call Sign: W6DLM
David L Miller
6381 Huron Shore Rd
Rogers City MI 49779

Call Sign: K8ZED
David L Miller
6381 Huron Shore Rd
Rogers City MI 49779

Call Sign: KC8TGI
William N Smith
920 Linden St
Rogers City MI 49779

Call Sign: K8CXG
William N Smith
920 Linden St
Rogers City MI 49779

Call Sign: N8HGD
James R Carr
8586 M 68
Rogers City MI 49779

Call Sign: KA8SMM
Gregory E Erno
359 N 1st St
Rogers City MI 49779

Call Sign: KC8EUG
Julie A Morrill
594 N Bradley Hwy
Rogers City MI
497791509

Call Sign: N8UHK
Lawrence E Kamyszek
1660 N Ward Branch
Rd
Rogers City MI 49779

Call Sign: KC8JHT
Michael L Lietzow
4670 Nagel Hwy
Rogers City MI 49779

Call Sign: AA8PP
Robert A Hughes
706 S 2nd
Rogers City MI 49779

Call Sign: AA8PH
Stefan Knutsson
1046 St Paul St
Rogers City MI 49779

Call Sign: W6OTI
Stefan Knutsson
1046 St Paul St
Rogers City MI 49779

Call Sign: AB8SW
William N Smith
2840 US 23 N
Rogers City MI 49779

Call Sign: WD8KDB
Steve L Porter
7717 US 23 N
Rogers City MI 49779

Call Sign: N8IFW

Randall D Martens
385 W Michigan Ave
Rogers City MI 49779

Call Sign: KC8TXU
Dale H Quade
2849 Wenzel Hwy
Rogers City MI 49779

FCC Amateur Radio Licenses in Roosevelt Park

Call Sign: AB9GD
Craig D Harris
1423 Marlboro Rd
Roosevelt Park MI
49441

FCC Amateur Radio Licenses in Roscommon

Call Sign: KD8EGY
Shane B Major
1150 Ausable Trl
Roscommon MI 48653

Call Sign: KD8ADC
Robert M Clark
243 Ballanger Apt 25
Roscommon MI 48653

Call Sign: KC8SBS
Kelly C Baines
8716 Baptist Dr
Roscommon MI 48653

Call Sign: KC8SNZ
Ronda G Baincs
8716 Baptist Dr
Roscommon MI 48653

Call Sign: KD8GGE
Richard S Aardema
103 Black Bear Cir
Roscommon MI 48653

Call Sign: N9YAQ
Brett M Sprtel
11934 Crossing Deer
Ct
Roscommon MI 48653

Call Sign: KC8GXT
Pamela S Clement
11988 Crossing Deer
Ct
Roscommon MI 48653

Call Sign: KC8GXU
Robert A Clement
11988 Crossing Deer
Ct
Roscommon MI 48653

Call Sign: KD8ADJ
Derek A Nelson
10689 Deerwood Trl
Roscommon MI 48653

Call Sign: KB8LKA
Earl D Swanson
851 Doyle Tr
Roscommon MI 48653

Call Sign: WA8RLI
Thomas M Duggan
100 Duggan Dr
Roscommon MI 48653

Call Sign: AA8DO
Constance E Creighton
206 Elm Ave
Roscommon MI 48653

Call Sign: KC8ZRO
Joseph R Baldwin
1642 Fuller Dr
Roscommon MI 48653

Call Sign: KC8OUC
Christopher R
Mclaughlin
1105 B Helen St
Roscommon MI 48653

Call Sign: WB8WVZ
John J Steigerwald
204 Hillsdale Dr
Roscommon MI 48653

Call Sign: W8MKO
Stanley T Cooke
218 Jackson Blvd
Roscommon MI 48653

Call Sign: N8BWD

Frank E Gates
534 Jefferson Blvd
Roscommon MI 48653

Call Sign: KC8NJN
Louiko S Johnson
231 Lake St
Roscommon MI 48653

Call Sign: KB8UPI
Thela C Ostling
1340 Maplehurst Dr
Roscommon MI 48653

Call Sign: KD8ODD
Crawford Eoc Club
11734 Marber Dr
Roscommon MI 48653

Call Sign: WD7CRA
Crawford ARES Races
Emcomm Group
11734 Marber Dr
Roscommon MI 48653

Call Sign: N8FVM
Edward H Bassett
11734 Marber Dr
Roscommon MI 48653

Call Sign: KA8WWG
Louis Ona
213 Marywood Dr
Roscommon MI
486538755

Call Sign: KB8UES
Raoul J Meyer Jr
203 N 3rd St
Roscommon MI 48653

Call Sign: WA8CUP
Franz C Achard
8105 N Harrison Rd
Roscommon MI 48653

Call Sign: N8AVB
Mark F Lockwood
8039 N Higgins Lake
Dr
Roscommon MI
486539003

Call Sign: KB8QXK

Gerald L Schwartz
2770 N M 18
Roscommon MI 48653

Call Sign: KB8SPY
Robert L Schwartz
2819 N M 18
Roscommon MI 48653

Call Sign: N8YUE
Joanne C Johnson
4070 N M 18
Roscommon MI 48653

Call Sign: N8KHC
Jack T Johnson
4070 N M 18
Roscommon MI
486539631

Call Sign: N8VHK
James I Hall
204 Nancy Sue Dr
Roscommon MI 48653

Call Sign: KA8NAT
Joe G Myers
100A Norway R 3 Box
78
Roscommon MI 48653

Call Sign: N8JHN
Scott F Ludwig
4407 Norwood Dr
Roscommon MI 48653

Call Sign: WO8N
Scott F Ludwig
4407 Norwood Dr
Roscommon MI 48653

Call Sign: KC8QBC
Frank L Bitner Jr
446 Pine Acres
Roscommon MI 48653

Call Sign: N8ORX
Frank H Michelson
209C Pine Bluffs Rd
Roscommon MI 48653

Call Sign: N8KHV
James L Mobarak Sr
10803 Pines Tr

Roscommon MI 48653

Call Sign: N8JEN
Raymond Foulkrod Jr
212 Rising Fawn Trl
Roscommon MI 48653

Call Sign: KC8OWA
Brad A Livingston
242 Rising Fawn Trl
Roscommon MI 48653

Call Sign: N8ZKC
Dolores I Lim
10101 S Grayling Rd
Roscommon MI 48653

Call Sign: WB8CHC
Garland G Griffith Sr
10101 S Grayling Rd
Roscommon MI
486539417

Call Sign: KC8DMC
Joyce F Carson
11195 S Grayling Rd
Roscommon MI 48653

Call Sign: KE8CB
Howard A Carson
11195 S Grayling Rd
Roscommon MI 48653

Call Sign: KD8FSM
Daniel M Collins
10875 Sam Ellsworth
Ridge
Roscommon MI 48653

Call Sign: K9KSR
Daniel M Collins
10875 Sam Ellsworth
Ridge
Roscommon MI 48653

Call Sign: N8IPV
Roger D Whitlock
220 Spruce Ave
Roscommon MI 48653

Call Sign: KC0MDL
James R Mathewson
102 Village Pl Dr Apt
B

Roscommon MI 48653

Call Sign: N8JEM
Dan W Alschbach
2338 W Burdell
Roscommon MI 48653

Call Sign: N8SCX
Richard J Bonk
327 W Burdell Rd
Roscommon MI 48653

Call Sign: KC8DMD
Charles E Groh
2585 W Doyle Trl
Roscommon MI 48653

Call Sign: KD8OTI
Sharon M Zacny
10667 Wheeler Rd
Roscommon MI 48653

Call Sign: K8SSZ
Darius D Dustman
124 Whispering Pines
Ct
Roscommon MI 48653

Call Sign: K8CZG
Ralph W Linley
600 Winchester Ave
Roscommon MI 48653

Call Sign: N8OHF
Sandra J Cywinski
Roscommon MI 48653

Call Sign: N8ORV
Thomas R Cywinski
Roscommon MI 48653

Call Sign: KC8APO
James B Burgan Jr
Roscommon MI 48653

**FCC Amateur Radio
Licenses in Rose City**

Call Sign: KC8WPT
Michael D Connors
1044 Abbot Rd
Rose City MI 48654

Call Sign: KC8YDD

Casey M Connors
1044 Abbott Rd
Rose City MI 48654

Call Sign: KC8YBY
Cody L Connors
1044 Abbott Rd
Rose City MI 48654

Call Sign: N8RRP
John R Boring
1628 Abbott Rd
Rose City MI 48654

Call Sign: KG8A
Roy A Wilcox
4691 Beechwood Rd
Rose City MI
486549794

Call Sign: KC8OEI
Wally E Snyder
4691 Beechwood Rd
Rose City MI
486549794

Call Sign: N8PSC
Rex L Suttles
5734 Beechwood Rd
Rose City MI 48654

Call Sign: KD8HGM
Jason E Benjamin
1215 Carlisle Dr
Rose City MI 48654

Call Sign: N8QAG
John I Rukavina
176 E Hughes Lake Rd
Rose City MI 48654

Call Sign: WA8YVM
Carter W Rae
126 E Main St
Rose City MI 48654

Call Sign: K8ING
Richard A King Jr
5238 E Twin Lakes Trl
Rose City MI 48654

Call Sign: KA8SKV
Carl A Shoup
3579 Grandjean Rd

Rose City MI 48654

Call Sign: W8COP
Christopher A Barbb
1140 Lorenze Ct
Rose City MI 48654

Call Sign: KC8ZOG
Charles W Herbst
2141 M 33
Rose City MI 48654

Call Sign: KB8VLO
Maxwell L Garnett
4870 M 33
Rose City MI 48654

Call Sign: K8YKR
Robert L Van Tiflin
332 Maplewood Rd
Rose City MI 48654

Call Sign: KD8ACY
David M Saelens
5164 Mt Tom Rd
Rose City MI 48654

Call Sign: KD8BF
Robert N Sanback
4312 N Campbell Rd
Rose City MI 48654

Call Sign: K8ZKG
Robert F Bragg
575 W Esmond Rd
Rose City MI
486549781

Call Sign: KD8QB
Bernard L Chandler
447 W Heath Rd
Rose City MI 48654

Call Sign: N8RBF
Jeffrey M Sanders
Rose City MI 48654

Call Sign: KC8WTH
Susan E King
Rose City MI 48654

**FCC Amateur Radio
Licenses in Rothbury**

Call Sign: KC8JNL
Patrick J Healey
1043 E Yale Rd
Rothbury MI 49452

Call Sign: KC8ZRR
Jodi M Harper
6106 S 100th St
Rothbury MI 49452

Call Sign: W8TML
Thomas M Lau
8615 S 116th Ave
Rothbury MI
494528085

Call Sign: KD8BGP
Linda J Wishman
5541 S 120th Ave
Rothbury MI 49452

Call Sign: KC8VRH
Lynn L Warren
6208 S Oceana Dr
Rothbury MI 49452

Call Sign: N8HE
Lynn L Warren
6208 S Oceana Dr
Rothbury MI 49452

Call Sign: KC8NCD
David W Miller
2942 W McKinley Rd
Rothbury MI 49452

Call Sign: WA8NQO
John E Mears
2875 W McKinley Rd
Rothbury MI 49452

Call Sign: KD8GQF
Carlos H Canales
2847 Winston Rd
Rothbury MI 49452

Call Sign: AA8KA
Michael K Chappell
7911 Wood Ave
Rothbury MI 49452

**FCC Amateur Radio
Licenses in Rudyard**

Call Sign: KA8TTY
Richard D Brown
Rr 1 Box 775B
Rudyard MI 49780

Call Sign: KC8LXQ
Michael K Feighner
10765 McDowell St
Rudyard MI 49780

Call Sign: N8QYF
Jennifer J Lovegrove
N Elliott St
Rudyard MI 49780

Call Sign: KC8MLD
Marvin L De Witt
15197 S Centerline
Rudyard MI 49780

Call Sign: KC8NEC
Charlene B Dewitt
15197 S Centerline
Rudyard MI 49780

Call Sign: KB8ODA
Carol J Vandermate
10481 W 17 Mile Rd
Rudyard MI 49780

Call Sign: KC8PSD
Benjamin O Saint
Louis
Rudyard MI 49780

**FCC Amateur Radio
Licenses in Rumely**

Call Sign: KC8DTE
Coral A Howe
Rumely MI 49826

Call Sign: KC8QWP
Brenda A Howe
Rumely MI 49826

Call Sign: KD8CGI
Kristy A Howe
Rumley MI 49826

**FCC Amateur Radio
Licenses in Sagola**

Call Sign: KB8HDT

Anthony C Hoynacke
II
W7985 Welles Grade
Rd
Sagola MI 498810061

Call Sign: N8BBI
Joseph E Grosser
10511 Beaver Dr
Saint Helen MI 48656

Call Sign: N8KFV
Richard H Baden
10901 Beaver Dr
Saint Helen MI 48656

Call Sign: KE8FX
Robert D Hall Jr
4230 Brenda Ct
Saint Helen MI
486560156

Call Sign: KF8PA
Harry W Kubert
1534 Cactus Ct
Saint Helen MI 48656

Call Sign: KC8EM
Frederick P Stocking
Sr
7480 Campground Rd
Saint Helen MI 48656

Call Sign: N8NHU
Nancy A Carter
6900 Jessie Dr
Saint Helen MI 48656

Call Sign: KC8PXS
Marcus J Rodgers Sr
9552 Kewaene Rd
Saint Helen MI 48656

Call Sign: AB8WR
Marcus J Rodgers Sr
9552 Kewaunee Rd
Saint Helen MI
486569526

Call Sign: N8SMK

Richard G Wilson
1018 Leeward Ln
Saint Helen MI 48656

Call Sign: KB8WJC
Michael A Loop
1321 Leeward Ln
Saint Helen MI 48656

Call Sign: KC8IFF
Thomas C Drake
1657 Lolich
Saint Helen MI 48656

Call Sign: N8RSK
Matthew Gruza
9035 Michigan Ave
Saint Helen MI 48656

Call Sign: KC8ADD
Henry J Jaguszewski
9033 N Saint Helen Rd
Saint Helen MI 48656

Call Sign: KC8QYD
Wendy M Greer
9115 N St Helen Rd
Saint Helen MI 48656

Call Sign: KD8JSJ
Edward L Wolfe Sr
5068 Nestel Rd E
Saint Helen MI 48656

Call Sign: KD8JSK
Londa J Olson
5068 Nestel Rd E
Saint Helen MI 48656

Call Sign: KC8EDV
Tim A Steinhauer
1565 Shoshone Ln
Saint Helen MI 48656

Call Sign: KC8HXN
Euna M Steinhauer
1565 Shoshone Ln
Saint Helen MI 48656

Call Sign: KC8IAR
Martin L Steinhauer
1565 Shoshone Ln
Saint Helen MI 48656

Call Sign: KF8SY
Edward H Westlake
6451 Sundown Ln
Saint Helen MI
486569544

Call Sign: KC8EDU
Shawn V Dunn
9209 Sunshine Ct
Saint Helen MI 48656

Call Sign: KB8KAP
Frank D Turnage
1116 Tanglewood Dr
Saint Helen MI 48656

Call Sign: K8UOF
Frank A Schloss
Saint Helen MI 48656

Call Sign: N8ORW
Dennis Galleck
Saint Helen MI
486560216

Call Sign: KB8TVJ
Walter Groves Jr
181 Boundary Line Rd
Saint Ignace MI 49781

Call Sign: N8QZA
Robert L Lindley
414 Ellsworth
Saint Ignace MI 49781

Call Sign: KC8FAS
Troy A Huskey
259 Fitch St
Saint Ignace MI 49781

Call Sign: N8UNE
Gregory S Cheeseman
325 Graham Ave
Saint Ignace MI 49781

Call Sign: N8QYX
Charles E Goudreau Sr
100 Gros Cap Rd
Saint Ignace MI 49781

Call Sign: KD8QJB
Patrick M Fenlon
251 Keightley St
Saint Ignace MI 49781

Call Sign: KC8JJZ
Gary P Laysell
340 McCann St
Saint Ignace MI 49781

Call Sign: W8JFB
James F Bishop
W 1142 Pointe La
Barbe Rd
Saint Ignace MI 49781

Call Sign: WA8HSM
James F Bishop
332 Pte La Barbe Rd
Saint Ignace MI 49781

Call Sign: K8HEW
John L Stephenson
710 S State St
Saint Ignace MI 49781

Call Sign: WB8MNU
Barbara A Stephenson
710 S State St
Saint Ignace MI 49781

Call Sign: W8JU
James E Laakko
360 Spring St
Saint Ignace MI 49781

Call Sign: KD8CW
Leon B Westover
121 Stockbridge St
Saint Ignace MI 49781

Call Sign: W8DHH
Louis M Ozak
Saint Ignace MI 49781

Call Sign: WZ8W
Charles D Blaksmith
2756 Avery Rd
Saint Johns MI 48879

Call Sign: KD8PSH
Thomas E Herrmann
1003 E Cass St
Saint Johns MI 48879

Call Sign: KC8POF
David R Richmond Sr
711 E Gibbs St Apt 13
Saint Johns MI 48879

Call Sign: WB8ZYZ
Kenneth G Hude
1132 E Maple Rapids
Rd
Saint Johns MI 48879

Call Sign: K8RNQ
Robert W Remer
1780 E Maple Rapids
Rd
Saint Johns MI 48879

Call Sign: KC8YQG
Robert J Andretz
4189 E Pratt Rd
Saint Johns MI
488798125

Call Sign: KC8NJJ
Steven S Campos
4803 E Pratt Rd
Saint Johns MI 48879

Call Sign: N8SHS
Dean A Gill
2525 E Price Rd
Saint Johns MI 48879

Call Sign: KA8UUF
Robert A Gill
2730 E Price Rd
Saint Johns MI 48879

Call Sign: KC8LRM
William H Coon
2286 E Steel Rd
Saint Johns MI 48879

Call Sign: KD8IEI
Ccarpsc
1347 E Townsend Rd
Saint Johns MI 48879

Call Sign: WA8RZJ

William S Russell
304 E Walker St
Saint Johns MI 48879

Call Sign: KC8VVP
Charles P Graham
1202 Glastonbury Dr
Saint Johns MI 48879

Call Sign: KC8NBN
Michael L Porter
1205 Hampshire Dr
Saint Johns MI 48879

Call Sign: KC8NBO
Chris J Porter
1205 Hampshire Dr
Saint Johns MI 48879

Call Sign: KC8VZQ
Martin A Minnick
1212 Lincolnshire
Saint Johns MI 48879

Call Sign: KB8LJB
Paul D Minnick
1212 Lincolnshire Dr
Saint Johns MI 48879

Call Sign: KC8UWF
Clinton County
Amateur Radio
Association
2765 N Airport Rd
Saint Johns MI 48879

Call Sign: KC8RVI
Lawrence R St George
2765 N Airport Rd
Saint Johns MI 48879

Call Sign: N8SG
Lawrence R St George
2765 N Airport Rd
Saint Johns MI 48879

Call Sign: N8IWM
Robert L Walker
6204 N Dewitt Rd
Saint Johns MI 48876

Call Sign: KC8TJD
Melissa S Brenner
3790 N Harmon Rd

Saint Johns MI 48879

Call Sign: KC8ODQ
Richard Carnicom
906 N Oakland
Saint Johns MI 48879

Call Sign: N8NBP
Donald J Moore
902 N Oakland St
Saint Johns MI 48879

Call Sign: KA3DUA
Karl F Gruber
8343 N Williams Rd
Saint Johns MI 48879

Call Sign: KC8VDV
Karl F Gruber
8343 N Williams Rd
Saint Johns MI 48879

Call Sign: W8QW
David R Leisman
8501 N Williams Rd
Saint Johns MI 48879

Call Sign: N8HJQ
Kay L L Mclaughlin
6200 Paxton
Saint Johns MI 48879

Call Sign: WB8TOE
Richard E Mclaughlin
Jr
6200 Paxton
Saint Johns MI 48879

Call Sign: KB8YEC
Frank L Hart
701 S Banker
Saint Johns MI 48879

Call Sign: KD8BTC
Mark A Mox
5217 S De Witt Rd
Saint Johns MI 48879

Call Sign: WD8PHX
Kenneth A Gilson
601 S Oakland
Saint Johns MI 48879

Call Sign: WB8PHX

Kenneth A Gilson
601 S Oakland
Saint Johns MI 48879

Call Sign: KC8JXF
Lewis C Moldenhauer
306 S Scott Rd
Saint Johns MI 48879

Call Sign: W7ITB
Harold F Tolles
1101 S Scott Rd 69
Saint Johns MI 48879

Call Sign: W8KWO
Kenneth D Harris Sr
1103 S Scott Rd Apt
207
Saint Johns MI 48879

Call Sign: KC8PII
Steven L Lehman
5200 S St Clair Rd
Saint Johns MI 48879

Call Sign: KD8RMQ
Levi J Hebert
3707 Saint Clair Rd
Saint Johns MI 48879

Call Sign: KD8INX
William A Smith
4172 W French Rd
Saint Johns MI 48879

Call Sign: KB8NUU
Perry G Patterson
3898 W Parks Rd
Saint Johns MI 48879

Call Sign: KB8VHQ
Richard A Hale
2207 W Taft Rd
Saint Johns MI 48879

Call Sign: WB8YYF
Peter E Niska
1510 Yallup Rd
Saint Johns MI 48879

Call Sign: N8SUA
Jon F Seaver
Saint Johns MI 48879

Call Sign: N8NQY
John W Rogers
4055 Applewood Dr
Saint Joseph MI 49085

Call Sign: KB8VIM
Gary D Wallis
1809 Arcadia Dr
Saint Joseph MI 49085

Call Sign: KB8EEG
Ann M Stoub
1823 Arcadia Dr
Saint Joseph MI 49085

Call Sign: N8JTZ
Marvin Stoub
1823 Arcadia Dr
Saint Joseph MI 49085

Call Sign: KC8QHL
David E Mitchell
2267 Autumn Ridge
Saint Joseph MI 49085

Call Sign: N8QP
David E Mitchell
2267 Autumn Ridge
Saint Joseph MI 49085

Call Sign: KD8SAN
Joseph C Campbell
3336 Bacon School Rd
Saint Joseph MI 49085

Call Sign: KC8ZPO
Joel L Kamerer
4065 Bacon School Rd
Saint Joseph MI 49085

Call Sign: K8ZPO
Joel L Kamerer
4065 Bacon School Rd
Saint Joseph MI 49085

Call Sign: WB8BWA
Ronald W Holling
3733 Blenheim Rd
Saint Joseph MI 49085

Call Sign: KD8FGE
Michael R Webster
3515 Bluegrass Way
Saint Joseph MI 49085

Call Sign: KA8GIX
James R Lersch
1770 Briarcliff Dr
Saint Joseph MI 49085

Call Sign: KD8DU
Wallace E Jersey
1866 Briarcliff Dr
Saint Joseph MI 49085

Call Sign: KD8OMI
David C Rudi
3461 Bridle Path
Saint Joseph MI 49085

Call Sign: KB8EGC
Cheri L Parren
712 Broad St
Saint Joseph MI 49085

Call Sign: WA8ZVO
Edward A Mosher
1442 Cardinal Dr
Saint Joseph MI 49085

Call Sign: WK8B
Rankin W Tippins
1028 Carley Ln
Saint Joseph MI 49085

Call Sign: N8JHY
Edwin J Smith
2840 Carrie Ln
Saint Joseph MI 49085

Call Sign: N8JID
Robert E Smith
2840 Carrie Ln
Saint Joseph MI 49085

Call Sign: W8LRM
Albert K Rea
706 Church St
Saint Joseph MI 49085

Call Sign: W8RLF
Saint Joseph High Sch
Amat Rad Club
Alumni Assn

706 Church St
Saint Joseph MI
490851304

Call Sign: N8AUU
Kally J Bergstrom
684 Clemens Ave
Saint Joseph MI 49085

Call Sign: KB8RFR
Jeffery M Beam
1002 Court St 2
Saint Joseph MI 49085

Call Sign: WA3UDV
John R Bentley
4217 Courtney St
Saint Joseph MI 49085

Call Sign: W8EEF
Norman H Bradshaw
646 E Glenlord Rd
Saint Joseph MI 49085

Call Sign: KC8YSX
Connie D Kepner
684 E Glenlord Rd
Saint Joseph MI 49085

Call Sign: N8QNQ
Greg R Smith
2713 E Yukon
Saint Joseph MI 49085

Call Sign: KB8SKY
James F Sokol
1861 Edison Dr
Saint Joseph MI 49085

Call Sign: WB9CLQ
Gary L Ilker
3172 Estates Ct
Saint Joseph MI 49085

Call Sign: N9CQB
Douglas J Schmutte
1526 Fetke Dr
Saint Joseph MI 49085

Call Sign: W8SIO
Saint Joseph High Sch
Amat Rad Clb Alumni
Assn
1108 Flanders Pl

Saint Joseph MI 49085

Call Sign: KL7XX
William A Preston
1108 Flanders Pl
Saint Joseph MI 49085

Call Sign: K8SJ
William A Preston
1108 Flanders Pl
Saint Joseph MI 49085

Call Sign: KC8AFW
Kevin D Pounders
3768 Glen Haven
Saint Joseph MI 49085

Call Sign: KB8GXF
Shirley A Hackney
1419 Glenwood Dr
Saint Joseph MI 49085

Call Sign: N8HXB
Ronald E Hackney
1419 Glenwood Dr
Saint Joseph MI 49085

Call Sign: N9KCQ
Steven J Gillis
524 Granada Ave
Saint Joseph MI 49085

Call Sign: AB8GK
Wilfred C Stapley
4118 Grandwood Cir
Saint Joseph MI 49085

Call Sign: KA8UYL
James E Pabis Sr
1310 Harrison Ave
Saint Joseph MI
490851724

Call Sign: KA8AGB
Edward H Getz
1337 Harrison Ave
Saint Joseph MI 49085

Call Sign: KB8UKP
Mike W Knapp
1216 Hillcrest Ave
Saint Joseph MI 49085

Call Sign: KC8YSY

Marsha K Laya
429 Howard
Saint Joseph MI 49085

Call Sign: N8KHH
Jerry J Stelling
992 Jean Ann
Saint Joseph MI 49085

Call Sign: WB8ZCV
Paul E Simonton
3160 Kevin St
Saint Joseph MI 49085

Call Sign: KB8GXH
Robert F Plante
711 Kingsley Ave
Saint Joseph MI 49085

Call Sign: W9SAT
R Bryce Glenn
920 Kingsley Ave
Saint Joseph MI
490852018

Call Sign: N8NQX
Mark L Herman
3919 Kristine St
Saint Joseph MI 49085

Call Sign: KB8EKX
Jerry E Tomaszewski
536 La Salle
Saint Joseph MI 49085

Call Sign: WA6UPT
William G
Stringfellow
2616 Lake Bluff Ter
Saint Joseph MI
490859204

Call Sign: KE8CR
James C Folk
1301 Lake Blvd
Saint Joseph MI
490851547

Call Sign: KA8VBI
Jo Anne Gustafson
325 Lake Ct
Saint Joseph MI 49085

Call Sign: WB8ERG

Conrad A Reichert
2720 Lake Pine Path
Apt 110
Saint Joseph MI 49085

Call Sign: KB8EGD
Iris J De Morrow
503 Lake St
Saint Joseph MI 49085

Call Sign: WB8DNQ
John F Sullivan
3001 Lakeshore Dr
Apt 248
Saint Joseph MI 49085

Call Sign: KA8UYF
Ronald L Edwards
2708 Lakeshore Dr
Apt 305
Saint Joseph MI 49085

Call Sign: N8HLI
William T Moore
3005 Lakeshore Dr
Apt 314
Saint Joseph MI 49085

Call Sign: KC8HLO
Travis A Cole
2704 Lakeshore Dr
Apt 401
Saint Joseph MI 49085

Call Sign: N8UUV
Dan L McElwain
3612 Lakeshore Dr
Apt D12
Saint Joseph MI 49085

Call Sign: KA8OXX
Lloyd F Sanborn
2618 Lakeview Ave
Saint Joseph MI 49085

Call Sign: N8VXI
Charles W Berk
2803 Lakeview Ave
Saint Joseph MI 49085

Call Sign: KC8KKB
Brad E Carr
3746 Lane Ct
Saint Joseph MI 49085

Call Sign: N8XXK
Daniel H Conklin
514 Lasalle Ave
Saint Joseph MI 49085

Call Sign: KD8NOF
Ronald D Sortland
1016 Lausman Dr
Saint Joseph MI 49085

Call Sign: WA8LFI
Gordon P McFaul
3033 Lincoln Ave
Saint Joseph MI 49085

Call Sign: KE4FKL
John W Helsley Jr
715 Lincoln Pines Pl
Saint Joseph MI 49085

Call Sign: N3WXF
Douglas K Sluss
3617 Lincoln Pines St
Saint Joseph MI 49085

Call Sign: KC8MNF
Gary J Hirsch
516 Lions Park Dr
Saint Joseph MI 49085

Call Sign: WD8AOK
Bruce U Capes
916 Lions Pk Dr
Saint Joseph MI 49085

Call Sign: KD8ALP
Robert A Neel Jr
3427 Locust Ln
Saint Joseph MI
490853716

Call Sign: KD8RMN
Stephen P Zanto
4799 Luther Path
Saint Joseph MI 49085

Call Sign: N7AJU
Edward J Pomeroy
1075 Lydia Dr
Saint Joseph MI 49085

Call Sign: KB8YNK
Jason D Bromberek

741 Maiden Ln
Saint Joseph MI 49085

Call Sign: N8KLY
Lars F Maaseidvaag
907 Michigan Ave
Saint Joseph MI 49085

Call Sign: N8OEI
John T Hammond
3390 Middlebrook Dr
Saint Joseph MI 49085

Call Sign: W8ORM
Albert F Carpenter
750 Miller Ln
Saint Joseph MI
490853616

Call Sign: W8DOR
Robert E Van Dyke
822 Miller Ln
Saint Joseph MI 49085

Call Sign: K8POW
Ray E Zebell Jr
1224 Mohawk Ln
Saint Joseph MI 49085

Call Sign: K8BAU
Leroy F Champagne
1011 Morrison Ave
Saint Joseph MI 49085

Call Sign: KD8ZB
Matthew M Adrian
1792 Nash Dr
Saint Joseph MI 49085

Call Sign: KD8IIX
Michael D Thieneman
1417 Newberry Hills
Ln
Saint Joseph MI 49085

Call Sign: WA8WTS
J Thomas Butler
1802 Niles Ave
Saint Joseph MI 49085

Call Sign: W8MNB
Douglas W Smith
2563 Niles Rd
Saint Joseph MI 49085

Call Sign: KC8UXI
Jonathan D Gephart
3867 Niles Rd
Saint Joseph MI 49085

Call Sign: KB8QAL
Jonathan L Kovarik
1575 Oak Ter
Saint Joseph MI 49085

Call Sign: N8XSD
Lynn P Kovarik
1575 Oak Ter
Saint Joseph MI 49085

Call Sign: N8CBA
Jeffrey M Hopwood
765 Oakridge Dr
Saint Joseph MI 49085

Call Sign: KD8ALO
Marlene E Koehl
1454 Old Farm Ln
Saint Joseph MI 49085

Call Sign: W8KTL
Raymond B Comfort
1561 Old Hickory Ln
Saint Joseph MI 49085

Call Sign: KD8PN
George C Sparke
690 Park Den St
Saint Joseph MI 49085

Call Sign: N8DKP
Arthur J Schmidt Jr
517 Petrie Ave
Saint Joseph MI
490851927

Call Sign: KG8LO
Thomas E Hollowell
Sr
2405 Pine Hill Ct
Saint Joseph MI 49085

Call Sign: KB8DRA
Onam Smith
2619 Pixley Ave
Saint Joseph MI 49085

Call Sign: WB8WLS

Howard M Hutchinson
601 Port St Apt 1408
Saint Joseph MI 49085

Call Sign: WA8WNX
Allen G Haughey
333 Rainbow Dr
Saint Joseph MI 49085

Call Sign: W9JXM
Mark M Senninger
501 Ridgeway St
Saint Joseph MI 49085

Call Sign: W8JAN
Thomas C Yeager
544 Ridgeway St
Saint Joseph MI 49085

Call Sign: NN8T
John W Helsley Sr
2339 Riverside Pointe
Saint Joseph MI 49085

Call Sign: KC8TWD
Roger T Morrissett
1222 Riverwood Ter
Saint Joseph MI
490852118

Call Sign: WB0CEY
Stephen L Hempel
301 S Bluffwood Ter
Saint Joseph MI 49085

Call Sign: WA8KEW
Raymond A Nelson
1769 S Cambridge
Saint Joseph MI 49085

Call Sign: N8KUJ
Brian C Fritz
227 S Sunnybank
Saint Joseph MI 49085

Call Sign: KD8EOF
Michael B Bradley
1554 Saint Joseph Cir
Saint Joseph MI 49085

Call Sign: WD9BDP
Mark D Holloway
3822 Southfield Dr
Saint Joseph MI 49085

Call Sign: KD8ALN
Robert R Conrad
1452 St Joseph Cir
Saint Joseph MI 49085

Call Sign: KC8JX
Lawrence P Knapp
1509 St Joseph Cir
Saint Joseph MI 49085

Call Sign: W8UVK
Carl F Heald
1510 St Joseph Cir
Saint Joseph MI 49085

Call Sign: KG1Z
Robert L Clark
717 St Joseph Dr
Saint Joseph MI 49085

Call Sign: W8JFW
Robert T Hatch
1100 State St
Saint Joseph MI 49085

Call Sign: W8JMS
John M Stafford
4297 Sunnymeade Dr
Saint Joseph MI
490859341

Call Sign: KD8NW
Gareth H Dominy
2019 Sunset Dr
Saint Joseph MI 49085

Call Sign: KC8FZC
John W Weil
4661 Terra Ln
Saint Joseph MI 49085

Call Sign: N8WFK
Mark W Weil
4661 Terra Ln
Saint Joseph MI 49085

Call Sign: KD8FFO
Joseph A Agay
2825 Thayer Dr
Saint Joseph MI 49085

Call Sign: KD8FFN
Milton A Agay

2825 Thayer Dr
Saint Joseph MI 49085

Call Sign: KD4YIW
Paul A Freye
1508 Trebor Rd
Saint Joseph MI
490853723

Call Sign: KD8MNH
Duane F Horton
1431 Ventnor Ave
Saint Joseph MI 49085

Call Sign: N3UXN
Richard L Stern
4736 Vince Ct
Saint Joseph MI 49085

Call Sign: N1CKG
Gordon L Helm
1023 Vineland
Saint Joseph MI 49085

Call Sign: KC8YPP
Mark L Parren
1051 Vinewood Dr
Saint Joseph MI
490853236

Call Sign: KB8WJS
Brian D Weackler
1526 W Marquette
Woods Rd
Saint Joseph MI 49085

Call Sign: KB8PVB
Richard J Williamson
906 W Napier Ave
Saint Joseph MI 49085

Call Sign: NQ8A
Larry A Schrader
3266 W Valley View
Dr
Saint Joseph MI
490859479

Call Sign: W8IWO
Frederick A Rogers
3381 W Valley View
Dr
Saint Joseph MI 49085

Call Sign: WD8AOA
Gary J Huff
3067 Washington Ave
Saint Joseph MI 49085

Call Sign: KC8FHN
Steve M Baydowicz
1086 Wedgewood Rd
Saint Joseph MI 49085

Call Sign: KA8UYK
Joan S Kleaveland
2602 Willa Dr
Saint Joseph MI 49085

Call Sign: WB8IMD
Joseph F Montella
2719 Willa Dr
Saint Joseph MI 49085

Call Sign: KG4EDK
Matthew T Severin
2814 Willa Dr
Saint Joseph MI 49085

Call Sign: N8TFU
Douglas M Bonham
2819 Willa Dr
Saint Joseph MI 49085

Call Sign: KD8CZN
Caroline A Morris
528 Winchester Ave
Saint Joseph MI
490851663

Call Sign: KA8RCW
David S Schmitt
535 Winchester Ave
Saint Joseph MI 49085

Call Sign: KM8V
Frederick L Brutsche
3811 Windermere Dr
Saint Joseph MI
490859416

Call Sign: KC8HBT
Cam E Utsman
2973 Windsor Dr
Saint Joseph MI 49085

Call Sign: WA8JBW
Thomas W Smith

Saint Joseph MI 49085

Call Sign: W8TWS
Thomas W Smith
Saint Joseph MI 49085

Call Sign: W8MAI
Blossomland Amateur
Radio Association
Saint Joseph MI 49085

Call Sign: KA5GLP
Roger J Kinnavy Jr
Saint Joseph MI 49085

Call Sign: KD8IRV
Steven P Foster
Saint Joseph MI 49085

Call Sign: KC8LTW
Philip M Hudson
8189 20 Mile Rd
Sand Lake MI 49343

Call Sign: W8PHL
Philip M Hudson
8189 20 Mile Rd
Sand Lake MI 49343

Call Sign: N8KMD
Kerry B Terpenning
6371 21 Mile Rd
Sand Lake MI 49343

Call Sign: N8LUE
Dawn R Branch
Terpenning
6371 21 Mile Rd
Sand Lake MI 49343

Call Sign: KA8ACZ
Wanda H Raymond
3400 22 Mile Rd
Sand Lake MI 49343

Call Sign: KA8ADA
Farrand F Raymond Sr
3400 22 Mile Rd
Sand Lake MI 49343

Call Sign: KC8JBX
Jon J Brown
27 6th St
Sand Lake MI
493430094

Call Sign: KC8OPT
Jennifer L Gunneson
82 Cedar St
Sand Lake MI 49343

Call Sign: KC8YTC
Kenneth R Meksula
5575 Coan NE
Sand Lake MI 49343

Call Sign: WD8AMI
Randolph O Johnson
22155 Leota Dr
Sand Lake MI 49343

Call Sign: NO8R
Delos R Byrne
12801 Maston Lake Dr
NE
Sand Lake MI 49343

Call Sign: KC8FDM
Ruth A Tallman
16200 Myers Lake
Ave
Sand Lake MI
493439549

Call Sign: KD8PWG
Jerilyn A Bell
3022 Rau Dr
Sand Lake MI 49343

Call Sign: KD8EOI
Milton L Weeks
16987 Shawano
Sand Lake MI 49343

Call Sign: KD8EVY
Nicholas J Andres
1544 W County Line
Rd
Sand Lake MI 49343

Call Sign: KD8CPJ
Clair A Andres
1544 W County Line
Rd

Sand Lake MI 49343

Call Sign: AC8IY
Clair A Andres
1544 W County Line
Rd
Sand Lake MI 49343

Call Sign: KD8PIV
John J Hannon
18950 W South
County Line Rd
Sand Lake MI 49343

Call Sign: KC8PQF
Jack D Ryan Jr
6670 Bliss Rd
Saranac MI 48881

Call Sign: KC8REF
Wanda J Ryan
6670 Bliss Rd
Saranac MI 48881

Call Sign: KC8TTD
Delma E Pitchford
5382 Grand Rider Ave
Saranac MI 48881

Call Sign: N8TSJ
Jerry W Pitchford
5382 Grand River
Saranac MI 48881

Call Sign: K8TSJ
Delma E Pitchford
5382 Grand River Ave
Saranac MI 48881

Call Sign: KD8QGT
Lucas J Falsetta
6777 Jackson Rd
Saranac MI 48881

Call Sign: W8BRB
Lucas J Falsetta
6777 Jackson Rd
Saranac MI 48881

Call Sign: KC8IMH
Paul P Hunter

1690 Johnson Rd
Saranac MI 48881

Call Sign: KD8PVL
Dana Q Proctor
2061 Johnson Rd
Saranac MI 48881

Call Sign: KD8KLN
John T Vogelzang
8408 Macarthur Rd
Saranac MI 48881

Call Sign: N8GLZ
Craig J Spanberger
5670 Nash Hwy
Saranac MI 48881

Call Sign: W9AJC
Hubert R Nelsen
768 Paradise Park
Saranac MI 48881

Call Sign: KC8NTR
Art W Jones
7621 Parsonage Rd
Saranac MI 48881

Call Sign: KD8LZS
Brian D Bergy
6971 Regan Dr
Saranac MI 48881

Call Sign: KD8NEY
Brayton R Grant
9055 Rickert Rd
Saranac MI 48881

Call Sign: KC8ZTK
Paul L Woodward
2042 S Johnson Rd
Saranac MI 48881

Call Sign: KB8YJA
Arthur C Hotchkiss
7067 Sayles Rd
Saranac MI 488819419

Call Sign: WB8HNI
Jack L Finley
320 Summit St Apt
210
Saranac MI 488819526

Call Sign: KC8PFW
Michelle L Bush
62 Washington Ave
Saranac MI 48881

Call Sign: KD8MDN
Elizabeth A Bush
62 Washington Ave
Saranac MI 48881

Call Sign: KD8MDS
Richard C Bush III
62 Washington Ave
Saranac MI 48881

Call Sign: KC8IMT
Ionia County ARC
136 Washington Ave
Saranac MI 488819506

Call Sign: KC8NDA
Richard C Bush II
62 Washington St
Saranac MI 48881

Call Sign: KC8ZTU
Edward E Cadieux
Saranac MI 48881

Call Sign: KD8OSH
Helen M Smith
Saranac MI 48881

Call Sign: N8MRC
Michael R Carigon
Saranac MI 48881

**FCC Amateur Radio
Licenses in Saugatuck**

Call Sign: WA8ERG
Martin G Raebel II
3460 64th St
Saugatuck MI 49453

Call Sign: KD8HRE
James J Nee
3515 66th St
Saugatuck MI 49453

Call Sign: KD8HRD
Kathy S Nee
3515 66th St
Saugatuck MI 49453

Call Sign: KD8LNL
Eli Ramos
6139 Blue Star Hwy
Saugatuck MI 49453

Call Sign: W9MPW
Gilbert J Vollink
257 Brook St
Saugatuck MI 49453

Call Sign: KD8JNZ
Richard J Ruckauf
6424 Destin Ct
Saugatuck MI 49453

Call Sign: W8BVR
Emil E Kubanek
6298 Old Allegan Rd
Saugatuck MI 49453

Call Sign: KF8DV
Scott L Siebelink
6418 Otis Rd
Saugatuck MI 49453

Call Sign: N8NXA
Barbara J Siebelink
6418 Otis Rd
Saugatuck MI 49453

Call Sign: N8TLP
David J Andersen
Saugatuck MI 49453

Call Sign: KC8CDL
Thomas D Rexius
Saugatuck MI
494530339

**FCC Amateur Radio
Licenses in Sault
Sainte Marie**

Call Sign: KC8JLG
Andrew J Armstrong
2654 Ashmun St
Sault Sainte Marie MI
497833712

Call Sign: N5FSH
Edward Cowen
813 Bingham Ave

Sault Sainte Marie MI
49783

Call Sign: W8LQX
George A Rohrer
1135 Bingham Ave
Sault Sainte Marie MI
49783

Call Sign: K8ZSM
Clare M Smith
200 Bluewater Dr
Sault Sainte Marie MI
49783

Call Sign: K8QJA
Frank J Kowalesky
Hc 46 Box 120
Sault Sainte Marie MI
49783

Call Sign: KB8WTV
Floyd T Mills
R 1 Box 158Aaa
Sault Sainte Marie MI
49783

Call Sign: KC8AOP
Mike H Rousseau
Rt 1 Box 158Aaa
Sault Sainte Marie MI
49783

Call Sign: KC8EUX
Jared S Swartz
Rr 2 Box 179
Sault Sainte Marie MI
49783

Call Sign: KC8HHT
Joseph D Samp
724 Buchanen Dr
Sault Sainte Marie MI
49783

Call Sign: KE6CNZ
Dennis J Henry
5355 Cedar Dr
Sault Sainte Marie MI
49783

Call Sign: KC8KTA
Susan A Johnson
724 Cedar St

Sault Sainte Marie MI
497832410

Call Sign: W8CCY
Lawrence F Davis
1327 Charwood Cir
Sault Sainte Marie MI
49783

Call Sign: KC8MBH
Emma J Fowler
1814 Chestnut St
Sault Sainte Marie MI
49783

Call Sign: AC8FA
Tony P Lelieveld
1616 Davitt St
Sault Sainte Marie MI
49783

Call Sign: K8DWI
Tony P Lelieveld
1616 Davitt St
Sault Sainte Marie MI
49783

Call Sign: KB8SKC
James M Callon
1616 Davitt St
Sault Sainte Marie MI
49783

Call Sign: KD8QYQ
Harvey M Hammock
1606 E 10th Ave
Sault Sainte Marie MI
49783

Call Sign: W8HRV
Harvey M Hammock
1606 E 10th Ave
Sault Sainte Marie MI
49783

Call Sign: KB8ZUI
Scott M Bartz
6577 E 12 Mile Rd
Sault Sainte Marie MI
49783

Call Sign: KC8MCD
Susan J Bartz
6577 E 12 Mile Rd

Sault Sainte Marie MI
49783

Call Sign: N0SZB
David H Broten
122 E 25 Ave
Sault Sainte Marie MI
49783

Call Sign: KD8TDR
Todd D Roe
1287 E 3 Mile Rd
Sault Sainte Marie MI
49783

Call Sign: KC8HEO
Robert E McKechnie
1299 E 3 Mile Rd
Sault Sainte Marie MI
49783

Call Sign: N8QBY
Patrick W Bernard
2664 E 3 Mile Rd
Sault Sainte Marie MI
49783

Call Sign: WB8BIX
Robert J Proulx
4750 E 6 Mi
Sault Sainte Marie MI
49783

Call Sign: KA8DGT
Leroy A Fake
1019 E 8th Ave
Sault Sainte Marie MI
49783

Call Sign: KC8PSF
Stanley E Newill
307 E Spruce St
Sault Sainte Marie MI
49783

Call Sign: KC8NTT
James A Davison
409 E Spruce St
Sault Sainte Marie MI
497832136

Call Sign: KD8NVV
Oliver F Fernander
907 E Spruce St

Sault Sainte Marie MI
49783

Call Sign: N8VVV
Mary E Lamoreaux
662 Ford Dr
Sault Sainte Marie MI
49783

Call Sign: KD8DTI
Sault Area Contesting
Klub
220 Hursley
Sault Sainte Marie MI
49783

Call Sign: KA8F
Sault Area Contesting
Klub
220 Hursley
Sault Sainte Marie MI
49783

Call Sign: WA8OLD
David P Deatrick
220 Hursley
Sault Sainte Marie MI
49783

Call Sign: KC8YPY
Kristopher B Deatrick
220 Hursley St
Sault Sainte Marie MI
497832227

Call Sign: W8UOM
Kristopher B Deatrick
220 Hursley St
Sault Sainte Marie MI
497832227

Call Sign: W8EUP
Eastern Upper
Peninsula Amateur
Radio
220 Hursley St
Sault Sainte Marie MI
49783

Call Sign: KC8PSE
James M O Gorman
809 John St
Sault Sainte Marie MI
49783

Call Sign: W8JZG
Gerard A Roy
1215 John St
Sault Sainte Marie MI
49783

Call Sign: KC8HEM
Gerald F Lalonde
207 Johnston
Sault Sainte Marie MI
49783

Call Sign: AB8CB
Lyle H Willette
752 Kimball St
Sault Sainte Marie MI
49783

Call Sign: KC8PAF
Scott E Ford
911 Kimball St
Sault Sainte Marie MI
49783

Call Sign: WH6ADE
Arn M Heggers
1012 Kimball St
Sault Sainte Marie MI
49783

Call Sign: KC8NUT
Beverly R Tankersley
2621 Lake Blvd The
Shallows
Sault Sainte Marie MI
497831001

Call Sign: KG8QA
Margaret E Pearce
3468 Lakeshore Dr
Sault Sainte Marie MI
49783

Call Sign: N8LNG
David B Pearce
3468 Lakeshore Dr
Sault Sainte Marie MI
49783

Call Sign: WB8JQM
Ronald J Pattison
915 Lizzie St

Sault Sainte Marie MI
49783

Call Sign: KE8IG
Charles G Dickinson
1125 Mann Dr
Sault Sainte Marie MI
497832546

Call Sign: KD8OOP
Todd D Roe
417 Maple St
Sault Sainte Marie MI
49783

Call Sign: KC8SIZ
Algoma Chippewa
ARES Races Network
1412 Minneapolis
Sault Sainte Marie MI
49783

Call Sign: WA8UFK
Louis J Montero
2910 Minneapolis
Sault Sainte Marie MI
49783

Call Sign: N8JIS
Evan L Schemm
1412 Minneapolis St
Sault Sainte Marie MI
49783

Call Sign: KC8LKD
Jerry J Timm
623 Myrtle Elliott Cir
23
Sault Sainte Marie MI
49783

Call Sign: KC8JLB
Dennis A Earhart
623 Myrtle Elliott Cir
Apt 26
Sault Sainte Marie MI
49783

Call Sign: KC8LXS
Brian P Lavey
508 N Ravine St
Sault Sainte Marie MI
49783

Call Sign: KC8BLA
Dennis A Earhart
821 N Wescott Ln
Sault Sainte Marie MI
49783

Call Sign: WL7BKR
David M Myton
1100 Parnell Ave
Sault Sainte Marie MI
49783

Call Sign: KC8HEJ
Benjamin N Myton
1100 Parnell Ave
Sault Sainte Marie MI
497832756

Call Sign: W8BEN
Benjamin N Myton
1100 Parnell Ave
Sault Sainte Marie MI
497832756

Call Sign: W8SOO
Ken R Demaray
1011 Prospect St
Sault Sainte Marie MI
49783

Call Sign: KC8MJW
Lloyd J Gibbs
605 Ridge St
Sault Sainte Marie MI
49783

Call Sign: KC8LXR
Carl J Stutzner
2565 Riverside Dr
Sault Sainte Marie MI
49783

Call Sign: KB8WTW
Betty J Mills
8020 S Lower Haylake
Rd
Sault Sainte Marie MI
49783

Call Sign: KC8RVV
Michael R Worley
8372 S M 129
Sault Sainte Marie MI
49783

Call Sign: W8JQ
Charles C Richardson
16652 S M 129
Sault Sainte Marie MI
49783

Call Sign: KC8QAK
Jeffrey P Sullivan
9244 S Mackinaw Trl
Sault Sainte Marie MI
49783

Call Sign: W8ICE
Jeffrey P Sullivan
9244 S Mackinaw Trl
Sault Sainte Marie MI
49783

Call Sign: KD8BDW
Doreen P Freeborn
4421 S Nicolet Rd
Sault Sainte Marie MI
49783

Call Sign: WA8UAA
Kenneth E Lake
3142 S Sun Glo Dr
Sault Sainte Marie MI
49783

Call Sign: N8IZ
Timothy A Switzer
3466 S Westshore Dr
Sault Sainte Marie MI
497838829

Call Sign: K8JMC
James M Callon Jr
5861 Scenic Dr
Sault Sainte Marie MI
49783

Call Sign: KB0OTT
Kathryn M Callon
5861 Scenic Dr
Sault Sainte Marie MI
49783

Call Sign: WA8IXD
John W Mackey
606 Sheridan Dr
Sault Sainte Marie MI
49783

Call Sign: N8GMC
Robert J Hovie
607 Sheridan Dr
Sault Sainte Marie MI
49783

Call Sign: KC8WYR
Carlton G Rich
3104 Sherman Park Dr
Sault Sainte Marie MI
49783

Call Sign: N7DSJ
James E Haglund
3301 Sherman Park Dr
Sault Sainte Marie MI
49783

Call Sign: WA8HHE
Clyde B Beale
918 Summit St
Sault Sainte Marie MI
49783

Call Sign: KB8FHL
John P Beale
918 Summit St
Sault Sainte Marie MI
49783

Call Sign: KD8EOV
David M Theut
1001 Superior St
Sault Sainte Marie MI
49783

Call Sign: KB7UEX
Daniel M Workenaour
2524 Tahoma Way
Sault Sainte Marie MI
49783

Call Sign: KB8HPO
Sara B Ames
110 W 10th Ave
Sault Sainte Marie MI
49783

Call Sign: KC8HEK
Floyd F Bricker Jr
121 W 11th Ave
Sault Sainte Marie MI
49783

Call Sign: N8IMT
Betty J Bricker
124 W 12 Ave
Sault Sainte Marie MI
49783

Call Sign: N8IFH
Robert C Voorhees
124 W 12 Ave
Sault Sainte Marie MI
49783

Call Sign: WD8KUC
Daniel M Harwood
1933 W 14th St
Sault Sainte Marie MI
49783

Call Sign: W8BEP
David Gregg Sr
2117 W 3rd Ave
Sault Sainte Marie MI
49783

Call Sign: KC8FHJ
Stacey E Swartz
66 W 6 Mile
Sault Sainte Marie MI
49783

Call Sign: WD8KUD
Janie A Harwood
1701 W 8th Ave
Sault Sainte Marie MI
49783

Call Sign: KC8QIB
Ora C Mccready III
614 Washington Way
Sault Sainte Marie MI
49783

Call Sign: W8OCM
Ora C Mccready III
614 Washington Way
Sault Sainte Marie MI
49783

Call Sign: KC0KVL
Denis R James Sr
1711 Young St
Sault Sainte Marie MI
49783

Call Sign: N8XQQ
William B Mac Millan
Sault Sainte Marie MI
49783

Call Sign: KB8PGX
Juergen M Pilz
Sault Sainte Marie MI
49783

Call Sign: W8BZ
Robert E Heath
Sault Sainte Marie MI
49783

Call Sign: K8OTL
William B Mac Millan
Sault Sainte Marie MI
49783

Call Sign: N8XQP
Roy P Brockelbank
Sault Sainte Marie MI
49783

Call Sign: K1EYQ
James A Withers
Sault Sainte Marie MI
49783

Call Sign: KC8LKE
Bruce J Lenton
Sault Sainte Marie MI
49783

FCC Amateur Radio Licenses in Sawyer

Call Sign: WR8R
Lee G Lull
5407 Browntown Rd
Sawyer MI 49125

Call Sign: K8YRT
John E Olson
6374 Harbert Rd
Sawyer MI 49125

Call Sign: KC8IEC
Ernest S Brandon
6002 S Wolcott Ave
Sawyer MI 49125

Call Sign: WD8IAR
Leo Segar
12829 Sand Ridge Rd
Sawyer MI 49125

Call Sign: KC8HBV
Phillip U Castelluccio
5940 Sawyer Rd
Sawyer MI 49125

Call Sign: N8RCP
Donald J Skorupa Sr
5991 Sawyer Rde
Sawyer MI 49125

Call Sign: KD8GOQ
Glenn D Gustafson
12370 Tower Hill Rd
Sawyer MI 49125

Call Sign: W5GDG
Glenn D Gustafson
12370 Tower Hill Rd
Sawyer MI 49125

FCC Amateur Radio Licenses in Schoolcraft

Call Sign: KC8YEU
Grant Johnston
2221 Crimora
Schoolcraft MI 49087

Call Sign: N8DVY
Donald P Stephens
211 E Clay St
Schoolcraft MI 49087

Call Sign: KA8GAK
Collette R Rice
13429 S 14th St
Schoolcraft MI 49087

Call Sign: KC8OOE
Theresa A O'Neil Cook
11386 S 2nd St
Schoolcraft MI 49087

Call Sign: WS8H
Richard W Carpenter
5287 W R Ave
Schoolcraft MI 49087

Call Sign: KD8AAF
Molly M Buckham
6508 W R Ave
Schoolcraft MI 49087

Call Sign: WA8PLW
William L Nichols
5746 W Vw Ave
Schoolcraft MI 49087

Call Sign: KD8NPW
John M Jacobs
6344 W Vw Ave
Schoolcraft MI 49087

Call Sign: KD8JU
Sandra K Leversee
754 W W Ave
Schoolcraft MI 49087

Call Sign: KD8VC
Douglas C Leversee
754 W W Ave
Schoolcraft MI 49087

Call Sign: KA5DIE
Raymond L
Hendriksma
124 West St
Schoolcraft MI
490877409

FCC Amateur Radio Licenses in Scotts

Call Sign: KD8RHB
Bret C White
8449 33rd St S
Scotts MI 49088

Call Sign: KC8IYC
Jesse L Burns
7592 E Op Ave
Scotts MI 49088

Call Sign: KC0OQP
Dinah J Hoke
10487 E Q Ave
Scotts MI 49088

Call Sign: N8IDE
Betty J Tripp
8154 Greenfield
Shores

Scotts MI 49088

Call Sign: W8MP
Oliver R Woods
8354 Greenfield
Shores
Scotts MI 49088

Call Sign: KB8KNP
Dennis M Watson
9401 S 32nd St
Scotts MI 49088

Call Sign: KC8TQN
Edward L Purk
6742 S 34th St
Scotts MI 49088

Call Sign: KC8GXQ
Marty A Johnson
8630 S 36th St
Scotts MI 49088

Call Sign: KD8CIG
Gary P Hurt
11355 T Ave E
Scotts MI 49088

Call Sign: KC8H
Gary P Hurt
11355 T Ave E
Scotts MI 49088

Call Sign: KC8TQL
Gregory B Boer
9484 Woodin St
Scotts MI 49088

Call Sign: KB8CJH
Freddie L Webster
Scotts MI 490880071

Call Sign: N8IVM
Alex Barvicks
104 E 5th St
Scottville MI 49454

Call Sign: K8AXL
Charles C Chadwick
306 E 5th St
Scottville MI 49454

Call Sign: KD8DOD
Richard D Heglund
412 E Decker Rd
Scottville MI
494549653

Call Sign: KC8DCP
John L Frane
144 Ivan St
Scottville MI 49454

Call Sign: AB8CY
Robert R Merkey
2400 N Darr Rd
Scottville MI
494549654

Call Sign: W8NBH
Roger A Vitucki
2963 N US Hwy 31
Scottville MI 49454

Call Sign: KC8DCO
Jeff L Budzynski
717 S Gordon Ave
Scottville MI 49454

Call Sign: N8YOE
Kirk W Narmore
400 W 3rd At 402
Scottville MI 49454

Call Sign: N8WEV
Adam Jurkowski
1529 W Hansen Rd
Scottville MI 49454

Call Sign: KC8TTG
Bradley S Manor
2008 W Hansen Rd
Scottville MI 49454

Call Sign: N8KHX
Sylvia A Maki
302 W Maple Ave
Scottville MI 49454

Call Sign: WW8U
Richard L Maki
302 W Maple Ave
Scottville MI 49454

Call Sign: WB8KQX

Henry J De Good
1238 W Sugar Grove
Rd
Scottville MI 49454

Call Sign: WB8HFI
Aldis G Wagner
1473 W US 10
Scottville MI 49454

Call Sign: K8DXF
Mason County Radio
Club
1644 W US 10
Scottville MI 49454

Call Sign: KA9DIO
Susan L Kaiser
Scottville MI
494540162

Call Sign: N8XQG
John D Reiman
4108 Deer Run Ln
Sears MI 49679

Call Sign: KC8QOX
James P Darlington
5366 Logging Trl
Sears MI 49679

Call Sign: KC8UUP
Arthur W Damman
3485 N Shore Dr
Sears MI 49679

Call Sign: KB8IGN
Robert D Boger
4991 Washington St
Sears MI 49679

Call Sign: NK8G
Albert N Seccia
1540 W M 28
Seney MI 49883

Call Sign: N8OSD
Daniel L De Shetler

Seney MI 49883

Call Sign: KD8IGS
Jesse H Bowman
271 1st St
Shelby MI 49455

Call Sign: WD8DJI
Mike Bokulich
52811 Antoinette Dr
Shelby MI 48316

Call Sign: KB8YNM
Janet L Swanson
252 E Johnson
Shelby MI 49455

Call Sign: N8HKN
Ted H Swanson
252 E Johnson
Shelby MI 49455

Call Sign: KC8WIZ
Susan R Mussell
1670 E Shelby Rd
Shelby MI 49455

Call Sign: N8LPN
Harold R Marsh
286 N 88th Ave
Shelby MI 49455

Call Sign: N8NJI
Maxine L Marsh
286 N 88th Ave
Shelby MI 49455

Call Sign: KA8VEF
Daniel E Carrico
1693 S 58th Ave
Shelby MI 49455

Call Sign: W8OGN
George B Hallack
455 S Oceana Dr
Shelby MI 49455

Call Sign: KB8ULP
Paul K Pearl
687 S Oceana Dr
Shelby MI 49455

Call Sign: N8NMB
Arthur F Hagstrom
1172 S Oceana Dr
Shelby MI 49455

Call Sign: AJ1P
Thomas P West Jr
637 S Point Rd
Shelby MI 49455

Call Sign: N8JGS
Robert E Howey
779 S Point Rd
Shelby MI 49455

Call Sign: KC8GED
Michael R Green
4217 Scenic Dr
Shelby MI 49455

Call Sign: N8ODU
William G Brown
2005 W Buchanan
Shelby MI 49455

Call Sign: K8HJ
John C Huffman
7371 W Buchanan Rd
Shelby MI 49455

Call Sign: KC8OEQ
Walter W Walsh
8254 W Shelby Rd
Shelby MI 49455

Call Sign: KD8NOK
Warren E Wentzloff
8550 W Shelby Rd
Shelby MI 49455

Call Sign: KE8DB
Jeff T Rairigh
12000 12 Mile Rd
Shelbyville MI 49344

Call Sign: KE8DD
Janine M Rairigh
12000 12 Mile Rd
Shelbyville MI 49344

Call Sign: N8WUM
Keith W Larsen
858- 125th Ave Unit 1
Shelbyville MI 49344

Call Sign: WD8NME
Thomas P McInerney
442 126th Ave
Shelbyville MI 49344

Call Sign: N9CNM
John C Babrick
750 126th Ave
Shelbyville MI 49344

Call Sign: KC8RKH
Kevin A Stephenson
2466 4th St
Shelbyville MI 49344

Call Sign: N8OFX
Emmett H Kadwell Jr
2794 6th St
Shelbyville MI 49344

Call Sign: W8TZA
William C Kirks
12859 9 Mile Rd
Shelbyville MI 49344

Call Sign: W8WKD
Sharon L Kirks
12859 9 Mile Rd
Shelbyville MI 49344

Call Sign: WB8SCJ
Andrew Vander Meer
11888 England Dr
Shelbyville MI 49344

Call Sign: W8RXR
Walter J McDonald
4282 Lynden Rd
Shelbyville MI 49344

Call Sign: K8TJH
August M Wickland
4960 Marsh Rd R1
Shelbyville MI
493449626

Call Sign: W8RR
Gary F Kaser

2364 Patterson Rd
Shelbyville MI 49344

Call Sign: K8KOR
Dan M Hausermann
2414 Pearl St
Shelbyville MI 49344

Call Sign: KD8DZT
Ronald J Betz
3200 Condensery
Sheridan MI 48884

Call Sign: KD8DQA
Blaine A Jenks
648 Condensery Rd
Sheridan MI 48884

Call Sign: KC8VXD
David B Mccomb
4329 Condensery Rd
Sheridan MI 48884

Call Sign: KA8ZPO
Michael S Alexander
1503 County Farm Rd
Sheridan MI 48884

Call Sign: K8BOQ
Wilfred F Wieczorek
Jr
481 Dorothy Bowen
Dr
Sheridan MI 48884

Call Sign: WB8WYK
Martha J Wieczorek
481 Dorothy Bowen
Dr
Sheridan MI 48884

Call Sign: K8HE
Harry W Eldridge
3402 E Boyer Rd
Sheridan MI 48884

Call Sign: KD8FSV
Tandalaya M Neve
3485 E Condensery Rd
Sheridan MI 48884

Call Sign: KC8ZTP
James L Bovee
381 E Holland Lake Dr
Box 314
Sheridan MI 48884

Call Sign: K8HE
Harry W Eldridge
935 E Sidney Rd
Sheridan MI 48884

Call Sign: NR8Y
Century Club Truckers
Club
3902 E Sidney Rd
Sheridan MI 48884

Call Sign: NZ0F
Century Club Truckers
Club
3902 E Sidney Rd
Sheridan MI 48884

Call Sign: WM8P
Harry W Eldridge
3902 E Sidney Rd
Sheridan MI 48884

Call Sign: KD8DCA
Sheila M Eldridge
3303 Log Cabin Trl
Sheridan MI 48884

Call Sign: KD8DBP
Thomas A Eldridge
3303 Log Cabin Trl
Sheridan MI 48884

Call Sign: KD8LMO
Jodi L Cole
4231 Miller Rd
Sheridan MI 48884

Call Sign: WD8BWE
John W Billett
6170 Peck Rd
Sheridan MI 48884

Call Sign: KA8LDL
Richard L Blackmer
401 S Main St
Sheridan MI 48884

Call Sign: KC8ZPF

Clifford J Searles
7075 S Stevenson Rd
Sheridan MI
488849710

Call Sign: KC8KCU
Robert L Macdonald Jr
6934 S Vickeryville
Rd
Sheridan MI 48884

Call Sign: WB8DXV
Don E Ralph
6037 Stevenson Rd
Sheridan MI 48884

Call Sign: KD8AFJ
Patricia A Searles
7075 Stevenson Rd SE
Sheridan MI
488849710

Call Sign: WA8FJF
Henry Rydahl
2806 W Carson City
Rd
Sheridan MI 48884

Call Sign: N8YJQ
Gerald W Hoye 2Nd
2836 W Kroman
Sheridan MI 48884

Call Sign: K8CRD
Paul Horn
2693 W Muskrat Rd
Sheridan MI
488849459

Call Sign: WD8KFE
Larry L Vos
4625 W Wise Rd
Sheridan MI 48884

**FCC Amateur Radio
Licenses in Sherwood**

Call Sign: KC8ETK
Christopher S Noel
228 N Wheatfield Rd
Sherwood MI 49089

**FCC Amateur Radio
Licenses in
Shingleton**

Call Sign: W8UPS
Roland Karklin
N7775 H 58
Shingleton MI 49884

Call Sign: KC8HE
Donald R Nord
N9992 Nevins Lake Dr
Shingleton MI 49884

**FCC Amateur Radio
Licenses in Sidnaw**

Call Sign: N8OXZ
Paul A Jacobson
Sidnaw MI 49961

**FCC Amateur Radio
Licenses in Sidney**

Call Sign: KC8BME
Don A Wittkopp
2138 S Derby Rd
Sidney MI 48885

Call Sign: N8GTU
Daniel L Nash Jr
3502 S Holland Rd
Sidney MI 48885

Call Sign: KA8ZCT
Robert J Kline
5305 Woods Rd
Sidney MI 48885

**FCC Amateur Radio
Licenses in Six Lakes**

Call Sign: N8VWF
Rex N De Vree
681 Coolidge
Six Lakes MI 48886

Call Sign: KD8FSX
Christine S Nelsen
2226 Dewey Rd
Six Lakes MI 48886

Call Sign: KD8FSW

Morgan L Anderson
116 E Vesta St
Six Lakes MI 48886

Call Sign: KB8KFA
Peter M Voss
1410 Judy Dr
Six Lakes MI 48886

Call Sign: WA8DLI
Gregory J Hiscock
5802 Keeney Rd
Six Lakes MI 48886

Call Sign: KB8OQU
Martha K Burrill
2652 Lucille St
Six Lakes MI 48886

Call Sign: KE8KA
Lloyd J Brothers Jr
2652 Lucille St
Six Lakes MI 48886

Call Sign: N8BMC
Ernest E Cornell
10750 Miles Rd
Six Lakes MI 48886

Call Sign: KD8FST
Sherry A Nickerson
9675 Nevins Rd
Six Lakes MI 48886

Call Sign: KD8DBW
Kristina L King
2226 W Dewey Rd
Six Lakes MI 48886

Call Sign: K9EMM
Kristina L King
2226 W Dewey Rd
Six Lakes MI 48886

Call Sign: KD8IXY
Willie D Smith
1750 W Edgar Rd
Six Lakes MI 48829

Call Sign: N8HVY
Ronald K Estill
1136 W Felck Rd
Six Lakes MI 48886

Call Sign: KD8ICN
Phillip E Cole
3500 W Yankee Rd
Six Lakes MI 48886

Call Sign: N8KKV
Richard A Longstreet
Six Lakes MI 48886

**FCC Amateur Radio
Licenses in Skandia**

Call Sign: KC8DHZ
Christopher E Girard
2626 CR 456
Skandia MI 49885

Call Sign: KD8JIR
Michael A Beltz
703 CR 545 N
Skandia MI 49885

Call Sign: KC8JPV
Nicholas A Hautamaki
1125 CR 545 S
Skandia MI 49885

Call Sign: KD8NPI
Peter J Johnson
1183 CR 545 S
Skandia MI 49885

Call Sign: N4ILC
Pierre R Leach
496 Dalton Rd
Skandia MI 49885

Call Sign: KB8PPE
Andrew J Larsen
1801 Engman Lake Rd
Skandia MI 49885

Call Sign: KD8IAW
James A Kirkpatrick
495 Selma Rd
Skandia MI 49885

Call Sign: KC8ABW
Daniel P Dillinger
165 Town Line Rd
Skandia MI 498850137

Call Sign: W8LSY
Edward J Keto

9148 US Hwy 41 S
Skandia MI 49885

Call Sign: K8XE
Thomas E Lenon
10599 US Hwy 41 S
Skandia MI 498859559

Call Sign: N8MKA
Lemuel P Smyth
682 W M 94
Skandia MI 49885

Call Sign: W8WCC
Clifton K Jasper
Skandia MI 49885

Call Sign: KD8IAU
Kathren H Kirkpatrick
Skandia MI 49885

FCC Amateur Radio Licenses in Skanee

Call Sign: KD8DBD
Thomas R Collins
Hcr 1 Box 723
Skanee MI 49962

Call Sign: KD8ACQ
Mark G Buzenski
5880 N Huron Rd
Skanee MI 49962

FCC Amateur Radio Licenses in Sodus

Call Sign: N8VWM
Aric W Street
5963 Hillandale
Sodus MI 49126

Call Sign: KD8BUV
Patrick M Nolan
3241 Hillandale Rd
Sodus MI 49126

Call Sign: N8SIB
Keith A Kerbs
5962 Hillandale Rd
Sodus MI 49126

Call Sign: N8ZQP
Craig S Fair

3633 Townline Rd
Sodus MI 49126

FCC Amateur Radio Licenses in South Boardman

Call Sign: WB8TNX
Glen W Gerring
5359 Boardman St SW
South Boardman MI
49680

Call Sign: KC8SPR
Wesley R Szumera
5159 Creighton Rd SW
South Boardman MI
496800055

Call Sign: KC8HJS
Justin J Prough
925 Gregg Rd
South Boardman MI
49680

Call Sign: KB8ZPB
Margery E Bernholtz
1291 Gregg Rd
South Boardman MI
49680

Call Sign: KB8UTJ
Jeffrey C Kloepfer
4595 Ludlow
South Boardman MI
49680

Call Sign: KF4HZN
Barbara A Cram
4919 Session Dam Rd
South Boardman MI
49680

Call Sign: KB8SJT
Noel D Shrum
4919 Session Dam Rd
South Boardman MI
49680

Call Sign: KB8SJU
David V Shrum
4919 Session Dam Rd
South Boardman MI
49680

Call Sign: KF4FEB
Leonard E Cram
4919 Session Dam Rd
South Boardman MI
49680

Call Sign: N8PU
David V Shrum
4919 Session Dam Rd
South Boardman MI
49680

Call Sign: KC8HNE
Cynthia K Sleight
343 SW Montgomery
Rd
South Boardman MI
49680

FCC Amateur Radio Licenses in South Branch

Call Sign: K8VF
Mark A Kenward
7059 Chain Lake Dr
South Branch MI
48761

Call Sign: KA8UWT
Jimmie P Rice
7266 East Dr
South Branch MI
48761

Call Sign: KC8GXW
James E Harbin
7711 Nicole Dr
South Branch MI
48761

Call Sign: KC8HNR
Judith J Harbin
7711 Nicole Dr
South Branch MI
48761

Call Sign: KB8BLS
Catherine A McCubbin
South Branch MI
48761

Call Sign: N8FBX

Judy L Noell
South Branch MI
48761

Call Sign: N8GNI
Harry G Kauffman
South Branch MI
48761

FCC Amateur Radio Licenses in South Haven

Call Sign: W8BUD
Buddy L Coulter
7053 107th Ave
South Haven MI 49090

Call Sign: NO8Q
Buddy L Coulter
7053 107th Ave R2
South Haven MI 49090

Call Sign: W8LSV
Buddy L Coulter
7053 107th Ave R2
South Haven MI 49090

Call Sign: KA8VMI
Nancy J Hubley
70887 16th Ave
South Haven MI 49090

Call Sign: KL7EZ
Lewis E Parsell Sr
75641 16th Ave 20
South Haven MI 49090

Call Sign: KA8LEU
Howard A Hubley
70887 16th Ave Box
52A
South Haven MI 49090

Call Sign: WA8QGV
Maxwell E Seely
75641 16th Ave Lot 30
South Haven MI 49090

Call Sign: AB5VD
Robert L Dotson Jr
73647 26th St
South Haven MI 49090

Call Sign: KC8EWZ
Robert R Garvison
14502 64th St
South Haven MI 49090

Call Sign: KD8SBP
Jon A Clark
376 65th St
South Haven MI 49090

Call Sign: KB8QYL
Eugene D Slotman
1012 68th St
South Haven MI 49090

Call Sign: N0DZN
Leonard H Mack
6865 68th St
South Haven MI 49090

Call Sign: KA8YWP
Clayton R Kinney
18658 77th St
South Haven MI 49090

Call Sign: WA8PQN
Charles G Wenban
61245 8th Ave
South Haven MI 49090

Call Sign: N8UUW
Daniel L Hosier
68611 8th Ave
South Haven MI 49090

Call Sign: N5MGJ
Phillip H De Ruiter
71463 8th Ave Apt 2
South Haven MI
490909016

Call Sign: W8XI
Frank J Forsyth III
234 Bailey Ave
South Haven MI 49090

Call Sign: WA8LUQ
Anthony Rumiez
7309 Baseline Rd
South Haven MI 49090

Call Sign: KD8IUH
Ryan J Holbein

230 Baseline Rd Apt
E8
South Haven MI 49090

Call Sign: WA8ZXR
Rita A Wenban
230 Baseline Rd Apt
K1
South Haven MI 49090

Call Sign: WD4MZR
Joseph E Miles
67222 Becky Ln
South Haven MI 49090

Call Sign: WB7NKH
Wenda K Shaltry
4933 Cecilia Dr Apt
508
South Haven MI
490907142

Call Sign: KD8HXD
John A Shaul
620 Church St
South Haven MI 49090

Call Sign: KD8BQZ
Michael J Forrest
67833 CR 380
South Haven MI 49090

Call Sign: KA8NKT
Allen E Collins
74800 CR 380
South Haven MI 49090

Call Sign: KB8VZC
Mark D Peterson
76522 CR 380
South Haven MI 49090

Call Sign: KD8AHE
Robert J Torsten Jr
67300 CR 384
South Haven MI 49090

Call Sign: KC8NHK
William C Spratt
67663 CR 388 Lot 13
South Haven MI 49090

Call Sign: N8BOA
Patrick S Coady S

12730 CR 687
South Haven MI 49090

Call Sign: WD8JWX
James R Wolf
8679 CR 689
South Haven MI 49090

Call Sign: N8ARE
Henry R Bessler
1002 E Wilson Rd
South Haven MI 49090

Call Sign: N8QHD
Jeffrey R Bessler
1002 E Wilson Rd
South Haven MI 49090

Call Sign: WD8MEU
Loren G Soergel
1008 E Wilson Rd
South Haven MI 49090

Call Sign: K8NKO
Ludwig J Baldauf
316 Jones Ave
South Haven MI 49090

Call Sign: KB9SDS
Dennis A McCurine
767 Kalamazoo St
South Haven MI 49090

Call Sign: KA9JME
Martin J Graber
31 Lincoln Ave
South Haven MI 49090

Call Sign: WA8CSR
Duane H Wood
67654 M 43 Hwy
South Haven MI 49090

Call Sign: KA8JNG
George D Hooper
72524 M 43 Hwy
South Haven MI 49090

Call Sign: N8NFX
Katherine A Button
72560 M 43 Hwy
South Haven MI 49090

Call Sign: WD8MEV

Shirley A Hooper
72560 M 43 Hwy
South Haven MI 49090

Call Sign: WD8AGC
George C Hooper
72560 M 43 Hwy
South Haven MI
490909701

Call Sign: KC8AAI
Nicholas B Trenkle
88 Michigan Ave
South Haven MI 49090

Call Sign: N8GCA
Phillip H Rock
428 Michigan Ave
South Haven MI 49090

Call Sign: N8MHZ
Bryan L Lundgren
714 Michigan Ave
South Haven MI 49090

Call Sign: KC8UOC
Daniel E Eidem
805 Monroe Blvd
South Haven MI 49090

Call Sign: N8QHE
Douglas H Torp
1316 Monroe Blvd
South Haven MI 49090

Call Sign: NQ8R
Paul C Hogan
811 Phoenix St
South Haven MI 49090

Call Sign: WB8WXE
George Bartholomew
67945 Ridgewood Dr
South Haven MI 49090

Call Sign: K8DIA
George Bartholomew
67945 Ridgewood Dr
South Haven MI 49090

Call Sign: WB8WXE
George Bartholomew
67945 Ridgewood Dr
South Haven MI 49090

Call Sign: KC8WBK
Paul K Vandenbosch
757 Superior St
South Haven MI 49090

Call Sign: KC8ZEN
John E Schneider
842 Wilson St
South Haven MI 49090

Call Sign: KC8ZRQ
Lisa R Schneider
842 Wilson St
South Haven MI 49090

Call Sign: WB8HAY
Marvin J Winkel
South Haven MI 49090

FCC Amateur Radio
Licenses in South
Range

Call Sign: KL7AHI
Joseph A Prebelich
43 2nd St
South Range MI 49963

Call Sign: WB8WHU
Lee R Taube
70 3rd St Box 250
South Range MI 49963

Call Sign: KC8FSO
John R Manninen
29 6th St
South Range MI 49963

Call Sign: KD8MFP
James M Pidgeon
South Range MI 49963

Call Sign: KD8ALC
Jordan J Deforge
South Range MI 49963

Call Sign: KC8VPE
Tim J Hulinek
South Range MI 49963

FCC Amateur Radio
Licenses in Spalding

Call Sign: KD8BVZ
Elaine M Harter
3676 Ashland
Spalding MI 49886

Call Sign: KD8BVY
Harry J Ackerman
3676 Ashland St
Spalding MI 49886

FCC Amateur Radio
Licenses in Sparta

Call Sign: KD8DQB
Charles A Mikowski
1339 12 Mile Rd
Sparta MI 49345

Call Sign: KC8VUB
Pamela L Anderson
1484 12 Mile Rd NW
Sparta MI 49345

Call Sign: KC8MIL
Chris W Anderson
1484 12 Mile Rd NW
Sparta MI 49345

Call Sign: N6CWA
Chris W Anderson
1484 12 Mile Rd NW
Sparta MI 49345

Call Sign: KC8MIL
Chris W Anderson
1484 12 Mile Rd NW
Sparta MI 49345

Call Sign: N8VWJ
Roy B Brown Jr
3776 13 Mile Rd NW
Sparta MI 49345

Call Sign: W8UF
Roy B Brown Jr
3776 13 Mile Rd NW
Sparta MI 49345

Call Sign: N8VWJ
Roy B Brown Jr
3776 13 Mile Rd NW
Sparta MI 49345

Call Sign: K8KYU

Hugh W Larson
3051 14 Mile Rd
Sparta MI 49345

Call Sign: K8WZ
Michael L Partridge
3130 14 Mile Rd NE
Sparta MI 493458501

Call Sign: WD8NFG
Joyce L Partridge
3130 14 Mile Rd NE
Sparta MI 493459850

Call Sign: KC8MVO
Darryl M Gender
2381 15 Mile Rd NE
Sparta MI 493459517

Call Sign: WA8LQV
Paul E Kitchka
357 15 Mile Rd NW
Sparta MI 49345

Call Sign: KC8NWF
Paul B Crowley
88 Alma St
Sparta MI 49345

Call Sign: KB8QAQ
James E Van Malsen
300 Blake St
Sparta MI 49345

Call Sign: KC8TTC
Timothy M Arends
319 Blake St
Sparta MI 49345

Call Sign: KB8FRK
Richard D Greenman
29 Centennial St
Sparta MI 49345

Call Sign: KB8OGJ
Daniel A Kurtz
1421 Country View Ct
Sparta MI 49345

Call Sign: KD8BPK
William Robbins
8754 Country View Dr
Sparta MI 49345

Call Sign: KD8MDH
Charles L Burden
8823 Country View Dr
Sparta MI 49345

Call Sign: W8WTN
Charles L Burden
8823 Country View Dr
Sparta MI 49345

Call Sign: KC8LCA
Floyd A Moline II
325 Doris Dr
Sparta MI 49345

Call Sign: N8OAT
Dennis J Purtee
362 E Gardner
Sparta MI 49345

Call Sign: WA8VLB
Jay T Dean
786 Indian Lakes Rd
Sparta MI 49345

Call Sign: KC8CLA
Kevin P Nester
986 Indian Lakes Rd N
E
Sparta MI 49345

Call Sign: N8EOK
Jay W Shoemaker
306 Indian Lakes Rd
NW
Sparta MI 49345

Call Sign: KC8IJQ
Craig A Bailey
12269 Long Lk Dr
Sparta MI 49345

Call Sign: N8MND
Rhonda L Bowen
10320 Martindale NW
Sparta MI 49345

Call Sign: KF6EML
Wayne E Moore Jr
11955 N Division Ave
Sparta MI 49345

Call Sign: KB8IMU
Marty O Wolverton

332 N Elm St
Sparta MI 49345

Call Sign: KD8PZK
William C Hayes
278 N Union
Sparta MI 49345

Call Sign: KB9PAK
Mark A Oberg
904 Olin Meadows Dr
Sparta MI 49345

Call Sign: KB8AXV
Robert D Greenman
71 Orchard Dr
Sparta MI 49345

Call Sign: KC8DOC
Brian J Scholten
8570 Peach Ridge Ave
Sparta MI 49345

Call Sign: AB8MS
Mark J Scholten
8570 Peach Ridge Ave
NW
Sparta MI 49345

Call Sign: N8GS
Gale A Scholten
8530 Peach Ridge NW
Sparta MI 49345

Call Sign: KB8AXY
Rowland E Hill
10056 Peachridge
Sparta MI 49345

Call Sign: KD8RVN
Bryan D Rader
12585 Phelps Ave
Sparta MI 49345

Call Sign: KD8CDH
Philip J Stritzinger
9950 Pine Island Dr
Sparta MI 493459329

Call Sign: KD8LNN
Ryan J Hayes
138 S State St
Sparta MI 49345

Call Sign: WA8MQO
Edward E Carpenter
11469 Tebeau Dr
Sparta MI 49345

Call Sign: KB8FH
Raymond H Munson
8437 Thome Dr
Sparta MI 49345

Call Sign: KD8RPW
Teresa K Ripley
8669 Thome Dr
Sparta MI 49345

Call Sign: KB8PRA
Boyd F Newman
84 Traveler Dr
Sparta MI 49345

Call Sign: KB8MNI
Harold R Allen
56 Washington St
Sparta MI 49345

Call Sign: K8MEK
William E Bundy
947 White Pine St
Sparta MI 49345

**FCC Amateur Radio
Licenses in Spring
Lake**

Call Sign: KD8BHW
Michael D Dawes Sr
17525 144th St Apt B
Spring Lake MI
494568807

Call Sign: N8JFN
Peter A Carney
17561 148th Ave
Spring Lake MI 49456

Call Sign: W9DBE
Brent Ensign
15223 152nd Ave
Spring Lake MI 49456

Call Sign: W9LBE
Leta G Ensign
15223 152nd Ave
Spring Lake MI 49456

Call Sign: W8VLE
Russell A Johnson
16168 152nd Ave
Spring Lake MI 49456

Call Sign: WD8BNJ
Herbert Koedoot
17855 168th Ave
Spring Lake MI 49456

Call Sign: KB8ZBT
Heath M Blondin
17728 170th Ave
Spring Lake MI 49456

Call Sign: KF4OAX
Dale H Scott
17686 Allen Ave
Spring Lake MI 49456

Call Sign: N8FQ
Joseph J Veldhuis
18273 Alpine Ct Apt 1
Spring Lake MI
494569745

Call Sign: KB8VPX
Frederick L Kincaid
17226 Arthur Ct
Spring Lake MI 49456

Call Sign: KL7FHI
Garnet L Levandoski
16000 Baird Dr
Spring Lake MI 49456

Call Sign: KL7FHK
Martin F Levandoski
16000 Baird Dr
Spring Lake MI 49456

Call Sign: KB8NFT
Verle D Winningham
II
117 Barber Ct
Spring Lake MI 49456

Call Sign: KF8VN
Alan B Groenleer
17635 Bayberry
Spring Lake MI 49456

Call Sign: AB8CD

Daniel K Anderson
17235 Benjamin Ave
Spring Lake MI 49456

Call Sign: W0EJD
Bernard D Miller
14961 Brookside Dr
Spring Lake MI 49456

Call Sign: KB8NLN
Phyllis A Simmons
17818 Channel View
Dr
Spring Lake MI 49456

Call Sign: N8RXC
Roger L Simmons
17818 Channel View
Dr
Spring Lake MI 49456

Call Sign: KB8QAR
Karen D Stano
17880 Channel View
Dr
Spring Lake MI 49456

Call Sign: W8RAS
Randolph A Stano
17880 Channel View
Dr
Spring Lake MI 49456

Call Sign: KC0ECT
Russell Y Cox
18003 Charokee Dr
Spring Lake MI
494569123

Call Sign: K8AR
Bernhard H Docter
18152 Cherokee Ct
Spring Lake MI 49456

Call Sign: WB0DGF
Roger A Cox
18003 Cherokee Dr
Spring Lake MI
494569123

Call Sign: KA0DWH
Gayle J Y Cox
18003 Cherokee Dr
Spring Lake MI 49456

Call Sign: KD8KAL
Susan A Weishaar
15361 Concord Dr
Spring Lake MI 49456

Call Sign: KB8TOF
Ramon C Mulder
15470 Cricket St
Spring Lake MI 49456

Call Sign: KB8NM
John M De Grazia
14835 Cross Ln
Spring Lake MI 49456

Call Sign: K8BGP
Russell J Ronning
217 De Witt Ln Apt
211
Spring Lake MI 49456

Call Sign: N8BGP
Edith L Ronning
217 De Witt Ln Apt
211
Spring Lake MI 49456

Call Sign: W8BXW
Lawrence I Abbott
217 Dewitt Ln Apt 310
Spring Lake MI 49456

Call Sign: KD8RQR
Kenneth D Giese
17634 Dustin Dr
Spring Lake MI 49456

Call Sign: KC8NGC
Christopher M Bunda
1281 E Pontaluna Lot
95
Spring Lake MI 49456

Call Sign: KC8NHR
Joshua A Carlisle
223 E Savidge
Spring Lake MI 49456

Call Sign: WB8DWG
Arthur E Graham
510 E Savidge St
Spring Lake MI 49456

Call Sign: WA8JDF
Edward L Passenger
526 Ferry St
Spring Lake MI 49456

Call Sign: KD8EFG
Timothy S O Donnell
540 Ferry St
Spring Lake MI 49456

Call Sign: KC8OJX
James C Dufford
17274 Franklin Ave
Spring Lake MI 49456

Call Sign: KB8WXN
Douglas L Walton
18760 Fruitport Rd
Spring Lake MI 49456

Call Sign: N8WDX
David G Keizer
14141 Garfield Rd
Spring Lake MI 49456

Call Sign: KA8ZNF
Randolph B Daley
19045 Glendale Cir
Spring Lake MI 49456

Call Sign: KC8WHT
Patrick T Poponea
16887 Highland Ave
Spring Lake MI 49456

Call Sign: N8UKX
Andrea J Lobbezoo
16076 Highland Dr
Spring Lake MI 49456

Call Sign: WB8YOO
Lee D Sherman
18725 Hopi Ct
Spring Lake MI 49456

Call Sign: N8UKW
Michael A Happel
15175 Krueger Dr
Spring Lake MI 49456

Call Sign: KC8DR
Daniel S Ruiter
16865 Lake Rd
Spring Lake MI 49456

Call Sign: KD8HRB
Ronald L Meschke
15913 Leonard
Spring Lake MI 49456

Call Sign: KC8WCR
Richard A Klecka
15787 Leonard Rd
Spring Lake MI 49456

Call Sign: KC5TXW
Sindy L Matus
15885 Leonard Rd
Spring Lake MI 49456

Call Sign: KC8DFD
William W Brewer
17046 Lloyds Bayou
311
Spring Lake MI 49456

Call Sign: K9RMJ
William W Brewer
17046 Lloyds Bayou
Dr Apt 425
Spring Lake MI 49456

Call Sign: KB8HEX
Owen D Hansen
18116 Lovell Park Rd
Spring Lake MI 49456

Call Sign: W8IQE
Paul E Zellar
207 N Division
Spring Lake MI 49456

Call Sign: AB8XS
Eric A Hultman
15253 N Scenic Dr
Spring Lake MI 49456

Call Sign: KB8TOC
Scott A Hill
19142 N Shore Rd
Spring Lake MI 49456

Call Sign: KE8OI
Preston B Wells
17388 Oak Crest Pky
Spring Lake MI 49456

Call Sign: N8GPI

Christy R Vanderwall
15295 Oak Point Dr
Spring Lake MI 49456

Call Sign: KC8THN
Craig R Christilaw
15386 Oak Point Dr
Spring Lake MI 49456

Call Sign: KD8CBI
Lee G Veurink
15395 Oak Point Dr
Spring Lake MI 49456

Call Sign: KC8TOH
Michael F O Brien
17518 A Parkwood
Spring Lake MI 49456

Call Sign: KA1ERE
Guy H Reece
15231 Pruin St
Spring Lake MI 49456

Call Sign: K7DGX
Ronald R Gervenack
7176 Quimby Dr
Spring Lake MI 49456

Call Sign: N8QZE
James E Sutliff
16451 Ranch Ln
Spring Lake MI 49456

Call Sign: KR8N
V Dale Maxam
17529 Reitsma Ln
Spring Lake MI 49456

Call Sign: W8UMP
David T Holmes Jr
17561 Reitsma Ln
Spring Lake MI 49456

Call Sign: W8PQW
Richard L Jones
2908 Rennells Rd
Spring Lake MI 49456

Call Sign: KC8GYL
Gerald A Bogner
215 River
Spring Lake MI 49456

Call Sign: N8LBG
Woodrow S Aldrich
120 S Lake Ave
Spring Lake MI
494561984

Call Sign: W0OU
Lowell E Blevins
214 S Lake Ave
Spring Lake MI 49456

Call Sign: KB8HU
Charles H Osborn
408 S Lake Ave
Spring Lake MI 49456

Call Sign: WA8YES
Rick L Hansen
18796 Sioux Dr
Spring Lake MI 49456

Call Sign: WB8ASI
Herbert A Blue Jr
17706 Spahr St
Spring Lake MI 49456

Call Sign: WB8AVK
Jerry J Brower
15073 State Rd
Spring Lake MI
494569588

Call Sign: KD8FCU
Mark E Stern
16277 Suffolk Dr
Spring Lake MI 49456

Call Sign: K8MAZ
Mark E Stern
16277 Suffolk Dr
Spring Lake MI 49456

Call Sign: KA8ZEX
Henry Miller
615 Summer St
Spring Lake MI 49456

Call Sign: KC8CWU
Ira De Jager
732 Summer St
Spring Lake MI 49456

Call Sign: W8JRM
James R Miller

16762 Taft Rd
Spring Lake MI 49456

Call Sign: KC8SRS
Alan E Freeman
15002 Thoroughbred
Run
Spring Lake MI 49456

Call Sign: N8KYO
Louis W Meisch
18097 Trillium Dr
Spring Lake MI 49456

Call Sign: W8LLA
John F Van Kuiken
17348 Villa Park St
Spring Lake MI 49456

Call Sign: KC8ZCP
Michael C Grzyb
15900 Vine Crest
Spring Lake MI 49456

Call Sign: W8FH
Frank W Hannum
15761 Vine St
Spring Lake MI 49456

Call Sign: KD8OKI
Richard L Anderson
312 W Exchange St
Spring Lake MI 49456

Call Sign: KC8FQH
Jeffrey G Olson
18725 W Spring Lake
Rd
Spring Lake MI 49456

Call Sign: N8UKG
Glen Gilson
18525 W Spring Lake
Rd
Spring Lake MI 49456

Call Sign: KA8QFX
Jason W Vinkemulder
19102 Walden Dr
Spring Lake MI 49456

Call Sign: WW8T
Gregory J Munski
15052 Waterleaf Ct

Spring Lake MI 49456

Call Sign: KC8ULC
Thomas H Fischer
112 Williams
Spring Lake MI 49456

Call Sign: K8OOO
Thomas H Fischer
112 Williams
Spring Lake MI 49456

Call Sign: KC8THM
David W Fischer
112 Williams St
Spring Lake MI 49456

Call Sign: KC8ZCR
George R Dood
1089 Wilson Rd
Spring Lake MI 49456

Call Sign: KC8ZCQ
Robert L Jernstadt
586 Wind Drift Ln
Spring Lake MI 49456

Call Sign: W9BWC
James F Wolter
15480 Wisteria
Spring Lake MI 49456

Call Sign: KB8ODD
Stacy E Van Buren
15437 Wisteria Ln
Spring Lake MI 49456

Call Sign: W8SEV
Stacy E Van Buren
15437 Wisteria Ln
Spring Lake MI
494561146

Call Sign: W0PGV
Jules P Bernd
17676 Woodbridge
Spring Lake MI 49456

Call Sign: KC8PWQ
Fenton T Daniel III
18330 10 Woodland
Ridge Dr
Spring Lake MI 49456

Call Sign: KB8DBM
Edward H Hoisington
Spring Lake MI 49456

FCC Amateur Radio
Licenses in
Springfield

Call Sign: KD8PWB
Lorie J Nierman
355 Ave A
Springfield MI 49037

Call Sign: N7KUT
Edward J Lakies
360 Ave A
Springfield MI
490377839

Call Sign: NG8I
Keith A Storm
937 Betterly Rd
Springfield MI
490154817

Call Sign: KD8CDS
Billy W Booth Sr
4 Cinderella Cir
Springfield MI 49015

Call Sign: KD8RVW
Cynthia G Coffman
240 N 21st St
Springfield MI 49037

Call Sign: N8KLI
Milford A Mellon II
26 Royal Rd
Springfield MI 49015

FCC Amateur Radio
Licenses in Spruce

Call Sign: N8FOT
Richard J Bremer
4495 Detroit Ave
Spruce MI 48762

Call Sign: KD8AOX
Michelle R Labonte
1470 E Spruce Rd
Spruce MI 48762

Call Sign: WA8UKW

James H Angus
5701 Franklin Ave
Spruce MI 48762

Call Sign: KD8BRI
Colin D Scott
6252 Hansen Rd
Spruce MI 48762

Call Sign: KD8GFL
Gary W Saranen
5030 Hubbard Lk Rd
Spruce MI 48762

Call Sign: KB8ZZB
Richard D Van Dam
3200 N Hilltop
Spruce MI 48762

Call Sign: KC8DOO
Clark N Van Dam
3200 N Hilltop Pkwy
Spruce MI 48762

Call Sign: KC8BJF
Rich J Van Dam
3200 N Hilltop Pky
Spruce MI 48762

Call Sign: N8VJR
Gary J Butkovich
4929 N Hubbard Lakr
Rd
Spruce MI 48762

Call Sign: KC8KPU
Ryan T Stevens
5191 Pine Grove Dr
Spruce MI 487629530

Call Sign: KC8KPV
Russell A Stevens
5191 Pine Grove Dr
Spruce MI 487629530

Call Sign: KC8NGS
Carol L Stevens
5191 Pine Grove Dr
Spruce MI 487629530

Call Sign: KD8BXD
Mark A Palmer
464 W Main St
Spruce MI 48762

Call Sign: KD8IML
Emily A Palmer
464 W Main St
Spruce MI 48762

Call Sign: KD8IMM
Zachary T Palmer
464 W Main St
Spruce MI 48762

**FCC Amateur Radio
Licenses in
Stambaugh**

Call Sign: KB8BK
John R Lappala
15 19th St
Stambaugh MI 49964

Call Sign: N8ZHE
Larry Ballinger
601 6th St
Stambaugh MI 49964

Call Sign: N8LVQ
Clarence A
Hendrickson
Stambaugh MI 49964

Call Sign: W8RFH
Robert F Harding
Stambaugh MI
499640172

Call Sign: KB8VYK
Joseph L Tousignant
Stambaugh MI 49964

Call Sign: N8XTC
Kenneth W Hookenson
Stambaugh MI 49964

Call Sign: W8FOA
Albert J Todey
Stambaugh MI 49964

Call Sign: KC8NIF
Grace M Serbinski
Stambaugh MI 49964

**FCC Amateur Radio
Licenses in Standish**

Call Sign: KD8HGO
Judith D Swanson
2162 E Wenonah Dr
Standish MI 48658

Call Sign: KD8JNU
Arenac Standish
Emergency
Commission Ass
340 Hickory Island Rd
Standish MI
486589723

Call Sign: WI8Z
Arenac Standish
Emergency
Communication
Association
340 Hickory Island Rd
Standish MI
486589723

Call Sign: KA8WOT
Charles A Young
342 Hickory Island Rd
Standish MI 48658

Call Sign: W1ORG
Oriance R Godfroy
3915 Irwin Rd
Standish MI 48658

Call Sign: K8JKC
Oliver C Porter
4825 La Clair Rd
Standish MI 48658

Call Sign: WN8IJD
Kenneth W Waldie
831 Langdon Rd
Standish MI 48658

Call Sign: KD8EUG
Kristie M Damron
5199 Lincoln
Standish MI 48658

Call Sign: KA8UMZ
Bruce R Hartman
5052 Melita Rd
Standish MI 48658

Call Sign: KB8MGV
Debra K Hartman

5052 Melita Rd
Standish MI 48658

Call Sign: K8TXW
Ralph M Jackson
216 N Forest
Standish MI 48658

Call Sign: KB8TTY
Duane L Hadley
105 N Grove St
Standish MI 48658

Call Sign: N2ULT
Aaron V Hoyt
330 Orchard St
Standish MI 48658

Call Sign: KC8QMG
Donald T Spresny
3333 Palmer Rd
Standish MI 48658

Call Sign: WD8PYK
Michael J Beson
3970 S Huron Rd
Standish MI 48658

Call Sign: KC8NZH
Thomas D Page
3457 State Rd
Standish MI 48658

Call Sign: KC8PLQ
Robert A Hunter Sr
54 W Conrad Rd
Standish MI 48658

Call Sign: KC8NJU
Melody J Grosinsky
455 W Mills 9
Standish MI 48658

Call Sign: KA8JYR
Bernard L Reinhart
5653 W Worth
Standish MI 48658

Call Sign: N8VCW
Leona M Reinhart
5653 W Worth Rd
Standish MI 48658

Call Sign: KC8YYW

Charles L Rood
4726 Wheeler Rd
Standish MI 48658

Call Sign: AB8SY
Charles L Rood
4726 Wheeler Rd
Standish MI 48658

Call Sign: N8XTQ
Charles L Hundley
Standish MI 48658

Call Sign: N8ZEJ
Thelrene I Hundley
Standish MI 48658

Call Sign: KD8ERJ
Richard L Gould
Standish MI 48658

FCC Amateur Radio Licenses in Stanton

Call Sign: KC8TBW
Lyle L Bennett
5798 Briggs Rd NW
Stanton MI 488889779

Call Sign: KB8ZGW
Arthur S Wirtz
960 Cedar Lake
Stanton MI 488889579

Call Sign: N8STE
Charles H Zilch
1600 Cedar Lake Rd NE
Stanton MI 48888

Call Sign: N8VYZ
Michelle E Heinlen
146 E 4th St
Stanton MI 48888

Call Sign: KC8XG
Richard L Evans
1020 E Main St
Stanton MI 48888

Call Sign: KD8FQD
W Michael Steere
375 E Pakes Rd
Stanton MI 48888

Call Sign: N8YJB
Everett L Burkey
441 Lakeside Dr
Stanton MI 48888

Call Sign: N8SXA
Carolyn L Zilch
1600 N Cedar Lake Rd
Stanton MI 48888

Call Sign: KC8CGG
Richard C Shindorf
2702 N Greenville Rd
Stanton MI 48888

Call Sign: KD8KOV
Billy J Wright Sr
1102 N Hillman Rd
Stanton MI 48888

Call Sign: KD8NOC
Duane D Beshada
1251 N Nevins Rd
Stanton MI 48888

Call Sign: N8YJW
Jimmie E Doolittle
301 NE Vickeryville Rd
Stanton MI 48888

Call Sign: KD8DRM
Brandon P C Langford
363 Potter Pl
Stanton MI 48888

Call Sign: K8ZAA
Randy E Brace
19 S Beechwood Dr
Stanton MI 48888

Call Sign: KB8TOU
Randall J Hillebrand
1030 S Brown Rd
Stanton MI 48888

Call Sign: W8JWE
Robert J Leyrer
561 Spring Grove
Stanton MI 48888

Call Sign: KX8W
Harry W Eldridge

1804 Town Hall Rd
Stanton MI 48888

Call Sign: AA8OM
Harry W Eldridge
1804 Town Hall Rd
Stanton MI 48888

Call Sign: K8BOO
Edward L Dilno
359 W Main St
Stanton MI 48888

Call Sign: KA8FKU
Margaret L Cross
650 W Shore Dr
Stanton MI 48888

Call Sign: KD8NXL
Lester D Stowell II
750 W Shore Dr
Stanton MI 48888

Call Sign: KC8WGB
Kevin R Keeler
2304 Wyman Rd
Stanton MI 48888

Call Sign: KC8ACO
Leon F Salisbury
Stanton MI 48888

FCC Amateur Radio Licenses in Stanwood

Call Sign: KD8EXL
Clair A Bono
18710 10 Mile Rd
Stanwood MI 49346

Call Sign: W8NCZ
Clair A Bono
18710 10 Mile Rd
Stanwood MI 49346

Call Sign: N8PHZ
Gerald D Covey
7774 140th Ave
Stanwood MI 493469716

Call Sign: KC8TTB
Charles A Tennant
23635 8 Mile Rd

Stanwood MI 493069164

Call Sign: WA8WVI
Ralph Le Roy
11296 Alpine Rd
Stanwood MI 49346

Call Sign: KC8AFZ
James G Patteson
11069 Birwood Dr
Stanwood MI 49346

Call Sign: WA8KEP
Charles E Boboltz
23630 Buchanan Rd
Stanwood MI 49346

Call Sign: KB8ZET
Michael L Harvell Jr
11995 Cape Breton Rd
Stanwood MI 49346

Call Sign: KD8EJE
Robert S Tennant
12140 Dubois Dr
Stanwood MI 493469606

Call Sign: WD8AUL
Dale E Colby
10119 Eagle Pass
Stanwood MI 49346

Call Sign: KG8LX
Michael L Harvell Jr
9805 Golf Port Dr
Stanwood MI 49346

Call Sign: KC8QWU
Robert B Lewis
12159 Highland Trl
Stanwood MI 49346

Call Sign: KC8DNN
Ray A Fuller
11259 Lake Rd
Stanwood MI 49346

Call Sign: KC8WGD
John A May
20129 Lincoln Rd
Stanwood MI 49346

Call Sign: K8PAO
Kenneth C Bakhaus
8847 Longview Dr
Stanwood MI 49346

Call Sign: WD8EHT
Channing H Lintz
8867 Longview Dr
Stanwood MI 49346

Call Sign: KB8WXI
Mark A Thurston
10101 Mtn View Trl
Stanwood MI 49346

Call Sign: KB8ZEP
Gerald M Flessland
10121 Mtn View Trl
Stanwood MI
493469792

Call Sign: N8HDD
Walter R Nevill
10261 Mtn View Trl
Stanwood MI 49346

Call Sign: WA8YIA
Kenneth O Runnels
10767 Otahnagon Dr
Stanwood MI 49346

Call Sign: W8KOR
Kenneth O Runnels
10767 Otahnagon Dr
Stanwood MI 49346

Call Sign: KB8ZEJ
David S Young
12221 Trail Creek Dr
Stanwood MI 49346

Call Sign: N8OMG
William F Windhorst
10878 W Royal Rd
Stanwood MI
493469760

Call Sign: KC8RSM
Diana M Jarnutowski
N 7231 Butchli Dr

Stephenson MI 49887

Call Sign: W9AMZ
Robert J Jarnutowski
N 7231 Butchli Dr
Stephenson MI
498878606

Call Sign: K8RJ
Robert J Jarnutowski
N 7231 Butchli Dr
Stephenson MI
498878606

Call Sign: KB0RCW
Andrew D Stonina
N7907 Church Rd J 3
Stephenson MI 49887

Call Sign: KA8UVP
Mary A Peterson
N7950 Church Rd J3
Stephenson MI
498879395

Call Sign: K8NB
Noel A Beardsley
W 7021 CR 356
Stephenson MI 49887

Call Sign: N8RSA
Lisa M Beardsley
W 7021 CR 356
Stephenson MI 49887

Call Sign: KD8LQB
Derek D Hockin
W5507 CR G12
Stephenson MI 49887

Call Sign: WD8OSE
Thomas J Horvath
E 411 Division St Box
158
Stephenson MI 49887

Call Sign: W9JTL
Jason M Lauzer
N9927 K 1 Rd
Stephenson MI 49887

Call Sign: KB6AV
Edward G Freis
N6735 N 3 Rd

Stephenson MI 49887

Call Sign: KC8WJO
James H Voss
N8879 Santosa Ln
Stephenson MI 49887

Call Sign: KC8QNF
Richard T Philpot
2717 9 Mile Rd
Sterling MI 48659

Call Sign: KD8DRV
Keith A Rebischke Sr
2045 Adams Rd
Sterling MI 48659

Call Sign: KC8YHW
Paul B Mulford
1362 Bishop Rd
Sterling MI 48659

Call Sign: KC8CFB
Elaine I Freeman
333 Jefferson St
Sterling MI 48659

Call Sign: N8ZE
John T Freeman
333 Jefferson St
Sterling MI 48659

Call Sign: KC8HTF
Eugene Ignatowski
800 M 76
Sterling MI 48659

Call Sign: KD8HGP
Maryjane S Honner
1305 M 76
Sterling MI 48659

Call Sign: KC8EBW
Brian T Freeman
310 N Saginaw St
Sterling MI 48659

Call Sign: KD8JSS
Jacqueline M Leonard
741 N School Rd
Sterling MI 48659

Call Sign: W8ERK
Clifford L Williams Jr
2026 S School Rd
Sterling MI 48659

Call Sign: KC8CFW
Frank C Ferrero
33632 Sebastian
Sterling MI 48312

Call Sign: KA8VSF
Stephen A Holechko
4933 W Main St Rd
Sterling MI 48659

Call Sign: N8RBS
George R Babcock
Sterling MI 48659

Call Sign: W8FZU
Murray E Nichols
3138 Birchwood
Stevensville MI 49127

Call Sign: K9IUL
James E Boardman
5921 Clearbrook Dr
Stevensville MI 49127

Call Sign: KD8CZO
Annie L Kaeding
5965 Clearbrook Dr
Stevensville MI 49127

Call Sign: W8ALK
Annie L Kaeding
5965 Clearbrook Dr
Stevensville MI 49127

Call Sign: K8TMK
Arlington R Kaeding
5965 Clearbrook Dr
Stevensville MI
491271370

Call Sign: KC8OCN
Heathkit Amateur
Radio Group
5965 Clearbrook Dr

Stevensville MI
491271370

Call Sign: W8KIT
Heathkit Amateur
Radio Group
5965 Clearbrook Dr
Stevensville MI
491271370

Call Sign: K8TJZ
Richard S Johns
6019 Clearbrook Dr
Stevensville MI 49127

Call Sign: KC9PQP
Stephen E Mueller
4130 Cottage Path
Stevensville MI 49127

Call Sign: KC8HVL
Paul R Pugh
5668 Dennis
Stevensville MI
491279502

Call Sign: KE3K
Robert C Bash
5849 Echo Rdg
Stevensville MI
491271319

Call Sign: N8IZA
Paul E Bell
4171 Elizabeth Dr
Stevensville MI 49127

Call Sign: N8XSG
Christian G Jantz
2557 Glenlord
Stevensville MI 49127

Call Sign: K8MAB
Norbert J Rybarczyk Jr
5667 Hiawatha
Stevensville MI 49127

Call Sign: K8NKS
Norbert J Rybarczyk Jr
5667 Hiawatha
Stevensville MI 49127

Call Sign: K8MAB
Norbert J Rybarczyk Jr

5667 Hiawatha
Stevensville MI 49127

Call Sign: KB8NZW
George D Godush
3019 Mansueto Dr
Stevensville MI 49127

Call Sign: K7ZB
Robert E Houf
5308 N Alpine Ridge
Stevensville MI 49127

Call Sign: N8RYC
Walter L McTague I
1831 N Donna Dr
Stevensville MI 49127

Call Sign: W0TCF
Patricia L Lotfi
1832 N Donna Dr
Stevensville MI 49127

Call Sign: W8JBA
William G Wheeler
1832 N Donna Dr
Stevensville MI 49127

Call Sign: K8MYC
Ben M Dziegel
1861 N Donna Dr
Stevensville MI 49127

Call Sign: N8BPY
Ronnald E Ballard
1850 N Sierra Way
Stevensville MI 49127

Call Sign: KC8JUD
William D Spicer
2854 Oak St
Stevensville MI 49127

Call Sign: KC8POY
Neil W Conlon
1966 Orchard Dr
Stevensville MI 49127

Call Sign: KD8ALS
Donald J Meyer
5858 Red Arrow Hwy
B1
Stevensville MI 49127

Call Sign: KC8MND
David E Gotsch
4419 Redarrow Hwy
Apt E4
Stevensville MI 49127

Call Sign: KD8BMU
Candice J Warnke
5726 Ridge Rd 22
Stevensville MI 49127

Call Sign: WA8UOC
Michael P Krieger
2419 Ridgewood Dr
Stevensville MI 49127

Call Sign: KD8ALR
Connie S Kyncl
2833 Robin Hood Dr
Stevensville MI 49127

Call Sign: KC8ODM
John W Castle Sr
2833 Robin Hood Dr
Stevensville MI 49127

Call Sign: K8NKS
Norbert J Rybarczyk
Sr
5684 Roosevelt Rd
Stevensville MI 49127

Call Sign: WD8MTG
Randall L Fife
4862 S Cleveland
Stevensville MI 49127

Call Sign: N8ZUL
Daniel T Cooper
1671 S Riviera Dr
Stevensville MI
491279621

Call Sign: KC8GPQ
Carl L Krause III
5445 S San Martine
Stevensville MI 49127

Call Sign: KB8EJM
Larry G Bollman
5458 S San Martine
Stevensville MI 49127

Call Sign: KB8ANW

Jacob D Spencer
1811 S Sierra Way
Stevensville MI 49127

Call Sign: W8REQ
Donald L Fife
1856 S Sierra Way
Stevensville MI 49127

Call Sign: K8TXD
Clifford L Deschaaf
1662 S Teakwood
Stevensville MI 49127

Call Sign: W8TXX
James R Isham
1733 Santa Maria
Stevensville MI 49127

Call Sign: N8UUU
Craig R Peacock
1830 Santa Maria
Stevensville MI 49127

Call Sign: N8CZY
Thurlo O Looney
2196 Shiawasee Ln
Stevensville MI 49127

Call Sign: W8FKG
Wallace Correll
1868 Sierraway S
Stevensville MI 49127

Call Sign: W8OT
Earl D Harris Jr
5854 St Joseph Ave
Stevensville MI 49127

Call Sign: KC8UVV
Marcia M Harris
5854 St Joseph Ave
Stevensville MI 49127

Call Sign: W3XYL
Marcia M Harris
5854 St Joseph Ave
Stevensville MI 49127

Call Sign: W8HAT
Richard M Kramer
5888 St Joseph Ave
Stevensville MI 49127

Call Sign: W1BLE
William I Basser
2248 W Glenlord Rd
Stevensville MI 49127

Call Sign: KC8ODJ
Robert T Tripp
406 W John Beers Rd
Stevensville MI 49127

Call Sign: N8GKS
Ervin H Brooks
1150 W John Beers Rd
Stevensville MI 49127

Call Sign: W4GKS
Ervin H Brooks
1150 W John Beers Rd
Stevensville MI 49127

Call Sign: KD8MBM
Nathan T Dumminger
4348 W Velvet St
Stevensville MI 49127

Call Sign: KC8MGD
Thomas M Dumminger
4348 W Velvet St
Stevensville MI 49127

Call Sign: KC8SMC
Beth M Dumminger
4348 W Velvet St
Stevensville MI 49127

Call Sign: KD8ALQ
Josh J Dumminger
4348 W Velvet St
Stevensville MI 49127

Call Sign: KA8BNC
Robert L Sturch
2720 Wildwood Ln
Stevensville MI 49127

Call Sign: N8BQO
Jack L Aaron
2975 Windward Path
Stevensville MI 49127

Call Sign: KB8VF
Joseph T Novak
Stevensville MI
491270165

Call Sign: W8NDG
Robert D Fernau
Stevensville MI 49127

**FCC Amateur Radio
Licenses in Sturgis**

Call Sign: N4VHZ
Harold L Miller
1855 Alder Ln Apt 3
Sturgis MI 49091

Call Sign: WB1ASJ
Donald E Davies
71048 Aldrich Lake
Rd
Sturgis MI 49091

Call Sign: KC9DJ
J Herbert Bazur
61828 Bayshore Dr
Sturgis MI 49091

Call Sign: WB9THG
John A Wigren
61842 Bayshore Dr
Sturgis MI 49091

Call Sign: N9DFA
Paul D Van Briggle
61902 Bayshore Dr
Sturgis MI 49091

Call Sign: KB8PEA
James D Ralston
1021 Cato Ln Apt A3
Sturgis MI 49091

Call Sign: N8KYQ
John E Steele
505 Cherry Ave
Sturgis MI 490912202

Call Sign: WA8OKA
John E Raifsnider
704 E Chicago Rd
Sturgis MI 49091

Call Sign: W8JER
John E Raifsnider
704 E Chicago Rd
Sturgis MI 49091

Call Sign: KI8BQ
Gary V Martin
29875 E Fawn River
Rd
Sturgis MI 49091

Call Sign: AC8Z
Girard Schilbach
437 E South St
Sturgis MI 49091

Call Sign: KB8SOA
Selenia C Stiles
700 E West St
Sturgis MI 49091

Call Sign: AE8EA
William J Douglas
30205 Fawn River Rd
Sturgis MI 49090

Call Sign: W8LTQ
William J Douglas
30205 Fawn River Rd
Sturgis MI 49091

Call Sign: AB8HF
William J Douglas
30205 Fawn River Rd
Sturgis MI 49091

Call Sign: AE8K
William J Douglas
30205 Fawn River Rd
Sturgis MI 49091

Call Sign: KE8ZX
Robert W Littke
30531 Fawn River Rd
Sturgis MI 49091

Call Sign: N9OVJ
Curtis A De Witt
27370 Findley Rd
Sturgis MI 49091

Call Sign: KF4YZP
Richard L Mead
720 Friar Tuck
Sturgis MI 49091

Call Sign: KC8OFY
Douglas L Souter Jr
402 George St

Sturgis MI 49091

Call Sign: KD8CGT
Thaddeus F Juszczak
III
1201 Independence
Sturgis MI 49091

Call Sign: KD8CGS
Thad F Juszczak Jr
1201 Independence St
Sturgis MI 490912307

Call Sign: AJ8T
Thad F Juszczak Jr
1201 Independence St
Sturgis MI 490912307

Call Sign: KD8RM
Joseph H Zonyk
61439 Irongate Dr
Sturgis MI 49091

Call Sign: KG0ZN
Thomas J Angellotti
25495 Ironwood Dr
Sturgis MI 49091

Call Sign: KD8LSM
Greg S Carlin
25369 Kimberly Rd
Sturgis MI 49091

Call Sign: KB8ESG
Shawn D Gingerich
66361 Klinger Lake
Rd
Sturgis MI 49091

Call Sign: N8XFK
Jerry C Metzger
69872 Krontz Rd
Sturgis MI 49091

Call Sign: KB8ESH
Richard F Byers
24621 M 86
Sturgis MI 49091

Call Sign: N8JJJ
Siegfried H Loetz
113 McKee St
Sturgis MI 49091

Call Sign: W8FRL
Donald B Loetz
113 McKee St
Sturgis MI 490911080

Call Sign: N8YGO
Christopher G Fisher
201 McKee St
Sturgis MI 49091

Call Sign: KB8HCO
John R Conrad
920 Merryview
Sturgis MI 49091

Call Sign: N8YBP
Dean C Whims
803 Michigan Ave
Sturgis MI 49091

Call Sign: KC8ZKL
Steven L Ammer
70747 Miller Rd
Sturgis MI 49091

Call Sign: KC8IJY
Doreen K Leo
25150 Mintdale
Sturgis MI 49091

Call Sign: KC8ZKK
Andy L Johnson
25890 Mintdale
Sturgis MI 49091

Call Sign: N8PSE
John M Carlin
224 N Lakeveiw
Sturgis MI 49091

Call Sign: KD8CBX
Donald L Roehrig III
66339 N Lakeview
Sturgis MI 49091

Call Sign: KB8PRB
Russell L Parker
110 N Ohio Ct
Sturgis MI 49091

Call Sign: KA8VLW
Kenneth E De Busk
511 N Prospect St
Sturgis MI 490911160

Call Sign: N8ABZ
Michael W Tribbett
63530 Nottawa Rd
Sturgis MI 49091

Call Sign: KC8EPE
Jake A Carlin
27366 Oak Dr
Sturgis MI 49091

Call Sign: WA8DCF
Philip E Thrasher
1208 Oak Wood Dr
Sturgis MI 49091

Call Sign: N8VBO
Orin C Evans
69850 Pamela Dr
Sturgis MI 49091

Call Sign: WA8LCL
Douglas Van Meter
28097 Robin Hood Tr
Sturgis MI 49091

Call Sign: WD8PER
Jeffery Owen
326 Rose Cir
Sturgis MI 49091

Call Sign: KB8PTK
Clayton F Howe
310 S Jefferson St
Sturgis MI 49091

Call Sign: W8EGX
Clayton F Howe
310 S Jefferson St
Sturgis MI 49091

Call Sign: WB8MWV
Roberta A Carroll
209.5 S Maple Rd
Sturgis MI 49091

Call Sign: KB8ERM
Adrienne R Heitger
315 S Monroe
Sturgis MI 49091

Call Sign: W7KNK
Ronald L King
69945 S Nottawa

Sturgis MI 49091

Call Sign: WA8L
Robert A Machan
67785 Shimmel Rd
Sturgis MI 49091

Call Sign: KB8OGC
Ricky L Bunnell
65240 Shimmel Rd Rr
3
Sturgis MI 49091

Call Sign: WA8GJS
Richard L Bunnell
65240 Shimmel Rd Rr
3
Sturgis MI 49091

Call Sign: KB8GTQ
Giovanni M Iannotti
417 Sturgis Ave
Sturgis MI 49091

Call Sign: N8JGG
Dennis E Eagan
507 Sturgis Ave
Sturgis MI 49091

Call Sign: KB8NMA
Toni E Jones
307 Texas Ave Apt B1
Sturgis MI 49091

Call Sign: KB8PTJ
Troy M Walsh
307 Texas Ave Apt B8
Sturgis MI 49091

Call Sign: KD8RN
Robert W Pufall
67531 Thunderbird Dr
Sturgis MI 49091

Call Sign: N7GPA
Sean K Peterson
605 Virginia Ave
Sturgis MI 49091

Call Sign: N8XFL
Corey J Aulbach
322 W Jerolene St
Sturgis MI 49091

Call Sign: W8SAT
Ralph E Herzler
1423 W Rishel Rd
Sturgis MI 49091

Call Sign: KC8DEE
David L Boggs
115 Washington St
Sturgis MI 490911047

Call Sign: KA8FEP
Michael Van Meter
69692 White School
Rd
Sturgis MI 49091

Call Sign: KB8HBZ
Donald C Andrews
26135 Wyndham Rd
Sturgis MI 49091

Call Sign: WA0ZMY
Beverly M Andrews
26135 Wyndham Rd
Sturgis MI 49091

Call Sign: N8VTM
Thomas C Perry
Sturgis MI 49091

**FCC Amateur Radio
Licenses in Sunfield**

Call Sign: N1RTU
Steven E St Laurent
210 Dunham St
Sunfield MI 48890

Call Sign: KB8ZY
Karl C Weinner
5895 Grand Ledge
Hwy Rt 1
Sunfield MI 48890

Call Sign: N8THX
John F Sandborn II
13575 Keefer Hwy
Sunfield MI 48890

Call Sign: N8YED
Lisa A Vogel
Sunfield MI 48890

Call Sign: KD8ONC

Brian R Wellwood
Sunfield MI 48890

Call Sign: KB7ZJT
Norman T Kjome
10730 E Fort Rd
Suttons Bay MI 49682

Call Sign: KB8QOJ
Chris D Vant Hof
11090 E McKeese
Suttons Bay MI 49682

Call Sign: N8KVE
Sharon M Curtin
12070 E Sugar Maple
Ct
Suttons Bay MI 49682

Call Sign: KC8OLG
Michael T Butler
90 N Nanagosa Tl
Suttons Bay MI 49682

Call Sign: AD8W
Charles S Secrest
4033 NW Bay Shore
Dr
Suttons Bay MI 49682

Call Sign: KC8CTL
Harold M Gardner Jr
3633 S Bay Ridge Ln
Suttons Bay MI 49682

Call Sign: KC8PVS
Harold P Freeman Jr
1200 S Bay View Trl
Suttons Bay MI 49682

Call Sign: KD8CQJ
Eric R Lind
1981 S Cherry
Blossom Ln
Suttons Bay MI 49682

Call Sign: N8RSS
Thomas M Kelly
1601 S Maple Bluffs
Ct

Suttons Bay MI 49682

Call Sign: N8STR
Anne W Kelly
1601 S Maple Bluffs
Ct
Suttons Bay MI 49682

Call Sign: KB8WPU
John M Klang
1166 S Peck Rd
Suttons Bay MI 49682

Call Sign: WB8JRX
Richard A Blake II
990 S Ridgeview Trl
Suttons Bay MI 49682

Call Sign: KB8EBA
Brian K Wales
1117 S Westbay Shore
Dr
Suttons Bay MI 49682

Call Sign: WB8TPR
Gregory G North
6330 S Westwood
Pkwy
Suttons Bay MI 49682

Call Sign: KD8EWM
Bruce W Harlton
6363 S Westwood
Pkwy
Suttons Bay MI 49682

Call Sign: W8MSE
Bruce W Harlton
6363 S Westwood
Pkwy
Suttons Bay MI 49682

Call Sign: KC8OUA
Laurel Chapman
Suttons Bay MI 49682

Call Sign: KC8VWU
Brian K Nelson
Suttons Bay MI 49682

Call Sign: N8SWS
Devern E York
1054 4th St
Tawas City MI 48763

Call Sign: KD8JWV
Calvin E Williams
1143 Anderson Rd
Tawas City MI 48763

Call Sign: N8EDW
Robert M Sherbino
711 Cedar St
Tawas City MI 48763

Call Sign: KA8CMS
Carol Ann Burgis
122 Dean Rd
Tawas City MI 48763

Call Sign: KA8CMW
Earl E Burgis
122 Dean Rd
Tawas City MI 48763

Call Sign: W8MYZ
Neil B Ericsson
1733 Douglas Dr
Tawas City MI 48763

Call Sign: KC8GMQ
David L Wentworth
1929 Douglas Dr
Tawas City MI 48763

Call Sign: KC8UP
Alan C Bingham
560 E M 55 Unit 204
Tawas City MI 48763

Call Sign: KC8KEC
Raymond S Boldizar
1201 Harris Ave
Tawas City MI 48763

Call Sign: KC8KPZ
John O Bellinger
1008 Meadow
Tawas City MI 48763

Call Sign: KC8MZG
Kristy A Bellinger
1008 Meadow Rd
Tawas City MI 48763

Call Sign: KC8EYO
Edward M Keller
2915 Miller Rd
Tawas City MI 48763

Call Sign: KB8GFC
Donald H Mac Leod
963 Nanette St
Tawas City MI 48763

Call Sign: KD8PFQ
Richard M Rujan
1655 Oates Rd
Tawas City MI 48763

Call Sign: N8SJP
Scott M Gingerich
228 S Plank Rd
Tawas City MI 48763

Call Sign: KC8HNS
Betty L Sells
2054 S US 23
Tawas City MI 48763

Call Sign: KC8HBD
Floyd L Sells Jr
2054 S US 23
Tawas City MI 48763

Call Sign: W8SIZ
Donald R Ingalls
726 Sparton
Tawas City MI 48763

Call Sign: KC8AHZ
Gary L Fairfield
120 Spring St
Tawas City MI 48763

Call Sign: KB8VLP
Michael J O Dea
311 Tawas River
Trailer Park
Tawas City MI 48763

Call Sign: WA8CQD
Eli W Ruja
411 Tawas River
Trailer Park
Tawas City MI 48763

Call Sign: KC8MZF

James C Ancel
910 W Lake St
Tawas City MI 48764

Call Sign: N8IIG
Terry T Bronson
1365 W M 55
Tawas City MI 48763

Call Sign: KD8KNR
James R Shoemaker
2818 W M 55
Tawas City MI 48763

Call Sign: AC8GC
James R Shoemaker
2818 W M 55
Tawas City MI 48763

Call Sign: W8YO
Kenneth M Spahr II
2300 W Miller Rd
Tawas City MI
487639644

Call Sign: WD8OAH
Arnold B Boudreau
Tawas City MI 48763

FCC Amateur Radio Licenses in Tekonsha

Call Sign: KD8AGZ
Andrew S Glenn
1240 Bell Rd
Tekonsha MI 49092

Call Sign: W8CSS
Andrew S Glenn
1240 Bell Rd
Tekonsha MI 49092

Call Sign: KD8JEK
Timothy J Miner
1201 Dean Rd
Tekonsha MI 49092

Call Sign: KD8IXZ
Jerri A Onjukka
398 Hyannis Hill Dr
Tekonsha MI 49092

Call Sign: KD8IXT
Tommy R Onjukka

398 Hyannis Hills Dr
Tekonsha MI 49092

Call Sign: KC8NCM
Benjamin E Vincent
19311 T Dr S
Tekonsha MI 49092

Call Sign: KC8QNV
Samuel D Mcfadden
Tekonsha MI 49092

FCC Amateur Radio Licenses in Thompson

Call Sign: KA8RTO
Cynthia S Miller
Thompson MI 49889

Call Sign: KA8RTP
Paul A Miller II
Thompson MI 49889

FCC Amateur Radio Licenses in Thompsonville

Call Sign: N8DEJ
Calvin A Scott
Rt 1 Box 260 Lindy Rd
Thompsonville MI
49683

Call Sign: KC8JJL
Frank J Pracher
15260 Homestead
Thompsonville MI
49683

Call Sign: WD8MSY
Betty L Scott
18440 Lindy Rd
Thompsonville MI
496839760

Call Sign: WD8PCZ
Michael T Petersen
14694 Woods Trl
Thompsonville MI
49683

Call Sign: KA8SAS
Victoria Mueller

Thompsonville MI
49683

FCC Amateur Radio Licenses in Three Oaks

Call Sign: K9WPU
Richard J Benedick
14418 3 Oaks Rd
Three Oaks MI 49128

Call Sign: KA9NCQ
Herbert D Anderson
16967 3 Oaks Rd
Three Oaks MI 49128

Call Sign: KD8BYE
Edward T Killips
14720 Bell Ave
Three Oaks MI
491289137

Call Sign: N8WMJ
Gary E Schmaltz
14510 Brown Rd
Three Oaks MI 49128

Call Sign: KD8CXR
Charles F Osburn
504 Hickory St
Three Oaks MI
491281055

Call Sign: KA8CYH
Eldon F Lee
305 Locust St Apt 5
Three Oaks MI
491281291

Call Sign: WA0TAQ
Jonathan C White
6116 Long Rd
Three Oaks MI 49128

Call Sign: KD8BTJ
Paul A Taylor
24.5 N Elm St
Three Oaks MI 49128

Call Sign: NW9R
Seth Walker Jr
19498 S Martin Rd
Three Oaks MI 49128

Call Sign: KC8DUC
Richard D Snow
17248 S Schwark
Three Oaks MI 49128

Call Sign: KA9ZNS
Richard P Matt
4029 W Kruger Rd
Three Oaks MI 49128

Call Sign: KC8QXK
Richard P Matt
4029 W Kruger Rd
Three Oaks MI 49128

Call Sign: N9HLC
Patrick F Pellouchoud
6063 W Kruger Rd
Three Oaks MI
491289702

Call Sign: W9KRU
Timothy E Krueger
6992 W US Hwy 12
Lot 69
Three Oaks MI 49128

FCC Amateur Radio Licenses in Three Rivers

Call Sign: KB8ESF
Dawn M Martinka
56895 7 Hills Rd
Three Rivers MI 49093

Call Sign: N8EOX
Warren L Harder
14820 Broadway Rd
Three Rivers MI
490939503

Call Sign: WD8EIW
Barton J Carrel
12502 Coon Hollow
Rd
Three Rivers MI
490939117

Call Sign: KB9NWU
Dean J Schlabach
13399 Coon Hollow
Rd

Three Rivers MI 49093

Call Sign: KD8JSF
Thomas M Gahan
11046 Cory Lake Rd
Three Rivers MI 49093

Call Sign: N8ZSG
George J Dibble
18841 E M 60 Hwy
Three Rivers MI 49093

Call Sign: N8SAA
Stan H Santow
58502 E Pleasant View
Ct
Three Rivers MI 49093

Call Sign: N8IYW
Cheryl D Miller
57542 Gearhart
Landing Rd
Three Rivers MI 49093

Call Sign: N8IYX
Randall L Miller
57542 Gearhart
Landing Rd
Three Rivers MI 49093

Call Sign: K8OMQ
Eugene L Childress
57580 Gearharts
Landing Rd
Three Rivers MI 49093

Call Sign: N8NJU
James L Gage
56805 Haines Rd
Three Rivers MI 49093

Call Sign: KA8VIA
George B Gunter
17701 Hoshel Rd
Three Rivers MI 49093

Call Sign: KI4OZJ
Robert L Barton
22460 Klines Resort
Rd
Three Rivers MI 49093

Call Sign: KB8SVH
Janet M Squires

22460 Klines Resort
Rd 235
Three Rivers MI 49093

Call Sign: W8WKD
Robert E De Korte
22460 Klines Resort
Rd Box 253
Three Rivers MI 49093

Call Sign: AA4RV
James W Hope
22460 Klines Resort
Rd Lot 235
Three Rivers MI 49093

Call Sign: KF4EEG
Wilma M Hope
22460 Klines Resort
Rd Lot 235
Three Rivers MI 49093

Call Sign: WA8STV
Donald M Squires
22460 Klines Resort
Rd Lot 235
Three Rivers MI
490939690

Call Sign: K8ALP
Avery L Playford
22460 Klines Resort
Rd Lot 45
Three Rivers MI 49093

Call Sign: W8VIB
Glenn W Godshalk
204 N Erie
Three Rivers MI 49093

Call Sign: W8YBL
Margaret A Godshalk
204 N Erie
Three Rivers MI 49093

Call Sign: WA8TMN
Herbert G Gibson
312 N Grant Ave
Three Rivers MI 49093

Call Sign: WD8OGR
Michael J Westfall
626 N Main St
Three Rivers MI 49093

Call Sign: K8SGV
Gilbert Jackson Jr
16191 Null Rd
Three Rivers MI 49093

Call Sign: KC8FMR
Jonathan W Rice
429 Portage Ave
Three Rivers MI 49093

Call Sign: N8ZXG
John P Kison Jr
51288 Pulver Rd
Three Rivers MI 49093

Call Sign: KB8JLO
John D Huston
18895 Riverview Dr
Three Rivers MI 49093

Call Sign: WB8WJY
Jerry W Sample
60351 Roberts Rd
Three Rivers MI 49093

Call Sign: W8ZAP
Jerry W Sample
60351 Roberts Rd
Three Rivers MI 49093

Call Sign: W8WUT
Avis E Miracle
114 S Hooker Ave
Three Rivers MI 49093

Call Sign: W8WUU
Wilfred R Miracle
114 S Hooker Ave
Three Rivers MI 49093

Call Sign: WA8ZET
James H Wagner
501 S Hooker Ave
Three Rivers MI 49093

Call Sign: K8SUV
Harold J Barton
622 S Hooker Ave
Three Rivers MI 49093

Call Sign: KD8BYP
Eric W Kaup
11305 S Horseshoe Dr

Three Rivers MI 49093

Call Sign: KD8ADB
Richard A Osborn
218 S Lincoln Ave
Three Rivers MI 49093

Call Sign: KC8FMU
Michael P Glide
20984 Schweitzer Rd
Three Rivers MI 49093

Call Sign: N8TGD
Evertt P Pritchard
21799 Schweitzer Rd
Three Rivers MI 49093

Call Sign: KC8GOU
Eric J Forsyth
56940 Tamarac Ln
Three Rivers MI 49093

Call Sign: KB8IBH
Ronald E Ward
1099 W Mi Ave 105
Three Rivers MI
490932800

Call Sign: KB8ERL
Rodney W Mesick
814 West St
Three Rivers MI 49093

Call Sign: N8LAP
Loretta L Mesick
814 West St
Three Rivers MI 49093

Call Sign: KJ8D
Roger D Kibby
53717 Wilbur Rd
Three Rivers MI 49093

Call Sign: K8LKC
Joseph A Medsker
55940 Wilbur Rd
Three Rivers MI 49093

Call Sign: KD8AYE
Kirk P Graham
20119 Wilson Blvd
Three Rivers MI 49093

Call Sign: KC8MIY

Jonathan M Lancaster
56026 Woodridge
Three Rivers MI 49093

Call Sign: KA8HQR
Wesley E Maatta
3616 Artic Cir Rd
Toivola MI 49965

Call Sign: KA8WAL
Marvin J W Mattson
Hc 01 Box 93 Bb
Toivola MI 49965

Call Sign: W8MZB
Donald A Arnson
40341 N Hwy M2B
Toivola MI 499650007

Call Sign: WD8IPG
Dennis W Stark
Toivola MI 49965

Call Sign: K8BIP
Madelyn H Moore
662 Giauque
Topinabee MI 49791

Call Sign: KD8QEZ
Ronald J Brown
Topinabee MI 49791

Call Sign: KC8WUW
Timothy A Morley
Topinabee MI
497910396

Call Sign: KC8NVJ
Kenneth A Repke
7156 Veihl Rd
Tower MI 49792

Call Sign: KD8BOY
David J Schaefer
E3262 H44 Rd
Traunik MI 49891

Call Sign: KD8BOZ
Erika A Schaefer
E3262 H44 Rd
Traunik MI 49891

Call Sign: N8JZM
Joel E Asher
N3283 Ladoga Rd
Traunik MI 49891

Call Sign: KA8YLK
Thomas P Waclawski
5975 Donna Ct
Traverse MI 49684

Call Sign: KC8HJP
Gary M Carscadden
632 George St
Traverse MI 49686

Call Sign: KC8RLY
Rudy A Gavaldon
1504 River Rd W
Traverse MI 49686

Call Sign: KB8RDG
Todd M Olson
414 W 7th
Traverse MI 49684

Call Sign: KD8DYB
Grand Traverse County Arpsc
4283 3 Mile Rd
Traverse City MI
49686

Call Sign: N7LMJ
Michael Dell
4283 3 Mile Rd N

Traverse City MI
49686

Call Sign: KB8RDD
Kitty Z Gauss
325 6th St
Traverse City MI
49684

Call Sign: KB9BTD
Timothy M Dunn
612 Airport Access 1
Traverse City MI
49684

Call Sign: KD8NEK
Daniel B Hartman
3122 Andys Ln
Traverse City MI
49684

Call Sign: K8ZZ
Edwin E Eklin
2960 Arborview Dr
Apt 12
Traverse City MI
49684

Call Sign: KB8VAY
George C Ferrar
2026 Arrowhead Dr
Traverse City MI
49686

Call Sign: KD8CQE
Paul R Welser
9781 Avondale Ln
Traverse City MI
49684

Call Sign: KD8CQF
Laurie S Welser
9781 Avondale Ln
Traverse City MI
49684

Call Sign: K8NVH
William E Lively
9965 Avondale Ln
Traverse City MI
49684

Call Sign: N8KAP
Dennis J De Marco

1540B Barlow St
Traverse City MI
49684

Call Sign: KC8CBD
Donald C Andersen
1251 Bass Lake Rd
Traverse City MI
49684

Call Sign: KC8LTN
Kim L Andersen
1251 Bass Lake Rd
Traverse City MI
49684

Call Sign: KB8OYX
Thomas M Barnhart
2789 Bayway Ct 202
Traverse City MI
49684

Call Sign: KD8BZO
Ann Drury
1661 Birmley Rd
Traverse City MI
49686

Call Sign: KD8BZP
Dennis J Lautner
1661 Birmley Rd
Traverse City MI
49686

Call Sign: N8GAJ
William J Dwyer
3553 Blair Valley Rd
Traverse City MI
49684

Call Sign: W8LDR
William J Dwyer
3553 Blair Valley Rd
Traverse City MI
49684

Call Sign: W8FVH
James R Hoogesteger
558 Bloomfield Rd
Traverse City MI
49684

Call Sign: KB8FDG
Dorothy J Van Farowe

10505 Bluff Rd
Traverse City MI
49686

4901 Buckhorn Dr
Traverse City MI
49684

11422 Cedar Run Rd
Traverse City MI
49684

10565 Cherry Bend Rd
Traverse City MI
496845245

Call Sign: NZ8H
George C Van Farowe
10505 Bluff Rd
Traverse City MI
49686

Call Sign: N8PZY
Kenneth R Snyder
760 Calla Lilly Ln
Traverse City MI
49684

Call Sign: W8LVZ
James C Fenton
11476 Cedar Run Rd
Traverse City MI
49684

Call Sign: AB8BN
Ralph A Posnik Jr
4425 Cherry Ln
Traverse City MI
49684

Call Sign: KC8HU
Laurence P Ducheny
830 Boon St
Traverse City MI
49686

Call Sign: W8FIK
Thomas D Mang
988 Callalilly Ln
Traverse City MI
49684

Call Sign: KD8RTE
Deborah A Hanchett
20320 Cedar Run Rd
Traverse City MI
49684

Call Sign: KC8ILI
Ian K Kennedy
9664 Cherrybend Rd
Traverse City MI
49684

Call Sign: N8RTC
Carol L Pearce
896 Boon St
Traverse City MI
49684

Call Sign: WA8VKJ
John M Patrick
2198 Cambridge Dr
Traverse City MI
49686

Call Sign: KJ4KFJ
David J Hanchett
20320 Cedar Run Rd
Traverse City MI
49684

Call Sign: N8MLL
James R Black
1702 Comanche
Traverse City MI
49686

Call Sign: N8KJB
Ronald W L Pearce
896 Boon St
Traverse City MI
49684

Call Sign: KA8WWN
Ivan J Porter Jr
1206 Carl Rd
Traverse City MI
49684

Call Sign: KB8HBL
Rich M Wunsch
9167 Center Rd
Traverse City MI
49684

Call Sign: KC8VST
Mark G Baranski
1703 Comanche
Traverse City MI
49686

Call Sign: KD8CQK
Dmytko R Daciuk
1569 Braemar
Traverse City MI
49686

Call Sign: KD8AZF
Michelle G Drapeau
915 Carlisle Rd
Traverse City MI
49686

Call Sign: KB8HCA
Richard E Wunsch
9167 Center Rd
Traverse City MI
49684

Call Sign: KC8AUH
Dennis E Miller
4034 Coors Dr
Traverse City MI
49684

Call Sign: WB8CCA
David K Sanger
1699 Braemar Dr
Traverse City MI
49686

Call Sign: W8FAP
Clarence R Lamoreaux
826 Carver St
Traverse City MI
49684

Call Sign: N8KVZ
Louise J Wunsch
9167 Center Rd
Traverse City MI
49684

Call Sign: KD8JPY
James D Haldaman
3615 Courtney Pl
Traverse City MI
49684

Call Sign: KD8CVN
John J Mcclay
8555 Brown Bridge Rd
Traverse City MI
49686

Call Sign: N8RBV
Christopher A Miller
3946 Cedar Run Rd
Traverse City MI
49684

Call Sign: KC4CNU
F Richard Schantz
9965 Center Rd
Traverse City MI
49684

Call Sign: K8JDH
James D Haldaman
3615 Courtney Pl
Traverse City MI
49684

Call Sign: KC8GCK
Christopher S Wood
4536 Brunson Pl
Traverse City MI
49684

Call Sign: N8ZWS
Daniel J Hills
7175 Cedar Run Rd
Traverse City MI
49684

Call Sign: KC8PHM
Alex R Malocha
820 Centre St
Traverse City MI
49686

Call Sign: W8QDS
William M Keely
1251 Coyote Crossing
Traverse City MI
49686

Call Sign: KC8RNT
David D Beery

Call Sign: KB8HCE
Bill C Fenton

Call Sign: WA8ABL
Robert C Korb

Call Sign: N8RDD
Eugene R Crocker

6208 Cranbrook Trl
Traverse City MI
49684

Call Sign: W8TVI
Noel D Shrum
2516 Crossing Cir Apt
A 303
Traverse City MI
49684

Call Sign: KF8RU
Robert E Stuedemann
10258 Deerpath N
Traverse City MI
49685

Call Sign: KD8JMC
Thomas R Bell
5861 Dover Ln
Traverse City MI
49684

Call Sign: WA8VLY
William W Lipscomb
6073 Dover Ln
Traverse City MI
49684

Call Sign: KC8IHA
Patrick J Carolan
1282 Downhill Ln
Traverse City MI
49686

Call Sign: KC8REO
John H Peters
749 Dyer Lake Rd
Traverse City MI
49684

Call Sign: N8PVS
Daniel F Garvin
240 E 9th St
Traverse City MI
49684

Call Sign: W8JUZ
Laura E Steinberger
907 E Arbutus Lake
Rd
Traverse City MI
49696

Call Sign: KC8TDG
Bernard Hanchett
9762 E Avondale Ln
Traverse City MI
49684

Call Sign: KD8LCJ
Russell R Riker
2385 E Carriage Hill
Dr
Traverse City MI
49686

Call Sign: W8LSX
Leo R Hepner
7040 E Fouch Rd
Traverse City MI
49684

Call Sign: KC8NEI
Ngaire M Hepner
7040 E Fouch Rd
Traverse City MI
49684

Call Sign: KC8JXT
Andrew C Pachmayer
9210 E Grandview Rd
Traverse City MI
49684

Call Sign: W8FOV
Gary L Randall
3633 E Hammond Rd
Traverse City MI
49684

Call Sign: WB8APT
David L Poinsett
9770 E Harbor Hills Dr
Traverse City MI
49684

Call Sign: KE8KX
Thomas R Dundon
9994 E Harbor Hills Dr
Traverse City MI
496965046

Call Sign: KC8GOS
Denice S Whaley
2805 E Ironwood Dr
Traverse City MI
49684

Call Sign: KC8KGG
Northwest Michigan
ARC
3113 E Long Lake Rd
Traverse City MI
49684

Call Sign: W8TVC
David A Dell
3113 E Long Lake Rd
Traverse City MI
49684

Call Sign: KC8PCQ
Betty L Dell
3113 E Long Lake Rd
Traverse City MI
49684

Call Sign: WI0OK
Northwest Michigan
ARC
3113 E Long Lake Rd
Traverse City MI
49684

Call Sign: KC8NJQ
Betty R Wrasse
4861 E Red Oaks Dr
Traverse City MI
49684

Call Sign: KB8MQX
Michael R Popp
1984 E Silver Lake Rd
Traverse City MI
49684

Call Sign: KB8RDF
Phyllis E Nicholson
719 E Silver Lake Rd
N
Traverse City MI
49684

Call Sign: KC8ITF
Scott J Swan
849 E State St
Traverse City MI
49686

Call Sign: KB8IID
Frederick H Tank Jr

1026 E State St
Traverse City MI
49684

Call Sign: NS8K
Thomas J Peterson
9198 E Tottenham Dr
Traverse City MI
49684

Call Sign: N8IYG
Sally J Peterson
9198 E Tottenham Dr
Traverse City MI
49684

Call Sign: K5FNT
Joseph E Brown Jr
1415 Eastern Ave
Traverse City MI
49686

Call Sign: KD8REH
Michael J Vandermey
19121 Eastern Rd
Traverse City MI
49686

Call Sign: W8EQK
William H Cruse
513 Eastwood Shore
Traverse City MI
49684

Call Sign: W8PQ
Michael F Leger
9563 Echo Valley Dr
Traverse City MI
49684

Call Sign: W8LQZ
John P Mesch
9793 Edgewood Ave
Traverse City MI
49684

Call Sign: WD8BZP
Shirley Mesch
9793 Edgewood Ave
Traverse City MI
49684

Call Sign: W8SGR
Wendell C Mellberg

9906 Edgewood Ave
Traverse City MI
49684

Call Sign: WS8N
Paul H Miller
422 Fairlane Dr
Traverse City MI
49684

Call Sign: WA8HNW
Douglas L Schrag
2914 Feiger Ln
Traverse City MI
49684

Call Sign: N8LPO
Svea R Nepote
802 Fern St
Traverse City MI
49684

Call Sign: KA8HIB
Paul J Nepote
802 Fern St
Traverse City MI
49686

Call Sign: K8HIB
Paul J Nepote
802 Fern St
Traverse City MI
49686

Call Sign: KB5BSS
Jon J Lapekas
2412 Field Rd
Traverse City MI
49684

Call Sign: KC8DOF
Molly J Van Oordt
10422 Fishers Run
Traverse City MI
49684

Call Sign: N8ZUT
Scott R Van Oordt
10422 Fishers Run
Traverse City MI
49684

Call Sign: W8EXO
Eugene J Hansknecht

891 Fitzhugh Apt 10
Traverse City MI
49684

Call Sign: WD8JHU
Mary E Ferris
601 Fitzhugh Dr Apt
135D
Traverse City MI
49684

Call Sign: W8FFG
George D Ferris
601 Fitzhugh Dr Apt
D135
Traverse City MI
49684

Call Sign: N8OUZ
Joseph R Erlewein
830 Floresta St
Traverse City MI
49686

Call Sign: KC8EKR
Dennis D Howard
1758 Forest Ridge Dr
Traverse City MI
496864799

Call Sign: K8DAG
David A Gary
632 George St
Traverse City MI
49686

Call Sign: W8CLF
Harry W Ansorge
540 Georgetown Dr
Apt 27
Traverse City MI
49684

Call Sign: KD8DWI
Michael J Matthews
8865 Gilbert Trl
Traverse City MI
49684

Call Sign: W8TCX
Michael J Matthews
8865 Gilbert Trl
Traverse City MI
49685

Call Sign: K8LYB
Maurice E Stanwick
808 Glenview Ave
Traverse City MI
49686

Call Sign: KC8NEK
William D Dow
3536 Glorianne Dr
Traverse City MI
49684

Call Sign: K8ATM
William D Dow
3536 Glorianne Dr
Traverse City MI
49685

Call Sign: KD8RSZ
Lucas T Cross
4466 Goldenrod Dr
Traverse City MI
49685

Call Sign: KE6PHJ
Elizabeth A Cyran
2820 Hakala Hills Dr
Traverse City MI
49686

Call Sign: KA6AYJ
Ann E Cyran
2820 Hakala Hills Dr
Traverse City MI
49686

Call Sign: N8RSO
Karen L Powell
430 Hamilton St
Traverse City MI
49686

Call Sign: N8RSR
Richard L Powell
430 Hamilton St
Traverse City MI
496862917

Call Sign: WB8DX
Bay Area Dxers
2663 Hammond
Highlands Dr

Traverse City MI
49686

Call Sign: KA8HYE
Edgar A Bringman
3930 Hammond Rd
Traverse City MI
49684

Call Sign: KA8OGC
Jean E Bringman
3930 Hammond Rd
Traverse City MI
49684

Call Sign: KB8ALS
Holly Bringman
3930 Hammond Rd
Traverse City MI
49684

Call Sign: KA8REU
John L Finfrock
924 Hannah Ave
Traverse City MI
49686

Call Sign: KB6AJB
Lisa J Annable
9845 Harbor Hills Dr
Traverse City MI
49684

Call Sign: KB6AJC
Craig J Annable
9845 Harbor Hills Dr
Traverse City MI
49684

Call Sign: N8STW
Joan A Van Dyke
1158 Hemingway Ln
Traverse City MI
49684

Call Sign: KD8BWP
Traverse City Dx Club
5562 Heritage Way
Traverse City MI
49684

Call Sign: NS8A
Traverse City Dx Club
5562 Heritage Way

Traverse City MI
49684

Traverse City MI
49686

Traverse City MI
49686

Traverse City MI
49686

Call Sign: K9JP
Jeffrey E Peters
5562 Heritage Way
Traverse City MI
49685

Call Sign: NF8T
Norman E Risk
48 Highview Rd
Traverse City MI
49686

Call Sign: WB2LHP
James J Marco
198 Island View Dr
Traverse City MI
49696

Call Sign: WB8NVR
Susan K Leishman
4459 Lakeview Trl
Traverse City MI
49686

Call Sign: N8LYG
Scott A Niedecken
182 High Lake Rd
Traverse City MI
49696

Call Sign: W8IAS
Frank A Smith
412 Highview Rd
Traverse City MI
496869466

Call Sign: KA8EVM
John S Woodrow
2450 Jorae Dr
Traverse City MI
49684

Call Sign: KC8DFG
Theodore V Zachman
9118 Lawrence Dr
Traverse City MI
49684

Call Sign: N8NKQ
Shannon M Niedecken
182 High Lake Rd
Traverse City MI
49696

Call Sign: W8GJH
Francis E Gary
7149 Hilltop Ave
Traverse City MI
49684

Call Sign: KA8EXD
Ernestine M Woodrow
2450 Jorae Dr
Traverse City MI
49684

Call Sign: W8BNL
Tom J Garrisi
4146 Lilac Ln
Traverse City MI
49684

Call Sign: KB8RIV
Harry M Liebziet
1615 High St
Traverse City MI
49684

Call Sign: KC8UPR
Frank H Rutherford
2986 Holiday Rd
Traverse City MI
49686

Call Sign: NX8E
Gary M Routsong
932 Kelley St
Traverse City MI
49684

Call Sign: KB8DEU
Juris Ozols
1101 Lindale Dr
Traverse City MI
49684

Call Sign: KC8BQL
Lyle J Powers
5016 Highland Dr
Traverse City MI
49684

Call Sign: AA8YJ
Angela M Nehs
3146 Horseshoe Dr
Traverse City MI
49684

Call Sign: KD8NEH
Evrid D Potter
1156 Knollcrest Ct
Traverse City MI
49686

Call Sign: KD8EDC
Mark Tosiello
6148 London Dr
Traverse City MI
49684

Call Sign: KC8JJJ
June E Thaden
520 Highland Park Dr
Traverse City MI
49686

Call Sign: KB8SKA
Timothy C Havens
809 Indian Trl
Traverse City MI
49684

Call Sign: KD8POG
George F Ammann
537 Lake 5 Dr
Traverse City MI
49696

Call Sign: KC8LTP
Daniel C Ahrns
14668 Mallard Dr
Traverse City MI
49686

Call Sign: NW2E
John Thaden
520 Highland Park Dr
Traverse City MI
496862849

Call Sign: KB8HAH
Randolph S Averill
820 Indian Trl Blvd
Traverse City MI
49684

Call Sign: WB3KMP
Bruce G Walker
831 Lake George Trl
Traverse City MI
49686

Call Sign: KB8FDT
David G Heydlauff
4308 Manhattan E
Traverse City MI
49684

Call Sign: KB8WZU
Samuel D Falk
553 Highland Pk Dr
Traverse City MI
48686

Call Sign: KD8IQQ
Richard B Woodbury
3020 Ishpeming Trl
Traverse City MI
49686

Call Sign: W8SYQ
Anael T Kirkby
4206 Lakeview Trl
Traverse City MI
49684

Call Sign: N8STT
Martha A Dundon
7345 Maple Ter
Traverse City MI
49684

Call Sign: N8JJC
Carolyn S Risk
48 Highview Rd

Call Sign: KD8LCK
Debby J Stevens
120 Island View

Call Sign: K8XX
John R Leishman
4459 Lakeview Trl

Call Sign: KA8UCQ
David B Crawford
1891 McRae Hill Rd

Traverse City MI
49684

Call Sign: WA8LEP
Sylvia C Kekic
802 Minkin Dr
Traverse City MI
49684

Call Sign: N8SSY
Lawrence M
Thompson
18680 Mission Rd
Traverse City MI
49686

Call Sign: W8LBP
E David Rollert
6442 Mission Ridge
Traverse City MI
49684

Call Sign: KC8QOB
Charles A Brackett
6688 Mission Ridge
Traverse City MI
49686

Call Sign: KG8PK
Michael W Wood
3850 Morningside Dr
Traverse City MI
49684

Call Sign: KB8HOO
Shari A Freeman
1143 Mulberry Dr
Traverse City MI
496855064

Call Sign: WB8FUZ
Jan A White
710 N Birchwood Ave
Traverse City MI
49686

Call Sign: NW8Y
Dennis H Markey
1110 N Carriage Hill
Traverse City MI
49686

Call Sign: KG8BD
Jon S Rinckey

4334 N Curry Dr
Traverse City MI
49684

Call Sign: W8JSR
Jon S Rinckey
4334 N Curry Dr
Traverse City MI
49684

Call Sign: N8RSY
Tony P Paddock
131 N Elmwood
Traverse City MI
49684

Call Sign: N8STP
Bob W Sprenger
619 N Elmwood
Traverse City MI
49684

Call Sign: KA8SOC
Marc T Greenlaw
912 N Forest Ln
Traverse City MI
49684

Call Sign: N8YCO
Jerry J Williams
8871 N Long Lake Rd
Traverse City MI
49684

Call Sign: N8ZWX
Madonna J Williams
8871 N Long Lake Rd
Traverse City MI
49684

Call Sign: KD8DVW
William C Williston
11113 N Long Lake
Rd
Traverse City MI
49684

Call Sign: W8LBS
Morris A Booth
629 N Monroe St
Traverse City MI
496841420

Call Sign: KC8KVW

Thomas A Borsos
201 N Oak St
Traverse City MI
49684

Call Sign: KA8IAT
Lester G Swain
312 N South Long
Lake Rd
Traverse City MI
49684

Call Sign: W8RNQ
Elgen W Walt
121 N Spruce St
Traverse City MI
49684

Call Sign: KA8WFL
Michael J Whipple
902 Nakoma Dr
Traverse City MI
49684

Call Sign: W8CJT
William M Duckwitz
770 Neahtawanta Rd
Traverse City MI
49686

Call Sign: N8JEH
Manfred W Grunwaldt
2831 North Dr
Traverse City MI
496848723

Call Sign: KF9JC
Howard W Kiser
1466 Oban Way
Traverse City MI
49686

Call Sign: KC8CLS
Matthew C Salon Md
2777 Old Farm Ln
Traverse City MI
49684

Call Sign: KG8AO
Jonathan F
Schumacher
4381 Old Orchard Tr
Traverse City MI
49684

Call Sign: N8UL
Jonathan F
Schumacher
4381 Old Orchard Tr
Traverse City MI
49684

Call Sign: KD8AGJ
Diana K Lyon
Schumacher
4381 Old Orchard Tr
Traverse City MI
49684

Call Sign: W8DKL
Diana K Lyon
Schumacher
4381 Old Orchard Tr
Traverse City MI
49684

Call Sign: KD8KFF
Ernest E Abel
1600 Outer Dr
Traverse City MI
49684

Call Sign: K8RCT
Ernest E Abel
1600 Outer Dr
Traverse City MI
49684

Call Sign: K8GTC
Traverse Bay Amateur
Radio Emer
Communications
Group
1600 Outer Dr W
Traverse City MI
49685

Call Sign: KD8OXV
Traverse Bay Amateur
Radio Emergency
Communications
Group
1600 Outer Dr W
Traverse City MI
49685

Call Sign: N8SCZ
Bill R Gauthier

934 Peninsula Dr
Traverse City MI
49684

Call Sign: N8WK
R Edward Kuhn
1114 Peninsula Dr
Traverse City MI
49686

Call Sign: KC8QLE
Carol A Kuhn
1114 Peninsula Dr
Traverse City MI
49686

Call Sign: K8CAK
Carol A Kuhn
1114 Peninsula Dr
Traverse City MI
49686

Call Sign: N8KUT
Adam C McClay
6330 Peninsula Dr
Traverse City MI
49686

Call Sign: N8KXJ
Gloria M McClay
6330 Peninsula Dr
Traverse City MI
49686

Call Sign: KD8CQO
Thomas H Cowell
6449 Peninsula Dr
Traverse City MI
49685

Call Sign: KC8SSD
Donald F Strzynski
6518 Peninsula Dr
Traverse City MI
49686

Call Sign: N8QX
Donald F Strzynski
6518 Peninsula Dr
Traverse City MI
49686

Call Sign: N8HKQ
Arthur F Dundon

7236 Peninsula Dr
Traverse City MI
49686

Call Sign: N8KVY
Jacqueline A Dundon
7236 Peninsula Dr
Traverse City MI
496861750

Call Sign: W8QKP
Kenneth H Musson
9680 Peninsula Dr
Traverse City MI
49686

Call Sign: N8HLK
Patricia M Musson
9680 Peninsula Dr
Traverse City MI
496869201

Call Sign: KG8GT
Frederick H Doelker
11432 Peninsula Dr
Traverse City MI
49686

Call Sign: KA8UMR
Arthur G Sherman III
12006 Peninsula Dr
Traverse City MI
49686

Call Sign: N8PJY
Kent W Ackerman
3865 Perimeter Dr
Traverse City MI
49684

Call Sign: KB8UFJ
Thomas I Wyant Jr
1153 Piccadilly Rd
Traverse City MI
49684

Call Sign: KC8ZXD
Janice L Wyant
1153 Piccadilly Rd
Traverse City MI
49684

Call Sign: KC8OTZ
Norma A Loper

150 Pine Apt 802
Traverse City MI
49684

Call Sign: N8ZWQ
Richard M Daniels
150 Pine St Apt 602
Traverse City MI
49684

Call Sign: KC8GCH
Todd W McManus
686 Potter Rd W
Traverse City MI
49686

Call Sign: N8CN
David L Erlewein
2738 Ra Wa Si Ave
Traverse City MI
49684

Call Sign: W8TCM
Cherryland ARC
2738 Ra Wa Si Ave
Traverse City MI
49684

Call Sign: KD8IYT
Cherryland ARC
2738 Ra Wa Si Ave
Traverse City MI
49684

Call Sign: KC8IUQ
Thomas G Scott
904 Randolph St
Traverse City MI
49684

Call Sign: KD8MZG
B W Bura
6254 Red Fox Run
Traverse City MI
49686

Call Sign: N8HHA
Douglas H Lape
6264 Red Fox Run
Traverse City MI
496862067

Call Sign: K8TVC
Douglas Lape

6264 Red Fox Run
Traverse City MI
496862067

Call Sign: KC8LFM
Michael R Shevy
3514 Red Pine Dr
Traverse City MI
49684

Call Sign: KB8WZH
Gerald K Wick
853 Rennie Lk Rd
Traverse City MI
49686

Call Sign: KI8AZ
Gary J Wick
853 Rennie Lk Rd
Traverse City MI
49686

Call Sign: N8KP
Gary J Wick
853 Rennie Lk Rd
Traverse City MI
49686

Call Sign: KD8SBB
Roger A Racine
4317 Ridgemoor Dr
Traverse City MI
49684

Call Sign: KD8BXL
Gary L Hilts
4312 Ridgemoor Dr
Traverse City MI
49684

Call Sign: N0YWO
William P Vockel
4797 Ridgewater Run
Traverse City MI
49684

Call Sign: KD8RDU
John T Woods
1542 River Dr
Traverse City MI
49696

Call Sign: W8NGH
Robert A Van Dyke

632 River Rd E
Traverse City MI
49684

Call Sign: AA8SN
R Hope Francisco
1500 River Rd W
Traverse City MI
49686

Call Sign: KC8RLZ
Peter M Francisco
1500 River Rd W
Traverse City MI
49686

Call Sign: KD8BOD
Gilbert D Francisco
1500 River Rd W
Traverse City MI
49686

Call Sign: KD8BOA
Katie A Francisco
1500 River Rd W
Traverse City MI
49686

Call Sign: KD8BOE
Gabriela D Gavaldon
1504 River Rd W
Traverse City MI
49686

Call Sign: N8JUS
Mark D Styles
6083 Robert Dr
Traverse City MI
49684

Call Sign: KC8PUT
Michael J Culberson
934 Rose Ct
Traverse City MI
49686

Call Sign: KC8WNS
Charles E Ohearn
937 Rose Ct
Traverse City MI
49686

Call Sign: KA8WYY
Pat A Mullen

710 Rose St
Traverse City MI
49684

Call Sign: KB8KTU
Rhoda F Ackerman
76 S Airport Rd E
Traverse City MI
49684

Call Sign: N8LLU
Karin C Ackerman
76 S Airport Rd E
Traverse City MI
49684

Call Sign: N8LNM
Keith A Ackerman
76 S Airport Rd E
Traverse City MI
49684

Call Sign: KF8CW
Bernard K Ackerman
76 S Airport Rd E
Traverse City MI
496864827

Call Sign: KB8ZHH
Jennifer J Dobek
3753 S Airport Rd W
Traverse City MI
49684

Call Sign: WB6UTW
Michael C Peron
11018 S Blue Ridge Ln
Traverse City MI
49684

Call Sign: W8DXH
Donald A Campbell
4448 S Curry Dr
Traverse City MI
49684

Call Sign: KD8CQI
Keith F Forton
10221 S Dalzell Rd
Traverse City MI
49684

Call Sign: KD8BWQ

Grand Traverse
Independent Radio
League For Girls
4852 S Flamingo Dr
Traverse City MI
49684

Call Sign: K8GRL
Grand Traverse
Independent Radio
League For Girls
4852 S Flamingo Dr
Traverse City MI
49684

Call Sign: KC8ZSW
Mary E Schoech
4852 S Flamingo Dr
Traverse City MI
49684

Call Sign: KC8UPS
Scott T Schoech
4852 S Flamingo Dr
Traverse City MI
49684

Call Sign: KC8ZAR
William H Koucky
972 S Forest Ln Dr
Traverse City MI
49686

Call Sign: KB8ACM
Danny H Brewer
1638 S Garfield Ave
Traverse City MI
49686

Call Sign: N8STS
Norman L Dill
39 S Hobbs Hwy
Traverse City MI
496868794

Call Sign: KC8IBG
John T Hock
180 S Hobbs Hwy
Traverse City MI
49686

Call Sign: KD8FGZ
Michael G Engle

8371 S Lake Leelanau
Dr
Traverse City MI
49684

Call Sign: W8SEF
Scott E Ford
785S S Long Lake Rd
Traverse City MI
49685

Call Sign: N8LRU
Robert L Chouinard
410 S Long Lake Rd N
Traverse City MI
49684

Call Sign: N8XMC
Gregory S Hatfield
2427 S M 37 Apt 1
Traverse City MI
496846966

Call Sign: W1WOW
Jason S Hulet
1920 S Quail Ct
Traverse City MI
49686

Call Sign: N8RRR
Janet L Novak
201 S Spruce St
Traverse City MI
49684

Call Sign: W8TVT
Joseph W Novak
201 S Spruce St
Traverse City MI
496842331

Call Sign: KI8MET
Frederick V Gnich
9177 S Tottenham Dr
Traverse City MI
49685

Call Sign: WA8CYG
John L C Kinnucan
10530 S Weisler Rd
Traverse City MI
49684

Call Sign: W8CVU

Walter C Mayer
7222 S Westbay Shore
Dr
Traverse City MI
49684

Call Sign: KB8VAZ
Jon E Fessant
1935 Sawyer Rd
Traverse City MI
49684

Call Sign: N8RTB
Mary Anne Bartlett
4716 Scharmen Rd
Traverse City MI
49684

Call Sign: N8STZ
Thomas A Bartlett Sr
4716 Scharmen Rd
Traverse City MI
49684

Call Sign: KB8WBE
Jason A Stringham
1093 Sharkey Rd
Traverse City MI
49686

Call Sign: N8KSB
Carol A Larson
2671 Shenandoah Dr
Traverse City MI
49684

Call Sign: K8OTF
Gwen C Sanford
2671 Shenandoah Dr
Traverse City MI
496848922

Call Sign: K8GWN
Gwen C Sanford
2671 Shenandoah Dr
Traverse City MI
496848922

Call Sign: WA8NLZ
William R Davy
14713 Shipman Rd
Traverse City MI
49686

Call Sign: KC8BWN
John J Jeffrey Jr
9044 Shorter Lake Rd
Traverse City MI
49684

Call Sign: WA8OWS
John J Jeffrey Sr
9044 Shorter Lake Rd
Traverse City MI
49684

Call Sign: KC8KVX
Dale A Inman
3325 Silver Farms Ln
Traverse City MI
49684

Call Sign: N8VX
Dale A Inman
3325 Silver Farms Ln
Traverse City MI
49684

Call Sign: KB8UZM
Alfa J Spooner
2990 Silver Lake Rd
Traverse City MI
49684

Call Sign: N8RTA
Mike Wardin
10100 Skiver Rd
Traverse City MI
49684

Call Sign: KD8RTB
Elizabeth C Rought
1181 Smith Rd
Traverse City MI
49696

Call Sign: KA8SMA
Robert S Rought
1181 Smith Rd
Traverse City MI
49696

Call Sign: KB8ZPE
Michael P Rinckey
1217 Smith Rd
Traverse City MI
49686

Call Sign: KG8AU
Lyle P Rinckey
1217 Smith Rd
Traverse City MI
49686

Call Sign: N4RNI
Antonios Kekalos
989 Snow Apple Dr
Traverse City MI
49684

Call Sign: KB8RTT
Albert N Deaner
326 State Rd
Traverse City MI
49684

Call Sign: KB8GUD
James E Vasher Jr
871 State St
Traverse City MI
49684

Call Sign: KC8ZAQ
Robert A Ripley
3769 Stone Bridge Dr
Traverse City MI
49684

Call Sign: W9VUE
Andrew V Kiselius
8960 SW Bay Shore
Dr
Traverse City MI
49684

Call Sign: KA8JIT
Gary W Cornell
3999 Swaney Rd
Traverse City MI
49686

Call Sign: W8POX
Michael J Kurta
1349 Terrace Bluff Dr
Traverse City MI
49686

Call Sign: N8BRI
Brian L Paterson
4884 Thornapple Ln
Traverse City MI
49684

Call Sign: N8UV
Brian L Paterson
4884 Thornapple Ln
Traverse City MI
49684

Call Sign: KB1HXZ
M Montgomery Plough
443 Timber Crest Dr
Traverse City MI
49686

Call Sign: W8SOK
Wallace W McKim
2391 US 31 N
Traverse City MI
49684

Call Sign: KC8KCS
Elaine R Campbell
3793 Vale Dr
Traverse City MI
49686

Call Sign: KD8LPB
Brian C Nuszkowski
1303 Valley Dr
Traverse City MI
49685

Call Sign: KC8RKK
Michael T Lopacki
4282 Vance Rd
Traverse City MI
49684

Call Sign: KD8CQH
Steven L Wyckoff
1158 Vega Dr
Traverse City MI
49686

Call Sign: N8RSU
Jane N Schnack
220 W 10th St
Traverse City MI
49684

Call Sign: KD8CQG
Glen W Rauth
323 W 11th
Traverse City MI
49684

Call Sign: WB8BPO
Glen W Rauth
323 W 11th
Traverse City MI
49684

Call Sign: KA8NXX
Richard A Skendzel
222 W 11th St
Traverse City MI
49684

Call Sign: WD8IIR
Francis J Hughes Jr
210 W 13th St
Traverse City MI
49684

Call Sign: KB8JTK
Richard A Fidler
401 W 15th St
Traverse City MI
49684

Call Sign: K8RUS
Russell R Riker
503 W 15th St
Traverse City MI
49684

Call Sign: KB8GGK
John W McClellan
321 W 16th St
Traverse City MI
49684

Call Sign: N8RST
Gerry D McClellan
321 W 16th St
Traverse City MI
49684

Call Sign: AB8G
Gregory R Hodge
411 W 16th St
Traverse City MI
49684

Call Sign: N8DUW
Francis A Jackson
415 W 16th St
Traverse City MI
49684

Call Sign: N8KWN
Fitch R Williams
12599 W Bay Shore Dr
Traverse City MI
49684

Call Sign: W8KAN
Warren D Lange
11900 W Bayshore
Traverse City MI
49684

Call Sign: N6NTS
Cheryl L Archer
8439 W Bayshore Dr
Traverse City MI
49684

Call Sign: KD8MKW
Jeff A Weatherwax
2345 W Carriage Hill
Traverse City MI
49686

Call Sign: W8LKR
Clarence S Rasmussen
2365 W Carriage Hill
Dr
Traverse City MI
49686

Call Sign: KC8IAS
Cary J Sweet
893 W Forest Ln
Traverse City MI
49684

Call Sign: W8TVQ
Frank X Shumsky III
893 W Forest Ln
Traverse City MI
49686

Call Sign: KC8NJR
Patricia L Shumsky
893 W Forrest Ln
Traverse City MI
49686

Call Sign: W8FGA
Homer L Gifford
673 W Orchard Dr

Traverse City MI
49684

Call Sign: KC8RLV
Anthony R Gavaldon
1504 W River Rd
Traverse City MI
49686

Call Sign: AA8YI
Thomas I Shikoski
416 W Sleights Rd
Traverse City MI
49686

Call Sign: KC8ZST
Mary C Shikoski
416 W Sleights Rd
Traverse City MI
49686

Call Sign: KB8RDS
Donald J Shikoski
474 W Sleights Rd
Traverse City MI
49686

Call Sign: KI8KR
Donald J Shikoski
474 W Sleights Rd
Traverse City MI
49686

Call Sign: KI8IE
Thomas L Boynton
222 Washington 2
Traverse City MI
49684

Call Sign: KD8CVP
Eric N Anderson
857 Washington St
Traverse City MI
49686

Call Sign: WX1J
W Scott Pyles
919 Washington St
Traverse City MI
49686

Call Sign: N8FCA
Jack H Peterson

752 Watch Hill Ln Apt
B3
Traverse City MI
49684

Call Sign: N8NV
Leonard A Mohr
216 Waxwing Dr
Traverse City MI
49696

Call Sign: N8NPJ
Leonard A Mohr
216 Waxwing Dr
Traverse City MI
496868514

Call Sign: N8NPN
Theresa A Mohr
216 Waxwing Dr
Traverse City MI
496868514

Call Sign: K8NV
Theresa A Mohr
216 Waxwing Dr
Traverse City MI
496968514

Call Sign: KB8IJF
Lindsay A Mack
3793 Wemple Rd
Traverse City MI
49684

Call Sign: N8UGV
Vance J Stringham
3968 Wemple Rd
Traverse City MI
49686

Call Sign: N8ZWV
Jeannie M Stringham
3968 Wemple Rd
Traverse City MI
49686

Call Sign: KD8CKO
Samantha W
Stringham
3968 Wemple Rd
Traverse City MI
49686

Call Sign: KC8KVY
Anthony J Kortokrax
2522 Westward Dr
Traverse City MI
49684

Call Sign: N8XQK
Larry D Kortokrax
2522 Westward Dr
Traverse City MI
49685

Call Sign: KD8PRN
Elisa K Stroh
7284 Westwind Rd
Traverse City MI
49686

Call Sign: KG6LHF
Lloyd M Houlden
2784 White Hill Ln
Apt 101
Traverse City MI
49686

Call Sign: KD8IHH
Dean A Tobias
2505 Woodcock Ln
Traverse City MI
49684

Call Sign: W8DTC
Dean A Tobias
2505 Woodcock Ln
Traverse City MI
49684

Call Sign: KB8MKQ
Arthur M Gibson III
725 Woodcreek Blvd
Traverse City MI
49686

Call Sign: KB8QFH
Phillip J Gibbs
527 Woodland Dr
Traverse City MI
48686

Call Sign: K8WPE
David J Wilcox
3196 Zimmerman Rd
Traverse City MI
49684

Call Sign: KC8TVI
Matthew D Wilcox
3196 Zimmerman Rd
Traverse City MI
49684

Call Sign: KB8RDR
Mark A Thomas
Traverse City MI
49685

Call Sign: KC8PBX
Houghton County
Communications
Authority
Traverse City MI
49685

Call Sign: KC8WYK
John M Grindel
Traverse City MI
49685

Call Sign: AB8RV
John M Grindel
Traverse City MI
49685

Call Sign: K8KWG
Donald A McMillan
Traverse City MI
49685

Call Sign: KC8RLU
Joseph C Schnaidt
Traverse City MI
49696

Call Sign: KD8QPC
James P Bolinski
Traverse City MI
49696

Call Sign: KD8KXJ
Jeffrey A Godin
Traverse City MI
49696

Call Sign: KC8JJH
James M Palmer
Traverse City MI
496850103

Call Sign: K8OJP
James M Palmer
Traverse City MI
496850103

Call Sign: N8YCR
Calvin J Lamie
Traverse City MI
496850996

Call Sign: KC8IBE
Aaron K Bowron
Traverse City MI
496851067

Call Sign: N8TNT
Robert J Benko
Traverse City MI
496965128

Call Sign: KJ7HS
Matthew Kula
Traverse City MI
496965247

Call Sign: KD8FWK
Terry Augustyn
N2131 Coaster Rd
Trenary MI 49891

Call Sign: WD8CSZ
Allan Augustyn
N2131 Coaster Rd
Trenary MI 49891

Call Sign: W8FYZ
Allan Augustyn
N2131 Coaster Rd
Trenary MI 49891

Call Sign: W5TJC
Freddie J Miller
E3157 Gilliland Rd
Trenary MI 49891

Call Sign: KC8WPK
Douglas J Bosscher
E2398 H44 Rd
Trenary MI 49891

Call Sign: KC0OBU

Danny M Stegner
Trenary MI 49891

Call Sign: K8NAD
Danny M Stegner
Trenary MI 49891

Call Sign: W8DCD
Arne E Kangas
Rt Box 9
Trout Creek MI 49967

Call Sign: WD8LHS
Bill J Besonen
6893 E One Mile Rd
Trout Creek MI 49967

Call Sign: N8DHL
Patrick R Martin
338 Wilwin Rd
Trout Lake MI 49793

Call Sign: N8IZO
Nora I Martin
338 Wilwin Rd
Trout Lake MI 49793

Call Sign: KB8BDN
Angela M Adams
304 Black Rd
Trufant MI 49347

Call Sign: KB8PWK
James C Christensen
11530 Dickerson Lake
Rd
Trufant MI 49347

Call Sign: KB8MEC
Myron C Jorgensen
125 F St
Trufant MI 49347

Call Sign: KA8SRH
Richard A Lesher
12842 Hillis Rd
Trufant MI 49347

Call Sign: KB8YYX
Deborah A Sutter
13278 Stanton Rd
Trufant MI 49347

FCC Amateur Radio Licenses in Turner

Call Sign: KC8NUZ
Timothy S Miller
318 E Main St
Turner MI 48765

Call Sign: KD8HLI
Reuben R Swartz
1378 Edmonds Rd
Turner MI 48765

Call Sign: AB8CV
Ronald D Swartz
2166 Turner Rd
Turner MI 48765

Call Sign: KC8EOX
Lucretia A Swartz
2166 Turner Rd
Turner MI 48765

FCC Amateur Radio Licenses in Tustin

Call Sign: N8GG
Jonathan P Hutchins
19292 130th Ave
Tustin MI 49688

Call Sign: KC8GZF
Alison N Beydoun
22746 150 Ave
Tustin MI 49688

Call Sign: KB9FBG
David S Bolduc
14625 20 Mile Rd
Tustin MI 49688

Call Sign: KC8SFU
Donald W Ruswick
17617 20 Mile Rd

Tustin MI 49688

Call Sign: K8BLE
Donald W Dibble
18217 20 Mile Rd
Tustin MI 496889701

Call Sign: WA8LKV
Alan E Van Antwerp
23204 20 Mile Rd
Tustin MI 49688

Call Sign: KD8LE
Lawrence A Erickson
18806 200th Ave
Tustin MI 49688

Call Sign: K8TSO
Winford P Guthrie
208 E Church
Tustin MI 49688

Call Sign: KB8GC
Mark E Schmidt
120 E Church 73
Tustin MI 49688

Call Sign: KX8XX
Mark E Schmidt
120 E Church 73
Tustin MI 49688

Call Sign: KD8SBC
David L Ostrander
300 E Church St
Tustin MI 49688

Call Sign: N8JCQ
Jean C Hutchins
8344 N 130 Ave
Tustin MI 49688

Call Sign: N8DKM
Robert J Kramer
12581 N 210 Ave
Tustin MI 49688

Call Sign: NI9R
Robin E Corbin
7330 N Asplund Rd
Tustin MI 49688

Call Sign: W8IQB
Lowell D Corbin

7330 N Asplund Rd
Tustin MI 49688

Call Sign: N8DMJ
Richard G Alexa
20637 Pine Rd
Tustin MI 49688

Call Sign: KA8UUU
Raymond C Drouillard
8221 Raymond Rd
Tustin MI 49688

FCC Amateur Radio Licenses in Twin Lake

Call Sign: KC8MDI
K C Juntunen
3280 4th St
Twin Lake MI 49457

Call Sign: KC8QJI
Michael J Moore
5074 Austin Rd
Twin Lake MI 49457

Call Sign: KB8VOX
Garry R Bruckner
2446 Beech St
Twin Lake MI 49457

Call Sign: KC8WSE
Flora Jean Young
6240 Beverly Way
Twin Lake MI 49457

Call Sign: AC8AR
Flora Jean Young
6240 Beverly Way
Twin Lake MI 49457

Call Sign: N8MUS
Jonathan L Greenwood
9095 Blue Lake Rd
Twin Lake MI 49457

Call Sign: KC8TAL
Betty A Klingel
4220 Brickyard Rd
Twin Lake MI 49457

Call Sign: KC5RRU
William L Klingel

4220 Brickyard Rd
Twin Lake MI 49457

Call Sign: N8YEK
Kenneth C Howe
3546 Cedar Rd
Twin Lake MI 49457

Call Sign: KB8YNO
April P Howe
3546 Cedar Rd
Twin Lake MI 49457

Call Sign: KD8PWV
Annette R Vida
4291 Dalson Rd
Twin Lake MI 49457

Call Sign: KC8AGB
Michael D Hittle
5065 Dalson Rd
Twin Lake MI 49457

Call Sign: KD8NNF
Donald E Petrie III
5791 Dalson Rd
Twin Lake MI 49457

Call Sign: KB8UNF
Mark A Verhoeven
981 Danc Dr
Twin Lake MI 49457

Call Sign: KB8VXY
David A Bakos
2374 Duff Rd
Twin Lake MI 49457

Call Sign: KB8UFE
William H Mills
7765 E Lake Rd
Twin Lake MI 49457

Call Sign: KA8QAK
Larry W Boxer
2290 E Michillinda Rd
Twin Lake MI 49457

Call Sign: WB9FRU
Paul E Haubner
8155 E Ruprecht Rd
Twin Lake MI 49457

Call Sign: WB6YEH

Ernest W Brinser Sr
7080 E Ryerson Rd
Twin Lake MI 49457

Call Sign: KC8GOP
Victoria K Halverson
6565 E Sweeter Rd
Twin Lake MI 49457

Call Sign: N8WKR
Jeffrey M Halverson
6565 E Sweeter Rd
Twin Lake MI 49457

Call Sign: N8JKR
Terry L Hinkelman
5830 Holton Rd
Twin Lake MI 49457

Call Sign: KC8RZP
Guy D Zak
2750 Holton Whitehall
Rd
Twin Lake MI 49457

Call Sign: KC8RZQ
Marilyn E Zak
2750 Holton Whitehall
Rd
Twin Lake MI 49457

Call Sign: KR8P
Bradley A Hulce
6633 Lake Rd
Twin Lake MI 49457

Call Sign: N8RGN
David J Bukala
4434 Manchester Ln
Twin Lake MI 49457

Call Sign: KC8JNK
Colleen B Walsh
5930 Meeuwenberg Dr
Twin Lake MI 49457

Call Sign: AC8BK
Colleen B Walsh
5930 Meeuwenberg Dr
Twin Lake MI 49457

Call Sign: KC8PGB
Lois L Wood
5815 N Maple

Twin Lake MI 49457

Call Sign: K8ROH
Elmer L Wood Jr
5815 N Maple Rd
Twin Lake MI 49457

Call Sign: W8ROH
Lois L Wood
5815 N Maple Rd
Twin Lake MI 49457

Call Sign: KC8EGE
Rodney J Sprader
3117 N Riverwood Dr
Twin Lake MI 49457

Call Sign: WD8QGL
Robert A O Grady
3242 N Riverwood Dr
Twin Lake MI 49457

Call Sign: W8DCT
Dennis D Harriss
2448 Oak Rd
Twin Lake MI 49457

Call Sign: AB8QD
Dennis D Harriss
2448 Oak Rd
Twin Lake MI 49457

Call Sign: N8CTT
Dennis D Harriss
2448 Oak Rd
Twin Lake MI 49457

Call Sign: KD8PWN
Angela B Blakley
2370 Oak St
Twin Lake MI 49457

Call Sign: KI4VUO
Jason C Blakley
2370 Oak St Lot 15
Twin Lake MI 49457

Call Sign: K8LIO
James J Henry
2306 Riverwood Dr
Twin Lake MI 49457

Call Sign: KD8KGW
Steven E Schrader

8083 Russell Rd
Twin Lake MI 49457

Call Sign: W8OSR
Boy Scouts Of
America Owasippe
Scout Reservation
9900 Russell Rd
Twin Lake MI 49457

Call Sign: N8JMM
Jack N Otteren
6757 Staple Rd
Twin Lake MI 49457

Call Sign: KA8SFE
Frank A Anthony
7200 Sweeter Rd
Twin Lake MI 49457

Call Sign: W8EBV
Robert E Sullivan
8101 Sweeter Rd
Twin Lake MI 49457

Call Sign: KD8MDF
Katie A Whelpley
449 W Ashland Rd
Twin Lake MI 49457

Call Sign: KD8MDE
Richard A Whelpley
449 W Ashland Rd
Twin Lake MI 49457

Call Sign: K8COP
James C Duram
2010 W Lake Rd
Twin Lake MI 49457

Call Sign: KA8ROP
Barbara K Duram
2010 W Lake Rd
Twin Lake MI 49457

Call Sign: N8CUH
Christopher J Duram
2010 W Lake Rd
Twin Lake MI 49457

Call Sign: KC8NRD
Jessica R Duram
2010 W Lake Rd
Twin Lake MI 49457

Call Sign: KC8EGN
Rachelle L Hadley
995 W Lakewood Rd
Twin Lake MI 49457

Call Sign: AK8C
Michael A O Grady
3329 Whitetail Ln
Twin Lake MI 49457

Call Sign: KB8AHG
Marna R O Grady
3329 Whitetail Ln
Twin Lake MI 49457

Call Sign: N8KUL
Lynn E Califf
Twin Lake MI 49457

**FCC Amateur Radio
Licenses in Twining**

Call Sign: KF8MY
Michael S Bilacic
700 Bessinger Rd
Twining MI 48766

Call Sign: KC8VGY
Colleen K Rittenberg
681 N Crawford Rd
Twining MI 48766

Call Sign: KC8UYD
James E Rittenberg
681 N Crawford Rd
Twining MI 48766

Call Sign: KA8PWH
James E Rittenberg
681 N Crawford Rd
Twining MI 48766

Call Sign: KD8MAF
Wilhelmina F Nickell
1718 N Fire Rd
Twining MI 48766

Call Sign: KA8GIN
Robert L Rittenberg
302 Park St
Twining MI 48766

Call Sign: KC8EXV

Wilford C Cuty Sr
412 W Main St
Twining MI 48766

Call Sign: WD8MZJ
Herman C Whipple
2651 W Maple Ridge
Rd
Twining MI 48766

Call Sign: KC8FLN
Shannon M St Cyr
97 W Mason Rd
Twining MI 48766

FCC Amateur Radio Licenses in Union

Call Sign: KC8BM
James A Leers
15871 Guyer
Union MI 49130

Call Sign: N9GEF
Roger L Rohrer
70604 Kessington Rd
Union MI 49130

Call Sign: KA8JSU
Mikel D Ruple
15765 Mason St
Union MI 49130

Call Sign: W8GUG
Robert L Peffley
16314 Wayne Rd
Union MI 49130

Call Sign: KB8HZA
Matthew J Smiley
14183 Wayne St
Union MI 49130

Call Sign: N8XSX
Bobbie G Marbaugh
16873 Wayne St
Union MI 49130

Call Sign: KD8CSX
Kerry J Bathe
Union MI 49130

Call Sign: KE8RRY
Kerry J Bathe

Union MI 49130

FCC Amateur Radio Licenses in Union City

Call Sign: KD8CYZ
Leo J Wilson
1881 9 Mile Rd
Union City MI 49094

Call Sign: KD8EPV
Corliss J Fleming
1064 Bell Rd
Union City MI 49094

Call Sign: KC8YUN
Jacob W Ash
1064 Bell Rd
Union City MI 49094

Call Sign: K8DKT
Carl W King
1065 Bell Rd Box 400
Union City MI 49094

Call Sign: WD8RDK
Robert L Cook
1268 Burlington Rd
Union City MI 49094

Call Sign: K8AOP
William S Miller
300 Calhoun St
Union City MI 49094

Call Sign: WB8ZSK
Leo B Wilson
1626 Case Dr
Union City MI 49094

Call Sign: KC8JCU
Charles J Osten
1319 Prairie Rose Ln
Union City MI 49094

Call Sign: N8MXT
John H Horton
1329 Prairie Rose Ln
Union City MI 49094

Call Sign: WB8WXL
Lewis J Frye
418 St Joseph St

Union City MI 49094

Call Sign: W8JST
Russell C Mercer
611 Thomas St
Union City MI 49094

Call Sign: KE8HH
Richard A Adams
Union City MI
490940151

FCC Amateur Radio Licenses in Union Pier

Call Sign: WX8O
William D Hewitt
9434 Community Hall
Rd
Union Pier MI 49129

Call Sign: K9LT
Harcourt S Patterson Jr
8833 W Elm Valley Rd
Union Pier MI 49129

FCC Amateur Radio Licenses in Vandalia

Call Sign: KB8FEJ
Janet L Whiteman
14955 Birch Lakeshore
Dr
Vandalia MI 49095

Call Sign: KC8PUK
Larry M Bergen
16774 M 60
Vandalia MI 49095

FCC Amateur Radio Licenses in Vanderbilt

Call Sign: KB8WFL
Thomas K Serino
7178 Airport Rd
Vanderbilt MI 49795

Call Sign: N8OFZ
Thomas A Serino
7178 Airport Rd
Vanderbilt MI 49795

Call Sign: KD8AOW
Kris S Morey
1189 Alexander Rd
Vanderbilt MI 49795

Call Sign: KD8JMB
Sherry M Morey
1189 Alexander Rd
Vanderbilt MI 49795

Call Sign: KD8IHK
Charles L Chewning
6800 Birch Valley Tr
Vanderbilt MI 49795

Call Sign: KD8CYO
Debra L Matthew
3017 Coash Rd
Vanderbilt MI 49795

Call Sign: KD8DHL
Marlene G Guerin
3017 Coash Rd
Vanderbilt MI 49795

Call Sign: WS8J
Terry M Spencer
4951 Coash Rd
Vanderbilt MI 49795

Call Sign: KB8TNY
Jeffery S Morey
1059 E Alexander Rd
Vanderbilt MI 49795

Call Sign: KD8QNF
Good Ol Boys ARC
1189 E Alexander Rd
Vanderbilt MI 49795

Call Sign: K9ACE
Good Ol Boys ARC
1189 E Alexander Rd
Vanderbilt MI 49795

Call Sign: WD8DX
Jeffery S Morey
1189 E Alexander Rd
Vanderbilt MI 49795

Call Sign: KA8QWE
Thomas R Kellogg

3487 E Sturgeon
Valley Rd
Vanderbilt MI 49795

Call Sign: N8KCK
Ralph A Robinson
1508 E Sturgeon Vly
Vanderbilt MI 49795

Call Sign: KD8CAB
Mathew D Matewicz
121 E Thumb Lake Rd
Vanderbilt MI 49795

Call Sign: KD8FDE
Allyne N Green
11856 Jewell Rd
Vanderbilt MI 49795

Call Sign: N8YCQ
Robert D Mac Gregor
III
1961 Mac Gregor Rd
Vanderbilt MI 49795

Call Sign: KB8IZM
Timothy J Holliday
8273 Mill St
Vanderbilt MI 49795

Call Sign: KC8JJK
William J Walther
8336 S Shire Rd
Vanderbilt MI 49795

Call Sign: KD8FRA
Earl R Geikowski Jr
3387 Sturgeon Valley
Rd E
Vanderbilt MI 49795

Call Sign: KI4UTM
Scott D Cikalo
8540 Sunshine Trl
Vanderbilt MI 49795

Call Sign: KB4BKI
Alethea M Roberts
8074 Washington St
Vanderbilt MI 49795

Call Sign: N8KTQ
Rebekah L Roberts
8074 Washington St

Vanderbilt MI 49795

Call Sign: WA8IJS
Ray R Kalamay
6377 Whitehouse
Vanderbilt MI 49795

Call Sign: KD8HNG
Kurt A Willis
623 Allegan Rd
Vermontville MI
49096

Call Sign: KD8HNH
Kevin A Willis
623 Allegan Rd
Vermontville MI
49098

Call Sign: KB8TI
Richard K Waara
8270 Carlisle
Vermontville MI
49096

Call Sign: AB8NR
Roy G Decker
8760 Kelly Hwy
Vermontville MI
49096

Call Sign: KA8FCN
Daniel L Childs
10066 N Ionia Rd
Vermontville MI
49096

Call Sign: KD8FPE
Richard W Stokes
9021 Nashville Hwy
Vermontville MI
49096

Call Sign: KC8WKC
Rodney L Harmon
360 S Main St
Vermontville MI
490969404

Call Sign: WK8H

Rodney L Harmon
360 S Main St
Vermontville MI
490969404

Call Sign: KC8DWF
Edward J Palmer
6370 Caris Rd
Vestaburg MI 48891

Call Sign: WA8FCP
Edward J Palmer
6370 Caris Rd
Vestaburg MI 48891

Call Sign: KC0LTD
David E Passons
7434 E Howard City
Edmore Rd
Vestaburg MI 48891

Call Sign: KC8PDF
Dale D Markowski
10275 Edgar Rd
Vestaburg MI 48891

Call Sign: KB8BJZ
Marilyn A Chamberlin
202 Lincoln St
Vestaburg MI 48891

Call Sign: WD8OZI
Thomas A Chamberlin
202 Lincoln St
Vestaburg MI 48891

Call Sign: KB8JSL
Duane L Dishong
8650 N Blackmer Rd
Vestaburg MI 48891

Call Sign: KB8ZGT
Jane E Miller
5600 N Bollinger Rd
Vestaburg MI 48891

Call Sign: KB8ZGU
Tim I Miller
5600 N Bollinger Rd
Vestaburg MI
488919740

Call Sign: KB8ZGV
Ralph H Mullard
4501 N Douglas
Vestaburg MI 48891

Call Sign: KB0NI
Edward G Wigle
8457 N Pine Grove Rd
Vestaburg MI 48891

Call Sign: WA8YLO
Wayne L Pletcher
671 N Rocklake Rd
Vestaburg MI 48891

Call Sign: N8STB
Nancy J Nixon
8244 Pine Grove Rd
Vestaburg MI 48891

Call Sign: N8VOB
Kenneth V Nixon
8244 Pine Grove Rd
Vestaburg MI 48891

Call Sign: KC8DND
Gail J Platt
421 S Rock Lake Rd
Vestaburg MI 48891

Call Sign: KC8DNF
Duane A Platt
421 S Rock Lake Rd
Vestaburg MI 48891

Call Sign: KC8MUG
Allen B Campbell
441 Yoder Ln
Vestaburg MI 48891

Call Sign: KD8FWW
Arthur R Papworth
12981 Bayview
Vicksburg MI 49097

Call Sign: KD8GOB
Cody A Sharpe
12936 Bayview Dr
Vicksburg MI 49097

Call Sign: K8DPS
Donald P Shoup
11117 E Indian Lake
Dr
Vicksburg MI
490979320

Call Sign: K8NJS
Norma J Shoup
11117 E Indian Lake
Dr
Vicksburg MI
490979320

Call Sign: KD8ODU
Chris E Cathcart
511 E S Ave
Vicksburg MI 49097

Call Sign: N8NXY
Guy D Pound Jr
6212 E S Ave
Vicksburg MI 49097

Call Sign: WD8AXB
Charles R Pfister
410 E State St
Vicksburg MI
490971230

Call Sign: KD8OXP
Gary W Robertson
5965 E T Ave
Vicksburg MI 49097

Call Sign: K8POU
Donald J Dobbin
6233 E T Ave
Vicksburg MI 49097

Call Sign: K8DJ
Donald J Dobbin
6233 E T Ave
Vicksburg MI 49097

Call Sign: KD8FK
Thomas R Parish
4577 E T U Ave
Vicksburg MI 49097

Call Sign: KC8VGE
Robert J Jackson
5891 E Uv Ave
Vicksburg MI 49097

Call Sign: W8JRI
Clyde M Covell
2681 E W Ave
Vicksburg MI 49097

Call Sign: KC8MHK
Andrew A De Vries
350 E Xy Ave
Vicksburg MI 49097

Call Sign: AB7L
Thomas J Thamann
5727 E Y Ave
Vicksburg MI 49097

Call Sign: KC8NSM
Michael G Barton
138 Mill St
Vicksburg MI 49097

Call Sign: KD8DW
Marc Skippers
139 N Kalamazoo St
Vicksburg MI
490971204

Call Sign: KB8CMF
Kevin L Bell
12071 S 26th St
Vicksburg MI 49097

Call Sign: KC8VPH
David W Duke
14904 S 33rd
Vicksburg MI 49097

Call Sign: N8MJ
Melbourne O Jaquays
13300 S 34th St
Vicksburg MI
490977506

Call Sign: W8HAA
Zigmont L Werbinski
10010 Sprinkle Rd
Vicksburg MI 49097

Call Sign: WD8NTX
John P Simpson
10296 Sprinkle Rd
Vicksburg MI 49097

Call Sign: KD8JNC

Stephanie L Pfister
410 State St
Vicksburg MI 49097

Call Sign: KE8ED
Ellery W Mann
13641 Tremblay
Vicksburg MI 49097

Call Sign: KD8OWZ
Anthony D Sirotti
810 Vicker St
Vicksburg MI 49097

Call Sign: WB8RMJ
Russell J Morrison
7969 Victory St
Vicksburg MI 49097

Call Sign: AA8WF
James L Stevens
8076 Victory St
Vicksburg MI
490979300

Call Sign: KH6IG
Gaylord A Rich
8115 Victory St
Vicksburg MI 49097

Call Sign: W8GLS
Gregory L Setina
15420 W Barton Lake
Dr
Vicksburg MI
490979775

Call Sign: KA8QIC
David A Ouvry
204 W Washington
Vicksburg MI 49097

Call Sign: KD8OXQ
Dennis L Windle
4132 Waterview
Vicksburg MI 49097

Call Sign: KC8QNW
Ken G Thompson
407 Xy Ave
Vicksburg MI 49097

Call Sign: KA8NQY
Jodell J Cutler

3051 Z Ave
Vicksburg MI 49097

Call Sign: N8DDU
Dennis R Cutler
3051 Z Ave
Vicksburg MI 49097

FCC Amateur Radio Licenses in Vulcan

Call Sign: KD8DJK
Joseph F Schutte
W2251 Alfredson Rd
Vulcan MI 49892

Call Sign: KD8QEX
Perry M Amicangelo
N 1182 Ball Rd
Vulcan MI 49892

Call Sign: KA8ABK
Henry A Stephens
N1537 Ball Rd
Vulcan MI 49892

Call Sign: KB8EYG
Genny T Thoresen
Rte 1 Box 179
Vulcan MI 49892

Call Sign: KB8ETN
Melissa J Lewis
W5007 Brickyard Rd
Vulcan MI 49892

Call Sign: KE9LK
Arthur A Caswell
W5007 Brickyard Rd
Vulcan MI 49892

Call Sign: KD8KUE
Douglas J Bacon
W5007 Brickyard Rd
Vulcan MI 49892

Call Sign: KC8LRP
Marjorie G Meyers
N 637 Thaler Dr
Vulcan MI 49892

Call Sign: WA8FXQ
Robert J Meyers
N637 Thaler Dr

Vulcan MI 49892

Call Sign: KC8UVX
Mich A Con ARC
W3821 Waucedah Rd
Vulcan MI 49892

Call Sign: KA1DDB
Michael F Bray
W3821 Waucedah Rd
Vulcan MI 49892

Call Sign: K8DDB
Michael F Bray
W3821 Waucedah Rd
Vulcan MI 49892

Call Sign: KC8VC
Mich A Con ARC
W3821 Waucedah Rd
Vulcan MI 49892

FCC Amateur Radio Licenses in WAFB Oscoda

Call Sign: KB8MYS
Nathaniel E Pierce
8304 F Hawaii St
WAFB Oscoda MI
48753

FCC Amateur Radio Licenses in Wakefield

Call Sign: W9OC
David L Johnson
1002 Charles St
Wakefield MI 49968

Call Sign: AB8BK
John M Grasso
505 Chicago Mine Rd
Wakefield MI 49968

Call Sign: KC8TGA
Douglas R Freeman
812 Hwy 519
Wakefield MI 49968

Call Sign: KC8SZC
William N Watson
3403 Pierce St
Wakefield MI 49968

Call Sign: WD8LVH
Lawrence R Anderson
212 Smith St
Wakefield MI 49968

Call Sign: W8CJW
Lawrence R Anderson
212 Smith St
Wakefield MI 49968

Call Sign: KD8NLO
Thomas J Wagner
Wakefield MI 49968

FCC Amateur Radio Licenses in Walhala

Call Sign: KC8TSI
Kim W Cloud
Walhalla MI 49458

Call Sign: KD8FXB
Allen J Michels
Walhalla MI 49458

FCC Amateur Radio Licenses in Walker

Call Sign: KA8SAU
David L Fuhrmann Sr
4310 4 Mile Rd NW
Walker MI 495049403

Call Sign: KD8JB
Michael P Hood
600 Faircrest Ave NW
Walker MI 49534

Call Sign: KC8ZDH
Stanley J Bydalek
2608 Falcon Woods Dr
Walker MI 49534

Call Sign: N8EOD
John R Boluyt
3625 Leonard
Walker MI 49534

Call Sign: N0JS
John J Streyle
1487 Maderia SW
Walker MI 49504

Call Sign: W8QZ
John J Streyle
1487 Maderia SW
Walker MI 49534

Call Sign: KB8UNO
Sarah A Klamer
2395 O Brien
Walker MI 49544

Call Sign: W8BM
David C Laug Jr
2147 Pheasant Ave
NW
Walker MI 495342384

Call Sign: AB8UT
David C Laug Jr
2147 Pheasant Ave
NW
Walker MI 495342384

Call Sign: KC8TTE
Hayden E Butcher
4071 Richmond NW
Walker MI 49544

Call Sign: K8CCA
Eric K Moore
1417 Stark NW
Walker MI 49504

Call Sign: N8ZVB
Louis R White
1713 Vinecroft NW
Walker MI 49504

Call Sign: N8XPR
Michael D Mason
4256 W Grand
Walker MI 49504

Call Sign: N9RNK
Gregory A Jacques
557 Westway NW
Walker MI 49544

Call Sign: KC8OKC
Anthony W Driza
1028 White Pine Dr
SW
Walker MI 49544

Call Sign: KA8VOK

Ernst J Otto
1268 Wilson SW
Walker MI 49504

FCC Amateur Radio Licenses in Walkerville

Call Sign: KB8OXF
Joe R Jonassen
9096 N 188th Ave
Walkerville MI 49459

Call Sign: KA8QEL
James C Nelson
9396 N 192 Ave
Walkerville MI 49459

FCC Amateur Radio Licenses in Wallace

Call Sign: KC8ZVD
Elizabeth A Pearson
W5380 CR 342
Wallace MI 49893

Call Sign: KC8YZA
James J Pearson
W5380 CR 342
Wallace MI 49893

Call Sign: KS8O
James J Pearson
W5380 CR 342
Wallace MI 49893

Call Sign: KD8EXZ
Menominee River
Radio Club
W5380 CR 342
Wallace MI 49893

Call Sign: K8MRR
Menominee River
Radio Club
W5380 CR 342
Wallace MI 49893

Call Sign: KD8HZD
Yacht Young Amateur
Contest Ham Team
W5380 CR 342
Wallace MI 49893

Call Sign: K8KDZ
Yacht Young Amateur
Contest Ham Team
W5380 CR 342
Wallace MI 49893

Call Sign: KB6BNI
Donald H Polen Sr
W6041 CR G 08
Wallace MI 49893

Call Sign: WB6UVG
M Earlane Polen
W6041 CR G 08
Wallace MI 49893

Call Sign: KC8RGE
Patricia J Douville
W 5942 G 08 Rd
Wallace MI 49893

Call Sign: KC8YZC
Ronald M Dolivo
N6133 Shore Dr
Wallace MI 49893

FCC Amateur Radio Licenses in Walloon Lake

Call Sign: KD8QJC
James W Biglane
Walloon Lake MI
49796

Call Sign: N8JWB
James W Biglane
Walloon Lake MI
49796

FCC Amateur Radio Licenses in Waters

Call Sign: KC8KZM
Robert T Smith
10835 Beaver
Waters MI 49797

Call Sign: KB8WZX
Bradley A Baker
6955 N Kolka Creek
Rd
Waters MI 497970306

Call Sign: KB8TGN
Mark A Fahler
Waters MI 49797

Call Sign: KC8PKI
Marshall D Woods
Waters MI 49797

FCC Amateur Radio Licenses in Watersmeet

Call Sign: WB9OJM
Harold W Neumann Jr
N4747 2nd St
Watersmeet MI 49969

Call Sign: N8BYE
Hayden U S Hall Jr
E 23859 A Ave
Watersmeet MI 49969

Call Sign: N9KPQ
Susan A Holloway
N 3899 Maplewood Rd
Watersmeet MI 49969

Call Sign: WD0GKD
Eleanor L Nystrom
4692 Marion Lake Rd
Watersmeet MI 49969

Call Sign: WD0FSV
Marvin L Nystrom
4692 Marion Lk Rd
Watersmeet MI 49969

Call Sign: KB8ZHF
Mary J Congdon
E 19882 Thousand
Island Lake Rd
Watersmeet MI 49969

Call Sign: N9NQX
Jack L Congdon
E19882 Thousand
Island Lake Rd
Watersmeet MI 49969

Call Sign: KC8IDU
Russell W Moulton
E 21800 Wold Lake
Rd
Watersmeet MI 49969

Call Sign: KC8ASL
Breton L Alberty
1800 Wolf Lake Rd
Watersmeet MI 49969

Call Sign: KC8BLT
Jeremy R Tanner
Box One E 21800
Wolf Lake Rd
Watersmeet MI 49969

Call Sign: KB8VOA
Steve A Moerman
E 21800 Wolf Lake Rd
Watersmeet MI 49969

Call Sign: KB8ZAR
Craig M Roberts
E 21800 Wolf Lake Rd
Watersmeet MI 49969

Call Sign: KC8ASN
Nathan Petroski
E 21800 Wolf Lake Rd
Watersmeet MI 49969

Call Sign: KC8BMZ
John A Tanner
E 21800 Wolf Lake Rd
Watersmeet MI 49969

Call Sign: KC8BNA
Leon K Tan
E 21800 Wolf Lake Rd
Watersmeet MI 49969

Call Sign: KC8DDZ
Wayne J Berry II
E 21800 Wolf Lake Rd
Watersmeet MI 49969

Call Sign: KC8DEB
John I Nix
E 21800 Wolf Lake Rd
Watersmeet MI 49969

Call Sign: KC8DJB
Daniel G Moulton
E 21800 Wolf Lake Rd
Watersmeet MI 49969

Call Sign: KC8EIM
Ben A Mirecki

E 21800 Wolf Lake Rd
Watersmeet MI 49969

Call Sign: KC8HHB
Matthew S Lindquist
E 21800 Wolf Lake Rd
Watersmeet MI 49969

Call Sign: KC8HQO
Nathan A Jongsma
E 21800 Wolf Lake Rd
Watersmeet MI 49969

Call Sign: KC8IDQ
Patricia L Chapman
E 21800 Wolf Lake Rd
Watersmeet MI 49969

Call Sign: KC8IDR
Steve G Nix
E 21800 Wolf Lake Rd
Watersmeet MI 49969

Call Sign: KC8IDS
Carla E Nix
E 21800 Wolf Lake Rd
Watersmeet MI 49969

Call Sign: KC8IDT
Debbie C Moulton
E 21800 Wolf Lake Rd
Watersmeet MI 49969

Call Sign: KC8IDV
Byrton M Herring Jr
E 21800 Wolf Lake Rd
Watersmeet MI 49969

Call Sign: KC8IDW
Heather R Tuplin
E 21800 Wolf Lake Rd
Watersmeet MI 49969

Call Sign: KC8LBV
Patrick J Chapman
E 21800 Wolf Lake Rd
Watersmeet MI 49969

Call Sign: KC8LBW
Aaron J Jongsma
E 21800 Wolf Lake Rd
Watersmeet MI 49969

Call Sign: KD6RRK

Daniel W Chapman
E 21800 Wolf Lake Rd
Watersmeet MI 49969

Call Sign: KC8NCL
Paul D Bell
E 21800 Wolf Lake Rd
Watersmeet MI 49969

Call Sign: KC8NCN
Isaac P Reichardt
E 21800 Wolf Lake Rd
Watersmeet MI 49969

Call Sign: KC8NCO
Andrew Van Essen
E 21800 Wolf Lake Rd
Watersmeet MI 49969

Call Sign: KC8NCQ
Matt P Barber
E 21800 Wolf Lake Rd
Watersmeet MI 49969

Call Sign: KC8GCP
Jonathan L Bendickson
E 21800 Wolf Lake Rd
Watersmeet MI 49969

Call Sign: KC8DJD
Joseph A Nix
E 21800 Wolf Lake Rd
Watersmeet MI 49969

Call Sign: KC8FIN
Thomas W Exstrum
E21800 Wolf Lake Rd
Watersmeet MI 49669

Call Sign: KB8VTG
Matthew Petroski
E21800 Wolf Lake Rd
Watersmeet MI 49969

Call Sign: KC8DJC
Thomas W Chapman
E21800 Wolf Lake Rd
Watersmeet MI 49969

Call Sign: KC8FIM
Benjamin L Chapman
E21800 Wolf Lake Rd
Watersmeet MI 49969

Call Sign: KC8FIP
Joshua D Knaak
E21800 Wolf Lake Rd
Watersmeet MI 49969

Call Sign: KC8FIQ
Anna J Knight
E21800 Wolf Lake Rd
Watersmeet MI 49969

Call Sign: KC8FIR
Andrew T Leonhard
E21800 Wolf Lake Rd
Watersmeet MI 49969

Call Sign: KC8FIS
Steven D Lindberg
E21800 Wolf Lake Rd
Watersmeet MI 49969

Call Sign: KC8FIT
Kevin C Staples
E21800 Wolf Lake Rd
Watersmeet MI 49969

Call Sign: KC8GAP
Rebekah C Helland
E21800 Wolf Lake Rd
Watersmeet MI 49969

Call Sign: KC8GCX
Jonathan R Knight
E21800 Wolf Lake Rd
Watersmeet MI 49969

Call Sign: KC8JNP
David J Fishback
E21800 Wolf Lake Rd
Watersmeet MI 49969

Call Sign: KC8JNQ
Like A Kujacznski
E21800 Wolf Lake Rd
Watersmeet MI 49969

Call Sign: KC8JNR
Timothy P Mirecki
E21800 Wolf Lake Rd
Watersmeet MI 49969

Call Sign: KC8JNS
Justin H Swartz
E21800 Wolf Lake Rd
Watersmeet MI 49969

Call Sign: KC8LUK
Aaron M Childress
E21800 Wolf Lake Rd
Watersmeet MI 49969

Call Sign: KC8MIZ
Timothy J Ferry
E21800 Wolf Lake Rd
Watersmeet MI 49969

Call Sign: KC8MJA
Stephen J Hough
E21800 Wolf Lake Rd
Watersmeet MI 49969

Call Sign: KC8MJB
Andrew W Whitaker
E21800 Wolf Lake Rd
Watersmeet MI 49969

Call Sign: KC8MJC
Justin B Tanner
E21800 Wolf Lake Rd
Watersmeet MI 49969

Call Sign: KC8MJD
Riley R Irvin
E21800 Wolf Lake Rd
Watersmeet MI 49969

Call Sign: KC8OAP
David Bair
E21800 Wolf Lake Rd
Watersmeet MI 49969

Call Sign: KC8OAQ
Tim P Anderson
E21800 Wolf Lake Rd
Watersmeet MI 49969

Call Sign: KC8OAR
Cory S Finch
E21800 Wolf Lake Rd
Watersmeet MI 49969

Call Sign: KC8OAS
Joe H Snow IV
E21800 Wolf Lake Rd
Watersmeet MI 49969

Call Sign: KC8OHL
Joshua B Skaggs
E21800 Wolf Lake Rd

Watersmeet MI 49969

Call Sign: KC8OSO
Daniel J Minnich
East 21800 Wolf Lake
Rd
Watersmeet MI 44969

Call Sign: KC8OSI
Royce D Bradford
East 21800 Wolf Lake
Rd
Watersmeet MI 49969

Call Sign: KC8OSK
Stephen R Dagarin
East 21800 Wolf Lake
Rd
Watersmeet MI 49969

Call Sign: KC8OSL
Jesse P Gates
East 21800 Wolf Lake
Rd
Watersmeet MI 49969

Call Sign: KC8OSM
Joshua T Inman
East 21800 Wolf Lake
Rd
Watersmeet MI 49969

Call Sign: KC8OSN
Geoff S Mcgrath
East 21800 Wolf Lake
Rd
Watersmeet MI 49969

Call Sign: KC8OSP
Christian J Norris
East 21800 Wolf Lake
Rd
Watersmeet MI 49969

Call Sign: KC8OSR
Misha J Randolph
East 21800 Wolf Lake
Rd
Watersmeet MI 49969

Call Sign: KC8OSS
Timothy K Toews
East 21800 Wolf Lake
Rd

Watersmeet MI 49969

Call Sign: KC8OST
Brian E Tuplin
East 21800 Wolf Lake
Rd
Watersmeet MI 49969

Call Sign: KC8OSU
Frederick R Van Til
East 21800 Wolf Lake
Rd
Watersmeet MI 49969

Call Sign: KC8OSV
Andy Wirt
East 21800 Wolf Lake
Rd
Watersmeet MI 49969

Call Sign: KC8OHM
Christopher R Ekstrom
E2100 Wolflake Rd
Watersmeet MI 49969

Call Sign: KC8JNO
Caleb J Boyette
E21800 Wolflake Rd
Watersmeet MI 49969

Call Sign: KC8OHN
Benjamin B Foged
E21800 Wolflake Rd
Watersmeet MI 49969

FCC Amateur Radio Licenses in Watervliett

Call Sign: N8XTZ
Mark E Zepik
8325 Carmody Rd
Watervliet MI 49098

Call Sign: KF8PN
Harold R Barrett
9325 Dwight Boyer Rd
Watervliet MI 49098

Call Sign: WA8ZSE
Robert S Stearns
7606 Florence Ave
Watervliet MI 49098

Call Sign: W8MGY
Robert H Ashton
7855 Forest Beach
Watervliet MI 49098

Call Sign: W9VH
Thys J Van Hout
8616 High St
Watervliet MI 49098

Call Sign: KD8MLA
Carlton G Schooley
7565 Hill Rd
Watervliet MI 49098

Call Sign: KD8CGS
Carlton G Schooley
7565 Hill Rd
Watervliet MI 49098

Call Sign: KB8RSB
Matthew R Quinn
4702 M 140
Watervliet MI 49098

Call Sign: K8VBL
Thomas M Turner
8530 N Branch Rd
Watervliet MI 49098

Call Sign: KA8EHE
Norma K Turner
8530 N Branch Rd
Watervliet MI 49098

Call Sign: KA8WOW
Daniel J Malburg
6816 N County Line
Rd
Watervliet MI 49098

Call Sign: N8RMP
Russell J Goyer
8014 Shore Ln
Watervliet MI 49098

Call Sign: N8CSO
Mary E Harrell
414 W Parsons Ave
Watervliet MI 49098

Call Sign: N8DZL
Michael J Drake
414 W Parsons Ave

Watervliet MI 49098

Call Sign: N8DZP
Brian C Drake
414 W Parsons Ave
Watervliet MI 49098

Call Sign: WD8MEY
Charles A Harrell
414 W Parsons Ave
Watervliet MI 49098

Call Sign: KD8FFQ
Carla M Baldwin
Watervliet MI 49098

FCC Amateur Radio Licenses in Watton

Call Sign: N8FDL
Herman Kinnunen
Rfd 1 Box 14
Watton MI 49970

Call Sign: N8CSE
Gerald E Nopola
R-1 Box 7
Watton MI 499709705

Call Sign: WA8RJH
Roy W Mannikko
Rt 1 Box 9
Watton MI 49970

Call Sign: WD8LIP
James W Leppala
26192 Korpi Rd
Watton MI 49970

FCC Amateur Radio Licenses in Wayland

Call Sign: WD8REX
Kenneth W Thede
4321 11th St
Wayland MI 49348

Call Sign: N8YJV
Bruce E Hess
220 133rd Ave
Wayland MI 49348

Call Sign: KC8BIV
Charles R Fenton

482 137th St
Wayland MI 49348

Call Sign: KB8WKA
Reuben K Dozeman
1335 138th Ave
Wayland MI 49348

Call Sign: N8WKL
Michael L Osborne
3494 13th St
Wayland MI 49348

Call Sign: N8QEN
Douglas F Kimble
704 140th Ave
Wayland MI 49348

Call Sign: N8IMH
Steven P Werkema
320 141st Ave
Wayland MI 49348

Call Sign: KD8PCC
James C Williams
945 146th Ave
Wayland MI 49348

Call Sign: KD8DBX
Jill M Westra
2596 1st St
Wayland MI 49348

Call Sign: KG8CA
Keith A Vandenbergh
3442 4th St
Wayland MI 49348

Call Sign: KG8DL
Elane M Vandenbergh
3442 4th St
Wayland MI 49348

Call Sign: N8NIH
Orien A Vandenbergh
3442 4th St
Wayland MI 49348

Call Sign: WB8RAF
Bernard L Clark Sr
12910 Barry Ln
Wayland MI 49348

Call Sign: KD8LDW

William J Byers
224 Church St
Wayland MI 49348

Call Sign: KC8IMG
Bryan K Swift
1651 Creek Side Ct
Wayland MI 49348

Call Sign: N8NDZ
Kevin R Rinard
4483 Division St
Wayland MI 49348

Call Sign: N8PGV
R Mark Barnett
316 E Maple St
Wayland MI 49348

Call Sign: KD8POL
Brian W Crittendon
427 E Maple St D7
Wayland MI 49348

Call Sign: N8PQN
Michael M Wilde
312 E Superior St
Wayland MI 49348

Call Sign: N8PQM
Ian M Wilde
145 Hanlon Ct
Wayland MI 49348

Call Sign: WD9GTT
Joseph J Sobiesczyk
323 Hickory Dr
Wayland MI 49348

Call Sign: KB8VBZ
Patricia J Fettig Vora
418 Hill Lake
Wayland MI 49348

Call Sign: KB8QGR
Andrej A Sensnovis
320 N Locust
Wayland MI 49348

Call Sign: N8SUV
Robert B Fuller
4289 Oxford St
Wayland MI
484308937

Call Sign: N8DDB
Dale D Bonnema
12692 Park Dr
Wayland MI 49348

Call Sign: KC8LD
Steven R Salisbury
1906 Parker Dr
Wayland MI
493489312

Call Sign: N8MED
Craig D Smith
4292 Plymouth Ave
Wayland MI 49348

Call Sign: W8SQL
Gerald H Fitzgerald
3407 Sandy Beach Rd
Wayland MI 49348

Call Sign: KB8RWX
Todd R Foote
12863 Valley Dr
Wayland MI 49348

Call Sign: KB8QON
Roger H Bont
129 W Maple Ave
Wayland MI 49348

Call Sign: KD8AUV
Jennifer R Parker
3574 Windsor Woods
Wayland MI 49348

Call Sign: W8CTB
Donald P Hartman
1205 Woodland Dr
Wayland MI 49348

Call Sign: WA8BQT
Clare R Seplinski
Wayland MI
493480131

Call Sign: WD8RTH
John W Anderson
5736 Main St
Wells MI 498940295

Call Sign: KD8YQ
Homer D Remsberg
5780 Main St
Wells MI 49894

Call Sign: KD8HOR
Justin T Poquette
6321 S 9th St
Wells MI 49894

Call Sign: KD8LBL
Jackie W Kaufman Jr
17035 2nd St
Wellston MI 49689

Call Sign: KD8MTR
Jimmy D Morris
21170 Caberfae Hwy
Wellston MI 49689

Call Sign: KD8MTS
Sharon D Morris
21170 Caberfae Hwy
Wellston MI 49689

Call Sign: K8UKC
Jack R Hengartner
12873 Cedar Creek Rd
Wellston MI 49689

Call Sign: WB8VOF
Douglas E Almquist
22714 Hoxeyville Rd
Wellston MI 49689

Call Sign: KC8WKN
Mary Ann Almquist
22714 Hoxeyville Rd
Wellston MI 49689

Call Sign: KD8ATS
Ronald J Webber
663 Seamon Rd
Wellston MI 49689

Call Sign: KA8QFW
Leo C Quillen
16554 Stineberg Rd
Wellston MI 49689

Call Sign: KC8QYC
Michael S Dixon
3351 Bella Ln
West Branch MI 48661

Call Sign: WB8UXJ
Roy O Eagle
2301 Birchcrest
West Branch MI
486619503

Call Sign: KC8DMA
Harold L Partlo
1103 Brick Rd
West Branch MI 48661

Call Sign: K8YBU
Harold L Partlo
1103 Brick Rd
West Branch MI 48661

Call Sign: KC8JOY
Cory D Messer
1300 Brick Rd
West Branch MI 48661

Call Sign: W8JOC
Joe L Collins
976 Clear Lake Rd
West Branch MI 48661

Call Sign: WA8TDA
Howard L Schroeder
646 Court St Apt A8
West Branch MI 48661

Call Sign: KA8NCV
Dianne M Miller
4863 Diebold Ranch
Rd
West Branch MI 48661

Call Sign: KC8RGI
David L Kimble
3651 Dill Dr
West Branch MI 48661

Call Sign: KC8DYH
Patrick C Ernst Sr
850 E Engle Rd

West Branch MI 48661

Call Sign: KC8YRE
Dennis C Wisebaker
473 E Tawas Rd
West Branch MI 48661

Call Sign: WD8MHZ
Bernard C Fisher
2727 Flowage Lake Rd
West Branch MI 48661

Call Sign: WD8MQX
Ruth A Fisher
2727 Flowage Lake Rd
West Branch MI 48661

Call Sign: KD8IRX
Tracey A Wood
184 Fremont St
West Branch MI 48661

Call Sign: KD8IRZ
Cheryl A Moyer
840 Gerald Miller Rd
West Branch MI 48661

Call Sign: KD8IRY
James E Thompson
840 Gerald Miller Rd
West Branch MI 48661

Call Sign: KD8DBO
Timothy W Vogan
1165 Gerald Miller Rd
West Branch MI 48661

Call Sign: K8TWV
Timothy W Vogan
1165 Gerald Miller Rd
West Branch MI 48661

Call Sign: N8PGQ
Vito Michelozzi
2970 Hansen Rd
West Branch MI 48661

Call Sign: KD8GOK
Donald B Dean
3820 Ironwood Ln
West Branch MI 48661

Call Sign: N9AGO
Roman J Bender

3168 Jobin Dr
West Branch MI 48661

Call Sign: KD8BDB
West Branch Repeater
2937 Maes Rd
West Branch MI 48661

Call Sign: K8WBR
West Branch Repeater
2937 Maes Rd
West Branch MI 48661

Call Sign: KD8FJV
Yvonne M Mussleman
2937 Maes Rd
West Branch MI 48661

Call Sign: KA8SCM
William R Hall Jr
2136 Marjorie Ann Dr
West Branch MI 48661

Call Sign: KD8RVZ
Damon Dx Association
2708 McGregor Rd
West Branch MI 48661

Call Sign: K8DDX
Damon Dx Association
2708 McGregor Rd
West Branch MI 48661

Call Sign: KD8IQX
David A Burnell
2708 McGregor Rd
West Branch MI 48661

Call Sign: AC8CZ
David A Burnell
2708 McGregor Rd
West Branch MI 48661

Call Sign: K8BD
David A Burnell
2708 McGregor Rd
West Branch MI 48661

Call Sign: W4PDJ
Ivan R Doxey
313 N 5th St
West Branch MI 48661

Call Sign: KD8EUE

James R Hall
150 N Burgess
West Branch MI 48661

Call Sign: KC8TSC
William K Evilsizer
105 N Burgess St
West Branch MI 48661

Call Sign: KD8OIW
Lisa K Gibson
243 N Burgess St
West Branch MI 48661

Call Sign: KA8NKD
Dean L Coleman
5051 N Fairview
West Branch MI 48661

Call Sign: W8BUH
Dean L Coleman
5051 N Fairview
West Branch MI 48661

Call Sign: KB8KSC
Glenn E Stantiford
4664 Oak Rd
West Branch MI 48661

Call Sign: W8YBU
Arvid A McPherson
134 S 2nd St
West Branch MI
486611432

Call Sign: KD8RCL
Jonathan J Berns
2133 S Gray Rd
West Branch MI 48661

Call Sign: K8OD
Loren J Hintz Jr
33 S Mud Lake Rd
West Branch MI 48661

Call Sign: KC8NNV
William L Allen
1954 S Ogemaw Trl
West Branch MI 48661

Call Sign: KD8EUC
Melodie M Allen
356 State St 6
West Branch MI 48661

Call Sign: KA8MVO
Kenneth P Spencer
3248 Sunset Dr
West Branch MI 48661

Call Sign: WA8LTH
Alton J Kott
1946 Tomahawk Ct
West Branch MI 48661

Call Sign: WD8MQY
Ronald G Hodges
1120 W Airport Rd
West Branch MI 48661

Call Sign: KX8DX
Ronald G Hodges
1120 W Airport Rd
West Branch MI 48661

Call Sign: KC8JOZ
Tyler H Rosebrugh
750 W M 55
West Branch MI 48661

Call Sign: WB8KIK
Charles M Schwab
1040 W M 55
West Branch MI 48661

Call Sign: N8NYT
William D Radtke
5725 W M 76
West Branch MI 48661

Call Sign: W8WDR
William D Radtke
5725 W M 76
West Branch MI 48661

Call Sign: WD7G
Anthony J Brent
607 W Peters Rd
West Branch MI 48661

Call Sign: KC8MFO
Edward M Zupan
3770 W Rose City Rd
West Branch MI 48661

Call Sign: KD8PBH
Donald H Carros
1426 Wallin Lake Dr

West Branch MI 48661

Call Sign: KX8G
Robert D Robarts
569 Weiler Rd
West Branch MI 48661

Call Sign: N8IFY
Chris T Schmidt
355 White Ridge Trl
West Branch MI 48661

Call Sign: KD8EPT
Cindy L Papworth
Schmidt
355 White Ridge Trl
West Branch MI
486619405

Call Sign: N8PKI
Mark W Maisonville
West Branch MI 48661

Call Sign: N8CJM
Dennis L Musselman
West Branch MI 48661

Call Sign: N8YMM
Yvonne M Musselman
West Branch MI 48661

Call Sign: KC8NPD
Paul F Lebzelter
West Branch MI
486610678

Call Sign: K8PFL
Paul F Lebzelter
West Branch MI
486610678

Call Sign: KA8UXW
Judi L De Jonge
8695 160th Ave
West Olive MI 49460

Call Sign: KC8JVZ
Jim P McCaleb
12014 160th Ave
West Olive MI 49460

Call Sign: KC8VBX
Dan H Hendricks
11558 88th Ave
West Olive MI 49460

Call Sign: KC8OPD
Matt S Jones
12570 90th Ave
West Olive MI 49460

Call Sign: WA3LVS
L Lamar Styer
16525 Blair St
West Olive MI
494609733

Call Sign: W8TNJ
Anthony W Driza
6262 Brooklyn
West Olive MI
494609114

Call Sign: KC8QDF
William M Vanslooten
9450 Buchanan St
West Olive MI 49460

Call Sign: KD8GMP
Lori M Scholten
9545 Buchanan St
West Olive MI 49460

Call Sign: KC8WCT
Thomas M Lau
8995 Champlain Pl
West Olive MI 49460

Call Sign: WA8QHK
Johan K Rademaker
14561 Croswell St
West Olive MI 49460

Call Sign: KB8LOI
Francis R Harlow
16075 Croswell St
West Olive MI
494609378

Call Sign: KC8SKT
Jeffrey A Anderson
10900 Derick Dr
West Olive MI 49460

Call Sign: N8ONR
Kurt A Sokoly
17099 Donahue Woods
Dr
West Olive MI 49460

Call Sign: KC8LCP
Ottawa County
Emergency
Communications
12220 Fillmore St
West Olive MI 49460

Call Sign: KC8TKG
James E Marsh
12705 Fillmore St
West Olive MI 49460

Call Sign: KB8JGK
James C De Witt
6345 Lakeshore Dr
West Olive MI 49460

Call Sign: N8PFB
Harold A Fitzgerald II
10145 Lakeshore Dr
West Olive MI 49460

Call Sign: KC8TOB
Irene M Rasey
14419 Lawton Stn
West Olive MI 49460

Call Sign: KC8TOC
Howard L Rasey
14419 Lawton Stn
West Olive MI 49460

Call Sign: KD8RQQ
Theodore H Rigterink
16435 Pierce St
West Olive MI 49460

Call Sign: WB8NED
Theodore H Rigterink
16435 Pierce St
West Olive MI 49460

Call Sign: WD8NHA
Michael R Cole
10559 Rich St
West Olive MI 49460

Call Sign: WA8MTI

Richard J Anderson
10338 Rich St Pvt
West Olive MI 49460

Call Sign: KD8GMO
Curtis J Koop
9420 S Cedar Dr
West Olive MI 49460

Call Sign: KC8PZD
Benjamin S Westrate
9701 S Cedar Dr
West Olive MI 49460

Call Sign: KC8WYL
Gary L Greenert II
16052 Taylor St
West Olive MI 49460

Call Sign: KC8BKU
Kirk L Dykstra
15032 Van Buren St
West Olive MI 49460

Call Sign: N9JZJ
Rick S George
15610 Van Buren St
West Olive MI 49460

Call Sign: KD8ISX
Zachary J Vonduinen
9080 Warner St
West Olive MI 49460

Call Sign: KC8EWR
Eric M Heyboer
8681 Wood Wren Dr
West Olive MI 49460

Call Sign: KB8GDC
Beverly A Thomas
Hcr 1 Box 641
Wetmore MI 49895

Call Sign: KD8BKM
Alger ARC
N3253 Buckhorn Rd
Wetmore MI 49895

Call Sign: KC8BAN
Alger ARC

N3253 Buckhorn Rd
Wetmore MI 49895

Call Sign: K8KIT
Alger ARC
N3253 Buckhorn Rd
Wetmore MI 49895

Call Sign: W8RDR
Raoul D Revord
N3253 Buckhorn Rd
Wetmore MI 49895

Call Sign: WA8I
Angela M Le Veque
E 9586 Cedar St
Wetmore MI 49895

Call Sign: WB8Q
William E Le Veque
E 9586 Cedar St
Wetmore MI 49895

Call Sign: KA8PCB
Mary A Verbeke
14567 CR 33
Wetmore MI 49895

Call Sign: KD8LYU
Larry A Martin
16820 Kk 6 Ln
Wetmore MI 49895

Call Sign: KD8NFF
Charles N Bouth
E8917 Lostlake Rd
Wetmore MI 49895

Call Sign: K8RR
John R Sheller
5633 N Eastpointe Rd
Wetmore MI 49895

Call Sign: WD8RMV
David J Nelson
Wetmore MI 49895

FCC Amateur Radio Licenses in White Cloud

Call Sign: KC8NJY
Timothy J Looy
4692 2 Mile Rd E

White Cloud MI 49349

Call Sign: KB8IFE
James F Maike Jr
977 8th St
White Cloud MI 49349

Call Sign: W8WUB
Marolyn E Gwinn
6255 E 29th St Rt 3
White Cloud MI 49349

Call Sign: KB8ZEL
Michael L Fetterley
5960 E 4 Mile
White Cloud MI 49349

Call Sign: KB8ZSQ
Craig A Verburg
1232 E 40th
White Cloud MI 49349

Call Sign: KB8JCK
Judy Maike
977 E 8th Ave
White Cloud MI 49349

Call Sign: N8PXL
Robin L Maike
977 E 8th Ave
White Cloud MI 49349

Call Sign: N8PXQ
Randall E Trimm
2160 E 8th Ave
White Cloud MI 49349

Call Sign: KC8FUV
Verne A Williams
1315 E Pine Hill Ave
White Cloud MI 49349

Call Sign: N9SYR
Cynthia J Petrie
6335 E Valley Ave
White Cloud MI
493499304

Call Sign: N8PXN
Wayne C Harvatich
1470 E Van Buren
White Cloud MI 49349

Call Sign: KC8JEY

Mark A Bankus Sr
570 Mohawk Ave
White Cloud MI 49349

Call Sign: N8PXO
Robert L Bulson
610 Mohawk Dr
White Cloud MI 49349

Call Sign: KB8OVL
James D Calhoun
107 Morgan
White Cloud MI 49349

Call Sign: KB8OVO
Jane Calhoun
107 Morgan
White Cloud MI 49349

Call Sign: KB8JPS
Shirley M Glover
1580 N Evergreen
White Cloud MI 49349

Call Sign: KB8JPT
James E Robinson Jr
1580 N Evergreen
White Cloud MI 49349

Call Sign: KD8KQB
James E Buttleman
980 N Meadowbrook
White Cloud MI 49349

Call Sign: N8SRY
Rufus M Spillman
2346 N Poplar
White Cloud MI
493499626

Call Sign: N8PXI
Twila J Silman
1020 Poplar Ave
White Cloud MI 49349

Call Sign: N8PXK
Loren R Silman
1020 Poplar Ave
White Cloud MI 49349

Call Sign: N8PQO
Marshall T Major
90 W Jackson
White Cloud MI 49349

Call Sign: KC8PKQ
Roger E Silverthorn
White Cloud MI 49349

FCC Amateur Radio Licenses in White Pigeon

Call Sign: KC8YEC
Douglas G Birky
12959 Barker Rd
White Pigeon MI
49099

Call Sign: KB8M
Douglas G Birky
12959 Barker Rd
White Pigeon MI
49099

Call Sign: KD8CXS
Lori A Birky
12959 Barker Rd
White Pigeon MI
49099

Call Sign: N8HCL
Christopher L
Hostetler
305 E Peck Ave
White Pigeon MI
49099

Call Sign: KB8LWW
Howard T Bargwell
105 E Vermont
White Pigeon MI
49099

Call Sign: W8EN
Caleb F Enix
200 E Vermont Ave
White Pigeon MI
49099

Call Sign: KB8FBJ
Carl A Rehm
68121 Edgewater
Beach Rd
White Pigeon MI
49099

Call Sign: WW8C

Roger M Tepfer
18970 Fairview Ct
White Pigeon MI
490999777

Call Sign: KD8HBT
Joy F Thomas
19013 Fawn River Rd
Lot 27
White Pigeon MI
49099

Call Sign: KD8CEE
Danny E Thomas
19013 Fawn River Rd
Lot 27
White Pigeon MI
49099

Call Sign: WD8RZF
Rosanne E Brothers
17028 Fish Lake Rd
White Pigeon MI
49099

Call Sign: N8YGP
Michael R Baumer
204 Murray St
White Pigeon MI
49099

Call Sign: WB8DXS
Dale A Randall
307 N Kalamazoo
White Pigeon MI
49099

Call Sign: NT8R
Eddie L Shearer
12420 River Side Dr
White Pigeon MI
49099

Call Sign: K8IPX
Lawrence J Abbott
206 S Athletic Dr Box
281
White Pigeon MI
49099

Call Sign: K8KCE
Delvin S Hendricks
71092 Scott Rd

White Pigeon MI
49099

Call Sign: KA0DFJ
Kenneth D Willems
70940 Sevison Rd
White Pigeon MI
49099

Call Sign: N9ZSZ
Jeffrey J Wyatt
71379 Sevison Rd
White Pigeon MI
49099

Call Sign: KD8HBZ
Raymond L Hammons
9764 State Line Rd
White Pigeon MI
49099

Call Sign: KB8ZU
Donald R Reilly
68932 Vistula Rd
White Pigeon MI
490999458

Call Sign: AF8FU
John D Bransford
106 W Michigan Ave
White Pigeon MI
49099

Call Sign: KC8WTX
Michiana ARC
106 W Michigan Ave
White Pigeon MI
49099

Call Sign: WQ8TV
Michiana ARC
106 W Michigan Ave
White Pigeon MI
49099

Call Sign: K8CCN
Michiana ARC
106 W Michigan Ave
White Pigeon MI
49099

Call Sign: WM8CC
Michiana ARC
106 W Michigan Ave

White Pigeon MI
49099

Call Sign: W8ZHW
John D Bransford
106 W Michigan Ave
White Pigeon MI
49099

Call Sign: KC8NAE
Robert A Bransford
106 W Michigan Ave
White Pigeon MI
49099

Call Sign: KO1PF
John D Bransford
106 W Michigan Ave
White Pigeon MI
49099

Call Sign: N8SI
John D Bransford
106 W Michigan Ave
White Pigeon MI
49099

Call Sign: AJ4DB
John D Bransford
106 W Michigan Ave
White Pigeon MI
49099

Call Sign: AJ8T
John D Bransford
106 W Michigan Ave
White Pigeon MI
49099

Call Sign: N8SI
John D Bransford
106 W Michigan Ave
White Pigeon MI
49099

Call Sign: AB8O
John D Bransford
106 W Michigan Ave
White Pigeon MI
49099

Call Sign: KV8O
John D Bransford
106 W Michigan Ave

White Pigeon MI
49099

Call Sign: WY8R
John D Bransford
106 W Michigan Ave
White Pigeon MI
49099

Call Sign: AC8YY
John D Bransford
106 W Michigan Ave
White Pigeon MI
49099

Call Sign: K8LPQ
John D Bransford
106 W Michigan Ave
White Pigeon MI
49099

Call Sign: NI2S
John D Bransford
106 W Michigan Ave
White Pigeon MI
49099

Call Sign: WM8V
John D Bransford
106 W Michigan Ave
White Pigeon MI
49099

Call Sign: KA8MMA
David L Bresson
White Pigeon MI
49099

Call Sign: KD8FWX
James W Bathe
White Pigeon MI
49099

Call Sign: KD8GQH
Patricia L Bathe
White Pigeon MI
49099

**FCC Amateur Radio
Licenses in White
Pine**

Call Sign: W9HI
G Allan Stewart

1 Cherry St
White Pine MI 49971

Call Sign: N8GRM
Kenneth C Bjurstrom
Sr
25 Oak St
White Pine MI
499710186

Call Sign: KF4PQG
Victor A Karlson
1011 Riverview Dr
White Pine MI
499710124

Call Sign: KC8NQZ
Ross W Reishus
White Pine MI 49971

Call Sign: KC8OLT
James T Richardson
White Pine MI 49971

Call Sign: KC8QMC
Carl L Ott
White Pine MI 49971

FCC Amateur Radio Licenses in Whitehall

Call Sign: KC8SFZ
Michael D Schmalz
2935 Alice St
Whitehall MI 49461

Call Sign: W8MKG
Michael D Schmalz
2935 Alice St
Whitehall MI 49461

Call Sign: KD8KAO
Raymond M Cole Jr
2550 Benston Rd
Whitehall MI 49461

Call Sign: KC8DOE
Damien E Rostar
7731 Carefree Dr
Whitehall MI 49461

Call Sign: KD8KGR
Bethany A Duram
922 Colby St Apt 8A

Whitehall MI 49461

Call Sign: N8TIJ
Janet M Grady
4141 Creekside Dr
Whitehall MI 49461

Call Sign: N8TIK
Gerald R Grady
4141 Creekside Dr
Whitehall MI 49461

Call Sign: KD8KGU
Eric L Fleet
1115 Crystal Lake Rd
Whitehall MI 49461

Call Sign: KC8MDG
Wayne S Jackson
4613 Doug Dr
Whitehall MI 49461

Call Sign: W8KID
Richard G Hathaway
2040 Duck Lake Rd
Whitehall MI 49461

Call Sign: KD8FWZ
Alan J Graham
2841 Duck Lake Rd
White Hall MI 49461

Call Sign: WA8RGA
John P Grabenstetter
5020 Duck Lake Rd
Whitehall MI 49461

Call Sign: KD8MRX
Brandon K Parsons
5765 Duck Lake Rd
Whitehall MI 49461

Call Sign: WA8DUC
Rozella L Holmstrom
701 E Alice St
Whitehall MI 49461

Call Sign: KC8PLL
Alfred E Ronning
1121 E Colby
Whitehall MI 49461

Call Sign: KC8TEH
Kathy L Ronning

1121 E Colby Apt 401
White Hall MI 49461

Call Sign: K8AER
Alfred E Ronning
1121 E Colby
Whitehall MI 49461

Call Sign: W8WPD
Whitehall Police
Department
405 E Colby St
Whitehall Pd
Whitehall MI
494611147

Call Sign: KA8YZC
Carol J Crevier
821 E Spring St
Whitehall MI 49461

Call Sign: K8PY
Dale F Crevier
821 E Spring St
Whitehall MI 49461

Call Sign: W8CJC
Carol J Crevier
821 E Spring St
Whitehall MI 49461

Call Sign: K8VJW
Frank L Warren
1312 King St
Whitehall MI 49461

Call Sign: KA8QYM
James E Hain Sr
415 Lake St
Whitehall MI
494610302

Call Sign: KA9MFJ
Mary Kay Specht
5200 Lakewood Rd
Whitehall MI 49461

Call Sign: W9GBL
James R Specht
5200 Lakewood Rd
Whitehall MI 49461

Call Sign: W8JCO
Bernard L Weidner

612 Mary St
Whitehall MI 49461

Call Sign: KC8WSC
Tim A Lohman
316 Mill Pond Rd
Whitehall MI 49461

Call Sign: W8KMA
Tim A Lohman
316 Mill Pond Rd
Whitehall MI 49461

Call Sign: N8GZR
Raymond J Veeder Jr
420 Muskegon Ave
Whitehall MI 49461

Call Sign: KC8DWJ
Scott M Ogborn Jr
212 N Elizabeth
Whitehall MI 49461

Call Sign: N8UEK
Ronald R Mahal Jr
3673 N Jay Rd
Whitehall MI
494619776

Call Sign: K8PYY
Dale F Crevier
6016 N Zellar Rd
Whitehall MI 49461

Call Sign: KD8KZC
Timothy J Harris
3134 Orshal Rd
Whitehall MI 49461

Call Sign: KC8SIC
Larry A Cain
5160 Orshal Rd
Whitehall MI 49461

Call Sign: NF8D
Alan C Stover
600 River St
Whitehall MI 49461

Call Sign: KA8RPY
Rebecca R Stover
636 Riverview Ct
Whitehall MI 49461

Call Sign: KD8NBH
Clint T Leatrea
1312 S Division St
Whitehall MI 49461

Call Sign: KD8CJY
Michael B Hain
6366 S Durham Rd
Whitehall MI 49461

Call Sign: KA9NZP
William G Haines
520 S Livingston St
Whitehall MI 49461

Call Sign: KA8RWY
William S Pitkin
108 S Mears Ave Apt
2
Whitehall MI 49461

Call Sign: KB8WOR
Luke D Cole
4700 Sandy Ln
Whitehall MI 49461

Call Sign: W8OQY
Harry M Barrett
5230 Scenic Dr
Whitehall MI
494619620

Call Sign: WA8NSK
James V Morford
1219 Shore Walk Ln
Whitehall MI 49461

Call Sign: WB8PFA
Darrel E Cardy
9925 Silver Creek Rd
Whitehall MI 49461

Call Sign: KB9NHE
Hubert Widner
6520 Todd Rd
Whitehall MI 49461

Call Sign: W8OBU
Levi D Huffman
106 Tulgeywood Ln
Whitehall MI 49461

Call Sign: KD8PWR
Jeffery T Abram

858 W Crystal Lake
Rd
Whitehall MI 49461

Call Sign: WA8YJE
Duane L Simonson
4411 W Lakewood Rd
Whitehall MI 49461

Call Sign: W1HPT
Francis F Paul
204 W Lewis St Apt D
Whitehall MI
494611561

Call Sign: W8NWF
Daniel A Krupp
5616 Weber Rd
Whitehall MI 49461

Call Sign: KD8KMV
Brian T Stevens
2351 White Lake Dr
Whitehall MI 49461

Call Sign: KC8UWM
Stanley D Buxton
4241 White Lake Dr
Whitehall MI 49461

Call Sign: KC8UWN
Stuart W Buxton
4241 White Lake Dr
Whitehall MI 49461

Call Sign: K8JVX
Francis A Witt
7808 Whitehall Rd
Whitehall MI 49461

Call Sign: KB8QJV
Per Malmbak
Whitehall MI 49461

Call Sign: KD8QEU
William F Mcadams
6807 Alabaster Rd
Whittemore MI 48770

Call Sign: N8WMB

Morrison W Whetstone
Jr
1349 Kelly Rd
Whittemore MI 48770

Call Sign: N8GNH
Harlan R Bero
6860 Legget Rd
Whittemore MI 48770

Call Sign: K8MKF
Merrill W Carlton
5647 M 55
Whittemore MI 48770

Call Sign: W2HHL
Rupert A Bentley Jr
6759 Old State Rd
Whittemore MI 48770

Call Sign: KA8AIP
John L Hanley III
489 S Towerline Rd
Whittemore MI 48770

Call Sign: KA8UAJ
Barbara J Hanley
489 S Towerline Rd
Whittemore MI 48770

Call Sign: KD8CLN
Paul L Birkenbach
2741 S Towerline Rd
Whittemore MI 48770

Call Sign: KD8GIX
Ernest L Reinhardt
6880 School St Apt 2
Whittemore MI 48770

Call Sign: KA0EOF
Daniel J Anderson
10120 Amos Wood Dr
Williamsburg MI
49690

Call Sign: KA8FEW
Harold B Vincent
5875 Andorra Dr 18

Williamsburg MI
49690

Call Sign: WD8MQC
Gary A Roberts
6250 Applewood Ln
Williamsburg MI
49690

Call Sign: N8KAO
Patricia L Wagner
7566 Bates Rd
Williamsburg MI
49690

Call Sign: K8KUA
James E Peacock
8220 Bates Rd
Williamsburg MI
49690

Call Sign: N8WMG
Mark A Bak
4211 Broomhead Rd
Williamsburg MI
49690

Call Sign: N8YCU
Michelle L Bak
4211 Broomhead Rd
Williamsburg MI
49690

Call Sign: KB8SJX
Jim O Lawrence Jr
11896 Cabana Shores
Williamsburg MI
49690

Call Sign: KB8SJY
Jacqueline K Lawrence
11896 Cabana Shores
Williamsburg MI
49690

Call Sign: KF8CU
John M Harlan
7769 Clearwater Dr
Williamsburg MI
49690

Call Sign: KB8STO
Fredrick E Myers
15371 Clearwater Pt

Williamsburg MI
49690

Call Sign: KM8D
George E Webster
6882 Cook Rd
Williamsburg MI
49690

Call Sign: KA8NZK
Mary L Doran
7632 Cook Rd
Williamsburg MI
49690

Call Sign: W8OKN
Sean P Doran
7632 Cook Rd
Williamsburg MI
49690

Call Sign: KC8WMH
Timothy E Doran
7632 Cook Rd
Williamsburg MI
49690

Call Sign: K8GYZ
Wallace E Weir
7792 Cook Rd
Williamsburg MI
49690

Call Sign: KA8KNK
Steven W Sanborn
6984 Cram Rd
Williamsburg MI
49690

Call Sign: KB8WZG
Mark R Wilson
8250 Cram Rd
Williamsburg MI
49690

Call Sign: WA8UOM
Marvin L Grahn
8409 Crisp Rd
Williamsburg MI
49690

Call Sign: KC8QEJ
Benjamin B Schnurr
6793 Deepwater Pt Rd

Williamsburg MI
49690

Call Sign: K8QXZ
Ray S Swan
7113 Deepwater Pt Rd
Williamsburg MI
49690

Call Sign: KC8KEN
Ben E Hammer
7686 Elk Lake Rd
Williamsburg MI
49690

Call Sign: KC8JBF
Philip M Wells
9490 Elk Lake Rd
Williamsburg MI
496909505

Call Sign: N8VYR
Timothy A
Arbenowske
6408 Elk View Dr
Williamsburg MI
49690

Call Sign: KG8WF
Vincenzo J Festa
4593 Hampshire Dr
Williamsburg MI
49690

Call Sign: KD8BNN
Tawyna L Festa
4593 Hampshire Dr
Williamsburg MI
49690

Call Sign: WB8BJV
Peter H Lawrie
10930 Lakeshore Rd
Williamsburg MI
49690

Call Sign: KC8NTZ
Alan D Lawcock
5877 Linderleaf Ln
Williamsburg MI
49690

Call Sign: AA9BA
Terry L Witt

5936 Linderleaf Ln
Williamsburg MI
49690

Call Sign: KB8MZD
Carey A Witt
5936 Linderleaf Ln
Williamsburg MI
49690

Call Sign: N9VVF
Lydia A Witt
5936 Linderleaf Ln
Williamsburg MI
49690

Call Sign: WS9T
Dave W Witt
5936 Linderleaf Ln
Williamsburg MI
49690

Call Sign: KB8WZK
Joseph V Schott
5483 Millbrook Dr
Williamsburg MI
49690

Call Sign: KB8VTF
Brian A Haskin Jr
4938 Moore Rd
Williamsburg MI
49690

Call Sign: KB8VGK
Micah P Kohler
7609 N Bates Rd
Williamsburg MI
496909526

Call Sign: KC8HNB
Jared J Kohler
7609 N Bates Rd
Williamsburg MI
496909526

Call Sign: KC8HNC
Josiah P Kohler
7609 N Bates Rd Rt 2
Williamsburg MI
49690

Call Sign: KC8HNA
Ariel J Kohler

7609 N Bates Rd Rt 2
Williamsburg MI
49690

Call Sign: KB8RDE
Nathan A Moore
7575 Skegemog Point
Rd
Williamsburg MI
49690

Call Sign: KB8GNH
Dorothy M Poniatoski
8610 Skegemog Point
Rd
Williamsburg MI
49690

Call Sign: KB8GHE
Anthony W Poniatoski
8610 Skegenog Point
Rd
Williamsburg MI
49690

Call Sign: WX8R
Charles W Perry
11690 US 31 S
Williamsburg MI
49690

Call Sign: KB8TYE
Thomas E Finch
5756 Vinton Rd
Williamsburg MI
49690

Call Sign: N8KHY
Joseph C Grenchik
5661 Williamsburg Rd
Williamsburg MI
49690

Call Sign: KB8WZJ
Walter G Thompson
3533 Woodland Tr
Williamsburg MI
49690

Call Sign: KF8BD
Kenneth A Gallo
Williamsburg MI
49690

Call Sign: WD8CFN
Llewelyn A Bone
Williamsburg MI
49690

Call Sign: KB9POO
Sally D Cronce
N16395 Bellefeuil Ln
Wilson MI 49896

Call Sign: KB9QNM
Daniel L Cronce
N16395 Bellefeuil Ln
Wilson MI 49896

Call Sign: KD8IGV
Clay Laveau
N15480 Cedarview Dr
Wilson MI 49896

Call Sign: KB8FCS
Timothy L Murray Sr
W1018 N 34 5 Rd
Wilson MI 49896

Call Sign: KC8IHQ
William H Marcotte
9836 Afton Rd
Wolverine MI 49799

Call Sign: W8OLE
Thomas R Maskus
3625 Wurm Rd
Wolverine MI 49799

Call Sign: KC8NUQ
Mark A Pierce
3803 Wurm Rd
Wolverine MI 49799

Call Sign: KA8NCL
Walter W Stephenson
Wolverine MI 49799

Call Sign: KA8REG

Betty J Carey
6361 Davenport Rd
Woodland MI 48897

Call Sign: KC8LGE
Tony A Velte
4700 Velte Rd
Woodland MI 48897

Call Sign: KG4UAM
Jonathan E Reid
6338 Velte Rd
Woodland MI 48897

Call Sign: K8JER
Jonathan E Reid
6338 Velte Rd
Woodland MI 48897

Call Sign: WB8MHJ
Thomas L Smith
2663 Woodland Rd
Woodland MI 48897

Call Sign: KD8RVO
Mike D Vanhouten
766 26th St
Wyoming MI 49509

Call Sign: K8EMD
Erin M Donat
772 26th St SW
Wyoming MI 49509

Call Sign: N8VWE
Richard J Keizer
1919 28th St
Wyoming MI 49509

Call Sign: WA8YFA
James L Levandowski
2450 30th St
Wyoming MI 49519

Call Sign: KF8E
Joseph L Swanson
123 32nd St SE
Wyoming MI 49548

Call Sign: N8UMP
James D Beaudoin

129 32nd St SW
Wyoming MI 49548

Call Sign: KD8GJJ
Helene A Castle
719 32nd St SW
Wyoming MI 49509

Call Sign: KD8KOW
William F Castle Jr
719 32nd St SW
Wyoming MI 49509

Call Sign: KC8PFX
David L Walton
103 35th St SE
Wyoming MI 49548

Call Sign: WD8OTT
Donald G Wenger
138 35th St SE
Wyoming MI 49548

Call Sign: KC8YDQ
Janette M Young
814 35th St SW
Wyoming MI 49509

Call Sign: KB8WGB
Jason L Hessey
2317 38th St SW
Wyoming MI 49519

Call Sign: N8VLN
Michael R Gage
1136 40th SW
Wyoming MI 49509

Call Sign: K8QP
Eugene I Batchelder
1635 41st SW
Wyoming MI 49509

Call Sign: KB8KGH
Joseph L Robinson Jr
144 Abbie St
Wyoming MI 49509

Call Sign: KB8DWE
Joseph L Robinson
144 Abbie St SE
Wyoming MI 49548

Call Sign: KC8FQG

Jeffery A Bishop
2411 Ancient SW
Wyoming MI 49509

Call Sign: N8IOC
Gerald S Ambrose
2330 Arden SW
Wyoming MI 49509

Call Sign: K3SPV
William W Henry
2380 Aurora Pond Dr
217
Wyoming MI 49519

Call Sign: KC8RWN
Glenn L Schuette
2380 Aurora Pond Dr
Apt 225
Wyoming MI 49519

Call Sign: KD8NRC
Paul J Aseltine
39 Avonlea SW
Wyoming MI 49548

Call Sign: K8UAZ
Jess W Conlon
3221 Badger Ave SW
Wyoming MI 49509

Call Sign: KB8RHX
William E Craig
3352 Badger SW
Wyoming MI 49509

Call Sign: N8MJF
Michael J Fusaro
5880 Bayberry Farms
Dr 10
Wyoming MI 49418

Call Sign: WD8OAD
Frank J Kovalcsik Jr
5856 Bayberry Farms
Dr Apt 10
Wyoming MI 49418

Call Sign: KD8MDR
Tyler J Sturgis
5856 Bayberry Farms
Dr SW Apt 6
Wyoming MI 49418

Call Sign: KD8FSU
William J Sturgis
5856 Bayberry Farms
Dr SW Apt 6
Wyoming MI 49418

Call Sign: K8WJS
William J Sturgis
5856 Bayberry Farms
Dr SW Apt 6
Wyoming MI 49418

Call Sign: WA8CWK
Laurence R Brown
934 Beech SW
Wyoming MI 49509

Call Sign: WD8DIJ
Robert G Gross
1704 Belden SW
Wyoming MI 49509

Call Sign: KD8JWI
Benjamin R Momber
2300 Berwyn Ave SW
Wyoming MI 49519

Call Sign: KC8ZTQ
David R Corey
953 Blanchard St
Wyoming MI
495092811

Call Sign: N8UZX
John Van Solkema Jr
1907 Blandford SW
Wyoming MI 49509

Call Sign: KC8CWE
Melinda J Mennega
3821 Bonne SW
Wyoming MI 49509

Call Sign: W8DDU
Edwin J Vander Ploeg
3539 Boone Ave SW
Wyoming MI
495193215

Call Sign: KC8NJX
Jason M Stewart
4546 Buchanan Ave
Wyoming MI 49548

Call Sign: K8NFJ
Harry M Bodbyl
1282 Buckingham
Wyoming MI 49509

Call Sign: K2COP
Harry M Bodbyl
1282 Buckingham
Wyoming MI 49509

Call Sign: KB8UFH
Deborah L Verwoerd
821 Buckingham SW
Wyoming MI 49509

Call Sign: KG8UH
Donald N Verwoerd Sr
821 Buckingham SW
Wyoming MI 49509

Call Sign: WD8LDL
Gary J Ritzema
1188 Bunkerway Dr
SW
Wyoming MI 49509

Call Sign: KC8RQX
Mohamed H Elrahimy
4115 Burr Ave SW
Wyoming MI 49509

Call Sign: N8SFI
Angela K Washer
2260 Byron Center 14
Wyoming MI 49509

Call Sign: KC8OAO
Matthew O Gommesen
2539 Byron Center
Ave
Wyoming MI
495092113

Call Sign: KA8JVZ
Keith E Sharp
2532 Byron Center
Ave SW
Wyoming MI 49509

Call Sign: N8NII
Jeffrey P Ansley
5148 Carson St SW
Wyoming MI 49548

Call Sign: KC8AFX
Delwin G Milarch
5120 Carson SW
Wyoming MI 49548

Call Sign: KB8WXF
Lisa C Ansley
5148 Carson SW
Wyoming MI 49548

Call Sign: KF8OR
James K Wirsing
4632 Caspian Dr SW
Wyoming MI 49519

Call Sign: N8YJZ
Cheryl L Wirsing
4632 Caspian Dr SW
Wyoming MI 49519

Call Sign: KD8GZH
James H Richards
5787 Charolais Dr SW
Wyoming MI 49418

Call Sign: KD8JHR
James H Richards
5787 Charolais Dr SW
Wyoming MI 49418

Call Sign: K8JHR
James H Richards
5787 Charolais Dr SW
Wyoming MI 49418

Call Sign: KB8UYW
Steven J La Huis
2201 Clarion SW
Wyoming MI 49509

Call Sign: KC8UOX
Russell G Taber
1952 Cleveland Ave
SW
Wyoming MI
495091455

Call Sign: N8JSN
Jeffrey S Nawrot
2851 Clyde Park
Wyoming MI 49509

Call Sign: KC8BII
Phiip G Beech

3238 Clyde Park SW
Wyoming MI
495093555

Call Sign: KA8RPJ
Jerrine J Van Splintern
3741 Colby SW
Wyoming MI 49509

Call Sign: WB8ZUH
William J Van
Splintern
3741 Colby SW
Wyoming MI 49509

Call Sign: WD8EMF
Lee A Moore
3924 Colby SW
Wyoming MI 49509

Call Sign: KD8RVX
Gloria A Everts
3522 Collingwood Ave
SW
Wyoming MI 49519

Call Sign: KD8IAK
Michael J Everts
3522 Collingwood SW
Wyoming MI 49519

Call Sign: N8EZH
Michael S Vincent
3903 Collingwood SW
Wyoming MI 49509

Call Sign: KC8SWU
Dennis R Brailey
1100 Colrain
Wyoming MI 49509

Call Sign: KD8IYQ
William L Aurner Sr
135 Colrain St SW
Wyoming MI 49548

Call Sign: WA8DOA
Clarence J Vander
Ploeg
1061 Cricklewood St
SW
Wyoming MI 49509

Call Sign: KD8RBV

Marc J Edgcombe
4105 Crooked Tree
Apt 5
Wyoming MI 49519

Call Sign: N8IMP
Richard H Burmeister
302 Crown St SW
Wyoming MI 49548

Call Sign: KC8FFV
Jeffrey S Nawrot
2653 Dehoop
Wyoming MI 49509

Call Sign: KC8VGD
Erin M Donat
2653 Dehoop
Wyoming MI 49509

Call Sign: KC8TSY
William G Willyard
4358 Del Mar Dr
Wyoming MI 49418

Call Sign: KA8YXH
Robert J Sterenberg
706 Den Hertog St SW
Wyoming MI 49509

Call Sign: KC8DCQ
Elisabeth A Ricker
4115 Emma Ave SW
Wyoming MI 49509

Call Sign: KB8SEY
Robert J Sieberlink Jr
1851 Farragut
Wyoming MI 49509

Call Sign: NE8L
Richard A Roersma
4290 Flamingo Ave
SW
Wyoming MI 49509

Call Sign: KC8EKH
Rickey W Ainsworth
Jr
4255 Flamingo SW
Wyoming MI 49509

Call Sign: N8MNV
Wanda S Roersma

4290 Flamingo SW
Wyoming MI 49509

Call Sign: N8AGK
Andrew G Keuhs
129 Floyd St SW
Wyoming MI
495483121

Call Sign: K8SMK
Jack N Billingsley
1530 Floyd St SW
Wyoming MI 49509

Call Sign: WA7RXU
Jonathan D Griswold
2445 Forest Grove Ave
SW
Wyoming MI 49509

Call Sign: W8DTI
Albert L Thomson
2645 Forest Grove Ave
SW
Wyoming MI 49509

Call Sign: N8IAU
Susan C Thomson
2645 Forest Grove SW
Wyoming MI 49509

Call Sign: KD8MCV
Michael S Miller
4436 Forest Park Dr
SW
Wyoming MI 49519

Call Sign: WD8NZZ
David R Jenista
4386 Forest Park SW
Wyoming MI 49509

Call Sign: W8HLT
Melvyn C Keesler
2000 Frontier Ct SW
Wyoming MI 49509

Call Sign: N8IMC
Betty J Swieringa
3232 Gladiola SW
Wyoming MI 49519

Call Sign: WD8BWH
Roger D Swieringa

3232 Gladiola SW
Wyoming MI 49519

Call Sign: KB8WXH
Hugh E Lingg
2524 Glenbrook SW
Wyoming MI 49509

Call Sign: WH6XS
Daniel L Richardson
3563 Goodman Ave
SW
Wyoming MI 49519

Call Sign: N8LAS
Robert A Van Rhee
2386 Greenview Dr
Wyoming MI 49519

Call Sign: W8GEP
Grant E Pearce
4849 Grenadier Dr SW
Wyoming MI 49509

Call Sign: WA8SIA
Robert D Tacoma
4034 Groveland SW
Wyoming MI 49509

Call Sign: KB5LBO
Richard L Straight II
5641 Haughey Ave
Wyoming MI 49548

Call Sign: WD8IDY
Dan P Joyce
3865 Havana SW
Wyoming MI 49509

Call Sign: KB8TUN
Schaefer A Arnould
3901 Hazelwood Ave
SW
Wyoming MI 49509

Call Sign: N8LBA
Scott D Guthrie
4114 Herman
Wyoming MI 49509

Call Sign: KD8NNO
Kenneth J Bartolome
5771 Hickory Ridge
Dr SW

Wyoming MI 49418

Call Sign: KC8GON
Dave L Ausema
2821 Highgate SW
Wyoming MI 49509

Call Sign: WB8YRB
Robert D Underwood
1926 Holliday Dr SW
Wyoming MI 49509

Call Sign: KD8IYR
Thomas L Dutkiewicz
3728 Illinois Ave SW
Wyoming MI 49509

Call Sign: W8QAW
Richard B Smith
3943 Illinois Ave SW
Wyoming MI 49509

Call Sign: KD8MDM
David A Sweet
3101 Jefferson SE
Wyoming MI 49548

Call Sign: K8TDV
David A Sweet
3101 Jefferson SE
Wyoming MI 49548

Call Sign: KB8OSZ
Jeffrey J Shrontz
1020 Joosten SW
Wyoming MI 49509

Call Sign: N8SFK
Sean E Regts
1277 Joosten SW
Wyoming MI 49509

Call Sign: KD8CWN
David J Wittkowski
48 Jordan SW
Wyoming MI 49548

Call Sign: KD8IUI
Lee L Rice
5191 Kaufman Greens
Ln SW
Wyoming MI 49509

Call Sign: AC8IC

Lee L Rice
5191 Kaufman Greens Ln SW
Wyoming MI 49509

Call Sign: KA8ONJ
Hans Pechler
2411 Kentfield SW
Wyoming MI 49509

Call Sign: KC8LOI
Russell W Povenz Jr
2400 Lamar Ave SW
Wyoming MI 49519

Call Sign: K8LO
Arie P Helder
2443 Lamar Ave SW
Wyoming MI 49519

Call Sign: W8PD
Arie P Helder
2443 Lamar Ave SW
Wyoming MI 49519

Call Sign: KD8CSJ
Peter A Helder
2443 Lamar Ave SW
Wyoming MI 49519

Call Sign: KB8QAT
Thomas E Pikaart
2187 Lee St SW
Wyoming MI 49509

Call Sign: KB8RHV
Roxanne M Pikaart
2187 Lee St SW
Wyoming MI 49509

Call Sign: N8PMM
Gerald F Frye
3859 Llewellyn Ct
Wyoming MI 49509

Call Sign: W8RVF
Charles J Holbrook
3104 Longstreet SW
Wyoming MI 49509

Call Sign: KC8AVQ
Terry C Mesler
3858 Loraine Ave SW

Wyoming MI
495483127

Call Sign: KC8VJT
Joseph M Cunningham Jr
216 Luther St SW
Wyoming MI 49548

Call Sign: AB8XY
Joseph M Cunningham Jr
216 Luther St SW
Wyoming MI 49548

Call Sign: K8JC
Joseph M Cunningham Jr
216 Luther St SW
Wyoming MI 49548

Call Sign: KB8TXD
Daniel J Bowen
552 Marcia St SW
Wyoming MI 49509

Call Sign: N8SFH
Darwin L Rinks
1425 Marquette St SW
Wyoming MI 49509

Call Sign: KB8VUD
Robert E Lay
1779 Mayflower Dr SW
Wyoming MI 49519

Call Sign: KD8IYP
Jeff G Corey
5385 Meadow Run Dr SW
Wyoming MI 49509

Call Sign: KA8GFW
James R Nash
4216 Michael SW
Wyoming MI 49509

Call Sign: N8QFC
Timothy B Zimmer
3808 Milan SW
Wyoming MI 49509

Call Sign: KB8FTH

Rebecca L Anglin
3856 Minnie SW
Wyoming MI 49509

Call Sign: KD8QIJ
Robert C Richards
1139 Mulligan Ct SW
Wyoming MI 49509

Call Sign: N8SFJ
Dan J Huizinga
2951 Nancy Ct S W
Wyoming MI 49418

Call Sign: KC8RJN
Linden A Ream
2619 Noel Ave SW
Wyoming MI 49509

Call Sign: KB8MFZ
Daniel C Strube
2515 Noel SW
Wyoming MI 49509

Call Sign: KD8DLB
Frederick W Davison
3161 Nursery Ave SW
Wyoming MI 49519

Call Sign: KD8IUK
Michelle De Zwaan
893 Oakcrest St SW
Wyoming MI 49509

Call Sign: W8MJD
Michelle De Zwaan
893 Oakcrest St SW
Wyoming MI 49509

Call Sign: K8YES
Donald A Andrews
5168 Olsen Springs Ct SW
Wyoming MI 49509

Call Sign: KC8YGN
Shirley B Andrews
5168 Olsen Springs Ct SW
Wyoming MI 49509

Call Sign: KB8SXS
Candace A Woodbeck
3468 Opal Ave SW

Wyoming MI 49548

Call Sign: KC8NKA
Richard H Douglas
3903 Oriole Ave SW
Wyoming MI 49509

Call Sign: KD8EMI
Joyce M Douglas
3903 Oriole Ave SW
Wyoming MI 49509

Call Sign: KD8IYN
David F Clark
2467 Palm Dale Dr SW
Wyoming MI 49418

Call Sign: KD8ATQ
Vincent E Axley
1875 Parkcrest Dr Apt 2
Wyoming MI 49519

Call Sign: KC8UMA
Romulo P Campos
3650 Perry Ave SW
Wyoming MI 49509

Call Sign: N8PV
Romulo P Campos
3650 Perry Ave SW
Wyoming MI 49509

Call Sign: KB8VXW
Donald R Fletcher
2584 Picadilly Ct
Wyoming MI 49418

Call Sign: KD8RPR
Martha A June
4439 Pinehurst Ave SW
Wyoming MI 49548

Call Sign: W8IJD
Gordon D Aldrich
1537 Plas SW
Wyoming MI 49509

Call Sign: KD8BPL
James D Mckinney Jr
1833 Prairie Pkwy SW Apt F

Wyoming MI 49519

Call Sign: KD8RPU
Nicki D Van Noord
1660 R W Berends Apt
8
Wyoming MI 49519

Call Sign: KD8FSZ
Alex M Bouwman
2691 Regina
Wyoming MI 49519

Call Sign: K8WJR
Dennis M Roossien
4549 Rhodes Ave SW
Wyoming MI 49508

Call Sign: KD8FAM
Kevin J Andres
4322 Ridge Ln SW
Wyoming MI 49519

Call Sign: N8LLV
Jo A Church
4329 Ridge Ln SW
Wyoming MI 49509

Call Sign: KC8EWX
Yuttana Sirisang
Mongkol
3487 Robin SW
Wyoming MI 49509

Call Sign: KC8OVU
Steve J Holiday
812 Royal Oak
Wyoming MI 49509

Call Sign: KC8QKD
Steve J Holiday
812 Royal Oak
Wyoming MI 49509

Call Sign: N8SJH
Steven J Holiday
812 Royal Oak
Wyoming MI 49509

Call Sign: KA8ZBK
Terence G Marion
1130 Royal Oak
Wyoming MI 49509

Call Sign: KC8THS
Laura L Holiday
812 Royal Oak St SW
Wyoming MI 49509

Call Sign: KD8IAB
Emilee Zandbergen
2711 Sarnia St SW
Wyoming MI 49519

Call Sign: K8IEZ
Emilee Zandbergen
2711 Sarnia St SW
Wyoming MI 49519

Call Sign: KA8LPD
Deborah Dubis
2867 Sharon Ave SW
Wyoming MI 49519

Call Sign: WD8JMC
Ronald I Shoemaker
2867 Sharon Ave SW
Wyoming MI 49519

Call Sign: KB8RHU
Bryan C Lundberg
3187 Stratford Dr
Wyoming MI 49509

Call Sign: K8BPT
Gerald E Goeldel
3738 Taft SW
Wyoming MI 49509

Call Sign: KB8OKK
Jan A Lichtig
5337 Tahoe Pine Ct
SW
Wyoming MI 49509

Call Sign: KC8MRT
Ben J Brinks
4311 Thorndyke SW
Wyoming MI 49548

Call Sign: KC8MRU
James R Brinks
4311 Thorndyke SW
Wyoming MI 49548

Call Sign: K9JSH
Acil L Couch
2319 Thornwood St

Wyoming MI 49509

Call Sign: KB9DTK
William P Cahill
4310 Timber Ridge Trl
SW Apt 3
Wyoming MI
495094288

Call Sign: N8XPN
John R Westphal
2523 Valley View
Wyoming MI 49509

Call Sign: N8TYY
Kenneth E Westphal
2523 Valley View SW
Wyoming MI 49509

Call Sign: KB8SVZ
Gene D Thorpe
4751 Valleyridge
Wyoming MI
495094516

Call Sign: K8LIR
Gilbert J Hiddema
5207 Village Dr SW
Wyoming MI 49509

Call Sign: AJ8W
Charles J Nowak
5240 Virginia Ln SW
Wyoming MI 49418

Call Sign: KC8LTT
Aaron P Schreiber
2960 W Ave SW
Wyoming MI 49509

Call Sign: K8APS
Aaron P Schreiber
2960 W Ave SW
Wyoming MI 49509

Call Sign: N8XQH
Barton K Bechtel
1688 W Berends Dr
SW Apt 3
Wyoming MI
495194979

Call Sign: KD8NSU
Erin A Ammons

1688 R W Berends Dr
SW Apt 3
Wyoming MI 49519

Call Sign: KC8LOJ
Alan K Gittins
3043 W SW
Wyoming MI 49509

Call Sign: N9TSR
Christopher M Leaver
937 Walcott SW
Wyoming MI
495091950

Call Sign: KB8OOB
William J Batchelder
2142 Waldron St SW
Wyoming MI 49509

Call Sign: W8KRP
Karl R Palma
2124 Waldron SW
Wyoming MI 49519

Call Sign: KA8ZBP
Joseph C Roszell
155 Walter SE
Wyoming MI 49508

Call Sign: WB8EUK
Raymond R Roszell
155 Walter SE
Wyoming MI 49548

Call Sign: KD8GJN
Kenneth R Kaminski
4460 Walton SW
Wyoming MI 49548

Call Sign: WB8PTM
Robert F Ruhf
3789 Wentworth Dr
SW
Wyoming MI 49509

Call Sign: KD8CWO
Keith A E Gittins
3043 West Ave
Wyoming MI 49509

Call Sign: WY8D
Stewart N Ausema
339 Wilber SE

Wyoming MI
495483330

Call Sign: WD8RKG
Anthony Snarski II
3576 Wilex SW
Wyoming MI 49509

Call Sign: KD8HG
Peter T Klein
4279 Windcrest S W
Wyoming MI 49418

Call Sign: KD8GTE
David S Hodge
1531 Woodhill Ct SW
Wyoming MI 49509

Call Sign: KC8PBY
Wyoming Amateur
Radio Association
2781 Woodlake Rd
SW 4
Wyoming MI 49509

Call Sign: KI8W
Wyoming Amateur
Radio Association
2781 Woodlake Rd
SW 4
Wyoming MI 49509

Call Sign: N8ELS
Deborah A Truskoski
2581 Woodlake Rd
SW Apt 4
Wyoming MI 49519

Call Sign: KC8LLX
Don B Kuiper
6711 Woodspointe Ct
SW
Wyoming MI 49509

Call Sign: KB8OGT
James R Spicer
2857 Woodward SW
Wyoming MI 49509

Call Sign: KA8LOS
Jay A Van Sweden
2437 Wyoming Ave
Wyoming MI
495192231

Call Sign: KA8DHW
James A Carey
2607 Wyoming Ave
Wyoming MI 49509

Call Sign: WD8ONH
Daniel K Saz
2208 Wyoming Ave
SW
Wyoming MI 49519

Call Sign: KD8PVY
Robert E Smith
2528 Wyoming Ave
SW
Wyoming MI 49519

**FCC Amateur Radio
Licenses in Wyoming
City**

Call Sign: WB8KGA
Richard A Tolar
1724 Glenvale SW
Wyoming City MI
49509

**FCC Amateur Radio
Licenses in Zeeland**

Call Sign: KD8EKV
Zeeland Schools ARC
3390 100th Ave
Zeeland MI 49464

Call Sign: KC8RQT
Christopher D Dandrea
3499 146th Ave
Zeeland MI 49464

Call Sign: KC8LZG
Dale F Demerest
774 40th Ave
Zeeland MI 494649321

Call Sign: N8RML
Beverly S Bareman
4681- 64th Ave
Zeeland MI 49464

Call Sign: W8PRN
Roger F Cole
3421 64th Ave Rr 2

Zeeland MI 49464

Call Sign: KB8SWB
Jonathan R Brockmeier
1900 72nd Ave
Zeeland MI 49464

Call Sign: W8QPP
Jonathan R Brockmeier
1900 72nd Ave
Zeeland MI 49464

Call Sign: WB8ZBD
James D Dolson
2475 72nd Ave
Zeeland MI 49464

Call Sign: K8DDV
James D Dolson
2475 72nd Ave
Zeeland MI 49464

Call Sign: KB8PYR
Scott W Piper
761 78th Ave
Zeeland MI 49464

Call Sign: N8FHM
Gordon L Van Haitsma
889 80th Ave
Zeeland MI 49464

Call Sign: N8FHP
Karen Van Haitsma
889 80th Ave
Zeeland MI 49464

Call Sign: KC8EPG
Brian T Haskin
6819 80th Ave
Zeeland MI 49464

Call Sign: KD8DEG
Thomas R Wilson
7830 80th Ave
Zeeland MI 49464

Call Sign: KD8DDZ
Bernie Johnson
6333 84th St
Zeeland MI 49464

Call Sign: N8GGO
Richard D Elushik

4105 88th Ave
Zeeland MI 49464

Call Sign: KB8TDX
Jack H Datema
4141 88th Ave
Zeeland MI 49464

Call Sign: KC8TT
Timothy M Jersey
8543 88th Ave
Zeeland MI 49464

Call Sign: KC8SRN
Chris W Kaminsky
9801 92nd Ave
Zeeland MI 49464

Call Sign: N8RMK
Etta M Van Dyke
9835 92nd Ave
Zeeland MI 49464

Call Sign: WB8YQU
Robert P Van Dyke
9835 92nd Ave
Zeeland MI 49464

Call Sign: KD8GKF
Brent Hoogerhyde
9911 92nd Ave
Zeeland MI 49464

Call Sign: W8ZHS
Zeeland Schools ARC
3333 96th Ave
Zeeland MI 49464

Call Sign: W8HA
Chester L Uncapher
2638 Airpark Dr
Zeeland MI 49464

Call Sign: WB8IXK
Patti M Uncapher
2638 Airpark Dr
Zeeland MI 49464

Call Sign: N9BU
Richard M Castle
1520 Ashtyn Woods
Pkwy
Zeeland MI 49464

Call Sign: WA8ARA
Marvin T Hoekstra
8950 Barry St
Zeeland MI 49464

Call Sign: N8SAK
Barbara J Prince
9408 Bingham St
Zeeland MI 49464

Call Sign: N8SAO
Kevin J Prince
9408 Bingham St
Zeeland MI 49464

Call Sign: N8KVJ
David M Fackler
10502 Bridgewater Dr
Zeeland MI 49464

Call Sign: KC8SNN
Kenton D Van
Klompenberg
10465 Brookview Dr
Zeeland MI 49464

Call Sign: KD8EMH
Adam W Heyboer
1660 Cedar Creek Dr
Zeeland MI 49464

Call Sign: WD8ANR
Rex E Bowers
3171 Crestbrook
Zeeland MI 49464

Call Sign: KD8KGP
Adolfo Barreto
3416 Danielle Ct
Zeeland MI 49464

Call Sign: W8KOP
Adolfo Barreto
3416 Danielle Ct
Zeeland MI 49464

Call Sign: KA9KIM
Michael J Sims
10662 Deer Ridge Ct
Zeeland MI 49464

Call Sign: KC8QDB
Amy L Sims
10662 Deer Ridge Ct

Zeeland MI 49464

Call Sign: KB8YPX
Kenneth D Post
104 E Central
Zeeland MI 49464

Call Sign: AA8CH
Christopher J Polena
2733 E Chester Dr
Zeeland MI 49464

Call Sign: AB2OS
Alan J Beagley
2768 E Chester Dr
Zeeland MI 49464

Call Sign: NV8A
Alan J Beagley
2768 E Chester Dr
Zeeland MI 49464

Call Sign: KD8CHS
Jeanette A Beagley
Koolhaas
2768 E Chester Dr
Zeeland MI 49464

Call Sign: K8JBK
Jeanette A Beagley
Koolhaas
2768 E Chester Dr
Zeeland MI 49464

Call Sign: KC8ZCO
Jonathan A Beagley
2768 E Chester Dr
Zeeland MI 49464

Call Sign: K8DAA
Holland ARC
2866 E Chester Dr
Zeeland MI 49464

Call Sign: WA8RSA
David L Lamer
2866 E Chester Dr
Zeeland MI 49464

Call Sign: KC8OOW
Floyd J Peplinski
3466 E Wind Trl
Zeeland MI 49464

Call Sign: KA8FQS
John E Tiggleman
2782 Floral Dr
Zeeland MI 49464

Call Sign: KD8FVA
Brett A Tiggleman
2782 Floral Dr
Zeeland MI 49464

Call Sign: KG8IC
Dennis D Peasley
2560 Gay Paree
Zeeland MI 49464

Call Sign: KA8YIN
Duane E Cook
3185 Gray Fox Ct
Zeeland MI 49464

Call Sign: N8PUC
Michael G Hathaway
10292 Hannah Dr
Zeeland MI 49464

Call Sign: KD8EMG
Joshua D Swett
10364 Hannah Dr
Zeeland MI 49464

Call Sign: KD8LDX
Bryan T Leenheer
9099 Hillcrest Dr Lot
34
Zeeland MI 49464

Call Sign: KC8PMF
William J Macauley
3254 Hillcrest Way
Zeeland MI 49464

Call Sign: W9RPE
Ronald P Emerson
3290 Hillcrest Way
Zeeland MI 49464

Call Sign: W8RPE
Ronald P Emerson
3290 Hillcrest Way
Zeeland MI 49464

Call Sign: WD8T
Ronald P Emerson
3290 Hillcrest Way

Zeeland MI 49464

Call Sign: KA8UYD
Jeffrey W Karger
10589 Hunters Creek
Dr
Zeeland MI 49464

Call Sign: WB8YXY
Bruce W Karger
10589 Hunters Creek
Dr
Zeeland MI 49464

Call Sign: WA8RWP
Christen Baarman
256 Interlaken Ct
Zeeland MI 49464

Call Sign: N8XPQ
Michael J Koetje
10841 James St
Zeeland MI 49464

Call Sign: WB8VYZ
Alan J Waterway
2043 Lakeview Dr
Zeeland MI 49464

Call Sign: KC8VBW
Levi D Scott
10510 Lauren Dr
Zeeland MI 49464

Call Sign: WA8RMV
Glenn A Hamburg
8684 Maple Ln
Zeeland MI 49464

Call Sign: W8IQQ
Stanley J Hamburg
8684 Maple Ln
Zeeland MI 494649157

Call Sign: N8WVN
John E Bok
24 N Centennial St
Zeeland MI 494641306

Call Sign: N8QEM
Charles R Gregory
359 N Jefferson St
Zeeland MI 49464

Call Sign: KF8EV
Edwin W Heyboer
356 N Lindy Ave
Zeeland MI 49464

Call Sign: W8DTB
John Bremer
8515 N Maple Ct
Zeeland MI 49464

Call Sign: KA8YFR
Brian R Ransler
10524 Northfield Dr
Zeeland MI 49464

Call Sign: WB0CRK
Lenard D Heath
222 Parkside Dr
Zeeland MI 494642049

Call Sign: W8FIZ
Hollis A Roels
340 Parkside Dr
Zeeland MI 49464

Call Sign: WB8OAW
Dewey L Ferman
500 Parkside Dr 233
Zeeland MI 49464

Call Sign: NW9A
Rodger H Dalman
500 Parkside Dr Apt
142
Zeeland MI 49464

Call Sign: KB9MQF
Danny R Woods
3321 Partridge Ave
Zeeland MI 49464

Call Sign: KD8QCJ
David R Kiekintveld
10691 Paw Paw Dr
Zeeland MI 49464

Call Sign: KB8RFW
Marilyn K Newman
17 Pine St
Zeeland MI 494641617

Call Sign: W8KZB
J Arnold Newman
17 Pine St

Zeeland MI 494641617

Call Sign: KC8AFY
James L Wood
9720 Platinum Pt
Zeeland MI 49464

Call Sign: KC8BKS
Brian T Harvey
8332 S Maple Ct
Zeeland MI 49464

Call Sign: KA8OFL
Michael S Walters
8546 S Maple Ct
Zeeland MI 494649376

Call Sign: KB8YNG
John P Pettinga
8555 S Maple Ct
Zeeland MI 49464

Call Sign: W8NBT
Douglas Elzinga
9161 S Maple Lake Dr
Zeeland MI 49464

Call Sign: W8LTY
William J Gras
220 S Taft
Zeeland MI 49464

Call Sign: KB8IVQ
Michelle R Batema
2530 Spring Ct
Zeeland MI 49464

Call Sign: KD8QPB
Evan R Van Heukelom
10366 Springwood Dr
Zeeland MI 49464

Call Sign: KV8U
Jack A Van Voorst
8737 Summit Ct
Zeeland MI 49464

Call Sign: KD8OOZ
Joseph W Dekock
451 W Central Ave
Zeeland MI 49464

Call Sign: AC8JD
Joseph W Dekock

451 W Central Ave
Zeeland MI 49464

Call Sign: N8ZTB
Craig S Borst
2656 W Chester
Zeeland MI 49464

Call Sign: K0TWB
Arthur L Van Wyhe
2641 W Chester Dr
Zeeland MI 49464

Call Sign: KB8DYU
Kent L Pollard
324 W Garfield
Zeeland MI 49464

Call Sign: W8IAB
A Le Roy Rediger
430 W Lawrence Hwy
Zeeland MI 49464

Call Sign: KD8DAG
Donald G Stephens
56 W Main St
Zeeland MI 49464

Call Sign: KC8WYS
Christopher J Stephens
56 W Main St
Zeeland MI 49464

Call Sign: KC8DRM
George S Whitcomb
1393 Wiersma Dr
Zeeland MI 49464

Call Sign: N8YEL
Peter C Venlet
1348 Woodfield Dr
Zeeland MI 494642207

Call Sign: AC8PV
Peter C Venlet
1348 Woodfield Dr
Zeeland MI 494642207

Call Sign: N8YEL
Peter C Venlet
1348 Woodfield Dr
Zeeland MI 494642207

Call Sign: KD8CAO

Douglas C Papay
1383 Woodfield Dr
Zeeland MI 494642201

Call Sign: KC8LYZ
Timothy J Derks
1439 Woodfield Ln
Zeeland MI 49464

Call Sign: KD8JBM
Craig S Coleman
357 Woodward St
Zeeland MI 49464